Federal Income Tax

Federal Income Tax

A Problem-Solving Approach

Cases and Materials

Toni Robinson

QUINNIPIAC UNIVERSITY SCHOOL OF LAW

Mary Ferrari

QUINNIPIAC UNIVERSITY SCHOOL OF LAW

CAROLINA ACADEMIC PRESS

Durham, North Carolina

ISBN 10: 0-89089-900-2
ISBN 13: 978-0-89089-900-7
LCCN: 2007924137

Carolina Academic Press
700 Kent Street
Durham, North Carolina 27701
Telephone (919) 489-7486
Fax (919) 493-5668
www.cap-press.com

Printed in the United States of America

Contents

III. Who Is the "Proper" Taxpayer?

VII. Additional Transactional Problems

Table of Cases

Table of Internal Revenue Code Sections

Table of Treasury Regulations

Table of Revenue Rulings

Table of Miscellaneous Authorities

A Note to Students

Many students, maybe including you, view the income tax course with hesitation (or horror). You may be concerned that tax is nothing but numbers, business, economics, finance, and accounting, *i.e.*, not only incomprehensible but, even worse, unbelievably boring to the liberal arts majors that many of you are. Don't panic! You need neither math, business, nor accounting expertise to succeed in this course. What you do need is an open mind to the reality that, when you enter law practice, your clients will come to you for assistance in solving problems of everyday living: divorce, real estate, family property matters, small business, tort claims—all of which involve issues requiring a basic understanding of business, finance, and taxation, a basic understanding without which you cannot communicate effectively with and successfully counsel your clients.

We believe that the study of federal tax law is essential because tax is the one subject that pervades almost every other substantive area of law practice in which you may eventually engage. The study of basic federal income tax requires you to begin to become life and business literate. We believe that good lawyers know more than the rules of law: they are true generalists who know something about business, finance, and accounting, and, equally important, a great deal about life. To borrow from Justice Cardozo in *Welch v. Helvering*, tax cases are unique (and far from boring) in that they deal with "life in all its fullness." We have found that tax is an ideal medium through which to introduce students to basic business concepts and to discuss such basic business and financial matters as borrowing and lending, the time value of money, basic intra-family financial dealings, and the different types of business entities.

Even those of you who come to this course with business, accounting, or science backgrounds, and who think you do not have much to gain from this course because you took a tax course in college, or because you are good with numbers, have much to learn from the basic tax course. We have found that we can impart to you an appreciation of words. After all, statutes are written in words—words that must be read slowly and carefully, words that may not mean what you think they do. Numbers are important, but you can't be an effective lawyer without developing facility with the "language" of statutes. We hope to demonstrate to you that a lawyer's approach to tax is far different from that of a number cruncher.

Thus, we believe that the basic tax course has something to teach all law students from whatever background. Liberal arts majors need confidence in demystifying numbers, business, and finance; and business and science majors often need to be sensitized to the power of words and their creative possibilities. It is the confluence of numbers and words that makes the study of tax law so vital for all our students and so challenging for us who teach it.

We believe that to encourage students to study tax is also pedagogically sound. In the first year you studied the development of the common law through analysis of appellate decisions. After your first year, however, it is imperative that you become more focused on the study of statutes. We have found the course in federal income taxation to be an ideal medium through which to teach rigorous statutory reading and analysis and methods of statutory interpretation (employed by courts and used by tax planners). The federal income tax course also introduces you to the sources of law and the legislative and administrative processes that are vital to virtually all areas of law practice. Further, through the federal income tax course, we can help you learn more about the Constitution, federalism, and the basic structure of the federal government.

Although we believe that it should be the goal of the basic federal income tax course to impart to students an understanding of the wide impact of the Internal Revenue Code on many legal problems that do not seem to have tax consequences, we know that it is impossible to give students a complete overview of the Code in a three or four credit survey course. There are, however, some foundational topics and cases that you should know. It is also vital for you to read the Code, to learn about the various authorities that interpret the Code, and to learn about the administrative process. If you do that, you will be able to read any statute—tax or otherwise—and you will know more about the administrative process (in which lawyers frequently engage in practice).

This book will give you an overview of the basic income tax calculation formula without examining in detail every single inclusion, exclusion, deduction, and credit. Our pedagogical goal is to assist you in creating for yourselves a sense of the structure of the whole by focusing on fundamental principles so you will be able to deal in the future with Code sections that you have not read before, and to deal with legislative changes (which in tax occur with unusual frequency.) It is approach and methodology we are trying to impart to you, not to overwhelm you with minutia.

This book is, we hope, unique among traditional casebooks. The teaching method we use here reflects what we have learned, during many years of teaching tax to many types of students, about how students learn tax. We have tried very hard to remember how we felt as beginners in the study of tax law. Thus, we conduct a colloquy with you as you proceed through the materials and present a series of problems designed to illustrate tax issues (and associated policy, procedure, and ethical issues) that affect real taxpayers in their everyday lives. This approach has helped our students feel more engaged with (and less intimidated by) the materials. At the end of the book we present a series of "transactional problems." Because most of you have not had much experience in the technique of integrating multiple sources of law: cases, statutes, legislative histories, administrative regulations and other administrative communications, we have found that the best way for students to develop this critical skill is to apply what you have learned in the early parts of this book to these transactional problems.

Many of us who have practiced law, especially tax law, remember (with some chagrin) that the most difficult part of solving a tax problem was often identifying it. Because your client will tell you a "story" without identifying the particular issues (legal or tax), it will be up to you to make the identification. Some of you (we hope) will become tax lawyers. It will be up to you to both identify and solve the tax problems of your clients. But even those of you who pursue some other area of practice must be able at least to identify (not necessarily solve) those ever-lurking tax issues. We hope this book will provide you with a solid foundation in federal income tax no matter what legal career path you choose.

We look forward to working with you. Now, let's begin.

Professor Toni Robinson
Professor Mary Ferrari

Acknowledgments

We are grateful to many people for aiding in the creation of this book. Among those who gave us invaluable assistance are our present or former colleagues Paul Feinberg, Stuart Filler, and Mary Moers Wenig, and especially Alexander M. Meiklejohn for his tireless work in educating us about real estate, help in developing the real estate problems, and insightful comments on various drafts.

We also had the assistance of Quinnipiac's fine law library staff, in particular Christina DeLucia and Larry Raftery, and its technology department, especially Maritza Ramirez and Robin Levitz. For getting us started technologically, we are also indebted to Valerie Jablonowski and Scott Barnett.

Many students assisted us over the years as researchers and proofreaders, especially Nichole Framularo, John Ghidini, Jennifer Golas, James and Susan Hartford, Matthew Jalowiec, Matthew Jaumann, Charlene Jones, Karen Mayer, Thomas McCabe, Jennifer Nelson, Donovan Riley, and Dawn Vigue. Jamie and Susan also made the final production possible through their painstaking rereading of the entire manuscript (double checking with the original sources). Dawn's readiness to help and knowledge of the library were second only to Jamie and Susan's. Joseph Hurley, Dawn Vigue, Tricia White, and John Williams made their class notes available to us so that we could "see" whether we were making sense. We also owe a debt to the many students whose comments, feedback, and identification of typos greatly improved the manuscript.

Without the secretarial help of Rosemary Golia and Sue Passander, this book would still be a stack of notes and tapes. They were indefatigable and handled our (rare) impatience and word processing ineptitude with good humor and grace. Laurie Hurston and Don Nylander always made sure that, no matter how late we gave them the next chapter, they had copies ready for distribution to our students the next morning (and sometimes the same day!).

Deans Neil Cogan, David King, and Brad Saxton were generous with their support, financial and otherwise. We have benefited greatly from the availability of research assistance and other essentials they provided.

Thanks, especially, to several "generations" of Quinnipiac students who, although required to take tax, did so with (mostly) good humor, never complaining that their three-ring binders were bulging with yet another handout.

We also acknowledge, with thanks, the authors, publishers, and copyright holders who have granted us permission to reproduce materials from the following works:

American Law Institute, *Restatement of the Law Third, Restatement of the Law of Property (Mortgages)*, 1997, American Law Institute. Reproduced with Permission. All rights reserved.

Alan J. Auerbach, Kevin A. Hassett, and William G. Gale, Editors, *Toward Fundamental Tax Reform*, 2005. Reprinted with the permission of the American Enterprise Institute for Public Policy Research, Washington, D.C.

Sheldon I. Banoff and Richard Lipton, "More on Historic Homers: Do Auction Prices Control?," 90 J. Tax'n 189 (1999), Warren, Gorham and Lamont.

Sheldon I. Banoff and Richard Lipton, "McGwire's 62nd Home Run: IRS Bobbles the Ball," 89 J. Tax'n 253 (1998), Warren, Gorham and Lamont.

Bruce Bartlett, "Why the Correct Capital Gains Tax Rate Is Zero", 84 Tax Notes 1411 (1999), Tax Analysts, Inc.

Berger and Johnstone, *Land Transfers and Finance: Cases and Materials, Fourth Edition*, 1993. Reprinted with the permission of Aspen Law & Business.

Ira Berkow, "McGwire's 70th Homer Still Defying Gravity," The New York Times, January 13, 1999.

Boris I. Bittker, "Tax Shelters, Nonrecourse Debt, and the Crane Case," 33 Tax L. Rev. 227 (1978), Tax Law Review, New York University School of Law.

Boris I. Bittker, "Federal Income Taxation and the Family," 27 Stan. L. Rev. 1389 (1975), Stanford Law Review.

Boris I. Bittker and Martin J. McMahon, Jr., *Federal Income Taxation of Individuals*, 1995, Warren, Gorham and Lamont.

Black's Law Dictionary, 6th ed., 1990. Reprinted with the permission of The West Group.

Steven Bradford and Gary Ames, *Basic Accounting Principles for Lawyers*, 1997, Anderson Publishing Company.

Marvin Chirelstein, *Federal Income Taxation, Eighth Edition*, 1999, Foundation Press.

Noel B. Cunningham and Deborah H. Schenk, "The Case for a Capital Gains Preference," 48 Tax L. Rev. 319 (1993), The Tax Law Review, New York University School of Law.

Bill Dedman, "Fan Snaring No. 62 Faces Big Tax Bite," The New York Times, September 7, 1998.

Kip Dellinger, "Home Run Balls and Nettlesome Tax Problems," 1998 TNT 177–178 (September 14, 1998), Tax Analysts, Inc. Used with Permission.

Joseph M. Dodge, *The Logic of Tax*, 1989. Reprinted with the permission of The West Group.

Jesse Dukeminier, "A Modern Guide to Perpetuities," 74 Cal. L. Rev. 1867 (1986), California Law Review.

William E. Elwood and Cynthia A. Moore, *Employee Fringe Benefits*, 394—3rd T. M. 1101 (1996), Tax Management Portfolio (U.S.) Series, Bureau of National Affairs.

Pamela Gann, "Abandoning Marital Status as a Factor in Allocating Income Tax," 59 Tex. L. Rev. 1 (1980), Texas Law Review.

Michael J. Graetz, *The U.S. Income Tax: What It Is, How It Got That Way, and Where We Go From Here*, 1999, W.W. Norton & Co.

Robert E. Hall and Alvin Rabushka, *The Flat Tax, Second Edition*. Reprinted with the permission of the publisher, Hoover Institution Press, copyright (c) 1995 by the Board of Trustees of the Leland Stanford, Junior University

Mary Heen, "Plain Meaning, the Tax Code, and Doctrinal Incoherence," 48 Hastings L.J. 771 (1997).

Kohler's Dictionary for Accountants, Sixth Edition, 1983, Prentice-Hall, Inc., Pearson Education.

Stephen Labaton, "Scientologists Granted Tax Exemptions by the U.S.," The New York Times, October 14, 1993.

John W. Lee, "Capital Gains Myths," 67 Tax Notes 809 (1995), Tax Analysts, Inc.

Elizabeth MacDonald, "Scientologists and IRS Settled for $12.5 Million," The Wall Street Journal, December 30, 1997.

Paul R. McDaniel and Stanley Surrey, "The Tax Expenditure Concept: Current Developments and Emerging Issues," 20 B.C. L. Rev. 225 (1979), Boston College Law Review.

McIntyre, et. al., *Readings in Federal Taxation, Second Edition*, (1983), Foundation Press.

Matthew Miller, "A Tax None Will Touch," U.S. News and World Report, August 4, 1997.

Joseph A. Pechman, *Federal Tax Policy, Fifth Edition*, 1987, Brookings Institution Press.

Burgess J.W. Raby and William L. Raby, "Religious Tuition as Charitable Contribution," 88 Tax Notes 215 (2000), Tax Analysts, Inc.

Gail Richmond, *Federal Tax Research, Fifth Edition*, 1997, and *Sixth Edition*, 2002, Foundation Press.

David E. Rosenbaum, "The Fine Print: The Tax Bills; When Lawmakers Look Homeward," The New York Times, July 21, 1999.

St. Petersburg Times, "Sellout to Scientology," excerpt from editorial, January 6, 1998.

Henry C. Simons, *Personal Income Taxation: The Definition of Income as a Problem of Fiscal Policy*, 1938, The University of Chicago Press.

Dan Throop Smith, "High Progressive Tax Rates: Inequity and Immorality?," 20 U. Fla. L. Rev. 451 (1968), University of Florida, Frederic Levin College of Law.

Joseph J. Cordes, Robert D. Ebel, and Jane G. Gravelle, Editors, *The Encyclopedia of Taxation & Tax Policy, CD-ROM Edition*, C. Eugene Steuerle, "Tax reform, federal," 1999, The Urban Institute Press.

Paul Streckfus, "Scientology Case Redux," 87 Tax Notes 1414 (2000), Tax Analysts, Inc.

Lawrence A. Zelenak and Martin J. McMahon, Jr., "Taxing Baseballs and Other Found Property," 84 Tax Notes 1299 (1999), Tax Analysts, Inc.

Federal Income Tax

Introduction

We begin with the most fundamental question: Why tax? Oliver Wendell Holmes answered, simply, that "Taxes are what we pay for civilized society...."[1] But having decided that civilization is desirable and requires government revenues, the legislature[2] has many types of tax among which to choose. The choice will often be guided not only by policy, but by practicality as well. Among the types of tax that a given legislature might enact are income, export, import, sales, excise, and wealth or consumption taxes.

A country may choose one or more of these types of tax to accomplish various government policies or for ease of administration. For example, many European countries impose very high taxes on gasoline to discourage consumption. In contrast, a developing country that exports oil may choose to impose an export tax on its primary export, oil. This type of tax is both easy to administer and will produce a substantial portion of the revenues the country needs for its operations. An economically developed country may, however, adopt a broad range of taxes, including an income tax.

In the United States, the individual states reap substantial revenues from income taxes and from other types of taxes as well, principally sales taxes. Localities depend most heavily for their revenues on property taxes, both real and personal.[3] The federal government depends upon a self-administered[4] income tax system to produce the largest percentage of federal government revenues. The following graphic shows the federal government's sources of income and categories of outlays for fiscal year 2000.[5]

---

1. *Compania General de Tobacos de Filipinas v. Collector*, 275 U.S. 87, 100 (1927) (Holmes J., dissenting).

2. Our use of the term "legislature" is in its broadest sense, *i.e.*, the body, whatever it may be officially designated, that has the authority to make law for any given political unit. Thus, such term, as used here, encompasses legislative bodies as complex as the United States Congress and as simple as a small town council.

3. Can you define the difference between a "real" property and a "personal" property tax?

4. What do you think "self-administered" means in this context?

5. Each year, the instruction book that accompanies the individual income tax return (Form 1040) presents two similar pie charts showing the major categories of federal revenue and outlays for the prior fiscal year.

Major Categories of Federal Income and Outlays for Fiscal Year 2000

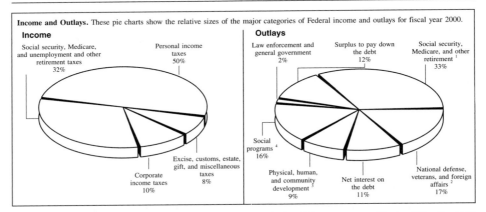

Income and Outlays. These pie charts show the relative sizes of the major categories of Federal income and outlays for fiscal year 2000.

On or before the first Monday in February of each year, the President is required by law to submit to the Congress a budget proposal for the fiscal year that begins the following October. The budget plan sets forth the President's proposed receipts, spending, and the surplus or deficit for the Federal Government. The plan includes recommendations for new legislation as well as recommendations to change, eliminate, and add programs. After receiving the President's proposal, the Congress reviews it and makes changes. It first passes a budget resolution setting its own targets for receipts, outlays, and the surplus or deficit. Next, individual spending and revenue bills that are consistent with the goals of the budget resolution are enacted.

In fiscal year 2000 (which began on October 1, 1999, and ended on September 30, 2000), Federal income was $2,025 billion and outlays were $1,789 billion, leaving a surplus of $236 billion.

Footnotes for Certain Federal Outlays

1. Social security, Medicare, and other retirement: These programs provide income support for the retired and disabled and medical care for the elderly.

2. National defense, veterans, and foreign affairs: About 14% of outlays were to equip, modernize, and pay our armed forces and to fund other national defense activities; about 2% were for veterans benefits and services; and about 1% were for international activities, including military and economic assistance to foreign countries and the maintenance of U.S. embassies abroad.

3. Physical, human, and community development: These outlays were for agriculture; natural resources; environment; transportation; aid for elementary and secondary education and direct assistance to college students; job training; deposit insurance, commerce and housing credit, and community development; and space, energy, and general science programs.

4. Social programs: About 11% of total outlays were for Medicaid, food stamps, temporary assistance for needy families, supplemental security income, and related programs; and 5% for health research and public health programs, unemployment compensation, assisted housing, and social services.

Note. The percentages on this page exclude undistributed offsetting receipts, which were $43 billion in fiscal year 2000. In the budget, these receipts are offset against spending in figuring the outlay totals shown above. These receipts are for the U.S. Government's share of its employee retirement programs, rents and royalties on the Outer Continental Shelf, and proceeds from the sale of assets.

Now compare the pie chart above to the pie chart below that shows the federal government's sources of income and categories of outlays for fiscal year 2004.

Major Categories of Federal Income and Outlays for Fiscal Year 2004

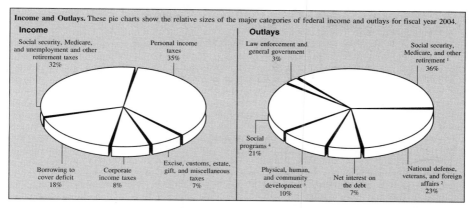

Income and Outlays. These pie charts show the relative sizes of the major categories of federal income and outlays for fiscal year 2004.

Income

Social security, Medicare, and unemployment and other retirement taxes 32%

Personal income taxes 35%

Borrowing to cover deficit 18%

Corporate income taxes 8%

Excise, customs, estate, gift, and miscellaneous taxes 7%

Outlays

Law enforcement and general government 3%

Social security, Medicare, and other retirement[1] 36%

Social programs[4] 21%

Physical, human, and community development[3] 10%

Net interest on the debt 7%

National defense, veterans, and foreign affairs[2] 23%

On or before the first Monday in February of each year, the President is required by law to submit to the Congress a budget proposal for the fiscal year that begins the following October. The budget plan sets forth the President's proposed receipts, spending, and the surplus or deficit for the Federal Government. The plan includes recommendations for new legislation as well as recommendations to change, eliminate, and add programs. After receiving the President's proposal, the Congress reviews it and makes changes. It first passes a budget resolution setting its own targets for receipts, outlays, and the surplus or deficit. Next, individual spending and revenue bills that are consistent with the goals of the budget resolution are enacted.

In fiscal year 2004 (which began on October 1, 2003, and ended on September 30, 2004), federal income was $1.9 trillion and outlays were $2.3 trillion, leaving a deficit of $0.4 trillion.

Footnotes for Certain Federal Outlays

1. **Social security, Medicare, and other retirement:** These programs provide income support for the retired and disabled and medical care for the elderly.

2. **National defense, veterans, and foreign affairs:** About 19% of outlays were to equip, modernize, and pay our armed forces and to fund other national defense activities; about 3% were for veterans benefits and services; and about 1% were for international activities, including military and economic assistance to foreign countries and the maintenance of U.S. embassies abroad.

3. **Physical, human, and community development:** These outlays were for agriculture; natural resources; environment; transportation; aid for elementary and secondary education and direct assistance to college students; job training; deposit insurance, commerce and housing credit, and community development; and space, energy, and general science programs.

4. **Social programs:** About 14% of total outlays were for Medicaid, food stamps, temporary assistance for needy families, supplemental security income, and related programs; and the remaining outlays were for health research and public health programs, unemployment compensation, assisted housing, and social services.

Note. The percentages on this page exclude undistributed offsetting receipts, which were $59 billion in fiscal year 2004. In the budget, these receipts are offset against spending in figuring the outlay totals shown above. These receipts are for the U.S. Government's share of its employee retirement programs, rents and royalties on the Outer Continental Shelf, and proceeds from the sale of assets.

The United States government is limited in its choice of tax systems by certain provisions of the United States Constitution. Although Article I, section 8 of the Constitution authorizes Congress to "lay and collect taxes," it was not until the passage of the Sixteenth Amendment in 1913 that Congress could fully exercise this power by imposing a tax on "income from whatever source derived."

Prior to 1913, of course, the federal government did impose various taxes, most importantly, excise and tariff taxes.[6] Indeed, Alexander Hamilton, the first secretary of the Treasury, "convinced Congress to impose [the first federal] taxes on distilled spirits and carriages"....[7] In the years that followed, Congress added taxes on real estate and slaves. These taxes became increasingly unpopular and difficult to enforce, leading to the defeat of John Adams and the election of Thomas Jefferson in 1800. By 1802, only tariffs

---

6. Don't forget that the Revolution was triggered in part by resentment of the "high-handed" imposition of taxes by the British government ("no taxation without representation"), culminating in the Boston Tea Party. Also, remember that the Constitution prohibits the imposition of export taxes.

7. Michael J. Graetz, *The U.S. Income Tax, What It Is, How It Tax Got That Way, and Where We Go From Here* 13 (W.W. Norton & Co. 1999).

and the tax on salt remained.[8] But the War of 1812 made clear the need for additional sources of revenue and Congress revived many of the old taxes. In 1815, the Treasury secretary proposed the first income and inheritance taxes. But Congress failed to act on these proposed new taxes prior to the War's end in 1815. From the end of the War of 1812 until the Civil War, "the government financed all of its activities from customs duties and sales of public lands."[9]

It was not until the Civil War that Congress first imposed an income tax in order to finance that war.[10] The new income and inheritance taxes, signed by President Lincoln on July 1, 1862, survived a constitutional challenge.[11] Congress later repealed both, the inheritance tax in 1870 and the income tax in 1872. It then reinstated the income tax in 1894, modeled after the Civil War income tax.[12] In 1895, however, in contrast to its view of the Civil War tax, the Supreme Court struck down the tax in its entirety, holding that it was a direct tax not apportioned among the states as required by Article I section 2 of the Constitution.[13] Although the Supreme Court later approved of a corporate income tax, reasoning that it was an excise tax on the privilege of doing business,[14] it took a constitutional amendment to provide the necessary authorization for imposition of a personal income tax.

No sooner had the Sixteenth Amendment become effective on February 25, 1913, than Congress passed the 1913 Tariff Act on October 3, 1913, with an effective date of 1916. This too was challenged; but the Supreme Court held that the new income tax on the net incomes of individuals and corporations was, indeed, constitutionally permissible as a consequence of the new amendment.[15] Thus, the Sixteenth Amendment authorized Congress to choose "income" as the proper base upon which to impose what would become the most important source of federal revenues.

Although the Sixteenth Amendment identifies income as the proper base upon which to impose the tax, it does not define the term "income." Immediately after the adoption of the Sixteenth Amendment, Congress passed the Tariff Act of 1913 which provided:

> there shall be levied, assessed, collected and paid annually upon the entire net income arising or accruing from all sources in the preceding calendar year to every citizen of the United States, whether residing at home or abroad, and to every person residing in the United States, though not a citizen thereof, a tax of 1 per centum per annum upon such income....[16]

---

8. We are indebted for this description to the far more complete history of the income tax that appears in Professor Graetz's 1999 book and at greater length in Michael J. Graetz and Deborah H. Schenk, *Federal Income Taxation: Principles and Policies* 4–15 (3d ed., Foundation Press 1995).

9. Graetz and Schenk at 6.

10. The Civil War income tax applied to all income in excess of $600 at the rate of 3% up to incomes of $10,000. On incomes over $10,000, the rate rose to 5% on the amount of income in excess of $10,000. Graetz and Schenk at 6.

11. *Springer v. United States*, 102 U.S. 586 (1880). Opponents of the income tax contended that it was a "direct" tax and, therefore, must be "apportioned among the several states" as provided in Article I section 2 of the Constitution.

12. The 1894 income tax applied to all income in excess of $4,000 at the rate of 2%. Thus, one might say that the 1894 income tax was the first American "flat" income tax.

13. *Pollack v. Farmers' Loan & Trust Co.*, 158 U.S. 601 (1895).

14. *Flint v. Stone Tracy Co.*, 220 U.S. 107 (1911). The Tariff Act of 1909 imposed a tax of 1% on corporate net income in excess of $5,000.

15. *Brushaber v. Union Pacific Railroad*, 240 U.S. 1 (1916).

16. 38 Stat. 114, 166, c.16 Section II. A (1913).

This language embodies Congress's choice of the basic framework necessary for the determination of the income tax. This language answers the four questions that are fundamental to the construct of any income tax. How does the Tariff Act answer these four questions? **Identify the specific language of the Act that answers each question.**[17]

(1) What is the proper *rate*? °/o a unit is taxed

(2) What is the proper *tax base*? amount that can be taxed / minimum

(3) What is the proper *tax-paying unit*? individual or group

(4) What is the proper *time period*?

Although far longer and more complicated than the Tariff Act of 1913, the income tax provisions of the Internal Revenue Code of 1986[18] reflect these same four choices.

___

17. As noted in the first paragraph of this Introduction, the legislature has many types of tax among which to choose in order to raise revenue. In addition to an income tax, it may choose to impose, for example, as some have recently suggested, a tax on sales or consumption, or to impose a tax on the increase in the value of goods and services at each stage of production, that is, a "value-added tax." Further discussion of these alternatives to the income tax appears later in the text. Without, for the moment, considering the arguments for or against these alternatives, can you formulate how the four questions concerning an income tax might or might not apply to these alternatives?

18. The Internal Revenue Code (hereinafter the "Code"), constitutes Title 26 of the United States Code. (You probably remember looking at Title 28 when you studied Civil Procedure and perhaps Title 18 when you studied Criminal Law.) When Congress enacts and the President signs tax legislation, the bill, like any other law of a session of Congress, receives a public law number. The public law number includes the session of Congress that adopted the legislation and the number of the act. For example, the Tax Reform Act of 1986 is designated "P.L. 99-514," which means that it was the 514th act that the 99th Congress passed. (You can convert easily between the year of enactment and which Congress passed the act by applying the following formulas: (1) to convert from the 99th Congress to the year, multiply times 2 and add 1787; (2) to convert from the year to the Congress, subtract 1787 and divide by 2. Both of these may need adjustment for the fact that each Congress meets for two years—beginning in an odd year. The formula will always produce the first year of the Congress. Thus, 99 x 2 = 198 + 1787 = 1985. Therefore, the formula is somewhat imperfect in that it requires you to know that the tax act actually passed in the second year of that Congress: 1986. But tax lawyers use this method as a short hand way of converting between sessions of Congress and the years of tax legislation. This is particularly important to tax lawyers because of the frequency with which Congress amends the Code.)

The text of the public law (the "sessions law") actually consists of a set of instructions for amending Title 26. Those instructions tell the editors of the United States Code how to edit the Internal Revenue Code to reflect the changes, additions, or deletions made by the public law. The public law usually contains some additional material that does not become part of the Code itself, such as effective dates and, sometimes, transition rules. Therefore, the public law often is important apart from the actual changes it makes to the language of the Code. For example, section 121 of P.L. 99-514 (the Tax Reform Act of 1986) provides as follows:
SEC. 121. TAXATION OF UNEMPLOYMENT COMPENSATION.

Section 85 (relating to unemployment compensation) is amended to read as follows:
"SEC. 85. UNEMPLOYMENT COMPENSATION.

"(a) GENERAL RULE.—In the case of an individual, gross income includes unemployment compensation.

"(b) UNEMPLOYMENT COMPENSATION DEFINED.—For purposes of this section, the term 'unemployment compensation' means any amount received under a law of the United States or of a State which is in the nature of unemployment compensation."
A different section of P.L. 99-514, section 151(b), prescribes the effective rate of the change (which does not become part of the Code:
SEC. 151. EFFECTIVE DATES.

. . .
(b) UNEMPLOYMENT COMPENSATION.—The amendment made by section 121 shall apply to amounts received after December 31, 1986, in taxable years ending after such date.

. . .

LOOK at section
1(j)(2)(A)
through
(E)

ns 1(a) through 1(d) and 1(i) of the Internal Revenue Code of 1986,
after the "Code").[19]

provisions reflect the first three[20] of the choices set forth above:

rate: *graduated rates ranging from 10% to 35%*;[21]

(2) the proper tax base: *taxable income*; and

(3) the proper tax-paying unit: *married individuals who file joint returns and surviving spouses; heads of households; all other unmarried individuals; and married individuals who file separate returns.*

One normally reads a book from beginning to end (sometimes sneaking a peek at the end to see what happens). The first lesson that a novice reader learns about reading the Code is that its beginning, section 1, previews the end of the story rather than introducing its outline. Before we can apply section 1, we must examine in detail the four factors that constitute the fundamental framework necessary for its application. Our examination of the four fundamental questions constitutes a large part of what we will do in this course.

Let's begin with an outline that will sketch out where we will go through the semester in this course. This outline should help you conceptualize, from the beginning, the broad outline of the individual income tax provisions of the Code. It is like the picture on the cover of a jigsaw puzzle box and you will find that each piece will fit into that picture as the course progresses. We present this to you now because many of us need to see the whole picture before being able to understand the relationships among the parts.[22]

---

19. All section references unless otherwise noted, are to the Internal Revenue Code of 1986, as amended.

20. You will note that the "time period" question is not answered in section 1. In tax, as in life, timing is important. Be alert as we proceed through the course to timing issues as they arise in various contexts.

21. In the spring of 2001, Congress (once again) amended the section 1 tax rate tables applicable to taxable incomes beginning in tax year 2001. When complete, the new rates were to range from 10% to 35% (compared to the pre-Act range of 15% to 39.6%). The changes did not apply in their entirety in 2001; rather, the changes were to phase in over a period of years from 2001 through 2006. The Jobs and Growth Tax Relief Reconciliation Act of 2003 (hereinafter the "2003 Act") accelerated the effective date of the reduction so that the rates scheduled to take effect in 2006 became effective in 2003. See section 1(i).

22. Those of you who prefer to put all the pieces of the puzzle together before looking at the picture may be tempted to skip this diagram and come back to it at the end of the course. But a quick glance should not spoil the challenge to you of creating the picture yourself.

CALCULATION OF INCOME TAX PAYABLE BY INDIVIDUALS

Step 1. Determine **GROSS INCOME** (Section 61).

Includes, but is not limited to, items enumerated in section 61(a)(1) through (15), as well as those items specifically included in sections 71 through 90. *Excludes* items provided in sections 101 through 139A.

Step 2. Determine **ADJUSTED GROSS INCOME** (Section 62).

Determine by *subtracting* from GROSS INCOME the deductions "described" in section 62(a)(1) through (a)(20). (Deductions are "authorized" in other sections of the Code.)

Step 3. Determine **TAXABLE INCOME** (Section 63).

Determine by *subtracting* from ADJUSTED GROSS INCOME the following two items:

A. *Either* the "standard deduction" as adjusted for inflation (section 63(c)(1) through (4)) *or* "itemized deductions" (section 63(d) as limited by sections 67 and 68), whichever of the two is *greater*; *and*

B. The deduction for the relevant number of "personal exemptions" (section 151(a) through (d)(2) as adjusted for inflation (section 151(d)(4)) and as limited by section 151(d)(3)).

Step 4. Determine **TOTAL TAX LIABILITY**.

A. Determine TENTATIVE TAX LIABILITY under the applicable filing status as set forth in section 1 (sections 1(a) through 1(d)), by applying the applicable rate to TAXABLE INCOME (sections 1(a) through 1(d) and 1(i), as adjusted for inflation (section 1(f)), and for net capital gain (section 1(h)));

B. *Subtract* from the TENTATIVE TAX LIABILITY any applicable "credits against tax" set forth in sections 21 through 53; and

C. *Add* to the TENTATIVE TAX LIABILITY certain "other taxes", such as the alternative minimum tax (section 55) and the tax on self-employment income (section 1401).

The outline set forth above may be summarized (and simplified) as follows:

GROSS INCOME Section 61

Minus:	Deductions described in section 62
Equals:	**ADJUSTED GROSS INCOME**
Minus:	Deductions described in section 63: Greater of either "standard" or "itemized" deductions plus Personal exemption(s) deduction
Equals:	**TAXABLE INCOME**
Multiplied by:	Applicable section 1 rate
Equals:	**TENTATIVE TAX LIABILITY**
Minus:	Applicable credits against tax
Plus:	Other applicable taxes
Equals:	**TOTAL TAX LIABILITY**

As you proceed through the course, you may wish to use these outlines as a way of organizing the material that the course covers. As is usual for a survey course, the materials will not be exhaustive but illustrative. Nevertheless, at the end of the semester, you will have learned not only quite a bit about the basics of federal income tax, but you will also have learned a great deal about the federal legislative and administrative process, and the techniques for reading and interpreting statutes that you will be able to apply to all statutory material, tax and non-tax, with which you will inevitably be confronted in practice.

I. Defining the "Proper" Rate

Chapter 1

Possible Rate Structures

Since the Tariff Act of 1913,[1] the history of the individual income tax has been one of almost constant rate revisions, but with a consistent reliance on a rate structure that could generally be described as "graduated" or "progressive." As noted, the Civil War tax did not apply to the first $1 of income; rather, the first $600 was free from tax. Then, income up to $10,000 was taxed at one rate; income in excess of $10,000 at a higher rate.[2]

From time to time, policy makers and others (notably politicians) return to the idea that a so-called "flat" tax system would offer a simpler, fairer method of calculating tax than the current "progressive" system. Not only as a lawyer, but, maybe even more importantly, as a tax-paying, voting citizen, you should be able to understand and evaluate these proposals. Before it is possible to do so, however, it is necessary for you to understand the variety of tax rate structures and the benefits and problems associated with each.

A progressive system of tax applies an increasing rate of tax to increasing incremental amounts of income. Therefore, as a taxpayer's income increases, the rate applicable to each incremental amount of income increases. Since 1913,[3] the federal income tax system of the United States has reflected the adoption by Congress of a progressive rate system. But both the different rates and the increments to which they apply have varied widely over the almost 90 years since 1913. Compare the current six-bracket rate schedule you have seen already to the rate schedule for tax year 1944. In 1944, the Code imposed a "normal tax" of 3% of net income and, in addition, a twenty-four bracket "sur-

---

1. 38 Stat. 114, c. 16 (1913).

2. Some commentators have even regarded the 1894 income tax as a graduated tax; although only one rate applied, the first $4,000 of income was free of tax. Therefore, the rates were graduated from 0% to 2%. *See* Robert E. Hall and Alvin Rabushka, *The Flat Tax* 53–54 (2d ed., Hoover Inst. Press 1995).

3. Not only did the Tariff Act of 1913 impose, in section II.A., a tax of "1 per centum per annum" on "entire net income" (referred to as the "normal income tax"), the Act also imposed six additional brackets (referred to as the "additional tax") of 1% each on increasing levels of income as follows:

> 1 per centum per annum upon the amount by which the total net income exceeds $20,000 and does not exceed $50,000, and 2 per centum per annum upon the amount by which the total net income exceeds $50,000 and does not exceed $75,000, 3 per centum per annum upon the amount by which the total net income exceeds $75,000 and does not exceed $100,000, 4 per centum per annum upon the amount by which the total net income exceeds $100,000 and does not exceed $250,000, 5 per centum per annum upon the amount by which the total net income exceeds $250,000 and does not exceed $500,000, and 6 per centum per annum upon the amount by which the total net income exceeds $500,000.

c. 16, 38 Stat. at 166, Section II. A. Subdivision 2.

Thus, the top rate imposed by the Tariff Act of 1913 was 7%.

tax," ranging from 20% to 91%. Therefore, in 1944, the top tax rate was 94%, as shown in the following table:

1944 →

If surtax net income is:	The surtax shall be:
Not over $2,000...................	20% of the surtax net income
Over $2,000 but not over $4,000	$400, plus 22% of excess over $2,000
Over $4,000 but not over $6,000	$840, plus 26% of excess over $4,000
Over $6,000 but not over $8,000	$1,360, plus 30% of excess over $6,000
Over $8,000 but not over $10,000	$1,960, plus 34% of excess over $8,000
Over $10,000 but not over $12,000	$2,640, plus 38% of excess over $10,000
Over $12,000 but not over $14,000	$3,400, plus 43% of excess over $12,000
Over $14,000 but not over $16,000	$4,260, plus 47% of excess over $14,000
Over $16,000 but not over $18,000	$5,200, plus 50% of excess over $16,000
Over $18,000 but not over $20,000	$6,200, plus 53% of excess over $18,000
Over $20,000 but not over $22,000	$7,260, plus 56% of excess over $20,000
Over $22,000 but not over $26,000	$8,380, plus 59% of excess over $22,000
Over $26,000 but not over $32,000	$10,740, plus 62% of excess over $26,000
Over $32,000 but not over $38,000	$14,460, plus 65% of excess over $32,000
Over $38,000 but not over $44,000	$18,360, plus 69% of excess over $38,000
Over $44,000 but not over $50,000	$22,500, plus 72% of excess over $44,000
Over $50,000 but not over $60,000	$26,820, plus 75% of excess over $50,000
Over $60,000 but not over $70,000	$34,320, plus 78% of excess over $60,000
Over $70,000 but not over $80,000	$42,120, plus 81% of excess over $70,000
Over $80,000 but not over $90,000	$50,220, plus 84% of excess over $80,000
Over $90,000 but not over $100,000	$58,620, plus 87% of excess over $90,000
Over $100,000 but not over $150,000	$67,320, plus 89% of excess over $100,000
Over $150,000 but not over $200,000	$111,820, plus 90% of excess over $150,000
Over $200,000...................	$156,820, plus 91% of excess over $200,000

Those who champion the progressive rate structure rely principally on the arguments that as income increases, taxpayers are increasingly able to pay higher taxes and that increased taxes on upper-income taxpayers accomplishes a desirable redistribution of wealth. There is no one explanation for the appeal of a progressive rate structure, although several justifications support its widespread acceptance: the idea that it is fair to tax higher income individuals at a higher rate on their additional dollars, and the idea that the additional dollars mean less to higher income individuals, to name just two. These ideas are often summed up in the phrase "vertical equity."[4]

---

4. Many articles applaud, explain, or criticize a progressive rate structure. Students who are interested might want to begin with Walter J. Blum and Henry Kalven Jr., "The Uneasy Case for Progressive Taxation," 19 U. Chi. L. Rev. 417 (1952). For additional articles of interest, see Donna M. Byrne, "Locke, Property, and Progressive Taxes," 78 Neb. L. Rev. 700 (1999); and Martin J. McMahon and Alice G. Abreu, "Winner-Take-All Markets: Easing the Case for Progressive Taxation," 4 Fla. Tax Rev. 1 (1998).

Adoption of a progressive rate also creates the need to understand the difference between a taxpayer's "effective" (or "average") rate of tax and her "marginal" rate of tax.
To calculate her effective (or average) rate, the taxpayer figures out the total tax due on
her income, and, then, what percentage the tax represents of that income. For example,
Jayne, an unmarried taxpayer whose taxable income for 2006 was $100,000 (assuming
no applicable credits or additional taxes), would find by looking at section 1(c) of the
Code that her total tax liability was $26,522. That, however, would not be Jayne's actual
tax liability for 2006. Read section 1(f), which requires an annual adjustment to the tax
tables set forth in sections 1(a) through (e) so that inflation will not result in tax increases (a phenomenon known as "bracket creep"). Can you explain how bracket creep
occurs?

Section 1(f) provides that the "Secretary shall prescribe tables which shall apply in
lieu of the tables contained in subsections (a), (b), (c), (d), and (e)...." Who is the
"Secretary"? How does the Secretary "prescribe" the tables? Look at sections
7701(a)(11) and 7805(a). Review, for example, Revenue Procedure 2005-70, 2005-47
I.R.B 979, portions of which are set forth below, showing the Secretary's inflation adjustments for tax year 2006. (Because the inflation adjustments require publication of
new tables every tax year, a revenue procedure setting forth the new rate schedule appears late in every year for the following tax year.) The revenue procedure appearing
below is illustrative of the one Treasury issues each year. Compare the rates that appear
in section 1 of your Code with the rates in Revenue Procedure 2005-70. How are they
different?

REVENUE PROCEDURE 2005-70
2005-47 I.R.B. 979

SECTION 1. PURPOSE

This revenue procedure sets forth inflation adjusted items for 2006.

...

SECTION 3. 2006 ADJUSTED ITEMS

.01 Tax Rate Tables. For taxable years beginning in 2006, the tax rate tables under § 1
are as follows:

TABLE 1—*Section 1(a)*.—Married Individuals Filing Joint Returns and Surviving Spouses

If Taxable Income Is:	The Tax Is:
Not over $ 15,100	10% of the taxable income
Over $ 15,100 but not over $ 61,300	$ 1,510 plus 15% of the excess over $ 15,100
Over $ 61,300 but not over $ 123,700	$ 8,440 plus 25% of the excess over $ 61,300
Over $ 123,700 but not over $ 188,450	$ 24,040 plus 28% of the excess over $ 123,700
Over $ 188,450 but not over $ 336,550	$ 42,170 plus 33% of the excess over $ 188,450
Over $ 336,550	$ 91,043 plus 35% of the excess over $ 336,550

TABLE 2—*Section 1(b)*.—Heads of Households

If Taxable Income Is:	The Tax Is:
Not over $ 10,750	10% of the taxable income

Over $ 10,750 but not over $ 41,050	$ 1,075 plus 15% of the excess over $ 10,750
Over $ 41,050 but not over $ 106,000	$ 5,620 plus 25% of the excess over $ 41,050
Over $ 106,000 but not over $ 171,650	$ 21,857.50 plus 28% of the excess over $ 106,000
Over $ 171,650 but not over $ 336,550	$ 40,239.50 plus 33% of the excess over $ 171,650
Over $ 336,550	$ 94,656.50 plus 35% of the excess over $ 336,550

TABLE 3 — *Section 1(c).* — Unmarried Individuals (other than Surviving Spouse and Heads of Households).

If Taxable Income Is:	The Tax Is:
Not over $ 7,550	10% of the taxable income
Over $ 7,550 but not over $ 30,650	$ 755 plus 15% of the excess over $ 7,550
Over $ 30,650 but not over $ 74,200	$ 4,220 plus 25% of the excess over $ 30,650
Over $ 74,200 but not over $ 154,800	$ 15,107.50 plus 28% of the excess over $ 74,200
Over $ 154,800 but not over $ 336,550	$ 37,675.50 plus 33% of the excess over $ 154,800
Over $ 336,550	$ 97,653 plus 35% of the excess over $ 336,550

TABLE 4 — *Section 1(d).* — Married Individuals Filing Separate Returns

If Taxable Income Is:	The Tax Is:
Not over $ 7,550	10% of the taxable income
Over $ 7,550 but not over $ 30,650	$ 755 plus 15% of the excess over $ 7,550
Over $ 30,650 but not over $ 61,850	$ 4,220 plus 25% of the excess over $ 30,650
Over $ 61,850 but not over $ 94,225	$ 12,020 plus 28% of the excess over $ 61,850
Over $ 94,225 but Not over $ 168,275	$ 21,085 plus 33% of the excess over $ 94,225
Over $ 168,275	$ 45,521.50 plus 35% of the excess over $ 168,275

...

.10 Standard Deduction.

(1) In general. For taxable years beginning in 2006, the standard deduction amounts under $ 63(c)(2) are as follows:

Filing Status	Standard Deduction
Married Individuals Filing Joint Returns and Surviving Spouses ($ 1(a))	$ 10,300
Heads of Households ($ 1(b))	$ 7,550
Unmarried Individuals (other than Surviving Spouses and Heads of Households) ($ 1(c))	$ 5,150
Married Individuals Filing Separate Returns ($ 1(d))	$ 5,150

(2) Dependent. For taxable years beginning in 2006, the standard deduction amount under § 63(c)(5) for an individual who may be claimed as a dependent by another taxpayer may not exceed the greater of (i) $ 850, or (ii) the sum of $ 300 and the individual's earned income.

(3) Aged and blind. For taxable years beginning in 2006, the additional standard deduction amounts under § 63(f) for the aged and for the blind are $ 1,000 for each. These amounts are increased to $ 1,250 if the individual is also unmarried and not a surviving spouse.

.11 Overall Limitation on Itemized Deductions. For taxable years beginning in 2006, the "applicable amount" of adjusted gross income under § 68(b), above which the amount of otherwise allowable itemized deductions is reduced under § 68, is $ 150,500 (or $ 75,250 for a separate return filed by a married individual).

. . .

.17 Personal Exemption.

(1) Exemption amount. For taxable years beginning in 2006, the personal exemption amount under § 151(d) is $ 3,300.

(2) Phase out. For taxable years beginning in 2006, the personal exemption amount begins to phase out at, and is completely phased out after, the following adjusted gross income amounts:

Filing Status	AGI— Beginning of Phaseout	AGI— Exemption Fully Phased Out
Married Individuals Filing Joint Returns and Surviving Spouses § 1(a))	$ 225,750	$ 348,250
Heads of Households (§ 1(b))	$ 188,150	$ 310,650
Unmarried Individuals (other than Surviving Spouses and Heads of Households) (§ 1(c))	$ 150,500	$ 273,000
Married Individuals Filing Separate Returns (§ 1(d))	$ 112,875	$ 174,125

. . .

SECTION 4. EFFECTIVE DATE

.01 General Rule. Except as provided in section 4.02, this revenue procedure applies to taxable years beginning in 2006.

After applying the inflation adjustments contained in Revenue Procedure 2005-70, you should find[5] that Jayne's total tax liability for 2006 is $22,331.50.[6] Thus, her *effective* (or *average)* tax rate was $22,331.50 divided by $100,000, or 22.33%.

But, because of the progressive rate structure, Jayne must also know at what rate additional dollars of income will be taxed. This rate is called her "marginal" rate of tax: the rate of tax that will apply to her *next* dollar of taxable income. What was Jayne's marginal rate? Why is it important for a taxpayer (or the taxpayer's advisor) to know the taxpayer's marginal rate?[7] For example, suppose that Jayne's employer had offered her the opportunity to do some extra work that would increase her taxable income by $10,000. How would she analyze the tax effect of the extra income? At what rate would the extra $10,000 be taxed? Might the tax consequences affect her decision whether or not to do the work?

Those who argue for a proportional structure claim that it is unfair to the more productive taxpayers of society to require them to pay a larger percentage of their additional income, and thus, each taxpayer should pay tax at the same proportional rate no matter what her level of income.[8] The current proposals for a flat tax are, in reality, proposals for a proportional tax, although most of the recent public rhetoric focuses on the

---

5. You will find Revenue Procedure 2005-70 in the Internal Revenue Bulletin (hereinafter "I.R.B.") for the 47th week of 2005 at page 979. The I.R.B. provides timely information to taxpayers and their advisors. It is but one of a variety of publications that communicate important tax information. Twice a year, the Government Printing Office binds the weekly I.R.B.'s into Cumulative Bulletin volumes, designating those for the first half of the year with the year followed by "-1" and those for the second half with the year followed by "-2." (Note, however, that some items contained in the weekly bulletin do not become part of the cumulative compilations.) The first Cumulative Bulletin volume for tax year 2005 would be cited 2005-1 C.B. (page). On occasion, the Government Printing Office will issue a third (or even fourth) volume of the cumulative bulletin in order to publish important legislative materials. This occurs most frequently when Congress enacts major tax legislation.

6. **Look at section 3.01, Table 3, of Revenue Procedure 2005-70, which provides the inflation-adjusted section 1(c) tax table for tax year 2006.** (Note: before the changes made by Congress in the spring of 2001, the lowest rate of tax was 15% and the highest was 39.6%, as reflected in section 1 of the Code.) To compute Jayne's federal income tax for 2006, the table shows that if her taxable income was "[o]ver $74,200 but not over $ 154,800" her tax was "$ 15,107.50 plus 28% of the excess over $ 74,200...." Thus, her total tax of $22,331.50 consisted of the sum of two components: (1) $15,107.50 plus (2) $7,224. The first component, $15,107.50, equals the sum of the amount of her tax at each of the successive rates below 28%. In other words, the table does much of the work for the taxpayer. Instead of having to compute the tax at 10% on the first $7,500.50 of income, adding the tax at 15% on the next $23,100 of income (the difference between the first $7,550, and $30,650, the amount of income at which the rate rises to 15%), and adding the tax at 25% on the next $43,550 (the difference between $30,650 and $74,200, the amount of income at which the rate rises to 28%), the total tax on the first $74,200 is built into the table. The second component equals 28% of $25,800, the amount by which her taxable income of $100,000 exceeded $74,200. Calculate Jayne's tax liability for the current year using the revenue procedure applicable to this year.

7. Taxpayers and their advisors use "marginal rate analysis" in determining the "after-tax value" of income-producing investments or activities. Determining a taxpayer's marginal rate will also be important when we discuss the "after-tax value" to a taxpayer of a deduction later on in the course when we deal with deductions in Part II, Chapter 3.

8. President Ronald Reagan was a recent outspoken proponent of the view. During his administration, Congress twice "flattened" the tax rate schedule, first in 1981, by lowering the maximum rate of tax from 70% to 50%, and again in 1986, by reducing the number of rates to just two, 15% and 28%. Under President George Bush, and despite his pledge on the day he accepted his party's nomination for President, Congress, with his agreement, added an additional rate of 31% in 1990. Under President Bill Clinton, Congress added two additional rates: 36% and 39.6%. Under President George W. Bush, Congress added a 10% rate and lowered the top rate gradually from 39.6% to 35%. See note 21 of Introduction.

dercut whatever redistributive policies a society may be pursuing. For example, a special surcharge on high income taxpayers could offset, on the average, the disproportionate benefits that high income taxpayers typically obtain from tax preferences. But the surcharge would be more favorable than a tax base correction to high income taxpayers with above average tax preference income and would unfairly penalize members of that class with below average tax preference income—while exacerbating whatever undesirable economic side effects are produced by high marginal tax rates. Exemptions to all taxpayers, such as the personal exemption, or exemptions granted to a clearly defined income class, such as the low income allowance, need not undercut redistributive policies, since such measures are functionally equivalent to rate adjustments.

A progressive income tax is one that redistributes taxable income in favor of low- and/or middle-income taxpayers by imposing proportionally higher taxes on upper-income taxpayers. This contrasts sharply with a regressive income tax, which imposes proportionally higher taxes on low-and/or middle-income groups. A proportional income tax, the third possibility, seeks to preserve intact whatever inequalities in income distribution existed prior to its imposition.

. . .

Most commentators believe that a personal income tax worthy of respect would exempt the poor from taxation. Low-income relief can take the form of a deduction, a credit, a zero tax rate, or some combination of the above, but whatever its form, it is best understood as a tax rate adjustment, since the purpose and effect of low-income relief is to redistribute tax relevant economic goods in favor of the poor. Thus the proper debate over progressive rates is over the degree of progressivity, not over progressivity itself. Some commentators would impose steeply graduated rates on upper-middle-class and high-income taxpayers in order to reduce the great disparities in economic well-being almost inevitably produced by an economy that rewards individuals for the relative scarcity of the goods and services they are able to offer for sale in the market place. Other commentators suggest that redistribution (except in favor of the poor) is an improper governmental function. The middle position would be to tax the great mass of middle-income taxpayers at a flat rate and to reserve graduated rates for those at the extremes of the income spectrum.[17]

What do the authors mean by the term "tax preferences"? What might the authors mean by "redistributive policies"? What do the authors mean when they say "[l]ow income relief can take the form of a deduction, a credit, a zero tax rate ... but whatever its form, it is best understood as a tax rate adjustment"? **Clue: Look at the income tax calculation outline.**

The debate between a graduated schedule and a flat tax regime has spawned extensive disagreement among legal scholars and economists. But true agreement would require acceptance of common views of morality, philosophy, political economy, and even feminism. Such agreement is unlikely. But, the wide acceptance of a graduated rate schedule probably reflects the intuitive reactions of most of the public. Consider the following anecdote related first by Dan Throop Smith:

---

17. McIntyre, et al., *Readings in Federal Taxation* 74–75 (2d ed., Foundation Press 1983).

The equity and economic issues [of progressivity] were stated in a condensed form by three children in a one-room school in Montana where the author had the challenge of discussing tax policy at the invitation of his daughter, the teacher. In response to the question: What would be a fair tax on a family with an income of 5,000 dollars if a family with 2,000 dollars income paid 200 dollars? The first child said, "500 dollars," thereby showing a predisposition for proportional burdens and perhaps a desire to make use of a newly-acquired familiarity with percentages. A second child immediately disagreed, with the comment that the payment should be more than 500 dollars because "each dollar isn't so important" to the family with the larger income. A third child agreed but with the reservation that the additional tax over 500 dollars shouldn't be "too much more or they won't work so hard." Elaborate theoretical structures concerning diminishing utility and incentives and disincentives are all really refinements of the quasi-intuitive opinions of those children and may not lead to any greater certainty.[18]

Two of the most daunting problems preventing widespread support for the substitution of a flat tax for the current graduated schedule have been the inability of proponents to demonstrate that a flat tax bearing a reasonable rate could produce sufficient revenue to fund government programs, and the remaining suspicion among a substantial number of voters who agree with the second child in Professor Smith's anecdote. Thus, none of the major tax bills of recent years has adopted a flat tax rate, though the number of rates has declined.

---

18. Dan Throop Smith, "High Progressive Tax Rates: Inequity and Immorality?," 20 U. Fla. L. Rev. 451, 452 (1968).

Chapter 2

Current Rate Structure and Some Recent Proposals

From the passage of the first post-Sixteenth Amendment income tax bill, the Tariff Act of 1913, until today, the United States income tax has incorporated a progressive rate structure. At different periods of time since 1913, the federal income tax has been highly progressive—so much so that during certain periods, in tax year 1964, for example, there have been over 30 different rates applicable to increasing amounts of a taxpayer's taxable income; and the top marginal rate on income has been as high as 94%. Recall the 1944 surtax rate schedule.

In 1981, as part of the Economic Recovery Tax Act,[1] Congress lowered the maximum marginal rate to 50%. In 1986, in the name of "tax simplification," Congress amended the rate structure again, providing for only two rates: 15 and 28%.[2] (Query for you to consider during this course: Does a reduction in tax rates necessarily result in simplification?)[3] Since 1986, through a series of amendments, Congress has once again increased the number and progressivity of the rates. After passage of the 2003 Act, section 1 included six basic rates: 10, 15, 25, 28, 33, and 35%.[4]

---

1. P.L. 97-34. (Hereinafter the "1981 Act.")

2. The Tax Reform Act of 1986, P.L. 99-514. (Hereinafter the "1986 Act.")

3. Even though section 1 of the Code, as amended by the 1986 Act, imposed only two rates, 15% and 28%, the 15% rate was phased out gradually for higher income taxpayers so that once a taxpayer's taxable income exceeded a certain level ($113,300 in the case of an individual taxable under section 1 (c)), the taxpayer was paying a flat rate of 28% on any taxable income above that level. This gradual phase-out had the effect of creating a hidden third marginal rate of 33% for certain taxpayers. Old section 1(g) imposed a surtax on high income taxpayers. For these taxpayers, the surtax had the effect of "recapturing" the amount of income that had been taxed at 15%, and, instead, taxing it at 28%. But in order to accomplish that result, certain dollars of earnings were actually taxed at 33%. While a taxpayer's use of the 15% rate was phased out, she, in fact, paid tax at the rate of 33% (28% plus the 5% surtax) on an amount equal to the amount that had been taxed at 15%. Thereafter, her additional income was taxed at 28%. The overall effect was as though her total income had been taxed at 28%.

4. The new rates were part of the Economic Growth and Tax Relief Reconciliation Act of 2001, P.L. 107-16 (hereinafter the "2001 Act"), enacted by Congress in the spring of 2001 and signed into law by President George W. Bush on June 7, 2001, and the Jobs and Growth Tax Relief Reconciliation Act of 2003, P.L. 108-27 (hereinafter the "2003 Act"), enacted by Congress in the spring of 2003 and signed into law by President George W. Bush on May 28, 2003. The 2001 Act changes in tax rates were to occur over a period of years, becoming fully effective by 2006. For 2006 and thereafter the rates were to be 10%, 15%, 25%, 28%, 33%, 35%. The 2003 Act accelerated these rate reductions, making the 2006 rates effective in 2003. All provisions enacted under the 2001 and 2003 Acts sunset for taxable years beginning after December 31, 2010. *See* section 901(a)-(b) of the 2001 Act and section 107 of the 2003 Act. Therefore, for tax years beginning January 1, 2011 or later, tax rates effective prior to the 2001 Act will again apply, unless Congress takes further action. **Review the**

During the 1996 presidential campaign, candidate Steve Forbes proposed replacing the progressive rate structure with a "flat" tax on income varying from 10 to 19%. Candidate Bob Dole proposed revising the current rate structure by enacting an "across-the-board" 15% reduction in rates. (Neither candidate won.) Also during the 1996 campaign, the former Chairman of the House Ways and Means Committee,[5] Bill Archer of Texas, championed scrapping the income tax code entirely and replacing it with some form of "consumption" tax like a national sales tax.[6] Shortly after the success of the George W. Bush administration in achieving passage of the 2001 Act, various reliable news organizations reported that the administration had initiated an examination of various proposals for possible simplification of the current progressive rate tax system or for scrapping the present tax system and replacing it with either a flat tax or a consumption tax system. What do you think would be the effect of these proposals on government revenue? What other objectives might be served by such proposals? In early 2005, President Bush convened a bipartisan Advisory Panel on Federal Tax Reform to explore and recommend options for reform of the current income tax system.[7]

Many tax policy experts believe that "income" is not the appropriate base on which a taxpayer's contribution to the government should be based. Many advocate a "consumption" tax which would tax taxpayers only on the value of what they consume (*i.e.*, purchase) during the year. The advocates of such a system believe that a consumption tax would encourage more saving and would be easier to administer. Critics contend that consumption taxes discriminate against lower-income taxpayers who, frequently, must spend all their incomes. Critics also worry that an even larger underground economy could develop as taxpayers attempt to evade paying a sales tax.

The impetus for many of these recent proposals appears primarily to be simplification of what is, admittedly, a very complex statute. But it may be difficult to reconcile the goal of simplicity with other goals currently reflected in the Code. In addition to raising revenue, the Code has incorporated, almost since its inception, a variety of policy aims:

---

rates in **Revenue Procedure 2005-70**, *supra*, Chapter 1. **and in section 1.** As of this writing Congress is debating whether to make the rate reductions made by the 2001 and 2003 Acts permanent.

In addition, The Taxpayer Relief Act of 1997 amended section 1(h) of the Code. (Hereinafter the "1997 Act.") Prior to the 1997 Act, section 1(h) limited the tax on "net capital gain" to 28%. (We will discuss the meaning of this term later in the course.) Section 1(h), after the 1997 Act and subsequent amendments, now imposes tax on "net capital gain" at different rates ranging from 5% to 28% (0% to 28% beginning in 2008 until 2010), depending upon the nature of the asset that produced the capital gain.

5. Look at section 7 of Article I of the United States Constitution. The traditional starting point for tax legislation has been, because of the Constitution's directive that all revenue bills originate in the House of Representatives, the Ways and Means Committee of the House. In recent years, other committees of the House, including the Budget Committee, and, indeed, the Senate and the executive branch have played an equal, and in some cases, more important role in originating tax legislation. The Senate has sometimes attached riders or made substitutions in bills unrelated to revenue, and, thereby avoided technical violation of Article I, section 7. The President using the bully pulpit, or the Treasury (on its own or at the direction of the President) has created congressional interest in tax legislation. Moreover, recent tax legislation has often been the by-product of the budget process.

6. For citations to scholarly works on the flat tax and a consumption tax, see footnotes 2, 9, and 10, *supra*, ch. 1.

7. Executive Order 13369, issued January 7, 2005, amended June 16, 2005. The Advisory Panel issued its final recommendation on November 1, 2005. You will find its final report and the written testimony of the many experts who appeared at the hearings the Panel conducted throughout the country during the course of its work on its website: *www.taxreformpanel.gov.*

[handwritten: Policy aims]

*[handwritten: } * 3 goals]*

Taxation is a major instrument of social and economic policy. It has three goals: to transfer resources from the private to the public sector; to distribute the cost of government fairly by income classes (vertical equity) and among people in approximately the same economic circumstances (horizontal equity); and to promote economic growth, stability, and efficiency. From these standpoints, the U.S. tax system is both a source of satisfaction and an object of criticism.... The federal part of the tax system is progressive, thus placing a proportionately heavier burden on those who have greater ability to pay, but the degree of progression is modest.... Some say the system is not progressive enough; others believe that the burdens at the top of the income scale, which are mainly due to the taxes on property incomes, are too heavy. But there is a consensus in favor of at least *some* progression in the overall tax burden.... Tax policy is generally regarded as a legitimate device for promoting economic growth and stability, provided the particular measures chosen can accomplish their objectives and do not permit individuals and corporations to escape tax entirely. Within these broad areas of agreement, there is considerable controversy about the relative emphasis that should be placed on equity and economic objectives.

[handwritten: 4th goal – transparency! administrability]

These issues involve difficult, technical questions of law, accounting, and economics. They are often obscured by misunderstanding, lack of information, and even misrepresentation. Yet they have important implications for the welfare of every citizen and for the vitality of the economy.[8]

It is practically a certainty that debate will continue. Because the federal Treasury projected a substantial surplus for the foreseeable future at the end of Bill Clinton's presidency, Congress enacted, at the urging of the George W. Bush administration, a large multi-year tax cut.[9] Then, despite rising budget deficits, Congress again enacted substantial tax cuts in 2003 to stimulate the sluggish economy. As the most recent tax legislation demonstrates, in addition to policy considerations, tax legislation will almost certainly continue to reflect budgetary concerns and the impact of special interests.[10] Moreover, it is certain that the current legislation will not be the last to affect the rate structure of the federal income tax. During your lifetimes, it is likely that Congress will raise or lower rates applicable to taxable income in light of perceptions of fairness and revenue needs, and may even supplement or replace the current tax system with an alternative.

---

8. Joseph A. Pechman, *Federal Tax Policy* 5–7 (5th ed., The Brookings Institution 1987).

9. *See supra* note 4 and accompanying text.

10. For example, section 1529 of the 1997 Act, P.L. 105-34, overruled case law that interpreted section 104(a)(1) of the Code. The issue in these cases was whether certain police officers and fire fighters were entitled to exclude from their gross incomes the amount of disability pay they received because of heart disease or hypertension. These former officers were entitled to receive retirement pay without having to prove that their disabilities were job related. The Internal Revenue Service (hereinafter "the Service") had successfully argued that these amounts did not constitute "amounts received under workmen's compensation acts as compensation for personal injuries or sickness." In addition to pursuing their cause in court, these officers undertook an extensive lobbying campaign to inform their members of Congress of what they perceived as an unfair application of the law by the courts.

II. Defining the "Proper" Tax Base

Introduction

As an eminent analyst of federal income tax policy has noted:

> The basic structure of the federal income tax is simple. Taxpayers add up their income from all taxable sources, subtract certain allowable deductions and exemptions for themselves, their spouses, their children, and other dependents, then apply the tax rates to the remainder, and finally deduct any applicable tax credits.[1]

While accurate, this misleadingly simple statement only hints at the investigation upon which you are just embarking that will introduce you to the broad sweep of the definition of income and some, but by no means all, the allowable exclusions and deductions in this Part. Indeed, much of what you will learn in this course deals with the rules in the Code that govern what is includible in, and excludible from the taxpayer's income, and what the taxpayer may properly subtract from that income in the form of deductions to arrive at "taxable income," the base under our income tax system to which the taxpayer applies the rates. (And yet, there are many items that we will be unable to study. Nevertheless, by the end of this course, you will have the tools to read the Code and understand sections to which you have not been formally introduced or that Congress has added since the date of your course.)

Re-examine the income tax calculation outline we gave you in the Introduction. The structure of individual federal income tax is really no more complicated than this outline. Indeed, in many ways, this outline mirrors in large part the Form 1040 on which individuals report their tax liability to the government every April 15th.[2]

We do not want to leave you with the impression, however, that what you will learn in this course is how to fill out a Form 1040. That is not our purpose. Unlike tax return preparers, who fill in the numbers on 1040s for taxpayers, the tax lawyer's task is very different. Tax lawyers do not generally fill out tax returns[3]; they work (and grapple) directly with primary authorities — the Code, Treasury Regulations, and cases — to prevent and solve tax problems for their clients.[4] For example, they plan the most favorable tax outcome (within the bounds of ethics and the law) for their clients' business or personal financial transactions; they advise their clients whether and how to report specific

---

1. Joseph A. Pechman, *Federal Tax Policy* 64 (5th ed., The Brookings Institution 1987).

2. Recall that in the Introduction to this book, we characterized our federal tax system as "self-administered." The annual voluntary filing of the Form 1040 (or its variations, Forms 1040A and 1040EZ) by a taxpayer is the act that places our self-administered system in motion. (You can find copies of Forms 1040, 1040A, 1040EZ, and certain other forms we refer to in the Forms Appendix to this book. You can find all IRS forms and instructions at the IRS website: *www.irs.gov*).

3. Many tax lawyers do fill out returns from time to time, but it is not the principal focus of their work.

4. What is "primary authority"? If there is "primary authority," is there "secondary authority"?

items on their 1040s; and, when certain items on their clients' returns are challenged by the Internal Revenue Service (hereinafter "the Service"), they formulate arguments in support of the validity of those positions, and they frequently represent these clients at both the administrative level and in court.

In short, our purpose is to impart to you the lawyer's perspective on federal income tax. Our principal focus will be on how to work with the primary tax authorities. As you proceed through the materials during the rest of this course, you will find that what is challenging about federal income tax, from the lawyer-in-training's point of view, is to learn:

(1) to read the Code;

(2) to identify and resolve the interpretive problems and possibilities presented by the words of the Code;

(3) to appreciate the significance of facts;

(4) to learn when and how to use other materials in interpreting the Code; and

(5) to understand and relate legal consequences to basic business transactions.

The goal of this book is to help you learn, practice, and integrate these essential skills that all lawyers, not only tax lawyers, use in their work every day. Our hope is that you will learn to work with the Code (and any other statute) from the inside out, rather than mechanically following instructions for filling out a Form 1040. (Of course, by the end of the semester if you were tempted to do your own tax return for the first time, we wouldn't be surprised to hear that what you have learned this semester enables you to do it with confidence!)

Chapter 1

Some Characteristics of Income

Recall that section 1 of the Code imposes certain rates of tax on a taxpayer's "taxable income." **Refer now to the income tax calculation outline.** Notice that a taxpayer cannot calculate taxable income without first determining gross income. **Now turn to section 61 of the Code: Gross Income Defined.**[1]

Section 61(a) contains a "general definition"[2] followed by a list of 15 illustrative (but not exclusive) items that constitute gross income. Reading 61(a) is not difficult.[3] What *is* difficult is that section 61(a) violates the cardinal rule you learned in first grade: that you should not use the term itself to define the term; *i.e.*, how can the definition of "gross income" be defined by reference to "all income"? Circular, isn't it? Therefore, the materials in the first chapter of this part will help you formulate your own definition of what gross income is by reference to the various authorities that interpret the word "income."

[handwritten note: GI = all income]

---

1. The titles of sections are not part of the statute.

2. Section 61(a), which contains the general definition of gross income, begins with the words "[e]xcept as otherwise provided in this subtitle...." What is "this subtitle"? **Examine the Table of Contents of the Code.** Notice that the Code, like all codes, has a structure. Understanding the structure is vital for reading the Code properly. For example, the definition of gross income in section 61 is applicable only to the subtitle in which section 61 appears, *i.e.*, Subtitle A. If the term "gross income" were to appear in any other subtitle of the Code, you could not assume that its definition would be the same for purposes of the other subtitle. Moreover, grasping the structure at the outset will assist you in understanding how the various provisions fit within the outline. See tax calculation outline.

3. You will find that you can understand many sections of the Code without reference to other materials. To do so, you must begin by reading that section carefully and, if necessary, outlining the section in your own words. Many sections of the Code share a similar organization: subsection (a) contains the general rule and the subsections that follow contain special rules, limitations, and definitions. Once you have read and reread, and, if necessary, outlined the Code section, the first outside source you should consult for assistance in understanding the meaning of the Code is the appropriate Treasury Regulation (hereinafter cited as "Treas. Reg." and sometimes referred to as "regulation"). The Office of Associate Chief Counsel of the Service, and the Assistant Secretary of the Treasury for Tax Policy and the Office of Tax Legislative Counsel of the Department of the Treasury draft and issue regulations that appear in Title 26 of the Code of Federal Regulations (hereinafter "C.F.R."). (Note that the title of the C.F.R. that contains treasury regulations, Title 26, is the same numbered title of the United States Code that contains the Internal Revenue Code, Title 26.) Regulations are designated by reference to the section of the Code to which they apply. For example, regulations pertaining to section 61 of the Code are designated 1.61-. **Find Treasury Regulation §1.61-1(a).**

A. *Glenshaw Glass*: A Working Definition?

Perhaps the most famous case that defines what gross income is for purposes of the definition of section 61(a) is the following one, decided in 1955 by the United States Supreme Court. Although the first year of law school may lead new law students to think that the most significant law is made in the appellate courts, that is rarely true in federal income tax; the most important interpretations of the Code come from other sources, as you will soon learn.

Nevertheless, certain tax cases do reach the appellate courts, including the Supreme Court, and many of those cases, especially those decided by the high Court, have lasting importance despite the trouble that the Supreme Court often has in dealing with tax issues. This is particularly true of a number of early Supreme Court decisions that deal with basic principles. As you read these cases, however, do not be afraid to be critical of the reasoning that the majority (or minority) uses in deciding a tax case.

COMMISSIONER v. GLENSHAW GLASS CO.[4]
348 U.S. 426 (1955)

MR. CHIEF JUSTICE WARREN delivered the opinion of the Court.

This litigation involves two cases with independent factual backgrounds yet presenting the identical issue.... The common question is whether money received as exemplary damages for fraud or as the punitive two-thirds portion of a treble-damage antitrust recovery must be reported by a taxpayer as gross income under §22 (a) of the Internal Revenue Code of 1939. In a single opinion ... the Court of Appeals affirmed the Tax Court's separate rulings in favor of the taxpayers.... Because of the frequent recurrence of the question and differing interpretations by the lower courts of this Court's decisions bearing upon the problem, we granted the Commissioner of Internal Revenue's ensuing petition for certiorari....

The facts of the cases were largely stipulated and are not in dispute. So far as pertinent they are as follows:

Commissioner v. Glenshaw Glass Co. — The Glenshaw Glass Company, a Pennsylvania corporation, manufactures glass bottles and containers. It was engaged in protracted litigation with the Hartford-Empire Company, which manufactures machinery of a character used by Glenshaw. Among the claims advanced by Glenshaw were demands for exemplary damages for fraud and treble damages for injury to its business by reason of Hartford's violation of the federal antitrust laws. In December, 1947, the parties concluded a settlement of all pending litigation, by which Hartford paid Glenshaw approximately $800,000. Through a method of allocation which was approved by the Tax Court, ... it was ultimately determined that, of the total settlement, $324,529.94 represented payment of punitive damages for fraud and antitrust violations. Glenshaw did not report this portion of the settlement as income for the tax year involved. The Commissioner determined a deficiency claiming as taxable the entire sum....

---

4. We have edited the cases in this book to reduce the amount of reading in order to enable you to focus on the important points. We have retained only those footnotes that aid in understanding the points we intend the cases to illustrate. To avoid confusing case footnotes with those in the text, we have placed the footnotes to a case at the end of the case.

Commissioner v. William Goldman Theatres, Inc. — William Goldman Theatres, Inc., a Delaware corporation operating motion picture houses in Pennsylvania, sued Loew's, Inc., alleging a violation of the federal antitrust laws and seeking treble damages. After a holding that a violation had occurred, ... [i]t was found that Goldman had suffered a loss of profits equal to $125,000 and was entitled to treble damages in the sum of $375,000.... Goldman reported only $125,000 of the recovery as gross income and claimed that the $250,000 balance constituted punitive damages and as such was not taxable....

It is conceded ... that there is no constitutional barrier to the imposition of a tax on punitive damages. Our question is one of statutory construction: are these payments comprehended by § 22 (a)?

The sweeping scope of the controverted statute is readily apparent:

"SEC. 22. GROSS INCOME.

"(a) GENERAL DEFINITION. — 'Gross income' includes gains, profits, and income derived from salaries, wages, or compensation for personal service ... of whatever kind and in whatever form paid, or from professions, vocations, trades, businesses, commerce, or sales, or dealings in property, whether real or personal, growing out of the ownership or use of or interest in such property; also from interest, rent, dividends, securities, or the transaction of any business carried on for gain or profit, *or gains or profits and income derived from any source whatever....*"

This Court has frequently stated that this language was used by Congress to exert in this field "the full measure of its taxing power." ... Respondents contend that punitive damages, characterized as "windfalls" flowing from the culpable conduct of third parties, are not within the scope of the section. But Congress applied no limitations as to the source of taxable receipts, nor restrictive labels as to their nature. And the Court has given a liberal construction to this broad phraseology in recognition of the intention of Congress to tax all gains except those specifically exempted.... Thus, the fortuitous gain accruing to a lessor by reason of the forfeiture of a lessee's improvements on the rented property was taxed in *Helvering v. Bruun*, 309 U.S. 461.... Such decisions demonstrate that we cannot but ascribe content to the catchall provision of § 22 (a), "gains or profits and income derived from any source whatever." The importance of that phrase has been too frequently recognized since its first appearance in the Revenue Act of 1913 to say now that it adds nothing to the meaning of "gross income."

...

Here we have instances of undeniable accessions to wealth, clearly realized, and over which the taxpayers have complete dominion. The mere fact that the payments were extracted from the wrongdoers as punishment for unlawful conduct cannot detract from their character as taxable income to the recipients. Respondents concede, as they must, that the recoveries are taxable to the extent that they compensate for damages actually incurred. It would be an anomaly that could not be justified in the absence of clear congressional intent to say that a recovery for actual damages is taxable but not the additional amount extracted as punishment for the same conduct which caused the injury. And we find no such evidence of intent to exempt these payments.

It is urged that re-enactment of § 22 (a) without change since the Board of Tax Appeals held punitive damages nontaxable in *Highland Farms Corp.*, 42 B. T. A. 1314, indicates congressional satisfaction with that holding. Re-enactment — particularly without the slightest affirmative indication that Congress ever had the *Highland Farms* decision before it — is an unreliable indicium at best.... Moreover, the Commissioner promptly published his nonacquiescence in this portion of the *Highland Farms* holding and has, before and since, consistently maintained the position that these receipts are taxable. It therefore cannot be said with certitude that Congress intended to carve an exception out of § 22 (a)'s pervasive coverage. Nor does the 1954 Code's legislative history, with its reiteration of the proposition that statutory gross income is "all-inclusive," give support to respondents' position. The definition of gross income has been simplified, but no effect upon its present broad scope was intended. (Footnote 11) Certainly punitive damages cannot reasonably be classified as gifts, ... nor do they come under any other exemption provision in the Code. We would do violence to the plain meaning of the statute and restrict a clear legislative attempt to bring the taxing power to bear upon all receipts constitutionally taxable were we to say that the payments in question here are not gross income....

Reversed.

FOOTNOTES:

11. In discussing § 61 (a) of the 1954 Code, the House Report states:

"This section corresponds to section 22 (a) of the 1939 Code. While the language in existing section 22 (a) has been simplified, the all-inclusive nature of statutory gross income has not been affected thereby. Section 61 (a) is as broad in scope as section 22 (a). *transition to §61*

"Section 61 (a) provides that gross income includes 'all income from whatever source derived.' This definition is based upon the 16th Amendment and the word 'income' is used in its constitutional sense." H. R. Rep. No. 1337....

Consider the following questions about *Glenshaw Glass.*

1. What are "exemplary damages"? Look back at the case: how does the Court describe these damages? Are they different from the treble damages mentioned?

2. How much did Hartford pay Glenshaw? How did Glenshaw treat this payment for tax purposes?

3. How much did Loew's pay William Goldman Theatres? Did William Goldman Theatres treat its receipt in the same manner as Glenshaw?

4. What issue did the Court decide? Can you find the language in which the Court describes the issue?

5. If section 61 defines "gross income," why does the Supreme Court refer to section 22?

6. What were the precise words of section 22 that the Court interpreted in deciding this case? Are the words in section 61 similar enough to the words construed by the Court in section 22 to make it reasonable to conclude that the same interpretation applies today to section 61?

7. What is the significance of the Court's discussion of "re-enactment"?

8. Can you venture a guess as to what it means when the Commissioner[5] publishes a "nonacquiescence"? You should be able to based on the plain meaning of the word.

---

5. Who is the "Commissioner"? **Glance at section 7803(a).**

Whenever a court renders a decision adverse to the position of the Service, a special office in the Office of the Chief Counsel issues a written statement, informing the public whether the Service will acquiesce or nonacquiesce in the result. Nonacquiescence indicates that the Service will continue to litigate the issue.

9. What factors did the Court rely on to determine whether the receipts constituted gross income?

Keep these factors in mind as you go on in this chapter and ask yourself whether these factors are as useful in identifying items of income as is implied in the Court's opinion.

1. Accessions to Wealth

Suppose that you are a practicing lawyer. A person you have never met before (she found your name in the yellow pages where you advertise that you prepare simple wills for $1,000), comes to your office one day and asks you to draft a will for her. You prepare her will and she pays you $1,000 in cash. Have you had an "accession to wealth"? Look back to the decision of the Supreme Court in *Glenshaw Glass*. How would you define "an accession to wealth"? Is there anything in section 61(a) that helps you answer this gross income question? Is there anything in the section 61 regulations?

Would your answer change if she paid you by check? Suppose she tells you that she does not have the money to pay you, but she has a bond worth $1,000? What is a "bond"? Suppose instead of paying you anything, you ask her to pay to your dentist the $1,000 you owe him for a root canal? You never receive the money. Can you have an "accession to wealth"? Consider the facts and arguments in the following case.

OLD COLONY TRUST CO. v. COMMISSIONER
279 U.S. 716 (1929)

MR. CHIEF JUSTICE TAFT delivered the opinion of the Court.

. . .

No. 130 comes here by certificate from the Circuit Court of Appeals for the First Circuit. The action in that court was begun by a petition to review a decision of the United States Board of Tax Appeals. The petitioners are the executors of the will of William M. Wood, deceased. On June 27, 1925, before Mr. Wood's death, the Commissioner of Internal Revenue notified him by registered mail of the determination of a deficiency in income tax against him for the years 1919 and 1920, under the Revenue Act of 1918. The deficiency was revised by the Commissioner August 18, 1925. An appeal was taken to the Board of Tax Appeals.... The Board approved the action of the Commissioner and found a deficiency in the federal income tax return of Mr. Wood for the year 1919 of $708,781.93, and for the year 1920 of $350,837.14....

[handwritten margin note: "deficiency"]

The facts certified to us are substantially as follows:

William M. Wood was president of the American Woolen Company during the years 1918, 1919 and 1920. In 1918 he received as salary and commissions from the company $978,725, which he included in his federal income tax return for 1918. In 1919 he received as salary and commissions from the company $548,132.27, which he included in his return for 1919.

August 3, 1916, the American Woolen Company had adopted the following resolution, which was in effect in 1919 and 1920:

"Voted: That this company pay any and all income taxes, State and Federal, that may hereafter become due and payable upon the salaries of all the officers of the company, including the president, William M. Wood; ... to the end that said persons and officers shall receive their salaries or other compensation in full without deduction on account of income taxes, State or Federal, which taxes are to be paid out of the treasury of this corporation."

This resolution was amended on March 25, 1918, as follows:

"Voted: That, in referring to the vote passed by this board on August 3, 1916, in reference to income taxes, State and Federal, payable upon the salaries or compensation of the officers and certain employees of this company, the method of computing said taxes shall be as follows, viz:

"'The difference between what the total amount of his tax would be, including his income from all sources, and the amount of his tax when computed upon his income excluding such compensation or salaries paid by this company.'"

Pursuant to these resolutions, the American Woolen Company paid to the collector of internal revenue Mr. Wood's federal income and surtaxes due to salary and commissions paid him by the company, as follows:

Taxes for 1918 paid in 1919 . . . . . . $ 681,169.88
Taxes for 1919 paid in 1920 . . . . 351,179.27

The decision of the Board of Tax Appeals here sought to be reviewed was that the income taxes of $681,169.88 and $351,179.27 paid by the American Woolen Company for Mr. Wood were additional income to him for the years 1919 and 1920.

The question certified by the Circuit Court of Appeals for answer by this Court is:

"Did the payment by the employer of the income taxes assessable against the employee constitute additional taxable income to such employee?"

. . .

Coming now to the merits of this case, we think the question presented is whether a taxpayer, having induced a third person to pay his income tax or having acquiesced in such payment as made in discharge of an obligation to him, may avoid the making of a return thereof and the payment of a corresponding tax. We think he may not do so. The payment of the tax by the employers was in consideration of the services rendered by the employee and was a gain derived by the employee from his labor. The form of the payment is expressly declared to make no difference.... It is therefore immaterial that the taxes were directly paid over to the Government. The discharge by a third person of an obligation to him is equivalent to receipt by the person taxed. The certificate shows that the taxes were imposed upon the employee, that the taxes were actually paid by the employer and that the employee entered upon his duties in the years in question under the express agreement that his income taxes would be paid by his employer. This is evidenced by the terms of the resolution passed August 3, 1916, more than one year prior to the year in which the taxes were imposed. The taxes were paid upon a valuable consideration, namely, the services rendered by the employee and as part of the compensation therefor. We think therefore that the payment constituted income to the employee.

. . .

Nor can it be argued that the payment of the tax in No. 130 was a gift. The payment for services, even though entirely voluntary, was nevertheless compensation within the statute. This is shown by the case of *Noel v. Parrott*, 15 F. 2d 669. There it was resolved that a gratuitous appropriation equal in amount to $3 per share on the outstanding stock of the company be set aside out of the assets for distribution to certain officers and employees of the company and that the executive committee be authorized to make such distribution as they deemed wise and proper. The executive committee gave $35,000 to be paid to the plaintiff taxpayer. The court said, p. 672:

"In no view of the evidence, therefore, can the $35,000 be regarded as a gift. It was either compensation for services rendered, or a gain or profit derived from the sale of the stock of the corporation, or both; and, in any view, it was taxable as income."

It is next argued against the payment of this tax that if these payments by the employer constitute income to the employee, the employer will be called upon to pay the tax imposed upon this additional income, and that the payment of the additional tax will create further income which will in turn be subject to tax, with the result that there would be a tax upon a tax. This it is urged is the result of the Government's theory, when carried to its logical conclusion, and results in an absurdity which Congress could not have contemplated.

In the first place, no attempt has been made by the Treasury to collect further taxes, upon the theory that the payment of the additional taxes creates further income, and the question of a tax upon a tax was not before the Circuit Court of Appeals and has not been certified to this Court. We can settle questions of that sort when an attempt to impose a tax upon a tax is undertaken, but not now.... It is not, therefore, necessary to answer the argument based upon an algebraic formula to reach the amount of taxes due. The question in this case is, "Did the payment by the employer of the income taxes assessable against the employee constitute additional taxable income to such employee?" The answer must be "Yes."

Consider the following questions about *Old Colony*.

1. Describe in your own words the arrangement between the taxpayer, William M. Wood, and his employer, the American Woolen Company, during the tax years in question.

2. Was this arrangement the same as the usual withholding and payment of federal income and FICA taxes that employers are required to do on behalf of their employees? **Recall withholding and FICA discussion in Part I, Chapter 1.** Does *Old Colony* have any applicability to withholding?

3. Can you formulate the rule set forth by the Court in *Old Colony*?

4. Why did the taxpayer argue that the payment by the American Woolen Company was a gift? **Glance at section 102(a).**

5. What do you think is meant by the phrase "determination of a deficiency"? Who "determined" the "deficiency"? Who "found" a "deficiency"?

Look at sections 6211(a), 6212(a), and 6213(a). These sections introduce you to one of the ways, procedurally, that a tax dispute begins. A hint to help you: the Board of Tax Appeals, sometimes referred to as "the Board," the court in which the *Old Colony* litigation began, is the predecessor to the United States Tax Court (usually referred to as the

"Tax Court"), the trial-level court in which most tax litigation occurs.) Make sure as you read the cases that you pay attention to the procedural history. By focusing on procedural history, you can learn a lot about tax litigation, which is somewhat different from other federal litigation with which you may be familiar.

In reality, a potential tax dispute begins much earlier than the litigation stage. In order for you to understand fully the procedural history of the cases you will read during this course, we must take a short detour to examine a brief outline of federal tax procedure.[6]

A Brief Introduction to Federal Tax Procedure

we file returns annually

In the Introduction to this book, we noted that the current system of federal income tax is "self-administered." Review Introduction, footnote 4 and accompanying text. Remember that section 1 of the Code imposes a tax on each person's "taxable income." The Code grants authority to the Service to formulate appropriate forms to enable taxpayers to calculate taxable income and report it to the Service.[7] For most individual taxpayers, the Service requires completion of one of the variations of Form 1040; *e.g.,* Form 1040, 1040A, 1040EZ. (You can find copies of Forms 1040, 1040A, 1040EZ, and certain other forms we refer to in the Forms Appendix to this book or at the IRS website: *www.irs.gov*). **Examine blank copies of Forms 1040, 1040A, and 1040EZ in the Forms Appendix.** The final step in completing the return is the calculation of the amount of tax due. Find the appropriate line on Form 1040. When a taxpayer completes and files one of these tax returns showing a tax liability due, she is said to have "self-assessed" that liability. She must then satisfy the liability through some combination of payments, including amounts withheld and paid over by her employer, estimated payments made by the taxpayer during the tax year, and payments made with the filing of the return.

As you will soon learn, the determination of tax can be quite complex for some taxpayers. You might wonder, therefore, why the government would allow taxpayers such broad authority in assessing their own taxes. Does this authorization give taxpayers an

---

6. The procedural provisions of the Code appear in "Subtitle F—Procedure and Administration." Because of its complexity, many tax lawyers consider tax procedure as a specialty unto itself. The introduction that we provide you with here gives you only a bare outline to aid your understanding of the cases.

7. Section 6001 provides: "Every person liable for any tax imposed by this title, or for the collection thereof, shall keep such records, render such statements, make such returns, and comply with such rules and regulations as the Secretary may from time to time prescribe...." Section 6011(a) further provides:

> When required by regulations prescribed by the Secretary any person made liable for any tax imposed by this title, or with respect to the collection thereof, shall make a return or statement according to the forms and regulations prescribed by the Secretary. Every person required to make a return or a statement shall include therein the information required by such forms or regulations.

Other countries have utilized other methods for calculating and reporting income and collecting tax but none has achieved as great a level of compliance as the United States.

incentive to underestimate their tax liabilities? Even though this would seem to be the case, in fact, it is not. One of the responsibilities of the Service is to insure that taxpayers engage in the process of self-assessment in a manner that produces the correct tax result.[8] The Service fulfills part of its responsibility for administering the collection of taxes through the audit process.

The Service has no right to collect any taxes until those taxes have been "assessed." But the Service can only assess taxes as a consequence of the taxpayer's self-assessment or through the audit process.[9] Although "assessment" is nothing more than the ministerial act of recording a taxpayer's tax liability, it is, nonetheless, the key to the collection of taxes.

It also divides review of a taxpayer's proper tax liability into two parts. That is, it is proper to regard the review process as having two phases: one before assessment, in which review is made by the Service and the United States Tax Court, and one after assessment, in which review is generally available only in the federal district court or the Claims Court.[10]

---

8. To insure that taxpayers include items of income on their returns, the Code imposes reporting requirements on many payors to report payments made. In some cases, the Code goes a step farther and requires the payor to withhold a part of the payment and turn it over to the Service as an advance payment of tax on behalf of the payee. Most well-known of these is, of course, the withholding requirement imposed on employers under sections 3401–3404. But the Code also requires, for example, payors of more than $5,000 of gambling winnings to withhold 28% of the payments, section 3402(q), and payors of interest to non-resident aliens to withhold a portion for tax, section 1441. These provisions, requiring the withholding of tax from income at its source, help insure that the Service will both know about the payments and have a better chance of collection of taxes.

9. In addition to her original return, although there is no specific provision in the Code allowing the procedure, the Service has long allowed a taxpayer to file an amended return on Form 1040X. **See Form 1040X in the Forms Appendix.** If the amendment reflects an additional amount of tax due, she has "self-assessed" this additional amount and the Service may then assess and collect this additional amount. If the amended return claims a smaller amount of tax was actually due, the Service treats the amended return as a claim for refund. If the Service accepts the taxpayer's amended return as accurate, the Service revises the taxpayer's record. If the taxpayer has paid the amount of tax shown on the original return in full, the Service will refund the excess amount of tax, provided the taxpayer files the amended return by the later of two years from the time she paid the tax or three years from the day the return was "filed." See section 6511(a). For this purpose, the return is "filed" on the later of the date it was due or the date on which it was, in fact, filed. See section 6513. If the Service does not agree with the taxpayer's amended return that claims a refund, it will deny the claim. In that case, the taxpayer may seek judicial review. See *infra*, text at notes 19–23.

10. The Internal Revenue Service Restructuring and Reform Act of 1998, P.L. 105-206 (hereinafter the "1998 Act"), added sections 6320 and 6330 to the Code. The new sections amend the collection process in order to provide taxpayers with additional protections from the perceived harshness of the lien and levy procedures. In sum, the taxpayer now has the right to a "fair hearing," similar to the fair hearings allowed by other federal statutes, *e.g.*, disability benefits, Medicaid benefits. The new sections grant broad authority to the Tax Court and district courts to review determinations made by the Service as to the appropriateness of the proposed collection activities. Because the statutory language and legislative history are quite sweeping, the extent of the new review authorization will probably remain unclear for some years until interpreted by the courts. Prior to the 1998 legislation, the Service already had certain limited post-assessment review procedures. These include the practice of the Service of referring returns to the audit division when a taxpayer files a claim for refund and the ability of a taxpayer to seek administrative review of the assessment of certain penalties. (For example, the Service may impose a negligence penalty.)

Each year the Service selects a number of returns for audit.[11] Most audits of individual taxpayer returns are either "correspondence" or "office" audits.[12] Correspondence audits generally involve one or more issues for which the Service seeks verification that a taxpayer can supply easily through correspondence. If the issues are more complex or will require extensive documentation, the Service will summon the taxpayer to an office audit. The taxpayer has the burden of proving each item on her return.[13] Rarely, however, does the Service require proof of all items;[14] rather, it generally identifies certain

---

11. Audits range from "tattle-tale" and "infection" audits (in which the return is selected based upon the identity of the preparer or the results of another taxpayer's audit, for example) to so called "DIF" score audits (in which the Service selects the return for audit based upon the high "DIF" score the return received). The Service has developed a scoring system, the "DIF" system ("discriminant information function") representing the high probability of error on the return as a consequence of its variation from returns of similarly situated taxpayers. The Service guards the criteria it applies in the "DIF" selection process with extraordinary zeal. It does, however, reveal some information concerning the number of random audits it carries out at various levels of income and the identity of specific audit projects directed at certain types of taxpayer activity. The 1998 Act required the Service to incorporate in one of the publications it makes available to the public, Publication 1, "Your Rights As A Taxpayer," in simple language, the criteria it uses for selecting returns for audit. **Examine Publication 1.** (You can find Publication 1 and certain others in the Publications Appendix to this book. You can find all IRS publications at the IRS web site: *www.irs.gov*). For more information on examinations, see Publication 556.

12. The Service frequently audits business taxpayers at their business locations because the relevant records are generally too voluminous to bring into an Internal Revenue Service office. This type of audit is called a "field" audit.

13. The burden of proof has long been a subject of controversy and became a "hot-button" issue during Congress's deliberations of the 1998 Act. The traditional rule has always been that the taxpayer bears the burden of proof in civil tax controversies. Why? Because in our self-administered system, the taxpayer files a return based upon information that is in the hands of the taxpayer-preparer. Therefore, the argument went, the appropriate party to justify what was on the return was the taxpayer. During the debate on the 1998 Act, various committees and subcommittees of the Congress held public hearings, many of which focussed on the complaints of taxpayers and exposure of the Service's real and perceived misdeeds. Widely reported by a by-and-large uncritical media, these hearings produced greater excoriation of the agency by legislators than at any time in at least recent memory. One change that, therefore, gained wide public and legislative support was reversal of the burden of proof. The tax bar, in contrast, opposed the reversal, citing the obvious opportunities reversal would create for avoidance or even evasion. In the end, Congress enacted a provision, section 7491, that appears to grant the public what it wanted: reversal of the burden of proof. But, in reality, the new provision may prove a trap for the unwary: the burden does not shift until the controversy reaches a court and then only if the taxpayer has complied with the requirements to substantiate items on the return, has maintained all records required, and has cooperated with reasonable requests by the Service for witnesses, information, documents, meetings, and interviews. **Read section 7491.** Therefore, the taxpayer who now thinks that the shift in the burden of proof relieves him of the obligation to keep adequate records to substantiate all items on the return may be in for an unpleasant shock when he is to produce the "credible evidence" in court, required by section 7491 to shift the burden of proof.

14. Until 1988, the Service periodically conducted taxpayer compliance management program (hereinafter "TCMP") audits in which randomly selected taxpayers of all income levels were required to prove each item on their returns. The Service used the information it gained from these audits to develop the DIF scoring system that it used to identify returns that had a high probability of error. Taxpayers, not surprisingly, often found the TCMP audits to be more onerous than ordinary audits. Taxpayer complaints about these audits led to unfavorable comments by important members of Congress. As a result, the Service suspended its conduct of TCMP audits, abandoning its plan to conduct a new round in 1994.

In 2002, the Service began to implement a new audit program, the National Research Program (hereinafter "NRP"), to measure taxpayer compliance. The stated goal of the program is to gather the data needed to measure compliance, but to minimize the burden on taxpayers. The Service will use the data it collects through the NRP to update its return-selection formulas. Unlike the burdensome TCMP audits, which required line-by-line substantiation by taxpayers, NRP audits are con-

items that may appear unusual for the type of taxpayer involved and it asks the taxpayer to prove her entitlement to those items.

Upon completion of an audit, the examining agent may recommend that there be no changes to the return or, in many cases, the agent may propose certain adjustments that result in either a refund to the taxpayer or, more likely, an increase in the taxpayer's tax liability. If the agent proposes an increase in the taxpayer's tax liability, the difference in tax liability between what the taxpayer reported on her return and what the agent has proposed is known as a "deficiency" in tax. If the agent proposes an increase in tax liability, the taxpayer has two choices: agree or disagree. If the taxpayer agrees with the agent's adjustments, she will sign a Form 870, allowing the Service to assess and collect the additional tax liability. **See Form 870 in the Forms Appendix.** If the taxpayer disagrees with the agent's adjustments, the Service will send her a formal notice of its proposed adjustments (called a "30-day letter"). The taxpayer then has 30 days to "protest" the findings and request a review by an appeals officer.[15]

If the taxpayer does nothing in response to the 30-day letter, or if the appeals officer concurs with the original auditor's proposed adjustments (or finds new adjustments), the taxpayer will receive a Notice of Deficiency (called a "90-day letter"). The 90-day letter will set forth the proposed adjustments that result in a change in tax liability. **See Notice of Deficiency in the Forms Appendix.** These adjustments may be the same as those proposed by the initial auditor or may be the result of different conclusions at the appeals level.

The 90-day letter is commonly referred to as a taxpayer's "Ticket to the Tax Court" because the taxpayer has 90 days from the date of mailing of the notice to petition the United States Tax Court[16] for a redetermination of her tax liability for the year in question.[17] **See copy of Petition to the Tax Court in the Forms Appendix.** The Service is required to send the taxpayer a 90-day letter before it may assess a deficiency in tax.[18]

---

ducted through the use of information contained in the Service's databases, so the audits will cover only the lines on selected returns that the Service is unable to verify. Thus, some items will be examined without the need to contact the taxpayer; some will be examined through correspondence only; and those returns requiring face-to-face examination will focus only on certain lines on the return. According to the Service, very few of the returns selected under the NRP will be subject to the same face-to-face, line-by-line scrutiny that caused so much criticism of the TCMP audits. In June, 2007, the Service announced plans to conduct a new NRP reporting compliance study, beginning in October, 2007. It plans to examine approximately 13,000 randomly selected 2006 tax returns, and similar numbers in subsequent years. The Service hopes that using a rolling three-year period will enable it to "make annual updates to compliance estimates and develop more efficient workload plans on an annual basis, after the initial three annual studies." IR-2007-113, June 6, 2007.

15. A "protest" is not simply a letter stating that the taxpayer disagrees. If the amount in controversy is less than $2,500, the taxpayer may make an oral request for a conference. If, however, the amount is $2,500 or more, a "brief written statement of disputed issues" is required if the taxpayer seeks a conference. For amounts exceeding $10,000, the taxpayer must submit a lengthier written document, similar to a brief, including a statement of facts and a statement outlining the law or other authority supporting the taxpayer's position. See 26 C.F.R. sections 601.105, -106. **For further information on the appeals process and protest requirements see Publication 5 in Publications Appendix.**

16. The Code grants the Tax Court jurisdiction to hear only cases for which the taxpayer requests a redetermination within the 90-day period. (If a notice of deficiency is addressed to a person outside the United States, she has 150 days to file a petition for redetermination with the Tax Court.) The Court has no power to extend these periods no matter how sympathetic the taxpayer's reasons for failing to file a timely petition.

17. The Tax Court does not simply conduct a review of what the Service did during the audit process. Rather, the Court conducts a *de novo* review of the taxpayer's return for the year at issue.

18. The general rule of section 6501(a) of the Code requires the Service to assess taxes within three years of the filing of a taxpayer's return. (Section 6501(b)(1) provides that if a taxpayer files her

Thus, the Tax Court offers a taxpayer a pre-assessment opportunity for judicial review of her tax liability before she is required to pay the tax.

If the taxpayer fails to petition the Tax Court within the 90-day period, the Service may assess and then collect the amount of additional tax shown on the 90-day notice. In this event, until the Internal Revenue Service Restructuring and Reform Act of 1998 (hereinafter the "1998 Act"), the only further judicial review available to the taxpayer was through a suit brought against the United States for a refund in either the federal district court or the United States Court of Federal Claims (hereinafter the "Claims Court").[19] (A refund suit in either court, as its name implies, already requires full payment of the additional tax as a prerequisite to the court's jurisdiction.[20] Whether the taxpayer or the Service has the burden of proof in cases before the Tax Court, the federal district court, or the Claims Court, generally depends upon the taxpayer's earlier compliance with the requirements of section 7491,[21] except with respect to certain special issues. The Service always bears the burden of proof concerning fraud and on new issues it raises in the Tax Court.)

The 1998 Act added sections 6320 and 6330 to the Code, called the "Collection Due Process" (or CDP) provisions, which give a taxpayer who did not actually receive a notice of deficiency or did not otherwise have an opportunity to dispute the liability, an opportunity for a fair hearing and to later appeal an adverse determination to the Tax Court. The Act does not clearly define what these conditions entail. It may, therefore, be some time before the outlines of this new procedure emerge with any clarity. Until then, it is likely that the Service and the Tax Court will be besieged by taxpayers who claim rights under these new rules.[22]

Either the taxpayer or the government may appeal an adverse ruling to one of the circuit courts of appeal. Appeals from Tax Court go to the circuit in which the taxpayer resided at the time she filed her Tax Court petition. Appeals from the district court will also, generally, go to the circuit in which the taxpayer resides because most taxpayers who sue in the district court do so in the one closest to home.[23] All appeals from the

---

return before the statutory due date, the return is deemed filed on the statutory due date.) Because the Service must comply with the procedural requirement of issuing a 90-day letter before it may assess a deficiency, the Service must, as a practical matter, complete the audit process within the three-year statute of limitations period. The mailing of a 90-day letter suspends the running of the statute of limitations on assessments for the 90-day period that the taxpayer may file a Tax Court petition, and, if the taxpayer files a petition, until 60 days after the Tax Court decision becomes final. Section 6501(c) and (e) contain exceptions to the general three year rule. **Look at section 6501.**

19. Some taxpayers may choose voluntarily not to petition the Tax Court for review. They may prefer to file a claim for refund in federal district court in order to secure a jury trial. A jury trial is unavailable to petitioners in the Tax Court or claimants in the Claims Court where issues of fact are decided by judges. Does this violate the Seventh Amendment to the United States Constitution? **Read the Seventh Amendment.**

20. Although the issue is not free from doubt, there is considerable authority requiring full payment of all interest and penalties, as well as the additional tax, before a taxpayer may sue for a refund. *See Flora v. United States*, 357 U.S. 63 (1958), *on reh'g*, 362 U.S. 145 (1960). For taxpayers who are unable to pay a deficiency that the Service proposes, it is imperative that they respond timely to the 90-day letter because the Tax Court, commonly known as the "poor man's court," is the only pre-payment forum for judicial review. If a taxpayer fails to respond properly to a 90-day letter, the Service can assess and collect the deficiency, leaving the taxpayer with no further pre-payment recourse for review.

21. *See supra* note 13.

22. For an excellent summary and critique of the CDP provisions, *see* Leslie Book, "The Collection Due Process Rights: A Misstep or a Step in the Right Direction?", 41 Hous. L. Rev. 1145 (2004).

23. Title 28 U.S.C. section 1402 requires as a general rule that suits against the United States be brought in the judicial district in which the plaintiff resides.

Claims Court go to the Federal Circuit.[24] Further appeal by either the taxpayer or the government from any of the federal circuit courts must follow the usual procedure for seeking review in the United States Supreme Court, *i.e.*, by petitioning for a writ of certiorari. See 28 U.S.C. section 1254. The Supreme Court accepts very few petitions for certiorari each year. It generally accepts only those important issues that have created a split among the circuit courts.

———————

Now, let's return to *Old Colony* for a few more observations. In *Old Colony* and in the hypotheticals above, there was no issue regarding the value of the property the payor transferred. Suppose the value is unknown. For example, how would your answer to the questions posed above change, if at all, if, instead of giving you cash or a check for preparing her will, your client gave you a diamond ring she bought at Tiffany's?[25] What are the methods you might use to determine the fair market value of the ring? Is the following definition helpful? "The fair market value is the price at which the property would change hands between a willing buyer and a willing seller, neither being under any compulsion to buy or to sell and both having reasonable knowledge of relevant facts." Treas. Reg. section 20.2031-1(b). Would the result be the same using the following definition? "[T]he fair market value ... is the amount that an individual would have to pay for the [item] in an arm's-length transaction." Treas. Reg. section 1.61-21(b)(2).[26]

Suppose instead of a ring, your client gives you a painting by a well-known artist. Would the issue be different if the client (who is not known as an artist) gave you a painting that she herself had painted?

Suppose your client has no current assets that you are willing to accept in payment, so she gives you an unsecured promissory note. What is an "unsecured promissory note"? What factors would affect the value of the note?

Next, consider the results in the following revenue ruling.[27]

———————

24. The Claims Court is located in Washington, D.C. Therefore, any taxpayer who chooses to sue the United States for a refund in the Claims Court will have to suffer the possible inconvenience of litigating in Washington. The Federal Circuit is also located in Washington, D.C.

25. Does the fact that you receive something other than cash mean that you do not have income? **Look closely at Treasury Regulation section 1.61-1(a) and 1.61-2(d).**

26. These definitions appear in Treasury regulations, the first for the purpose of determining the fair market value of assets in a decedent's estate for estate tax purposes, the second for the purpose of determining the value of an employer-provided fringe benefit. The first of these is the most often cited because it reflects the common law definition of "fair market value" that lawyers and courts often apply in many contexts, *e.g.*, real estate.

27. A revenue ruling is one of the many types of communication that the Service uses to inform taxpayers of its interpretation of the Code. It is different from a Treasury Regulation. In general, a Treasury Regulation represents the Service's interpretation or, in certain instances, expansion of a particular Code provision. The courts, generally, grant great deference to Treasury Regulations. In a revenue ruling, on the other hand, the Service applies one or more Code sections, Treasury Regulations, and cases to a particular set of hypothetical facts in order to inform Service personnel and the taxpaying public with respect to the Service's position on the tax consequences of those facts. A revenue ruling represents only the statement of the Service's position; it has not, traditionally, been considered authoritative by the courts. The Service publishes revenue rulings in its weekly magazine-like publication, the Internal Revenue Bulletin (hereinafter "I.R.B."). Each I.R.B. bears the designation of the week of its publication. For example, the I.R.B. for the fifth week of 1999 will bear the designation: I.R.B. 1999-5. Twice a year the Service compiles most of the contents of the I.R.B.'s in a bound volume called the Cumulative Bulletin (hereinafter "C.B."). The volume for the first half of the year is designated with the year and the number one; the volume for the second half of the year is designated with the year and the number two. For example, the I.R.B.'s for the first half of

"barter revenue ruling"
REVENUE RULING 79-24
1979-1 C.B. 60

FACTS

Situation 1. In return for personal legal services performed by a lawyer for a house painter, the house painter painted the lawyer's personal residence. Both the lawyer and the house painter are members of a barter club, an organization that annually furnishes its members a directory of members and the services they provide. All the members of the club are professional or trades persons. Members contact other members directly and negotiate the value of the services to be performed.

Situation 2. An individual who owned an apartment building received a work of art created by a professional artist in return for the rent-free use of an apartment for six months by the artist.

LAW

The applicable sections of the Internal Revenue Code of 1954 and the Income Tax Regulations thereunder are 61(a) and 1.61-2, relating to compensation for services.

Section 1.61-2(d)(1) of the regulations provides that if services are paid for other than in money, the fair market value of the property or services taken in payment must be included in income. If the services were rendered at a stipulated price, such price will be presumed to be the fair market value of the compensation received in the absence of evidence to the contrary.

 HOLDINGS

Situation 1. The fair market value of the services received by the lawyer and the house painter are includible in their gross incomes under section 61 of the Code.

Situation 2. The fair market value of the work of art and the six months fair rental value of the apartment are includible in the gross incomes of the apartment-owner and the artist under section 61 of the Code.

––––––––––––

Consider the following questions about Revenue Ruling 79-24.

1. Can you draw a diagram of the transactions described in Revenue Ruling 79-24? It is frequently helpful to diagram a transaction described in a case or a ruling. Sometimes stripping a transaction down to its essentials, in visual terms, makes the transaction come alive and makes it much easier to "see" what happened.

2. How would you formulate the rule set forth in the ruling?

3. Based on your formulation of the rule, do the parties in each of the respective transactions have the same or differing amounts of income?

4. Is there any doubt that the parties on both sides of each of the transactions in Revenue Ruling 79-24 enjoy "accessions to wealth"? If your answer is no, consider whether

––––––––––––

1999 will appear in C.B. 1999-1; the I.R.B.'s for the second half of 1999 will appear in C.B. 1999-2. The Service occasionally issues an additional volume of the cumulative bulletin during a particular year to publish the legislative history of significant tax legislation.

Now look at Table 2 below:

Table 2
Present Value of $1 Payable After n Periods in the Future

No. of periods	3%	4%	5%	6%	7%	8%	10%	12%	15%
1	.9709	.9615	.9524	.9434	.9346	.9259	.9091	.8929	.8696
2	.9426	.9246	.9070	.8900	.8734	.8573	.8264	.7972	.7561
3	.9151	.8890	.8638	.8396	.8163	.7938	.7513	.7118	.6575
4	.8885	.8548	.8227	.7921	.7629	.7350	.6830	.6355	.5718
5	.8626	.8219	.7835	.7473	.7130	.6806	.6209	.5674	.4972
6	.8375	.7903	.7462	.7050	.6663	.6302	.5645	.5066	.4323
7	.8131	.7599	.7107	.6651	.6227	.5835	.5132	.4523	.3759
8	.7894	.7307	.6768	.6274	.5820	.5403	.4665	.4039	.3269
9	.7664	.7026	.6446	.5919	.5439	.5002	.4241	.3606	.2843
10	.7441	.6756	.6139	(.5584)	.5083	.4632	.3855	.3220	.2472
15	.6419	.5553	.4810	.4173	.3624	.3152	.2394	.1827	.1229
20	.5537	.4564	.3769	.3118	.2584	.2145	.1486	.1037	.0611
25	.4776	.3751	.2953	.2330	.1842	.1460	.0923	.0588	.0304

Table 2 shows the present value of a lump-sum payment due at the end of n periods. Again, using the same 6% rate of interest, find the place in Table 2 that states the present value of $1 payable at the end of 10 years. What is the present value of Adams Adverts' promise to pay a lump-sum at the end of 10 years? *$156,352 — PV of $280,000 payable in 10 yrs at 6%*

Suppose you decide to take the lump-sum payment of $100,000 today. The present value of this amount is, of course, $100,000.

Now look at Table 3 below:

Table 3
Future Value After n Periods of $1 Invested Today

No. of periods	3%	4%	5%	6%	7%	8%	10%	12%	15%
1	1.0300	1.0400	1.0500	1.0600	1.0700	1.0800	1.1000	1.1200	1.1500
2	1.0609	1.0816	1.1025	1.1236	1.1449	1.1664	1.2100	1.2544	1.3225
3	1.0927	1.1249	1.1576	1.1910	1.2250	1.2597	1.3310	1.4049	1.5209
4	1.1255	1.1699	1.2155	1.2625	1.3108	1.3605	1.4641	1.5735	1.7490
5	1.1593	1.2167	1.2763	1.3382	1.4026	1.4693	1.6105	1.7623	2.0114
6	1.1941	1.2653	1.3401	1.4185	1.5007	1.5869	1.7716	1.9738	2.3131
7	1.2299	1.3159	1.4071	1.5036	1.6058	1.7138	1.9487	2.2107	2.6600
8	1.2668	1.3686	1.4775	1.5938	1.7182	1.8509	2.1436	2.4760	3.0590
9	1.3048	1.4233	1.5513	1.6895	1.8365	1.9990	2.3579	2.7731	3.5179
10	1.3439	1.4802	1.6289	(1.7908)	1.9672	2.1589	2.5937	3.1058	4.0456
15	1.5580	1.8009	2.0789	2.3966	2.7590	3.1722	4.1772	5.4736	8.1371
20	1.8061	2.1911	2.6533	3.2071	3.8697	4.6610	6.7275	9.6466	16.3665
25	2.0938	2.6658	3.3864	4.2919	5.4274	6.8485	10.8347	17.0001	32.9190

Table 3 shows the future value after n periods of $1 invested today. To compare the results with the value of the stream of payments, you must choose the same 6% rate of interest. Find the place in Table 3 where a period of 10 years intersects with 6% interest. So, what is the future value of the $100,000 lump-sum payment? How does that amount compare with the offer of $280,000 paid at the end of 10 years?

Which method of payment should you choose? Well, if you base your decision solely on the basis of comparing the three results, which will produce a higher total sales price for your company? Are there other factors that might affect your decision?

Suppose you choose the $100,000 immediate payment option, what is your accession to wealth this year? Does the *Raytheon* court make any statements that affect your answer to this question?

When Adams Adverts buys your business for $100,000, it has made an "investment" of that amount. Suppose shortly after the purchase, Adams learns that environmental regulations require it to do a costly job to the plumbing system of the building it acquired as part of the purchase of your business. The repair will cost $5,000. Adams sues you for failing to disclose the plumbing problem and recovers the full $5,000 from you. Has Adams had an accession to its wealth as a result of its receipt of the $5,000? Consider the following revenue ruling.

REVENUE RULING 81-277
1981-2 C.B. 14

ISSUE

Does payment by a contractor of a sum of money to a buyer in exchange for a release of the buyer's claims against the contractor for failure to fulfill a contract result in income to the buyer or a return of capital?

FACTS

In 1969 corporation M agreed to construct a nuclear generating plant for corporation P at a price of $250x$ dollars. The construction contract specified that M would provide, at no additional cost to P, any additional items that later were determined to be necessary to deliver a complete, safe, licensable, fully operational plant. During the construction period regulatory agencies imposed stricter environmental safeguards on nuclear generating plants than were in effect at the time the contract was signed. Disputes arose between M and P over M's obligation to provide for stricter safeguards and to include them as part of the delivered plant at the original contract price. To the date of the dispute, P has paid M $230x$ dollars of the contract price of $250x$ dollars.

The parties eventually settled their dispute by agreeing that the terms of the 1969 contract must be met by both parties. They also agreed that M was responsible to deliver a plant that met the stricter environmental safeguards and that it would cost an additional $40x$ dollars. P was required to forward $20x$ dollars to M to complete P's payment obligation under the contract.

In light of these agreements, P paid M $20x$ dollars, the value of the work performed under the contract but unpaid at the time of the settlement agreement. M paid P $40x$ dollars representing the estimated cost to satisfy the stricter environmental standards rather than completing the plant's construction. Both parties then executed general releases to each other and M ceased its construction activities.

adopted, an amount equivalent to the par value of the proposed new stock was transferred accordingly, and the new stock duly issued against it and divided among the stockholders.

Defendant in error, being the owner of 2,200 shares of the old stock, received certificates for 1,100 additional shares, of which 18.07 per cent, or 198.77 shares, par value $19,877, were treated as representing surplus earned between March 1, 1913, and January 1, 1916. She was called upon to pay, and did pay under protest, a tax imposed under the Revenue Act of 1916, based upon a supposed income of $19,877 because of the new shares; and an appeal to the Commissioner of Internal Revenue having been disallowed, she brought action against the Collector to recover the tax. In her complaint she alleged the above facts, and contended that in imposing such a tax the Revenue Act of 1916 violated Art. I, §2, cl. 3, and Art. I, §9, cl. 4, of the Constitution on the United States, requiring direct taxes to be apportioned according to population, and that the stock dividend was not income within the meaning of the Sixteenth Amendment. A general demurrer to the complaint was overruled upon the authority of *Towne v. Eisner*, 245 U.S. 418; and, defendant having failed to plead further, final judgment went against him. To review it, the present writ of error is prosecuted.

The case was argued at the last term, and reargued at the present term, both orally and by additional briefs.

We are constrained to hold that the judgment of the District Court must be affirmed: First, because the question at issue is controlled by *Towne v. Eisner, supra*; secondly, because a reexamination of the question, with the additional light thrown upon it by elaborate arguments, has confirmed the view that the underlying ground of that decision is sound, that it disposes of the question here presented, and that other fundamental considerations lead to the same result.

In *Towne v. Eisner*, the question was whether a stock dividend made in 1914 against surplus earned prior to January 1, 1913, was taxable against the stockholder under the Act of October 3, 1913, ... which provided ... that net income should include "dividends," and also "gains or profits and income derived from any source whatever." Suit having been brought by a stockholder to recover the tax assessed against him by reason of the dividend, the District Court sustained a demurrer to the complaint.... The court treated the construction of the act as inseparable from the interpretation of the Sixteenth Amendment; and ... proceeded very properly to say ... : "It is manifest that the stock dividend in question cannot be reached by the Income Tax Act, and could not, even though Congress expressly declared it to be taxable as income, unless it is in fact income." ...'A stock dividend really takes nothing from the property of the corporation, and adds nothing to the interests of the shareholders. Its property is not diminished, and their interests are not increased.... The proportional interest of each shareholder remains the same. The only change is in the evidence which represents that interest, the new shares and the original shares together representing the same proportional interest that the original shares represented before the issue of the new ones.'... In short, the corporation is no poorer and the stockholder is no richer than they were before.... If the plaintiff gained any small advantage by the change, it certainly was not an advantage of $417,450, the sum upon which he was taxed.... What has happened is that the plaintiff's old certificates have been split up in effect and have diminished in value to the extent of the value of the new."

This language aptly answered not only the reasoning of the District Court but the argument of the Solicitor General in this court, which discussed the essential nature of a stock dividend. And if, for the reasons thus expressed, such a dividend is not to be regarded as "income" or "dividends" within the meaning of the Act of 1913, we are unable to see how it can be brought within the meaning of "incomes" in the Sixteenth Amendment; it being very clear that Congress intended in that act to exert its power to the extent permitted by the Amendment. In *Towne v. Eisner* it was not contended that any construction of the statute could make it narrower than the constitutional grant; rather the contrary.

... In *Peabody v. Eisner*, ... we observed that the decision of the District Court in *Towne v. Eisner* had been reversed "only upon the ground that it related to a stock dividend which in fact took nothing from the property of the corporation and added nothing to the interest of the shareholder, but merely changed the evidence which represented that interest;" and we distinguished the *Peabody Case* from the *Towne Case* upon the ground that "the dividend of Baltimore & Ohio shares was not a stock dividend but a distribution *in specie* of a portion of the assets of the Union Pacific."

We adhere to the view then expressed, and might rest the present case there; not because that case in terms decided the constitutional question, for it did not; but because the conclusion there reached as to the essential nature of a stock dividend necessarily prevents its being regarded as income in any true sense.

Nevertheless, in view of the importance of the matter, and the fact that Congress in the Revenue Act of 1916 declared ... that a "stock dividend shall be considered income, to the amount of its cash value," we will deal at length with the constitutional question, incidentally testing the soundness of our previous conclusion.

The Sixteenth Amendment must be construed in connection with the taxing clauses of the original Constitution and the effect attributed to them before the Amendment was adopted. In *Pollock v. Farmers' Loan & Trust Co.*, 158 U.S. 601, under the Act of August 27, 1894, c. 349, § 27, 28 Stat. 509, 553, it was held that taxes upon rents and profits of real estate and upon returns from investments of personal property were in effect direct taxes upon the property from which such income arose, imposed by reason of ownership; and that Congress could not impose such taxes without apportioning them among the States according to population, as required by Art. I, § 2, cl. 3, and § 9, cl. 4, of the original Constitution.

Afterwards, and evidently in recognition of the limitation upon the taxing power of Congress thus determined, the Sixteenth Amendment was adopted, in words lucidly expressing the object to be accomplished: "The Congress shall have power to lay and collect taxes on incomes, from whatever source derived, without apportionment among the several States, and without regard to any census or enumeration." As repeatedly held, this did not extend the taxing power to new subjects, but merely removed the necessity which otherwise might exist for an apportionment among the States of taxes laid on income....

...

In order, therefore, that the clauses cited from Article I of the Constitution may have proper force and effect, save only as modified by the Amendment, and that the latter also may have proper effect, it becomes essential to distinguish between what is and what is not "income," as the term is there used; and to apply the distinction, as cases arise, according to truth and substance, without regard to form. Congress cannot by any definition it may adopt conclude the matter, since it cannot by legislation alter the Constitution, from which alone it derives its power to legislate, and within whose limitations alone that power can be lawfully exercised.

The fundamental relation of "capital" to "income" has been much discussed by economists, the former being likened to the tree or the land, the latter to the fruit or the crop;

the former depicted as a reservoir supplied from springs, the latter as the outlet stream, to be measured by its flow during a period of time. For the present purpose we require only a clear definition of the term "income," as used in common speech, in order to determine its meaning in the Amendment; and, having formed also a correct judgment as to the nature of a stock dividend, we shall find it easy to decide the matter at issue.

After examining dictionaries in common use (Bouv. L.D.; Standard Dict.; Webster's Internat. Dict.; Century Dict.), we find little to add to the succinct definition adopted in two cases arising under the Corporation Tax Act of 1909 (*Stratton's Independence v. Howbert*, 231 U.S. 399, 415; *Doyle v. Mitchell Bros. Co.*, 247 U.S. 179, 185) "Income may be defined as the gain derived from capital, from labor, or from both combined," provided it be understood to include profit gained through a sale ... of ... assets, to which it was applied in the *Doyle Case* (pp. 183, 185).

Brief as it is, it indicates the characteristic and distinguishing attribute of income essential for a correct solution of the present controversy. The Government, although basing its argument upon the definition as quoted, placed chief emphasis upon the word "gain," which was extended to include a variety of meanings; while the significance of the next three words was either overlooked or misconceived. "*Derived—from—capital*";—"the *gain—derived—from—capital*," etc. Here we have the essential matter: *not* a gain *accruing to* capital, not a *growth* or *increment* of value *in* the investment; but a gain, a profit, something of exchangeable value *proceeding from* the property, *severed from* the capital however invested or employed, and *coming in*, being "*derived*," that is, *received* or *drawn by* the recipient (the taxpayer) for his *separate* use, benefit and disposal;—*that* is income derived from property. Nothing else answers the description.

The same fundamental conception is clearly set forth in the Sixteenth Amendment—"incomes, *from* whatever *source derived*"—the essential thought being expressed with a conciseness and lucidity entirely in harmony with the form and style of the Constitution.

Can a stock dividend, considering its essential character, be brought within the definition? To answer this, regard must be had to the nature of a corporation and the stockholder's relation to it. We refer, of course, to a corporation such as the one in the case at bar, organized for profit, and having a capital stock divided into shares to which a nominal or par value is attributed.

Certainly the interest of the stockholder is a capital interest, and his certificates of stock are but the evidence of it. They state the number of shares to which he is entitled and indicate their par value and how the stock may be transferred. They show that he or his assignors, immediate or remote, have contributed capital to the enterprise, that he is entitled to a corresponding interest proportionate to the whole, entitled to have the property and business of the company devoted during the corporate existence to attainment of the common objects, entitled to vote at stockholders' meetings, to receive dividends out of the corporation's profits if and when declared, and, in the event of liquidation, to receive a proportionate share of the net assets, if any, remaining after paying creditors. Short of liquidation, or until dividend declared, he has no right to withdraw any part of either capital or profits from the common enterprise; on the contrary, his interest pertains not to any part, divisible or indivisible, but to the entire assets, business, and affairs of the company. Nor is it the interest of an owner in the assets themselves, since the corporation has full title, legal and equitable, to the whole. The stockholder has the right to have the assets employed in the enterprise, with the incidental rights mentioned; but, as stockholder, he has no right to withdraw, only the right to persist, subject to the risks of the enterprise, and looking only to dividends for his return. If he desires to dissociate himself from the company he can do so only by disposing of his stock.

For bookkeeping purposes, the company acknowledges a liability in form to the stockholders equivalent to the aggregate par value of their stock, evidenced by a "capital stock account." If profits have been made and not divided they create additional bookkeeping liabilities under the head of "profit and loss," "undivided profits," "surplus account," or the like. None of these, however, gives to the stockholders as a body, much less to any one of them, either a claim against the going concern for any particular sum of money, or a right to any particular portion of the assets or any share in them unless or until the directors conclude that dividends shall be made and a part of the company's assets segregated from the common fund for the purpose. The dividend normally is payable in money, under exceptional circumstances in some other divisible property; and when so paid, then only (excluding, of course, a possible advantageous sale of his stock or winding-up of the company) does the stockholder realize a profit or gain which becomes his separate property, and thus derive income from the capital that he or his predecessor has invested.

In the present case, the corporation had surplus and undivided profits invested in plant, property, and business, and required for the purposes of the corporation, amounting to about $45,000,000, in addition to outstanding capital stock of $50,000,000. In this the case is not extraordinary. The profits of a corporation, as they appear upon the balance sheet at the end of the year, need not be in the form of money on hand in excess of what is required to meet current liabilities and finance current operations of the company. Often, especially in a growing business, only a part, sometimes a small part, of the year's profits is in property capable of division; the remainder having been absorbed in the acquisition of increased plant, equipment, stock in trade, or accounts receivable, or in decrease of outstanding liabilities. When only a part is available for dividends, the balance of the year's profits is carried to the credit of undivided profits, or surplus, or some other account having like significance. If thereafter the company finds itself in funds beyond current needs it may declare dividends out of such surplus or undivided profits; otherwise it may go on for years conducting a successful business, but requiring more and more working capital because of the extension of its operations, and therefore unable to declare dividends approximating the amount of its profits. Thus the surplus may increase until it equals or even exceeds the par value of the outstanding capital stock. This may be adjusted upon the books in the mode adopted in the case at bar—by declaring a "stock dividend." This, however, is no more than a book adjustment, in essence not a dividend but rather the opposite; no part of the assets of the company is separated from the common fund, nothing distributed except paper certificates that evidence an antecedent increase in the value of the stockholder's capital interest resulting from an accumulation of profits by the company, but profits so far absorbed in the business as to render it impracticable to separate them for withdrawal and distribution. In order to make the adjustment, a charge is made against surplus account with corresponding credit to capital stock account, equal to the proposed "dividend"; the new stock is issued against this and the certificates delivered to the existing stockholders in proportion to their previous holdings. This, however, is merely bookkeeping that does not affect the aggregate assets of the corporation or its outstanding liabilities; it affects only the form, not the essence, of the "liability" acknowledged by the corporation to its own shareholders, and this through a readjustment of accounts on one side of the balance sheet only, increasing "capital stock" at the expense of "surplus"; it does not alter the preexisting proportionate interest of any stockholder or increase the intrinsic value of his holding or of the aggregate holdings of the other stockholders as they stood before. The new certificates simply increase the number of the shares, with consequent dilution of the value of each share.

A "stock dividend" shows that the company's accumulated profits have been capitalized, instead of distributed to the stockholders or retained as surplus available for distribution in money or in kind should opportunity offer. Far from being a realization of profits of the stockholder, it tends rather to postpone such realization, in that the fund represented by the new stock has been transferred from surplus to capital, and no longer is available for actual distribution.

The essential and controlling fact is that the stockholder has received nothing out of the company's assets for his separate use and benefit; on the contrary, every dollar of his original investment, together with whatever accretions and accumulations have resulted from employment of his money and that of the other stockholders in the business of the company, still remains the property of the company, and subject to business risks which may result in wiping out the entire investment. Having regard to the very truth of the matter, to substance and not to form, he has received nothing that answers the definition of income within the meaning of the Sixteenth Amendment.

. . .

We are clear that not only does a stock dividend really take nothing from the property of the corporation and add nothing to that of the shareholder, but that the antecedent accumulation of profits evidenced thereby, while indicating that the shareholder is the richer because of an increase of his capital, at the same time shows he has not realized or received any income in the transaction.

It is said that a stockholder may sell the new shares acquired in the stock dividend; and so he may, if he can find a buyer. It is equally true that if he does sell, and in doing so realizes a profit, such profit, like any other, is income, and so far as it may have arisen since the Sixteenth Amendment if taxable by Congress without apportionment. The same would be true were he to sell some of his original shares at a profit. But if a shareholder sells dividend stock he necessarily disposes of a part of his capital interest, just as if he should sell a part of his old stock, either before or after the dividend. What he retains no longer entitles him to the same proportion of future dividends as before the sale. His part in the control of the company likewise is diminished. Thus, if one holding $60,000 out of a total $100,000 of the capital stock of a corporation should receive in common with other stockholders a 50 per cent. stock dividend, and should sell his part, he thereby would be reduced from a majority to a minority stockholder, having six-fifteenths instead of six-tenths of the total stock outstanding. A corresponding and proportionate decrease in capital interest and in voting power would befall a minority holder should he sell dividend stock; it being in the nature of things impossible for one to dispose of any part of such an issue without a proportionate disturbance of the distribution of the entire capital stock, and a like diminution of the seller's comparative voting power — that "right preservative of rights" in the control of a corporation. Yet, without selling, the shareholder, unless possessed of other resources, has not the wherewithal to pay an income tax upon the dividend stock. Nothing could more clearly show that to tax a stock dividend is to tax a capital increase, and not income, than this demonstration that in the nature of things it requires conversion of capital in order to pay the tax.

Throughout the argument of the Government, in a variety of forms, runs the fundamental error already mentioned — a failure to appraise correctly the force of the term "income" as used in the Sixteenth Amendment, or at least to give practical effect to it. Thus, the Government contends that the tax "is levied on income derived from corporate earnings," when in truth the stockholder has "derived" nothing except paper certificates which, so far as they have any effect, deny him present participation in such earnings. It contends that the tax may be laid when earnings "are received by the stockholder," whereas he has received none; that the profits are "distributed by means of a stock dividend," although a stock dividend distributes no profits; that under the Act of 1916 "the tax is on the stockholder's share in corporate earnings," when in truth a stockholder has no such share, and receives none in a stock dividend; that "the profits are segregated from his former capital, and he has a separate certificate representing his invested profits or gains," whereas there has been no segregation of profits, nor has he any separate certificate representing a personal gain, since the certificates, new and old, are alike in what they represent—a capital interest in the entire concerns of the corporation.

We have no doubt of the power or duty of a court to look through the form of the corporation and determine the question of the stockholder's right, in order to ascertain whether he has received income taxable by Congress without apportionment. But, looking through the form, we cannot disregard the essential truth disclosed; ignore the substantial difference between corporation and stockholder; treat the entire organization as unreal; look upon stockholders as partners, when they are not such; treat them as having in equity a right to a partition of the corporate assets, when they have none; and indulge the fiction that they have received and realized a share of the profits of the company which in truth they have neither received nor realized. We must treat the corporation as a substantial entity separate from the stockholder, not only because such is the practical fact but because it is only by recognizing such separateness that any dividend—even one paid in money or property—can be regarded as income of the stockholder. Did we regard corporation and stockholders as altogether identical, there would be no income except as the corporation acquired it; and while this would be taxable against the corporation as income under appropriate provisions of law, the individual stockholders could not be separately and additionally taxed with respect to their several shares even when divided, since if there were entire identity between them and the company they could not be regarded as receiving anything from it, any more than if one's money were to be removed from one pocket to another.

. . .

It is said there is no difference in principle between a simple stock dividend and a case where stockholders use money received as cash dividends to purchase additional stock contemporaneously issued by the corporation. But an actual cash dividend, with a real option to the stockholder either to keep the money for his own or to reinvest it in new shares, would be as far removed as possible from a true stock dividend, such as the one we have under consideration, where nothing of value is taken from the company's assets and transferred to the individual ownership of the several stockholders and thereby subjected to their disposal.

. . .

Thus, from every point of view, we are brought irresistibly to the conclusion that neither under the Sixteenth Amendment nor otherwise has Congress power to tax without apportionment a true stock dividend made lawfully and in good faith, or the accumulated profits behind it, as income of the stockholder. The Revenue Act of 1916, in so far as it imposes a tax upon the stockholder because of such dividend, contravenes the provisions of Article I, § 2, cl. 3, and Article I, § 9, cl. 4, of the Constitution, and to this extent is invalid notwithstanding the Sixteenth Amendment.

Judgment affirmed.

FOOTNOTES:

1. TITLE I—INCOME TAX

PART I—ON INDIVIDUALS

Sec. 2(a). That, subject only to such exemptions and deductions as are hereinafter allowed, the net income of a taxable person shall include gains, profits, and income derived..., also from interest, rent, dividends, securities, or the transaction of any business carried on for gain or profit, or gains or profits and income derived from any source whatever: *Provided*, That the term "dividends" as used in this title shall be held to mean any distribution made or ordered to be made by a corporation, ... out of its earnings or profits accrued since March first, nineteen hundred and thirteen, and payable to its shareholders, whether in cash or in stock of the corporation, ... which stock dividend shall be considered income, to the amount of its cash value.

...

MR. JUSTICE BRANDEIS, dissenting, delivered the following opinion, ...

Financiers, with the aid of lawyers, devised long ago two different methods by which a corporation can, without increasing its indebtedness, keep for corporate purposes accumulated profits, and yet, in effect, distribute these profits among its stockholders. One method is a simple one. The capital stock is increased; the new stock is paid up with the accumulated profits; and the new shares of paid-up stock are then distributed among the stockholders *pro rata* as a dividend. If the stockholder prefers ready money to increasing his holding of the stock in the company, he sells the new stock received as a dividend. The other method is slightly more complicated. Arrangements are made for an increase of stock to be offered to stockholders *pro rata* at par and, at the same time, for the payment of a cash dividend equal to the amount which the stockholder will be required to pay to the company, if he avails himself of the right to subscribe for his *pro rata* of the new stock. If the stockholder takes the new stock as is expected, he may endorse the dividend check received to the corporation and thus pay for the new stock. In order to ensure that all the new stock so offered will be taken, the price at which it is offered is fixed far below what it is believed will be its market value. If the stockholder prefers ready money to an increase of his holdings of stock, he may sell his right to take new stock *pro rata*, which is evidenced by an assignable instrument. In that event the purchaser of the rights repays to the corporation, as the subscription price of the new stock, an amount equal to that which it had paid as a cash dividend to the stockholder.

Both of these methods of retaining accumulated profits while in effect distributing them as a dividend had been in common use in the United States for many years prior to the adoption of the Sixteenth Amendment. They were recognized equivalents. Whether a particular corporation employed one or the other method was determined sometimes by requirements of the law under which the corporation was organized; sometimes it was determined by preferences of the individual officials of the corporation; and sometimes by stock market conditions. Whichever method was employed the resultant distribution of the new stock was commonly referred to as a stock dividend....

...

It thus appears that among financiers and investors the distribution of the stock by whichever method effected is called a stock dividend; that the two methods by which accumulated profits are legally retained for corporate purposes and at the same time distributed as dividends are recognized by them to be equivalents; and that the financial results to the corporation and to the stockholders of the two methods are substantially the same—unless a difference results from the application of the federal income tax law.

...

It is conceded that if the stock dividend paid to Mrs. Macomber had been made by the more complicated method ... that is, issuing rights to take new stock *pro rata* and paying to each stockholder simultaneously a dividend in cash sufficient in amount to enable him to pay for this *pro rata* of new stock to be purchased—the dividend so paid to him would have been taxable as income, whether he retained the cash or whether he returned it to the corporation in payment for his *pro rata* of new stock. But it is contended that, because the simple method was adopted of having the new stock issued direct to the stockholders as paid-up stock, the new stock is not to be deemed income, whether she retained it or converted it into cash by sale. If such a different result can flow merely from the difference in the method pursued, it must be because Congress is without power to tax as income of the stockholder either the stock received under the latter method or the proceeds of its sale; for Congress has, by the provisions in the Revenue Act of 1916, expressly declared its purpose to make stock dividends, by whichever method paid, taxable as income.

...

... It surely is not clear that the enactment exceeds the power granted by the Sixteenth Amendment. And, as this court has so often said, the high prerogative of declaring an act of Congress invalid, should never be exercised except in a clear case. "It is but a decent respect due to the wisdom, the integrity and the patriotism of the legislative body, by which any law is passed, to presume in favor of its validity, until its violation of the Constitution is proved beyond all reasonable doubt." *Ogden v. Saunders*, 12 Wheat. 213, 270.

...

———————

Consider the following questions about *Eisner v. Macomber.*

1. In *Eisner v. Macomber*, Justice Pitney, speaking for the majority, stated in the first paragraph, "This case presents the question whether, by virtue of the Sixteenth Amendment, Congress has the power to tax, as income of the stockholder and without apportionment, a stock dividend made lawfully and in good faith against profits accumulated by the corporation since March 1, 1913." Did the majority correctly characterize the issue in this case? Consider the following brief description of the treatment of corporations as separate taxable entities.

A corporation is a separate juridical[43] and taxpaying entity. As we noted earlier, for each accounting period, the corporation prepares several forms of financial statements in order to report its operating results and current financial position to its shareholders; to other interested parties, such as lenders; and, in the case of a public corporation, to the public. **Reread first footnote in Question 6 following *Kirby Lumber*.** A corporation reports its income and expenses on its income statement. It must then account for its income statement results on its balance sheet. If it earns a profit, after all expenses, including taxes, the balance sheet will show the income after expenses as an asset on the asset side and a matching entry on the liabilities and shareholders' equity side, probably

———————

43. What does "juridical" mean?

denoted "retained earnings," until the corporation decides to use these earnings for one of a number of possible corporate purposes.

Tracy's Problem

As a simple example, suppose that Tracy took $10 out of his savings account. He created a corporation,[44] "T Corp.," and "contributed" his $10 to it in return for 10 shares of common stock, par value $1/share (remember our discussion of "par value" following the *Kirby Lumber* case.) **Look back at question 2 following *Kirby Lumber*.** For tax purposes, there are now two "persons," Tracy and T Corp. Construct the opening balance sheet for T Corp.

Now, assume that T Corp. used $7 of its capital to acquire a parcel of raw land. It "net leased"[45] the land to a local gun club to use for hunting. In year 1, the hunt club paid $12 in real estate taxes on behalf of T Corp. and $106 in rent to T Corp. What was T Corp.'s gross income in year 1?

As you will learn later in this course, T Corp. may deduct the real estate taxes paid on its behalf by its tenant. Therefore, T Corp.'s taxable income for year 1 was $106. Assume that T Corp. paid income tax at a 15% rate, or $16, on its taxable income. Thus, T Corp.'s net income for year 1 was $90. Construct the balance sheet at the end of year 1. Has the value of Tracy's stock changed? Does he have an accession to wealth? If so, would he have gross income if you applied the rule of *Glenshaw Glass*? How did the Supreme Court answer this question in *Eisner v. Macomber*?

Return for a moment to T Corp.'s balance sheet. It now has an increase of $90 on the asset side at the end of year 1, (presumably in the form of cash or a bank deposit) (and, as noted above, the value of Tracy's equity has increased by the same amount). What might T Corp. decide to do with the $90 increase in the value of its assets? It could invest in additional parcels of real estate or other assets. Or, it could hold the cash (in some interest-bearing form) until needed. Or, it could decide to distribute a cash dividend to its sole shareholder, Tracy. If T Corp. distributed a cash dividend to Tracy, what result to him? **Look at section 61(a)(7).**[46]

Suppose T Corp. decides to retain the additional amount of assets in a money market account until it decides on a corporate use for the funds. Remember, T Corp. originally issued 10 shares with a par value of $1 each to Tracy. How much is each of Tracy's 10 shares now worth? When the value of a corporation's shares has increased substantially, the corporation may decide that, as a business matter, the value of each share is too high.[47] What would the corporation then do in order to reduce the value of each

---

44. How does he "create" the corporation?

45. What is a "net lease"? A net lease requires the lessee to pay the expenses associated with the property. Therefore, the lessor receives a "net rent." How much income does the lessor report for tax purposes? **Hint: recall *Old Colony*.**

46. The traditional rule under section 61(a)(7) was that dividends were includible in gross income and were subject to the section 1 rate of tax applicable in general to the taxpayer's taxable income. In the 2003 Act, Congress enacted section 1(h)(11) which makes the special lower rate we noted in our earlier discussion of the "proper rate" as applicable to "net capital gain" also applicable to "qualified dividend income."

47. Consider, for example, that the shares of IBM have, at times, exceeded $300 per share in value. Because most investors prefer to buy a "round lot" of stock, that is, a multiple of 100 shares (because the commission rate is lower on round lots), a single round lot at that price would exceed $30,000 in cost.

share? Suppose T Corp. decides to issue an additional 90 shares to Tracy. Has the value of his stock ownership in T Corp. changed? What is his basis in his T Corp. shares after the dividend? **Hint: remember TOAD.**

2. Note that the Supreme Court stated in *Eisner v. Macomber* that the meaning of "income" under the Sixteenth Amendment is as follows: "… the gain derived from capital, from labor, or from both combined…." Recall the exemplary damages at issue in *Glenshaw Glass*. Were they derived from capital, from labor, or from both combined? Suppose you win $20,000,000 in the lottery this evening? Is that gain derived from capital, from labor, or from both combined? Or is it derived from chance? Do your lottery winnings constitute gross income to you? If so, what is the remaining validity of *Eisner v. Macomber*?

––––––––––––

Now consider this: suppose your parents offer to let you use their house while they go off to Florida for a year. As soon as you move in, you remember that your parents do not have cable TV. Desperate for your favorite programs, you call the local cable company, which agrees to come the next day and install the service. Because you are so far from an existing cable, the connection will cost $250. Any result to your parents as they enjoy themselves in sunny Florida? Have they realized an accession to wealth? Consider the following case.

HELVERING v. BRUUN
309 U.S. 461 (1940)

MR. JUSTICE ROBERTS delivered the opinion of the Court.

The controversy had its origin in the petitioner's assertion that the respondent realized taxable gain from the forfeiture of a leasehold, the tenant having erected a new building upon the premises. The court below held that no income had been realized. Inconsistency of the decisions on the subject led us to grant certiorari.

The Board of Tax Appeals made no independent findings. The cause was submitted upon a stipulation of facts. From this it appears that on July 1, 1915, the respondent, as owner, leased a lot of land and the building thereon for a term of ninety-nine years.

The lease provided that the lessee might, at any time, upon giving bond to secure rentals accruing in the two ensuing years, remove or tear down any building on the land, provided that no building should be removed or torn down after the lease became forfeited, or during the last three and one-half years of the term. The lessee was to surrender the land, upon termination of the lease, with all buildings and improvements thereon.

In 1929 the tenant demolished and removed the existing building and constructed a new one which had a useful life of not more than fifty years. July 1, 1933, the lease was cancelled for default in payment of rent and taxes and the respondent regained possession of the land and building.

The parties stipulated "that as at said date, July 1, 1933, the building which had been erected upon said premises by the lessee had a fair market value of $64,245.68 and that the unamortized cost of the old building, which was removed from the premises in 1929 to make way for the new building, was $12,811.43, thus leaving a net fair market value as at July 1, 1933, of $51,434.25, for the aforesaid new building erected upon the premises by the lessee."

On the basis of these facts, the petitioner determined that in 1933 the respondent realized a net gain of $51,434.25. The Board overruled his determination and the Circuit Court of Appeals affirmed the Board's decision.

The course of administrative practice and judicial decision in respect of the question presented has not been uniform. In 1917 the Treasury ruled that the adjusted value of improvements installed upon leased premises is income to the lessor upon the termination of the lease. The ruling was incorporated in two succeeding editions of the Treasury Regulations. In 1919 the Circuit Court of Appeals for the Ninth Circuit held in *Miller v. Gearin*, 258 F. 225, that the regulation was invalid as the gain, if taxable at all, must be taxed as of the year when the improvements were completed.

The regulations were accordingly amended to impose a tax upon the gain in the year of completion of the improvements, measured by their anticipated value at the termination of the lease and discounted for the duration of the lease. Subsequently the regulations permitted the lessor to spread the depreciated value of the improvements over the remaining life of the lease, reporting an aliquot part each year, with provision that, upon premature termination, a tax should be imposed upon the excess of the then value of the improvements over the amount theretofore returned.

In 1935 the Circuit Court of Appeals for the Second Circuit decided in *Hewitt Realty Co. v. Commissioner*, 76 F.2d 880, that a landlord received no taxable income in a year, during the term of the lease, in which his tenant erected a building on the leased land. The court, while recognizing that the lessor need not receive money to be taxable, based its decision that no taxable gain was realized in that case on the fact that the improvement was not portable or detachable from the land, and if removed would be worthless except as bricks, iron, and mortar. It said (p. 884): "The question as we view it is whether the value received is embodied in something separately disposable, or whether it is so merged in the land as to become financially a part of it, something which, though it increases its value, has no value of its own when torn away."

This decision invalidated the regulations then in force.

… [T]he petitioner's contention that gain was realized when the respondent, through forfeiture of the lease, obtained untrammeled title, possession and control of the premises, with the added increment of value added by the new building, runs counter to the decision in the *Miller* case and to the reasoning in the *Hewitt* case.

The respondent insists that the realty,—a capital asset at the date of the execution of the lease,—remained such throughout the term and after its expiration; that improvements affixed to the soil became part of the realty indistinguishably blended in the capital asset; that such improvements cannot be separately valued or treated as received in exchange for the improvements which were on the land at the date of the execution of the lease; that they are, therefore, in the same category as improvements added by the respondent to his land, or accruals of value due to extraneous and adventitious circumstances. Such added value, it is argued, can be considered capital gain only upon the owner's disposition of the asset. The position is that the economic gain consequent upon the enhanced value of the recaptured asset is not gain … realized within the meaning of the Sixteenth Amendment and may not, therefore, be taxed without apportionment.

We hold that the petitioner was right in assessing the gain as realized in 1933.

…

The respondent can not successfully contend that the definition of gross income in § 22 (a) of the Revenue Act of 1932 is not broad enough to embrace the gain in question.... He relies upon what was said in *Hewitt Realty Co. v. Commissioner, supra,* ... to the effect that gain derived from capital must be something of exchangeable value proceeding from property, severed from the capital, however invested or employed, and received by the recipient for his separate use, benefit, and disposal. He emphasizes the necessity that the gain be separate from the capital and separately disposable....

While it is true that economic gain is not always taxable as income, it is settled that the realization of gain need not be in cash derived from the sale of an asset. Gain may occur as a result of exchange of property, payment of the taxpayer's indebtedness, relief from a liability, or other profit realized from the completion of a transaction. The fact that the gain is a portion of the value of property received by the taxpayer in the transaction does not negative its realization.

Here, as a result of a business transaction, the respondent received back his land with a new building on it, which added an ascertainable amount to its value. It is not necessary to recognition of taxable gain that he should be able to sever the improvement begetting the gain from his original capital. If that were necessary, no income could arise from the exchange of property; whereas such gain has always been recognized as realized taxable gain.

Judgment reversed.

Consider the following questions about *Helvering v. Bruun.*

1. Outline in chronological order the different administrative and judicial approaches to the timing of gross income.

2. Locate the portion of the opinion that describes the Supreme Court's view of the "clearly realized" prong of the three-prong test set forth in *Glenshaw Glass.*

3. Once you conclude that the lessor should have gross income as a result of the lessee's construction of a building that remained on the lessor's property at the termination of the lease, what are the alternatives as to *when* the lessor should realize the income and *how* the income should be valued?[48]

4. If you work for the Internal Revenue Service, would you prefer to have the taxpayer report the income at the earliest or the latest time? What position did the Service take in the case? Is it what you would have predicted?

5. Suppose you are the taxpayer, would your answer change? Why might the Service and the taxpayer have differing interests with respect to the timing of the income?

6. Why is the name of the Commissioner of Internal Revenue and sometimes the name of the taxpayer listed first in the tax cases decided by the Supreme Court?

7. In *Eisner v. Macomber,* the Supreme Court focused on the word "derived" in the Sixteenth Amendment. Recall the following quote from the case.

----

48. Just as Congress ultimately responded to *Burnet v. Sanford & Brooks,* it also amended the Code in response to *Helvering v. Bruun.* **Glance at section 109.** How would the taxpayer have fared had section 109 been in effect? Would the improvements ever have been taxed? **Glance at the first sentence of section 1019.**

Here we have the essential matter: *not* a gain *accruing* to capital, not a *growth* or *increment* of value *in* the investment; but a gain, a profit, something of exchangeable value *proceeding from* the property, *severed from* the capital however invested or employed, and *coming in*, being "*derived*," that is, *received* or *drawn by* the recipient (the taxpayer) for his *separate* use, benefit and disposal;—that is, income derived from property. Nothing else answers the description.

In *Helvering v. Bruun*, however, the Supreme Court stated something that seems to contradict what it had said earlier in *Eisner v. Macomber*. See following quote from *Bruun*. "It is not necessary to recognition of taxable gain that he should be able to sever the improvement begetting the gain from his original capital."

In light of the discussions of the concept of "realization" in *Eisner*[49] and *Bruun*, formulate a definition of "realization" that would accommodate the outcomes of both cases.[50]

In *Burnet v. Sanford & Brooks*, *Helvering v. Bruun*, and *Eisner v. Macomber*, the issue of timing of income is important. As you probably gathered from our earlier questions, as a general proposition, it is in the taxpayer's interest to defer the reporting of income for as long as possible, and it is in the government's interest to require a taxpayer to report income at the earliest time possible. Why?

This proposition is one of the basic illustrations of the "time value of money" game that has been played by taxpayers and the government over the decades. Simply stated, the object for the taxpayer of the "time value of money" game is to hold on to her money as long as possible in order to put it to productive use.[51] (What does "productive use" mean in this context?) Conversely, the object for the government is to collect that money as soon as possible so as to put it to its own productive use.

Considerations other than time value of money sometimes influence the timing strategies of taxpayers and the government. As you read the *United States v. Lewis*

---

49. In general, one should not shorten the name of a tax case to just the name of the Commissioner of Internal Revenue (in view of the fact that each Commissioner has been involved in many cases during his or her period of service)(see *infra*, footnote 50). For example, one would never say the "Helvering" case. But, for some reason, many tax lawyers make an exception to this rule for *Eisner v, Macomber* and do call it the "Eisner" case. It is, of course, always proper to refer to it by its full name!

50. At the beginning of this section on realization, we told you that the Code does not contain a definition of "realize." **Look, however, at section 1001(a).** This section prescribes one type of realization, the type the Supreme Court was talking about in *Eisner v. Macomber*. A taxpayer will "realize" gain or loss upon the "sale or other disposition of property." Does section 1001(a) address the realization issues raised in *Bruun* and *Glenshaw Glass*?

51. For example, even at a simple interest rate of 6%, a taxpayer would have an additional $6 at the end of the period if she could postpone payment of $100 for one year.

As you know, state lotteries report the jackpot winnings in the form of gross value (without reduction for the fact that the winner does not collect all at one time). Now, however, some lotteries, New York for example, permit the ticket holder to choose a lump-sum amount instead of yearly installments. How would you calculate the value of $10 million payable over 20 years? Suppose New York offered to pay you $4,909,050 in a lump sum instead of $500,000 per year for 20 years. (Remember, if you accept installments, you will not receive the first one until the end of the year, then successive ones on the yearly anniversary.) Is that a "good deal?" Suppose the amount were $6,795,150? Look back to the time value of money tables. If this sounds familiar (or, even if it doesn't, although it should), **refer back to the Adams Adverts problem following *Raytheon*.**

and *Cesarini v. United States* cases, which are set forth in sections 3 and 4 below, think about what may have motivated the timing strategies of the parties in those cases.

3. Complete Dominion

Suppose your grandmother paid you $100 to weed her garden five years ago but she told you not to spend the $100 until your 25th birthday. Did you have income when she paid you? Would your answer change if, instead of paying you when you did the weeding and imposing a moral obligation on you not to spend the money until a later date, she held the money until your 25th birthday? Suppose she gave you a postdated check? Does the following case assist you in analyzing these questions?

UNITED STATES v. LEWIS
340 U.S. 590 (1951)

MR. JUSTICE BLACK delivered the opinion of the Court.

Respondent Lewis brought this action in the Court of Claims seeking a refund of an alleged overpayment of his 1944 income tax. The facts found by the Court of Claims are: In his 1944 income tax return, respondent reported about $22,000 which he had received that year as an employee's bonus. As a result of subsequent litigation in a state court, however, it was decided that respondent's bonus had been improperly computed; under compulsion of the state court's judgment he returned approximately $11,000 to his employer. Until payment of the judgment in 1946, respondent had at all times claimed and used the full $22,000 unconditionally as his own, in the good faith though "mistaken" belief that he was entitled to the whole bonus.

On the foregoing facts the Government's position is that respondent's 1944 tax should not be recomputed, but that respondent should have deducted the $11,000 as a loss in his 1946 tax return. See G.C.M. 16730, XV-1 Cum. Bull. 179 (1936). The Court of Claims, however, ... held that the excess bonus received "under a mistake of fact" was not income in 1944 and ordered a refund based on a recalculation of that year's tax.... We granted certiorari, 340 U.S. 903, because this holding conflicted ... with principles announced in *North American Oil v. Burnet*, 286 U.S. 417.

In the *North American Oil* case we said: "If a taxpayer receives earnings under a claim of right and without restriction as to its disposition, he has received income which he is required to return, even though it may still be claimed that he is not entitled to retain the money, and even though he may still be adjudged liable to restore its equivalent." 286 U.S. at 424. Nothing in this language permits an exception merely because a taxpayer is "mistaken" as to the validity of his claim.... [I]n *Commissioner v. Wilcox, supra,* we held that receipts from embezzlement did not constitute income, distinguishing *North American Oil* on the ground that an embezzler asserts no "bona fide legal or equitable claim." 327 U.S. at 408.

Income taxes must be paid on income received (or accrued) during an annual accounting period.... [S]ee *Burnet v. Sanford & Brooks Co.*, 282 U.S. 359, 363. The "claim of right" interpretation of the tax laws has long been used to give finality to that period, and is now deeply rooted in the federal tax system.... We see no reason why the Court should depart from this well-settled interpretation merely because it results in an advantage or disadvantage to a taxpayer. (Footnote *)

Reversed.

FOOTNOTES:

* It has been suggested that it would be more "equitable" to reopen respondent's 1944 tax return. While the suggestion might work to the advantage of this taxpayer, it could not be adopted as a general solution because, in many cases, the three-year statute of limitations would preclude recovery....

MR. JUSTICE DOUGLAS, dissenting.

The question in this case is not whether the bonus had to be included in 1944 income for purposes of the tax. Plainly it should have been because the taxpayer claimed it as of right. Some years later, however, it was judicially determined that he had no claim to the bonus. The question is whether he may then get back the tax which he paid on the money.

Many inequities are inherent in the income tax. We multiply them needlessly by nice distinctions which have no place in the practical administration of the law. If the refund were allowed, the integrity of the taxable year would not be violated. The tax would be paid when due; but the Government would not be permitted to maintain the unconscionable position that it can keep the tax after it is shown that payment was made on money which was not income to the taxpayer.

Consider the following questions about *Lewis*.

1. In what court did Lewis bring his claim?

2. In what year did Lewis receive the bonus? Did he have an accession to wealth as a consequence? What limitation, if any, did the employer impose on the bonus?

3. Why did Lewis return part of the bonus and in what year?

4. There were two possible methods for adjusting Lewis's tax returns for the bonus and its partial repayment. Which method did Lewis choose and why? Which method did the government want him to use and why? Which method did the Court decide was appropriate and why? Upon which two principles did the Court rely in making its decision? Can you find the language in the decision where the Court refers to these rules and the cases from which they come?[52]

5. How would Lewis report the income from a bonus if he were told in 1944 that he was to receive a bonus based on the profitability of the company for 1944 but he did not actually receive the bonus until the profits of the company were known with certainty in 1945? Would Lewis enjoy an accession to wealth in 1944? Was it realized?

6. How would Lewis report a bonus that he was told about in 1944 but did not receive until 1945 because he forgot to pick up the check before going home on December 31st? That is, did he have complete dominion? (Should the taxpayer be able to "manip-

---

52. The Court's references to the "claim of right" and "annual accounting period" concepts come from two oft-cited, early decisions: *North American Oil v. Burnet*, 286 U.S. 417 (1932) and, *Burnet v. Sanford & Brooks Co.*, 282 U.S. 359 (1931). Why does the name "Burnet" appear in both case names? Many of the well-known Supreme Court tax cases include the name "Helvering," for the same reason these two cases both include the name "Burnet." (Note that Congress has substantially modified the result in *Lewis* through enactment of section 1341.)

ulate" the date on which he gains dominion over an item of income and, thereby, manipulate the year for which he must report the item as income?)[53]

7. Why would it make a difference to an employee in what year he includes the bonus in income? Suppose, for example, that Neil, a single taxpayer, received a bonus of $12,000 in 1998 when his taxable income (his gross income after all deductions but without the bonus), was $50,000. Suppose he does not receive the bonus until 1999 when his taxable income is the same as in 1998. Does it matter to him in which year he receives the bonus? Suppose he does not receive the bonus until 1999 and his taxable income has declined to $20,000?

In *Lewis*, the Supreme Court stated that "receipts from embezzlement [do] not constitute income ... on the ground that an embezzler asserts no 'bona fide legal or equitable claim.'" 340 U.S. at 591–92 (citation to *Wilcox* omitted). Does this mean that the embezzler never has to pay tax on embezzled money? Should that be the result using our three-prong test for income: accession to wealth, clearly realized, and complete dominion?

In what way, if at all, is the position of the embezzler different from that of Lewis in 1944? Is there a difference, or should there be a difference, between the tax treatment of an embezzler and a borrower of money?

How might you distinguish the difference between a true borrower and the employee bookkeeper who, facing some financial stress, decides to "borrow" some of her employer's money until she can pay it back at a later date when her finances improve? How does the following case address these issues?

JAMES v. UNITED STATES[54]
366 U.S. 213 (1961)

MR. CHIEF JUSTICE WARREN announced the judgment of the Court and an opinion in which MR. JUSTICE BRENNAN and MR. JUSTICE STEWART concur.

The issue before us in this case is whether embezzled funds are to be included in the "gross income" of the embezzler in the year in which the funds are misappropriated under §22(a) of the Internal Revenue Code of 1939 (Footnote 1) and §61(a) of the Internal Revenue Code of 1954. (Footnote 2)

The facts are not in dispute. The petitioner is a union official who, with another person, embezzled in excess of $738,000 during the years 1951 through 1954 from his employer union and from an insurance company with which the union was doing business. (Footnote 3) Petitioner failed to report these amounts in his gross income in those years and was convicted for willfully attempting to evade the federal income tax due for each of the years 1951 through 1954 in violation of §145(b) of the Internal Revenue Code of 1939 (Footnote 4) and §7201 of the Internal Revenue Code of 1954. (Footnote 5) He was sentenced to a total of three years' imprisonment. The Court of Appeals affirmed. 273 F.2d 5. Because of a conflict with this Court's decision in *Commissioner v.*

---

53. The timing of income requires further discussion. We will take it up in greater detail in Part IV, What is the Proper Time Period? There we will elaborate on the issue of "constructive receipt," begun here, and will also consider other timing and tax accounting issues in detail.

54. This extract of the case presents three opinions, written by Chief Justice Warren, Justice Black, and Justice Whittaker, respectively. The footnotes, which are noted in parentheses, follow each opinion.

Wilcox, 327 U.S. 404, a case whose relevant facts are concededly the same as those in the case now before us, we granted certiorari....

In *Wilcox*, the Court held that embezzled money does not constitute taxable income to the embezzler in the year of the embezzlement under §22(a) of the Internal Revenue Code of 1939. Six years later, this Court held, in *Rutkin v. United States*, 343 U.S. 130, that extorted money does constitute taxable income to the extortionist in the year that the money is received under §22(a) of the Internal Revenue Code of 1939. In *Rutkin*, the Court did not overrule *Wilcox*, but stated:

"We do not reach in this case the factual situation involved in *Commissioner v. Wilcox*, 327 U.S. 404. We limit that case to its facts. There embezzled funds were held not to constitute taxable income to the embezzler under §22(a)." *Id.*, at 138. (Footnote 6)

However, examination of the reasoning used in *Rutkin* leads us inescapably to the conclusion that *Wilcox* was thoroughly devitalized.

The basis for the *Wilcox* decision was "that a taxable gain is conditioned upon (1) the presence of a claim of right to the alleged gain and (2) the absence of a definite, unconditional obligation to repay or return that which would otherwise constitute a gain. Without some bona fide legal or equitable claim, even though it be contingent or contested in nature, the taxpayer cannot be said to have received any gain or profit within the reach of §22(a)." *Commissioner v. Wilcox, supra*, at p. 408. Since Wilcox embezzled the money, held it "without any semblance of a bona fide claim of right," *ibid.*, and therefore "was at all times under an unqualified duty and obligation to repay the money to his employer," *ibid.*, the Court found that the money embezzled was not includible within "gross income." But, Rutkin's legal claim was no greater than that of Wilcox. It was specifically found "that petitioner had no basis for his claim ... and that he obtained it by extortion." *Rutkin v. United States, supra*, at p. 135. Both Wilcox and Rutkin obtained the money by means of a criminal act; neither had a bona fide claim of right to the funds. (Footnote 7) Nor was Rutkin's obligation to repay the extorted money to the victim any less than that of Wilcox. The victim of an extortion, like the victim of an embezzlement, has a right to restitution. Furthermore, it is inconsequential that an embezzler may lack title to the sums he appropriates while an extortionist may gain a voidable title. Questions of federal income taxation are not determined by such "attenuated subtleties." ... Thus, the fact that Rutkin secured the money with the consent of his victim, *Rutkin v. United States, supra*, at p. 138, is irrelevant. Likewise unimportant is the fact that the sufferer of an extortion is less likely to seek restitution than one whose funds are embezzled. What is important is that the right to recoupment exists in both situations.

Examination of the relevant cases in the courts of appeals lends credence to our conclusion that the *Wilcox* rationale was effectively vitiated by this Court's decision in *Rutkin*. (Footnote 8) Although this case appears to be the first to arise that is "on all fours" with *Wilcox*, the lower federal courts, in deference to the undisturbed *Wilcox* holding, have earnestly endeavored to find distinguishing facts in the cases before them which would enable them to include sundry unlawful gains within "gross income." (Footnote 9)

It had been a well-established principle, long before either *Rutkin* or *Wilcox*, that unlawful, as well as lawful, gains are comprehended within the term "gross income." Section II B of the Income Tax Act of 1913 provided that "the net income of a taxable person shall include gains, profits, and income ... from ... the transaction of any *lawful* business carried on for gain or profit, or gains or profits and income derived from any source whatever...." (Emphasis supplied.) 38 Stat. 167. When the statute was amended in 1916, the one word "lawful" was omitted. This revealed, we think, the obvious intent of that Congress to tax income derived from both legal and illegal sources, to remove the incongruity of having the gains of the honest laborer taxed and the gains of the dishonest immune. *Rutkin v. United States, supra*, at p. 138; *United States v. Sullivan*, 274 U.S. 259, 263. Thereafter, the Court held that gains from illicit traffic in liquor are includible within "gross income." *Ibid....* And, the Court has pointed out, with approval, that there "has been a widespread and settled administrative and judicial recognition of the taxability of unlawful gains of many kinds," *Rutkin v. United States, supra*, at p. 137. These include protection payments made to racketeers, ransom payments paid to kidnappers, bribes, money derived from the sale of unlawful insurance policies, graft, black market gains, funds obtained from the operation of lotteries, income from race track bookmaking and illegal prize fight pictures. *Ibid.*

The starting point in all cases dealing with the question of the scope of what is included in "gross income" begins with the basic premise that the purpose of Congress was "to use the full measure of its taxing power." *Helvering v. Clifford*, 309 U.S. 331, 334. And the Court has given a liberal construction to the broad phraseology of the "gross income" definition statutes in recognition of the intention of Congress to tax all gains except those specifically exempted.... The language of § 22(a) of the 1939 Code, "gains or profits and income derived from any source whatever," and the more simplified language of § 61(a) of the 1954 Code, "all income from whatever source derived," have been held to encompass all "accessions to wealth, clearly realized, and over which the taxpayers have complete dominion." *Commissioner v. Glenshaw Glass Co.*, 348 U.S. 426, 431. A gain "constitutes taxable income when its recipient has such control over it that, as a practical matter, he derives readily realizable economic value from it." *Rutkin v. United States, supra*, at p. 137. Under these broad principles, we believe that petitioner's contention, that all unlawful gains are taxable except those resulting from embezzlement, should fail.

When a taxpayer acquires earnings, lawfully or unlawfully, without the consensual recognition, express or implied, of an obligation to repay and without restriction as to their disposition, "he has received income which he is required to return, even though it may still be claimed that he is not entitled to retain the money, and even though he may still be adjudged liable to restore its equivalent." *North American Oil v. Burnet, supra*, at p. 424. In such case, the taxpayer has "actual command over the property taxed — the actual benefit for which the tax is paid." ... This standard brings wrongful appropriations within the broad sweep of "gross income"; it excludes loans. When a law-abiding taxpayer mistakenly receives income in one year, which receipt is assailed and found to be invalid in a subsequent year, the taxpayer must nonetheless report the amount as "gross income" in the year received. *United States v. Lewis, supra....* We do not believe that Congress intended to treat a law-breaking taxpayer differently. Just as the honest taxpayer may deduct any amount repaid in the year in which the repayment is made, the Government points out that, "If, when, and to the extent that the victim recovers back the misappropriated funds, there is of course a reduction in the embezzler's income." Brief for the United States, p. 24.

Petitioner contends that the *Wilcox* rule has been in existence since 1946; that if Congress had intended to change the rule, it would have done so; that there was a general revision of the income tax laws in 1954 without mention of the rule; that a bill to change it (Footnote 11) was introduced in the Eighty-sixth Congress but was not acted upon; that, therefore, we may not change the rule now. But the fact that *re-enactment* Congress has remained silent or has re-enacted a statute which we have construed, or that congressional attempts to amend a rule announced by this Court have failed, does not necessarily debar us from re-examining and correcting the Court's own errors.... There may have been any number of reasons why Congress acted as it did.... One of the reasons could well be our subsequent decision in *Rutkin* which has been thought by many to have repudiated *Wilcox*. Particularly might this be true in light of the decisions of the Courts of Appeals which have been riding a narrow rail between the two cases and further distinguishing them to the disparagement of *Wilcox*. See notes 8 and 9, *supra*.

We believe that *Wilcox* was wrongly decided and we find nothing in congressional *Wilcox wrongly decided* history since then to persuade us that Congress intended to legislate the rule. Thus, we believe that we should now correct the error and the confusion resulting from it, certainly if we do so in a manner that will not prejudice those who might have relied on it.... We should not continue to confound confusion, particularly when the result would be to perpetuate the injustice of relieving embezzlers of the duty of paying income taxes on the money they enrich themselves with through theft while honest people pay their taxes on every conceivable type of income.

But, we are dealing here with a felony conviction under statutes which apply to any person who "willfully" fails to account for his tax or who "willfully" attempts to evade his obligation. In *Spies v. United States*, 317 U.S. 492, 499, the Court said that § 145(b) of the 1939 Code embodied "the gravest of offenses against the revenues," and stated that willfulness must therefore include an evil motive and want of justification in view *Willfulness specific intent* of all the circumstances. *Id.*, at 498. Willfulness "involves a specific intent which must be proven by independent evidence and which cannot be inferred from the mere understatement of income." *Holland v. United States*, 348 U.S. 121, 139.

We believe that the element of willfulness could not be proven in a criminal prosecution for failing to include embezzled funds in gross income in the year of misappropriation so long as the statute contained the gloss placed upon it by *Wilcox* at the time the *** alleged crime was committed. Therefore, we feel that petitioner's conviction may not stand and that the indictment against him must be dismissed.

Since MR. JUSTICE HARLAN, MR. JUSTICE FRANKFURTER, and MR. JUSTICE CLARK agree with us concerning *Wilcox*, that case is overruled. MR. JUSTICE BLACK, MR. JUSTICE DOUGLAS, and MR. JUSTICE WHITTAKER believe that petitioner's conviction must be reversed and the case dismissed for the reasons stated in their opinions.

Accordingly, the judgment of the Court of Appeals is reversed and the case is remanded to the District Court with directions to dismiss the indictment.

It is so ordered.

FOOTNOTES:

1. § 22. *Gross Income.*

"(a) *General Definition.* — 'Gross income' includes gains, profits, and income derived from salaries, wages, or compensation for personal service ... of whatever kind and in whatever form paid, or from professions, vocations, trades, businesses, commerce, or sales, or dealings in property, whether real or personal, growing out of the ownership or use of or interest in such property; also from interest, rent, dividends, securities, or the transaction of any business carried on for gain or profit, or gains or profits and income derived from any source whatever...." (26 U.S.C. (1952 ed.) § 22(a).)

2. § 1. *Gross Income Defined.*

"(a) *General Definition.*—Except as otherwise provided in this subtitle, gross income means all income from whatever source derived...." (26 U.S.C. § 61(a).)

3. Petitioner has pleaded guilty to the offense of conspiracy to embezzle in the Court of Essex County, New Jersey.

4. § 145. *Penalties.*

"(b) *Failure to Collect and Pay Over Tax, or Attempt to Defeat or Evade Tax.*—Any person required under this chapter to collect, account for, and pay over any tax imposed by this chapter, who willfully fails to collect or truthfully account for and pay over such tax, and any person who willfully attempts in any manner to evade or defeat any tax imposed by this chapter or the payment thereof, shall, in addition to other penalties provided by law, be guilty of a felony and, upon conviction thereof, be fined not more than $10,000 or imprisoned for not more than five years, or both, together with the costs of prosecution." (26 U.S.C. (1952 ed.) § 145(b).)

5. § 7201. Attempt to Evade or Defeat Tax.

"Any person who willfully attempts in any manner to evade or defeat any tax imposed by this title or the payment thereof shall, in addition to other penalties provided by law, be guilty of a felony and, upon conviction thereof, shall be fined not more than $10,000, or imprisoned not more than 5 years, or both, together with the costs of prosecution." (26 U.S.C. § 7201.)

6. The dissenters in *Rutkin* stated that the Court had rejected the *Wilcox* interpretation of § 22(a). *Id.*, at 140.

7. The Government contends that the adoption in *Wilcox* of a claim of right test as a touchstone of taxability had no support in the prior cases of this Court; that the claim of right test was a doctrine invoked by the Court in aid of the concept of annual accounting, to determine when, not *whether*, receipts constituted income. See *North American Oil v. Burnet*, 286 U.S. 417; *United States v. Lewis*, 340 U.S. 590.... In view of our reasoning set forth below, we need not pass on this contention. The use to which we put the claim of right test here is only to demonstrate that, whatever its validity as a test of *whether* certain receipts constitute income, it calls for no distinction between *Wilcox* and *Rutkin*.

8. In *Marienfeld v. United States*, 214 F.2d 632, the Eighth Circuit stated, "We find it difficult to reconcile the Wilcox case with the later opinion of the Supreme Court in Rutkin...." *Id.*, at 636. The Second Circuit announced, in *United States v. Bruswitz*, 219 F.2d 59, "It is difficult to perceive what, if anything, is left of the Wilcox holding after Rutkin...." *Id.*, at 61. The Seventh Circuit's prior decision in *Macias v. Commissioner*, 255 F.2d 23, observed, "If this reasoning [of Rutkin] had been employed in Wilcox, we see no escape from the conclusion that the decision in that case would have been different. In our view, the Court in Rutkin repudiated its holding in Wilcox; certainly it repudiated the reasoning by which the result was reached in that case." *Id.*, at 26.

9. For example, *Kann v. Commissioner*, 210 F.2d 247, was differentiated on the following grounds: the taxpayer was never indicted or convicted of embezzlement; there was no adequate proof that the victim did not forgive the misappropriation; the taxpayer was financially able to both pay the income tax and make restitution; the taxpayer would have likely received most of the misappropriated money as dividends. In *Marienfeld v. United States, supra*, the court believed that the victim was not likely to repudiate. In *United States v. Wyss*, 239 F.2d 658, the distinguishing factors were that the district

judge had not found as a fact that the taxpayer embezzled the funds and the money had not as yet been reclaimed by the victim....

11. H.R. 8854, 86th Cong., 1st Sess.

MR. JUSTICE BLACK, whom MR. JUSTICE DOUGLAS joins, concurring in part and dissenting in part.

On February 25, 1946, fifteen years ago, this Court, after mature consideration, and in accordance with what at that time represented the most strongly supported judicial view, held, in an opinion written by Mr. Justice Murphy to which only one Justice dissented, that money secretly taken by an embezzler for his own use did not constitute a taxable gain to him under the federal income tax laws. *Commissioner v. Wilcox*, 327 U.S. 404. The Treasury Department promptly accepted this ruling in a bulletin declaring that the "mere act of embezzlement does not of itself result in taxable income," although properly urging that "taxable income may result to the embezzler, depending on the facts in the particular case." (Footnote 11) During the fifteen years since *Wilcox* was decided, both this Court and Congress, although urged to do so, have declined to change the *Wilcox* interpretation of statutory "income" with respect to embezzlement. In this case, however, a majority of the Court overrules *Wilcox*. Only three of the members of the Court who decided the *Wilcox* case are participating in this case—MR. JUSTICE FRANKFURTER, MR. JUSTICE DOUGLAS, and myself. MR. JUSTICE DOUGLAS and I dissent from the Court's action in "overruling" *Wilcox*.... We think *Wilcox* was sound when written and is sound now.

. . .

II.

We think *Wilcox* was right when it was decided and is right now. It announced no new, novel doctrine. One need only look at the Government's briefs in this Court in the *Wilcox* case to see just how little past judicial support could then be mustered had the Government sought to send *Wilcox* to jail for his embezzlement under the guise of a tax evasion prosecution. The Government did cite many cases from many courts saying that under the federal income tax law gains are no less taxable because they have been acquired by illegal methods. This Court had properly held long before *Wilcox* that there is no "reason why the fact that a business is unlawful should exempt it from paying the taxes that if lawful it would have to pay." We fully recognized the correctness of that holding in *Wilcox*:

> "Moral turpitude is not a touchstone of taxability. The question, rather, is whether the taxpayer in fact received a statutory gain, profit or benefit. That the taxpayer's motive may have been reprehensible or the mode of receipt illegal has no bearing upon the application of § 22(a)."

The Court today by implication attributes quite a different meaning or consequence to the *Wilcox* opinion. One opinion argues at length the "well-established principle ... that unlawful, as well as lawful, gains are comprehended within the term 'gross income.'" *Wilcox* did not deny that; we do not deny that. This repeated theme of our Brethren is wholly irrelevant since the *Wilcox* holding in no way violates the sound principle of treating "gains" of honest and dishonest taxpayers alike. The whole basis of the *Wilcox* opinion was that an embezzlement is not in itself "gain" or "income" to the embezzler within the tax sense, for the obvious reason that the embezzled property still belongs, and is known to belong, to the rightful owner. It is thus a mistake to argue that petitioner's contention is "that all unlawful gains are taxable except those resulting from embezzlement."

... The whole picture can best be obtained from the court's opinion in *McKnight v. Commissioner*, written by Judge Sibley, one of the ablest circuit judges of his time. He recognized that the taxpayer could not rely upon the unlawfulness of his business to defeat taxation if he had made a "gain" in that business. He pointed out, however, that the ordinary embezzler "got no title, void or voidable, to what he took. He was still in possession as he was before, but with a changed purpose. He still had no right nor color of right. He claimed none." Judge Sibley's opinion went on to point out that the "first takings [of an embezzler] are, indeed, nearly always with the intention of repaying, a sort of unauthorized borrowing. It must be conceded that no gain is realized by borrowing, because of the offsetting obligation." Approaching the matter from a practical standpoint, Judge Sibley also explained that subjecting the embezzled funds to a tax would amount to allowing the United States "a preferential claim for part of the dishonest gain, to the direct loss and detriment of those to whom it ought to be restored." He was not willing to put the owner of funds that had been stolen in competition with the United States Treasury Department as to which one should have a preference to get those funds.

It seems to us that Judge Sibley's argument was then and is now unanswerable. The rightful owner who has entrusted his funds to an employee or agent has troubles enough when those funds are embezzled without having the Federal Government step in with its powerful claim that the embezzlement is a taxable event automatically subjecting part of those funds (still belonging to the owner) to the waiting hands of the Government's tax gatherer. We say part of the *owner's* funds because it is on the supposed "gain" from them that the embezzler is now held to be duty-bound to pay the tax and history probably records few instances of independently wealthy embezzlers who have had nonstolen assets available for payment of taxes.

There has been nothing shown to us on any of the occasions when we have considered this problem to indicate that Congress ever intended its income tax laws to be construed as imposing what is in effect a property or excise tax on the rightful owner's embezzled funds, for which the owner has already once paid income tax when he rightfully acquired them. In our view, the Court today does Congress a grave injustice by assuming that it has imposed this double tax burden upon the victim of an embezzlement merely because someone has stolen his money, particularly when Congress has refused requests that it do so. The owner whose funds have been embezzled has done nothing but entrust an agent with possession of his funds for limited purposes, as many of us have frequent occasion to do in the course of business or personal affairs. Ordinarily the owner is not, and has no reason to be, at all aware of an embezzlement until long after the first misuse occurs. If Congress ever did manifest an intention to select the mere fact of embezzlement as the basis for imposing a double tax on the owner, we think a serious question of confiscation in violation of the Fifth Amendment would be raised. All of us know that with the strong lien provisions of the federal income tax law an owner of stolen funds would have a very rocky road to travel before he got back, without paying a good slice to the Federal Government, such funds as an embezzler who had not paid the tax might, perchance, not have dissipated. An illustration of what this could mean to a defrauded employer is shown in this very case by the employer's loss of some $700,000, upon which the Government claims a tax of $559,000.

It seems to be implied that one reason for overruling *Wilcox* is that a failure to hold embezzled funds taxable would somehow work havoc with the public revenue or discriminate against "honest" taxpayers and force them to pay more taxes. We believe it would be impossible to substantiate either claim. Embezzlers ordinarily are not rich people against whom judgments, even federal tax judgments can be enforced. Judging from the meager settlements that those defrauded were apparently compelled to make with the embezzlers in this very case, it is hard to imagine that the Treasury will be able to collect the more than $500,000 it claims. And certainly the *Wilcox* case does not seem to have been one in which the Government could have collected any great amount of tax. The employer's embezzled $11,000 there went up in gambling houses. The scarcity of cases involving alleged taxes due from embezzlers is another indication that the Government cannot expect to make up any treasury deficits with taxes collected from embezzlers and thieves, especially when the cost to the Government of investigations and court proceedings against suspected individuals is considered. And, as already indicated, to the extent that the Government could be successful in collecting some taxes from embezzlers, it would most likely do so at the expense of the owner whose money had been stolen.

It follows that, except for the possible adverse effect on rightful owners, the only substantial result that one can foresee from today's holding is that the Federal Government will, under the guise of a tax evasion charge, prosecute people for a simple embezzlement. But the Constitution grants power to Congress to get revenue not to prosecute local crimes. And if there is any offense which under our dual system of government is a purely local one which the States should handle, it is embezzlement or theft. The Federal Government stands to lose much money by trying to take over prosecution of this type of local offense. It is very doubtful whether the further congestion of federal court dockets to try such local offenses is good for the Nation, the States or the people. Here the embezzler has already pleaded guilty to the crime of embezzlement in a state court, although the record does not show what punishment he has received. Were it not for the novel formula of applying the Court's new law prospectively, petitioner would have to serve three years in federal prison in addition to his state sentence. This graphically illustrates one of the great dangers of opening up the federal tax statutes, or any others, for use by federal prosecutors against defendants who not only can be but are tried for their crimes in local state courts and punished there. If the people of this country are to be subjected to such double jeopardy and double punishment, despite the constitutional command against double jeopardy, it seems to us it would be far wiser for this Court to wait and let Congress attempt to do it.

...

FOOTNOTES:

1. G.C.M. No. 24945, 1946-2 Cum. Bull. 27, 28. This was precisely in accord with this Court's statement of the proper rule in the *Wilcox* opinion:

"Taxable income may arise, to be sure, from the use or in connection with the use of such [embezzled] property.... But apart from such factors the bare receipt of property or money wholly belonging to another lacks the essential characteristics of a gain or profit within the meaning of §22(a)." 327 U.S., at 408.

MR. JUSTICE WHITTAKER, whom MR. JUSTICE BLACK and MR. JUSTICE DOUGLAS join, concurring in part and dissenting in part.

The starting point of any inquiry as to what constitutes taxable income must be the Sixteenth Amendment, which grants Congress the power "to lay and collect taxes on incomes, from whatever source derived...." It has long been settled that Congress' broad statutory definitions of taxable income were intended "to use the full measure of [the Sixteenth Amendment's] taxing power." *Helvering v. Clifford*, 309 U.S. 331, 334; ... equally well settled is the principle that the Sixteenth Amendment "is to be taken as written and is not to be extended beyond the meaning clearly indicated by the language used." ... The language of the Sixteenth Amendment, as well as our prior controlling decisions, compels me to conclude that the question now before us—whether an embezzler receives taxable income at the time of his unlawful taking—must be answered negatively. Since the prevailing opinion reaches an opposite conclusion, I must respectfully dissent from that holding, although I concur in the Court's judgment reversing petitioner's conviction. I am convinced that *Commissioner v. Wilcox*, 327 U.S. 404, which is today overruled, was correctly decided on the basis of every controlling principle used in defining taxable income since the Sixteenth Amendment's adoption.

THE CHIEF JUSTICE's opinion, although it correctly recites *Wilcox*'s holding that "embezzled money does not constitute taxable income to the embezzler *in the year of the embezzlement*" (emphasis added), fails to explain or to answer the true basis of that holding. *Wilcox* did not hold that embezzled funds may never constitute taxable income to the embezzler. To the contrary, it expressly recognized that an embezzler may realize a taxable gain to the full extent of the amount taken, if and when it ever becomes his. The applicable test of taxable income, *i.e.*, the "presence of a claim of right to the alleged gain," of which *Wilcox* spoke, was but a correlative statement of the factor upon which the decision placed its whole emphasis throughout, namely, the "absence of a definite, unconditional obligation to repay or return [the money]." ... In holding that this test was not met at the time of the embezzlement, the *Wilcox* opinion repeatedly stressed that the embezzler had no "bona fide legal or equitable claim" to the embezzled funds, *ibid.*; that the victim never "condoned or forgave the taking of the money and still holds him liable to restore it," ... and that the "debtor-creditor relationship was definite and unconditional." ... These statements all express the same basic fact—the fact which is emphasized most strongly in the opinion's conclusion explaining why the embezzler had not yet received taxable income: "Sanctioning a tax under the circumstances before us would serve only to give the United States an unjustified preference as to part of the money which *rightfully and completely belongs to the taxpayer's employer*."

However, *Wilcox* plainly stated that "if the unconditional indebtedness is canceled or retired, taxable income may adhere, under certain circumstances, to the taxpayer." ... More specifically, it recognized that had the embezzler's victim "condoned or forgiven any part of the [indebtedness], the [embezzler] might have been subject to tax liability to that extent," ... *i.e.*, in the tax year of such forgiveness.

These statements reflect an understanding of, and regard for, substantive tax law concepts solidly entrenched in our prior decisions. Since our landmark case of *United States v. Kirby Lumber Co.*, 284 U.S. 1, it has been settled that, upon a discharge of indebtedness by an event other than full repayment, the debtor realizes a taxable gain in the year of discharge to the extent of the indebtedness thus extinguished. Such gains are commonly referred to as ones realized through "bargain cancellations" of indebtedness, and it was in this area, and indeed, in *Kirby Lumber Co.* itself, that the "accession" theory or "economic gain" concept of taxable income, upon which THE CHIEF JUSTICE's opinion today mistakenly relies, found its genesis. In that case, the taxpayer, a corporation, had reduced a portion of its debt, with a corresponding gain in assets, by purchasing its bonds in the open market at considerably less than their issue price. Mr. Justice Holmes, who wrote the Court's opinion, found it unnecessary to state the elementary principle that, so long as the bonds remained a fully enforceable debt obligation of the taxpayer, there could be no taxable gain. However, when the taxpayer retired the debt by purchasing the bonds for less than their face value, it "made a clear [taxable] gain" and "realized within the year an accession to income" in the amount of its bargain....

This doctrine has since been reaffirmed and strengthened by us, ... and by the lower federal courts in numerous decisions involving a variety of "bargain cancellations" of indebtedness, as by a creditor's release condoning or forgiving the indebtedness in whole or in part, or by the running of a Statute of Limitations barring the legal enforceability of the obligation. In none of these cases has it been suggested that a taxable gain might be realized by the debtor at any time *prior* to the effective date of discharge, and as *Wilcox* recognized, there is no rational basis on which to justify such a rule where the debt arises through embezzlement.

An embezzler, like a common thief, acquires not a semblance of right, title, or interest in his plunder, and whether he spends it or not, he is indebted to his victim in the full amount taken as surely as if he had left a signed promissory note at the scene of the crime. Of no consequence from any standpoint is the absence of such formalities as (in the words of the prevailing opinion) "the consensual recognition, express or implied, of an obligation to repay." The law readily implies whatever "consensual recognition" is needed for the rightful owner to assert an immediately ripe and enforceable obligation of repayment against the wrongful taker. These principles are not "attenuated subtleties" but are among the clearest and most easily applied rules of our law. They exist to protect the rights of the innocent victim, and we should accord them full recognition and respect.

The fact that an embezzler's victim may have less chance of success than other creditors in seeking repayment from his debtor is not a valid reason for us further to diminish his prospects by adopting a rule that would allow the Commissioner of Internal Revenue to assert and enforce a prior federal tax lien against that which "rightfully and completely belongs" to the victim. *Commissioner v. Wilcox*.... THE CHIEF JUSTICE's opinion quite understandably expresses much concern for "honest taxpayers," but it attempts neither to deny nor justify the manifest injury that its holding will inflict on those honest taxpayers, victimized by embezzlers, who will find their claims for recovery subordinated to federal tax liens. Statutory provisions, by which we are bound, clearly and unequivocally accord priority to federal tax liens over the claims of others, including "judgment creditors." (Footnote 4)

However, if it later happens that the debtor-creditor relationship between the embezzler and his victim is discharged by something other than full repayment, such as by the running of a Statute of Limitations against the victim's claim, or by a release given for less than the full amount owed, the embezzler at that time, but not before, will have made a clear taxable gain and realized "an accession to income" which he will be required under full penalty of the law to report in his federal income tax return for that year. No honest taxpayer could be harmed by this rule.

The inherent soundness of this rule could not be more clearly demonstrated than as applied to the facts of the case before us. Petitioner, a labor union official, concededly embezzled sums totaling more than $738,000 from the union's funds, over a period extending from 1951 to 1954. When the shortages were discovered in 1956, the union at once filed civil actions against petitioner to compel repayment. For reasons which need not be detailed here, petitioner effected a settlement agreement with the union on July 30, 1958, whereby, in exchange for releases fully discharging his indebtedness, he repaid to the union the sum of $13,568.50. Accordingly, at least so far as the present record discloses, petitioner clearly realized a taxable gain in the year the releases were executed, to the extent of the difference between the amount taken and the sum restored. However, the Government brought the present action against him, not for his failure to report this gain in his 1958 return, but for his failure to report that he had incurred "income" from—actually indebtedness to—the union in each of the years 1951 through 1954. It is true that the Government brought a criminal evasion prosecution rather than a civil deficiency proceeding against petitioner, but this can in no way alter the substantive tax law rules which alone are determinative of liability in either case.

There can be no doubt that until the releases were executed in 1958, petitioner and the union stood in an absolute and unconditional debtor-creditor relationship, and, under all of our relevant decisions, no taxable event could have occurred until the indebtedness was discharged for less than full repayment. Application of the normal rule in such cases will not hinder the efficient and orderly administration of the tax laws, any more than it does in other situations involving "bargain cancellations" of indebtedness. More importantly, it will enhance the creditor's position by assuring that prior federal tax liens will not attach to the subject of the debt when he seeks to recover it.

. . .

There is still another obvious and important distinction between embezzlement and the varieties of illegal activity listed by the prevailing opinion—one which clearly calls for a different tax treatment. Black marketeering, gambling, bribery, graft and like activities generally give rise to no legally enforceable right of restitution—to no debtor-creditor relationship which the law will recognize. (Footnote 6) Condemned either by statute or public policy, or both, such transactions are *void ab initio*. Since any consideration which may have passed is not legally recoverable, its recipient has realized a taxable gain, an "accession to income," as clearly as if his "indebtedness" had been discharged by a full release or by the running of a Statute of Limitations. As we have already shown at length, quite the opposite is true when an embezzlement occurs; for then the victim acquires an immediately ripe and enforceable claim to repayment, and the embezzler assumes a legal debt equal to his acquisition.

To reach the result that it does today, THE CHIEF JUSTICE's opinion constructs the following theory for defining taxable income:

> "When a taxpayer acquires earnings, lawfully or unlawfully, without the consensual recognition, express or implied, of an obligation to repay and without restriction as to their disposition, 'he has received income which he is required to return, even though it may still be claimed that he is not entitled to retain the money, and even though he may still be adjudged liable to restore its equivalent.' *North American Oil v. Burnet*, . . . in such case, the taxpayer has 'actual command over the property taxed—the actual benefit for which the tax is paid.'. . . This standard brings wrongful appropriations within the broad sweep of 'gross income'; it excludes loans. When a law-abiding taxpayer mistakenly receives income in one year, which receipt is assailed and found to be invalid in a subsequent year, the taxpayer must nonetheless report the amount as 'gross income' in the year received. *United States v. Lewis, supra....*

This novel formula finds no support in our prior decisions, least of all in those which are cited.... *North American Oil v. Burnet*, 286 U.S. 417, is the case which introduced the principle since used to facilitate uniformity and certainty in annual tax accounting procedure, *i.e.*, that a taxpayer must report in gross income, in the year in which received, money or property acquired under a "claim of right"—a colorable claim of the right to *exclusive possession* of the money or property. Thus, in its complete form, the sentence in *North American Oil* from which the above-quoted fragment was extracted reads: "If a taxpayer receives *earnings under a claim of right* and without restriction as to its *[sic]* disposition, he has received income which he is required to return, even though it may still be claimed that he is not entitled to retain the money, and even though he may still be adjudged liable to restore its equivalent." *Id.*, at 424 (Emphasis added.) But embezzled funds, like stolen property generally, are not "earnings" in any sense and are held without a vestige of a colorable claim of right; they constitute the principal of a debt. Of no significance whatever is the formality of "consensual recognition, express or implied" of an obligation to repay. By substituting this meaningless abstraction in place of the omitted portion of the *North American Oil* test of *when* a receipt constitutes taxable income, the prevailing opinion today goes far beyond overruling *Wilcox*—it reduces a substantial body of tax law into uncertainty and confusion. The above-cited case of *United States v. Lewis*, 340 U.S. 590, decided 19 years after *North American Oil*, demonstrates the truth of this. For there we said:

> "The 'claim of right' interpretation of the tax laws has long been used to give finality to [the accounting] period, and is now deeply rooted in the federal tax system.... We see no reason why the Court should depart from this well-settled interpretation merely because it results in an advantage or disadvantage to a taxpayer." 340 U.S., at 592.

...

FOOTNOTES:

4. 26 U.S.C. § 6321-6323, 6331; ...

6. Restatement, Contracts, § 598; 6 Corbin, Contracts, § 1373 et seq. (1951)....

Consider the following questions about *James.*

1. After *James, w*hat is the rule with respect to income from embezzled funds?

2. Would the Court have decided differently if it had not already decided *Lewis, i.e.,* because it would be anomalous to make Lewis include his bonus in income but let a lawbreaker off the hook? Or, did the Court believe its earlier opinions concerning embezzlers were wrong and that ill-gotten funds should have been income from the beginning?

3. Unlike the taxpayer in *Raytheon*, James lost the battle, but won the war. Why? Why did the Court order a dismissal of the indictment?

4. Can you articulate the arguments put forth by Justices Black and Whittaker in their opinions? Why did the Court have so much trouble deciding this case? Among the views of the Chief Justice and the dissenters, who is "right"?

5. Both Justices Black and Whittaker mention the power of "federal tax liens" that would make it difficult for the rightful owner to obtain her funds. What is a "federal tax lien"?

6. How justifiable is the view of Justice Black that because Congress knew about the decision of the Supreme Court in *Wilcox* and rejected attempts to amend the income tax rules to reverse *Wilcox*, it must agree with the outcome in *Wilcox*?

Consider Justice Black's dissent. Should the Supreme Court be bound by anything other than its own earlier interpretation of the words of the Code? That is, when the Court has already interpreted those words in another case, should *stare decisis* be outweighed by other sources to which the court might turn for aid in interpreting the Code, for example, maxims of statutory interpretation or legislative history?

In this case, the majority and the minority advance, in effect, two different maxims of statutory interpretation: the majority points to the inaction of Congress after the *Wilcox* decision; the dissent points to the re-enactment by Congress of the existing Code provision. Does one maxim seem more likely than the other to reflect the "real" intent of Congress?

4. Applying the Three-Prong Test

Suppose you are walking along the beach in Hawaii. You trip over something that turns out to be a packet of money. You are an honest person so you go to the local police station and report your find. The police have no record of the serial numbers (thus, the money is not associated with a known crime). The police tell you that if no one claims the money in three months, they will turn it over to you. Do you have income and, if so, when? Would your answer change if the packet contained a gold watch? Consider the following case (keeping in mind the definition you formulated for "realization" following Eisner v. *Macomber* and *Helvering v. Bruun*). **Look again at question 7 following *Bruun*.**

CESARINI v. UNITED STATES
296 F. Supp. 3 (N.D. Ohio 1969)

YOUNG, District Judge:

This is an action by the plaintiffs as taxpayers for the recovery of income tax payments made in the calendar year 1964. Plaintiffs contend that the amount of $836.51 was erroneously overpaid by them in 1964, and that they are entitled to a refund in that amount, together with the statutory interest from October 13, 1965, the date which they made their claim upon the Internal Revenue Service for the refund....

... In 1957, the plaintiffs purchased a used piano at an auction sale for approximately $15.00, and the piano was used by their daughter for piano lessons. In 1964, while cleaning the piano, plaintiffs discovered the sum of $4,467.00 in old currency, and since have retained the piano instead of discarding it as previously planned. Being unable to ascertain who put the money there, plaintiffs exchanged the old currency for new at a bank, and reported the sum of $4,467.00 on their 1964 joint income tax return as ordinary income from other sources. On October 18, 1965, plaintiffs filed an amended return with the District Director of Internal Revenue in Cleveland, Ohio, this second return eliminating the sum of $4,467.00 from the gross income computation, and requesting a refund in the amount of $836.51, the amount allegedly overpaid as a result of the former inclusion of $4,467.00 in the original return for the calendar year of 1964. On January 18, 1966, the Commissioner of Internal Revenue rejected taxpayers' refund claim in its entirety, and plaintiffs filed the instant action in March of 1967.

Plaintiffs make ... alternative contentions in support of their claim that the sum of $836.51 should be refunded to them. First, that the $4,467.00 found in the piano is not includable in gross income under Section 61 of the Internal Revenue Code.... Secondly, even if the retention of the cash constitutes a realization of ordinary income under Section 61, it was due and owing in the year the piano was purchased, 1957, and by 1964, the statute of limitations provided by ... § 6501 had elapsed.... The Government ... asserts that the amount found in the piano is includible in gross income under Section 61(a) ... that the money is taxable in the year it was actually found, 1964....

After a consideration of the pertinent provisions of the Internal Revenue Code, Treasury Regulations, Revenue Rulings, and decisional law in the area, this Court has concluded that the taxpayers are not entitled to a refund of the amount requested....

The starting point in determining whether an item is to be included in gross income is, of course, Section 61(a) ... and that section provides in part:

"Except as otherwise provided in this subtitle, *gross income means all income from whatever source derived*, including (but not limited to) the following items:...."

Subsections (1) through (15) of Section 61(a) then go on to list fifteen items specifically included in the computation of the taxpayer's gross income, and Part II of Subchapter B of the 1954 Code (Sections 71 *et seq.*) deals with other items expressly included in gross income. While neither of these listings expressly includes the type of income which is at issue in the case at bar, Part III of Subchapter B (Sections 101 *et seq.*) deals with items specifically *excluded* from gross income, and found money is not listed in those sections either. This absence of express mention in any of the code sections necessitates a return to the "all income from whatever source" language of Section 61(a) of the code, and the express statement there that gross income is "not limited to" the following fifteen examples. Section 1.61-1(a) of the Treasury Regulations, the corresponding section to Section 61(a) in the 1954 Code, reiterates this broad construction of gross income, providing in part:

"Gross income means all income from whatever source derived, unless excluded by law. *Gross income includes income realized in any form*, whether in money, property, or services...."

The decisions of the United States Supreme Court have frequently stated that this broad all-inclusive language was used by Congress to exert the full measure of its taxing power under the Sixteenth Amendment to the United States Constitution. Commissioner of ~~Internal Revenue v. Glenshaw Glass Co.~~, 348 U.S. 426, 429.... *GG*

In addition, the Government in the instant case cites and relies upon an I.R.S. Revenue Ruling which is undeniably on point:

"The finder of treasure-trove is in receipt of taxable income, for Federal income tax purposes, to the extent of its value in United States currency, for the taxable year in which it is reduced to undisputed possession." Rev. Rul. 61, 1953-1, Cum. Bull. 17.

The plaintiffs argue that the above ruling does not control this case for two reasons. The first is that subsequent to the Ruling's pronouncement in 1953, Congress enacted Sections 74 and 102 of the 1954 Code, <u>§ 74 expressly *including* the value of prizes and gifts in gross income in most cases, and § 102 specifically *exempting* the value of gifts received from gross income.</u> From this, it is argued that Section 74 was added because prizes might otherwise be construed as nontaxable gifts, and since no such section was passed expressly taxing treasure trove, it is therefore a gift which is non-taxable under Section 102. This line of reasoning overlooks the statutory scheme previously alluded to, whereby income from all sources is taxed unless the taxpayer can point to an express exemption. Not only have the taxpayers failed to list a specific exclusion in the instant case, but also the Government has pointed to express language covering the found money, even though it would not be required to do so *§ 74 § 102* under the broad language of Section 61(a) and the foregoing Supreme Court decisions interpreting it.

The second argument of the taxpayers in support of their contention that Rev. Rul. 61, 1953-1 should not be applied in this case is based upon the decision of Dougherty v. Commissioner, 10 T.C.M. 320 ... (1951). In that case the petitioner was an individual who had never filed an income tax return, and the Commissioner was attempting to determine his gross income by the so-called "net worth" method. Dougherty had a substantial increase in his net worth, and attempted to partially explain away his lack of reporting it by claiming that he had found $31,000.00 in cash inside a used chair he had purchased in 1947. The Tax Court's opinion deals primarily with the factual question of whether or not Dougherty actually *did* find this money in a chair, finally concluding that he did not, and from this petitioners in the instant case argue that if such found money is clearly gross income, the Tax Court would not have reached the fact question, but merely included the $31,000.00 as a matter of law. Petitioners argue that since the Tax Court did not include the sum in Dougherty's gross income until they had found as a fact that it *was not* treasure trove, then by implication such discovered money is not taxable. This argument must fail for two reasons. First, the *Dougherty* decision precedes Rev. Rul. 61, 1953-1 by two years, and thus was dealing with what then was an uncharted area of the gross income provisions of the Code. Secondly, the case cannot be read as authority for the proposition that treasure trove is not includable in gross income, even if the revenue ruling had not been issued two years later. (Footnote 1)

In partial summary, then, the arguments of the taxpayers which attempt to avoid the application of Rev. Rul. 61, 1953-1 are not well taken. The *Dougherty* case simply does not hold one way or another on the problem before this Court, and therefore petitioners' reliance upon it is misplaced. The other branch of their argument, that found money must be construed to be a gift under Section 102 of the 1954 Code since it is not expressly included as are prizes in Section 74 of the Code, would not even be effective were it being urged at a time prior to 1953, when the ruling had not yet been promulgated. In addition to the numerous cases in the Supreme Court which uphold the broad sweeping construction of Section 61(a) found in Treas. Reg. § 1.61-1(a), other courts and commentators writing at a point in time before the ruling came down took the position that windfalls, including found monies, were properly includable in gross income under Section 22(a) of the 1939 Code, the predecessor of Section 61(a) in the 1954 Code.... While it is generally true that revenue rulings may be disregarded by the courts if in conflict with the code and the regulations, or with other judicial decisions, plaintiffs in the instant case have been unable to point to any inconsistency between the gross income sections of the code, the interpretation of them by the regulations and the courts, and the revenue ruling which they herein attack as inapplicable. On the other hand, the United States *has* shown a consistency in letter and spirit between the ruling and the code, regulations, and court decisions.

Although not cited by either party, and noticeably absent from the Government's brief, the following Treasury Regulation appears in the 1964 Regulations, the year of the return in dispute:

"§ 1.61-14 Miscellaneous items of gross income.

"(a) In general. In addition to the items enumerated in section 61(a), there are many other kinds of gross income.... *Treasure trove, to the extent of its value in United States currency, constitutes gross income for the taxable year in which it is reduced to undisputed possession."* ...

Identical language appears in the 1968 Treasury Regulations, and is found in all previous years back to 1958. This language is the same in all material respects as that found in Rev. Rul. 61-53-1, Cum. Bull. 17, and is undoubtedly an attempt to codify that ruling into the Regulations which apply to the 1954 Code. This Court is of the opinion that Treas. Reg. § 1.61-14(a) is dispositive of the major issue in this case if the $4,467.00 found in the piano was "reduced to undisputed possession" in the year petitioners reported it, for this Regulation was applicable to returns filed in the calendar year of 1964.

...

This brings the Court to the second contention of the plaintiffs: that if any tax was due, it was in 1957 when the piano was purchased, and by 1964 the Government was blocked from collecting it by reason of the statute of limitations. Without reaching the question of whether the voluntary payment in 1964 constituted a waiver on the part of the taxpayers, this Court finds that the $4,467.00 sum was properly included in gross income for the calendar year of 1964. Problems of when title vests, or when possession is complete in the field of federal taxation, in the absence of definitive federal legislation on the subject, are ordinarily determined by reference to the law of the state in which the taxpayer resides, or where the property around which the dispute centers is located. Since both the taxpayers and the property in question are found within the State of Ohio, Ohio law must govern as to when the found money was "reduced to undisputed possession" within the meaning of Treas. Reg. § 1.61-14 and Rev. Rul. 61, 1953-1, Cum. Bull. 17.

...

In Ohio, there is no statute specifically dealing with the rights of owners and finders of treasure trove, and in the absence of such a statute the common-law rule of England applies, so that "title belongs to the finder as against all the world except the true owner." Niederlehner v. Weatherly, 78 Ohio App. 263, 69 N.E. 2d 787 (1946).... The *Niederlehner* case held, *inter alia*, that the owner of real estate upon which money is found does not have title as against the finder. Therefore, in the instant case if plaintiffs had resold the piano in 1958, not knowing of the money within it, they later would not be able to succeed in an action against the purchaser who did discover it. Under Ohio law, the plaintiffs must have actually *found* the money to have superior title over all but the true owner, and they did not discover the old currency until 1964. Unless there is present a specific state statute to the contrary, the majority of jurisdictions are in accord with the Ohio rule. Therefore, this Court finds that the $4,467.00 in old currency was not "reduced to undisputed possession" until its actual discovery in 1964, and thus the United States was not barred by the statute of limitations from collecting the $836.51 in tax during that year.

... Since it appears to the Court that the income tax on these taxpayers' gross income for the calendar year of 1964 has been properly assessed and paid, this taxpayers' suit for a refund in the amount of $836.51 must be dismissed, and judgment entered for the United States. An order will be entered accordingly.

FOOTNOTES:

1. The Dougherty Court, after carefully considering the evidence before it on the factual question of whether or not the taxpayer actually found the $31,000.00 as claimed, stated:

"In short, we do not believe the money was in the chair when the chair was acquired by the petitioner.

"Where the petitioner got the money which he later took from the chair and in what manner it was obtained by him, we do not know. It is accordingly impossible for us to conclude and hold the $31,000 here in question was not acquired by him in a manner such as would make it income to him within the meaning of the statute. Such being the case, *we do not reach the question whether money, if acquired in the manner claimed by the petitioner, is income under the statute.*" 10 T.C.M. 320 at 323. (1951)

How do you apply the principles of *Glenshaw Glass* in the context of the following issues raised by *Cesarini*?

1. Why did the Cesarinis report the $4,467 found in the piano as income? (What was the importance, if any, of the fact that what they found was "old currency"?)

2. The Cesarinis first argued that the money was not income at all. Why did they advance as an alternative argument that the money was includable in gross income in 1957, the year they purchased the piano, rather than in 1964, the year they found the money? **Look again at section 6501(a).**

3. Suppose instead of money, the Cesarinis found a diamond ring in the piano that was worth $5,000. How does the finder ascertain that its value is $5,000? Would that change the result in the case?

Issues involving "treasure trove" arise more often than you might think and in many contexts — some of them quite surprising to the participants. For example, according to the "treasure trove" regulation, beachcombers who successfully search the beach with metal detectors have income; divers who successfully search for underwater treasure have income.[55] But the doctrine applies well beyond these common illustrations.

Suppose you purchase a ticket to see a baseball game, hoping that this will be the game in which the leading home run hitter breaks the record for home runs and that you will be the lucky fan who catches the ball. Your dream comes true! Do you have income? Apply the test of *Glenshaw Glass*: do you have an accession to wealth, clearly realized, over which you have complete dominion?

In fact, as the excitement built during the 1998 baseball season concerning the likelihood that either Mark McGwire or Sammy Sosa would "break" Roger Maris' season home run record, discussions erupted over the tax fate of the catcher of the tie-breaking ball.[56] A September 7, 1998, article, by a New York Times reporter, was typical of the media furor:

---

55. You may be thinking to yourself, "Yeah, right. But, how will the Service ever find out?" Remember our discussion of your ethical obligations as a lawyer when we discussed barter transactions. **Review footnote 29 in question 6 following Revenue Ruling 79-24.** Even non-lawyers should not risk omitting such income; remember also our citation to section 7201 of the Code, the criminal evasion statute.

56. As this book goes to press, allegations of steroid use have called into question the legitimacy of home run records set by McGuire in 1998 and Barry Bonds in 2001 and (imminently) in 2007. The steroid controversy notwithstanding, it is the authors' view that the panoply of tax issues raised by the historic baseballs continues to be relevant and deserving of study.

Fan Snaring No. 62 Faces Big Tax Bite[57]

If a fan catches the ball that breaks baseball's home-run record and generously gives it to the slugger, it could be more than a great baseball event. It could be the taxable event of a lifetime.

Fans attending games featuring Mark McGwire and Sammy Sosa might want to buy extra tickets for their accountants. According to the Internal Revenue Service, the bleacher bum who paid $6 to $10 for a ticket — not the multimillionaire slugger — could owe Federal gift tax. For a fan giving a million-dollar ball to McGwire or Sosa, the Federal tax could reach $150,000 or more. And states also have gift taxes.

The person receiving a gift owes no tax.

The gift tax applies to "any property" worth $10,000 or more, according to I.R.S. regulations. It makes no difference under the tax code whether the gift is cash, a diamond necklace or a record-setting baseball. The tax is computed on the fair market value of the gift.

It remains to be seen whether the new, customer-friendly I.R.S. has the chutzpah to try to collect the tax from, say, a 12-year-old baseball fan.

"I can confirm your understanding of how the gift tax works," an I.R.S. spokesman ... said today. "The giver of the gift is required to file the gift tax return. We'd have to take a look at all the circumstances: the value of the gift and who owns the baseball."

A ball that breaks Roger Maris's record of 61 homers could fetch $1 million or more, sports collectors say. Already a donor who asked to remain anonymous has offered to pay $1 million for the ball to publicize the cause of three American nuns and a lay worker who were murdered in El Salvador in 1980.

The ball is the property of Major League Baseball until it leaves the field. Then whoever catches it owns it. The tax permutations are more complicated than figuring a slugging percentage, but tax experts lay out several options:

- If the fan keeps the ball, the fan owes no tax now. But the ball would become part of the fan's estate, taxable after death.

- The only way to avoid tax entirely is to give the ball to a charity. Any charity could then sell the ball for a profit, which would not be taxed.

- If the fan sells the ball, the fan owes tax on the profit, just as the seller of any property would. The transaction would put the fan in the highest tax bracket, with 39.6 percent due. The tax on a million-dollar ball would be $396,000.

"It's not a taxable event when the fan catches the ball, but it is if he sells the ball or gives it away," said ... a certified public accountant ... in Manhattan. "If a fan catches a ball, it's worth what the market will pay at auction. You'd probably want to get three appraisals."

...

If the fan gives the ball to the player or the baseball team, the gift tax is triggered....

---

57. Bill Dedman, "Fan Snaring No. 62 Faces Big Tax Bite," N.Y. Times, Sept. 7, 1998, at D1.

... So a person giving away a ball worth $1 million would owe ... a tax of $150,000.

People often avoid gift taxes by not filing the gift tax return. In this case, however, it would be quite a trick for the fan who catches the ball to remain anonymous.

Couldn't the fan and the player make a deal to have the player pay the gift tax? "If the player pays your gift tax for you, then you'll have to pay income tax on the gift tax you received," said [a] Professor ... who teaches tax law.

...

McGwire and Sosa have said they would not pay for a baseball. "I'm a baseball player," Sosa said, "not a baseball fan." McGwire has warned, "I wouldn't pay a dime for it."

Both players, however, have said they would accept the ball if a fan gave it to them.

...

Query: Did the reporter accurately describe the federal income tax consequences? (Might you observe that he had not recently reviewed *Glenshaw Glass* or Treasury Regulation section 1.61-14?)[58]

When McGwire (of the St. Louis Cardinals), finally broke the record, hitting his 62nd home run of the year, the ball was caught on the club grounds by an employee of the club. The media (and the public) were abuzz; would the poor guy be hit with a huge gift tax, despite his intention to give the ball back to McGwire?[59]

Service Commissioner Rossotti, following a distressed call from Senator William V. Roth, Chair of the Senate Finance Committee, quickly assured the public that there would be no gift tax; Bill Thomas, Congressman from California, introduced H.R. 4522 to make sure there would be none. Other legislators quickly turned the occasion into an opportunity to bash the present tax system. Would they have been equally critical of the Code if the same day, the Cardinal employee went home, checked his lottery numbers, and found that he had won $3 million? In fact, the person who caught the 70th (the record ball for the year) sold the ball in January of 1999 for more than $3 million at auction. And, at the same auction, a number of other balls were also sold for startling prices. The following article appeared in the New York Times on January 13, 1999:

McGwire's 70th Homer Still Defying Gravity[60]

To begin with, this baseball that has been called the Hope Diamond of sports collectibles — the Holy Grail, the fan's equivalent of a Picasso or a Renoir — is not even in mint condition. It is defaced in two places, one where Mark McGwire's bat bashed it for his record-setting 70th and final home run of last season. The other bruise oc-

---

58. Note that the income tax is separate from the gift and estate tax that may apply to transmissions of wealth during a donor's lifetime or at death. Recall the landlord in Revenue Ruling 79-24, the barter ruling. The landlord had income for federal income tax purposes on receipt of the painting in an amount equal to the then fair market value of the painting. Had he chosen immediately thereafter to give the painting as a gift to another person or entity, he would also have incurred a gift tax unless one of the statutory exemptions applied or he donated it to a charitable organization.

59. At first, no one seemed to mention the possibility of an income tax!

60. Ira Berkow, "McGwire's 70th Homer Still Defying Gravity," N.Y. Times, Jan. 13, 1999, at D2.

curred when the ball hit a wall in a left-field upper-deck box in Busch Stadium in St. Louis. And rumor had it that someone was going to pay $1 million or more for this used ball?

That was absolutely ridiculous. It defied common sense. So, of course, someone last night paid $2.7 million for it. (The total sale was $3,005,000 after adding the auction house's commission.)

In a baseball memorabilia auction in the Theater in Madison Square Garden, the bidding for this first of 41 items began at $400,000 and rose in increments of $50,000 and $100,000—the large crowd buzzing as it did—to that king's ransom. The recipient of the ball was "Anonymous," who was bidding by phone, perhaps with a team of therapists at his side.

The ball was struck on Sept. 27, the last day of the season and McGwire's final at-bat.... It was nine homers beyond Roger Maris's single-season record and 10 past the Babe. No. 70 was recovered in that left-field box by a ... 26-year-old medical researcher in St. Louis ... who stands to take home all but about $400,000 of the bid—the auction house has to make a living, too....

This ball, which was encased, as were the others in the auction, in glass, may very well drip with sentimental value for one so inclined for such things.

But on close observation it looks like any other of the 70,000 dozen major league baseballs used last season—white horsehide and red stitching—and one that you could pick up in any sporting goods [store] for $9.95.

"The 70th home run ball is the most valuable sports artifact in history," said ... the owner of the Manhattan auction house running the event. He was also the one who described the ball as the Hope Diamond, the Holy Grail, etc. In the auction program, [the] condition of McGwire ball No. 70 is described as very clean, but with "Two semicircular marks approximately 1/8" in diameter in clear area. Slight smudge on lettering 'Center' (Cushion Cork Center) and 's' (in Rawlings logo.)"

[The fan who caught the ball] had attended the game that fateful night with about a hundred people from his company. "I just went to see a game," he said. "I never dreamed of catching a home run ball. I'd never caught one before, and I've been to many games."

So he's sitting up there enjoying things when suddenly this missile is heading in his direction ... bounces under a metal bench.

[He] then reaches down and plucks up the ball and the rest is hysteria. He got an agent, he got a lawyer, he's made so many media appearances for his 107 days and 15 minutes of fame that on the morning of the auction he was an hour and a half late for an interview.

... [H]e is no financial dunce. The man who caught McGwire's 62nd—the homer that broke the record held by Roger Maris—gave it back to the slugger for some bats, balls and a jersey. [This fan] was able to figure out—maybe with the help of a newly acquired accountant—that $50 worth of equipment was less than the estimated $1 million plus.

Others who experienced windfalls from McGwire's retrieved homers Nos. 63, 67 and 68 suffered in comparison.... The highest of those three went for an embarrassing $50,000. Also sold was Sammy Sosa's 66th and final homer in what was a remarkable slugging tandem with McGwire last season. Sosa's ball went for $150,000.

...

Regarding home run ball No. 70, the auction program also notes: "The current owner of the baseball … retains the right to produce 70 Cibachrome prints and 7,000 posters of the baseball, both numbered and signed."

―――――――

Can there be any question that this kind of good luck should produce income tax consequences based on all you have learned so far: recall the criteria of *Glenshaw Glass*. One of the Senators, Christopher Bond of Missouri, who commented publicly on the income tax issue observed that, in his opinion, a smart employee of the Service who was also a baseball fan should be able to advise the Service on how to avoid imposing the income tax on the lucky catcher. Here are some of the remarks that Senator Bond made on the floor of the Senate on September 8, 1998:[61]

Mr. President, I rise today as a proud St. Louis Cardinals baseball fan.…

This weekend we saw the fabulous Mark McGwire hit runs 60 and 61.…

   …

I will tell you something else that America can be proud of, the young men who caught the home runs 60 and 61. When they were asked, "Are you going to sell it for a million dollars?" They said, "No, we are going to give it back to Mark McGwire." And this selfless act, giving the ball back to the guy who hit it so he could give it to Cooperstown, epitomizes the spirit. But you have to know, the Grinch appears.

   …

Now, get a life. The IRS spokesman has confirmed that the person who gives the ball back to Mark McGwire might be facing a gift tax of $150,000. The young man who caught number 60 is just out of college and he works in the promotion department of the Rams. The guy who caught number 61 is the catering manager who had to go to work at 4:30 this morning. They are going to have to pay $150,000? Now, that is about as ludicrous as anything I have seen. If the IRS wants to know why they are the most feared, disliked agency in town, this is the classic example.

   …

… I know there is a strong, bipartisan enthusiasm for the support of baseball. And for the Commissioner to tolerate somebody saying that a fan who gives the ball back to Mark McGwire could owe a $150,000 gift tax is outrageous.

The IRS needs to lighten up.… [I]t is absolutely ridiculous that the IRS would seriously consider imposing a tax on a generous fan who happens to catch the historic ball and return it. Get a life. Surely there are baseball fans among the clever lawyers and accountants at the IRS who can devise reasons why this good deed should go unpunished.…

―――――――

Was Senator Bond correct? Recall *Cesarini*. What arguments did you suggest in answer to question 3 above for why the Cesarinis might not have to report income imme-

―――――――

61. 1998 TNT 181-35 (Sept. 18, 1998).

diately if they found, instead of cash, a diamond ring in the piano? Were those arguments successful? Wasn't the real issue one of valuation, not timing?[62]

Recall that the catcher of the 62nd home run was an employee of the St. Louis Cardinals. Assume that as an employee, he had an obligation to return the ball to the club. Did he have income? **Review *Lewis*.**

Suppose you were a member of a group of six who had agreed that each one of you would buy a ticket to the ballpark in hopes of catching the record-breaking home run ball. The six members of your group also had agreed in advance that in the event one of you caught the ball, you would all share its ownership. You are the lucky one. Do you have income and, if so, how much? Can you argue that you never had a "right" to more than one-sixth of the ball's value? **Review *Lewis*.**

After all the hoopla concerning the gift tax died down, a number of commentators published articles more soberly analyzing the tax consequences of this kind of treasure trove. Although the home run ball tax controversy "caught" the national interest as a sidebar to the record-breaking event itself, it also provided tax professionals with the opportunity to engage in an analysis of the many tax issues the home run ball created. The following articles illustrate the discussion that raged in the professional tax press:

Home Run Balls and Nettlesome Tax Problems[63]

In reviewing the press coverage, it's interesting to note that the question of the income tax consequences of "catching the ball" (a skill possibly involving combat abilities, based on recent observations of fans going after McGwire home run balls) is one that the Internal Revenue Service did not initially address. Clearly, to complete the economic cycle, if one uses his or her baseball fan skills to obtain a preferred seat and catch or recover the ball, it is akin to winning a game of skill or, at least, cashing in on the lottery. Receipts from both activities are, of course, fully taxable. (Footnote 1) But rue the world in which the poor fourth outfielder, having experienced the glory of grasping

---

62. Of course, in most cases of treasure trove, the issue of valuation disappears because the finder of the treasure liquidates it immediately. Therefore, the sales price clearly establishes the fair market value. The more troublesome cases arise when the finder does not want to sell the item immediately but must value it for income tax purposes as of the date on which it is "reduced to [his] undisputed possession." **Review Treasury Regulation section 1.61-14.** For example, suppose the fan who caught the McGwire ball in 1998 decided not to sell it in 1998, (as, in fact, was the case). He would, nevertheless, have to value it for 1998 income tax reporting. He might look to an anonymous offer to purchase the home run ball for $1 million. But, could he, in the alternative, take the position that the ball could not be accurately valued and that, therefore, he could postpone all income until he eventually sold it? The answer is almost certainly, "No!" The Code generally disfavors so-called "open transactions" but in *rare and extraordinary* circumstances, the regulations do allow a taxpayer to postpone income recognition when the total value of the property cannot be determined with reasonable certainty. For example, when a taxpayer makes an installment sale, where the amount realized is contingent and will only become certain sometime in the future, the Code will permit the taxpayer to defer recognition "[o]nly in those rare and extraordinary cases ... in which the fair market value ... cannot reasonably be ascertained...." Treasury Regulation section 15A.453-1(d)(2)(iii).

63. Kip Dellinger, "Home Run Balls and Nettlesome Tax Problems," 1998 TNT 177-78 (Sept. 14, 1998).

Mark McGwire's 62nd home run record-setting baseball, is now told to cough up perhaps $450,000 in federal and state income taxes and another $80,000 in gift tax if she
"gives" the ball back to McGwire.

...

About the IRS getting involved in the tax aspects of an historic sports event one
might, at the very least, ask this question: Did it ever occur to the IRS that, before releasing its "partial edict" on the tax aspects of the McGwire Home Run Ball, perhaps it
first should have spoken to the Treasury Department, the White House, key congressional leaders, and a public relations consultant and recommended that the law be
amended for this situation? In other words, why hasn't the IRS yet figured out how to
show its "kinder, gentler" side?

So as the crescendo of congressional and public outrage peaked over the IRS's initial statement on the tax treatment of taxpayers who catch historic home run balls,
the agency—acting like a pitcher on his way to the showers after a bad game—
sheepishly recanted its earlier statements and indicated that no gift or income tax
consequences would arise if a fan returned a baseball to McGwire.... And while the
IRS remained silent on the tax implications involved if a fan kept the ball, many readers of news accounts interpreted the agency's position to mean that no tax consequences would arise if a fan retained possession of the ball for future gift or sale or
charitable donation.

But it would be pure folly for the IRS to suggest that a fan catching the ball owes no
tax immediately. (Footnote 3) Unless, of course, it is making up the law as it goes along.

On the other hand, perhaps making it up as life goes along isn't so far-fetched. (Footnote 4) Having screwed up the initial public relations aspect of the baseball issue, the
agency then proclaimed there would be no tax consequences. Most fans probably cheered
the outcome. But others are questioning whether it has any foundation in the law.

...

Looking at the handling of the McGwire Home Run Ball situation, one can only conclude that the application of tax law depends very much on the individual involved or
the public relations fallout from a taxable transaction. (Footnote 6) Is this the message
taxpayers should be receiving about the operation of our tax system? Is this the new
IRS? ... I continue to hope that ... the IRS will start hitting at least a few doubles instead
of leading all federal agencies in strikeouts.

FOOTNOTES:

1. Is there really any question that the receipt of property valued at $1 million is some-
how beyond the reach of *section 61*? Clearly, it cannot be excluded under the "exceptions" listed in section 74—"Prizes and Awards."

3. Let's take the example of a U.S. citizen/treasure seeker who finds gold bullion in a
sunken vessel. Is the value of the "find" income tax-free? This writer ventures to argue
that it is not and that there is much analogous case law, statutory authority, and regulatory history to require inclusion of the fair market value of "the find" in income immediately. Ignoring this outcome would essentially represent the validation of all kinds of deferral transactions against which the IRS has long argued. There is little, if any, underlying
difference between finding gold bullion and Mark McGwire's 62nd home run ball.

4. As in: Since when did property received as income need be reduced to cash before it
becomes taxable?

6. As history played itself out in St. Louis on the evening of September 8, McGwire hit a 341-foot chip shot that cleared the left field fence but fell short of the stands. The ball was recovered by a fellow St. Louis Cardinal employee, a groundskeeper who immediately stated that the ball would be given to McGwire. Thus it is arguable that this individual was acting on behalf of McGwire and was simply returning the ball to him. And with that ball destined for its rightful owner, the National Baseball Hall of Fame, McGwire himself was simply acting as an agent "for the game and its fans." So destiny produced a happy ending and Congress and the IRS were relieved of dealing with an admittedly dicey situation.

McGwire'S 62nd Home Run:
IRS Bobbles the Ball[64]

Millions of baseball aficionados shared a dream on the night of September 8th: to be the lucky person to catch Mark McGwire's 62nd home run, which would break Roger Maris's record for most home runs in a single season. You field the ball and are interviewed on television. In a scene broadcast to millions around the world, you hand the souvenir to Mark McGwire, who graciously expresses his thanks for the ball's return.

Then the dream turns into a nightmare when an IRS agent grabs the microphone and announces in front of the international audience that you have just received $1 million of taxable income (resulting in combined federal and state income taxes of $450,000) and have also made a $1 million taxable gift to McGwire (resulting in your owing as much as another $550,000 of gift taxes), all $1 million of taxes being payable next April 15. The ultimate Catch-22 (or, in this case, Catch-62)!

Sound farfetched? ... According to comments attributed to [an] IRS spokesman ... if a fan were to return the record-setting ball to McGwire, the fan might be asked to pay a federal gift tax—even if the fan doesn't get any money for it....

...

... [G]ift taxes are only one issue. The first concern, of course, should be whether the receipt of the ball itself is a taxable event, on which the recipient will owe income taxes. (The IRS spokesman's reported comments did not include any discussion of the income tax consequences to the ball catcher.)

There appears to be a good argument that getting the ball *is* a taxable event. Although the effort involved may be relatively meager (possibly as little as reaching down to pick up a ball lying momentarily at one's feet, although scrambling and grabbing have been more like it), the effort appears to generate income under Section 61(a)—gross income includes all income from whatever source derived....

---

64. Sheldon I. Banoff and Richard M. Lipton, "McGwire's 62nd Home Run: IRS Bobbles the Ball," 89 J. Tax'n 253, 253-55 (1998).

Good luck *can* result in income—it takes little effort to purchase a lottery ticket, but lottery winnings clearly are taxable income; why should bending down for the prized ball be any different? Prizes awarded in contests requiring a modicum of skill are similarly taxable. Moreover, "finding" the ball at one's feet is functionally similar to finding treasure, which has long been held taxable under Section 61. See, e.g., *Cesarini*, 428 F.2d 812 ... (CA-6, 1970). The "treasure" is taxable not when first converted into cash but rather as soon as the property is in the finder's "undisputed possession" (see Reg. 1.61-14(a)).

Even though the "treasure trove" and lottery ticket analogies are strong, there may be some counter arguments. For example, if a taxpayer pays $5 to go to a swap meet and there finds and purchases for $10 a Van Gogh painting worth millions, there is no question of the taxpayer's having income—he has a cost basis in the painting. When a fan pays $12 to sit in the bleachers at Busch Stadium, has she paid for the "right" to find any stray baseballs which just happen to come her way? Under this analysis, the fan has "purchased" the baseball and has no income on its receipt. Of course, payment of any contest entry fee or purchase of a ticket to win the lottery is functionally the same "price of admission," and therefore taxability of the "winnings" under Section 61 may not be avoided. The distinction might be, however, that a winning lottery ticket is equivalent to cash, whereas the baseball is clearly property.

What if the fan who catches one of McGwire's historic home runs sells the ball? The sale would establish the value of the ball (assuming an arm's-length transaction, e.g., a sports memorabilia auction sale).... Although the income recognized by our fan would be taxable at ordinary income rates of 39.6%, she at least would be able to keep the other 60.4% (disregarding state and local income taxes), and wouldn't have to worry about the feds hounding her for gift taxes, as initially threatened by the IRS if the ball had been returned to McGwire!

If the fan wishes to avoid being out-of-pocket for the tax liability but wanted the ball to go to Cooperstown, she might attempt to sell it to the Hall of Fame for a price which, on an after-tax basis, would exactly offset her potential tax liabilities. Depending on the fan's marginal income and unified transfer tax rates, this would have cost the Hall of Fame a very substantial amount. More important, Hall of Fame director of communications John Ralph stated the Hall can't buy or sell artifacts.

How else might our fan (lucky in fielding prowess but unlucky in taxes) avoid this dilemma? If McGwire's intent was to donate the ball to the Baseball Hall of Fame in Cooperstown, soon after his receipt, our fan would be better off to retain ownership but (for p.r. purposes) make a joint presentation with McGwire to the Hall. So long as the gift goes to such an organization, no gift tax should be imposed on the donor. If McGwire never obtains the benefits and burdens of ownership of the ball, but merely makes a joint appearance with our fan to donate the ball to the Hall of Fame, the ball catcher would avoid the adverse gift tax results.

   ...

This tax nightmare ended on September 8th. Collapsing under a barrage of public (including congressional and White House) criticism, Commissioner Rossotti acknowledged in a press release (IR-98-56, 9/8/98) just hours before McGwire's historic 62nd homer that the ball catcher "would not have taxable income" *if* the ball were returned right away. According to this information release, the ball catcher who promptly returned the ball would not have taxable income "based on an analogy to principles of tax law that apply when someone immediately declines a prize or returns unsolicited merchandise." The release further states that there would likewise be no gift tax in these circumstances. The Service's backtracking was politically expedient, even if not founded in the tax law; the Commissioner admitted that "sometimes pieces of the tax code can be as hard to understand as the infield fly rule."

Of course, as readers know, it was not a fan but rather Busch Stadium groundskeeper Tim Forneris who that night retrieved the 62nd home run ball in the outfield tunnel beyond the left field fence. Forneris gave the ball to his supervisor, as he presumably did with all other baseballs that came his way (and as undoubtedly was required by St. Louis Cardinals practices and procedures applicable to the grounds crew). It would seem that the receipt and disposition of the ball were part of Forneris's everyday business, so that there would be no income tax consequences to him. Likewise, the supervisor followed orders in returning the ball to the team that employed him, so he should be off the hook. This leaves all of the potential tax consequences to Mark McGwire when the ball is returned to him by his employer. Has McGwire received compensation of $1 million under Section 83 as a result of the receipt of property? IR-98-56 is not designed to protect McGwire. Even if he can get (and make full use of) an offsetting deduction for donating the ball to Cooperstown, is it likely that the Cardinals will withhold a portion of his salary? Will McGwire and the Cardinals each pay health insurance taxes (1.45%) on the value of the property?

Forneris presented the ball to McGwire during a post-game ceremony. Perhaps having received wise tax counsel (and apparently unaware of the Service's backtracking hours earlier), the 22-year-old Forneris said, "It's *McGwire's* ball. He lost it and I found it for him".... Since the ball was never "owned" by McGwire the batter (but rather was initially the property of Major League Baseball), Forneris's characterization is technically inaccurate—but most unlikely to lead to a tax evasion conviction in light of the Commissioner's pro-taxpayer position reflected in IR-98-56.

. . .

The taxability of catching a historic and highly valued ball raises further questions. It has long been the practice at Wrigley Field for fans in the bleachers to throw back onto the field home runs hit by Cubs opponents. One of your Shop Talk editors, a long-suffering season ticket holder at Wrigley, verifies that over the last two decades every homer he has witnessed that was hit by an opponent has been thrown back. (Peer pressure, which includes duress and threat of severe bodily harm by both sober and intoxicated Bleacher Bums, usually generates this result within seconds of the catch.)

If McGwire were to hit a historic homer in Wrigley Field, would the fan who caught the ball have to recognize taxable income because the ball was "reduced to [his] undisputed possession," even though he abandoned ownership of the ball moments later? Would it not be income to him under Commissioner Rossotti's edict because the ball was "returned right away"? Does the ball have to be returned *to McGwire* to avoid income taxation, or merely abandoned? The rejection of the ball clearly comes within the "unwanted merchandise" analogy discussed in the Service's pro-taxpayer press release. But the owner of the ball before it left the field was Major League Baseball—not McGwire. Can one validly "reject merchandise" when property is in one's "undisputed possession" by giving it to a *third party* (i.e., McGwire), not the owner? In this context is McGwire an agent of Major League Baseball (for federal tax purposes)? ...

. . .

More on Historic Homers: Do Auction Prices Control?[65]

On January 12, an unprecedented auction of numerous historic baseballs was held in New York's Madison Square Garden. The auction was widely publicized, the bidding fast and furious....

Prior to this year, the record price for a baseball sold at auction was $126,500 for Babe Ruth's first home run at Yankee Stadium. At the January 12 auction, McGwire's 63rd, 67th, and 68th home run balls of 1998, along with Sosa's 61st, 64th, and 66th homers of the same year were sold—Sosa's 66th reportedly being purchased by an anonymous telephone bidder for $172,000. That same bidder paid a record-smashing $3,005,000 for McGwire's 70th homer, far exceeding the highest price previously paid for *any* sports item.

For those few lucky historic home run ball catchers who sold their balls in the January sale, interesting income tax issues arise as to the timing of income recognized. Under the long-standing "treasure trove doctrine" in Reg. 1.61-14(a), found treasure is taxable not when first converted into cash but rather as soon as the property is in the finder's "undisputed possession." Although an argument might be made that purchasing a ticket to the game makes the receipt of the ball itself not a taxable event (i.e., the fan paid $12 to sit in the bleachers for the "right" to find any stray baseballs that just happen to come his or her way), the better view is that recovering the historic homer is a taxable event on receipt.... Thus, for baseballs caught in 1998, the proper year for reporting income is 1998, in an amount equal to the FMV of the ball at the time caught.

... [T]here *was* a substantial change in value between the income tax valuation date and the auction date, as the value actually paid at auction far exceeded the speculative value of the ball at the moment caught just months earlier. Prior to the fateful day that [The fan] caught the 70th home run ball, there previously had never been an auction of such historic baseball memorabilia. The Second Circuit has ruled in *Saltzman*, 131 F.3d 87, 80 AFTR2d 97-8365 (CA-2, 1997), that, in order for a subsequent sale price to be probative of FMV, the subsequent sale itself must have been foreseeable on the valuation date.... Therefore, the ball's value arguably would be established based on the "willing buyer-willing seller" principle, which by definition would exclude an unforeseeable "feeding frenzy" auction price. Thus, a bona fide offer for McGwire's 70th "tater" (baseball slang for a home run) at $1 million, outstanding at the time of the catch, would tend to set a floor on value. Unsubstantiated offers of $1 million or more were reported in the press, but such offers are disregarded for valuation purposes. As a general rule, unaccepted offers have no more than limited probative weight in estimating value.... An argument can be made, however, that the FMV was not substantially greater than the reported offer.

In contrast, the facts indicate that the value of the historic ball increased substantially due to subsequent events, such as the activities of the auction house and the auctioneer in negotiating the sale of a number of historic baseballs all in one "superstar" auction that caught the public's imagination (and incidentally, boundless press coverage).... IRS

---

65. Sheldon I. Banoff and Richard M. Lipton, "More on Historic Homers: Do Auction Prices Control?," 90 J. Tax'n 189, 189–91 (1999).

More telling than the authorities that have cited the treasure trove regulation are the many situations in which the ruling has been ignored. The finding of valuable property is not an uncommon event; many people devote considerable effort to searching for valuable property. Under the treasure trove regulation, they should realize gross income when the find is "reduced to undisputed possession." These taxable finders would include commercial fishermen, big game hunters, prospectors and miners, and professional treasure hunters. Yet there are no cases or rulings in which the IRS has attempted to apply the treasure trove regulation to tax any of these finds before conversion to cash, and there is substantial authority ... implying the finds are *not* taxable on reduction to undisputed possession.

It is true that these situations generally involve looked-for-found property rather than pure windfall, but that does not serve to distinguish the baseball case, even in the unlikely event the baseballs were pure windfall to the lucky fans. (Footnote 19) Nothing in the regulation indicates a tax difference between stumbled-over and searched-for treasure trove, and under Glenshaw Glass ("Congress applied no limitations as to the source of taxable receipts") (Footnote 20) there should be no difference. (Footnote 21) If it is IRS practice not to apply the treasure trove regulation to sought-after finds, there is no justification for different treatment of windfalls.

III. Why Practice Is Right & the Regulation Is Wrong

A. Found Property & the Scope of Gross Income

One can describe the scope of gross income under section 61 from either of two starting points. The usual approach among tax theorists is to start from the sweeping Haig-Simons definition of income as including all consumption and all increase in asset values during a taxable period,(Footnote 48) and then to describe the ways in which section 61 retreats from that definition. The two most important retreats are the failures to tax unrealized appreciation and imputed income. Congress has never found it necessary to provide explicit statutory authority for either of these departures from Haig-Simons income. It is clear nevertheless, that gross income includes neither mere increase in value of property, (Footnote 49) nor any of the various forms of imputed income—the value of self-performed services, self-created property, and the use value of one's property. (Footnote 50)

It is also possible to grab the other end of the stick, and start with the observation that basically what the income tax is about is the inclusion of the receipt of *cash* in gross income, (Footnote 51) and then describe the ways in which section 61 extends beyond cash receipts. The logic here is that a cash-based tax system has the "attainable virtues" of ease of valuation and of liquidity, and that the only reason to extend the tax base beyond cash—to exchanges of property, (Footnote 53) to noncash compensation for services, (Footnote 54) and to barter generally (Footnote 55)—is to discourage tax-induced replacements of cash with in-kind transfers. It is necessary to tax noncash compensation to prevent wholesale tax avoidance by employees asking employers to do all their shopping for them, instead of paying them cash; the same reasoning explains why the amount realized on the sale of property must include the fair market value of property received. (Footnote 56) Without a tax incentive for in-kind transfers, such transfers will be rare, and the vast majority of the tax base will be cash. The point of taxing in-kind transfers is not to raise revenue from the tax on those transfers; it is to protect the cash tax base. Since the idea is to tax noncash *transactions* (to channel those transactions into cash), (Footnote 58) the noncash benefits that remain untaxed are those that involve *no transaction*. This obviously includes the standard tax-free categories of unrealized appreciation and imputed income, but what has not been articulated (although in practice it has been understood at some less than fully conscious level) is that it also includes found property.

An important kind of imputed income, universally understood to be outside the scope of section 61, is self-created property. For example, an IRS Publication tells farmers not to deduct the cost of raising produce for personal consumption, (Footnote 59) for the reason (which is so clear as not to require an explanation) that the self-consumed produce is imputed income, (Footnote 60)and the cost of producing tax exempt income is not deductible. (Footnote 61) The exclusion of self-created property applies not only when the taxpayer consumes the property, but also when the taxpayer simply holds the property—as with a work of art, patent, or copyright. (Footnote 62) In those cases, of course, tax will be imposed (on the amount realized, less any costs of production) if the taxpayer later sells property.

Given the universal understanding that self-*created* property is not taxable unless and until it is sold, why would anyone think that the tax treatment of self-*found* [property] should be any different? As with created property, found property should never be taxed if it is consumed by the taxpayer (fish or game, for example), and should be taxed only on disposition if the taxpayer eventually sells it (sunken treasure, or the McGwire baseball). The supposed distinction makes no sense, but its likely source is confusion about the reason for the nontaxation of self-created property. Perhaps the exclusion is hung on the doctrinal peg of unrealized appreciation, instead of or in addition to imputed income. Thus when Robert Rauschenberg applies paint to canvas, the result is viewed as unrealized appreciation in the paint and canvas. But this analysis will not work to exclude found property from income; getting something when a moment before one had nothing does not fit the mold of unrealized appreciation.

The tax distinction between created and found property does not survive careful examination, because unrealized appreciation fails to explain the exclusion of many kinds of self-created property. Severing crops from land and then eating them is certainly dramatic enough to qualify as a realization event, even under the exacting standards of *Eisner v. Macomber*. (Footnote 63) And patents and copyrights are intangible assets, separate and distinct from the paper or hard drive on which the information is recorded. They cannot be viewed as unrealized appreciation in a physical asset; they have the same *ex nihilo* quality as found property. If found property must be taxed because the finding is a realization event, self-created intangible assets must be taxed because the creation is a realization event.

The current tax treatment of self-created property is correct. It is just the understanding of the reason for the treatment—and the resulting distinction between created and found property—that needs reconsideration. To use the standard tools of analysis, the key to the nontaxation of self-created property is imputed income, not unrealized appreciation. Although harvesting and eating crops, or creating intangible assets out of nothing, seem sufficiently dramatic to constitute realizations, there should still be no tax because there has been no transaction. These are benefits one confers on oneself, and as such they are tax-free imputed income. Those benefits may never be taxed, or they may be taxed on a later sale, but they are not taxed now. The analysis for found property is identical; it should also be excluded from section 61 as imputed income. (Footnote 64)

An alert reader may have an objection to this approach. If anything one finds for oneself is excluded as imputed income, for want of a transaction, then even found *cash* should be tax free. But that would be nonsense, since neither liquidity nor valuation concerns give any policy reason for not taxing found cash. It would also be contrary to *Cesarini*, the only case that has actually included anything in income based on the treasure trove regulation. We think found cash is and should be taxable. (We also think that self-created cash—if such a thing were possible—should be taxable.) The case of found cash presents an analytical problem only if one starts from Haig-Simons income and then works toward gross income by subtraction of unrealized appreciation and imputed income. But if one starts from cash receipts as the core of section 61, and then works outward to include in-kind *transfers*, everything falls into place nicely. Found cash is taxable simply because it is cash and cash is at the core of gross income; other found property is excluded because it is not necessary to tax nontransferred in-kind property to protect the cash tax base.

Neither the exclusion of self-created property nor the exclusion of found property threatens significant erosion of the cash tax base. Only a very limited range of consumption needs and wants can be satisfied by consuming self-created or found property. Most created or found property must be sold to finance consumption (or investment diversification), and the Treasury can afford to wait for the sale—and the resulting disappearance of valuation and liquidity concerns—to impose tax. (Footnote 66) There is not the danger, as there would be if in-kind-*transfers* were tax-free, of wholesale avoidance by selling one's services or property in exchange for satisfaction of one's shopping list. If anything, the extent of permanent tax avoidance with found property is even less than with self-created property; probably most people can create more items for their own consumption than they can find. Permanent exclusion of found property may apply to little more then trout and venison.

B. The Special Case of Finding Liquid Property

How should the tax system treat the finder of liquid property, such as gold bullion, foreign currency, or (now almost extinct) bearer bonds? A possible answer is that there is no good reason to exclude found property from income in the absence of valuation and liquidity problems, so found liquid property should be taxed just as found cash is taxed. That is a defensible position, but we are led to the opposite answer by the analogy to unrealized appreciation. Although the deferral of tax on unrealized appreciation in bullion, foreign *currency*, goes beyond the valuation and liquidity rationales for not taxing unrealized appreciation, the tax law does not draw a doctrinal line between appreciation in liquid and illiquid assets.

To be consistent, the system should also not draw a distinction between findings of liquid and illiquid property. Instead of a tax at the moment of finding, the tax should be deferred until the finder sells or otherwise disposes of the property. In the case of found foreign currency, taxable dispositions would include both exchanging the currency for dollars (or other currencies) and using the currency to buy property. Although this treatment may be rather generous, it poses no threat to the integrity of the tax base; there are few, if any, large scale opportunities to find liquid property. With the possible exception of foreign currency the number of significant finds of liquid assets must be vanishingly small, and what finds there are must be overwhelmingly of the stumbled-over variety. We would not expect the favorable tax treatment of found liquid property to lead to large numbers of people quitting their jobs to devote their lives to searching for abandoned Krugerrands and bearer bonds.

C. Back to Baseball: The Right Doctrinal Peg

Some commentators on the baseball tax problem have suggested (although without much conviction) that a lucky fan might avoid income tax on the value of a record-breaking baseball by treating it as unrealized appreciation in the fan's ticket to the game (which implicitly includes the right to keep any baseballs that happen to come one's way). (Footnote 71) This approach leads to some unappealing results. First, it results in radically different tax—treatment—with no apparent policy justification—between the fan who catches a record ball in the bleachers, and one who recovers a record ball in the street outside the ballpark. (As it happens, this is not just a hypothetical; Brendon Cunningham emerged from a scuffle on Waveland Avenue, just outside of Wrigley Field, with home run ball number 62 of Sammy Sosa.) (Footnote 72) Perhaps more importantly, it implies that any in-kind prize where one pays a price to play the game should be treated as unrealized appreciation in the bingo card, raffle ticket, or the like. But that result is wrong, both under current law and under the analysis set forth above. (Footnote 73) In a real raffle, as opposed to the pseudo-raffle of the record breaking baseball, the prize is received *as a transfer* from another, rather than being found by oneself, and so it is taxable.

Although treating the baseball as unrealized appreciation in the ticket happens to reach the right result in the Ozersky case, it reaches the wrong result for both the Waveland Avenue baseball and the true raffle prize. In terms of the standard categories, the key to the nontaxability of the baseball is imputed income—the absence of a transfer—and-not unrealized appreciation.

IV. Conclusion

Despite the support in both IRS practice and basic income tax principles for not taxing found property, there remains the problem of the clear statement of taxability in the treasure trove regulation. The choice among reasonable interpretations of tax statutes belongs to the agency charged with writing interpretive regulations, not to the courts. (Footnote 75) A court that would not have interpreted section 61 to include found property in gross income might nevertheless defer to the treasure trove regulation as being barely within the range of reasonable interpretations. Or it might not. (Footnote 76) In the leading case discussing challenges to the validity of tax regulations, the Supreme Court noted that three important considerations are whether the regulation was "substantially contemporaneous" with the enactment of the provision it interprets, the "consistency of the Commissioner's interpretation," and "the degree of scrutiny Congress has devoted to the regulation during subsequent re-enactments of the statute." (Footnote 77) The treasure trove regulation fairs poorly on all three counts. It dates from only 1957, so it is not entitled to the particular deference given to contemporaneous regulations. There has been ongoing inconsistency between the interpretation in the regulation and IRS practice with respect to found property. And because in practice the IRS has not taxed found property, Congress has had no occasion to scrutinize the regulation during subsequent re-enactments. (The furor over the baseball tax suggests the treasure trove regulation would not fare well, were it subjected to congressional scrutiny.) (Footnote 79)

As long as the treasure trove regulation remains on the books, taxpayers who find property must worry about the validity of the regulation, and if the IRS ever tries to apply it a court will have to decide the issue. But Treasury can and should moot the question by officially sanctioning the IRS practice of not taxing found property—that is, by simply removing the regulation from the books. It should do so quickly, before someone breaks the McGwire home run record.[67]

---

67. In fact, Treasury did not follow the advice of Zelenak and McMahon. Barry Bonds of the San Francisco Giants did break McGwire's record on October 7, 2001, and will soon break Henry Aaron all-time record in 2007. The Regulation remains in effect.

The Bonds baseball did not raise tax questions as had the McGwire balls. Rather, the controversy that arose from the Bonds ball concerned its ownership. Shortly after he "lost" the ball to a different fan, Alex Popov brought suit against Patrick Hayashi, claiming that Hayashi knocked the ball from his hands. After a year of legal wrangling, a judge ordered the ball sold and the proceeds split equally between the two men. At the subsequent auction sale, Todd McFarlane, who had earlier

FOOTNOTES:

5. *Id.* His statement accurately reflects current IRS practice. An IRS publication states that a prize won in "a lucky number drawing, television or radio quiz program, beauty contest, or other event," is ordinarily taxable, but that inclusion in gross income can be avoided by refusing to accept the prize. IRS Publication 525, *Taxable and Nontaxable Income* 13 (1998). The authority for the position is Rev. Rul. 57-374, 1957-2 C.B. 69 (setting forth the conclusion without explaining the rationale). This is a sensible response to the concern that including the fair market value of a prize in income might result in a tax bill greater than the subjective value of the prize to the recipient....

In the case of unsolicited merchandise, it is IRS practice not to impose tax unless the taxpayer gives away the merchandise and claims a charitable deduction. *Compare* Rev. Rul. 70-498, 1970-2 C.B. 6 (including in gross income "under the specific facts described" the value of unsolicited books donated to charity and with respect to which a charitable contribution deduction was claimed) *with* Rev. Rul. 70-330, 1970-1 C.B. 14, superseded by Rev. Rul. 70-498, *supra* (unsolicited books donated to charity were included in gross income "since the value of the books is not excluded from the taxpayer's gross income by any provision of the code and in view of the broad scope of section 61(a)"). A court has described the IRS practice as being based on an administrative decision to be concerned with the taxation of unsolicited samples only when failure to tax those samples would provide taxpayers with "double tax benefits." *Haverly v. United States*, 513 F.2d 224, 227 (7th Cir.)....

7. H. R. 4522, 105th Cong., 2d Sess., September 9, 1998 (Reps. Thomas, Bonilla, Gibbons, Franks, Boehner, and Jones). Narrowly drafted to target the perceived problem, the bill applied only to "a baseball which is a home run ball hit during the 1998 baseball season if the batter of the baseball hit at least 61 home runs during such season." The precision was less than laser-like, however, since the language covered *all* 1998 home runs by McGwire and Sosa, not just the record-breaking balls.

13. We must confess an error of our own. We uncritically accepted the validity of the treasure trove regulation when we wrote that jewelry found in a vase purchased at a flea market would be taxed in the year it was discovered, under the authority of the regulation. Martin J. McMahon, Jr. & Lawrence Zelenak, *Teacher's Manual to Federal Income Taxation of Individuals Study Problems* 6 (2d ed. 1996). We are older and wiser now.

14. The taxpayer might or might not have basis to recover on the taxable sale, depending on whether the taxpayer incurred any costs in finding the property. In Ozersky's case, there may be a factual issue as to whether he bought his ticket for the purpose of trying to catch a McGwire home run ball, but even if he did his basis would be trivial compared to his amount realized.

15. Our argument is limited to property that truly is "found" or otherwise acquired by happenstance without an express intentional transfer from another person. It does not extend to prizes and awards taxable under section 74, a rule with which we do not take issue.

---

bought McGwire's record-breaking ball for $3,005,000, paid only $450,000 for the Bonds ball. The rival claimants then discovered, to their mutual chagrin, that each one's half did not cover his legal costs! Each would have been better off had they decided to play Solomon on their own without the assistance of their lawyers and the judge.

16. *Cesarini v. U.S.*, 296 F. Supp. 3 (N.D. Ohio 1969), *aff'd per curiam* 428 F.2d 812 (6th Cir. 1970).

17. *Collins v. Commissioner*, T.C. Memo. 1992-478.... The taxpayer in the case was a cashier at an off-track betting parlor, who had stolen tickets from his employer, most of which turned out to be losers. He suggested the analogy to the finder of the sweepstakes ticket, hoping that the court would agree that the finder would have no income. Unfortunately for the taxpayer, the court accepted the analogy but disagreed as to the tax consequences to the finder.

19. Most likely the fans who caught the valuable balls went to the games and selected their seat locations with the possibility of retrieving a McGwire or Sosa home run ball very much in mind.

20. *Commissioner v. Glenshaw Glass Co.*, 348 U.S. 426, 429 (1955).

21. Until the Supreme Court decided *Glenshaw Glass*, there was an argument for a tax difference between stumbled-over and searchedfor treasure, based on the Supreme Court's previous definition of income as "the gain derived from capital, from labor, or from both combined." *Eisner v. Macomber*, 252 U.S. 189, 207 (1920). Under this definition, stumbled-over treasure might have been viewed as derived from neither labor nor capital and so not income, whereas searched-for treasure would have been within the income definition. In any event, after *Glenshaw Glass* this distinction is of only historical interest.

48. Henry C. Simons, Personal Income Taxation: The Definition of Income as a Problem of Fiscal Policy 50 (1938).

49. Although the Supreme Court once considered the realization doctrine to be constitutionally required, *Eisner v. Macomber*, 252 U.S. 189, 219 (1920), the Court's current view is that the doctrine is based on mere "administrative convenience." *Cottage Sav. Ass'n. v. Commissioner*, U.S. 554, 563, 91 TNT 85-2 (1991) quoting *Helvering v. Horst*, 311 U.S. 112, 116 (1940)).

50. Despite the absence of a statutory exclusion for imputed income, the "congressional silence on the subject is clearly tantamount to an affirmative grant of immunity." Boris I. Bittker & Martin J. McMahon, Jr., [Federal Income Taxation of Individuals] para. 3.3[1] (2d ed. 1995).

51. Reduced by basis in the case of property transactions. Sections 61(a)(3), 1001(a).

53. Treas. reg. section 1.1001-1(a) (an "exchange of property for other differing materially either in kind or in extent" is a taxable event).

54. Treas. reg. section 1.61-2(d) (if services are paid for with property or other services, the value of the services or property received must be included in gross income).

55. *See. E.g.*, *Rooney v. Commissioner*, 88 T.C. 523, 88 TNT 7712 (1987) (bartering of services results in gross income equal to fair market value of services received); Rev. Rul. 79-24, 1979-1 C.B. 60 (same); Rev. Rul. 80-52, 1980-1 C.B. 100 (credits earned in a barter club are includable in gross income).

56. Like most rules of broad application, the taxation of in-kind transfers will occasionally apply to situations beyond the policy justification for the rule. Perhaps the classic example is *Wills v. Commissioner*, 411 F.2d 537 (9th Cir. 1969). Maury Wills was taxed on the fair market value of the jewel-encrusted "Hickok belt" awarded to him (not by his employer) as the outstanding professional athlete of 1962. It was not something he would have bought on his own, and although he could have sold it that would have been rude. The court almost weeps as it rules against Wills, and hints that Congress might craft a rule ex-

When Susan borrowed, she acquired both an asset (the property purchased with the loan), and a liability. Therefore, her net worth did not change as a result of the borrowing. When she repays all or part of the loan, she reduces both her assets and her liabilities by the amount of the repayment. Again, her net worth does not change as a result of the repayment. Now, look again. What is the net change in the value of her assets?[75]

Can you calculate Susan's income using the *Glenshaw Glass* test? If your initial response was to add her $31,000 spending to the increase in her net worth, that too would be incorrect. Recall our earlier discussion, following *Kirby Lumber* and the questions following case, of the effect of borrowing on a taxpayer's balance sheet. As noted above, when Susan borrowed, she acquired both an asset (the loan or the property purchased with the loan), and a liability. Therefore, she did not have income; there was no accession to her wealth and her net worth did not change as a result of the borrowing. When she repays all or part of the loan, she reduces both her assets and her liabilities by the amount of the repayment. Again, her net worth does not change as a result of the repayment. So, what then is the difference between the Haig-Simons definition and the *Glenshaw Glass* definition? Remember the second test of *Glenshaw Glass*: income must be clearly realized. But here, the change in the market values of her house and car are not yet "realized." Could these changes then be part of her income under *Glenshaw Glass*?

Why have most tax experts concluded that the *Glenshaw Glass* formulation is the more practical one?[76] In not including changes in net worth in income until a realization event occurs, and because it does not reflect the value of what is termed "imputed income," the *Glenshaw Glass* definition is narrower than that of Haig-Simons. "Imputed income" is the term economists apply to the value of such things as uncompensated services provided to one's self or the family unit, *e.g.* homemaker services and home repairs. It also includes the rental value of the home that the owner herself occupies. While economists recognize that these items truly constitute income in the sense of accretions to wealth, the practical problems, most particularly problems of valuation, have discouraged attempts to include these items in income for federal income tax purposes.

The definition adopted by accountants reflects in part the Haig-Simons' view but is somewhat more elaborate[77] and involves some differences in timing that result from the emphasis placed on realization and the matching of income and expense.[78]

---

75. It is unlikely that the increase in the value of her clothing is due to an increase in the value of the clothes that she owned at the start of the period. Rather, it is more likely that the change represents the net decrease in the value of the clothes she had at both the beginning and the end of the period plus the value of new clothes acquired during the period.

76. Section 1001 clearly adopts the policy that unrealized gains are not included in income. The justification for this rule has always been that it is cumbersome and impractical to require taxpayers to revalue their assets at the end of each tax year. But, what about publicly-traded securities? For example, the New York Stock Exchange reports an exact closing price as of the close of business on the last trading day of the tax year. The Code now requires dealers in securities to "realize" their gains or losses on some of their securities at the end of each tax year. This requirement, called "mark-to-market accounting", may result in a gain in one year and a loss in the next (or vice versa) on the same security. The rule, contained in section 475 of the Code, clearly alters the realization rule of *Glenshaw Glass* and section 1001.

77. "[The] money or money equivalent *earned* or *accrued* during an accounting period, increasing the total of previously existing net assets, and arising from sales and rentals of any type of goods or services ... and windfalls from any outside source." *Kohler's, Dictionary for Accountants* 253–54 (6th ed. 1983).

78. The accountant's definition does not require valuation of the increase in existing net assets. Rather, this definition does not include these increases in value until disposition, *i.e.*, until "realiza-

It also does not include imputed income. The purpose of the primary reports prepared by accountants, the income statement, balance sheet, and the sources and uses of funds statement,[79] is fundamentally different from the need to define income for tax purposes, however. The three primary types of accounting statement deliver information about the financial condition and operations of a profit-seeking activity for the benefit of third parties. The combined role of these documents is far broader than simply to measure the single factor of income for the purpose of imposing a tax. Therefore, although the accountant's definition of income refers to the concept of realization in a way that traditional economic definitions do not, there are many important differences between "income" for accounting purposes and "income" for section 61 purposes.[80]

---

tion." In fact, on financial statements, accountants show assets at their "historic" costs, that is, their costs at acquisition.

79. Recall our earlier discussion in footnote 31, *supra.*

80. For those who wish to investigate the various theories of income in greater depth, see Victor Thuronyi, "The Concept of Income," 46 Tax L. Rev. 45 (1991).

Chapter 2

Exclusions from Gross Income

Section 61 of the Code defines gross income as "all income from whatever source derived." In *Glenshaw Glass*, the Supreme Court noted "the sweeping scope of the ... statute." The Court went on to reiterate its view that the "language was used by Congress to exert in this field 'the full measure of its taxing power.'" **Recall the text of the Sixteenth Amendment.** The Supreme Court interpreted the words of section 61 (which echo the Sixteenth Amendment) as reflecting the intention of Congress to set forth an unlimited definition of income. The Court stated: "Congress applied no limitations as to the source of taxable receipts, nor restrictive labels as to their nature. And the [Supreme] Court has given a liberal construction to this broad phraseology in recognition of the intention of Congress to tax all gains except those specifically exempted."

The Service has incorporated the language of the Supreme Court in Treasury Regulation section 1.61-1(a), which provides that "[g]ross income means all income from whatever source derived, unless excluded by law." Thus, any receipt that otherwise meets the broad three-prong test for gross income must be included in gross income unless there is a specific provision in the Code that excludes the item from income.

Congress has, in fact, chosen to exclude certain items from the broad sweep of section 61. Most of these items are found in Part III, Subchapter B of Chapter 1, sections 101 *et seq.* of the Code.[1] (What is "Part III"? What is "Subchapter B"? How do you find out? Recall our earlier discussions about the Code's table of contents. Examine the portion of the table of contents that shows Part III of Subchapter B of Chapter 1.) In a survey course such as this, which is intended to teach you the basic conceptual framework of the income tax provisions applicable to individuals, there is not enough time to study each statutory exclusion in detail. In the materials that follow, we will focus only on a few selected exclusions.[2] Although these materials do not cover all the listed exclusions,

---

1. It may sound contradictory to state that an item of gross income must be excluded by a statutory exclusion, but also to state that only "most" of the exclusions are found in Part III of Subchapter B, which is entitled "Items Specifically Excluded From Gross Income." Part II of Subchapter B, which is entitled "Items Specifically Included in Gross Income" actually contains at least two provisions that, in a backward fashion, exclude items that might otherwise be includible in gross income. Look at sections 79 and 86. Both sections purport to include certain items in gross income, but in doing so, they also exclude a portion as well. What is included and what is excluded in sections 79 and 86?

2. From this moment, make sure that you begin to be precise in your tax terminology. Do not confuse the concept of an "exclusion" from gross income with the concept of a "deduction" from gross income. See tax calculation outline. An "exclusion" is an item that meets the definition of gross income under the *Glenshaw Glass* formulation that we have learned, but that Congress has chosen to allow taxpayers to exclude from gross income by means of a specific exclusion contained in the Code. An item excluded from gross income by a provision of the Code never makes it into the tax calculation.

it is a good idea for you to scan sections 101 through 139A in the table of contents to get an idea of the types of items that are excluded from gross income.

All the items specifically excluded from income by sections 101 through 139A clearly would be income within the broad definition of section 61. Why has Congress chosen to exclude these items? There is no single reason. The reason for excluding one might differ from the reason for excluding another. Congress chose some exclusions for policy reasons, some for ease of administration, and others for just plain political reasons. But, in all cases, the fact that these statutory exclusions represent exceptions to the broad sweep of section 61—as the courts have noted, exclusions from gross income are matters of "legislative grace"—means that courts will narrowly construe them to maximize the taxation of any accession to wealth.[3]

A. Gifts, Bequests, Devises, and Inheritances

Recall the question we considered in Chapter 1[4] following the *Cesarini* case, concerning a computer that you obtained through a "bargain" purchase from your employer. When we applied the three-prong *Glenshaw Glass* test to your purchase of the computer, we concluded that you had an accession to wealth, clearly realized, over which you had complete dominion. As a result, we concluded that you had gross income in the amount of the difference between the value of the computer and the amount you paid for it, *i.e.*, the "bargain element." Consider whether the result would have been any different had you purchased the computer from your mother for the same price. **Look at section 102.**

Suppose your father gives you a gift of $1,000 in cash. Apply the three-prong test of *Glenshaw Glass*: (1) Accession to wealth? (2) Clearly realized? (3) Complete dominion? Why then exclude gifts (and bequests, inheritances, and devises as well) from gross income?[5] A simple answer is that Congress does not wish to impede the transmission of gratuitous economic benefits from one to another.[6] But this is not a satisfactory explanation because, in fact, Congress imposes either a gift or an estate tax on many transmissions of property.[7] Whatever Congress's original intent, treating "property acquired

---

A "deduction," on the other hand, as shown schematically on the taxing formula diagram, is subtracted from gross income for reasons that we will learn in the next chapter.

3. *See New Colonial Ice Co. v. Helvering*, 292 U.S. 435, 440 (1934), and *Robinson v. Commissioner*, 102 T.C. 116, 125 (1994).

4. Question 1, following Zelenak and McMahon article in Part II., Chapter 1.

5. Congress has excluded gifts and bequests from income since the Tariff Act of 1913. 38 Stat. 114 at 167, c. 16, Section II. B.

6. There is no explicit expression of the policy underlying the original exclusion of gifts and bequests, however, in the legislative history of the Tariff Act of 1913.

7. As mentioned briefly in connection with the tax controversy that erupted when Mark McGwire was vying for the home run title, the federal estate tax, 26 U.S.C. sections 2001 *et seq.*, and its companion, the federal gift tax, 26 U.S.C. sections 2501 *et seq.*, impose a tax on the transfer of property by an individual to others either upon death or during his lifetime. These taxes are known as the federal transfer taxes and they are levied on *donors* of property for the privilege of transferring their property to others.

As part of the 2001 Act, Congress adopted a gradual repeal of the federal estate tax. It accomplished the phased-in repeal by increasing the amount of an estate that will not be subject to tax. Complete repeal occurs at the end of 2009; that is, decedents dying after December 31, 2009, will be able to pass their entire estates tax-free, provided they die before January 1, 2011. This strange twist stems from the fact that *all* the provisions of the 2001 Act expire at the end of 2010. This bizarre bit

by gift, bequest, devise, or inheritance" as income would create nightmarish problems of administration. While non-cash property passing at death can often be identified easily because the administrator or executor[8] must record the new ownership, how would the tax authorities police the 25 cents (or whatever the current going rate) that a child has received from the tooth fairy? An extreme example, but one that illustrates the enormous administrative problems in treating gifts as income.

Deciding that gifts are excluded from gross income is only one part of the inquiry, however. Once we decide that gifts are excluded from gross income, we must be able to identify a gift. How do we know which transfers are "gifts?" Perhaps in your first year property class you learned that a "gift" is a voluntary transfer of cash or property from one to another gratuitously and without consideration. Is that the definition of "gift" for purposes of the income tax? Consider the following case.

COMMISSIONER v. DUBERSTEIN

363 U.S. 278 (1960)

MR. JUSTICE BRENNAN delivered the opinion of the Court.

These two cases concern the provision of the Internal Revenue Code which excludes from the gross income of an income taxpayer "the value of property acquired by gift." (Footnote 1) They pose the frequently recurrent question whether a specific transfer to a taxpayer in fact amounted to a "gift" to him within the meaning of the statute. The importance to decision of the facts of the cases requires that we state them in some detail.

No. 376, *Commissioner v. Duberstein.* The taxpayer, Duberstein,(Footnote 2) was president of the Duberstein Iron & Metal Company, a corporation with headquarters in Dayton, Ohio. For some years the taxpayer's company had done business with Mohawk Metal Corporation, whose headquarters were in New York City. The president of Mohawk was one Berman. The taxpayer and Berman had generally used the telephone to

---

of lawmaking results from the intersection of tax legislation and budget-setting legislation. The budget bill that made the 2001 Act possible expires at the end of 10 years. Therefore, the tax provisions in the separate 2001 Act must also expire. Many observers think it likely that Congress will amend the 2001 Act before the date it is scheduled to expire, or extend it through later legislative action.

For purposes of this course, in which we are focusing only on the individual income tax provisions of the Code, it is important for you to differentiate between an "income" tax and a "gift or estate tax" that taxes the person who transfers property to another through a lifetime gift or at death. The income and transfer tax systems are separate systems of taxation that tax different things. Do not be confused when you hear that there is a tax on a gift. Under section 102, there is no income tax on the recipient of a gift, but there may be a gift tax on the donor of the gift. It is the *donor* who is responsible for paying the gift tax. Note that the 2001 Act repealed only the federal estate tax after 2009; the Act did not repeal the federal gift tax; it merely increased the amount of gifts exempt from tax and lowered the rate applicable to taxable gifts.

8. When someone dies, the procedure to be followed for disposing of the decedent's assets (and paying any liabilities) varies, depending upon whether the decedent left a will. If there is a will, the local probate court will be asked by the executor named in the will to admit the will for probate, *i.e.*, to allow the executor to carry out the instructions in the will. If there is no will, a person willing to handle the affairs of the decedent, often a close member of the decedent's family, will apply to the probate court for appointment as "administrator" or (in the old-fashioned term for a female administrator) "administratrix." Of course, many survivors are not well-advised, and do not follow these procedures, particularly when the assets of the decedent do not require probate court action for transfer of ownership because they pass by operation of law, *e.g.*, property that is jointly owned with a right of survivorship, or *de facto* transfer, *e.g.*, clothing and other personal property.

transact their companies' business with each other, which consisted of buying and selling metals. The taxpayer testified, without elaboration, that he knew Berman "personally" and had known him for about seven years. From time to time in their telephone conversations, Berman would ask Duberstein whether the latter knew of potential customers for some of Mohawk's products in which Duberstein's company itself was not interested. Duberstein provided the names of potential customers for these items.

One day in 1951 Berman telephoned Duberstein and said that the information Duberstein had given him had proved so helpful that he wanted to give the latter a present. Duberstein stated that Berman owed him nothing. Berman said that he had a Cadillac as a gift for Duberstein, and that the latter should send to New York for it; Berman insisted that Duberstein accept the car, and the latter finally did so, protesting however that he had not intended to be compensated for the information. At the time Duberstein already had a Cadillac and an Oldsmobile, and felt that he did not need another car. Duberstein testified that he did not think Berman would have sent him the Cadillac if he had not furnished him with information about the customers. It appeared that Mohawk later deducted the value of the Cadillac as a business expense on its corporate income tax return.

Duberstein did not include the value of the Cadillac in gross income for 1951, deeming it a gift. The Commissioner asserted a deficiency for the car's value against him, and in proceedings to review the deficiency the Tax Court affirmed the Commissioner's determination. It said that "The record is significantly barren of evidence revealing any intention on the part of the payor to make a gift.... The only justifiable inference is that the automobile was intended by the payor to be remuneration for services rendered to it by Duberstein." The Court of Appeals for the Sixth Circuit reversed. 265 F.2d 28.

No. 546, *Stanton v. United States.* The taxpayer, Stanton, had been for approximately 10 years in the employ of Trinity Church in New York City. He was comptroller of the Church corporation, and president of a corporation, Trinity Operating Company, the church set up as a fully owned subsidiary to manage its real estate holdings, which were more extensive than simply the church property. His salary by the end of his employment there in 1942 amounted to $22,500 a year. Effective November 30, 1942, he resigned from both positions to go into business for himself. The Operating Company's directors, who seem to have included the rector and vestrymen of the church, passed the following resolution upon his resignation: "BE IT RESOLVED that in appreciation of the services rendered by Mr. Stanton ... a gratuity is hereby awarded to him of Twenty Thousand Dollars, payable to him in equal installments of Two Thousand Dollars at the end of each and every month commencing with the month of December, 1942; provided that, with the discontinuance of his services, the Corporation of Trinity Church is released from all rights and claims to pension and retirement benefits not already accrued up to November 30, 1942."

The Operating Company's action was later explained by one of its directors as based on the fact that, "Mr. Stanton was liked by all of the Vestry personally. He had a pleasing personality. He had come in when Trinity's affairs were in a difficult situation. He did a splendid piece of work, we felt. Besides that ... he was liked by all of the members of the Vestry personally." And by another: "[W]e were all unanimous in wishing to make Mr. Stanton a gift. Mr. Stanton had loyally and faithfully served Trinity in a very difficult time. We thought of him in the highest regard. We understood that he was going in business for himself. We felt that he was entitled to that evidence of good will."

On the other hand, there was a suggestion of some ill-feeling between Stanton and the directors, arising out of the recent termination of the services of one Watkins, the Operating Company's treasurer, whose departure was evidently attended by some acrimony. At a special board meeting on October 28, 1942, Stanton had intervened on Watkins' side and asked reconsideration of the matter. The minutes reflect that "resentment was expressed as to the 'presumptuous' suggestion that the action of the Board, taken after long deliberation, should be changed." The Board adhered to its determination that Watkins be separated from employment, giving him an opportunity to resign rather than be discharged. At another special meeting two days later it was revealed that Watkins had not resigned; the previous resolution terminating his services was then viewed as effective; and the Board voted the payment of six months' salary to Watkins in a resolution similar to that quoted in regard to Stanton, but which did not use the term "gratuity." At the meeting, Stanton announced that in order to avoid any such embarrassment or question at any time as to his willingness to resign if the Board desired, he was tendering his resignation. It was tabled, though not without dissent. The next week, on November 5, at another special meeting, Stanton again tendered his resignation which this time was accepted.

The "gratuity" was duly paid. So was a smaller one to Stanton's (and the Operating Company's) secretary, under a similar resolution, upon her resignation at the same time. The two corporations shared the expense of the payments. There was undisputed testimony that there were in fact no enforceable rights or claims to pension and retirement benefits which had not accrued at the time of the taxpayer's resignation, and that the last proviso of the resolution was inserted simply out of an abundance of caution. The taxpayer received in cash a refund of his contributions to the retirement plans, and there is no suggestion that he was entitled to more. He was required to perform no further services for Trinity after his resignation.

The Commissioner asserted a deficiency against the taxpayer after the latter had failed to include the payments in question in gross income. After payment of the deficiency and administrative rejection of a refund claim, the taxpayer sued the United States for a refund in the District Court for the Eastern District of New York. The trial judge, sitting without a jury, made the simple finding that the payments were a "gift," (Footnote 3) and judgment was entered for the taxpayer. The Court of Appeals for the Second Circuit reversed. 268 F.2d 727.

The Government, urging that clarification of the problem typified by these two cases was necessary, and that the approaches taken by the Courts of Appeals for the Second and the Sixth Circuits were in conflict, petitioned for certiorari in No. 376, and acquiesced in the taxpayer's petition in No. 546. On this basis, and because of the importance of the question in the administration of the income tax laws, we granted certiorari in both cases. 361 U.S. 923.

The exclusion of property acquired by gift from gross income under the federal income tax laws was made in the first income tax statute (Footnote 4) passed under the authority of the Sixteenth Amendment, and has been a feature of the income tax statutes ever since. The meaning of the term "gift" as applied to particular transfers has always been a matter of contention. (Footnote 5) Specific and illuminating legislative history on the point does not appear to exist. Analogies and inferences drawn from other revenue provisions, such as the estate and gift taxes, are dubious.... The meaning of the statutory term has been shaped largely by the decisional law. With this, we turn to the contentions made by the Government in these cases.

First. The Government suggests that we promulgate a new "test" in this area to serve as a standard to be applied by the lower courts and by the Tax Court in dealing with the numerous cases that arise. (Footnote 6) We reject this invitation. We are of opinion that the governing principles are necessarily general and have already been spelled out in the opinions of this Court, and that the problem is one which, under the present statutory framework, does not lend itself to any more definitive statement that would produce a talisman for the solution of concrete cases. The cases at bar are fair examples of the settings in which the problem usually arises. They present situations in which payments have been made in a context with business overtones—an employer making a payment to a retiring employee; a businessman giving something of value to another businessman who has been of advantage to him in his business. In this context, we review the law as established by the prior cases here.

The course of decision here makes it plain that the statute does not use the term "gift" in the common-law sense, but in a more colloquial sense. This Court has indicated that a voluntary executed transfer of his property by one to another, without any consideration or compensation therefor, though a common-law gift, is not necessarily a "gift" within the meaning of the statute. For the Court has shown that the mere absence of a legal or moral obligation to make such a payment does not establish that it is a gift. *Old Colony Trust Co. v. Commissioner*, 279 U.S. 716, 730. And, importantly, if the payment proceeds primarily from "the constraining force of any moral or legal duty," or from "the incentive of anticipated benefit" of an economic nature, *Bogardus v. Commissioner*, 302 U.S. 34, 41, it is not a gift. And, conversely, "[w]here the payment is in return for services rendered, it is irrelevant that the donor derives no economic benefit from it." *Robertson v. United States*, 343 U.S. 711, 714. (Footnote 7) A gift in the statutory sense, on the other hand, proceeds from a "detached and disinterested generosity," *Commissioner v. LoBue*, 351 U.S. 243, 246; "out of affection, respect, admiration, charity or like impulses." *Robertson v. United States, supra*, at 714. And in this regard, the most critical consideration, as the Court was agreed in the leading case here, is the transferor's "intention." *Bogardus v. Commissioner*, 302 U.S. 34, 43. "What controls is the intention with which payment, however voluntary, has been made." *Id.*, at 45 (dissenting opinion).

The Government says that this "intention" of the transferor cannot mean what the cases on the common-law concept of gift call "donative intent." With that we are in agreement, for our decisions fully support this. Moreover, the *Bogardus* case itself makes it plain that the donor's characterization of his action is not determinative—that there must be an objective inquiry as to whether what is called a gift amounts to it in reality. 302 U.S., at 40. It scarcely needs adding that the parties' expectations or hopes as to the tax treatment of their conduct in themselves have nothing to do with the matter.

It is suggested that the *Bogardus* criterion would be more apt if rephrased in terms of "motive" rather than "intention." We must confess to some skepticism as to whether such a verbal mutation would be of any practical consequence. We take it that the proper criterion, established by decision here, is one that inquires what the basic reason for his conduct was in fact—the dominant reason that explains his action in making the transfer. Further than that we do not think it profitable to go.

Second. The Government's proposed "test," while apparently simple and precise in its formulation, depends frankly on a set of "principles" or "presumptions" derived from the decided cases, and concededly subject to various exceptions; and it involves various corollaries, which add to its detail. Were we to promulgate this test as a matter of law, and accept with it its various presuppositions and stated consequences, we would be passing far beyond the requirements of the cases before us, and would be painting on a large canvas with indeed a broad brush. The Government derives its test from such propositions as the following: That payments by an employer to an employee, even though voluntary, ought, by and large, to be taxable; that the concept of a gift is inconsistent with a payment's being a deductible business expense; that a gift involves "personal" elements; that a business corporation cannot properly make a gift of its assets. The Government admits that there are exceptions and qualifications to these propositions. We think, to the extent they are correct, that these propositions are not principles of law but rather maxims of experience that the tribunals which have tried the facts of cases in this area have enunciated in explaining their factual determinations. Some of them simply represent truisms: it doubtless is, statistically speaking, the exceptional payment by an employer to an employee that amounts to a gift. Others are overstatements of possible evidentiary inferences relevant to a factual determination on the totality of circumstances in the case: it is doubtless relevant to the over-all inference that the transferor treats a payment as a business deduction, or that the transferor is a corporate entity. But these inferences cannot be stated in absolute terms. Neither factor is a shibboleth. The taxing statute does not make nondeductibility by the transferor a condition on the "gift" exclusion; nor does it draw any distinction, in terms, between transfers by corporations and individuals, as to the availability of the "gift" exclusion to the transferee. The conclusion whether a transfer amounts to a "gift" is one that must be reached on consideration of all the factors.

Specifically, the trier of fact must be careful not to allow trial of the issue whether the receipt of a specific payment is a gift to turn into a trial of the tax liability, or of the propriety, as a matter of fiduciary or corporate law, attaching to the conduct of someone else. The major corollary to the Government's suggested "test" is that, as an ordinary matter, a payment by a corporation cannot be a gift, and, more specifically, there can be no such thing as a "gift" made by a corporation which would allow it to take a deduction for an ordinary and necessary business expense. As we have said, we find no basis for such a conclusion in the statute; and if it were applied as a determinative rule of "law," it would force the tribunals trying tax cases involving the donee's liability into elaborate inquiries into the local law of corporations or into the peripheral deductibility of payments as business expenses. The former issue might make the tax tribunals the most frequent investigators of an important and difficult issue of the laws of the several States, and the latter inquiry would summon one difficult and delicate problem of federal tax law as an aid to the solution of another. (Footnote 9) ... These considerations, also, reinforce us in our conclusion that while the principles urged by the Government may, in nonabsolute form as crystallizations of experience, prove persuasive to the trier of facts in a particular case, neither they, nor any more detailed statement than has been made, can be laid down as a matter of law.

Third. Decision of the issue presented in these cases must be based ultimately on the application of the fact-finding tribunal's experience with the mainsprings of human conduct to the totality of the facts of each case. The nontechnical nature of the statutory standard, the close relationship of it to the data of practical human experience, and the multiplicity of relevant factual elements, with their various combinations, creating the necessity of ascribing the proper force to each, confirm us in our conclusion that primary weight in this area must be given to the conclusions of the trier of fact....

This conclusion may not satisfy an academic desire for tidiness, symmetry and precision in this area, any more than a system based on the determinations of various fact-finders ordinarily does. But we see it as implicit in the present statutory treatment of the exclusion for gifts, and in the variety of forums in which federal income tax cases can be tried. If there is fear of undue uncertainty or overmuch litigation, Congress may make more precise its treatment of the matter by singling out certain factors and making them determinative of the matter, as it has done in one field of the "gift" exclusion's former application, that of prizes and awards. (Footnote 12) Doubtless diversity of result will tend to be lessened somewhat since federal income tax decisions, even those in tribunals of first instance turning on issues of fact, tend to be reported, and since there may be a natural tendency of professional triers of fact to follow one another's determinations, even as to factual matters. But the question here remains basically one of fact, for determination on a case-by-case basis.

One consequence of this is that appellate review of determinations in this field must be quite restricted. Where a jury has tried the matter upon correct instructions, the only inquiry is whether it cannot be said that reasonable men could reach differing conclusions on the issue.... Where the trial has been by a judge without a jury, the judge's findings must stand unless "clearly erroneous." Fed. Rules Civ. Proc., 52(a). "A finding is 'clearly erroneous' when although there is evidence to support it, the reviewing court on the entire evidence is left with the definite and firm conviction that a mistake has been committed." *United States v. United States Gypsum Co.*, 333 U.S. 364, 395. The rule itself applies also to factual inferences from undisputed basic facts, *id.*, at 394, as will on many occasions be presented in this area....

Fourth. A majority of the Court is in accord with the principles just outlined. And, applying them to the *Duberstein* case, we are in agreement, on the evidence we have set forth, that it cannot be said that the conclusion of the Tax Court was "clearly erroneous." It seems to us plain that as trier of the facts it was warranted in concluding that despite the characterization of the transfer of the Cadillac by the parties and the absence of any obligation, even of a moral nature, to make it, it was at bottom a recompense for Duberstein's past services, or an inducement for him to be of further service in the future. We cannot say with the Court of Appeals that such a conclusion was "mere suspicion" on the Tax Court's part. To us it appears based in the sort of informed experience with human affairs that fact-finding tribunals should bring to this task.

As to *Stanton*, we are in disagreement. To four of us, it is critical here that the District Court as trier of fact made only the simple and unelaborated finding that the transfer in question was a "gift." (Footnote 14) To be sure, conciseness is to be strived for, and prolixity avoided, in findings; but, to the four of us, there comes a point where findings become so sparse and conclusory as to give no revelation of what the District Court's concept of the determining facts and legal standard may be.... Such conclusory, general findings do not constitute compliance with Rule 52's direction to "find the facts specially and state separately ... conclusions of law thereon." While the standard of law in this area is not a complex one, we four think the unelaborated finding of ultimate fact here cannot stand as a fulfillment of these requirements. It affords the reviewing court not the semblance of an indication of the legal standard with which the trier of fact has approached his task. For all that appears, the District Court may have viewed the form of the resolution or the simple absence of legal consideration as conclusive. While the judgment of the Court of Appeals cannot stand, the four of us think there must be further proceedings in the District Court looking toward new and adequate findings of fact. In this, we are joined by MR. JUSTICE WHITTAKER, who agrees that the findings were inadequate, although he does not concur generally in this opinion.

Accordingly, in No. 376, the judgment of this Court is that the judgment of the Court of Appeals is reversed, and in No. 546, that the judgment of the Court of Appeals is vacated, and the case is remanded to the District Court for further proceedings not inconsistent with this opinion.

It is so ordered.

FOOTNOTES:

1. The operative provision in the cases at bar is § 22(b)(3) of the 1939 Internal Revenue Code. The corresponding provision of the present Code is § 102(a).

2. In both cases the husband will be referred to as the taxpayer, although his wife joined with him in joint tax returns.

3. See note 14, *infra.*

4. § II.B., c. 16, 38 Stat. 167.

5. The first case of the Board of Tax Appeals officially reported in fact deals with the problem. *Parrott v. Commissioner*, 1 B.T.A. 1.

6. The Government's proposed test is stated: "Gifts should be defined as transfers of property made for personal as distinguished from business reasons."

7. The cases including "tips" in gross income are classic examples of this. See, *e.g., Roberts v. Commissioner*, 176 F.2d 221.

9. Justice Cardozo once described in memorable language the inquiry into whether an expense was an "ordinary and necessary" one of a business: "One struggles in vain for any verbal formula that will supply a ready touchstone. The standard set up by the statute is not a rule of law; it is rather a way of life. Life in all its fullness must supply the answer to the riddle." *Welch v. Helvering*, 290 U.S. 111, 115. The same comment well fits the issue in the cases at bar.

12. I.R.C., §74, which is a provision new with the 1954 Code. Previously, there had been holdings that such receipts as the "Pot O' Gold" radio giveaway, *Washburn v. Commissioner*, 5 T.C. 1333, and the Ross Essay Prize, *McDermott v. Commissioner*, 80 U.S. App. D.C. 176, 150 F.2d 585, were "gifts." Congress intended to obviate such rulings. S. Rep. No. 1622, 83d Cong., 2d Sess., p. 178. We imply no approval of those holdings under the general standard of the "gift" exclusion....

14. The "Findings of Fact and Conclusions of Law" were made orally, and were simply: "The resolution of the Board of Directors of the Trinity Operating Company, Incorporated, held November 19, 1942, after the resignations had been accepted of the plaintiff from his positions as controller of the corporation of the Trinity Church, and the president of the Trinity Operating Company, Incorporated, whereby a gratuity was voted to the plaintiff, Allen [sic] D. Stanton, in the amount of $20,000 payable to him in monthly installments of $2,000 each, commencing with the month of December, 1942, constituted a gift to the taxpayer, and therefore need not have been reported by him as income for the taxable years 1942, or 1943."

MR. JUSTICE BLACK concurring and dissenting.

I agree with the Court that it was not clearly erroneous for the Tax Court to find as it did in No. 376 that the automobile transfer to Duberstein was not a gift, and so I agree with the Court's opinion and judgment reversing the judgment of the Court of Appeals in that case.

I dissent in No. 546, *Stanton v. United States*. The District Court found that the $20,000 transferred to Mr. Stanton by his former employer at the end of ten years' service was a gift and therefore exempt from taxation under I.R.C. of 1939, § 22(b)(3) (now I.R.C. of 1954, § 102(a)). I think the finding was not clearly erroneous and that the Court of Appeals was therefore wrong in reversing the District Court's judgment. While conflicting inferences might have been drawn, there was evidence to show that Mr. Stanton's long services had been satisfactory, that he was well liked personally and had given splendid service, that the employer was under no obligation at all to pay any added compensation, but made the $20,000 payment because prompted by a genuine desire to make him a "gift," to award him a "gratuity." ... The District Court's finding was that the added payment "constituted a gift to the taxpayer, and therefore need not have been reported by him as income...." The trial court might have used more words, or discussed the facts set out above in more detail, but I doubt if this would have made its crucial, adequately supported finding any clearer. For this reason I would reinstate the District Court's judgment for petitioner.

MR. JUSTICE FRANKFURTER, concurring in the judgment in No. 376 and dissenting in No. 546.

As the Court's opinion indicates, we brought these two cases here partly because of a claimed difference in the approaches between two Courts of Appeals but primarily on the Government's urging that, in the interest of the better administration of the income tax laws, clarification was desirable for determining when a transfer of property constitutes a "gift" and is not to be included in income for purposes of ascertaining the "gross income" under the Internal Revenue Code.

As soon as this problem emerged after the imposition of the first income tax authorized by the Sixteenth Amendment, it became evident that its inherent difficulties and subtleties would not easily yield to the formulation of a general rule or test sufficiently definite to confine within narrow limits the area of judgment in applying it. While at its core the tax conception of a gift no doubt reflected the non-legal, non-technical notion of a benefaction unentangled with any aspect of worldly requital, the diverse blends of personal and pecuniary relationships in our industrial society inevitably presented niceties for adjudication which could not be put to rest by any kind of general formulation.

Despite acute arguments at the bar and a most thorough re-examination of the problem on a full canvass of our prior decisions and an attempted fresh analysis of the nature of the problem, the Court has rejected the invitation of the Government to fashion anything like a litmus paper test for determining what is excludable as a "gift" from gross income. Nor has the Court attempted a clarification of the particular aspects of the problem presented by these two cases, namely, payment by an employer to an employee upon the termination of the employment relation and non-obligatory payment for services rendered in the course of a business relationship. While I agree that experience has shown the futility of attempting to define, by language so circumscribing as to make it easily applicable, what constitutes a gift for every situation where the problem may arise, I do think that greater explicitness is possible in isolating and emphasizing factors which militate against a gift in particular situations.

Thus, regarding the two frequently recurring situations involved in these cases — things of value given to employees by their employers upon the termination of employment and payments entangled in a business relation and occasioned by the performance of some service — the strong implication is that the payment is of a business nature. The problem in these two cases is entirely different from the problem in a case where a payment is made from one member of a family to another, where the implications are directly otherwise. No single general formulation appropriately deals with both types of cases, although both involve the question whether the payment was a "gift." While we should normally suppose that a payment from father to son was a gift, unless the contrary is shown, in the two situations now before us the business implications are so forceful that I would apply a presumptive rule placing the burden upon the beneficiary to prove the payment wholly unrelated to his services to the enterprise. The Court, however, has declined so to analyze the problem and has concluded "that the governing principles are necessarily general and have already been spelled out in the opinions of this Court, and that the problem is one which, under the present statutory framework, does not lend itself to any more definitive statement that would produce a talisman for the solution of concrete cases."

The Court has made only one authoritative addition to the previous course of our decisions. Recognizing *Bogardus v. Commissioner*, 302 U.S. 34, as "the leading case here" and finding essential accord between the Court's opinion and the dissent in that case, the Court has drawn from the dissent in *Bogardus* for infusion into what will now be a controlling qualification, recognition that it is "for the triers of the facts to seek among competing aims or motives the ones that dominated conduct." 302 U.S. 34, 45 (dissenting opinion). All this being so in view of the Court, it seems to me desirable not to try to improve what has "already been spelled out" in the opinions of this Court but to leave to the lower courts the application of old phrases rather than to float new ones and thereby inevitably produce a new volume of exegesis on the new phrases.

Especially do I believe this when fact-finding tribunals are directed by the Court to rely upon their "experience with the mainsprings of human conduct" and on their "informed experience with human affairs" in appraising the totality of the facts of each case. Varying conceptions regarding the "mainsprings of human conduct" are derived from a variety of experiences or assumptions about the nature of man, and "experience with human affairs," is not only diverse but also often drastically conflicting. What the Court now does sets fact-finding bodies to sail on an illimitable ocean of individual beliefs and experiences. This can hardly fail to invite, if indeed not encourage, too individualized diversities in the administration of the income tax law. I am afraid that by these new phrasings the practicalities of tax administration, which should be as uniform as is possible in so vast a country as ours, will be embarrassed. By applying what has already been spelled out in the opinions of this Court, I agree with the Court in reversing the judgment in *Commissioner v. Duberstein*.

But I would affirm the decision of the Court of Appeals for the Second Circuit in *Stanton v. United States*. I would do so on the basis of the opinion of Judge Hand and more particularly because the very terms of the resolution by which the $20,000 was awarded to Stanton indicated that it was not a "gratuity" in the sense of sheer benevolence but in the nature of a generous lagniappe, something extra thrown in for services received though not legally nor morally required to be given. This careful resolution, doubtless drawn by a lawyer and adopted by some hardheaded businessmen, contained a proviso that Stanton should abandon all rights to "pension and retirement benefits." The fact that Stanton had no such claims does not lessen the significance of the clause as something "to make assurance doubly sure." 268 F.2d 728. The business nature of the payment is confirmed by the words of the resolution, explaining the "gratuity" as "in appreciation of the services rendered by Mr. Stanton as Manager of the Estate and Comptroller of the Corporation of Trinity Church throughout nearly ten years, and as President of Trinity Operating Company, Inc." The force of this document, in light of all the factors to which Judge Hand adverted in his opinion, was not in the least diminished by testimony at the trial. Thus the taxpayer has totally failed to sustain the burden I would place upon him to establish that the payment to him was wholly attributable to generosity unrelated to his performance of his secular business functions as an officer of the corporation of the Trinity Church of New York and the Trinity Operating Co. Since the record totally fails to establish taxpayer's claim, I see no need of specific findings by the trial judge.

Consider the following questions about *Duberstein*.

1. What kind of test does *Duberstein* create for identifying which transfers are gifts and which are something else? What are the benefits and problems with this type of test?

2. Given the nature of the necessary inquiry for determining the existence of a gift after *Duberstein*, how would you advise your clients who wish to make gifts? Would you require different information or documentation depending on the identity of the donee?

3. If a transfer does not constitute a gift, in what other ways might you characterize it? (Clue: consider the identities of and relationship between the transferor and the transferee.) Would all the alternatives you suggest constitute income based upon the characteristics of income we have studied?

4. Reconsider taxpayer Stanton in the *Duberstein* case. Why are both cases decided in one opinion? Would Stanton have been able to assert that the transfer was a gift after the enactment of section 102(c)? **Look at section 102(c).**

5. Suppose Julie is employed by her mother and her mother gives her $5,000. In light of section 102(c), how would you characterize the transfer from mother to daughter? Would you need additional facts? **Read the following proposed regulation, Treasury Regulation section 1.102-1(f).**[9]

In interpreting this proposed regulation, you must answer the following questions: (1) What is an "extraordinary transfer"?; (2) Who are "the natural objects of an employer's bounty"?; and (3) How might an employee show that "the transfer was not made in recognition of the employee's employment"?

6. How would you advise an employer to document a transfer in order to escape section 102(c) and come within the proposed amendment to the regulation?[10]

Consider Justice Frankfurter's concern, expressed in his concurrence to the Duberstein portion of the Supreme Court's opinion:

> What the Court now does sets fact-finding bodies to sail on an illimitable ocean of individual beliefs and experiences. This can hardly fail to invite, if indeed not encourage, too individualized diversities in the administration of the income tax law. I am afraid that by these new phrasings the practicalities of tax administration, which should be as uniform as is possible in so vast a country as ours, will be embarrassed.

363 U.S. at 397.

---

9. What is the legal effect of a proposed regulation? What is its practical effect?

10. To what extent can you feel confident in advising your client to rely on a proposed regulation? The Service might alter the proposal before adoption in final form. Consider the difference between a proposed regulation and a temporary regulation. **Glance at Treasury Regulation section 1.71-1T.** This is an example of a temporary regulation. Notice its interesting question and answer (Q/A) format.

An interesting manifestation of Justice Frankfurter's concern occurred in the case that follows. (As you read the case, recall Mr. James, the embezzler from Part II Chapter 1, whose embezzled funds the Supreme Court characterized as gross income. Why was he not guilty of tax evasion for failing to report the embezzled funds as gross income?)

UNITED STATES v. HARRIS
942 F.2d 1125 (7th Cir. 1991)

ESCHBACH, Senior Circuit Judge:

David Kritzik, now deceased, was a wealthy widower partial to the company of young women. Two of these women were Leigh Ann Conley and Lynnette Harris, twin sisters. Directly or indirectly, Kritzik gave Conley and Harris each more than half a million dollars over the course of several years. For our purposes, either Kritzik had to pay gift tax on this money or Harris and Conley had to pay income tax. The United States alleges that, beyond reasonable doubt, the obligation was Harris and Conley's. In separate criminal trials, Harris and Conley were convicted of willfully evading their income tax obligations regarding the money, (Footnote 1) and they now appeal.

Under *Commissioner v. Duberstein, 363 U.S. 278 ... (1960)*, the donor's intent is the "critical consideration" in distinguishing between gifts and income. We reverse Conley's conviction and remand with instructions to dismiss the indictment against her because the government failed to present sufficient evidence of Kritzik's intent regarding the money he gave her. We also reverse Harris' conviction. The district court excluded as hearsay letters in which Kritzik wrote that he loved Harris and enjoyed giving things to her. These letters were central to Harris' defense that she believed in good faith that the money she received was a nontaxable gift, and they were not hearsay for this purpose.

We do not remand Harris' case for retrial, however, because Harris had no fair warning that her conduct might subject her to criminal tax liability. Neither the tax code, the Treasury Regulations, or Supreme Court or appellate cases provide a clear answer to whether Harris owed any taxes or not. The closest authority lies in a series of Tax Court decisions—but these cases *favor* Harris' position that the money she received was not income to her. Under this state of the law, Harris could not have formed a "willful" intent to violate the statutes at issue. For this reason, we remand with instructions that the indictment against Harris be dismissed. The same conclusion applies to Conley, and provides an alternative basis for reversing her conviction and remanding with instructions to dismiss the indictment.

Insufficiency of the Evidence as to Conley

Conley was convicted on each of four counts for violating *26 U.S.C. §7203*, which provides,

> Any person ... required ... to make a [tax] return ... who willfully fails to ... make such return ... shall, in addition to other penalties provided by law, be guilty of a misdemeanor....

Conley was "required ... to make a return" only if the money that she received from Kritzik was income to her rather than a gift. Assuming that the money was income, she acted "willfully," and so is subject to criminal prosecution, only if she knew of her duty to pay taxes and "voluntarily and intentionally violated that duty." *Cheek v. United States, 498 U.S. 192 ... (1991)*. The government met its burden of proof if the jury could have found these elements beyond a reasonable doubt, viewing the evidence in the light most favorable to the government. *See, e.g., United States v. Lamon, 930 F.2d 1183, 1190 (7th Cir. 1991)*.

The government's evidence was insufficient to show either that the money Conley received was income or that she acted in knowing disregard of her obligations. "Gross income" for tax purposes does not include gifts, which are taxable to the donor rather than the recipient. *26 U.S.C. §§ 61, 102(a), 2501(a)*. In *Commissioner v. Duberstein, 363 U.S. 278 ... (1960),* the Supreme Court stated that in distinguishing between income and gifts the "critical consideration ... is the transferor's intention." A transfer of property is a gift if the transferor acted out of a "detached and disinterested generosity, ... out of affection, respect, admiration, charity, or like impulses." *Id.* By contrast, a transfer of property is income if it is the result of "the constraining force of any moral or legal duty, constitutes a reward for services rendered, or proceeds from the incentive of anticipated benefit of an economic nature."

Regarding the "critical consideration" of the donor's intent, the only direct evidence that the government presented was Kritzik's gift tax returns. On those returns, Kritzik identified gifts to Conley of $ 24,000, $ 30,000, and $ 36,000 for the years 1984–6, respectively, substantially less than the total amount of money that Kritzik transferred to Conley. This leaves the question whether Kritzik's other payments were taxable income to Conley or whether Kritzik just underreported his gifts. The gift tax returns raise the question, they do not resolve it. (Footnote 3)

This failure to show Kritzik's intent is fatal to the government's case. Without establishing Kritzik's intent, the government cannot establish that Conley had any obligation to pay income taxes. Further, Conley could not have "willfully" failed to pay her taxes unless she knew of Kritzik's intent. Even if Kritzik's gift tax returns proved anything, the government presented no evidence that Conley knew the amounts that Kritzik had listed on those returns. Absent proof of Kritzik's intent, and Conley's knowledge of that intent, the government has no case.

The government's remaining evidence consisted of a bank card that Conley signed listing Kritzik in a space marked "employer" and testimony regarding the form of the payments that Conley received. The bank card is no evidence of Kritzik's intent and even as to Conley is open to conflicting interpretations—she contends that she listed Kritzik as a reference and no more. As to the form of the payments, the government showed that Conley would pick up a regular check at Kritzik's office every week to ten days, either from Kritzik personally or, when he was not in, from his secretary. According to the government, this form of payment is that of an employee picking up regular wages, but it could just as easily be that of a dependent picking up regular support checks.

...

[I]n the present case, the bare facts of Kritzik's gift tax return, the bank card, and the form of the payments are as consistent with an inference of innocence as one of guilt. The evidence does not support a finding of guilt beyond a reasonable doubt, and we reverse Conley's conviction and remand with instructions to dismiss the indictment against her.

The Admissibility of Kritzik's Letters

Harris was convicted of two counts of willfully failing to file federal income tax returns under *26 U.S.C. § 7203* (the same offense for which Conley was convicted) and two counts of willful tax evasion under *26 U.S.C. § 7201*. (Footnote 4) At trial, Harris tried to introduce as evidence three letters that Kritzik wrote, but the District Court excluded the letters as hearsay. The District Court also suggested that the letters would be inadmissible under *Fed. R. Evid. 403* because the possible prejudice from the letters exceeded their probative value. We hold that the letters were not hearsay because they were offered to prove Harris' lack of willfulness, not for the truth of the matters asserted. We further hold that the critical nature of the letters to Harris' defense precludes their exclusion under Rule 403, and so reverse her conviction.

The first of the letters at issue was a four page, handwritten letter from Kritzik to Harris, dated April 4, 1981. In it, Kritzik wrote that he loved and trusted Harris and that, "so far as the things I give you are concerned—let me say that I get as great if not even greater pleasure in giving than you get in receiving." Def. Ex. 201, p. 2. He continued, "I love giving things to you and to see you happy and enjoying them." *Id.* In a second letter to Harris of the same date, Kritzik again wrote, "I ... love you very much and will do all that I can to make you happy," and said that he would arrange for Harris' financial security. Def. Ex. 202, p. 3. In a third letter, dated some six years later on May 28, 1987, Kritzik wrote to his insurance company regarding the value of certain jewelry that he had "given to Ms. Lynette Harris as a gift." Kritzik forwarded a copy of the letter to Harris.

These letters were hearsay if offered for the truth of the matters asserted—that Kritzik did in fact love Harris, enjoyed giving her things, wanted to take care of her financial security, and gave her the jewelry at issue as a gift. But the letters were not hearsay for the purpose of showing what Harris believed, because her belief does not depend on the actual truth of the matters asserted in the letters. Even if Kritzik were lying, the letters could have caused Harris to believe in good faith that the things he gave her were intended as gifts. *See generally, Fed. R. Evid. 801(a); United States v. Mejia, 909 F.2d 242, 247 (7th Cir. 1990).* This good faith belief, in turn, would preclude any finding of willfulness on her part.

In general, hearsay problems like this—evidence being admissible for one purpose but not for another—still leave the District Court discretion. Jurors are not robots, after all, and can rarely consider evidence strictly for a single purpose to the exclusion of other, often more obvious purposes. For this reason, we will usually defer to a trial judge's conclusion that, under *Fed. R. Evid. 403*, otherwise admissible evidence is likely to do more harm than good....

In this case, however, the letters were too important to Harris' defense to be excluded. Her belief about Kritzik's intent decides the issue of willfulness, which is an element of the offense, and she had no other objective means of proving that belief. True, admitting the letters would probably lead to some prejudice to the government's case. The jury would be hard pressed to consider the letters only for the permissible issue of what Harris thought of Kritzik's intent, and not for the impermissible issue of what Kritzik actually intended. The alternative, however, is to strip Harris of evidence that we believe was essential to a fair trial. In these circumstances, we hold that the District Court abused its discretion in excluding the letters and so reverse Harris' conviction.

The Tax Treatment of Payments to Mistresses

Our conclusion that Harris should have been allowed to present the letters at issue as evidence would ordinarily lead us to remand her case for retrial. We further conclude, however, that current law on the tax treatment of payments to mistresses provided Harris no fair warning that her conduct was criminal. Indeed, current authorities favor Harris' position that the money she received from Kritzik was a gift. We emphasize that we do not necessarily agree with these authorities, and that the government is free to urge departure from them in a noncriminal context. But new points of tax law may not be the basis of criminal convictions. For this reason, we remand with instructions that the indictment against Harris be dismissed. Although we discuss only Harris' case in this section, the same reasoning applies to Conley and provides an alternative basis for dismissal of the indictment against her.

Again, the definitive statement of the distinction between gifts and income is in the Supreme Court's *Duberstein* decision, which applies and interprets the definition of income contained in *26 U.S.C. §61*. But as the Supreme Court described, the *Duberstein* principles are "necessarily general." It stated, "'One struggles in vain for any verbal formula that will supply a ready touchstone. The standard set up ... is not a rule of law; it is rather a way of life. Life in all its fullness must supply the answer to the riddle.'" *Id., quoting Welch v. Helvering, 290 U.S. 111, 115, 78 L. Ed. 212, 54 S. Ct. 8 (1933).* Along these lines, Judge Flaum's concurrence properly characterizes *Duberstein* as "eschew[ing] ... [any] categorical, rule-bound analysis" in favor of a "case-by-case" approach. Concurrence, at 1136.

Duberstein was a civil case, and its approach is appropriate for civil cases. But criminal prosecutions are a different story. These must rest on a violation of a clear rule of law, not on conflict with a "way of life". If "defendants [in a tax case] ... could not have ascertained the legal standards applicable to their conduct, criminal proceedings may not be used to define and punish an alleged failure to conform to those standards." *United States v. Mallas, 762 F.2d 361, 361 (4th Cir. 1985).* This rule is based on the Constitution's requirement of due process and its prohibition on *ex post facto* laws; the government must provide reasonable notice of what conduct is subject to criminal punishment. *See id., at 363; see also Kucharek v. Hanaway, 902 F.2d 513, 518 (7th Cir. 1990), cert. denied, 498 U.S. 1041, 112 L. Ed. 2d 702, 111 S. Ct. 713 (1991).* The rule is also statutory in tax cases, because only "willful" violations are subject to criminal punishment. *Mallas, 762 F.2d at 363; see Cheek v. United States, 498 U.S. 192 ... (1991).* In the tax area, "willful" wrongdoing means the "voluntary, intentional violation of a known" — and therefore knowable — "legal duty." *Cheek, 111 S. Ct. at 610, quoting United States v. Bishop, 412 U.S. 346 ... (1973).* If the obligation to pay a tax is sufficiently in doubt, willfulness is impossible as a matter of law, and the "defendant's actual intent is irrelevant." *United States v. Garber, 607 F.2d 92, 98 (5th Cir. 1979)* (en banc), *quoting United States v. Critzer, 498 F.2d 1160, 1162 (4th Cir. 1974).* (Footnote 6)

We do not doubt that *Duberstein's* principles, though general, provide a clear answer to many cases involving the gift versus income distinction and can be the basis for civil as well as criminal prosecutions in such cases. We are equally certain, however, that *Duberstein* provides no ready answer to the taxability of transfers of money to a mistress in the context of a long term relationship. The motivations of the parties in such cases will always be mixed. The relationship would not be long term were it not for some respect or affection. Yet, it may be equally clear that the relationship would not continue were it not for financial support or payments.

. . .

The most pertinent authority lies in several civil cases from the Tax Court, but these cases *favor* Harris' position. At its strongest, the government's case against Harris follows the assertions that Harris made, but now repudiates, in a lawsuit she filed against Kritzik's estate. According to her sworn pleadings in that suit, "all sums of money paid by David Kritzik to Lynette Harris ... were made ... in pursuance with the parties' express oral agreement." Government Exhibit 22, p. 4. As Harris' former lawyer testified at her trial, the point of this pleading was to make out a "palimony" claim under the California Supreme Court's decision in *Marvin v. Marvin, 18 Cal. 3d 660 ... (1976)*. Yet, the Tax Court has likened Marvin-type claims to amounts paid under antenuptial agreements. Under this analysis, these claims are *not* taxable income to the recipient:

> In an antenuptial agreement the parties agree, through private contract, on an arrangement for the disposition of their property in the event of death or separation. *Occasionally, however, the relinquishment of marital rights is not involved. These contracts are generally enforceable under state contract law. See Marvin v. Marvin, 18 Cal. 3d 660, 557 P.2d 106, 134 Cal. Rptr. 815 (1976).* Nonetheless, transfers pursuant to an antenuptial agreement are generally treated as gifts between the parties, because under the gift tax law the exchanged promises are not supported by full and adequate consideration, in money or money's worth.

Green v. Commissioner, T.C. Memo 1987-503 (emphasis added). We do not decide whether Marvin-type awards or settlements are or are not taxable to the recipient. The only point is that the Tax Court has suggested they are not. Until contrary authority emerges, no taxpayer could form a willful, criminal intent to violate the tax laws by failing to report Marvin-type payments. Reasonable inquiry does not yield a clear answer to the taxability of such payments.

Other cases only reinforce this conclusion. *Reis v. Commissioner, T.C. Memo 1974-287* is a colorful example. The case concerned the tax liability of Lillian Reis, who had her start as a 16 year old nightclub dancer. At 21, she met Clyde "Bing" Miller when he treated the performers in the nightclub show to a steak and champagne dinner. As the Tax Court described it, Bing passed out $ 50 bills to each person at the table, on the condition that they leave, until he was alone with Reis. Bing then offered to write a check to Reis for any amount she asked. She asked for $ 1,200 for a mink stole and for another check in the same amount so her sister could have a coat too.

The next day the checks proved good; Bing returned to the club with more gifts; and "a lasting friendship developed" between Reis and Bing. For the next five years, she saw Bing "every Tuesday night at the [nightclub] and Wednesday afternoons from approximately 1:00 p.m. to 3:00 p.m.... at various places including ... a girl friend's apartment and hotels where [Bing] was staying." He paid all of her living expenses, plus $ 200 a week, and provided money for her to invest, decorate her apartment, buy a car, and so on. The total over the five years was more than $ 100,000. The Tax Court held that this money was a gift, not income, despite Reis' statement that she "earned every penny" of the money. Similarly, in *Libby v. Commissioner, T.C. Memo 1969-184 (1969)*, the Tax Court accorded gift treatment to thousands of dollars in cash and property that a young mistress received from her older paramour. And in *Starks v. Commissioner, T.C. Memo 1966-134*, the Tax Court did the same for another young woman who received cash and other property from an older, married man as part of "a very personal relationship."

The Tax Court did find that payments were income to the women who received them in *Blevins v. Commissioner, T.C. Memo 1955-211*, and in *Jones v. Commissioner, T.C. Memo 1977-329*. But in *Blevins*, the taxpayer was a woman who practiced prostitution and "used her home to operate a house of prostitution" in which six other women worked. Nothing suggested that the money at issue in that case was anything other than payments in the normal course of her business. Similarly in *Jones*, a woman had frequent hotel meetings with a married man, and on "*each* occasion" he gave her cash.

(emphasis added). Here too, the Tax Court found that the relationship was one of prostitution, a point that was supported by the woman's similar relationships with other men.

If these cases make a rule of law, it is that a person is entitled to treat cash and property received from a lover as gifts, as long as the relationship consists of something more than specific payments for specific sessions of sex. What's more, even in *Blevins*, in which the relationship was one of raw prostitution, the Tax Court rejected the IRS' claim that a civil fraud penalty should be imposed. Nor was a fraud penalty applied in *Jones*, the other prostitution case, although there the issue apparently was not raised. The United States does not allege that Harris received specific payments for specific sessions of sex, so *Reis*, *Libby*, and *Starks* support Harris' position.

Judge Flaum argues in his concurrence that these cases turn on their particular facts and do not make a rule of law. Concurrence, slip. op. at 18, 19. Fair enough (although the cases do cite each other in a manner that suggests otherwise). We need not decide this issue. We only conclude that a reasonably diligent taxpayer is entitled to look at the reported cases with the most closely analogous fact patterns when trying to determine his or her liability. When, as here, a series of such cases favors the taxpayer's position, the taxpayer has not been put on notice that he or she is in danger of crossing the line into criminality by adhering to that position. These Tax Court cases can turn entirely on their facts, yet together show that the law provided no warning to Harris that she was committing a criminal act in failing to report the money that she received. It is also worth noting that Judge Flaum's argument has no application to the case of *Green v. Commissioner, T.C. Memo 1987-503*, which, as discussed at the start of this section, suggests that Marvin-type palimony payments are not taxable income as a matter of law.

Besides Harris' prior suit, the United States also presented evidence regarding the overall relationship between Harris and Kritzik. Testimony showed that Harris described her relationship with Kritzik as "a job" and "just making a living." Trial Transcript, p. 338. She reportedly complained that she "was laying on her back and her sister was getting all the money," described how she disliked when Kritzik fondled her naked, and made other derogatory statements about sex with Kritzik. *Id.*, at 232, 337.

This evidence still leaves Harris on the favorable side of the Tax Court's cases. Further, this evidence tells us only what Harris thought of the relationship. Again, the Supreme Court in *Duberstein* held that the *donor's* intent is the "critical consideration" in determining whether a transfer of money is a gift or income. *Commissioner v. Duberstein, 363 U.S. 278 … (1960)*. If Kritzik viewed the money he gave Harris as a gift, or if the dearth of contrary evidence leaves doubt on the subject, does it matter how mercenary Harris' motives were? *Duberstein* suggests that Harris' motives may not matter, but the ultimate answer makes no difference here. As long as the answer is at least a close call, and we are confident that it is, the prevailing law is too uncertain to support Harris' criminal conviction.

> …

In short, criminal prosecutions are no place for the government to try out "pioneering interpretations of tax law." *United States v. Garber, 607 F.2d 92, 100 (5th Cir. 1979)* (en banc). The United States has not shown us, and we have not found, a single case finding tax liability for payments that a mistress received from her lover, absent proof of specific payments for specific sex acts. Even when such specific proof is present, the cases have not applied penalties for civil fraud, much less criminal sanctions. The broad principles contained in *Duberstein* do not fill this gap. Before she met Kritzik, Harris starred as a sorceress in an action/adventure film. She would have had to be a real life sorceress to predict her tax obligations under the current state of the law.

Conclusion

For the reasons stated, we REVERSE Harris and Conley's convictions and remand with instructions to DISMISS the indictments against them.

FOOTNOTES:

1. Harris was sentenced to ten months in prison, to be followed by two months in a halfway house and two years of supervised release. She was also fined $ 12,500.00 and ordered to pay a $ 150.00 special assessment. Conley was sentenced to five months in prison, followed by five months in a halfway house and one year supervised release. She was also fined $ 10,000.00 and ordered to pay a $ 100.00 assessment.

4. *26 U.S.C. § 7201* provides:

Any person who willfully attempts in any manner to evade or defeat any tax imposed by this title or the payment thereof shall, in addition to other penalties provided by law, be guilty of a felony....

6. *See also James v. United States, 366 U.S. 213 ... (1961).* In *James*, the Supreme Court held that embezzled funds are income to the recipient, formally overruling its prior decision in *Commissioner v. Wilcox, 327 U.S. 404 ... (1946)*, a case that had been all but overruled in *Rutkin v. United States, 343 U.S. 130 ... (1952)*. A plurality of the *James* Court decided that its new holding would only apply prospectively, and reversed the defendant's conviction because "the element of willfulness *could not* be proven in a criminal prosecution" given the unsettled state of the case law, apparently regardless of the defendant's actual reliance on that case law. *Id., 366 U.S. at 221–22* (emphasis added). On this point, the plurality was joined by Justices Black and Douglas, forming a majority. *Id., at 224; see United States v. Garber, 607 F.2d 92, 98–9 & n. 4 (5th Cir. 1979)* (en banc) (discussing *James*).

FLAUM, Circuit Judge, concurring.

The majority has persuasively demonstrated why Leigh Ann Conley's conviction is infirm and why the district court abused its discretion in excluding the Kritzik letters. I therefore join that portion of its opinion.

I further agree that Lynnette Harris' conviction must be reversed as well. To convict Harris for violating § 7201 and *§ 7203 of the Internal Revenue Code*, the government had to establish beyond a reasonable doubt that Harris had a legal duty to file a tax return.... It failed, in my view, to meet this burden; no reasonable juror could have found beyond a reasonable doubt that Kritzik's payments to Harris were income rather than gifts.

I am troubled, however, by the path the majority takes to reach this result, and thus concur only in the court's judgment with respect to the reversal of Harris' conviction. I part company with the majority when it distills from our gift/income jurisprudence a rule that would tax only the most base type of cash-for-sex exchange and categorically exempt from tax liability all other transfers of money and property to so-called mistresses or companions. After citing several decisions of the tax court, the majority concludes that a person "is entitled to treat cash and property received from a lover as gifts, as long as the relationship consists of something more than specific payments for specific sessions of sex." *Ante at 1133–34.* I respectfully disagree. In *Commissioner v. Duberstein, 363 U.S. 278 ... (1960)*, the font of our analysis of the gift/income distinction, the Supreme Court expressly eschewed the type of categorical, rule-bound analysis propounded by the majority. *See id. at 289* ("while the principles urged by the Government may, in nonabsolute form as crystallizations of experience, prove persuasive to the trier of facts in a particular case, neither they, nor any more detailed statement than has been made, can be laid down as a matter of law"). The Court counseled instead that in distinguishing gifts from income we should engage in a case-by-case analysis, the touchstone of which is "the 'transferor's intention.'" *Id. at 285–86* (quoting *Bogardus v. Commissioner, 302 U.S. 34 ... (1937))*. After reading *Duberstein*, a reasonable taxpayer would conclude that payments from a lover were taxable as income if they were made "in return for services rendered" rather than "out of affection, respect, admiration, charity or like impulses." *Id.* at 285 (quoting *Robertson v. United States, 343 U.S. 711 ... (1952))*.

Viewed in this light, I suggest that the bulk of the tax court cases cited by the majority offer no more than that the transferors in those particular cases harbored a donative intent. In my view, one cannot convincingly fashion a rule of law of general application from such a series of necessarily fact-intensive inquiries. That other taxpayers were found to have a donative intent does not bear on whether Harris had a duty to pay taxes on the monies she received from Kritzik. Whether Harris had such a duty is, under *Duberstein*, a question of Kritzik's intent, a question whose answer can be found only upon analysis of her particular circumstances. If Kritzik harbored a donative intent, then Harris was not obligated to pay taxes on his largess; if, however, he did not—if he was paying Harris for her services—then she was under a duty to do so.

It appears that the majority at once agrees and disagrees with this analysis. The majority acknowledges ... that *Duberstein's* principles "though general, provide a clear answer to many cases involving the gift versus income distinction and can be the basis for civil as well as criminal prosecutions in such cases." The majority is "equally certain," however, that "*Duberstein* provides no ready answer to the taxability of transfers of money to a mistress in the context of a long-term relationship." *Ante* at 1132. It takes this view because tax court cases have characterized similar payments made to other mistresses and companions as gifts rather than income. While apparently nodding to *Duberstein*, the majority contends that the state of the law is such that no reasonable mistress or companion could *ever*, with sufficient certainty, conclude that the payments she received were income rather than gifts and hence taxable.

How the majority can agree that the focal point of our inquiry is properly the transferor's intent and yet establish what amounts to a rule of law effectively preempting such inquiries I find perplexing. Putting aside this problem, I am unpersuaded by the majority's argument that *Duberstein's* guidance is categorically no guidance at all. Consider the following example. A approaches B and offers to spend time with him, accompany him to social events, and provide him with sexual favors for the next year if B gives her an apartment, a car, and a stipend of $ 5,000 a month. B agrees to A's terms. According to the majority, because this example involves a transfer of money to a "mistress in the context of a long-term relationship", A could never be charged with criminal tax evasion if she chose not to pay taxes on B's stipend. I find this hard to accept; what A receives from B is clearly income as it is "in return for services rendered." *363 U.S. at 285*. To be sure, there will be situations—like the case before us—where the evidence is insufficient to support a finding that the transferor harbored a "cash for services" intent; in such cases, criminal prosecutions for willful tax evasion will indeed be impossible as a matter of law. That fact does not, however, condemn as overly vague the analysis itself.

I am thus prompted to find Harris' conviction infirm because of the relative scantiness of the record before us, not because mistresses are categorically exempt from taxation on the largess they receive. Simply put, the record before us does not establish beyond a reasonable doubt that Kritzik's intent was to pay Harris for her services, rather than out of affection or charitable impulse. As the majority relates, the record does contain evidence showing that Harris thought their relationship to be of the "cash-for-services" kind. Such evidence is, in my view, probative—to some degree—of Kritzik's intent. *See Olk v. United States, 536 F.2d 876, 879 (9th Cir. 1976)* ("The manner in which a [transferee] may regard [that which is transferred] is, of course, not the touchstone for determining whether the receipt is excludable from gross income. It is, however, a reasonable and relevant inference."). But not sufficiently so to support a criminal conviction. Absent even a scintilla of direct evidence of Kritzik's intent, I cannot conclude, on the basis of Harris' perception of the relationship alone, that the government proved the nature of Kritzik's payments to be income rather than gift beyond a reasonable doubt.

Consider the following questions.

1. What does the court mean when it says: "'Gross income' for tax purposes does not include gifts, which are taxable to the donor rather than the recipient."? **Hint: Review footnote 7 in this Chapter 2.A.**

2. Why did the court reverse the convictions of the two women?

3. Why did the court cite the *James* case in footnote 6 of its opinion?

4. What does the word "willfully" mean for purposes of 26 U.S.C. sections 7201 and 7203?

5. Why does Judge Flaum disagree with the majority?

Suppose the donee receives a gift of property other than cash. Is the fair market value of the property included in gross income? **Review section 102.** What is the donee's basis in that property? Think back to the discussion of capital investment (*i.e.*, "basis"). **Find the portions of Revenue Ruling 81-277 that discuss basis and adjustments to basis, and review the Adams Adverts problem following *Raytheon*.** Recall that section 1012 sets forth the basic rule that the basis of property is its cost, and that Treas. Reg. section 1.1012-1(a) provides that the cost of property is "the amount paid for such property in cash or other property."

Recall too the concept of TOAD (or basis) that we discussed in connection with the computer you bought in a "bargain" purchase from your employer. **Review question 1 following the Zelenak and McMahon article in Part II, Chapter 1.** When the donee receives a gift of property, section 102(a) excludes it from her gross income. Has she "paid" for it? What was its "cost" in the section 1012 sense? Is her basis then $0? Can you justify assigning her a basis of other than $0? Consider the following case.

TAFT v. BOWERS
278 U.S. 470 (1929)

Mr. JUSTICE McREYNOLDS delivered the opinion of the Court.

Petitioners, who are donees of stocks, seek to recover income taxes exacted because of advancement in the market value of those stocks while owned by the donors. The facts are not in dispute. Both causes must turn upon the effect of paragraph (2), §202, Revenue Act, 1921, (c. 136, 42 Stat. 227) which prescribes the basis for estimating taxable gain when one disposes of property which came to him by gift. The records do not differ essentially and a statement of the material circumstances disclosed by No. 16 will suffice.

During the calendar years 1921 and 1922, the father of petitioner Elizabeth C. Taft, gave her certain shares of Nash Motors Company stock then more valuable than when acquired by him. She sold them during 1923 for more than their market value when the gift was made.

The United States demanded an income tax reckoned upon the difference between cost to the donor and price received by the donee. She paid accordingly and sued to recover the portion imposed because of the advance in value while the donor owned the stock. The right to tax the increase in value after the gift is not denied.

Abstractly stated, this is the problem—

In 1916 A purchased 100 shares of stock for $1,000 which he held until 1923 when their fair market value had become $2,000. He then gave them to B who sold them during the year 1923 for $5,000. The United States claim that, under the Revenue Act of 1921, B must pay income tax upon $4,000, as realized profits. B maintains that only $3,000—the appreciation during her ownership—can be regarded as income; that the increase during the donor's ownership is not income assessable against her within intendment of the Sixteenth Amendment.

The District Court ruled against the United States; the Circuit Court of Appeals held with them.

Act of Congress approved November 23, 1921, Chap. 136, 42 Stat. 227, 229, 237—

"Sec. 202. (a) That the basis for ascertaining the gain derived or loss sustained from a sale or other disposition of property, real, personal, or mixed, acquired after February 28, 1913, shall be the cost of such property; except that—

"(1) ...

"(2) In the case of such property, acquired by gift

after December 31, 1920, the basis shall be the same as that which it would have in the hands of the donor or the last preceding owner by whom it was not acquired by gift. If the facts necessary to determine such basis are unknown to the donee, the Commissioner shall, if possible, obtain such facts from such donor or last preceding owner, or any other person cognizant thereof. If the Commissioner finds it impossible to obtain such facts, the basis shall be the value of such property as found by the Commissioner as of the date or approximate date at which, according to the best information the Commissioner is able to obtain, such property was acquired by such donor or last preceding owner. In the case of such property acquired by gift on or before December 31, 1920, the basis for ascertaining gain or loss from a sale or other disposition thereof shall be the fair market price or value of such property at the time of such acquisition;"

"Sec. 213. That for the purposes of this title (except as otherwise provided in section 233) the term 'gross income'—

"(a) Includes gains, profits, and income derived from salaries, wages, or compensation for personal service ... or gains or profits and income derived from any source whatever. The amount of all such items (except as provided in subdivision (e) of section 201) shall be included in the gross income for the taxable year in which received by the taxpayer, unless, under methods of accounting permitted under subdivision (b) of section 212, any such amounts are to be properly accounted for as of a different period; but

"(b) Does not include the following items, which shall be exempt from taxation under this title;

"(1) ... (2) ...

"(3) The value of property acquired by gift, bequest, devise, or descent (but the income from such property shall be included in gross income); ..."

We think the manifest purpose of Congress expressed in paragraph (2), Sec. 202, *supra*, was to require the petitioner to pay the exacted tax.

The only question subject to serious controversy is whether Congress had power to authorize the exaction.

It is said that the gift became ... [the] asset of the donee to the extent of its value when received and, therefore, when disposed of by her no part of that value could be treated as taxable income in her hands.

The Sixteenth Amendment provides—

"The Congress shall have power to lay and collect taxes on incomes from whatever source derived, without apportionment among the several States, and without regard to any census or enumeration."

Income is the thing which may be taxed—income from any source. The Amendment does not attempt to define income or to designate how taxes may be laid thereon, or how they may be enforced.

Under former decisions here the settled doctrine is that the Sixteenth Amendment confers no power upon Congress to define and tax as income without apportionment something which theretofore could not have been properly regarded as income.

Also, this Court has declared—"Income may be defined as the gain derived from capital, from labor, or from both combined, provided it be understood to include profit gained through a sale or conversion of capital assets." *Eisner v. Macomber*, 252 U.S. 189, 207. The "gain derived from capital," within the definition, is "not a gain accruing to capital, nor a growth or increment of value in the investment, but a gain, a profit, something of exchangeable value proceeding from the property, severed from the capital however invested, and coming in, that is, received or drawn by the claimant for his separate use, benefit and disposal." *United States v. Phellis*, 257 U.S. 156, 169.

If, instead of giving the stock to petitioner, the donor had sold it at market value, the excess over the capital he invested (cost) would have been income therefrom and subject to taxation under the Sixteenth Amendment. He would have been obliged to share the realized gain with the United States. He held the stock—the investment—subject to the right of the sovereign to take part of any increase in its value when separated through sale or conversion and reduced to his possession. Could he, contrary to the express will of Congress, by mere gift enable another to hold this stock free from such right, deprive the sovereign of the possibility of taxing the appreciation when actually severed, and convert the entire property into a capital asset of the donee, who invested nothing, as though the latter had purchased at the market price? And after a still further enhancement of the property, could the donee make a second gift with like effect, etc.? We think not.

In truth the stock represented only a single investment of capital—that made by the donor. And when through sale or conversion the increase was separated therefrom, it became income from that investment in the hands of the recipient subject to taxation according to the very words of the

Sixteenth Amendment. By requiring the recipient of the entire increase to pay a part into the public treasury, Congress deprived her of no right and subjected her to no hardship. She accepted the gift with knowledge of the statute and, as to the property received, voluntarily assumed the position of her donor. When she sold the stock she actually got the original sum invested, plus the entire appreciation; and out of the latter only was she called on to pay the tax demanded.

The provision of the statute under consideration seems entirely appropriate for enforcing a general scheme of lawful taxation. To accept the view urged in behalf of petitioner undoubtedly would defeat, to some extent, the purpose of Congress to take part of all gain derived from capital investments. To prevent that result and insure enforcement of its proper policy, Congress had power to require that for purposes of taxation the donee should accept the position of the donor in respect of the thing received. And in so doing, it acted neither unreasonably nor arbitrarily.

The power of Congress to require a succeeding owner, in respect of taxation, to assume the place of his predecessor is pointed out by *United States v. Phellis*, 257 U.S. 156, 171—

"Where, as in this case, the dividend constitutes a distribution of profits accumulated during an extended period and bears a large proportion to the par value of the stock, if an investor happened to buy stock shortly before the dividend, paying a price enhanced by an estimate of the capital plus the surplus of the company, and after distribution of the surplus, with corresponding reduction in the intrinsic and market value of the shares, he were called upon to pay a tax upon the dividend received, it might look in his case like a tax upon his capital. But it is only apparently so. In buying at a price that reflected the accumulated profits, he of course acquired as a part of the valuable rights purchased the prospect of a dividend from the accumulations—bought 'dividend on' as the phrase goes—and necessarily took subject to the burden of the income tax proper to be assessed against him by reason of the dividend if and when made. He simply stepped into the shoes, in this as in other respects, of the stockholder whose shares he acquired, and presumably the prospect of a dividend influenced the price paid, and was discounted by the prospect of an income tax to be paid thereon. In short, the question whether a dividend made out of company profits constitutes income of the stockholder is not affected by antecedent transfers of the stock from hand to hand."

There is nothing in the Constitution which lends support to the theory that gain actually resulting from the increased value of capital can be treated as taxable income in the hands of the recipient only so far as the increase occurred while he owned the property....

The judgments below are

Affirmed.

———————

Consider the following questions about *Taft v. Bowers*.

1. What was the argument made by the donees of the stocks?

2. **Look again at the words of section 1001(a).** Do any of the words apply or potentially apply to the donor of property?

3. What rule does the Supreme Court set forth in *Taft v. Bowers*? **Look at section 1015(a).** Is this section consistent or inconsistent with the case?

4. Based on the outcome of *Taft v. Bowers*, does section 1001(a) apply to the donor of property?[11] In other words, does a gift constitute an "other disposition" within the meaning of section 1001(a)?

5. Suppose a donee wants to dispose of a gift sometime after its receipt. For example, suppose your mother made a gift to you last year of her Rembrandt drawing when it was worth $50,000. She paid $12,000 for it many years ago. What tax consequences to you at the time of the gift? What tax consequences to her? Recall Situation 2 in Revenue Ruling 79-24, the "barter" revenue ruling. Query: What tax consequences to the professional artist who transferred a work of art to her landlord in exchange for "rent-free use" of her apartment? Are the tax consequences the same for your mother as for the artist?

6. You now want to sell the drawing; its fair market value is $75,000. What section(s) of the Code govern(s) the tax consequences of your sale of the drawing?[12]

7. Suppose that right before you sell the drawing, you discover that it is not, in fact, a Rembrandt.[13] Therefore, the value of the drawing when your mother gave it to you was only $10,000[14] and you are able to sell it for only $4,000. What result? What if you sell it for $11,000? $15,000? **Reconsider section 1015(a).**

8. Now, consider the consequences if, instead of giving you the drawing as a gift, your mother decides to keep it until she dies and leaves it to you in her will. What are the tax consequences to you if you receive the drawing (which is a Rembrandt worth

---

11. Recall our discussion of *Eisner v. Macomber*. We concluded that the Supreme Court in *Eisner v. Macomber* was really dealing with a "realization" case, although it characterized the issue as a Constitutional one of "income." As we noted earlier, section 1001(a) codifies the requirement of "realization." Section 1001 identifies a "sale or other disposition" as the realization event for measuring gain or loss on property. If the calculation under section 1001 produces a gain, section 1001(c) generally requires that it be "recognized," and section 61(a)(3) requires the taxpayer to include it in gross income. We will return to the question of what happens if the calculation under section 1001 produces a loss when we consider deductions in Chapter 3.

12. When doing your calculations you may disregard the effect of section 1015(d), which provides an increase in the donee's basis to reflect gift tax the donor paid upon on transfer of the gift. Section 1015(d) prescribes different basis increases depending on the date of the gift. For gifts made between September 2, 1958, and December 31, 1976, a donee may increase her basis by the amount of the gift tax the donor paid on the gift. Section 1015(d)(1). For gifts made after December 31, 1976, the donee's basis increase is limited to the portion of the donor's gift tax that reflects the net appreciation of the property in the hand of the donor. Section 1015(d)(6).

13. Experts have recently determined that many supposed Rembrandts were not actually painted by Rembrandt. Indeed, in 1995, the Metropolitan Museum of New York mounted an exhibit entitled "Rembrandt/Not Rembrandt," which attracted a large number of viewers. Scholars now attribute only about half of the more than 600 paintings once attributed to Rembrandt to the artist himself. But those that have been discredited are rarely the result of actual attempts at deception, true fakes. Rather, most appear to be the work of students or followers of Rembrandt who attempted to emulate the work of the master. For more about the exhibit, see Michael Kimmelman, "Sincerest Flattery: Imitations and Rembrandt," N.Y. Times, October 13, 1995; and William Grimes, "An Enigma Sometimes Wrapped in a Fake," N.Y. Times, October 1, 1995.

14. Although the drawing is not a Rembrandt, it is probably the product of one of Rembrandt's followers so it still has substantial value, though it is worth far less than if it were, indeed, a Rembrandt.

$75,000) as a result of a specific bequest[15] in her will? Should your basis in the drawing be the same when you receive it by inheritance as it would be if you had received it by gift? **Compare section 1014(a) with section 1015(a).**[16]

9. Suppose your aging mother tells you she wants to give you the Rembrandt drawing before she dies so she can enjoy your enjoyment and so you can thank her in person. What might you suggest to her (ever so subtly and tactfully!)?

10. Section 1014 presents obvious opportunities for tax avoidance. **Look at section 1014(e).** What sort of scheme does it address? Does it solve the problem? Would there be another way to address the problem?

B. Employee Benefits

1. Meals and Lodging

Suppose your employer has a policy of giving every employee a fruitcake at Christmas time. Is it income when you apply the three-prong test? Well, then, is the fruitcake a gift to you and thereby excluded from gross income by section 102 of the Code? **Recall section 102(c).** Remember, exclusions are a matter of legislative grace. Therefore, you must find a specific exclusion; you cannot imply one.

Suppose instead of a fruitcake, your employer requires you to attend an office Christmas party. The party is on the premises and is catered by a famous local caterer. The value of the dinner you eat at the party is $75. Income? Does your answer change if the employer does not require you to attend?

Compare the following two cases.

---

15. What is a "specific bequest"?

16. Will the difference in the fair market value of the drawing from the time your mother bought it until the date of her death ever be taxed? Section 1014 represents an important exception to the general rule that you can only increase your basis in an asset by increasing your investment. (Thus, the general rule is that the only two ways to increase your basis in an asset are to "pay for it or die!")

Of course, you are the decedent by the time section 1014 results in an increase in the basis of your asset. Therefore, the benefit of this "step-up" goes to your estate and your successor in interest. Note, however, that there is a price for this "step-up": the basis increases (or decreases) to the fair market value of the asset on the date of death or the alternate date for the valuation of the estate six months after death. Therefore, the value of the estate will reflect any increase in value which may increase the amount of estate tax due.

Note in this connection, however, that with some regularity, Congress has debated the wisdom of retaining the estate tax. Although the estate tax raises only a small amount of revenue, it represents an application of the redistributive philosophy that supports the adoption of a progressive rate schedule: imposing a greater tax burden on those who have a greater ability to pay. Recall McIntyre quote in Part I, Chapter 1. The newest revision, made by the 2001 Act, repeals the estate tax, but not until 2010. At that point, a carryover basis (similar to section 1015(a)) will apply under new section 1022(a), except to the extent that new section 1022(b) or (c) permit a partial step-up of basis in certain cases. See section 1022.

What happens under section 1014 if the value of the asset has declined prior to your mother's death? **Review section 1014(a).**

BENAGLIA v. COMMISSIONER

36 B.T.A. 838 (1937)

The Commissioner determined a deficiency in the petitioners' joint income tax for 1933 of $856.68, and for 1934 of $1,001.61, and they contest the inclusion in gross income each year of the alleged fair market value of rooms and meals furnished by the husband's employer.

FINDINGS OF FACT.

The petitioners are husband and wife, residing in Honolulu, Hawaii, where they filed joint income tax returns for 1933 and 1934.

The petitioner has, since 1926 and including the tax years in question, been employed as the manager in full charge of the several hotels in Honolulu owned and operated by Hawaiian

Hotels, Ltd., a corporation of Hawaii, consisting of the Royal Hawaiian, the Moana and bungalows, and the Waialae Golf Club. These are large resort hotels, operating on the American plan. Petitioner was constantly on duty, and, for the proper performance of his duties and entirely for the convenience of his employer, he and his wife occupied a suite of rooms in the Royal Hawaiian Hotel and received their meals at and from the hotel.

Petitioner's salary has varied in different years, being in one year $25,000. In 1933 it was $9,625, and in 1934 it was $11,041.67. These amounts were fixed without reference to his meals and lodging, and neither petitioner nor his employer ever regarded the meals and lodging as part of his compensation or accounted for them.

OPINION.

STERNHAGEN: The Commissioner has added $7,845 each year to the petitioner's gross income as "compensation received from Hawaiian Hotels, Ltd.", holding that this is "the fair market value of rooms and meals furnished by the employer." … The deficiency notice seems to hold that the rooms and meals were not in fact supplied "merely as a convenience to the hotels" of the employer.

From the evidence, there remains no room for doubt that the petitioner's residence at the hotel was not by way of compensation for his services, not for his personal convenience, comfort or pleasure, but solely because he could not otherwise perform the services required of him. The evidence of both the employer and employee shows in detail what petitioner's duties were and why his residence in the hotel was necessary. His duty was continuous and required his presence at a moment's call. He had a lifelong experience in hotel management and operation in the United States, Canada, and elsewhere, and testified that the functions of the manager could not have been performed by one living outside the hotel, especially a resort hotel such as this. The demands and requirements of guests are numerous, various, and unpredictable, and affect the meals, the rooms, the entertainment, and everything else about the hotel. The manager must be alert to all these things day and night. He would not consider undertaking the job and the owners of the hotel would not consider employing a manager unless he lived there. This was implicit throughout his employment, and when his compensation was changed from time to time no mention was ever made of it. Both took it for granted. The corporation's books carried no accounting for the petitioner's meals, rooms, or service.

Under such circumstances, the value of meals and lodging is not income to the employee, even though it may relieve him of an expense which he would otherwise bear. In *Jones v. United States, supra*, the subject was fully considered in determining that neither the value of quarters nor the amount received as commutation of quarters by an Army officer is included within his taxable income. There is also a full discussion in the English case of *Tennant v. Smith*, H.L. (1892) App. Cas. 150, III British Tax Cases 158. A bank employee was required to live in quarters located in the bank building, and it was held that the value of such lodging was not taxable income. The advantage to him was merely an incident of the performance of his duty, but its character for tax purposes was controlled by the dominant fact that the occupation of the premises was imposed upon him for the convenience of the employer. The Bureau of Internal Revenue has almost consistently applied the same doctrine in its published rulings.

The three cases cited by the respondent, *Ralph Kitchen*, 11 B.T.A. 855; *Charles A. Frueauff*, 30 B.T.A. 449; and *Fontaine Fox*, 30 B.T.A. 451, are distinguishable entirely upon the ground that what the taxpayer received was not shown to be primarily for the need or convenience of the employer. Of course, as in the *Kitchen* case, it can not be said as a categorical proposition of law that, where an employee is fed and lodged by his employer, no part of the value of such perquisite is income. If the Commissioner finds that it was received as compensation and holds it to be taxable income, the taxpayer contesting this before the Board must prove by evidence that it is not income. In the *Kitchen* case the Board held that the evidence did not establish that the food and lodging were given for the convenience of the employer. In the present case the evidence clearly establishes that fact, and it has been so found.

The determination of the Commissioner on the point in issue is reversed.

ARNOLD, dissenting: I disagree with the conclusions of fact that the suite of rooms and meals furnished petitioner and his wife at the Royal Hawaiian Hotel were entirely for the convenience of the employer and that the cash salary was fixed without reference thereto and was never regarded as part of his compensation.

Petitioner was employed by a hotel corporation operating two resort hotels in Honolulu—the Royal Hawaiian, containing 357 guest bed rooms, and the Moana, containing 261 guest bed rooms, and the bungalows and cottages in connection with the Moana containing 127 guest bed rooms, and the Waialae Golf Club. His employment was as general manager of both hotels and the golf club.

His original employment was in 1925, and in accepting the employment he wrote a letter to the party representing the employer, with whom he conducted the negotiations for employment, under date of September 10, 1925, in which he says:

Confirming our meeting here today, it is understood that I will assume the position of general manager of both the Royal Waikiki Beach Hotel (now under construction) and the Moana Hotel in Honolulu, at a yearly salary of $10,000.00, payable monthly, together with living quarters, meals, etc., for myself and wife. In addition I am to receive $20.00 per day while travelling, this however, not to include any railroad or steamship fares, and I [am] to submit vouchers monthly covering all such expenses.

While the cash salary was adjusted from time to time by agreement of the parties, depending on the amount of business done, it appears that the question of living quarters, meals, etc., was not given further consideration and was not thereafter changed. Petitioner and his wife have always occupied living quarters in the Royal Hawaiian Hotel and received their meals from the time he first accepted the employment down through the years before us. His wife performed no services for the hotel company.

This letter, in my opinion, constitutes the basic contract of employment and clearly shows that the living quarters, meals, etc., furnished petitioner and his wife were understood and intended to be compensation in addition to the cash salary paid him. Being compensation to petitioner in addition to the cash salary paid him, it follows that the reasonable value thereof to petitioner is taxable income. . . .

Conceding that petitioner was required to live at the hotel and that his living there was solely for the convenience of the employer, it does not follow that he was not benefited thereby to the extent of what such accommodations were reasonably worth to him. His employment was a matter of private contract. He was careful to specify in his letter accepting the employment that he was to be furnished with living quarters, meals, etc., for himself and wife, together with the cash salary, as compensation for his employment. Living quarters and meals are necessities which he would otherwise have had to procure at his own expense. His contract of employment relieved him to that extent. He has been enriched to the extent of what they are reasonably worth.

The majority opinion is based on the finding that petitioner's residence at the hotel was solely for the convenience of the employer and, therefore, not income. While it is no doubt convenient to have the manager reside in the hotel, I do not think the question here is one of convenience or of benefit to the employer. What the tax law is concerned with is whether or not petitioner was financially benefited by having living quarters furnished to himself and wife. He may have preferred to live elsewhere, but we are dealing with the financial aspect of petitioner's relation to his employer, not his preference. He says it would cost him $3,600 per year to live elsewhere.

It would seem that if his occupancy of quarters at the Royal Hawaiian was necessary and solely for the benefit of the employer, occupancy of premises at the Moana would be just as essential so far as the management of the Moana was concerned. He did not have living quarters or meals for himself and wife at the Moana and he was general manager of both and both were in operation during the years before us. Furthermore, it appears that petitioner was absent from Honolulu from March 24 to June 8 and from August 19 to November 2 in 1933, and from April 8 to May 24 and from September 3 to November 1 in 1934—about 5 months in 1933 and 32 months in 1934. Whether he was away on official business or not we do not know. During his absence both hotels continued in operation. The $20 per day travel allowance in his letter of acceptance indicates his duties were not confined to managing the hotels in Honolulu, and the entire letter indicates he was to receive maintenance, whether in Honolulu or elsewhere, in addition to his cash salary.

At most the arrangement as to living quarters and meals was of mutual benefit, and to the extent it benefited petitioner it was compensation in addition to his cash salary, and taxable to him as income.

The Court of Claims in the case of *Jones v. United States*, relied on in the majority opinion, was dealing with a governmental organization regulated by military law where the compensation was fixed by law and not subject to private contract. The English case of *Tennant v. Smith*, involved the employment of a watchman or custodian for a bank whose presence at the bank was at all times a matter of necessity demanded by the employer as a condition of the employment.

The facts in both these cases are so at variance with the facts in this case that they are not controlling in my opinion.

COMMISSIONER v. KOWALSKI
434 U.S. 77 (1977)

MR. JUSTICE BRENNAN delivered the opinion of the Court.

This case presents the question whether cash payments to state police troopers, designated as meal allowances, are included in gross income under §61(a) of the Internal Revenue Code of 1954, 26 U.S.C. §61(a), and, if so, are otherwise excludable under §119 of the Code, 26 U.S.C. §119. (Footnote 2)

I

The pertinent facts are not in dispute. Respondent (Footnote 3) is a state police trooper employed by the Division of State Police of the Department of Law and Public Safety of the State of New Jersey. During 1970, the tax year in question, he received a base salary of $8,739.38, and an additional $1,697.54 designated as an allowance for meals.

The State instituted the cash meal allowance for its state police officers in July 1949. Prior to that time, all troopers were provided with midshift (Footnote 5) meals in kind at various meal stations located throughout the State. A trooper unable to eat at an official meal station could, however, eat at a restaurant and obtain reimbursement. The meal-station system proved unsatisfactory to the State because it required troopers to leave their assigned areas of patrol unguarded for extended periods of time. As a result, the State closed its meal stations and instituted a cash-allowance system. Under this system, troopers remain on call in their assigned patrol areas during their midshift break. Otherwise, troopers are not restricted in any way with respect to where they may eat in the patrol area and, indeed, may eat at home if it is located within that area. Troopers may also bring their midshift meal to the job and eat it in or near their patrol cars.

The meal allowance is paid biweekly in advance and is included, although separately stated, with the trooper's salary. The meal-allowance money is also separately accounted for in the State's accounting system. Funds are never commingled between the salary and meal-allowance accounts. Because of these characteristics of the meal-allowance system, the Tax Court concluded that the "meal allowance was not intended to represent additional compensation." 65 T.C. 44, 47 (1975).

Notwithstanding this conclusion, it is not disputed that the meal allowance has many features inconsistent with its characterization as a simple reimbursement for meals that would otherwise have been taken at a meal station. For example, troopers are not required to spend their meal allowances on their midshift meals, nor are they required to account for the manner in which the money is spent. With one limited exception not relevant here, no reduction in the meal allowance is made for periods when a trooper is not on patrol because, for example, he is assigned to a headquarters building or is away from active duty on vacation, leave, or sick leave. In addition, the cash allowance for meals is described on a state police recruitment brochure as an item of salary to be received in addition to an officer's base salary and the amount of the meal allowance is a subject of negotiations between the State and the police troopers' union. Finally, the amount of an officer's cash meal allowance varies with his rank and is included in his gross pay for purposes of calculating pension benefits.

On his 1970 income tax return, respondent reported $9,066 in wages. That amount included his salary plus $326.45 which represented cash meal allowances reported by

ployer doctrine, but indeed endorsed the doctrine shorn of the confusion created by Mim. 6472 and cases like *Doran*. Respondent further argues that, by negative implication, the technical appendix to the Senate Report creates a class of noncompensatory cash meal payments that are to be excluded from income. We disagree.

The Senate unquestionably intended to overrule *Doran* and rulings like Mim. 6472. Equally clearly the Senate refused completely to abandon the convenience-of-the-employer doctrine as the House wished to do. On the other hand, the Senate did not propose to leave undisturbed the convenience-of-the-employer doctrine as it had evolved prior to the promulgation of Mim. 6472. The language of § 119 quite plainly rejects the reasoning behind rulings like O.D. 514, see n. 15, *supra*, which rest on the employer's characterization of the nature of a payment. (Footnote 28) This conclusion is buttressed by the Senate's choice of a term of art, "convenience of the employer," in describing one of the conditions for exclusion under § 119. In so choosing, the Senate obviously intended to adopt the meaning of that term as it had developed over time, except, of course, to the extent § 119 overrules decisions like *Doran*. As we have noted above, *Van Rosen v. Commissioner*, 17 T.C. 834 (1951), provided the controlling court definition at the time of the 1954 recodification and it expressly rejected the *Jones* theory of "convenience of the employer"—and by implication the theory of O.D. 514—and adopted as the exclusive rationale the business-necessity theory. See 17 T.C., at 838–840. The business-necessity theory was also the controlling administrative interpretation of "convenience of the employer" prior to Mim. 6472. See *supra*, at 85–86, and n. 19. Finally, although the Senate Report did not expressly define "convenience of the employer" it did describe those situations in which it wished to reverse the courts and create an exclusion as those where "an employee must accept ... meals or lodging in order properly to perform his duties." S. Rep. No. 1622, *supra*, at 190.

As the last step in its restructuring of prior law, the Senate adopted an additional restriction created by the House and not theretofore a part of the law, which required that meals subject to exclusion had to be taken on the business premises of the employer. Thus § 119 comprehensively modified the prior law, both expanding and contracting the exclusion for meals and lodging previously provided, and it must therefore be construed as its draftsmen obviously intended it to be—as a replacement for the prior law, designed to "end [its] confusion."

Because § 119 replaces prior law, respondent's further argument—that the technical appendix in the Senate Report recognized the existence under § 61 of an exclusion for a class of noncompensatory cash payments—is without merit. If cash meal allowances could be excluded on the mere showing that such payments served the convenience of the employer, as respondent suggests, then cash would be more widely excluded from income than meals in kind, an extraordinary result given the presumptively compensatory nature of cash payments and the obvious intent of § 119 to narrow the circumstances in which meals could be excluded. Moreover, there is no reason to suppose that Congress would have wanted to recognize a class of excludable cash meal payments. The two precedents for the exclusion of cash—O.D. 514 and *Jones v. United States*—both rest on the proposition that the convenience of the employer can be inferred from the characterization given the cash payments by the employer, and the heart of this proposition is undercut by both the language of § 119 and the Senate Report. *Jones* also rests on *Eisner v. Macomber*, 252 U.S. 189 (1920), but Congress had no reason to read *Eisner's* definition of income into § 61 and, indeed, any assumption that Congress did is squarely at odds with *Commissioner v. Glenshaw Glass Co.*, 348 U.S. 426 (1955).... Finally, as petitioner suggests, it is much

more reasonable to assume that the cryptic statement in the technical appendix—
"cash allowances ... will continue to be includable in gross income to the extent that
such allowances constitute compensation"—was meant to indicate only that meal
payments otherwise deductible under § 162(a)(2) of the 1954 Code were not affected
by § 119.

...

Finally, respondent argues that it is unfair that members of the military may exclude
their subsistence allowances from income while respondent cannot. While this may be
so, arguments of equity have little force in construing the boundaries of exclusions and
deductions from income many of which, to be administrable, must be arbitrary. In any
case, Congress has already considered respondent's equity argument and has rejected it
in the repeal of § 120 of the 1954 Code. That provision as enacted allowed state troopers
like respondent to exclude from income up to $5 of subsistence allowance per day. Sec-
tion 120 was repealed after only four years, however, because it was "inequitable since
there are many other individual taxpayers whose duties also require them to incur subsistence expenditures regardless of the tax effect. Thus, it appears that certain police officials by reason of this exclusion are placed in a more favorable position taxwise than
other individual income taxpayers who incur the same types of expense...." H.R. Rep.
No. 775, 85th Cong., 1st Sess., 7 (1957).

Reversed.

FOOTNOTES:

2. "§ 119. Meals or lodging furnished for the convenience of the employer.

"There shall be excluded from gross income of an employee the value of any meals
or lodging furnished to him by his employer for the convenience of the employer, but
only if—

"(1) in the case of meals, the meals are furnished on the business premises of
the employer....

"In determining whether meals ... are furnished for the convenience of the employer, the
provisions of an employment contract or of a State statute fixing terms of employment
shall not be determinative of whether the meals or lodging are intended as compensation."

3. References to "respondent" are to Robert J. Kowalski. Nancy A. Kowalski, also a respondent, is a party solely because she filed a joint return with her husband for the 1970
tax year.

5. While on active duty, New Jersey troopers are generally required to live in barracks.
Meals furnished in kind at the barracks before or after a patrol shift are not involved in
this case. Nor is the meal allowance intended to pay for meals eaten before or after a
shift in those instances in which the trooper is not living in the barracks. However, because of the duration of some patrols, a trooper may be required to eat more than one
meal per shift while on the road.

8. On October 1, 1970, the Division of State Police began to withhold income tax from
amounts paid as cash meal allowances. No claim has been made that the change in the
Division's withholding policy has any relevance for this case.

11. See *Wilson v. United States,* 412 F.2d 694 (CA1 1969) (troopers' subsistence allowance taxable); *United States v. Keeton,* 383 F.2d 429 (CA10 1967) (*per curiam*)
(troopers' subsistence allowance nontaxable); *United States v. Morelan,* 356 F.2d 199

(CA8 1966) (same); *United States v. Barrett*, 321 F.2d 911 (CA5 1963) (same); *Magness v. Commissioner*, 247 F.2d 740 (CA5 1957) (troopers' subsistence allowance taxable), cert. denied, 355 U.S. 931 (1958); *Saunders v. Commissioner*, 215 F.2d 768 (CA3 1954) (troopers' meal allowance nontaxable). See also *Ghastin v. Commissioner*, 60 T.C. 264 (1973) (troopers' subsistence allowance taxable); *Hyslope v. Commissioner*, 21 T.C. 131 (1953) (troopers' meal allowance taxable).

14. Substantially identical language appeared in the income tax regulations on the date of the 1954 recodification of the Internal Revenue Code. See Treas. Regs. 111, § 29.22(a)-3 (1943); Treas. Regs. 118, § 39.22(a)-3 (1953).

15. "'Supper money' paid by an employer to an employee, who voluntarily performs extra labor for his employer after regular business hours, *such payment not being considered additional compensation and not being charged to the salary account*, is considered as being paid for the convenience of the employer...." (Emphasis added.)

17. "Where, from the location and nature of the work, it is necessary that employees engaged in fishing and canning be furnished with lodging and sustenance by the employer, the value of such lodging and sustenance may be considered as being furnished for the convenience of the employer and need not, therefore, be included in computing net income...." O.D. 814, 4 Cum. Bull. 84, 84–85 (1921).

18. "Where the employees of a hospital are subject to immediate service on demand at any time during the twenty-four hours of the day and on that account are required to accept quarters and meals at the hospital, the value of such quarters and meals may be considered as being furnished for the convenience of the hospital and does not represent additional compensation to the employees. On the other hand, where the employees ... could, if they so desired, obtain meals and lodging elsewhere than in the hospital and yet perform the duties required of them by such hospital, the ratable value of the board and lodging furnished is considered additional compensation." O.D. 915, 4 Cum. Bull. 85, 85–86 (1921).

19. "3. As a general rule, the test of 'convenience of the employer' is satisfied if living quarters or meals are furnished to an employee who is required to accept such quarters and meals in order to perform properly his duties." 1940-1 Cum. Bull., at 15, citing O.D. 915, *supra*, n. 18.

21. "The better and more accurate statement of the reason for the exclusion from the employee's income of the value of subsistence and quarters furnished in kind is found, we think, in *Arthur Benaglia*, 36 B.T.A. 838, where it was pointed out that, on the facts, the subsistence and quarters were not supplied by the employer and received by the employee 'for his personal convenience[,] comfort or pleasure, but solely because he could not otherwise perform the services required of him.' In other words, though there was an element of gain to the employee, in that he received subsistence and quarters which otherwise he would have had to supply for himself, he had nothing he could take, appropriate, use and expend according to his own dictates, but rather, the ends of the employer's business dominated and controlled, just as in the furnishing of a place to work and in the supplying of the tools and machinery with which to work. The fact that certain personal wants and needs of the employee were satisfied was plainly secondary and incidental to the employment." *Van Rosen v. Commissioner*, 17 T.C., at 838.

22. Van Rosen was a civilian ship captain employed by the United States Army Transportation Corps. *Id.*, at 834. In this capacity, his pay and subsistence allowances were determined by the Marine Personnel Regulations of the Transportation Corps of the

Army. *Id.*, at 837. His principal argument in the Tax Court was the factual similarity of his case to *Jones v. United States*, 60 Ct. Cl. 552 (1925). See 17 T.C., at 837.

25. "Sec. 120. STATUTORY SUBSISTENCE ALLOWANCE RECEIVED BY POLICE.

"(a) GENERAL RULE.—Gross income does not include any amount received as a statutory subsistence allowance by an individual who is employed as a police official...."

"(b) LIMITATIONS.—

"(1) Amounts to which subsection (a) applies shall not exceed $5 per day.

"(2) If any individual receives a subsistence allowance to which subsection (a) applies, no deduction shall be allowed under any other provision of this chapter for expenses in respect of which he has received such allowance, except to the extent that such expenses exceed the amount excludable under subsection (a) and the excess is otherwise allowable as a deduction under this chapter." 68A Stat. 39.

28. We do not decide today whether, notwithstanding § 119, the "supper money" exclusion may be justified on other grounds. See, *e.g.*, Treasury Department, Proposed Fringe Benefit Regulations, 40 Fed. Reg. 41118, 41121 (1975) (example 8). Nor do we decide whether sporadic meal reimbursements may be excluded from income. Cf. *United States v. Correll*, 389 U.S. 299 (1967).

MR. JUSTICE BLACKMUN, with whom THE CHIEF JUSTICE joins, dissenting.

...

I have no particular quarrel with the conclusion that the payments received by the New Jersey troopers constituted income to them under § 61. I can accept that, but my stance in *Morelan* leads me to disagree with the Court's conclusion that the payments are not excludable under § 119. The Court draws an in-cash or in-kind distinction. This has no appeal or persuasion for me because the statute does not speak specifically in such terms. It does no more than refer to "meals ... furnished on the business premises of the employer," and from those words the Court draws the in-kind consequence. I am not so sure. In any event, for me, as was the case in *Morelan*, the business premises of the State of New Jersey, the trooper's employer, are wherever the trooper is on duty in that State. The employer's premises are statewide.

The Court in its opinion makes only passing comment, with a general reference to fairness, on the ironical difference in tax treatment it now accords to the paramilitary New Jersey state trooper structure and the federal military. The distinction must be embarrassing to the Government in its position here, for the Internal Revenue Code draws no such distinction. The Commissioner is forced to find support for it—support which the Court in its opinion in this case does not stretch to find—only from a regulation, Treas. Reg. § 1.61-2(b), 26 CFR § 1.61-2(b) (1977), excluding subsistence allowances granted the military, and the general references in 37 U.S.C. § 101 (25) (1970 ed., Supp. V), added by Pub. L. 93-419, § 1, 88 Stat. 1152, to "regular military compensation" and "Federal tax advantage accruing to the aforementioned allowances because they are not subject to Federal income tax." This, for me, is thin and weak support for recognizing a substantial benefit for the military and denying it for the New Jersey state trooper counterpart.

I fear that state troopers the country over, not handsomely paid to begin with, will never understand today's decision. And I doubt that their reading of the Court's opinion—if, indeed, a layman can be expected to understand its technical wording—will convince them that the situation is as clear as the Court purports to find it.

Consider the following questions about *Benaglia* and *Kowalski*.

1. If, on your behalf, your employer pays your monthly rent to your landlord and your weekly grocery bill to your grocer, do you have gross income? Apply the *Glenshaw Glass* test. Recall Treasury Regulation section 1.61-1(a), which provides that gross income can take many forms. Recall also *Old Colony*.

2. Would Mr. Benaglia's Royal Hawaiian meals and lodging have met the *Glenshaw Glass* test for gross income?[17] Why did the court allow Mr. Benaglia to exclude the value of the meals and lodging from gross income? Did the court rely on a statutory exclusion? How should the court have analyzed the meals and lodging that Mrs. Benaglia enjoyed?

3. *Kowalski* refers to section 119 of the Code. **Look at section 119.** What does the Court in *Kowalski* say regarding the survival of a common law exclusion from income for meals as expressed in *Benaglia*?

4. Compare the type of rulemaking you see in section 119 with the type of rulemaking you saw in section 102. Is it the same? Is it different?[18]

5. Suppose the employee is not a state trooper. What aspect(s) of section 119 do you think will be the most difficult to satisfy? Suppose your client wants his employees to eat lunch on his premises because there is no nearby eating establishment; he would rather give the employees 3/4 hour to eat in the company-funded cafeteria than have them away from their duties for an hour and a half. Would this satisfy the requirements of section 119? Is it clear that the meals are provided "in-kind" and on the business premises of the employer as required by section 119(a)? How do you determine whether such an arrangement is for the "convenience of the employer"? What is the test? The Supreme Court stated in *Kowalski* that the enactment of section 119 in 1954 was intended by Congress to replace the common law doctrine that the Board of Tax Appeals had applied in *Benaglia*.

6. Now that the statute expressly requires satisfaction of a "convenience of the employer" test, where would you look first for guidance in defining this statutory term? **Study Treasury Regulation section 1.119-1.**

How does subsection 1.119-1(a)(1) of the regulation restate the requirements for exclusion under section 119 of the Code for the value of meals furnished to an employee? How does the regulation direct you to determine whether the meals are furnished for the convenience of the employer? Where do you find the "tests described in subdivisions (i) and (ii) of this subparagraph"? **Identify the appropriate part of the regulations.**

7. What is the test for "convenience of the employer" as stated in Treasury Regulation section 1.119-1(a)(2)(i)?

8. How do you determine whether a meal is furnished for a "substantial noncompensatory business reason of the employer"? What does this mean? **Identify the appropriate part of Treasury Regulation section 1.119-1(a)(2)(i).**

Notice that Treasury Regulation section 1.119-1(a)(2)(i) represents another example of a "facts and circumstances test" for fitting within a provision of the Code. How can you be sure that your case will meet this type of test? The problem with this type of test is that while a tax advisor can make an informed prediction based on the particular

---

17. Note that *Benaglia* pre-dates *Glenshaw Glass*.
18. If you believe it is different, how would you define that difference? What are the benefits and problems with the type of rulemaking found in section 119?

facts of the situation, she cannot guarantee the outcome; the ultimate determination can only be made by the trier of fact as discussed in *Duberstein*. Locate the discussion of role of triers of fact in *Duberstein*.

Recognizing this problem for taxpayers and their advisors, the Service frequently provides guidance in several different formats, one of which is by including examples in regulations.[19] For instance, Treasury Regulation section 1.119-1(a)(2)(ii) sets forth "some of the substantial noncompensatory business reasons which occur frequently and which justify the conclusion that meals furnished for such a reason are furnished for the convenience of the employer."[20]

In Treasury Regulation section 1.119-1(a)(2)(iii), the regulations set forth "some of the business reasons which are considered to be compensatory and which, in the absence of a substantial noncompensatory business reason, justify the conclusion that meals furnished for such a reason are not furnished for the convenience of the employer."[21]

Now that you have carefully studied Treasury Regulation section 1.119-1(a)(2), use it to analyze the following problems:

1. Return to the problem involving the law firm office Christmas party at the beginning of this section B. 1. Fully analyze (using systematic statutory analysis technique) the problem under Code section 119 and Treasury Regulation section 1.119-1.

2. Now, suppose you are an associate of a law firm. The only convenient time for all members of the firm to meet and discuss their cases is over lunch. The firm arranges with a local caterer to provide lunch every day in the conference room. The firm requires all members who are not out of the office on business (*e.g.*, court or client meeting) or on vacation to attend. Do you have income?

3. Suppose it is impractical to have the lunches in the office because the office is too far from the courts where the members spend most of their days. Therefore, the firm decides to have the lunches every day in the private dining room of a restaurant near the courts. Locate the portion of Treasury Regulation section 1.119-1 that deals with business premises. Again, every member of the firm is required to attend. Does the location change the result? Would the result change if the firm gave each lawyer a cash allowance to purchase meals?

4. Note that section 119(a)(2) imposes the additional requirement for lodging that the employee "is required to accept such lodging ... as a condition of his[22] employment." How would you apply this additional requirement to the foregoing alternatives? Where would you look for guidance in Treasury Regulation section 1.119-1? Treasury Regulation section 1.119-1(b) provides that "the employee is required to accept such

---

19. Among the other types of format the Service uses to transmit information and guidance to taxpayers and their advisors are revenue rulings and private letter rulings.

20. Treas. Reg. section 1.119-1(a)(2)(i).

21. *Id.*

22. Does the use of the word "his" mean that women cannot take advantage of this exclusion? Although section 7701 of the Code provides a number of definitions applicable throughout the Code, it does not contain a definition, as do many modern statutes, that says "man" includes "woman" and "he" or "his" includes "she" and "her." See section 7701. Section 1031(e) says that livestock of different sexes are not property of like-kind. What is the danger of reasoning from this provision that "he" does not include "she"?

lodging as a condition of his employment means that he be required to accept the lodging in order to enable him properly to perform the duties of his employment." If this sentence still leaves some doubt, where would you look? Does the regulation contain any examples? **Review Treasury Regulation section 1.119-1(b).**

Recall that *Benaglia* predates the adoption of section 119. How would the Benaglias fare under section 119 and its regulations with respect to the excludibility of their lodging?

The following case analyzes the three requirements for the excludibility of lodging under section 119.

ADAMS v. UNITED STATES
585 F.2d 1060 (Ct. Cl. 1978)

PER CURIAM:

The issue in this tax refund suit is whether the fair rental value of a Japanese residence furnished the plaintiffs by the employer of plaintiff Faneuil Adams, Jr., is excludable from their gross income under Section 119 of the Internal Revenue Code of 1954.

Plaintiffs Faneuil Adams, Jr. and Joan P. Adams are husband and wife who filed joint federal income tax returns for 1970 and 1971 with the Office of the Director of the Office of International Operations, Internal Revenue Service, Washington, D. C. In 1970 and 1971, Faneuil Adams [hereinafter "plaintiff"] was president of Mobil Sekiyu Kabushiki Kaisha ("Sekiyu"), a Tokyo-based Japanese corporation which was wholly owned by Mobil Oil Corporation ("Mobil"). During those years, Sekiyu employed about 1,500 persons in Japan with sales between $400–700 million each year. It had several thousand service stations in Japan and was also involved in two joint ventures with Japanese companies which owned and operated four refineries.

In order to attract qualified employees for foreign service and to maintain an equitable relationship between its domestic and American foreign-based employees, thereby preventing any employee from gaining a benefit or suffering a hardship from serving overseas, Mobil maintained a compensation policy for its American employees assigned outside the United States. One of the components of the policy involved the procurement by Mobil of housing for such employees, regardless of their position or duties. Mobil first calculated a "U.S. Housing Element" for each American foreign-based employee, based on a survey of the Bureau of Labor Statistics, which reflected the approximate average housing costs in the United States at various family sizes and income levels. Mobil then subtracted from that employee's salary the amount of his particular U.S. Housing Element. If Mobil provided housing to the employee, the employee would include in his gross income for federal tax purposes the U.S. Housing Element amount. If the employee instead obtained his own housing abroad, Mobil reimbursed him for the full amount, subject to certain predetermined limitations based upon reasonableness, and the employee would then include the full amount reimbursed in his gross income.

Pursuant to the above policy, Mobil provided plaintiff with a residence for the years in question. The three-level house, which was built and owned by Sekiyu, was 3 miles from headquarters and consisted of a large living room, dining room, pantry and kitchen, three bedrooms, a den, two bathrooms, two maid's rooms, two garage areas, and a garden and veranda. By American standards the house was not large, but it was apparently choice. Sekiyu felt that it was important to house its chief executive officer in prestigious surroundings because, particularly in Japan, there is less of a distinction than in the United States between business activities and social activities. The effectiveness of a president of a company in Japan is influenced by the social standing and regard accorded to him by the Japanese business community. If the president of Sekiyu had not resided in a residence equivalent to the type provided the plaintiff, it would appear that he would have been unofficially downgraded and slighted by the business community and his effectiveness for Sekiyu correspondingly impaired. Sekiyu, therefore, provided such a house to plaintiff and required him to reside there as a matter of company policy.

The house was also designed so that it could accommodate the business activities of the plaintiff. The den was built specifically for the conduct of business, and the kitchen and living room were sufficiently large for either business meetings or receptions. Plaintiff worked in the house in the evenings and on weekends and held small meetings there for mixed business and social purposes. He regularly used the telephone for business purposes from his home after regular working hours, both for business emergencies and also for communicating with persons in the United States because of the time difference. In addition, he regularly discharged his business entertainment responsibilities in the residence, generally averaging about 35–40 such occasions in a normal year. In 1970 his entertaining declined considerably because of the absence of his wife from Japan for 10 months, but it resumed again in 1971. Plaintiff was provided with two maids, only one of whom was needed for his family's personal requirements.

Plaintiff included in his gross income for federal tax purposes, as the value of the housing furnished him by his employer, the U.S. Housing Element amounts which had been subtracted from his gross salary. Those amounts which were designed to approximate the average housing costs of a similarly situated person in the United States during 1970 and 1971, totalled $4,439 for 1970 and $4,824 for 1971. However, because the cost of housing in Tokyo in those years was considerably higher than that in the United States, it is agreed by the parties that the fair rental value of the residence furnished plaintiff by Sekiyu was $20,000 in 1970 and $20,599.09 in 1971. Accordingly, upon audit of plaintiff's 1970 and 1971 income tax returns, the Internal Revenue Service, among other adjustments, increased the amounts reported by plaintiff as the value of the housing furnished by Sekiyu to $20,000 in 1970 and $20,599.09 in 1971. Plaintiff has filed suit to recover the sum of $914.24 plus assessed interest as a result of the Internal Revenue Service's inclusion in his gross income of the amounts in excess of the U.S. Housing Element for the 2 years in suit.

Gross income means all income from whatever source derived, including compensation for services. I.R.C. §61(a). It includes income realized in any form. Section 1.61-2(d)(1) of Treasury Regulations ... states, "If services are paid for other than in money, the fair market value of the property or services taken in payment must be included in income."

Presumably, then, if the lodging furnished to plaintiff was compensation to him, the fair rental value of the lodging would be includable in his gross income unless excludable under another provision of the Code....

Plaintiff contends that the fair rental value of the residence supplied to him by Sekiyu in 1970 and 1971 is excludable from his gross income because of Section 119 of the 1954 Code. Alternatively, plaintiff asserts that the excess of the fair rental value of the residence over the U.S. Housing Element amount represented a benefit to his employer and not a benefit to him, and therefore is not gross income to him. Finally, plaintiff contends that even if the fair rental value of the residence is income to him, it should be measured by the amount plaintiff would have spent for housing in the United States, rather than the fair rental value in Japan. Because we hold that the conditions of Section 119 of the 1954 Code and the Regulations promulgated thereunder have been met, we do not address the other arguments of plaintiff.

Section 119 of the 1954 Code provides in part:

> There shall be excluded from gross income of an employee the value of any meals or lodging furnished to him by his employer for the convenience of the employer, but only if—
>
> …
>
> (2) in the case of lodging, the employee is required to accept such lodging on the business premises of his employer as a condition of his employment.

Thus, in order to qualify for the exclusion of Section 119, each of three tests must be met:

(1) the employee must be required to accept the lodging as a condition of his employment;

(2) the lodging must be furnished for the convenience of the employer; and

(3) the lodging must be on the business premises of the employer. [Treas.Reg. § 1.119-1(b) (1956).]

The Regulations further provide that the first test is met where the employee is "required to accept the lodging in order to enable him properly to perform the duties of his employment." …

It is clear that the first requirement of the statute has been met because the plaintiff was explicitly required to accept the residence provided by Sekiyu as a condition of his employment as president of the company. Sekiyu's goal was twofold: first, it wanted to insure that its president resided in housing of sufficiently dignified surroundings to promote his effectiveness within the Japanese business community. Secondly, Sekiyu wished to provide its president with facilities which were sufficient for the conduct of certain necessary business activities at home. Since at least 1954 Sekiyu had required that its chief executive officer reside in the residence provided to plaintiff, as a condition to appointment as president.

With respect to this first test of Section 119, then, this case is as compelling as *United States Junior Chamber of Commerce v. United States*, 334 F.2d 660, 167 Ct. Cl. 392 (1964). In that case, the court found that it was not *necessary* for the taxpayer-president to reside in the Chamber's "White House" during his term of office so long as he lived in the Tulsa area. But, as a practical matter, for the convenience of his employer and as a condition of his tenure, the president was *required* to live there. Therefore, it was held that the "condition of employment" test was met. The court noted that the "condition of employment" test is met if

> due to the nature of the employer's business, a certain type of residence for the employee is required and that it would not be reasonable to suppose that the employee would normally have available such lodging for the use of his employer. 334 F.2d at 664, 167 Ct.Cl. at 399.

Here, because the size and style of one's residence had an important effect upon the Japanese business community, a certain type of residence was both required by Mobil and Sekiyu for the plaintiff and necessary for the proper discharge of his duties in Sekiyu's best interests.

① required to accept the condition of employment

In contrast, the Tax Court in *James H. McDonald*, 66 T.C. 223 (1976), found that the taxpayer was not expressly required to accept his accommodations as a condition of his employment in Tokyo. Moreover, the court noted that the apartment provided to the taxpayer was not integrally related to the various facets of the employee's position. In the present case, plaintiff was required to accept the housing, and the residence was directly related to plaintiff's position as president, both in terms of physical facilities and psychic significance. It is held, therefore, that plaintiff was required to accept the lodging in order to enable him properly to perform the duties of his employment.

As to the "for the convenience of the employer" test, in *United States Junior Chamber of Commerce v. United States*, ... the court stated,

> "There does not appear to be any substantial difference between the ...'convenience of the employer' test and the 'required as a condition of his employment' test."

Since it has already been determined that the condition of employment test has been satisfied, on that basis alone it could be held that the convenience of the employer test has also been met.

In *James H. McDonald*, ... the court stated that the convenience of the employer test is satisfied where there is a direct nexus between the housing furnished the employee and the business interests of the employer served thereby. In *McDonald*, the taxpayer was a principal officer of Gulf who was furnished an apartment by his employer which totalled only about 1,500 square feet of living space. The taxpayer was not required to live in the apartment, and it was found that the only benefit Gulf received in maintaining the apartment was the flexibility it afforded Gulf in personnel transfers. There was no prestige consideration. The court held that there was an insufficient nexus between the apartment and the employer's business interests to meet the convenience of the employer test requirements. Moreover, the court further noted that:

> While its practice of maintaining various leasehold interests for assignment to expatriate employees may have accorded Gulf a benefit in terms of flexibility in personnel transfers, that is not to conclude that the assignments of these lodgings to petitioners at a discount similarly served the interests of Gulf; that is, although convenience may have dictated the form in which the leasehold arrangements were structured, the convenience of Gulf did not require it to subsidize the assignments. 66 T.C. at 229.

Here there was a sufficiently direct relationship between the housing furnished the plaintiff by Sekiyu and Sekiyu's business interests to meet the convenience of the employer test. The lodging had been built and was owned by Sekiyu. It was specially identified with the business of Sekiyu, for the house had served as the home of its presidents since at least 1954. If Sekiyu's president had not resided in housing comparable to that supplied plaintiff, Sekiyu's business would have been adversely affected. The house had been designed for this purpose to accommodate substantial business activities, and therefore further served Sekiyu's business interests.

Moreover, the fact that Sekiyu subsidized plaintiff's use of the house was also in its best business interests. Sekiyu was interested in attracting a qualified person as its chief executive officer. Because of the unusual housing situation in Tokyo during the years in question, a person would have had to pay up to four times his U.S. housing costs to obtain comparable housing in Tokyo. Certainly, such a factor would have been a strong deterrent to any qualified person's interest in Sekiyu's presidency, absent a housing subsidy from Sekiyu. Furthermore, it was clearly in Mobil-Sekiyu's best business interests to maintain an equitable compensation relationship between its domestic employees and its American foreign-based ones. The housing subsidy was designed to accomplish that.

That the plaintiff also incurred a benefit from this residence and that it was, in part, a convenience to him, does not disturb the conclusion. As noted in *William I. Olkjer,* ... :

> No doubt the facilities furnished benefited the employee also. The test which the statute provides, however, is that of convenience to the employer. There is no provision to the effect that the employee is to be deprived of his right to exclude from gross income the value of food and lodging otherwise excludable because he, too, is convenienced....

The third and final test is whether the lodging was on the business premises of the employer. Observe first that "[t]he operative framework of [the clause 'on the business premises'] is at best elusive and admittedly incapable of generating any hard and fast line." *Jack B. Lindeman,* 60 T.C. 609, 617 (1973) (Tannenwald, J., concurring). This question is largely a factual one requiring a commonsense approach. The statute should not be read literally. As noted by the Tax Court in *Lindeman,* ... :

> [T]he statutory language ordinarily would not permit any exclusion for lodging furnished a domestic servant, since a servant's lodging is rarely furnished on "the business premises of his employer"; yet the committee report ... shows a clear intention to allow the exclusion where the servant's lodging is furnished in the employer's home.

In the original version of the 1954 Code, as enacted in the House, the term that was used in Section 119 was "place of employment." The Senate changed the wording to "business premises", which was accepted by the House. However, the change was without substance, for the House Conference Report stated that "[t]he term 'business premises of the employer' is intended, in general, to have the same effect as the term 'place of employment' in the House bill." H.Conf.Rep. No. 2543, 83d Cong., 2d Sess. 27.... The pertinent Treasury regulation similarly provides that "business premises" generally refers to the place of employment of the employee. Treas.Reg. Sec. 1.119-1(c)(1) (1956). The phrase, then, is not to be limited to the business compound or headquarters of the employer. Rather, the emphasis must be upon the place where the employee's duties are to be performed. See *Comm'r. of Internal Revenue v. Anderson,* 371 F. 2d 59, 64 (6th Cir. 1966), *cert. denied,* 387 U.S. 906 ... (1967). In *United States Junior Chamber of Commerce v. United States,* ... the court stated, "We think that the business premises of Section 119 means premises of the employer on which the duties of the employee are to be performed." The phrase has also been construed to mean either (1) living quarters that constitute an integral part of the business property, or (2) premises on which the company carries on some substantial segment of its business activities. *Gordon S. Dole,* 43 T.C. 697, 707 (1965), *aff'd per curiam,* 351 F.2d 308 (1st Cir. 1965).

In *United States Junior Chamber of Commerce, supra,* the taxpayer-president had an office in the employer-owned "White House" which he used at night for the conduct of business meetings. In addition, he used his residence for business entertainment purposes. The court held that, because of these two factors, the White House constituted a part of the business premises of the employer, though not physically contiguous to headquarters. In this case plaintiff, although he had an office at the employer's headquarters, worked in his residence in the evenings and on weekends, had business meetings and performed required business telephone calls from there which could not be made during normal business hours, and conducted regular business entertaining in the residence. In this sense plaintiff's residence was a part of the business premises of his employer, for it was a "premises on which the duties of the employee are to be performed", ... and a "premises on which the company carries on some of its business activities." ...

Interpretations of the phrase which are limited to the geographic contiguity of the premises or to questions of the quantum of business activities on the premises are too restrictive.... Rather, the statutory language "on the business premises of the employer" infers a functional rather than a spatial unity. In Rev.Rul. 75-540, 1975-2 Cum. Bull. 53, it was determined that the fair rental value of the official residence furnished a governor by the state is excludable from the governor's gross income under Section 119 of the Code. The Ruling noted that the business premises test was met because the residence provided by the state enabled the governor to carry out efficiently the administrative, ceremonial, and social duties required by his office. The governor's mansion, thus, served an important business function in that it was clearly identified with the business interests of the state. It was, in short, an inseparable adjunct. Similarly, in *United States Junior Chamber of Commerce, supra*, one of the main objectives of the employer was to promote and foster the growth of civic organizations in the United States. The White House, as official residence of the president of the organization, served a significant public relations function in furtherance of the organization's goals. In the present case, even apart from the strictly business activities which took place in plaintiff's residence, the house was a symbol to the Japanese business community of the status of Sekiyu's chief executive officer and a place where he officially entertained for business purposes. As such, it influenced plaintiff's effectiveness in the business community and directly served a business function for Sekiyu.

The situation, thus, is not the same as in *James H. McDonald*, 66 T.C. 223 (1976). In that case, the court found the quantum of business activities performed by the taxpayer in his home to be insignificant. There was no suggestion of prestige value to the employer or of its use for significant business entertainment. Also, the court held that the rental apartment supplied to the taxpayer was not closely identified with the business interests of his employer. Here, because plaintiff was the highest-ranking officer of his company, his status in the business community was extremely important to his employer. The residence supplied to him was closely identified with Sekiyu's business interests and was used to advance those interests.

... [W]e are persuaded that where, as here, (1) the residence was built and owned by the employer, (2) it was designed, in part, to accommodate the business activities of the employer, (3) the employee was required to live in the residence, (4) there were many business activities for the employee to perform after normal working hours in his home because of the extensive nature of the employer's business and the high-ranking status of the employee, (5) the employee did perform business activities in the residence, and (6) the residence served an important business function of the employer, then the residence in question is a part of the business premises of the employer.

The three statutory requisites for exclusion are met. Accordingly, pursuant to Section 119 ... the fair rental value of the residence is excludable from plaintiff's gross income.[23] ...

---

23. Code Section 911 provides an exclusion from gross income for salaries and housing allowances for certain U.S. citizens or residents living abroad. For some corporate executives, like Mr. Adams, this provision, if applicable, could eliminate the issue in this case or reduce the amount of gross income he would have to include as a result of employer-provided housing.

Consider the following additional questions.

1. Reconsider question 3 before *Adams*. Would your answer change based on what the court held in *Adams*?

2. Suppose you are a teacher at a private boarding school. As part of your duties, you are required to live on the school grounds in an apartment that is at one end of a student dormitory and eat with the students in the cafeteria. Do you have gross income equal to the value of your rent and meals? Again, fully analyze under section 119 and its regulations, using systematic statutory analysis technique.

3. Suppose instead, that you are required to live just off campus and the school gives you a housing allowance to pay your rent. Income? Review section 119 and Treasury Regulation section 1.119-1.

Why are some employees able to exclude the value of meals and lodging from gross income if they meet the requirements of section 119? Can you formulate a defensible policy argument for treating some employees differently from others? Consider the following excerpt from a noted economist:

> Let us consider here another of Kleinwächter's conundrums. We are asked to measure the relative incomes of an ordinary officer serving with his troops and a *Flügeladjutant* to the sovereign.... He accompanies the prince to theater and opera, and, in general, lives royally at no expense to himself and is able to save generously from his salary. But suppose, as one possible complication, that the *Flügeladjutant* detests opera and hunting.
>
> The problem is clearly hopeless. To neglect all compensation in kind is obviously inappropriate. On the other hand, to include the perquisites as a major addition to the salary implies that all income should be measured without regard for the relative pleasurableness of different activities—which would be the negation of measurement. There is hardly more reason for imputing more income to the *Flügeladjutant* on account of his luxurious wardrobe than for bringing into account the prestige and social distinction of a (German) university professor.[24]

2. Other Fringe Benefits

Of course, "free" meals and lodging are not the only in-kind employment benefits that raise compensation issues under section 61. Reconsider the fruitcake that your employer gives everyone at Christmas time. Consider too the executive who gets free use of a company car, or who can hitch a ride to a business meeting in Chicago or to a vacation spot in Hawaii on the corporate jet. What about the computer your employer gives you to work on in your office, the secretarial services you receive, and the heat, light, and air-conditioning in your office? Do any of these items constitute in-kind compensatory benefits that should be included in gross income?

---

24. Simons, *Personal Income Taxation: The Definition of Income as a Problem of Fiscal Policy* 53 (U. of Chicago Press 1938).

Consider first the common benefits that many employees enjoy based on the type of business in which they work. Airline employees fly free; department store employees buy merchandise at a discount; and university employees get free tuition. Are any of these benefits gross income under the three-prong test for income in *Glenshaw Glass*? By this point, do you have any doubt?

Neither free flights, nor discounted merchandise, nor free tuition, however, are excluded from gross income under section 119, the section we examined that excludes employer-provided meals and lodging. But such "perks," traditionally, have been considered tax-free "fringe benefits," and the availability of such benefits frequently induces taxpayers to engage in certain lines of work.

Fringe benefits, however, create problems for an income tax system. **Recall the Zelenak and McMahon article at the end of Chapter 1.** For example, as you observed in *Old Colony*, it would be rather easy for an employee to arrange with the employer to provide all items of personal consumption, *i.e.*, food, clothing, shelter, transportation, and entertainment, in the form of in-kind benefits. Such an arrangement, obviously, would be extreme; it does, however, illustrate the problem that results for an income tax system when employees arrange with their employers to receive as much compensation as possible in the form of in-kind "fringe benefits."

Consider the following excerpt from the explanation of a discussion draft of proposed regulations under section 61 that the Service proposed in 1975 governing the taxation of in-kind fringe benefits.[25] Notice, in particular, the approach that the Service adopted in these proposed regulations. The Service "intended that the proposed regulations be viewed as broad principles suggesting a rationale and path to a reasonable solution in particular cases."[26] Thus, the Service emphasized that the proposed regulations were "essentially different from those highly technical provisions of the Code and regulations intended to deal definitively with all aspects of a narrow problem."[27]

Summary and Explanation of Discussion Draft of Proposed Regulations on Fringe Benefits[28]

The following document contains a discussion draft of proposed regulations dealing with the subject of fringe benefits. In general, the proposed regulations codify practices that have grown up over more than 60 years. Those practices and precedents constitute a practical interpretation of statutory language which is so elastic that it provides only general guidance. With the definition of "income"—as in the case of other broad concepts such as "due process" or "equal protection"—most of the law must be discovered in a study of the ways in which the language has been interpreted. Thus, for example, official

---

25. 40 Fed. Reg. 41118 (Sept. 5, 1975).

26. *Id.*

27. *Id.*

28. From Treasury News Release, Sept. 2, 1975, *quoted in* William E. Elwood and Cynthia A. Moore, 394—3rd T.M., *Employee Fringe Benefits*, B 1101–1106, (1996). We have chosen to retain only selected footnotes within the discussion draft. In the actual discussion draft, footnotes are designated by asterisks. For easier reference, we have replaced the asterisks with numbers and placed the footnotes to the discussion draft at the end of the draft.

interpretations outstanding for decades hold that such things as travel passes for railroad employees or supper money for employees who work overtime are not to be included in income. These conclusions are carried forward into the proposed regulations, although a logical argument to the contrary could be made if we were writing on a clean slate.

...

The following summary and discussion are published in the hope that an explanation of the considerations underlying the precedents and the proposed rules will better focus public discussion.

I. *Summary*

General rules.

(1) Employees do not have taxable compensation where the benefit is on hand anyway, it costs nothing additional to provide it, and it is not limited to top executives.

(2) If a benefit does not qualify under (1), then its tax status is determined by looking at all of the facts and circumstances. Among the factors indicating whether or not a benefit is not taxable are:

- Whether the employer incurs a substantial and identifiable cost.
- Whether the expense is clearly related to the employer's business.
- Whether the benefit is exact reimbursement of an unusually large personal expense incurred by the employee on account of the employer's business.
- Whether the benefit is limited to top executives.

(3) Small amounts are not taxed.

Some examples illustrating the general rules.

(1) Airline employees and travel agents are not taxed on travel passes.

(2) Store employees are not taxed on merchandise discounts.

(3) An interior decorator is not taxed on the purchase of furniture for personal use at wholesale prices.

(4) Use of a business jet is not taxed where employees and their guests use otherwise empty seats. But a flight made only for personal entertainment purposes of an executive and spouse is taxed.

(5) Benefits to insure safety are not taxed. Examples are taxi fare home at night from a plant in an unsafe area and bodyguards after a threat by terrorists.

(6) Cars are not taxed to the extent required for the job. A specific example deals with and exempts transportation provided the President, and those cabinet officers, ambassadors, and consuls, for whom Congress has impliedly recognized that transportation to and from home is "official." Officials not covered by Congressional authorization are taxable on the personal use of government cars, including commuting between their homes, and offices. Another example covers officials such as fire chiefs, who must be on duty at all hours.

Also not taxed are cars for outside salesmen who pay for gas for personal use.

Cars are not taxed where they are provided to take an executive from his office to business appointments, but there is tax to the extent the car is used for commuting. The use of "demonstrators" by employees of an auto agency who do not primarily use the car for business is taxed.

(7) Free parking spaces in a company garage are not taxed under most circumstances.

(8) Having one's secretary type a personal letter is not taxed.

(9) Payment of bar association dues by a law firm is not taxed.

(10) Periodic social functions of a firm are not taxed to employees.

. . .

II. Discussion.

The taxation of economic benefits which individuals receive in kind has been troublesome since our income tax system began in 1913. Fringe benefits have proliferated as our industries and working conditions have grown ever more complex. Generalized principles have been slow to develop, and there has inevitably been nonuniformity of treatment of different taxpayers in similar situations.

The statutory definition of "gross income"—like most broad and sweeping definitions—fails to provide certainty in a multitude of individual situations. As a result, interpreting and applying the definitions have become major tasks for the courts and administrative officials. As in the case of such other broad phrases as "due process" and "equal protection," a substantial gloss on the statutory language has evolved and become a part of the law.

Our Anglo-American system of law rests firmly on precedent, but as precedents amass, it has been the role of jurists and scholars to rationalize the accumulation and to seek the threads of underlying principle. In the process, some precedents are discarded as defective; others are recognized as correct conclusions, but for reasons different from those advanced at the time; and the entire process is subject to constant revision for, as Cardozo said, "If we were to state the law today as well as human minds can state it, new problems, arising almost overnight, would encumber the ground again." (Footnote 1) This constant and dynamic search for organizing principles is the genius of our legal system. The proposed regulations represent a limited effort to apply that process to a narrow but vexing area of the tax law, in which more than half a century of judicial and administrative precedent have produced considerable confusion and uncertainty.

There are no general principles which will accommodate every judicial decision and administrative action that has occurred in the last 62 years, for a number of those decisions and actions are inconsistent with each other and with the general lines of precedent that have developed. The attempt has been to discover those organizing principles which best conform to the body of precedent and which themselves represent sound and equitable policies.

The proposals are presented with the awareness that the principles expressed are not all-encompassing and that the principles will themselves require modification in time, for it is no doubt necessary to a sound and practical income tax that the content of "income" should remain somewhat fluid, so that the application of the tax can keep pace with changing conditions. (Footnote 2)

It is intended that the proposed regulations be viewed as broad principles suggesting a rationale and path to a reasonable solution in particular cases. They are essentially different from those highly technical provisions of the Code and regulations intended to deal definitively with all aspects of a narrow problem. They are not to be construed or applied in a narrow and literal fashion to exclude every situation which fails to be described by the precise language employed. "As in other sciences, so in politics, it is impossible that all things should be precisely set down in writing; for enactments must be universal, but actions are concerned with particulars." (Footnote 3)

The Definition of "Income."

The Internal Revenue Code states simply that Gross income means all income from whatever source derived....

As a definition, that language has an obvious defect, for to say that gross income includes income still fails to tell us what income is. The statutory language should be viewed rather as broad authorization to reach such items as may be appropriate, in the context of our overall system. It is clearly broad enough to encompass almost any economic benefit, but it is equally clear that it has not been construed to do so. To the uninitiated layman the language may appear sufficient. For perhaps the great majority of taxpayers, no ambiguities exist. Income from wages and salaries, dividends, interest from savings deposits, and the like are universally regarded as income under any definition, and for the majority that appears to take care of all of the problems. But students of the tax law know better, and most of the hundreds of pages of the Internal Revenue Code were written to help draw the lines between what will and what will not be treated as income.

Even for theoretical economists, there has been great confusion as to exactly what constitutes income. The classic work on the subject is Professor Simons', *Personal Income Taxation* (1938), which comments on the task of defining "income":

> Many writers have undertaken to formulate definitions, and with the most curious results. Whereas the word is widely used in discussions of justice in taxation and without evident confusion, the greatest variety and dissimilarity appear, as to both content and phraseology, in the actual definitions proposed by particular writers. The consistent recourse to definition in terms which are themselves undefinable (or undefined or equally ambiguous) testifies eloquently to the underlying confusion. (Footnote 4)

Professor Simons' own theoretical definition of income (generally known as the Haig-Simons definition) has become the definition perhaps most widely accepted among economists.

... It is sometimes asserted simply that income includes any "economic benefit" received, and "economic benefit" is the germ of the more elegant theoretical definition which Professor Simons developed. But the concept of "economic benefit" does not explain 60 years of actual experience. Nor does it conform to public understanding and custom. The fact that economic logic and theory are separated by a substantial gap from the legal rules that have actually developed is neither unique nor undesirable, for as Justice Holmes said:

> The life of the law has not been logic: it has been experience. The felt necessities of the time, the prevalent moral and political theories, intuitions of public policy, avowed or unconscious, even the prejudices which judges share with their fellow-men, have had a good deal more to do than the syllogism in determining the rules by which men should be governed. (Footnote 5)

A few examples will suffice to show that the concept of "economic benefit" does not explain the law:

(1) Social security, welfare, and unemployment compensation payments are not taxable as income under our system. There is no section of the Code which so provides. The exclusion grew up as a result of administrative action, undoubtedly in response to what Justice Holmes called "the felt necessities of the times."

(2) Persons who purchase life insurance pay premiums which are in effect invested on their behalf. Income from those investments is not taxed to the purchaser, notwithstanding that they clearly represent economic benefits.

(3) Taxpayers who invest money in the purchase of a house realize income in kind consisting of the right to live in the house. That income is not taxed under our tax system although there is nothing in the Code which expressly excludes it. (Such income has been taxed at various times under other systems.) A taxpayer who invests the same money in stocks or bonds with the intention of using the income to rent a house, on the other hand, must pay tax on the income from the stocks and bonds, which reduces the amount available to pay rent.

(4) Meals and lodging provided to taxpayers by their employers clearly constitute an economic benefit but are not taxable to the extent they are provided "for the convenience of the employer." This exclusion was initiated early by administrative ruling and existed for 40 years on that basis. In 1954, it was written into the Internal Revenue Code in somewhat modified fashion.

(5) Entertainment, meals, travel, and lodging received in a business context are in large part untaxed under current statutory provisions. At the higher levels of today's business communities, individuals' personal and business lives tend to meld into an indistinguishable whole, and many persons spend much of their lives in such activities. It is a legitimate conjecture whether the restaurant and resort industries would be decimated without these provisions.

(6) Large elaborate officers [sic] for executives, attended with employees and accompanied by working conditions designed to provide every creature comfort and convenience are commonplace and obviously constitute an economic benefit which has both personal and business aspects. Those benefits are not taxed.

(7) A great variety of miscellaneous benefits provided by employers have been held administratively not to constitute income. Examples include group-term life insurance and compensation for tornado damage.

None of the economic benefits in the foregoing examples was originally excluded from income because of a clear and specific statutory exclusion. Nor were they excluded because of insurmountable administrative considerations. For the billions of dollars of additional revenues which could be obtained from these sources, it would obviously be possible to devise workable administrative rules.

The results are better explained by what Justice Holmes called "the prevalent moral and political theories," than by strict theory. The attitude of labor unions on some of these items is interesting as an expression of one view as to "prevalent theories." Justice Goldberg speaking in his earlier role as General Counsel, CIO, took the following position:

> The line between [compensation and conditions of employment] is, perhaps, not susceptible of precise definition. The reason it is not is because the line is really an institutional and sociological one. It depends very much on what our current conception of the relative responsibilities of employer and employee happen to be. The question is whether the benefit in question is one which we regard as a proper responsibility which employers should supply for employees as a condition of employment wholly apart from the compensation for their work. And the answers to that question vary from time to time. To the extent that benefits are usually or normally provided by employers, even though they may involve a saving to an employee over alternative methods of providing this

facility by himself, then, to that extent the provision of such benefits should not be considered as compensation to the employee but as the provision of improved conditions of work.

Applying these views to employer-provided insurance, he concluded the benefit to be nontaxable, stating:

> How about insurance? With this principle in mind, are the insurance programs negotiated by unions just a disguised way of paying compensation, or are they offered on a service basis as a condition of employment? Clearly the latter. (Footnote 6)

The Internal Revenue Code as presently interpreted by the regulations and the better reasoned case law requires more than a finding that an employee enjoyed an economic benefit. Section 61(a)(1) of the Code speaks of "compensation *for* services." The regulations condition taxability upon finding a situation where "services are *paid for* other than in money." Treas. Reg. Sec. 1.61-2(d)(1). And, in the Supreme Court's words, section 61 "is broad enough to include in taxable income any economic or financial benefit conferred on the employee *as compensation.*" *Comm'r v. Smith*, 324 U.S. 177, 181 (1945) (emphasis added). The notion of a bargain between employer and employee—that there must be a payment *in exchange for* services—has been added as an essential element for the taxation of compensation, including fringe benefits.

Policy Considerations.

In sum, there is no easy or entirely satisfactory answer as to how all economic benefits should be taxed or not taxed. Professor Simons says with respect to income in kind:

> There is here an essential and insuperable difficulty, even in principle. The problem ... certainly is not amenable to reasonable solution on the basis of simple rules which could be administered by revenue agents.... At all events, let it be recognized that one faces here one of the real imponderables of income definition. (Footnote 7)

The principles governing the taxation of fringe benefits inescapably involve a large degree of judgment not reducible to a single formulistic test or tests. Simple mechanical formulas are not possible. In reaching the judgments embodied in the proposed regulations, the following policy considerations were taken into account.

(1) *Present practices in general are codified.* Sixty-two years of experience must be given great weight. The practices which have developed provide a reasonable and pragmatic guide to which economic benefits are appropriate for taxation. The general rules of the proposed regulations excluding benefits inherent in the employer's business under certain circumstances deal with a category of clear economic benefits that have not been generally taxed and which, we believe, generally should not be taxed. The first eight factors set out in the proposed regulations are distillations of principles from experience and are applications of the ninth factor, which states that an item is not taxed if it is not thought of as constituting compensation paid for services. While these factors necessarily lack particularity in many respects, they are much more specific than the statutory language and far preferable to some simplistic theory (such as "economic benefit") that is at odds with our national conception of what realistically constitutes taxable compensation for services. In some instances, where precedent was slim, or unconvincing, questions have been resolved in favor of taxpayers. In other cases, rules were resolved against taxpayers even though good arguments would be made for a contrary result. For example, in the case of executive transportation furnished by employers, it might arguably have been reasonable to hold that private transportation was not taxable

to the extent it was furnished to permit the executive to perform work while commuting. However, the line of precedent with respect to commuting expense is so extensive and so firmly established that such a rule did not appear to be an administrative option.

(2) *Statutory authority is broad but not mandatorily all-encompassing.* The statutory definition of income is very broad. That broad scope provides the residual authority to deal with new forms of compensation and other income generally as they develop without having to amend the statute each time. Inherent in that authority is the flexibility and, indeed, the necessity to distinguish between economic benefits which should be taxed and those which should not. The draft regulations do not extend the reach of the income tax to fringe benefits so far as they could legally, but only so far as they may practically.

(3) *Equity among taxpayers.* As indicated earlier, many high-income persons, particularly those whose business and personal lives are in effect melded, enjoy major economic benefits in the form of meals, lodging, travel, and entertainment, much of which goes untaxed under rules that are statutory. When this is occurring in so widespread a fashion, it seems particularly unfair, for example, to tax ordinary airline employees for traveling in otherwise empty seats or to tax retail clerks for discounts received on goods purchased from their employers.

If all taxpayers had fringe benefits or other benefits in kind and those benefits were roughly in proportion to their other income, then the uniform exclusion of all such benefits from tax would be as equitable as tax matters are likely ever to be and would probably contribute to a more efficient and effective tax system, as it would avoid the valuation and withholding problems discussed below. But the non-uniform exclusion of such benefits—exclusions for some but not others—would be clearly inequitable. Thus, in drafting the proposed regulations a special effort was made to be sure that ordinary taxpayers in the lower and middle income classes were treated in a fashion as generous as that which very high income taxpayers already enjoy, subject to the overriding principle that the integrity of the system must be protected.

(4) *Valuation problems.* Valuation of benefits in kind is extremely difficult in many, if not most cases, and the necessity for valuation vastly complicates the tax law. What is the value to a stewardess of riding in an otherwise empty seat? In most cases the privilege would not be worth to her the retail price of a ticket, i.e., she would not make the trip if she had to pay for it. Thus, in *Reginald Turner*, 13 T.C.M. 462 (1954), the court dealt with taxpayers who had won a free trip to South America and stated:

> The winning of the tickets did not provide them with something which they needed in the ordinary course of their lives and for which they would have made an expenditure in any event, but merely gave them an opportunity to enjoy a luxury otherwise beyond their means. Their value to the petitioners was not equal to their retail cost.

Similarly, how would one tax free or subsidized medical and recreational services and facilities for employees? Or company cafeteria meals provided at prices less than the prices prevailing in comparable restaurants? Valuation of such items comes very close to valuing working conditions as such, an undertaking that would encounter almost insurmountable difficulties. (Footnote 8) In general, it is desirable to avoid the complications of taxing such items, unless their omission constitutes a serious threat to the tax base or creates inequities that are significant in the context of the system as a whole.

(5) *Withholding considerations.* Our system relies on wage withholding to collect most of the personal income tax. In 1972, $91 billion of $110 billion personal income tax col-

lected was withheld from wages. The system works well only because almost all of the tax is collected automatically on cash payments. Withholding involves only easy arithmetic applied to unambiguous dollar amounts. Audit of withheld amounts is easy. If we should attempt to include in the withholding base every economic benefit enjoyed by great numbers of employees, the operation of the system would be seriously jeopardized. Taxpayers would have many ingenious theories to justify exclusion from gross income and, when taxed, there would be an infinity of valuation problems, of the kind referred to above.

This reliance on a simple self-executing system to collect most income tax leads to the policy judgment that, as a general rule, only those fringe benefit cases which threaten the integrity of the basic system should be taxed. Thus, the proposed regulations reach private junkets on corporate aircraft, personal use of company cars (and drivers) by executives, and discriminatory use of company facilities generally. While the proposed regulations reach these obvious cases, they do not involve the esoteric problems of taxing, and thus valuing, for example, the right to occupy an otherwise empty seat on a commercial flight. Employee discounts and free travel for airline flight attendants do not threaten the integrity of our income tax system. There is a great risk that trying to tax these and similar items would threaten the continued success of our self-assessment system.

...

Conclusion.

The proposed regulations are published for discussion as an attempt to provide guidelines that will afford greater degrees of certainty, uniformity, and fairness in an area which has become steadily more significant. They will not provide simple formulas which can be mechanically applied by revenue agents. That is not a defect, as present law provides no such formula either, except insofar as the broad sweep of the existing statutory language may in practicality give a revenue agent the personal discretion to include anything and everything that appears to result in economic benefit to the employee—an obviously unsatisfactory state of affairs. There is no way to avoid judgments in this difficult area, and we can only work to insure that those judgments are as sound and uniform as possible. The draft regulations are published in the hope that they will provide the basis for prescribing better guidelines to that end.

Office of the
Assistant Secretary for Tax Policy
September 2, 1975

FOOTNOTES:

1. Cardozo, "The Growth of the Law" (1924), p. 19. These lectures, addressed in part to the then current effort of the American Law Institute to "restate" the law in a number of areas, contain a discussion of this process.

2. Cf. Surrey and Warren, *Federal Income Taxation*, 1972, vol. 1, p. 115.

3. Aristotle, *Politics*, Book II, quoted by Cardozo, op. cit.

4. pp. 41–42.

5. Holmes, *The Common Law*, p. 1.

6. Quoted in Surrey and Warren, op. cit., p. 139.

7. Simons, op. cit., pp. 123–24.

8. See Vickrey, Agenda for Progressive Taxation (1947), p. 123.

The 1975 proposed regulations drew extensive comment and criticism. Indeed, in 1978, Congress enacted, and then on several successive occasions extended, a moratorium on the issuance of fringe benefit regulations by the Service. In 1984, Congress finally acted itself to fill in the perceived statutory gap in the fringe benefit area by enacting section 132 as part of the Tax Reform Act of 1984. Section 132 represents Congress's attempt to impose coherence on the taxation of common employee fringe benefits. The Joint Committee on Taxation[29] explained the reasons for Congress' action:

Tax Treatment of Fringe Benefits[30]

Prior Law

General rules

The Internal Revenue Code defines gross income for purposes of the Federal income tax as meaning "all income from whatever source derived," and specifies that it includes "compensation for services" (sec. 61). Treasury regulations provide that gross income includes compensation for services paid other than in money (Reg. sec. 1.61-1(a)). Further, the U.S. Supreme Court has stated that Code section 61 "is broad enough to include in taxable income any economic or financial benefit conferred on the employee as compensation, whatever the form or mode by which it is effected."

The social security and unemployment insurance payroll taxes (FICA and FUTA, respectively) and income tax withholding apply to "wages," defined in the Code as all remuneration for employment, including the cash value of all remuneration paid in any medium other than cash (secs. 3121(a), 3306(b), and 3401(a)).... Regulations applicable to these statutory provisions specify that the value of any noncash item is to be determined by the excess of its fair market value over any amount paid by the recipient for the item (see, e.g., Reg. sec. 31.3121(a)-1(e)).

Certain employee benefits, such as health plan benefits, are specifically excluded by statute from gross income and wages....

Employer-provided housing

Section 119 excludes from an employee's gross income the value of lodging provided by the employer if (1) the lodging is furnished for the convenience of the employer, (2)

---

29. The Joint Committee on Taxation, as the name implies, is a committee of Congress that consists of members of both the Senate Finance Committee and the House Ways and Means Committee, the tax-writing committees of Congress. After the passage of any significant tax legislation, the professional staff of the Joint Committee publishes a "General Explanation" of the provisions of the new legislation. As in the case of the other reports prepared by the various committees and by both houses of Congress in connection with the passage of tax legislation, the Government Printing Office in Washington, D.C. publishes the General Explanation. (Tax professionals often refer to the General Explanation as "the Blue Book" because it has a blue cover.) Although the General Explanation of any new tax legislation does not constitute the official legislative history of the legislation — the committee reports of the respective Senate and House committees, the reports of the House and Senate, and the report of the House/Senate Conference Committee constitute legislative history-tax professionals view the Blue Book as a valuable source of insight into the purposes and effects of the new legislation.

30. Joint Committee on Taxation, *General Explanation of the Revenue Provisions of the Deficit Reduction Act of 1984* (JCS-41-84), Dec. 31, 1984.

the lodging is on the business premises of the employer, and (3) the employee is required to accept the lodging as a condition of employment. Several court decisions have held that on-campus housing furnished to faculty or other employees by an educational institution under the circumstances involved in those cases did not satisfy the section 119 requirements, and hence that the fair rental value of the housing (less any amounts paid for the housing by the employee) was includible in the employee's gross income and constituted wages for income tax withholding and employment tax purposes.

Moratorium on issuance of certain income-tax regulations

In 1975, the Treasury Department issued a discussion draft of proposed regulations which contained a number of rules for determining whether various types of nonstatutory fringe benefits constitute taxable compensation. In general, these benefits involve the acquisition by an employee of goods or services that are regularly sold to the public by the employer, or the use by an employee of property or facilities of the employer, on terms more favorable than those available to the public.

Public Law 95-427, enacted in 1978, prohibited the Treasury Department from issuing, prior to 1980, final regulations under section 61 of the Internal Revenue Code relating to the income tax treatment of fringe benefits....

Public Law 96-167, enacted in 1979, extended the moratorium on issuance of fringe benefit regulations through May 31, 1981. That extension prohibited the Treasury Department from issuing, prior to June 1, 1981, final regulations under section 61 relating to the income tax treatment of fringe benefits....

The Economic Recovery Tax Act of 1981 (Public Law 97-34) extended the moratorium on issuance of fringe benefit regulations through December 31, 1983. Under the 1981 Act, the Treasury Department was prohibited from issuing, prior to January 1, 1984, final regulations under section 61 relating to the income tax treatment of fringe benefits....

Reasons for Change

In providing statutory rules for exclusion of certain fringe benefits for income and payroll tax purposes, the Congress struck a balance between two competing objectives.

First, the Congress was aware that in many industries, employees may receive, either free or at a discount, goods and services which the employer sells to the general public. In many cases, these practices are long established, and generally have been treated by employers, employees, and the Internal Revenue Service as not giving rise to taxable income.

Although employees receive an economic benefit from the availability of these free or discounted goods or services, employers often have valid business reasons, other than simply providing compensation, for encouraging employees to avail themselves of the products which those employees sell to the public. For example, a retail clothing business will want its salespersons to wear, when they deal with customers, the clothing which it seeks to sell to the public, rather than clothing sold by its competitors. In addition, where an employer has only one line of business, the fact that the selection of goods and services offered in that line of business may be limited in scope makes it appropriate to provide a limited exclusion, when such discounts are generally made available to employees, for the income employees realize from obtaining free or reduced-cost goods or services. By contrast, allowing tax-free discounts for all lines of business of a conglomerate organization, where the employee might have unlimited choices among many products and services which individuals normally consume or use on a regular basis, would be indistinguishable in economic effect from allowing tax-free compensation in the form of cash or gift certificates. Also, the noncompensatory element involved in providing discounts on the particular products or services that the employee sells to the public may be marginal or absent where an employer offers discounts across all lines of business.

The Congress believed, therefore, that many present practices under which employers may provide to a broad group of employees, either free or at a discount, the products and services which the employer sells or provides to the public do not serve merely to replace cash compensation. These reasons support the decision to codify the ability of employers to continue many of these practices without imposition of income or payroll taxes.

The second objective of the new statutory rules is to set forth clear boundaries for the provision of tax-free benefits. Because of the moratorium on the issuance of fringe benefit regulations, the Treasury Department has been precluded from clarifying the tax treatment of many of the forms of noncash compensation commonly in use. As a result, the administrators of the tax law have not had clear guidelines in this area, and hence taxpayers in identical or comparable situations have been treated differently. The in-equities, confusion, and administrative difficulties for businesses, employees, and the Internal Revenue Service resulting from this situation have increased substantially in re-cent years. The Congress believed that it would be unacceptable to allow these condi-tions—which had existed since 1978—to continue.

In addition, the Congress was concerned that without any well-defined limits on the ability of employers to compensate their employees tax-free by providing noncash ben-efits having economic value to the employee, new practices will emerge that could shrink the income tax base significantly. This erosion of the income tax base results be-cause the preferential tax treatment of fringe benefits serves as a strong motivation to employers to substitute more and more types of benefits for cash compensation. A sim-ilar shrinkage of the base of the social security payroll tax could also pose a threat to the viability of the social security system above and beyond the adverse projections which the Congress addressed in the Social Security Amendments of 1983. In addition, con-tinuation of the dramatic growth in noncash forms of compensation in recent years— at a rate exceeding the growth in cash compensation—could further shift a dispropor-tionate tax burden to those individuals whose compensation is in the form of cash.

Finally, an unrestrained expansion of noncash compensation would increase in-equities among employees in different types of businesses, because not all employers can or will provide comparable compensation packages. For example, consumer-goods retail stores can offer their employees discounts on clothing, hardware, etc.; by contrast, a manufacturer of aircraft engines cannot give its workers compensation in the form of tax-free discounts on its products. Similarly, an unlimited exclusion for noncash bene-fits discriminates among employers. For example, if tax-free discounts were allowed across all lines of business of an employer, a large employer with many types of busi-nesses (e.g., department store, hotel, airline, etc.) would be given a favorable edge by the tax system in competing for employees as compared with a small firm having one line of business (e.g., a specialty clothing store). Also, a failure to put any limits on the untaxed status of fringe benefits would encourage employers to provide further non-cash forms of compensation and thus, in effect, restrict the employees' freedom of choice over how to spend or save their compensation.

Accordingly, the Congress determined that specific rules of exclusion should be set forth in the Code, with limitations on the availability, applicability, and scope of these statutory exclusions. These general limitations include a nondiscrimination rule, the line of business limitation, and the limitation on exclusions to benefits provided to the employee and the employee's spouse and dependent children. In addition, specific limitations apply to particular types of benefits.

The nondiscrimination rule is an important common thread among the types of fringe benefits which are excluded under the Act from income and employment taxes. Under the Act, most fringe benefits may be made available tax-free to officers, owners, or highly compensated employees only if the benefits are also provided on substantially equal terms to other employees. The Congress believed that it would be fundamentally unfair to provide tax-free treatment for economic benefits that are furnished only to highly paid executives. Further, where benefits are limited to the highly paid, it is more likely that the benefit is being provided so that those who control the business can receive compensation in a nontaxable form; in that situation, the reasons stated above for allowing tax-free treatment would not be applicable. Also, if highly paid executives could receive free from taxation economic benefits that are denied to lower-paid employees, while the latter are compensated only in fully taxable cash, the Congress was concerned that this situation would exacerbate problems of noncompliance among taxpayers. In this regard, some commentators argued that the prior-law situation—in which the lack of clear rules for the tax treatment of nonstatutory fringe benefits—encouraged the nonreporting of many types of cash income which are clearly taxable under present-law rules, such as interest and dividends.

In addition to enacting specific statutory exclusions covering many fringe benefit practices, the tax treatment of which had been uncertain under prior law, the Congress provided amendments in the Act to Code section 61, defining gross income, and to comparable employment tax provisions. These amendments made clear that any fringe benefit that does not qualify for exclusion under a specific Code provision is includible in the recipient's gross income, and in wages for withholding and other employment tax purposes, at the excess of the fair market value of the benefit over any amount paid by the recipient for the benefit.

The Congress recognized that the inclusion of taxable fringe benefits at fair market value raises valuation issues. However, the problem has been ameliorated because the Act exempts from any taxation a significant portion of benefits made available under existing practices. In addition, the Congress has directed the Treasury to issue regulations, to the extent feasible, setting forth appropriate and helpful rules for the valuation of taxable fringe benefits, to assist both employers, employees, and the Internal Revenue Service.

Also, the Congress understood that valuation issues inherently arise whenever compensation is paid in the form of noncash benefits. For example, both under prior law and the Act, the personal use by an employee (including use by members of the employee's family) of an employer-provided car or plane is includible in income, thereby necessitating a determination of the fair market value of the personal use. While it is understood that as a matter of practice, some taxpayers have not been reporting the full fair market value of such benefits, and that the Internal Revenue Service may not have been actively pursuing the matter on audit, the Congress anticipated that with the enactment in the Act of statutory rules delineating exclusions for fringe benefits, the Internal Revenue Service will be more effective in assuring that all sources of income and wages are properly reported on employer and employee tax returns. The Congress believed that this will help achieve a greater fairness in the tax law, by treating alike employees having equivalent economic income.

In summary, the Congress believed that by providing rules which essentially codify many present practices under which employers provide their own products or services tax-free to a broad group of employees whose work involves those products or services, and by ending the uncertainties arising from a moratorium on the Treasury Department's ability to clarify the tax treatment of these benefits, the Act substantially improves the equity and administration of the tax system.

––––––––––

Now let's study section 132, the Code provision that finally emerged. **Begin by reading section 132(a).** Section 132(a) excludes from gross income eight categories of common fringe benefits. **Examine the eight categories and study the definitions of each category contained in subsections (b) through (g) and (m) and (n).**[31]

Compare the section Congress adopted with the description of the regulations the Service proposed. Do they seem to reflect two different kinds of rulemaking? How would you characterize the difference?[32]

Identify an example of each of the eight types of fringe benefits. What do sections 132(h) and 132(j)(1) add to your analysis?

Why did Congress choose each of these eight categories? Is the justification the same for all?[33] Can you identify examples of common fringe benefits that section 132(a) does not cover? Identify other provisions in Part III of subchapter B that exclude any of the benefits you identified as *not* covered by section 132. Which of these do you believe represents the biggest revenue loss to the Treasury? Can you suggest some policy arguments for and against these exclusions?

Recall our examination of section 119. What is the relationship between section 119 and section 132? Do they overlap? If you conclude that both provisions might apply to a particular fringe benefit, which section would you apply? Does it matter? **See section 132(l).**

Congress enacted section 119 as part of the Internal Revenue Code of 1954 to codify the common law doctrine of "the convenience of the employer" developed by the courts and the Treasury Department. In contrast, Congress enacted section 132 after many years of controversy and study in an attempt to codify a diverse body of administrative and judicial rules. As a result, Congress appears to have attempted to cover all possible common variations in fringe benefits not otherwise covered by other provisions of the Code. (Nevertheless, Congress has subsequently amended section 132 five times since 1992, first to add two additional categories of excludable fringe benefits, sections 132(a)(5), and 132(a)(6), and four times again in 1997, 1998, 2001, and 2003 to increase the excludible amount of transportation fringe, and add two more categories, sections 132(a)(7) and (8).)

Note also the presence in section 132 of subsection (o) that authorizes the Secretary to "prescribe such regulations as may be necessary or appropriate to carry out the purposes

––––––––––

31. Section 132 contains a ninth (hidden) category of common fringe benefits. Can you find it?

32. Most rulemaking (regulatory or statutory) reflects either the "broad brush" approach of the proposed regulations or the very specific rules of section 132. What are the benefits and problems of each type? Which is likely to produce more litigation? Which is likely to produce worthy cases that do not quite satisfy the rule? Think back to the difference between the facts and circumstances test for determining a gift under *Duberstein* and the very precise anti-abuse bright-line rule under section 1014(e). **Find the appropriate language in *Duberstein*; then review Code section 1014(e).**

33. Note that, as originally enacted, section 132 excluded the fringe benefits, and only the fringe benefits, described in sections 132(a)(1) through (4). Congress has amended section 132(a) four times since 1992 to add subsections (5) through (8). The Joint Committee Blue Book explanation (that you have just read), explains the reasons underlying sections 132(a)(1) through (4) only. Can you think of reasons why Congress enacted subsections (5) through (8) of section 132(a)?

of this section." Has the Secretary utilized this authority? How? Did the Secretary need the explicit authorization contained in section 132(o) in order to promulgate regulations? **Look again at section 7805(a).** How does the Secretary go about promulgating regulations? To explain this requires a brief foray into the mysterious realm of administrative law.

The Treasury Department is one of the administrative bodies that form the executive branch of our tri-partite federal government. Congress has delegated authority for the administration of the Code to the Secretary of the Treasury as head of the Treasury Department.[34] The Secretary exercises this power through the various branches of the Treasury Department, one of which is the Internal Revenue Service, headed by the Commissioner of Internal Revenue.[35] One of the peculiarities of our system of administrative law is that within one administrative agency, such as the Treasury, various parts of the agency function as interpreters (almost quasi-legislators) and enforcers of the Code, and, in addition, quasi-adjudicators in disputes between taxpayers and Treasury Department personnel. Thus, the Service, as one agency, mirrors the tri-partite functions of our Federal constitutional government inasmuch as it performs, within the agency, executive, legislative, and judicial functions.

Many commentators have noted that section 7805(a) constitutes authorization to the Secretary to issue "interpretive-type" regulations. In contrast, a section, such as 132(o), constitutes specific authority to issue "legislative-type" regulations. If you have studied administrative law, you may have learned that the Administrative Procedure Act governs the method for adoption of "legislative-type" regulations, but not "interpretive" ones.[36] You may also have learned, however, that it is not always easy to distinguish between the two. Nevertheless, courts and commentators frequently observe that while "legislative-type" regulations have the force of law, "interpretive" ones do not.

In the realm of tax regulations this distinction is probably inaccurate. Courts do view "legislative-type" regulations as having the force of law. Therefore, a taxpayer will find it impossible to overturn a "legislative-type" regulation unless she can show that the regulation exceeds the specific grant of authority by Congress or is unconstitutional. Courts may give taxpayers the impression that overturning an "interpretive-type" regulation will be easier. In fact, it is almost as unlikely that the taxpayer will succeed in attacking one of these regulations because the uniform view of the courts is to grant deference to the agency charged with administration of the statute. Therefore, the Secretary's interpretation of the statute need only be reasonable. It need not be the only reasonable interpretation; it need only be one reasonable interpretation.[37] Thus, the difference between the two types of regulations may be a distinction without a difference.

In any event, the regulations that the Service has promulgated under the specific authority of section 132(o) are extensive. They are necessary, however, because although section 132, on its face, appears to provide exhaustive regulation of the area, as you read its provisions, you will realize that the statute itself leaves many questions unanswered. Many of the unanswered questions are answered in the regulations. Thus, in order to interpret properly any question under section 132, it is necessary to consult the statute first, then the regulations.

---

34. See section 7801(a).
35. See section 7801(a).
36. 5 U.S.C. section 553 (1997).
37. See, generally, *Chevron U.S.A. Inc. v. Natural Resources Defense Council, Inc.*, 467 U.S. 837 (1984).

Shawn's Problem

Consider whether or to what extent the benefits listed below are includible or excludible from Shawn's gross income. Support each of your conclusions with *specific citations of authority* from the statute and/or the regulations. (Pay careful attention to whether the statute and regulations answer all the issues or whether further amplification is necessary. If so, what might you consult for further amplification?)

1. Shawn is an employee of a national chain of clothing stores. She is entitled to purchase clothes at a discount of 20% from retail. The corporation's gross sales for the year total $2,500,000; its total costs for those sales are $1,750,000.[38]

2. Suppose Shawn usually works at corporate headquarters. As a corporate officer, she is entitled to a parking space in the adjoining garage (not affiliated with the company for which she works). The usual monthly charge for the parking space is $350, but because her company rents a number of spaces, the owner of the garage charges the company only $150. Shawn pays nothing.

3. The company sends Shawn to New York on business. She spends 3 nights at the Waldorf Astoria Hotel. Her company pays the $200 per night for three nights even though Shawn has finished her business assignment by the end of day 2. Suppose the company also pays for her meals at the rate of $100 per day. Does Treasury Regulation section 1.162-2 help you answer this question?[39] **Read Treasury Regulation section 1.162-2.** How can a regulation pertaining to section 162 help you in understanding Code section 132?

4. Shawn flies home on United Airlines after her business trip. As a result of this and other business trips, she has enough frequent flyer miles for a free round-trip ticket to California worth $300. She decides to fly to California for her summer vacation.

5. In order to look her best, Shawn works out at the company gym which is on the employer's premises and is free for employees.

6. In order to go to the gym in the evenings, she has to take her mother. She pays a reduced membership fee of $25 per month for her mother (usual rate is $50 per month). Suppose you conclude that the mother's discounted $25 access to the gym is not an excludible fringe benefit within section 132. Who must include its value in income? **Read Treasury Regulation section 1.61-21(a)(4) and review section 102.**

7. Suppose that Shawn's job is as a full-time lawyer in the division of her employer that manufactures clothes. But her employer owns a second division that owns and

---

38. Section 132(b) defines a "no-additional-cost service" "[f]or purposes of this section." What is "this section?" Recall our earlier advice that a close reading of the Code is essential. Only a close reading will make clear, for example, to which rules a particular definition applies. In contrast to the limited applicability of the section 132(b) definition (only to "this section"), section 2(b)(1) of the Code defines a head-of-household "[f]or purposes of this subtitle." What is "this subtitle"?

Despite the broad application of the definition of "head-of-household" in the first part of section 2(b)(1), the flush language following section 2(b)(1)(what's the "flush language"?), defines when an individual is considered to be maintaining a household solely "[f]or purposes of this paragraph!" What does "paragraph" mean in the context of a statute that is not written in traditional prose form?

Section 2(c) provides that under the circumstances listed, an individual shall be treated as not married "[f]or purposes of this part." To what sections of the Code does this rule apply, *i.e.*, what sections constitute "this part"?

39. *See also* section 274(c).

injured party. For example, damages (other than punitive damages) received by an individual on account of a claim for loss of consortium due to the physical injury or physical sickness of such individual's spouse are excludable from gross income. In addition, damages (other than punitive damages) received on account of a claim of wrongful death continue to be excludable from taxable income as under present law.

The House bill also specifically provides that emotional distress is not considered a physical injury or physical sickness. Thus, the exclusion from gross income does not apply to any damages received (other than for medical expenses as discussed below) based on a claim of employment discrimination or injury to reputation accompanied by a claim of emotional distress. (Footnote 56) Because all damages received on account of physical injury or physical sickness are excludable from gross income, the exclusion from gross income applies to any damages received based on a claim of emotional distress that is attributable to a physical injury or physical sickness. In addition, the exclusion from gross income specifically applies to the amount of damages received that is not in excess of the amount paid for medical care attributable to emotional distress.

origin #2

RE: emotional distress

No inference is intended as to the application of the exclusion to damages prior to the effective date of the House bill in connection with a case not involving a physical injury or physical sickness.

FOOTNOTES:

54. The Supreme Court recently agreed to decide whether punitive damages awarded in a physical injury lawsuit are excludable from gross income. *O'Gilvie v. U.S.*, 66 F.3d 1550 (10th Cir. 1995), cert. granted, 64 U.S.L.W. 3639 (U.S. March 25, 1996) (No. 95-966). Also, the Tax Court recently held that if punitive damages are not of a compensatory nature, they are not excludable from income, regardless of whether the underlying claim involved a physical injury or physical sickness. *Bagley v. Commissioner*, 105 T.C. No. 27 (1995).

55. *Schleier v. Commissioner*, 115 S.Ct. 2159 (1995)....

56. It is intended that the term emotional distress includes symptoms (e.g., insomnia, headaches, stomach disorders) which may result from such emotional distress.

———————

defamation

Now assume that Sam did not suffer a physical injury; rather, Sam sued his former employer for defamation after receiving a poor job recommendation. The jury awarded Sam damages as follows:

all included in GI

Loss of future earnings[47]	$ 80,000
Emotional Distress	150,000
Punitive damages	450,000
TOTAL	$680,000

Has Sam suffered a personal injury? How much, if any, of his damages may Sam exclude from income under section 104(a)(2)?

———————

Now read sections 105 and 106. Suppose in the first problem, instead of receiving medical expenses as damages, Sam receives payment from a medical insurance plan in the amount of $15,000. He also receives $10,000 under the plan as compensation for the loss of his fingers. Suppose Sam paid for his own medical insurance. How do these sec-

———————

47. He did not, of course, get the new job and was unemployed for nine months.

tions, taken together with section 104, affect his inclusion in or exclusion from income of the amount he receives on account of medical expenses? What result to Sam of the compensation for the loss of his fingers?

In the alternative, suppose Sam's employer pays for his medical insurance premiums. Does that change in facts affect Sam's obligation to include in or his right to exclude from income the amount he receives for medical expenses and/or compensation for the loss of his fingers?

––––––––––––

This chapter has not, of course, exhausted the list of exclusions. Rather, we have looked at some of the exclusions that are most important to the individual taxpayer.[48] Among other exclusions that are of interest to a significant number of taxpayers is the exclusion of interest on certain bonds issued by municipal governments or agencies, the exclusion of certain scholarships, and the exclusion of foster care expenses. It is not necessary to examine in this introductory course every exclusion contained in Part III of Subchapter B. (We will, however, touch on a few additional ones in the transactional problem section of this book.) But note, once again, the organization of the Code. Also note, most importantly, that each of these items represents gross income under the three-prong *Glenshaw Glass* test and would be includible in section 61 Gross Income had Congress not specifically chosen to exclude the item from income. But remember: exclusions (like deductions, which we will cover next), are a matter of legislative grace, and what Congress giveth, Congress can taketh away!

––––––––––––

48. Along the way, you also began to learn the important skill of reading statutes and regulations.

Chapter 3

Deductions

Introduction and Problem

Exclusions are, as their designation implies, items that as a result of Congressional fiat are not included in a taxpayer's gross income. In contrast, deductions are, as their designation implies, items that a taxpayer subtracts from her gross income to arrive, first, at adjusted gross income, and, second, at taxable income. Therefore, while both exclusions and deductions in effect reduce both the adjusted gross income and the taxable income of the taxpayer, exclusions come before the calculation of gross income, reduce the amount of a taxpayer's gross income,[1] and are not part of the taxing formula. In contrast, deductions do not reduce gross income; they are subtracted from it. These items, frequently, at least in the case of a cash basis taxpayer,[2] consist of cash expenditures.

---

1. For example, Code section 61(a)(2) requires an inclusion in "gross income of gross income derived from business." Treasury Regulation section 1.61-3(a) provides that gross income means total sales, less the cost of goods sold." Thus, cost-of-goods sold (of principal concern to taxpayers who manufacture goods) is an exclusion for business taxpayers and reduces the business taxpayer's gross income. A similar rule applies to inventory. *See infra, Smith v. Commissioner*, 9 T.C. 1150 (1947).

2. What is a "cash basis taxpayer"? Recall our discussions regarding "timing" issues. Section 441 of the Code, in essence, codifies the rule set forth in *Burnet v. Sanford & Brooks Co.* that a taxpayer must compute taxable income based on her "taxable year" consisting of an annual accounting period. Section 441, however, does not specify how a taxpayer determines to which taxable year she assigns items of income and deduction. (This process of assigning items of income and deduction to particular taxable periods is known generally as "tax accounting.") Section 446 specifies the methods that taxpayers may use (the "permissible methods") to account for items of income and deduction.

One of the permissible methods of accounting section 446(c) specifies is the cash receipts and disbursements method." Treasury Regulation section 1.446-1(c)(1)(i) provides that "under the cash receipts and disbursements method ... all items which constitute gross income (whether in the form of cash, property, or services) are to be included for the taxable year in which actually ... received. Expenditures are to be deducted for the taxable year in which actually made." Thus, the cash method of accounting, the simplest of tax accounting methods, used by the majority of individual taxpayers, follows a simple cash in/cash out approach.

The other common permissible method of accounting is the accrual method. Taxpayers who use this method account for income ("accrue income") as soon as all the events have occurred that fix the right to receive the income and the amount of the income can be determined with reasonable accuracy." They account for expenses ("accrue expenses") when "all the events have occurred that establish the fact of the liability, the liability can be determined with reasonable accuracy, and economic performance has occurred with respect to the liability." *See* Treasury Regulation section 1.446-1(c)(1)(ii). Thus, cash flow in or out is irrelevant for accrual method accounting. Many busi-

A number of different rationales have prompted Congress to enact a variety of deductions. Some of these rationales enjoy widespread support, *e.g.*, deducting the cost of earning income from the income. Most people would agree that a business should be able to deduct from income the expenses paid or incurred to produce it.

———————

Suppose, for example, that your business is as a lawyer in private practice. You charge a client $1,000 for a will, but the cost of producing the will includes the salary you paid to your secretary in the amount of $250, the rent you paid to maintain your office in the amount of $150, and stationery supplies that cost you $15. How much "income" should you be taxed on for the will? What is your actual accession to wealth?

Section 162(a) of the Code, which allows taxpayers to deduct expenses attributable to a trade or business, would allow the attorney in the example described above to deduct $415 from the $1,000 fee as the expenses required to produce the income. **Read section 162(a).** Thus, the attorney's accession to wealth is $1,000 minus $415, or $585.

Section 212 allows taxpayers similar deductions for their expenses attributable to earning income from various investment activities. Suppose, for example, the same lawyer rents a house to a tenant who pays you rent of $750 per month. **Look at section 212.**[3] But the costs of maintaining the house are $75 for monthly lawn service, $100 for real estate taxes, and $10 for water.[4]

On the other hand, section 262 states that a taxpayer may not deduct the cost of "personal, living, or family expenses." **Read section 262.** Thus, in general, a taxpayer may only deduct expenses that are directly associated with a trade or business or with the production of income. Nevertheless, for various policy reasons, Congress has chosen to allow taxpayers to deduct certain personal expenses. Many of these personal expense deductions enjoy widespread support if they benefit a large number of taxpayers. For example, section 163(h)(3) allows a homeowner to deduct mortgage interest even though the expense is clearly a "personal, living, or family expense." Others of these personal expense deductions do not enjoy widespread support. Moreover, many tax policy experts argue that deductions for personal expenses defeat the integrity of the taxing system and represent unappropriated subsidies to favored taxpayers.[5]

———————

ness taxpayers use the accrual method, however, because it is a more accurate matching of the income and expenses of the business (and, in this respect, more closely resembles financial accounting than does the cash method).

We will study tax accounting issues in greater detail in Part IV, Chapter 1.

3. Note that section 212 provides an interesting deviation from the usual structure of a Code section. Most Code sections have subsections denominated "(a)," "(b)," "(c)," etc. In contrast, section 212's subsections are denominated by numbers, *i.e.*, "(1)," "(2)," and "(3)."

4. This amount does not, of course, take into account the cost of the property, *i.e.*, your investment in it. To recover that investment, you would also be permitted to claim deductions for depreciation. Ignore depreciation here.

5. Professor Stanley Surrey first named these "subsidies" "tax expenditures" when he was serving as Assistant Secretary of the Treasury for Tax Policy. Professor Surrey served from 1961 to 1969. In 1968, he oversaw the *Tax Expenditure Study*, published first in 1968 in the *Secretary of the Treasury Annual Report of the State of the Finances For Fiscal Year 1968* 326–340. Professor Surrey then wrote about the concept of tax expenditures in his article, "Federal Income Tax Reform: The Varied Approaches Necessary to Replace Tax Expenditures with Direct Governmental Assistance", 84 Harv. L. Rev. 352 (1970). We will examine the concept of tax expenditures in greater depth later in this chapter.

...

Legal and Litigation-Related Expenses

Petitioners claimed deductions under section 162 for legal fees, costs, and litigation-related expenses (hereinafter legal and litigation-related expenses) for taxable years 1983, 1984, 1985, 1986, and 1988. (Footnote 21) ... [R]espondent determined that, for taxable years 1985, 1986, and 1988, the deductions were improperly reported on Schedule C....

In deciding whether and to what extent the legal expenses and litigation-related expenses are deductible, we must consider the following issues: Initially, we must decide whether such expenses are deductible in general; ... and finally, we must decide whether any allowable deductions should be taken as itemized expenses.

We first consider the issue of the general deductibility of the legal and litigation-related expenses. We must consider the context in which the expenses are incurred. See secs. 162, 212, 262, 263. If the expenses relate to the taxpayer's employment, then the deductibility of the expenses will turn on whether the expenses were paid or incurred in the course of the taxpayer's business. Sec. 162. It is well settled that an individual may engage in the trade or business of rendering services as an employee. *O'Malley v. Commissioner*, 91 T.C. 352, 363–364 (1988); *Primuth v. Commissioner*, 54 T.C. 374, 377 (1970). Consequently, an employee's business expenses may be deductible under section 162. *O'Malley v. Commissioner*, *supra* at 363–364; *Primuth v. Commissioner*, *supra* at 377–378; ... It makes no difference whether the employee is defending himself in actions that challenge his activities as a corporate officer or the employee is bringing a suit against his former employer. (Footnote 23)

Petitioner's legal and litigation-related expenses were incurred in the course of carrying on his trade or business as a corporate executive at Ashland. Accordingly, petitioner's expenses are deductible, if at all, under section 162.... In the instant case, petitioner's expenses were incurred in the trade or business of being an employee....

...

We next consider the issue of whether petitioners' deductions must be itemized. Petitioners contend that, because the deductions were incurred in a trade or business, the deductions are not itemized deductions but instead are deductions which should be taken under section 162 to arrive at adjusted gross income. We disagree. Section 62, which defines adjusted gross income, lists the deductions from gross income which are allowed for the purpose of computing adjusted gross income. Section 62(1) states the general rule that trade or business deductions are allowed for the purpose of computing adjusted gross income only "if such trade or business does not consist of the performance of services by the taxpayer as an employee". (Footnote 27) Consequently, for employed individuals, section 162 trade and business deductions ordinarily are itemized deductions. Secs. 161 and 162.

... For taxable years beginning after 1986, for the purpose of computing adjusted gross income, section 62(a)(2) only allows employees (other than performing artists) deductions for reimbursed expenses.

To reiterate, petitioner was in the trade or business of being an employee.... [W]e hold that petitioners must itemize their deductions for legal and litigation-related expenses for 1984, 1985, 1986, and 1988 on Schedule A rather than on Schedule C. (Footnote 29)

Section 67(a) imposes a 2-percent floor on the miscellaneous itemized deductions of individuals for all taxable years beginning after December 31, 1986. Miscellaneous itemized deductions are defined in section 67(b) as those itemized deductions that are not specifically enumerated in section 67(b). As section 162 itemized deductions are not included in section 67(b), they are limited by the 2-percent floor. Sec. 1.67-1T(a)(1)(i), Temporary Income Tax Regs., 53 Fed. Reg. 9875 (Mar. 28, 1988). Accordingly, we further hold that petitioners' deductions for 1988 are limited by the 2-percent floor under section 67(a).

FOOTNOTES:

21. On their 1983 tax return, petitioners claimed these deductions as employee business expenses on Form 2106. For all other years in issue, petitioner claimed the deductions on Schedule C.

23. The cases do not distinguish between the situation in which a taxpayer is defending himself and the situation in which a taxpayer initiates the suit. The expenses are deductible under sec. 162 so long as the transaction or transactions subject to litigation arose in the context of the taxpayer's trade or business. See *Butler v. Commissioner*, 17 T.C. 675, 681 (1951) (litigation expenses for defending a corporate officer for actions directly connected with his employment are ordinary and necessary and therefore, deductible); *McKeague v. United States*, 12 Cl. Ct. 671 (1987) (litigation expenses for bringing suit against former employer for lost wages originated in trade or business and are deductible), affd. without published opinion 852 F.2d 1294 (Fed. Cir. 1988).

27. For taxable years beginning after Dec. 31, 1986, sec. 62(1) was renumbered as sec. 62(a)(1).

29. Nonetheless, as petitioner's 1983 business expenses are reimbursed employee expenses allowed under sec. 62(2)(A), they were properly deducted for the purpose of computing adjusted gross income, and were properly reported on Form 2106.

Consider the following additional questions about Carole's problem.

4. Does section 68 have any applicability to Carole?[12] **Read section 68.**

5. Every person is "born" with a personal exemption. At one time, the personal exemption was regarded as representing a subsistence amount of income to which a taxpayer was entitled free of income tax. As the cost of living has increased, however, Congress's increases to the amount of the personal exemption have failed to keep pace with those costs. Moreover, the original view that the personal exemption represents an amount of tax-free income available to every taxpayer has been eroded by the phase-out provision Congress added to the Code in 1990.[13]

What is the amount of Carole's *personal exemption* deduction for the current year? **Look at sections 151(a); 151(b); and 151(d)(1), (d)(3), and (d)(4).**[14] Notice that

---

12. Note that the 2001 Act provides for the gradual phase-out of the section 68 limitations on itemized deductions. Section 68 is scheduled to terminate in 2010.

13. This provision and the addition of section 68 were both part of the 1990 tax act which also increased the highest tax bracket from 28% to 31%. These tax increases, signed into law by President George Bush, may have helped defeat him in the 1992 election. You may recall his famous remark during the campaign: "Read my lips: no new taxes."

14. Note that the 2001 Act provides for the gradual phase-out of the section 151(d)(3) phase-out of the personal exemption amount. Section 151(d)(3) is scheduled to terminate in 2010.

the combination of the standard deduction and the personal exemption(s)[15] may eliminate a taxpayer's taxable income. That is, many low-income taxpayers are not subject to income tax at all after reducing their adjusted gross incomes by the standard deduction and the personal exemption.[16] Can you reconcile a personal exemption deduction with section 262(a)'s prohibition on the deductibility of personal living costs?

6. What is Carole's TI for the current year?

7. What is her *tentative tax liability* for the current year (assuming no credits)? In order to calculate her income tax liability you will have to separate any portion of her income that is subject to a special rate of tax applicable to net capital gain under section 1(h)(11). **Look at section 1(h)(11).** Might any item of Carole's income enjoy a special rate of tax? Do you need more information in order to determine her eligibility? Now that you have examined section 1(h)(11), assume for the purposes of your calculations that the dividend received by Carole is not "qualified dividend income."

8. Assume Carole's employer withheld $10,000 from her salary for federal income tax. Where does this withheld amount fit into the income tax calculation outline? **Examine section 31.**

9. What is her *FICA tax liability* for the current year?

10. What is Carole's *marginal rate* of tax? What is her *effective (average)* rate?

11. Would her marginal or effective rates of tax be higher or lower without sections 68 and 151(d)(3)? Based on your answer, how would you describe the effect of sections 68 and 151(d)(3) on Carole's rate of tax? Why do you think Congress chose to enact sections 68 and 151(d)(3) rather than to adjust the tax rate tables? Was enactment of these provisions a good policy choice?[17]

A. Personal Itemized Deductions

As noted above, section 262(a) provides that "no deduction shall be allowed for personal, living, or family expenses." The section begins, however, with the important phrase "Except as otherwise expressly provided in this chapter." In the problem we have just completed you examined briefly some of the exceptions to the general rule of section 262(a). Each of these exceptions represents a departure from the concept that deductions should only be allowed to the extent that they represent the costs of producing items of income.

---

15. Section 151(c) permits a taxpayer to claim an additional exemption for each "dependent" who meets certain other requirements. Section 152 defines a "dependent." **Look at sections 151(c) and 152.**

16. Remember that a taxpayer with earned income must pay the FICA or SECA tax described earlier without regard to income tax liability.

17. *See* footnotes 12 and 14, *supra*, describing the gradual phase-out and termination of sections 68 and 151(d)(3) in connection with questions 4 and 5, *supra*. In its *Study of the Overall State of the Federal Tax System and Recommendations for Simplification, Pursuant to section 8022(3)(B) of the Internal Revenue Code of 1986* (JCS-3-01), Apr. 2001 (hereinafter "*Study*"), the Staff of the Joint Committee on Taxation recommended the elimination of these phaseouts. *Study*, vol. 2 at 89.

In the sections that follow we will examine in greater detail several exceptions to the general rule of section 262(a). Remember that each of these provisions has the effect of reducing the amount of tax a taxpayer would otherwise pay. Therefore, as you go through these provisions, consider the policy reasons that supporters might advance in justification of their continuation, and opponents might advance in justification of their repeal.

For example, Code section 164 permits a taxpayer to deduct certain types of taxes, including state income taxes.[18] Can you suggest a policy reason for allowing a taxpayer to deduct state income tax before calculating federal taxable income? Another deduction important to many taxpayers is the deduction provided by section 219 for contributions to Individual Retirement Accounts. Can you speculate as to what policy dictates that the deductible amount is limited?

Professor Stanley Surrey first described the Code's preferential treatment of certain items as "tax expenditures" in 1967. Professors Surrey and McDaniel have defined the concept of a "tax expenditure" by first analyzing the two distinct elements of an income tax.

> The first element contains the structural provisions necessary for implementation of a normal income tax. These structural provisions include the definition of net income; the specification of accounting periods; the determination of the entities subject to tax; and the specification of the rate schedule and exemption levels. These provisions compose the revenue raising aspects of the tax.
> The second element consists of the special preferences found in every income tax system. These special preferences, often called tax incentives or tax subsidies, are departures from the normal tax structure, designed to favor a particular industry, activity, or class of persons. Tax subsidies partake of many forms, such as permanent exclusions from income, deductions, deferrals of tax liabilities, credits against tax, or special rates. Whatever their form, these departures from the "normative" income tax structure essentially represent government spending for the favored activities or groups through the tax system rather than through direct grants, loans, or other forms of government assistance.[19]

As a consequence of Professor Surrey's work, the Treasury Department published its first "tax expenditure" budget in 1968.[20] The Congressional Budget and Impoundment Control Act of 1974 directs the President to provide, as part of the annual budget presented to Congress, an estimate of "tax expenditures." The Treasury Department publishes its estimates of tax expenditures (as prepared by the Office of Management and budget) as part of the budget that the President submits to Congress.[21] The staff of the Joint Committee on Taxation prepares a separate estimate of tax expenditures for use by the House Ways and Means and Budget Committees and the Senate Finance and Budget Committees in connection with Congress's budget deliberations. The respective Executive and Congressional tax expenditure budgets detail the revenue the federal government foregoes each year as a result of preferential tax provisions.[22] Table 1 shows the Joint Committee's tax expenditure estimates for fiscal years 2006–2010.

---

18. We will examine the deductibility of real estate taxes in the context of a real estate transactional problem in Part VI.

19. Stanley S. Surrey and Paul R. McDaniel, "The Tax Expenditure Concept: Current Developments and Emerging Issues," 20 B.C. L. Rev. 225, 227–228 (1979).

20. *Secretary Of The Treasury Annual Report On The State Of The Finances For Fiscal Year 1968* 326–40 (1969).

21. *See, e.g.,* Office of Management and Budget, "Tax Expenditures," *in Budget of the United States Government: Analytical Perspectives Fiscal Year 2001*, 107–139, Feb. 7, 2000.

22. According to the Joint Committee on Taxation, the four largest tax expenditures for the 5-

Table 1.—Tax Expenditure Estimates by Budget Function, Fiscal Years 2006–2010
[Billions of dollars]

Function	Corporations					Individuals					Total 2006–10
	2006	2007	2008	2009	2010	2006	2007	2008	2009	2010	
National Defense											
Exclusion of benefits and allowances to Armed Forces personnel						2.8	2.8	2.9	3.0	3.0	14.5
Exclusion of military disablty benefits						0.1	0.1	0.1	0.1	0.1	0.4
Deduction for overnight-travel expenses of National Guard and Reserve Members						0.1	0.1	0.1	0.1	0.1	0.3
International Affairs											
Exclusion of income earned abroad by U.S. citizens						3.8	4.0	4.2	4.4	4.6	21.0
Exclusion of certain allowances for Federal employees abroad						0.6	0.6	0.7	0.7	0.8	3.4
Exclusion of extraterritorial income	3.9	1.9	0.1	0.1	0.1	0.1	(¹)	(¹)	(¹)	(¹)	6.2
Deferral of active income of controlled foreign corporations	3.4	5.8	6.4	7.0	7.5						30.1
Inventory property sales source rule exception	6.2	6.4	6.6	6.8	7.0						33.0
Deferral of certain active financing income	1.1	1.7									2.8
General Science, Space, and Technology											
Expensing of research and experimental expenditures	2.0	3.7	5.5	6.0	5.8	(¹)	0.1	0.1	0.1	0.1	29.4
Energy											
Expensing of exploration and development costs:											
Oil and gas	1.1	1.6	1.2	0.8	0.6	(¹)	(¹)	(¹)	(¹)	(¹)	5.4
Other fuels	(¹)	(¹)	(¹)	(¹)	(¹)	(¹)	(¹)	(¹)	(¹)	(¹)	0.2
Excess of percentage over cost depletion:											
Oil and gas	1.0	1.0	0.9	0.9	0.9	(¹)	(¹)	(¹)	(¹)	(¹)	4.7
Other fuels	0.1	0.1	0.1	0.1	0.1	(²)	(¹)	(¹)	(¹)	(¹)	0.6
Tax credit and deduction for small refiners with capital costs associated with EPA sulfur regulation compliance	(¹)	(¹)	(¹)	(¹)	(¹)						0.1
Tax credit for production of non-conventional fuels	2.7	3.2	1.2	(¹)	(¹)	1.0	1.0	0.2	(¹)	(¹)	8.8
Tax credit for alcohol fuels [2]	(¹)	(¹)	(¹)	(¹)	(¹)						0.2
Tax credit for biodiesel fuels [3]	(¹)	0.1	0.1	(¹)							0.2
Exclusion of interest on State and local government qualified private activity bonds for energy production facilities	(¹)	(¹)	(¹)	(¹)	(¹)	0.1	0.1	0.1	0.1	0.1	0.5
Exclusion of energy conservation subsidies provided by public utilities						(¹)	(¹)	(¹)	(¹)	(¹)	0.1
Energy credit (Section 48)	(¹)	0.1	(¹)	(¹)	(¹)	(¹)	(¹)	(¹)	(¹)	(¹)	0.2
Tax credit for electricity production from renewable resources	2.0	3.7	5.5	6.0	5.8	0.1	0.1	0.1	0.1	0.1	29.4
Deferral of gain from the disposition of electric transmission property to implement Federal Energy Regulatory Commission restructuring policy	0.6	0.5	(⁴)	-0.3	-0.3						0.4
Tax credit for holders of clean renewable energy bonds	(¹)	(¹)	(¹)	(¹)	(¹)	(¹)	(¹)	(¹)	(¹)	(¹)	0.2
Tax credits for investments in clean coal power generation facilities	(¹)	0.1	0.1	0.2	0.2						0.5
Expensing of the cost of property used in the refining of liquid fuels	(¹)	(¹)	0.1	0.2	0.3						0.7
Amortization of geological and geophysical costs associated with oil and gas exploration	(⁴)	0.1	0.2	0.2	0.1	(⁴)	(¹)	0.1	0.1	(¹)	0.8
Deduction for expenditures on energy-efficient commercial building property	(¹)	0.1	(¹)	(⁴)	(⁴)	(¹)	0.1	(¹)	(⁴)	(⁴)	0.3
Tax credit for the purchase of qualified energy efficiency improvements to existing homes						0.1	0.3	0.2			0.6
Tax credit for the production of energy-efficient appliances	0.1	0.1									0.2
Tax credits for alternative technology vehicles	0.1	0.1	(¹)	(¹)	(¹)	0.2	0.2	0.1	0.1	(¹)	0.8

Table 1.—Tax Expenditure Estimates by Budget Function, Fiscal Years 2006–2010—Continued
[Billions of dollars]

Function	Corporations					Individuals					Total 2006–10
	2006	2007	2008	2009	2010	2006	2007	2008	2009	2010	
Tax credit for clean-fuel vehicle refueling property	[1]	[1]	[1]	[1]	[1]	[1]	[1]	[1]	[1]	[1]	0.1
Five-year carryback period for certain net operating losses of electric utility companies	0.1	[1]	[1]	[4]	[4]						0.1
Natural Resources and Environment											
Expensing of exploration and development costs, nonfuel minerals	0.1	0.1	0.1	0.1	0.1	[1]	[1]	[1]	[1]	[1]	0.4
Excess of percentage over cost depletion, nonfuel minerals	0.1	0.1	0.1	0.1	0.1	0.1	0.1	0.1	0.1	0.1	1.0
Expensing of timber-growing costs	0.2	0.2	0.2	0.2	0.2	[1]	[1]	[1]	[1]	[1]	1.1
Exclusion of interest on State and local government qualified private activity bonds for sewage, water, and hazardous waste facilities	0.2	0.2	0.2	0.2	0.2	0.4	0.4	0.5	0.5	0.5	3.3
Special rules for mining reclamation reserves	[1]	[1]	[1]	[1]	[1]	[1]	[1]	[1]	[1]	[1]	0.2
Special tax rate for nuclear decommissioning reserve funds	0.5	0.6	0.7	0.8	0.8						3.4
Exclusion of contributions in aid of construction for water and sewer utilities	[1]	[1]	[1]	[1]	[1]						0.2
Amortization of certified pollution control facilities	[1]	[1]	0.1	0.1	0.1						0.3
Amortization and expensing of reforestation expenditures	[1]	[1]	[1]	[1]	[1]	0.1	0.1	0.1	0.1	0.1	0.6
Agriculture											
Expensing of soil and water conservation expenditures	[1]	[1]	[1]	[1]	[1]	[1]	[1]	[1]	[1]	[1]	0.2
Expensing of fertilizer and soil conditioner costs	[1]	[1]	[1]	[1]	[1]	0.2	0.1	0.1	0.1	0.1	0.7
Expensing of the costs of raising dairy and breeding cattle	[1]	[1]	[4]	[4]	[1]	0.1	[1]	[4]	[4]	[1]	0.2
Exclusion of cost-sharing payments	[1]	[1]	[1]	[1]	[1]	[1]	[1]	[1]	[1]	[1]	0.1
Exclusion of cancellation of indebtedness income of farmers						0.1	0.1	0.1	0.1	0.1	0.4
Income averaging for farmers and fishermen						[1]	[1]	[1]	[1]	[1]	0.1
Five-year carryback period for net operating losses attributable to farming	[1]	[1]	[1]	[1]	[1]	[1]	[1]	[1]	[1]	[1]	0.1
Commerce and Housing											
Financial institutions:											
Exemption of credit union income	1.7	1.8	1.9	2.0	2.1						9.3
Insurance companies:											
Exclusion of investment income on life insurance and annuity contracts	2.5	2.5	2.6	2.7	2.7	25.5	26.1	26.8	27.5	28.2	147.1
Small life insurance company taxable income adjustment	0.1	0.1	0.1	0.1	0.1						0.3
Special treatment of life insurance company reserves	1.9	2.0	2.0	2.1	2.2						10.2
Deduction of unpaid property loss reserves for property and casualty insurance companies	3.4	3.4	3.5	3.6	3.6						17.5
Special deduction for Blue Cross and Blue Shield companies	0.9	1.0	1.0	1.0	1.0						5.0
Housing:											
Deduction for mortgage interest on owner-occupied residences						69.4	75.6	80.7	85.9	91.1	402.7
Deduction for property taxes on owner-occupied residences						19.9	13.8	13.5	13.4	13.2	73.8
Exclusion of capital gains on sales of principal residences						24.1	25.2	25.7	26.3	27.1	128.4
Exclusion of interest on State and local government qualified private activity bonds for owner-occupied housing	0.3	0.4	0.4	0.4	0.4	0.9	1.0	1.0	1.1	1.1	7.0

Table 1.—Tax Expenditure Estimates by Budget Function, Fiscal Years 2006–2010—Continued
[Billions of dollars]

Function	Corporations					Individuals					Total 2006–10
	2006	2007	2008	2009	2010	2006	2007	2008	2009	2010	
Exclusion of interest on State and local government qualified private activity bonds for rental housing	0.2	0.2	0.2	0.2	0.2	0.5	0.5	0.5	0.6	0.6	3.7
Depreciation of rental housing in excess of alternative depreciation system	0.4	0.5	0.6	0.7	0.8	4.0	4.6	5.3	6.1	7.0	29.9
Tax credit for low-income housing	3.4	3.6	3.8	4.1	4.4	1.4	1.5	1.6	1.7	1.9	27.4
Tax credit for rehabilitation of historic structures	0.3	0.3	0.3	0.3	0.3	0.1	0.1	0.1	0.1	0.1	2.2
Tax credit for rehabilitation of structures, other than historic structures	(1)	(1)	(1)	(1)	(1)	0.1	0.1	0.1	0.1	0.1	0.5
Additional exemption for housing provided to individuals displaced by Hurricane Katrina	.....	.....	.....	.....	.....	0.1	(1)	.....	.....	.....	0.1
Tax credit for Gulf Opportunity Zone employers providing in-kind lodging for employees and income exclusion for the employees	0.1	(1)	.....	.....	.....	0.1	(1)	.....	.....	.....	0.2
Other business and commerce:											
Reduced rates of tax on dividends and long-term capital gains	.....	.....	.....	.....	.....	92.2	94.5	101.7	99.6	50.2	438.1
Exclusion of capital gains at death	.....	.....	.....	.....	.....	50.9	51.9	53.2	69.7	64.5	290.2
Carryover basis of capital gains on gifts	.....	.....	.....	.....	.....	5.4	5.5	5.7	7.6	56.1	80.3
Deferral of gain on non-dealer installment sales	0.6	0.7	0.7	0.7	0.8	0.5	0.5	0.5	0.6	0.6	6.2
Deferral of gain on like-kind exchanges	2.0	2.1	2.2	2.4	2.5	0.8	0.8	0.9	0.8	1.0	15.5
Depreciation of buildings other than rental housing in excess of alternative depreciation system	0.4	0.6	0.8	1.1	1.4	0.4	0.5	0.7	1.0	1.3	8.3
Depreciation of equipment in excess of the alternative depreciation system	5.7	11.0	17.7	23.4	27.7	-2.2	0.1	2.2	4.3	6.1	96.0
Expensing under section 179 of depreciable business property	0.6	0.6	-0.1	-0.4	-0.2	2.8	2.6	0.1	-0.8	-0.4	4.8
Amortization of business startup costs	(1)	(1)	(1)	(1)	(1)	0.7	0.7	0.8	0.8	0.9	3.9
Reduced rates on first $10,000,000 of corporate taxable income	4.3	4.3	4.3	4.3	4.3	.....	.....	.....	.....	.....	21.6
Permanent exemption from imputed interest rules	(1)	(1)	(1)	(1)	(1)	0.4	0.4	0.4	0.4	0.5	2.1
Expensing of magazine circulation expenditures	(1)	(1)	(1)	(1)	(1)	(1)	(1)	(1)	(1)	(1)	0.1
Special rules for magazine, paperback book, and record returns	(1)	(1)	(1)	(1)	(1)	(1)	(1)	(1)	(1)	(1)	0.2
Completed contract rules	0.3	0.3	0.4	0.4	0.5	(1)	(1)	(1)	(1)	(1)	1.9
Cash accounting, other than agriculture	(1)	(1)	(1)	(1)	(1)	0.8	0.8	0.8	0.9	0.9	4.2
Exclusion of interest on State and local government small-issue qualified private activity bonds	0.1	0.1	0.1	0.1	0.1	0.3	0.3	0.3	0.4	0.4	2.3
Exception from net operating loss limitations for corporations in bankruptcy proceedings	0.6	0.6	0.6	0.6	0.6	.....	.....	.....	.....	.....	3.0
Tax credit for employer-paid FICA taxes on tips	0.2	0.2	0.2	0.2	0.3	0.3	0.4	0.4	0.4	0.5	3.1
Deduction of certain film and television production costs	0.1	0.1	0.1	(1)	(1)	(1)	(1)	(1)	(1)	(1)	0.3
Production activity deduction	2.7	3.9	5.5	5.9	7.4	0.9	1.3	1.8	2.0	2.6	34.0
Tax credit for the cost of carrying tax-paid distilled spirits in wholesale inventories	(1)	(1)	(1)	(1)	(1)	.....	.....	.....	.....	.....	0.1
Partial expensing of Gulf Opportunity Zone clean-up costs	(1)	(1)	(1)	(4)	(4)	(1)	(1)	(1)	(4)	(4)	0.1
Additional first-year depreciation for Gulf Opportunity Zone property	0.9	0.9	0.4	-0.1	-0.2	0.4	0.4	0.2	(4)	-0.1	2.9
Ten-year carryback period for casualty losses of public utility property attributable to Hurricane Katrina	0.2	(1)	(4)	(4)	(4)	.....	.....	.....	.....	.....	0.2

DEDUCTIONS

Table 1.—Tax Expenditure Estimates by Budget Function, Fiscal Years 2006–2010—Continued
[Billions of dollars]

Function	Corporations					Individuals					Total 2006–10
	2006	2007	2008	2009	2010	2006	2007	2008	2009	2010	
Five-year carryback period for casualty losses of public utility property attributable to Hurricane Katrina	0.1	(1)	(4)	(4)	(4)						0.1
Five-year carryback period for losses attributable to various expenses related to Hurricane Katrina	1.0	0.3	−0.1	−0.2	−0.2						0.9
Tax credit for employers for retention of employees affected by Hurricanes Katrina, Rita, and Wilma	(1)	(1)	(1)	(1)	(1)	(1)	(1)	(1)	(1)		0.2
Transportation											
Exclusion of interest on State and local government qualified private activity bonds for highway projects and rail-truck transfer facilities	(1)	(1)	(1)	(1)	(1)	(1)	(1)	(1)	(1)	(1)	0.1
Provide a 50-percent tax credit for certain expenditures for maintaining railroad tracks	0.1	0.1	0.1	0.1	(1)						0.4
Deferral of tax on capital construction funds of shipping companies	0.1	0.1	0.1	0.1	0.1						0.4
Exclusion of employer-paid transportation benefits						4.2	4.3	4.4	4.5	4.7	22.1
Community and Regional Development											
New York City Liberty Zone tax incentives	0.4	0.2	0.1	(4)	−0.1	−0.1	0.2	0.1	0.2	0.1	1.0
Empowerment zone tax incentives	0.3	0.4	0.4	0.4	0.2	0.4	0.4	0.4	0.5	0.3	3.7
Renewal community tax incentives	0.2	0.2	0.2	0.2	0.2	0.3	0.4	0.4	0.4	0.3	2.9
New markets tax credit	0.2	0.3	0.4	0.3	0.3	0.3	0.4	0.5	0.5	0.4	3.7
Exclusion of interest on State and local qualified private activity bonds for green buildings and sustainable design projects	(1)	(1)	(1)	(1)	(1)	(1)	(1)	(1)	(1)	(1)	0.1
Exclusion of interest on State and local government qualified private activity bonds for private airports, docks, and mass-commuting facilities	0.3	0.3	0.3	0.3	0.4	0.7	0.8	0.8	0.9	0.9	5.8
Education, Training, Employment, and Social Services											
Education and training:											
Tax credits for tuition for post-secondary education						4.9	5.2	5.1	5.0	5.0	25.2
Deduction for interest on student loans						0.8	0.9	0.9	0.9	1.0	4.5
Exclusion of tax on earnings of Coverdell education savings accounts						0.1	0.1	0.1	0.2	0.2	0.7
Exclusion of interest on educational savings bonds						(1)	(1)	(1)	(1)	(1)	0.1
Exclusion of tax on earnings of qualified tuition programs						0.7	0.8	0.9	1.0	1.0	4.3
Exclusion of scholarship and fellowship income						1.5	1.6	1.7	1.8	1.9	8.5
Exclusion of income attributable to the discharge of certain student loan debt and NHSC Educational Loan repayments						(1)	(1)	(1)	(1)	(1)	0.1
Exclusion of employer-provided education assistance benefits						0.8	0.9	0.9	0.9	0.9	4.4
Exclusion of employer-provided tuition reduction benefits						0.2	0.2	0.2	0.2	0.2	1.0
Parental personal exemption for students age 19 to 23						0.5	0.2	0.2	0.1	(1)	1.0
Exclusion of interest on State and local government qualified private activity bonds for student loans	0.1	0.1	0.1	0.1	0.1	0.3	0.3	0.3	0.4	0.4	2.3
Exclusion of interest on State and local government qualified private activity bonds for private nonprofit and qualified public educational facilities	0.4	0.5	0.5	0.5	0.5	1.1	1.2	1.2	1.3	1.3	8.4

Table 1.—Tax Expenditure Estimates by Budget Function, Fiscal Years 2006-2010—Continued
[Billions of dollars]

Function	Corporations					Individuals					Total 2006-10
	2006	2007	2008	2009	2010	2006	2007	2008	2009	2010	
Tax credit for holders of qualified zone academy bonds	0.1	0.1	0.1	0.1	0.1						0.5
Deduction for charitable contributions to educational institutions	0.7	0.7	0.7	0.8	0.8	5.3	5.9	6.3	6.8	7.1	35.1
Employment:											
Exclusion of employee meals and lodging (other than military)						0.9	0.9	0.9	1.0	1.0	4.9
Exclusion of benefits provided under cafeteria plans[5]						27.9	30.6	33.4	36.6	40.0	168.5
Exclusion of housing allowances for ministers						0.5	0.5	0.5	.0.6	0.6	2.7
Exclusion of miscellaneous fringe benefits						6.6	6.8	7.0	7.2	7.7	35.2
Exclusion of employee awards						0.2	0.2	0.2	0.2	0.2	0.9
Exclusion of income earned by voluntary employees' beneficiary associations						3.3	3.4	3.5	3.7	3.8	17.6
Special tax provisions for employee stock ownership plans (ESOPs)	0.8	0.9	0.9	1.0	1.1	0.3	0.3	0.3	0.3	0.3	6.2
Work opportunity tax credit	0.2	0.1	0.1	[1]	[1]	[1]	[1]	[1]	[1]	[1]	0.8
Welfare-to-work tax credit	[1]	[1]	[1]	[1]	[1]	[1]	[1]	[1]	[1]		0.2
Deferral of taxation and capital gains treatment on spread on acquisition of stock under incentive stock option plans and employee stock purchase plans[6]						0.4	0.4	0.4	0.2	0.1	1.5
Social services:											
Tax credit for children under age 17[7]						46.0	45.9	46.1	46.0	46.0	230.0
Tax credit for child and dependent care and exclusion of employer-provided child care[8]						3.1	2.7	2.7	2.6	2.5	13.5
Tax credit for employer-provided dependent care	[1]	[1]	[1]	[1]	[1]	[1]	[1]	[1]	[1]	[1]	0.2
Exclusion of certain foster care payments						0.6	0.6	0.7	0.7	0.8	3.4
Adoption credit and employee adoption benefits exclusion						0.4	0.5	0.5	0.5	0.5	2.4
Deduction for charitable contributions, other than for education and health	1.7	1.7	1.7	1.8	1.8	29.1	31.9	34.2	36.8	38.4	179.1
Tax credit for disabled access expenditures	[1]	[1]	[1]	[1]	[1]	0.1	0.1	0.1	0.1	0.1	0.4
Health											
Exclusion of employer contributions for health care, health insurance premiums, and long-term care insurance premiums[9]						90.6	99.7	107.0	114.5	122.2	534.0
Exclusion of medical care and TRICARE medical insurance for military dependents, retirees, and retiree dependents						1.9	2.0	2.1	2.3	2.5	10.9
Deduction for health insurance premiums and long-term care insurance premiums by the self-employed						3.8	4.2	4.5	4.9	5.2	22.6
Deduction for medical expenses and long-term care expenses						7.3	8.2	9.5	10.7	12.1	47.8
Exclusion of workers' compensation benefits (medical benefits)						6.5	6.9	7.4	8.0	8.5	37.3
Health savings accounts						0.1	0.3	0.6	0.9	1.2	3.2
Exclusion of interest on State and local government qualified private activity bonds for private nonprofit hospital facilities	0.6	0.7	0.7	0.8	0.8	1.7	1.8	1.9	2.0	2.1	13.1
Deduction for charitable contributions to health organizations	0.8	0.8	0.9	0.9	0.9	3.7	4.0	4.3	4.7	4.8	25.8
Tax credit for orphan drug research	0.2	0.3	0.3	0.3	0.3						1.4
Tax credit for purchase of health insurance by certain displaced persons						0.2	0.2	0.2	0.2	0.3	1.2
Medicare											
Exclusion of Medicare benefits:											
Hospital insurance (Part A)						18.5	20.7	22.5	24.5	26.7	112.9
Supplementary medical insurance (Part B)						12.5	14.2	15.4	16.7	18.1	76.9

DEDUCTIONS

Table 1.—Tax Expenditure Estimates by Budget Function, Fiscal Years 2006–2010—Continued
[Billions of dollars]

Function	Corporations					Individuals					Total 2006-10
	2006	2007	2008	2009	2010	2006	2007	2008	2009	2010	
Prescription drug insurance (Part D)						3.4	6.2	7.5	8.3	9.5	34.9
Exclusion of certain subsidies to employers who maintain prescription drug plans for Medicare enrollees	0.7	1.2	1.4	1.5	1.6						6.3
Income Security											
Exclusion of workers' compensation benefits (disability and survivors payments)						2.5	2.6	2.7	2.7	2.8	13.2
Exclusion of damages on account of personal physical injuries or physical sickness						1.4	1.5	1.5	1.5	1.5	7.4
Exclusion of special benefits for disabled coal miners						0.1	0.1	(¹)	(¹)	(¹)	0.2
Exclusion of cash public assistance benefits						3.4	3.6	3.7	3.9	4.0	18.6
Net exclusion of pension contributions and earnings:											
Employer plans						104.1	110.2	115.2	120.8	126.7	577.1
Individual retirement plans						11.2	14.0	15.5	16.9	18.4	76.0
Plans covering partners and sole proprietors (sometimes referred to as "Keogh plans")						9.4	10.3	10.8	11.3	11.6	53.4
Tax credit for certain individuals for elective deferrals and IRA contributions						0.9	0.6	(¹)			1.5
Tax credit for new retirement plan expenses of small businesses	(¹)	(¹)	(¹)	(¹)	(¹)	(¹)	(¹)	(¹)	(¹)	(¹)	0.1
Exclusion of other employee benefits:											
Premiums on group term life insurance						2.5	2.6	2.6	2.7	2.7	13.1
Premiums on accident and disability insurance						2.6	2.8	2.9	3.0	3.1	14.4
Additional standard deduction for the blind and the elderly						1.6	1.6	1.7	1.7	1.8	8.4
Tax credit for the elderly and disabled						(¹)	(¹)	(¹)	(¹)	(¹)	0.1
Deduction for casualty and theft losses						0.7	0.8	0.3	0.3	0.3	2.4
Earned income credit (EIC)						42.1	42.8	43.5	44.5	45.4	218.3
Exclusion of cancellation of indebtedness income of Hurricane Katrina victims						0.2	0.1				0.3
Social Security and Railroad Retirement											
Exclusion of untaxed social security and railroad retirement benefits						23.1	24.1	24.8	25.9	27.2	125.1
Veterans' Benefits and Services											
Exclusion of veterans' disability compensation						3.6	3.8	3.9	4.0	4.0	19.2
Exclusion of veterans' pensions						0.1	0.1	0.1	0.1	0.1	0.6
Exclusion of veterans' readjustment benefits						0.2	0.3	0.3	0.3	0.3	1.3
Exclusion of interest on State and local government qualified private activity bonds for veterans' housing	(¹)	(¹)	(¹)	(¹)	(¹)	(¹)	(¹)	(¹)	(¹)	(¹)	0.3
General Purpose Fiscal Assistance											
Exclusion of interest on public purpose State and local government bonds	7.3	7.8	8.2	8.6	9.0	18.7	20.1	21.1	22.1	23.1	146.0
Deduction of nonbusiness State and local government income, sales, and personal property taxes (¹⁰)						36.8	27.3	27.3	28.1	28.9	148.5
Tax credit for Puerto Rico and possession income, and Puerto Rico economic activity	0.3										0.3
Interest											
Deferral of interest on savings bonds						1.1	1.1	1.2	1.2	1.2	5.8

¹ Positive tax expenditure of less than $50 million.
² In addition, the credit from excise tax for alcohol fuels results in a reduction in excise tax receipts, net of income tax effect, of $11.1 billion over the fiscal years 2006 through 2010.
³ In addition, the credit from excise tax for biodiesel results in a reduction in excise tax receipts, net of income tax effect, of less than $50 million in each of the fiscal years 2006 through 2010.
⁴ Negative tax expenditure of less than $50 million.
⁵ Estimate includes amounts of employer-provided health insurance purchased through cafeteria plans and employer-provided child care purchased through dependent care flexible spending accounts. These amounts are also included in other line items in this table.
⁶ Tax expenditure estimate does not include offsetting denial of corporate deduction for qualified stock option compensation.
⁷ Tax expenditure estimate includes refundable amounts, amounts used to offset income taxes, and amounts used to offset other taxes. The amount of refundable child tax credit and earned income tax credit used to offset taxes other than income tax or paid out as refunds is: $50.1 billion in 2006, $51.5 billion in 2007, $51.4 billion in 2008, $52.2 billion in 2009, and $53.2 in 2010.
⁸ Estimate includes employer-provided child care purchased through dependent care flexible spending accounts.
⁹ Estimate includes employer-provided health insurance purchased through cafeteria plans.
¹⁰ Deduction for state and local sales taxes expires after December 31, 2005.
Note.—Details may not add to totals due to rounding.
Source: Joint Committee on Taxation.

Not all commentators, however, agree with the Surrey-McDaniel view. They argue that because there are no universally agreed-upon structural models, there is no such thing as a "normative income tax structure."[23]

Consider the following questions.

1. How can an exclusion from income or a deduction "represent government spending"?[24]

2. Congress both enacts the special so-called tax expenditure provisions of the Code and all direct spending bills. Why then, would Congress choose to benefit favored activities or groups through one method rather than the other? Consider the following article that appeared in the New York Times, on July 21, 1999, during the debate in the House concerning the Republican-proposed tax reductions in July of 1999:

The Fine Print: The Tax Bills; When Lawmakers Look Homeward[25]

Buried deep in the giant tax-cut bill that the Senate Finance Committee began debating today is fine print that could turn chicken droppings into a tax shelter.

On the other side of the Capitol, the House of Representatives is planning to vote on Wednesday on a companion bill that includes a section removing the excise tax on fishing-tackle boxes.

Like most other tax bills before Congress in recent years, the measures in the Senate and House this year contain dozens of narrow provisions like these benefitting one particular interest or another B or, to put it another way, benefitting one particular constituent or another of an important Senator or Representative.

In the case of the chicken droppings, the important lawmaker is Senator William V. Roth Jr., the Delaware Republican who is the chairman of the Finance Committee. The nugget he inserted in the Senate bill would give tax credits to companies that convert waste from chicken coops into electricity.

This has long been a dream on the Delmarva Peninsula—Delaware and the eastern shore of Maryland and Virginia—where chicken farming is the largest agricultural en-

---

year period spanning FY 2006–2010 are: $577.1 billion for the exclusion from gross income of pension contributions and earnings in employer plans; $534 billion for the exclusion from gross income of employer-provided health care benefits; $438.1 billion for the reduced rate of tax on dividends and long-term capital gains; and $402.7 billion for the deduction of mortgage interest on owner-occupied residences. Table 1, Joint Committee on Taxation, *Estimates of Federal Tax Expenditures for Fiscal Years 2006–2010* (JCS-2-06), April 26, 2006.

23. *See, e.g.,* Douglas A. Kahn and Jeffrey S. Lehman, "Tax Expenditures Budgets: A Critical View," 54 Tax Notes 1661 (1992); *and* Boris I. Bittker, "Accounting for Federal 'Tax Subsidies' in the National Budget," 22 Nat'l Tax J. 244 (1969).

24. To assist you in answering this question, you may wish to read Roberta F. Mann, "The (Not So) Little House on the Prairie: The Hidden Costs of the Home Mortgage Interest Deduction," 32 Ariz. St. L.J. 1347 (2000).

25. David E. Rosenbaum, "The Fine Print: The Tax Bills; When Lawmakers Look Homeward," N.Y. Times, July 21, 1999, at A18.

terprise and where producers like Perdue Farms and Tyson Foods have big processing plants and thousands of employees.

Nowadays, chicken droppings are used for fertilizer. But this has become a major source of pollution, and all three states have new laws that will eventually ban this source of fertilizer.

So the question ... is becoming how to dispose of the 800 tons of chicken droppings produced on the peninsula every year. The technology has long existed for producing electricity by burning chicken manure. The problem is that it has never seemed profitable, so it has never been tried in the United States.

A tax credit might help in this regard. But the chicken farmers and producers on the Delmarva Peninsula should not get their hopes up.

Representative Bill Archer of Texas, the Republican who is chairman of the House Ways and Means Committee, is not wild about the measure, staff assistants said, and will probably fight it in the conference committee to resolve differences between the Senate and House tax bills. The reason: The tax credit could put chicken droppings in competition with oil and gas as [a] source of energy.

In fact, Mr. Archer, whose district is in Houston, put into the House bill several tax breaks for his constituents in the petroleum industry. One, for example, allows more favorable tax treatment for Americans who have income from foreign oil and gas. Another allows new write-offs for wells that are marginally productive.

The tackle box provision in the House bill approved last week by the Ways and Means Committee owes its existence to Speaker J. Dennis Hastert. One of the nation's largest manufacturers of tackle boxes, the Plano Molding Company of Plano, Ill., is in Mr. Hastert's district.

For years the president of the company has been coming to Washington trying to persuade lawmakers to repeal the 10 percent excise tax on tackle boxes. He even hired a lobbyist....

But [they] had no success until this year, when Mr. Hastert became Speaker.

This is their argument: A 1984 law placed a 10 percent Federal tax on fishing equipment. The money goes into the Sport Fishing Account of the Aquatic Resources Trust Fund and is returned to the states to pay for hatcheries, water-safety measures and other sport fishing activities. The program is popular among fisherman.

Plano Molding's problem is that the plastic tackle boxes it makes are indistinguishable from containers made by other manufacturers that are called tool boxes or sewing boxes and are not subject to the tax. Side by side on a shelf at Walmart, Plano's boxes are more expensive, and the company believes that is unfair.

This argument may not carry in the Senate.

Besides Mr. Hastert's influence, Representative Jerry Weller, a Republican from an adjacent district in Illinois who has many constituents who work for [Plano Molding] is a member of the Ways and Means Committee.

But [the lobbyist] said he had not been able to get a comparable provision in the Senate bill. The Finance Committee has no members from Illinois. And no one on the panel ... was prepared to take on the cause of Plano Molding.

That may have been because they were too busy taking care of their own.

For example, Senator Frank H. Murkowski, a Republican, was able to get several tax breaks for his constituents in Alaska.

One would exempt Alaskans from the requirement that dye be put in diesel fuel.

Under Federal law, all other distributors of diesel fuel must dye it to distinguish it from home heating oil, which is otherwise the same product. Diesel fuel is taxed as a motor fuel, and heating oil is not.

Alaskans contend that it is impractical for remote villages in Alaska to have two storage tanks, one with diesel fuel and the other with heating oil. But without the dye, collecting the proper tax on diesel fuel would be problematic.

Another Murkowski measure would allow Eskimo whaling captains to claim charitable deductions of up to $7,500 to offset the cost of whale hunts.

The argument is that the captains pick up the costs for people in their villages to go on whale hunts that are allowed under international whaling agreements. They then divide the whale meat, called muktuk, among the villagers, who rely on it for subsistence. Since the captains give the muktuk away, the argument goes, it should be treated no differently from any other charitable donation.

A similar measure was passed by the Senate in 1994 but died in the House. Environmentalists said it would encourage more whaling.

Professor Surrey was clearly motivated in part by a belief that requiring the preparation of the tax expenditure budget would expose to public scrutiny what he viewed as subsidies that should, instead, be measured against other direct spending programs of the government. But, even if he were correct in his view, has the publication of a tax expenditure budget had the desired educational effect? It may be that articles like the one reprinted above have a greater likelihood of informing the public than the preparation of the tax expenditure budget will have.

The cases and materials that follow are intended to provide you with more familiarity with the issues that arise under certain of these personal deduction provisions.

1. Extraordinary Expenses

Certain personal deduction provisions of the Code reflect the philosophy that when a taxpayer incurs involuntary extraordinary expenses, the funds she expends to cover the costs of these events have never been part of her discretionary disposable income. The Code, therefore, allows deductions for certain of these types of expenses, generally, in an amount in excess of a floor, as you earlier saw in Carole's case. We will examine two of the most common and important examples of this type of variation from the general rule that personal expenses are not deductible.

a. Section 213: Medical Expenses

Read section 213, focusing specifically on subsection (d)(1), and Treasury Regulation section 1.213-1(e) in connection with your consideration of the following revenue rulings, administrative advice, and case.

REVENUE RULING 73-200
1973-1 C.B. 140

A taxpayer purchased birth control pills for her personal use under a prescription provided by her physician.

Held, the amount expended for the birth control pills is an amount paid for medical care, as defined in section 213(e) of the Internal Revenue Code of 1954, and is deductible under section 213 of the Code subject to the limitations provided for therein.

Revenue Ruling 67-339, 1967-2 C.B. 126, which deals with the deductibility as a medical expense of the cost of oral contraceptives purchased by a taxpayer for his wife who almost died during childbirth, is hereby superseded, since its substance is incorporated in this Revenue Ruling.

REVENUE RULING 79-162
1979-1 C.B. 116

ISSUE

Is the cost of completing a course designed to help people stop smoking deductible under section 213 of the Internal Revenue Code of 1954?

FACTS

A, an individual, at the suggestion of *A*'s physician, participated in a nine-week program that consisted of weekly meetings designed to help cigarette smokers stop smoking by altering their personal habits that encouraged smoking. *A*'s participation in the program was not for the purpose of curing any specific ailment or disease, but for the purpose of improving *A*'s general health and sense of well being.

LAW AND ANALYSIS

Section 213 of the Code allows a deduction in computing taxable income for expenses paid during the taxable year, not compensated for by insurance or otherwise, for medical care of the taxpayer, the taxpayer's spouse, or a dependent, subject to certain limitations. The term "medical care" is defined to include amounts paid for the diagnosis, cure, mitigation, treatment, or prevention of disease, or for the purpose of affecting any structure or function of the body, or for transportation primarily for and essential to these purposes.

Section 1.213-1(e)(1)(ii) of the Income Tax Regulations provides, in part, that deductions for expenditures for medical care allowable under section 213 of the Code will be confined strictly to expenses incurred primarily for the prevention or alleviation of a physical or mental defect or illness. However, an expenditure which is merely beneficial to the general health of an individual is not an expenditure for medical care.

Section 262 of the Code provides that, except as otherwise expressly provided by the Code, no deduction shall be allowed for personal, living, or family expenses.

Rev. Rul. 55-261, 1955-1 C.B. 307, question 9 at page 310, holds that ordinarily, fees paid to a health institute where the taxpayer takes exercise, rubdowns, etc., are personal expenses. Such fees may be deductible as medical expenses only when the treatments by the institute are prescribed by a physician and are substantiated by a statement by the physician to be necessary for the alleviation of a physical or mental defect or illness of the individual receiving the treatment. Furthermore, Rev. Rul. 55-261, question 16 at page 312, holds that amounts expended for the preservation of general health or for the alleviation of a physical or mental discomfort that is unrelated to some particular disease or defect are not expenses for medical care.

HOLDING

A's cost for completing the program to stop smoking is not deductible as a medical expense under section 213 of the Code, but is an expense the deduction of which is prohibited by section 262.

REVENUE RULING 99-28

1999-1 C.B. 1269

ISSUE

Are uncompensated amounts paid by taxpayers for participation in a smoking-cessation program, for prescribed drugs designed to alleviate nicotine withdrawal, and for nicotine gum and nicotine patches that do not require a prescription, expenses for medical care that are deductible under § 213 of the Internal Revenue Code?

FACTS

Taxpayers A and B were cigarette smokers. A participated in a smoking-cessation program and purchased nicotine gum and nicotine patches that did not require a prescription. A had not been diagnosed as having any specific disease, and participation in the program was not suggested by a physician. B purchased drugs that required a prescription of a physician to alleviate the effects of nicotine withdrawal. A's and B's costs were not compensated for by insurance or otherwise.

LAW AND ANALYSIS

Section 213(a) allows a deduction for uncompensated expenses for medical care of an individual, the individual's spouse or a dependent to the extent the expenses exceed 7.5 percent of adjusted gross income. Section 213(d)(1) provides, in part, that medical care means amounts paid for the diagnosis, cure, mitigation, treatment, or prevention of disease, or for the purpose of affecting any structure or function of the body.

Under § 213(b), a deduction is allowed for amounts paid during the taxable year for medicine or a drug only if the medicine or drug is a prescribed drug or insulin. Section 213(d)(3) defines a "prescribed drug" as a drug or biological that requires a prescription of a physician for its use by an individual.

Section 1.213-1(e)(1)(ii) of the Income Tax Regulations provides, in part, that the deduction for medical care expenses will be confined strictly to expenses incurred primarily for the prevention or alleviation of a physical or mental defect or illness. An expense that is merely beneficial to the general health of an individual is not an expense for medical care.

Section 262 provides that, except as otherwise expressly provided by the Code, no deduction is allowed for personal, living, or family expenses.

Rev. Rul. 79-162, 1979-1 C.B. 116, holds that a taxpayer who has no specific ailment or disease may not deduct as a medical expense under § 213 the cost of participating in a smoking-cessation program. However, the Internal Revenue Service has held that treatment for addiction to certain substances qualifies as medical care under §213. *See* Rev. Rul. 73-325, 1973-2 C.B. 75 (alcoholism); Rev. Rul. 72-226, 1972-1 C.B. 96 (drug addiction).

A report of the Surgeon General, *The Health Consequences of Smoking: Nicotine Addiction* (1988), states that scientists in the field of drug addiction agree that nicotine, a substance common to all forms of tobacco, is a powerfully addictive drug. Other reports of the Surgeon General have concluded, based on numerous studies, that a strong causal link exists between smoking and several diseases. *See, e.g., Tobacco Use Among U.S. Racial/Ethnic Minority Groups* (1998); *Preventing Tobacco Use Among Young People* (1994); *The Health Benefits of Smoking Cessation* (1990). Scientific evidence has thus established that nicotine is addictive and that smoking is detrimental to the health of the smoker.

Under the facts provided, the smoking-cessation program and the prescribed drugs are treatment for *A*'s and *B*'s addiction to nicotine. Accordingly, *A*'s costs for the smoking-cessation program and *B*'s costs for prescribed drugs to alleviate the effects of nicotine withdrawal are amounts paid for medical care under §213(d)(1). However, under section 213(b), *A*'s costs for nicotine gum and nicotine patches are not deductible because they contain a drug (other than insulin) and do not require a prescription of a physician.

HOLDING

Uncompensated amounts paid by taxpayers for participation in a smoking-cessation program and for prescribed drugs designed to alleviate nicotine withdrawal are expenses for medical care that are deductible under §213, subject to the 7.5 percent limitation. However, amounts paid for drugs (other than insulin) not requiring a prescription, such as nicotine gum and certain nicotine patches, are not deductible under §213.

EFFECT ON OTHER DOCUMENTS

Rev. Rul. 79-162 is revoked.

REVENUE RULING 2002-19
2002-16 I.R.B. 778

ISSUE

Are uncompensated amounts paid by individuals for participation in a weight-loss program as treatment for a specific disease or ailment (including obesity) diagnosed by a physician and for diet food items expenses for medical care that are deductible under §213 of the Internal Revenue Code?

FACTS

Taxpayer A is diagnosed by a physician as obese. A does not suffer from any other specific disease. Taxpayer B is not obese but suffers from hypertension. B has been directed by a physician to lose weight as treatment for the hypertension.

A and B participate in the X weight-loss program. A and B are required to pay an initial fee to join X and an additional fee to attend periodic meetings. At the meetings participants develop a diet plan, receive diet menus and literature, and discuss problems encountered in dieting. A and B also purchase B brand reduced-calorie diet food items. Neither A's nor B's costs are compensated by insurance or otherwise.

LAW

Section 213(a) allows a deduction for uncompensated expenses for medical care of an individual, the individual's spouse or a dependent, to the extent the expenses exceed 7.5 percent of adjusted gross income. Section 213(d)(1) provides, in part, that medical care means amounts paid for the diagnosis, cure, mitigation, treatment, or prevention of disease, or for the purpose of affecting any structure or function of the body.

Under § 1.213-1(e)(1)(ii) of the Income Tax Regulations, the deduction for medical care expenses will be confined strictly to expenses incurred primarily for the prevention or alleviation of a physical or mental defect or illness. An expense that is merely beneficial to the general health of an individual is not an expense for medical care. Whether an expenditure is primarily for medical care or is merely beneficial to general health is a question of fact.

Section 262 provides that, except as otherwise expressly provided by the Code, no deduction is allowed for personal, living, or family expenses.

Rev. Rul. 79-151, 1979-1 C.B. 116, holds that a taxpayer who participates in a weight reduction program to improve the taxpayer's appearance, general health, and sense of well-being, and not to cure a specific ailment or disease, may not deduct the cost as a medical expense under § 213.

Rev. Rul. 55-261, 1955-1 C.B. 307, holds that medical care includes the cost of special food if (1) the food alleviates or treats an illness, (2) it is not part of the normal nutritional needs of the taxpayer, and (3) the need for the food is substantiated by a physician. However, special food that is a substitute for the food the taxpayer normally consumes and that satisfies the taxpayer's nutritional needs is not medical care.

ANALYSIS

Amounts paid for the primary purpose of treating a disease are deductible as medical care. Obesity is medically accepted to be a disease in its own right. The National Heart, Lung, and Blood Institute, part of the National institutes of Health, describes obesity as a "complex, multifactorial chronic disease." Clinical Guidelines on the Identification, Evaluation, and Treatment of Overweight and Obesity in Adults (1998), page vii. This report is based on an evaluation by a panel of health professionals of scientific evidence published from 1980 to 1997.

Other government and scientific entities have reached similar conclusions. For example, in a preamble to final regulations the Food and Drug Administration states "obesity is a disease." 65 Fed. Reg. 1027, 1028 (Jan. 6, 2000). The World Health Organization states that "[o]besity is now well recognized as a disease in its own right…." Press Release 46 (June 12, 1997).

In the present case, a physician has diagnosed A as suffering from a disease, obesity, Therefore, the cost of A's participation in the X weight-loss program as treatment for A's obesity is an amount paid for medical care under § 213(d)(1). Although B is not suffering from obesity, B's participation in X is part of the treatment for B's hypertension. Therefore, B's cost of participating in the program is also an amount paid for medical care. A and B may deduct under § 213 (subject to the limitations of that section) the fees to join the program and to attend periodic meetings. These situations are distinguishable from the facts of Rev. Rul. 79-151, in which the taxpayer was not suffering from any specific disease or ailment and participated in a weight-loss program merely to improve the taxpayer's general health and appearance. However, A and B may not deduct any portion of the cost of purchasing reduced-calorie diet foods because the foods are substitutes for the food A and B normally consume and satisfy their nutritional requirements.

HOLDING

Uncompensated amounts paid by individuals for participation in a weight-loss program as treatment for a specific disease or diseases (including obesity) diagnosed by a physician are expenses for medical care that are deductible under §213, subject to the limitations of that section. The cost of purchasing diet food items is not deductible under §213.

CHIEF COUNSEL ADVICE 200603025

January 20, 2006

This Chief Counsel Advice responds to your request for assistance dated February 4, 2005. This advice may not be used or cited as precedent.

. . .

ISSUE

Whether the taxpayer's costs for male-to-female gender reassignment surgery (and related medications, treatments, and transportation) paid during Year 6 may be deducted as medical expenses under I.R.C. *§213*.

CONCLUSION

Without an unequivocal expression of Congressional intent that expenses of this type qualify under *section 213*, allowing the medical expense deduction is not justified in this case.

FACTS

The subject non-docketed case is currently under consideration by the [TEXT REDACTED] Office of Appeals. On the taxpayer's Year 6 return, the taxpayer reported medical and dental expenses for an amount exceeding $ [TEXT REDACTED]. After applying the 7.5% limitation to adjusted gross income, the taxpayer claimed a deduction for medical and dental expenses in the amount of $ [TEXT REDACTED]. The expenses included payments for various doctors, prescriptions, health insurance, transportation and lodging in connection with the taxpayer's gender reassignment surgery (GRS).

In a report dated July 2, Year 8, the Revenue Agent disallowed the expenses on the ground that they were for cosmetic surgery and nondeductible pursuant to *I.R.C. section 213(d)(9)*.

. . . Based on documents provided by the taxpayer's representative to the Appeals Officer, including letters prepared by medical professionals who treated the taxpayer, the following is a synopsis of the taxpayer's medical condition and treatments:

1. The taxpayer grew up with a condition known as Gender Identity Disorder (GID).

2. It is not clear from the records when the taxpayer first realized that he had some type of disorder, but it was suggested that the taxpayer had gender issues dating back to childhood.

3. Beginning in Year 1, the taxpayer sought psychotherapy from a licensed social worker, Social Worker A.

4. During the course of treatment, Social Worker A formally diagnosed the taxpayer as meeting the criteria for Gender Identity Disorder.

5. In September, Year 2, subsequent to the diagnosis, the taxpayer began hormone treatment under the care of an endocrinologist.

6. In March, Year 5, the taxpayer began living as a full-time female.

7. In March, Year 5, the taxpayer legally changed his name from Taxpayer Name 2 to Taxpayer Name 1.

8. In July, Year 6, Social Worker A, in accordance with medical standards that were followed for treatment of Gender Identity Disorder, recommended the taxpayer for Gender Reassignment Surgery (GRS).

9. In July, Year 6, the taxpayer met with Doctor B to be evaluated as to whether GRS was an appropriate treatment for his diagnosed GID.

10. Doctor B considered the taxpayer's GID to be profound. Several alternative treatments were considered and dismissed. Doctor B ultimately opined that the taxpayer was in need of GRS.

11. Prior to surgery, the taxpayer complied with the preparatory requirements for sex reassignment surgery. These standards are known as the Harry Benjamin Standards. See Harry Benjamin International Gender Dysphoria Association's Standards of Care for Gender Identity Disorders (6th Ed.)

12. In October Year 6, the taxpayer underwent GRS.

LAW AND ANALYSIS

I.R.C. §213(d)(1)(A) defines the term "medical care" as amounts paid for the diagnosis, cure, mitigation, treatment, or prevention of disease, or for the purpose of affecting any structure or function of the body. See also *Treas. Reg. §1.213-1(e)(1)(i)*. Although not amended to take into account tax law changes since 1981, (including the cosmetic surgery limitation discussed below), *Treas. Reg. §1.213-1(e)(1)(ii)* [TEXT REDACTED] provides that amounts paid for legal operations or treatments affecting any portion of the body are deemed to be for the purpose of affecting any structure or function of the body and are therefore paid for medical care. *Treas. Reg. §1.213-1(e)(1)(ii)* also provides that deductions for expenditures for medical care will be confined strictly to expenses incurred primarily for the prevention or alleviation of a physical or mental defect or illness. Finally, *Treas. Reg. §1.213-1(e)(1)(ii)* provides that an expenditure which is merely beneficial to the general health of an individual, such as an expenditure for a vacation, is not an expenditure for medical care.

I.R.C. §213(d)(9)(A) provides that the term "medical care" does not include cosmetic surgery or other similar procedures, unless the surgery or procedure is necessary to ameliorate a deformity arising from, or directly related to, a congenital abnormality, a personal injury resulting from an accident or trauma, or a disfiguring disease. I.R.C. §213 (d)(9)(B) defines "cosmetic surgery" as any procedure that is directed at improving the patient's appearance and does not meaningfully promote the proper function of the body or treat illness or disease.

Legislative History

A detailed analysis of the legislative history is instructive on Congressional intent regarding the cosmetic surgery limitation.

The legislative history to the Omnibus Budget Reconciliation Act of 1990, P.L. 101-508, 104 Stat. 1388, section 11342, indicates that, by 1990, Congress was aware that the Internal Revenue Service was interpreting the term "medical care" to include procedures that permanently alter any structure of the body, even if the procedure generally was considered to be an elective, purely cosmetic treatment (such as removal of hair by electrolysis and face-lift operations). H.R. Rep. No. 101-964, at 1031. Therefore, Congress enacted *I.R.C. §213(d)(9)*, with the Omnibus Budget Reconciliation Act of 1990.

The Omnibus Budget Reconciliation Act of 1990 was initiated in the House of Representatives (101st Cong., 2d Sess.) as H.R. 5835. However, H.R. 5835 as initially passed by the House contained no provision restricting cosmetic surgery from the definition of medical care in *section 213*.

The bill was considered by the Senate as S. 3209. Section 7463(b)(2) of S. 3209 was the genesis of the cosmetic surgery limitation. Section 7463(b)(2)(A) provided the general rule (ultimately enacted as *I.R.C. §213(d)(9)(A)*) eliminating a deduction for "cosmetic surgery or other similar procedures." Section 7463(b)(2)(B) specifically defined cosmetic surgery as "any procedure which is directed at improving the patient's appearance and does not meaningfully promote the proper function of the body or prevent or treat illness or disease." Because this exact language was ultimately enacted as *I.R.C. §213(d)(9)(B)*, it is important to analyze the Senate Report regarding this provision.

As printed in the Congressional Record of October 18, 1990 at p. S 15711, the Senate Budget Committee determined that expenses for cosmetic surgery should not be eligible for the medical expense deduction absent certain circumstances clearly not present in the case of GRS (i.e., a congenital abnormality, an accident or trauma, or a disfiguring disease). The Senate Report states that expenses for purely cosmetic procedures that are not medically necessary are, in essence, voluntary personal expenditures, which like other personal expenditures (e.g., food and clothing) generally should not be deductible in computing taxable income. Id. In discussing the types of surgery which are deemed to be medically necessary, the Senate Report lists only: (1) procedures that are medically necessary to promote the proper function of the body and which only incidentally affect the patient's appearance; and (2) procedures for treatment of a disfiguring condition arising from a congenital abnormality, personal injury, trauma, or disease (such as reconstructive surgery following the removal of a malignancy). Id.

From the material submitted the taxpayer has not satisfactorily demonstrated that the expenses incurred for the taxpayer's GRS fit within the strict boundaries discussed above. There is nothing to substantiate that these expenses were incurred to promote the proper function of the taxpayer's body and only incidentally affect the taxpayer's appearance. The expenses also were not incurred for treatment of a disfiguring condition arising from a congenital abnormality, personal injury, trauma, or disease (such as reconstructive surgery following the removal of a malignancy).

Whether gender reassignment surgery is a treatment for an illness or disease is controversial. For instance, Johns Hopkins Hospital has closed its gender reassignment clinic and ceased performing these operations. See, Surgical Sex, Dr. Paul McHugh, 2004 First Things 147 (November 2004) 34–38. To our knowledge, there is no case law, regulation, or revenue ruling that specifically addresses medical expense deductions for GRS or similar procedures. In light of the Congressional emphasis on denying a deduction for procedures relating to appearance in all but a few circumstances and the controversy surrounding whether GRS is a treatment for an illness or disease, the materials submitted do not support a deduction. Only an unequivocal expression of Congressional intent that expenses of this type qualify under *section 213* would justify the allowance of the deduction in this case. Otherwise, it would seem we would be moving beyond the generally accepted boundaries that define this type of deduction.

CASE DEVELOPMENT, HAZARDS AND OTHER CONSIDERATIONS

[TEXT REDACTED]

OCHS v. COMMISSIONER
195 F.2d 692 (2d Cir. 1952)

AUGUSTUS N. HAND, Circuit Judge.

The question raised by this appeal is whether the taxpayer Samuel Ochs was entitled under Section 23(x) of the Internal Revenue Code to deduct the sum of $1,456.50 paid by him for maintaining his two minor children in day school and boarding school as medical expenses incurred for the benefit of his wife. The pertinent sections of the Internal Revenue Code and the Regulations are set forth in the margin.

The Tax Court made the following findings:

"During the taxable year petitioner was the husband of Helen H. Ochs. They had two children, Josephine age six and Jeanne age four.

"On December 10, 1943, a thyroidectomy was performed on petitioner's wife. A histological examination disclosed a papillary carcinoma of the thyroid with multiple lymph node metastases, according to the surgeon's report. During the taxable year the petitioner maintained his two children in day school during the first half of the year and in boarding school during the latter half of the year at a cost of $1,456.50. Petitioner deducted this sum from his income for the year 1946 as a medical expense under section 23(x) of the Internal Revenue Code.

"During the taxable year, as a result of the operation on December 10, 1943, petitioner's wife was unable to speak above a whisper. Efforts of petitioner's wife to speak were painful, required much of her strength, and left her in a highly nervous state. Petitioner was advised by the operating surgeon that his wife suffered from cancer of the throat, a condition which was fatal in many cases. He advised extensive X-ray treatment after the operation. Petitioner became alarmed when, by 1946, his wife's voice had failed to improve, and believed that the irritation and nervousness caused by attempting to care for the children at a time when she could scarcely speak above a whisper might cause a recurrence of the cancer. Petitioner and his wife consulted a reputable physician and were advised by him that if the children were not separated from petitioner's wife she would not improve and her nervousness and irritation might cause a recurrence of the cancer. Petitioner continued to maintain his children in boarding school after the taxable year here involved until up to the end of five years following the operation of December 10, 1943, petitioner having been advised that if there was no recurrence of the cancer during that time his wife could be considered as having recovered from the cancer.

"During the taxable year petitioner's income was between $5,000 and $6,000. Petitioner's two children have not attended private school but have lived at home and attended public school since a period beginning five years after the operation of December 10, 1943. Petitioner's purpose in sending the children to boarding school during the year 1946 was to alleviate his wife's pain and suffering in caring for the children by reason of her inability to speak above a whisper and to prevent a recurrence of the cancer which was responsible for the condition of her voice. He also thought it would be good for the children to be away from their mother as much as possible while she was unable to speak to them above a whisper.

"Petitioner's wife was employed part of her time in 1946 as a typist and stenographer. On account of the impairment which existed in her voice she found it difficult to hold a position and was only able to do part-time work. At the time of the hearing of this proceeding in 1951, she had recovered the use of her voice and seems to have entirely recovered from her throat cancer."

The Tax Court said in its opinion that it had no reason to doubt the good faith and truthfulness of the taxpayer and that his devotion and consideration for his wife were altogether admirable, but it nevertheless held that the expense of sending the children to school was not deductible as a medical expense under the provisions of Section 23(x) and the Treasury Regulations herein referred to.

In our opinion the expenses incurred by the taxpayer were non-deductible family expenses within the meaning of section 24(a)(1) of the Code rather than medical expenses. Concededly the line between the two is a difficult one to draw, but this only reflects the fact that expenditures made on behalf of some members of a family unit frequently benefit others in the family as well. The wife in this case had in the past contributed the services—caring for the children—for which the husband was required to pay because, owing to her illness, she could no longer care for them. If, for example, the husband had employed a governess for the children, or a cook, the wages he would have paid would not be deductible. Or, if the wife had died, and the children were sent to a boarding school, there would certainly be no basis for contending that such expenses were deductible. The examples given serve to illustrate that the expenses here were made necessary by the loss of the wife's services, and that the only reason for allowing them as a deduction is that the wife also received a benefit. We think it unlikely that Congress intended to transform family expenses into medical expenses for this reason. The decision of the Tax Court is further supported by its conclusion that the expenditures were to some extent at least incurred while the wife was acting as a typist in order to earn money for the family. We do not think that the decisions discussed in the opinion of the Tax Court and the briefs of the parties have any real bearing upon the issues involved in this appeal.

The decision is affirmed.

FRANK, Circuit Judge (dissenting).

Humane considerations in revenue laws are undeniably exceptional. But there is no good reason why, when, for once, Congress, although seeking revenue, shows it has a heart, the courts should try to make it beat feebly. Here is a man earning between $5,000 and $6,000 a year. His wife was operated on for cancer three years earlier and has still not regained the use of her voice. The doctor says that she will not get any better—may indeed have a recurrence of the cancer, this time surely fatal—unless she is separated from her two children, aged six and four. The children are young, healthy, active and irrepressible; their mother cannot speak above a whisper without pain. She becomes ever more nervous and irritable when they are around; her voice does not improve when it should. The father (instead of sending her to a sanitarium) sends the children away to school and seeks to deduct the cost therefor as a "medical expense."

The Commissioner, the Tax Court, and now my colleagues, are certain Congress did not intend relief for a man in this grave plight. The truth is, of course, no one knows what Congress would have said if it had been faced with these facts. The few paltry sentences of Congressional history for § 23(x) do not lend strong support—indeed any support at all—to a strict construction theory: "This allowance is granted in consideration of the heavy tax burden that must be borne by industry during the existing emergency and of the desirability of maintaining the present high level of public health and morale.... The term 'medical care' is broadly defined to include amounts paid for the diagnoses, cure, mitigation, treatment, or prevention of disease, or for the purpose of affecting any structure or function of the body. It is not intended, however, that a deduction should be allowed for any expense that is not incurred primarily for the prevention or alleviation of a physical or mental defect of illness." (Footnote 1)

I think that Congress would have said that this man's expense fell within the category of "mitigation, treatment, or prevention of disease," and that it was for the "purpose of affecting [a] structure or function of the body." The Commissioner argued, successfully in the Tax Court, that, because the money spent was only indirectly for the sake of the wife's health and directly for the children's maintenance, it could not qualify as a "medical expense." Much is made of the fact that the children themselves were healthy and normal—and little of the fact that it was their very health and normality which were draining away the mother's strength. The Commissioner seemingly admits that the deduction might be a medical expense if the wife were sent away from her children to a sanitarium for rest and quiet, but asserts that it never can be if, for the very same purpose, the children are sent away from the mother—even if a boarding-school for the children is cheaper than a sanitarium for the wife. I cannot believe that Congress intended such a meaningless distinction, that it meant to rule out all kinds of therapeutic treatment applied indirectly rather than directly even though the indirect treatment be "primarily for the ... alleviation of a physical or mental defect or illness." The cure ought to be the doctor's business, not the Commissioner's.

The only sensible criterion of a "medical expense"—and I think this criterion satisfies Congressional caution without destroying what little humanity remains in the Internal Revenue Code—should be that the taxpayer, in incurring the expense, was guided by a physician's bona fide advice that such a treatment was necessary to the patient's recovery from, or prevention of, a specific ailment.

... (Footnote 3)

In the final analysis, the Commissioner, the Tax Court and my colleagues all seem to reject Mr. Ochs' plea because of the nightmarish spectacle of opening the floodgates to cases involving expense for cooks, governesses, baby-sitters, nourishing food, clothing, frigidaires, electric dish-washers—in short, allowances as medical expenses for everything "helpful to a convalescent housewife or to one who is nervous or weak from past illness." I, for one, trust the Commissioner to make short shrift of most such claims. The tests should be: Would the taxpayer, considering his income and his living standard, normally spend money in this way regardless of illness? Has he enjoyed such luxuries or services in the past? Did a competent physician prescribe this specific expense as an indispensable part of the treatment? Has the taxpayer followed the physician's advice in most economical way possible? Are the so-called medical expenses over and above what the patient would have to pay anyway for his living expenses, i.e., room, board, etc? Is the treatment closely geared to a particular condition and not just to the patient's general good health or well-being?

My colleagues are particularly worried about family expenses, traditionally nondeductible, passing as medical expenses. They would classify the children's schooling here as a family expense, because, they say, it resulted from the loss of the wife's services. I think they are mistaken. The Tax Court specifically found that the children were sent away so they would not bother the wife, and not because there was no one to take care of them. Ochs' expenditures fit into the Congressional test for medical deductions because he was compelled to go to the expense of putting the children away primarily for the benefit of his sick wife. Expenses incurred solely because of the loss of the patient's services and not as a part of his cure are a different thing altogether. Wendell v. Commissioner, 12 T.C. 161, for instance, disallowed a deduction for the salary of a nurse engaged in caring for a healthy infant whose mother had died in childbirth. The case turned on the simple fact that, where there is no patient, there can be no deduction.

Thus, even here, expense attributed solely to the education, at least of the older child, should not be included as a medical expense.... Nor should care of the children during that part of the day when the mother would be away, during the period while she was working part-time.... The same goes for any period when the older child would be away at public school during the day. In so far as the costs of this private schooling are thus allocable, I would limit the deductible expense to the care of the children at the times when they would otherwise be around the mother. If my views prevailed, this might require a remand to the Tax Court for such allocation.

Line-drawing may be difficult here as everywhere, but that is what courts are for. See Lavery v. Purssell, 399 Ch.D. 508, 517: "... courts of justice ought not to be puzzled by such old scholastic questions as to where a horse's tail begins and where it ceases. You are obliged to say, this is a horse's tail at some time."

FOOTNOTES:

1. Sen.Rep.1631, 77th Cong., 2d Sess. (1942) 95–96.

3. The majority of §23(x) cases seems to have dealt, strangely enough, with Florida or Arizona winter vacations. One taxpayer closed up his business after a coronary occlusion and, in effect, retired to Florida. He wanted to deduct his year's rent and payment to a cleaning woman; Brody v. Commissioner, 8 T.C.M. 288. A second taxpayer and his wife took an extended holiday in the sunshine as an aftermath of ulcers and pneumonia; Keller v. Commissioner, 8 T.C.M. 685. Dobkin v. Commissioner, 15 T.C. 886, concerned a heart patient who took annual Florida vacations. Havey v. Commissioner, 12 T.C. 409, involved another heart patient who returned to old vacation haunts in New Jersey and Arizona as late as two years after the attack. All these five taxpayers were halted by the same stumbling block: None of them could show a direct relation between (1) the heart condition or the ulcers and (2) the Florida sunshine. The inference was unavoidable that the patient enjoyed a relief from the cold winds of winter for his general well-being; in some cases, he might very well have made the trip anyway according to his long-established vacation practices. The Commissioner and the Tax Court, on the other hand, have sanctioned deductions of funds paid for southern exposures in cases where the patients went South for relief from asthma, hay fever, or respiratory infections, i.e., where a direct relation was proved between the southern climate and treatment of the disease. Stringham v. Commissioner, 12 T.C. 580, affirmed 6 Cir., 183 F.2d 579.

———————

Consider the following questions.

1. Why are the expenses for birth control pills in Revenue Ruling 73-200 deductible whereas the expenses for boarding school in *Ochs v. Commissioner* were not? Is there statutory justification for the distinction?

2. Why did the Service alter its position between the date of issuance of Revenue Ruling 79-162 and the date of issuance of Revenue Ruling 99-28? Is there statutory justification for the alteration? Why did it take the Service so long?

3. Which previsions of section 213 and its regulations support the taxpayer's deduction of the cost of his gender reassignment surgery? Why did the Chief Counsel disallow the deduction? Who is correct?

4. In his dissent in *Ochs*, Judge Frank comments that "Humane considerations in revenue laws are undeniably exceptional." Should our income tax system be based in part on humane considerations? (Would Professor Surrey question whether humane considerations are outside the bounds of a normative income tax structure?)

5. The floor, that is, the amount of medical expenses that are not deductible, has increased over the years. At the outset, Congress permitted deduction of the total amount of medical expenses. As you have noted, the current version of section 213 permits deduction only of expenses in excess of seven and one half percent of AGI. What might be the policy justification for allowing deduction only of the amount of expenses that exceed the floor?

6. Note that because the floor is based on a taxpayer's AGI, a taxpayer whose AGI is $10,000 can deduct medical expenses that exceed $750 whereas a taxpayer whose AGI is $100,000 may deduct only amounts that exceed $7,500. What might be the policy justification for this disparity?[26]

7. Recall our discussion in Chapter 2.C., in this part, of the damages Sam received for the loss of his fingers. Among the items for which he received an award was past medical expenses that he deducted in the year of his injury. Now that you have studied the medical expense deduction permitted by section 213, can you explain why section 104(a) would not permit Sam to exclude from income amounts previously deducted as medical expenses? Can you prove that he would be getting a double benefit?

Consider carefully the tax effect on Sam if he can both deduct the amount in one year and exclude it in a later year? The concept, termed the "tax benefit rule," applies when an event occurs in a later year that is inconsistent with the deduction of an item in an earlier year.[27] The tax benefit rule applies in a wide variety of circumstances but only when the deduction in the earlier year produced a tax benefit.[28] So,

---

26. Under Professor Surrey's tax expenditure view, the medical expense deduction would be characterized as an expenditure based upon some estimate of the amount of tax revenue lost to the Treasury in a particular year due to the deduction (*i.e.*, an estimate of how much tax taxpayers would have paid if the deduction had not been available). In his view, this "lost" revenue is the equivalent of the taxpayer receiving that amount as a direct subsidy. Thus, section 213 might be viewed as a government health insurance program. But, unlike our usual view of medical insurance, the program benefits the wealthy, high income taxpayer more than the moderate income taxpayer and does not benefit the poor (or those who do not itemize their deductions) at all. One argument for retention of the medical expense deduction rests on one of the reasons often advanced for the desirability of a graduated rate schedule. If the goal of our tax policy (in adopting a graduated rate), is to tax those with a greater ability to pay, the argument is that taxing people after deduction of extraordinary medical expenses is a better measure of ability to pay.

27. *Hillsboro National Bank v. Commissioner*, 460 U.S. 370 (1983). To determine whether a later event is inconsistent with an earlier's year's deduction, ask whether the deduction would be allowed if both events had occurred in one year. So, for example, if Sam's payment of medical expenses had occurred in the same year as the year in which he received the damages, he would not have had any out-of-pocket expenses to deduct (and would not, of course, had a deduction).

28. Section 111 of the Code confirms that the tax benefit rule only operates when there has been, in fact, a tax benefit in the earlier year.

for example, if Sam could not (or did not) deduct medical expenses in the earlier year, he had no benefit in the earlier year and could exclude the damage recovery in the later year. If, however, he did claim the deduction, he benefited by doing so and cannot benefit again by claiming an exclusion in the later year. Commentators call this "double-dipping."

As you read the following materials on another of these special deductions, reconsider the policy questions we have raised with respect to medical expenses.

b. Section 165(c)(3): Casualty Losses

Read section 165(a), (b), (c), (d), (h)(1), (h)(2)(A), and (h)(4)(A) and (E). Read also Treasury Regulation section 1.165-7(a) and (b)(1), (2), and (3). Now read the following revenue ruling and two cases.

REVENUE RULING 72-592
1972-2 C.B. 101

The Service will follow the decision in *John P. White*, holding that an accidental loss of property may qualify as a "casualty loss."

In view of the decision of the Tax Court of the United States in *John P. White v. Commissioner*, 48 T.C. 430 (1967), reconsideration has been given to the meaning of the term "casualty" for purposes of section 165(c)(3) of the Internal Revenue Code of 1954. That section of the Code provides that an individual may deduct:

(3) losses of property not connected with a trade or business, if such losses arise from fire, storm, shipwreck or other casualty ... [but] only to the extent that the amount of loss to such individual arising from each casualty ... exceeds $100....

The provision allowing this deduction for losses from "other casualty" has been part of the Federal tax law since the enactment of the Revenue Act of 1916. However, there is neither statutory definition of the term "other casualty," nor legislative history expressing Congressional intent as to its meaning.

The courts have consistently upheld the Internal Revenue Service position that an "other casualty" is limited to casualties analogous to fire, storm, or shipwreck. The Service position has been that a casualty is the complete or partial destruction of property resulting from an identifiable event of a sudden, unexpected, and unusual nature.

In the *White* case, however, the Tax Court found that property that was accidentally and irretrievably lost could, under the circumstances described, be the basis for a casualty loss deduction under section 165(c)(3) of the Code. The Service has acquiesced in the decision of the Tax Court in the *White* case, C.B. 1969-1, 21.

In the *White* case, the taxpayer-husband accidentally slammed the car door on his wife's hand after helping her alight from the car. Her diamond engagement ring absorbed the full impact of the blow, which broke two flanges of the setting holding the diamond in place. His wife quickly withdrew her injured hand, shaking it vigorously, and the diamond dropped or flew out of the broken setting. The uninsured diamond was never found, and the taxpayer claimed a casualty loss deduction for its value in the year it was lost.

The Tax Court, convinced that the diamond was irrevocably and irretrievably lost, sustained the taxpayer's claim, indicating that the diamond was completely removed from the enjoyment of its owner and that it had no value to the owner after the loss.

The Service, in acquiescing in the decision, agreed that property that is accidentally and irretrievably lost can be the basis for a casualty loss deduction under section 165(c)(3) of the Code if it otherwise qualifies as a casualty loss.

In other words, the Service position is altered only to the extent that the accidental loss of property can now qualify as a casualty. Such losses must, of course, qualify under the same rules as must any other casualty; namely, the loss must result from some event that is (1) identifiable, (2) damaging to property, and (3) sudden, unexpected, and unusual in nature. The meaning of the terms "sudden, unexpected, and unusual," as developed in court decisions, is set forth below.

To be "sudden" the event must be one that is swift and precipitous and not gradual or progressive.

To be "unexpected" the event must be one that is ordinarily unanticipated that occurs without the intent of the one who suffers the loss.

To be "unusual" the event must be one that is extraordinary and nonrecurring, one that does not commonly occur during the activity in which the taxpayer was engaged when the destruction or damage occurred, and one that does not commonly occur in the ordinary course of day-to-day living of the taxpayer.

KEENAN v. BOWERS
91 F. Supp. 771 (E.D.S.C. 1950)

WYCHE, Chief Judge.

. . .

On March 15, 1945, the taxpayers, husband and wife, filed a joint federal income tax return for the tax year 1944, and in their computation of net taxable income claimed a deduction of $1,300 under Section 23(e)(3), Internal Revenue Code, ... for the loss of two diamond rings not compensated for by insurance, which deduction was disallowed by the Commissioner, and an assessment made for additional taxes in the amount of $972.02, plus $180.38 interest, which was paid under protest by plaintiffs. A claim for refund was duly filed by plaintiffs and disallowed.

The stipulation by the parties and the affidavit of Mrs. Keenan, which was agreed to be considered as testimony for the plaintiff, disclose the following facts: On or about May 4, 1944, Mr. and Mrs. W. J. Keenan, the plaintiffs herein, were en route to visit their son at Grenada, Mississippi, prior to his departure overseas with the 94th Infantry, and they stopped and spent the night at the Bankhead Hotel in Birmingham, Alabama; they had never spent the night in said hotel before and the surroundings were strange to both of them; their hotel room had single beds with a small lamp table between the beds. This arrangement differed from that in their home where they had bed tables on each side. On this night, Mr. Keenan prepared for bed, and being bothered with a nose irritation, placed a box of kleenex tissues on his side of the bed table and went to sleep prior to Mrs. Keenan. Subsequent to this, his wife retired. Customarily, when retiring at home, Mrs. Keenan removed her rings and placed them on or in her bureau, but this night she did not do so. However, during the night, she found her rings uncomfortable, and recalling the box of kleenex on the table, she reached out in the dark and unbeknown to her husband, took a piece of kleenex and wrapped her rings in it, and placed them wrapped on her side of the small table; she wrapped them in kleenex tissue with the thought in mind that this would be a possible precaution against the theft of the rings; during the night, Mr. Keenan awoke several times, used pieces of kleenex tissues to blow his nose, and having no convenient waste basket at hand, placed these balls of tissue on the table, intending to dispose of them upon rising; the next morning, Mr. Keenan arose early and prior to his wife's awakening, hastily preparing for an early departure, swept the used tissues up, not knowing that some of them contained the rings, balled them up, went to the bathroom and disposed of them in the toilet, flushing it forthwith; about a half an hour after Mr. Keenan's actions, Mrs. Keenan realized what had happened and immediately communicated with the hotel manager who called in the hotel engineer. A search of the trap was to no avail and then later the City of Birmingham's engineer went into the large trap in the sewer into which the hotel refuse emptied but all efforts to recover the rings were unavailing. The value of these rings, less the maximum amount of insurance which could be collected, was $1,300.

Section 23(e)(3) of the Internal Revenue Code ... upon which the claim for deduction is based, provides as follows: In computing net income there shall be allowed as deductions: "In the case of an individual, losses sustained during the taxable year and not compensated for by insurance or otherwise— ... of property not connected with the trade or business, if the loss arises from fires, storms, shipwreck, *or other casualty*, or from theft...." (Emphasis added)

The question for decision is whether or not the phrase 'other casualty' in the statute can be construed so as to cover the loss of jewelry under the foregoing agreed statement of facts.

It is well-established that deductions are a matter of legislative grace and no deductions will be allowed for losses unless the alleged loss falls within one of the categories enumerated in the statute. The taxpayer must show he comes within the terms of the provisions of the statute allowing deductions. New Colonial Ice Co., Inc. v. Helvering, 292 U.S. 435, 440; ...

Generally, the words "other" and "any other" following an enumeration of particular classes of things in a statute, must be read as meaning "other such like" and include only words of like kind or character. Bigger v. Unemployment Compensation Commission, 4 Terry (Del.) 274, 46 A.2d 137, 142.

The word "other" in a statute means of like kind and character. Twin Falls County v. Hulbert, 66 Idaho 128, 156 P.2d 319, 324.

The word "casualty" has been defined as follows: "An accident or casualty, according to common understanding, proceeds from an unknown cause or is an unusual effect of a known cause. Either may be properly said to occur by chance and unexpectedly." Chicago, St. Louis & N.O.R. Co. v. Pullman Co., 139 U.S. 79...."Casualty" has also been defined as "an event due to some sudden, unexpected, or unusual cause," Matheson, Exec. v. Comm., 2 Cir., 54 F.2d 537, 539; and embraces losses arising through the action of natural physical forces and which occur suddenly, unexpectedly, and without design on the part of the one who suffers the loss. However, it is now recognized that a human agency can constitute or cause the sudden turn of events resulting in the loss. Ray Durden, 3 T.C. 1; Robert L. Stephens v. Commissioner, 3 T.C. 1.

The words "other casualty" were added by the 1916 Act, and the Treasury at first took the view that "other casualty" must be incident similar to fires, storms or shipwreck arising from a natural cause and not due to negligence. In Shearer v. Anderson, 2 Cir., 16 F.2d 995, 996, this construction was held to be erroneous and the court, in allowing a deduction for damage to the taxpayer's pleasure automobile sustained when it overturned on an icy road, stated: " ... as 'casualty' expresses rather the result than the cause of the damage, that is, the wreck itself rather than the lightning, storm, or the negligence of fault of some person, so the 'other casualty' is at least as clearly ejusdem generis (of the same kind) with shipwreck as with fire or storm." The court's modification of the Treasury Regulations in the case of Shearer v. Anderson, 2 Cir., 16 F.2d 995, does not change the Treasury's construction that the phrase means *or other like casualty*, because the court, in allowing a deduction for the damages resulting from the automobile was similar to a shipwreck and was a casualty of the same kind.

Some of the losses which have been held to be deductible as from "other casualty" are as follows: loss occasioned by freezing and bursting of water pipes in a residence during the absence of the occupant; loss occasioned by the bursting of a boiler used in heating a taxpayer's residence; damage to a factory from an earthquake; an extensive deep sinking of land caused by a subterranean disturbance; damage to trees caused by a sleet and ice storm; loss from violent quarry blasting operations.

Examples of losses that have been held not be from "other casualty" are as follows: damage to buildings caused by termites; loss of a ring when there was no evidence or testimony establishing that the ring was stolen rather than mislaid, and the taxpayer did not attempt to establish the fair market value of the ring as of the date of disappearance; loss of a ring when it slipped from taxpayer's finger and was lost in a muddy water when he was trying to retrieve a decoy while duck hunting; damage to a residence caused by excavations on property adjoining that of the taxpayer; loss occasioned by rusting and corrosion of the re-enforcing steel used in the ... island; damage on account of injuries caused to one who trips over a wire stretched in front of the taxpayer's residence; loss of household goods either in storage or in transit; and loss of a bird dog which disappeared when released for exercise by its handler and was never seen again. Mertens, Law of Federal Income Taxation, §28.57, pp. 215, 216, and the 1950 Cumulative Pocket Supplement, p. 98.

The section of the statute involved herein has been construed as authorizing the deduction only of losses caused by fires, storms, shipwreck, or other *like* casualty. Ray Durden, 3 T.C. 1; Stephens, 3 T.C. 1. Under the doctrine of ejusdem generis it is necessary to define the word "casualty" in connection with the words "fires, storms, shipwreck" immediately preceding it. By the rule of ejusdem generis, where general words follow the enumeration of particular classes of things, the general words should be construed as applicable only to those of the same general nature or class as those enumerated. Merchants' National Bank v. United States, 42 Ct. Cl. 6, 19. The rule is based on the reason that, if the Legislature had intended the general words to be used in their unrestricted sense, there would have been no mention of the particular classes.

In the case of United States v. Rogers, 122 F.2d 485, the Circuit Court of Appeals for the Ninth Circuit said: "The meaning of the word 'casualty' as used in the statute depends upon the context. The doctrine of ejusdem generis requires the statute to be construed as though it read 'loss by fires, storms, shipwrecks, or other casualty of the same kind.'" ...

So, the question here is whether or not the loss of the two diamond rings by the taxpayers may be classified as a casualty of the same kind as a loss by "fires, storms, shipwreck".

The case nearest in point is Stevens v. Commissioner, decided July 8, 1947, where the taxpayer, while duck hunting and in the act of retrieving a decoy, a ring belonging to him, slipped off his finger and dropped into muddy water several feet deep. Although he was conscious of the fact at the moment the ring slipped from his finger, it disappeared into the muddy water making all efforts to recover it futile. In this case the Tax Court disallowed the deduction and said: "The loss here was not like that resulting from the collision of an automobile, Shearer v. Anderson, supra; W. S. Bronson, 9 B.T.A. 1008; or a flood, Ferguson v. Commissioner, 10 Cir., 59 F.2d 893; or an ice storm, Federick H. Nash, 22 B.T.A. 482; or subterranean disturbances, Harry Johnston Grant, 30 B.T.A. 1028. The petitioner merely permitted his ring to drop from his finger, by his own carelessness, we must presume, without the intervention of any sudden or destructive force. It was much the same kind of loss as might result from the loss of one's purse, or any other article of value. Certainly, if Congress had intended to allow the deduction of such losses it would have expressed its aim in language much simpler and more appropriate to that end than is to be found in section 23(e)(3)."

In the instant case it may be conceded that the loss of the rings was due to an unexpected and unusual cause and was not an intentional act on the taxpayers' part, but the loss lacks the element of suddenness. The primary cause of the loss was the placing of the rings in the kleenex tissue. The loss was caused by a chain of events on the part of Mrs. Keenan and Mr. Keenan. There was no intervening sudden force, cause or occurrence which brought on the event such as would ever be present in a casualty arising from fires, storms or shipwreck. I cannot say that the event or accident resulting in the loss was of the same kind as would be caused by fire, storm or shipwreck.

Therefore, judgment must be entered for the defendant, and it is so ordered.

NEWTON v. COMMISSIONER
57 T.C. 245 (1971)

DAWSON, *Judge*: Respondent determined a deficiency of $715.59 in petitioners' Federal income tax for the year 1968.

[The question presented] for our decision: ...

(2) Are petitioners entitled to a casualty loss deduction in 1968 with respect to their damaged automobile? ...

FINDINGS OF FACT

Some of the facts have been stipulated and are found accordingly.

...

In 1967, Ellery W. Newton received a 10-year-old Chevrolet automobile, which was then in very good condition, as his share of a real estate commission. The estimated value of the automobile at that time was $500. Sometime during 1968 the motor burned out while the car was being driven on the highway. The damage was caused by "metal fatigue." The car was sold by petitioners for $25 as junk. Petitioners claimed a casualty loss of $475 on their 1968 Federal income tax return which was disallowed by respondent.

...

OPINION

...

2. *Claimed casualty loss deduction.*—On their Federal income tax return for 1968 the petitioners claimed a casualty loss deduction of $475, based upon a "burned out" motor in their 1957 Chevrolet sedan.

Section 165(c), I.R.C. 1954, allows a deduction for "casualty" losses. Damage to an automobile under circumstances similar to those present in this case does not constitute a deductible casualty loss within the meaning of section 165(c)(3). It is well established that the term "casualty" as used in the statute means "an accident, a mishap, some sudden invasion by a hostile agency; it excludes the progressive deterioration of property through a steadily operating cause." *Fay v. Helvering*, 120 F. 2d 253 (C.A. 2, 1941); *United States v. Rogers*, 120 F. 2d 244 (C.A. 9, 1941). The automobile engine here did not suffer serious internal damage which was the result of sudden invasion by an external or hostile agency. It obviously resulted from a progressive deterioration of the engine through a steadily operating cause. In Ellery Newton's own words, the motor just stopped because of "metal fatigue." Therefore, we hold that the petitioners have not established that the claimed loss resulted from a "casualty" within the purview of section 165(c)(3).

Now consider the following questions.

1. What is the definition of "other casualty"? In *Keenan v. Bowers*, the court stated that the term is "ejusdem generis" to the other events described in section 165(c)(3). What does that mean?

2. What distinguished the husband's actions in the *White* case from those of the husband in *Keenan v. Bowers*? How did the wives in both cases consider the loss of their rings? A "casualty"?

3. Suppose you bought a house in 1987 that you have used as your personal residence since that time. You bought it for $150,000. As a result of the economic conditions in the area of the country in which you live, you find out that it is now worth only $20,000. If you sold it for its current fair market value, what would be the amount of your loss? To what Code section must you refer to determine the amount of your loss?

4. Can you take a casualty loss deduction? (To you, its loss in value is certainly a casualty, is it not?)

Reread section 1001(c). Your initial reading might lead you to the false impression that a taxpayer must "recognize" all "realized" gains and, conversely, may "recognize" all "realized" losses. In fact, the Code treats "realized" gains and losses differently. In general, a taxpayer must recognize all realized gains unless she can point to a specific Code provision that permits her to exclude or defer recognition. In contrast, a taxpayer may recognize losses (that is, deduct them), only if the Code provides a specific provision allowing the recognition (that is, the deduction), of the loss. In the case of dispositions of property, that section is section 165.

Although section 165(a) allows the deduction of all losses "sustained during the taxable year and not compensated for by insurance or otherwise," section 165(c) significantly limits that broad statement in the case of an individual taxpayer. **Read section 165(c).** An individual may deduct a loss on the sale or other disposition of property only if one of the paragraphs of subsection 165(c) specifically authorizes deduction of that loss. Note in particular, that an individual taxpayer may not deduct any loss on any "personal use property"[29] that does not result from a "casualty."

---

29. Is "personal use property" the same as "personal property"? This distinction will become important later in the course. For now, note that section 165(c) allows individuals to deduct losses with respect to three types of property: (c)(1) covers losses incurred through dealings in property held for use in a trade or business, (c)(2) covers losses incurred through dealings in property held in

5. Suppose Jeremiah is a Civil War buff who participates on weekends in reenactments of Civil War battles. He purchased a Civil War uniform at a flea market for $1,000. A fire unfortunately destroyed the uniform at a time when its fair market value was $5,000. The insurance company paid Jeremiah the $5,000 fair market value of the uniform. Would Jeremiah have a loss deductible under section 165? Explain your answer.

6. Suppose, instead, that Jeremiah had forgotten to pay his insurance premium and the insurance coverage had lapsed. What result? (Hint: look carefully at the Code and regulations for instructions as to how Jeremiah must calculate the amount of his loss.)

7. Can Jeremiah deduct his loss under section 165?

8. Assume Amanda was driving to work one morning. An 18-wheeler truck veered into Amanda, forcing her into the center barrier. She was fortunate enough to escape from the car, but the impact ruptured her gas tank and her car was consumed by fire. The only item other than the car that Amanda lost in the fire was her antique viola da gamba. She had originally bought her viola da gamba for $5,000. Her homeowner's insurance company paid her the $12,000 fair market value. She had intended to obtain insurance coverage for her brand new Ferrari, but had not been able to reach her insurance agent. As a consequence, at a time when her adjusted basis in the Ferrari and its fair market value were $100,000, she had no insurance coverage at all for her loss. What result if her adjusted gross income were $100,000?

9. Note that both Jeremiah and Amanda failed to insure fully their property. Some critics of section 165 have opined that this section functions as a "back-up" insurance policy that might, in fact, act as a disincentive to the acquisition of private insurance by property owners. Should taxpayers "subsidize" Jeremiah's and Amanda's losses?[30]

Before we conclude our examination of the medical expense and casualty loss deductions, let's go back to one of the two important maxims of tax policy that we introduced you to earlier. Perhaps the most universally accepted maxim of tax policy is that a fair income tax system should treat similarly-situated taxpayers the same. This maxim is denoted "horizontal equity." But repeating the maxim is far easier than applying it to particular taxpayers. The simple example of two single taxpayers each of whom has income of $50,000 appears to illustrate similarity. But, for example, is the family of four in which only one parent is employed with an income of $50,000 similarly situated to a single individual with an income of $50,000? Is a two-adult household in which each earns $50,000 for a total of $100,000 similarly situated to a single individual of $50,000?

Despite the difficulties, however, the broad general acceptance of the desirability of horizontal equity may play a part in the continuation of personal deduction provisions like section 213 and 165(c)(3). How would you explain the idea that the goal of horizontal equity supports these Code provisions?

---

connection with investment activities, and (c)(3) covers casualty losses of personal use property. Section 165(c) thus represents three of the four categories of property ownership. The fourth category is inventory.

30. The same policy arguments that make the medical expense deduction controversial apply as well to the casualty loss deduction.

2. Favored Activities and Groups—Section 170: Charitable Contributions

Provisions granting special treatment to favored activities or groups interlace the Code.[31] For example, many provisions in the Code treat elderly taxpayers in special ways. Another important group of beneficiaries of these provisions is employees. Among the provisions favoring employees are those permitting before-tax contributions to retirement plans and the exclusion from income of employer-provided medical insurance.

To get a quick idea of how many groups enjoy special benefits, glance at the portion of the Table of Contents of Code Sections in your Code volumes listing the credits available under Part IV of Subchapter A, the exclusions available in Part III of subchapter B, and the deductions available under Part VII of Subchapter B.[32] So too, the Code includes many provisions favoring (or disfavoring) various activities. For example, as you learned in Carole's problem, section 163(h)(3) allows homeowners to deduct the interest they pay on their home mortgages (subject to some limits). Can you suggest a policy reason for this deduction?

A deduction that perfectly illustrates the use of the Code to favor both activities and groups is section 170, which allows a taxpayer to deduct a "charitable contribution." Because it is such a good example of this type of personal itemized deduction and has a long history, we will examine some portions, but not all, of what is an extremely long and complicated section of the Code. Therefore, rather than asking you to read the entire Code provision, **read only, but carefully, section 170(a)(1) and (c). Also read section 501(a). Compare the organizations listed in section 170(c)(2)-(5) with those listed in section 501(c)(3),(8), (10), (13), and (19).** What is the relationship among the foregoing subsections of 170 and 501? Consider the following case.

HERNANDEZ v. COMMISSIONER
490 U.S. 680 (1989)

JUSTICE MARSHALL delivered the opinion of the Court.

Section 170 of the Internal Revenue Code of 1954 (Code), 26 U. S. C. §170, permits a taxpayer to deduct from gross income the amount of a "charitable contribution." The Code defines that term as a "contribution or gift" to certain eligible donees, including entities organized and operated exclusively for religious purposes. (Footnote 1) We granted certiorari to determine whether taxpayers may deduct as charitable contributions payments made to branch churches of the Church of Scientology (Church) in order to receive services known as "auditing" and "training." We hold that such payments are not deductible.

I.

Scientology was founded in the 1950's by L. Ron Hubbard. It is propagated today by a "mother church" in California and by numerous branch churches around the world.

---

31. Review the "Fine Print" article from the New York Times reporting the special provisions included in the 1999 House-passed tax cut proposal.

32. Another reason for looking at the Table of Contents of the Code over and over again is to deepen your understanding of the organization and structure of the Code.

The mother Church instructs laity, trains and ordains ministers, and creates new congregations. Branch churches, known as "franchises" or "missions," provide Scientology services at the local level, under the supervision of the mother Church. *Church of Scientology of California v. Commissioner*, 823 F. 2d 1310, 1313 (CA9 1987), cert. denied, 486 U.S. 1015 (1988).

Scientologists believe that an immortal spiritual being exists in every person. A person becomes aware of this spiritual dimension through a process known as "auditing." Auditing involves a one-to-one encounter between a participant (known as a "preclear") and a Church official (known as an "auditor"). An electronic device, the E-meter, helps the auditor identify the preclear's areas of spiritual difficulty by measuring skin responses during a question and answer session. Although auditing sessions are conducted one on one, the content of each session is not individually tailored. The preclear gains spiritual awareness by progressing through sequential levels of auditing, provided in short blocks of time known as "intensives." 83 T. C. 575, 577 (1984), aff'd, 822 F. 2d 844 (CA9 1987).

The Church also offers members doctrinal courses known as "training." Participants in these sessions study the tenets of Scientology and seek to attain the qualifications necessary to serve as auditors. Training courses, like auditing sessions, are provided in sequential levels. Scientologists are taught that spiritual gains result from participation in such courses. 83 T. C., at 577.

The Church charges a "fixed donation," also known as a "price" or a "fixed contribution," for participants to gain access to auditing and training sessions. These charges are set forth in schedules, and prices vary with a session's length and level of sophistication. In 1972, for example, the general rates for auditing ranged from $625 for a 12½-hour auditing intensive, the shortest available, to $4,250 for a 100-hour intensive, the longest available. Specialized types of auditing required higher fixed donations: a 12½-hour "Integrity Processing" auditing intensive cost $750; a 12½-hour "Expanded Dianetics" auditing intensive cost $950. This system of mandatory fixed charges is based on a central tenet of Scientology known as the "doctrine of exchange," according to which any time a person receives something he must pay something back. *Id.*, at 577–578. In so doing, a Scientologist maintains "inflow" and "outflow" and avoids spiritual decline. 819 F. 2d 1212, 1222 (CA1 1987).

The proceeds generated from auditing and training sessions are the Church's primary source of income. The Church promotes these sessions not only through newspaper, magazine, and radio advertisements, but also through free lectures, free personality tests, and leaflets. The Church also encourages, and indeed rewards with a 5% discount, advance payment for these sessions. 822 F. 2d, at 847. The Church often refunds unused portions of prepaid auditing or training fees, less an administrative charge.

Petitioners in these consolidated cases each made payments to a branch church for auditing or training sessions. They sought to deduct these payments on their federal income tax returns as charitable contributions under §170. Respondent Commissioner, the head of the Internal Revenue Service (IRS), disallowed these deductions, finding that the payments were not charitable contributions within the meaning of §170.

Petitioners sought review of these determinations in the Tax Court.... Before trial, the Commissioner stipulated that the branch churches of Scientology are religious organizations entitled to receive tax-deductible charitable contributions under the relevant sections of the Code. This stipulation isolated as the sole statutory issue whether payments for auditing or training sessions constitute "contribution[s] or gift[s]" under §170.

The Tax Court held a 3-day bench trial during which the taxpayers and others testified and submitted documentary exhibits describing the terms under which the Church promotes and provides auditing and training sessions. Based on this record, the court up-held the Commissioner's decision. 83 T. C. 575 (1984). It observed first that the term "charitable contribution" in §170 is synonymous with the word "gift," which case law had defined "as a *voluntary transfer* of property by the owner to another *without consideration* therefor." *Id.*, at 580, … It then determined that petitioners had received consideration for their payments, namely, "the benefit of various religious services provided by the Church of Scientology." 83 T. C., at 580. The Tax Court also rejected the taxpayers' con-stitutional challenges based on the Establishment and Free Exercise Clauses of the First Amendment.

        …

II

For over 70 years, federal taxpayers have been allowed to deduct the amount of con-tributions or gifts to charitable, religious, and other eleemosynary institutions.… Sec-tion 170, the present provision, was enacted in 1954; it requires a taxpayer claiming the deduction to satisfy a number of conditions. The Commissioner's stipulation in this case, however, has narrowed the statutory inquiry to one such condition: whether peti-tioners' payments for auditing and training sessions are "contribution[s] or gift[s]" within the meaning of §170.

The legislative history of the "contribution or gift" limitation, though sparse, reveals that Congress intended to differentiate between unrequited payments to qualified recip-ients and payments made to such recipients in return for goods or services. Only the former were deemed deductible. The House and Senate Reports on the 1954 tax bill, for example, both define "gifts" as payments "made with no expectation of a financial re-turn commensurate with the amount of the gift." S. Rep. No. 1622, 83d Cong., 2d Sess., 196 (1954); H. R. Rep. No. 1337, 83d Cong., 2d Sess., A44 (1954). Using payments to hospitals as an example, both Reports state that the gift characterization should not apply to "a payment by an individual to a hospital *in consideration of* a binding obliga-tion to provide medical treatment for the individual's employees. It would apply only if there were no expectation of any quid pro quo from the hospital." S. Rep. No. 1622, *supra*, at 196 (emphasis added); H. Rep. No. 1337, *supra*, at A44 (emphasis added).

In ascertaining whether a given payment was made with "the expectation of any quid pro quo," S. Rep. No. 1622, *supra*, at 196; H. Rep. No. 1337, *supra*, at A44, the IRS has customarily examined the external features of the transaction in question. This practice has the advantage of obviating the need for the IRS to conduct imprecise inquiries into the motivations of individual taxpayers. The lower courts have generally embraced this structural analysis.…

In light of this understanding of §170, it is readily apparent that petitioners' pay-ments to the Church do not qualify as "contribution[s] or gift[s]." As the Tax Court found, these payments were part of a quintessential *quid pro quo* exchange: in return for their money, petitioners received an identifiable benefit, namely, auditing and training sessions. The Church established fixed price schedules for auditing and training sessions in each branch church; it calibrated particular prices to auditing or training sessions of particular lengths and levels of sophistication; it returned a refund if auditing and training services went unperformed; it distributed "account cards" on which persons who had paid money to the Church could monitor what prepaid services they had not yet claimed; and it categorically barred provision of auditing or training sessions for free. Each of these practices reveals the inherently reciprocal nature of the exchange.

Petitioners do not argue that such a structural analysis is inappropriate under §170, or that the external features of the auditing and training transactions do not strongly suggest a *quid pro quo* exchange. Indeed, the petitioners in the consolidated *Graham* case conceded at trial that they expected to receive specific amounts of auditing and training in return for their payments. 822 F.2d, at 850. Petitioners argue instead that they are entitled to deductions because a *quid pro quo* analysis is inappropriate under §170 when the benefit a taxpayer receives is purely religious in nature. Along the same lines, petitioners claim that payments made for the right to participate in a religious service should be automatically deductible under §170.

We cannot accept this statutory argument for several reasons. First, it finds no support in the language of §170. Whether or not Congress could, consistent with the Establishment Clause, provide for the automatic deductibility of a payment made to a church that either generates religious benefits or guarantees access to a religious service, that is a choice Congress has thus far declined to make. Instead, Congress has specified that a payment to an organization operated exclusively for religious (or other eleemosynary) purposes is deductible *only* if such a payment is a "contribution or gift." 26 U. S. C. §170(c). The Code makes no special preference for payments made in the expectation of gaining religious benefits or access to a religious service.... The House and Senate Reports on §170, and the other legislative history of that provision, offer no indication that Congress' failure to enact such a preference was an oversight.

Second, petitioners' deductibility proposal would expand the charitable contribution deduction far beyond what Congress has provided. Numerous forms of payments to eligible donees plausibly could be categorized as providing a religious benefit or as securing access to a religious service. For example, some taxpayers might regard their tuition payments to parochial schools as generating a religious benefit or as securing access to a religious service; such payments, however, have long been held not to be charitable contributions under §170.... Taxpayers might make similar claims about payments for church-sponsored counseling sessions or for medical care at church-affiliated hospitals that otherwise might not be deductible. Given that, under the First Amendment, the IRS can reject otherwise valid claims of religious benefit only on the ground that a taxpayers' alleged beliefs are not sincerely held, but not on the ground that such beliefs are inherently irreligious, see *United States v. Ballard*, 322 U.S. 78 (1944), the resulting tax deductions would likely expand the charitable contribution provision far beyond its present size. We are loath to effect this result in the absence of supportive congressional intent....

Finally, the deduction petitioners seek might raise problems of entanglement between church and state. If framed as a deduction for those payments generating benefits of a religious nature for the payor, petitioners' proposal would inexorably force the IRS and reviewing courts to differentiate "religious" benefits from "secular" ones. If framed as a deduction for those payments made in connection with a religious service, petitioners' proposal would force the IRS and the judiciary into differentiating "religious" services from "secular" ones. We need pass no judgment now on the constitutionality of such hypothetical inquiries, but we do note that "pervasive monitoring" for "the subtle or overt presence of religious matter" is a central danger against which we have held the Establishment Clause guards....

Accordingly, we conclude that petitioners' payments to the Church for auditing and training sessions are not "contribution[s] or gift[s]" within the meaning of that statutory expression.

. . .

IV

We turn, finally, to petitioners' assertion that disallowing their claimed deduction is at odds with the IRS' longstanding practice of permitting taxpayers to deduct payments made to other religious institutions in connection with certain religious practices. Through the appellate stages of this litigation, this claim was framed essentially as one of selective prosecution. The Courts of Appeals for the First and Ninth Circuits summarily rejected this claim, finding no evidence of the intentional governmental discrimination necessary to support such a claim. 822 F.2d, at 853 (no showing of "the type of hostility to a target of law enforcement that would support a claim of selective enforcement"); 819 F. 2d, at 1223 (no "discriminatory intent" proved).

In their arguments to this Court, petitioners have shifted emphasis. They now make two closely related claims. First, the IRS has accorded payments for auditing and training disparately harsh treatment compared to payments to other churches and synagogues for their religious services: Recognition of a comparable deduction for auditing and training payments is necessary to cure this administrative inconsistency. Second, Congress, in modifying §170 over the years, has impliedly acquiesced in the deductibility of payments to these other faiths; because payments for auditing and training are indistinguishable from these other payments, they fall within the principle acquiesced in by Congress that payments for religious services are deductible under §170.

Although the Commissioner demurred at oral argument as to whether the IRS, in fact, permits taxpayers to deduct payments made to purchase services from other churches and synagogues, Tr. of Oral Arg. 30–31, the Commissioner's periodic revenue rulings have stated the IRS' position rather clearly. A 1971 ruling, still in effect, states: "Pew rents, building fund assessments, and periodic dues paid to a church ... are all methods of making contributions to the church, and such payments are deductible as charitable contributions within the limitations set out in section 170 of the Code." Rev. Rul. 70-47, 1970-1 Cum. Bull. 49 (superseding A.R.M. 2, Cum. Bull. 150 (1919)). We also assume for purposes of argument that the IRS also allows taxpayers to deduct "specified payments for attendance at High Holy Day services, for tithes, for torah readings and for memorial plaques." *Foley v. Commissioner*, 844 F. 2d, at 94, 96.

The development of the present litigation, however, makes it impossible for us to resolve petitioners' claim that they have received unjustifiably harsh treatment compared to adherents of other religions. The relevant inquiry in determining whether a payment is a "contribution or gift" under §170 is, as we have noted, not whether the payment secures religious benefits or access to religious services, but whether the transaction in which the payment is involved is structured as a *quid pro quo* exchange. To make such a determination in this case, the Tax Court heard testimony and received documentary proof as to the terms and structure of the auditing and training transactions; from this evidence it made factual findings upon which it based its conclusion of nondeductibility, a conclusion we have held consonant with §170 and with the First Amendment.

Perhaps because the theory of administrative inconsistency emerged only on appeal, petitioners did not endeavor at trial to adduce from the IRS or other sources any specific evidence about other religious faiths' transactions. The IRS' revenue rulings, which merely state the agency's conclusions as to deductibility and which have apparently never been reviewed by the Tax Court or any other judicial body, also provide no specific facts about the nature of these other faiths' transactions. In the absence of such facts, we simply have no way (other than the wholly illegitimate one of relying on our personal experiences and observations) to appraise accurately whether the

IRS' revenue rulings have correctly applied a *quid pro quo* analysis with respect to any or all of the religious practices in question. We do not know, for example, whether payments for other faiths' services are truly obligatory or whether any or all of these services are generally provided whether or not the encouraged "mandatory" payment is made.

The IRS' application of the "contribution or gift" standard may be right or wrong with respect to these other faiths, or it may be right with respect to some religious practices and wrong with respect to others. It may also be that some of these payments are appropriately classified as partially deductible "dual payments." With respect to those religions where the structure of transactions involving religious services is established not centrally but by individual congregations, the proper point of reference for a *quid pro quo* analysis might be the individual congregation, not the religion as a whole. Only upon a proper factual record could we make these determinations. Absent such a record, we must reject petitioners' administrative consistency argument.

Petitioners' congressional acquiescence claim fails for similar reasons. Even if one assumes that Congress has acquiesced in the IRS' ruling with respect to "[p]ew rents, building fund assessments, and periodic dues," Rev. Rul. 70-47, 1970-1 Cum. Bull. 49, the fact is that the IRS' 1971 ruling articulates no broad principle of deductibility, but instead merely identifies as deductible three discrete types of payments. Having before us no information about the nature or structure of these three payments, we have no way of discerning any possible unifying principle, let alone whether such a principle would embrace payments for auditing and training sessions.

V

For the reasons stated herein, the judgments of the Courts of Appeals are hereby

Affirmed.

FOOTNOTE:

1. Section 170 provides in pertinent part:

"(a) Allowance of deduction

"(1) General Rule

"There shall be allowed as a deduction any charitable contribution (as defined in subsection (c)) payment of which is made within the taxable year. A charitable contribution shall be allowable as a deduction only if verified under regulations prescribed by the Secretary.

. . .

"(c) Charitable contribution defined

"For purposes of this section, the term "charitable contribution" means a contribution or gift to or for the use of—

. . .

"(2) A corporation, trust, or community chest, fund, or foundation—

"(A) created or organized in the United States or in any possession thereof, or under the law of the United States, any State, the District of Columbia, or any possession of the United States;

"(B) organized and operated exclusively for religious, charitable, scientific, literary, or educational purposes, or to foster national or international amateur sports competition (but only if no part of its activities involve the provision of athletic facilities or equipment), or for the prevention of cruelty to children or animals;

"(C) no part of the net earnings of which inures to the benefit of any private shareholder or individual; and

"(D) which is not disqualified for tax exemption under section 501(c)(3) by reason of attempting to influence legislation, and which does not participate in, or intervene in (including the publishing or distributing of statements), any political campaign on behalf of any candidate for public office...."

JUSTICE O'CONNOR, with whom JUSTICE SCALIA joins, dissenting.

The Court today acquiesces in the decision of the Internal Revenue Service (IRS) to manufacture a singular exception to its 70-year practice of allowing fixed payments indistinguishable from those made by petitioners to be deducted as charitable contributions. Because the IRS cannot constitutionally be allowed to select which religions will receive the benefit of its past rulings, I respectfully dissent.

The cases before the Court have an air of artificiality about them that is due to the IRS' dual litigation strategy against the Church of Scientology (Church).... [T]he IRS has successfully argued that the mother Church of Scientology was not a tax-exempt organization from 1970 to 1972 because it had diverted profits to the founder of Scientology and others, conspired to impede collection of its taxes, and conducted almost all of its activities for a commercial purpose. See *Church of Scientology of California v. Commissioner*, 83 T. C. 381 (1984), aff'd, 823 F. 2d 1310 (CA9 1987), cert. denied, 486 U.S. 1015 (1988). In the cases before the Court today, however, the IRS decided to contest the payments made to Scientology under 26 U. S. C. §170 rather than challenge the tax-exempt status of the various branches of the Church to which the payments were made. According to the Deputy Solicitor General, the IRS challenged the payments themselves in order to expedite matters. Tr. of Oral Arg. 26–29.... As part of its litigation strategy in these cases, the IRS agreed to several stipulations which, in my view, necessarily determine the proper approach to the questions presented by petitioners.

The stipulations, relegated to a single sentence by the Court ... established that Scientology was at all relevant times a religion; that each Scientology branch to which payments were made was at all relevant times a "church" within the meaning of §170(b)(1)(A)(i); and that Scientology was at all times a "corporation" within the meaning of §170(c)(2) and exempt from general income taxation under 26 U. S. C. §501(a).... 83 T. C. 575, 576 (1984), aff'd, 822 F. 2d 844 (CA9 1987). As the Solicitor General recognizes, it follows from these stipulations that Scientology operates for "'charitable purposes'" and puts the "public interest above the private interest." Brief for Respondent 30.... Moreover, the stipulations establish that the payments made by petitioners are fixed donations made by individuals to a tax-exempt religious organization in order to participate in religious services, and are not based on "market prices set to reap the profits of a commercial moneymaking venture." ... The Tax Court, however, appears to have ignored the stipulations. It concluded, perhaps relying on its previous opinion in *Church of Scientology*, that "Scientology operates in a commercial manner in providing [auditing and training]. In fact, one of its articulated goals is to make money." 83 T. C., at 578. The Solicitor General has duplicated the error here, referring on numerous occasions to the commercial nature of Scientology in an attempt to negate the effect of the stipulations. See Brief for Respondent 13–14, 23, 25, 44.

It must be emphasized that the IRS' position here is *not* based upon the contention that a portion of the knowledge received from auditing or training is of secular, commercial, nonreligious value. Thus, the denial of a deduction in these cases bears no resemblance to the denial of a deduction for religious-school tuition up to the market value of the secularly useful education received.... Here the IRS denies deductibility solely on the basis that the exchange is a *quid pro quo*, even though the *quid* is exclusively of spiritual or religious worth. Respondent cites no instances in which this has been done before, and there are good reasons why.

When a taxpayer claims as a charitable deduction part of a fixed amount given to a charitable organization in exchange for benefits that have a commercial value, the allowable portion of that claim is computed by subtracting from the total amount paid the value of the physical benefit received. If at a charity sale one purchases for $1,000 a painting whose market value is demonstrably no more than $50, there has been a contribution of $950. The same would be true if one purchases a $1,000 seat at a charitable dinner where the food is worth $50. An identical calculation can be made where the *quid* received is not a painting or a meal, but an intangible such as entertainment, so long as that intangible has some market value established in a noncontributory context. Hence, one who purchases a ticket to a concert, at the going rate for concerts by the particular performers, makes a charitable contribution of zero even if it is announced in advance that all proceeds from the ticket sales will go to charity. The performers may have made a charitable contribution, but the audience has paid the going rate for a show.

It becomes impossible, however, to compute the "contribution" portion of a payment to a charity where what is received in return is not merely an intangible, but an intangible (or, for that matter a tangible) that is not bought and sold except in donative contexts so that the only "market" price against which it can be evaluated is a market price that always includes donations. Suppose, for example, that the charitable organization that traditionally solicits donations on Veterans Day, in exchange for which it gives the donor an imitation poppy bearing its name, were to establish a flat rule that no one gets a poppy without a donation of at least $10. One would have to say that the "market" rate for such poppies was $10, but it would assuredly not be true that everyone who "bought" a poppy for $10 made no contribution. Similarly, if one buys a $100 seat at a prayer breakfast—receiving as the *quid pro quo* food for both body and soul—it would make no sense to say that no charitable contribution whatever has occurred simply because the "going rate" for all prayer breakfasts (with equivalent bodily food) is $100. The latter may well be true, but that "going rate" *includes* a contribution.

Confronted with this difficulty, and with the constitutional necessity of not making irrational distinctions among taxpayers, and with the even higher standard of equality of treatment among *religions* that the First Amendment imposes, the Government has only two practicable options with regard to distinctively religious *quids pro quo*: to disregard them all, or to tax them all. Over the years it has chosen the former course.

Congress enacted the first charitable contribution exception to income taxation in 1917. War Revenue Act of 1917, ch. 63, §1201(2), 40 Stat. 330. A mere two years later, in A.R.M. 2, 1 Cum. Bull. 150 (1919), the IRS gave its first blessing to the deductions of fixed payments to religious organizations as charitable contributions:

> "[T]he distinction of pew rents, assessments, church dues, and the like from basket collections is hardly warranted by the act. The act reads 'contributions' and 'gifts.' It is felt that all of these come within the two terms.

"In substance it is believed that these are simply methods of contributing although in form they may vary. Is a basket collection given involuntarily to be distinguished from an envelope system, the latter being regarded as 'dues'? From a technical angle, the pew rents may be differentiated, but in practice the so-called 'personal accommodation' they may afford is conjectural. It is believed that the real intent is to contribute and not to hire a seat or pew for personal accommodation. In fact, basket contributors sometimes receive the same accommodation informally."

The IRS reaffirmed its position in 1970, ruling that "[p]ew rents, building fund assessments and periodic dues paid to a church ... are all methods of making contributions to the church and such payments are deductible as charitable contributions." Rev. Rul. 70-47, 1970-1 Cum. Bull. 49. Similarly, notwithstanding the "form" of Mass stipends as fixed payments for specific religious services, see infra, at 709, the IRS has allowed charitable deductions of such payments. See Rev. Rul. 78-366, 1978-2 Cum. Bull. 241.

These rulings, which are "official interpretation[s] of [the tax laws] by the [IRS]," Rev. Proc. 78-24, 1978-2 Cum. Bull. 503, 504, flatly contradict the Solicitor General's claim that there "is no administrative practice recognizing that payments made in exchange for religious benefits are tax deductible." Brief for Respondent 16. Indeed, an Assistant Commissioner of the IRS recently explained in a "question and answer guidance package" to tax-exempt organizations that "[i]n contrast to tuition payments, religious observances generally are not regarded as yielding private benefits to the donor, who is viewed as receiving only incidental benefits when attending the observances. The primary beneficiaries are viewed as being the general public and members of the faith. Thus, payments for saying masses, pew rents, tithes, and other payments involving fixed donations for similar religious services, are fully deductible contributions." IRS Official Explains New Examination-Education Program on Charitable Contributions to Tax-Exempt Organizations, BNA Daily Report for Executives, Special Report No. 186, J-1, J-3 (Sept. 26, 1988). Although this guidance package may not be as authoritative as IRS rulings, ... in the absence of any contrary indications it does reflect the continuing adherence of the IRS to its practice of allowing deductions for fixed payments for religious services.

There can be no doubt that at least some of the fixed payments which the IRS has treated as charitable deductions, or which the Court assumes the IRS would allow taxpayers to deduct, ante, at 690–691, are as "inherently reciprocal," ante, at 692, as the payments for auditing at issue here. In exchange for their payment of pew rents, Christians receive particular seats during worship services. See Encyclopedic Dictionary of Religion 2760 (1979). Similarly, in some synagogues attendance at the worship services for Jewish High Holy Days is often predicated upon the purchase of a general admission ticket or a reserved seat ticket. See J. Feldman, H. Fruhauf, & M. Schoen, Temple Management Manual, ch. 4, p. 10 (1984). Religious honors such as publicly reading from Scripture are purchased or auctioned periodically in some synagogues of Jews from Morocco and Syria. See H. Dobrinsky, A Treasury of Sephardic Laws and Customs 164, 175–177 (1986). Mormons must tithe their income as a necessary but not sufficient condition to obtaining a "temple recommend," i.e., the right to be admitted into the temple. See The Book of Mormon, 3 Nephi 24:7–12 (1921); Reorganized Church of Jesus Christ of Latter-day Saints, Book of Doctrine and Covenants §106:1b (1978); Corporation of Presiding Bishop of Church of Jesus Christ of Latter-day Saints v. Amos, 483 U.S. 327, 330, n. 4 (1987). A Mass stipend—a fixed payment given to a Catholic priest, in consideration of which he is obliged to apply the fruits of the Mass for the intention of the donor—has similar overtones of exchange. According to some Catholic theologians, the nature of the pact between a priest and a donor who pays a Mass stipend is "a bilateral contract known as do ut facias. One person agrees to give while the other party agrees to do something in return." 13 New Catholic Encyclopedia, Mass Stipend, p. 715 (1967). A finer example of a quid pro quo exchange would be hard to formulate.

. . .

There is no discernible reason why there is a more rigid connection between payment and services in the religious practices of Scientology than in the religious practices of the faiths described above. Neither has respondent explained why the benefit received by a Christian who obtains the pew of his or her choice by paying a rental fee, a Jew who gains entrance to High Holy Day services by purchasing a ticket, a Mormon who makes the fixed payment necessary for a temple recommend, or a Catholic who pays a Mass stipend, is incidental to the real benefit conferred on the "general public and members of the faith," BNA Daily Report, at J-3, while the benefit received by a Scientologist from auditing is a personal accommodation. If the perceived difference lies in the fact that Christians and Jews worship in congregations, whereas Scientologists, in a manner reminiscent of Eastern religions, see App. 78–83 (testimony of Dr. Thomas Love), gain awareness of the "immortal spiritual being" within them in one-to-one sessions with auditors, *ante*, at 684–685, such a distinction would raise serious Establishment Clause problems....

. . .

In my view, the IRS has misapplied its longstanding practice of allowing charitable contributions under §170 in a way that violates the Establishment Clause. It has unconstitutionally refused to allow payments for the religious service of auditing to be deducted as charitable contributions in the same way it has allowed fixed payments to other religions to be deducted. Just as the Minnesota statute at issue in *Larson v. Valente*, 456 U.S. 228 (1982), discriminated against the Unification Church, the IRS' application of the *quid pro quo* standard here—and only here—discriminates against the Church of Scientology. I would reverse the decisions below.

Consider the following questions about *Hernandez*.

1. Why do you think the Commissioner stipulated that "the branch churches of Scientology are religious organizations entitled to receive tax-deductible charitable contributions under the relevant sections of the Code"?

2. Based on your reading of *Hernandez*, can you define the term "charitable contribution?"

3. What is the relationship, if any, between the definition of "gift" under section 102(a) as set forth by the Supreme Court in *Duberstein* and that of the term "gift" under section 170(c) as set forth by the Court in *Hernandez*?

4. Suppose you contributed $100 for a raffle ticket to a qualified donee under section 501(c)(3). Is your "contribution" deductible?

5. Suppose you contributed $2,000,000 to your law school, which is a qualified donee under section 501(c)(3), and, in return, the law school named a wing of its building after you.[33] Is your "contribution" deductible?

---

33. Section 170 contains a type of limit that you have not studied before. Section 170(b) places an upper limit on the amount any taxpayer may deduct in a single year. **See the flush language of**

6. Suppose you are a lawyer and you volunteer ten hours of your time each week to the local legal services office (which is a qualified donee under section 501(c)(3)). Can you deduct the value of your time? **Look at Treasury Regulation section 1.170A-1(g).** What might be the rationale for the regulation's treatment of donated services?

7. Suppose you contributed $365 to your local public television station (which is a qualified donee under section 501(c)(3)). In return you receive a video tape of a performance by the Three Irish Tenors, which the station tells you has a retail value of $25. What is the amount, if any, of your deduction?

8. Can you articulate the position of Justices O'Connor and Scalia, who dissented in this case? Does the majority address their concerns adequately?

––––––––––

At about the same time as *Hernandez* was proceeding through the courts, another aspect of the relationship between the Church of Scientology and federal tax law was unfolding elsewhere. Despite the Commissioner's concession in *Hernandez* that the church met the definition of a religious organization under the definition of section 501(c)(3), the church was not necessarily exempt from tax. Rather than dispute whether an organization is actually a religion, the Service instead investigates activities carried on by the organization to ascertain that it does not operate in ways prohibited by the Code. Two examples constituting prohibited behavior are the use of its assets by an exempt organization for the benefit of any individual or use of its efforts or assets in political campaigns.

In *Church of Scientology of California v. Commissioner*, 83 T.C. 381 (1984), the Tax Court held that Scientology's mother church (in California) failed to qualify as tax exempt under section 501(c)(3) of the Code because it diverted assets to the church's founder, L. Ron Hubbard, and others; conspired to avoid taxes; and operated for a substantial, non-exempt, commercial purpose. The Ninth Circuit affirmed the Tax Court, but rested its decision solely on the ground that the church's profits inured to the benefit of private individuals.[34]

But the story does not end there; subsequent developments in the on-going conflict between the Church of Scientology and the Internal Revenue Service are both interesting and provocative. In 1993, the Service surprised almost everyone by reversing its position. As reported by the *New York Times* on October 13, 1993:

Scientologists Granted Tax Exemption by the U.S.[35]

The Government said today that it had agreed to grant a tax exemption to the Church of Scientology and more than 150 of its related corporations, ending one of the longest-running tax disputes in American history.

––––––––––

section 170(b)(1). This type of limit is known as a "ceiling." Do you recall which deductions contain a "floor"? The limit depends upon the nature of the donor, the donee, and the gift. In general, these limitations do not permanently bar the deduction of the gift, but simply postpone the deduction of the balance to a future tax year or years (a so-called "carryover"). For individuals, the limitation is usually 50 percent of AGI. Few taxpayers are affected by this limitation, and you may ignore it for purposes of this problem.

34. 823 F.2d 1310 (9th Cir. 1987), *cert. denied*, 486 U.S. 1015 (1988).

...

Officials at the Internal Revenue Service and the Scientology group declined to spell out the details of the settlement and would not explain why it had finally been reached after four decades of costly and bitter court fights.

People familiar with the group's closely held finances said the tax exemptions could save the organization at least tens of millions of dollars a year in taxes.

The exemptions were granted as part of a larger settlement between the Government and the Scientology organizations that end legal disputes that go back to the founding of the church 39 years ago....

Officials at the Internal Revenue Service said the decision granting the Scientologists tax-exempt status does not change the standards for determining when an institution is to be considered religious for tax purposes....

The church's California branch had a Federal tax exemption at one point but lost it 26 years ago, and most of the other related organizations never had exemptions. For decades, the Government has said that although Scientology can be considered a religion, its affiliated organizations had operated as businesses for the financial gain of the church's leaders, most notably L. Ron Hubbard.

Mr. Hubbard, who founded the group in the 1950's after his book "Dianetics" became a best seller, responded to the Internal Revenue Service's challenge by making anti-Government statements that became part of the church's dogma. And after Mr. Hubbard died in 1986, other Scientology leaders ... continued to preach against the Government and the tax collectors.

...

The ruling means that the church and the more than 150 related educational and counseling groups will no longer have to pay Federal income taxes. Church members may also deduct their membership dues from their taxes....

[The president of one of the Scientology organizations] was unusually conciliatory toward the I.R.S. today. He said that the church had prevailed after what he called "an objective review." ...

...

The Federal Government recognized the Church of Scientology of California as a tax-exempt religious organization in 1957, but revoked that exemption in 1967. Its decision led to a wave of litigation by the church and the Government over various issues, like the church's request under the Freedom of Information Act for Government files, to the Government's attempts to assess the organization.

In 1984, a Tax Court concluded that the church had "made a business out of selling religion," and that Mr. Hubbard and his family had diverted millions of dollars of church funds....

Court documents showed that the church had an extensive project to infiltrate Government agencies in the United States and more than 30 countries to suppress investigations of the organization. Ultimately, 11 church leaders, including Mr. Hubbard's wife, Mary Sue, served prison terms for the wiretap of an Internal Revenue Service office and other crimes.

---

35. Stephen Labaton, "Scientologists Granted Tax Exemption by the U.S.," N.Y. Times, Oct. 14, 1993, at A1.

The Service's reversal of position was contained in a "closing agreement" it entered into with the church.[36] The Service refused to disclose the closing agreement; it remained confidential until its text was leaked to the Wall Street Journal in December 1997. As reported by Elizabeth MacDonald:

Scientologists and IRS Settled for $12.5 Million[37]

The Church of Scientology paid the federal government $12.5 million as part of a broad 1993 settlement with the Internal Revenue Service under which the church's main branch secured its tax-exempt status.

According to a copy of the settlement, details of which have never before been made public, the church also agreed to set up a special "church tax-compliance committee," composed of high-level church officials, to monitor its adherence to the pact and to laws governing nonprofit organizations.

Further, the church agreed to drop thousands of lawsuits filed against the IRS in courts around the country and to stop assisting people or groups suing the agency based on claims prior to Oct. 1, 1993, the settlement date. Any Scientology member or organization that sues based on those claims could face IRS penalties.

The 1993 agreement was nearly unprecedented and brought an end to an extraordinary battle. Starting in 1967, the IRS had argued that the main Scientology church should lose its tax-exempt status because it was a for-profit business that enriched church officials. The church's response was an all-out attack: filing suits against the IRS, feeding negative stories abut the agency to news organizations, and supporting IRS whistle-blowers.

The church's $12.5 million payment was intended to cover the church's payroll, income and estate-tax bills for an undisclosed number of years prior to 1993. It is unclear how much money the IRS originally sought.

More Provisions

Other major provision of the settlement:

---

36. Section 7121 provides a methodology for settling disagreements between the Service and taxpayers. The section provides:
  (a) AUTHORIZATION.—The Secret is authorized to enter into an agreement in writing with any person relating to the liability of such person ... in respect of any internal revenue tax for any taxable period.
  (b) FINALITY.—If such agreement is approved by the Secretary ... such agreement shall be final and conclusive, and, except upon a showing of fraud or malfeasance, or misrepresentation of a material fact—
  (1) the case shall not be reopened as to the matters agreed upon or the agreement modified by any officer, employee, or agent of the United States, and
  (2) in any suit, action, or proceeding, such agreement, or any determination, assessment, collection, payment, abatement, refund, or credit made in accordance therewith, shall not be annulled, modified, set aside, or disregarded.
37. Elizabeth MacDonald, "Scientologists and IRS Settled For $12.5 Million," Wall St. J., Dec. 30, 1997, at A12.

- The IRS canceled the payroll taxes and penalties it had assessed against certain church entities and seven church officials, including church leader David Miscavige. (The pact doesn't specify the amount of these bills). It also dropped liens and levies it had filed against these entities and officials for these bills.

- The church tax-compliance committee was required to give the IRS annual reports for 1992 through 1995 disclosing how much the church paid its 20 top-compensated officials, as well as the finances of 23 member churches, businesses and organizations. Failure to file the reports could result in penalties of as much as $75,000 for each committee member.

- The IRS can impose as much as $50 million in penalties on certain church entities if the IRS finds that they repeatedly spend church funds on noncharitable purposes, including enriching themselves. The penalties would be in effect through 1999.

- The IRS dropped its audits of 13 Scientology organizations, including the mother church, the Church of Scientology International, and agreed not to audit the church for any year prior to 1993. The IRS also dropped litigation to enforce summonses for church records.

Regulating the activities of churches has long been a prickly area for the IRS. The First Amendment generally prohibits the government from determining what is and isn't a valid church; yet the tax-collection agency is charged with making certain that churches don't abuse their tax-exempt status, since taxpayers effectively subsidize their operations. The Scientology settlement shows just how difficult it is to walk that line.

IRS officials refused to discuss the settlement, citing confidentiality rules. Spokesman Frank Keith said the IRS granted Scientology tax-exempt status "because the church provided adequate documentation and information to us to enable us to make the determination that they met the legal standards under the law and that they were legally entitled to tax-exempt status."

Monique Yingling, a lawyer for the church, declined to comment on details of the agreement but said the church "does comply with the tax laws." She added that the church "received a more in-depth standard of scrutiny than other religions." Ms. Yingling also said that the church's $12.5 million payment was not a tax bill but was "meant to resolve all outstanding disputes" between the church and the IRS.

"At one time the IRS asserted [that the church owed] hundreds of millions of dollars, [and] it might have gone as high as a billion dollars," "Ms. Yingling said. The IRS so far has not assessed any penalties against the church as spelled out in the agreement, she said.

Some tax experts worry the settlement may prove it pays to harass the tax agency. "The IRS normally settles on tax issues alone," said Robert Fink, a New York tax lawyer who reviewed the agreement. "What the IRS wanted was to buy peace from the Scientologists. You never see the IRS wanting to buy peace."

Established in 1954

The Church of Scientology was established in Los Angles in 1954 and was granted tax-exempt status in 1957. But 10 years later, the IRS pulled the tax exemption for the main church in California, although not for any other branches, according to church officials. The IRS claimed that founder L. Ron Hubbard and his family were enriching themselves with church funds. Subsequently, courts also noted that the church makes money from the sale of Scientology books and materials, as well as its "sacrament" of "auditing," in which members generally are required to pay church-trained "auditors" to hook them up to a device that is supposed to purge negative thoughts.

The settlement, which lets Scientologists deduct on their individual tax returns "auditing" fees as donations, supersedes the IRS's earlier rule denying such deductions—a position that was backed by the U.S. Supreme Court.

The church owns an estimated $300 million in assets; between 1988 and 1992, according to church documents filed with the IRS, its revenues totaled about $1.1 billion. In a separate IRS filing, the church said it may spend an estimated $114 million for a variety of church-related activities, including designing titanium time capsules to hold Mr. Hubbard's "scriptures." Mr. Hubbard died in 1986.

A trust that oversees the church's 7,056 ton, 440-foot cruise ship, Freewinds, also got tax-exempt status. According to church filings with the IRS unrelated to the pact, the church uses the ship, which is docked in Curacao and "has sailed almost exclusively in the Caribbean," as a "seagoing religious retreat" for church parishioners. The church bought the ship with $5 million in donations in 1986.

The Service's reversal of position, its acceptance of a relatively small settlement payment, and its secrecy in both the negotiation process and the details of the closing agreement elicited criticism from the media, as well as from tax professionals. Representative of the criticism is an editorial from the St. Petersburg Times of January 6, 1998:

Sellout to Scientology[38]

For 25 years, the Internal Revenue Service held all of the cards against the Church of Scientology. The IRS steadfastly refused to give Scientology a much-coveted tax exemption, and the courts consistently sided with the agency. Then the IRS abruptly folded in 1993, granting the tax exemption while refusing to disclose the details of the agreement. Amid such secrecy, taxpayers could only wonder what Scientology offered to persuade the IRS to abandon more than two decades of policy.

The answer turns out to be a relative pittance.

The secret agreement, obtained by the Wall Street Journal, indicates Scientology bought its way out of potentially hundreds of millions of dollars in taxes for $12.5-million. In return, the IRS granted tax-exempt status to 114 Scientology-related organizations, dismissed tax penalties and liens against some church groups and stopped audits of 13 Scientology entities. That is not a deal; it is a sellout by an IRS that has been accused of running roughshod over less threatening taxpayers.

The tax-exempt status gave Scientology something even more important than avoiding millions of dollars in tax bills. It gave members a powerful weapon to use in their ceaseless public relations campaign to be considered a legitimate religion. When Germany fights Scientology and labels it a business, the church waves its IRS ruling. The impact also was felt in Pinellas County [Florida], where the ruling forced the property appraiser to treat Scientology "like any other religion" and give up a long court battle over whether Scientology's local properties should be exempt from property taxes. Now about $20-million of Scientology's $30-million worth of property in the Clearwater area is exempt from taxes. Taxpayers have the IRS to thank.

---

38. Editorial, "Sellout to Scientology," St. Petersburg Times, Jan. 6, 1998, at 8A.

With details of the Scientology agreement now public, there is every reason to question whether IRS officials were more interested in avoiding harassment than in sound tax policy. The agreement called for Scientology to drop its lawsuits against the IRS and agency officials and to stop helping church members who had filed similar lawsuits. That could have affected some 2,200 lawsuits. The New York Times also has reported about Scientology's hiring of private investigators to look for code violations at a building owned by IRS officials, and about an IRS whistle-blowers group financed by the church. Scientology was not the typical taxpayer quarreling over its tax bill, and it did not receive typical treatment.

When Scientology's tactics were disclosed last year, no one heard a peep from Congress. Since then, members of Congress from both political parties have treated the IRS as a punching bag. Perhaps news of the $12.5-million settlement finally will prod someone in Washington to ask the agency some tough questions about this one-sided agreement. To most taxpayers, $12.5-million would be a stiff penalty. For the Church of Scientology, it was the small cost of doing business.

Shortly after the Service's reversal of position, it issued Revenue Ruling 93-73, 1993-2 C.B. 172, authorizing the deduction of fees paid to the Church of Scientology for training and auditing, in effect reversing the holding of the *Hernandez* case. How could the Service overrule the United States Supreme Court? Although the reasoning of the Service is not entirely clear, it may have based its reversal on congressional enactment of section 170(f)(8). Congress enacted that provision in 1993, three months prior to issuance of the new Revenue Ruling. **Read section 170(f)(8).**

The difficulty with this argument is that the new section does not clearly overrule the holding in *Hernandez* that an intangible religious benefit may be a *quid-pro-quo*. Rather, section 170(f)(8) requires that the donee of a contribution of $250 or more give the donor an acknowledgment of the gift, indicating whether there is any *quid-pro-quo* element. But, the donee need not value the *quid-pro-quo* element if it is in the form of an intangible religious benefit.[39] Relieving the donee of the need to value the intangible religious benefit does not automatically free the benefit from *quid-pro-quo* status. That is, an intangible religious benefit is, nevertheless, under the statute, "goods or services" received.

The Service's reversal of its decision on the issue of auditing and training fees led some commentators to wonder "if Scientologists can deduct for religious training, why can't Catholics and Jews [and, presumably, members of other religious denominations] deduct the costs of their children's religious training in schools that either teach religion exclusively or as part of a secular education?"[40] Consider the following case:

SKLAR v. COMMISSIONER

T.C. Memo. 2000-118

NAMEROFF, Special Trial Judge: Respondent determined a deficiency in petitioners' Federal income tax for the taxable year 1994 of $3,696 plus an addition to tax under

---

39. An intangible religious benefit is one "provided by an organization organized exclusively for religious purposes and which generally is not sold in a commercial transaction outside the donative context." Section 170(f)(8)(B)(iii), flush language. *See also* section 6115(b).

40. Paul Streckfus, "Scientology Case Redux," 87 Tax Notes 1414 (June 5, 2000). Mr. Streckfus is the editor of Paul Streckfus' EO Tax Journal. ("EO" is "exempt organization.")

section 6651(a)(1) of $408.20. In the notice of deficiency, respondent disallowed petitioners' claimed charitable contribution deductions of $13,240. The explanation in the notice of deficiency stated: "Since these costs are personal tuition expenses, they are not deductible." In a timely filed petition, petitioners contend that they are entitled to the claimed charitable contribution deductions on the grounds that the amounts in question are similar to those paid for auditing to the Church of Scientology, which petitioners allege the Internal Revenue Service (IRS) has allowed as charitable contributions. Thus petitioners contend that respondent's position is a violation of the Establishment Clause of the First Amendment to the Constitution of the United States.

Background

Some of the facts have been stipulated and are so found....

On their 1994 joint Federal income tax return, which was filed on November 27, 1995, petitioners claimed a deduction for charitable contributions in the amount of $23,996. Petitioners' 1994 return was examined by respondent, and the charitable contribution deduction was questioned. During the examination, petitioners provided copies of checks totaling $10,756 that qualified as charitable contributions, and this amount was not disallowed.

In addition, petitioners provided copies of checks totaling $7,000 paid as tuition to the Yeshiva Rav Isacsohn Torath Emeth Academy (Yeshiva Rav Isacsohn). Petitioners also provided checks totaling $17,146 in tuition payments to the Emek Hebrew Academy (Emek). Yeshiva Rav Isacsohn and Emek are collectively referred to as the schools. The amounts paid to the schools in 1994 total $24,146.

In July 1996, during the examination of their 1994 return, petitioners presented letters from each school which acknowledge receipt of the amounts paid and state unequivocally that the payments were applied toward the tuition of petitioners' children for their religious and secular education. Each letter also states that the school estimates that the total education comprised 55 percent religious education and 45 percent secular education. According to petitioners, they calculated their claimed 1994 "religious education" deduction in the amount of $13,240 by multiplying by 55 percent the total tuition payments to the schools.

Emek and Yeshiva Rav Isacsohn are organizations recognized to be exempt from Federal income tax under section 501(c)(3). They are classified for Federal income tax purposes as organizations that are not private foundations as defined in section 509(a) because they are organizations described in section 170(b)(1)(A)(ii). In short, they are orthodox Jewish day schools, and their students receive a complete dual curriculum in religious and secular studies. Both schools issue academic grades in their secular and religious education programs. During 1994, three of petitioners' minor children attended Emek and one minor child attended Yeshiva Rav Isacsohn.

The schools establish annually the amount of tuition for each student, payment of which is mandatory. There are also other mandatory payments for, inter alia, special events and application processing. Partial scholarships are provided for students with financial needs. Tuition payments are recorded as such in the schools' books, and charitable contributions to the schools are recorded as "donations".

In the petition, petitioners make no allegations in connection with the addition to tax for delinquency. In petitioners' response to a motion for summary judgment filed by respondent and subsequently denied, petitioners state:

> The primary reason for filing after October 16, 1995, was lack of sufficient
> time to correctly prepare the return due to high work-related volume peti-

tioner Michael Sklar, who is the petitioner knowledgeable in the taxable affairs of petitioners and regularly prepares petitioners' returns. The reason this was not stated in the original petition is that petitioners felt that it was a moot point as, in the opinion of petitioners, there is no deficiency.

Petitioners presented no further evidence on this issue.

Discussion

The law is well settled that tuition paid for the education of the children of the taxpayer is a family expense, not a charitable contribution to the educating institution. See *DeJong v. Commissioner,* ... 309 F.2d 373, 376 (9th Cir. 1962), affg.... 36 T.C. 896 (1961). A tuition payment to a parochial school is generally not considered a charitable contribution because the taxpayer making the payment receives something of economic value, i.e., educational benefits, in return. See *Winters v. Commissioner,* ... 468 F.2d 778, 781 (2d Cir. 1972), affg.... T.C. Memo. 1971-290. The payment proceeds primarily from the incentive of anticipated benefits to the payor beyond the satisfaction which flows from the performance of a generous act. See *DeJong v. Commissioner, supra* at 376. The Court of Appeals for the Ninth Circuit further stated:

> The value of a gift may be excluded from gross income only if the gift proceeds from a "detached and disinterested generosity" or "out of affection, admiration, charity or like impulses" and must be included if the claimed gift proceeds primarily from "the constraining force of any moral or legal duty" or from "the incentive of anticipated benefit of an economic nature." We must conclude that such criteria are clearly applicable to a charitable deduction under § 170.

Id, at 379.

It is clear in this case that petitioners' payments to the schools were not made out of detached and disinterested generosity or out of affection, admiration, charity, or like impulses. They were intended as payment in the nature of tuition for petitioners' children, a personal expense. These mandatory payments were received as payments for tuition by the schools. Therefore, they do not qualify as charitable contribution deductions.

In *Hernandez v. Commissioner,* ... 490 U.S. 680 (1989), the Supreme Court held on the record presented that payments for "auditing" to the Church of Scientology were not deductible as charitable contributions because they represented a quid pro quo; i.e., the payor was receiving goods or services in return for the payment. The taxpayer in *Hernandez* had argued, inter alia, that the disallowance of the auditing payments represented an impermissible failure by the IRS to consistently enforce section 170, relying on various revenue rulings, such as Rev. Rul. 70-47, 1970-1 C.B. 49, pertaining to such things as pew rents, building fund assessments, and periodic dues.... However, the Supreme Court rejected this contention because the record therein did not support it.

Petitioners contend that the terms of a closing agreement between the Commissioner and the Church of Scientology are relevant and will show that the Commissioner has agreed to allow charitable contributions for all or a percentage of auditing payments, and that the disallowance of the charitable contribution deductions herein in light of the settlement with the Church of Scientology is in violation of the First Amendment....

In her dissenting opinion in *Hernandez v. Commissioner,* ... Justice O'Connor stated:

It must be emphasized that the IRS' position here is *not* based upon the contention that a portion of the knowledge received from auditing or training is of a secular, commercial, nonreligious value. Thus, the denial of a deduction in these cases bears no resemblance to the denial of a deduction for a religious-school tuition up to the market value of the secularly useful education received. See *Oppewal v. Commissioner*, ... 468 F.2d 1000 (1st Cir. 1972); *Winters v. Commissioner*, ... 468 F.2d 778 (2d Cir. 1972); *DeJong v. Commissioner*, 309 F.2d 373 (9th Cir. 1962)....

There is nothing in the record to show that petitioners' situation is analogous to that of the members of the Church of Scientology. The Church of Scientology and the schools involved in this case are not identical in their organization, structure, or purpose. Auditing, as defined in *Hernandez v. Commissioner*, ... is not the same as a general education, which may include some percentage for religious education. Thus we perceive no denominational preference to require any inquiry into a purported violation of the Establishment Clause. As stated earlier, deductions have been generally disallowed for payments made in exchange for educational benefits, regardless of faith. See *Oppewal v. Commissioner*, ... 468 F.2d 1000 (1st Cir. 1972), affg.... T.C. Memo. 1971-273; *Winters v. Commissioner*, supra; *DeJong v. Commissioner*, supra. The taxpayers in those cases were similarly situated with petitioners, and petitioners have not established that they are similarly situated with the members of the Church of Scientology who make payments for auditing. Petitioners' reliance on *Hernandez* and the concept of consistent interpretation and enforcement is rejected.

We now turn to the question of whether petitioners are liable for the addition to tax for delinquency under section 6651(a)(1). Unless shown to be for reasonable cause and not due to willful neglect, failure to file a return on the due date generally results in an addition to tax of 5 percent for each month during which such failure continues, but not exceeding 25 percent in the aggregate. See sec. 6651(a)(1).

Petitioners contend that petitioner Michael Sklar was simply too busy to timely file their tax return for 1994. After extensions, their tax return was due on October 15, 1995, but was not filed until November 16, 1995. Accordingly, in the notice of deficiency, respondent determined the delinquency addition to tax based on 10 percent of the deficiency. On the tax return, petitioner Michael Sklar is identified as a C.P.A., while petitioner Marla Sklar is identified as a teacher. Petitioner's argument that he was simply too busy to file his Federal income tax return for 1994 by October 15, 1995, does not constitute reasonable cause for his failure to file....

Decision will be entered for respondent.

Consider the following questions about *Sklar*.

1. Notice that the citation for *Sklar* is "T.C. Memo 2000-118."[41] Look back at the cite for the case *McKay v. Commissioner*, which you read in connection with Carole's problem. The Tax Court decided both cases. Why do they have different forms of citation?

The Tax Court publishes certain opinions in its official reporter ("Tax Court Reports," designated, "T.C."). Those opinions appearing in the official reporter involve,

---

41. The United States Court of Appeals for the Ninth Circuit affirmed the Tax Court's decision. *Sklar v. Commissioner*, 279 F.3d 697; amended 282 F.3d 610 (9th Cir. 2002).

generally, legal issues of first impression. (The Chief Judge determines which will appear in the official reporter.) Those that do are considered binding precedent. *McKay*, as is revealed by its "T.C." cite, appears in the official reporter.

The Tax Court also issues two other types of opinions that do not appear in its official reporter: memorandum and summary opinions. Memorandum opinions deal generally with the application of established legal rules to new sets of facts. These decisions, designated "Tax Court Memorandum" decisions, are not precedential; they apply only to the particular taxpayer. They are, however, published by commercial publishers, and they are valuable despite their lack of binding precedential value. They are important guides to taxpayers and the Service. *Sklar*, with its designation "T.C. Memo.," is an example of a memorandum decision.

The Tax Court issues summary opinions only in cases in which the taxpayer has elected to have her case proceed according to the procedure provided by section 7463. That provision permits taxpayers involved in controversies with the Service where the amount in controversy is $50,000 or less, to elect a stream-lined, simplified procedure that allows the case to reach the docket more quickly based on pleadings easily prepared by the taxpayer herself in pen. These cases are designated "S" cases. Summary opinions have no precedential value.

A second distinction between the two cases is that *McKay* was decided by Judge Wells, one of the nineteen "regular" judges of the Tax Court.[42] In contrast, *Sklar* was decided by Judge Nameroff, a "special" trial judge of the Tax Court. Regular Tax Court judges are appointed by the President (with the advice and consent of the Senate), and serve for a term of 15 years.[43] They may be reappointed indefinitely until they reach the age of 70, when they must retire.[44] After retirement, however, the Chief Judge may recall them.[45]

Regular Tax Court judges may preside over any matter coming before the Tax Court. They are referred to as "Article I" judges. Why?

Section 7443A(a) authorizes the Chief Judge of the Tax Court to appoint special trial judges. Special trial judges generally preside over a limited list of cases unless designated by the Chief Judge.[46] The most important function of special trial judges is to preside over the "S" cases.

---

2. What does Judge Nameroff mean when he says, "[s]ome of the facts have been stipulated and are so found"? Section 7459(b) requires judges to include findings of fact in regular and memorandum opinions. As you learned in other courses, it is the function of the finder of fact to make these determinations. Because there is no jury in the Tax Court, the judge must make factual determinations. What are the methods by which litigants seek to influence the fact finder's factual determinations?

One of the distinguishing features of Tax Court practice is the Court's reliance on the stipulation process. Facts, once stipulated by both sides, are considered established and

---

42. Section 7443(a).
43. Section 7443(b); section 7443(e).
44. Section 7447(b)(1).
45. Section 7447(c).
46. Section 7443A(b).

cannot be contested except in the most extraordinary circumstances. The Tax Court also relies heavily on other aspects of pre-trial discovery common in other federal courts. Because the Tax Court regards the pre-trial process as extremely important to the narrowing of issues and the elimination of unnecessary controversy, it has issued the following standing pre-trial order, applicable to all Tax Court litigants.

United States Tax Court Washington, D.C.
Standing Pre-Trial Order

To the parties in the Notice of Trial to which this Order is attached:

Policies

You are expected to begin discussions as soon as practicable for purposes of settlement and/or preparation of a stipulation of facts. Valuation cases and reasonable compensation cases are generally susceptible of settlement, and the Court expects the parties to negotiate in good faith with this objective in mind. All minor issues should be settled so that the Court can focus on the issue(s) needing a Court decision.

If difficulties are encountered in communicating with another party, or in complying with this Order, you should promptly advise the Court in writing, with copy to each other party, or in a conference call among the parties and the trial judge.

Continuances will be granted only in exceptional circumstances. See Rule 134, Tax Court Rules of Practice and Procedure. Even joint motions for continuance will not routinely be granted.

If any unexcused failure to comply with this Order adversely affects the timing or conduct of the trial, the Court may impose appropriate sanctions, including dismissal, to prevent prejudice to the other party or imposition on the Court. Such failure may also be considered in relation to disciplinary proceedings involving counsel. See Rule 202(a).

Requirements

To effectuate the foregoing policies and an orderly and efficient disposition of all cases on the trial calendar, it is hereby

ORDERED that all facts shall be stipulated to the maximum extent possible. All documentary and written evidence shall be marked and stipulated in accordance with Rule 91(b), unless the evidence is to be used to impeach the credibility of a witness. Objections may be preserved in the stipulation. If a complete stipulation of facts is not ready for submission at trial, and if the Court determines that this is the result of either party's failure to cooperate fully in the preparation thereof, the Court may order sanctions against the uncooperative party. Any documents or materials which a party expects to utilize in the event of trial (except for impeachment), but which are not stipulated, shall be identified in writing and exchanged by the parties at least 15 days before the first day of the trial session. The Court may refuse to receive in evidence any document or material not so stipulated or exchanged, unless otherwise agreed by the parties or allowed by the Court for good cause shown. It is further

ORDERED that unless a basis of settlement has been reached, each party shall prepare a Trial Memorandum substantially in the form attached hereto and shall submit it directly to the undersigned and to the opposing party not less than fifteen (15) days before the first day of the trial session. It is further

ORDERED that witnesses shall be identified in the Trial Memorandum with a brief summary of the anticipated testimony of such witnesses. Witnesses who are not identified will not be permitted to testify at the trial without leave of the Court upon sufficient showing of cause. Unless otherwise permitted by the Court upon timely request, expert witnesses shall prepare a written report which shall be submitted directly to the undersigned and served upon each other party at least 30 days before the first day of the trial session. An expert witness' testimony may be excluded for failure to comply with this Order and the provisions of Rule 143(f). It is further

ORDERED that, where a basis of settlement has been reached, stipulated decisions shall be submitted to the Court prior to the first day of the trial session. Additional time for filing of settlement documents will be granted only where it is clear that settlement has been approved by both parties, and the parties shall be prepared to state for the record the basis of settlement and the reasons for delay in filing documents. The Court will specify the date by which settlement documents will be due and expect proposed decisions to be submitted by such date. It is further

ORDERED that all parties shall be prepared for trial at any time during the term of the trial session unless a specific date has been previously set by the Court. It is further

ORDERED that every pleading, motion, letter or other document submitted to the Court by any party subsequent to the date of the notice of trial shall be served upon every other party or counsel for a party and shall contain a certificate of service as specified in Rule 21(b).

Judge

Dated: Washington, D.C.

Trial Calendar:

Date:

TRIAL MEMORANDUM FOR (Petitioner/Respondent)
Please type or print legibly
This form may be expanded as necessary)

NAME OF CASE   DOCKET NO. (S).
ATTORNEYS:

Petitioner: Respondent:

Tel. No. :   Tel. No. :

AMOUNTS IN DISPUTE:

Year(s)   Deficiencies   Additions   Damages

STIPULATION OF FACTS: Completed: In Process

ISSUES:

WITNESS(ES) YOU EXPECT TO CALL (Name and brief summary of expected testimony)

CURRENT ESTIMATE OF TRIAL TIME:

SUMMARY OF FACTS

(Attach separate pages, if necessary, to inform Court of facts in chronological narrative form)

BRIEF SYNOPSIS OF LEGAL AUTHORITIES

(Attach separate pages, if necessary, to discuss fully your legal position)

EVIDENTIARY PROBLEMS

DATE:

        Petitioner/Respondent

Return to: Judge _____

                      United States Tax Court

                      Room

                      400 Second Street, N.W.

                      Washington, D.C. 20217

                      (202) 606-

3. How can the Tax Court in *Sklar* cite *Hernandez* as controlling the outcome but ignore the fact that the 1993 closing agreement and Revenue Ruling make it clear that the Service is no longer applying *Hernandez*? Consider the following article.

Scientology Case Redux[47]

Back in 1989, the U.S. Supreme Court concluded, as part of the IRS's extensive litigation with the Church of Scientology, that certain payments to the church from its members for training or "auditing" services are not deductible as charitable contributions. *Hernandez v. Commissioner*, 490 U.S. 680 (1989). But in a 1993 closing agreement with the church, later leaked to the press, the IRS agreed "not to contest the deductibility of Church of Scientology fixed donations in connection with qualified religious services." Imagine if, after the *Brown v. School Board* decision in 1954, the Executive Branch had decided to ignore this case and not enforce the law of the land! Yet this has been the approach of both the Bush and Clinton administrations in regard to *Hernandez*....

Over the years, many have argued that the Scientology closing agreement has resulted in a situation where Scientologists are treated better than adherents of other religious faiths. If Scientologists can deduct for religious training, why can't Catholics and Jews deduct the costs of their children's religious training in schools that either teach religion exclusively or as part of a secular education? In the latter situation, parents would bifurcate their tuition payments and deduct only the portion attributable to religious training.

Well, some of us have been waiting for a Catholic or a Jew to do this, be audited, and then go to court. We finally have [our] champion[s],[the Sklars]....

To the dismay of those of us who care about the integrity of the tax laws, the Tax Court, in a recent memorandum opinion (*Sklar v. Commissioner*, T.C. Memo. 2000-118 ... *2000 TNT 67-11*), glossed over the significance of the Scientology closing agreement and even confused the IRS's refusal to enforce the *Hernandez* decision with the decision itself....

---

47. Paul Streckfus, "Scientology Case Redux," *supra* note 40.

Unfortunately, Michael Sklar brought the case *pro se* and the likelihood of an appeal, much less an effective appeal, is doubtful, unless he can get some outside backing.

It's interesting that the field service advice directed to this case (FSA 2000-12633 ...) spends a great deal of time citing *Hernandez*, but neglects to mention that the IRS does not follow *Hernandez*! Sort of reminds me of the old *Saturday Night Live* skit where Roseanne Roseannadanna, after being told she is spouting nonsense, says, "Never mind." I hope we will get a case one of these days where the IRS is forced to defend its indefensible position. I've often wondered why Catholic and Jewish organizations have not mounted a legal challenge to the IRS's position. Could it be because many parents already deduct tuition payments and, in this day of few audits, no one is getting caught? Are organizations concluding, "Why upset the apple cart if we are getting, in effect, the same deal as the Scientologists?" Is there, as I'm starting to suspect, a major conspiracy of silence between the major religions in this country and the IRS on this issue?

———————

4. The *Sklar* case involved both the substantive issue of the deductibility of the taxpayers' parochial school tuition payments, and also whether the Sklars were subject to the addition to tax provided by section 6651(a)(1). **Read section 6651(a)(1).** Where does that section appear in the Code?

A Brief Introduction to Penalties and Interest

The Code imposes civil penalties on taxpayers who fail to comply with its requirements.[48] These requirements pertain primarily to the filing of a timely and accurate return.[49] The most common of these penalties are those for failing to file a return at all or on time, the omission of items of income, and the claiming of improper deductions. Knowledge of the various penalty provisions appearing in the Code requires an exhaustive examination of a multitude of specialized rules. This type of examination is beyond the scope of an introductory course in federal income tax. Nevertheless, it is important for you to know of the existence of some of these penalties. Even if you do not advise clients on tax matters, properly preparing your own return necessitates some familiarity with the risks of taking uncertain positions on your own return.

———————

48. Taxpayers and tax practitioners commonly refer to these additions to the tax as "penalties." The Code, however, terms them "additions to tax." We have chosen to use the word "penalties" here. But when you refer to the cited Code sections, you will see the phrase "additions to the tax."

The self-administered nature of our tax system, reinforced by this array of penalties has, until now, made the tax system of the United States the most successful in the world. As stated by the Supreme Court in *Spies v. United States*:

> The United States has relied for the collection of its income tax largely upon the taxpayer's own disclosures.... This system can function successfully only if those within and near taxable income keep and render true accounts. In many ways, taxpayers' neglect or deceit may prejudice the orderly and punctual administration of the system as well as the revenues themselves. Congress has imposed a variety of sanctions for the protection of the system and the revenues.

317 U.S. 492, 495 (1943).

49. The Code also imposes criminal penalties in certain cases. Recall *James*. We will not deal extensively with them. But, note that a failure to abide by the rules of the Code may produce in some cases a civil penalty, in others a criminal penalty, and in some cases both.

Perhaps one of the most common errors made by taxpayers that results in penalties is the failure to file a return on time. In general, section 6012 of the Code requires a taxpayer to file a return if her gross income exceeds the sum of the standard deduction and the personal exemption amount. Although this error is generally easy to avoid (due to the generous rules for filing a return up to four months late based on an extension), many taxpayers incur penalties for late filing. In addition to the penalty imposed by section 6651(a)(1) for late filing, a failure to file (or late filing) affects the running of the statute of limitations.[50]

The penalty for late filing (or failure to file) is based on a percentage of the amount of tax due. These amounts can add up quickly; the rate is set at 5% per month of the amount of tax that should have been shown on the return that has not been filed (with a maximum of 25%).[51] Because the penalty is calculated based on the amount of tax that should be shown on the return (and has not been paid), many taxpayers who are expecting a refund do not believe they have an obligation to file a timely return. But, there is also a statute of limitations on refunds. In order to obtain a refund, a taxpayer must request it. Filing a return is one method of requesting a refund. If the taxpayer fails to make a proper request within the statutory time, the refund is barred.[52]

As you saw in the *Sklar* case, however, the taxpayer is not liable for the failure to file penalty if she can show that her failure was "due to reasonable cause and not due to willful neglect."[53] Mr. Sklar advanced the excuse that he was unable to file his return due to "lack of sufficient time ... due to high work-related volume." The court said that Mr. Sklar's argument that "he was simply too busy to file ... does not constitute reasonable cause for his failure to file." To satisfy the statute's dual requirement of both reasonable cause and the absence of willful neglect, it is usually sufficient to show reasonable cause. (The reverse is not true, however; merely showing an absence of willful neglect does not satisfy the statute.) According to the regulations, the test is objective.[54] A plethora of cases has defined a number of bases that now appear in the Internal Revenue Manual as acceptable excuses.[55] These include serious illness, mental or physical; death of the taxpayer or a member of his immediate family; destruction of the taxpayer's records by fire or other casualty; and inability to obtain the proper forms due to shortages.

A second common omission that produces a penalty is a taxpayer's failure to pay the tax. This penalty is separate from and in addition to the penalty for failure to file.[56] The

---

50. We first introduced you to the Code's statute of limitations rules in the Brief Introduction to Tax Procedure in Part II, Chapter 1. Remember that if a taxpayer files no return, the statute of limitations for examination by the Service will never expire. Section 6501(c)(3). Late filing extends the period because the statute does not begin to run until the date the return is actually filed. Section 6501(a).

51. Section 6651(a)(1). Note that courts and practitioners often refer to the penalties imposed by section 6651 as the "delinquency" penalties.

52. Section 6511. Furthermore, even a taxpayer who is due a refund is subject to audit; and, if she files no return, the statute of limitations on that audit will never expire.

53. Section 6651(a)(1).

54. Treas. Reg. section 301.6651-1(c)(1). Reading this regulation carefully is vital to preparing a successful claim that a taxpayer's failure was due to reasonable cause.

55. I.R.M. 120.1.1.3.1. The Internal Revenue Manual is a multi-volume set of materials, prepared by the Internal Revenue Service, primarily for the guidance of employees of the Service. It was unavailable to the public until passage of the Freedom of Information Act, and even now, some sections are unavailable to the public. It is useful in both planning and litigation because a taxpayer can often ascertain the position of the Service on an issue (that may be otherwise unavailable). It does not, unfortunately, include a very helpful index.

56. Section 6651(a)(2).

penalty for failure to pay is .5% per month up to a total of 25%. Thus, the penalty for failure to file is substantially more severe than the penalty for failure to pay. For this reason, a taxpayer who cannot pay her tax should, nevertheless, file her return on time.[57]

Again, as in failure to pay, a taxpayer can avoid the penalty if she shows that the failure is due to reasonable cause and not to willful neglect. Again, the regulations apply an objective standard. To show reasonable cause for a failure to pay, a taxpayer must demonstrate that "he exercised ordinary business care and prudence in providing for payment of his tax liability and was nevertheless either unable to pay the tax or would suffer an undue hardship ... if he paid on the due date."[58] Again, the test is a dual one: the taxpayer must satisfy both prongs. The taxpayer must show that she exercised ordinary care and prudence and that she was either unable to pay the tax or would have suffered an undue hardship. To show an inability to pay, the Service will analyze the taxpayer's living expenses in relation to her income. (And, those living expenses cannot be lavish!).[59] The Service will view "undue hardship" quite narrowly; payment cannot be merely inconvenient; there must be substantial financial loss.[60]

A third important civil penalty provision, section 6662, imposes a hefty addition to tax in several situations. Entitled the "accuracy-related penalty," this section includes negligence or disregard of rules and regulations, substantial understatements of income tax, and substantial valuation misstatements. Subsections of section 6662 define further each of these categories. The penalty is imposed at the rate of 20% of the tax attributable to the item. But, the maximum penalty is 20%, even if the inaccuracy is attributable to more than one of the covered categories. Section 6664(c) relieves the taxpayer from accuracy related penalties if the taxpayer shows that she had reasonable cause and that she acted in good faith.

Section 6662(c) defines "negligence" as including "any failure to make a reasonable attempt to comply with the provisions" of the Code, and "disregard" includes "any careless, reckless, or intentional disregard" of rules or regulations. A reading of Treasury Regulation section 1.6662-3 will provide you with a better understanding of the view of the Service of what constitutes negligence and disregard. As with all civil penalties (except the fraud penalty of section 6663), the taxpayer has the burden of proof.[61] Therefore, it is up to the taxpayer to demonstrate the absence of negligence or disregard.

Section 6662(d)(1)(A) defines "a substantial understatement of income tax" as failing to state on a return an amount that exceeds the greater of 10% of the tax that should have been shown on the return or $5,000. This type of understatement of tax can easily result from omission of items of income or the claiming of improper deductions. A tax-

---

57. There have been many cases in which a taxpayer delayed filing due to inability to pay. Deferring filing and paying can then become the basis for criminal prosecution. Sections 7201; 7202; and 7203.

58. Treas. Reg. section 301.6651-1(c)(1).

59. *Id.*

60. Treas. Reg. section 1.6161-1(b).

61. Note that in court proceeding, section 7491(c) places the burden of production on the Secretary. But, the burden of production means that the Service must merely produce enough evidence to resist a motion to dismiss. It is not the same as the burden of persuasion.

payer may avoid a penalty in this case, however, if (1) she can show that there was substantial authority for her position,[62] or (2) she disclosed the relevant facts and there is a reasonable basis for her treatment of the item(s).[63]

Section 6662(e)(1)(A) defines "a substantial valuation misstatement" as one where the taxpayer claims a value for any property or a basis for any property that is 200% or more of the amount determined to be the correct value or basis.[64] But, there is no penalty unless the additional tax resulting from the overvaluation or excess basis exceeds $5,000.[65]

The final civil penalty provision that requires attention here is section 6663(a), which imposes an addition to tax at the rate of 75% of any part of an underpayment due to fraud. The classic statement of the conduct that constitutes fraud for tax purposes appears in the opinion of the United States Supreme Court in its 1943 decision in *Spies v. United States*.[66] The Court said.

> [W]e would think affirmative willful attempt [to evade tax]may be inferred from conduct such as keeping a double set of books, making false entries or alterations, or false invoices or documents, destruction of books or records, concealment of assets or covering up sources of income, handling of one's affairs to avoid making the records usual in transactions of the kind, and any conduct, the likely effect of which would be to mislead or to conceal. If the tax-evasion motive plays any part in such conduct the offense may be made out even though the conduct may also serve other purposes such as concealment of other crime.[67]

The burden of proof regarding fraud rests initially on the government to show its existence.[68] Once the Service has satisfied its burden, the burden shifts to the taxpayer to show that any portion of the underpayment is not due to fraud.[69]

---

62. Treasury Regulation section 1.6662-4(d)(3) provides that "[t]here is substantial authority for the tax treatment of an item only if the weight of authorities supporting the treatment is substantial in relation to the weight of authorities supporting contrary treatment." The regulation goes on to list the sources that constitute "authority" for measuring the existence of "substantial authority."

63. Section 6662(d)(2)(B)(ii).

64. Section 6662(h) doubles the penalty to 40% if the overvaluation or excess basis exceeds the amount of value or basis determined to be correct by 400%.

65. Section 6662(e)(2).

66. 317 U.S. 492 (1943). *Spies* involved a criminal tax evasion statute. The Code does not define either civil or criminal fraud. A definition of civil fraud does appear in *Mitchell v. Commissioner*, 118 F.2d 308 (5th Cir. 1941). In that case, the Fifth Circuit said: "Negligence, whether slight or great, is not equivalent to the fraud with intent to evade tax named in the statute. The fraud meant is actual, intentional wrongdoing, and the intent required is the specific purpose to evade a tax believed to be owing." 118 F.2d at 310. Despite the absence of the phrase "with the intent to evade tax," from the "badges of fraud" identified in *Spies* are appropriate in identifying both civil and criminal fraud under the current Code.

67. 317 U.S. at 499. Note that a taxpayer's efforts to "avoid tax" through skillful planning is not the same thing as a taxpayer's effort to "evade tax," which involves deceptive and misleading conduct. Note also that one important basis for a charge of fraud is the failure to file a return with the intent to evade tax. Section 6651(f) imposes the fraud penalty for a fraudulent failure to file a return. The penalty is 15% per month (up to a maximum of 75%) of the tax that should have been shown on the return. (The section 6663 fraud penalty can only apply when the taxpayer has actually filed a return.)

68. Section 7454(a).

69. Section 6663(b).

Remember that this is a civil fraud penalty. There are also criminal fraud penalties for which the Service bears the burden of proof.[70] One important difference between the civil fraud penalty and the criminal fraud penalty is the standard of proof. For civil fraud, the standard of proof is clear and convincing evidence; for criminal fraud, the standard of proof is beyond a reasonable doubt. One consequence of the existence of both penalties and the difference in the standards of proof is that a taxpayer who is convicted of criminal fraud will be collaterally estopped from claiming he is innocent of civil fraud. But, a taxpayer who is not guilty of criminal fraud may, nevertheless, be guilty of civil fraud.

It is impossible to state with any accuracy a guide for when the Service is likely to attempt to impose a fraud penalty, rather than one of the lesser penalties. Recall, however, our discussion of the statute of limitations. One important consequence of a fraud penalty (rather than a lesser one), is its effect on the statute of limitations. Remember, the statute of limitations does not expire at any time in the case of fraud.[71] Therefore, the existence of fraud will allow the Service to examine a return and propose changes that produce additional income tax long after the normal three-year period has expired.

Section 6601(a) of the Code requires a taxpayer to pay interest on any tax not paid by the date it is due.[72] The rate of interest varies quarterly and is based on the short-term federal interest rate.[73] The interest is compounded daily.[74] The underlying objective of imposing interest at a rate that bears a reasonable relationship to current market rates of interest is to compensate the government for the loss of the use of the tax monies owed but unpaid. The statutory provision for regular rate adjustments represents a more sophisticated view of the time value of money than the predecessor provision, under which the interest rate remained at a simple rate of 6% for many years despite extreme market fluctuations.

It is also important to note that interest accrues on penalties, as well as on the unpaid tax. It, too, compounds daily. The Service can forgive penalties and if it does, the interest that would otherwise have accrued on that penalty also disappears. (But, the Service cannot forgive the statutorily imposed interest on unpaid tax except in very rare circumstances.)[75]

As you learned earlier, a taxpayer may petition the Tax Court for a redetermination of any proposed deficiency in her taxes asserted by the Service after an examination. As noted, one of the advantages of seeking review in the Tax Court, rather than in a district court or the Claims Court, is the ability of the taxpayer to obtain judicial review without first paying the tax. But it is important to note that, in the event of a loss in the Tax Court, the price of not having paid the tax in advance is the imposition of interest

---

70. The prosecution always bears the burden of proof in criminal cases.

71. Section 6501(c)(1).

72. For most taxpayers whose income is subject to withholding, any tax that has not been withheld by an employer is due on the date the return is due. For those taxpayers whose incomes are not subject to withholding by an employer or other third party, taxes are normally due on a quarterly basis (together with an estimated return).

73. Section 6621 provides that the interest rate will be determined by the Secretary based on the federal short-term rate plus 3%. (The interest rate is the same on refunds.)

74. Section 6622(a).

75. But see section 6404(g), which provides that interest and penalties are suspended after eighteen months for an individual taxpayer who files a timely return if the Service fails to provide a notice to the taxpayer that there is a tax due.

for the full period from the date the tax was due until it is later paid.[76] Taxpayers who seek review in a district court or the Claims Court must, of course, pay the tax in advance. Therefore, they will not incur additional interest for the period of the litigation.

The government, too, must pay interest. If the taxpayer has overpaid her taxes, she is entitled to interest at the same rate of interest as is applicable to unpaid tax.[77] The interest runs from the date of overpayment.

———————

The *Sklar* case highlights another important area of concern for tax practitioners: ethics. As the Rabys express it in the following article, the $64 million question is how to advise your clients. Can an ethical tax lawyer justify being associated with a tax return on which such deductions appear?

Religious Tuition as Charitable Contribution[78]

The result in *Michael Sklar v. Commissioner*, ... seemed to some commentators a foregone conclusion. Thus, John L. Norman Jr., in the June 2000 *Bisk Audio Tax Report* noted in regard to *Sklar*, "my child gets to come because I pay the money, and as a benefit to my child, the benefit being the education, it can't possibly be tax-deductible." To which his colleague, E. Lynn Nichols, replied, "We need to give the client the *Sklar* case and let them read it before they insist that we deduct it." What Norman and Nichols are telling practitioners is that there is no justification for taxpayers taking charitable contribution deductions for amounts paid for religious education, and thus no justification for tax practitioners being associated with returns claiming such deductions.

An Indefensible Position?

But not everyone would agree. For example, Paul Streckfus, of the *EO Tax Journal*, bemoaning that Sklar was acting *pro se* and probably would not even appeal, wrote "I hope we will get a case one of these days where the IRS is forced to defend its indefensible position." ...

...

... [Streckfus has] raised the question that is the $64 million question to those concerned with ethics and tax practice, and could result in *Sklar* precipitating confrontations between clients and practitioners. "Could it be," Streckfus asked, "[that] many parents already deduct tuition payments and, in this day of few audits, no one is getting caught?" If so, and if *Sklar* forces practitioners to face the fact that such deductions lack any authoritative support, what are practitioners to do? Norman and Nichols suggested

———————

76. To prevent the accrual of interest during the period of Tax Court litigation, the Service developed a procedure to allow a taxpayer to make a "deposit" against the tax that could be due in the event of a loss in the Tax Court. Because it is a "deposit" and not the actual "payment" of the tax, it does not destroy the jurisdiction of the Tax Court. The Tax Court has limited jurisdiction to hear only cases in which there is a claimed deficiency in taxes (and certain other cases dealing with collections). The term "deficiency" is a term of art; a deficiency cannot exist if the amount of additional tax the Service claims the taxpayer owes has been paid. In the 2004 Jobs Act, Congress codified, in new Code section 6603, the longstanding administrative deposit procedure.

77. Section 6611.

78. Burgess J.W. Raby and William L. Raby, "Religious Tuition as Charitable Contribution," 88 Tax Notes 215 (July 10, 2000).

that the practitioner hand the client a copy of the *Sklar* opinion. In the face of *Sklar*, they imply, how can any ethical tax practitioner justify being associated with a tax return on which such deductions are being claimed? How can any law-abiding taxpayer attempt to claim such deductions?

Do the Sklars Have an Argument?

The situation may not be that black and white, however. Our purpose in this article is to explore the grey areas involving deductions for religious education and see if, perhaps, there is more to the Sklar position than Judge Nameroff was willing to concede.

We start with several propositions:

(1) payments made to a section 501(c)(3) organization may contain both deductible and nondeductible omponents;

(2) receipt of an "intangible religious benefit" is not

considered receipt of a quid pro quo for purposes of treating a payment to a section 501(c)(3) organization as nondeductible;

(3) an "intangible religious benefit" is a benefit received from or through a religious organization which is not sold in a commercial context outside of the donative context;

(4) taxpayers should not be allowed charitable contribution deductions for what are essentially consumption expenditures in transactions with religious organizations, when essentially the same goods or services are available on the private market.

The Scientology Situation

Hernandez v. Commissioner, 490 U.S. 680 (1989), involved the deductibility of payments made to the Church of Scientology for "auditing" and "training" services. That auditing and training, however, are not quite what those words normally mean, at least not in the world of CPAs and attorneys. Scientology "auditing," as described in *Hernandez,* consists of one-to-one encounter sessions between a participant and a church official, or "auditor," during which the participant's areas of spiritual difficulty are identified; and "training" consists of doctrinal courses in which participants seek to attain the qualifications necessary to serve as auditors. Scientology has a tenet called the doctrine of exchange. Any time one receives something one must pay something back. Therefore, the church charges fixed "donations" for auditing and training sessions. Price schedules are established in each Scientology branch church, calibrated according to the length and level of sophistication of the sessions.

In *Hernandez,* the Supreme Court majority attempted to fit the Scientology approach to financing the church into the Internal Revenue Code's approach to allowing charitable contribution deductions for payments to churches. Said the Court, "The legislative history of the 'contribution or gift' limitation, though sparse, reveals that Congress intended to differentiate between unrequited payments to qualified recipients and payments made to such recipients in return for goods or services. Only the former were deemed deductible." The Court used the example of payments to hospitals. If the payment is in exchange for the hospital's "binding obligation" to provide medical service, it would not be deductible. "In ascertaining whether a given payment was made with 'the expectation of any quid pro quo,'" added the Court, "the IRS has customarily examined the external features of the transaction in question. This practice has the advantage of obviating the need for the IRS to conduct imprecise inquiries into the motivations of individual taxpayers. The lower courts have generally embraced this structural analysis."

Adequate Consideration?

...

In the context of *Sklar*, it is also interesting to note what the Supreme Court did not decide in *Hernandez*. In footnote 10, the Court commented that "[p]etitioners have not argued here that their payments qualify as 'dual payments' under IRS regulations and that they are therefore entitled to a partial deduction to the extent their payments exceeded the value of the benefit received. See *American Bar Endowment*, 477 U.S., at 117 (citing Rev. Rul. 67-246, 1967-2 Cum. Bull. 104). We thus have no occasion to decide this issue." Yet that is, in a sense, what the Sklars were trying to do. They subtracted from the total amount they paid the value of the secular education being received by their children and claimed a deduction for the amount they paid for the religious education. Since such intangible benefits as those represented by a religious education that prepares one to be part of a religious community are not normally sold in commercial transactions outside of a religious context, the Sklars were really arguing that the religious education had no fair market value as that term is normally used.

Two Developments in 1993

That was 1989. In 1993, two developments occurred. First, Congress passed the Revenue Reconciliation Act of 1993. This included section 170(f)(8), imposing new substantiation requirements for charitable contributions of $250 or more. Later in 1993, the IRS entered into a closing agreement with the Church of Scientology. Among other things, that agreement apparently committed the IRS to allowing charitable contribution deductions for the same auditing and training payments that the Supreme Court had ruled to be nondeductible in *Hernandez*.

Section 170(f)(8), and its legislative history, contained some interesting language in the context of this discussion. The donor must obtain from the recipient charitable organization an acknowledgment of the amount contributed and a statement as to whether the donee organization provided any goods or services in exchange for the donation. If there were goods or services, the donee must either provide a "description and good faith estimate of the value" of those goods or services or a statement that the goods or services consisted solely of "intangible religious benefits." According to the code, "the term 'intangible religious benefit' means any intangible religious benefit which is provided by an organization organized exclusively for religious purposes and which generally is not sold in a commercial transaction outside the donative context." That is, receipt of an intangible religious benefit is not regarded as the receipt of a quid pro quo for purposes of the substantiation requirements of section 170(f)(8). In a footnote, the conference report to the 1993 act points out that "This exception [for intangible religious benefits] does not apply, for example, to tuition for education leading to a recognized degree, travel services, or consumer goods. However, the Senate committee explanation states that it is intended that *de minimis* tangible benefits furnished to contributors that are incidental to a religious ceremony (such as wine) generally may be disregarded."

The Supreme Court in *Hernandez* had only four years earlier commented on the dangers of trying to define religious benefits as distinguished from secular benefits. The Court had said that "the deduction petitioners seek might raise problems of entanglement between church and state. If framed as a deduction for those payments generating benefits of a religious nature for the payor, petitioners' proposal would inexorably force the IRS and reviewing courts to differentiate 'religious' benefits from 'secular' ones. If framed as a deduction for those payments made in connection with a religious service, petitioners' proposal would force the IRS and the judiciary into differentiating 'religious' services from 'secular' ones. We need pass no judgment now on the constitutionality of such hypothetical inquiries, but we do note that 'pervasive monitoring' for 'the subtle or overt presence of religious matter' is a central danger against which we have held the Establishment Clause guards. *Aguilar v. Felton*, 473 U.S. 402, 413 (1985)...." It appears to us that section 170(f)(8), if "monitored," might some day force "the IRS and reviewing courts to differentiate 'religious' benefits from 'secular' ones." It also seems to us that there is at least an inference in the 1993 act that "intangible religious benefits" should not be considered to have any fair market value for charitable contribution purposes, thus avoiding the even more intrusive problem of trying to put a price tag on something outside the normal commercial marketplace.

The O'Connor Dissent in *Hernandez*

Some dissents are more interesting than the majority opinions with which they disagree, and some prove prophetic as to what is to come. Justice Sandra Day O'Connor, joined by Justice Antonin Scalia, focused in her *Hernandez* dissent on the duality inherent in many contributions, in language quite similar to the section 170(f)(8) approach that Congress adopted four years later. "When a taxpayer claims as a charitable deduction part of a fixed amount given to a charitable organization in exchange for benefits that have a commercial value," explained Justice O'Connor, "the allowable portion of that claim is computed by subtracting from the total amount paid the value of the physical benefit received. If at a charity sale one purchases for $1,000 a painting whose market value is demonstrably no more than $50, there has been a contribution of $950.... An identical calculation can be made where the quid received is not a painting or a meal, but an intangible such as entertainment, so long as that intangible has some market value established in a noncontributory context...."

"It becomes impossible, however, to compute the 'contribution' portion of a payment to a charity where what is received in return is not merely an intangible, but an intangible (or, for that matter a tangible) that is not bought and sold except in donative contexts so that the only 'market' price against which it can be evaluated is a market price that always includes donations. Suppose, for example, that the charitable organization that traditionally solicits donations on Veterans Day, in exchange for which it gives the donor an imitation poppy bearing its name, were to establish a flat rule that no one gets a poppy without a donation of at least $10. One would have to say that the 'market' rate for such poppies was $10, but it would assuredly not be true that everyone who 'bought' a poppy for $10 made no contribution. Similarly, if one buys a $100 seat at a prayer breakfast receiving as the quid pro quo food for both body and soul it would make no sense to say that no charitable contribution whatever has occurred simply because the 'going rate' for all prayer breakfasts (with equivalent bodily food) is $100. The latter may well be true, but that 'going rate' includes a contribution."

To what conclusion did this line of thought lead Justice O'Connor? "Confronted with this difficulty, and with the constitutional necessity of not making irrational distinctions among taxpayers, and with the even higher standard of equality of treatment among religions that the First Amendment imposes, the government has only two practicable options with regard to distinctively religious quids pro quo: to disregard them all, or to tax them all." The road taken has been to disregard them all.

Administrative Inconsistency

Which leads us to the administrative consistency issue. Note that the majority in *Hernandez* did not so much reject the idea that administrative inconsistency was a relevant argument as it rejected the idea that the record below provided a basis for finding that the IRS treated some religions differently from others....

But the Court certainly did not rule out the possibility that given a different set of facts, it might reach a different result. "The IRS' application of the 'contribution or gift' standard may be right or wrong with respect to these other faiths," observed the Court, "or it may be right with respect to some religious practices and wrong with respect to others. It may also be that some of these payments are appropriately classified as partially deductible 'dual payments'.... Only upon a proper factual record could we make these determinations. Absent such a record, we must reject petitioners' administrative consistency argument."

Religious Education

The leading cases dealing with religious education are probably *Oppewal v. Commissioner*, 468 F. 2d 1000 (1st Cir. 1972); *Winters v. Commissioner*, 468 F. 2d 778 (2d Cir. 1972); and *DeJong v. Commissioner*, 309 F. 2d 373 (9th Cir. 1962). All three involved parochial schools. In all three, the courts could be viewed as using a quid pro quo approach. What was the cost of providing an equivalent education in a nonreligious school setting? A deduction was then allowed for the excess paid over the value of the education received. The courts wisely refrained from any attempt to quantify the value of the religious benefits being obtained. In her dissent, Justice O'Connor dismissed these cases as irrelevant to the Scientology issue. Denial of a deduction in the Scientology cases, she wrote, "bears no resemblance to the denial of a deduction for religious school tuition up to the market value of the secularly useful education received."

Religious education is a tricky topic. Presbyterians, for example, call their clergy "teaching elders" while their lay people in leadership positions are called "ruling elders." That may say something about what they see as the focus of the church. But they are not alone. We would guess that religious education and religious worship are the two dominant activities of any church, of any religion, in the minds of most lay people. Some denominations happen to have parochial schools. Some educate their children through Sunday school classes, vacation bible schools, and confirmation classes. Whether members of one religious group contribute to the church and send their children to confirmation classes, for which no specific charge is made, or whether the Sklars prepare their children for their religious life as adults by sending them to Orthodox Jewish day schools, should not make that big a tax difference. The purely religious component of the education should not be treated as a quid pro quo received for what was paid to the religious organization, but rather should be considered to be a charitable contribution. Otherwise, what we are doing is establishing one set of tax rules for deductibility of the costs of religious education for some of our children and another set for other children and for almost all adults....

Conclusion

Is Streckfus right in arguing that the Sklars should have prevailed on the ground of administrative consistency because the IRS routinely allows charitable contributions for Scientology audit and training payments? Or are Nichols and Norman right, and no self-respecting practitioner can be associated with preparing a return on which a charitable contribution deduction is claimed for any part of the tuition paid for religious education? We do not really think either is right.

The Scientology payments are analogous to religious school tuition only in that they are fixed amounts. The audit process is not so much education as it is a religious experience. The training process, since it prepares one to be an auditor, is somewhat akin to an on-the-job type of seminary training. The *Sklar* case deals with educating the taxpayer's children while the Scientology situation deals with the taxpayer's own activity. There are similarities as well, of course, but we doubt whether a court would necessarily find them compelling.

That does not, however, mean to us that practitioners cannot be associated with returns that claim charitable contribution deductions for tuition paid for religious education. We think that the gross inconsistency in the approaches taken to measuring charitable contributions and in identifying how much of dual purpose payments may be deductible has created substantial confusion as to the meaning of the law. If we accept the *Hernandez* majority's statement that "[t]he *sine qua non* of a charitable contribution is a transfer of money or property without adequate consideration," we have to ask what was received for what was given.

A plausible argument can be put together that intangible religious benefits should not be considered to be a quid (as in quid pro quo) for payments made to religious organizations. It can also be plausibly argued that religious education of children aimed at preparing them to participate in adult religious life is the provision of an intangible religious benefit to the parents of those children. Is there substantial authority for such a conclusion? Probably not. Is it frivolous? Definitely not. Can a practitioner be associated with a return taking such a position without violating the ethics of the profession? We think so, so long as there is adequate disclosure of what is being deducted such as through attaching a Form 8275. [See discussion in the next section.]

What *are* a lawyer's ethical obligations when she advises a client on whether to take a reporting position on a return? Read the following section.

A Brief Introduction to Ethics in Federal Tax Practice

Tax lawyers have obligations to both their clients and to the tax law. Their obligations to their clients result primarily from the rules of ethics to which all lawyers must subscribe. Even non-lawyers are familiar with the commandment that lawyers must represent their clients zealously. But a lawyer also owes a duty to represent his clients within the bounds of the law. Thus, a tax lawyer must perform his work by carefully balancing the desire of his client to minimize or eliminate ("avoid") tax without exceeding the boundary of the tax law.

The most important source guiding a tax lawyer's duty to his client is Formal Opinion 85-352, issued by the Committee on Ethics and Professional Responsibility of the American Bar Association. That opinion provides in part:

> [A] lawyer, in representing a client in the course of the preparation of the client's tax return, may advise the statement of positions most favorable to the client if the lawyer has a good faith belief that those positions are warranted in existing law or can be supported by a good faith argument for an extension, modification or reversal of existing law. A lawyer can have a good faith belief in this context even if the lawyer believes the client's position probably will not prevail. However, good faith requires that there be some realistic possibility of success if the matter is litigated....

Thus, where a lawyer has a good faith belief in the validity of a position in accordance with the standard stated above that a particular transaction does not result in taxable income or that certain expenditures are properly deductible as expenses, the lawyer has no duty to require as a condition of his or her continued representation that riders be attached to the client's tax return explaining the circumstances surrounding the transaction or the expenditures.

In the role of advisor, the lawyer should counsel the client as to whether the position is likely to be sustained by a court if challenged by the IRS, as well as of the potential penalty consequences to the client if the position is taken on the tax return without disclosure.[79] Section [6662(d)(2)(B)] of the Internal Revenue Code imposes a penalty for substantial understatement of tax liability which can be avoided if the facts are adequately disclosed if there is or was substantial authority for the position taken by the taxpayer. Competent representation of the client would require the lawyer to advise the client fully as to whether there is or was substantial authority for the position taken in the tax return. If the lawyer is unable to conclude that the position is supported by substantial authority, the lawyer should advise the client of the penalty the client may suffer and of the opportunity to avoid such penalty by adequately disclosing the facts in the return or in a statement attached to the return. If after receiving such advice the client decides to risk the penalty by making no disclosure and to take the position initially advised by the lawyer in accordance with the standard stated above, the lawyer has met his or her ethical responsibility with respect to the advice....

In summary, a lawyer may advise reporting a position on a return even where the lawyer believes the position probably will not prevail, there is no "substantial authority" in support of the position, and there will be no disclosure of the position in the return. However, the position to be asserted must be one which the lawyer in good faith believes is warranted in existing law or can be supported by a good faith argument for an extension, modification or reversal of existing law. This requires that there is some realistic possibility of success if the matter is litigated. In addition, in his role as advisor, the lawyer should refer to potential penalties and other legal consequences should the client take the position advised.[80]

Thus, the lawyer, in zealously representing his client, may counsel the client to take positions that may be inconsistent with the view of the Service, provided the client does so based on complete information as to the risks. But, as stated above, the lawyer also has a duty to the law.

Formal Opinion 85-352 recognizes this duty and provides: "In all cases ... with regard both to the preparation of returns and negotiating administrative settlements, the lawyer is under a duty not to mislead the Internal Revenue Service deliberately, either by misstatements or by silence or by permitting the client to mislead."[81]

The Service's view of the responsibility of the tax lawyer appears in Circular 230.[82] Circular 230 covers a lawyer's eligibility to practice before the Service, and her duties re-

---

79. At the end of their article, the Rabys mention attachment of Form 8275 to a return, disclosing a possibly controversial position. **See Form 8275 in Forms Appendix.** Attachment of a rider or this form may protect the taxpayer from a penalty if his position is not ultimately sustained.

80. Formal Opinion 85-352, July 7, 1985.

81. *Id.*

82. Circular No. 230, 31 C.F.R. Pt.10.

lating to and restrictions on that practice. It also provides rules applicable to violations of Circular 230.[83] Circular 230's rules apply to client representation in both planning and litigating tax matters. In some respects, the rules expressed in Circular 230 are not quite the same as those contained in Formal Opinion 85-352. For example, Circular 230's rule for advising a client provides a two-prong test.[84] First, a lawyer may advise a client to take a position that shows a realistic possibility of being sustained on the merits. A realistic possibility of being sustained on the merits exists if an analysis by a person expert in the tax law would lead that person to conclude that the position has a one-in-three or greater likelihood of being sustained on the merits. In the alternative, if the position does not satisfy the one-in-three test, the lawyer may advise the client to take a non-frivolous position, so long as he advises the client of any opportunity to avoid the accuracy-related penalty of section 6662 by adequate disclosure.[85] In advising a client to take a position on a tax return, the lawyer must advise the client of any penalties that are likely to apply and of the opportunities to avoid penalties by proper disclosure.

Circular 230, as revised effective June 20, 2005, adopts the following requirements for written advice that does not constitute a "covered opinion": (1) a practitioner may not give written advice based on unreasonable factual or legal assumptions; (2) may not unreasonably rely upon taxpayer representations; (3) must consider all relevant facts; and (4) may not take into account "the possibility that a tax return will not be audited, that an issue will not be raised on audit, or that an issue will be resolved through settlement."[86] In addition, revised Circular 230 contains a list of aspirational "best practices" to insure that tax advisers provide clients with high quality representation.[87] Best practices include the following: (1) communicating clearly with a client regarding the scope of representation; (2) establishing relevant facts, evaluating the reasonableness of assumptions and representations, and arriving at a conclusion based on the law and facts; (3) advising a client regarding the consequences of conclusions, including advice as to whether a client may avoid accuracy-related penalties if she acts in reliance on the advice; and (4) acting "fairly and with integrity" in practice before the Service.[88]

---

83. Note that although our discussion is limited to a lawyer's ethical obligations in advising a client generally, a special set of rules applies to advising a client on a tax shelter. After a long period of consideration and public discussion, the Service amended Circular 230, effective June 20, 2005. The changes were intended primarily to affect opinions covering tax shelters. Because the incidence of shelters attractive to individual taxpayers has declined markedly in recent years for all but the super-wealthy, we have chosen to omit what would otherwise be a lengthy discussion of this complex set of rules. We note, however, that the rules governing these so-called "covered opinions" are quite broad; they govern written advice to clients involving issues not necessarily thought of as rising to the level of tax shelters. Many practitioners believe that the rules governing "covered opinions" are so broad that they encompass virtually all written communication (including electronic communication) from a tax advisor to a client. Any communication that meets the technical definition of a "covered opinion" and that fails to meet the complex requirements governing these opinions must contain a prominent legend that informs a client that the communication was not written and cannot be used for the purpose of avoiding penalties. Because of the all-encompassing definition of a "covered opinion" a tax lawyer must be thoroughly familiar with this portion of Circular 230. *See*, generally, Circular No. 230, 31 C.F.R. section 10.35.

84. Circular No. 230, 31 C.F.R. section 10.34.

85. Refer back to the discussion, in the section on penalties and interest, of the section 6662 accuracy-related penalty.

86. Circular No. 230, 31 C.F.R. section 10.37(a). *See* discussion of "covered opinions" in footnote 83, *supra*.

87. Preamble to amendments to Circular No. 230, published in T.D. 9165, 69 F.R. 75839–75845.

88. Circular No. 230, 31 C.F.R. section 10.33(a).

The standard contained in Formal Opinion 85-352 contains no mathematical guidelines for assessing a "realistic possibility of being sustained;" Circular 230 does. Do you think that providing a mathematical measurement aids the practitioner in determining the ethical outer limits? The ABA Special Task Force Report on Formal Opinion 85-352[89] attempts to provide some clarification. It states: "[a] position having only a 5% or 10% likelihood of success, if litigated, should not meet the new standard. A position having a likelihood of success closely approaching one-third should meet the standard."[90] But, this leaves uncertain whether a likelihood between 10% and almost one-in-three satisfies the standard, even if a tax lawyer can possibly reduce this type of prognosis to a percentage.

The Task Force Report also provides, however: "[o]rdinarily, there would be some realistic possibility of success where the position is supported by 'substantial authority,'[91] as that term is used in section [6662] of the Code and applicable regulations."[92] For many tax lawyers, the difficulty of trying to quantify the likelihood that a position will be sustained has led to the widespread practice of advising clients to attach disclosure statements to their returns. A client who attaches a statement to a return may take a position that has less than a realistic possibility of being sustained without incurring either a substantial understatement or a negligence penalty if there is a reasonable basis for the position. The section 6662 regulations define a reasonable basis as "a relatively high standard of tax reporting, that is, significantly higher than not frivolous or not patently improper. The reasonable basis standard is not satisfied by a return position that is merely arguable or is merely a colorable claim."[93] Thus, the standards frequently make tax lawyers wary of advising their clients to take any but positions clearly settled by law.

But, recall the Rabys' article. What is a position clearly settled with respect to the deduction of a portion of the tuition paid to a parochial school? Remember that the *Sklar* case was decided in a memorandum decision by a single special trial judge of the Tax Court. The three cases he relied on disallowed a deduction of parochial school tuition but without an explicit finding of fact or discussion of whether a portion of the payment represented secular education and a portion religious education.[94] Had there been evidence of the possible bifurcation of these two amounts, might the courts have allowed a deduction for the religious portion based on the argument that an intangible religious benefit does not constitute a *quid-pro-quo* and is, therefore, charitable in nature?[95] This appears to be the argument of the Rabys. The Rabys appear to accept the proposition that an intangible religious benefit does not constitute a *quid-pro-quo* and, therefore, a contribution made in exchange for this type of consideration may produce a charitable deduction. Does the *Hernandez* case support this proposition?

Consider the Tax Court's discussion of these issues in a second, more recent, case involving the Sklars' deduction, for a different tax year, of parochial school tuition.[96]

---

89. Reprinted in 39 Tax Lawyer 635 (1986).

90. *Id.* at 638–39.

91. Refer back to the discussion of the section 6662 accuracy-related penalty.

92. *Id.* at 639.

93. Treas. Reg. section 1.6662-3(b)(3).

94. See *Oppewal v. Commissioner*, 468 F.2d 1000 (1st Cir. 1972); *Winters v. Commissioner*, 468 F.2d 778 (2d Cir. 1972); *DeJong v. Commissioner*, 309 F.2d 373 (9th Cir. 1962).

95. Compare the majority.

96. You might wonder how the Sklars were able to litigate the same issue regarding the deductibility of their children's parochial school tuition before the Tax Court. In *Commissioner v. Sunnen*, 333 U.S. 591, 598–599 (1948) the Supreme Court stated:

SKLAR v. COMMISSIONER

125 T.C. 281 (2005)

COLVIN, Judge:

...

FINDINGS OF FACT

...

Petitioners deducted 55 percent of their payments to Emek and Yeshiva Rav Isacsohn as a charitable contribution deduction for 1994. Petitioners described the deduction on a Form 8275, Disclosure Statement, attached to their 1994 return. Respondent examined petitioners' 1994 tax return and disallowed the charitable contribution deduction. Litigation relating to petitioners' 1994 return is discussed below at paragraph E.

...

Petitioners timely filed their 1995 Federal income tax return on October 15, 1996. Petitioners deducted $ 24,421 as a charitable contribution for 1995, including $ 15,000 which petitioners attributed to the cost of their children's religious education at Emek and Yeshiva Rav Isacsohn during 1995. That amount ($ 15,000) is 54.97 percent (referred to here as 55 percent) of the total amount of tuition and fees that petitioners paid to Emek and Yeshiva Rav Isacsohn during 1995. Petitioners did not file a Form 8275 or otherwise describe their payment on their 1995 return. Respondent had petitioners' 1994 return under examination when petitioners filed their 1995 return.

Pursuant to petitioner's request, Emek and Yeshiva Rav Isacsohn issued letters to petitioner dated November 5 and November 10, 1997, respectively, in which each school estimated that 45 percent of the education provided to petitioners' children was secular and 55 percent was religious.

E. Litigation Relating to Petitioners' 1994 Return

Petitioners filed a petition with the Court challenging respondent's notice of deficiency for 1994. In *Sklar v. Commissioner, T.C. Memo. 2000-118* (Sklar I), this Court held that petitioners could not deduct as charitable contributions amounts for tuition and fees that they paid for their children's religious education that year. Our decision was affirmed on appeal by the U.S. Court of Appeals for the Ninth Circuit in *Sklar v. Commissioner, 282 F.3d 610 (9th Cir. 2002)*, amending and superseding *279 F.3d 697 (9th Cir. 2002)*.

OPINION

A. Whether Petitioners May Deduct Tuition and Fees They Paid to Orthodox Jewish Day Schools During 1995

Income taxes are levied on an annual basis.

Each year is the origin of a new liability and a separate cause of action. Thus, if a claim of liability or non-liability relating to a particular year is litigated, a judgment on the merits is *res judicata* as to any subsequent proceeding involving the same claim and the same tax year. But if the later proceeding is concerned with a similar or unlike claim relating to a different tax year, the prior judgment acts as a collateral estoppel only as to those matters in the second proceeding which were actually presented and determined in the first suit....

... [Collateral estoppel] is designed to prevent repetitious lawsuits over matters which have once been decided and which have remained substantially static, factually and legally.

1. Petitioners' Contentions

Petitioners contend that they may deduct as a charitable contribution $ 15,000 of the $ 27,283 they paid to Emek and Yeshiva Rav Isacsohn in 1995. They deducted about 55 percent of those payments because that was the portion of the school day that each school estimated was devoted to religious studies.

Petitioners contend that: (a) The religious education that Emek and Yeshiva Rav Isacsohn provided their children is an "intangible religious benefit" as defined in sections 170(f)(8) and 6115, and payments for intangible religious benefits are made deductible by those sections; and (b) respondent's disallowance of their charitable contribution deduction for tuition and fees violates the Establishment Clause of the First Amendment to the U.S. Constitution because the Commissioner allows members of the Church of Scientology to deduct as charitable contributions "auditing" and "training" payments.

2. Whether Petitioners' Tuition Payments Qualify for Deduction Under Section 170 Pursuant to a Dual Payment Analysis

a. Introduction

To put our consideration of petitioners' contentions in context, we first consider whether petitioners' payment of tuition and fees is deductible under a dual payment analysis to the extent the payments exceed the value of the secular education received by their children. See *United States v. Am. Bar Endowment, 477 U.S. 105 (1986); Sklar v. Commissioner, supra at 612, 614 n.3, 621.* We initially consider that issue without regard to the enactment of sections 170(f)(8) and 6115 in 1993 and the Commissioner's settlement with the Church of Scientology on October 1, 1993. We then consider the effect (if any) of those developments on our analysis.

b. Background

In 1967, the Commissioner issued *Rev. Rul. 67-246, 1967-2 C.B. 104,* in response to:

> an increasing number of instances in which the public has been erroneously advised in advertisements or solicitations by sponsors that the entire amounts paid for tickets or other privileges in connection with fund-raising affairs for charity are deductible.

> ...

The examples that the Commissioner cited included tickets for charitable events such as banquets, balls, bazaars, concerts, and athletic events. In *Rev. Rul. 67-246,* supra, the Commissioner ruled that, where a taxpayer receives an item of value for a payment to a charitable organization, (1) the payment is not deductible unless the taxpayer intends to make a gift; and (2) any deduction is limited to the excess of the payment over the fair market value of what is received in exchange.

Courts have also applied those two requirements. Thus, a portion of a payment is deductible as a charitable contribution under section 170 if the following two conditions are met: "First, the payment is deductible only if and to the extent it exceeds the market value of the benefit received. Second, the excess payment must be 'made with the intention of making a gift.'" *United States v. Am. Bar Endowment, supra at 117–118,* (quoting *Rev. Rul. 67-246, 1967-2 C.B. at 105); Sklar v. Commissioner, supra at 621.*

In *United States v. Am. Bar Endowment, supra at 118,* the Supreme Court said:

> The sine qua non of a charitable contribution is a transfer of money or property without adequate consideration. The taxpayer, therefore, must at a mini-

mum demonstrate that he purposely contributed money or property in excess
of the value of any benefit he received in return....

A taxpayer may not deduct a payment as a charitable contribution if the taxpayer receives a substantial benefit for a payment to a charitable organization. *Id. at 116–117;
Ottawa Silica Co. v. United States, 699 F.2d 1124, 1131 (Fed. Cir. 1983); Singer Co. v.
United States, 196 Ct. Cl. 90, 449 F.2d 413, 420, 422 (1971);* S. Rept. 1622, 83d Cong., 2d
Sess. 196 (1954). If the size of a taxpayer's payment to a charity is clearly out of proportion to the benefit received, the taxpayer may claim a charitable contribution equal to
the difference between a payment to the charitable organization and the market value of
the benefit received in return on the theory that the payment has the "dual character" of
a purchase and a contribution. *United States v. Am. Bar Endowment, supra at 117.* To be
deductible, a charitable contribution must be a gift; i.e., a transfer of property without
adequate consideration. *Sec. 170(c); United States v. Am. Bar Endowment, supra at 118;
Sklar v. Commissioner, supra at 612.*

c. Dual Payment Theory and Tuition Paid for a Secular and Religious Education

It is well established that tuition paid to schools which provide both secular and religious education is not deductible as a charitable contribution because it is not paid with
detached and disinterested generosity and because the payor expects a substantial benefit
in return. *Oppewal v. Commissioner, 468 F.2d 1000 (1st Cir. 1972),* affg. T.C. Memo. 1971-
273; *Winters v. Commissioner, 468 F.2d 778, 780–781 (2d Cir. 1972),* affg T.C. Memo. 1971-
290; *DeJong v. Commissioner, 309 F.2d 373, 377–378 (9th Cir. 1962),* affg. 36 T.C. 896
(1961)....

In *DeJong v. Commissioner, supra,* decided by the Court of Appeals for the Ninth
Circuit, the taxpayer made payments to a religious organization which operated a
school which imposed no explicit tuition charges. Part of the payment was deductible as a charitable contribution because the payment exceeded the amount apparently expected to be paid by the parent to cover the school's estimated cost per
student of operating the secular and religious educational programs of the school. *Id.
at 379.* That kind of excess is not in dispute here; the only amounts in dispute here
were paid for tuition and fees. The Court of Appeals in DeJong did not allow a charitable contribution deduction for tuition paid for either the secular or the religious
education.

d. Absence of Charitable Intent

Like the taxpayers in the cases just cited, petitioners received a substantial benefit for
their tuition payments. We next consider whether petitioners had any charitable intent
in paying their children's tuition. See *United States v. Am. Bar Endowment, 477 U.S. at
117–118; Sklar v. Commissioner, 282 F.3d at 612.* Petitioners do not so claim; and, as discussed next, the record shows they could not have made that claim successfully.

In *Sklar v. Commissioner, supra at 621,* the Court of Appeals said that petitioners did
not show that "any dual payments they may have made exceeded the market value of
the secular education their children received"; i.e., "the cost of a comparable secular education offered by private schools". The Court of Appeals also said petitioners had
"failed to show that they intended to make a gift by contributing any such 'excess payment'" and thus could not prevail under *United States v. Am. Bar Endowment, supra.* Id.

The parties introduced into evidence information about tuition costs and qualitative
aspects of private schools, primarily in the Los Angeles area. The record supports the
conclusion that tuition at Emek and Yeshiva Rav Isacsohn is higher than the average tu-

ition at Los Angeles area Catholic schools, but equal to or lower than average tuition at other Los Angeles area Orthodox Jewish schools..., other Jewish day schools, and private schools which do not provide religious education.

Petitioners' expert opined about the market value of a secular education provided by Emek and Yeshiva Rav Isacsohn. He apparently was proceeding from the assumption that a dual payments analysis applies in this case; i.e., that petitioners may deduct the excess of the tuition they paid over the market value of a secular education at Emek and Yeshiva Rav Isacsohn. However, more fundamentally, the record speaks to whether a dual payments analysis applies in this case at all.

Petitioners must have a charitable intent to be entitled to a deduction under section 170 for part of their tuition payments. See *Sklar v. Commissioner, supra at 612;* see also sec. 170(c); *United States v. Am. Bar Endowment, 477 U.S. at 117–118.* On the basis of evidence in the record regarding tuition at various Los Angeles area schools we conclude: (1) Some schools charge more tuition than Emek and Yeshiva Rav Isacsohn, and some charge less; and (2) the amount of tuition petitioners paid is unremarkable and is not excessive for the substantial benefit they received in exchange; i.e., an education for their children. Thus, petitioners have not shown that any part of their tuition payments was a charitable contribution, and this case is indistinguishable from those cited....

3. Whether Sections 170(f)(8) and 6115 Authorize Charitable Contribution Deductions for Tuition Payments to Schools Providing Religious and Secular Education

Petitioners contend that, under sections 170(f)(8) and 6115 as enacted in 1993, a portion of tuition payments to schools providing a religious and secular education is deductible as a charitable contribution.

a. Background

Sections 170(f)(8) and 6115 were enacted under the Omnibus Budget Reconciliation Act of 1993, Pub. L. 103-66, secs. 13172 and 13173, 107 Stat. 455, to address "difficult problems of tax administration" associated with taxpayers' deductions of charitable contributions in connection with fund-raising events involving quid pro quo transactions. To enhance taxpayer compliance in this area, Congress imposed (a) a new substantiation requirement under section 170(f)(8), and (b) a new disclosure requirement on charitable organizations under section 6115.

Section 170(f)(8) generally requires a taxpayer claiming a charitable contribution deduction greater than $ 250 to substantiate the deduction by obtaining a contemporaneous written acknowledgment of the contribution from the charitable organization, including an estimate of the value of any goods or services that the charitable organization provided to the taxpayer. Under section 6115, a charitable organization that receives a quid pro quo payment in excess of $ 75 must inform the taxpayer that any charitable contribution deduction is limited to the difference between the value of any money or property transferred to the charitable organization and the value of any goods or services that the taxpayer received from the charitable organization.

Sections 170(f)(8) and 6115 except certain intangible religious benefits from the substantiation and disclosure requirements described above. Sections 170(f)(8) and 6115 provide, inter alia, that if a charitable organization is organized exclusively for religious purposes and provides solely an intangible religious benefit to a taxpayer in exchange for a payment, the charitable organization need not assign a value to the intangible religious benefit.

b. Petitioners' Contentions

Petitioners contend that (1) sections 170(f)(8) and 6115 make tuition payments to religious schools deductible to the extent the payments relate to religious education, (2) the religious education that Emek and Yeshiva Rav Isacsohn provided to their children was an intangible religious benefit as defined in those sections, and (3) their tuition payments are deductible to the extent that the payments exceed the value of the secular education their children received.(Footnote 11) Petitioners also contend that they need not show that they intended to make a gift or contribution to Emek and Yeshiva Rav Isacsohn.

c. Analysis

We disagree. Congress did not change what is deductible under section 170 in these 1993 statutory changes. Neither sections 170(f)(8) and 6115 nor the accompanying legislative history suggests that Congress intended to expand the types of payments that are deductible as charitable contributions under section 170 (Footnote 12) or that Congress intended to overturn the long line of cases (cited above) holding that no part of tuition paid to religious schools is deductible as a charitable contribution.(Footnote 13) We believe that, if Congress had intended to overturn decades of caselaw disallowing charitable contribution deductions for tuition payments to schools providing a religious and secular education, Congress would have made such an intention clear. It did not.

The exception to the substantiation and disclosure requirements in sections 170(f)(8) and 6115 for intangible religious benefits does not apply to the educational services at issue here. The exception applies only where the organization is organized exclusively for religious purposes. Petitioners contend that Emek and Yeshiva Rav Isacsohn were organized and existed solely for the religious purpose of allowing Jewish parents to fulfill their religious obligation to teach their children Torah, which includes providing a secular education in an Orthodox Jewish environment.

We disagree that Emek and Yeshiva Rav Isacsohn were organized exclusively for religious purposes. Emek and Yeshiva Rav Isacsohn were organized and operated to provide both a secular and a religious education. The Commissioner granted both schools exemptions from tax under section 501(c)(3), and both schools qualify as charitable organizations described in section 170(b)(1)(A)(ii), which pertains to educational organizations. A substantial part of each day was spent on secular studies. Petitioners concede that the education their children received in 1995 at Emek and Yeshiva Rav Isacsohn met educational requirements imposed by the State of California. Both schools were accredited by nonreligious accrediting agencies based in part on their secular educational programs.

Petitioners contend that Emek and Yeshiva Rav Isacsohn were organized exclusively as religious organizations because respondent excused both from filing Forms 990, Return of Organization Exempt From Income Tax. We disagree. Organizations exempt from tax under section 501(a) generally are required to file Forms 990. Sec. 6033(a)(1). However, churches, exempt organizations with gross receipts of not more than $ 5,000, and exclusively religious activities of any religious order are exempt from that requirement. The Commissioner may relieve any exempt organization from filing a return where the Commissioner determines that filing is not necessary to the efficient administration of the internal revenue laws. Sec. 6033(a)(2)(B).

Emek and Yeshiva Rav Isacsohn do not qualify for the exception to the general filing requirement provided in section 6033(a)(2)(A). Neither school is a church, an exempt organization with gross receipts of not more than $ 5,000, or a religious order. Given that Emek and Yeshiva Rav Isacsohn were treated as charitable organizations described in section 170(b)(1)(A)(ii), i.e., educational organizations, we infer that the Commissioner exercised discretion under section 6033(a)(2)(B) to except Emek and Yeshiva Rav Isacsohn from filing Forms 990.

Emek and Yeshiva Rav Isacsohn provided a religious and secular education for their students. Regardless of petitioners' reasons for choosing to educate their children at Emek and Yeshiva Rav Isacsohn, those schools did not provide exclusively religious services.

4. Whether the Agreement Reached Between the Internal Revenue Service and the Church of Scientology in 1993 Affects the Result in This Case

In *Hernandez v. Commissioner, 490 U.S. 680, 702 (1989)*, the U.S. Supreme Court held that the record did not support the taxpayer's claim of entitlement to deduct as charitable contributions payments to the Church of Scientology for what the Church of Scientology calls auditing and training. However, the parties stipulated that an agreement dated October 1, 1993, between the Commissioner and the Church of Scientology settled several longstanding issues. According to a letter sent to petitioners in 1994 from the chief of the adjustments branch, Fresno Service Center, the settlement agreement between the Commissioner and the Church of Scientology allows individuals to claim, as charitable contributions, 80 percent of the cost of qualified religious services.

Petitioners contend that, because of that closing agreement, the Commissioner is constitutionally required to allow a deduction for tuition paid to schools that provide religious and secular education to the extent that the tuition paid exceeds the value of the secular education. Petitioners contend that the religious education that the Jewish day schools provide in exchange for tuition is jurisprudentially indistinguishable from the auditing and training that the Church of Scientology provides to its members in exchange for a fixed fee.

The U.S. Court of Appeals for the Ninth Circuit previously rejected petitioners' arguments about the Church of Scientology in *Sklar v. Commissioner, 282 F.3d at 619–620*. Petitioners' tuition payments were made to schools that in part provide secular educational services, not to exclusively religious organizations. Thus, the analysis in *United States v. Am. Bar Endowment, 477 U.S. 105 (1986)*, controls here. We conclude that the agreement reached between the Internal Revenue Service and the Church of Scientology referred to in the letter sent to petitioners in 1994 from respondent's Fresno Service Center does not affect the result in this cases.(Footnote 16)

...

6. Conclusion

We conclude that petitioners are not entitled to a charitable contribution deduction under section 170 for any part of the tuition, including the fee for Mishna classes, they paid to Emek or Yeshiva Rav Isacsohn in 1995.

FOOTNOTES:

11. Petitioners aver:

> if a taxpayer pays $ 100 to his church and receives in return a book that could be purchased in any bookstore for $ 20 plus the right to sit in a certain pew at the church, $ 80 is deductible as a charitable contribution to the church, regardless of whether having the right to sit in that pew is worth $ 80 or more to the taxpayer, because that right is only an intangible religious benefit. Similarly here, to the extent petitioners' dual payments to the schools exceeded the value

of the secular studies they purchased, those payments are deductible as charitable contributions notwithstanding that petitioners received religious educations for their children worth that excess, because those religious educations are only intangible religious benefits.

12. See H. Conf. Rept. 103-213, at 566 (1993), *1993-3 C.B. 393, 444*, stating that the *sec. 6115* disclosure requirement "does not apply to transactions that have no donative element (e.g., sales of goods by a museum gift shop that are not, in part, donations)." Thus, a charitable organization need not make a *sec. 6115* disclosure if the taxpayer did not intend to make a gift.

13. See H. Conf. Rept. 103-213, supra at 566 n. 34, 1993-3 C.B. at 444, stating that the exception to the substantiation requirement for an intangible religious benefit "does not apply, for example, to tuition for education leading to a recognized degree, travel services, or consumer goods." Along the same lines, H. Rept. 103-111, supra at 786 n. 170, 1993-3 C.B. at 362, states:

> The committee intends that, in the case of religious organizations, a quid pro quo contribution (for purposes of the substantiation and disclosure requirements) is limited to an exchange of goods or services that are generally available on a commercial basis, or advertised for an established price (e.g., tuition, travel and entertainment, and consumer goods). No inference is intended, however, whether or not any contribution outside of the scope of the bill's substantiation or reporting requirements is deductible (in full or in part) under the present-law requirements of *section 170*.

16. In *Sklar v. Commissioner, 282 F.3d 610, 612 n. 3 (9th Cir. 2002)*, affg. *T.C. Memo. 2000-118*, the U.S. Court of Appeals said it is strongly inclined to the view that *sec. 170* was not amended in 1993 to permit deductions for which the consideration is intangible religious benefits, and that *Hernandez v. Commissioner, 490 U.S. 680, 702 (1989)*, is still controlling. That court also said that it need not rule definitively on this point because petitioners' claims did not meet the requirements for partial deductibility of dual payments established by *United States v. Am. Bar Endowment, 477 U.S. 105 (1986)*. Similarly, we have decided this case by applying *United States v. Am. Bar Endowment, supra*.

Now that you have read *Sklar I* and *Sklar II*, and the commentary in between, how would you advise your client who asks you whether she can deduct the parochial school tuition she pays for her children? Does the precipitous decline in the number of audits in the last several years affect your advice to your client?[97] (That is, should you advise your client to play the audit lottery?)

Before we leave personal deductions, one final aspect of personal itemized deductions deserves investigation: the variation in the benefit of the deductions to taxpayers who are not similarly situated. For example, suppose Aaron has income that is taxed at a marginal rate of 15% while Mary Ellen has income that is taxed at a marginal rate of 35%. Each contributes $1,000 to a qualified donee under section 170(c). How much will each one's contribution really "cost" the taxpayer? In other words,

---

97. Recall the Streckfus article.

how much revenue will the federal treasury forego as a result of each contribution?[98] Might you characterize this foregone revenue as a subsidy to the recipient of the contribution? Can you now see why Professor Surrey labeled this type of subsidy as a "tax expenditure"? Why does Professor Surrey refer to these expenditures as "upside-down subsidies"?

As you have already read, both exclusions from gross income and deductions are "matters of legislative grace." Why has the legislature, *i.e.*, Congress, "graced" the foregoing expenses with special treatment? In most discussions about the flat tax, the replacement of the current progressive rate structure with a relatively low flat rate of tax is conditioned upon the repeal of many, if not all, of the personal itemized deductions we have just examined. Why would advocates of the flat tax want to repeal such cultural icons as the charitable contribution deduction, the casualty loss deduction, or the medical expense deduction? What effects might the repeal of such provisions have on the nonprofit or medical community?

B. Profit-Making Activities: The Relationship among Sections 162, 212, 183, and 262

As we stated in the introduction to this chapter, most people consider it fair to deduct the costs of producing income from the gross amount of that income; expenses incurred in connection with income-producing activities are essential to producing the income. But, no similarly agreed-upon policy supports the deduction of personal expenses.

In contrast to the expenses that must be borne to produce income, many personal expenses are discretionary in nature a taxpayer makes many of these personal outlays out of choice, not necessity.[99] For example, a movie maker may deduct the costs of her movie from the income the movie produces. But should the Code allow a deduction for the cost of a movie ticket purchased for personal enjoyment? The United States Supreme Court has noted with approval, the formulation by two prominent tax theorists of the Code's approach to deductions:

> For income tax purposes Congress has seen fit to regard an individual as having two personalities: "one is [as] a seeker after profit who can deduct the expenses incurred in that search; the other is [as] a creature satisfying his needs

---

98. Taxpayers often analyze the "after-tax cost" of certain outlays. Some people refer to this as the "value of a deduction." If the deduction for a contribution were not available to Aaron and Mary Ellen, might that influence either Aaron's or Mary Ellen's decision to contribute to the organization?

99. There are, however, many personal expenditures that taxpayers do not make out of personal choice. For example, medical expenses, casualty loss expenses, and state and local income taxes are not discretionary. As you observed in Part A of this chapter, section 262(a) of the Code prohibits the deduction of most personal expenses. But Congress has chosen to recognize the unavoidability and financial impact of some of these expenses by overriding the general rule and authorizing the deduction of some personal expenses. No uniform policy dictates Congress's choice. Indeed, in some cases, it is difficult to identify any clear policy objective. Nevertheless, there is strong popular support for the continuation of these deductions.

as a human and those of his family but who cannot deduct such consumption and related expenditures."[100]

Thus, as a general rule, the costs associated with income-producing activities are deductible, whereas costs associated with day-to-day living are not. **Compare Code sections 162(a) and 212(1) and (2)[101] with section 262.** The distinction between income-producing and personal activities, however, is not always so clear. Nevertheless, the discussion and cases that follow should provide you with a basic analytical framework for distinguishing between the two types of activities.

After determining that the taxpayer is engaged in an income-producing activity, sections 162(a) and 212 of the Code introduce an additional distinction between two types of income-producing activities: those that constitute the active "carrying on [of] any trade or business," and those that constitute more passive profit-seeking investment activities "for the production or collection of income; ... for the management, conservation, or maintenance of property held for the production of income...." We will defer discussion of this distinction to section 2 below.

1. Section 162(a): "Carrying on any Trade or Business": Distinguishing a Trade or Business from a Hobby or a Personal Activity

Section 162(a) allows a taxpayer to deduct "all the ordinary and necessary expenses paid or incurred during the taxable year in carrying on any trade or business...." **Review section 162(a).** It is readily apparent that determination of a taxpayer's right to claim a deduction under section 162(a) will require solving a number of issues. For example, what is "ordinary and necessary"? What are "expenses"? What does "paid or incurred" mean? What does "carrying on" mean? And, most important, what is a "trade or business"? **Reread section 162(a).** What words do not require interpretation?[102]

Let's begin with an analysis of the fundamental requirement of section 162(a), *i.e.*, that a taxpayer must engage in a "trade or business." Consider the following scenarios as you attempt to define this critical statutory term:

Jack's Problem

Jack works full-time (60 hours per week) as a partner at a law firm. Is Jack engaged in a trade or business? What is it?

---

100. *United States v. Gilmore*, 372 U.S. 39, 44 (1963) (footnote omitted), (citing Surrey and Warren, *Cases on Federal Income Taxation*, 272 (1960)).

101. Section 212(3) contains an additional category of deductible expenses: those paid or incurred "in connection with the determination, collection, or refund of any tax." **Look at section 212(3).** Does this category of deductible expense seem consistent with the general rule that expenses associated with income-producing activities are deductible while those associated with personal activities are not?

102. Once again, note that you cannot read a statute in the same way that you read a case. You cannot skip *any* words and you must be certain that you can define each one.

Jack is very concerned about all the reports he has heard about bacterial contamination of chickens and eggs. Jack decides to keep a few chickens to produce the eggs that he likes to eat for breakfast before work. He soon discovers that he has more eggs than he can eat so he brings the four to six extra eggs that his hens lay per day to the office and gives them to several co-workers. How might you characterize Jack's egg-producing activity? Assuming he satisfies the other requirements of section 162(a), does his production of eggs constitute "a trade or business" so that he can deduct the expenses associated with the production of his eggs? Does he have any income against which to deduct the expenses? Does it matter?

Word spreads about how good Jack's eggs are. Jack decides to expand his flock of chickens in order to produce more eggs and to sell them to people in the office. Instead of four to six eggs per day, Jack is soon selling three dozen eggs per day. Does this change the nature of his egg-producing activity? Now he has income from the sale of eggs. Can he deduct the expenses associated with the production of his eggs?

Again, finding that he cannot keep up with demand, Jack expands his flock in order to produce twelve dozen extra eggs per day. Does this make a difference? *12 doz eggs / day*

His customers love his eggs, but Jack finds that he cannot keep up with his law practice and his egg production activities. Jack decides to give up his law practice, to expand his number of chickens again, and to sell more eggs. Is Jack now engaged in a trade or business? What is it?

It was not until 1987 that the United States Supreme Court articulated a definition of "trade or business." Read the following extract from *Commissioner v. Groetzinger*, 480 U.S. 23 (1987), and identify the proper test that Jack should apply to determine if he is engaged in an income-producing activity that constitutes a "trade or business."

The phrase "trade or business" has been in § 162(a) and in that section's predecessors for many years. Indeed, the phrase is common in the Code, for it appears in over 50 sections and 800 subsections and in hundreds of places in proposed and final income tax regulations.... The concept thus has a well-known and almost constant presence on our tax-law terrain. Despite this, the Code has never contained a definition of the words "trade or business" for general application, and no regulation has been issued expounding its meaning for all purposes. Neither has a broadly applicable authoritative judicial definition emerged. Our task in this case is to ascertain the meaning of the phrase....

...

If a taxpayer, as Groetzinger is stipulated to have done in 1978, devotes his full-time activity [6 days per week, 60 to 80 hours per week] to gambling, and it is his intended livelihood source, it would seem that basic concepts of fairness (if there be much of that in the income tax law) demand that his activity be regarded as a trade or business just as any other readily accepted activity, such as being a retail store proprietor or, to come closer categorically, as being a casino operator or as being an active trader on the exchanges....

Of course, not every income-producing and profit-making endeavor constitutes a trade or business. The income tax law, almost from the beginning, has distinguished between a business or trade, on the one hand, and "transactions entered into for profit but not connected with ... business or trade," on the *income = producing*

other.... Congress "distinguished the broad range of income or profit producing activities from those satisfying the narrow category of trade or business."
Whipple v. Commissioner, 373 U.S., at 197. We accept the fact that to be engaged in a trade or business, the taxpayer must be involved in the activity with
continuity and regularity and that the taxpayer's primary purpose for engaging
in the activity must be for income or profit. A sporadic activity, a hobby, or an
amusement diversion does not qualify.[103]

(margin, handwritten: Trade/ Business definition)

What about a taxpayer who devotes long hours to an activity without making a
profit? Suppose a taxpayer enjoys gourmet food. He travels the world, eating at the great
restaurants of the world. He publishes a book reviewing the restaurants he has visited.
Is he engaged in a trade or business under the *Groetzinger* test? What is it?

What is the significance to the Service and to the taxpayer of the distinction between
an activity that constitutes a trade or business and one that does not? The answer lies in
the proposition set forth in the beginning of this section: that it is reasonable to allow a
taxpayer to deduct the expenses of producing income, but not reasonable to allow a taxpayer to deduct expenses of personal consumption.

Review the income tax calculation outline and reread section 62(a)(1) of the Code.
Note that trade or business expenses deductible as a result of section 162 (other than unreimbursed employee business expenses) reduce gross income. These expenses are important adjustments that lead to "adjusted gross income." As noted earlier, these expenses, and the other adjustments to gross income listed in section 62(a), are referred to
as "above the line deductions." Therefore, these expenses reduce gross income dollar-for-
dollar.[104] In contrast, most expenses incurred for personal consumption do not qualify
under section 62(a), and do not enter the taxing formula until after calculation of adjusted gross income.

Section 183 of the Code reflects the problem of distinguishing between a trade or
business activity and a "hobby." **Read section 183 and Treasury Regulation section
1.183-2.** Then recall our discussion of Jack. In further analyzing the characterization of
Jack's egg-producing activities as a trade or business, read the following case.

SMITH v. COMMISSIONER
9 T.C. 1150 (1947)

Respondent determined a deficiency in petitioner's income and victory tax for the
year ended December 31, 1943, in the amount of $884.07. The deficiency results from
respondent's disallowance of certain deductions claimed for farm losses in 1942 and

----

103. 480 U.S. at 27, 33–35 (footnotes omitted).

104. As you learned in Carole's problem, "adjusted gross income" constitutes the basis for calculating a number of percentage limitations that apply to below the line itemized deductions, *e.g.*, the
limit on the deduction of medical expenses to the amount that exceeds 7 1/2% of adjusted gross income.

1943. The question for determination is whether such losses are deductible and that question in turn depends on whether the farm was operated for profit....

FINDINGS OF FACT.

Petitioner is an executive of Chicopee Manufacturing Corporation and Johnson & Johnson Co.

In 1933 petitioner bought an 118-acre farm on South Middlebush Road near Middlebush, New Jersey. He paid $13,000 for it. A reasonable allocation of the cost is residence $5,000, tenant house $1,000, farm buildings $1,500, and land $5,500. He acquired the farm for the purpose of occupying the main house thereon as a permanent home for himself and family and to operate the farm to supplement his income and increase his financial security. The dwelling house occupied by petitioner and his family was situated in one corner of the farm about 300 feet from the main highway on one side and about 300 feet from a side road on the other side. The farm and its buildings were in a run-down condition when acquired by petitioner. He spent $5,000 improving the main residence and $1,400 improving the tenant house.

For the first year or two petitioner rented the farm to a tenant farmer. This arrangement proved unprofitable and was discontinued. Petitioner then took over the farm, employed a farmer, purchased farm equipment, and endeavored to operate the farm himself. This arrangement likewise proved unprofitable. Petitioner next tried poultry raising and general farming. Later on he tried raising hogs and sheep and in about 1938 or 1939 he began raising and breeding beef cattle. All of the above activities were undertaken with the view to profit, but none proved profitable. In 1945 petitioner was unable to get sufficient help and sold off most of his cattle. He is now raising wheat, corn, and hay. Petitioner has also spent time and study to improve the soil and for this purpose has grown clover and legumes and has put lime and fertilizer on the land. He has reclaimed several eroded fields. He has increased the acreage devoted to agricultural uses from about 75 to 95 acres. Petitioner devotes considerable time on week ends actually working about the farm. On week days he usually confers 10 or 15 minutes with the hired help.

Petitioner sells the produce from his farm. He sells principally to a few local butchers and grocerymen. Some sales result from purchasers stopping by and picking up eggs and chickens. Occasionally petitioner has sold cattle to the Delaware Packing Co. at Trenton. Petitioner usually makes the selling arrangements except in instances when purchasers stop by the farm to buy eggs or chickens. Petitioner and his family also consume some produce of the farm. The amount so consumed is usually about 10 per cent of the produce raised or a little less. It is included in farm income at prevailing market rates. The capital and operating expenses of the residence are and have been segregated from the farm expenses.

Petitioner has never made a profit from farm operations. His net losses for the years indicated have been as follows:

1934	$ 494.00
1940	2,000.00
1941	1,200.00
1942	1,086.50
1943	2,035.89
1944	2,800.00
1945	386.69
1946	1,100.00

Petitioner's farm inventory for income computation for 1942 was shown on Form 1040F as follows:

Description (kind of livestock, crops or other products)	On hand beginning of year Quantity	On hand beginning of year Inventory value	Purchased during year Quantity	Purchased during year Amount paid	Raised during year Quantity	Raised during year Inventory value
Poultry	120	$ 120	300	$ 66		
Turkeys	70	280	300	152		
Cows	2	170				
Beef cattle	14	1,395	1	200	6	
Wheat	180	180			240	
Oats	170	102			300	
Corn	600	450			700	
Barley	120	84			198	
Soy bean					36	
Hay	85	128			9	
Eggs					1,937	
Milk					1,000	
Total		2,909		418		

	Consumed or lost during year Quantity	Consumed or lost during year Inventory value	Sold during year Quantity	Sold during year Amount received	On hand at end of year Quantity	On hand at end of year Inventory value
Poultry		$ 50	230	$ 161.00	140	$ 140
Turkeys		50	265	1,114.00	55	266
Cows					2	170
Beef cattle			4	562.25	17	1,620
Wheat	240				180	180
Oats	270				200	120
Corn	600				700	525
Barley	168				150	105
Soy bean	6				30	45
Hay	10				7	105
Eggs			1,937	732.90		
Milk	500		500	150.00		
Total				2,720.15		3,276

Farm expenses for 1942 were shown as follows:

Labor hired	$ 1,290.00
Feed purchased	532.29
Seed, plants and trees purchased	172.57
Machine hire	132.00
Supplies purchased	173.05
Cost of repairs and maintenance	282.17
Fertilizers and lime	172.02
Veterinary and medicine for livestock	45.00
Gasoline, other fuel and oil for farm business	135.23
Insurance on property (except dwelling)	113.25

Water rent, electricity, and telephone	33.15
Spray material	13.56
Total	3,094.29

Depreciation on buildings and machinery was taken in the amount of $661.36. The above designated items of expense in the total amount of $3,094.29 were ordinary and necessary expenses paid by petitioner in 1942 in the operation of his farm and $661.36 was a reasonable amount to be allowed as depreciation on the farm buildings and machinery. Petitioner sustained a net loss in 1942 of $1,086.50 in the operation of the farm.

Petitioner's farm inventory for income tax purposes for 1943 is shown on Form 1040F as follows:

Description (kind of livestock, crops, or other products)	On hand at beginning of year		Purchased during year		Raised during year	
	Quantity	Inventory value	Quantity	Amount paid	Quantity	Inventory value
Poultry	140	$ 140	500	$ 200		
Turkeys	55	266	300	165		
Cows	2	140				
Beef cattle	17	1,620			11	
Wheat	180	180			220	$ 220
Oats	200	120			250	175
Corn	700	525			250	200
Barley	150	105				
Soy bean	30	45			50	100
Hay	7	105			15	450
Eggs					2,152 (doz.)	
Milk					900 (gal.)	
Total		3,276		365		

	Consumed or lost during year		Sold during year		On hand at end of year	
	Quantity	Inventory value	Quantity	Amount received	Quantity	Inventory value
Poultry	80		230	$ 323	330	$ 264
Turkeys	50		295	1,706	10	48
Cows					2	170
Beef cattle			4	524	24	1,970
Wheat	340	$ 340			60	60
Oats	400	260			50	35
Corn	900	685			50	40
Barley	150	105				
Soy bean	30	45			50	100
Hay	20	495			2	60
Eggs			2,152	968		
Milk	500		400	120		
Total				3,641		2,747

Farm expenses for 1943 were shown as follows:

Labor hired	$ 1,483.50
Feed purchased	1,005.12
Seed, plants and trees purchased	225.00
Machine hire	125.00
Supplies purchased	66.21
Cost of repairs and maintenance	685.07
Veterinary and medicine for livestock	34.00
Gasoline, other fuel and oil for farm business	177.13
Taxes, property (1/2)	173.00
Interest on farm notes and mortgages, Federal L. B. mort. (1/2)	45.00
Water rent, electricity, and telephone	44.00
Miscellaneous	1.75
Registration fees	41.25
Total	4,104.03

Depreciation on buildings and machinery was taken in the amount of $678.86. The above designated items of expense in the total amount of $4,104.03 were ordinary and necessary expenses paid by petitioner in 1943 in the operation of his farm and $678.86 was a reasonable amount to be allowed as depreciation on the farm buildings and machinery. Petitioner sustained a net loss in 1943 of $2,035.89.

...

Petitioner has spent money beautifying his residence and has used it for normal social purposes. His residential expenses have, however, been segregated from his farm expenses. The farm itself, excluding the residence, is not used for social purposes.

The farm, separate and apart from the residence, was operated by the petitioner during the years herein involved for profit and its operation constituted a business regularly carried on for profit during such years.

OPINION

HILL, *Judge*: The question is whether petitioner operated the farm as a trade or business or for profit, on the one hand, or for recreational purposes or as a hobby, on the other. As is implicit or stated in the cases cited by both petitioner and respondent, the answer to this question lies in determining petitioner's intention from all of the evidence. We have concluded that the facts show that the petitioner's intent in operating the farm was primarily for the purpose of making a profit.

Respondent bases his argument that petitioner had no intent to operate the farm as a trade or business or for profit on the following points: (1) That the operation of the farm resulted in a series of uninterrupted losses, (2) that petitioner's purchase of the farm was essentially motivated by his desire to have a country estate for his home, and (3) that petitioner operated the farm in order to supply his family with food for home consumption.

It is true that the petitioner has experienced continuous annual losses from the operation of his farm since its acquisition in 1933 and through the taxable years in question. Moreover, the record discloses that after the taxable years involved here there were further losses in 1944, 1945, and 1946. The fact that the operation of the farm has resulted in a series of losses, however, is not controlling if the other evidence shows there is a true intention of eventually making a profit.... Respondent cites the case of *Thacher v. Lowe*, 282 Fed. 1944, to support his argument. The court in that case stated: ... it is difficult to imagine how a farm which has been running the number of years which this had could be thought capable of turning a deficiency of 90 percent into a profit.

On the facts in the instant case, however, we can not say that there is no reasonable expectation of realizing a profit.

We do not agree with the respondent that petitioner purchased the farm primarily to satisfy his desire to live on a country estate. It may be true that petitioner experienced pleasure from residing in a country home, but this fact alone does not negative his intent to operate the farm for profit.... Nor is such intent negatived by the fact assumed by respondent that petitioner, as a business executive, has received an annual salary sufficiently high to indicate no need to supplement his income by the farm operation.

We are convinced from the record that it has at all times been petitioner's intention to operate the farm for profit, and that he had reasonable expectations of accomplishing that result. His efforts to make a profit have included increasing the land in cultivation and in pasturage from 75 to 95 acres, renting the farm, employing an experienced farmer to operate it under his supervision, improving the land by reclamation practices and fertilization and soil conservation methods, and engaging at various times in a number of diversified types of farming. He spends most of his week ends working on the farm, performing such odd jobs as repairing buildings or equipment, feeding poultry, and spraying orchards. On week days he usually consults with his employee for 10 or 15 minutes each morning in connection with problems related to the operation of the farm. In addition he has expended a great deal of money in repairing farm buildings and buying farm equipment, all of which was for utilitarian rather than beautification purposes. He has always considered the farm separate from his home, he has segregated the capital and operating expenses of the residence from the farm expenses, and he has not used the farm for any social or recreational purposes, nor does it have any such facilities.

This leaves for our consideration respondent's argument that petitioner operated the farm primarily for the purpose of providing wholesome food for his family. It should be noted, first, that petitioner and his family consumed at the most only 10 per cent of the farm products on the average and that all of those used were included and reported in the farm income at regular prices. The other approximately 90 per cent of the farm produce was sold by the petitioner to local butchers and grocerymen, to purchasers stopping by the farm, and occasionally to the Delaware Packing Co. at Trenton. In addition to that, the types of products raised by petitioner included poultry, eggs, cattle, sheep, wheat, corn and hay, many of which are not readily adaptable to home consumption, and such of them as were so adaptable were produced in far greater quantities than his home consumption requirements. The petitioner's primary intention, therefore, was not to produce good food for home consumption....

We hold that petitioner's farm operations during the taxable period here involved were a business regularly carried on by him for profit and that the losses in question resulted from ordinary and necessary expenses paid during such taxable period in carrying on such business and, therefore, are deductible for income tax purposes.

It follows that respondent erred in his determination.

Consider the following questions about *Smith*.

1. What does the Tax Court mean by the phrase "farm losses"? How much were Smith's losses for each of 1942 and 1943? How did he calculate them? Were they incurred in connection with his operation of the business or with a specific transaction?

Section 165 governs only those losses that arise from a particular event, for example, a sale or abandonment. In the words of the Treasury Regulation, losses allowable under section 165 have to be "evidenced by closed and completed transactions, fixed by identifiable events." Treas. Reg. section 1.165-1(b). In contrast, operating losses occur when the expenses of carrying on the activity exceed the income from the activity.[105] The taxpayer must, of course, report the entire income from the activity. She may deduct the expenses attributable to that activity only to the extent that a particular section of the Code authorizes the deduction and no other provision of the Code limits or prohibits that deduction. For example, in the commercial real estate problem in Part VI, you will encounter one of the provisions, section 469, that limits otherwise allowable deductions associated with a commercial real estate venture.

2. **Return to the case *McKay v. Commissioner* that you read in connection with Carole's problem.** Review the Tax Court's discussion of McKay's trade or business. Based on that discussion, how would you characterize Smith's trade or business? Was it that of being a corporate executive? Could he also have been in the trade or business of farming? Can a taxpayer have more than one trade or business? How many can a taxpayer have? What is the test for a trade or business?

3. The Tax Court decided *Smith* before Congress enacted Code section 183. Therefore, Treasury had not yet promulgated Treasury Regulation section 1.183-2. **Read section 183 and study Treasury Regulation section 1.183-2.** How would you analyze Mr. Smith's farming activity under the *Groetzinger* test, section 183, and Treasury Regulation section 1.183-2?

4. What is the real difference to a taxpayer like Mr. Smith if his activity is characterized as a hobby rather than as a trade or business? (To answer this one, you don't have to do the numbers, just describe the difference conceptually.)

Mary Alice's Problem

Suppose Mary Alice decides to grow organic vegetables in her back yard. She sells all her vegetables to a local natural foods store. Her gross income from the sale of the vegetables is $5,000 and her expenses are as follows:

Organic fertilizer	$2,000
Seeds	2,000
Water	500
Part-time help	1,500
Property tax	600[106]

What difference will it make to Mary Alice if her activity is characterized as a hobby rather than as a trade or business? **Compare section 162 and section 183(b).** Note care-

---

105. Recall the case of *Burnet v. Sanford & Brooks Company*, 282 U.S. 359 (1931), in Part II, Chapter 1.A.1.

106. She owns a one-acre lot. Her real estate property tax on the land alone is $2,400. But she uses only one-quarter of the land for her organic gardening operations.

fully that section 183(b)(1) allows some deductions while section 183(b)(2) allows others. If her vegetable-producing activity is characterized as a hobby, which of these expenses can she deduct under section 183(b)(1) and which under section 183(b)(2)? Do sections 67 and 68 apply to limit her deductions? **Review sections 67 and 68.** What is the location of her deduction? **Review section 62(a).**

The introduction to this section sets forth the proposition that it is reasonable to allow a taxpayer to deduct the expenses of producing income, but not reasonable to allow a taxpayer to deduct expenses attributable to personal consumption. Section 183(b) represents a limited concession by Congress with respect to the deductibility of what are essentially personal expenses—those associated with hobbies. This concession, however, is limited to hobbies that produce income and only to the extent that the hobby produces income that exceeds deductions[107] that a taxpayer may take without regard to profit motive.[108] In effect, therefore, section 183 represents a midpoint on the continuum between profit-making activities and personal activities.

Returning again to the idea that expenses associated with producing income should be deducted from that income while expenses associated with personal activities should not, leads to questions of identification, not always easily accomplished. Sometimes it is difficult to distinguish business expenses from personal consumption. There is frequently an uncertain boundary, as the following two cases demonstrate.

SMITH v. COMMISSIONER
40 B.T.A. 1038 (1939)

OPPER: Respondent determined a deficiency of $23.62 in petitioner's 1937 income tax. This was due to the disallowance of a deduction claimed by petitioners, who are husband and wife, for sums spent by the wife in employing nursemaids to care for petitioners' young child, the wife, as well as the husband, being employed. The facts have all been stipulated and are hereby found accordingly.

Petitioners would have us apply the "but for" test. They propose that but for the nurses the wife could not leave her child; but for the freedom so secured she could not pursue her gainful labors; and but for them there would be no income and no tax. This thought evokes an array of interesting possibilities. The fee to the doctor, but for whose healing service the earner of the family income could not leave his sickbed; the cost of the laborer's raiment, for how can the world proceed about its business unclothed; the very home which gives us shelter and rest and the food which provides energy, might all by an extension of the same proposition be construed as necessary to the operation of business and to the creation of income. Yet these are the very essence of those "personal" expenses the deductibility of which is expressly denied. Revenue Act of 1936, section 24(a).

We are told that the working wife is a new phenomenon. This is relied on to account for the apparent inconsistency that the expenses in issue are now a commonplace, yet

---

107. As you noticed above, however, section 67 limits these deductions to the amount that exceeds 2% of adjusted gross income. Therefore, a taxpayer whose adjusted gross income is high may not be able to deduct under section 183(b)(2) any of the expenses associated with her hobby.

108. For example, as in the case of Mary Alice, a taxpayer may deduct her real property tax payments under section 164(a)(1) for her personal residence.

have not been the subject of legislation, ruling, or adjudicated controversy. But if that is true it becomes all the more necessary to apply accepted principles to the novel facts. We are not prepared to say that the care of children, like similar aspects of family and household life, is other than a personal concern. The wife's services as custodian of the home and protector of its children are ordinarily rendered without monetary compensation. There results no taxable income from the performance of this service and the correlative expenditure is personal and not susceptible of deduction.... Here the wife has chosen to employ others to discharge her domestic function and the services she performs are rendered outside the home. They are a source of actual income and taxable as such. But that does not deprive the same work performed by others of its personal character nor furnish a reason why its cost should be treated as an offset in the guise of a deductible item.

We are not unmindful that, as petitioners suggest, certain disbursements normally personal may become deductible by reason of their intimate connection with an occupation carried on for profit. In this category fall entertainment, ... and traveling expenses, ... and the cost of an actor's wardrobe,.... The line is not always an easy one to draw nor the test simple to apply. But we think its principle is clear. It may for practical purposes be said to constitute a distinction between those activities which, as a matter of common acceptance and universal experience, are "ordinary" or usual as the direct accompaniment of business pursuits, on the one hand; and those which though they may in some indirect and tenuous degree relate to the circumstances of a profitable occupation, are nevertheless personal in their nature, of a character applicable to human beings generally, and which exist on that plane regardless of the occupation, though not necessarily of the station in life, of the individuals concerned. See *Welch v. Helvering*, 290 U.S. 111.

In the latter category, we think, fall payments made to servants or others occupied in looking to the personal wants of their employers.... And we include in this group nursemaids retained to care for infant children.

Decision will be entered for the respondent.[109]

MOSS v. COMMISSIONER
758 F.2d 211 (7th Cir. 1985)

POSNER, Circuit Judge.

The taxpayers, a lawyer named Moss and his wife, appeal from a decision of the Tax Court disallowing federal income tax deductions of a little more than $1,000 in each of two years, representing Moss's share of his law firm's lunch expense at the Cafe Angelo in Chicago. 80 T.C. 1073.... The Tax Court's decision in this case has attracted some attention in tax circles because of its implications for the general problem of the deductibility of business meals....

Moss was a partner in a small trial firm specializing in defense work, mostly for one insurance company. Each of the firm's lawyers carried a tremendous litigation caseload, averaging more than 300 cases, and spent most of every working day in courts in

---

109. **Now look at sections 21 and 129.** What does each section do?

Chicago and its suburbs. The members of the firm met for lunch daily at the Cafe Angelo near their office. At lunch the lawyers would discuss their cases with the head of the firm, whose approval was required for most settlements, and they would decide which lawyer would meet which court call that afternoon or the next morning. Lunchtime was chosen for the daily meeting because the courts were in recess then. The alternatives were to meet at 7:00 a.m. or 6:00 p.m., and these were less convenient times. There is no suggestion that the lawyers dawdled over lunch, or that the Cafe Angelo is luxurious.

The framework of statutes and regulations for deciding this case is simple, but not clear. Section 262 of the Internal Revenue Code (Title 26) disallows, "except as otherwise expressly provided in this chapter," the deduction of "personal, family, or living expenses." Section 119 excludes from income the value of meals provided by an employer to his employees for his convenience, but only if they are provided on the employer's premises; and section 162(a) allows the deduction of "all the ordinary and necessary expenses paid or incurred during the taxable year in carrying on any trade or business, including— ... (2) traveling expenses (including amounts expended for meals ...) while away from home...." Since Moss was not an employee but a partner in a partnership not taxed as an entity, since the meals were not served on the employer's premises, and since he was not away from home (that is, on an overnight trip away from his place of work, see *United States v. Correll*, 389 U.S. 299 ... (1967)), neither section 119 nor section 162(a)(2) applies to this case. The Internal Revenue Service concedes, however, that meals are deductible under section 162(a) when they are ordinary and necessary business expenses (provided the expense is substantiated with adequate records, see section 274(d)) even if they are not within the express permission of any other provision and even though the expense of commuting to and from work, a traveling expense but not one incurred away from home, is not deductible. Treasury Regulations on Income Tax §1.262-1(b)(5)....

The problem is that many expenses are simultaneously business expenses in the sense that they conduce to the production of business income and personal expenses in the sense that they raise personal welfare. This is plain enough with regard to lunch; most people would eat lunch even if they didn't work. Commuting may seem a pure business expense, but is not; it reflects the choice of where to live, as well as where to work. Read literally, section 262 would make irrelevant whether a business expense is also a personal expense; so long as it is ordinary and necessary in the taxpayer's business, thus bringing section 162(a) into play, an expense is (the statute seems to say) deductible from his income tax. But the statute has not been read literally. There is a natural reluctance, most clearly manifested in the regulation disallowing deduction of the expense of commuting, to lighten the tax burden of people who have the good fortune to interweave work with consumption. To allow a deduction for commuting would confer a windfall on people who live in the suburbs and commute to work in the cities; to allow a deduction for all business-related meals would confer a windfall on people who can arrange their work schedules so they do some of their work at lunch.

Although an argument can thus be made for disallowing *any* deduction for business meals, on the theory that people have to eat whether they work or not, the result would be excessive taxation of people who spend more money on business meals because they are business meals than they would spend on their meals if they were not working. Suppose a theatrical agent takes his clients out to lunch at the expensive restaurants that the clients demand. Of course he can deduct the expense of their meals, from which he derives no pleasure or sustenance, but can he also deduct the expense of his own? He can, because he cannot eat more cheaply; he cannot munch surreptitiously on a peanut butter and jelly sandwich brought from home while his client is wolfing down tournedos Rossini followed by souffle au grand marnier. No doubt our theatrical agent, unless concerned for his longevity, derives personal utility from his fancy meal, but probably less than the price of the meal. He would not pay for it if it were not for the business benefit; he would get more value from using the same money to buy something else; hence the meal confers on him less utility than the cash equivalent would. The law could require him to pay tax on the fair value of the meal to him; this would be (were it not for costs of administration) the economically correct solution. But the government does not attempt this difficult measurement; it once did, but gave up the attempt as not worth the cost, ... The taxpayer is permitted to deduct the whole price, provided the expense is "different from or in excess of that which would have been made for the taxpayer's personal purposes." *Sutter v. Commissioner*, 21 T.C. 170, 173 (1953).

Because the law allows this generous deduction, which tempts people to have more (and costlier) business meals than are necessary, the Internal Revenue Service has every right to insist that the meal be shown to be a real business necessity. This condition is most easily satisfied when a client or customer or supplier or other outsider to the business is a guest. Even if Sydney Smith was wrong that "soup and fish explain half the emotions of life," it is undeniable that eating together fosters camaraderie and makes business dealings friendlier and easier. It thus reduces the costs of transacting business, for these costs include the frictions and the failures of communication that are produced by suspicion and mutual misunderstanding, by differences in tastes and manners, and by lack of rapport. A meeting with a client or customer in an office is therefore not a perfect substitute for a lunch with him in a restaurant. But it is different when all the participants in the meal are coworkers, as essentially was the case here (clients occasionally were invited to the firm's daily luncheon, but Moss has made no attempt to identify the occasions). They know each other well already; they don't need the social lubrication that a meal with an outsider provides at least don't need it daily. If a large firm had a monthly lunch to allow partners to get to know associates, the expense of the meal might well be necessary, and would be allowed by the Internal Revenue Service. See *Wells v. Commissioner*, 36 T.C.M. 1698, 1699 (1977), aff'd without opinion, 626 F.2d 868 (9th Cir. 1980). But Moss's firm never had more than eight lawyers (partners and associates), and did not need a daily lunch to cement relationships among them.

It is all a matter of degree and circumstance (the expense of a testimonial dinner, for example, would be deductible on a morale-building rationale); and particularly of frequency. Daily—for a full year—is too often, perhaps even for entertainment of clients, as implied by *Hankenson v. Commissioner*, 47 T.C.M. 1567, 1569 (1984), where the Tax Court held nondeductible the cost of lunches consumed three or four days a week, 52 weeks a year, by a doctor who entertained other doctors who he hoped would refer patients to him, and other medical personnel.

We may assume it was necessary for Moss's firm to meet daily to coordinate the work of the firm, and also, as the Tax Court found, that lunch was the most convenient time. But it does not follow that the expense of the lunch was a necessary business expense. The members of the firm had to eat somewhere, and the Cafe Angelo was both convenient and not too expensive. They do not claim to have incurred a greater daily lunch expense than they would have incurred if there had been no lunch meetings. Although it saved time to combine lunch with work, the meal itself was not an organic part of the meeting, as in the examples we gave earlier where the business objective, to be fully achieved, required sharing a meal.

The case might be different if the location of the courts required the firm's members to eat each day either in a disagreeable restaurant, so that they derived less value from the meal than it cost them to buy it, cf. *Sibla v. Commissioner*, 611 F.2d 1260, 1262 (9th Cir. 1980); or in a restaurant too expensive for their personal tastes, so that, again, they would have gotten less value than the cash equivalent. But so far as appears, they picked the restaurant they liked most. Although it must be pretty monotonous to eat lunch the same place every working day of the year, not all the lawyers attended all the lunch meetings and there was nothing to stop the firm from meeting occasionally at another restaurant proximate to their office in downtown Chicago; there are hundreds.

An argument can be made that the price of lunch at the Cafe Angelo included rental of the space that the lawyers used for what was a meeting as well as a meal. There was evidence that the firm's conference room was otherwise occupied throughout the working day, so as a matter of logic Moss might be able to claim a part of the price of lunch as an ordinary and necessary expense for work space. But this is cutting things awfully fine; in any event Moss made no effort to apportion his lunch expense in this way.

AFFIRMED.

Noted tax scholar, Professor Marvin Chirelstein, has remarked that:

> The distinction between personal expenses and business expenses presents what may be the hardest classification problem in the entire tax field.... The reason for the difficulty ... is that the notion of a sharp division between pleasure-seeking and profit-seeking is alien to human psychology and essentially unrealistic. Everybody combines work with pleasure to some degree; no one is able to separate and quantify the two elements at every point, nor even always to state which objective is predominant. But the tax law cannot embrace this comfortable commonplace; it *must* proceed as if individual behavior were divisible into two parts, because the concept of net (taxable) income depends directly on the idea that one's business and one's personal life can be distinguished. The problem, then, is how to draw a dividing line that is equitable and meaningful—one, moreover, that can be administered without resort to truth serum.[110]

Professor Chirelstein warns that the effort to distinguish between business and personal deductions is so difficult that one is left to "proceed by rote rather than by attempting to articulate general principles."[111] For those of you who like to know "the rules," the following are examples of the most common troublesome business/personal expenses and their tax treatment:[112]

1. **Child Care.** *Smith* says not deductible. See, however, section 21, which allows a tax credit for dependent care expenses if the conditions of the statute are satisfied.[113]

---

110. Marvin A. Chirelstein, *Federal Income Taxation* 103–104 (9th ed., 2002). What does Professor Chirelstein mean by his final comment abut "truth serum"?

111. *Id.* at 97.

112. Business/personal issues also arise when a taxpayer uses property for both business and personal purposes, for example an office in her principal residence or use of her car for both business and personal purposes. We will address these issues when we discuss depreciation and in a transactional problem.

113. **Look back at the income tax calculation outline.** We have not discussed credits in detail thus far. For now, it is sufficient to point out that credits represent dollar-for-dollar reductions in the amount of tax due. Therefore, credits are far more valuable than deductions. Why? The child

2. **Food and Lodging.** Food and shelter are essential to basic human existence and are, thus, inherently personal in nature and, therefore, not generally deductible.

Section 162(a)(2), however, allows a taxpayer to deduct the cost of food and lodging if the taxpayer is traveling "away from home" in pursuit of his trade or business.[114] **Look at section 162(a)(2).** To be "away from home," a taxpayer must be away long enough to require sleep or rest, *U.S. v. Correll*, 389 U.S. 299 (1967), but may not be away longer than one year because then she is not temporarily "away from home" (section 162(a), last sentence in flush language[115]). In effect, in such a case, the taxpayer has, by staying away for more than a year, established a new tax home.

Correll involved a traveling salesman who worked for a wholesale grocery company in Tennessee. He left home early each working morning, ate breakfast and lunch on the road, and returned each evening in time to eat dinner at home. He attempted to deduct the cost of the meals he ate on the road, breakfast and lunch, on the theory that he was "away from home" in pursuit of his business. The Supreme Court denied him the deductions as a result of its approval of the Commissioner's long-standing administrative position that no deduction is available unless the taxpayer is away from home long enough to require a period of "sleep or rest." The Court stated:

> [T]he Commissioner has avoided the wasteful litigation and continuing uncertainty that would inevitably accompany any purely case-by-case approach to the question of whether a particular taxpayer was "away from home" on a particular day. Rather than requiring "every meal-purchasing taxpayer to take pot luck in the courts," the Commissioner has consistently construed travel "away from home" to exclude all trips requiring neither sleep nor rest, regardless of how many cities a given trip may have touched, how many miles it may have covered, or how many hours it may have consumed. By so interpreting the statutory phrase, the Commissioner has achieved not only ease and certainty of application but also substantial fairness, for the sleep or rest rule places all one-day travelers on a similar tax footing, rather than discriminating against intracity travelers and commuters, who of course cannot deduct the cost of the meals they eat on the road.
>
> Any rule in this area must make some arbitrary distinctions....[116]

Recall our discussion about rule-making. See Question 4 following *Kowalski*. We noted there the benefits and burdens of choosing either a facts and circumstances test or a safe-harbor test. The former produces uncertainty that can only be made certain by a court but allows for the many possible but unforeseen factual variations that inevitably arise. The latter produces certainty but no elasticity to include on the favorable side of the line a worthy but unanticipated variation from the norm. In *Correll*, the Court chose the certainty of a safe-harbor test. Who benefits most from the choice made by the Court?

The issue of what constitutes a taxpayer's "home" and, therefore, the question of when she is away from it have spawned a number of cases. One of the most-cited is

---

care credit is but one of several pro-family credits that we will take up later in the course. Also note section 129, which excludes certain child care fringe benefits from gross income.

114. Recall our earlier discussion of section 132(a)(3), working condition fringe benefits, in Shawn's fringe benefit problem.

115. What does the phrase "flush language" mean? **Look for the portion of section 162(a) that begins at the margin.**

116. 389 U.S. at 302–03 (footnotes and citations omitted).

Hantzis v. Commissioner, 638 F.2d 248 (1st Cir. 1981). In *Hantzis*, the taxpayer, a law student, accepted a summer job at a law firm in New York City, leaving her husband in Boston, where he was employed and where she attended school. She attempted to deduct the cost of living in New York City, including rental of an apartment and meals, under section 162(a)(2). She claimed that she was "away from home." The First Circuit disallowed her deduction, noting that the:

> traveling expense deduction obviously is not intended to exclude from taxation every expense incurred by a taxpayer who, in the course of business, maintains two homes. Section 162(a)(2) seeks rather "to mitigate the burden of the taxpayer who, *because of the exigencies of his trade or business, must* maintain two places of abode and thereby incur additional and duplicate living expenses." ... [T]he ultimate allowance or disallowance of a deduction is a function of the court's assessment of the reason for a taxpayer's maintenance of two homes. If the reason is perceived to be personal, the taxpayer's home will generally be held to be his place of employment rather than his residence and the deduction will be denied.... If the reason is felt to be business exigencies, the person's home will usually be held to be his residence and the deduction will be allowed.[117]

The court held that the taxpayer's "*trade or business* did not require that she maintain a home in Boston as well as one in New York."[118] The court viewed her business home as New York; although she was a student in Boston, she had no business connection there. Thus, her decision to keep two homes was "a choice dictated by personal ... considerations and not a business or occupational necessity."[119]

At the other end of the "away from home" spectrum is a taxpayer who has been "temporarily" assigned to a distant job site. When does the assignment cease to be temporary and become permanent so that the taxpayer is no longer "away from home"? This issue caused extensive litigation. The courts decided these cases on a case-by-case basis. Therefore, a taxpayer never knew if she would be audited as a consequence of deducting putative "away from home" expenses and whether she would ultimately prevail in the courts. Congress eventually amended section 162(a), second-to-last sentence of the flush language, to draw a line between temporary assignments away and permanent establishment of a new tax home at the one year point. Thus, Congress chose the bright-line approach rather than a facts and circumstances test in order to provide certainty and limit litigation.

A taxpayer may deduct the cost of certain business meals under the *Sutter* rule, discussed in *Moss*, even if the taxpayer is not away from home.[120] The rule requires, how-

---

117. 638 F.2d at 253 (citation omitted).

118. *Id.* at 254.

119. *Id.* at 254. Another interesting case is *Rosenspan v. United States*, 438 F.2d 905 (2d Cir. 1971). The case concerned a traveling salesman who had no permanent residence. The Second Circuit held that without a permanent residence, he could never be "away from home."

120. A lawyer may, of course, deduct the cost of his client's meal if he meets the requirements of sections 162(a) and 274(a)(1)(A). **Read section 274(a).** A special section of the Code limits the deduction for all meal costs to 50% of the cost, however. **Recall section 274(n).** Moreover, to sustain the deduction, the taxpayer must comply with the requirement of section 274(a)(1)(A) that the expense be "directly related to" or "associated with" the active conduct of a trade or business. In addition, section 274(d) requires meticulous record-keeping. The issue in *Moss* was whether the lawyer could deduct a meal when he was unaccompanied by a client. The issue to which Judge Posner ad-

ever, that the expense of the meal be greater than what the taxpayer usually spends on food. What is Judge Posner's rationale for endorsing this rule? Does it have anything to do with Kleinwächter's conundrum?

Would the *Moss* case have had a different outcome if the meals had been served on the law firm's premises? **Recall section 119 and** *Kowalski*. In recent testimony before Congress, a board member of the National Restaurant Association reported that many patrons who use his restaurant for business meals are consultants or small business owners: "[E]ach [one of them] 'considers my restaurant his or her conference room.... [F]or many of these small-business people ... this is the best and sometimes the only way for them to do business."[121] Could the lawyers in *Moss* have made an argument under section 119 for exclusion from income of the value of the meals served to them?[122]

   3. **Commuting Expenses.** Not deductible. Treasury Regulation sections 1.162-2(e), 1.212-1(f), and 1.262-1(b)(5). A taxpayer's work day begins when he arrives at the office, not when he leaves home, and ends when he leaves the office, not when he arrives back at home. Commuting means traveling to and from work; any travel a taxpayer undertakes in connection with work does not constitute non-deductible commuting expenses.[123] The travel a taxpayer undertakes in connection with work includes both local travel and "away from home" travel. Therefore, a taxpayer may have deductible travel expenses if he travels from his office to that of his client, whether his client is across town or across the country.[124]

   It is not uncommon today for a taxpayer to have more than one job. Although commuting from home to the first job is not, commuting from one job to another is a business expense. So too, commuting between two job locations of a single job is deductible but going to and from are not. The Service has attempted to diagram the various permutations for the benefit of taxpayers as shown in the following schematic.[125]

---

dresses his observation is the case of a meeting between a service provider and his client in which the service provider seeks to deduct the cost of his own meal, as well as that of his client.

   121. Statement of Jim Wordsworth, the owner of a restaurant in Tysons Corner, Virginia, quoted in Alison Mitchell, "Tax-Cut Bill Could Well Revive a Thing of the Past: The 'Three-Martini Lunch'", N.Y. Times, Jul. 24, 1999, at A9.

   122. Of course, in *Kowalski*, as you recall, the problem was not that the meals were not served on the employer's premises. Rather, the fatal feature was that they were not provided in kind.

   123. For those who are interested in the source of this rule, see *Commissioner v. Flowers*, 326 U.S. 465 (1946).

   124. But, recall Treasury Regulation section 1.162-2(a), dealing with mixed business and personal travel. **Review Treasury Regulation section 1.162-2(a) and Question 3 in Shawn's fringe benefit problem.**

   125. The diagram appears in Publication 463

When Are Transportation Expenses Deductible?
Most employees and self-employed persons can use this chart.
(Do not use this chart if your home is your principal place of business.
See *Office in the home.*)

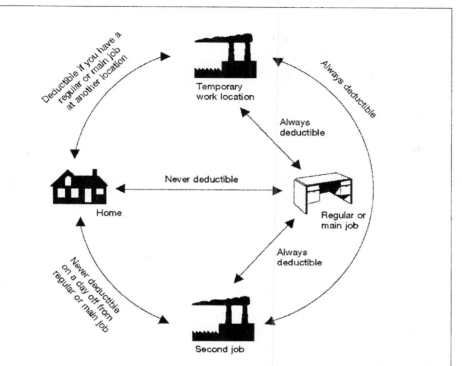

Home: The place where you reside. Transportation expenses between your home and your main or regular place of work are personal commuting expenses.

Regular or main job: Your principal place of business. If you have more than one job, you must determine which one is your regular or main job. Consider the time you spend at each, the activity you have at each, and the income you earn at each.

Temporary work location: A place where your work assignment is realistically expected to last (and does in fact last) one year or less. Unless you have a regular place of business, you can only deduct your transportation expenses to a temporary work location <u>outside</u> your metropolitan area.

Second job: If you regularly work at two or more places in one day, whether or not for the same employer, you can deduct your transportation expenses of getting from one workplace to another. You cannot deduct your transportation costs between your home and a second job on a day off from your main job.

4. **Clothing.** Not deductible if the clothing is adaptable to ordinary wear. *Pevsner v. Commissioner*, 628 F.2d 467 (5th Cir. 1980). Therefore, if an employer requires a special uniform that is not adaptable to ordinary wear, the taxpayer will be able to deduct its cost. But the fact that an employer requires an employee to wear a type of clothing the employee would not ordinarily purchase or wear, *e.g.*, a business suit, does not make the expense of purchasing the clothing deductible because it is adaptable to ordinary wear.

5. **Educational Expenses. Read Treasury Regulation section 1.162-5.** Only certain educational expenses are deductible. Are your law school expenses deductible? What about the expenses of an LL.M. degree? How would you analyze the deductibility of these expenses under the regulation? What impact does the statutory requirement of "carrying on" under section 162(a) have on your answers?

Code sections 221 and 222 allow above the line deductions of interest on certain student loans and of higher education tuition expenses, respectively. **Look at sections 221 and 222.** Are they consistent with the rationale contained in the Treasury Regulation that denies deduction of many educational expenses? Sections 221 and 222 are provisions Congress added as part of the 1997 and 2001 Acts to strengthen educational opportunities. (Section 222 terminated for tax years beginning after December 31, 2005. Congress then revived it as part of the Tax Relief and Health Care Act of 2006, P.L. 109-432. The new provision applies to tax years 2006 and 2007.) In addition to sections 221 and 222, the Code now also contains section 25A, providing credits for certain higher education expenses, the so-called Hope and Life-time Learning credits. **Look at section 25A.** Like the dependent care credit, these credits represent dollar-for-dollar reductions in income tax and are far more valuable than deductions. Are they consistent with the general rule expressed in the Treasury Regulation? What is the policy (if any) justifying these deductions and credits?

2. Section 212 Activities

If a taxpayer is involved in an income-producing activity with an intent to make a profit, but her level of activity does not rise to the level of a "trade or business" under the definition as set forth in *Groetzinger* (engaged in with continuity and regularity), she may deduct expenses connected with the activity under section 212. Because the *Groetzinger* test presupposes active involvement in an income-producing activity, section 212 generally covers the types of activities more commonly thought of as passive investment activities-ones in which the taxpayer is not actively involved.

But the case that led Congress to enact the predecessor to section 212 in 1942 illustrates that this simple statement of the dividing line between an active trade or business and a passive investment is misleading. In *Higgins v. Commissioner*, 312 U.S. 212 (1941), the Supreme Court held that a wealthy investor who maintained an office and staff in New York to manage his investment portfolio under his direction while he was living in Paris was not engaged in the active conduct of a trade or business under the predecessor to section 162 of the Code. Later, in *Groetzinger*, the Supreme Court articulated the test for the active conduct of a trade or business as requiring regular and continuous involvement. But the fact that an investor is engaged in managing his own portfolio with regularity and continuity is not enough; in *Groetzinger*, the Supreme Court carefully enunciated its intention not to over-rule *Higgins*. The Supreme Court stated:

> We do not overrule or cut back on the Court's holding in *Higgins* when we
> conclude that if one's gambling activity is pursued full time, in good faith, and

with regularity, to the production of income for a livelihood, and is not a mere hobby, it is a trade or business within the meaning of the statutes with which we are here concerned. Respondent Groetzinger satisfied that test in 1978. Constant and large-scale effort on his part was made. Skill was required and was applied. He did what he did for a livelihood, though with a less-than-successful result. This was not a hobby or a passing fancy or an occasional bet for amusement.

We therefore adhere to the general position of the Higgins Court, taken 46 years ago, that resolution of this issue "requires an examination of the facts in each case." 312 U.S. at 217. This may be thought by some to be a less-than-satisfactory solution, for facts vary....[126]

Note here that the Supreme Court endorsed a facts and circumstances test, rather than a safe harbor test, despite the likelihood that a facts and circumstances standard will lead to more litigation.

Now that the Supreme Court has affirmed the continuing viability of *Higgins*, can you formulate a rationale to justify its holding? Can a taxpayer who manages her own investments ever be engaged in the active conduct of a trade or business? The Supreme Court in *Groetzinger* seems to draw a distinction between the activities of someone who gambles on cards, sports, horses, and the like, at casinos or elsewhere, and an investor in securities which some may also characterize as "gambling." Is this a reasonable distinction? What about a "day-trader"?

Look at Treasury Regulation sections 1.212-1(f)-(m), containing examples of deductible and nondeductible expenses under section 212. Read those portions of the regulations. Do they help clarify the line, on the one hand between expenses associated with the conduct of an active trade or business and those associated with a passive investment, and the line on the other hand between those expenses associated with a non-profit seeking activity and those associated with a passive investment?

Try to formulate for yourself an understanding of the types of activities covered by section 212. Query: If you determine that an expense is deductible under section 212, is it an above the line or below the line deduction? Does section 212 tell you? If a section 212 expense is a below the line deduction, is it considered a miscellaneous itemized deduction under section 67? **Review section 67(b).**

3. The Meaning of "Ordinary and Necessary"

Section 162(a) and 212 both require that a deductible expense must be "ordinary and necessary." Read the following famous case and try to articulate Justice Cardozo's formulations of these two statutory requirements.

WELCH v. HELVERING
290 U.S. 111 (1933)

MR. JUSTICE CARDOZO delivered the opinion of the Court.

The question to be determined is whether payments by a taxpayer, who is in business as a commission agent, are allowable deductions in the computation of his income if

---

126. 480 U.S. at 35–36.

made to the creditors of a bankrupt corporation in an endeavor to strengthen his own standing and credit.

In 1922 petitioner was the secretary of the E. L. Welch Company, a Minnesota corporation, engaged in the grain business. The company was adjudged an involuntary bankrupt, and had a discharge from its debts. Thereafter the petitioner made a contract with the Kellogg Company to purchase grain for it on a commission. In order to reestablish his relations with customers whom he had known when acting for the Welch Company and to solidify his credit and standing, he decided to pay the debts of the Welch business so far as he was able. In fulfillment of that resolve, he made payments of substantial amounts during five successive years. In 1924, the commissions were $18,028.20; the payments $3,975.97; in 1923, the commissions $31,377.07; the payments $11,968.20; in 1926, the commissions $20,925.25, the payments $12,815.72; in 1927, the commissions $22,119.61, the payments $7,379.72; and in 1928, the commissions $26,177.56, the payments $11,068.25. The Commissioner ruled that these payments were not deductible from income as ordinary and necessary expenses, but were rather in the nature of capital expenditures, an outlay for the development of reputation and good will. The Board of Tax Appeals sustained the action of the Commissioner (25 B.T.A. 117), and the Court of Appeals for the Eighth Circuit affirmed. 63 F.(2d) 976. The case is here on certiorari.

"In computing net income there shall be allowed as deductions ... all the ordinary and necessary expenses paid or incurred during the taxable year in carrying on any trade or business." Revenue Act of 1924.... [predecessor section to I.R.C. §162(a).]

We may assume that the payments to creditors of the Welch Company were necessary for the development of the petitioner's business, at least in the sense that they were appropriate and helpful. *McCulloch v. Maryland*, 4 Wheat. 316. He certainly thought they were, and we should be slow to override his judgment. But the problem is not solved when the payments are characterized as necessary. Many necessary payments are charges upon capital. There is need to determine whether they are both necessary and ordinary. Now, what is ordinary, though there must always be a strain of constancy within it, is none the less a variable affected by time and place and circumstance. Ordinary in this context does not mean that the payments must be habitual or normal in the sense that the same taxpayer will have to make them often. A lawsuit affecting the safety of a business may happen once in a lifetime. The counsel fees may be so heavy that repetition is unlikely. None the less, the expense is an ordinary one because we know from experience that payments for such a purpose, whether the amount is large or small, are the common and accepted means of defense against attack.... The situation is unique in the life of the individual affected, but not in the life of the group, the community, of which he is a part. At such times there are norms of conduct that help to stabilize our judgment, and make it certain and objective. The instance is not erratic, but is brought within a known type.

The line of demarcation is now visible between the case that is here and the one supposed for illustration. We try to classify this act as ordinary or the opposite, and the norms of conduct fail us. No longer can we have recourse to any fund of business experience, to any known business practice. Men do at times pay the debts of others without legal obligation or the lighter obligation imposed by the usages of trade or by neighborly amenities, but they do not do so ordinarily, not even though the result might be to heighten their reputation for generosity and opulence. Indeed, if language is to be read in its natural and common meaning (*Old Colony R. Co. v. Commissioner*, 284 U.S. 552, 560), ... we should have to say that payment in such circumstances, instead of being ordinary is in a high degree extraordinary. There is nothing ordinary in the stimulus evoking it, and none in the response. Here, indeed, as so often in other branches of the law, the decisive distinctions are those of degree and not of kind. One struggles in vain for any verbal formula that will supply a ready touchstone. The standard set up by the statute is not a rule of law; it is rather a way of life. Life in all its fullness must supply the answer to the riddle.

The Commissioner of Internal Revenue resorted to that standard in assessing the petitioner's income, and found that the payments in controversy came closer to capital outlays than to ordinary and necessary expenses in the operation of a business. His ruling has the support of a presumption of correctness, and the petitioner has the burden of proving it to be wrong.... Unless we can say from facts within our knowledge that these are ordinary and necessary expenses according to the ways of conduct and the forms of speech prevailing in the business world, the tax must be confirmed. But nothing told us by this record or within the sphere of our judicial notice permits us to give that extension to what is ordinary and necessary. Indeed, to do so would open the door to many bizarre analogies. One man has a family name that is clouded by thefts committed by an ancestor. To add to his own standing he repays the stolen money, wiping off, it may be, his income for the year. The payments figure in his tax return as ordinary expenses. Another man conceives the notion that he will be able to practice his vocation with greater ease and profit if he has an opportunity to enrich his culture. Forthwith the price of his education becomes an expense of the business, reducing the income subject to taxation. There is little difference between these expenses and those in controversy here. Reputation and learning are akin to capital assets, like the good will of an old partnership.... For many, they are the only tools with which to hew a pathway to success. The money spent in acquiring them is well and wisely spent. It is not an ordinary expense of the operation of a business.

Many cases in the federal courts deal with phases of the problem presented in the case at bar. To attempt to harmonize them would be a futile task. They involve the appreciation of particular situations, at times with borderline conclusions....

The decree should be *Affirmed*.

Consider the following questions about *Welch v. Helvering*.

1. What did the taxpayer do that caused the tax controversy in the case?

2. What was the issue in the case?

3. What was the Service's position? What was the taxpayer's position?

4. How did Justice Cardozo define the term "necessary"? Is his standard strict or broad? Why?

5. The more difficult part of this opinion involves Justice Cardozo's definition of the term "ordinary." How would you articulate his formulation of the term? If an expense has to be "common and accepted" in order to be considered ordinary, what about business expenses that represent innovative ways of doing things? For example, an article in The New York Times recently described the increasingly popular business practice of hiring ministers, priests, rabbis, and other spiritual advisors to counsel employees. Would Justice Cardozo's formulation sanction a deduction of the expense by the first firm that hired a rabbi?[127]

---

127. The taxpayer in *Trebilcock v. Commissioner*, 64 T.C. 852 (1975), *aff'd per curiam*, 557 F. 2d 1226 (6th Cir. 1977), hired an ordained minister "primarily to minister spiritually to petitioner and his employees." The minister conducted prayer meetings "at which he tried to raise the level of spir-

4. Ordinary Expenses Versus Capital Expenditures: Sections 162(a)/212 versus Section 263

Consider the possibility that there might be another way to interpret Justice Cardozo's discussion of the meaning of "ordinary" in *Welch v. Helvering*. Reconsider the Service's position in the case. The Service contended that the taxpayer's payments "were not deductible from income as ordinary and necessary expenses, but were rather in the nature of capital expenditures, an outlay for the development of reputation and good will." **(Recall the *Raytheon* case and the concept of goodwill as a continuing asset of a business.)**

The Service classified the payments in *Welch v. Helvering* as "capital expenditures." **Read section 263(a)(1) (first sentence before exceptions).** What does it provide? This is the first time you have encountered the concept of a capital expenditure in the statute.[128] Note that section 263 is entitled "Capital Expenditures." Note too that section 162(a) deals with the deductibility of "ordinary ... expenses." Does Justice Cardozo's decision with respect to the "ordinariness" of the expenses in the case make more sense in the context of this distinction?[129]

Because the distinction between an ordinary expense and a capital expenditure is critical in determining its current deductibility, it is critical for you to be able to distinguish one from the other. **Read carefully Treasury Regulation sections 1.263(a)-1 and -2.** In addition, read the following cases.

MIDLAND EMPIRE PACKING COMPANY v. COMMISSIONER
14 T.C. 635 (1950)

... The issue presented for decision is whether or not the sum of $4,868.81 expended by the petitioner in oilproofing the basement of its meat-packing plant during the tax-

---

itual awareness of the participants, and counseled petitioner and individual employees concerning their business and personal problems." The court denied the taxpayer a deduction for the expense of these services because the taxpayer was unable to show that the minister's services were "ordinary," *i.e.*, "of common or frequent occurrence," in the taxpayer's type of business. Might the result be different today if the taxpayer were able to introduce evidence supporting the statement in the New York Times article.

128. We did, however, touch tangentially on the concept of capital expenditures when we discussed Revenue Ruling 81-277 early in the course. Recall that in the ruling, a contractor paid the owner of a power plant 40X dollars in damages for breach of contract for failing to complete the plant as agreed. The owner of the plant later had to pay 50X dollars to complete the plant. The ruling cited section 1016(a)(1) of the Code which provides that "[p]roper adjustment in respect of the [basis of] property shall in all cases be made ... for expenditures, receipts ... properly chargeable to capital account...." The ruling characterized the owner's receipt of the 40X dollars as a return of capital, a "receipt" that caused a reduction in the plant's basis under section 1016(a)(1). Conversely, the 50X dollars that the owner had to expend to finish construction were "expenditures" that caused an increase in the plant's basis under section 1016(a)(1). Thus, the 50X dollars expenditures, which increased basis, were "properly chargeable to capital account," and are characterized as capital expenditures.

129. In *Commissioner v. Tellier*, 383 U.S. 687, 689–690 (1966), the Supreme Court explained that: "The principal function of the term 'ordinary' in §162(a) is to clarify the distinction, often difficult, between those expenses that are currently deductible and those that are in the nature of capital expenditures, which, if deductible at all, must be amortized over the life of the asset."

able year 1943 is deductible as an ordinary and necessary business expense under section 23 (a) of the Internal Revenue Code....

...

FINDINGS OF FACT.

The petitioner, herein sometimes referred to as Midland, is a Montana corporation and the owner of a meat-packing plant which is located adjacent to the city of Billings, Yellowstone County, State of Montana....

The basement rooms of petitioner's plant were used by it in its business for the curing of hams and bacon and for the storage of meat and hides. These rooms have been used for such purposes since the plant was constructed in about 1917. The original walls and floors, which were of concrete, were not sealed against water. There had been seepage for many years and this condition became worse around 1943. At certain seasons of the year, when the water in the Yellowstone River was high, the underground water caused increased seepage in the plant. Such water did not interfere with petitioner's use of the basement rooms. They were satisfactory for their purpose until 1943.

The Yale Oil Corporation, sometimes referred to herein as Yale, was the owner of an oil-refining plant and storage area located some 300 yards upgrade from petitioner's meat-packing plant. The oil plant was constructed some years after petitioner had been in business in its present location. Yale expanded its plant and storage from year to year and oil escaping from the plant and storage facilities was carried to the ground surrounding the plant of petitioner. In 1943 petitioner found that oil was seeping into its water wells and into water which came through the concrete walls of the basement of its packing plant. The water would soon drain out through the sump, leaving a thick scum of oil on the basement floor. Such oil gave off a strong odor, which permeated the air of the entire plant. The oil in the basement and fumes therefrom created a fire hazard. The Federal meat inspectors advised petitioner to oilproof the basement and discontinue the use of the water wells or shut down the plant.

As soon as petitioner discovered that oil had begun to seep into its water wells and into the basement of its plant, its officers conferred with the officers of the Yale Oil Corporation and informed Yale that they intended to hold it liable for all damage caused by the oil which had saturated the ground around its packing plant. They informed the officials of Yale that they believed this condition constituted a legal nuisance, which condition they expected would continue to exist for future years, and that they were discontinuing the use of their water wells. The officials of Yale were also informed that the Federal inspectors were requiring petitioner to oilproof the basement.

...

The original walls and floor of petitioner's plant were of concrete construction. For the purpose of preventing oil from entering its basement, petitioner added concrete lining to the walls from the floor to a height of about four feet, and also added concrete to the floor of the basement. Since the walls and floor had been thickened, petitioner now had less space in which to operate. Petitioner had this work done by independent contractors, supervised by Jacoby, in the fiscal year ended November 30, 1943, at a cost of $4,868.81. Petitioner paid for this work during that year.

The oilproofing work was effective in sealing out the oil. While it has served the purposes for which it was intended down to the present time, it did not increase the useful life of the building or make the building more valuable for any purpose than it had been before the oil had come into the basement. The primary object of the oilproofing operation was to prevent the seepage of oil into the basement so that the petitioner could use the basement as before in preparing and packing meat for commercial consumption.

...

Midland charged the $4,868.81 to repair expense on its regular books and deducted that amount on its tax returns as an ordinary and necessary business expense for the fiscal year 1943. The Commissioner, in his notice of deficiency, determined that the cost of oilproofing was not deductible, either as an ordinary and necessary expense....

OPINION.

ARUNDELL, *Judge*: The issue in this case is whether an expenditure for a concrete lining in petitioner's basement to oilproof it against an oil nuisance created by a neighboring refinery is deductible as an ordinary and necessary expense under section 23 (a) of the Internal Revenue Code, on the theory it was an expenditure for a repair,....

The respondent has contended, in part, that the expenditure is for a capital improvement and should be recovered through depreciation charges and is, therefore, not deductible as an ordinary and necessary business expense or as a loss.

It is none too easy to determine on which side of the line certain expenditures fall so that they may be accorded their proper treatment for tax purposes. Treasury Regulations 111 [the predecessor to Treasury Regulation section 1.162-4] ... is helpful in distinguishing between an expenditure to be classed as a repair and one to be treated as a capital outlay. In *Illinois Merchants Trust Co., Executor*, 4 B.T.A. 103, at page 106, we discussed this subject in some detail and in our opinion said:

> It will be noted that the first sentence of the [regulation] relates to repairs, while the second sentence deals in effect with replacements. In determining whether an expenditure is a capital one or is chargeable against operating income, it is necessary to bear in mind the purpose for which the expenditure was made. To repair is to restore to a sound state or to mend, while a replacement connotes a substitution. A repair is an expenditure for the purpose of keeping the property in an ordinarily efficient operating condition. It does not add to the value of the property, nor does it appreciably prolong its life. It merely keeps the property in an operating condition over its probable useful life for the uses for which it was acquired. Expenditures for that purpose are distinguishable from those for replacements, alterations, improvements, or additions which prolong the life of the property, increase its value, or make it adaptable to a different use. The one is a maintenance charge, while the others are additions to capital investment which should not be applied against current earnings.

It will be seen from our findings of fact that for some 25 years prior to the taxable year petitioner had used the basement rooms of its plant as a place for the curing of hams and bacon and for the storage of meat and hides. The basement had been entirely satisfactory for this purpose over the entire period in spite of the fact that there was some seepage of water into the rooms from time to time. In the taxable year it was found that not only water, but oil, was seeping through the concrete walls of the basement of the packing plant and, while the water would soon drain out, the oil would not, and there was left on the basement floor a thick scum of oil which gave off a strong odor that permeated the air of the entire plant, and the fumes from the oil created a fire hazard. It appears that the oil which came from a nearby refinery had also gotten into the water wells which served to furnish water for petitioner's plant, and as a result of this whole condition the Federal meat inspectors advised petitioner that it must discontinue the use of the water from the wells and oilproof the basement, or else shut down its plant.

To meet this situation, petitioner during the taxable year undertook steps to oilproof the basement by adding a concrete lining to the walls from the floor to a height of about four feet and also added concrete to the floor of the basement. It is the cost of this work which it seeks to deduct as a repair. The basement was not enlarged by this work, nor did the oilproofing serve to make it more desirable for the purpose for which it had been used through the years prior to the time that the oil nuisance had occurred. The evidence is that the expenditure did not add to the value or prolong the expected life of the property over what they were before the event occurred which made the repairs necessary. It is true that after the work was done the seepage of water, as well as oil, was stopped, but, as already stated, the presence of the water had never been found objectionable. The repairs merely served to keep the property in an operating condition over its probable useful life for the purpose for which it was used.

While it is conceded on brief that the expenditure was "necessary," respondent contends that the encroachment of the oil nuisance on petitioner's property was not an "ordinary" expense in petitioner's particular business. But the fact that petitioner had not theretofore been called upon to make a similar expenditure to prevent damage and disaster to its property does not remove that expense from the classification of "ordinary" for, as stated in *Welch v. Helvering*, 290 U.S. 111, "ordinary in this context does not mean that the payments must be habitual or normal in the sense that the same taxpayer will have to make them often.... [t]he expense is an ordinary one because we know from experience that payments for such a purpose, whether the amount is large or small, are the common and accepted means of defense against attack.... The situation is unique in the life of the individual affected, but not in the life of the group, the community, of which he is a part." Steps to protect a business building from the seepage of oil from a nearby refinery, which had been erected long subsequent to the time petitioner started to operate its plant, would seem to us to be a normal thing to do, and in certain sections of the country it must be a common experience to protect one's property from the seepage of oil. Expenditures to accomplish this result are likewise normal.

In *American Bemberg Corporation*, 10 T. C. 361, we allowed as deductions, on the ground that they were ordinary and necessary expenses, extensive expenditures made to prevent disaster, although the repairs were of a type which had never been needed before and were unlikely to recur. In that case the taxpayer, to stop cave-ins of soil which were threatening destruction of its manufacturing plant, hired an engineering firm which drilled to the bedrock and injected grout to fill the cavities where practicable, and made incidental replacements and repairs, including tightening of the fluid carriers. In two successive years the taxpayer expended $734,316.76 and $199,154.33, respectively, for such drilling and grouting and $153,474.20 and $79,687.29, respectively, for capital replacements. We found that the cost (other than replacement) of this program did not make good the depreciation previously allowed, and stated in our opinion:

> In connection with the purpose of the work, the Proctor program was intended to avert a plant-wide disaster and avoid forced abandonment of the plant. The purpose was not to improve, better, extend, or increase the original plant, nor to prolong its original useful life. Its continued operation was endangered; the purpose of the expenditures was to enable petitioner to continue the plant in operation not on any new or better scale, but on the same scale and, so far as possible, as efficiently as it had operated before. The purpose was not to rebuild or replace the plant in whole or in part, but to keep the same plant as it was and where it was.

The petitioner here made the repairs in question in order that it might continue to operate its plant. Not only was there danger of fire from the oil and fumes, but the presence of the oil led the Federal meat inspectors to declare the basement an unsuitable place for the purpose for which it had been used for a quarter of a century. After the expenditures were made, the plant did not operate on a changed or larger scale, nor was it thereafter suitable for new or additional uses. The expenditure served only to permit petitioner to continue the use of the plant, and particularly the basement for its normal operations.

In our opinion, the expenditure of $4,868.81 for lining the basement walls and floor was essentially a repair and, as such, it is deductible as an ordinary and necessary business expense....

The question of whether an item constitutes a capital expenditure would not seem to be problematic when the taxpayer acquires an asset. In fact, if the taxpayer purchases, for example, a building, the acquisition certainly constitutes a capital expenditure. But, suppose the "acquisition" does not occur through a simple purchase of a single asset for a fixed price? What expenses associated with the acquisition are part of the "cost" of the asset and, therefore, a capital expenditure, and which are not? Consider the following two cases:

WOODWARD v. COMMISSIONER
397 U.S. 572 (1970)

MR. JUSTICE MARSHALL delivered the opinion of the Court.

This case ... involve[s] the tax treatment of expenses incurred in certain appraisal litigation.

Taxpayers owned or controlled a majority of the common stock of the Telegraph-Herald, an Iowa publishing corporation. The Telegraph-Herald was incorporated in 1901, and its charter was extended for 20-year periods in 1921 and 1941. On June 9, 1960, taxpayers voted their controlling share of the stock of the corporation in favor of a perpetual extension of the charter. A minority stockholder voted against the extension. Iowa law requires "those stockholders voting for such renewal ... [to] purchase at its real value the stock voted against such renewal." ...

Taxpayers attempted to negotiate purchase of the dissenting stockholder's shares, but no agreement could be reached on the "real value" of those shares. Consequently, in

1962 taxpayers brought an action in state court to appraise the value of the minority stock interest. The trial court fixed a value, which was slightly reduced on appeal by the Iowa Supreme Court,.... In July 1965, taxpayers purchased the minority stock interest at the price fixed by the court.

During 1963, taxpayers paid attorneys', accountants', and appraisers' fees of over $25,000, for services rendered in connection with the appraisal litigation. On their 1963 federal income tax returns, taxpayers claimed deductions for these expenses, asserting that they were "ordinary and necessary expenses paid ... for the management, conservation, or maintenance of property held for the production of income" deductible under §212 of the Internal Revenue Code of 1954, *26 U. S. C. §212*. The Commissioner of Internal Revenue disallowed the deduction "because the fees represent capital expenditures incurred in connection with the acquisition of capital stock of a corporation." The Tax Court sustained the Commissioner's determination, with two dissenting opinions, 49 T.C. 377 (1968), and the Court of Appeals affirmed, 410 F.2d 313 (C.A. 8th Cir. 1969). We granted certiorari,.... We affirm.

Since the inception of the present federal income tax in 1913, capital expenditures have not been deductible. (Footnote 2) See Internal Revenue Code of 1954, §263. Such expenditures are added to the basis of the capital asset with respect to which they are incurred, and are taken into account for tax purposes either through depreciation or by reducing the capital gain (or increasing the loss) when the asset is sold. If an expense is capital, it cannot be deducted as "ordinary and necessary," either as a business expense under §162 of the Code or as an expense of "management, conservation, or maintenance" under §212. (Footnote 3)

It has long been recognized, as a general matter, that costs incurred in the acquisition or disposition of a capital asset are to be treated as capital expenditures. The most familiar example of such treatment is the capitalization of brokerage fees for the sale or purchase of securities, as explicitly provided by a longstanding Treasury regulation, Treas. Reg. on Income Tax §1.263(a)-2(e), and as approved by this Court in *Helvering v. Winmill*, 305 U.S. 79 (1938), and *Spreckels v. Commissioner*, 315 U.S. 626 (1942). The Court recognized that brokers' commissions are "part of the acquisition cost of the securities," *Helvering v. Winmill, supra*, at 84, and relied on the Treasury Regulation, which had been approved by statutory re-enactment, to deny deductions for such commissions even to a taxpayer for whom they were a regular and recurring expense in his business of buying and selling securities.

The regulations do not specify other sorts of acquisition costs, but rather provide generally that "[t]he cost of acquisition ... of ... property having a useful life substantially beyond the taxable year" is a capital expenditure. Treas. Reg. on Income Tax §1.263(a)-2(a). Under this general provision, the courts have held that legal, brokerage, accounting, and similar costs incurred in the acquisition or disposition of such property are capital expenditures. See, *e. g., Spangler v. Commissioner*, 323 F.2d 913, 921 (C.A. 9th Cir. 1963); *United States v. St. Joe Paper Co.*, 284 F.2d 430, 432 (C. A. 5th Cir. 1960).... The law could hardly be otherwise, for such ancillary expenses incurred in acquiring or disposing of an asset are as much part of the cost of that asset as is the price paid for it.

More difficult questions arise with respect to another class of capital expenditures, those incurred in "defending or perfecting title to property." Treas. Reg. on Income Tax §1.263 (a)-2(c). In one sense, any lawsuit brought against a taxpayer may affect his title to property—money or other assets subject to lien. The courts, not believing that Congress meant all litigation expenses to be capitalized, have created the rule that such expenses are capital in nature only where the taxpayer's "primary purpose" in incurring them is to defend or perfect title. See, *e. g., Rassenfoss v. Commissioner,* 158 F.2d 764 (C.A. 7th Cir. 1946); *Industrial Aggregate Co. v. United States,* 284 F.2d 639, 645 (C.A. 8th Cir. 1960). This test hardly draws a bright line, and has produced a melange of decisions, which, as the Tax Court has noted, "[i]t would be idle to suggest ... can be reconciled." *Ruoff v. Commissioner,* 30 T.C. 204, 208 (1958).

Taxpayers urge that this "primary purpose" test, developed in the context of cases involving the costs of defending property, should be applied to costs incurred in acquiring or disposing of property as well. And if it is so applied, they argue, the costs here in question were properly deducted, since the legal proceedings in which they were incurred did not directly involve the question of title to the minority stock, which all agreed was to pass to taxpayers, but rather was concerned solely with the value of that stock.

We agree with the Tax Court and the Court of Appeals that the "primary purpose" test has no application here. That uncertain and difficult test may be the best that can be devised to determine the tax treatment of costs incurred in litigation that may affect a taxpayer's title to property more or less indirectly, and that thus calls for a judgment whether the taxpayer can fairly be said to be "defending or perfecting title." Such uncertainty is not called for in applying the regulation that makes the "cost of acquisition" of a capital asset a capital expense. In our view application of the latter regulation to litigation expenses involves the simpler inquiry whether the origin of the claim litigated is in the process of acquisition itself.

A test based upon the taxpayer's "purpose" in undertaking or defending a particular piece of litigation would encourage resort to formalisms and artificial distinctions. For instance, in this case there can be no doubt that legal, accounting, and appraisal costs incurred by taxpayers in *negotiating* a purchase of the minority stock would have been capital expenditures. See *Atzingen-Whitehouse Dairy Inc. v. Commissioner,* 36 T.C. 173 (1961). Under whatever test might be applied, such expenses would have clearly been "part of the acquisition cost" of the stock. *Helvering v. Winmill, supra.* Yet the appraisal proceeding was no more than the substitute that state law provided for the process of negotiation as a means of fixing the price at which the stock was to be purchased. Allowing deduction of expenses incurred in such a proceeding, merely on the ground that title was not directly put in question in the particular litigation, would be anomalous.

Further, a standard based on the origin of the claim litigated comports with this Court's recent ruling on the characterization of litigation expenses for tax purposes in *United States v. Gilmore,* 372 U.S. 39 (1963). This Court there held that the expense of defending a divorce suit was a nondeductible personal expense, even though the outcome of the divorce case would affect the taxpayer's property holdings, and might affect his business reputation. The Court rejected a test that looked to the consequences of the litigation, and did not even consider the taxpayer's motives or purposes in undertaking defense of the litigation, but rather examined the origin and character of the claim against the taxpayer, and found that the claim arose out of the personal relationship of marriage.

The standard here pronounced may, like any standard, present borderline cases, in which it is difficult to determine whether the origin of particular litigation lies in the process of acquisition. This is not such a borderline case. Here state law required taxpayers to "purchase" the stock owned by the dissenter. In the absence of agreement on the price at which the purchase was to be made, litigation was required to fix the price.

Where property is acquired by purchase, nothing is more clearly part of the process of acquisition than the establishment of a purchase price. (Footnote 8) Thus the expenses incurred in that litigation were properly treated as part of the cost of the stock that the taxpayers acquired.

Affirmed.

FOOTNOTES:

2. See § II B of the Income Tax Act of 1913, 38 Stat. 167.

3. The two sections are *in pari materia* with respect to the capital-ordinary distinction, differing only in that § 212 allows deductions for the ordinary and necessary expenses of nonbusiness profitmaking activities. See *United States v. Gilmore*, 372 U.S. 39, 44–45 (1963)....

8. Taxpayers argue that "purchase" analysis cannot properly be applied to the appraisal situation, because the transaction is an involuntary one from their point of view—an argument relied upon by the District Court in the *Smith Hotel Enterprises* case, *supra*, n. 1. In the first place, the transaction is in a sense voluntary, since the majority holders know that under state law they will have to buy out any dissenters. More fundamentally, however, wherever a capital asset is transferred to a new owner in exchange for value either agreed upon or determined by law to be a fair *quid pro quo*, the payment itself is a capital expenditure, and there is no reason why the costs of determining the amount of that payment should be considered capital in the case of the negotiated price and yet considered deductible in the case of the price fixed by law. See *Isaac G. Johnson & Co. v. United States*, 149 F.2d 851 (C.A. 2d Cir. 1945) (expenses of litigating amount of fair compensation in condemnation proceeding held capital expenditures).

ENCYCLOPAEDIA BRITANNICA, INC. v. COMMISSIONER
685 F.2d 212 (7th Cir. 1982)

POSNER, Circuit Judge.

Section 162(a) of the Internal Revenue Code of 1954 ... allows the deduction of "all the ordinary and necessary expenses paid or incurred during the taxable year in carrying on any trade or business...," but this is qualified (see 26 U.S.C. § 161) by section 263(a) of the Code, which forbids the immediate deduction of "capital expenditures" even if they are ordinary and necessary business expenses. We must decide in this case whether certain expenditures made by Encyclopaedia Britannica, Inc. to acquire a manuscript were capital expenditures.

Encyclopaedia Britannica decided to publish a book to be called *The Dictionary of Natural Sciences*. Ordinarily it would have prepared the book in-house, but being temporarily short-handed it hired David-Stewart Publishing Company "to do all necessary research work and to prepare, edit and arrange the manuscript and all illustrative and other material for" the book. Under the contract David-Stewart agreed "to work closely with" Encyclopaedia Britannica's editorial board "so that the content and arrangement of the Work (and any revisions thereof) will conform to the idea and desires of [Encyclopaedia Britannica] and be acceptable to it"; but it was contemplated that David-Stewart would turn over a complete manuscript that Encyclopaedia Britannica would copyright, publish, and sell, and in exchange would receive advances against the royalties that Encyclopaedia Britannica expected to earn from the book.

Encyclopaedia Britannica treated these advances as ordinary and necessary business expenses deductible in the years when they were paid, though it had not yet obtained any royalties. The Internal Revenue Service disallowed the deductions and assessed deficiencies. Encyclopaedia Britannica petitioned the Tax Court for a redetermination of its tax liability, and prevailed. The Tax Court held that the expenditures were for "services" rather than for the acquisition of an asset and concluded that therefore they were deductible immediately rather than being, as the Service had ruled, capital expenditures. "The agreement provided for substantial editorial supervision by [Encyclopaedia Britannica]. Indeed, David-Stewart's work product was to be the embodiment of [Encyclopaedia Britannica's] ideas and desires. David-Stewart was just the vehicle selected by [Encyclopaedia Britannica] to assist ... with the editorial phase of the Work." Encyclopaedia Britannica was "the owner of the Work at all stages of completion" and "the dominating force associated with the Work." The Service petitions for review of the Tax Court's decision....

As an original matter we would have no doubt that the payments to David-Stewart were capital expenditures regardless of who was the "dominating force" in the creation of *The Dictionary of Natural Sciences*. The work was intended to yield Encyclopaedia Britannica income over a period of years. The object of sections 162 and 263 of the Code, read together, is to match up expenditures with the income they generate. Where the income is generated over a period of years the expenditures should be classified as capital, contrary to what the Tax Court did here. From the publisher's standpoint a book is just another rental property; and just as the expenditures in putting a building into shape to be rented must be capitalized, so, logically at least, must the expenditures used to create a book. It would make no difference under this view whether Encyclopaedia Britannica hired David-Stewart as a mere consultant to its editorial board, which is the Tax Court's conception of what happened, or bought outright from David-Stewart the right to a book that David-Stewart had already published. If you hire a carpenter to build a tree house that you plan to rent out, his wage is a capital expenditure to you. See *Commissioner of Internal Revenue v. Idaho Power Co.*, 418 U.S. 1 ... (1974).

We are not impressed by Encyclopaedia Britannica's efforts to conjure up practical difficulties in matching expenditures on a book to the income from it. What, it asks, would have been the result if it had scrapped a portion of the manuscript it received from David-Stewart? Would that be treated as the partial destruction of a capital asset, entitling it to an immediate deduction? We think not. The proper analogy is to loss or breakage in the construction of our hypothetical tree house. The effect would be to increase the costs of construction, which are deductible over the useful life of the asset. If the scrapped portion of the manuscript was replaced, the analogy would be perfect. If it was not replaced, the tax consequence would be indirect: an increase or decrease in the publisher's taxable income from the published book.

What does give us pause, however, is a series of decisions in which authors of books have been allowed to treat their expenses as ordinary and necessary business expenses that are deductible immediately even though they were incurred in the creation of long-lived assets — the books the authors were writing. The leading case is *Faura v. Commissioner*, 73 T.C. 849 (1980); it was discussed with approval just recently by a panel of the Tenth Circuit in *Snyder v. United States*, 674 F.2d 1359, 1365 (10th Cir. 1982), and was relied on heavily by the Tax Court in the present case.

We can think of a practical reason for allowing authors to deduct their expenses immediately, one applicable as well to publishers though not in the circumstances of the present case. If you are in the business of producing a series of assets that will yield income over a period of years—which is the situation of most authors and all publishers—identifying particular expenditures with particular books, a necessary step for proper capitalization because the useful lives of the books will not be the same, may be very difficult, since the expenditures of an author or publisher (more clearly the latter) tend to be joint among several books. Moreover, allocating these expenditures among the different books is not always necessary to produce the temporal matching of income and expenditures that the Code desiderates, because the taxable income of the author or publisher who is in a steady state (that is, whose output is neither increasing nor decreasing) will be at least approximately the same whether his costs are expensed or capitalized. Not the same on any given book—on each book expenses and receipts will be systematically mismatched—but the same on average. Under these conditions the benefits of capitalization are unlikely to exceed the accounting and other administrative costs entailed in capitalization.

Yet we hesitate to endorse the *Faura* line of cases: not only because of the evident tension between them and *Idaho Power, supra,* where the Supreme Court said that expenses, whatever their character, must be capitalized if they are incurred in creating a capital asset, but also because *Faura,* and cases following it such as *Snyder,* fail in our view to articulate a persuasive rationale for their result. *Faura* relied on cases holding that the normal expenses of authors and other artists are deductible business expenses rather than nondeductible personal expenses, and on congressional evidence of dissatisfaction with the Internal Revenue Service's insistence that such expenses be capitalized. See 73 T.C. at 852–61. But most of the cases in question [including all those at the court of appeals] are inapposite, because they consider only whether the author's expenditures are deductible at all—not whether, if they are deductible, they must first be capitalized.

...

Yet despite all this we need not decide whether *Faura* is good law, and we are naturally reluctant to precipitate a conflict with the Tenth Circuit. The Tax Court interpreted Faura too broadly in this case. As we interpret *Faura* its principle comes into play only when the taxpayer is in the business of producing a series of assets that yield the taxpayer income over a period of years, so that a complex allocation would be necessary if the taxpayer had to capitalize all his expenses of producing them. This is not such a case. The expenditures at issue are unambiguously identified with *The Dictionary of Natural Sciences.* We need not consider the proper tax treatment of any other expenses that Encyclopaedia Britannica may have incurred on the project—editorial expenses, for example—as they are not involved in this case. Those expenses would be analogous to author Faura's office and travel expenses; they are the normal, recurrent expenses of operating a business that happens to produce capital assets. This case is like *Idaho Power, supra.* The expenditure there was on transportation equipment used in constructing capital facilities that Idaho Power employed in its business of producing and distributing electricity, and was thus unambiguously identified with specific capital assets, just as Encyclopaedia Britannica's payment to David-Stewart for the manuscript of *The Dictionary of Natural Sciences* was unambiguously identified with a specific capital asset.

It is also relevant that the commissioning of the manuscript from David-Stewart was somewhat out of the ordinary for Encyclopaedia Britannica. Now the word "ordinary" in section 162 of the Internal Revenue Code has two different uses: to prevent the deduction of certain expenses that are not normally incurred in the type of business in which the taxpayer is engaged ("ordinary" in this sense blends imperceptibly into "necessary"), *Deputy v. du Pont,* 308 U.S. 488 ... (1940); ... and to clarify the distinction be-

tween expenses that are immediately deductible and expenses that must first be capitalized, *Commissioner v. Tellier*, 383 U.S. 687 ... (1966).... Most of the "ordinary," in the
sense of recurring, expenses of a business are noncapital in nature and most of its capital expenditures are extraordinary in the sense of nonrecurring. Here, as arguably in
Idaho Power as well—for Idaho Power's business was the production and distribution
of electricity, rather than the construction of buildings—the taxpayer stepped out of its
normal method of doing business. In this particular project Encyclopaedia Britannica
was operating like a conventional publisher, which obtains a complete manuscript from
an author or in this case a compiler. The conventional publisher may make a considerable contribution to the work both at the idea stage and at the editorial stage but the
deal is for a manuscript, not for services in assisting the publisher to prepare the manuscript itself....

There is another point to be noted about the distinction between recurring and nonrecurring expenses and its bearing on the issue in this case. If one really takes seriously the
concept of a capital expenditure as anything that yields income, actual or imputed, beyond
the period (conventionally one year, *United States v. Wehrli*, 400 F.2d 686, 689 (10th Cir.
1968)) in which the expenditure is made, the result will be to force the capitalization of
virtually every business expense. It is a result courts naturally shy away from.... It would
require capitalizing every salesman's salary, since his selling activities create goodwill for
the company and goodwill is an asset yielding income beyond the year in which the salary
expense is incurred. The administrative costs of conceptual rigor are too great. The distinction between recurring and nonrecurring business expenses provides a very crude but
perhaps serviceable demarcation between those capital expenditures that can feasibly be
capitalized and those that cannot be. Whether the distinction breaks down where, as in the
case of the conventional publisher, the firm's entire business is the production of capital assets, so that it is literally true that all of its business expenses are capital in nature, is happily not a question we have to decide here, for it is clear that Encyclopaedia Britannica's
payments to David-Stewart were of a nonnormal, nonrecurrent nature.

    ...

REVERSED AND REMANDED.

Now that you have read the applicable regulations and three of the important cases
dealing with the subject, how would you define a capital expenditure?

Midland Empire, *Woodward*, and *Encyclopaedia Britannia* illustrate the tension that
results from the differing tax treatment of capital expenditures and ordinary expenses
under the Code. As you learned, beginning with the power plant revenue ruling, Revenue Ruling 81-277, expenses characterized as "capital," increase the capital account.
Rather than deducting them fully in the year paid or incurred, the taxpayer must recover them over a period of time, or, upon disposition.

Note the observation by Judge Posner in *Encyclopedia Britannica* that if a capital expenditure is anything that yields income substantially beyond the taxable year "the result will be to force the capitalization of virtually every business expense." Judge Posner notes that courts "shy away" from this result. Courts appear to use a rule of
reason. In a recent pronouncement on capital expenditures, the Supreme Court stated:

> In exploring the relationship between deductions and capital expenditures,
> this Court has noted the "familiar rule" that "an income tax deduction is a

matter of legislative grace and that the burden of clearly showing the right to the claimed deduction is on the taxpayer." ... *New Colonial Ice Co. v. Helvering, 292 U.S. 435, 440* ... (1934). The notion that deductions are exceptions to the norm of capitalization finds support in various aspects of the Code. Deductions are specifically enumerated and thus are subject to disallowance in favor of capitalization. See §§ 161 and 261. Nondeductible capital expenditures, by contrast, are not exhaustively enumerated in the Code; rather than providing a "complete list of nondeductible expenditures," *Lincoln Savings, 403 U.S. at 358,* § 263 serves as a general means of distinguishing capital expenditures from current expenses. See *Commissioner v. Idaho Power Co., 418 U.S. at 16.* For these reasons, deductions are strictly construed and allowed only "as there is a clear provision therefor." *New Colonial Ice Co. v. Helvering, 292 U.S. at 440.* ...

The Court also has examined the interrelationship between the Code's business expense and capital expenditure provisions. (Footnote omitted.) In so doing, it has had occasion to parse § 162(a) and explore certain of its requirements. For example, in *Lincoln Savings,* we determined that, to qualify for a deduction under § 162(a), "an item must (1) be 'paid or incurred during the taxable year,' (2) be for 'carrying on any trade or business,' (3) be an 'expense,' (4) be a 'necessary' expense, and (5) be an 'ordinary' expense." *403 U.S. at 352.* ... The Court has recognized, however, that the "decisive distinctions" between current expenses and capital expenditures "are those of degree and not of kind," *Welch v. Helvering, 290 U.S. at 114,* and that because each case "turns on its special facts" *Deputy v. Dupont, 308 U.S. at 496,* the cases sometimes appear difficult to harmonize. ...

INDOPCO, Inc. v. Commissioner, 503 U.S. 79, 83–86 (1992).

A measure of fairness to which there is universal agreement is that if the government elects to impose an income tax on profit-seeking activities, the expenses associated with the production of the income from that activity should be deducted from the gross receipts before the imposition of the tax. When a taxpayer incurs expenses that relate only to the income arising in a single tax period, the proper period for accounting for that expense is undisputed. But, suppose the taxpayer incurs an expense that will aid in the production of a stream of income over a period of years (a so-called "capital expenditure"). There is no dispute that the expense relates to the income to be produced; the only question is one of timing. When should the taxpayer deduct the expense?

5. The Concept of Cost Recovery/Depreciation: Sections 167, 168, 179, 195, 197, and 1016(a)(2)

The section we have just examined, section 263(a), provides that capital expenditures are not deductible. Treasury Regulation section 1.263(a)-2(a) sets forth the most common examples of capital expenditures: "buildings, machinery and equipment, furniture and fixtures, and similar property having a useful life substantially beyond the taxable year."

Suppose a taxpayer constructs or purchases a building, a machine, furniture, or some other asset that she uses in connection with her income-producing activities. Why does section 263(a) proscribe deduction of the cost of that asset from the income that the asset assists in producing? Does section 263(a) contradict the generally-agreed-to proposition that it is "fair" for a taxpayer to subtract from income the costs of producing that income? It may appear to at first. To quote the King of Siam: "Is a puzzlement."[130] (Maybe it's even a conundrum!) Can you, as drafters of the tax code, reconcile these seemingly inconsistent principles?

Brian's Problem

Suppose Brian decides to start a business. He wants to run a facility that specializes in exercising the muscles of the hand and arm. (He plans to rent the space initially.) At the beginning of the tax year, he acquires vise grips, arm curl equipment, juggling sets, large mirrors, and exercise mats. Are these expenditures ordinary and necessary expenses? Do these purchases meet the definition of capital expenditures? Should the Code permit him to deduct the costs of these modest pieces of equipment, clearly necessary for the conduct of his trade or business? Assume that your answer is "yes." What are some of the ways that the Code might permit Brian to deduct these costs?

(1) Suppose you suggest that Brian should be able to deduct the full cost of this equipment in the year he acquires it. What are the consequences for Brian and the tax system of letting him deduct the full cost in year one?

(2) Are there alternate plans you might suggest for requiring Brian to spread the deduction over more than one year? How many years? How much per year? What are the consequences to Brian and the tax system of each alternative you suggest?

The Code solves this conundrum under the provisions of sections 167 and 168. **Read section 167(a).** What does it provide? To what kind of property does it apply? Section 167(a) purports to provide a "reasonable allowance" for the "exhaustion, wear and tear (including ... obsolescence)" of property. This statutory description leads you to the inference that the tax concept of depreciation is similar to the commonly accepted notion that depreciation is tied to a decline in the value of property.

Although it is obvious that some property a taxpayer uses in her income-producing activities does indeed decline in value, that is not always the case. The aim of the depreciation deduction in the federal income tax is *not* to track the decline in the value of an asset (although in some cases it does).[131] Rather, the current system of depreciation represents Congress's choice of methods for allowing Brian to deduct the cost of assets that he uses in his business and that are necessary to produce the income but which have "a useful life substantially beyond the taxable year." Moreover, the depreciation rules make clear the true meaning of section 263(a): a taxpayer may not deduct a capital expenditure in a single year; rather, the taxpayer must spread the cost over the period of its use in producing income.[132] If a taxpayer makes certain types of capital "expenditures" for

---

130. Oscar Hammerstein II, *The King and I*, act I, sc. 3.

131. Prior to Congress's adoption of section 168, depreciation was based on the "useful life" of the asset. When that was the case, depreciation came closer to tracking the actual decline in the value of the asset. But the frequent litigation resulting from the use of this facts and circumstances determination of an asset's useful life led Congress to adopt a system of categories of assets. A taxpayer now deducts the basis of an asset over the period of time prescribed for the category into which the asset falls. Far more arbitrary than the old system that attempted to predict the actual useful life of the asset, this system is another example of Congress choosing a bright-line, safe-harbor rule to promote certainty.

132. This is not meant to imply that a taxpayer may deduct the cost of all capital expenditures. Suppose a taxpayer pays $100,000 for her personal residence. Does section 167(a) authorize her to

use in connection with her income-producing activities, she cannot deduct them under section 162(a) because they are not "expenses." She can, however, deduct the cost of the "expenditures" *over time* as depreciation deductions under section 167(a).

Thus, the concept of depreciation under the federal income tax is better conceived of as a timing mechanism with respect to the deductibility (or recovery) of the cost of certain property used in connection with income-producing activities. Section 263(a), then, does not act as a total bar to the deduction of capital expenditures; it acts merely as a timing device.

If the Code allowed Brian to deduct the full cost of his equipment in the first year, it might, at first, have appeared advantageous to him. But on reflection, you probably noted that this would mean Brian has no remaining deductions to reduce his future income from the business. To allow a deduction all in one year, therefore, would produce a significant distortion in the results of his operation. As noted earlier, the original depreciation rules under section 167(a) required a taxpayer to deduct the cost of the asset over the "useful life" of the asset. This resulted in a rough "matching" of the expense against the income it assisted in producing.

Suppose at the beginning of the tax year Brian purchased a machine for his business, at a cost of $10,000, that exercises the rotator cuff of baseball pitchers. If the machine had a useful life in the business of 5 years, Brian could not deduct the full $10,000 cost of the machine as a current "expense" in the year of purchase under section 162(a) because it was a capital expenditure under section 263(a); it had a life in the business substantially beyond the taxable year of purchase. Brian was able, however, to deduct the cost of the machine by means of depreciation deductions under section 167(a) over its 5-year useful life.

Can you think of an appropriate way Brian might have allocated the cost of the machine over its life?[133] Two of the most common methods are described in Treasury Regulation sections 1.167(b)-1 and -2. **Read those regulations and see if you can apply them to determine the appropriate depreciation deductions for the machine for years 1 through 5.**[134]

In 1981, the rules and some of the underlying conceptual rationales of depreciation changed dramatically, as the following case makes clear.

SIMON v. COMMISSIONER
68 F.3d 41 (2d Cir. 1995)

WINTER, Circuit Judge:

This appeal from the Tax Court raises the question whether professional musicians may take a depreciation deduction for wear and tear on antique violin bows under the Accelerated Cost Recovery System ("ACRS") of the Economic Recovery Tax Act of 1981 ("ERTA"), ... although the taxpayers cannot demonstrate that the bows have a "determinable useful life."

The parties agree that under the pre-ERTA Internal Revenue Code of 1954 and the Treasury Department regulations interpreting that Code, the bows would be considered

---

deduct the cost of the residence over the useful life prescribed for residential real estate by section 168(c)(1)? Can she ever recover the cost?

133. Can you identify the proper recovery period?

134. You might also want to read Treasury Regulation sections 1.167(a)-1(a), (b), and (c)(1); -2; and -3 to more fully understand the original depreciation rules.

depreciable property only if the taxpayers could demonstrate a determinable useful life. The issue here is to what extent, if any, the ACRS modified the determinable useful life requirement.

BACKGROUND

The facts are essentially undisputed. Richard and Fiona Simon are highly skilled professional violinists. Richard Simon began to play and study the violin at the age of 7. He received a bachelor of music degree from the Manhattan School of Music in 1956 and subsequently pursued his master's degree in music at the Manhattan School of Music and Columbia University. In 1965, Mr. Simon joined the New York Philharmonic Orchestra ("Philharmonic") as a member of its first violin section. Since then, he has also been a soloist, chamber music player, and teacher. Mr. Simon was a full-time performer with the Philharmonic throughout the relevant tax year.

Fiona Simon has played and studied the violin since the age of 4. She studied at the Purcell School in London from 1963 to 1971 and at the Guildhall School of Music from 1971 to 1973. Ms. Simon joined the first violin section of the Philharmonic in 1985. She, too, has been a soloist, chamber music player, teacher, and free-lance performer. Ms. Simon was a full-time performer with the Philharmonic throughout the pertinent tax year.

The business property at issue consists of two violin bows ("the Tourte bows") made in the nineteenth century by Francois Tourte, a bowmaker renowned for technical improvements in bow design. These bows were purchased by the Simons in 1985 and were in a largely unused condition at the time. The Tax Court found that "[o]ld violins played with old bows produce exceptional sounds that are superior to sounds produced by newer violins played with newer bows." *Simon v. Commissioner*, 103 T.C. 247, 250, ... (1994). The Tax Court also found that violin bows suffer wear and tear when used regularly by performing musicians. With use, a violin bow will eventually become "played out," producing an inferior sound. *Id.* at 252, 253.... However, a "played out" Tourte bow retains value as a collector's item notwithstanding its diminished utility. The Simons' Tourte bows, for example, were appraised in 1990 at $45,000 and $35,000, even though they had physically deteriorated since their purchase by the Simons in 1985 for $30,000 and $21,500, respectively.

The Simons use the Tourte bows regularly in their trade. In 1989, the tax year in question, the Simons performed in four concerts per week as well as numerous rehearsals with the Philharmonic. *Id.* at 249.... Their use of the Tourte bows during the tax year at issue subjected the bows to substantial wear and tear. *Id.* at 252.... Believing that they were entitled to depreciate the bows under the ACRS, the Simons claimed depreciation deductions for the two bows on their 1989 Form 1040 in the amount of $6,300 and $4,515. The parties stipulated that these amounts represent the appropriate ACRS deductions if deductions are allowable.

The Tax Court agreed with the Simons and allowed the depreciation deductions. The Commissioner brought the present appeal. (Footnote 1)

DISCUSSION

This appeal turns on the interpretation of the ACRS provisions of I.R.C. §168, (Footnote 2) which provide a depreciation deduction for "recovery property" placed into service after 1980. Recovery property is defined by that section as "tangible property of a character subject to the allowance for depreciation" when "used in a trade or business, or ... held for the production of income." I.R.C. §168(c)(1). The record establishes that the Simons' Tourte bows were tangible property placed in service after 1980 and used in the taxpayers' trade or business. The Commissioner contends, however, that the bows are not "property of a character subject to the allowance for depreciation."

The parties agree that Section 168's phrase "of a character subject to depreciation" must be interpreted in light of the I.R.C. §167(a) allowances for "exhaustion, wear and tear, and ... obsolescence." The Simons and the Tax Court maintain that, when read in conjunction with the plain language of Section 167, Section 168 requires only that the Tourte bows suffer wear and tear in the Simons' trade to qualify as "recovery property." ... The Commissioner, on the other hand, argues that because all property used in a trade or business is necessarily subject to wear and tear, the Simons' construction of Section 168 would effectively render Section 168's phrase "of a character subject to the allowance for depreciation" superfluous, a result that Congress presumably could not have intended. *See United States v. Nordic Village, Inc.*, 503 U.S. 30 ... (1992) (It is a "settled rule that a statute must, if possible, be construed in such a fashion that every word has some operative effect."). Therefore, Section 168's requirement that the property be "of a character subject to the allowance for depreciation" must include an element beyond wear and tear, namely the "determinable useful life" requirement embodied in 26 C.F.R. §1.167(a)-1, a Treas. Reg. of pre-ERTA vintage.

We do not agree with the Commissioner's premise because some tangible assets used in business are not exhausted, do not suffer wear and tear, or become obsolete. For example, paintings that hang on the wall of a law firm merely to be looked at — to please connoisseur clients or to give the appearance of dignity to combative professionals — do not generally suffer wear or tear. More to the point, the Simons' Tourte bows were playable for a time precisely because they had been kept in a private collection and were relatively unused since their manufacture. Indeed, it appears that one had never been played at all. Had that collection been displayed at a for-profit museum, the museum could not have depreciated the bows under ERTA because, although the bows were being used in a trade or business, they were not subject to wear and tear. The Tourte bows are not unlike numerous kinds of museum pieces or collectors' items. The Commissioner's textual argument thus fails because there are tangible items not subject to wear and tear.

The Commissioner next argues that Congressional intent and the notion of depreciation itself require that Section 168's statutory language be supplemented by reading into the word "character" a requirement that tangible property have a demonstrable useful life. To address that issue, we must briefly examine the history of the depreciation allowance.

The tax laws have long permitted deductions for depreciation on certain income-producing assets used in a trade or business.... The original rationale for the depreciation deduction was to allow taxpayers to match accurately, for tax accounting purposes, the cost of an asset to the income stream that the asset produced. *See Massey Motors, Inc. v. United States*, 364 U.S. 92, 104, ... (1960) ("it is the primary purpose of depreciation accounting to further the integrity of periodic income statements by making a meaningful allocation of the cost entailed in the use ... of the asset to the periods to which it contributes"). In its traditional incarnation, therefore, the pace of depreciation deductions was determined by the period of time that the asset would produce income in the taxpayer's business. As the Supreme Court noted in *Massey*, "Congress intended by the depreciation allowance not to make taxpayers a profit thereby, but merely to protect them from a loss.... Accuracy in accounting requires that correct tabulations, not artificial ones, be used." *Id.* at 101....

To implement this accurate tax accounting, the concept of a determinable useful life was necessary because, without such a determination, one could not calculate the proper annual allowance—"the sum which should be set aside for the taxable year, in order that, at the end of the useful life of the plant in the business, the aggregate of the sums set aside will (with the salvage value) suffice to provide an amount equal to the original cost." *United States v. Ludey*, 274 U.S. 295 ... (1927). The regulation that the Commissioner now relies upon was promulgated under the 1954 Internal Revenue Code and reflects the rationale underlying the accounting scheme in effect just prior to ERTA. *See* Treas. Reg. § 1.167(a)-1 (1972)....

ERTA, however, altered the depreciation scheme for two reasons other than sound accounting practice that are not consistent with the Commissioner's argument. First, the ACRS introduced accelerated depreciation periods as a stimulus for economic growth. H.R. Conf. Rep. No. 215, 97th Cong., 1st Sess. 206 (1981) ... S.Rep. No. 144, 97th Cong., 1st Sess. 47 (1981).... Under ACRS, the cost of an asset is recovered over a predetermined period unrelated to—and usually shorter than—the useful life of the asset. Moreover, the depreciation deductions do not assume consistent use throughout the asset's life, instead assigning inflated deductions to the earlier years of use. *See* I.R.C. § 168(b). Therefore, the purpose served by the determinable useful life requirement of the pre-ERTA scheme—allowing taxpayers to depreciate property over its actual use in the business—no longer exists under the ACRS. *See generally Massey*, 364 U.S. 92.... Because the ACRS is different by design, there is no logic in the Commissioner's suggestion that depreciation practice under the old Section 167 calls for the imposition of a determinable useful life requirement after ERTA.

A second congressional purpose embodied in ERTA also militates against reading a determinable useful life prerequisite into Section 168. In addition to stimulating investment, Congress sought to simplify the depreciation rules by eliminating the need to adjudicate matters such as useful life and salvage value, which are inherently uncertain and result in unproductive disagreements between taxpayers and the Internal Revenue Service. S.Rep. No. 144 at 47. Indeed, the legislation specifically sought to "de-emphasize" the concept of useful life. *Id.* On this point, we agree with the Tax Court that:

> [The Commissioner's] argument that a taxpayer must first prove the useful life of personal property before he or she may depreciate it over the 3-year or 5-year period would bring the Court back to pre-ERTA law and reintroduce the disagreements that the Congress intended to eliminate by its enactment of ERTA.

103 T.C. at 263,....

We also cannot accept the Commissioner's suggestion that her proposed interpretation de-emphasizes useful life by requiring establishment of a demonstrable useful life for only a "narrow category" of property. Insofar as the Commissioner seeks to do this by singling out usable antiques and other business property likely to appreciate in real economic value, she relies on a concept that has nothing whatsoever to do with the useful life of the asset in the business. As the Supreme Court noted in *Massey*, "useful life is measured by the use in a taxpayer's business, not by the full abstract economic life of the asset in any business." Massey, 364 U.S. at 97.... Nor, a fortiori, does the concept of useful life bear on the asset's eligibility under the ACRS. Indeed, the Commissioner's position that deductions for depreciation may not be taken for property that retains value after use in a business seems designed to avoid the consequences of ERTA's explicit rejection of "salvage value." ... (Footnote 5)

The Commissioner's strongest support for her claim that Congress intended to maintain Section 1.167(a)-1's determinable useful life requirement comes from the House Conference Report, which noted that

Under present law, assets used in a trade or business or for the production of income are depreciable if they are subject to wear and tear, decay or decline from natural causes or obsolescence. Assets that do not decline in value on a predictable basis or that do not have a determinable useful life, such as land, goodwill, and stock, are not depreciable.

H.R. Conf. Rep. No. 215 at 206,.... The Simons unsuccessfully attempt to recharacterize this statement as an inartful catalogue of assets that are not subject to exhaustion, wear and tear, or obsolescence. The House report means what it says but gives us slight pause. In light of the overriding legislative intent to abandon the unnecessarily complicated rules on useful life, we cannot employ two sentences in a legislative report to trump statutory language and a clearly stated legislative purpose. Continued reliance on 26 C.F.R. §1.167(a)-1 is in sharp conflict with the overall legislative history of ERTA, which definitively repudiates the scheme of complex depreciation rules, including "current regulations." S. Rep. No. 144 at 47. We are thus not persuaded by the Commissioner's call for us to interpret a statute that abrogates a current regulatory regime as in fact incorporating the details of that scheme. In particular, we reject the argument that we should retain regulatory provisions now divorced from their functional purpose.

When a coherent regulatory system has been repudiated by statute—as this one has—it is inappropriate to use a judicial shoehorn to retain an isolated element of the now-dismembered regulation. We thus hold that, for the purposes of the "recovery property" provisions of Section 168, "property subject to the allowance for depreciation" means property that is subject to exhaustion, wear and tear, or obsolescence.

Our decision does not conflict with that of the Ninth Circuit in *Browning v. Commissioner*, 890 F.2d 1084 (9th Cir. 1989). In *Browning*, a taxpayer musician sought to claim depreciation deductions for three violins: a Ruggieri, a Stradivarius, and a Gabrielli. Browning claimed an ACRS deduction for only one of these violins, the Gabrielli. *Browning v. Commissioner*, 55 T.C.M. (CCH) 1232, ... (1988). Judge Hamblen's Tax Court memorandum noted Browning's Section 168 claim in the introduction but did not discuss that section or differentiate it from the pre-ERTA claims in any way. On review, the Ninth Circuit mentioned neither Section 168, ERTA, nor the ACRS. In addition, all citations to Section 167(a) and discussion in the Ninth Circuit opinion refer to the 1954 Code. Finally, the Ninth Circuit's discussion of the Gabrielli violin explicitly referred to its salvage value, a concept that was eliminated for recovery property under the ACRS. See I.R.C. §168(f)(9). *Browning* was thus decided as a pre-ERTA case.

We acknowledge that the result of our holding may give favorable treatment to past investment decisions that some regard as wasteful, such as a law firm's purchase of expensive antique desks, the cost of which could have been quickly depreciated under our current ruling. However, Congress wanted to stimulate investment in business property generally, and it is not our function to draw subjective lines between the wasteful and the productive. Moreover, courts should take care that the Commissioner's role as revenue maximizer does not vitiate Congress's intent to sacrifice revenue to generate economic activity....

One should not exaggerate the extent to which our holding is a license to hoard and depreciate valuable property that a taxpayer expects to appreciate in real economic value. (Footnote 7) The test is whether property will suffer exhaustion, wear and tear, or obsolescence in its use by a business. Even without a determinable useful life requirement, a business that displayed antique automobiles, for example, and kept them under near-ideal, humidity-controlled conditions, would still have difficulty demonstrating the requisite exhaustion, wear and tear, or obsolescence necessary to depreciate the automobiles as recovery property.... Nor is valuable artwork purchased as office ornamentation apt to suffer anything more damaging than occasional criticism from the tutored or untutored, ... and it too would probably fail to qualify as recovery property. Indeed, even a noted artwork that serves as a day-to-day model for another artist's work cannot be depreciated as recovery property if it does not face exhaustion, wear and tear, or obsolescence in the pertinent business....

For the foregoing reasons, we affirm.

FOOTNOTES:

1. The Third Circuit has recently held for the taxpayers in a companion case raising the same issues presented here. *See Liddle v. Commissioner*, 65 F.3d 329 (3d Cir. 1995), *aff'g* 103 T.C. 285, ... (1994).

2. For purposes of this appeal, we apply the Internal Revenue Code as it existed prior to the Tax Reform Act of 1986, Pub. L. No. 99-514, 100 Stat. 2085. The relevant portions of Section 168 read as follows:

> (a) *Allowance of deduction.* There shall be allowed as a deduction for any taxable year the amount determined under this section with respect to recovery property.
>
> ...
>
> (c) *Recovery Property.* For purposes of this title—
>
> (1) *Recovery property defined.* Except as provided in subsection (e), the term "recovery property" means tangible property of a character subject to the allowance for depreciation—
>
> (A) used in a trade or business,
>   or
>
> (B) held for the production of income.

5. We accept the Tax Court's finding that the bows have no "determinable useful life." That finding is based on the assumption that there is no distinction between the value of the bows to professional violinists and their value as antiques after they are no longer functional.

ERTA's abandonment of the concept of salvage value may be the rub that causes the Commissioner to take the position that the Tourte bows have no determinable useful life and are not depreciable. If salvage value could be used to offset depreciation, the Commissioner could, without loss to the Treasury, concede that the bows could be used to play the violin for only so long and simply offset the depreciation deduction by their continued value as antiques. The bows had been sparingly used, or not used at all, before they were purchased by the Simons and, having been used extensively, now have much less value as business property while retaining substantial value as antiques. The Commissioner may thus lean upon the thin reed of a supposed continuing determinable useful life requirement because Congress's intent to do away with the concept of salvage value is indisputable. In doing so, however, she fails to distinguish between a useful life as property used in a particular business—playing the violin as a professional—and value as non-functioning antiques.

7. We note that our decision today is limited to "recovery property," a concept that was deleted from the statute in the Tax Reform Act of 1986, Pub. L. No. 99-514, 100 Stat.

2085. Moreover, ACRS' depreciation deductions first became available in 1981. There-fore, this opinion applies only to property placed in service between January 1, 1981 and January 1, 1987.

OAKES, Senior Circuit Judge, dissenting:

I cannot believe that Congress, in changing the depreciation deduction from the Asset Depreciation Range System ("ADRS") for recovery of assets placed in service after De-cember 31, 1980, to the Accelerated Cost Recovery System ("ACRS") whereby the cost of an asset is recovered over a predetermined period shorter than the useful life of the asset or the period the asset is used to produce income, intended to abandon the concept un-derlying depreciation, namely, that to permit the deduction the property must have a useful life capable of being estimated.... I find no indication in either the changes of statutory language or the well-documented legislative history that Congress intended such a radical change.... Indeed, it seems to me that the statutory language and the leg-islative history—consistent with the dual congressional purpose of simplification and stimulating economic growth by permitting accelerated depreciation periods—retained the fundamental principle that, in order to depreciate, the asset involved must have a de-terminable useful life.

. . .

Under the majority's interpretation, however, the only criterion necessary to obtain a deduction under section 168(c) is that the property be subject to wear and tear. Thus, a car buff in the trade or business of buying, collecting, and selling antique automobiles, who drives his autos to auto shows may obtain a depreciation deduction, or the law of-fice that buys fine Sheraton or Chippendale desks or chairs for office use can take a de-duction, though in each case the auto or furniture is actually appreciating in value and has no determinable useful life.

As for legislative history, the majority candidly admits that House Conference Re-port 97-215, which states that "assets that do not decline in value on a predictable basis or that do not have a determinable useful life, such as land, goodwill, and stock, are not depreciable," "means what it says," see Maj. Op. at 46 (citing H.R. Conf. Rep. No. 215 at 206, ...). The majority then adds that the Report "gives us slight pause."

The majority of this court joins the Tax Court majority and the Third Circuit in hold-ing that section 168(c)(1) applies to all tangible property that is subject to "wear and tear." I agree with the Commissioner that such an interpretation renders meaningless the phrase in section 168(c)(1) "of a character subject to the allowance for depreciation," since all tangible property used in a trade or business is necessarily subject to wear and tear. See Commissioner's Rep. Br. at 3–4 (citing to U.S. v. Nordic Village, Inc., 503 U.S. 30, 35, ... (1992) ("a statute must, if possible, be construed in such fashion that every word has some operative effect")). This point is confirmed by the General Explanation of the Economic Recovery Tax Act of 1981 which states that section 168 "does not change the determination under prior law as to whether property is depreciable or non-deprecia-ble." Staff of Joint Comm. On Taxation, 97th Cong., 1st Sess. 77 (Comm. Print 1981).

Nor can reliance be placed, as it is by the majority, upon the fact that section 168(f)(9) changed prior law by removing "salvage value" from the depreciation calculus. The fact that Congress eliminated salvage value while simultaneously defining the term "recovery property" as "tangible property of a character subject to the allowance for de-preciation," cannot support the conclusion that section 168 eliminated the threshold re-quirement that taxpayers establish a determinable useful life for their property. Had

Congress intended otherwise, the statute simply would have defined "recovery property" as "tangible property used in a trade or business" rather than as "tangible property of a character subject to the allowance for depreciation," and not specified that the recovery property be "section 1245 property," which, as stated, refers us back to section 167.

Since, concededly, taxpayers Richard and Fiona Simon have not established that the bows in question have determinable useful lives, the bows do not qualify for the depreciation deduction. It is a long way from the dual purpose of section 168 (to shorten the depreciation periods for property that would have been depreciable under section 167 in order to stimulate investment and to simplify the complex series of rules and regulations pertaining to useful lives by substituting a four-tier system of three-year, five-year, ten-year, and fifteen-year property), to abandonment of the underlying concept of depreciable property altogether. In my view, the decision of the Tax Court should be reversed and accordingly I hereby dissent.

Consider the following questions concerning *Simon*.

1. Why did the court in *Simon* apply the pre-1986 version of the depreciation rule? *See* footnote 2 of the case.

2. If the opinion in *Simon* applies only to property placed in service between January 1, 1981, and January 1, 1987, as the court states, would the taxpayers prevail under the current version of section 168? *See* footnote 7 of the case.

The general rules of the depreciation system Congress has adopted appear in sections 167 and 168. **Look first at section 167(a).** What is the general rule? To what kind of property does it apply?

Now look at section 167(b). What is its significance? **Look at section 168(a).** To what property does section 168 apply? To what property does it not apply?

Once you have decided that section 168 applies to the particular property you are seeking to depreciate, what questions does section 168(a) require you to answer? Where are the answers found?

Consider first the answer to the question, "what is the applicable depreciation method?" **Read section 168(b) carefully.** Suppose you are seeking to advise Brian on the proper depreciation of his machine. Does section 168(b) provide Brian with any choice of method? That is, is there more than one proper method? What is the "straight line" method? What is a "declining balance" method? **Reread Treasury Regulation sections 1.167(b)-1 and -2.**

Now consider the question of "what is the applicable recovery period?" **Look at section 168(c).** Note that in order to determine the applicable recovery period under section 168(c), you must first determine the character of Brian's machine. Is it, for example, "3-year property," "5-year property," or "7-year property,"? Where do you find a definition for "3-year property," "5-year property," and "7-year property"?

Note that the organization of section 168 is akin to the organization of section 132 (at which you looked in connection with our study of fringe benefits). That section began with a general rule and continued with a subsection dealing with each of the types of fringe benefits. To find definitions, you had to look farther in the statute. Here too, to find the important definitions, you will have to look farther than sections 168(a) through (d). But, if you do so in a systematic way and keep in mind the need to solve the mystery of the allowable depreciation for Brian's machine, you will succeed.

Section 168 evolved from the asset depreciation range ("ADR") system the Service had developed when section 167 provided a facts and circumstances test for depreciation. Prior to enactment of section 168, section 167 required a taxpayer to determine the useful life and the salvage value of an asset before claiming depreciation. To make life simpler for business taxpayers with multiple classes of assets and multiple assets within each class, the Service developed the ADR system. That system established a list of thousands of business assets and a range of useful lives for each. Taxpayers, therefore, did not have to examine each asset within a class and determine its useful life.

Although enactment of section 168 made the process of determining the useful life far simpler for most assets by grouping items into broad categories (and including a default provision for those that did not fit into one of the categories), section 168 retains a reference to the ADR system in section 168(e)(1). **Read carefully section 168(e)(1).** Section 168(e)(1) classifies property, "3-year property" or "5-year property," based on its "class life." **Look at section 168(i)(1).** Section 168(i)(1) defines class life as those set forth by the Treasury under the ADR system that applied prior to enactment of section 168. Revenue Procedure 87-56, 1987-2 C.B. 674, lists class lives for a number of specific items and items used in various activities. If the property at issue is specifically listed in Revenue Procedure 87-56, the listed class life determines the character of the property under section 168(e)(1), which in turn determines the applicable recovery period under section 168(c). If it is not, the Revenue Procedure also lists assets used in specific types of activities. If the asset is used in a listed activity, the taxpayer uses the listed class life for all assets used in that activity.

For example, suppose the taxpayer wanted to identify the proper recovery period for a piano. She must first consult the Revenue Procedure to see if a piano has a listed class life.[135] There is no specific category for a piano. But, set forth below is the portion of the Revenue Procedure listing the only type of activity within which a piano might (arguably) fall.

Asset Class	Description of assets included	Recovery Periods (in years)		
		Class Life (in years)	General Depreciation System	Alternative Depreciation System
79.0	**Recreation:** Includes assets used in the provision of entertainment services on payment of a fee or admission charge, as in the operation of bowling alleys, billiard and pool establishments, theaters, concert halls, and miniature golf courses. Does not include amusement and theme parks and assets which consist primarily of specialized land improvements or structures, such as golf courses, sports stadia, race tracks, ski slopes and buildings which house the assets used in entertainment services.	10	7	10

---

135. If, however, the property has both a class life and is listed in either section 168(e)(2) or section 168(e)(3), e.g., real property or automobiles, section 168(e)(2) or section 168(e)(3) takes precedence over the class life listed in the Revenue Procedure. Note also that many of the recovery periods the new rules produce are unrelated to the true economic life of the asset (the old concept of "useful life.")

Unless the taxpayer can identify a class life by examination of the Revenue Procedure, she will next consult section 168(e) again, in order to determine the character of the property and, hence, its recovery period under section 168(c). **Reread section 168(e) focussing on subsections (e)(2) through (e)(5).** If she is unable to identify a period under sections 168(e)(2) through (e)(5),[136] she will have to treat the piano as "7-year property" pursuant to the default rule contained in section 168(e)(3)(C)(iv)(I). Depending upon the circumstances of the taxpayer, she may wish to argue for a shorter (or, perhaps, even a longer) life than seven years. Can she do that in this case?

But, what about Brian's machine? Reprinted below are more class lives that appear in Revenue Procedure 87-56.

Asset Class	Description of assets included	Recovery Periods (in years)		
		Class Life (in years)	General Depreciation System	Alternative Depreciation System
00.11	**Office Furniture, Fixtures and Equipment:** Includes furniture and fixtures that are not a structural component of a building. Includes such assets as desks, files, safes, and communications equipment. Does not include communications equipment that is included in other classes.	10	7	10
00.12	**Information Systems:** Includes computers and their peripheral equipment used in administering normal business transactions and the maintenance of business records, their retrieval and analysis. Information systems are defined as: 1) Computers: A computer is a programmable electronically activated device capable of accepting information, applying prescribed processes to the information, and supplying the results of these processes with or without human intervention. It usually consists of a central processing unit containing extensive storage, logic, arithmetic, and control capabilities. Excluded from this category are adding machines, electronic desk calculators, etc., and other equipment described in class 00.13. 2) Peripheral equipment consists of the auxiliary machines which are designed to be placed under control of the central processing unit. Nonlimiting exam	6	5*	5*

---

136. Sections 168(e)(2) through 168(e)(5) list special rules for certain types of property.

	ples are: Card readers, card punches, magnetic tape feeds, high speed printers, optical character readers, tape cassettes, mass storage units, paper tape equipment, keypunches, data entry devices, teleprinters, terminals, tape drives, disc drives, disc files, disc packs, visual image projector tubes, card sorters, plotters, and collators. Peripheral equipment may be used on-line or off-line. Does not include equipment that is an integral part of other capital equipment that is included in other classes of economic activity, i.e., computers used primarily for process or production control, switching, channeling, and automating distributive trades and services such as point of sale (POS) computer systems. Also, does not include equipment of a kind used primarily for amusement or entertainment of the user.			
80.0	**Theme and Amusement Parks:** Includes assets used in the provision of rides, attractions, and amusements in activities defined as theme and amusement parks, and includes appurtenances associated with a ride, attraction, amusement or theme setting within the park such as ticket booths, facades, shop interiors, and props, special purpose structures, and buildings other than warehouses, administration buildings, hotels, and motels. Includes all land improvements for or in support of park activities (e.g., parking lots, sidewalks, waterways, bridges, fences, landscaping, etc.) and support functions (e.g., food and beverage retailing, souvenir vending and other nonlodging accommodations) if owned by the park and provided exclusively for the benefit of park patrons. Theme and amusement parks are defined as combinations of amusements, rides, and attractions which are permanently situated on park land and open to the public for the price of admission. This guideline class is a composite of all assets used in this industry except transportation equipment (general purpose trucks,	12.5	7	12.5

	cars, airplanes, etc., which are included in asset guidelines classes with the prefix 00.2), assets used in the provision of administrative services (asset classes with the prefix 00.1), and warehouses, administration buildings, hotels and motels.			

*Property described in asset class 00.12 which is qualified technological equipment as defined in section 168(i)(2) is assigned a recovery period of 5 years notwithstanding its class life....

Do any of the lives appear to encompass Brian's machine? If so, you may go on to the final issue, what is the proper convention. If not, you must go back to sections 168(e)(2) and 168(e)(3). The only way to be sure, is to proceed step-by-step through the categories. Most important: do not guess about the meaning of a category. As noted above, definitions may appear in other parts of the section. Look for them!

The final piece of information you need in order to calculate Brian's depreciation is the identity of the proper convention. What is a "convention" in the context of a depreciation allowance? **Look at section 168(d).** What is the proper convention for rental real estate? What is the proper convention for Brian's machine? What does use of a convention accomplish? (You may assume that section 168(d)(3)(A) does not apply. To whom would it apply?)

Now, at last, you are ready to calculate Brian's depreciation allowance.

You should be able to do this using either a straight-line or an accelerated method.[137] To do this accurately, you must write out a table, showing the recovery period, the starting basis for each period, the amount of depreciation for that period, and, when you are using an accelerated method, when to switch to straight-line.[138]

Once Brian knows the amount of depreciation the Code permits him to claim as a deduction, are there any other adjustments he must make? (Remember that when we looked at capital expenditures, we noted that they increase a taxpayer's capital account, and are adjustments to basis pursuant to section 1016.) Once you decide the appropri-

---

137. As noted earlier, the Treasury Regulations, sections 1.167-1(b)-1 and -2, describe the method of calculating yearly depreciation using the straight-line and declining balance methods. These regulations were issued in connection with section 167. What adjustments do you have to make to utilize them in connection with section 168? To make it easier for taxpayers the Treasury has also issued Revenue Procedure 87-57, 1987-2 C.B. 687, setting forth the percentage allowed for each year. You must be careful, when using the Revenue Procedure, to apply the percentage for the year *to the unadjusted basis* of the asset. We think it is important for you to learn how to do the actual calculations based on the words of the statute itself. After doing so, however, you may compare your results with those the table would produce.

138. Note that if Brian had acquired his machine after September 10, 2001, and before September 11, 2004, and if the recovery period for the machine were 20 years or less, he would have been eligible for a "bonus depreciation" deduction for the first year under section 168(k) before he computed the amount of the deduction under the regular rules. Congress enacted section 168(k) as part of the Jobs Creation and Worker Assistance Act of 2002, P.L. 107-147 (hereinafter the "2002 Act"), which was aimed at spurring the economy after the September 11 terrorist attacks. Congress increased the bonus for property acquired after September 10, 2001, and before January 1, 2005, as part of the Jobs and Growth Tax Relief Reconciliation Act of 2003, P.L. 108-27 (hereinafter the "2003 Act"). The 2004 Jobs Act extended the benefits of section 168(k) to certain property placed in service before January 1, 2006. The extension does not apply to Brian's machine, however. Section 168(k) demonstrates the type of special provision, in this case intended as a stimulus, that makes the present Code so complex.

ate method to allocate the cost and, thus, what the appropriate deduction should be for each of years 1–5, section 1016(a)(2) requires Brian to take some further action. What is it? **Read section 1016(a)(2).** What is the function of section 1016(a)(2)? Why does it direct you to do what it does? Recall our reference to the first of two "bedrock" postulates quoted from Professor Joseph M. Dodge: "The same dollars should not be taxed *to the same taxpayer* more than once."[139] Professor Dodge also sets forth a second "bedrock" concept of income: "The same dollars should not be deducted by *the same taxpayer* more than once.[140] Does section 1016(a)(2) effectuate this principle?

Suppose Brian then purchased a building, on March 11, for $5,000,000 to house his operations. What would be the appropriate cost recovery deduction under section 168 for this year?[141] For next year?

Suppose a taxpayer decides not to claim depreciation, or mistakenly fails to claim it. Read the following case.

ESPINOZA v. COMMISSIONER
T.C. Memo 1999-269

PARR, Judge:

...

After concessions, (Footnote 1) the issues for decision are: (1) Whether petitioners realized capital gain in 1991 from the involuntary conversion of their property used in a trade or business. We hold they did to the extent set out below. (2) Whether petitioners are liable for the addition to tax for failure to timely file their 1991 Federal income tax return. We hold they are. (3) Whether petitioners are liable for the accuracy-related penalty pursuant to section 6662(a) either for negligence or disregard of rules or regulations or for the substantial understatement of their 1991 income tax. We hold petitioners are liable for the penalty for negligence or disregard of rules or regulations.

...

FINDINGS OF FACT

In the second half of the 1980's, petitioner was frequently away from home while working in the construction industry. Petitioner thought that it would be more economical to buy a used Greyhound bus and convert it into a motor home, which he would live in when he was working away from home, than to pay for commercial lodging and food. Accordingly, in March 1985, petitioners purchased a previously owned 1962 GMC Coach (bus) for $14,359.

The bus required repairs to the clutch and transmission, which were made shortly after purchase. The first item that petitioners purchased as part of the conversion

---

139. Joseph M. Dodge, *The Logic of Tax* 20 (West Pub. Co. 1989).

140. *Id.*

141. You may assume that Brian bought only the building, not the land under it. If he had bought both, he would have to allocate a portion of the purchase price to the land. How would he make the allocation? Why would he have to allocate? Recall the *Simon* case. Is there a difference between land and a building? **Look at Treasury Regulation sections 1.167(a)-2 and -5.**

process was a generator. During 1985, petitioner painted the body, completed the bed-room, and added wood paneling, lights, curtains, chairs, a couch, and bathroom plumbing, including holding tanks for potable and waste water. By the end of 1986, pe-titioner had replaced the front bumper, repainted the body, added a furnace, and com-pleted the bathroom and the kitchen, including cabinets.

Petitioners placed the bus in service as a business vehicle in 1985. Petitioners re-ported that they made improvements totaling $2,099 in 1985 and $2,883 in 1986. Peti-tioners claimed deductions totaling $18,517 between 1985 and 1989 for depreciation, including a $2,099 deduction in 1985 pursuant to section 179.

In December 1990, the bus was destroyed by fire. In early 1991, petitioners received $58,475 from their insurance provider for the replacement value of the converted bus. Rather than repeat the conversion process on a different bus, petitioners used the insur-ance proceeds to buy land.

Petitioners filed their 1991 tax return on January 26, 1993. Petitioners did not re-quest an extension of time to file their income tax return for the year in issue. Petition-ers never reported any gain or loss from the disposition of the bus.

OPINION

Issue 1. Whether Petitioners Realized Capital Gain

Respondent determined that petitioners' adjusted basis in the bus was $824, and that petitioners realized $18,517 of section 1245 gain and $39,134 of capital gain from its disposition. Petitioners concede the section 1245 gain; however, they assert that they did not realize any capital gain from the conversion as their basis in the bus was equal to the amount of the insurance proceeds received. Petitioners' argument essentially is that their adjusted basis in their depreciable property is not decreased by depreciation that they did not claim as a deduction on their Federal income tax returns.

...

Petitioner testified that he constantly made improvements to the bus that he did not report or depreciate. Petitioners kept most of the receipts pertaining to the conversion in the bus. Thus, when the bus burned, the receipts were destroyed. However, peti-tioners were able to submit a few receipts for materials used in the conversion that total $2,231.02 for 1985 and $431.74 for 1986. At trial, petitioners submitted a list they pre-pared of the conversion items and their approximate costs. We found petitioner to be a credible witness and accept his testimony with respect to these items and their cost.

Petitioners placed the bus in service in 1985. According to petitioner, most of the ex-penditures for the listed conversion items were made in 1985. The expenditures for the conversion items in that year total $21,400; however, on their return petitioners re-ported only $2,099 for improvements to the bus, which they deducted pursuant to sec-tion 179.

During 1986 petitioners expended a total of $4,600 to recondition the front bumper, install the furnace, repaint the body, and finish the kitchen and the bathroom. On their return for 1986, petitioners reported only $2,883 as the cost of improvements made to the bus in that year.

For purposes of calculating depreciation, petitioners' bus is 5-year property. See sec. 168(c)(2)(B), I.R.C. 1954 (as amended); (Footnote 4) Rev. Proc. 83-35, 1983-1 C.B. 745, 746. It appears from the returns that petitioners' method of accounting for depreciation was to recover the acquisition and improvement costs reported in 1985 separately from the improvement costs reported in 1986. Petitioners expended a total of $40,359 during 1985 and 1986 to acquire and convert the bus into a motor home; however, they claimed only $18,517 in total depreciation from 1985 through 1989. (Footnote 5)

Pursuant to section 1011(a), the adjusted basis for determining the gain or loss from the sale or other disposition of property is the cost of the property determined under section 1012 adjusted as provided in section 1016. Section 1016(a)(2) provides, in effect, that the basis of the property shall be adjusted by the amount of depreciation previously allowed, but not less than the amount allowable, with respect to the property. Depreciation "allowed" is the amount actually deducted by the taxpayer and not challenged by the Commissioner.... Consequently, the taxpayer's basis in a depreciable asset is reduced by the greater of the amount of depreciation that is allowed or allowable in a tax year.

The expenditures that petitioners made in 1985 to acquire and improve the bus would have been recovered completely in 1989. See sec. 168(b)(1), I.R.C. 1954 (as amended). Although it may seem a harsh result as petitioners did not claim the full amount of depreciation allowable, these costs provide petitioners no basis in 1990. The expenditures that petitioners made in 1986 to improve the bus would have been recovered completely in 1990; however, as the bus was destroyed in that year, no deduction is allowed. See sec. 168(d)(2)(B), I.R.C. 1954 (as amended). Accordingly, we find that petitioners had an adjusted basis in the bus at the time of the involuntary conversion that is equal to the percentage of the costs incurred during 1986 allowable for recovery in 1990. That basis and the consequent amount of gain that petitioners must recognize can be determined by the parties in their Rule 155 calculations.

Issue 2. Addition to Tax for Failure to Timely File

Respondent determined that petitioners are liable for the addition to tax pursuant to section 6651(a)(1) for 1991. Section 6651(a)(1) imposes an addition to tax for failure to file a return on the date prescribed (determined with regard to any extension of time for filing), unless the taxpayer can establish that such a failure is due to reasonable cause and not due to willful neglect. The addition to tax is 5 percent of the amount required to be reported on the return for each month or fraction thereof during which such failure to file continues, but not to exceed 25 percent in the aggregate. See sec. 6651(a)(1). Because petitioners are calendar year taxpayers, their 1991 return was due on April 15, 1992. See sec. 6072(a). Petitioners stipulated that they did not request an extension of time to fife their 1991 income tax return and that it was filed on January 26, 1993. Petitioners' return was not timely filed. Therefore, unless petitioners can show that their failure to timely file their return was due to reasonable cause and not due to willful neglect, respondent's determination will be sustained.

The term "reasonable cause" as set forth in section 6651(a)(1) has been defined as the exercise of ordinary business care and prudence. See sec. 301.6651-1(c)(1), Proced. & Admin. Regs. "Willful neglect" means a "conscious, intentional failure or reckless indifference." See *United States v. Boyle...*, 469 U.S. 241, 245, (1985). The question of whether a failure to file a timely return is due to reasonable cause and not willful neglect is one of fact, on which petitioners bear the burden of proof....

Petitioner testified that he thought he was entitled to a tax refund, and that taxpayers who are entitled to a refund are not required to request an extension if they file after the due date. Petitioner's testimony included the statement "I don't know where I came up with that idea".

Petitioners' erroneous belief that no taxes are due does not constitute reasonable cause for the failure to timely file their income tax return.... Under these circumstances, we conclude that petitioners' failure to timely file their income tax return for 1991 was not due to reasonable cause. Accordingly, we hold that the addition to tax pursuant to section 6651(a) is properly imposed.

Issue 3. Accuracy-Related Penalty

Respondent determined that petitioners are liable for an accuracy-related penalty pursuant to section 6662(a) for ... negligence or disregard of rules or regulations.... Section 6662 provides for the imposition of a penalty equal to 20 percent of the portion of an underpayment which is attributable to negligence or disregard of rules or regulations. See sec. 6662(a) and (b)(1). For purposes of this section, the term "negligence" includes any failure to make a reasonable attempt to comply with the provisions of the internal revenue laws, to exercise ordinary and reasonable care in the preparation of a tax return, and to keep adequate books and records or to substantiate items properly. See sec. 1.6662-3(b)(1), Income Tax Regs. The term "disregard" includes any careless, reckless, or intentional disregard of rules or regulations. See sec. 6662(c).

The burden is on the taxpayer to prove the Commissioner's imposition of the penalty is in error.... Except for petitioner's testimony that he thought the insurance proceeds were not taxable because they were compensation for the casualty loss, petitioners did not address this issue at trial.

Section 6664(c)(1) provides that the penalty under section 6662(a) shall not apply to any portion of an underpayment if it is shown that there was a reasonable cause for the taxpayer's position with respect to that portion and that the taxpayer acted in good faith with respect to that portion. See sec. 6664(c)(1).

The determination of whether a taxpayer acted with reasonable cause and good faith within the meaning of section 6664(c)(1) is made on a case-by-case basis, taking into account all pertinent facts and circumstances. See sec. 1.6664-4(b)(1), Income Tax Regs. The most important factor is the extent of the taxpayer's efforts to assess the taxpayer's proper tax liability. See *id.*

In this case, petitioners were negligent and disregarded rules or regulations. Petitioners received $58,475 from the insurance company for their loss of the bus. The acquisition cost of the bus plus the cost of petitioners' listed items total no more than $40,359. Furthermore, petitioners claimed $18,517 of depreciation deductions, which decreased their basis in the bus.

Although the amount that petitioners received from the insurance company for the converted bus substantially exceeded their basis, even without considering the depreciation charges, petitioners never reported any portion of the insurance proceeds as income. In addition, although petitioner testified that he had no knowledge of tax law, petitioners apparently did not seek the advice of anyone who could have informed them of their proper tax liability.

It is evident from the record that petitioners did not make a reasonable attempt to comply with the internal revenue laws or to exercise ordinary and reasonable care in the preparation of their tax return. Finally, we do not find that there was reasonable cause for petitioners' reporting position or that they acted in good faith. Respondent is sustained on this issue.

To reflect the foregoing,

Decision will be entered under Rule 155.

FOOTNOTES:

1. Petitioners concede that they realized $18,517 of ordinary income in 1991. This is the total amount of the depreciation allowed previously on their involuntarily converted business property. See sec. 1245....

4. The bus was placed in service in 1985; thus, the method of accounting for the depreciation of the bus is the accelerated cost recovery system (ACRS) as provided by I.R.C. 1954 (as amended). Under ACRS, the depreciation deduction is calculated by multiplying the asset's unadjusted basis by the appropriate recovery percentage obtained from statutory tables for the taxable year in question. See sec. 168(b), I.R.C. 1954 (as amended).

5. Petitioners did not claim a depreciation deduction for 1990, the year the motor home was destroyed. No ACRS deduction is allowable for the taxable year in which a taxpayer disposes of property that is not real property or low-income housing. See sec. 168(d)(2)(B), I.R.C. 1954 (as amended).

Now look at sections 179(a), (b)(1)-(3), (c), and (d)(1). How does section 179 affect your analysis with respect to Brian's machine? What if the machine had cost Brian $145,000?

Is section 179 consistent with the principles of depreciation you have just studied? Congress added section 179 to the Code as part of the 1958 Act. Can you speculate as to its reasons for doing so? Section 179 represents just one of many provisions Congress has added to the Code from time to time to provide business incentives.[142]

What if Brian purchases a car for $35,000 to use in his business. How would Brian calculate his depreciation deduction? If he applies the regular rules of section 168, what is the applicable depreciation method and what is the applicable recovery period? **Review sections 168(b), 168(c), and 168(e).** If Brian elects to use the 200% declining balance method as the applicable method, he will be able to deduct a significant portion of the cost of the vehicle in the first several years, even after application of the applicable convention.

Congress was alarmed by the frequency with which high income taxpayers were able to use the new depreciation rules to purchase expensive vehicles claimed as a trade or business expense. In response, Congress enacted section 280F, limiting the depreciation deduc-

---

142. One section that deserves mention is section 199, added by the 2004 Jobs Act. Congress has long been concerned that U.S. businesses, especially corporations, are sometimes subject to higher rates of tax on profits than their foreign competitors. Congress has attempted to equalize treatment (in its view) through various special tax provisions, first through special taxation of domestic international sales corporations (DISC's), then special taxation of foreign sales corporations (FSC's), and finally by adding to the Code an extraterritorial income exclusion (ETI). But international trade bodies held each of these attempts to constitute an export subsidy that violated international trade agreements. Congress' latest attempt to address this perceived inequity is section 199. Section 199 adds a new deduction available to individuals as well as to business entities. The new provision allows, when fully phased in, a deduction of 9% of income attributable to U.S. production activities. Section 199 is complex, requiring close reading of a number of definitional and limitation provisions, and is beyond the scope a basic individual income tax course. Whether international trade groups will challenge section 199 is uncertain.

tion that would otherwise be allowed by section 168. **Look at section 280F(a).**[143] Would section 280F(a) apply to Brian's car? How much depreciation can Brian claim in each of the first three years of his ownership? How long will it take him to fully recover the cost of the car?

Now consider the interplay of the rules in sections 168 and 280F(a) with the rule of section 179. Can Brian escape the section 280F(a) limitations by making an election to apply section 179 (assuming he satisfies the other requirements of section 179)? **Look at section 280F(d)(1).**

Now suppose that what Brian buys is a Porsche Cayenne SUV for $100,000, which weighs 6600 pounds. Does section 280F(a) apply? What would be his depreciation allowance in the first year of his ownership?

Another basis for escaping some of the limitations of section 280F is to purchase a truck or van, rather than a car. Can you cite a provision that supports this statement?

———————

Look next at section 197(a)-(d). Look also at Treasury Regulation section 1.167(a)-3. Treasury Regulation section 1.167(a)-3 provides that goodwill is not depreciable. Yet goodwill is clearly a business asset that has a useful life beyond one year. Why then was it not depreciable? Note, however, that the same regulation provides that taxpayers may depreciate other intangibles. What makes those other intangibles different from goodwill?

How does section 197 affect traditional depreciation analysis under section 167(a)?[144] Recall the firm of Adams Adverts in Chapter 1 of this Part that purchased your successful advertising business for $100,000. Recall that the assets of the business amounted to a value of $25,000, yet Adams paid you $100,000. Why? How does section 197 affect this purchase?

Suppose that after Adams Adverts purchases your business, it decides to begin a new division that will specialize in Internet advertising. It names this branch, "Adams-On-Line," embarking on an extensive advertising campaign to publicize the new division and spending $20,000. How would Adams Adverts account for this expense? It decides to register "Adams-On-Line" as a trademark, which costs $25,000. How would it account for that cost?

———————

Suppose you use the proceeds of your sale to create a new business, incurring $20,000 in advertising expenses. **Look now at section 195(a).** That provision converts what might otherwise appear to be deductible expenses into non-deductible expenses when they are incurred in connection with the start-up of a business. The general rule of section 195 codifies two principles that appear in other sections of the Code: (1) section 162(a) allows the deduction of "expenses paid or incurred ... in *carrying on*

———————

143. **Examine the title of section 280F.** Section 280F(a) contains limitations on depreciation deductions for "luxury" automobiles. (Query: did Congress sensibly define what constitutes a "luxury" automobile?) Section 280F(b) contains a limitation on depreciation deductions for certain property where the taxpayer uses the property for both business and personal purposes. Remember that the cost of any property the taxpayer uses for personal purposes may not be recovered through depreciation or amortization.

144. The new provision does not, of course, allow a business that has created goodwill over the years that it has been in business to place a monetary value on that goodwill and begin recovering that value based on section 197. **See section 197(c)(2).**

any trade or business" (emphasis added); and (2) Treasury Regulation section 1.263(a)-2(a) (issued under section 263), states that creation of an asset that has "a useful life substantially beyond the taxable year" is a non-deductible capital expenditure. Therefore, the individual expenses the taxpayer incurs in the creation of her business are capital expenditures, made at a time when she is not yet carrying on the trade or business.

Now look at section 195(b). Section 195(b), as amended by the 2004 Jobs Act, provides a mechanism for the recovery of the cost of these expenses through a combination of an immediate deduction and amortization over a period of time. Suppose that prior to the time that Brian opens his new facility, he incurs expenses for investigating the likelihood that this type of business will be successful. He spends $4,000 consulting with a business advisor and $4,000 for an attorney. He also took a course in physical therapy at a local college at a cost of $2,400. How does section 195 control his treatment of these expenses? Would your answer change if the total of his start-up expenses were $52,000?

Think, finally, about this question. Suppose Brian buys a house that he will use as his personal residence. He paid $200,000, of which $50,000 was allocable to the land. Can Brian recover his cost, and if so, how?

In this Part II, you have examined the elements necessary to calculate taxable income. That is, you have observed the present choices of Congress in answering the question: What is the "proper" tax base? Then, as you saw in Carole's problem, section 1 imposes what Congress currently views as the "proper" rate. So, at this point, you are well prepared to think about the overall picture and to consider more deeply the problems with the current system that have provoked people to seek alternatives.

Further Words about Tax Policy and Tax Reform Ideas

Ever since the Tariff Act of 1913, there have been requests for changes based on various views of the ideal tax policy. As this book goes to press, the dissatisfaction with the current Code has become a view uniting liberals and conservatives. Early in this book, we gave you an excerpt describing the basic tenets of income tax policy.[145] The basic tenets have changed little in the intervening years since 1913. But, the structure of the income tax or an alternative that will most closely accomplish these goals continues to be a subject of dispute.

In early 2005, President George W. Bush issued an Executive Order. His Order initiated the appointment of an advisory panel that would study various alternatives and make recommendations for tax reform. Section 3 of the Order provides:[146]

---

145. Part I, Chapter 2, Joseph A. Pechman, *Federal Tax Policy* 5–7 (5th ed., the Brookings Institution 1987).

146. Executive Order 13369, issued January 7, 2005. The original Order required the panel to report by July 31, 2005. A later amendment, dated June 16, 2005, postponed the due date for the report to September 30, 2005.

Sec. 3. Purpose. The purpose of the Advisory Panel shall be to submit to the Secretary of the Treasury in accordance with this order a report with revenue neutral policy options for reforming the Federal Internal Revenue Code. These options should:

(a) simplify Federal tax laws to reduce the costs and administrative burdens of compliance with such laws; (b) share the burdens and benefits of the Federal tax structure in an appropriately progressive manner while recognizing the importance of homeownership and charity in American society; and (c) promote long-run economic growth and job creation, and better encourage work effort, saving, and investment, so as to strengthen the competitiveness of the United States in the global marketplace.

At least one option submitted by the Advisory Panel should use the Federal income tax as the base for its recommended reforms.

In response to the President's Order, the newly appointed panel issued the following statement on its website after a series of public hearings:[147]

During our examination of the existing system, several themes emerged from the public comments and testimony. These themes will guide our efforts as we consider options for reform:

- We have lost sight of the fact that the fundamental purpose of our tax system is to raise revenues to fund government.

- Tax provisions favoring one activity over another or providing targeted tax benefits to a limited number of taxpayers create complexity and instability, impose large compliance costs and can lead to an inefficient use of resources. A rational system would favor a broad tax base, providing special treatment only where it can be persuasively demonstrated that the effect of a deduction, exclusion, or credit justifies higher taxes paid by all taxpayers.

- The complex and unpredictable influences of the current tax system on how families and businesses arrange their affairs distorts economic decisions, leads to an inefficient allocation of resources, and hinders economic growth.

- The complexity of our tax code breeds a perception of unfairness and creates opportunities for manipulation of the rules to reduce tax. The profound lack of transparency means that individuals and businesses cannot easily understand their own tax obligations or be confident that their neighbors or competitors are paying their fair share.

- The tax system is both unstable and unpredictable. Frequent changes in the tax code, which often add to or undo previous policies, as well as the enactment of temporary provisions, result in uncertainty for businesses and households. This volatility is harmful to economic development and creates additional compliance costs.

The objectives of simplicity, fairness, and economic growth are interrelated and, at times, may be at odds with each other. Policymakers routinely make choices among these competing objectives, and, in the end, simplification is almost always sacrificed. Although these objectives at times are in tension, mean-

---

147. Statement by the Members of the President's Advisory Panel on Federal Tax Reform, reprinted on the Advisory Panel's website: *www.taxreformpanel.gov.*

ingful reform can deliver a system that is simpler, fairer, and more growth oriented than our existing tax code.

Few would disagree with these laudable themes, no matter where they stand on the political spectrum. But, as the efforts to implement proposals proceed, observers must remember that there is considerable disagreement on such issues as the amount of revenue the government needs. As has also been pointed out, fairness is "in the eyes of the beholder."[148] The lack of agreement on more than basic generalities makes agreement on concrete recommendations difficult to achieve.

Now consider Alan J. Auerbach's and Kevin A. Hassett's Introduction to the recent book *Toward Fundamental Tax Reform*:[149]

> As soon one accepts the self-evident proposition that individual welfare can be improved by government, the necessity of financing government becomes apparent. Conditional on a given level of government spending, the tax-design problem is conceptually simple, at least in its objectives. Government should seek to raise sufficient funds to finance the desired level of spending in a manner that does the least amount of damage possible, while distributing the tax burden equitably.[150]

Before taking up some of the proposals for reform, however, it makes sense to understand the dimensions of current and projected spending that require revenue:

> Since 1950, tax revenues have hovered between 16 and 20 percent of gross domestic product (GDP). Under current projections, however, government spending is expected to rise to about 27 percent of GDP by 2030 (Rivlin and Sawhill 2005). This increase is fueled mainly by rising entitlement spending for Social Security and especially Medicare and Medicaid, trends which are fueled in turn by increases in the number of elderly households and in health-care expenditures per capita. Unless the country is willing to make truly massive cuts in such expenditures relative to their projected values, a significant increase in revenues above 20 percent of GDP will be required.[151]

The substantial increase in needed revenue has prompted both liberals and conservatives to re-examine many of the programs representing legislatively creative entitlements. (Of course, there are some conservatives who believe that the appropriate goal of this re-examination should be to "starve the beast.") But, whether liberal or conservative, there is growing agreement that the federal government must make choices among expenditures or face a long-term future of large deficits.

---

148. William G. Gale, "Tax Reform Options in the Real World," Chapter 2, *Toward Fundamental Tax Reform* 34, Edited by Alan J. Auerbach and Kevin A. Hassett (American Enterprise Institute Press, 2005).

149. Auerbach and Hassett invited nine tax scholars with various viewpoints to prepare an article each expressing their views on tax reform. These views reflect the latest developments in academic literature.

150. *Id.* at 1–2. Notice that the Introduction discusses the first two of the questions we set forth as critical to a tax system. As you read a sampling of the tax reform proposals outlined *infra* by Eugene Steuerle, try to identify the discussions of these two and the other two questions.

151. William G. Gale, *supra* at 36.

The Auerbach and Hassett Introduction goes on to distill the current tax reform debate as follows:

> Although opinions differ in many other dimensions as well, it is a useful simplification to say that the tax-reform community has camps that are divided between two issues. In the first issue, some argue that marginal tax rates should be progressive, increasing along with incomes, while others believe that the equity benefit from significantly graduated rates is not worth the cost in efficiency and, accordingly, advocate a relatively flat rate structure. In the second, some hold that income is the best base for taxation, while others think the base should be consumption.[152]

Nevertheless, in their Conclusion to *Toward Fundamental Tax Reform*, Auerbach and Hassett observe that there is broad agreement that "a wide range of positive effects" would result from "either an income tax with a broader base and lower rates, or a consumption tax.[153]

It is rarely possible, however, within the political structure, to enact the necessary legislation; many powerful interest groups are usually able to shape legislation before final enactment. As Auerbach and Hassett also observe in their Conclusion:

What is Feasible?

> Both broad-based income taxes and broad-based consumption taxes would improve the overall efficiency of the economy because the current code does so much to undermine it. For example, an efficient tax code affects the decision of individuals as little as possible; yet the mortgage-interest deduction provides a very large subsidy to home ownership, and thus introduces a large economic distortion. If the political system is fully wedded to a virtually unlimited mortgage-interest deduction, any of the benefits of tax reform are unattainable. There are numerous other similar provisions in the code that are politically popular but have questionable economic merit.[154]

President Bush himself, in his Executive Order and later public statements, clearly communicated his wish for retention of both the home mortgage interest deduction and the deductibility of charitable contributions, seemingly tying the hands of his Advisory Panel on those issues. Nevertheless, whether liberal or conservative, tax policy experts seem to agree that the effort begun by President Bush's Executive Order marked an important opportunity for meaningful change.

Recall now that we began our study of the federal income tax by setting forth four questions:

(1) What is the proper rate?

(2) What is the proper tax base?

(3) What is the proper tax-paying unit?

(4) What is the proper time period?

---

152. *Id.* at 2–3.
153. Conclusion, *Toward Fundamental Tax Reform, supra* at 149–50.
154. *Id.* at 151.

Any discussion of tax policy logically requires consideration of these same four questions. As you read through the article that follows, ask yourself how the suggestions for alternatives reported by Eugene Steuerle of the Urban Institute, would answer each of these questions and how those answers would further or impede the basic tenets set forth by Pechman.[155]

Tax Reform, Federal[156]

A review of the federal government experience in reviewing and adjusting its revenue system to adjust to changes in the national economy, demography, and its institutional and political arrangements. The term usually refers to broad rather than piecemeal changes in law.

Changes to the tax laws are almost always labeled reforms, but reform as improvement, not merely amendment, generally is based upon bringing the law into closer adherence to certain principles or goals. The public finance principles of efficiency, growth, equal treatment of those in equal situations (horizontal equity or fairness), progressivity, and simplicity provide a useful listing around which tax changes can be analyzed.

Taxes generally are not good in and of themselves. They provide the means by which government is financed, and hence their benefits relate to the expenditure side of the budget. By themselves, taxes nearly always distort behavior, add complications to the lives of at least some taxpayers, and, in practice, create problems of equity between some who pay and some who are equally capable of paying, but from whom payment is more difficult to extract. Much of tax reform, therefore, is aimed at minimizing the costs of taxation — reducing the inefficiencies of taxation — more than at maximizing some efficiencies it somehow adds to society.

Historical context

At the end of the 19th century and the beginning of the 20th, many federal reform efforts were aimed at displacing or replacing old taxes with new taxes. During the 19th century, government was financed primarily through tariffs. Today large tariffs are generally viewed as both unfair and inefficient, but in the earlier period they could be assessed conveniently at the time that goods were transferred from sellers to buyers, and an accounting was engaged at the port or dock. With the rise of the corporation and the large organization, however, more elaborate accounting schemes allowed better assessment of returns to factors of production such as labor and capital. It was this development, more than any other, that allowed replacement of tariffs by income and wage taxes as the primary sources of revenues to the federal government.

As income taxes grew in size and importance, more and more attention was paid to their design, rather than their adoption, expansion, or contraction, as a major reform option. Many fights, of course, also ensued over the size of the tax system, but the revenue goal here was closely related to how large government expenditures should be, an issue that extends far beyond tax reform. But the issues were often combined and con-

---

155. Part I, Chapter 2, *Federal Tax Policy, supra.*
156. C. Eugene Steuerle, Tax reform, federal, *The Encyclopedia of Taxation & Tax Policy* 462–64, edited by Joseph J. Cordes, Robert D. Ebel, and Jane G. Gravelle (Urban Institute Press, C.D. Rom ed. 2000).

fused. In some periods, such as wartime, consensus on the need for expenditures left as a remaining debate only the issue of who should pay. In other periods, many policymakers argued for higher or lower taxes primarily on the basis of what expenditures could be financed. In these cases, the tax debate often could not be separated from the issue of size of government.

Another confusion in the tax reform debate often arose in considerations of the design of the tax base and its interaction with the progressivity of the system itself. While tax progressivity generally can be determined by the setting of tax rates, even under widely varying tax bases, reform often began with statutory rates themselves considered as fixed. Hence, when the base changed, the reform often had distributional consequences across income classes even if the initial goals of reform were unrelated to redistribution. For instance, barring offsetting changes in the tax rate structure, cutting back on a particular tax preference might be favored or opposed primarily on the grounds of what it did to the relative tax burdens of the rich or poor.

Still another source of confusion arose over use of the tax system for growth or macroeconomic purposes versus other improvements in well-being, such as might be achieved through more standard improvements in efficiency. In the United States, these issues arose particularly in tax reform debates in the post-World War II era. In tax reform options put forward in the early 1960s, for instance, President Kennedy made a strong pitch that tax reductions would help spur the economy and produce economic growth by expanding demand. At the same time, he proposed a number of changes to the tax base to make it more inclusive of different sources of income. The macroeconomic goal at the time was associated closely with Keynesian economics, and the argument put forward was that the additional money circulating in the economy would spur demand. In 1981, President Reagan put forward a tax reform proposal that also used macroeconomic arguments. Indeed, its primary features were very similar to those adopted during the Kennedy round of tax reform in the early 1960s: rate reduction and expansion of incentives for investment in physical capital, particularly equipment. In the 1981 round, however, the justification put forward was that lower tax rates would spur suppliers of labor and capital to work harder and save more; the term "supply side" was applied to this macroeconomic argument. Thus, a similarly designed tax change was justified in both cases by an appeal to macroeconomics, yet the theory or apologetics used were very different (Steuerly 1992).

When the macroeconomic justification was used, as it was for several tax reductions between the early 1960s and 1981, it often tended to dominate not only the debate but the outcome. In many of these years, tax reduction was thought to bring about an expansion of the economy, a higher rate of growth, or a quicker turn out of recession. Many of the gains were argued to be immediate in their effect. Defining the base properly, on the other hand, was a long-term objective that could always be put off until another day. Thus, in the 1960s round the question of definition was essentially abandoned and the macroeconomic goal given preference, while in 1981 almost no base broadening was proposed, and later congressional expansions tended to erode the base further.

For many tax reformers, the issues of defining the tax base in a way that would promote efficiency, fairness, and simplicity often were given far too little weight because of the greater attention given to size of revenues, progressivity of the system, and macroeconomic incentives to spur either supply or demand. To the reformers, the issues could be separated. Given a tax base, the level of revenues and degree of progressivity could be separated. Given a tax base, the level of revenues and degree of progressivity could be determined by adjusting the tax rate schedule, including allowances for low-income individuals. Hence, the issue of what would be included in the base for the most part was a separable issue. If a given deduction was eliminated, for instance, any revenue raised could be offset by a reduction in rates, and any effect on progressivity could be offset by a change in the rate schedule itself.

Base broadening to include more items of income, better compliance with respect to items that were reported poorly, and reductions in preferences began to receive much more attention after 1981. At that time, the issue was again driven by a concern that went beyond tax reform: large levels of government deficit. Several base-broadening reforms in the 1980s were enacted as part of deficit reduction bills. President Reagan's strong antipathy to raising tax rates, coupled with Congress's reluctance or inability to deal with entitlement types of spending, left base broadening not so much a popular option as one of the least unpopular of choices for reducing the deficit.

In 1984 to 1986, the nation engaged in an extensive debate over a tax reform that would center almost entirely on the tax base itself and the lower rates that might be possible if that base were appropriately expanded. The effort for the most part attempted to put aside the issues of total revenues, progressivity, and short-term macroeconomic incentives for growth. Thus, the reform was designed approximately to be "revenue neutral" and "distributionally neutral." A large number of deductions, exclusions, credits, and other preferences were either pared or eliminated. Rates were reduced significantly, but unlike either the Kennedy round of rate reductions or the Reagan 1981 round of rate reductions or the Reagan 1981 round, they were paid for through other tax changes. Like all reforms, the 1986 Tax Reform Act was made possible by a combination of opportunities: a president who especially disliked high tax rates, the rapid expansion of tax shelters, the increased income taxation of the poor, and growing concerns over taxation of the family.

By the time the act was signed into law, it involved the most comprehensive reform of this type ever achieved for the income tax. According to Witte (1991), "Of the 72 provisions which tightened tax expenditures, 14 tax expenditures were eventually repealed, a figure approximately equal to the total that had been repealed from 1913 to 1985." Treasury had advocated repeal of 38 tax expenditures. Another detailed analysis, by Neubig and Joulfaian (1988), indicated that under some simplifying assumptions, tax reforms produced the equivalent of $193 billion in tax expenditure reduction for the year 1988. Base broadening was directly responsible for $77 billion of this total, and the rate reduction it made possible indirectly reduced the value of tax expenditures by $1.6 billion.

Further reform options

Debate over federal tax reform will continue as long as there is a tax system. Many discussions in the modern era combine different reform options into a single package. Among the principal reforms suggested are the following:

Conversion of income tax to a consumption tax

Should the tax base be reduced to exclude all purchases of capital equipment and net saving? Many current proposals would begin, as a base, with a subtraction method value-added tax applied to business—that is, by taking current income and subtracting net purchases of assets (Bradford 1986). To this system would be added an individual tax—either on wages at the individual level, or a complementary consumption tax at the individual level—which essentially would attempt to allow subtraction of savings from income. Some versions of these more elaborate reforms would maintain or expand an estate tax (Aaron and Galper 1985), and thus could be considered more as extending the accounting period for the income tax from a year to a lifetime, rather than excluding from taxation any income that was not consumed by the person who earned it.

Value-added taxes

More narrow reforms would simply add a value-added tax (VAT) to the existing tax system. In many cases, the VAT would follow more traditional types of consumption taxes adopted in other countries. The motives are diverse—increasing revenues to support some expenditure like health care, increasing the share of government burden paid by the elderly, who now receive a substantial share of government expenditures, financing the reduction in taxes on labor or on capital, and adopting a tax with a border tax adjustment (rebate of taxes) for exports.

Flat rate taxes

Still other reforms would convert the tax system into one with a single rate of tax applying to most of the tax base. Strictly speaking, most of these proposals allow some income to be taxed at a zero rate, so they are not flat. Most current proposals also are consumption tax proposals in that they allow the cost of capital equipment to be written off (expensed) right away rather than depreciated over time (Hall and Rabushka 1985). If carried out throughout the tax structure, flat taxes have the advantage of dramatically reducing the requirements for individual filing. That is, if the same rate applies to all income, it is not necessary to know to whom the income accrues. A payer-employer, bank, corporation—could simply pay over a flat rate on the tax base, and the amount paid over or withheld on behalf of eventual recipients would be exactly equal to the final tax owed. No filing or reconciliation would be required. This goal might also be achieved in part through essentially flat taxes on particular items of income—a scheduler approach more popular in many other industrialized countries. Generally speaking, a flat rate tax would also reduce taxes for those with the highest incomes and increase the share of the tax burden borne by those with incomes in the middle range.

Income tax reform

Many reforms would expand the efforts of the 1980s to define the tax base in a manner considered appropriate. Often these involve eliminating social preferences, cutting back on the value of various exclusions or deductions, and eliminating the taxation of items that would not legitimately be included in a system that more purely taxed income once and only once. There might be a reduction in the special preferences applied to health insurance purchased by employers, for example. Or integration of corporate and personal income taxes would eliminate the double taxation of capital income earned and paid out to equity owners of corporations.

Integration of tax and transfer systems

In recent years, there has been increased realization not only that expenditures are hidden in the tax system, but that taxes are hidden in the expenditure system. Most transfers from the government involve some sort of implicit tax. The Social Security benefit formula, for instance, provides for lower returns on taxes of higher-income individuals. Welfare systems typically phase out benefits as income rises. Means testing may be applied to a variety of health benefits. Each of these tax systems tends to develop independently, leading to a combined tax system that is little understood or appreciated. Some reforms would aim themselves more directly at determining an integrated rate structure for the systems as a whole. Here, of course, tax and expenditure reform become inseparable.

Tax simplification

Seldom, if ever, has tax reform focused primarily upon simplification. Although it was one of the goals of the 1986 reform, it was achieved only in part for moderate-income taxpayers, while filing became more complex for many businesses or individuals with significant capital income. Simplification might be sought through one of the broader reforms listed above, or it could be pursued step by step within the existing income tax framework.

Which, if any, of the reform proposals outlined by Steuerle adequately satisfy the purpose stated by President Bush in his Executive Order? Do you think that one or more of these proposals is compatible with the themes described by the Advisory Panel?[157]

---

157. The Advisory Panel issued its final report on November 1, 2005. (You may find the full report reprinted on the Advisory Panel's website: *www.taxreformpanel.gov.*) The Panel recommended two approaches to reform, briefly described as follows, in its transmittal letter to Treasury Secretary Snow:

> We unanimously recommend two options to reform the tax code. We refer to one option as the Simplified Income Tax Plan and the other option as the Growth and Investment Tax Plan. Both of them are preferable to our current system. Both satisfy the President's directive to recommend options that are simple, fair, and pro-growth.
>
> The Simplified Income Tax Plan dramatically simplifies our tax code, cleans out targeted tax breaks that have cluttered the system, and lowers rates. It does away with gimmicks and hidden traps like the alternative minimum tax. It preserves and simplifies major features of our current tax code, including benefits for home ownership, charitable giving, and health care, and makes them available to all Americans. It removes many of the disincentives to saving that exist in our current code, and it makes small business tax calculations much easier. It also offers an updated corporate tax structure to make it easier for American corporations to compete in global markets.
>
> The second recommended option, the Growth and Investment Tax Plan builds on the Simplified Income Tax Plan and adds a major new feature: moving the tax code closer to a system that would not tax families or businesses on their savings or investments. It would allow businesses to expense or write-off their investments immediately. It would lower tax rates, and impose a single, low tax rate on dividends, interest, and capital gains.
>
> As directed by the President, our recommendations have been designed to raise approximately the same amount of money as the current tax system. The issue of whether the tax code should raise more or less revenue was outside of our mandate....

The Panel concluded its transmittal letter with the following admonition:

> The effort to reform the tax code is noble in its purpose, but it requires political willpower. Many stand waiting to defend their breaks, deductions, and loopholes, and to defeat our efforts. That is part of the legislative process. But the interests of a few should not stand in the way of the tax code's primary goal: to raise funds efficiently for the common defense, vital social programs, and other goals of shared purpose. If we agree the goals serve us all, we must also agree that the costs must be fairly borne by all.
>
> This report aims to give voice to the frustrated American taxpayer and to provide a blueprint for lasting reform. We look forward to a national debate and a better tax system....

As this book goes to press, neither the Bush administration nor Congress has furthered the national tax reform debate.

III. Who Is the "Proper" Taxpayer?

Introduction

Identification of the proper taxpayer on whom tax should be imposed is often free from doubt; indeed, it usually seems quite obvious. For example, most taxpayers rightfully assume that monies they earn from providing services represent their own incomes. Owners of property also assume that the income the property produces will be taxable, if at all, to them; dividends to the stockholder, interest income to the bondholder, rent to the landlord appear inarguably the income of the owners of those assets.

In many cases, however, taxpayers have sought to shift income through various devices in order to reduce the overall tax burden on the income. How can shifting income lower the overall tax burden on that income? **Recall the progressive rate schedule in section 1.** Furthermore, many tax theorists and policy-makers have argued that the proper "taxpayer" is not necessarily the individual, but either husband and wife or the family unit as a whole. We take up the broad category of assignment of income as the first of the issues relating to a broader definition of the "taxpayer." Although we consider assignment of income in this chapter in family settings, the issue also arises frequently in other cases involving related taxpayers, for example, a corporation and its subsidiary, or commonly controlled business entities. Whether in the family setting or in a business setting, the fundamental issue remains: who is the proper taxpayer.

Identification of particular transactions that taxpayers structure are also often free from doubt; when a landlord enters into a lease with a tenant, when a family sells its home in order to move to a new location, the substance of the transaction follows the form. But form and substance do not always coincide. Taxpayers often construct transactions to obtain the most desirable tax results.

When does the desire for a certain tax effect so overtake the substance of the transaction that form and substance diverge? For example, what appears to be a lease may, in reality, be a sale, and what appears to be a sale may, in reality, be merely an option to purchase at a later time. In these types of cases, the substance of the transaction is not what the designated form suggests. If the form determines the tax consequences, one outcome will follow; if the true substance determines the tax consequences, another outcome will ensue. In such a case, the taxpayer who chose the form almost certainly did so in order to attain the tax consequences dictated by the form, rather than by the substance. Creative tax planning of this type has produced substantial litigation.[1] Thus, we introduce you to the important doctrine of "substance over form," a doctrine that appears throughout the tax law. For now, we will consider it only in the context of the issue of who is the proper taxpayer. We will return to it in other guises later.

---

1. While in many cases, courts have forced the taxpayer to accept the tax consequences of the true substance of the transactions, in other cases, courts have forced the taxpayer to endure the results of the form that she herself chose.

Chapter 1

Assignment of Income

A. Basic Principles

Many of the instances in which the question arises regarding who is the proper taxpayer may be included in the broad category of the doctrine known as assignment of income. The Supreme Court addressed the doctrine in an important case involving a husband and wife prior to the enactment of special rates for filing a joint income tax return in 1948.[1] Note the date on which the taxpayers entered into their contractual arrangement. Can you identify their motivation for doing so?

LUCAS v. EARL
281 U.S. 111 (1930)

MR. JUSTICE HOLMES delivered the opinion of the Court.

This case presents the question whether the respondent, Earl, could be taxed for the whole of the salary and attorney's fees earned by him in the years 1920 and 1921, or should be taxed for only a half of them in view of a contract with his wife which we shall mention. The Commissioner of Internal Revenue and the Board of Tax Appeals imposed a tax upon the whole, but their decision was reversed by the Circuit Court of Appeals.... A writ of certiorari was granted by this Court.

By the contract, made in 1901, Earl and his wife agreed "that any property either of us now has or may hereafter acquire ... in any way, either by earnings (including salaries, fees, etc.), or any rights by contract or otherwise, during the existence of our marriage, or which we or either of us may receive by gift, bequest, devise, or inheritance, and all the proceeds, issues, and profits of any and all such property shall be treated and considered and hereby is declared to be received, held, taken, and owned by us as joint tenants, and not otherwise, with the right of survivorship." The validity of the contract is not questioned, and we assume it to be unquestionable under the law of the State of California, in which the parties lived. Nevertheless we are of opinion that the Commissioner and Board of Tax Appeals were right.

The Revenue Act of 1918 ... imposes a tax upon the net income of every individual including "income derived from salaries, wages, or compensation for personal ser-

---

1. Although the Code has permitted the filing of a joint return since 1918, no special rate table applied to joint returns until 1948.

vice ... of whatever kind and in whatever form paid,"... A very forcible argument is presented to the effect that the statute seeks to tax only income beneficially received, and that taking the question more technically the salary and fees became the joint property of Earl and his wife on the very first instant on which they were received. We well might hesitate upon the latter proposition, because however the matter might stand between husband and wife he was the only party to the contracts by which the salary and fees were earned, and it is somewhat hard to say that the last step in the performance of those contracts could be taken by anyone but himself alone. But this case is not to be decided by attenuated subtleties. It turns on the import and reasonable construction of the taxing act. There is no doubt that the statute could tax salaries to those who earned them and provide that the tax could not be escaped by anticipatory arrangements and contracts however skillfully devised to prevent the salary when paid from vesting even for a second in the man who earned it. That seems to us the import of the statute before us and we think that no distinction can be taken according to the motives leading to the arrangement by which the fruits are attributed to a different tree from that on which they grew.

Judgment reversed.

————————

Consider the following questions about *Lucas v. Earl*.

1. What was the nature of the contract entered into by Mr. and Mrs. Earl?

2. Explain Mr. Earl's position in the case. Explain the government's position. Why would the government care that Mr. Earl was paying tax on only one-half of his income? Mrs. Earl was presumably paying tax on the other half, so how did the government lose tax revenue on the deal?

3. How would you express the rule from this case?

4. How, if at all, is the fruit/tree analogy that Justice Holmes used in this case related to the fruit/tree analogy that Justice Pitney used in *Eisner v. Macomber*? See *Eisner v. Macomber*.

The phrase "assignment of income" includes diverse plans for transferring income from a higher-rate taxpayer to a lower-rate one. A common example is the parent who attempts to transfer his or her income to a child. While these schemes often involve an attempt to assign income from services, as in the case of *Lucas v. Earl*, they may also involve attempts to assign income from property.

————————

Reconsider the case of Taft v. Bowers. We read that case to learn that the donee of property steps into the shoes of the donor with respect to basis, preserving the potential gain—or loss—on the property.[2] But what follows from the basis rule established in *Taft v. Bowers* is that the father in the case was able to assign the income from the appre-

————————

2. Of course, *Taft v. Bowers* did not concern an unrecognized loss. The Court's reasoning was correct at the time the case was decided. Although the general rule would be the same, that is, that the basis rules would preserve the potential gain or loss, Congress has since inserted a special rule concerning the basis of gift property, limiting losses. If the value of gift property is less than its basis at the time of the gift, the donee must use the fair market value, rather than the donor's basis for purposes of determining a loss on a subsequent disposition. **See section 1015(a) and review the problems following Taft v. Bowers.**

ciation in the value of the property to his daughter. Read the following case and consider its result in comparison with *Taft v. Bowers* and *Lucas v. Earl*.

HELVERING v. HORST
311 U.S. 112 (1940)

MR. JUSTICE STONE delivered the opinion of the Court.

The sole question for decision is whether the gift, during the donor's taxable year, of interest coupons detached from the bonds, delivered to the donee and later in the year paid at maturity, is the realization of income taxable to the donor.

In 1934 and 1935 respondent, the owner of negotiable bonds, detached from them negotiable interest coupons shortly before their due date and delivered them as a gift to his son who in the same year collected them at maturity. The Commissioner ruled that under the applicable § 22 of the Revenue Act of 1934, ... the interest payments were taxable, in the years when paid, to the respondent donor who reported his income on the cash receipts basis. The Circuit Court of appeals reversed the order of the Board of Tax Appeals sustaining the tax.... We granted certiorari, because of the importance of the question in the administration of the revenue laws and because of an asserted conflict in principle of the decision below with that of *Lucas v. Earl*, 281 U.S. 111....

The court below thought that as the consideration for the coupons had passed to the obligor, the donor had, by the gift, parted with all control over them and their payment, and for that reason the case was distinguishable from *Lucas v. Earl*, supra, ... where the assignment of compensation for services had preceded the rendition of the services, and where the income was held taxable to the donor.

The holder of a coupon bond is the owner of two independent and separable kinds of right. One is the right to demand and receive at maturity the principal amount of the bond representing capital investment. The other is the right to demand and receive interim payments of interest on the investment in the amounts and on the dates specified by the coupons. Together they are an obligation to pay principal and interest given in exchange for money or property which was presumably the consideration for the obligation of the bond. Here respondent, as owner of the bonds, had acquired the legal right to demand payment at maturity of the interest specified by the coupons and the power to command its payment to others, which constituted an economic gain to him.

Admittedly not all economic gain of the taxpayer is taxable income. From the beginning the revenue laws have been interpreted as defining realization of income as the taxable event rather than the acquisition of the right to receive it. And realization is not deemed to occur until the income is paid. But the decisions and regulations have consistently recognized that receipt in cash or property is not the only characteristic of realization of income to a taxpayer on the cash receipts basis. Where the taxpayer does not receive payment of income in money or property realization may occur when the last step is taken by which he obtains the fruition of the economic gain which has already accrued to him. *Old Colony Trust Co. v. Commissioner*, 279 U.S. 716....

In the ordinary case the taxpayer who acquires the right to receive income is taxed when he receives it, regardless of the time when his right to receive payment accrued.

But the rule that income is not taxable until realized has never been taken to mean that the taxpayer, even on the cash receipts basis, who has fully enjoyed the benefit of the economic gain represented by his right to receive income, can escape taxation because he has not himself received payment of it from his obligor. The rule, founded on administrative convenience, is only one of postponement of the tax to the final event of enjoyment of the income, usually the receipt of it by the taxpayer, and not one of exemption from taxation where the enjoyment is consummated by some event other than the taxpayer's personal receipt of money or property.... This may occur when he has made such use or disposition of his power to receive or control the income as to procure in its place other satisfactions which are of economic worth. The question here is, whether because one who in fact receives payment for services or interest payments is taxable only on his receipt of the payments, he can escape all tax by giving away his right to income in advance of payment. If the taxpayer procures payment directly to his creditors of the items of interest or earnings due him, see *Old Colony Trust Co. v. Commissioner, supra*; ... *United States v. Kirby Lumber Co.*, 284 U.S. 1, or if he sets up a revocable trust with income payable to the objects of his bounty, ... he does not escape taxation because he did not actually receive the money. Cf.... *Helvering v. Clifford*, 309 U.S. 331.

Underlying the reasoning in these cases is the thought that income is realized by the assignor because he, who owns or controls the source of the income, also controls the disposition of that which he could have received himself and diverts the payment from himself to others as the means of procuring the satisfaction of his wants. The taxpayer has equally enjoyed the fruits of his labor or investment and obtained the satisfaction of his desires whether he collects and uses the income to procure those satisfactions, or whether he disposes of his right to collect it as the means of procuring them....

Although the donor here, by the transfer of the coupons, has precluded any possibility of his collecting them himself he has nevertheless, by his act, procured payment of the interest, as a valuable gift to a member of his family. Such a use of his economic gain, the right to receive income, to procure a satisfaction which can be obtained only by the expenditure of money or property, would seem to be the enjoyment of the income whether the satisfaction is the purchase of goods at the corner grocery, the payment of his debt there, or such non-material satisfactions as may result from the payment of a campaign or community chest contribution, or a gift to his favorite son. Even though he never receives the money he derives money's worth from the disposition of the coupons which he has used as money or money's worth in the procuring of a satisfaction which is procurable only by the expenditure of money or money's worth. The enjoyment of the economic benefit accruing to him by virtue of his acquisition of the coupons is realized as completely as it would have been if he had collected the interest in dollars and expended them for any of the purposes named....

In a real sense he has enjoyed compensation for money loaned or services rendered, and not any the less so because it is his only reward for them. To say that one who has made a gift thus derived from interest or earnings paid to his donee has never enjoyed or realized the fruits of his investment or labor, because he has assigned them instead of collecting them himself and then paying them over to the donee, is to affront common understanding and to deny the facts of common experience. Common understanding and experience are the touchstones for the interpretation of the revenue laws.

The power to dispose of income is the equivalent of ownership of it. The exercise of that power to procure the payment of income to another is the enjoyment, and hence the realization, of the income by him who exercises it. We have had no difficulty in applying that proposition where the assignment preceded the rendition of the services, *Lucas v. Earl, supra;* .... But it is the assignment by which the disposition of income is controlled when the service precedes the assignment, and in both cases it is the exercise of the power of disposition of the interest or compensation, with the resulting payment to the donee, which is the enjoyment by the donor of income derived from them.

This was emphasized in *Blair v. Commissioner,* 300 U.S. 5, on which respondent relies, where the distinction was taken between a gift of income derived from an obligation to pay compensation and a gift of income-producing property.... Since the gift was deemed to be a gift of the property the income from it was held to be the income of the owner of the property, who was the donee, not the donor refinement which was unnecessary if respondent's contention here is right, but one clearly inapplicable to gifts of interest or wages. Unlike income thus derived from an obligation to pay interest or compensation, the income of the trust was regarded as no more the income of the donor than would be the rent from a lease or a crop raised on a farm after the leasehold or the farm had been given away. *Blair v. Commissioner, supra,* [300 U.S. at 12].... We have held without deviation that where the donor retains control of the trust property the income is taxable to him although paid to the donee.... Cf. *Helvering v. Clifford, supra.*

The dominant purpose of the revenue laws is the taxation of income to those who earn or otherwise create the right to receive it and enjoy the benefit of it when paid.... The tax laid by the 1934 Revenue Act upon income derived from ... wages, or compensation for personal service, of whatever kind and in whatever form paid, ... ; also from interest ... therefore cannot fairly be interpreted as not applying to income derived from interest or compensation when he who is entitled to receive it makes use of his power to dispose of it in procuring satisfactions which he would otherwise procure only by the use of the money when received.

It is the statute which taxes the income to the donor although paid to his donee. *Lucas v. Earl, supra;* ... True, in those cases the service which created the right to income followed the assignment, and it was arguable that in point of legal theory the right to the compensation vested instantaneously in the assignor when paid, although he never received it; while here the right of the assignor to receive the income antedated the assignment which transferred the right and thus precluded such an instantaneous vesting. But the statute affords no basis for such attenuated subtleties. The distinction was explicitly rejected as the basis of decision in *Lucas v. Earl.* It should be rejected here, for no more than in the *Earl* case can the purpose of the statute to tax the income to him who earns, or creates and enjoys it be escaped by anticipatory arrangements however skillfully devised to prevent the income from vesting even for a second in the donor.

Nor is it perceived that there is any adequate basis for distinguishing between the gift of interest coupons here and a gift of salary or commissions. The owner of a negotiable bond and of the investment which it represents, if not the lender, stands in the place of the lender. When, by the gift of the coupons, he has separated his right to interest payments from his investment and procured the payment of the interest to his donee, he has enjoyed the economic benefits of the income in the same manner and to the same extent as though the transfer were of earnings; and in both cases the import of the statute is that the fruit is not to be attributed to a different tree from that on which it grew. See *Lucas v. Earl.* . . .

Reversed.

————————

Consider the following questions.

1. What is a coupon bond?

2. **Recall** *Eisner v. Macomber* **and** *Helvering v. Bruun.* What does *Horst* add to the *concept* of realization?

3. What is the difference between the father's gift in *Taft v. Bowers* and the father's gift in *Helvering v. Horst* that justifies the difference in outcomes with respect to the father's success (or lack of success) in assigning income from property?[3] Can you reconcile these two cases?

4. Can you reconcile the outcomes of *Taft v. Bowers*, *Helvering v. Horst*, and *Lucas v. Earl*?

The father in *Taft v. Bowers* transferred the stock to his daughter and, therefore, transferred as well the appreciation in the value of the stock that had accrued at the time of the transfer. Recognizing that appreciation in the value of an asset constitutes unrealized income, he was successful in transferring that income to his daughter. The income, when later realized, incurred a tax at the daughter's, rather than the father's, rate of tax. Thus, it seems clear that if the father in *Helvering v. Horst* had transferred ownership of the underlying asset, the bond, to his son, he would have been successful in transferring the interest income from the bond to his son as well. But read the following case.

SALVATORE v. COMMISSIONER

T.C. Memo 1970-30

FEATHERSTON, Judge: Respondent determined a deficiency in petitioner's income tax for 1963 in the amount of $31,016.60. The only issue presented for decision is whether petitioner is taxable on all or only one-half of the gain realized on the sale of certain real property in 1963.

Findings of Fact

Petitioner was a legal resident of Greenwich, Connecticut, at the time her petition was filed. She filed an individual Federal income tax return for 1963 with the district director of internal revenue, Hartford Connecticut.

————————

3. The Court also cited the case of *Helvering v. Clifford*, 309 U.S. 331 (1940). In that case, a taxpayer transferred income-producing property to a revocable trust and provided that the income be payable to his wife. The trust was to end in five years or on the earlier of his or his wife's death. The Court held that the income should be taxed to the grantor because he had retained both ownership through his creation of a short-term revocable trust and significant powers with respect to it (dominion and control).

Petitioner's husband operated an oil and gas service station in Greenwich, Connecticut, for a number of years prior to his death on October 7, 1948. His will, dated December 6, 1941, contained the following pertinent provisions:

SECOND: I give devise and bequeath all of my estate both real and personal of whatsoever the same may consist and wheresoever the same may be situated of which I may die possessed or be entitled to at the time of my decease, to my beloved wife, SUSIE SALVATORE, to be hers absolutely and forever.

I make no provision herein for my beloved children because I am confident that their needs and support will be provided for by my beloved wife.

. . .

FOURTH: I hereby give my Executors full power to sell any and all of my property in their discretion and to execute any and all necessary deed or deeds of conveyance of my said property or any part or parts thereof, and which said deed or deeds, conveyance or assignment so executed by my Executors shall be as good and effectual to pass the title to the property therein described and conveyed as if the same had been executed by me in my lifetime.

For several years after her husband's death petitioner's three sons, Amedeo, Eugene, and Michael, continued operating the

service station with the help of her daughter Irene, who kept the books of the business. Sometime prior to 1958, however, Michael left the service station to undertake other business endeavors; and in 1958 Eugene left to enter the real estate business, leaving Amedeo alone to manage and operate the service station.

During this period and until 1963, petitioner received $100 per week from the income of the service station. This sum was not based on the fair rental of the property, but was geared to petitioner's needs for her support. The remaining income was divided among the family members who worked in the business.

The land on which the service station was located became increasingly valuable. Several major oil companies from time to time made purchase proposals, which were considered by members of the family. Finally, in the early summer of 1963 representatives of Texaco, Inc. (hereinafter Texaco), approached Amedeo regarding the purchase of the service station property. Petitioner called a family conference and asked for advice on whether the property should be sold. Realizing that Amedeo alone could not operate the station at peak efficiency, petitioner and her children decided to sell the property if a reasonable offer could be obtained.

Amedeo continued his negotiations with Texaco and ultimately received an offer of $295,000. During the course of the negotiations Eugene discovered that tax liens in the amount of $8,000 were outstanding against the property. In addition, there was an outstanding mortgage, securing a note held by Texaco, on which approximately $50,000 remained unpaid. The family met again to consider Texaco's offer.

As a result of the family meeting (including consultation with petitioner's daughter Geraldine, who lived in Florida), it was decided that the proposal should be accepted and that the proceeds should be used, first, to satisfy the tax liens and any other outstanding liabilities. Second, petitioner was to receive $100,000, the estimated amount needed to generate income for her life of about $5,000 per year the approximate equivalent of the $100 per week she previously received out of the service station income. Third, the balance was to be divided equally among the five children. To effectuate this family understanding, it was agreed that petitioner would first convey a one-half interest in the property to the children and that deeds would then be executed by petitioner and the children conveying the property to Texaco.

On July 24, 1963, petitioner formally accepted Texaco's offer by executing an agreement to sell the property to Texaco for $295,000, the latter making a down payment of $29,500. Subsequently, on August 28, 1963, petitioner executed a warranty deed conveying an undivided one-half interest in the property to her five children. This deed was received for record on September 6, 1963. By warranty deeds dated August 28 and 30, 1963, and received for record on September 6, 1963, petitioner and her five children conveyed their interest in the property to Texaco; Texaco thereupon tendered $215,582.12, the remainder of the purchase price less the amount due on the outstanding mortgage.

Petitioner filed a Federal gift tax return for 1963, reporting gifts made to each of her five children on August 1, 1963, of a 1/10 interest in the property and disclosing a gift tax due in the amount of $10,744.35.

After discharge of the mortgage and the tax liens the remaining proceeds of the sale (including the down payment) amounted to $237,082, of which one-half, $118,541, was paid to petitioner. From the other half of the proceeds the gift tax of $10,744.35 was paid and the balance was distributed to the children.

In her income tax return for 1963 petitioner reported as her share of the gain from the sale of the service station property a long-term capital gain of $115,063 plus an ordinary gain of $665. Each of the children reported in his 1963 return a proportionate share of the balance of the gain.

In the notice of deficiency respondent determined that petitioner's gain on the sale of the service station property was $238,856, all of which was taxable as long-term capital gain. Thereafter each of petitioner's children filed protective claims for refund of the taxes which they had paid on their gains from the sale of the service station property.

Opinion

The only question is whether petitioner is taxable on all or only one-half of the gain realized from the sale of the service station property. This issue must be resolved in accordance with the following principle stated by the Supreme Court in *Commissioner v. Court Holding Co....*, 324 U.S. 331, 334 (1945):

> The incidence of taxation depends upon the substance of a transaction. The tax consequences which arise from gains from a sale of property are not finally to be determined solely by the means employed to transfer legal title. Rather, the transaction must be viewed as a whole, and each step, from the commencement of negotiations to the consummation of the sale, is relevant. *A sale by one person cannot be transformed for tax purposes into a sale by another by using the latter as a conduit through which to pass title.* To permit the true nature of a transaction to be disguised by mere formalisms, which exist solely to alter tax liabilities, would seriously impair the effective administration of the tax policies of Congress. [Footnote omitted. Emphasis added.]

The evidence is unmistakably clear that petitioner owned the service station property prior to July 24, 1963, when she contracted to sell it to Texaco. Her children doubtless expected ultimately to receive the property or its proceeds, either through gifts or inheritance, and petitioner may have felt morally obligated to pass it on to them. But at that time the children held no property interest therein. Petitioner's subsequent conveyance, unsupported by consideration, of an undivided one-half interest in the property to her children all of whom were fully aware of her prior agreement to sell the property was merely an intermediate step in the transfer of legal title from petitioner to Texaco; petitioner's children were only conduit[s] through which to pass title. That petitioner's conveyance to the children may have been a bona fide completed gift prior to the transfer of title to Texaco, as she contends, is immaterial in determining the income tax consequences of the sale, for the form of a transaction cannot be permitted to prevail over its substance. In substance, petitioner made an anticipatory assignment to her children of one-half of the income from the sale of the property.

The artificiality of treating the transaction as a sale in part by the children is confirmed by the testimony by petitioner's witnesses that the sum retained by her from the sale was a computed amount an amount sufficient to assure that she would receive income in the amount of approximately $5,000 annually. If the sales price had been less, petitioner would have retained a larger percentage of the proceeds; if more, we infer, she would have received a smaller percentage. (Footnote 2) While the children's desire to provide for their mother's care and petitioner's willingness to share the proceeds of her property with her children during her lifetime may be laudable, her tax liabilities cannot be altered by a rearrangement of the legal title after she had already contracted to sell the property to Texaco.

All the gain from sale of the service station property was taxable to petitioner....

Decision will be entered for the respondent.

FOOTNOTE:

2. Eugene Salvatore testified as follows:

Q. You stated that you wanted one hundred thousand dollars for your mother. That is, this was to be her share, more or less?

A. Yes.

Q. If the property was sold for one hundred thousand dollars would your mother have kept all the money?

A. She had to.

Q. She would have?

A. She would have kept all the money.

Q. Because she needed the money to live on the interest?

A. Because we felt she needed it to live on.

Q. The children would have got nothing?

A. If she got $90 a week the five children would have made up the difference. We felt she needed the money to live on.

Now consider the following questions about the case.

1. What is a warranty deed?

2. Construct a time-line of the relevant dates leading up to the transfer of title to Texaco. With what date should your chart begin?

3. Why did Mrs. Salvatore report only one-half the gain on the sale of the property?

4. Could Mrs. Salvatore have structured the transaction differently in order to accomplish her desired outcome? How would you have advised her to accomplish her plan?

5. Is this case more like *Helvering v. Horst* or more like *Taft v. Bowers*? Why?

6. The court states that "[i]n substance, petitioner made an anticipatory assignment to her children of one-half of the income from the sale of the property." Have you seen similar language in any other case? **Locate sentence in *Lucas v. Earl* that includes the phrase anticipatory arrangements.**

B. Intra-Family Transfers

It is, of course, understandable that a family member might want to make a gift to another member of the family. But suppose the motivation is, in part at least, the desire to reduce the tax burden that would otherwise apply to income from services or property? Intra-family transactions have created many classic examples of assignment of income. Both types of assignment of income: those involving income from the performance of services and those involving income from property, deserve discussion here.

1. The Kiddie Tax

Until the Tax Reform Act of 1986, a common planning device employed by parents and grandparents allowed them to transfer income-producing property to children in order to lower the tax rate applicable to the income from the property. The plan depended upon the fact that before 1987, children were treated as separate taxpayers. Therefore, the income on the property would be taxed at the child's lower rate of tax (instead of the parents' higher rate) despite the likelihood that the income would simply replace the need for parental income for the support of the child. Congress amended the Code by adding section 1(g), requiring that the unearned income[4] of a child under 14 be taxed at the parents' rate. Section 510 of the Tax Increase Prevention and Reconciliation Act of 2005 amended section 1(g); effective January 1, 2006, the section is applicable to the unearned income of children under the age of 18. Section 1(g), however, does not differentiate between income from property given to the child by the parent and other income; rather, it applies to all unearned income. Popularly known as the kiddie tax, section 1(g) represents another of those complicated provisions, applicable to many taxpayers but difficult for the average parent to comprehend, that can justifiably be characterized as a trap for the unwary.

Glance at section 1(g). Then consider the following form that a parent must complete in order to calculate the amount of the kiddie tax. (Note that the form does not reflect the recent amendment to section 1(g)(2)(A), which now makes the section applicable to the unearned income of children under the age of 18.)

_____

Consider the following questions.

1. Why did Congress extend the reach of section 1(g)?

_____

4. What is "unearned income"?

Form 8615

Department of the Treasury
Internal Revenue Service   (99)

**Tax for Children Under Age 14
With Investment Income of More Than $1,600**

▶ Attach only to the child's Form 1040, Form 1040A, or Form 1040NR.
▶ See separate instructions.

OMB No. 1545-0074

2005

Attachment
Sequence No. **33**

Child's name shown on return | Child's social security number

Before you begin: If the child, the parent, or any of the parent's other children under age 14 must use the Schedule D Tax Worksheet or has income from farming or fishing, see **Pub. 929**, Tax Rules for Children and Dependents. It explains how to figure the child's tax using the **Schedule D Tax Worksheet** or **Schedule J** (Form 1040).

A   Parent's name (first, initial, and last). **Caution:** See instructions before completing.

B Parent's social security number

C   Parent's filing status (check one):

☐ Single   ☐ Married filing jointly   ☐ Married filing separately   ☐ Head of household   ☐ Qualifying widow(er)

Part I	**Child's Net Investment Income**		
1	Enter the child's investment income (see instructions)	**1**	
2	If the child **did not** itemize deductions on **Schedule A** (Form 1040 or Form 1040NR), enter $1,600. Otherwise, see instructions	**2**	
3	Subtract line 2 from line 1. If zero or less, **stop;** do not complete the rest of this form but **do** attach it to the child's return	**3**	
4	Enter the child's **taxable income** from Form 1040, line 43; Form 1040A, line 27; or Form 1040NR, line 40	**4**	
5	Enter the **smaller** of line 3 or line 4. If zero, **stop;** do not complete the rest of this form but **do** attach it to the child's return	**5**	

Part II	**Tentative Tax Based on the Tax Rate of the Parent**		
6	Enter the parent's **taxable income** from Form 1040, line 43; Form 1040A, line 27; Form 1040EZ, line 6; Form 1040NR, line 40; or Form 1040NR-EZ, line 14. If zero or less, enter -0-	**6**	
7	Enter the total, if any, from Forms 8615, line 5, of **all other** children of the parent named above. **Do** not include the amount from line 5 above	**7**	
8	Add lines 5, 6, and 7 (see instructions)	**8**	
9	Enter the tax on the amount on line 8 based on the **parent's** filing status above (see instructions). If the Qualified Dividends and Capital Gain Tax Worksheet, Schedule D Tax Worksheet, or Schedule J (Form 1040) is used to figure the tax, check here ▶ ☐	**9**	
10	Enter the parent's tax from Form 1040, line 44; Form 1040A, line 28, minus any alternative minimum tax; Form 1040EZ, line 10; Form 1040NR, line 41; or Form 1040NR-EZ, line 15. **Do** not include any tax from **Form 4972** or **8814.** If the Qualified Dividends and Capital Gain Tax Worksheet, Schedule D Tax Worksheet, or Schedule J (Form 1040) was used to figure the tax, check here ☐	**10**	
11	Subtract line 10 from line 9 and enter the result. If line 7 is blank, also enter this amount on line 13 and go to **Part III**	**11**	
12a	Add lines 5 and 7	**12a**	
b	Divide line 5 by line 12a. Enter the result as a decimal (rounded to at least three places)	**12b**	× .
13	Multiply line 11 by line 12b	**13**	

Part III	**Child's Tax**—If lines 4 and 5 above are the same, enter -0- on line 15 and go to line 16.		
14	Subtract line 5 from line 4	**14**	
15	Enter the tax on the amount on line 14 based on the **child's** filing status (see instructions). If the Qualified Dividends and Capital Gain Tax Worksheet, Schedule D Tax Worksheet, or Schedule J (Form 1040) is used to figure the tax, check here ▶ ☐	**15**	
16	Add lines 13 and 15	**16**	
17	Enter the tax on the amount on line 4 based on the **child's** filing status (see instructions). If the Qualified Dividends and Capital Gain Tax Worksheet, Schedule D Tax Worksheet, or Schedule J (Form 1040) is used to figure the tax, check here ▶ ☐	**17**	
18	Enter the **larger** of line 16 or line 17 here and on the **child's** Form 1040, line 44; Form 1040A, line 28; or Form 1040NR, line 41	**18**	

For Paperwork Reduction Act Notice, see the instructions.   Cat. No. 64113U   Form **8615** (2005)

2. Does enactment of such a complicated provision to solve a rather simple problem represent a justifiable solution?[5] For a child subject to the rule of section 1(g), a parent has the choice of including the child's income on his or her own return (or their return if the parents file a joint return), or filing Form 8615 with the child's return. Because inclusion in the parent's own return might produce a higher tax on the child's income by pushing the parents into a higher marginal rate, many parents will prepare a Form 8615 to compare the results with the results if the income is included on the parent's own return.

3. Why does section 1(g) not apply to a child's earned income when it is equally likely that it, like unearned income, will be used to replace other family income for the support of the child?[6]

4. What would be some of the issues and problems Congress would face if it decided to treat the family, rather than the individual, as the taxable unit?

---

5. Once Congress enacts a complicated provision such as section 1(g), it becomes the task of the Service to implement the provision. If the provision requires taxpayer reporting, the Service must create the appropriate form or forms and the instructions necessary to aid taxpayers in complying with the law. The Service explains its form-drafting function as follows:

> We try to create forms and instructions that can be easily understood. Often this is difficult to do because our tax laws are very complex. For some people with income mostly from wages, filling in the forms is easy. For others who have businesses, pensions, stocks, rental income, or other investments, it is more difficult.

Form 1040 Instructions for tax year 2005 at 78.

In a recent press release, entitled "IRS Updates Tax Gap Estimates," the Service reported:

> Internal Revenue Service officials announced today that they have updated their estimates of the Tax Year 2001 tax gap....
>
> The updated estimate of the overall gross tax gap for Tax Year 2001 — the difference between what taxpayers should have paid and what they actually paid on a timely basis — comes to $345 billion....
>
> IRS enforcement activities, coupled with other late payments, recover about $55 billion of the tax gap, leaving a net tax gap of $290 billion for Tax Year 2001.
>
> "The vast majority of Americans pay their taxes accurately and are shortchanged by those who don't pay their fair share," said IRS Commissioner Mark W. Everson. "The magnitude of the tax gap highlights the critical role of enforcement in keeping our system of tax administration healthy."
>
> The complexity of the tax law is also a significant factor in causing the tax gap, which can be seriously addressed only in the context of fundamental tax reform and simplification.
>
> While no tax system can ever achieve 100 percent compliance, the IRS is committed to taking all reasonable steps to improve compliance through increased and better targeted enforcement and through increased taxpayer service and outreach efforts.
>
> "Helping taxpayers better understand their obligations under the current tax law will facilitate compliance, but simplifying the tax code would have a big impact on reducing the tax gap" said Everson.
>
> ...

IR-2006-28, Feb. 14, 2006.

Proponents of a flat tax frequently cite the complexity of compliance as a principal reason for abandoning the current system and adopting a flat tax. Robert E. Hall and Alvin Rabushka, *The Flat Tax* 6-19 (2d ed. Hoover Inst. Press) (1995).

6. Don't forget that even though section 1(g) does not apply to a child's earned income, a child of any age is a separate taxpayer and is taxable on his earned income if his gross income exceeds the amount applicable to him under section 6012. The difference between the earned and unearned income of a child under 14 is that the earned income is taxed at the child's own section 1(c) rate but section 1(g) requires that his unearned income be taxed at his parents' rate. (A child 18 or over is taxable at his own section 1(c) rate on both earned and unearned income if his gross income exceeds the applicable section 6012 amount.)

2. The Family Business

A frequent device for accomplishing intra-family assignments of income is the family business. The business may take the form of a general or limited partnership, a regular or Subchapter S corporation, or one of the newer forms of business entity, such as a limited liability company. For example, a parent may create a business entity in which her children have ownership interests in an effort to transfer to her children a portion of what would otherwise be her income from the performance of services. Or, a parent may create a trust whose beneficiaries are her children in an effort to transfer to her children the income from and appreciation in the value of the assets that she contributes to the trust.

As you examine the following materials, consider whether the motivation was primarily tax reduction or whether that was secondary to some greater purpose, for example, to provide resources for a child's future education. Also, consider whether the plan, if successful, would affect income from services or income from property or both.

FRITSCHLE v. COMMISSIONER
79 T.C. 152 (1982)

FAY, *Judge*: ... After concessions, (Footnote 2) the remaining issue [is] whether payments received in 1975, 1976, and 1977 by petitioner Helen R. Fritschle for assembling ribbons and rosettes are includable in petitioners' gross income;.... (Footnote 3)

FINDINGS OF FACT

...

Petitioners have 11 children. The 8 youngest children lived at home with their parents during the years in issue.

Since 1956, petitioner Robert T. Fritschle (Robert) has been employed by American Gold Label Co. (AGL), a sole proprietorship.... During the years in issue, Robert was general manager in charge of virtually every aspect of the business....

Prior to 1970, AGL was engaged in a printing business generally limited to letterheads and stationery. Beginning in 1970, the business expanded to include more specialized types of printing which included printing on metals and cloth. Specifically, new items printed included ribbons and rosettes, much like the ribbons seen at horse and dog shows or the ribbon awarded the prize bull at the county fair. Even though AGL employed 15 people, outside help was needed to assemble the ribbons when the printing was completed. Petitioner Helen R. Fritschel (Helen) agreed with Elsie Walsh Fabel, the owner of AGL, to assemble the ribbons at home. Accordingly, in 1970, Helen, with the help of their children then living at home, began assembling ribbons and rosettes for AGL. From 1970 through 1976, this piecework was done in the basement washroom. In 1977, production was moved to the furnace room. The work involved cutting, shaping, and stapling of things like streamers, bezels, and ribbons to form the final product.

All materials were furnished by AGL at no cost to Helen. When the work was completed, Helen submitted a bill and received payment accordingly. During the years in issue, Helen was paid 3 cents per ribbon and 15 cents to 25 cents per rosette. Total payments received during 1975, 1976, and 1977 were $9,429.74, $11,136.41, and $8,262, respectively.

The children performed approximately 70 percent of all the work. Robert, the father, did not participate. The children were not employees of either Helen or AGL, nor was there any other arrangement for them to share directly in the compensation paid to Helen by AGL.

...

Petitioners did not report the income received by Helen in 1975 and 1976 for assembling the ribbons and rosettes. In 1977, the income received by Helen was reported....

In his notice of deficiency, respondent determined petitioners must include in income all payments received by Helen for work performed in assembling the ribbons and rosettes....

OPINION

1. *Payments to Helen for Ribbons and Rosettes*

Helen and the children assembled the ribbons and rosettes in the basement of their home. There is no question that payments received for this work are income under section 61. The issue is who is taxable on those payments. Since a portion of the compensation was attributable to work performed by their children, petitioners argue that a proportionate amount of the payments should be included in the income of the children. Respondent contends Helen was responsible for, and retained total control over, the earnings, and, therefore, the income is properly includable in her income. We find for respondent.

It is axiomatic that income must be taxed to him who earns it. *Lucas v. Earl*, 281 U.S. 111 (1930).... Moreover, it is the command of the taxpayer over the income which is the concern of the tax laws.... Recognizing that the true earner cannot always be identified simply by pointing "to the one actually turning the spade or dribbling the ball," this Court has applied a more refined test that of who controls the earning of the income. *Johnson v. Commissioner*, 78 T.C. 882, 890 (1982). (Footnote 5) Applying this test, it is clear that, for purposes of taxation, Helen, and not the children, was the true earner of the income attributable to the work performed on the ribbons and rosettes.

Helen was solely responsible for the performance of all services. AGL contracted only with Helen, and no contract or agreement existed between AGL and any of the children. All checks were made payable to Helen, and the children received no direct payments or compensation for their work. Clearly, the compensation was made in payment purely for the services of Helen. Although the company knew the children were performing part of the work, that does not change the fact that AGL looked exclusively to Helen for performance of the services. (Footnote 6) In short, Helen managed, supervised, and otherwise exercised total control over the entire operation. It was she who controlled the capacity to earn the income, and it was she who in fact received the income. It does not necessarily follow that income is taxable to the one whose personal efforts produced it. Thus, despite the fact that a portion of the amounts received can be traced to work actually performed by their children, Helen is treated as the true earner of all such income for tax purposes. Accordingly, pursuant to section 61, petitioners must include all payments received in 1975, 1976, and 1977 for assembling the ribbons and rosettes in their gross income. (Footnote 7)

Nevertheless, petitioners argue section 73 mandates a result in their favor. Section 73(a) provides:

> SEC. 73(a). TREATMENT OF AMOUNTS RECEIVED.—Amounts received
> in respect of the services of a child shall be included in his gross income and

not in the gross income of the parent, even though such amounts are not received by the child.

Petitioners argue the language and meaning of section 73 are clear, and that the amounts received by Helen with respect to the services performed by the children clearly are included in the gross income of the children. However, when viewed in light of the origin and purpose of section 73, it is apparent that section was enacted in response to a different situation and, under these facts, does not purport to tax the children on a portion of the income at issue herein.

The purpose of section 73 is to provide, for Federal tax purposes, consistent treatment of compensation paid for the services of a minor child regardless of different rights conferred by State laws on parents' entitlement to such compensation. Prior to 1944, a parent was required to include in income all earnings of a minor child if, under the laws of the State where they resided, the parent had a right to those earnings.... Since parents in all States were not entitled to the earnings of their minor children and since even in those States following the common law doctrine of the parents' right to those earnings, a parent could lose such rights if the child had been emancipated, different tax results obtained depending on State law.... To eliminate this discrepancy in the tax treatment of the earnings of minor children, Congress, in 1944, enacted the predecessor to section 73 to provide a uniform rule that all amounts received "in respect of the services of a child" shall be included in the income of that child regardless of the fact that, under State law, the parent may be entitled to those amounts. Thus, section 73 operates to tax a minor child on income he is deemed, in the tax sense, to have earned. Section 73 does not purport to alter the broad principle of taxation that income is taxed to the earner. See *Lucas v. Earl*, 281 U.S. 111 (1930), and its progeny. As we have already held, Helen (the mother) is the true earner of the income, herein, for tax purposes. She contracted for and retained total control of the earning of the income.

If, on the other hand, we made a finding that it was the services of the children that were being contracted for and that the children were the true earners of the income, then section 73 would tax the children on that income.... This is so despite State law. (Footnote 10)

While from a literal reading of the statute, petitioners' argument has superficial appeal, petitioners incorrectly assume the children are the true earners of the income in the first instance. However, section 73 simply does not tax a child on income until and unless he is recognized as the earner thereof. Petitioners' argument that these amounts must be included in the children's gross income because the income can be traced to services performed by the children must be rejected. Carrying this argument to its logical extreme, any parent could exclude a portion of the income received for services if his children helped him in the performance of those services. Congress surely did not intend such a result. (Footnote 11)

In summary, we find Helen the true earner of all amounts received for the ribbons and rosettes, and section 73 does not operate to include any portion of those amounts in the gross incomes of the children. Accordingly, petitioners must include in their gross income all payments received for the ribbons and rosettes.

   ...

While we have disposed of the issues before us, we have really only touched the surface of this case. Respondent asserted fraud on the part of petitioners, the parents of an industrious and hardworking family of 13, none of whom has ever had a scrape with the law. First, the record shows petitioners are clear of any impropriety or bad faith. Second, it is apparent the fraud allegation had a deep and resounding effect on this family. The mere allegation of fraud can tarnish a man in the eyes of his neighbors and, more importantly, in his own eyes. We are not dealing here only with tax deficiencies and money; we are dealing with people's lives. Fraud should be asserted with discretion.

This Court spent over 9 hours listening to testimony and conducting discussions with the parties in chambers. By far, the largest portion of that time was devoted to the fraud issue, and it is apparent respondent had no chance of presenting a case sufficient to carry his burden of proof. Petitioners manifested a sincere willingness to settle this case if the fraud allegation was dropped. In reality, this case should never have come before this Court. Facing an ever-increasing backlog of cases, this Court's valuable time commands a better sense of responsibility by those practicing before it. (Footnote 13) The scars and wasted time are not undone by respondent's concession of the fraud issue on brief.

. . .

FOOTNOTES:

2. Respondent conceded the fraud issue on reply brief.

3. Also in issue is whether petitioners omitted from their 1975 gross income an amount in excess of 25 percent of the gross income stated on their 1975 Federal income tax return. If so, respondent is not barred from assessing the 1975 tax since the 6-year statute of limitations applies. See sec. 6501(e). Petitioners reported 1975 gross income of $9,540. Thus, in the event we find greater than $2,385 was omitted from petitioners' 1975 gross income, respondent will not be barred from assessing 1975 taxes.... The parties agree respondent is not barred from assessing 1976 and 1977 taxes.

5. Although *Johnson v. Commissioner*, 78 T.C. 882 (1982), arose in the context of the taxation of a professional service corporation (a basketball player), the principles enunciated therein are universally applicable....

6. We are given no reason to believe AGL intended to contract for the services of the children. Thus, we do not place controlling significance on the fact that, under applicable State law, minors may lack capacity to enter into valid contracts. Moreover, no trustee or legal guardian was appointed on behalf of the children.

7. In 1975, those payments totaled $9,429.74. Since this amount exceeds 25 percent of the gross income reported on petitioners' 1975 Federal income tax return, respondent is not barred from assessing the 1975 taxes. See note 3 *supra*....

Petitioners make no claim for a deduction with respect to the services rendered by the children. Indeed, no such deduction would be allowable since no payments to the children were made or set aside in some way for their services actually performed. The only benefit accruing to the children was an increased budget for general family and living expenses. See *Romine v. Commissioner*, 25 T.C. 859 (1956), wherein a taxpayer's expenditures on his son's behalf for clothing, insurance, and college were held to be nondeductible personal expenses and not payments for services actually rendered. Compare *Hundley v. Commissioner*, 48 T.C. 339 (1967), wherein a professional baseball player, Randy Hundley, was allowed a business expense deduction for paying over to his father 50 percent of the bonus he received for signing with the San Francisco Giants. See also *Roundtree v. Commissioner*, T.C. Memo. 1980-117.

10. Apparently, under the law of Missouri, a parent is entitled to the services and earnings of his child. See *Franklin v. Butcher*, 144 Mo. App. 660, 129 S.W. 428 (1910).

11. The Committee reports state: "Thus, even though the contract of employment is made directly by the parent and the parent receives the compensation for the services, for the purposes of the Federal income tax, the amounts would be considered to be taxable to the child because earned by him." H. Rept. 1365, 1944 C.B. 821, 838; S. Rept. 885, 1944 C.B. 858, 876. Citing these reports, petitioners argue it could not be clearer that the children are taxable on the amounts in issue. This language, however, merely recognizes parents must be the contracting party when, due to their legal incapacity, minor children cannot enter into valid contracts. It must still be shown that the services of the child were being contracted for and that the children controlled the earning of the income therefrom.

13. We will not hesitate to call attention to an unsettling situation when the time and effort expended by the parties and this Court in litigation are totally disproportionate to any requirement of justice. See *Buffalo Tool & Die Mfg. Co. v. Commissioner*, 74 T.C. 441, 451–452 (1980); *Scott v. Commissioner*, T.C. Memo. 1972-109 (Tannenwald, J.).

Consider the following questions.

1. Do you agree with the court that Helen was the true earner of the income? Does an affirmative answer imply that the children performed their services gratuitously?

2. The court states that "from a literal reading of [section 73], petitioners' argument has superficial appeal...." The court ultimately rejected that literal reading, however, and referred to the origin and purpose of section 73. In other words, the court declined to accept the conclusion dictated by the actual words of the statute. Courts have long complied with the general maxim of statutory interpretation that when the words of a statute are uncertain, the court may look to the legislative history in an effort to determine Congress's intent. Is a court justified in refusing to follow the words of a statute when those words are clear and unambiguous? What justification did the Tax Court advance for departing from the literal words of the statute? Before you answer, read the following:

A Brief Introduction to Statutory Interpretation

Judge Richard A. Posner has observed that few basic statutory courses, such as Federal Income Tax, "explore with the class the process by which the legislation is enacted, the political and economic forces that shaped it, or even the methods the courts use to interpret it, as distinct from the particular interpretations that the courts have made."[7] We agree. Throughout this text, we have sought to highlight aspects of the political and economic forces that have shaped tax legislation and some of the ideas that have shaped the tax law. We have also included an Introduction to Tax Policy. But, without a further introduction to statutory interpretation, the ability of the tax adviser to counsel a client

---

7. Richard A. Posner, "Statutory Interpretation—In the Classroom and in the Courtroom," 50 U. Chi. L. Rev. 800, 802 (1983).

would lack an essential dimension. The following excerpts present an introduction to statutory interpretation in general and the interpretation of tax statutes in particular.

Interpreting Statutory Language[8]

1. Sources for Interpreting Statutes

When litigation arises involving the meaning of a statute, someone must interpret it. Although Congress has delegated the authority to issue interpretive rules to the Treasury Department ... regulations rarely follow on the heels of a law's enactment....

In addition to administrative interpretations, or in their absence when none are available, courts may turn to legislative history documents ... as expressions of congressional intent. Legislative history materials take on particular significance if administrative rules are alleged to be unreasonable and the statute's "plain meaning" is in doubt. (Footnote 61)

2. Using Statutory Language

... [C]areful reading of Code provisions is a critical part of the research process. If the Code provides its own definition for a term, you must locate that definition. If a term is specifically defined for purposes of a particular Code subdivision (e.g., Code section 165(g)(2) ...), you cannot automatically use that definition for another subdivision.

a. Intra-Code Cross-Reference

Because a single Code section rarely governs a transaction, your research must include a search for other operative sections. Congress frequently offers guidance in accomplishing this task by providing cross-references between Code sections that govern the same transaction. (Footnote 62) Unfortunately, cross-references may appear in only one of the sections. (Footnote 63)

...

C. Limitations on Cross-References as Interpretive Aids

While cross-references are useful in locating relevant statutory material, they lack independent interpretive significance. Code section 7806(a) provides that "[t]he cross references in this title to other portions of the title, or other provisions of law, where the word 'see' is used, are made only for convenience, and shall be given no legal effect."

3. Selected Maxims of Construction

Judges cite various rules of statutory construction in the course of interpreting statutes. The decisions listed below state or repeat several of these rules. (Footnote 65) To appreciate their effect, you should read the opinions cited for each proposition....

- The fundamental principal of statutory construction, *expressio unius est exclusio alterius*, applies. There is a firm presumption that everything in the I.R.C. was intentionally included for a reason and everything not in the code was likewise excluded for a reason—the expression of one thing is the exclusion of another. Speers v. United States, 38 Fed. Cl. 197, 202 (1997).

---

8. Gail Levin Richmond, *Federal Tax Research* 52–56 (6th ed., Foundation Press) (2002).

- Under the principle of *ejusdem generis*, when a general term follows a specific one, the general term should be understood as a reference to subjects akin to the one with specific enumeration.... In the usual instance, the doctrine of *ejusdem generis* applies where a "catch-all" term precedes, or more often follows, an enumeration of specific terms in order to expand the list without identifying every situation covered by the statute. Host Marriott Corp. v. United States, 113 Supp.2d 790 (D. Md. 2000).

- [T]he presumption is against interpreting a statute in a way which renders it ineffective or futile. Matut v. Commissioner, 86 T.C. 686, 690 (1986).

- [T]he courts have some leeway in interpreting a statute if the adoption of a literal or usual meaning of its words "would lead to absurd results ... or would thwart the obvious purpose of the statute."…. Or, to put it another way, we should not adopt a construction which would reflect a conclusion that Congress had "legislate[d] eccentrically." Edna Louise Dunn Trust v. Commissioner, 86 T.C. 745, 755 (1986).

- We should avoid an interpretation of a statute that renders any part of it superfluous and does not give effect to all of the words used by Congress. Beisler v. Commissioner, 814 F.2d 1304, 1307 (9th Cir. 1987).

- [T]he whole of [the section's] various subparts should be harmonized if possible. Water Quality Association Employees' Benefit Corp. v. United States, 795 F.2d 1303, 1307 (7th Cir. 1986).

- In terms of statutory construction, the *context* from which the meaning of a word is drawn must of necessity be the words of the statute itself. Strogoff v. United States, 10 Cl. Ct. 584, 588 (1986).

- [H]eadings and titles are not meant to take the place of the detailed provisions of the text. Nor are they necessarily designed to be a reference guide or a synopsis. Where the text is complicated and prolific, headings and titles can do no more than indicate the provisions in a most general manner, ... Factors of this type have led to the wise rule that the title of a statute and the heading of a section cannot limit the plain meaning of the text. Stanley Works v. Commissioner, 87 T.C. 389, 419 (1986).

- When a statute does not define a term, we generally interpret that term by employing the ordinary, contemporary, and common meaning of the words that Congress used. Merkel v. Commissioner, 192 F.3d 844, 848 (9th Cir. 1999).

- As a matter of statutory construction, identical words used in different parts of the Internal Revenue Code are normally given the same meaning. Disabled American Veterans v. Commissioner, 94 T.C. 60, 71 (1990).

- Stated another way, Congress must make a clear statement that a double benefit is intended before we will construe a provision to allow this result. Transco Exploration Co. v. Commissioner, 949 F.2d 837, 841 (5th Cir. 1992).

FOOTNOTES:

61. Chevron U.S.A. Inc. v. Natural Resources Defense Council, Inc., 467 U.S. 837 (1984), and United States v. Mead Corp., 533 U.S. 218(2001),....

61. I.R.C. §§ 267 and 707(b) specifically refer to each other.

63. I.R.C. § 104 refers to I.R.C. § 213 but § 213 fails to mention § 104.

65. The Code also includes rules of construction: "No inference, implication, or presumption of legislative construction shall be drawn or made by reason of the location

or grouping of any particular section or provision or portion of this title, nor shall any table of contents, table of cross references, or similar outline, analysis, or descriptive matter relating to the contents of this title be given any legal effect." I.R.C. §7806(b).

What Professor Richmond summarizes are the traditional means courts have used to interpret tax statutes. But, a number of commentators have suggested that the Supreme Court has been moving in the direction of "textualism," that is, looking to the face of the statute to the exclusion of policy, economic effect, and legislative history and other sources of legislative intent. Below, Professor Mary L. Heen describes the "special dangers" the "plain meaning" approach to statutory construction of the Code creates:

> The Supreme Court has turned increasingly to a "plain meaning" approach in statutory interpretation cases. This approach poses special dangers for tax law because of the rich range of contextual and policy considerations that inform the Internal Revenue Code. Under the plain meaning approach, the Court relies on the meaning of the statutory words themselves rather than on legislative history, intent or purpose. This method of interpretation, closely associated with textualists such as Justice Antonin Scalia, is consistent with the view that the role of the judiciary is to interpret the text of the statute, enacted by Congress and signed into law by the President, and not to interpret the statute more generally in light of its legal or social context.
>
> Although the textualists do not command a majority on the Court, the Court as a whole utilitzes a plain meaning approach when the language of the statute is "unambiguous." In identifying such unambiguous or determinate language, the Court often refers to dictionary meanings of words, linguistic canons of construction, the way the specific provision being construed relates to the statute as a whole, or to other legislative enactments.
>
> ...
>
> Whatever the reasons for the Court's increased reliance on the plain meaning approach, its use depends upon a judicial determination that the statutory provision being interpreted is not ambiguous. Whether the language of a statute is ambiguous or not may depend upon the background and knowledge of the interpreter as well as the skill of the drafter. It may also depend upon the sources consulted to aid in interpretation.
>
> Statutes develop over a period of time and in response to the active interrelationship among decisions of the administrative agencies, the courts, and Congress. As Professor Edward Rubin and others point out, some statutes are directed to bureaucracies or agencies charged with enforcing complex regulatory provisions. Some are enacted in response to court decisions or with the legislative expectation that courts will fill in statutory gaps when unanticipated questions arise. A specialized interpretive community may rely on meanings for words or phrases that develop over time in a particular regulatory context.
>
> An acontextual determination by the Court of the threshold question of whether a statute is ambiguous presents the possibility that a complex statute may be misinterpreted by the Court. Therein lies the inherent limitation of the plain meaning approach. That limitation has been acknowledged even by de-

fenders of the plain meaning approach: "Plain meaning, quite simply, is a blunt, frequently crude, and certainly narrowing device, cutting off access to many features of some particular conversational or communicative or interpretive context that would otherwise be available to the interpreter or conversational participant."

The plain meaning approach also creates a heightened risk of error because of its relationship to agency deference under *Chevron, USA, Inc. v. Natural Resources Defense Council, Inc.* Under the Chevron doctrine, reviewing courts must defer to an agency's reasonable interpretation of an ambiguous statute. However, under the Court's expanding use of plain meaning analysis, the Court less frequently finds statutory language to be ambiguous. In the tax context, the plain meaning approach not only cuts the Court off from the Code's interpretive context and policy background but also makes deference to Treasury's expertise less likely.[9]

3. Section 73(c) defines the term parent. When did Congress enact this definition? Does the definition remain appropriate? Consider the dramatic changes that have occurred in the law relating to parents and children.

4. Note the court's excoriation of the Service's assertion of the penalty for civil tax fraud. Why did the Service assert fraud if, as appears likely from the opinion, its attempt would almost certainly fail? In what year did the family begin its operations? How far back could the Service assess additional taxes? **Review section 6501(a), -(b), -(c), and -(e).**

5. Although the case does not make clear the date on which the Service issued the notice of deficiency, it appears certain that it was more than three years after the date the return was due or filed. Under what authority could the Service assert additional taxes for 1975? **Review section 6501(e).**

a. Family Partnerships

Suppose, instead, that the Fritschle family had started with a plan to make the children part owners of the business. That is, suppose the Fritschles had intended to split the income from their business among Mrs. Fritschle and the eleven children. One method they could have employed is the family partnership.

Suppose the eleven children and Mrs. Fritschle each contributed $1 to a new partnership. As a business dependent upon personal services, the business would not require costly assets to begin operations. If the plan succeeds, each of the partners will be treated as having a share of the income. This flows from the fact that a partnership, although a juridical entity, is not a tax-paying one. Rather, it is referred to as a flow-through or pass-through entity; it reports its income and deductions on a special tax form and the results flow through to the actual partners who report their shares on their own tax returns.[10] Therefore, the partnership also supplies each partner with a

---

9. Mary L. Heen, "Plain Meaning, The Tax Code, and Doctrinal Incoherence," 48 Hastings L.J. 771, 771–775 (1997).

10. Subchapter K of the Code contains the complex rules governing the taxation of partnerships and partners. Each partner reports his or her share of partnership income and deductions. A partnership computes its operational income (or loss) in a fashion very similar to any other taxpayer. There are, however, certain partnership items that may affect each partner differently on his or her own return. These items must be reported separately because of special rules that apply to each individual taxpayer that may affect the individual partner's treatment of the item. For example, the Code imposes a limit (based on a percentage of AGI) on the amount of charitable contributions an individual taxpayer may deduct in a particular year. Therefore, the partnership's charitable contri-

special form, a Form K-1, reflecting the partner's share of income and deductions for the year. Thus, a partnership is merely a tax reporting entity. Should the Service respect the partnership? Suppose the eleven children were emancipated adults at the time of formation. Does their age make a difference in assessing the issue of whether the partnership should be respected for tax purposes? Consider the following case.

COMMISSIONER v. CULBERTSON
337 U.S. 733 (1949)

MR. CHIEF JUSTICE VINSON delivered the opinion of the Court.

This case requires our further consideration of the family partnership problem. The Commissioner of Internal Revenue ruled that the entire income from a partnership allegedly entered into by respondent and his four sons must be taxed to respondent, (Footnote 1) and the Tax Court sustained that determination. The Court of Appeals for the Fifth Circuit reversed. We granted certiorari....

Respondent taxpayer is a rancher. From 1915 until October 1939, he had operated a cattle business in partnership with R. S. Coon. Coon, who had numerous business interests in the Southwest and had largely financed the partnership, was 79 years old in 1939 and desired to dissolve the partnership because of ill health. To that end, the bulk of the partnership herd was sold until, in October of that year, only about 1,500 head remained. These cattle were all registered Herefords, the brood or foundation herd. Culbertson wished to keep these cattle and approached Coon with an offer of $65 a head. Coon agreed to sell at that price, but only upon condition that Culbertson would sell an undivided one-half interest in the herd to his four sons at the same price. His reasons for imposing this condition were his intense interest in maintaining the Hereford strain which he and Culbertson had developed, his conviction that Culbertson was too old to carry on the work alone, and his personal interest in the Culbertson boys. Culbertson's sons were enthusiastic about the proposition, so respondent thereupon bought the remaining cattle from the Coon and Culbertson partnership for $99,440. Two days later Culbertson sold an undivided one-half interest to the four boys, and the following day they gave their father a note for $49,720 at 4 per cent interest due one year from date. Several months later a new note for $57,674 was executed by the boys to replace the earlier note. The increase in amount covered the purchase by Culbertson and his sons of other properties formerly owned by Coon and Culbertson. This note was paid by the boys in the following manner:

Credit for overcharge.....................	$5,930
Gifts from respondent................	21,744
One-half of a loan procured by Culbertson & Sons partnership ...	30,000

The loan was repaid from the proceeds from operation of the ranch.

The partnership agreement between taxpayer and his sons was oral. The local paper announced the dissolution of the Coon and Culbertson partnership and the continuation of the business by respondent and his boys under the name of Culbertson & Sons. A bank account was opened in this name, upon which taxpayer, his four sons and a bookkeeper could check. At the time of formation of the new partnership, Culbertson's

---

bution is one of the separately reported items, and each partner separately determines whether she may deduct her full share in the current tax year.

oldest son was 24 years old, married, and living on the ranch, of which he had for two years been foreman under the Coon and Culbertson partnership. He was a college graduate and received $100 a month plus board and lodging for himself and his wife both before and after formation of Culbertson & Sons and until entering the Army. The second son was 22 years old, was married and finished college in 1940, the first year during which the new partnership operated. He went directly into the Army following graduation and rendered no services to the partnership. The two younger sons, who were 18 and 16 years old respectively in 1940, went to school during the winter and worked on the ranch during the summer. (Footnote 2)

The tax years here involved are 1940 and 1941. A partnership return was filed for both years indicating a division of income approximating the capital attributed to each partner. It is the disallowance of this division of the income from the ranch that brings this case into the courts.

First. The Tax Court read our [prior] decisions ... as setting out two essential tests of partnership for income-tax purposes: that each partner contribute to the partnership either vital services or capital originating with him. Its decision was based upon a finding that none of respondent's sons had satisfied those requirements during the tax years in question....

The Court of Appeals, on the other hand, was of the opinion that a family partnership entered into without thought of tax avoidance should be given recognition taxwise whether or not it was intended that some of the partners contribute either capital or services during the tax year and whether or not they actually made such contributions, since it was formed with the full expectation and purpose that the boys would, in the future, contribute their time and services to the partnership. We must consider, therefore, whether an intention to contribute capital or services sometime in the future is sufficient to satisfy ordinary concepts of partnership....

... The partnership sections of the Code are, of course, geared to the sections relating to taxation of individual income, since no tax is imposed upon partnership income as such. To hold that individuals carrying on business in partnership includes persons who contribute nothing during the tax period would violate the first principle of income taxation: that income must be taxed to him who earns it. *Lucas v. Earl*, 281 U.S. 111 (1930)....

... A partnership is ... an organization for the production of income to which each partner contributes one or both of the ingredients of income capital or services.... The intent to provide money, goods, labor, or skill sometime in the future cannot meet the demands of ... the Code that he who presently earns the income through his own labor and skill and the utilization of his own capital be taxed therefor. The vagaries of human experience preclude reliance upon even good faith intent as to future conduct as a basis for the present taxation of income. (Footnote 8)

Second. We turn next to a consideration of the Tax Court's approach to the family partnership problem.... [T]he ultimate question for decision, namely, whether the partnership is real within the meaning of the federal revenue laws....

... [T]he question whether the family partnership is real for income-tax purposes depends upon

> whether the partners really and truly intended to join together for the purpose
> of carrying on the business and sharing in the profits or losses or both. And
> their intention in this respect is a question of fact, to be determined from testi-

mony disclosed by their 'agreement, considered as a whole, and by their conduct in execution of its provisions.'... We see no reason why this general rule should not apply in tax cases where the Government challenges the existence of a partnership for tax purposes....

The question is not whether the services or capital contributed by a partner are of sufficient importance to meet some objective standard ... but whether, considering all the facts the agreement, the conduct of the parties in execution of its provisions, their statements, the testimony of disinterested persons, the relationship of the parties, their respective abilities and capital contributions, the actual control of income and the purposes for which it is used, and any other facts throwing light on their true intent the parties in good faith and acting with a business purpose intended to join together in the present conduct of the enterprise. (Footnote 11) There is nothing new or particularly difficult about such a test. Triers of fact are constantly called upon to determine the intent with which a person acted. (Footnote 12) ...

But the Tax Court did not view the question as one concerning the bona fide intent of the parties to join together as partners. Not once in its opinion is there even an oblique reference to any lack of intent on the part of respondent and his sons to combine their capital and services for the purpose of carrying on the business....

Unquestionably a court's determination that the services contributed by a partner are not vital and that he has not participated in management and control of the business or contributed original capital has the effect of placing a heavy burden on the taxpayer to show the bona fide intent of the parties to join together as partners. But such a determination is not conclusive, and that is the vice in the tests adopted by the Tax Court. It assumes that there is no room for an honest difference of opinion as to whether the services or capital furnished by the alleged partner are of sufficient importance to justify his inclusion in the partnership. If, upon a consideration of all the facts, it is found that the partners joined together in good faith to conduct a business, having agreed that the services or capital to be contributed presently by each is of such value to the partnership that the contributor should participate in the distribution of profits, that is sufficient....

Third. The Tax Court's isolation of original capital as an essential of membership in a family partnership [is] ... erroneous.... We [have not said] that the donee of an intra-family gift could never become a partner through investment of the capital in the family partnership, any more than we said that all family trusts are invalid for tax purposes in *Helvering v. Clifford.*... The facts may indicate, on the contrary, that the amount thus contributed and the income therefrom should be considered the property of the donee for tax, as well as general law, purposes....

But application of the *Clifford-Horst* principle does not follow automatically upon a gift to a member of one's family, followed by its investment in the family partnership. If it did, it would be necessary to define family and to set precise limits of membership therein. We have not done so for the obvious reason that existence of the family relationship does not create a status which itself determines tax questions, but is simply a warning that things may not be what they seem. It is frequently stated that transactions between members of a family will be carefully scrutinized. But, more particularly, the family relationship often makes it possible for one to shift tax incidence by surface changes of ownership without disturbing in the least his dominion and control over the subject of the gift or the purposes for which the income from the property is used. He is able, in other words, to retain the substance of full enjoyment of all the rights which previously he had in the property. *Helvering v. Clifford,* ...

The fact that transfers to members of the family group may be mere camouflage does not, however, mean that they invariably are.... [O]ne's participation in control and management of the business is a circumstance indicating an intent to be a bona fide partner despite the fact that the capital contributed originated elsewhere in the family. (Footnote 17) If the donee of property who then invests it in the family partnership exercises dominion and control over that property and through that control influences the conduct of the partnership and the disposition of its income he may well be a true partner. Whether he is free to, and does, enjoy the fruits of the partnership is strongly indicative of the reality of his participation in the enterprise.... [W]e [have] distinguished between active participation in the affairs of the business by a donee of a share in the partnership on the one hand, and his passive acquiescence to the will of the donor on the other. (Footnote 18) This distinction is of obvious importance to a determination of the true intent of the parties. It is meaningless if original capital is an essential test of membership in a family partnership.

The cause must therefore be remanded to the Tax Court for a decision as to which, if any, of respondent's sons were partners with him in the operation of the ranch during 1940 and 1941. As to which of them, in other words, was there a bona fide intent that they be partners in the conduct of the cattle business, either because of services to be performed during those years, or because of contributions of capital of which they were the true owners, as we have defined that term in the *Clifford* [and] *Horst* ... cases? No question as to the allocation of income between capital and services is presented in this case, and we intimate no opinion on that subject.

The decision of the Court of Appeals is reversed with directions to remand the cause to the Tax Court for further proceedings in conformity with this opinion.

Reversed and remanded.

FOOTNOTES:

1. Gladys Culbertson, the wife of W. O. Culbertson, Sr., is joined as a party because of her community of interest in the property and income of her husband under Texas law.

2. A daughter was also made a member of the partnership some time after its formation upon the gift by respondent of one-quarter of his one-half interest in the partnership. Respondent did not contend before the Tax Court that she was a partner for tax purposes.

8. The *reductio ad absurdum* of the theory that children may be partners with their parents before they are capable of being entrusted with the disposition of partnership funds or of contributing substantial services occurred in *Tinkoff v. Commissioner*, 120 F. 2d 564, where a taxpayer made his son a partner in his accounting firm the day the son was born.

11. This is not, as we understand it, contrary to the approach taken by the Bureau of Internal Revenue in its most recent statement of policy. I.T. 3845, 1947 Cum.Bull. 66, states at p. 67.

Where persons who are closely related by blood or marriage enter into an agreement purporting to create a so-called family partnership or other arrangement with respect to the operation of a business or income-producing venture, under which agreement all of the parties are accorded substantially the same treatment and consideration with respect to their designated interests and prescribed responsibilities in the business as if they were strangers dealing at arm's length; where the actions of the parties as legally responsible persons evidence an intent to carry on a business in a partnership relation; and where the terms of such agreement are substantially followed in the operation of the business or venture, as well as in the dealings of the partners or members with each other, it is the policy of the Bureau to disregard the close family relationship existing between the parties and to recognize, for Federal income tax purposes, the division of profits prescribed by such agreement. However, where the instrument purporting to create the family partnership expressly provides that the wife or child or other member of the family shall not be required to participate in the management of the business, or is merely silent on that point, the extent and nature of the services of such individual in the actual conduct of the business will be given appropriate evidentiary weight as to the question of intent to carry on the business as partners.

12. Nearly three-quarters of a century ago, Bowen, L.J., made the classic statement that the state of a man's mind is as much a fact as the state of his digestion. *Edgington v. Fitzmaurice*, 29 L.R.Ch.Div. 459, 483. State of mind has always been determinative of the question whether a partnership has been formed as between the parties....

17.... [P]articipation in control and management of the business, although given equal prominence with contributions of vital services and original capital as circumstances indicating an intent to enter into a partnership relation, was discarded by the Tax Court as a test of partnership. This indicates a basic and erroneous assumption that one can never make a gift to a member of one's family without retaining the essentials of ownership, if the gift is then invested in a family partnership. We included participation in management and control of the business as a circumstance indicative of intent to carry on business as a partner to cover the situation in which active dominion and control of the subject of the gift had actually passed to the donee. It is a circumstance of prime importance.

18. There is testimony in the record as to the participation by respondent's sons in the management of the ranch. Since such evidence did not fall within either of the tests adopted by the Tax Court, it failed to consider this testimony. Without intimating any opinion as to its probative value, we think that it is clearly relevant evidence of the intent to carry on business as partners.

Now consider the following questions.

1. Look at footnote 8 of the case. What does *reductio ad absurdum* mean?

2. As you have seen by reading the case, this case began in the Tax Court. What test did the Tax Court apply in reaching its decision? What test did the Fifth Circuit apply? What test did the Supreme Court apply?

3. Why did the Supreme Court remand the case to the Tax Court? Why didn't the Supreme Court simply decide itself whether Mr. Culbertson was in a partnership with one or more of his sons? Why not remand to the Fifth Circuit? What should the trial court, that is the Tax Court, do when it receives the case back from the Supreme Court?

4. **Study the two paragraphs that begin four paragraphs from the end of the case** (beginning with the phrase [b]ut application of the *Clifford-Horst* principle ...). What kind of evidence will the next taxpayer have to present to the Tax Court to prove the existence of a family partnership? **Read 12th paragraph** (beginning [t]he question is not whether the services or capital contributed by a partner ...) .

After the decision in *Culbertson*, Congress added section 704(e) to the Code. **Read section 704(e)**. Although the section confirms the possibility of a family partnership, the particular facts of each arrangement continue to be vital to recognition. A family can apparently use a partnership to split income if the children are old enough to contribute services.[11] (Compare, *Commissioner v. Culbertson* with *Tinkoff v. Commissioner*, 120 F. 2d 564 (7th Cir. 1941), in which the taxpayer sought to make his son a partner in his accounting firm on the day of the son's birth.) Moreover, a family can apparently use a partnership to split income if the children contribute capital.[12] That would appear to be the case even if the capital came originally from other family members as gifts or inheritances. (See section 704(e).) But, as in *Lucas v. Earl*, a plan will fail if it merely represents the assignment of income from services (as in *Tinkoff*) or property (as in *Clifford* and *Horst*).

Over the past twenty years, all the states have adopted a new business form, the limited liability company, or "LLC." An LLC offers its members protection from liabilities under state law similar to that enjoyed by shareholders of a corporation. But for tax purposes the LLC, in general, is treated as a partnership subject to only one level of tax at the member level.[13] Thus, the partnership rules of section 704(e) concerning proper allocations of income and deduction will govern a family LLC.

b. Family Corporations

Another device that families have utilized to spread income among members is the personal services corporation. Recall our discussion of *Eisner v. Macomber*. As we learned in *Eisner v. Macomber*, one of the characteristics of the traditional corporation is that earnings are taxed first at the corporate level and then again to the shareholders when dividends are distributed to them.[14] If, however, the corporation pays salaries, the corporation may deduct those salaries in computing its corporate income and, therefore, the earnings it uses to pay those salaries are not subject to tax at the corporate level. Rather, they are taxable to the recipient shareholders.

But, Congress created a second type of corporation in 1958 that in some ways more closely resembles a partnership or an LLC. Now, for tax law purposes, there are two primary types of corporations: those whose income is taxed both at the corporate and shareholder levels and those whose income flows through to the shareholders,

---

11. But the amount of income payable to each family member must represent reasonable compensation for the services provided by that family member.

12. As you have learned from the earliest days of this course, both capital and services can produce income. In some cases, the capital of the entity will produce income without requiring the provision of services as well; for example, capital placed in a bank account can produce interest income. In some cases, capital enables the entity to earn income that also requires the provision of services; for example, a contracting entity provides the equipment and tools necessary for the performance of the construction services.

13. The default tax classification for an LLC with more than one member is taxation as a partnership. Treas. Reg. section 301.7701-3(b)(1)(i). The default classification rules disregard as an entity an LLC with only one member, so an individual who creates a one-member LLC is taxed as a sole proprietorship. Thus, in most cases, LLC's will be pass-through entities for tax purposes.

14. Recall our earlier discussion of section 1(h)(11) which taxes qualifying dividends at the lower rate applicable to net capital gain. As this book goes to press, some members of Congress question whether dividends should be taxed at all.

much as in the case of a partnership or LLC[15] as described above. The first type is identified as a "C" corporation because the rules applicable to it appear in Subchapter C of the Code. The second is referred to as an "S" or "Subchapter S" corporation for the same reason.

From time to time, taxpayers seek to use the corporate form when individual income tax rates exceed corporate income tax rates. The idea is to retain some earnings at the corporate level (subject to the lower corporate rate of tax), while paying out some of the earnings to the shareholders as salaries (subject to the individual rates of tax). Thus, the total tax imposed on the income from the services will be less than if the full amount were taxed to the service-providing shareholder or shareholders at their individual rates. But the rules for partnerships with respect to attempts to assign personal services income are the same when the taxpayers use the corporate form instead. That is, although a corporation is generally a separate taxable entity, the Service need not respect the supposed entity if it appears that its shareholders created it merely to split income from services. In some circumstances, the Service will attack a corporation, though validly formed under state law, as a mere sham and seek to tax its income to the shareholder or shareholders who perform the services that produce the only income of the corporation. The courts and the Service have referred to this type of recharacterization as refusing to respect form over substance.

It is, nevertheless, possible to form a family corporation that will be recognized for tax purposes. In that event, the corporation will be a separate taxable entity. But the goal of assigning personal services income to members of the family who are not performing the services, to split the income from personal services among the family members in order to produce a lower overall tax burden, will probably be unachievable. A corporation cannot pay out its earnings in the form of salaries to those who do not perform services without risk of audit. And, the only way a "C" corporation can pay out corporate earnings to those who do not perform services is in the form of dividends. As noted above, however, dividends are subject to double taxation. Therefore, use of a "C" corporation will fail to produce the desired rate-splitting effect.

A family would probably fare no better in its attempt to split the income produced by one or more shareholder-service-providers with non-producing shareholders by employing an "S" corporation. Even if the corporation is recognized as a separate entity, the Service would still likely succeed in deeming the income to be the income of its producer through application of either the assignment of income doctrine or section 482 of the Code.[16] If the children actually participate, that is, provide services, to the corporation, however, the Service's attack might fail. Moreover, as in the case of a partnership, a family can use an "S" corporation to split the income among its members if the various members contribute capital. And, that capital can come from gifts or inheritances.

---

15. An LLC having more than one member can elect to be taxed as a C or an S corporation. Treas. Reg. section 301.7701-3(a).

16. Section 482 allows the Service to allocate gross income between two or more trades or businesses under common ownership if it determines that a reallocation is necessary to prevent evasion of taxes or clearly to reflect the income of the respective trades or businesses. The limits of this doctrine are far from clear. But the Service has taken the position that a personal services corporation and its service-provider-shareholder constitute two trades or businesses within the meaning of section 482. *See, e.g., Foglesong v. Commissioner,* 691 F.2d 848 (7th Cir. 1982).

Would you advise a client to utilize the corporate device if her children were all under the age of 18? Suppose they were all adults? Would the result in *Fritschle* have been different if the family had formed a corporation in which each of the children owned shares? Was the primary problem the failure to pay the children for their work or their lack of proprietary interest in the endeavor?

c. *Family Trusts*

Family members have also attempted to use various forms of trusts to transfer income or potential appreciation in the value of assets to children. As in the case of partnerships, trusts too are juridical entities that file tax returns. In some cases, trusts also pay tax. As described by Black's Law Dictionary:

"[A trust is a] legal entity created by a grantor for the benefit of designated beneficiaries under the laws of the state.... The trustee holds a fiduciary responsibility to manage the trust's corpus assets and income for the economic benefit of all of the beneficiaries."[17] Undergirding the attraction of trusts is the donor's desire to continue to control the assets, or at least to limit the beneficiaries' complete control over the assets. (Otherwise, the donor would simply make an outright gift of the assets.) But if the retained control is too great, the trust itself appears to be a sham.[18]

From a tax standpoint, a grantor sometimes establishes a trust in the hope of splitting the income so that some or all of the income will be taxed at a lower rate than the rate applicable to income of the grantor. Of course, an outright gift to the beneficiaries would accomplish this splitting. But a trust is useful if the donor does not want to make an outright gift, whether for tax or non-tax reasons. Congress established a set of complex rules to police these trusts, the so-called grantor trust rules.[19] The primary function of these rules is to differentiate between those trusts in which the grantor retains so much control that she should continue to be treated as the owner of either the assets or the income or both, from those to which the normal rules of trust taxation should apply.

The normal rules of trust taxation depend upon whether the trust is characterized as a simple trust or as a complex trust. A simple trust requires yearly distribution to the beneficiaries of all ordinary income, that is, interest, cash dividends, and the like. Those items are taxable to the trust but the trust receives an offsetting deduction for the distributions it makes to the beneficiaries, who then must report those amounts on their own returns and pay tax. The trust need not distribute capital gains[20] or extraordinary dividends of stock. They are generally retained (though taxed at the trust level) until the termination of the trust.

In contrast, all other trusts, deemed complex trusts, need not, but may, distribute all or part of their yearly earnings to the beneficiaries. Whether they receive distributions or not, beneficiaries will be taxable on their shares of the ordinary income of the trust but not on items of capital gain. When they later receive distributions of the income, they will not be subject to tax on it a second time.

---

17. *Black's Law Dictionary* 1508 (6th ed. 1990).

18. Recall the unsuccessful attempt of Mr. Clifford. See footnote in question 3 following *Horst*.

19. Code sections 671–79 contain these rules.

20. It is not necessary at this point to be able to differentiate between "ordinary income" and "capital gains". We will encounter the fascinating topic of capital gains in Part V.

The graduated rate schedule could, therefore, present a powerful inducement to the use of a trust to transfer income to a lower rate of tax that might apply to trust or beneficiary income.[21] Grantor trust rules constitute the guardian against possible manipulation. If the grantor retains too much control over the income, like Mr. Clifford, the income will be taxable to the grantor. In general, the Code defines the forbidden control as the power to designate the use or enjoyment of the income or corpus. For example, a donor may not have more than a very small reversionary interest, exercise significant administrative power or significant power to designate beneficiaries, or retain the power to revoke the trust or enjoy trust income. To the extent the donor possesses the forbidden power, that portion of the trust will be treated as owned by her. If the grantor retains too much control over the principal, capital gains will be taxable to the grantor. Thus, in recognition that the donor has not really given anything away, the donor will continue to report the ordinary and/or capital gains income of the trust on her own tax return.[22]

In addition to the grantor trust rules, recent changes in the graduated rate schedules have also eliminated some of the attraction of trusts because of the imposition of a sharply graduated rate schedule on trust income.[23] To the extent that income is taxable to the beneficiaries at their individual rates, the use of trusts remains attractive as an income splitting device. To the extent that income is taxable to the trust, the benefit largely disappears.

d. Intra-Family Loans

A final device for transferring income among family members that also led to restrictive legislation was the making of below-market interest rate loans. The idea prompting these loans was to make capital available to a related person, often a child in the family context, who could then use the capital to make an investment that could produce both current income and possible appreciation. As part of the Deficit Reduction Act of 1984, Congress added section 7872 to the Code. You will consider this provision in detail as part of the transactional problems. For now, however, it is enough to understand the extraordinary income shifting that could occur if these transactions succeeded.

---

21. But, note that the trust rate schedule 1(e) imposes a more sharply graduated rate schedule on trusts than the normal schedules for individuals. For example, for 2006, individuals are not subject to the top marginal rate of tax, 35%, until taxable income exceeds $336,550; whereas, trusts are subject to the 35% rate when taxable income exceeds $10,050! See section 1(e). Moreover, trusts do not enjoy a personal exemption or standard deduction in calculating taxable income. But they do receive a small allowance in lieu of personal exemptions under section 642(b).

22. These rules do not eliminate the usefulness of grantor trusts, however. An important use of them has been the growing trend of estate planners to establish revocable *inter vivos* trusts for the purpose of avoiding probate at death. The grantor establishes a trust into which she transfers most of her assets. She also drafts a simple will for the small amount of property she retains, for example, clothing and other personal property. She retains both complete control over the trust and the power to revoke it during her lifetime and, therefore, remains taxable as though no trust existed. But at death, the assets will pass to the beneficiaries without the need for formal probate of her estate. In some states, for example in California where this technique was pioneered, avoidance of probate can save the estate substantial amounts that would otherwise be spent on various expenses of probate and eliminates the delay that probate can create.

23. *See supra* note 19.

DEAN v. COMMISSIONER

35 T.C. 1083 (1961)

RAUM, *Judge*: ... An amended answer filed by the Commissioner claims increases in the deficiencies already determined.... Such increases raise a single issue, ... namely, whether petitioners realized taxable income to the extent of the alleged economic benefit derived from the interest-free use of funds which they had borrowed from a family corporation controlled by them....

...

Issue 2. Income From Interest-Free Loans.

The Commissioner's amended answer charged petitioners with income equal to interest at the alleged legal rate in Delaware (6 percent) with respect to loans which they had obtained upon non-interest-bearing notes from their controlled corporation, Nemours Corporation, and which were outstanding during 1955 and 1956. The theory of the amended answer was that the petitioners realized income to the extent of the economic benefit derived from the free use of borrowed funds from Nemours, and that such economic benefit was equal to interest at the legal rate in Delaware, alleged to be 6 percent per annum. However, the Commissioner's brief has reduced the amount of his additional claim so that the income thus attributed to petitioners is measured, not by the legal rate of interest, but by the prime rate, since it is stipulated that petitioners could have borrowed the funds at the prime rate. As thus reduced, the additional income which the Commissioner seeks to charge to petitioners is $65,648.79 for 1955 and $97,931.71 for 1956. The facts in relation to this issue have been stipulated as follows:

9. Prior to December 17, 1954 the entire issued and outstanding capital stock of Nemours Corporation, hereinafter referred to as Nemours, organized under the laws of the State of Delaware with principal office in Wilmington, Delaware, consisting of 36,172 shares of no par common, was owned by the petitioners, as follows:

J. Simpson Dean .... 7,249 shares
Paulina duPont Dean [Dean's wife] .... 28,923 shares

10. On December 17, 1954 each of the petitioners made a gift of 2,000 shares of the stock of Nemours to the above-mentioned trusts created by them in 1937 for the benefit of their children. In the years 1955 and 1956 the petitioners owned 32,172 shares of no par common of Nemours.

...

13. Petitioner J. Simpson Dean owed Nemours on non-interest bearing notes the following amounts:

Period	Amount
January 1, 1955 to January 10, 1955	$302,185.73
January 11, 1955 to December 31, 1955	223,861.56
January 1, 1956 to December 31, 1956	357,293.41

14. Petitioner Paulina duPont Dean owed Nemours on non-interest bearing notes the following amounts:

Period	Amount
January 1, 1955 to December 31, 1955	$1,832,764.71
January 1, 1956 to December 31, 1956	2,205,804.66

15. The following are the prime rates of interest and the dates on which changes were made in such rates at which the petitioners could have borrowed money during the years 1955 and 1956:

January 1, 1955 . . . . 3%
August 15, 1955 . . . . 3 1/4%
October 20, 1955 . . . . 3 1/2%
April 20, 1956 . . . . 3 3/4%
September 1, 1956 . . . . 4%
December 31, 1956 . . . . 4%

16. Interest computed at the prime rates shown in the preceding paragraph on the non-interest bearing notes of the petitioners for the taxable years 1955 and 1956 would be as follows:

Year 1955:	*Amount*
J. Simpson Dean	$7,203.98
Paulina duPont Dean	58,444.81
Total	$65,648.79

Year 1956:	*Amount*
J. Simpson Dean	$13,651.59
Paulina duPont Dean	84,280.12
Total	$97,931.71

...

The theory of the Commissioner's amended answer . . . undoubtedly had its origin in a statement by this Court in a Memorandum Opinion involving certain gift taxes of these tax payers, *Paulina duPont Dean*, T.C. Memo. 1960-54, on appeal (C.A. 3), where it was said:

> Viewed realistically, the lending of over two million dollars to petitioners without interest might be looked upon as a means of passing on earnings (certainly potential earnings) of Nemours in lieu of dividends, to the extent of a reasonable interest on such loans. . . .

The amended answer herein was filed within several months after the foregoing Memorandum Opinion had been promulgated. The statement quoted above was mere dictum and we have not been directed to any case holding or even suggesting that an interest-free loan may result in the realization of taxable income by the debtor, or to any administrative ruling or regulation taking that position. Although the question may not be completely free from doubt we think that no taxable income is realized in such circumstances.

In support of its present position, the Government relies primarily upon a series of cases holding that rent-free use of corporate property by a stockholder or officer may result in the realization of income. . . . *Paulina duPont Dean*, 9 T.C. 256 (rent-free use of corporation's house). . . . These cases bear a superficial resemblance to the present case, but reflection convinces us that they are not in point. In each of them a benefit was conferred upon the stockholder or officer in circumstances such that had the stockholder or officer undertaken to procure the same benefit by an expenditure of money such expenditure would not have been deductible by him. Here, on the other hand, had petitioners borrowed the funds in question on interest-bearing notes, their payment of interest would have been fully deductible by them under section 163, I.R.C. 1954. Not only would they not be charged with the additional income in controversy herein, but they would have a deduction equal to that very amount. We think this circumstance differentiates the various cases relied upon by the Commissioner, and perhaps explains why he has apparently never taken this position in any prior case.

We have heretofore given full force to interest-free loans for tax purposes, holding that they result in no interest deduction for the borrower, ... nor interest income to the lender,.... We think it to be equally true that an interest-free loan results in no taxable gain to the borrower, and we hold that the Commissioner is not entitled to any increased deficiency based upon this issue.

Reviewed by the Court.

...

OPPER, J., concurring: The necessity is not apparent to me of deciding more on the second issue than that there can be no deficiency. If petitioners were in receipt of some kind of gross income, ... the corresponding interest deduction would perhaps exactly offset and nullify it. But because that would mean that there is no deficiency, it would not necessarily follow that there was no gross income, as the present opinion, in my view, gratuitously holds. Certainly the statement that an interest-free loan results in no taxable gain to the borrower is much too broad a generalization to make here.

Suppose, for example, ... [that] the property made available without charge to the shareholder-officer was rented by him to another, instead of being occupied for personal use. Would the fact that he could presumably deduct as a business or nonbusiness expense the hypothetical rental value theoretically paid by him to the corporation, ... and thereby completely offset any gross income, lead us to conclude, as here, contrary to that whole line of cases, that there could be no gross income in the first place?

Or suppose the facts showed that the indebtedness was incurred ... to purchase or carry obligations ... the interest on which is wholly exempt from ... taxes. Sec. 265(2), I.R.C. 1954.

This being apparently a case of first impression, the present result seems peculiarly unfortunate in deciding a point that need not be passed on. To make matters worse, the burden here is on respondent, since the issue was first raised by his answer; and thus in this leading case all factual conclusions and inferences must be favorable to petitioners....

...

BRUCE, J., dissenting: I respectfully dissent from the opinion of the majority with respect to the second issue. In my opinion the present case is not distinguishable in principle from such cases as *Paulina duPont Dean*, 9 T.C. 256 ... and other cases cited by the majority, wherein it was held that the rent-free use of corporate property by a stockholder or officer resulted in the realization of income. Interest in the sense that it represents compensation paid for the use, forbearance, or detention of money, may be likened to rent which is paid for the use of property.

I agree with Judge Opper in his concurring opinion that the statement that 'an interest-free loan results in no taxable gain to the borrower' is much too broad a generalization to make here. I do not wish to infer that the interest-free loan of money should be construed as resulting in taxable income to the borrower in every instance. However, it is difficult to believe that the interest-free loan of in excess of $2 million ($2,563,098.07 throughout 1956) by a personal holding company to its majority stockholders (its only stockholders prior to December 17, 1954) did not result in any economic benefit to the borrower.

In my opinion, the statement that had petitioners borrowed the funds in question on interest-bearing notes, their payment of interest would have been fully deductible by them under section 163, I.R.C. 1954, is likewise too broad a generalization to make here.

Section 163(a) states the General Rule to be that there shall be allowed as a deduction all interest paid or accrued within the taxable year on indebtedness. Section 265(2) provides, however, that

No deduction shall be allowed for

...

(2) INTEREST. Interest on indebtedness incurred or continued to purchase or carry obligations ... the interest on which is wholly exempt from the taxes imposed by this subtitle.

Section 265(2) is specifically included in the cross references contained in subsection (c) of section 163 and is therefore clearly intended as an exception to, or limitation upon, section 163(a). For obligations, the interest on which is wholly exempt from taxes, see section 103 of the Internal Revenue Code of 1954.

It is recognized that the burden with respect to the issue here presented by his amended answer is upon the respondent. This burden, however, was, in my opinion, discharged by the stipulated facts presented. It was incumbent upon the petitioners, if such were the facts, to plead and establish that had they been required to pay interest on the loans in question they would have been entitled to deduct such interest from their gross income. They have done neither. It is well established that deductions are matters of legislative grace and must be clearly established.

On the record presented herein, I do not agree that had petitioners borrowed the funds in question on interest-bearing notes, their payment of interest would have been fully deductible by them under section 163, and that the inclusion in the gross income of the petitioners of an amount representing a reasonable rate of interest on the loans in question would therefore result in no deficiency.

Consider the following questions.

1. What is the prime rate? Is it the same as the legal rate?

2. What benefit did the recipient of the loan enjoy as a consequence of the Court's holding in *Dean*? Was it an accession to wealth?

3. The court draws a distinction between the rent-free use of a house and an interest-free loan, based on the deductibility of interest as an expense.[24] **Review the income tax calculation outline, and look at section 163. Is the court's distinction justified?** Note Judge Opper's concurrence and Judge Bruce's dissent.

4. If Dean had borrowed from an unrelated lender, *e.g.*, the First National Bank of New Haven, would he have been able to do so without paying interest on his borrowing? If the corporation had issued bonds, *i.e.*, borrowed money (**recall *Kirby Lumber***), could it have done so without paying interest to the holders of the bonds?

5. If a corporation intended to benefit its employee through the use of a non-cash benefit, what would be the proper characterization of that benefit to the employee? Re-

----

24. In fact, in a prior case involving the same taxpayers, the Tax Court held that the rent-free use of a house owned by the corporation was income. *Dean v. Commissioner*, 9 T.C. 256 (1947).

view section 61(a)(1) and Treasury Regulation section 1.61-2(d). To the employer? Review section 162(a)(1).

6. The borrower in *Dean* was a shareholder of the corporation making the loan. How would you characterize the corporation's motive for making an interest-free loan to a shareholder?

7. What if the lender in *Dean* had been a mother and the recipient of the interest-free loan her son? How might you characterize the making of an interest-free loan by a mother to a son? Is the motive the same as it was in *Dean*?

8. Recall our discussion of the time value of money in Part II, Chapter 1. **Review the Adams Adverts problem following *Raytheon*.** Can you better explain the concept that underlies that principle after having considered *Dean* and the foregoing questions?

The *Dean* case spurred continuing controversy and led to the multiplication of various schemes for transferring the income-producing capacity of capital. The Service, however, did not abandon its view that the benefit of an interest-free loan represented income to the donee. Rather than directly challenging the *Dean* decision, however, it focused on a different aspect of another intra-family, interest-free loan transaction in *Dickman v. Commissioner*, 465 U.S. 330 (1984). In *Dickman*, the Supreme Court held that the forgone interest was a transfer of economic value that constituted a gift (for gift tax purposes), when the interest-free loan occurred in an intra-family context. The Court observed:

The right to the use of $100,000 without charge is a valuable interest in the money lent, as much so as the rent-free use of property consisting of land and buildings. In either case, there is a measurable economic value associated with the use of the property transferred. The value of the use of money is found in what it can produce; the measure of that value is interest — "rent" for the use of the funds.

Id. at 337.

As noted earlier, Congress responded by adding section 7872 to the Code as part of the 1984 Act. Consider the following excerpts from the legislative history of section 7872. To what extent do you suspect that Congress was motivated by *Dean* and *Dickman*? Does it seem likely that Congress keeps up with the decisions of the federal courts dealing with tax issues? How would such decisions ultimately affect the legislative process?

General Explanation of the Revenue Provisions of the Deficit Reduction Act of 1984[25]

2. Below-market and Interest-free Loans (Sec. 172 of the Act and new sec. 7872 of the Code)

Prior Law

Transfers of income other than by interest-free or below-market interest rate loans

Direct assignments of income. Investment income is generally taxed to the owner of the income producing property, even if the owner of the property makes a gift of the

---

25. Joint Comm. on Taxation, 98th Cong., General Explanation of the Revenue Provisions of the Deficit Reduction Act of 1984, at 524 (Joint Comm. Print 1985).

right to receive the income prior to its receipt. The rationale for this rule is that the owner of the property realizes the income upon the exercise of control over its disposition. *Helvering v. Horst*, 311 U.S. 112 (1940)....

For example, if a cash method taxpayer detaches coupons from a bond and gives them to his or her son, without receiving fair value in exchange, and the son receives the interest represented by the coupons, the interest income would be included in income by the parent donor under the principles of Horst....

Transfers of income-producing property to trusts. In general, the income of a trust that is distributed by the trust to its beneficiaries is not taxed at the trust level. Rather, such income is taxed only to beneficiaries of the trust. In contrast, income retained by a trust is taxed to the trust. If, however, a transferor of property to a trust (a "grantor") is treated as the owner of the transferred property for Federal income tax purposes, income, deductions and credits of the trust are attributed directly to the grantor and not to either the trust or its beneficiaries.

In general, a grantor is treated as the owner of transferred property if he retains certain power over, or interest in, the trust....

Demand or term loans to family members

Under prior law, an interest-free or below-market interest rate loan (each of which is referred to herein as a "below-market loan") without consideration resulted in a gift from the lender to the borrower for Federal tax purposes. *Dickman v. Commissioner*, 465 U.S. ___ (1984), 52 U.S.L.W. 4222 (U.S. Feb. 22, 1984). In the case of a demand loan, the amount of the gift was the value of the right to the use of the money for "such portion of the year as the [lender] in fact allows the [borrower] the use of the money." ... Under this approach, the amount of the gift was calculable as of the last day of each calendar year during which the loan was outstanding.

In the case of a term loan, the amount of the gift was the excess, at the time of the exchange of the money and the note, of the amount of money borrowed over the present value of the principal and interest payments required to be made under the terms of the loan....

Under prior law, the Federal income tax consequences of these below-market loans were not clear. Prior to enactment of the provision, the courts had addressed only the gift tax consequences of the transactions.

Loans to employees or shareholders

Demand loans. Under prior law, the Internal Revenue Service consistently asserted that, in the case of a below-market demand loan to an employee or shareholder ... the borrower derived an economic benefit that should be included in income for Federal income tax purposes. Under the Service's position, the amount of the income was the excess of the interest that would have been charged by an independent lender over the interest, if any, that was actually charged under the terms of the loan.

Notwithstanding the Internal Revenue Service's position, the Tax Court consistently held that non-family below-market demand loans did not result in taxable income. In *J. Simpson Dean v. Commissioner*, 35 T.C. 1083 (1961), for example, the controlling shareholders of Nemours Corporation borrowed substantial sums of money from the corporation on a non-interest bearing basis. The Internal Revenue Service sought to impute interest income to the borrowers. The Tax Court, however, held that the transactions did not result in income to the borrowers on the grounds that had they "borrowed the funds in question on interest bearing notes, their payment of interest would have been fully deductible by them under section 163. (Footnote 7) ...

Term loans. Under prior law, the Federal tax treatment of non-family below-market term loans was unclear. In one case, the Tax Court held that shareholders of a corporation, who obtained an interest-free loan from the corporation in order to purchase the corporation's assets, received a distribution of earnings taxable to them as a dividend. Further, the Court held that the amount of the dividend was the excess of the fair market value of the property received over the present value of the taxpayer's note....

...

Reasons for Change

A below-market loan is the economic equivalent of a loan bearing a market rate of interest, and a payment by the lender to the borrower to fund the payment of interest by the borrower. The Congress believed that, in many instances, the failure of the tax laws to treat these transactions in accordance with their economic substance provided taxpayers with opportunities to circumvent well-established tax rules.

Under prior law, loans between family members (and other similar loans) were being used to avoid the assignment of income rules and the grantor trust rules. A below-market loan to a family member, for example, generally involves a gratuitous transfer of the right to use the proceeds of the borrowing until repayment is demanded (in the case of a demand loan) or until the end of the term of the loan (in the case of a term loan). If the lender had assigned the income from the proceeds to the borrower instead of lending the proceeds to the borrower, the assignment of income doctrine would have taxed the lender (and not the borrower) on the income. If the lender had transferred the principal amount to a trust established for the benefit of the borrower that was revocable at will (similar to a demand loan), or that would terminate at the end of a period of not more than 10 years (similar to a term loan with a term of not more than 10 years), the income earned on trust assets would have been taxed to the lender under the grantor trust provisions....

In addition, loans from corporations to shareholders were being used to avoid rules requiring the taxation of corporate income at the corporate level. A below-market loan from a corporation to a shareholder is the economic equivalent of a loan by the corporation to the shareholder requiring the payment of interest at a market rate, and a distribution by the corporation to the shareholder with respect to its stock equal to the amount of interest required to be paid under the terms of the loan. If a transaction were structured as a distribution and a loan, the borrower would have dividend income and an offsetting interest deduction. The lender would have interest income. Under prior law, if the transaction was structured as a below-market loan, the lender avoided including in income the interest that would have been paid by the borrower. As a result, the lender was in the same economic position as it would have been if it had deducted amounts distributed as dividends to shareholders.

Finally, loans to persons providing services were being used to avoid rules requiring the payment of employment taxes and rules restricting the deductibility of interest in certain situations by the person providing the services. A below-market loan to a person providing services is the economic equivalent of a loan requiring the payment of interest at a market rate, and a payment in the nature of compensation equal to the amount of interest required to be paid under the terms of the loan. Under prior law, a transaction structured as a loan and a payment in the nature of compensation often did not result in any tax consequences for either the lender or the borrower because each would have offsetting income and deductions. However, there were a number of situations in which the payment of compensation and a loan requiring the payment of interest at a market rate did not offset. For example, if a taxpayer used the proceeds of an arm's-length loan to invest in tax-exempt obligations, the deduction for interest paid on the loan would be disallowed under section 265. Similarly, if a term loan extended beyond the taxable year in which it was made, income and deductions did not offset because the compensation income was includible in the year the loan was made. In such circumstances, substantial tax advantages could have been derived by structuring the transaction as a below-market loan.

Explanation of Provision

Overview

The Act adds to the Code new section 7872 (relating to the tax treatment of loans that, in substance, result in a gift, payment of compensation, dividend, capital contribution, or other similar payment from the lender to the borrower). Loans that are subject to the provision and that do not require payment of interest, or require payment at a rate below the statutory rate (referred to as the "applicable Federal rate"), are recharacterized as an arm's-length transaction in which the lender made a loan to the borrower in exchange for a note requiring the payment of interest at the applicable Federal rate. This rule results in the parties being treated as if:

(1) The borrower paid interest to the lender that may be deductible to the borrower and is included in income by the lender; and

(2) The lender (a) made a gift subject to the gift tax (in the case of a gratuitous transaction), or (b) paid a dividend or made a capital contribution (in the case of a loan between a corporation and a shareholder), or (c) paid compensation (in the case of a loan to a person providing services), or (d) made some other payment characterized in accordance with the substance of the transaction.

The Congress intended that, in general, in the case of a loan subject to this provision, the amount of the deemed payment from the lender to the borrower is to be determined solely under this provision. Thus, in the case of a below-market loan from a parent to a child, the amount of the gift is to be determined under section 7872, and not under the decision in the *Dickman* case, *supra*, even if the applicable Federal rate is less than a fair market interest rate. Further, in the case of a loan from an employer to an employee, the amount of the compensation is to be determined under section 7872, and not under section 83, even if the applicable Federal rate is less than a fair market interest rate.

...

Loans subject to the provision

The provision applies to term or demand loans that are gift loans, compensation-related loans, corporation-shareholder loans, and tax avoidance loans. In addition, the Congress intended that, under regulations to be prescribed by the Treasury, the provision is to apply to other similar transactions (i.e., loan transactions that in substance affect a transfer from the lender to the borrower other than the transfer of the principal amount of the loan) if the interest arrangements have a significant effect on the tax liability of either the borrower or the lender.

Generally, it was intended that the term "loan" be interpreted broadly in light of the purposes of the provision. Thus, any transfer of money that provides the transferor with a right to repayment is a loan. For example, advances and deposits of all kinds are treated as loans.

Demand loans and term loans. A demand loan is any loan which is payable in full at any time upon the demand of the lender. A term loan is any loan which is not a demand loan.

Gift loans. A gift loan is any below-market loan where the foregone interest is in the nature of a gift. In general, there is a gift if property (including foregone interest) is transferred for less than full and adequate consideration under circumstances where the transfer is a gift for gift tax purposes. A sale, exchange, or other transfer made in the ordinary course of business (i.e., a transaction which is bona fide, at arm's length and free from any donative intent) generally is considered as made for and full and adequate consideration. A loan between unrelated persons can qualify as a gift loan.

It was intended that if a taxpayer makes a below-market demand loan to a trust and the loan is treated as a revocable transfer of property for purposes of Subpart E, the provisions of Subpart E govern.... (Footnote 8)

...

Compensation-related loans.—A compensation-related loan is any below-market loan made in connection with the performance of services directly or indirectly between (1) an employer and an employee, or (2) an independent contractor and a person for whom such independent contractor provides services.

The Congress intended that an arrangement be treated as a compensation-related loan if, in substance, there is a compensatory element arising from the transaction. Thus, for example, a below-market loan by an employer to a child of an employee generally will be recharacterized under the provision as a compensation-related loan by the employer to the employee and a gift loan by the employee to the child.

The Congress intended that if an employer makes a payment to an unrelated third-party lender to buy-down a mortgage loan for an employee and, taking into account all the facts and circumstances, the transaction is in substance (1) a loan at a market rate by a third-party lender to the employee, and (2) a payment by the employer to secure a valuable benefit for the employee, the payment by the employer to the lender is to be treated as compensation under generally applicable principles of tax law. To that extent, the below-market loan rules do not apply. However, if the transaction is in substance a loan by the employer made with the aid of services provided by the third-party lender acting as an agent of the employer, there is a compensation-related loan subject to this provision.

Also, if an employee receives payment from a customer for services rendered on behalf of an employer, and is permitted to retain the money for a period without paying interest at a rate equal to or greater than the applicable Federal rate, there is generally a compensation-related loan. For example, if an investment banker is permitted by an issuer to retain the proceeds from a public offering of stock or debt for a period without paying interest, there is a below-market loan from the issuer to the banker. To the extent the benefit is in lieu of a fee for services, the loan is a compensation-related loan. (Footnote 9)

In the case of a compensation-related loan, the deemed payment by the lender to the borrower is treated as wages for purposes of chapter 21 (the Federal Insurance Contributions Act), ... and chapter 23 (the Federal Unemployment Tax Act) of the Code. Further, unless otherwise provided in regulations, a payment must be included in gross income by the borrower, even if the borrower is likely to be entitled to an offsetting deduction.

The Act provides that demand loans are exempt from wage withholding under chapter 24. The Congress intended that term loans also be exempt from wage withholding. A technical amendment may be required to effectuate this intent. Finally, even though there is no wage withholding, the Congress intended that all deemed payments be reported under the appropriate information reporting provision.

Corporation-shareholder loans.—A corporation-shareholder loan is any below-market loan made directly or indirectly between a corporation and any shareholder of such corporation.

Tax avoidance loans.—A below-market loan is a tax-avoidance loan if one of the principal purposes of the interest arrangement is the avoidance of any Federal tax by either the borrower or the lender. Tax-avoidance is a principal purpose of the interest arrangement if it is a principal factor in the decision to structure the transaction as a below-market loan, rather than a loan requiring the payment of interest at a rate that equals or exceeds the applicable Federal rate and a payment by the lender to the borrower.

Other below-market loans.—A loan that is not a gift loan, compensation-related loan, corporation-shareholder loan or tax avoidance loan may be subject to these provisions under Treasury regulations if the interest arrangement has a significant effect on the tax liability of the borrower or the lender.

The interest arrangement of a below-market loan has an effect on the tax liability of the borrower or the lender if, among other things, it results in the conversion of a nondeductible expense into the equivalent of a deductible expense. Generally, there is such a conversion when a taxpayer makes a non-interest bearing refundable deposit in partial or total payment of the cost of a nondeductible item or expense. For example, if a member of a club makes a non-interest bearing refundable deposit to the club in lieu of part or all of his or her membership fee, the member is paying the fee with money that has not been included in his income (i.e., the investment income from the proceeds of the deposit), and has, in effect, converted the fee into the equivalent of a deductible expense.

    . . .

The Congress anticipated that in determining whether an effect is significant, the Treasury will consider all the facts and circumstances, including (1) whether items of income and deduction generated by the loan offset each other, (2) the amount of such items, (3) the cost to the taxpayer of complying with the provision, and (4) any non-tax reasons for deciding to structure the transaction as a below-market loan rather than a loan with interest at a rate equal to or greater than the applicable Federal rate and a payment by the lender to the borrower.

In general, the Congress did not intend that the provision apply to below-market loans in the form of interest-bearing or other accounts in a financial institution in the ordinary course of its trade or business, loans by a financial institution in the ordinary course of its trade or business, loans by an insurance company to a policyholder of the cash value of such policyholder's insurance policy, or to most loans subsidized by the government (such as government insured or guaranteed student loans or residential mortgages). Further, the Congress did not intend that the provision apply to any below-market program-related loan by a private foundation or other charitable organization. It was intended, however, that the rules generally applicable to compensation-related loans apply to below-market loans by banks to employees.

...

Applicable Federal rate

Under the Act, the adequacy of any stated interest, and the amount of any deemed payments are determined by reference to an applicable Federal rate as determined under section 1274(d). For any period beginning on or after January 1, 1985, there will be three such rates: a short-term rate; a mid-term rate; and a long-term rate. In the case of a demand loan, the relevant rate generally is the short-term rate. In the case of a term loan, the relevant rate is determined by reference to the term of the loan, as set forth below:

Term	Rate
3 years or less	The Federal short-term rate
Over 3 years but not over 9 years	The Federal mid-term rate
Over 9 years	The Federal long-term rate

These rates are to be determined by the Treasury within 15 days after the close of 6-month periods ending on September 30 and March 31, respectively, and are to reflect the average market yield during such 6-month periods on outstanding marketable obligations of the United States with comparable maturities.

...

De minimis exceptions

The Act provides specific de minimis rules. For purposes of applying these rules, all loans between the same parties are aggregated.

De minimis exception for gift loans between individuals.—As a general rule, no amount is treated as transferred by the lender to the borrower, or retransferred by the borrower to the lender, for any day during which the aggregate, outstanding amount of loans does not exceed $10,000....

...

Because a term gift loan is treated as a demand loan for purposes of determining the timing and amount of the deemed transfers by the borrower to the lender, generally no amount is deemed transferred by the borrower to the lender for any day on which the aggregate amount owed is $10,000 or less. Thus, if the balance of a term gift loan fluctuates, there may be income tax consequences for some days but not for other days.

De minimis exception for compensation related loans and corporation shareholder loans.—A de minimis exception is provided for loans between (1) an employer and an employee, or an independent contractor and a person for whom such independent contractor provides services, or (2) a corporation and a shareholder of such corporation. Under these rules, in the case of a demand loan, no amount is treated as transferred by the lender to the borrower, and retransferred by the borrower to the lender, for any day during which the aggregate outstanding amount owed by the borrower to the lender does not exceed $10,000. In the case of a term loan, no amount is treated as transferred or retransferred if on the day the loan is made the aggregate outstanding amount owed by the borrower to the lender does not exceed $10,000. However, in the event of a reduction in the outstanding balance of a term loan below $10,000, the provision continues to apply....

...

Special rules for gift loans. The amount treated as retransferred by the borrower to the lender for any day on which the aggregate outstanding amount of loans between the lender and the borrower does not exceed $10,000 is limited to the borrower's net investment income for the year....

The term net investment income has the same meaning as it does for purposes of section 163(d)(3). Thus, the term generally means the excess of investment income over investment expense....

In addition, if a borrower has less than $1,000 of net investment income for the year, such borrower's net investment income for the year is deemed to be zero. Thus, if the aggregate outstanding amount of loans from the lender to the borrower does not exceed $100,000 on any day during a year, and the borrower has less than $1,000 of net investment income for the year, no amount is treated as retransferred by the borrower to the lender for such year.

. . .

Regulations

Under the Act, the Treasury is directed to prescribe such regulations as may be necessary or appropriate to carry out the purposes of the section, including (but not limited to) regulations providing for the application of the section in cases involving varying rates of interest, conditional interest payments, waivers of interest, or other circumstances. For example, the Congress anticipated that regulations may provide that if a loan is made requiring the payment of interest and the interest is waived, cancelled, or reduced, the lender will have income if the waiver, cancellation, or reduction is in the nature of a gift, payment of compensation, dividend, contribution to capital or other similar payment.

. . .

The authority granted to the Treasury Department also includes the authority to issue regulations exempting from these provisions any class of transactions if the interest arrangements do not have a significant effect on the tax liability of the borrower or the lender. The Congress anticipated that, in appropriate circumstances, compensation-related loans, including employee-relocation loans, may be exempted by these regulations. The term "significant effect" has the same meaning for this purpose as it does for purposes of determining whether loans not otherwise covered by the provision should be subject to it under regulations.

Authority is also provided to issue regulations for the purpose of assuring that borrowers and lenders take consistent positions under this provision. In appropriate cases, these regulations may condition a deduction for imputed interest on adequate identification of the lender.

In addition, authority is provided to issue regulations concerning the tax consequences of a disposition by a lender or a borrower of his or her interest in a below-market loan, or the acquisition of an interest in such a loan.

FOOTNOTES:

7. The Tax Court distinguished this case from the cases involving rent-free use of corporate property by shareholders or officers ... on the grounds that rental payments would not have been deductible in those cases.

8. This result is required because it would be anomalous to give effect for tax purposes to a loan made by a taxpayer to himself or herself.

9. To the extent the benefit is not in lieu of a fee for services, such an arrangement nevertheless may have a significant effect on the tax liability of the lender or the borrower. If so, the loan may be treated under regulations as a loan subject to the provision.

Indeed, as the Joint Committee states, section 7872 recognizes the economic reality that when a lender makes a below-market interest loan, the forgone interest constitutes a transfer of value to the recipient of the loan. The section characterizes that value according to the relationship between the lender and the borrower. So, for example, the value transferred as a result of a below-market interest loan between an employer and an employee clearly represents compensation. Therefore, section 7872 characterizes it as compensation, includible in the gross income of the employee and deductible by the employer as a business expense. The value transferred between a corporation and a shareholder is treated as a distribution often characterized as a dividend, and section 7872 treats it as such.[26] The section would,[27] therefore, have required the taxpayer in *Dean* to report the benefit as a dividend; the employer corporation would not have been able to deduct it as an expense. Also, the section adopts the gift characterization of the Court in *Dickman* for intra-family loans. As a result (subject to certain de minimis rules you will see in detail in a later transactional problem), the section treats the benefit as a gift to the recipient.

To accomplish its purpose, the section adopts a fictional two-step process: the first step treats the transfer of value from lender ("L") to borrower ("B") characterized according to the motivation for the loan. The second step creates a transfer of that value back to the lender from the borrower as the payment of interest. The two-step process looks like this:

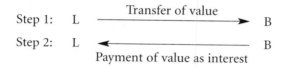

Therefore, in the case of *Dean*, the first step in section 7872 would treat the transfer of the value of the interest-free loan to the employee as additional compensation income; she would include it in her income and the employer would deduct it as a business expense. The second step would treat the employee as paying an equal amount in interest to the employer; the employee might be able to deduct the interest expense[28] and the employer would have interest income.

C. Statutorily Sanctioned Assignments: The Concept of Family

As the foregoing materials have demonstrated, our progressive rate structure invites income-splitting schemes because income splitting can produce a dramatically lower

---

26. Not all distributions from corporations to their shareholders are characterized as dividends. The distribution must be out of a corporation's "earnings and profits," *i.e.*, its previously taxed earnings. *See* section 316. Further discussion of the "earnings and profits" concept is beyond the scope of this text.

27. Certain de minimis rules apply to small loans and special rules differentiate between loans for a fixed period ("term loans") and those that may be called at any time ("demand loans").

28. Congress substantially tightened the rules for deducting interest in the Tax Reform Act of 1986. The deductibility of interest under section 163 now depends upon the reason for the borrowing. **Review section 163.** We will take this issue up in detail in the real estate problems.

overall tax burden. For that reason, taxpayers have been extremely creative in attempting to formulate schemes that will produce the desired effect. And, we have seen, the family is a perfect vehicle for employing many of these schemes. What the cases show is that splitting of income from services will not generally succeed; splitting of income from capital will, if carefully planned. There are, however, cases in which Congress has specifically sanctioned income splitting in the family context. As you go through these materials, consider what policies or practical considerations may underlie Congress' blessing of these types of assignment of income.

1. The Joint Return

For almost half the life of our present income tax system, the marital status of the taxpayer was nearly irrelevant. A single rate schedule measured the tax liability of both single and married taxpayers. Therefore, taxpayers calculated federal income tax on an individual basis and a single individual with an income of $10,000 paid the same tax as a married taxpayer with the same income and a non-working spouse. As a consequence, the progressive rates of tax led inevitably to various creative methods for "splitting" income. **Recall our discussion of** *Lucas v. Earl.*

Would the result have been different if the Earls had simply filed a joint return? The answer is that the Code did not permit married taxpayers, such as the Earls, to file the type of joint return that would result in a rate of tax calculated as though each spouse had earned one-half the income. Although the Code had permitted married taxpayers to file joint returns beginning in 1918, the tax on the joint income of the couple would be the same amount as it would have been had the total income been attributable to only one of the spouses. But at a time when few women worked outside the home, the couple's taxable income generally represented only that of the husband. Therefore, the filing of a joint return made no difference to the amount of tax due on the return from the amount that would have been due had the husband filed a separate return.

In the same year that the Supreme Court decided *Lucas v. Earl*, it also decided the case of *Poe v. Seaborn*, 282 U.S. 101 (1930). In *Poe v. Seaborn*, the Court recognized the ability of taxpayers in community property states to split one spouse's income as a result of the operation of community property laws.[29] The taxpayers in *Poe v. Seaborn* were a husband and wife who lived in a community property state.[30] Only one of the spouses had income, but the taxpayers took the position that the community property statute of their state meant that from the moment the income was earned by one, the other had a vested interest in one-half. That is, that the earner never had a right to more than one-half the income and, therefore, could not be taxed on more than one-half. The Supreme Court approved their splitting of the income so that each was taxable on one-half. Their total resulting tax bill was less than it would have been for a married couple in a common-law state.[31] Can you predict what happened next?

Many state legislatures considered adopting community property rules. Between 1939 and 1947, "[f]ive states and the territory of Hawaii abandoned their common-law

---

29. What is "community property"?
30. Which are the community property states?
31. What is a common law state? Why is it called a common-law state?

marital property systems and adopted community property regimes."[32] While other common-law states deliberated a change, some taxpayers attained a similar result by placing income-producing property in joint tenancies, family partnerships, or family trusts. These techniques did not accomplish the desired result for earned income, however. That took the action of Congress, which finally came in 1948 when Congress enacted the predecessor to section 6013(a).

The 1948 provision accomplished for all married taxpayers the result the Seaborns had achieved under the law of the State of Washington (but, because of a difference in state law, the Earls were unable to achieve under the law of the State of California[33]). The new provision allowed married taxpayers to file a joint return and use a table that resulted in a total tax to them equal to the amount it would have been if each spouse had one-half the total marital income. The 1948 legislation, therefore, constitutes an important example of congressionally sanctioned assignment of income, a reasonable outcome for those who argue that the proper taxpayer is the family unit.

Applies to Earl last

Consider the following questions.

1. Suppose Wendy is married to Hillel. **Look at section 7703 for the Code's directions for the determination of marital status.** Wendy has taxable income of $200,000 and Hillel, who is a student, has no income. What would be the couple's proper filing status under section 1? Is there more than one? What would be their total tentative federal income tax liability for this year under the relevant status?[35] Does section 1(a) accomplish the result that the Earls attempted to effect by their contract? What if Wendy and Hillel were not married, but lived together, would their total tax liability change?

2. What if Wendy and Hillel each had taxable income of $100,000. From a tax standpoint only, would they prefer to be married or not married? (After you have done the calculations for the various configurations of Wendy and Hillel's marriage/living arrangements, can you explain why tax policy experts, politicians, and some married couples decry the "marriage penalty" and why some couples enjoy a "marriage bonus"?)

---

32. Carolyn Jones, *Split Income and Separate Spheres: Tax Law and Gender Roles in the 1940s* 1 (Legal History Program, Inst. for Legal Studies, Univ. of Wisconsin—Madison Law School Working Paper 2:5, 1987).

33. If you listed California as one of the community property states, you may wonder why the Supreme Court treated the Earls differently from the Seaborns. The answer lies in the differences between the community property laws of the two states, California and Washington, as determined by the Court. In *United States v. Robbins*, 269 U.S. 315 (1926), the Court determined that under California's community property law, the wife had no more than "a mere expectancy" in community property. In contrast, in *Poe v. Seaborn*, 282 U.S. 101 (1930), the Court determined that under Washington's community property law, the wife had an immediate vested present interest in one-half the couple's joint income.

34. Because this result ensued regardless of whether the entire amount of the income was earned by one of the spouses or each earned a part, it was inevitable that unmarried taxpayers would complain. One single taxpayer argued to Congress that it was unfair to her that her income should be taxed at a higher rate than that of a married man with a non-earning wife simply because she was unable to find a husband! Congress responded once again, in 1969, by changing the rate structure in order to ameliorate this disparity.

35. **Look back at the income tax calculation outline in the Introduction to this book.** Remember that Wendy's and Hillel's final tax will be their tentative tax reduced by any credits to which they are entitled and increased by any other taxes (for example, social security tax).

The income-splitting effect of the joint return has been most beneficial to single-earner couples, creating a "marriage bonus," at times when the rates on ordinary income have been the highest. As the incomes of husband and wife become more equal and as the rate schedule becomes flatter, the value of the joint return declines. Indeed, the current rates of tax create a "marriage penalty" whereby a joint return may produce a higher total tax than the total tax that would be applicable to two single taxpayers. The marriage bonus or penalty occurs because of choices Congress makes for setting the relative rates for single and married taxpayers. As Professor Boris I. Bittker has observed: "we cannot simultaneously have (a) progression, (b) equal taxes on equal-income married couples, and (c) a marriage-neutral tax burden."[36]

Concern about the marriage penalty prompted Congress to amend the standard deduction provision and the rate tables beginning with the 2001 Act, which gradually increased the standard deduction for married joint filers beginning in 2005. Congress acted again in 2003, accelerating the gradual increase. Congress then superseded the gradual increases that were part of the 2001 and 2003 Acts as part of the Working Families Tax Relief Act of 2004 (hereinafter "the 2004 Working Families Act"). These 2001, 2003, and 2004 Working Families Acts changes attempted to ameliorate, at least in part, the marriage penalty.[37] Under these Acts, the standard deduction for married couples filing jointly increased to twice the amount of the standard deduction allowed a single taxpayer for tax years beginning in 2005.[38]

The 2001, 2003, and 2004 Working Families Acts also affected the rate tables. Under the 2001 and 2003 Acts the portion of the taxable income of married taxpayers filing jointly subject to the 15% rate was gradually to increase to twice the amount of taxable income of a single taxpayer subject to the 15% rate.[39] The 2004 Working Families Act also accelerated this process, making the increase in the amount of taxable income of married joint filers equal to twice the amount of taxable income of single

---

36. Boris I. Bittker, *Federal Income Taxation and the Family*, 27 Stan. L. Rev. 1389, 1396 (1975).

37. Although there are several hundred provisions in the Code that contain marriage penalties through their operation, the 2001, 2003, and 2004 Working Families Acts dealt only with a few of them.

38. Section 63(c)(2). For married taxpayers who file separately, however, the 2001 Act curiously provided that the standard deduction for each would equal the amount allowed for a single taxpayer beginning in 2005. (Former section 63(c)(2)(C)) Therefore, from 2005 until 2009, married taxpayers who filed separately would have had a total standard deduction that exceeded the standard deduction allowed a married couple filing jointly. Could Congress have intended to create a penalty for married taxpayers who chose to file jointly? Apparently not, because in the Job Creation and Worker Assistance Act of 2002, P.L. 107-147, (hereinafter the "2002 Act") Congress restored a separate standard deduction for married taxpayers filing separate returns after 2004. Married-filing-separate filers now have a standard deduction that is one-half the amount for joint filers.

Although there was little or no discussion during the debates regarding the increase in the standard deduction for married couples, the increase creates a substantial singles penalty. It was the dissatisfaction of some taxpayers with the singles penalty that prodded Congress to make changes to the rate schedules in 1969. There was also little discussion of the fact that more married taxpayers enjoyed a tax bonus under the pre-2001 Act than suffered a marriage penalty. The 2001, 2003, and 2004 Working Families Acts changes to the standard deduction for joint filers do not discriminate; the new provisions apply to all married joint filers. Therefore, those who enjoyed a married bonus under the old law will enjoy an even greater bonus after the changes.

39. Former section 1(f)(8). In 2003 and 2004, the 15% tax bracket for joint returns was twice (or 200% of) the amount taxable at the 15% rate applicable to single taxpayers. For 2005, the amount subject to the 15% rate for joint filers was to decline to 180% of the amount for single filers, gradually rising to 200% for 2008 and thereafter.

tax payers taxable at the 15% rate, effective in 2005.[40] Further, the amount of income subject to tax at the 15% rate for married taxpayers filing separately will be one-half the amount of income that would be subject to the 15% rate if they filed jointly.[41] Thus, as a result of the 2001, 2003, and 2004 Working Families Acts married taxpayers filing separately will use the same 15% rate schedule as single taxpayers in the 15% bracket.

As noted, the 2001, 2003, and 2004 Working Families Acts did not purport to correct the many other provisions of the Code that penalize married couples.[42] Reconsider Wendy and Hillel. After the changes made by the 2001, 2003 and 2004 Working Families Acts how do they fare? Recalculate, using each of the earlier alternatives.[43] How effective were Congress' efforts to eliminate the marriage penalty for them if they were married? What effect if they were unmarried?

Look next at section 6013, subsections (a) and (d)(3). What is the significance of section 6013(d)(3)?

Suppose Helen and Arthur file a joint federal income tax return in Year 1. They divorce in Year 2. In Year 3 the Service audits the joint return from Year 1 and finds a deficiency in tax in the amount of $25,000 attributable to Helen's disallowed business deductions. Arthur did not work in Year 1 and reported no income or deductions on the Year 1 return. Can the Service collect from Arthur (even though Arthur had nothing to do with causing the deficiency)? What result if Arthur and Helen's divorce decree contains a provision that provides as follows:

> Arthur and Helen acknowledge that they have filed a joint federal income tax return for Year 1. Arthur and Helen also acknowledge that all income and deductions on that return are attributable to Helen's business. In the event that the Internal Revenue Service determines a deficiency in income tax with respect to that return, Helen agrees to pay the deficiency and any penalties and interest due in full.

Many separation agreements or divorce decrees contain some kind of "indemnification" by one spouse to the other, sometimes in language similar to the foregoing provision.[44] Is Arthur "off the hook" for payment to the Service of any deficiency by virtue of

---

40. Section 1(f)(8)(A).

41. Section 1(f)(8)(B).

42. Recall that not all married taxpayers were penalized by the Code prior to revision by the 2001, 2003, and 2004 Working Families Acts. Most importantly, the more unequal a couple's incomes, the less likely they were to suffer a penalty. Indeed, couples with a single earner generally enjoyed a marriage bonus. The congressional hearings that produced the attempt at reform of the marriage penalty, vetoed by President Clinton in 2000, included several references to the effect of the proposed changes in tax rates and the standard deduction. As part of the 2001 Act, Congress adopted provisions not significantly different from those that were part of the earlier act. A reading of the hearings that preceded passage of that act reveals little congressional concern for the impact of the new rules on the marriage bonus or on single taxpayers.

43. A completely accurate calculation is, of course, impossible; the inflation adjustments to the rate schedules for the years between now and 2009 are unavailable. A comparison using the current rates will, however, graphically demonstrate the effect of the changes.

44. In fact, some might argue that a domestic relations lawyer would be remiss if he failed to include a provision of this type in the separation agreement. Another frequent error is to include the provision in the separation agreement but fail to include it in a decree that supersedes the separation agreement. A careful attorney can avoid this trap by specifically incorporating all or part of the separation agreement in the decree or providing in the decree that the separation agreement shall sur-

the provision in the decree? **Look again at section 6013(d)(3).** Does section 6013(d)(3) make the separation agreement provision illustrated above valueless?

Is it fair to impose "joint and several liability" on both the husband and the wife when, as in this example, one of the spouses has no income? Suppose the husband "knew" that the return was incorrect but signed it anyway?[45] Suppose he did not know but authorized his wife to sign his name for him? Can you formulate a justification for joint and several liability? In a 1998 report to Congress, Treasury quoted the following explanation from the legislative history of the Revenue Act of 1948 for Congress's enactment of the predecessor to section 6013(d)(3):

> Unless the husband and wife are to be held jointly and severally liable for the tax upon their aggregate net income, it will be necessary for the [Service] to require that their individual incomes and deductions shall be separately stated in the return, in order that their respective income-tax liability may be separately determined. Such a requirement would cause considerable hardship upon taxpayers with moderate incomes and would largely eliminate the advantage of the joint return.[46]

Now look at section 6015, enacted as part of the 1998 Act's Taxpayer Bill of Rights 3.[47] Does that section indemnify a spouse like Arthur? Section 6015, like its predecessor, section 6013(e), provides relief from joint and several liability under certain circumstances. Like its predecessor, section 6015 sets forth extremely complex rules that probably require a taxpayer to seek the advice of a tax professional.

In brief outline, section 6015 provides two broad categories of taxpayers with relief from joint and several liability. It also provides a third avenue for relief for taxpayers who do not qualify under the first two categories:

(1) A taxpayer who is "no longer married"[48] may elect to have his liability for additional taxes, interest, or penalties calculated based on his proportionate responsibility for the deficiency under section 6015(c); and/or

---

vive the decree. Remember that the cure for failure to carry out the terms of a decree is contempt; the cure for failure to carry out the terms of a contract is a breach of contract action. In some cases, the attorney may want to preserve both avenues of enforcement.

45. Note that in signing a return, the taxpayer certifies under the penalties of perjury that to the best of his knowledge and belief the return and accompanying schedules and statements are true, correct, and complete. **Look at the signature line of Form 1040 in the Forms Appendix.**

46. Department of the Treasury, *Report to the Congress on Joint Liability and Innocent Spouse Issues* 6–7, Feb. 9, 1998.

47. For a lengthier discussion of the provisions of new section 6015 and the legislative process that created it, see Toni Robinson and Mary Ferrari, "The New Innocent Spouse Provision: 'Reason and Law Walking Hand in Hand'?," 80 Tax Notes 835 (Aug. 17, 1998). For a discussion of the first cases decided under new section 6015, see Toni Robinson and Mary Ferrari, "Protecting the Innocent: Tax Court and Service 'One-up' Congress," 88 Tax Notes 1507 (Sept. 18, 2000).

48. Section 6015(c) defines individuals eligible to make the election as those who (1) at the time the election is filed are either no longer married or are legally separated or (2) at any time during the 12-month period ending on the date of election are not members of the same household as the spouse with whom he or she filed a joint return. Although the statute does not explicitly state that a widow or widower is eligible, the legislative history makes clear that these taxpayers are also covered. H.R. Conf. Rep. No. 105-599, at 252 n. 16 (1998).

(2) a taxpayer who qualifies may request treatment as an "innocent spouse" in order to be relieved of all liability for any deficiency in tax, interest, and penalties under section 6015(b)[49]; and/or

(3) those taxpayers who do not qualify for relief under either of these two provisions may seek relief through application of the equitable power granted to the Secretary under section 6015(f).[50]

Sections 6015(b) and 6015(c) require a deficiency or underpayment of tax. They do not apply in situations in which the taxpayer has shown the correct amount of tax on a return but has failed to pay it. Therefore, for joint return signers who have relied on their spouses to discharge the joint tax liability shown on a return, innocent spouse relief is not available under either subsection (b) or (c). The Service has issued Revenue Procedure 2003-61, 2003-32 I.R.B. 296, setting forth guidance on when it will grant equitable relief.

In the months immediately following passage of section 6015, thousands of taxpayers filed claims with the Service seeking administrative relief on one or more bases allowed by the new provision. Once the Service acted on these requests, more and more of those taxpayers whose requests the Service denied sought judicial relief. A significant change made by the 1998 legislation was its grant of jurisdiction to the Tax Court, pursuant to section 6015(e), to hear appeals of administrative denials of relief under subsections (b) and (c). But the statute was silent on appeals of denials under subsection (f). The earliest cases were of two types: those concerning the legal issue of whether the Service's denial of relief was correct, and those concerning the scope of the Tax Court's jurisdiction under section 6015(e). The Tax Court accepted jurisdiction over "(f)" cases both when the taxpayer had also made a claim under either (b) or (c) at the same time,[51] and in "stand-alone (f)" cases as well, but its expansive reading of the statute was rebuffed on appeal.[52] In 2006, Congress finally fixed the problem, amending section 6015(e) to explicitly extend Tax Court jurisdiction to "stand-alone (f)" cases.[53]

2. Alimony and Child Support

Examine sections 71(a), 215(a), and 62(a)(10). What is the relationship between the operation of these sections and the rule of *Lucas v. Earl*? These sections, like the 1948 joint return, accomplish for legally separated or divorced persons what Mr. Earl was unable to accomplish by contracting with his wife — they effect a statutorily authorized assignment of income. Since 1942, when Congress enacted the first alimony provisions as part of the Revenue Act of 1942, payments that qualify as "alimony" have been deductible by the payor and includible in gross income by the payee.

---

49. Section 6015(b) sets forth the requirements for qualitifcation as an "innocent spouse."

50. A taxpayer may seek relief under subsections (b) and (c) (and also (f)) on the same application, Form 8857.

51. *See Butler v. Commissioner*, 114 T.C. 276 (2000); and *Fernandez v. Commissioner*, 114 T.C. 324 (2000).

52. *See Ewing v. Commissioner*, 118 T.C. 494 (2002), *rev'd* 439 F.3d 1009 (9th Cir. 2006).

53. Section 408 of the Tax Relief and Health Care Act of 2006, P.L. 109-432, signed on December 20, 2006.

In enacting the predecessors to sections 71 and 215 of the Code in 1942, Congress overturned the 1917 case of *Gould v. Gould*.[54] In *Gould*, the Supreme Court had hewed to the accepted view that alimony represented a husband's continuing obligation to support his wife, a nondeductible personal expense. In reversing *Gould*, Congress apparently accepted the argument advanced by some taxpayers that the payor of alimony does not enjoy the use of funds paid in the form of support payments to a former spouse. Recall the Supreme Court's statement in *Helvering v. Horst*: "The power to dispose of income is the equivalent of ownership of it. The exercise of that power to procure the payment of income to another is the enjoyment, and hence the realization, of the income by him who exercises it."[55] Why is the payment of alimony different from the gift of income made by a father to his son in *Helvering v. Horst*?[56]

Another compelling argument that may have prompted Congress to allow a payor of alimony to deduct his payment, provided the payee included it in her income, was the result of the steeply progressive rates of tax in effect in 1942. At the time, divorce was far rarer than it is today. Moreover, there were many fewer working wives. Therefore, when a divorce did occur, it often resulted in the payment of alimony. Inclusion of these amounts first in the payors' incomes produced the anomalous result that high income husbands often found that their income tax liability exceeded their net earnings after payment of their alimony obligations.

Since enactment of the predecessors to sections 71 and 215, characterization of a payment made by a payor spouse (or former spouse) to a payee spouse (or former spouse) as "alimony" has had significant tax ramifications. If treated as alimony, the payment constitutes gross income to the payee spouse and is deductible by the payor spouse in calculating income. Thus, payment of alimony can produce tax savings through income shifting. This occurs when one taxpayer shifts income to another taxpayer, usually to take advantage of the lower rates applicable to the second taxpayer. When a high bracket payor is relieved of payments made to a lower bracket payee, the total tax bill of the two shrinks.

For example, assume that Jeffrey had income in tax year 2006 (ignoring deductions and personal exemptions) of $100,000, and Margaret had income of $10,000. Assume also that the only other item of tax significance was a $30,000 annual payment from Jeffrey to Margaret. If the payment qualified as alimony, Jeffrey's income would have been $70,000 and his tax liability (using 2006 section 1(c) rates)[57] would have been $14,057.50; Margaret's income would have been $40,000 and her tax liability would have been $6,557.50. Their combined tax liability would have been $20,615. If the payment was not alimony, Jeffrey's tax liability would have been $22,331.50; Margaret's tax liability would have been $1,122.50. Their combined tax liability would have been $23,454. Thus, if the payment was alimony, the payor's tax would have decreased and the payee's tax would have increased, but their overall tax savings would have been $2,839. These savings would have increased the total resources available to the parties and may have provided additional bargaining leverage to either or both spouses in the divorce negotiation process.

---

54. 245 U.S. 151 (1917).

55. 311 U.S. 112, 118 (1940).

56. Section 215 permits a payor to deduct expenses that qualify as "alimony" and that are included in income by the payee because the Code views these payments as being vested in the payee from the moment of receipt by the payor. That is, the Code views these amounts as never belonging to the payor. The payor's income, therefore, does not include these amounts. The placement of the deduction allowed by section 215 as an adjustment in section 62(a) carries out this intent.

57. You can find the section 1(c) rate table for tax year 2006 in Revenue Procedure 2005-70, 2005-47 I.R.B. 979, which we looked at in Part I.

Prior to the enactment of the current version of sections 71 and 215, taxpayers, the Service, and the courts had interpretive problems in defining "alimony." The tension resulted from the difference in treatment of payments for alimony, property settlements, and child support. Although payments of alimony were deductible, payments for lump-sum payments representing property settlements[58] and for child support were not. Property settlement payments made in a lump sum are arguably quite different from payments of alimony. But, what justification might you advance for the different treatment of child support?[59]

To qualify as alimony, the payments had to arise in discharge of the payor's marital obligation, and the payment had to be part of a "periodic" series. Both these requirements produced continuing controversy. Taxpayers frequently received different tax treatment because of different state law interpretations of marital obligations. The different treatment of alimony and lump sum payments sometimes gave taxpayers an incentive to attempt to convert otherwise nondeductible lump-sum divisions of marital property into deductible alimony by spreading the payments over a "series."

In 1984, and again in 1986, Congress enacted changes to sections 71 and 215 to simplify the characterization issues and to create a federal definition of alimony.

The following problems are intended to assist you in identifying the principal federal income tax issues attendant to divorce.

First, read carefully sections 71, 151, 152, and 215. Read also the regulations pertaining to section 71. Make a checklist of the elements a payment must satisfy to constitute alimony. How many items are on your list? Now, consider the problems and identify the interpretive problems that are raised.

1. Herb and Wanda have been married for 10 years. This year Herb falls in love with Mitzy, leaves Wanda and sets up house with Mitzy. Wanda files for divorce and a decree is issued dissolving the marriage. What are the tax consequences if:

a. The divorce decree provides that Herb will pay Wanda $2,000 per month ($24,000 per year) for 40 years.

b. Same facts as in (a) except that the divorce decree provides that on Wanda's death Herb will pay to her estate 1,000 shares of General Motors stock in lieu of the remaining monthly payments.

c. Same facts as in (a) except that Herb's lawyer properly advises him that he has no liability to make payments after Wanda's death as a matter of state law.

d. Same facts as in (a) and (c) except that two years later, Mitzy throws Herb out. Wanda agrees to let Herb move back into the house (separate bedrooms, of course) for 2 months while he looks for other living accommodations. Herb makes two payments to Wanda during this period.

e. Same facts as in (a) and (c) except that the divorce decree provides that the payments will not be included in Wanda's income.

---

58. Property settlements can take the form of a division of the actual property or a payment by one divorcing spouse to the other of the money value of the property.

59. As was the case for alimony prior to the 1942 legislation, Congress views child support as a parent's continuing obligation, a nondeductible personal expense.

f. Same facts as in (a) and (c) except that the agreement provides that $1,000 of each payment is for the support of Herb and Wanda's child, Little Herbie.

g. Same facts as in (a) and (c) except that the agreement provides that Herb's payments to Wanda will be reduced to $1,000 thirteen years from now. (Little Herbie was born five years ago.)

h. Same facts as in (a), (c), and (f) except that, one month, Herb is able to pay Wanda only $1,200 of the required $2,000.

One of the problems under the pre-1984 version of sections 71 and 215, as noted above, was that payor spouses attempted to disguise nondeductible/nontaxable property settlements by paying them out over a "series" of payments. Why would the payee agree to this fiction of making the payments look like alimony? Wouldn't that make the payments taxable to the payee rather than the payor?

When it amended the alimony provision, Congress also sought to eliminate the subjective (you guessed it) facts and circumstances test to determine which payments were alimony (versus lump-sum), and replace the test with an objective (safe-harbor) test. **Read section 71(f) carefully and apply it systematically to the following problem.**

2. Fred and Ethel were divorced in December of this year (Year 1). Fred is to make payments to Ethel that qualify as alimony pursuant to section 71(b). The payments are to be $36,000 per year, beginning next year (Year 2), and are to continue for 7 years. Fred makes the required $36,000 payment for year 2. The following year (Year 3), Fred is run over by Lucy and is unable to work for the entire year. Ethel, still having a soft spot in her heart for Fred, agrees to let him make the payment scheduled for Year 3 the next year (Year 4). Fred recovers, pays Ethel $72,000 in Year 4 (representing the Year 3 and Year 4 payments), and makes the remaining payments as scheduled. What are the tax consequences of these transactions? Suppose Fred's accident occurred instead in Year 4. He made the payments for Years 2 and 3, but none for Year 4. In Year 5, the year following his accident, he pays Ethel $72,000 (representing the Year 4 and Year 5 payments). Does this change the result?

3. Little Ricky is 8 years old at the time his parents, Fred and Ethel, divorce. Disregarding the assumptions in question 2, above, assume that Fred agrees to pay Ethel $36,000 in alimony per year until her death or remarriage and $12,000 per year for the support of Ricky, who lives with Ethel during the week and visits his father, Fred, on weekends.

a. Suppose that Ethel has no earnings. Who may claim Ricky as a dependent?

b. Does it matter whether Fred and Ethel have inserted a provision regarding claiming the exemption in their divorce instrument? If so, does it make a difference if the instrument grants the exemption to Ethel? In the alternative, if it grants the exemption to Fred? If a provision matters, need the couple or either of them take any other action?

c. Would your answers change if Ethel earns $24,000 per year?

d. Suppose that Ethel remarries. She has no income but her new spouse is very successful, earning more than $200,000 per year. Ricky (now 12) visits Fred less frequently because Fred has moved to a distant city. Fred (with Ethel's approval), discontinues paying child support (she says she no longer needs it after her remarriage). But Fred does pay the plane fare and other costs for Ricky to visit him for 2 weeks each summer. Who may claim the dependency exemption?

3. Transfers of Property Incident to Divorce

The second section of this Part C focussed primarily on one type of property transfer that occurs when parties divorce: the cash payment of alimony. But it also introduced you to the two other types of transfer: child support and property settlements. Although the second section of Part C presented justifications for the different tax treatments of alimony and child support, property settlements deserve separate consideration.

Once upon a time, when Alice married Harry, it was with an implicit agreement that except as a result of extremely adverse circumstances, she would spend the rest of her life as mate, maid, and mother. So too, in return for this implicit commitment on her part, Harry made an implicit commitment to bring home the bacon and, except as a result of extremely adverse circumstances, to protect Alice from the need to own and manage very much property. He might share title to the family home with her but little more. He often became a co-owner of any property she brought to the marriage and even managed it for Alice.

While the law encouraged Alice to rely on Harry for property ownership and management, the state did exhibit an interest in protecting Alice from beggarhood in the event of divorce. To protect Alice, in the case of divorce or widowhood, states adopted a number of devices: community property rules, spousal shares at death, and marital or dower rights. In fact, these rules did protect the Alices of some generations, at least in part. Community property laws created an immediately vested interest in each spouse for most property acquired during the marriage. In contrast, spousal shares and dower or curtesy rights generally did not create a vested interest in specific property for the non-titled spouse. Rather, these rules created an interest to be satisfied by a portion of the assets of the titled spouse, denominated usually in dollars.

In other common law states, however, should Alice and Harry divorce, she could expect no more than her portion of property in which she shared title with Harry. Courts lacked the power to require a transfer of property owned by Harry to Alice although Harry had acquired the property during the marriage.

The introduction of equitable distribution statutes in the latter part of this century by most of the non-community property states dramatically changed the common law rules. In the absence of agreement between Alice and Harry, these statutes enable a judge to order an equitable division of their property as part of Harry and Alice's property (including their separate property acquired during their marriage) as part of their decree of divorce.

As the Alice and Harry story demonstrates, an important part of any marital dissolution is the division of assets between the soon to be ex-spouses. The parties must agree on the division or, as numerous commentators have observed, risk litigation at an emotionally inopportune time. To their practical concerns about custody and visitation, levels of support and occupancy of the marital home, the law forces the parties to add the division of their possessions and the tax consequences of that division.

Property divisions of jointly-owned property represent a division of the assets of the marital unit. Because the division represents merely the drawing of a line between those assets that belong to the husband and those that will go to the wife, the division itself is not a taxable event. So, for example, the couple whose assets consist of a bank account with a balance of $20,000, 200 shares of stock, and 2 bonds, can easily divide the assets into two shares, each consisting of $10,000, 100 shares of stock, and one bond. The value of each of these assets represents taxed once already dollars. Therefore, the mere division of these assets produces no tax consequences.

The transfer of non-jointly-owned property, however, represents a constellation of different problems. First, not surprisingly, is the issue of valuing the various pieces of property and property rights in order to achieve an equitable division.

Although the following landmark case does not deal with marital property, it forms the foundation for both the tax consequences of exchanges of property and the valuing of property in many situations, including transfers of property incident to divorce. **In order to understand the case, it will be helpful to diagram the transaction and to review sections 1001 and 1012 of the Code.**[60]

PHILADELPHIA PARK AMUSEMENT CO. v. UNITED STATES
130 Ct. Cl. 166 (1954)

LARAMORE, *Judge*, delivered the opinion of the court:

... The issue presented in this case is whether or not the taxpayer is entitled to include as a part of the cost of its franchise, for purposes of determining depreciation and loss due to abandonment, the undepreciated cost of a bridge exchanged for a 10-year extension of the franchise. The facts which have been stipulated by the parties may be summarized as follows: The taxpayer's predecessor was granted on July 6, 1889, by the City of Philadelphia, a franchise to construct, operate, and maintain for 50 years a passenger railway in Fairmount Park at its own cost and expense. Upon the expiration of the 50-year term the franchise was to continue indefinitely for additional successive 10-year terms unless the City gave one year's written notice of its wish to terminate it at the end of the 50-year term or the 10-year term then in duration. Upon the termination of the license the City had the right to purchase all, but not just part of, the improvements; *i.e.*, railway cars, tracks, bridges, buildings, etc., made by the licensee at the cash value at the time of purchase, or in the event the City did not desire to purchase the assets the licensee had a specified period of time within which to remove them.

Pursuant to the franchise the taxpayer's predecessor constructed the bridge in question, commonly known as Strawberry Bridge, over the Schuylkill River at a cost of $381,000. The bridge was 79 ½ feet wide and carried pedestrian and vehicular traffic in addition to taxpayer's streetcars. The taxpayer's principal business was the operation of an amusement park and the street railway was employed in the transportation of customers to the park. With the increase in automobile transportation, the proportion of customers carried to the amusement park by the taxpayer's streetcars decreased over the years and during the latter years of its operation losses were sustained. Early in

---

60. Note that it was the predecessors to sections 1001 and 1012 that applied in this case. For your study, that distinction is not relevant.

1934 the City, in writing the taxpayer, pointed out that Strawberry Bridge was in need of extensive repairs, that it was taxpayer's obligation to make the repairs at taxpayer's expense, and threatened to close the bridge unless the repairs were made promptly. The taxpayer wrote the City explaining that its financial condition prevented the making of extensive repairs to the bridge and offered to transfer the ownership of the bridge to the City in exchange for a 10-year extension of the railway franchise. The City accepted the offer and on August 3, 1934, Strawberry Bridge was transferred to the City. The taxpayer reserved its right-of-way over the bridge for the duration of its franchise and agreed to maintain its facilities thereon. On November 14, 1934, the City amended the franchise and extended it from July 24, 1939, to July 24, 1949. The adjusted basis, *i.e.*, the undepreciated or unrecovered cost of Strawberry Bridge at the time of the exchange was $228,852.74. The taxpayer's bookkeeper ... promptly wrote the asset off the books by a direct debit to surplus of $228,852.74, without reporting any gain or loss on the exchange or adding the undepreciated cost or fair market value of the bridge to the cost of the franchise. From that time until 1946 the taxpayer's bookkeeper did not record on the taxpayer's books or claim a deduction on its returns for the amortization of this cost. He also failed to take the undisputed deduction for the amortization of the undepreciated portion, $50,000, of the original cost of the franchise.

...

On December 15, 1947, the taxpayer filed a claim for refund of 1944 taxes in the amount of $6,087.28 based on a claimed depreciation deduction of $15,218.21. This claim was founded upon the ground that the undepreciated cost of Strawberry Bridge, $228,852.74, was the cost of the 10-year extension of its franchise and, therefore, should be amortized over the remaining life of the franchise. On December 30, 1948, taxpayer filed a second claim for refund of 1944 income taxes. This claim was in the amount of $58,791.91 and was predicated on the following grounds: (1) net operating loss carryback deduction of $128,897.97 from 1946, (2) depreciation deduction of $3,816.66 as the 1944 proportion of the cost basis of taxpayer's original franchise, and (3) a repetition of the first claim for refund. On October 26, 1950, the Commissioner of Internal Revenue allowed $55,036.71 of the net operating loss carry back and $3,333.33 of the $3,816.66 claim for depreciation of the original cost of the franchise, but denied taxpayer's first claim for refund for 1944 and the repetition thereof in the second claim for a $15,218.21 depreciation deduction based upon the undepreciated cost of Strawberry Bridge. The Commissioner refunded to the taxpayer, on account of its 1944 taxes, $22,014.69 with interest thereon.

On December 30, 1948, taxpayer filed a claim for refund of income taxes for the year 1945 in the amount of $6,087.28, claiming a deduction of $3,816.66 as the depreciation deduction for the amortization of the cost of its original franchise and $15,218.21 as the depreciation deduction for the amortization of the cost of the 10-year extension of its franchise. On October 26, 1950, the Commissioner allowed $3,333.33 of the claimed deduction for the original cost of the franchise and, accordingly, refunded to taxpayer $1,282.05 with interest thereon, but denied the balance of the claim.

In its petition the taxpayer alleged that the Commissioner's rejection of all of its first claim for 1944, part of its second claim for 1944, and part of its claim for 1945 was erroneous.... [W]e are only concerned with the cost basis, if any, of the 10-year extension of taxpayer's franchise and the tax consequences thereof for the years 1944, 1945, and 1946.

It is clear that the cost of this type franchise can be amortized over its life by the taking of depreciation deduction under section 23(1) (Footnote 1) of the Code ... Therefore, the cost basis, if any, of the 10-year extension of the franchise should be depreciated over the remainder of the old term and over the new term.... It is also clear that when a franchise is abandoned prior to the end of its term the owner is entitled to deduct, under section 23(f) (Footnote 2) of the Code, as a loss in the year of abandonment, the undepreciated cost of the franchise at that time....

This brings us to the question of what is the cost basis of the 10-year extension of taxpayer's franchise. Although defendant contends that Strawberry Bridge was either worthless or not "exchanged" for the 10-year extension of the franchise, we believe that the bridge had some value, and that the contract under which the bridge was transferred to the City clearly indicates that the one was given in consideration of the other.... [I]t was a taxable exchange under section 112 (a)(Footnote 3) of the Code.

The gain or loss, whichever the case may have been, should have been recognized, and the cost basis under section 113 (a) (Footnote 4) of the Code, of the 10-year extension of the franchise was the cost to the taxpayer. The succinct statement in section 113 (a) that "the basis of property shall be the cost of such property," although clear in principle, is frequently difficult in application. One view is that the cost basis of property received in a taxable exchange is the fair market value of the property *given* in the exchange.

The other view is that the cost basis of property received in a taxable exchange is the fair market value of the property *received* in the exchange. As will be seen from the cases and some of the Commissioner's rulings, the Commissioner's position has not been altogether consistent on this question. The view that "cost" is the fair market value of the property given is predicated on the theory that the cost to the taxpayer is the economic value relinquished. The view that "cost" is the fair market value of the property received is based upon the theory that the term "cost" is a tax concept and must be considered in the light of the designed interrelationship of sections 111, 112, 113, and 114, and the prime role that the basis of property plays in determining tax liability. We believe that when the question is considered in the latter context that the cost basis of the property received in a taxable exchange is the fair market value of the property *received* in the exchange.

When property is exchanged for property in a taxable exchange the taxpayer is taxed on the difference between the adjusted basis of the property given in exchange and the fair market value of the property received in exchange. For purposes of determining gain or loss the fair market value of the property received is treated as cash and taxed accordingly. To maintain harmony with the fundamental purpose of these sections, it is necessary to consider the fair market value of the property received as the cost basis to the taxpayer. The failure to do so would result in allowing the taxpayer a stepped-up basis, without paying a tax therefor, if the fair market value of the property received is less than the fair market value of the property given, and the taxpayer would be subjected to a double tax if the fair market value of the property received is more than the fair market value of the property given. By holding that the fair market value of the property received in a taxable exchange is the cost basis, the above discrepancy is avoided and the basis of the property received will equal the adjusted basis of the property given plus any gain recognized, or that should have been recognized, or minus any loss recognized, or that should have been recognized.

Therefore, the cost basis of the 10-year extension of the franchise was its fair market value on August 3, 1934, the date of the exchange. The determination of whether the cost basis of the property received is its fair market value or the fair market value of the

ever (including but not by way of limitation, dower and all rights under the laws of testacy and intestacy)...." Pursuant to the above agreement which had been incorporated into the divorce decree, one-half of this stock was delivered in the tax year involved, 1955, and the balance thereafter. Davis' cost basis for the 1955 transfer was $74,775.37, and the fair market value of the 500 shares there transferred was $82,250....

I.

The determination of the income tax consequences of the stock transfer described above is basically a two-step analysis: (1) Was the transaction a taxable event? (2) If so, how much taxable gain resulted therefrom? Originally the Tax Court (at that time the Board of Tax Appeals) held that the accretion to property transferred pursuant to a divorce settlement could not be taxed as capital gain to the transferor because the amount realized by the satisfaction of the husband's marital obligations was indeterminable and because, even if such benefit were ascertainable, the transaction was a nontaxable division of property.... However, upon being reversed in quick succession by the Courts of Appeals of the Third and Second Circuits, ... the Tax Court accepted the position of these courts and has continued to apply these views in appropriate cases since that time, ... the Courts of Appeals reasoned that the accretion to the property was "realized" by the transfer and that this gain could be measured on the assumption that the relinquished marital rights were equal in value to the property transferred. The matter was considered settled until the Court of Appeals for the Sixth Circuit, in reversing the Tax Court, ruled that, although such a transfer might be a taxable event, the gain realized thereby could not be determined because of the impossibility of evaluating the fair market value of the wife's marital rights.... In so holding that court specifically rejected the argument that these rights could be presumed to be equal in value to the property transferred for their release. This is essentially the position taken by the Court of Claims in the instant case.

II.

We now turn to the threshold question of whether the transfer in issue was an appropriate occasion for taxing the accretion to the stock. There can be no doubt that Congress, as evidenced by its inclusive definition of income subject to taxation, *i.e.*, "all income from whatever source derived, including ... [g]ains derived from dealings in property," intended that the economic growth of this stock be taxed. The problem confronting us is simply *when* is such accretion to be taxed. Should the economic gain be presently assessed against taxpayer, or should this assessment await a subsequent transfer of the property by the wife? The controlling statutory language, which provides that gains from dealings in property are to be taxed upon "sale or other disposition," is too general to include or exclude conclusively the transaction presently in issue. Recognizing this, the Government and the taxpayer argue by analogy with transactions more easily classified as within or without the ambit of taxable events. The taxpayer asserts that the present disposition is comparable to a nontaxable division of property between two co-owners, (Footnote 6) while the Government contends it more resembles a taxable transfer of property in exchange for the release of an independent legal obligation. Neither disputes the validity of the other's starting point.

In support of his analogy the taxpayer argues that to draw a distinction between a wife's interest in the property of her husband in a common-law jurisdiction such as Delaware and the property interest of a wife in a typical community property jurisdiction would commit a double sin; for such differentiation would depend upon "elusive and subtle casuistries which ... possess no relevance for tax purposes," ... and would create disparities between common-law and community property jurisdictions in contradiction to Congress' general policy of equality between the two. The taxpayer's analogy, however, stumbles on its own premise, for the inchoate rights granted a wife in her husband's property by the Delaware law do not even remotely reach the dignity of co-ownership. The wife has no interest—passive or active—over the management or disposition of her husband's personal property. Her rights are not descendible, and she must survive him to share in his intestate estate. Upon dissolution of the marriage she shares in the property only to such extent as the court deems "reasonable." ... What is "reasonable" might be ascertained independently of the extent of the husband's property by such criteria as the wife's financial condition, her needs in relation to her accustomed station in life, her age and health, the number of children and their ages, and the earning capacity of the husband....

This is not to say it would be completely illogical to consider the shearing off of the wife's rights in her husband's property as a division of that property, but we believe the contrary to be the more reasonable construction. Regardless of the tags, Delaware seems only to place a burden on the husband's property rather than to make the wife a part owner thereof. In the present context the rights of succession and reasonable share do not differ significantly from the husband's obligations of support and alimony. They all partake more of a personal liability of the husband than a property interest of the wife. The effectuation of these marital rights may ultimately result in the ownership of some of the husband's property as it did here, but certainly this happenstance does not equate the transaction with a division of property by co-owners. Although admittedly such a view may permit different tax treatment among the several States, this Court in the past has not ignored the differing effects on the federal taxing scheme of substantive differences between community property and common-law systems. *e.g.*, *Poe v. Seaborn*, 282 U.S. 101 (1930)....

Our interpretation of the general statutory language is fortified by the long-standing administrative practice as sounded and formalized by the settled state of law in the lower courts. The Commissioner's position was adopted in the early 40's by the Second and Third Circuits and by 1947 the Tax Court had acquiesced in this view. This settled rule was not disturbed by the Court of Appeals for the Sixth Circuit in 1960 or the Court of Claims in the instant case, for these latter courts in holding the gain indeterminable assumed that the transaction was otherwise a taxable event. Such unanimity of views in support of a position representing a reasonable construction of an ambiguous statute will not lightly be put aside. It is quite possible that this notorious construction was relied upon by numerous taxpayers as well as the Congress itself, which not only refrained from making any changes in the statutory language during more than a score of years but re-enacted this same language in 1954.

III.

Having determined that the transaction was a taxable event, we now turn to the point on which the Court of Claims balked, *viz.*, the measurement of the taxable gain realized by the taxpayer. The Code defines the taxable gain from the sale or disposition of property as being the "excess of the amount realized therefrom over the adjusted basis...." I. R. C. (1954) § 1001(a). The "amount realized" is further defined as "the sum of any money received plus the fair market value of the property (other than money) received." I. R. C. (1954) § 1001(b). In the instant case the "property received" was the release of the wife's inchoate marital rights. The Court of Claims, following the Court of Appeals for the Sixth Circuit, found that there was no way to compute the fair market value of these marital rights and that it was thus impossible to determine the taxable gain realized by the taxpayer. We believe this conclusion was erroneous.

It must be assumed, we think, that the parties acted at arm's length and that they judged the marital rights to be equal in value to the property for which they were exchanged. There was no evidence to the contrary here. Absent a readily ascertainable value it is accepted practice where property is exchanged to hold, as did the Court of Claims in *Philadelphia Park Amusement Co. v. United States*, 130 Ct. Cl. 166, 172, 126 F.Supp. 184, 189 (1954), that the values "of the two properties exchanged in an arms-length transaction are either equal in fact, or are presumed to be equal." ... To be sure there is much to be said of the argument that such an assumption is weakened by the emotion, tension and practical necessities involved in divorce negotiations and the property settlements arising therefrom. However, once it is recognized that the transfer was a taxable event, it is more consistent with the general purpose and scheme of the taxing statutes to make a rough approximation of the gain realized thereby than to ignore altogether its tax consequences....

Moreover, if the transaction is to be considered a taxable event as to the husband, the Court of Claims' position leaves up in the air the wife's basis for the property received. In the context of a taxable transfer by the husband, (Footnote 7) all indicia point to a "cost" basis for this property in the hands of the wife. (Footnote 8) Yet under the Court of Claims' position her cost for this property, *i.e.*, the value of the marital rights relinquished therefor, would be indeterminable, and on subsequent disposition of the property she might suffer inordinately over the Commissioner's assessment which she would have the burden of proving erroneous, *Commissioner v. Hansen*, 360 U.S. 446, 468 (1959). Our present holding that the value of these rights is ascertainable eliminates this problem; for the same calculation that determines the amount received by the husband fixes the amount given up by the wife, and this figure, *i.e.*, the market value of the property transferred by the husband, will be taken by her as her tax basis for the property received.

...

FOOTNOTES:

6. Any suggestion that the transaction in question was a gift is completely unrealistic. Property transferred pursuant to a negotiated settlement in return for the release of admittedly valuable rights is not a gift in any sense of the term....

7. Under the present administrative practice, the release of marital rights in exchange for property or other consideration is not considered a taxable event as to the wife....

8. Section 1012 of the Internal Revenue Code of 1954 provides that: "The basis of property shall be the cost of such property, except as otherwise provided in this subchapter and subchapters C (relating to corporate distributions and adjustments), K (relating to partners and partnerships), and P (relating to capital gains and losses)...."

———————

Consider the following questions about *Davis*.

1. How is the diagram of this case different from the diagram you did for *Taft v. Bowers*? Recall that in the case of *Taft v. Bowers*, you learned that the donor of appreciated property is able to assign the potential income represented by the property appreciation to the donee. This results from the Supreme Court's holding that the donee "steps into the shoes" of the donor with respect to the donor's basis in the property. Code section 1015(a), the special basis rule for property acquired by gift, codifies the result in *Taft v. Bowers*.

Look at Footnote 6 in *Davis.* Does it help you answer this question?

2. Recall the difference noted in the introduction to the section on joint returns between a "common law" versus a "community property" jurisdiction. What type of marital property regime did the state of Delaware have? Why might the type of regime make a difference in the tax outcome?

3. Why did the Supreme Court refer to section 1001 for resolution of the case? What were Mr. Davis's tax consequences under section 1001? If Mr. Davis "sold or otherwise disposed of" his Dupont stock and received in exchange Mrs. Davis's marital rights, does the formula for gain in section 1001(a) apply to Mr. Davis? How would he calculate the "amount realized" on his "sale" of the Dupont stock? Is it now clear to you why it was important to read *Philadelphia Park* before reading *Davis*?

4. What were Mrs. Davis' tax consequences under section 1001? Why didn't Mrs. Davis also realize a gain on the transaction based on the principles of *Philadelphia Park*? **Look at footnote 7 of the case. Is it correct?**

5. At the conclusion of the transaction, Mrs. Davis owned the Dupont stock at issue. What was her basis in the stock? What did the Court say? Based on what you have so far learned about basis, is the Court correct?

———————

While the outcome in *Davis* might have been a surprise to Mr. Davis, the case represents the logical application of the long-standing tax rules you first encountered in Revenue Ruling 79-24, elaborated on when we introduced you to the concept of "TOAD" following Revenue Ruling 81-277, and expanded upon in questions 6 and 7 following *Cesarini*. **Review Revenue Ruling 79-24; Revenue Ruling 81-277; and *Cesarini*.**

First, an exchange constitutes as much a realization event as a sale for cash. **Recall the penultimate paragraph in *Helvering v. Bruun*.** Therefore, when Mr. Davis transferred appreciated stock to his wife for consideration (for marital rights), the transaction constituted a realization event. Second, when it is difficult to value the property on one side of the exchange (the consideration received, the marital rights), *Philadelphia Park* makes clear that it is perfectly appropriate to assign to it the value of the asset on the other side of the equation (the appreciated stock). Third, on a taxable exchange of property, the transferee takes a basis in the property received equal to its fair market value at the time of the transfer.

Mr. Davis's surprise marked only the first of many cries of pain through the years from 1962 to 1984 as divorcing asset owners transferred those assets to their soon to be ex-spouses. In the Deficit Reduction Act of 1984, Congress reversed the *Davis* result. **Read Section 1041(a).** Section 1041(a) states "No gain or loss shall be recognized on a transfer of property from an individual to ... (1) a spouse, or (2) a former spouse, but only if the transfer is incident to the divorce."

6. What would be the result of the *Davis* case today under section 1041? Which subsection of section 1041 would have applied to Mr. Davis and which to Mrs. Davis?

7. Would Mr. Davis's transfer be one that was "incident to the divorce"? Does the statute define that phrase? If you are dissatisfied with the statute's definition, where would you look for further clarification?

8. **Review section 1001 which part of section 1001, if any, does section 1041 affect?** Does section 1041 over-rule the general rule stated by section 1001(a)? What about section 1001(c)?

Can you speculate on what prompted Congress to enact section 1041, drastically altering the result of property transfers incident to divorce? Does application of section 1041 mean that the tax on the appreciation in the transferred property will never be paid?

The effect of the enactment of section 1041 was to change the result of the *Davis* case, making the transfer between spouses a "non-recognition event". Enactment of section 1041 coincided with the beginning of the drastic change in the laws of most common law states granting judicial power to order the transfer of "marital" property (or its equivalent value) from one spouse to the other to accomplish an equitable distribution. Prior to enactment of section 1041, under the property laws of most states, judges had no power to order such transfers. So, Congress and others saw section 1041 as a spur to encourage voluntary transfers that would no longer result in the harsh tax result of *Davis*: a taxable event without money to pay the tax. But, to a large extent, the advent of the equitable distribution statutes made enactment of section 1041 as an incentive to voluntary transfers unnecessary. The issue of immediate taxation on transfers remained, however.

This policy decision on the part of the legislature, to facilitate transfers incident to divorce from the spouse who has title to most of the property to the non-property owning spouse, necessarily shifts the tax burden to the non-property owning spouse, for payment at a later time. Of course, it also defers the recognition of loss.[61] In enacting section 1041, Congress transferred the tax consequences from the transferor to the transferee based on the perceived justification that at least the tax on the transferee was deferred until an actual disposition would produce cash in hand to pay the tax due. How does section 1041 accomplish this result? **Look at section 1041(b)(2).**

9. Suppose in 1990, Hakim and Moira bought a house for $65,000 that they used as their personal residence. This year they divorce and Moira agrees to transfer her one-half interest in the house to Hakim. At the time of the divorce the house was worth $400,000. What were the tax consequences to Hakim and Moira under section 1041? Who bore the burden of the tax on the appreciation in the house that occurred during the marriage?

Look now at section 121, especially subsections (a) and (b). Does section 121 affect the general rule of section 1001(c)? What, if any, is the difference between section 121 and section 1041? Does the location of each of these sections in the Code help you answer this question?

Suppose in problem 9 above, you represented Hakim. Now that you have studied section 121, what might you do to minimize H's potential future tax liability?

10. Return now to Charles and Bob in question 5 above. What tax consequences to Charles if he transfers his principal residence to Bob (instead of Blackacre, but with the same FMV and basis as Blackacre)? Charles has been living in his home for the past seven years. What is his basis in the stock he receives from Bob on the transfer?

11. Suppose Frances, a divorcing spouse, receives depreciated property incident to a divorce, that is, property whose value has declined. Would her basis in that property be the same as if she had received the property as a true gift? **Review section 1015(a).**

---

61. **Read section 1041(b).** Section 1041(b) treats the transfer as a "gift." Is that characterization incongruous in light of the *Duberstein* test when the transfer occurs as couples are divorcing? See "detached and disinterested generosity" language in *Duberstein*.

Once again, review the language of section 1001(c). Which words, if any, of that subsection authorize exceptions to its general rule? Section 1041 is just such an exception. In enacting section 1041, Congress did not, however, change the *Davis* rule for all section 1001 transactions; only for transactions involving interspousal transfers of appreciated or depreciated property.[62] "Common Nontaxable Exchanges." In Part IV of this book, we will study some additional provisions that appear in Part III of Subchapter O and thereby encounter some additional "non-recognition" transactions.

Moreover, although section 1041 appears straightforward and comprehensive, its very simplicity may mislead some taxpayers. Consider the following case, describing a very common method of settling competing claims to marital property when there is a divorce.

GODLEWSKI v. COMMISSIONER
90 T.C. 200 (1988)

STERRETT, *Chief Judge*: This case was assigned to and heard by Special Trial Judge Joan Seitz Pate pursuant to the provisions of section 7456 [Predecessor to section 7443A] of the Code.... The Court agrees with and adopts the Special Trial Judge's opinion which is set forth below.

OPINION OF THE SPECIAL TRIAL JUDGE

PATE, *Special Trial Judge*: Respondent determined a deficiency of $5,989 in petitioner's 1984 Federal income tax. After concessions by both parties, (Footnote 2) we need only determine the amount of gain realized by petitioner on the sale of a house transferred to him incident to his divorce.

FINDINGS OF FACT

Michael J. Godlewski (hereinafter petitioner)....

Petitioner was married to his former wife, Elizabeth Godlewski, on December 27, 1967. On July 13, 1973, they purchased a residence located at 1533 Sanden Ferry Drive in Decatur, Georgia, (hereinafter the house) for $32,200. The purchase was funded by a cash downpayment borrowed from petitioner's uncle and a first mortgage of $28,900. Mrs. Godlewski was named sole titleholder. (Footnote 3) On June 24, 1984, the fair market value of the ... house was appraised at $66,500 by Mrs. Godlewski's professional appraiser.

Petitioner and Mrs. Godlewski lived in the house until May 16, 1981, when petitioner moved out because of marital difficulties. By court order dated June 10, 1981, Mrs. Godlewski was granted exclusive use of the house and petitioner never lived there again. Mr. and Mrs. Godlewski obtained a final divorce on October 31, 1983, but the divorce decree expressly reserved the division of marital property for later determination.

Consequently, Mr. and Mrs. Godlewski executed an agreement dated July 13, 1984, (hereinafter agreement), purporting to settle "all their property rights, and all other rights and duties growing out of or rising out of the marriage relationship between the parties." Mrs. Godlewski signed the agreement on July 13th and petitioner signed it on

---

62. Note that section 1041 appears in Part III of Subchapter O of the Code. Subchapter O is entitled "Gain or Loss on Disposition of Property" and Part III is entitled "Common Nontaxable Exchanges." In Part IV of this book, we will examine some additional provisions that appear in Part III of Subchapter O and thereby encounter some additional "non-recognition transactions."

July 25th, 1984. Under its terms, Mrs. Godlewski was required to transfer title to the house to petitioner contemporaneously with the execution of the agreement, and petitioner was obligated to pay Mrs. Godlewski $18,000 within six months of the conveyance. If the payment was not made, the house was to be sold and one-half of the 'net equity' distributed to each spouse. On August 2, 1984, the Court entered a consent judgment adopting the agreement in its entirety.

Mrs. Godlewski executed a warranty deed transferring the house to petitioner on July 20, 1984, and the deed was recorded on September 5, 1984. There is no evidence in the record as to the actual delivery date of the deed to petitioner. Petitioner paid a total of $18,000 to Mrs. Godlewski in August and October 1984, consistent with the terms of the Agreement. Petitioner sold the house for $64,000 on October 26, 1984, and on December 3, 1984, he purchased a home in Lilburn, Georgia, for $75,000. Petitioner did not report the sale of the house or the acquisition of the Lilburn home on his 1984 income tax return.

Petitioner contends that respondent erred in computing the gain realized on the sale of the house by not increasing his basis to reflect the $18,000 he paid to Mrs. Godlewski. Respondent maintains that petitioner's basis in the house is its cost of $32,200 without adjustment for the $18,000 petitioner paid his ex-wife.

OPINION

The outcome of this case turns on whether section 1041 ... applies to the instant set of facts. The application of section 1041 is critical to our determination because it markedly changes the tax treatment accorded divorced spouses. Under section 1041, the transferor of appreciated property transferred incident to a divorce recognizes no gain and the transferee's basis in the property after transfer is the same as the transferor's basis before the transfer. In contrast, prior law provided that the transfer of appreciated property incident to a divorce resulted in the recognition of gain to the transferor and the transferee received a basis equal to the asset's fair market value at time of transfer. *United States v. Davis*, 370 U.S. 65 (1962). (Footnote 4) Moreover, prior law recognized gain on the sale of property between spouses even when transacted in connection with a divorce. See *McKinney v. Commissioner*, 64 T.C. 263, 268–269 (1975). Since these provisions result in materially disparate tax consequences, it is incumbent upon us to correctly determine which of these provisions apply to the transaction at issue. (Footnote 5)

In general, section 1041 applies to property transfers between former spouses incident to a divorce if such transfer took place after July 18, 1984, the enactment date of the Deficit Reduction Act of 1984.... However, by its terms, it does not apply "to transfers under any instrument in effect on or before the date of the enactment." Therefore, to determine whether section 1041 applies to the facts presented here, we must decide whether the house was "transferred" after July 18, 1984, and, if so, whether such transfer was made under any instrument in effect on or before July 18, 1984.

The answer to the first question is fairly straightforward. The house was titled in Mrs. Godlewski's name and she executed a warranty deed in favor of petitioner on July 20, 1984. Since Mrs. Godlewski executed the deed on July 20, 1984, the transfer necessarily occurred after July 18, 1984.

The answer to whether such transfer was made under any instrument in effect on or before July 18, 1984, is not nearly so easily determined. Although, admittedly, the transfer was incident to the divorce, (Footnote 7) the divorce decree specifically reserved the determination of property rights for later hearing. The inescapable conclusion, therefore, is that the transfer of the house was not "under" that "instrument."

Having eliminated the divorce decree, we next consider whether the agreement was the operative "instrument." The agreement was dated July 13, 1984, and was signed by Mrs. Godlewski on that date, clearly prior to the enactment date of July 18, 1984. However, the agreement was not executed by petitioner until July 25, 1984, obviously after the enactment of section 1041.

To be effective, an agreement settling marital rights between residents of Georgia must meet the same requisites of formation and enforceability as other contracts. See *Blum v. Morgan Guar. Trust Co. of New York*, 709 F.2d 1463, 1467 (11th Cir. 1983) (applying Georgia law for general litigation settlement); *McKie v. McKie*, 213 Ga. 582, ... (1957). Initially, there must be a meeting of minds between the parties concerning all the essential terms of the agreement. Ga. Code Ann. sec. 13-3-1 et seq. (1981). Moreover, under the Georgia statute of frauds, a contract transferring an interest in land must be in writing. Ga. Code Ann. sec. 13-5-30 (4) (1981); see *Stamps v. Ford Motor Co.*, 650 F. Supp. 390 (N.D. Ga., 1986); *Smith v. Cox*, 247 Ga. 563, ... (1981).

The record does not disclose any information surrounding the negotiation, preparation or execution of the agreement except that the $18,000, at least initially, was Mrs. Godlewski's "asking" figure based on the fair market value as determined by the June 1984 appraisal. Therefore, there is no evidence indicating a meeting of minds prior to petitioner's execution of the agreement on July 25, 1984. Further, even if there was, the statute of frauds would establish, as the effective date, the day the agreement was reduced to writing. The earliest date this could have occurred was when the agreement was signed by petitioner on July 25, 1984. Thus, we conclude that section 1041 is applicable to this transaction because the agreement became effective and the transfer of the house both occurred after July 18, 1984.

As previously stated, section 1041 provides that no gain or loss is recognized on a transfer of property between the taxpayer and his former spouse if the transfer is incident to the divorce. Sec. 1041(a)(2). Rather, the property is treated as if acquired by gift. Sec. 1041(b). Moreover, the "nonrecognition rule applies whether the transfer is for the relinquishment of marital rights, for cash or other property ... or for other consideration." H. Rept. 98-4170 (Pub. L. 369), 98th Cong., 2d Sess. 1491–1492 (1984).

Consequently, the basis to the transferee in the property is the adjusted basis of the transferor as contended by respondent. Sec. 1041(b)(2). Even so, petitioner argues that the transfer of the house was the result of a bona fide sale and, therefore, the $18,000 paid by petitioner to Mrs. Godlewski should rightfully be added to his basis to determine the amount of the gain he has to report. The temporary regulations, however, set out the unambiguous rule that—

In all cases, the basis of the transferred property in the hands of the transferee is the adjusted basis of such property in the hands of the transferor immediately before the transfer. *Even if the transfer is a bona fide sale, the transferee does not acquire a basis in the transferred property equal to the transferee's cost* (the fair market value). This carryover basis rule applies whether the adjusted basis of the transferred property is less than, equal to, or greater than its fair mark et value at the time of transfer (or the value of any consideration provided by the transferee) and applies for purposes of determining loss as well as a gain upon the subsequent disposition of the property by the transferee. Thus, this rule is different from the rule applied in section 1015(a) for determining the basis of property acquired by gift. [Sec. 1.1041-1T(d)A-11, Temporary Income Tax Regs., 49 Fed. Reg. 34452, 34453 (Aug. 31, 1984).... (Footnote 8)]

Since both the statute and regulations clearly provide that the $18,000 petitioner paid his former wife does not increase his basis in the house, we hold petitioner's basis in the house is $32,200. Sec. 1041(b)(2); sec. 1.1041 — 1T(d)A-11, Temporary Income Tax Regs., 49 Fed. Reg. 34452 (Aug. 31, 1984).

...

FOOTNOTES:

2. Respondent conceded all of the issues raised in the notice of deficiency except for the one at issue here. In addition, he conceded that ... the amount realized from the sale of the house should be reduced by sales expenses of $7,373.

3. Naming Mrs. Godlewski as titleholder was an attempt to shield the property from attachment or sale in the event petitioner was ever sued in his capacity as a physical education instructor. Petitioner is no longer employed in that capacity.

4. Exceptions to the general rule enunciated in *Davis* depended on State property and divorce law. E.g., *Bosch v. United States*, 590 F.2d 165 (5th Cir. 1979), cert. denied 444 U.S. 1044 (1980); *Serianni v Commissioner*, 80 T.C. 1090, 1100–1101 (1983), affd. 765 F.2d 1051 (11th Cir. 1985).

5. Although unclear, it appears from the record that the parties may have agreed that sec. 1041 would apply in this case. Nonetheless, it is well established that this Court may disregard stipulations of law. E.g., *Mead's Bakery v. Commissioner*, 364 F.2d 101, 106 (5th Cir. 1966), affg. on this point a Memorandum Opinion of this Court; *Estate of Di Marco v. Commissioner*, 87 T.C. 653, 663 n. 10 (1986); *Sivils v. Commissioner*, 86 T.C. 79, 82 (1986). Therefore, it is within the Court's power to determine the correct law to be applied even if the parties had knowingly agreed to such a stipulation....

7. For these purposes "transfer incident to divorce" means any transfer that occurs within one year after the date on which the marriage ceases or that is related to the cessation of the marriage. Sec. 1041(c). The transfer of the house in the instant case occurred within one year of the Oct. 31, 1983, divorce decree and, therefore, is a "transfer incident to divorce." Sec. 1041(c)(1).

8. These regulations were promulgated under the Treasury's general rule-making power as authorized by sec. 7805(a). They were in effect for the year in issue. While we recognize that the regulation involved is only temporary, we accord them the same weight as the final regulations. *Nissho Iwai American Corporation v. Commissioner*, 89 T.C. 765, 776 (1987); see *Zinniel v. Commissioner*, 89 T.C. 357 (1987).

Consider the following questions.

1. Who provided the original funding for the purchase of the house?

2. Who held title to it? What are some of the factors that may prompt a married couple to put title to the family home in the name of only one of the spouses?

3. If one spouse provides the funds to purchase the family home, does section 1041 provide tax-free treatment if title is placed in the name of the other spouse? Suppose the parties were unrelated and one provided the funds but the other took title. What result?

4. Why did Mr. Godlewski pay $18,000 to his former wife? (Can you calculate how they might have arrived at this number even though the opinion does not state what the mortgage balance was at the time of their negotiation?)

5. What was the transaction that brought this case to the Tax Court?

6. Why was the date "July 18, 1984" so important to the resolution of the case?

Note that section 421(d)(1) of the Deficit Reduction Act of 1984 set forth the effective date for new section 1041. (The case quotes section 421(d) in footnote 6.) You may look in vain at section 1041 itself for the effective date. As is customary, the effective date appears only in the session law, *i.e.*, the tax act itself, and not in the new provision. **Review footnote 18 in the Introduction to this book.** It describes the relationship between the session law and the United States Code provision. Effective dates are very important! As this case illustrates, in the words of the old song, "[w]hat a difference a day makes; 24 little hours...." Careful planning requires the taxpayer to take into account known changes in the law.

7. What was petitioner's position in the case? On what Code section did he rely? Did he prevail?

8. What was the court's reasoning supporting its decision?

Note that the court relied on a temporary regulation, 1.1041-1T(d)A-11, promulgated as Treasury Decision 7973 on August 30, l984, and published in proposed form in the Federal Register the following day at 49 Fed. Reg. 34452, 34453 (Aug. 31, 1984). It is common practice for the Treasury to issue proposed regulations in temporary form simultaneously with the issuance of the regulation in proposed form, particularly with respect to Code provisions that affect many individual taxpayers, as was the case with enactment of section 1041. Taxpayers may rely on temporary regulations until they are revoked or replaced. *Godlewski*, 90 T.C. at 206, n.8. In contrast, proposed regulations offer only guidance as to the thinking of the Treasury at the time the proposed regulation was issued (which may long precede issuance of the final regulation). A notice and comment period follows the publication of a proposed regulation. Note also that as this book goes to press, the proposed and temporary regulations, issued in 1984, have not been replaced by a final regulation.

9. Which judge decided this case?[63]

4. The Future?

You have now seen four examples of permissible assignments of income: (1) transfers of appreciated property by gift under the rule of *Taft v. Bowers* as codified by section 1015(a); (2) the joint return under section 6013(a); (3) alimony deductible by the payor and includible by the payee under sections 215 and 71; and (4) transfers of property between spouses (or former spouses) under section 1041.[64] All four present the question

---

63. Section 7443A has replaced section 7456, mentioned in the case. As noted in the material following the *Sklar* case, the new section allows the chief judge of the Tax Court to assign certain cases to "special trial judges." Section 7443A(b). The most important role for special trial judges at the United States Tax Court involves disputes involving $50,000 or less. In cases where the amount in controversy does not exceed $50,000, a taxpayer may elect an expedited procedure that results in a faster resolution, using a simplified procedure but without the possibility of appeal. Section 7463 is popular with taxpayers because they can write out their petitions by hand and represent themselves in a less formal proceeding.

64. Note that although we concentrated on the application of section 1041 to transfers of property incident to divorce, it also applies to transfers of property between spouses that are not incident to a divorce. See section 1041(a)(1).

of who is the proper taxpayer when the taxpayer is part of a family unit. The willingness of Congress to condone certain assignments of income between family members may result, at least in part, from the debate, ongoing almost since the inception of the income tax, as to what is the proper taxpaying unit within a family. As Professor Gann has stated:

> The primary justification for the present system [the joint return] is the assumption that the family or marital unit is an economic unit in which spouses equally share income, without regard to its actual source, for the joint and common good of the unit. This characterization, which results from the sociological aspects of marriage, is buttressed by the obligation of support imposed on family members. Thus, a spouse who earns income will not unilaterally treat that income as his or hers because, for social ... reasons, some of that income will benefit other members of the family.[65]

But, as we learned when we talked about the marriage penalty, adopting the family unit as the proper taxpayer sometimes disadvantages those who are not members of a traditional family. As stated by Professor Bittker:

> A persistent problem in the theory of income taxation is whether natural persons should be taxed as isolated individuals, or as social beings whose family ties to other taxpayers affect their taxpaying capacity. From its inception, the federal income tax law has permitted every taxpayer to file a personal return, embracing his or her own income but excluding the income of the taxpayer's spouse, children, and other relatives. On the other hand, married couples may elect to consolidate their income on a joint return, many exemptions and deductions take account of family links and responsibilities, and the income or property of one member of a family is sometimes attributed to another member for a variety of tax purposes. The Internal Revenue Code, in brief, is a patchwork, its history being a myriad of compromises fashioned to meet particular problems.
>
> While this tension between rugged individualism and family solidarity permeates the entire Code, four broad questions capture the major themes:
>
> – Should family members—husbands, wives, children, or others—be required, allowed, or forbidden to amalgamate their separate incomes in order to compute a joint tax liability?
>
> – If amalgamation is either permitted or required, what should be the relationship between the tax liability of a family on its amalgamated income and that of a person living outside any family unit on his or her individual income?
>
> – Should the taxpayer—whether an individual or a family entity—receive a tax allowance for supporting children, parents, or other relatives?
>
> – How should the tax law treat transfers, sales, and other financial and property arrangements between family members, and for what tax purposes (if any)should the law attribute the income or property of one family member to another?

The responses of today's law to these questions are, of course, influenced by the need for revenue, by the Internal Revenue Service's capacity to audit re-

---

65. Pamela B. Gann, "Abandoning Marital Status as a Factor in Allocating Income Tax Burdens," 59 Tex. L. Rev. 1, (1980).

turns and enforce the rules, by legislative and administrative efforts to minimize inconsistencies within the statute and regulations, and by other objectives, constraints, and values that are "internal" to the tax system. But the impact of these factors on Congress, the Treasury, and the public has always depended on a much more influential context—society's assumptions about the role of marriage and the family.

We are living in a period of unprecedented debate about the status of marriage and the family. Citizens, moral philosophers, political groups, legislators, and judges are questioning many traditional legal distinctions between men and women, between informal alliances and ceremonial marriage, between legitimate and illegitimate children, between the role of the family and the role of the state, and between the power of parents and the rights of children. In such an era, it is fatuous to expect the premises underlying the Internal Revenue Code to escape inquiry or to suppose that income taxation has a "logic" of its own capable of supplying certitudes to a society wracked by doubts.

For these reasons, the Internal Revenue Code's current answers to the questions set out above are ripe for reexamination....[66]

Professor Bittker authored the excerpt above more than thirty years ago. He suggested then that the underlying premises of the Code's treatment of the family were "ripe for re-examination". The following case demonstrates the effort (and result) of one taxpayer to persuade the Tax Court to re-examine the issue of defining the proper taxpaying unit.

MUELLER v. COMMISSIONER
T.C. Memo. 2000-132

LARO, Judge: ...

The issues for decision are:

(1) Whether petitioner is entitled to a filing status other than "single" in recognition of his claim that he has an "economic partnership" with a same-sex individual with whom he resided from 1989 to 1996; [and] (2) whether petitioner is liable for the additions to tax determined by respondent under section 6651(a)(1).... We hold for respondent on all issues.

...

FINDINGS OF FACT

... Petitioner did not file Federal income tax returns for any of the taxable years 1986 through 1995. During these years petitioner earned the bulk of his income by working as a computer programmer/consultant for various companies and hospitals....

...

Petitioner is homosexual. In 1989, petitioner began a relationship with another man whom petitioner describes as his roommate and partner. From 1989 through 1995 petitioner and his partner resided together and shared assets and income. Petitioner was

---

66. Boris I. Bittker, "Federal Income Taxation and the Family," 27 Stan. L. Rev., *supra* at 1391–92.

not married (to his partner or anyone else) as of December 31 for any of the taxable years 1986 through 1995. In the notice of deficiency mailed to petitioner, respondent determined that petitioner's proper filing status for income tax purposes for each year before the Court was single. Accordingly, respondent calculated the deficiencies and additions to tax using the tax rates applicable to unmarried individuals pursuant to section 1(c).

OPINION

Petitioner does not challenge the facts on which respondent's determinations are based. Petitioner's sole claim in this case is that he should be accorded married, rather than single, filing status on his tax returns for the years 1989 to 1995. Petitioner does not claim to have ever been married. Rather, petitioner argues that he had an "economic partnership" with his roommate and that he was unconstitutionally denied the opportunity to file a joint tax return with him in recognition of such partnership. Petitioner references a number of constitutional provisions, but we understand the crux of petitioner's constitutional claim to be that the tax code's unequal or differential treatment between married taxpayers and unmarried persons in an economic partnership constitutes a violation of the due process notions implicit in the Fifth Amendment and of the equal protection standards incorporated thereunder. (Footnote 2)

We have consistently denied constitutional challenges to marital classifications in the tax code. These have included challenges brought by disadvantaged married taxpayers, (Footnote 3) see *DeMars v. Commissioner...*, 79 T.C. 247 (1982); *Druker v. Commissioner...*, 77 T.C. 867 (1981), affd. on this issue and revd. in part ... 697 F.2d 46 (2d Cir. 1982); *Brady v. Commissioner...*, T.C. Memo. 1983-163, affd. without published opinion 729 F.2d 1445 (3d Cir. 1984), as well as by disadvantaged singles, see *Kellems v. Commissioner...*, 58 T.C. 556 (1972), affd. per curiam ... 474 F.2d 1399 (2d Cir. 1973). Other Federal courts have similarly upheld marital classifications in the tax code. See, e.g., *Mapes v. United States...*, 217 Ct. Cl. 115, 576 F.2d 896 (1978); *Jansen v. United States...*, 441 F.Supp. 20 (D. Minn. 1977), affd. per curiam ... 567 F.2d 828 (8th Cir. 1977); *Johnson v. United States...*, 422 F.Supp. 958 (N.D. Ind. 1976), affd. per curiam sub nom. *Barter v. United States...*, 550 F.2d 1239 (7th Cir. 1977).

Petitioner seeks to add a new gloss to these old challenges by identifying singles who share assets and income (whom he labels "economic partners") as a distinct class of taxpayers disadvantaged by marital classifications. For the reasons set forth below, we hold the tax code's distinctions between married taxpayers and unmarried economic partners to be constitutionally valid.

In evaluating whether a statutory classification violates equal protection, we generally apply a rational basis standard. See *Regan v. Taxation With Representation...*, 461 U.S. 540, 547 (1983). We apply a higher standard of review only if it is found that the statute (1) impermissibly interferes with the exercise of a fundamental right or (2) employs a suspect classification, such as race. See, e.g., *id; Harris v. McRae*, 448 U.S. 297, 322 (1980). Neither of these exceptions applies.

Petitioner does not directly identify any fundamental right impeded by the use of marital classifications in the tax code. Petitioner cites commentary addressing the right to marry. However, a law is considered to burden the right to marry only where the obstacle to marriage imposed by the law operates to preclude marriage entirely for a certain class of persons. See *DeMars v. Commissioner, supra* at 250. The classifications at issue in this case are a consequence, not a cause, of petitioner's nonmarried status, and thus do not burden the right to marry. See *Druker v. Commissioner...*, 697 F.2d at 50.

The marital classifications at issue also do not affect petitioner as a member of a suspect class. Petitioner claims discrimination not as a homosexual but as a person who shares assets and income with someone who is not his legal spouse. Petitioner therefore places himself in a class that includes nonmarried couples of the opposite sex, family members, and friends. We are aware of no authority that would render such group a suspect class. (Footnote 4)

Under the rational basis standard, a challenged classification is valid if rationally related to a legitimate government interest. See *City of Cleburne v. Cleburne Living Ctr., Inc.*, 473 U.S. 432, 440 (1985); *City of New Orleans v. Dukes*, 427 U.S. 297, 303 (1976). In *Kellems v. Commissioner...*, 58 T.C. 556 (1972), affd.... 474 F.2d 1399 (2d Cir. 1973), we addressed the constitutionality of the application of single return rates without the income-splitting benefit available to married taxpayers. We held therein that the classification between married and single taxpayers is founded upon a rational basis and was a permissible attempt to account for the greater financial burdens of married taxpayers and to equalize geographically their tax treatment. (Footnote 5) See *id.* at 558–559.

Our holding in *Kellems* is of no less application here. Congress had a rational basis for adopting marital classifications in the tax code. That conclusion is not altered by petitioner's claim that there are additional classifications that could have been made. Undoubtedly, certain inequalities persisted between married taxpayers and unmarried economic partners following the enactment of the joint filing provisions. However, legislatures have especially broad latitude in creating classification and distinctions in tax statutes. See *Regan v. Taxation With Representation, supra* at 547. Moreover, "reform may take one step at a time, addressing itself to the phase of the problem which seems most acute to the legislative mind." *Williamson v. Lee Optical Co.*, 348 U.S. 483, 489 (1955).

While petitioner makes several arguments on policy and sociological grounds, in the face of the cases cited above to the contrary, they have no legal bearing on the issues in this case. Whether policy considerations warrant narrowing of the gap between the tax treatment of married taxpayers and homosexual and other nonmarried economic partners is for Congress to determine in light of all the relevant legislative considerations. See *Druker v. Commissioner...*, 697 F.2d at 51.

Accordingly, we sustain the deficiencies determined by respondent. (Footnote 6)

2. Addition to Tax Under Section 6651(a)(1)

Respondent determined additions to tax under section 6651(a) for petitioner's failure to file his 1986 through 1995 Federal income tax returns. In order to avoid this addition to tax, petitioner must prove that his failure to file was: (1) Due to reasonable cause and (2) not due to willful neglect. See sec. 6651(a); Rule 142(a), *United States v. Boyle....* A failure to file a timely Federal income tax return is due to reasonable cause if the taxpayer exercised ordinary business care and prudence and, nevertheless, was unable to file the return within the prescribed time. See sec. 301.6651-1(c)(1), Proced. & Admin. Regs. Willful neglect means a conscious, intentional failure to file or reckless indifference....

Petitioner has offered no evidence to show that his failure to file was due to reasonable cause and not willful neglect. The evidence is clear that petitioner's actions were deliberate, intentional, and in complete disregard of the statutes and respondent's regulations. Petitioner made no attempt to file an authentic tax return for any of the years at issue.

Petitioner offers the "excuse" that his nonfiling was as an act of "non-violent civil disobedience" on a "human right's issue". As we stated in *Klunder v. Commissioner...*, T.C. Memo. 1991-489: "Petitioner wants the best of both worlds, to civilly disobey and also to be absolved of the additions to tax." Whether or not petitioner considers his nonfiling an act of civil disobedience, he must accept the consequences of actions knowingly taken....

Accordingly, we sustain respondent's determination under section 6651(a)(1) for the taxable years in issue.

...

FOOTNOTES:

2. The equal protection principles of the Fourteenth Amendment are encompassed within the Fifth Amendment as applied to Federal legislation....

3. Being accorded married status under the tax code is not always favorable. See U.S. General Accounting Office, Income Tax Treatment of Married and Single Individuals (Pub. No. GAO/GGD-96-175 (1996) (describing provisions in the tax code favoring single taxpayers over married taxpayers and vice versa); see also Cohen & Morris, "Tax Issues From 'Father Knows Best' To 'Heather Has Two Mommies'", 84 Tax Notes 1309 (Aug. 30, 1999) (describing the tax advantages and tax planning opportunities available to nonmarried couples).

4. Petitioner claims that the Federal tax laws specifically began to target homosexuals as a group after the enactment of the Defense of Marriage Act (DOMA), Pub. L. 104-199, 110 Stat. 2419 (1996). That law defines "marriage" in any act of Congress (which would include the Federal tax code) as a legal union "between one man and one woman" as husband and wife. The DOMA also defines the word "spouse" to mean only a person of the "opposite sex" who is a husband or wife. We decline to pass on the constitutionality of the DOMA because it was not effective for the years at issue in this case.

5. Prior to 1948 each individual was taxed on his or her own income regardless of marital status. However, under the Supreme Court's decision in *Poe v. Seaborn...*, 282 U.S. 101 (1930), married couples in community property States were permitted to split their community income evenly for Federal tax purposes regardless of the amounts each actually earned. See *Kellems v. Commissioner...*, 58 T.C. 556, 558–559 (1972), affd. per curiam ... 474 F.2d 1399 (2d Cir. 1973).

6. We also note that petitioner, as a nonfiler, would not be entitled to the relief he now seeks even if he had been married at the relevant times. Married taxpayers who fail to file returns are not entitled to application of the married filing jointly tax rates....

Consider the following questions about *Mueller*.

1. Might the taxpayer have fared better in the Tax Court if he had actually filed a joint return with his partner?

Remember family law is an area in which state law and federal tax law intersect. Although there have been some discussions at the state level of, for example, changing the state's treatment of couples in non-traditional relationships, thus far, only one state, Massachusetts, has changed state law to permit same-sex marriage. Vermont, Connecticut, New Jersey, and New Hampshire have come close, authorizing civil unions for same-sex couples; California has enacted a statute governing domestic partnerships; and New York City has authorized the registration of domestic partnerships for both same-sex and unmarried heterosexual couples. Other states and cities have adopted or are debating various measures to bestow benefits on either same-sex or unmarried heterosexual couples or both.

2. What if Mr. Mueller and his partner had been married under Massachusetts law?

Although the Code has always relied on whether a couple was "married" under state law, these state rules might not help future taxpayers like Mr. Mueller because of passage of the Federal Defense of Marriage Act, P.L. 104-199 (1996) ("DOMA"). With relatively little discussion, Congress, afraid of the possible consequences of a decision by a court in Hawaii that it was unconstitutional under that state's constitution to prohibit same-sex partners from marrying, enacted DOMA, the statute referred to in footnote 4 of *Mueller*.

In footnote 4 of its *Mueller* opinion the Tax Court recognized the passage of DOMA but declined to pass on DOMA's constitutionality because it was not effective for the years at issue in the case. The following year the Tax Court again addressed Mr. Mueller's claim that he was entitled to file a joint return with his partner, this time for 1996, after DOMA became effective. The Tax Court, again, ruled against him. *Mueller v. Commissioner*, T.C. Memo 2001-274. The court held that because Mr. Mueller was not married in 1996 under the laws of any state, DOMA did not actually apply.

3. Why did the Service file a return for Mr. Mueller?

Note that section 6020 authorizes the Service to file a return for a taxpayer when the taxpayer fails to file one for himself. When the Service does so, it employs the standard deduction and files either as "single" or, if it knows the taxpayer to be married, as "married filing separately." Of course, this methodology often produces a much higher tax than the taxpayer would have owed had she properly prepared her own return. There is no statute of limitations on audit when the Service files a section 6020(b) return; after all, the taxpayer has filed no return.

Note also footnote 6 of the opinion. The right to file a joint return depends upon the taxpayers' timely election under section 6013. As that footnote makes clear, a taxpayer who fails to make a timely election loses the right to file a joint return (even if married).

4. What does the court mean when it quotes the Supreme Court decision in *Williamson v. Lee Optical Co.*: "reform may take one step at a time, addressing itself to the phase of the problem which seems most acute to the legislative mind." … ?

5. Is it time for Congress to revisit the issue of what is the proper taxpaying unit?

Chapter 2

Form versus Substance

In a famous case involving corporate taxation, *Commissioner v. Court Holding Co.*, the Supreme Court stated that "[t]he incidence of taxation depends upon the substance of a transaction.... To permit the true nature of a transaction to be disguised by mere formalisms, which exist solely to alter tax liabilities, would seriously impair the effective administration of the tax policies of Congress."[1] In these few words, the Court summed up another important doctrine that pervades income tax. We take up here the concept of form versus substance as it affects the issue of identifying the proper taxpayer, *i.e.*, whether the identity the taxpayer seeks to claim is deserved. The doctrine arises in many types of transactions in income tax: for example, in sale versus lease cases. Also, recall *Salvatore v. Commissioner*. The taxpayers there attempted to arrange the transaction in the way that would achieve the most favorable tax treatment. They failed, however, to accomplish the intended result because the substance of the transaction simply did not coincide with its form. Whatever the transaction, however, the real issue is whether the taxpayer is entitled to the tax treatment the form of the transaction purports to produce.

Recall our earlier discussions of joint returns and the marriage penalty. **Also review section 7703(a)(1).** Consider the case of David and Angela Boyter set forth below. Why did the Boyters engage in their repeated divorces?

BOYTER v. COMMISSIONER
668 F.2d 1382 (4th Cir. 1981)

WINTER, Chief Judge:

Taxpayers (H. David Boyter and his sometime wife, Angela M. Boyter), both of whom are domiciled in Maryland, ask us to reverse the Tax Court and to rule that for the tax years 1975 and 1976 they successfully avoided the "marriage penalty" of the Internal Revenue Code. The "marriage penalty" results from the fact that a man and woman who are husband and wife on the last day of the taxable year, each having separate income, are taxed, in the aggregate, in a greater amount if they file either joint or separate income tax returns than would be the case if they were unmarried. The Tax Court ruled that the Boyters were legally married at the end of tax years 1975 and 1976, and therefore were subject to the higher tax rate, since their purported Haitian and Dominican Republic divorces (granted on December 8, 1975 and November 22, 1976, respectively) were invalid under the law of Maryland, the state of the Boyters' domicile. The Tax Court therefore sustained the Commissioner's deficiency assessments for unpaid taxes. In view of this conclusion the Tax Court apparently thought it unnecessary to decide the Commissioner's alternative argument that even if the divorces would be

---

1. 324 U.S. 331, 334 (1945).

recognized in Maryland, the taxpayers should not be treated as husband and wife for federal income tax purposes under the "sham" transaction doctrine.

…

… [W]e remand the case to the Tax Court for further findings as to the applicability of the sham transaction doctrine.

I.

Taxpayers were married in Maryland in 1966 and were domiciled in Maryland during the tax years in issue, 1975 and 1976. Both are employed as federal civil service employees and have not insubstantial earnings. They filed joint federal income tax returns and reported their income as married individuals filing separately from 1966 to 1974.

Probably as a result of dinner table conversation with a friend who had been recently divorced, taxpayers came to the realization that their combined federal income tax liability would be lower if they were able to report their respective incomes as unmarried individuals. They were also aware that the Internal Revenue Code provides that the determination of whether an individual is married shall be made as of the close of the taxable year.…

Taxpayers thus concluded that if they obtained a divorce decree at the end of the taxable year (here, December 31) they would be entitled to file their returns as unmarried individuals. It seems clear, as the Tax Court found, that at least through 1976 taxpayers never intended to and never did physically separate from each other prior to or subsequent to either of the divorces that they obtained. Rather, they continued to reside together through the tax years in question in the home they purchased in 1967.

Late in 1975 taxpayers traveled to Haiti. Through an attorney, whose name they had obtained from a Baltimore public library and who in correspondence had quoted them an attractive estimate of his fee and expenses, they obtained a decree of divorce. The action was instituted by Angela Boyter and the divorce decree was granted on the ground of incompatibility of character notwithstanding that the parties occupied the same hotel room prior to and immediately after the granting of the decree. Moreover, Angela Boyter testified before the Tax Court that her character was not incompatible to that of David Boyter. She testified also that the sole reason for her obtaining the divorce was "because the tax laws, as currently written, caused us to pay a penalty for being married." Indeed she testified that she advised her Haitian counsel "that we got along quite well and planned to continue to live together …" (Footnote 2) Shortly after the Haitian court granted the divorce, taxpayers returned to their matrimonial domicile in Maryland and were remarried in Howard County, Maryland on January 9, 1976. For the calendar year 1975 taxpayers filed separate income tax returns claiming the rates applicable to unmarried individuals.

In November of 1976 taxpayers traveled to the Dominican Republic where David Boyter, as the moving party, obtained a divorce decree on November 22, 1976. Again the parties traveled together to and from the Dominican Republic. Whether they occupied the same hotel room is not shown by the record. The record does show, however, that although the Dominican decree was granted on the ground of "incompatibilities of temperaments existing between [the parties] that has made life together unbearable," Angela Boyter denied that she had ever said anything which would serve as a basis for such a finding by the Dominican Republic court. David Boyter testified before the Tax Court that he would not characterize the grounds as "totally" true. As he explained it: "I understood that these were strictly legalistic terms."

The taxpayers returned to Maryland to their matrimonial domicile and they were re-married on February 10, 1977. For calendar year 1976 they filed separate federal income tax returns claiming the rates applicable to unmarried individuals.

The Commissioner determined a deficiency in income taxes for each of the taxpayers for 1975 and 1976 and taxpayers sought review in the Tax Court. The Tax Court sustained the deficiencies. Although the government argued that the divorce decrees should be disregarded for federal income tax purposes because a year-end divorce whereby the parties intend to and do in fact remarry early in the next year is a sham transaction, the Tax Court expressed no view on this argument. Rather, it undertook an elaborate analysis of Maryland law with respect to the validity of the divorce decrees and concluded that Maryland would not recognize the foreign divorces as valid to terminate the marriage. On this basis, the Tax Court entered judgment for the government.

II.

We agree with the government's argument that under the Internal Revenue Code a federal court is bound by state law rather than federal law when attempting to construe marital status.... The difficulty with this approach in this case, however, is that the Maryland authorities do not establish beyond peradventure of doubt that the two divorces with which we are concerned are invalid under Maryland law. As the Tax Court stated, "the law in Maryland with regard to the recognition of migratory divorces obtained in a foreign country by Maryland domiciliaries has not been explicitly declared by either the legislature or the highest court of that state," although, as the taxpayers have demonstrated, a number of Maryland trial courts, explicitly and implicitly, have recognized the validity of migratory foreign divorces.

In this ambiguous state of the Maryland law, we would ordinarily be disposed to invoke the certification procedure authorized by Ann. Code of Md., Cts. & Jud. Proc. § 12-601 (1980), and ask the Maryland Court of Appeals for a definitive pronouncement on the validity of these bilateral foreign migratory divorces. (Footnote 3)

But there are other factors which must be considered. The Commissioner has made it clear to us both in his brief and in oral argument that he intends to press the contention, advanced in the Tax Court but not decided by it, that under the sham transaction doctrine taxpayers must be treated as husband and wife in computing their federal income taxes for the years 1975 and 1976 even if Maryland recognizes the validity of their migratory foreign divorces. Of course, if the issue of their validity were certified to the Maryland Court of Appeals and that court ruled them invalid, that decision would decide this case. Significantly, however, if the Maryland Court of Appeals ruled them valid, further proceedings would still be necessary in a federal tribunal and those proceedings might result in an adjudication which would render the certification and the opinion of the Maryland court a futile, academic exercise with respect to final disposition of this case.

We think that certification is inappropriate here. Considerations of comity lead us to conclude that we ought not to request the Maryland Court of Appeals to answer a question of law unless and until it appears that the answer is dispositive of the federal litigation or is a necessary and inescapable ruling in the course of the litigation. Certainly we have discretion as to whether to employ the Maryland certification procedure.... We hold that that discretion ought not to be exercised to certify a question of state law where a question of federal law is present and undecided, the decision of which may be wholly dispositive of the case.

III.

We therefore turn to the question of whether in principle the sham transaction doctrine *may* be dispositive in this case. Although we hold that the doctrine *may* be applicable, we do not decide that the divorces in question are in fact shams.

The sham transaction doctrine has its genesis in *Gregory v. Helvering*, 293 U.S. 465, ... (1935)....

...

Gregory has been subsequently invoked by the courts to disregard the form of a variety of business transactions and to apply the tax laws on the basis of the substance or economic reality of the transactions. For example, in *Commissioner v. Tower*, 327 U.S. 280, ... (1946), the Court disregarded the formation of a partnership between a husband and a wife when its sole purpose was to divert income properly attributable to the husband to the wife and thus reduce the couple's overall tax burden. Similarly, in *Helvering v. Clifford*, 309 U.S. 331, ... (1940), the Court held that a husband could not escape tax liability on the income from a portfolio of securities by placing it in a trust for his wife's benefit while retaining in himself substantial dominion and control over the trust.... As the Court stated in *Minnesota Tea Co. v. Helvering*, "A given result at the end of a straight path is not made a different result because reached by following a devious path." 302 U.S. 609, 613, ... (1938).

In evaluating the substance of a transaction, the courts take care to examine the transaction as a whole, not as the sum of its component parts....

Although the sham transaction doctrine has been applied primarily with respect to the tax consequences of commercial transactions, personal tax consequences have often served as the motive for those transactions. *E.g.*, *Tower* 327 U.S. 289.... The principles involved, moreover, are fundamental to the system of income taxation in the United States and should be applicable generally. As Judge Learned Hand, the author of the *Gregory* opinion in the Court of Appeals, noted:

The question always is whether the transaction under scrutiny is in fact what it appears to be in form; a marriage may be a joke; a contract may be intended only to deceive others; an agreement may have a collateral defeasance. In such cases the transaction as a whole is different from its appearance. True, it is always the intent that controls; and we need not for this occasion press the difference between intent and purpose. We may assume that purpose may be the touchstone, but the purpose which counts is one which defeats or contradicts the apparent transaction, not the purpose to escape taxation which the apparent, but not the whole, transaction would realize....

Chisholm v. Commissioner, 79 F.2d 14, 15 (2d Cir. 1935) (citation omitted). Thus Revenue Ruling 76-255 applies the sham transaction doctrine to the divorce of taxpayers who promptly remarry. The underlying purpose of the transaction, viewed as a whole, is for the taxpayers to remain effectively married while avoiding the marriage penalty in the tax laws. It is the prompt remarriage that defeats the apparent divorce when assessing the taxpayers' liability.... Thus, the sham transaction doctrine may apply in this case if, as the record suggests, the parties intended merely to procure divorce papers rather than actually to effect a real dissolution of their marriage contract. (Footnote 7)

Having decided in principle that the sham transaction doctrine may apply to the conduct of the parties, we make no finding that the conduct in fact constituted a sham.

In our view, the Tax Court as the trier of fact is the only body competent to make that determination in the first instance.

It is generally held that whether a transaction lacks real substance and thus constitutes a sham is a question of fact reviewable only under the clearly-erroneous standard. *See Commissioner v. Court Holding, Inc.*, 324 U.S. 331, 333–34 (1945);.... It is the Tax Court which "has the primary function of finding the facts in tax disputes, weighing the evidence, and choosing from among conflicting inferences and conclusions those which it considers most reasonable." ... [W]e have "no power to change or add to these findings of fact or to reweigh the evidence." ...

In summary, we conclude that the correctness of the Tax Court's basis of decision cannot be determined under the present state of Maryland law without certifying the precise question to the Maryland Court of Appeals. Certification should not now be undertaken because there is present and undecided a federal issue which may be dispositive of the litigation, and it is proper that the federal issue be decided before certification is made. The sham transaction doctrine is not inapplicable to this case as a matter of law, but whether the two divorces with the subsequent marriages were shams for income tax purposes are questions of fact which must be determined by the Tax Court and not by us in the first instance.

Accordingly we remand the case to the Tax Court to determine whether the divorces, even if valid under Maryland law, are nonetheless shams and should be disregarded for federal income tax purposes for the years in question.

REMANDED.

FOOTNOTES:

2. The perspective in which the Boyters viewed their purported divorce further appears in the following testimony of Angela Boyter:

Q. You testified that you intended to be divorced, I think I understood you as saying, for all purposes of divorce even though your motivation was for purposes of tax reduction. Is that correct?

A. For all legal purposes, yes.

Q. Did you intend to physically separate from your spouse?

A. No.

Q. Did you continue to cohabit with your spouse throughout the period?

A. To what?

Q. Cohabit. Live together.

A. I suppose so, yes.

Q. You suppose so? You did? Is that correct?

A. Yes.

Q. Okay. Did you intend to separate your finances with respect to savings and checking accounts?

A. No.

Q. Investments?

A. Only in the kinds of property separations that automatically happen when you get divorced.

3. This option was not available to the Tax Court because the Maryland statute does not permit a certification from that tribunal.

7. Relevant to their intention is the evidence suggesting that they may have practiced fraud upon the tribunals granting the divorces.

Now consider the following questions:

1. The Boyters clearly hoped that their tax treatment would be based on the form of their actions. What was the outcome they sought?

2. In Revenue Ruling 76-255, 1976-2 C.B. 40, the Service announced that, in a case with facts very similar to those of the Boyters, it would assume the foreign divorce was valid. If the court assumed the Boyters' divorce was valid, could it have held, nevertheless, that the whole series of events constituted a "sham"?

3. Suppose the Boyters had not remarried early in the tax year following the year of their first divorce. Rather, they had simply resumed cohabitation. Assuming, as stated in Revenue Ruling 76-255, that the Service assumed their foreign divorce was valid, would the Service have challenged their status as single taxpayers?

4. Note that although it was issued after the Boyters' initial divorce and remarriage, and apparently in response to the actions of taxpayers like the Boyters, the Fourth Circuit cites Revenue Ruling 76-255. What is your reaction to the reliance of the court on the, in effect, retroactive application of the Revenue Ruling? How much deference does the court grant to the Ruling?

The Fourth Circuit identified the genesis of the "sham" doctrine as the case of *Gregory v. Helvering*, 293 U.S. 465 (1935). In that case, the Supreme Court examined a complicated business transaction. The taxpayer had structured the transaction to avoid taxation, rather than to accomplish a valid business purpose. The Court noted that although taxpayers are allowed to arrange their affairs as they wish, there must be an underlying purpose in the choice. If there is not, the transaction will not be respected. That is, the Court will look to the substance of the transaction and not be bound by its form. *Gregory v. Helvering* is known for the proposition that a taxpayer may choose the form of her transaction but only if the form chosen serves some non-tax purpose. As expressed by the great Learned Hand when the case was decided by the Second Circuit:

> [A] transaction, otherwise within an exception of the tax law, does not lose its immunity, because it is actuated by a desire to avoid, or, if one choose, to evade, taxation. Any one may so arrange his affairs that his taxes shall be as low as possible; he is not bound to choose that pattern which will best pay the Treasury; there is not even a patriotic duty to increase one's taxes.[2]

Thus, taxpayers must always walk a careful path, being prepared to explain the underlying substance of the transactions they wish to have recognized for tax purposes. At the time of the Boyters' first Tax Court appearance, there was extensive coverage of the plight that led them to their plan. The adverse decision may have prompted other taxpayers to be less daring but to, nevertheless, attempt to reduce their taxes, as the follow-

---

2. *Helvering v. Gregory*, 69 F.2d 809, 810 (2d Cir. 1934).

ing private letter ruling suggests. Remember that a private letter ruling (a "PLR"), is a request from a taxpayer to the Service for advice on the tax consequences of a certain set of actions.[3]

PRIVATE LETTER RULING 7835076
June 1, 1978

This document may not be used or cited as precedent. Section 6110((k)](3) of the Internal Revenue Code.

...

This is in reply to your letter dated February 27, 1978, in which you request a ruling as to your marital status, under the circumstances described below, for federal income tax purposes.

Briefly, the information submitted discloses that you were legally married in 1976; that you are planning to obtain a divorce; that you will get the divorce one time only and stay divorced; and, that you do not intend to remarry each other. However, you will be living together much of the time after the divorce. You are of the opinion that your divorce is legal under state law and is undertaken for a variety of personal reasons which would entitle you to file as single individuals for 1978 assuming your divorce is final in 1978.

Section [7703] of the Internal Revenue Code provides that the determination of whether an individual is married shall be made as of the close of the taxable year.

Section 6013(d) of the Code provides that an individual who is legally separated from his spouse under a decree of divorce shall not be considered married.

Revenue Ruling 67-442, 1967-2 C.B. 82, holds that, generally, for federal income tax purposes, the validity of any divorce decree will not be questioned until a court of competent jurisdiction declares the divorce to be invalid.

Revenue Ruling 76-255, 1976-2 C.B. 40, provides an example of a divorce that will not be recognized for federal income tax purposes even though a court did not declare the divorce to be invalid. As noted in the revenue ruling, it was concluded that the taxpayers involved did not intend the divorce to have any legal effect except to enable them to qualify as unmarried individuals who would be eligible to file separate returns. Further, the taxpayers intended to and did remarry each other early in the succeeding taxable year. Therefore, the divorce was not recognized for federal income tax purposes.

From the above you can appreciate that whether a couple is considered married for federal income tax purposes depends on the facts and circumstances present at the close of the taxable year. Thus, if a couple obtains a divorce that is not declared invalid by a court of competent jurisdiction and there are no factors present to indicate that the couple should not be considered as unmarried individuals, the Internal Revenue Service will recognize the divorce.

---

3. When an audit agent seeks advice, the reply is called a Technical Advice Memorandum ("TAM"). Although the origin of the requests is different, the replies, PLR or TAM, look virtually identical.

Accordingly, if you and your present spouse are legally divorced as of December 31, 1978, the Internal Revenue Service will consider you as unmarried individuals for purposes of section [7703] and 6013 of the Code, provided there are no factors present that would indicate otherwise.

Sincerely yours,

Mario E. Lombardo

Chief, Individual Income Tax Branch

Now consider the following questions:

1. What is the significance of a private letter ruling? Note that the ruling begins, citing section 6110[(k)](3) of the Code, "[t]his document may not be used or cited as precedent." See wording at top of ruling and then to section 6110(k)(3).

2. What does the ruling mean when it qualifies its recognition of the divorce by stating "there are no factors present to indicate that the couple should not be considered unmarried individuals"? What factor could be more compelling than continued cohabitation?

Note that the Fourth Circuit remanded the *Boyter* case to the Tax Court for a factual determination as to whether the plan was, in fact, a sham. See penultimate paragraph in *Boyter*. But, you will search in vain for a remand opinion. In 1982, the Service did not seek review of the decision of the Fourth Circuit. (And, in 1986, the Boyters and the Service finally settled the case.) Read the Action on Decision ("AOD") below that the Service issued in 1982.

Boyter v. Commissioner
Docket No. 80-1792

Decision: December 30, 1981

Tax: Income

Years: 1975 and 1976

$617.98 and $716.00.

ISSUE:

Whether taxpayers' year end divorces, which were obtained in foreign countries in order to render them unmarried for tax purposes, are valid for Federal income tax purposes.

DISCUSSION:

Plaintiffs filed their income tax returns for years prior to 1975 as a married couple. In November and December of 1975 and 1976, plaintiffs obtained divorces in the Republic of Haiti and the Dominican Republic, respectively, [they] were promptly remarried in

1976 and 1977. Plaintiffs filed their income tax returns for years 1975 and 1976 as single taxpayers claiming that they were unmarried individuals at the end of each of these years.

The Tax Court found that the divorces would not have been valid under Maryland law. The court, therefore, found plaintiffs to be married individuals for years 1975 and 1976 and should have filed their income tax returns as a married couple.

The Court of Appeals found that Maryland law is ambiguous regarding the validity of the divorces. Therefore, it would be necessary to utilize the certification procedures to refer this question to the Maryland Court of Appeals. The Court, however, decided not to exercise the option to utilize the certification procedure since the sham transaction doctrine under the federal income tax law could also dispose of this issue. The court, therefore, remanded this case to the Tax Court to decide on the sham transaction issue.

We do not believe that a petition for certiorari should be filed for the following reasons. First, while the Court declined to decide whether the divorces were in fact shams, it strongly implied that they were. Second, the Court's holding did not contradict the Government's position as articulated in Rev. Rul. 76-255, 1976-2 C.B. 40, in which the Service assumed the validity of foreign divorces under state law but ruled nonetheless that the divorces were invalid because of the sham transaction theory. Third, the issue presented in this case is one of first impression. Therefore, there is no conflict among the circuits regarding this issue.... In sum, this case should be viewed as a victory for the Government since the Court of Appeals did not find that the Tax Court's decision was erroneous. It merely directs the Tax Court to reconsider this case on an alternative basis.

> Recommendation:
> No certiorari.
> HENRY K. W. WOO
> Attorney
> Approved: KENNETH W. GIDEON
> Chief Counsel
> By: DANIEL F. FOLZENLOGEN
> Technical Assistant to
> the Chief Counsel

The Chief Counsel's office issues a public statement on its intentions with respect to an ongoing case. Whenever the Service loses an issue in a tax case, one of the divisions within the Chief Counsel's office prepares a recommendation on whether the Service should appeal. As in the case of "acquiescences," these "Actions on Decision" are made public.[4]

Although *Boyter* arose in a family context, as the Fourth Circuit noted in *Boyter*, substance versus form cases frequently arise in non-family commercial transaction cases. Read the following case. As with earlier cases, diagramming will help.

---

4. As Professor Richmond describes AODs: "A.O.D.s indicate the reasoning behind the Service's recommendation whether or not to appeal an adverse decision by a trial or appellate court and whether to acquiesce or nonacquiesce in that decision." Gail Levin Richmond, *Federal Tax Research* 98 (5th ed. 1997).

OESTERREICH v. COMMISSIONER
226 F.2d 798 (9th Cir. 1955)

LING, District Judge.

This case is here on petition to review a decision of the Tax Court relating to a deficiency assessment. The following facts are not in dispute.

Petitioner, Walburga Oesterreich, acquired three adjoining lots, 552, 553 and 554, in January, 1926. One of the lots was on the corner of Wilshire Boulevard and Hamilton Drive in Beverly Hills, California.

Wilshire Amusement Corporation was incorporated in 1929 by Albert H. and Albert J. Chotiner, father and son, for the purpose of building a motion picture theatre. They directed a real estate broker, operating in Beverly Hills, to find a suitable location which they could lease and on which they could construct a theatre. The broker learned from Walburga that she would be willing to enter into a lease for the three vacant lots which she owned and he arranged a meeting between the Chotiners and Walburga. After negotiations, Walburga and Wilshire Amusement Corporation entered into an agreement entitled "lease" dated September 11, 1929. The Chotiners decided, in the course of the negotiations, that additional land would be needed for the theatre which they desired to build and for that reason Wilshire Amusement Corporation purchased lot 555 and the northerly 40 feet of lot 556 at a total cost to it of $19,650. Wilshire conveyed that land to Walburga in the fall of 1929.

Walburga is referred to as lessor and Wilshire Amusement Corporation is referred to as lessee throughout the agreement of September 11, 1929. The "lease" agreement provides for payments called rent to be paid by lessee, Wilshire Amusement Corporation to lessor, the taxpayer. The lessee agreed to pay the lessor total rent of $679,380 payable in monthly installments for a period of 67 years and eight months beginning September 1, 1929 and ending the last day of April, 1997. The rental schedule provided for an annual rental of $7,500 for the first 10 years, $12,000 for the succeeding 18 years and amounts becoming progressively smaller so that the rental for the 68th year was $7,500. The lessee agreed to pay all taxes and similar charges on the property. The lessee agreed to erect a new building on the premises to cost not less than $300,000 and to be completed not later than July 1, 1930. The lessor agreed to join in the execution of notes or debentures and in a deed of trust or mortgage covering the leased premises to secure a loan not to exceed $225,000 to be used in constructing the building. The lessee agreed to take out adequate fire insurance on the building and insurance to protect lessor from claims arising out of the use of the premises. The agreement states that the lessee proposes to sublease a portion of the building for theatre purposes. The lease could be assigned by the lessee upon the terms stated therein and such an assignment would release the lessee of further obligations under the lease. The lessor could declare the lease terminated in case of default continuing longer than a period stated in the lease. The lessee had the right, but was not bound, to tear down any building which might be built on the premises for the purpose of reconstruction in accordance with the terms of the lease should the original building become obsolete or not suited to the purpose of the lessee. Any such replacement was to cost not less than $325,000.

One paragraph of the lease provided that when the lease expired and all conditions met, the "lessor promises and agrees that she will then, upon the payment to her of the further sum of ten dollars ($10.00) in hand, convey or cause to be conveyed by grant deed to the Lessee free and clear of all encumbrance, all of the real property herein leased, without further or other consideration."

The agreement was recorded in the Official Records of Los Angeles County.

Wilshire Amusement Corporation changed its name to Wilshire-Hamilton Properties, Inc., shortly after September 11, 1929. Wilshire Holding Corporation succeeded to the interest of Hamilton under the agreement of September 11, 1929, in August, 1935.

Wilshire Holding Corporation paid the taxpayer $12,000 in each of the years 1945 and 1946 in accordance with the agreement and entered the amounts so received as rental expense. The taxpayer, on her returns for 1945 and 1946, reported the $12,000 as income from rents. She received a letter from an Internal Revenue Agent in Charge indicating over assessments in her income tax for 1945 and 1946, and enclosing a report in which it was stated that she had reported rental income of $12,000 for the years 1945 and 1946, but investigation showed that the agreement under which these payments were made was "not a lease, but in effect an installment sale of realty ..." and she overstated her income for each year by $6,206.91 in that connection. She received another letter from the same source dated July 26, 1949, reversing the previous conclusion and stating that the rents were correctly reported as income on her previous tax returns.

The Commissioner determined a deficiency in income tax of $141.16 for 1946 against Walburga Oesterreich and deficiencies against Wilshire Holding Corporation of $1,584 in declared value excess profits tax, $3,097.83 in excess profits tax, for 1945, and $2,798.20 in income tax for 1946.

The Tax Court entered its decision sustaining the Commissioner's determination of deficiency in the taxpayer's income tax for the year 1946.

There is only one issue presented by this case. Is petitioner entitled to treat 'rental' payments made by "lessee" as long term capital gains [under section 1001] or must she treat them as ordinary income? Conversely, is lessee, the Wilshire Holding Corp., entitled to treat these payments as a deductible business expense ... or merely as non-deductible capital expenditures? The sole issue, therefore, is whether the agreement is a lease or a contract for the sale of land. The courts, in making determinations of this sort, commonly consider the intent of the parties and the legal effect of the instrument as written.

It seems well settled that calling such a transaction a 'lease' does not make it such, if in fact it is something else.... To determine just what it is the courts will look to see what the parties intended it to be.... Both petitioner and Wilshire Holding Corp. have at all times referred to the agreement as a lease and they have treated the payments as rental income and rental expense respectively.... However, the test should not be what the parties call the transaction nor even what they may mistakenly believe to be the name of such transaction. What the parties believe the legal effect of such a transaction to be should be the criterion. If the parties enter into a transaction which they honestly believe to be a lease but which in actuality has all the elements of a contract of sale, it is a contract of sale and not a lease no matter what they call it nor how they treat it on their books. We must look, therefore, to the intent of the parties in terms of what they intended to happen.

It is clear that it was intended that title to the premises was to pass to lessee at the end of the 68 year term. The testimony of the parties makes this explicit. Therefore, if the only test in determining whether it was a sale or lease was the passing of title, the parties intended a sale and not lease.

Testimony was offered to the effect that petitioner wanted the bulk of the consideration for the "lease" as soon as possible so that she could enjoy the money during her lifetime. Consequently, the agreement which provided for a tapering off of the rental payments in the later years was tailored to suit her needs and to what the lessees could afford to pay. This was the intent of the parties and this is what went into the agreement. Here we see that what the parties intended and the legal effect of the transaction were one and the same, so we should not consider the intent of the parties apart from the legal effect of the agreement.

The question before us remains whether petitioner is entitled to treat her rental payments as long term capital gains [under section 1001] rather than rental income and conversely whether Wilshire Holding Corporation is entitled to deduct the payment as rental expense as defined by Sec. 23(a)(1)(A) [the predecessor to action 162] which provide[d] as follows:

"In computing net income there shall be allowed as deductions:

"(a) Expenses

"(1) Trade or Business Expenses

"(A) In General. All the ordinary and necessary expenses paid or incurred during the taxable year in carrying on any trade or business, including * * * rentals or other payments required to be made as a condition to the continued use or possession, for purposes of the trade or business, of property to which the taxpayer has not taken *or is not taking title or in which he has no equity.*" ...

If Wilshire Holding Corporation is either taking title to the property or has acquired an equity, it cannot treat the payments from Wilshire as rental income. It is important to note that these two provisions of Sec. 23(a)(1)(A) are stated in the alternative and the deduction cannot be availed of if Wilshire Holding Corporation has brought itself into either category prohibited by statute....

It is not necessary to hold that by payment of the rental petitioner acquires an "equity", for that word is not easy to define; it is enough that the lease provides a right in the petitioners to take title to the premises for which the rental was paid.

... We find, therefore, that the Tax Court was in error for it ignored this alternative ground of taking title and based its decision on the ground that it believed Wilshire Holding Corporation had not yet acquired an equity in the premises.

There can be no doubt that Wilshire Holding Corporation is acquiring title to the premises. At the expiration of the lease it can acquire the premises now worth $100,000 for the token consideration of $10. Although there have been cases holding that a mere option to buy at the expiration of the time period does turn a lease into a contract of sale, ... it should be noted that in all of these cases, the option price constituted full consideration for the premises or goods acquired. In each of these cases it was always questionable whether or not the options would be exercised. Here there is virtually no question of this, for not only will Wilshire Holding Corporation acquire valuable land for a mere $10 but it will forfeit a $350,000 building now on the premises to the lessor if it does not decide to pay the $10 and take title. The testimony clearly shows that the Wilshire Holding Corporation during all of the original negotiations was very much concerned with what would happen to its building and the land after the lease expired and would not have agreed to the "lease" unless it provided that title would vest in Wilshire.

Another factor leading to the conclusion that the parties at the time of the transaction intended a sale is that the schedule of payments under the so-called lease was not commensurate to the benefit derived by Wilshire from the occupancy and use of the land, for instead of rising toward the end of the lease as the land on Wilshire Boulevard became more valuable the payments decreased.

The alternative criterion under Sec. 23(a)(1)(A) which would prevent Wilshire Holding Corporation from treating the payments as a business expense is whether an equity in the property was acquired. The Tax Court in applying this test held that since the amount due on the remaining portion of the lease greatly exceeded the appraisal value of the property, Wilshire Holding Corporation had not yet acquired an equity. We, however, do not believe that this method of determining whether an equity has been acquired is correct. From 1929 to 1946 Wilshire Holding Corporation paid approximately $160,000 to the lessor. In 1997 it will acquire property appraised at $100,000 in 1946 and worth perhaps ten times as much by 1997. Certainly a part of each payment is going toward the acquisition of this land and to this extent Wilshire Corporation does have an equity....

...

Looking at this transaction from a long range view we find that if the opinion of the Tax Court is affirmed, Wilshire Holding Corporation, at the expiration of the "lease", will have acquired a very valuable piece of property for payments written off entirely as business expense while petitioner will have, in effect, sold a valuable piece of property without having been able to treat the proceeds as a long term capital gain [under section 1001].

We are of opinion that the Tax Court erred in treating the question of intention of the parties as one of fact collateral to the written instrument. The document was not ambiguous, and evidence as to surrounding circumstances was not required to explain it. The intention of the parties, as expressed in the instrument, was cardinal, as has been said above. The document has here been construed in the light of the applicable statute. No question of fact was involved. One who contracts to purchase real property acquires an equity therein immediately on the signing of the contract to purchase and taking possession. This equity increases with every payment. No comparison of the value of the realty and the amount of rental paid at any given time has any validity.

The decision of the Tax Court is reversed.

Now consider the following questions about *Oesterreich*.

1. What form of transaction did the parties choose?

2. What did Walburga Oesterreich report on her tax returns for 1945 and 1946 with respect to this transaction?

3. What did Wilshire Holding Corporation, successor in interest to Wilshire Amusement Corporation, report on its tax returns for 1945 and 1946 with respect to this transaction?

4. Did the Ninth Circuit respect the form that the parties chose?[5] List the factors that the court relied upon in characterizing the transaction as it did.

---

5. Note that the court refers to the concept of "an installment sale of realty." In Part IV, you will learn that in certain circumstances a taxpayer may sell property and receive payments for it that extend over several tax periods. The taxpayer can then report the gain over the same tax periods. Each payment will represent in part a return of capital and in part a gain on the sale. The court also refers to "long term capital gains" versus "ordinary income." In Part V, you will learn that some section 1001 gains enjoy a special lower rate of tax than is applicable to other amounts of taxable income, such as rental income.

5. Based on the court's decision, what was the proper tax treatment of the recast transaction with respect to Walburga Oesterreich? With respect to Wilshire Holding Corporation?

6. Can you speculate why Walburga Oesterreich agreed to a form of transaction that led to less favorable tax results to her than those that the court determined would follow from the true substance of the transaction?

Did the taxpayers in *Oesterreich* fail to heed the advice above: that they must structure their transaction to satisfy the requirement of substance, rather than just complying with a chosen form, to accomplish their desired tax results? That is, did these taxpayers fail to "walk the line"?

Many real estate transactions have led to litigation concerning the nature of the transaction for tax purposes. *Oesterreich* introduced you to a common type of recharacterization. Now consider the following case:

FRANK LYON CO. v. UNITED STATES
435 U.S. 561 (1978)

MR. JUSTICE BLACKMUN delivered the opinion of the Court.

This case concerns the federal income tax consequences of a sale-and-leaseback in which petitioner Frank Lyon Company (Lyon) took title to a building under construction by Worthen Bank & Trust Company (Worthen) of Little Rock, Ark., and simultaneously leased the building back to Worthen for long-term use as its headquarters and principal banking facility.

I

The underlying pertinent facts are undisputed. They are established by stipulations, ... the trial testimony, and the documentary evidence, and are reflected in the District Court's findings.

A

Lyon is a closely held Arkansas corporation engaged in the distribution of home furnishings, primarily Whirlpool and RCA electrical products. Worthen in 1965 was an Arkansas-chartered bank and a member of the Federal Reserve System. Frank Lyon was Lyon's majority shareholder and board chairman; he also served on Worthen's board. Worthen at that time began to plan the construction of a multistory bank and office building to replace its existing facility in Little Rock. About the same time Worthen's competitor, Union National Bank of Little Rock, also began to plan a new bank and office building. Adjacent sites on Capitol Avenue, separated only by Spring Street, were acquired by the two banks. It became a matter of competition, for both banking business and tenants, and prestige as to which bank would start and complete its building first.

Worthen initially hoped to finance, to build, and to own the proposed facility at a total cost of $9 million for the site, building, and adjoining parking deck. This was to be accomplished by selling $4 million in debentures and using the proceeds in the acquisition of the capital stock of a wholly owned real estate subsidiary. This subsidiary would have formal title and would raise the remaining $5 million by a conventional mortgage loan on the new premises. Worthen's plan, however, had to be abandoned for two significant reasons:

1. As a bank chartered under Arkansas law, Worthen legally could not pay more interest on any debentures it might issue than that then specified by Arkansas law. But the proposed obligations would not be marketable at that rate.

2. Applicable statutes or regulations of the Arkansas State Bank Department and the Federal Reserve System required Worthen, as a state bank subject to their supervision, to obtain prior permission for the investment in banking premises of any amount (including that placed in a real estate subsidiary) in excess of the bank's capital stock or of 40% of its capital stock and surplus. (Footnote 1) ... Worthen, accordingly, was advised by staff employees of the Federal Reserve System that they would not recommend approval of the plan by the System's Board of Governors.

Worthen therefore was forced to seek an alternative solution that would provide it with the use of the building, satisfy the state and federal regulators, and attract the necessary capital. In September 1967 it proposed a sale-and-leaseback arrangement. The State Bank Department and the Federal Reserve System approved this approach, but the Department required that Worthen possess an option to purchase the leased property at the end of the 15th year of the lease at a set price, and the federal regulator required that the building be owned by an independent third party.

Detailed negotiations ensued with investors that had indicated interest, namely, Goldman, Sachs & Company; White, Weld & Co.; Eastman Dillon, Union Securities & Company; and Stephens, Inc. Certain of these firms made specific proposals.

Worthen then obtained a commitment from New York Life Insurance Company to provide $7,140,000 in permanent mortgage financing on the building, conditioned upon its approval of the titleholder. At this point Lyon entered the negotiations and it, too, made a proposal.

Worthen submitted a counterproposal that incorporated the best features, from its point of view, of the several offers. Lyon accepted the counterproposal, suggesting, by way of further inducement, a $21,000 reduction in the annual rent for the first five years of the building lease. Worthen selected Lyon as the investor. After further negotiations, resulting in the elimination of that rent reduction (offset, however, by higher interest Lyon was to pay Worthen on a subsequent unrelated loan), Lyon in November 1967 was approved as an acceptable borrower by First National City Bank for the construction financing, and by New York Life, as the permanent lender. In April 1968 the approvals of the state and federal regulators were received.

In the meantime, on September 15, before Lyon was selected, Worthen itself began construction.

B

In May 1968 Worthen, Lyon, City Bank, and New York Life executed complementary and interlocking agreements under which the building was sold by Worthen to Lyon as it was constructed, and Worthen leased the completed building back from Lyon:

1. Agreements between Worthen and Lyon. Worthen and Lyon executed a ground lease, a sales agreement, and a building lease.

Under the ground lease dated May 1, 1968, ... Worthen leased the site to Lyon for 76 years and 7 months through November 30, 2044. The first 19 months were the estimated construction period. The ground rents payable by Lyon to Worthen were $50 for the first 26 years and 7 months and thereafter in quarterly payments:

12/1/94 through 11/30/99 (5 years) — $100,000 annually
12/1/99 through 11/30/04 (5 years) — $150,000 annually
2/1/04 through 11/30/09 (5 years) — $200,000 annually
12/1/09 through 11/30/34 (25 years) — $250,000 annually
12/1/34 through 11/30/44 (10 years) — $10,000 annually.

Under the sales agreement dated May 19, 1968, ... Worthen agreed to sell the building to Lyon, and Lyon agreed to buy it, piece by piece as it was constructed, for a total price not to exceed $7,640,000, in reimbursements to Worthen for its expenditures for the construction of the building. (Footnote 2)

Under the building lease dated May 1, 1968, ... Lyon leased the building back to Worthen for a primary term of 25 years from December 1, 1969, with options in Worthen to extend the lease for eight additional 5-year terms, a total of 65 years. During the period between the expiration of the building lease (at the latest, November 30, 2034, if fully extended) and the end of the ground lease on November 30, 2044, full ownership, use, and control of the building were Lyon's, unless, of course, the building had been repurchased by Worthen.... Worthen was not obligated to pay rent under the building lease until completion of the building. For the first 11 years of the lease, that is, until November 30, 1980, the stated quarterly rent was $145,581.03 ($582,324.12 for the year). For the next 14 years, the quarterly rent was $153,289.32 ($613,157.28 for the year), and for the option periods the rent was $300,000 a year, payable quarterly.... The total rent for the building over the 25-year primary term of the lease thus was $14,989,767.24. That rent equaled the principal and interest payments that would amortize the $7,140,000 New York Life mortgage loan over the same period. When the mortgage was paid off at the end of the primary term, the annual building rent, if Worthen extended the lease, came down to the stated $300,000. Lyon's net rentals from the building would be further reduced by the increase in ground rent Worthen would receive from Lyon during the extension. (Footnote 3)

The building lease was a "net lease," under which Worthen was responsible for all expenses usually associated with the maintenance of an office building, including repairs, taxes, utility charges, and insurance, and was to keep the premises in good condition, excluding, however, reasonable wear and tear.

Finally, under the lease, Worthen had the option to repurchase the building at the following times and prices:

11/30/80 (after 11 years) — $6,325,169.85
11/30/84 (after 15 years) — $5,432,607.32
11/30/89 (after 20 years) — $4,187,328.04
11/30/94 (after 25 years) — $2,145,935.00

These repurchase option prices were the sum of the unpaid balance of the New York Life mortgage, Lyon's $500,000 investment, and 6% interest compounded on that investment.

2. Construction financing agreement. By agreement dated May 14, 1968, ... City Bank agreed to lend Lyon $7,000,000 for the construction of the building. This loan was secured by a mortgage on the building and the parking deck, executed by Worthen as well as by Lyon, and an assignment by Lyon of its interests in the building lease and in the ground lease.

3. Permanent financing agreement. By Note Purchase Agreement dated May 1, 1968, New York Life agreed to purchase Lyon's $7,140,000 6 3/4% 25-year secured note to be is-

sued upon completion of the building. Under this agreement Lyon warranted that it would lease the building to Worthen for a noncancelable term of at least 25 years under a net lease at a rent at least equal to the mortgage payments on the note. Lyon agreed to make quarterly payments of principal and interest equal to the rentals payable by Worthen during the corresponding primary term of the lease.... The security for the note was a first deed of trust and Lyon's assignment of its interests in the building lease and in the ground lease.... Worthen joined in the deed of trust as the owner of the fee and the parking deck.

In December 1969 the building was completed and Worthen took possession. At that time Lyon received the permanent loan from New York Life, and it discharged the interim loan from City Bank. The actual cost of constructing the office building and parking complex (excluding the cost of the land) exceeded $10,000,000.

C

Lyon filed its federal income tax returns on the accrual and calendar year basis. On its 1969 return, Lyon accrued rent from Worthen for December. It asserted as deductions one month's interest to New York Life; one month's depreciation on the building; interest on the construction loan from City Bank; and sums for legal and other expenses incurred in connection with the transaction.

On audit of Lyon's 1969 return, the Commissioner of Internal Revenue determined that Lyon was "not the owner for tax purposes of any portion of the Worthen Building," and ruled that "the income and expenses related to this building are not allowable ... for Federal income tax purposes." ... He also added $2,298.15 to Lyon's 1969 income as "accrued interest income." This was the computed 1969 portion of a gain, considered the equivalent of interest income, the realization of which was based on the assumption that Worthen would exercise its option to buy the building after 11 years, on November 30, 1980, at the price stated in the lease, and on the additional determination that Lyon had "loaned" $500,000 to Worthen. In other words, the Commissioner determined that the sale-and-leaseback arrangement was a financing transaction in which Lyon loaned Worthen $500,000 and acted as a conduit for the transmission of principal and interest from Worthen to New York Life.

All this resulted in a total increase of $497,219.18 over Lyon's reported income for 1969, and a deficiency in Lyon's federal income tax for that year in the amount of $236,596.36. The Commissioner assessed that amount, together with interest of $43,790.84, for a total of $280,387.20.

Lyon paid the assessment and filed a timely claim for its refund. The claim was denied, and this suit, to recover the amount so paid, was instituted in the United States District Court for the Eastern District of Arkansas within the time allowed by 26 U.S.C. §6532(a)(1).

After trial without a jury, the District Court, in a memorandum letter-opinion setting forth findings and conclusions, ruled in Lyon's favor and held that its claimed deductions were allowable.... It concluded that the legal intent of the parties had been to create a bona fide sale-and-leaseback in accordance with the form and language of the documents evidencing the transactions. It rejected the argument that Worthen was acquiring an equity in the building through its rental payments. It found that the rents were unchallenged and were reasonable throughout the period of the lease, and that the option prices, negotiated at arm's length between the parties, represented fair estimates of market value on the applicable dates. It rejected any negative inference from the fact that the rentals, combined with the options, were sufficient to amortize the New York

Life loan and to pay Lyon a 6% return on its equity investment. It found that Worthen would acquire an equity in the building only if it exercised one of its options to purchase, and that it was highly unlikely, as a practical matter, that any purchase option would ever be exercised. It rejected any inference to be drawn from the fact that the lease was a "net lease." It found that Lyon had mixed motivations for entering into the transaction, including the need to diversify as well as the desire to have the benefits of a "tax shelter."

...

The United States Court of Appeals for the Eighth Circuit reversed.... It held that the Commissioner correctly determined that Lyon was not the true owner of the building and therefore was not entitled to the claimed deductions. It likened ownership for tax purposes to a "bundle of sticks" and undertook its own evaluation of the facts. It concluded, in agreement with the Government's contention, that Lyon "totes an empty bundle" of ownership sticks.... It stressed the following: (a) The lease agreements circumscribed Lyon's right to profit from its investment in the building by giving Worthen the option to purchase for an amount equal to Lyon's $500,000 equity plus 6% compound interest and the assumption of the unpaid balance of the New York Life mortgage. (Footnote 5) (b) The option prices did not take into account possible appreciation of the value of the building or inflation. (Footnote 6) (c) Any award realized as a result of destruction or condemnation of the building in excess of the mortgage balance and the $500,000 would be paid to Worthen and not Lyon. (Footnote 7) (d) The building rental payments during the primary term were exactly equal to the mortgage payments. (Footnote 8) (e) Worthen retained control over the ultimate disposition of the building through its various options to repurchase and to renew the lease plus its ownership of the site. (Footnote 9) (f) Worthen enjoyed all benefits and bore all burdens incident to the operation and ownership of the building so that, in the Court of Appeals' view, the only economic advantages accruing to Lyon, in the event it were considered to be the true owner of the property, were income tax savings of approximately $1.5 million during the first 11 years of the arrangement. (Footnote 10) ... The court concluded ..."In sum, the benefits, risks, and burdens which [Lyon] has incurred with respect to the Worthen building are simply too insubstantial to establish a claim to the status of owner for tax purposes.... The vice of the present lease is that all of [its] features have been employed in the same transaction with the cumulative effect of depriving [Lyon] of any significant ownership interest." ...

We granted certiorari....

II

This Court, almost 50 years ago, observed that "taxation is not so much concerned with the refinements of title as it is with actual command over the property taxed—the actual benefit for which the tax is paid." *Corliss v. Bowers*, 281 U.S. 376, ... (1930). In a number of cases, the Court has refused to permit the transfer of formal legal title to shift the incidence of taxation attributable to ownership of property where the transferor continues to retain significant control over the property transferred. *E.g.*, ... *Helvering v. Clifford*, 309 U.S. 331. In applying this doctrine of substance over form, the Court has looked to the objective economic realities of a transaction rather than to the particular form the parties employed. The Court has never regarded "the simple expedient of drawing up papers," ... as controlling for tax purposes when the objective economic realities are to the contrary. "In the field of taxation, administrators of the laws, and the courts, are concerned with substance and realities, and formal written documents are not rigidly binding." ... Nor is the parties' desire to achieve a particular tax result necessarily relevant. *Commissioner v. Duberstein*, 363 U.S. 278, 286 (1960).

In the light of these general and established principles, the Government takes the position that the Worthen-Lyon transaction in its entirety should be regarded as a sham. The agreement as a whole, it is said, was only an elaborate financing scheme designed to provide economic benefits to Worthen and a guaranteed return to Lyon. The latter was but a conduit used to forward the mortgage payments, made under the guise of rent paid by Worthen to Lyon, on to New York Life as mortgagee. This, the Government claims, is the true substance of the transaction as viewed under the microscope of the tax laws. Although the arrangement was cast in sale-and-leaseback form, in substance it was only a financing transaction, and the terms of the repurchase options and lease renewals so indicate. It is said that Worthen could reacquire the building simply by satisfying the mortgage debt and paying Lyon its $500,000 advance plus interest, regardless of the fair market value of the building at the time; similarly, when the mortgage was paid off, Worthen could extend the lease at drastically reduced bargain rentals that likewise bore no relation to fair rental value but were simply calculated to pay Lyon its $500,000 plus interest over the extended term. Lyon's return on the arrangement in no event could exceed 6% compound interest (although the Government conceded it might well be less, ...). Furthermore, the favorable option and lease renewal terms made it highly unlikely that Worthen would abandon the building after it in effect had "paid off" the mortgage. The Government implies that the arrangement was one of convenience which, if accepted on its face, would enable Worthen to deduct its payments to Lyon as rent and would allow Lyon to claim a deduction for depreciation, based on the cost of construction ultimately borne by Worthen, which Lyon could offset against other income, and to deduct mortgage interest that roughly would offset the inclusion of Worthen's rental payments in Lyon's income. If, however, the Government argues, the arrangement was only a financing transaction under which Worthen was the owner of the building, Worthen's payments would be deductible only to the extent that they represented mortgage interest, and Worthen would be entitled to claim depreciation; Lyon would not be entitled to deductions for either mortgage interest or depreciation and it would not have to include Worthen's "rent" payments in its income because its function with respect to those payments was that of a conduit between Worthen and New York Life.

...

III

It is true, of course, that the transaction took shape according to Worthen's needs. As the Government points out, Worthen throughout the negotiations regarded the respective proposals of the independent investors in terms of its own cost of funds.... It is also true that both Worthen and the prospective investors compared the various proposals in terms of the return anticipated on the investor's equity. But all this is natural for parties contemplating entering into a transaction of this kind. Worthen needed a building for its banking operations and other purposes and necessarily had to know what its cost would be. The investors were in business to employ their funds in the most remunerative way possible. And, as the Court has said in the past, a transaction must be given its effect in accord with what actually occurred and not in accord with what might have occurred....

There is no simple device available to peel away the form of this transaction and to reveal its substance. The effects of the transaction on all the parties were obviously different from those that would have resulted had Worthen been able simply to make a mortgage agreement with New York Life and to receive a $500,000 loan from Lyon.... Here, however, and most significantly, it was Lyon alone, and not Worthen, who was liable on the notes, first to City Bank, and then to New York Life. Despite the facts that Worthen had agreed to pay rent and that this rent equaled the amounts due from Lyon to New York Life, should anything go awry in the later years of the lease, Lyon was primarily liable. (Footnote 12) No matter how the transaction could have been devised otherwise, it remains a fact that as the agreements were placed in final form, the obligation on the notes fell squarely on Lyon. (Footnote 13) Lyon, an ongoing enterprise, exposed its very business well-being to this real and substantial risk.

The effect of this liability on Lyon is not just the abstract possibility that something will go wrong and that Worthen will not be able to make its payments. Lyon has disclosed this liability on its balance sheet for all the world to see. Its financial position was affected substantially by the presence of this long-term debt, despite the offsetting presence of the building as an asset. To the extent that Lyon has used its capital in this transaction, it is less able to obtain financing for other business needs.

In concluding that there is this distinct element of economic reality in Lyon's assumption of liability, we are mindful that the characterization of a transaction for financial accounting purposes, on the one hand, and for tax purposes, on the other, need not necessarily be the same.... Accounting methods or descriptions, without more, do not lend substance to that which has no substance. But in this case accepted accounting methods, as understood by the several parties to the respective agreements and as applied to the transaction by others, gave the transaction a meaningful character consonant with the form it was given. Worthen was not allowed to enter into the type of transaction which the Government now urges to be the true substance of the arrangement. Lyon and Worthen cannot be said to have entered into the transaction intending that the interests involved were allocated in a way other than that associated with a sale-and-leaseback.

Other factors also reveal that the transaction cannot be viewed as anything more than a mortgage agreement between Worthen and New York Life and a loan from Lyon to Worthen. There is no legal obligation between Lyon and Worthen representing the $500,000 "loan" extended under the Government's theory. And the assumed 6% return on this putative loan—required by the audit to be recognized in the taxable year in question—will be realized only when and if Worthen exercises its options.

The Court of Appeals acknowledged that the rents alone, due after the primary term of the lease and after the mortgage has been paid, do not provide the simple 6% return which, the Government urges, Lyon is guaranteed.... Thus, if Worthen chooses not to exercise its options, Lyon is gambling that the rental value of the building during the last 10 years of the ground lease, during which the ground rent is minimal, will be sufficient to recoup its investment before it must negotiate again with Worthen regarding the ground lease. There are simply too many contingencies, including variations in the value of real estate, in the cost of money, and in the capital structure of Worthen, to permit the conclusion that the parties intended to enter into the transaction as structured in the audit and according to which the Government now urges they be taxed.

It is not inappropriate to note that the Government is likely to lose little revenue, if any, as a result of the shape given the transaction by the parties. No deduction was created that is not either matched by an item of income or that would not have been available to one of the parties if the transaction had been arranged differently. While it is true that Worthen paid Lyon less to induce it to enter into the transaction because Lyon anticipated the benefit of the depreciation deductions it would have as the owner of the building, those deductions would have been equally available to Worthen had it retained title to the building. The Government so concedes.... The fact that favorable tax consequences were taken into account by Lyon on entering into the transaction is no reason for disallowing those consequences. (Footnote 15) We cannot ignore the reality that the tax laws affect the shape of nearly every business transaction.... Lyon is not a corporation with no purpose other than to hold title to the bank building. It was not created by Worthen or even financed to any degree by Worthen.

The conclusion that the transaction is not a simple sham to be ignored does not, of course, automatically compel the further conclusion that Lyon is entitled to the items claimed as deductions. Nevertheless, on the facts, this readily follows. As has been noted, the obligations on which Lyon paid interest were its obligations alone, and it is entitled to claim deductions therefor under § 163(a)....

As is clear from the facts, none of the parties to this sale-and-leaseback was the owner of the building in any simple sense. But it is equally clear that the facts focus upon Lyon as the one whose capital was committed to the building and as the party, therefore, that was entitled to claim depreciation for the consumption of that capital. The Government has based its contention that Worthen should be treated as the owner on the assumption that throughout the term of the lease Worthen was acquiring an equity in the property. In order to establish the presence of that growing equity, however, the Government is forced to speculate that one of the options will be exercised and that, if it is not, this is only because the rentals for the extended term are a bargain. We cannot indulge in such speculation in view of the District Court's clear finding to the contrary. (Footnote 16) We therefore conclude that it is Lyon's capital that is invested in the building according to the agreement of the parties, and it is Lyon that is entitled to depreciation deductions, under § 167....

IV

We recognize that the Government's position, and that taken by the Court of Appeals, is not without superficial appeal. One, indeed, may theorize that Frank Lyon's presence on the Worthen board of directors; Lyon's departure from its principal corporate activity into this unusual venture; the parallel between the payments under the building lease and the amounts due from Lyon on the New York Life mortgage; the provisions relating to condemnation or destruction of the property; the nature and presence of the several options available to Worthen; and the tax benefits, such as the use of double declining balance depreciation, that accrue to Lyon during the initial years of the arrangement, form the basis of an argument that Worthen should be regarded as the owner of the building and as the recipient of nothing more from Lyon than a $500,000 loan.

We, however, as did the District Court, find this theorizing incompatible with the substance and economic realities of the transaction: the competitive situation as it existed between Worthen and Union National Bank in 1965 and the years immediately following; Worthen's undercapitalization; Worthen's consequent inability, as a matter of legal restraint, to carry its building plans into effect by a conventional mortgage and other borrowing; the additional barriers imposed by the state and federal regulators; the suggestion, forthcoming from the state regulator, that Worthen possess an option to purchase; the requirement, from the federal regulator, that the building be owned by an independent third party; the presence of several finance organizations seriously interested in participating in the transaction and in the resolution of Worthen's problem; the submission of formal proposals by several of those organizations; the bargaining process and period that ensued; the competitiveness of the bidding; the bona fide character of the negotiations; the three-party aspect of the transaction; Lyon's substantiality (Footnote 17) and its independence from Worthen; the fact that diversification was Lyon's principal motivation; Lyon's being liable alone on the successive notes to City Bank and New York Life; the reasonableness, as the District Court found, of the rentals and of the option prices; the substantiality of the purchase prices; Lyon's not being engaged generally in the business of financing; the presence of all building depreciation risks on Lyon; the risk, borne by Lyon, that Worthen might default or fail, as other banks have failed; the facts that Worthen could "walk away" from the relationship at the end of the 25-year primary term, and probably would do so if the option price were more than the then-current worth of the building to Worthen; the inescapable fact that if the building lease were not extended, Lyon would be the full owner of the building, free to do with it as it chose; Lyon's liability for the substantial ground rent if Worthen decides not to exercise any of its options to extend; the absence of any understanding between Lyon and Worthen that Worthen would exercise any of the purchase options; the nonfamily and nonprivate nature of the entire transaction; and the absence of any differential in tax rates and of special tax circumstances for one of the parties—all convince us that Lyon has far the better of the case. (Footnote 18)

In so concluding, we emphasize that we are not condoning manipulation by a taxpayer through arbitrary labels and dealings that have no economic significance. Such, however, has not happened in this case.

In short, we hold that where, as here, there is a genuine multiple-party transaction with economic substance which is compelled or encouraged by business or regulatory realities, is imbued with tax-independent considerations, and is not shaped solely by tax-avoidance features that have meaningless labels attached, the Government should honor the allocation of rights and duties effectuated by the parties. Expressed another way, so long as the lessor retains significant and genuine attributes of the traditional lessor status, the form of the transaction adopted by the parties governs for tax purposes. What those attributes are in any particular case will necessarily depend upon its facts. It suffices to say that, as here, a sale-and-leaseback, in and of itself, does not necessarily operate to deny a taxpayer's claim for deductions.

The judgment of the Court of Appeals, accordingly, is reversed.

FOOTNOTES:

1. Worthen, as of June 30, 1967, had capital stock of $4 million and surplus of $5 million....

2. This arrangement appeared advisable and was made because purchases of materials by Worthen (which then had become a national bank) were not subject to Arkansas sales tax....

3. The Government amounts payable would point out, however,

that the net amounts payable by Worthen to Lyon during the building lease's extended terms, if all are claimed, would approximate the amount required to repay Lyon's $500,000 investment at 6% compound interest....

5. Lyon here challenges this assertion on the grounds that it had the right and opportunities to sell the building at a greater profit at any time; the return to Lyon was not insubstantial and was attractive to a true investor in real estate; the 6% return was the

minimum Lyon would realize if Worthen exercised one of its options, an event the District Court found highly unlikely; and Lyon would own the building and realize a greater return than 6% if Worthen did not exercise an option to purchase.

6. Lyon challenges this observation by pointing out that the District Court found the option prices to be the negotiated estimate of the parties of the fair market value of the building on the option dates and to be reasonable....

7. Lyon asserts that this statement is true only with respect to the total destruction or taking of the building on or after December 1, 1980. Lyon asserts that it, not Worthen, would receive the excess above the mortgage balance in the event of total destruction or taking before December 1, 1980, or in the event of partial damage or taking at any time....

8. Lyon concedes the accuracy of this statement, but asserts that it does not justify the conclusion that Lyon served merely as a conduit by which mortgage payments would be transmitted to New York Life. It asserts that Lyon was the sole obligor on the New York Life note and would remain liable in the event of default by Worthen. It also asserts that the fact the rent was sufficient to amortize the loan during the primary term of the lease was a requirement imposed by New York Life, and is a usual requirement in most long-term loans secured by a long-term lease.

9. As to this statement, Lyon asserts that the Court of Appeals ignored Lyon's right to sell the building to another at any time; the District Court's finding that the options to purchase were not likely to be exercised; the uncertainty that Worthen would renew the lease for 40 years; Lyon's right to lease to anyone at any price during the last 10 years of the ground lease; and Lyon's continuing ownership of the building after the expiration of the ground lease.

10. In response to this, Lyon asserts that the District Court found that the benefits of occupancy Worthen will enjoy are common in most long-term real estate leases, and that the District Court found that Lyon had motives other than tax savings in entering into the transaction. It also asserts that the net cash after-tax benefit would be $312,220, not $1.5 million.

12. New York Life required Lyon, not Worthen, to submit financial statements periodically....

13. It may well be that the remedies available to New York Life against Lyon would be far greater than any remedy available to it against Worthen, which, as lessee, is liable to New York Life only through Lyon's assignment of its interest as lessor.

15. Indeed, it is not inevitable that the transaction, as treated by Lyon and Worthen, will not result in more revenues to the Government rather than less. Lyon is gambling that in the first 11 years of the lease it will have income that will be sheltered by the depreciation deductions, and that it will be able to make sufficiently good use of the tax dollars preserved thereby to make up for the income it will recognize and pay taxes on during the last 14 years of the initial term of the lease and against which it will enjoy no sheltering deduction.

16. The general characterization of a transaction for tax purposes is a question of law subject to review. The particular facts from which the characterization is to be made are not so subject....

17. Lyon's consolidated balance sheet on December 31, 1968, showed assets of $12,225,612, and total stockholders' equity of $3,818,671[.] Of the assets, the sum of $2,674,290 represented its then investment in the Worthen building....

18. Thus, the facts of this case stand in contrast to many others in which the form of the transaction actually created tax advantages that, for one reason or another, could not have been enjoyed had the transaction taken another form. See, *e.g., Sun Oil Co. v. Commissioner*, 562 F.2d 258 (CA3 1977) (sale-and-leaseback of land between taxpayer and tax-exempt trust enabled the taxpayer to amortize, through its rental deductions, the cost of acquiring land not otherwise depreciable)....

   MR. JUSTICE STEVENS, dissenting.

   ...

Petitioner has assumed only two significant risks. First, like any other lender, it assumed the risk of Worthen's insolvency. Second, it assumed the risk that Worthen might *not* exercise its option to purchase at or before the end of the original 25-year term. If Worthen should exercise that right *not* to repay, perhaps it would *then* be appropriate to characterize petitioner as the owner and Worthen as the lessee. But speculation as to what might happen in 25 years cannot justify the *present* characterization of petitioner as the owner of the building. Until Worthen has made a commitment either to exercise or not to exercise its option, I think the Government is correct in its view that petitioner is not the owner of the building for tax purposes. At present, since Worthen has the unrestricted right to control the residual value of the property for a price which does not exceed the cost of its unamortized financing, I would hold, as a matter of law, that it is the owner.

I therefore respectfully dissent.

——————————

Now consider the following questions.

1. The purported lease between Frank Lyon and Worthen was described as a "net lease." What is a "net lease"? (Recall Tracy's balance sheet when he created T Corp. in Part II, Chapter 1 following *Eisner v. Macomber*.)

Note that Frank Lyon and Worthen treated the land underlying the building and the building itself as two separate assets. The first of these, the land itself, initially belonged to Worthen. Worthen then leased the land by entering into a "ground lease," for a term of 76 years and 7 months, to Frank Lyon. In what case did you first encounter a ground lease? **Recall *Bruun*.**

Also note that Frank Lyon borrowed money in order to do the construction. What kind of loan was this called? What is the advantage to the lender of making this type of loan? As Worthen completed the various stages of the building, what did it do?

2. The issue in *Oesterreich* was whether the transaction constituted a sale or a lease by Walburga Oesterreich to Wilshire Amusement Corp. What was the issue in *Frank Lyon*?

3. What tax difference did the Court's view of the transaction make to Frank Lyon? What tax difference to the bank?

4. Why did the parties structure the transaction in *Frank Lyon* in the way they did? What was the benefit to each?

5. Can you identify one or more factors that might have convinced the Supreme Court not to respect the form of this transaction?

6. Can you identify one or more factors that convinced the Supreme Court to respect the form of this transaction?

——————————

It is not always easy to draw the line between a lease and a sale, or a sale and an option to purchase, to name only two of the types of cases that often lead to litigation. One reason for the plethora of litigation regarding these transactions is the heightened sensitivity of the tax authorities to identify cases in which taxpayers' self-interested attempts to minimize their taxes which leads them to attempt to put form over substance. (But, of course, not all cases that end in the courts are solely tax motivated. Even unwitting taxpayers can unhappily fall into a substance versus form controversy!)

Since the mid-1970's, more and more taxpayers have been involved in what the Service regards as tax-motivated transactions, that is, transactions that have no purpose other than to garner for the taxpayers who engage in them significant tax benefits. Many of these transactions are structured to meet the literal terms of the statute, but many lack a business purpose or economic substance. In 1999, the Joint Committee on Taxation reported on the judicial doctrines that have developed over the years to thwart attempts—like those of the Boyters—to exalt form over substance. As you read the Joint Committee's report below, recall our earlier discussion, in Chapter 1 of this Part, of the textualist method of statutory interpretation. Is textualism consistent with the judicial doctrines discussed below?

Description and Analysis of Present-Law Tax Rules and Recent Proposals Relating to Corporate Tax Shelters[6]

...

2. JUDICIAL DOCTRINES APPLICABLE TO TAX SHELTERS

a. OVERVIEW

... [O]ver the years the courts have developed several doctrines to deny certain tax-advantaged transactions their intended tax benefits. These doctrines are not entirely distinguishable, and their application to a given set of facts is often blurred by the courts and the IRS. There is considerable overlap among the doctrines, and typically more than one doctrine is likely to apply to a transaction. Because of these ambiguities, invocation of these doctrines can be seen as at odds with an objective, "rule-based" system of taxation. Nonetheless, the doctrines provide a useful tool under present law to police, at a minimum, the most egregious tax shelter abuses.

The Supreme Court has made it clear that "[t]he legal right of a taxpayer to decrease the amount of what otherwise would be his taxes, or altogether avoid them, by means which the law permits, cannot be doubted." (Footnote 17) When a taxpayer, however, "crosses the line" such that what was done, apart from tax motive, was not the thing which the statute intended, the tax advantage should be denied. (Footnote 18) The general doctrines used to deny such tax benefits are (1) the sham transaction doctrine, (2) the economic substance doctrine, (3) the business purpose doctrine, (4) the substance over form doctrine, and (5) the step transaction doctrine. (Footnote 19)

---

6. Joint Committee on Taxation, Description and Analysis of Present—law Tax Rules and Recent Proposals Relating to Corporate Tax Shelters (JCX-84-99), November 10, 1999.

b. SHAM TRANSACTION DOCTRINE

Sham transactions are those in which the economic activity that is purported to give rise to the desired tax benefits does not actually occur. The transactions have been referred to as "facades" or mere "fictions" (Footnote 20) and, in their most egregious form, one may question whether the transactions might be characterized as fraudulent.

At a minimum, the sham transaction doctrine can be said to apply to a "sham in fact." For example, where a taxpayer purported to buy Treasury notes for a small down payment and a financing secured by the Treasury notes in order to generate favorable tax benefits, but neither the purchase nor the loan actually occurred, the court applied the sham transaction doctrine to deny the tax benefits. (Footnote 21)

...

Although the sham transaction doctrine generally applies when the purported activity giving rise to the tax benefits does not actually occur, in certain circumstances, a transaction may be found to constitute a sham even when the purported activity does occur. For example, if a transaction is entered into to generate loss for the taxpayer, and the taxpayer actually has risk with respect to the transaction, but that risk has been eliminated through a guarantee by a broker that the broker will bear the market risk and that the only consequences to the taxpayer will be the desired tax benefits, such transaction may be found to be "in substance" a sham. (Footnote 22)

Finally, as discussed above, the delineation between this doctrine (particularly as applied to shams "in substance") and the "economic substance" and the "business purpose" doctrines (both discussed below) is not always clear. Some courts find that if transactions lack economic substance and business purpose, they are "shams" notwithstanding that the purported activity did actually occur. (Footnote 23)

c. ECONOMIC SUBSTANCE DOCTRINE

(i) IN GENERAL

The courts generally will deny claimed tax benefits where the transaction giving rise to those benefits lacks economic substance independent of tax considerations—notwithstanding that the purported activity did actually occur. The Tax Court recently described the doctrine as follows:

> The tax law ... requires that the intended transactions have economic substance separate and distinct from economic benefit achieved solely by tax reduction. The doctrine of economic substance becomes applicable, and a judicial remedy is warranted, where a taxpayer seeks to claim tax benefits, unintended by Congress, by means of transactions that serve no economic purpose other than tax savings. (Footnote 24)

The seminal authority most often credited for laying the foundation of the economic substance doctrine is the Supreme Court and Second Circuit decisions in *Gregory v. Helvering*. (Footnote 25) In *Gregory*, a transitory subsidiary was established to effectuate, utilizing the corporate reorganization provisions of the Code, a tax advantaged distribution from a corporation to its shareholder of appreciated corporate securities that the corporation (and its shareholder) intended to sell. Although the court found that the transaction satisfied the literal definition of a tax-free reorganization, the Second Circuit held (and the Supreme Court affirmed) that satisfying the literal definition was not enough:

> [T]he underlying presupposition is plain that the readjustment shall be undertaken for reasons germane to the conduct of the

venture in hand, not as an ephemeral incident, egregious to its prosecution. To dodge the shareholder's taxes is not one of the transactions contemplated as corporate "reorganizations." (Footnote 26)

Since the time of *Gregory*, several cases have denied tax benefits on the grounds that the subject transactions lacked economic substance. (Footnote 27) The economic substance doctrine can apply even when a taxpayer exposes itself to risk of loss and where there is some profit potential (i.e., where the transactions are real) if the facts suggest that the economic risks and profit potential were insignificant when compared to the tax benefits. (Footnote 28) In other words, the doctrine suggests a balancing of the risks and profit potential as compared to the tax benefits in order to determine whether the transactions had "purpose, substance or utility apart from their anticipated tax consequences." (Footnote 29)

...

(iii) SPECIAL APPLICATION: LEASING TRANSACTIONS

A line of authorities has developed addressing economic substance (and, as discussed below, business purpose) specifically in connection with leasing transactions. The focus with respect to leasing transactions (particularly leveraged leases and sale-leaseback transactions) is who should be entitled to the benefits of tax ownership such as depreciation deductions.

The determination of tax ownership sometimes overlaps with the determinations of whether the transactions have economic substance and business purpose. The Supreme Court articulated the standard as follows: "where ... there is a genuine multiple-party transaction with economic substance which is compelled or encouraged by business or regulatory realities, is imbued with tax-independent considerations, and is not shaped solely by meaningless labels attached, the Government should honor the allocation of rights and duties effectuated by the parties." (Footnote 58) The Fourth Circuit has interpreted *Frank Lyon* to require a two-prong analysis with respect to sale-leaseback transactions: namely, the court "must find that the taxpayer was motivated by no business purpose other than obtaining tax benefits in entering the transaction, and that the transaction has no economic substance because no reasonable possibility of profit exists." (Footnote 59) In analyzing the economic substance of a leasing transaction, the Tax Court found that economic substance was not supported where the discounted present value of the future rental income and sale proceeds would be less than the present value of the amount expended by the investors. (Footnote 60)

In addition to its application by the courts, economic substance is a component of the guidelines that were adopted in 1975 by the IRS for advance ruling purposes with respect to determining whether certain transactions purporting to be leases of property are, in fact, leases for Federal income tax purposes. (Footnote 61) The guidelines require that the lessor represent and demonstrate that it expects to receive a profit, apart from the value of or benefits obtained from tax deductions, allowances, credits, and other tax attributes arising from such transaction.

d. BUSINESS PURPOSE DOCTRINE

Another doctrine that overlays and is often considered together with (if not part and parcel of) the sham transaction and economic substance doctrines is the business purpose doctrine.... [T]he doctrine is not limited to cases where the relevant statutory provisions by their terms require a business purpose or profit potential. (Footnote 62)

In its common application, the courts use business purpose (in combination with economic substance, as discussed above) as part of a two-prong test for determining whether a transaction should be disregarded for tax purposes: (1) the taxpayer was motivated by no business purpose other than obtaining tax benefits in entering the transaction, and (2) the transaction lacks economic substance. (Footnote 63) In essence, a transaction will only be respected for tax purposes if it has "economic substance which is compelled or encouraged by business or regulatory realities, is imbued with tax-independent considerations, and is not shaped solely by tax-avoidance features that have meaningless labels attached." (Footnote 64)

The business purpose test is a subjective inquiry into the motives of the taxpayer—that is, whether the taxpayer intended the transaction to serve some useful nontax purpose.... (Footnote 65)

e. SUBSTANCE OVER FORM DOCTRINE

The concept of the substance over form doctrine is that the tax results of an arrangement are better determined based on the underlying substance rather than an evaluation of the mere formal steps by which the arrangement was undertaken. For instance, two transactions that achieve the same underlying result should not be taxed differently simply because they are achieved through different legal steps. The Supreme Court has found that a "given result at the end of a straight path is not made a different result because reached by following a devious path." (Footnote 67) However, many areas of income tax law are very formalistic and, therefore, it is often difficult for taxpayers and the courts to determine whether application of the doctrine is appropriate.

While tax cases have been decided both ways, the IRS generally has the ability to recharacterize a transaction according to its underlying substance. Taxpayers, however, are usually bound to abide by their chosen legal form. (Footnote 68) In *National Alfalfa Dehydrating & Mill & Co.*, the Supreme Court ruled as follows:

> This Court has observed repeatedly that, while a taxpayer is free to organize his affairs as he chooses, nevertheless, once having done so, he must accept the tax consequences of his choice, whether contemplated or not, [citations omitted], and may not enjoy the benefit of some other route he might have chosen to follow but did not. (Footnote 69)

...

f. STEP TRANSACTION DOCTRINE

An extension of the substance over form doctrine is the step transaction doctrine. The step transaction doctrine "treats a series of formally separate 'steps' as a single transaction if such steps are in substance integrated, interdependent, and focused toward a particular result." (Footnote 71) The courts have generally developed three methods of testing whether to invoke the step transaction doctrine: (1) the end result test, (2) the interdependence test, and (3) the binding commitment test.

The end result test is the broadest of the three articulations. The end result test examines whether it is apparent that each of a series of steps are undertaken for the purpose of achieving the ultimate result. (Footnote 72) The interdependence test attempts to prove that each of the steps were so interdependent that the completion of an individual step would have been meaningless without the completion of the remaining steps. The binding commitment test is the narrowest of the three articulations and looks to whether, at the time the first step is entered into, there is a legally binding commitment to complete the remaining steps. (Footnote 73)

In determining whether to invoke the step transaction doctrine, the courts have looked to two primary factors: (1) the intent of the taxpayer, (Footnote 74) and (2) the temporal proximity of the separate steps. If a taxpayer can provide evidence that at the time the first of a series of steps was undertaken, there was no plan or intention to effect the other steps, then the transactions should not be stepped together. An important factor that supports a taxpayer's lack of intent is found where subsequent steps are prompted by external, unexpected events that are beyond the taxpayer's control. Where there is no legally binding commitment to engage in subsequent steps after undertaking the initial transaction, the span of time between the events is an important measure in determining whether the transactions should be stepped together. A significant lapse of time between a series of transactions should prevent the application of the step transaction doctrine. (Footnote 75)

FOOTNOTES:

This document may be cited as follows: Joint Committee on Taxation, Description and Analysis of Present-law Tax Rules and Recent Proposals Relating to Corporate Tax Shelters (JCX-84-99), November 10, 1999.

17. *Gregory v. Helvering, 293 U.S. 465, 469 (1935),* aff'g *69 F.2d 809 (2d Cir. 1934).* In the lower court opinion with respect to this case, Judge Learned Hand stated this concept another way: "Anyone may so arrange his affairs that his taxes shall be as low as possible; he is not bound to choose that pattern which will best pay the Treasury; there is not even a patriotic duty to increase one's taxes." *69 F.2d at 810.*

18. *Gregory, 293 U.S. at 469.*

19. The *Gregory* case is often cited as the seminal case with respect to several of these doctrines, especially the sham transaction, economic substance, and business purpose doctrines. For a general discussion of these doctrines, see Alvin C. Warren, Jr., The Requirement of Economic Profit in Tax Motivated Transactions, 59 Taxes 985 (1981), and David P. Hariton, Sorting Out the Tangle of Economic Substance, 52 Tax Law. 235 (1999).

20. See, e.g., *Knetsch v. United States, 364 U.S. 361 (1960)* (disallowing deduction for prepaid interest on a nonrecourse, riskless loan used to purchase deferred-annuity savings bonds).

21. See *Goodstein v. Commissioner, 267 F.2d 127, 131* (1(st) Cir. 1959)....

22. See, e.g., *Yosha v. Commissioner, 861 F.2d 494* (7(th) Cir. 1988) (holding options straddles to be shams because the broker insured the clients against market risk).

23. See *United States v. Wexler, 31 F.3d 117, 124 (3d Cir. 1994).* In Wexler, the promoter of a tax shelter was brought up on criminal fraud charges. In the jury instructions, the court blurred the distinction between sham transactions and transactions having no business purpose or lacking economic substance.

24. *ACM, 73 T.C.M. at 2215.*

25. *293 U.S. 465 (1935),* aff'g *69 F.2d 809 (2d Cir. 1934).*

26. *Gregory, 69 F.2d at 811.*

27. See, e.g., *Knetsch v. United States, 364 U.S. 361 (1960); Goldstein v. Commissioner, 364 F.2d 734 (2d Cir. 1966)* (holding that an unprofitable, leveraged acquisition of T-bills, and accompanying prepaid interest deduction, lacks economic substance).... *Sheldon v. Commissioner, 94 T.C. 738 (1990)* (holding that a marginally profitable, leveraged acquisition of T-bills, and accompanying prepaid interest deduction, lacks economic substance, and imposing penalties); *Ginsburg v. Commissioner, 35 T.C.M. (CCH) 860 (1976)* (holding that a leveraged cattle-breeding program lacks economic substance).

28. See *Goldstein v. Commissioner, 364 F.2d 734, 739–40 (2d Cir. 1966)* (disallowing deduction even though taxpayer has a possibility of small gain or loss by owning T-bills)....

29. *Goldstein, 364 F.2d at 740.* Even this articulation of the economic substance doctrine will fall short in its application to some sets of facts. For example, taxpayers motivated solely by tax considerations have been permitted by the courts to time their recognition of accrued economic losses, notwithstanding that the IRS attacked such tax-motivated transactions as lacking economic substance. See, e.g., *Cottage Savings v. Commissioner, 499 U.S. 554 (1991)* (allowing losses, pursuant to *section 1001(a)*, on exchanges of substantially identical mortgages);....

30. *Frank Lyon Co. v. Commissioner, 435 U.S. 561, 583–84 (1978).*

59. *Rice's Toyota World v. Commissioner, 752 F.2d 89, 91–92 (4(th) Cir. 1985).*

60. *Hilton v. Commissioner, 74 T.C. 305, 353 n.23 (1980),* aff'd *671 F.2d 316, 317 (9(th) Cir. 1982).* The Tax Court arrived at the present value using a six-percent discount rate found in the estate tax regulations for purposes of making actuarial valuations. Although affirmed on appeal, the Ninth Circuit observed that the six-percent rate was illustrative only and that no suggestion of a minimum required rate of return is intended. See also *Estate of Franklin v. Commissioner, 544 F.2d 1045 (9(th) Cir. 1976).* In Estate of Franklin, property was overvalued when acquired by the lessor, and the lessor had no reasonable expectation of a residual value, so the court held that the lessor had no depreciable investment in the property and the nonrecourse debt was not true debt.

61. *Rev. Proc. 75-21, 1975-1 C.B. 715.*

62. ... *Goldstein, 364 F.2d at 736; Wexler, 31 F.3d at 122.*

63. *Rice's Toyota World, 752 F.2d at 91.*

64. *Frank Lyon Co., 435 U.S. at 561....*

65. See e.g., *Rice's Toyota World, 752 F.2d at 89....*

66. *Minnesota Tea Co. v. Helvering, 302 U.S. 609, 613 (1938).*

68. *Commissioner v. Danielson, 378 F.2d 771 (3d Cir. 1967),* cert. denied, *389 U.S. 858 (1967);* In the matter of: *Insilco Corporation v. United States, 53 F.3d 95 (5(th) Cir. 1995).*

69. *Commissioner v. National Alfalfa Dehydrating & Mill Co., 417 U.S. 134, 149 (1974)....*

71. *Penrod v. Commissioner, 88 T.C. 1415, 1428 (1987).*

72. *King Enterprises, Inc. v. United States, 418 F.2d 511, 516 (Ct. Cl. 1969).*

73. *Commissioner v. Gordon, 391 U.S. 83, 96 (1968).*

74. *McDonalds Restaurants of Ill. v. Commissioner, 688 F.2d 520 (7(th) Cir. 1982).*

75. *Cal-Maine Foods, Inc. v. Commissioner, 93 T.C. 181 (1989)* (by implication); Martin D. Ginsburg et al., Mergers, Acquisitions, and Buyouts, para. 608.2.2 (Apr. 1999 edition).

As you review the materials in this Part III, you may notice that, in fact, many of the cases we considered in Chapter 1 under the heading of "assignment of income" could, as easily have been included in Chapter 2, as "substance versus form" cases.[7] You also

---

7. Later, in Part VI, you will also see some of the cases the Joint Committee cites in its report when we take up the tax consequences of debt. (For those of you who continue on in your study of tax, the concepts of substance versus form, business purpose, economic substance, and the step transaction doctrine are very important in the context of business transactions.)

have seen, as the Joint Committee report states, that courts frequently interchange the phrases "form versus substance," "sham," "business purpose," and "economic substance" when criticizing a transaction. What is common to all these cases is the continuing vigilance of the courts in asking, "who is the proper taxpayer?"

IV. What Is the "Proper" Time Period?

Introduction

Review the quotation from the Tariff Act of 1913 in the Introduction to this book. In that Act, Congress imposed a tax on the "entire net income accruing from all sources *in the preceding calendar year....*" As became clear in Part II, however, a number of issues require solution before a taxpayer can complete her calculation of her entire net income for the preceding year. It is not sufficient to identify a taxpayer's items of gross income and eligibility for deductions. In addition, it is necessary to identify the proper time period for reporting that income and those deductions.

Although we learned early on in the case of *Burnet v. Sanford & Brooks Company* that the general rule in taxation is to compute taxable income on an annual basis, not all transactions begin and end within a single tax period. For example, suppose a taxpayer undertakes to construct a house "on spec."[1] Work begins in October of one tax year but the house is not completed until March of the following year. Although the taxpayer clearly has expenses in the year the work commences, the sale does not occur and no income is received until the following tax year. Yet, the taxpayer is clearly receiving a portion of the income for the work done in each of the two years. How should the taxpayer report the income and expenses of constructing and selling the house?

Suppose that in order to construct the house, the contractor has to purchase a brick-cutting machine that he will use not only in constructing this house but in constructing additional houses as well. Part II, Chapter 3.B.5. introduced you to depreciation as a method of recovering the cost of a machine, like the brick-cutting machine. We did not, however, focus on the issue of the timing of the depreciation deductions in relation to the income the capital investment enabled the taxpayer to produce. When and how should he account for the expense of purchasing the machine? What about replacement blades? Is there a difference between how he should account for major capital expenses, like purchasing the machine, and repetitive everyday expenses, like replacement blades?

Suppose the contractor decides after four years to "trade-in" the brick-cutting machine and replace it with a newer model.

How should he account for the amount he receives on the trade-in and his new investment? Suppose the machine is destroyed in a fire. He does or does not receive insurance but, in any event, must replace the machine. How does he account for the casualty to the old one and its replacement with a new one? (Remember Jeremiah, the Civil War buff, to whom we introduced you in Part II, Chapter 3.A.1.b. when we discussed personal itemized deductions, in particular section 165(c)(3)?)

The initial issues in determining the proper time period require an examination of the most common methods of accounting and some of the issues the choice of account-

---

1. What does "on spec" mean?

ing method might create. Whatever a taxpayer's method, however, an examination of the proper time period also requires us to explore some of the issues regarding recovery of basis. From the outset, a principle of this course has been TOAD and the rule that income should not be taxed twice to the same taxpayer. It is not enough, therefore, to determine the proper time period for reporting income and loss. The calculation itself requires some special rules. Once the taxpayer has determined the income or loss and the proper year for realization, the taxpayer will, of course, want to know whether any special rule permits avoidance of section 1001(c)'s recognition requirement. As you learned in Part III, Chapter 1, the Code contains certain exceptions to section 1001(c) which affect the timing of the recognition of realized gain. We will explore more of these exceptions in this Part.

Chapter 1

Methods of Accounting

Introduction

The short introduction at Part II, Chapter 3, footnote 2, introduced you to the two most common methods of accounting, the cash and accrual methods. We noted there that the cash basis method of accounting is the most common among individual taxpayers. Under this method, taxpayers include items of income in the year in which they receive them and deduct items of expense in the year in which they pay them. It was also noted there that for many business taxpayers, the cash method is both inaccurate and more difficult to administer.[1] The accrual method of accounting requires the taxpayer to treat an item of revenue as income for tax purposes once the right to receive it is fixed and to treat a liability as an expense for tax purposes only once it has become fixed. In the view of many commentators, the accrual method more accurately matches income and expenses and is, therefore, a more appropriate choice for most businesses. But, the choice of the accrual method does not solve all the problems of distortion that can result in the real world of business. Section 446(a) of the Code authorizes a taxpayer to compute "taxable income under the method of accounting on the basis of which the taxpayer regularly computes his income in keeping his books."

Whatever the method, the goal of the taxpayer's accounting method must be to "clearly reflect [the] income" of the taxpayer.[2] For most businesses, this does, in fact, require use of the accrual method. But, use of the cash method by a business is neither forbidden nor unknown. Once chosen, the method will dictate the timing of most items of income and deduction. As will be noted in the materials below, however, there are a number of special rules that require a variation in the treatment of certain items from what would be the expected treatment under the otherwise applicable accounting method. We begin with an examination of some of the common issues that arise under the cash method. After then taking up some of the common issues that arise under the accrual method, we will examine a few of the special variations, some of which are mandatory, some of which are available at the election of the taxpayer.

---

1. Business taxpayers do not necessarily keep track of income and expenses based on receipt of payment from purchasers and payments to suppliers. Rather, they keep track based upon the records they keep for financial accounting purposes. Financial accounting is almost identical to the accrual method of accounting for tax purposes.

2. Section 446(b). If the taxpayer's method does not clearly reflect income, the Secretary may require use of a different method.

A. Cash Method

1. Items of Income

Recall that the questions preceding and following *Old Colony* arose when a lawyer prepared a will for a client. In the simple case, you, no doubt, had no difficulty concluding that the cash payment for the will constituted an accession to wealth. You probably also saw immediately that payment through delivery of a bond also constituted an accession to wealth. The materials went on to raise questions about payment by delivery of a check or an unsecured promissory note. You probably also had no trouble concluding that those too created an accession to the wealth of the lawyer. You may have wondered, however, about the timing of that accession to wealth. Is delivery of a check an immediate accession to wealth as is the delivery of cash? Is the delivery of an unsecured promissory note an immediate accession to wealth?

Review Treasury Regulation section 1.446-1(c)(1)(i). It provides that "under the cash receipts and disbursements method in the computation of taxable income, all items which constitute gross income (whether in the form of cash, property, or services) are to be included for the taxable year in which actually or constructively received." By reading the following case, consider first the question raised above concerning payment through delivery of a check.

BRIGHT v. UNITED STATES
926 F.2d 383 (5th Cir. 1991)

PER CURIAM:

Plaintiff-Appellant R. Neal Bright, the executor of the estate of Elizabeth R. Cornell, appeals the district court's grant of summary judgment and entry of judgment in favor of Defendant-Appellee, the United States. The district court held that for income tax purposes the check that Cornell's employee received on December 27, 1985, constituted the receipt of cash or a cash equivalent by Bright on that date. We affirm.

OPERABLE FACTS

In 1970 Ms. Cornell entered into a trust agreement whereby the Elizabeth R. Cornell Trust was created for her benefit. The trust is a "grantor trust" for federal income tax purposes. Consequently, Cornell was treated as the owner of the trust and all income, gain, expenses and losses were taxable to her. Both Cornell and the trust used a calendar year as their taxable year, and both used the cash basis method of accounting. (Footnote 3) In 1985 and 1986 Cornell and Gilbert R. Bright (remaining trustee) served as trustees.

The trust owned 188,848 shares of stock of the Southland Royalty Company. Southland had agreed to merge with Burlington Northern, Inc. and M-R Holdings, Inc. (Holdings), a Burlington subsidiary. Pursuant to the merger agreement, Holdings offered to purchase all outstanding Southland shares. In early December 1985, the remaining trustee accepted Holding's offer of $3,210,416.00 for the trust's Southland shares. Pursuant to the purchase offer, the remaining trustee had the trust's bank, Inter-First Bank Dallas, N.A., located in Dallas, Texas, send the stock certificates to First Fidelity Bank, N.A., New Jersey, located in Newark, New Jersey. The remaining trustee made no arrangements with Fidelity or Holdings regarding the date of payment for the shares.

On Friday, December 27, 1985, an employee of Cornell's received the Holdings check from Fidelity at her office in Fort Worth. (Footnote 4) Neither Holdings, as maker of the check, nor Fidelity, as payor bank, placed any restrictions on the check's negotiability. Having informed the remaining trustee on the 27th of December that the check had arrived, Cornell's employee endorsed and mailed the check to InterFirst for deposit in the trust's account. InterFirst posted the check to the trust's account on Monday, December 30, 1985. On the 30th of December, Cornell's employee placed an order with InterFirst, as the remaining trustee had instructed, to buy government securities with the funds from the Holdings check. InterFirst, however, informed the employee that it would restrict the availability of the funds to the trust until InterFirst had collected the funds from Fidelity. Because of this restriction, InterFirst did not execute the purchase order until January 3, 1986.

In April 1986, both the taxpayer and the trust filed federal income tax returns for the 1985 taxable year. On these returns both the taxpayer and the trust included $1,284,166.40 in net capital gain recognized on the sale of the Southland shares. In July 1986, claiming that the gain on the sale of the shares should properly be reported in 1986, the taxpayer filed an amended 1985 tax return in which she claimed a refund of $674,187.36, plus interest, for a purported overpayment of her 1985 federal income tax.

Cornell died in December 1986. In August 1987, R. Neal Bright, the executor, instituted suit to recover the disputed overpayment. Bright contended that because InterFirst restricted the use of the funds until January 1986, Cornell neither actually nor constructively received in 1985 the funds from the sale of the stocks. The government maintained that the Holdings check was a "cash equivalent" that Cornell had actually received in 1985 and, in the alternative, that as the check's negotiability had no substantial restrictions placed on it, the income was constructively received in 1985. In either case, the income was, the government argued, includable in 1985.

After stipulating to the facts, both parties moved for summary judgment. On May 8, 1990, the district court denied the executor's and granted the government's summary judgment motion. Citing *Kahler v. Commissioner*, 18 T.C. 31, 34 (1952) for the proposition that once a check is honored, the date of payment relates back to the date of delivery, the district court stated that "[t]he check received by the Decedent's employee on December 27, 1985, constituted the receipt of cash or a cash equivalent by decedent on that date." After the district court denied the executor's timely motion for a new trial or, alternatively, for reconsideration, the executor appealed.

DISCUSSION

In declaring receipt of the Holdings check to be receipt of a cash equivalent, the district court relied solely upon *Kahler*, 18 T.C. 31 (1952). In *Kahler*, the tax court held that a check for approximately $4,300.00 which the taxpayer received from his employer after 5 p.m. on December 31st and cashed on January 2nd was a cash equivalent upon receipt. *Id.*; *see also Lavery v. Commissioner*, 158 F.2d 859, 860 (7th Cir.1946) (because taxpayer could have cashed check for $2,666.67 on Tuesday December 30th or on next day, check was equivalent of cash in year received). Even if cashing the check in the year in which drawn "might be impossible," stated the tax court, the check was still income in the year in which drawn if actual delivery occurred in that year. *Kahler*, 18 T.C. at 34.

The *Kahler* court recognized as "completely distinguishable" a situation in which a check was "subject to a substantial restriction" which the drawer had imposed on the check. *Id.* (distinguishing *Fischer v. Commissioner*, 14 T.C. 792 (1950)). The third circuit has also agreed that when the payor imposes a restriction upon the payee's use of a check, an exception exists to the general rule that ordinarily a check constitutes taxable income to a cash-basis taxpayer when he receives it. *Estate of Kamm v. Commissioner*, 349 F.2d 953, 955 (3rd Cir.1965). The court in *Kamm* refused, however, to admit the exception when the payee is responsible for the restrictions. *See id.* Such restrictions "emphasize the existence of dominion over the checks and unrestricted power to dispose of them." *Id.* at 956.

In *Kamm* the taxpayer's attorney received two checks on Friday December 30th after banking hours and deposited them in his trustee account that afternoon. On December 31st, the attorney drew checks on his account payable to the taxpayer and dated January 3rd, on which date the checks were deposited in the taxpayer's account in accordance with her instructions. The court acknowledged that "the time of receipt made it impracticable ... to convert the check into cash before the end of the taxable year." *Id.* The court, nevertheless, reasoned that because a certified check "has value and commercial utility so much like money, and its acceptance and convertibility into money are so routine," it is income upon receipt. *Id.* at 955–56 (citing *Kahler*, 18 T.C. 31).

The situation confronting the court in this appeal favors the cash-equivalent-upon-receipt rule even more than do the situations in *Kahler* and *Kamm*. As Cornell's employee received the Holdings check from Fidelity during business hours on Friday, December 27, 1985, Cornell had five calendar days and at least two business days before the end of the year in which to acquire access to the funds.

Furthermore, unlike the drawer of the check in *Fischer*, Fidelity, the payor bank, did not impose any restrictions on the negotiability of the check. In order not to confer preferential treatment on any holder of outstanding Southland stock, Fidelity sent the same type of check to all sellers who accepted Holdings' offer. Consequently, it would not wire same-day funds. Neither would it issue cashier's checks to cover the tender offer. But, crucially for the purposes of this appeal, Fidelity regarded the check drawn on it as "a cash transaction, thus same day funds." Had Cornell opened an account at Fidelity, she would have had immediate access to her funds.

The taxpayer's privies—either her employee, the remaining trustee, or, InterFirst, the trust's bank-imposed whatever restrictions that were imposed on accessibility to the funds. Cornell's employee informed the remaining trustee that the check had arrived. The latter instructed her to mail the check to InterFirst, the trust's bank, and to request InterFirst to purchase government securities with the funds. InterFirst accepted the check for deposit, but refused to purchase the securities until it had collected the funds from Fidelity. In ample time for the taxpayer or her privies to have access to same-day funds at Fidelity before the end of the year, InterFirst notified the employee of the restriction that it was imposing on the use of the funds until it had collected them from Fidelity.

Neither Cornell nor the remaining trustee chose to exercise the alternative option of immediate access to the funds through Fidelity. Instead, the taxpayer's agent or her trustee chose to deposit the check in InterFirst, which limited access to the funds. In doing so, Cornell "voluntarily subjected [her]self to a routine which delayed somewhat [her] personal receipt" of the funds. *See Kamm*, 349 F.2d at 956 (rejecting argument that taxpayer did not receive proceeds until January because attorney required to deposit check in trust account and not obliged to remit to taxpayer until checks had cleared)....

In conclusion, we agree with the district court that the check which the taxpayer's employee received in 1985 constituted taxable income in that year. Consequently, the judgment of the district court is AFFIRMED.

FOOTNOTES:

3. Section 451 of Title 26 of the United States Code states the general rule for determining the taxable year of inclusion of items of income. The regulations governing the cash receipts method of accounting are set forth in Section 1.446-1(c)(i) of title 26 of the Code of Federal Regulations.

4. The general rule that receipt by an agent constitutes receipt by the principal is normally followed in tax cases....

––––––––––

Consider the following questions concerning *Bright*.

1. Who received the check at issue? Is he or she a party in the case?

2. On what date was the check received?

3. When was the check posted by the bank to the checking account?

4. Although the taxpayer initially contended that the check proceeds should be included in gross income for 1985, she later filed an amended return claiming that the proper year was, in fact, 1986. Why? Did the court agree? What was the court's reasoning?

5. Would the result have been the same or different if the payor had sent the payee a post-dated check?

––––––––––

Suppose the payee's agent in *Bright* had received and mailed the check to the bank in 1985 but the check was lost in the mail. Would the payor have income in 1985? Might it depend upon whether the check ever reached the bank and was posted to the payee's account?

WALTER v. UNITED STATES
148 F.3d 1027 (8th Cir. 1998)

LOKEN, Circuit Judge.

Horace and Donna Walter farm and feed cattle in rural Clark County, South Dakota. By 1985 and 1986, the tax years in question, they were feeding and selling over 8,000 cattle per year and farming about 2,000 acres. In their joint federal income tax returns for those years, the Walters reported taxable income of $195,353 in 1985 and $204,513 in 1986. In 1988, the Commissioner of Internal Revenue audited the returns, increasing the Walters' taxable income to $393,817 in 1985 and $529,159 in 1986, and assessing negligence and substantial understatement penalties. *See* 26 U.S.C. (hereafter cited as "I.R.C.") §§ 6653, 6661. The Walters paid the amounts due and filed this refund lawsuit. Following trial, the district court entered judgment partially in favor of the Walters and partially in favor of the Commissioner. The Walters appeal, raising two issues: whether income received by check was taxable in 1986, the year a check was initially received and lost, and whether the Commissioner abused her discretion by refusing to waive part of the substantial understatement penalty. We affirm.

I. The Lost Check Issue.

During the 1988 audit, the IRS auditor discovered a document from a cattle buying customer in the Walters' business records. The document reported that the Walters sold 115 steers to IBP, Inc., in March 1986 for a net price of $77,441.83. The document appeared to be a "tear slip"—the top half of an IBP document that normally includes a business check which the recipient detaches for negotiation or deposit. The Walters' bank records for 1986 showed no such deposit. The Walters then contacted their customer. IBP advised that its March 1986 check for $77,441.83 had never been cashed and issued a new check in January 1988. The Walters included that amount in their 1988 taxable income. Some months later, the Commissioner issued an audit report contending that this income was taxable in 1986 under a theory of constructive receipt. The jury found that the first check was received in 1986 and then lost (presumably when the Walters mailed it to their bank for deposit), and that the Walters negligently failed to include the IBP payment in their 1986 income. On appeal, they argue the district court erred in not granting them judgment as a matter of law on their claim that the $77,441.83 was not taxable income until 1988.

For cash basis taxpayers like the Walters, an item of gross income "shall be included in the gross income for the taxable year in which received." I.R.C. §451(a). Because the timing of income receipt may have great tax significance, and because taxpayers are ingenious at devising ways to minimize taxes, the Commissioner has developed the concept of "constructive receipt," which the courts have uniformly endorsed. This concept is defined in the Commissioner's current regulations:

> Income although not actually reduced to a taxpayer's possession is constructively received by him in the taxable year during which it is credited to his account, set apart for him, or otherwise made available so that he may draw upon it at any time, or so that he could have drawn upon it during the taxable year if notice of intention to withdraw had been given. However, income is not constructively received if the taxpayer's control of its receipt is subject to substantial limitations or restrictions.

Treas. Reg. (26 C.F.R.) §1.451-2(a).

A check in the hands of a taxpayer ordinarily means that funds are immediately available. Therefore, the general rule is that a check constitutes taxable income to a cash-basis taxpayer *when received. See Avery v. Commissioner*, 292 U.S. 210, 215, 54 S.Ct. 674, 78 L.Ed. 1216 (1934); *Kahler v. Commissioner*, 18 T.C. 31, 1952 WL 112 (1952). There are some common sense exceptions to this rule, such as when the payor may be insolvent, *see Lavery v. Commissioner*, 158 F.2d 859, 860 (7th Cir. 1946), or has imposed substantial restrictions or conditions that prevent the taxpayer from receiving funds, *see Bright v. United States*, 926 F.2d 383, 386–87 (5th Cir. 1991).

Relying on a reference to negotiable instruments law in *Kahler*, 18 T.C. at 34, 1952 WL 112, the Walters argue that only if presentment is made and a check is honored should the date of payment relate back to its delivery. Therefore, a check that is lost and never honored should not be taxable income in the year the check was received. We agree that the law of negotiable instruments provides a useful backdrop, but it cannot trump the doctrine of constructive receipt as developed in the Internal Revenue Code and its implementing Treasury Regulations. The Walters received the check in 1986. IBP was not insolvent and placed no conditions or restrictions on its payment. Losing the check was a restriction on collection imposed by the Walters, the payees. No tax case has recognized an exception to the rule that receipt of a check is constructive receipt of the income when the restrictions on "the disposition of the proceeds were the payees' own." *Estate of Kamm v. Commissioner*, 349 F.2d 953, 955 (3d Cir. 1965); *accord Bright*, 926 F.2d at 386–87.... As we said in *Loose v. United States*, 74 F.2d 147, 150 (8th Cir. 1934):

> the strongest reason for holding constructive receipt of income to be within the statute is that for taxation purposes income is received or realized when it is made subject to the will and control of the taxpayer and can be, except for his own action or inaction, reduced to actual possession. So viewed, it makes no difference why the taxpayer did not reduce to actual possession. The matter is in no wise dependent upon what he does or upon what he fails to do. It depends solely upon the existence of a situation where the income is fully available to him.... Accordingly, the face amount of the check was income to the Walters when they received the check.

Consider the following questions.

1. How would you state the reasoning for the holding of the court in *Walter*?

2. Note that the Walters sought to rely on a rule of negotiable instruments law. To what extent must a court considering a tax issue be bound by nontax rules, like those of negotiable instruments?

Return now to the question concerning receipt of an unsecured promissory note. (What is an "unsecured promissory note"?) You have learned that in most cases, a check is the same as cash. Does the same rationale govern the treatment of promissory notes? Consider the following case.

COWDEN v. COMMISSIONER
289 F.2d 20 (5th Cir. 1961)

JONES, Circuit Judge.

We here review a decision of the Tax Court by which a determination was made of federal income tax liability of Frank Cowden, Sr., his wife and their children, for the years 1951 and 1952. In April 1951, Frank Cowden, Sr. and his wife made an oil, gas and mineral lease for themselves and their children upon described lands in Texas to Stanolind Oil and Gas Company. By related supplemental agreements, Stanolind agreed to make "bonus" or "advance royalty" payments in an aggregate amount of $511,192.50. On execution of the instruments $10,223.85 was payable, the sum of $250,484.31 was due "no earlier than" January 5 "nor later than" January 10, 1952, and $250,484.34 was stipulated to be paid "no earlier than" January 5 "nor later than" January 10, 1953. One-half of the amounts was to be paid to Frank Cowden, Sr. and his wife, and one-sixth was payable to each of their children. In the deferred payments agreements it was provided that:

> "This contract evidences the obligation of Stanolind Oil and Gas Company to make the deferred payments referred to in subparagraphs (b) and (c) of the preceding paragraph hereof, and it is understood and agreed that the obliga-

tion of Stanolind Oil and Gas Company to make such payments is a firm and absolute personal obligation of said Company, which is not in any manner conditioned upon development or production from the demised premises, nor upon the continued ownership of the leasehold interest in such premises by Stanolind Oil and Gas Company, but that such payments shall be made in all events."

On November 30, 1951, the taxpayer assigned the payments due from Stanolind in 1952 to the First National Bank of Midland, of which Frank Cowden, Sr. was a director. Assignments of the payments due in 1953 were made to the bank on November 20, 1952. For the assignment of the 1952 payments the bank paid the face value of the amounts assigned discounted by $257.43 in the case of Frank Cowden, Sr. and his wife, and $85.81 in the case of each of their children. For the amounts due in 1953 the discounts were $313.14 for Frank Cowden, Sr. and his wife, and $104.38 for each of their children. The taxpayers reported the amounts received by them from the assignments as long-term capital gains. The Commissioner made a determination that the contractual obligations of Stanolind to make payments in future years represented ordinary income, subject to depletion, to the extent of the fair market value of the obligations at the time they were created. The Commissioner computed the fair market value of the Stanolind obligations, which were not interest bearing, by the deduction of a discount of four per cent. on the deferred payments from the date of the agreements until the respective maturities. Such computation fixed a 1951 equivalent of cash value of $487,647.46 for the bonus payments, paid in 1951 and agreed to be paid thereafter, aggregating $511,192.50. The Commissioner determined that the taxpayers should be taxed in 1951 on $487,647.46, as ordinary income.

A majority of the Tax Court was convinced that, under the particular facts of this case, the bonus payments were not only readily but immediately convertible to cash and were the equivalent of cash, and had a fair market value equal to their face value. The Tax Court decided that the entire amounts of the bonus payments, $511,192.50, were taxable in 1951, as ordinary income. Cowden v. Commissioner of Internal Revenue, 32 T.C. 853. Two judges of the Tax Court dissented.

The Tax Court stated, as a general proposition, "that executory contracts to make future payments in money do not have a fair market value." The particular facts by which the Tax Court distinguishes this case from the authorities by which the general proposition is established are, as stated in the opinion of the majority

" ... that the bonus payors were perfectly willing and able at the time of execution of the leases and bonus agreements to pay such bonus in an immediate lump sum payment; to pay the bonus immediately in a lump sum at all times thereafter until the due dates under the agreements; that Cowden, Sr., believed the bonus agreements had a market value at the time of their execution; that a bank in which he was an officer and depositor was willing to and in fact did purchase such rights at a nominal discount; that the bank considered such rights to be bankable and to represent direct obligations of the payor; that the bank generally dealt in such contracts where it was satisfied with the financial responsibility of the payor and looked solely to it for payment without recourse to the lessor and, in short, that the sole reason why the bonuses were not immediately paid in cash upon execution of the leases involved was the refusal of the lessor to receive such payments."

These findings are, in some respects, challenged by the taxpayers as being unsupported by the evidence. Our review of the record has led us to the conclusion that the findings of fact made by the Tax Court are sustained by substantial evidence. However, we must observe that the statement of Frank Cowden, Sr. that the contract obligations had "some market value" is not to be regarded as binding upon him and other taxpayers with respect to the decisive issue in the case.

The dissenting opinion of the Tax Court minority states that the conclusion reached by the majority "is in effect that the taxpayers are not free to make the bargain of their choice," and one of the taxpayers' specifications of error is that the Tax Court "erred in holding that taxpayers are not free to make the bargain of their choice."

The Tax Court majority distinguishes the authorities cited and relied upon by the taxpayers upon several grounds. The Tax Court seemingly lays stress upon the fact, found to be here present, that the bonus payor was willing and able to make the entire bonus payment upon the execution of the agreement. It is said by the taxpayers that the Tax Court has held that a constructive receipt, under the equivalent of cash doctrine, resulted from the willingness of the lessee to pay the entire bonus on execution of the leases and the unwillingness of the taxpayers, for reasons of their own, (Footnote 1) to receive the full amount. If this be the effect of the Tax Court's decision there may be some justification for the criticism appearing in the opinion of the minority and the concern expressed elsewhere.

It was said in Gregory v. Helvering, 293 U.S. 465 ... and recently repeated in Knetsch v. United States, 364 U.S. 361, ..."The legal right of a taxpayer to decrease the amount of what otherwise would be his taxes, or altogether avoid them, by means which the law permits, cannot be doubted." ... As a general rule a tax avoidance motive is not to be considered in determining the tax liability resulting from a transaction.... The taxpayers had the right to decline to enter into a mineral lease of their lands except upon the condition that the lessee obligate itself for a bonus payable in part in installments in future years, and the doing so would not, of itself, subject the deferred payments to taxation during the year that the lease was made. Nor would a tax liability necessarily arise although the lease contract was made with a solvent lessee who had been willing and able to pay the entire bonus upon the execution of the lease.

While it is true that the parties may enter into any legal arrangement they see fit even though the particular form in which it was cast was selected with the hope of a reduction in taxes, it is also true that if a consideration for which one of the parties bargains is the equivalent of cash it will be subjected to taxation to the extent of its fair market value. Whether the undertaking of the lessee to make future bonus payments was, when made, the equivalent of cash and, as such, taxable as current income is the issue in this case. In a somewhat similar case, decided in 1941, the Board of Tax Appeals stated that "where no notes, bonds, or other evidences of indebtedness other than the contract were given, such contract had no fair market value." Kleberg v. Commissioner, 43 B.T.A. 277, quoting from Titus v. Commissioner, 33 B.T.A. 928. In 1959 the Tax Court held that where the deferred bonus payments were evidenced by promissory notes the equivalent of cash doctrine might be applicable. Barnsley v. Commissioner, 31 T.C. 1260. There the Tax Court said:

> "It is, of course, possible under an oil and gas lease containing proper provisions to have a bonus payable and taxable in installments, Alice K. Kleberg, 43 B.T.A. 277. The case before us does not constitute such an arrangement. In the Kleberg case the contractual agreement was to pay a named amount in two payments as bonus. It was not a case like the one here where cash and negotiable notes, the latter being the equivalent of cash, representing the bonus were received in the same year by the taxpayer."

The test announced in Kleberg, from which *Barnsley* does not depart, seems to be whether the obligation to make the deferred payments is represented by "notes, bonds, or other evidences of indebtedness other than the contract." In this case, the literal test of Kleberg is met as the obligation of Stanolind to the Cowdens was evidenced by an instrument other than the contract of lease. This instrument is not, however, one of the kind which fall into the classification of notes or bonds. The taxpayers urge that there can be no "equivalent of cash" obligation unless it is a negotiable instrument. Such a test, to be determined by the form of the obligation, is as unrealistic as it is formalistic. The income tax law deals in economic realities, not legal abstractions, and the reach of the income tax law is not to be delimited by technical refinements or mere formalism.

A promissory note, negotiable in form, is not necessarily the equivalent of cash. Such an instrument may have been issued by a maker of doubtful solvency or for other reasons such paper might be denied a ready acceptance in the market place. We think the converse of this principle ought to be applicable. We are convinced that if a promise to pay of a solvent obligor is unconditional and assignable, not subject to set-offs, and is of a kind that is frequently transferred to lenders or investors at a discount not substantially greater than the generally prevailing premium for the use of money, such promise is the equivalent of cash and taxable in like manner as cash would have been taxable had it been received by the taxpayer rather than the obligation. The principle that negotiability is not the test of taxability in an equivalent of cash case such as is before us, is consistent with the rule that men may, if they can, so order their affairs as to minimize taxes, and points up the doctrine that substance and not form should control in the application of income tax laws.

The Tax Court stressed in its findings that the provisions for deferring a part of the bonus were made solely at the request of and for the benefit of the taxpayers, and that the lessee was willing and able to make the bonus payments in cash upon execution of the agreements. It appears to us that the Tax Court, in reaching its decision that the taxpayers had received equivalent of cash bonuses in the year the leases were executed, gave as much and probably more weight to those findings than to the other facts found by it. We are persuaded of this not only by the language of its opinion but because, in its determination of the cash equivalent, it used the amounts which it determined the taxpayers could have received if they had made a different contract, rather than the fair market value cash equivalent (Footnote 8) of the obligation for which the taxpayers had bargained in the contracts which they had a lawful right to make. We are unable to say whether or not the Tax Court, if it disregarded, as we think it should have done, the facts as it found them as to the willingness of the lessee to pay and the unwillingness of the taxpayers to receive the full bonus on execution of the leases, would have determined that the equivalent bonus obligations were taxable in the year of the agreements as the equivalent of cash. This question is primarily a fact issue.... There should be a remand to the Tax Court for a reconsideration of the questions submitted in the light of what has been said here.

If the deferred bonus payments were the equivalent of cash and as such taxable as ordinary income during the year of receipt, the income so taxable would be subject to depletion....

. . .

For further proceedings in keeping with the conclusions here expressed, the decision of the Tax Court is reversed and the cause is remanded.

Reversed and remanded.

FOOTNOTES:

1. It is not denied that a desire to save taxes was the sole purpose for the taxpayers' insistence that payment be postponed.

8. Computed by the Commissioner by discounting the obligations at a 4 per cent rate....

Consider the following questions about *Cowden.*

1. What's an oil, gas, and mineral lease? Why would the Cowdens enter into such a lease with the oil company?

2. Once the Cowdens enter into such a lease, can they continue to use their property for other purposes?

3. Part of the agreement was that the oil company would pay advance royalty payments in a total amount $511,192.50, payable in three payments in 1951, 1952, and 1953. Why did the Cowdens assign the payments due in 1952 and 1953 to the bank?

4. Why would the bank agree to hand over substantial amounts of money to the Cowdens based on the unsecured promise of the oil company to pay in the future?

5. Would a bank do the same with respect to the unsecured promissory note received by the lawyer for drafting the will?

6. In what year did the court determine that the Cowdens had income?

7. Why did the Tax Court determine that the proper amount of the income of the Cowdens was less than the face value of the notes?

8. Describe the difference in approach between the Tax Court and the Fifth Circuit. (This case should remind you of the form versus substance materials in Part III.) Why did the Fifth Circuit remand the case to the Tax Court?

Another problem that arises when calculating the income of a cash basis taxpayer concerns the portion of the regulation quoted above that states: "items ... are to be included for the taxable year in which actually or *constructively* received." (Emphasis added.) This regulation raises the possibility that the common rule for the cash method income may not always apply. Under the general rule, a taxpayer includes items in gross income when received. But under the regulation, an item not actually received could, nevertheless, be includible in income by a cash basis taxpayer.

What problem justifies this variation from the general rules for the inclusion in income or the deduction of expenses by cash basis taxpayers? The general rules, in fact, make it possible for a taxpayer to manipulate both income and expense in certain cases. For example, the lawyer can decide not to send a bill to the client for the will until the next tax year, particularly if the lawyer drafts the will late in a tax year. So too, the lawyer can decide to pay her utility bill before the end of the tax year, rather than waiting until the start of the new year to do so. But just how far should such manipulations be permitted to go?

Suppose the lawyer drafts the will. She calls her client to come in to sign the will, which the client does, on December 27th. The client arrives, signs the will, and takes an envelope from his pocket containing $1,000 cash. But when he offers the cash to the lawyer, who uses a calendar year accounting period,[3] the lawyer refuses the cash and instructs the client to send it after the first of the year. In what year must the lawyer report the income? (**Hint: consult Treasury Regulation section 1.451-2(a).**)

Would your answer change if the client offered the lawyer a $1,000 check? What about an unsecured promissory note? Suppose the client offered to assign a bond to the lawyer?

Suppose that the client comes in and signs the will on the 27th but does not pay. Instead, he tells the lawyer he will send a check, which he does, on January 2nd. Does the lawyer have constructive receipt in this case? She certainly has an account receivable. Does she have a basis in the receivable? **Remember TOAD.** What happens when she receives the actual payment which extinguishes the receivable?

Note that the constructive receipt doctrine applies to such diverse situations as the taxpayer who does not take her savings account passbook to the bank to have the interest due recorded in the passbook and the employee awarded a bonus at the end of the year who delays picking up his check until the start of the next tax year. In both cases, the constructive receipt doctrine requires the taxpayer to report the income in the earlier year. As the Eighth Circuit stated the doctrine in *Loose v. United States*: a cash method taxpayer is in constructive receipt of income "when it is made subject to the will and control of the taxpayer and can be, except for his own action or inaction, reduced to actual possession."[4]

2. Items of Deduction

Treasury Regulation section 1.446-1(c)(1)(i) requires that "[e]xpenditures are to be deducted for the taxable year in which actually made." This language, like that relating to income, seems clear on its face. But, consider the obverse side of the issues that arise concerning the income of cash basis taxpayers. For example, if the lawyer sends a check to a creditor on December 31, but the payor bank does not post the check to the account of the payee until the following year (as in *Bright*), when did the lawyer make the payment? Based upon what you learned above about the receipt of checks, can you make a guess?[5]

Suppose the lawyer pays his telephone bill with a credit card on the last day of the tax year. Should that expense be charged to the year in which he gives the telephone company his credit card number? Should payment by credit card be the same or different from payment by check?[6]

How would you analyze the issue if the lawyer delivers a promissory note to his vendor? Suppose the lawyer borrows money from a bank to pay the vendor. Is his payment

---

3. **Look at section 441(a)** which requires that taxable income shall be computed in accordance with the taxpayer's tax year. **Look also at section 441(g)** which forces most individuals to use a calendar year for tax purposes.

4. 74 F.2d 147, 150 (8th Cir. 1934).

5. If you guessed that a check is like cash, you would be correct, provided the check is honored. A post-dated check, however, constitutes merely a promise to pay and is not a current payment.

6. In fact, credit card payments, like those made by check, are treated as made immediately, based on the rationale that when someone makes a payment by credit card, she immediately incurs a debt to the issuing bank. It is, therefore, exactly the same as if she borrowed the money from the bank and used it to discharge her obligation.

deductible in the year he makes it although he does so with borrowed funds? The answer is clearly, "yes." But when the lawyer pays with his own promissory note, he has made *no* payment until he actually discharges his obligation to make the payment required by the note. This is true even if the note constitutes a cash equivalent to the payee who, like *Cowden*, must include an amount in income in the year of receipt of the note.

Suppose the lawyer offers a bonus check to his secretary on December 31. She refuses to accept the check until the following tax year. She, of course, has income; she had constructive receipt of the check (the equivalent of cash). The lawyer, on the other hand, gets no deduction until the following year when the check is delivered to the secretary.

Why should the tax law create the inconsistency in treatment revealed by these last two examples? Note that in both cases, use of the cash method of accounting accelerates income inclusion but defers deduction of expenses. Recall our earlier discussion of the time value of money. Who is the winner in these last two examples of the application of the cash basis method of accounting?

One important exception to the general rule that a cash basis taxpayer deducts expenses in the year in which he pays them exists. Suppose the lawyer in our hypothetical leases his office for five years at the rate of $6,000 per year and prepays the $30,000 rent for all five years in the first year of the lease. As a cash basis taxpayer, one would expect that he could deduct the full amount of the rent paid in year one of the lease. Not so! Recall our discussion of capital expenditures and consider the following case.

COMMISSIONER v. BOYLSTON MARKET ASS'N
131 F.2d 966 (1st Cir. 1942)

MAHONEY, Circuit Judge.

The Board of Tax Appeals reversed a determination by the Commissioner of Internal Revenue of deficiencies in the Boylston Market Association's income tax of $835.34 for the year 1936, and $431.84 for the year 1938, and the Commissioner has appealed.

The taxpayer in the course of its business, which is the management of real estate owned by it, purchased from time to time fire and other insurance policies covering periods of three or more years. It keeps its books and makes its returns on a cash receipts and disbursements basis. The taxpayer has since 1915 deducted each year as insurance expenses the amount of insurance premiums applicable to carrying insurance for that year regardless of the year in which the premium was actually paid. This method was required by the Treasury Department prior to 1938 by G.C.M. 13148, XIII-1 Cum. Bull. 67 (1934). Prior to January 1, 1936, the taxpayer had prepaid insurance premiums in the amount of $6,690.75 and during that year it paid premiums in an amount of $1082.77. The amount of insurance premiums prorated by the taxpayer in 1936 was $4421.76. Prior to January 1, 1938, it had prepaid insurance premiums in the amount of $6148.42 and during that year paid premiums in the amount of $890.47. The taxpayer took a deduction of $3284.25, which was the amount prorated for the year 1938. The Commissioner in his notice of deficiency for the year 1936 allowed only $1082.77 and for the year 1938 only $890.47, being the amounts actually paid in those years, on the basis that deductions for insurance expense of a taxpayer on the cash receipts and disbursements basis is limited to premiums paid during the taxable year.

We are asked to determine whether a taxpayer who keeps his books and files his returns on a cash basis is limited to the deduction of the insurance premiums actually paid in any year or whether he should deduct for each tax year the pro rata portion of the prepaid insurance applicable to that year. The pertinent provisions of the statute are Sections 23 and 43 of the Revenue Act of 1936, (Footnote 1)....

This court in Welch v. DeBlois, 1 Cir., 1938, 94 F.2d 842, held that a taxpayer on the cash receipts and disbursements basis who made prepayments of insurance premiums was entitled to take a full deduction for these payments as ordinary and necessary business expenses in the year in which payment was made despite the fact that the insurance covered a three-year period. The government on the basis of that decision changed its earlier G.C.M. rule, supra, which had required the taxpayer to prorate prepaid insurance premiums. The Board of Tax Appeals has refused to follow that case in George S. Jephson v. Com'r, 37 B.T.A. 1117; Frank Real Estate & Investment Co., 40 B.T.A. 1382, unreported memorandum decision Nov. 15, 1939, and in the instant case. The arguments in that case in favor of treating prepaid insurance as an ordinary and necessary business expense are persuasive. We are, nevertheless, unable to find a real basis for distinguishing between prepayment of rentals, ... bonuses for the acquisition of leases, ... bonuses for the cancellation of leases, ... commissions for negotiating leases, ... and prepaid insurance. Some distinctions may be drawn in the cases ... on the basis of the facts contained therein, but we are of the opinion that there is no justification for treating them differently insofar as deductions are concerned. All of the cases ... are readily distinguishable from such a clear cut case as a permanent improvement to a building. This latter is clearly a capital expenditure.... In such a case there is the creation of a capital asset which has a life extending beyond the taxable year and which depreciates over a period of years. The taxpayer regardless of his method of accounting can only take deductions for depreciation over the life of the asset. Advance rentals, payments of bonuses for acquisition and cancellation of leases, and commissions for negotiating leases are all matters which the taxpayer amortizes over the life of the lease. Whether we consider these payments to be the cost of the exhaustible asset, as in the case of advance rentals, or the cost of acquiring the asset, as in the case of bonuses, the payments are prorated primarily because the life of the asset extends beyond the taxable year. To permit the taxpayer to take a full deduction in the year of payment would distort his income. Prepaid insurance presents the same problem and should be solved in the same way. Prepaid insurance for a period of three years may be easily allocated. It is protection for the entire period and the taxpayer may, if he desires, at any time surrender the insurance policy. It thus is clearly an asset having a longer life than a single taxable year. The line to be drawn between capital expenditures and ordinary and necessary business expenses is not always an easy one, but we are satisfied that in treating prepaid insurance as a capital expense we are obtaining some degree of consistency in these matters. We are, therefore, of the opinion that Welch v. DeBlois, supra, is incorrect and should be overruled.

The decision of Board of Tax Appeals is affirmed.

FOOTNOTES:

1. "§ 23. Deductions from Gross Income

"In computing net income there shall be allowed as deductions:

"(a) Expenses. All the ordinary and necessary expenses paid or incurred during the taxable year in carrying on any trade or business, including a reasonable allowance for salaries or other compensation for personal services actually rendered...."

"§ 43. Period for Which Deductions and Credits Taken

"The deductions and credits (other than the dividends paid credit provided in section 27) provided for in this title shall be taken for the taxable year in which 'paid or accrued' or 'paid or incurred', dependent upon the method of accounting upon the basis of which the net income is computed, unless in order to clearly reflect the income the deductions or credits should be taken as of a different period …".

Consider the following questions.

1. In *Boylston Market*, the Service took the position that the taxpayer should be allowed to deduct only amounts paid in a particular year. Do you think the Service would have taken that same position concerning our hypothetical prepaid rent?

2. What did the court hold and why with respect to the prepaid insurance premiums in the case?

3. The court mentions its earlier decision in *Welch v. DeBlois*, in which it held that a cash basis taxpayer was entitled to take a full deduction for prepayment of insurance premiums for three years' coverage as ordinary and necessary business expenses in the year of payment. The court also states that the Board of Tax Appeals (predecessor to the United States Tax Court), had refused to follow that decision in two of its cases. How could the Board of Tax Appeals refuse to follow the decision of a federal circuit court of appeals?

4. Suppose that the court is correct that the taxpayer's payments represent capital expenditures. What is the normal way in which you have learned a taxpayer accounts for capital expenses? Hint: recall Brian and his machine. Note, as a matter of interest, that when the capital expense is used for a nontangible asset, the method for accounting for the cost is called "amortization." But remember, that expenses for certain items are neither depreciable nor amortizable: the most important of these categories are land and personal use property.

An important rationale for the court's deviation from the normal cash basis rule in *Boylston Market* was its conclusion that the prepaid premiums were easily allocated over the period for which they were prepaid. As with insurance, interest is easily allocable to the period to which it relates. Nevertheless, until relatively recently, prepaid interest could be deducted in the year paid. In the heyday of tax shelters, one of the expenses that created "up front" deductions was the prepayment of interest. This treatment followed logically from the wording of section 163 of the Code and was approved by the Service until it issued Revenue Ruling 68-643, 1968-2 C.B. 76, which curtailed the practice when the advance payments extended for more than twelve months beyond the taxable year in which payment was made. Congress then enacted section 461(g) that now requires a cash basis taxpayer to account for interest as paid in the period to which it relates, regardless of its earlier payment. **Read section 461(g).**

B. Accrual Method

1. Items of Income

a. General Rule

The general rule for income inclusion by an accrual method taxpayer states that the proper time is the point when the taxpayer's right to the income becomes fixed and the amount can be determined with reasonable accuracy. **Read Treasury Regulation section 1.446-1(c)(1)(ii)(A)(first sentence).**

Recall once again the hypothetical of the lawyer drafting a will for a client. In that case, there was no issue concerning the amount of compensation to be received. But when have all events occurred fixing the client's obligation to pay the lawyer? Or, to put it the other way, when does the lawyer's right to receive the income become fixed? Does it become fixed when lawyer and client enter into the (oral) contract? Almost certainly not. **Look at Treasury Regulation section 1.446-1(c)(1)(ii)(A) again.** Can the lawyer have income before she has performed the services? What about at the moment the lawyer has completed the drafting of the will? There is a contract and there has been performance on the part of the lawyer. But, if two of the conditions implicit in the contract are: (1) review of the will by the client; and then (2) signing of the will by the client, have all events occurred prior to the happening of those events? **Look at Treasury Regulation section 1.451-1(a).**

In fact, the issue of timing rarely arises in service businesses because service businesses generally adopt the cash method. But the taxpayer has some flexibility to adopt a specific practice for reporting income within the accrual accounting method, provided his method is consistent with generally accepted accounting principles, is consistently applied from year to year, and is consistent with income tax regulations. **Read Treasury Regulation section 1.446-1(c)(1)(ii)(C), second and third sentences.** Notwithstanding the choice the Code grants to the taxpayer, the Code also grants to the Commissioner broad powers to require a taxpayer to use the method that most clearly reflects the taxpayer's income. (**Read Treasury Regulation section 1.446-1(c)(1)(ii)(C), first sentence.**) If the taxpayer does not choose a method or if the method chosen by the taxpayer does not clearly reflect income, the Secretary may exercise his or her statutory power to require a taxpayer to change from cash to accrual or vice versa or to adopt a particular treatment for certain items. **Read section 446(b) of the Code and Treasury Regulation section 1.446-1(b)(1).**

Remember, the key to income inclusion in an accrual accounting system is the right to receive income, rather than actual receipt of the income itself. Frequently, therefore, accrual accounting taxpayers must include in income amounts they have not yet received.[7] Suppose the lawyer in our will drafting example is an accrual basis taxpayer. He performs all services necessary to accrue gross income in year 1, but does not receive the actual $1,000 payment from the client until year 2. Under the accrual method, he will include $1,000 in income in year 1. What then happens when he actually receives the $1,000 in year 2? Can he possibly have gross income again? Of course not! **Recall our discussion of Treasury Regulation section 1.61-2(d)(2).** That regulation makes clear that when a taxpayer includes an item in gross income, he acquires a basis in that item equal to the amount he included in income. Thus, when our lawyer receives $1,000 in year 2, he is exchanging one asset for another: he is exchanging a receivable with a basis of $1,000 for $1,000 in cash. (Recall our discussion of this concept in connection with the bank that loaned money to Larry in Part II, Chapter 1.)

---

7. The accrual method taxpayer must accrue the income at its face value, not at the fair market value. *See* Revenue Ruling 79-292, 1979-2 C.B. 287. What would happen to the accrual method taxpayer if, after accruing the income, she does not receive any or all of the receivable? Should she amend her tax return for the year of accrual? **Recall *Lewis*.** She clearly requires some kind of correction. She makes that correction by claiming a bad debt deduction in the year in which all or part of the receivable becomes clearly uncollectible. **Look at section 166.**

b. Special Problems Relating to Prepayments

(1) Prepayments for Services

The general rule for inclusion of income by accrual basis taxpayers requires recognition in the year in which all events have occurred that fix the right to the income and its amount can be ascertained with reasonable certainty. Suppose an accrual basis taxpayer actually receives payment before performing the services for which the payments are made in advance? The normal rule for accrual accounting would suggest that the taxpayer does not have to report income until she performs the services. Now, consider the following case.

RCA CORPORATION v. UNITED STATES
664 F.2d 881 (2d Cir. 1981)

KEARSE, Circuit Judge:

This appeal requires us to determine whether the Commissioner of Internal Revenue ("Commissioner") properly exercised his discretion when he rejected as "not clearly reflect[ing] income" within the meaning of §446(b) of the Internal Revenue Code of 1954 ("I.R.C."), ... the accrual method of accounting used in 1958 and 1959 by plaintiff RCA Corporation ("RCA") to account for revenues received from the prepayment of fees associated with certain service contracts entered into with purchasers of its products. The ... District Court ... held ... that the Commissioner had abused his discretion in rejecting RCA's accrual method of accounting, and awarded judgment to RCA in the amount of $5,956,039.25, plus assessed deficiency interest and statutory interest, on its claim for a refund of corporate income taxes for the years 1958 and 1959. Believing that the Commissioner properly exercised his discretion, we reverse.

I

The ... facts are substantially undisputed. Since 1946 RCA has carried on a business, either directly or through its wholly-owned subsidiary RCA Service Company ("RCAS"), of servicing television sets and other consumer products it sold. In the typical service arrangement, the purchaser of an RCA product would contract, at the time of purchase, to receive service and repair of the product for a stated period in exchange for prepayment of a single lump sum. Under these agreements, service was available to the purchaser on demand at any time during the contract term, which might range from three to twenty-four months. Until 1958, this service business was conducted by RCAS. On December 31, 1957, however, RCAS was liquidated by means of its merger into RCA; thereafter RCA continued the business of RCAS through RCA's Service Company division.

RCAS, and later RCA, employed an accrual method of accounting for service contract revenues on their books. For each group of service contracts of a given duration entered into in a given month, the seller credited to current income a sum that represented the actual cost of selling and processing the contracts, plus a profit. The balance of the revenues derived from each group of contracts, i.e., the portion to be earned through future performance under them, was credited to a deferred income account. Each month thereafter, the seller journaled from the deferred income account to current income that proportion of the revenues from each group of contracts that the seller estimated had been earned in the month through actual performance. For the most part, the seller's estimates of its rate of performance for a particular class of contracts were based on its past experience in the business, and took into account such factors as seasonal repair patterns, variations in average daily workloads, and the number of working days in each month. (Footnote 2) Although these forecasts were not perfect and may have rested to some extent on untested assumptions, they matched service contract revenues and related expenses with reasonable accuracy.

Although RCAS accounted for service contract revenues on an accrual basis in keeping its own books, it employed a cash method of accounting for service contract income on its tax returns. (Footnote 3) For tax purposes, RCAS added to its gross taxable income for each year the amount by which the aggregate year-end balance in its deferred service contract income accounts exceeded the previous year's closing balance; if the accounts had decreased, RCAS subtracted the amount of the decrease from its gross taxable income.

After the liquidation of RCAS, RCA continued to employ RCAS's accrual method, based on reasonably accurate forecasts of monthly variations in the demand for service, in its book accounting for the prepaid service contract income of its Service Company division. For tax purposes, however, RCA discontinued RCAS's former practice of adjusting taxable income by the amount of the annual change in the deferred service contract income accounts. Instead, RCA reported the service contract income of the Service Company division on the same accrual basis used in its books, including in taxable gross income only those service contract revenues that it estimated it had earned during the taxable year by actual performance. Thus, although the aggregate balance of the deferred income accounts increased ... between December 31, 1957 and December 31, 1958, RCA did not add to its gross taxable income for 1958 the ... increase. Similarly, RCA did not include in its gross income for 1959 the ... increase ... that occurred in that year. In addition, in an adjustment designed to reconcile differences in book and taxable income, RCA reduced its 1958 taxable income ... thus eliminating from taxable income most of the ... balance in the RCAS deferred income accounts (on which RCAS had already paid taxes) that had been credited to RCA's book income accounts after the merger. RCA reduced its taxable income for 1959 ... through a similar adjustment. These accounting changes and adjustments had the effect of reducing RCA's 1958 income taxes by \$4,627,436.59 and its 1959 income taxes by \$1,328,602.66. In neither 1958 nor 1959 did RCA seek the Commissioner's permission, pursuant to I.R.C. §446(e), to adopt its accrual method of tax accounting for service contract income. (Footnote 4)

After an audit of RCA's tax returns for 1958 and 1959, the Internal Revenue Service ("IRS") required RCA to report its service contract revenues upon receipt, rather than deferring recognition of any portion of them. For 1958, this change from accrual to cash accounting increased RCA's taxable income ... and increased its tax liability.... For 1959, the adjustment increased taxable income ... and tax liability.... RCA paid these increased income taxes and filed timely administrative claims for refund of the disputed sums. RCA commenced this litigation ... and, after what seems to have been a lengthy interregnum of fruitless settlement talks, the case was tried in 1979.

At trial, RCA contended, first, that its accrual method of tax accounting for prepaid service contract revenues "clearly reflect[ed] income" within the meaning of I.R.C. §446(b), and that the Commissioner had therefore abused his discretion in rejecting that method. (Footnote 5) ... Finally, RCA asserted that its accrual method was acceptable because certain revenue rulings, Rev. Proc. 71-21, 1971-2 C.B. 549, and Rev. Rul. 71-299, 1971-2 C.B. 218, promulgated by the Commissioner in 1971 and permitting limited use of accounting procedures such as RCA's, are retroactive in effect. (Footnote 7)

For its part, the government argued that under a trio of Supreme Court Cases, *Automobile Club of Michigan v. Commissioner*, 353 U.S. 180, ... (1957), ("*Michigan*"); *Amer-*

ican Automobile Association v. United States, 367 U.S. 687, ... (1961) ("*AAA*"), and *Schlude v. Commissioner*, 372 U.S. 128, ... (1963) ("*Schlude*"), methods of accrual accounting based on projections of customers' demands for services do not "clearly reflect income," and that in view of these decisions the Commissioner did not abuse his discretion in rejecting RCA's method. The government also pressed a broader argument that accrual accounting is *never* permissible without express legislative authorization and the Commissioner's consent. In addition, the government contended that RCA was not entitled to a refund because its adoption of the accrual method was a change of accounting methods for which it was required to, but did not, obtain the Commissioner's consent under I.R.C. §446(e). Finally, the government argued that ... Rev. Proc. 71-21 and Rev. Rul. 71-299 are not retroactive.

After reviewing the stipulated facts and hearing the testimony of the one live witness, an accounting expert, the district court ruled for RCA. The court read *Michigan, AAA*, and *Schlude, supra*, to proscribe, as "not clearly reflect[ing] income," only those methods of deferring recognition of income that are not based on demonstrably accurate projections of future expenses required to earn the income.... Finding that RCA's accrual method matched service contract revenues and related expenses "with reasonable precision" and therefore "clearly reflect[ed] income," the court held that the Commissioner had abused his discretion under I.R.C. §446(b) in rejecting RCA's method and imposing on RCA a cash method of accounting.... In addition, the court rejected the government's argument that the Commissioner may disallow any deferred-income method of accounting that is not specifically authorized by statute, and it held that RCA was not barred from seeking a refund by its failure to secure the Commissioner's consent for its adoption of its accrual method. The court found it unnecessary, in view of its disposition of the other issues, to discuss the parties' contentions concerning the retroactivity of Rev. Proc. 71-21 and Rev. Rul. 71-299.

Accordingly, the district court entered judgment for RCA.... This appeal followed.... We conclude that the district court erred in holding ... that the Commissioner abused his discretion in rejecting RCA's accrual method of accounting for prepaid service contract revenues,....

II

This case well illustrates the fundamental tension between the purposes of financial accounting and those of tax accounting. As the Supreme Court has recognized, these two systems of accounting have "vastly different objectives":

> The primary goal of financial accounting is to provide useful information to management, shareholders, creditors, and others properly interested; the major responsibility of the accountant is to protect these parties from being misled. The primary goal of the income tax system, in contrast, is the equitable collection of revenue; the major responsibility of the Internal Revenue Service is to protect the public fisc. Consistently with its goals and responsibilities, financial accounting has as its foundation the principle of conservatism, with its corollary that "possible errors in measurement [should] be in the direction of understatement rather than overstatement of net income and net assets." In view of the Treasury's markedly different goals and responsibilities, understatement of income is not destined to be its guiding light.

Thor Power Tool Co. v. Commissioner, 439 U.S. 522, 542, ... (1979).... The case also highlights the fundamentally different perspective that courts must adopt when reviewing the propriety of an exercise of administrative discretion rather than deciding a naked question of substantive law. We conclude that the district court gave too little weight to the objectives of tax accounting and to the Commissioner's wide discretion in implementing those objectives.

Section 446 of the Internal Revenue Code of 1954 provides that "[t]axable income shall be computed under the method of accounting on the basis of which the taxpayer regularly computes his income in keeping his books," unless "the method used does not clearly reflect income"; in the latter event "the computation of taxable income shall be made under such method as, in the opinion of the Secretary [of the Treasury], does clearly reflect income." I.R.C. § 446(a), (b). It is well established that the Commissioner enjoys "broad discretion" to determine whether, "'in (his) opinion,'" a taxpayer's accounting methods clearly reflect income, *Thor Power Tool, supra*, 439 U.S. at 540, ... (quoting 26 C.F.R. § 1.446-1(a)(2)), and the Commissioner's exercise of his discretion must be upheld unless it is clearly unlawful:

> In construing § 446 and its predecessors, the Court has held that "[t]he Commissioner has broad powers in determining whether accounting methods used by a taxpayer clearly reflect income." *Commissioner v. Hansen*, 360 U.S. 446, 467, ... (1959). Since the Commissioner has "[m]uch latitude for discretion," his interpretation of the statute's clear-reflection standard "should not be interfered with unless clearly unlawful." *Lucas v. American Code Co.*, 280 U.S. 445, 449, ... (1930).... The task of a reviewing court, therefore, is not to determine whether in its own opinion RCA's method of accounting for prepaid service contract income "clearly reflect[ed] income," but to determine whether there is an adequate basis in law for the Commissioner's conclusion that it did not. Our review of the relevant decisions persuades us that the law adequately supports the Commissioner's action.

In *Michigan, supra*, the first Supreme Court ruling on tax accounting for income received in respect of services to be performed in the future upon demand, the taxpayer received income in the form of prepaid membership dues and promised, in exchange, to perform various services for its members upon demand at any time during the twelve-month term of the membership agreement. In order to match prepaid dues revenues with related expenses, the taxpayer assumed that members would demand services at a constant rate during the contract term and credited prepaid membership dues to current income on a monthly pro rata basis to match the hypothetical rate of demand for services. The Supreme Court upheld the Commissioner's rejection of this method, reasoning that it was "purely artificial and [bore] no relation to the services which [the taxpayer] may in fact be called upon to render." 353 U.S. at 189....

...

Subsequently, in *AAA, supra*, a Supreme Court case that involved a method of deferring recognition of prepaid membership dues income "substantially identical," 367 U.S. at 691, ... to that employed by the taxpayer in Michigan, the taxpayer argued that the Commissioner had abused his discretion in rejecting its deferral method of accounting because it had shown at trial that its method accorded with generally accepted accounting principles and was justified by its past experience in providing services. Despite this showing, the Court upheld the Commissioner's rejection of the method. The Court stated as follows:

> When [the] receipt [of prepaid dues] as earned income is recognized ratably over two calendar years, without regard to correspondingly fixed individual ex-

pense or performance justification, but consistently with overall experience, their accounting doubtless presents a rather accurate image of the total financial structure, but fails to respect the criteria of annual tax accounting and may be rejected by the Commissioner....

[F]indings merely reflecting statistical computations of average monthly cost per member on a group or pool basis are without determinate significance to our decision that the federal revenue cannot, without legislative consent and over objection of the Commissioner, be made to depend upon average experience in rendering performance and turning a profit.

Id. 367 U.S. at 692–93....

Finally, in *Schlude, supra,* the third Supreme Court case on the subject, the taxpayers, operators of a dance studio, contracted with some of their students to provide a specified number of dancing lessons in exchange for a prepaid fee; the lessons were to be given from time to time, as the student specified, during the contract term. For both tax and book accounting purposes, the taxpayers credited contract prepayments to a deferred income account, and then at the end of each fiscal period credited to current income for that period the fraction of the contract price that represented the fraction of the total number of hours of instruction available under the contract that the student had actually used during the period. In addition, if for more than a year a student failed to request any lessons, the taxpayer treated the contract as canceled and recognized gain to the extent of the amount of the student's prepayment. Despite the fact that the taxpayer's method of accounting was based largely on its actual performance of services during the taxable year, the court upheld the Commissioner's rejection of the method, viewing the case as "squarely controlled" by *AAA,* 372 U.S. at 134, ... because the taxpayer was required to perform services under its contracts only at the student's demand, *id.* at 135....

The policy considerations that underlie *Michigan, AAA,* and *Schlude* are quite clear. When a taxpayer receives income in the form of prepayments in respect of services to be performed in the future upon demand, it is impossible for the taxpayer to know, at the outset of the contract term, the amount of service that his customer will ultimately require, and, consequently, it is impossible for the taxpayer to predict *with certainty* the amount of net income, *i.e.,* the amount of the excess of revenues over expenses of performance, that he will ultimately earn from the contract. For purposes of financial accounting, this uncertainty is tolerable; the financial accountant merely estimates future demands for performance and defers recognition of income accordingly. Tax accounting, however, "can give no quarter to uncertainty." *Thor Power Tool, supra,* 439 U.S. at 543,.... The entire process of government depends on the expeditious collection of tax revenues. Tax accounting therefore tends to compute taxable income on the basis of the taxpayer's present ability to pay the tax, as manifested by his current cash flow, without regard to deductions that may later accrue.... By the same token, tax accounting is necessarily hostile to accounting practices that defer recognition of income, and thus payment of the tax on it, on the basis of estimates and projections that may ultimately prove unsound.

In view of the relevant Supreme Court decisions and the policies they reflect, we cannot say that the Commissioner abused his discretion in rejecting RCA's method of accounting for service contract income. Like the service agreements at issue in *Michigan, AAA,* and *Schlude,* RCA's service contracts obligated it to perform services only upon the customer's demand. Thus, at the beginning of the contract term, RCA could not know the extent of the performance that the customer might ultimately require, and it could not be certain of the amount of income that it would ultimately earn from the contract. The Commissioner was not required to subject the federal revenues to the vicissitudes of RCA customers' future demands for services. Accordingly, he acted within his discretion in requiring RCA to report its prepaid service contract income upon receipt....

Equally unpersuasive are RCA's efforts to distinguish *AAA* and *Schlude*. RCA contends that the accounting practices at issue in those cases, which were based on the past demand for services, differ significantly from its own, which was based on relatively scientific projections of the future demand for services, and that its accounting method was valid under *AAA* and *Schlude*.... We think, however, that the differences between RCA's method and the others are immaterial in the present context. As noted above, the vice of the systems treated in *AAA* and *Schlude* was their tendency to subject government revenues to the uncertainties inherent in prognostications about the rate at which customers would demand services in the future. RCA's system shared this vice. Although RCA's predictions may have been more accurate than those of the taxpayers in *AAA* and *Schlude*, they were predictions nonetheless, and the Commissioner was not required to accept them as determinants of the federal revenue.

RCA's other arguments on this score require but brief discussion. While the Commissioner has permitted certain forms of accrual accounting in Rev. Proc. 71-21, *supra*, and Rev. Rul. 71-299, *supra*, that does not necessarily mean, as RCA asserts, that the Commissioner has conceded the correctness of RCA's position in this litigation. As we have emphasized above, the Commissioner possesses considerable discretion in these matters, and he was at liberty to alter his stance toward the accounting practices at issue here in light of his greater experience with them and their effect on revenue collection. In addition, although the district court found that RCA's accounting practices did "clearly reflect income," we are not bound by that finding under the "clearly erroneous" standard of Fed. R. Civ. P. 52. The issue before the district court was not whether RCA's accounting method adequately reflected income, but whether the Commissioner abused his discretion in determining that it did not. The latter question is one of law, and for the reasons stated above we conclude that the Commissioner did not abuse his discretion. (Footnote 10)

III

...

Finally, we conclude that we need not decide whether Rev. Proc. 71-21 and Rev. Rul. 71-299 are retroactive. Both require the taxpayer to obtain the Commissioner's consent before employing the accounting procedures permissible under them. Rev. Proc. 71-21 at § 5.01. (Footnote 12) RCA has neither sought nor obtained the Commissioner's consent to adopt those procedures. Accordingly, it may not use them even if the Procedure and Ruling are retroactive.

IV

For the reasons stated above, we reverse the judgment of the district court and remand the matter with instructions to dismiss the complaint.

FOOTNOTES:

2. The companies had learned from experience that customers were more likely to seek service during certain seasons and on certain days of the week than they were at other

times. RCA's statistics projected future demand on the basis of observed variations in past demand.

3. Although RCAS had employed an accrual method of tax accounting for this income in 1946 and 1947, it adopted the cash method in 1948, after the Commissioner rejected its accrual method as not clearly reflecting income.

4. Section 446(e) provides as follows:

(e) Requirement respecting change of accounting method.—Except as otherwise expressly provided in this chapter, a taxpayer who changes the method of accounting on the basis of which he regularly computes his income in keeping his books shall, before computing his taxable income under the new method, secure the consent of the Secretary.

5. Sections 446(a) and (b) provide as follows:

(a) General rule.—Taxable income shall be computed under the method of accounting on the basis of which the taxpayer regularly computes his income in keeping his books.

(b) Exceptions.—If no method of accounting has been regularly used by the taxpayer, or if the method used does not clearly reflect income, the computation of taxable income shall be made under such method as, in the opinion of the Secretary, does clearly reflect income.

7. Section 3.02 of Revenue Procedure 71-21, on which RCA relies, provides, in relevant part:

An accrual method taxpayer who, pursuant to an agreement (written or otherwise), receives a payment in one taxable year for services, where all of the services under such agreement are required by the agreement as it exists at the end of the taxable year of receipt to be performed by him before the end of the next succeeding taxable year, may include such payment in gross income as earned through the performance of the services,....

Revenue Ruling 71-299 simply states that Revenue Procedure 71-21 supercedes several earlier revenue rulings to the extent that they are inconsistent with the new Revenue Procedure.

10. In view of our disposition of this issue, we do not address the government's argument that, absent express legislative authorization and the Commissioner's consent, deferring recognition of income items in accordance with the principles of accrual accounting is never permissible.

12. Section 5.01 provides:

Any change by a taxpayer from his present method of

including amounts in gross income to the method prescribed in section 3.02 of this Revenue Procedure is a change in method of accounting to which section 446 ... appl[ies].

Section 446(e), quoted in full at note 4, *supra*, provides that a taxpayer wishing to change his accounting method must obtain the consent of the Secretary of the Treasury.

———————

Consider the following questions concerning *RCA*.

1. Was RCA Corp. a cash or accrual basis taxpayer?

2. What type of income was at issue in the case?

3. How did RCA Corp. account for the income for tax purposes?

4. Why did the court state that there is a "fundamental tension" between the purposes of financial and tax accounting?

5. Why is tax accounting "necessarily hostile" to accounting practices that defer recognition of income?

6. Note the court's discussion of the trio of Supreme Court cases that began with *Automobile Club of Michigan v. Commissioner*, 353 U.S. 180 (1957). What are the key factors that led the Supreme Court to its decision in these three cases?

7. Suppose a taxpayer offered a service contract covering a period of three years that provided that if the customer required no service during that period, the taxpayer would refund the price of the contract less a 20% service fee. Would the result be the same as in RCA?

8. Suppose a service contract offered the right to three service calls per year for three years for a fixed price. Could the service provider allocate the income among the three years, one-third to each? Would your answer change if the three visits per year were mandatory? In *Artnell Co. v. Commissioner*, 400 F.2d 981 (7th Cir. 1968), the court distinguished the Supreme Court trilogy in a case involving prepaid baseball season tickets, prepaid parking permits, and broadcasting rights, good only on dates that were readily identifiable. The court accepted the taxpayer's argument that the future services would be rendered only on those certain identifiable dates. This case marks a rare exception to the Supreme Court trilogy. Moreover, the Supreme Court did not review the case.

9. The RCA case also cites Revenue Procedure 71-21, 1971-2 C.B. 549. That procedure provides that an accrual method taxpayer does not have to include advance payments in income until the services are performed, provided the services are performed no later than the end of the next tax year. (But, the Revenue Procedure specifically excludes prepayments of rent or interest.) Does that procedure mean that RCA could enter into a service contract shortly after the start of one tax year that will expire at the end of the following tax year and defer a portion of the income to the second year?

(2) Prepayments of Interest

Interest has always created special problems, no matter what the accounting method of the taxpayer. Although it might come as a surprise, the Service requires an accrual method taxpayer to report interest income in the year of its receipt, even if the interest relates to a later period.[8] The Service reasoned that even if the debtor might be entitled to a refund of all or part of the prepaid interest if he repaid the debt early, the lender receives the prepayment under claim of right and has complete dominion and control over it. (**Once again, remember *Lewis*.**)

In addition to the problems of prepayments of interest, another income item that has produced controversy concerns treatment of various types of discounts. A common example of this type of discount sometimes occurs in connection with the issuance of a mortgage loan. Suppose that the borrower must pay "points" at the initiation of a loan. What are points? They simply represent additional interest on the loan. In contrast to the normal method for calculating interest, however, points represent a percentage of the entire initial amount borrowed and are payable only once.

---

8. Revenue Ruling 58-225, 1958-1 C.B. 258.

The borrower may pay the points in several different ways. Of course, he is always free to take money out of his pocket to pay the points. But, the more common way is to pay the points out of the mortgage loan. In that case, the transaction may occur in one of two ways: (1) either the lender will deduct the points from the face amount of the loan and then issue a check for the balance to the borrower (who then endorses it to the property owner); or (2) the lender will issue a check for the full amount to the borrower who then issues a check back to the lender for the points and a check for the balance to the seller.

Whether the lender deducts the points before cutting the check for the balance of the loan or gives the borrower the full amount out of which the borrower pays the points, the borrower must still repay the full amount of the points plus the balance to the lender, the points representing interest. If the borrower draws an immediate check to his lender for the points, the lender must report that income immediately.[9] If, however, the loan is discounted, each payment by the borrower to the lender includes both regular interest on the loan and a partial payment of the points, as well as part principal.

A variation of this type of discount occurs in connection with the issuing of bonds. Suppose the issuer of the bond issues the bond for less than its face value. A common example of this is the so-called "zero-coupon bond" that is issued for a fraction of its face value but pays no interest during its term. In that case, when the bond is paid off, the investor receives the face value of the bond. How should she characterize the difference between the price she paid and the amount she receives? Remember, the borrower paid no interest during the period the bond was outstanding. If you answered that the difference constituted interest on the loan, you were correct. In other words, the lender (purchaser of the bond), lent the borrower (the issuer of the bond), a certain sum (the discounted amount), and the borrower paid it back with interest. Then how should the lender account for the interest, all in the year paid at retirement of the bond or over the period the bond was outstanding?

For many transactions involving discounts, including both the discounted points described above and these zero coupon bonds, Congress has adopted this latter view and in a series of very complicated statutory rules, called the "original issue discount" or "OID" rules, requires taxpayers to report the income over the life of the loan or the life of the bond.[10]

2. Items of Expense

a. General Rule

Treasury Regulation section 1.461-1(a)(2)(i) provides that an accrual method taxpayer deducts an expense "in the taxable year in which all the events have occurred that establish the fact of the liability, the amount of the liability can be determined with reasonable accuracy, and economic performance has occurred with respect to the liability."

---

9. Revenue Ruling 74-607, 1974-2 C.B. 149, provides that all the events occur that fix an accrual basis taxpayer's right to receive income when: (1) the required performance occurs, (2) payment is due, or (3) payment is made, whichever happens earliest.

10. See further discussion of the OID rules in Chapter 2.B. *infra*. For those who are interested in a fuller discussion of OID, *see* Marvin A. Chirelstein, *Federal Income Taxation*, 383 *et seq.* (9th ed. 2002).

The long-standing rule for accrual of expenses required satisfaction of only the first two of these three prongs: that all events had occurred to establish the fact of the liability and that the amount could be determined with reasonable accuracy. In a number of cases, these rules forced taxpayers to defer the accrual of an expense because of uncertainty as to the ultimate amount; in others, the issue was whether all the events had occurred that established the fact of the liability. Consider the following case.

PUTOMA CORP. v. COMMISSIONER
601 F.2d 734 (5th Cir. 1979)

SKELTON, Senior Judge.

This is an income tax case that involves an appeal by ... Putoma Corporation (Putoma), successor by merger of Pro-Mac Company (Pro-Mac), with J. M. Hunt and wife, Inez Hunt,....

At all times pertinent to this case, Putoma Corporation and Pro-Mac Company were Texas corporations using the accrual basis of accounting....

THE ISSUE PRESENTED BY THE TAXPAYERS IS:

... Whether the Tax Court erred in holding that said accrual basis corporations, which accrued certain compensation for their officer shareholders, Lee Roy Purselley and J. M. Hunt, under a fixed formula, but which was not paid, were not entitled to deduct such compensation on the ground that their obligation for same was conditional and not properly accruable during the years in question....

We consider first the ... issue involving the accrued compensation for officer-shareholders Purselley and Hunt, which was never paid but was deducted by the corporations.

I. DEDUCTIONS FOR ACCRUED UNPAID COMPENSATION.

The facts relevant to this appeal by taxpayers were found by the Tax Court as follows:

At a meeting of Putoma's directors held in July, 1964, Purselley's salary was set at $600 per month, retroactive from July 1, 1963. This salary was not to be paid, but was to accrue to his credit until such time as, in the judgment of the majority of directors, corporate earnings were sufficient to justify payment of the salary. In addition, as part of his compensation, Purselley was to receive 25 percent of the corporation's net profits. Compensation from July 1, 1964, was to be determined at a future meeting.

The minutes of the board of directors' meeting for Putoma held on August 23, 1965, contain the following statement relating to salary:

Upon motion duly made and seconded, the salary of Lee Roy Purselley for the current year was fixed at $2,000.00 per month plus 25% of the net profit of the corporation after deduction of the $2,000.00 monthly salary, but before deduction for any bonus or Federal income taxes. This salary is to be retroactive from July 1, 1965. Such salary in excess of the $2,000.00 per month is not to be paid but to accrue to his credit until such time as in the judgment of the majority of the directors of the company, the company has such cash reserve in order to pay the additional salary.

Upon further motion duly made and seconded, the salary of J. M. Hunt was established at 10% of the net income of the company before the deduction of any bonus or Federal income taxes. This salary is to be retroactive from July 1, 1965. Such salary is not to be paid, but to accrue to his credit until such time as in the judgment of the majority of the directors of the company, the company has sufficient cash reserve in order to pay the salary.

The compensation formula set out above remained unchanged until January 1, 1970. At a meeting of Putoma's directors held on December 10, 1969, bonuses for Purselley and Hunt were discontinued as of December 31, 1969, and Purselley's salary was set at $3,000 per month beginning January 1, 1970....

Pro-Mac was formed on December 1, 1966. Article V, Section 4 of Pro-Mac's by-laws provides that the salaries of corporate officers are to be fixed by the board of directors. The minutes of the organizational meeting of Pro-Mac's board of directors, however, contain no mention of officer compensation. Further, there were no board of directors' minutes for Pro-Mac during the period November 30, 1966, through July 18, 1969. Nevertheless, Pro-Mac's books and records for that period reflect that the corporation consistently recorded a salary expense of $1,000 per month for both Hunt and Purselley, and further recorded a bonus expense equal to 25 percent of profits for Purselley and bonus expense equal to 10 percent of profits for Hunt. The Tax Court found, however, that the salaries and bonuses for Purselley and Hunt recorded by Pro-Mac on its books were not payable until Pro-Mac's earnings were sufficient to permit payment.

The first minutes to discuss compensation for Pro-Mac's officers were those of a directors' meeting held December 10, 1969. At that time, it was decided to discontinue the bonuses for Purselley and Hunt and to fix Purselley's salary at $3,000 per month commencing January 1, 1970. At a subsequent meeting held August 27, 1970, a $1,000 per month salary was also voted for Hunt, retroactive to January 1, 1970. Due to the low cash condition of the corporation, Hunt's salary was to be recorded in his "accrued salary account," but was not to be paid until a later date when the corporation was "financially able."

...

At a meeting of Putoma's board of directors on July 9, 1970, a discussion was held concerning the current financial condition of the corporation. It was agreed that in order to reflect a better financial condition to creditors and potential lenders, Hunt and Purselley would be asked to forgive a portion of the salaries shown owing to them on the books. Substantially the same decision was made by Pro-Mac's board of directors in a meeting held the same day.

On September 15, 1970, Purselley and Hunt forgave the following items shown owing to them on the books and records of Putoma and Pro-Mac:

	PUTOMA	PRO-MAC
Lee Roy Purselley accrued salary	$ 89,109.06	$ 44,453.50
Hunt accrued salary	66,938.36	35,673.76
Hunt accrued interest	22,170.70	2,779.74
Hunt accrued commission	–	6,000.00
Total	$178,218.12	$88,907.00

On September 15, 1970, Purselley's accrued payroll account on Putoma's books showed a balance of $194,626.32, before forgiveness, and $106,017.26 after forgiveness. Hunt's accrued payroll account on Putoma's books and records showed a balance of $66,938.36 before forgiveness and $0 after forgiveness.

On September 15, 1970, Purselley's accrued payroll balance on Pro-Mac's books showed a balance of $72,064.09 before forgiveness and $27,610.59 after forgiveness. Hunt's accrued payroll account on Pro-Mac's books showed a balance of $37,673.76 before forgiveness and $2,000 after forgiveness.

On their returns for the years in issue, the taxpayer corporations claimed deductions for the salaries and bonuses for Purselley and Hunt which they had accrued on their corporate books. The Commissioner disallowed the deductions to the extent they represented accrued but unpaid salaries on the ground that taxpayers' liability for the accrued salaries and bonuses was contingent and not fixed during the years in question. The Tax Court, in a reviewed opinion with no dissents as to this issue, sustained the Commissioner's determination.

Ever since the Supreme Court rendered its opinion in *United States v. Anderson*, 269 U.S. 422, ... (1926), it has been the rule that accrual taxpayers, such as Putoma and Pro-Mac in the instant case, may deduct an expense in the taxable year in which "all the events" have occurred which determine the fact of liability and which fix with reasonable certainty the amount of such liability. In that case the court said:

> "Only a word need be said with reference to the contention that the tax upon munitions manufactured and sold in 1916 did not accrue until 1917. In a technical legal sense it may be argued that a tax does not accrue until it has been assessed and becomes due; but it is also true that in advance of the assessment of a tax, all the events may occur which fix the amount of the tax and determine the liability of the taxpayer to pay it. In this respect, for purposes of accounting and of ascertaining true income for a given accounting period, the munitions tax here in question did not stand on any different footing than other accrued expenses appearing on appellee's books. In the economic and bookkeeping sense with which the statute and Treasury decision were concerned, the taxes had accrued." 269 U.S. 440–441....

The "all events" test has been applied many times by various courts since the decision in *Anderson* was handed down.... In fact, the test is now included in the Treasury Regulations as follows:

> "Under an accrual method of accounting, an expense is deductible for the taxable year in which all the events have occurred which determine the fact of the liability and the amount thereof can be determined with reasonable accuracy." Treas. Reg. § 1.461-1(a)(2) (1970), promulgated by T.D. 6282, 1958-1 Cum. Bull. 215, ... 26 C.F.R. § 1.461-1(a)(2) (1970).

Stated conversely, the accrual of an item of expense is improper where the liability for such item in the taxable year is contingent upon the occurrence of future events.... The Supreme Court stated in *Brown [v. Helvering], supra*:

> "Except as otherwise specifically provided by statute, a liability does not accrue as long as it remains contingent...." 291 U.S. 200....

This court held in *Guardian Investment Corporation v. Phinney, supra*:

> "A contingent obligation may be a liability, but it is not a debt: and accrual is improper for tax deductions when the liability is contingent." 253 F.2d 329.

The Court of Claims held in *Union Pacific R. R. Co. v. United States, supra*:

> "So long as a liability remains contingent or if the liability has attached but the amount cannot be reasonably estimated, a business expense deduction is not allowed." 524 F.2d 1350....

The foregoing authorities show that without dispute the all-events test is incorporated in the law. The only question to be answered in this case is whether or not the test has been met. Putoma and Pro-Mac contend that the accrued salaries and bonuses were definite fixed obligations that were mathematically arrived at under an authorized and definite formula, and that only the payment was deferred. They argue that under these facts the all-events test has been complied with. We do not agree.

The minutes of Putoma's Board of Directors' meeting held on August 23, 1965, quoted above, show that the Board set Purselley's salary at $2,000 per month plus a bonus of 25% of the net profit of the corporation. However, the payment of the bonus was made conditional on the financial condition of the corporation by the following minutes:

> "Such salary in excess of the $2,000 per month is not to be paid but to accrue to his credit until such time as in the judgment of the majority of the directors of the company, the company has such cash reserve in order to pay the additional salary."

As a part of the same minutes, the Board set Hunt's salary at 10% of the net income of the corporation which was not to be paid, like Purselley's bonus, until such time as in the judgment of the directors, the corporation had sufficient cash reserve in order to pay the salary. In this regard, the minutes provided:

> "Upon further motion duly made and seconded, the salary of J. M. Hunt was established at 10% of the net income of the company before the deduction of any bonus or Federal income taxes. This salary is to be retroactive from July 1, 1965. Such salary is not to be paid, but to accrue to his credit until such time as in the judgment of the majority of the directors of the company, the company has sufficient cash reserve in order to pay the salary."

The compensation formula set out above remained unchanged until January 1, 1970. At a meeting of Putoma's directors held on December 10, 1969, bonuses for Purselley and Hunt were discontinued as of December 31, 1969, and Purselley's salary was set at $3,000 per month beginning January 1, 1970.

It is clear from these minutes of the Board that Putoma had no fixed obligation during the years involved to pay Hunt's salary or Purselley's bonus. Such obligation was not to come into being until sometime in the future when the directors determined that the corporation had sufficient cash reserve to make the payments.

Pro-Mac had a similar arrangement. Its books showed that Purselley was entitled to a bonus of 25% of the company's profits and that Hunt was entitled to a bonus of 10% of the profits of the company. The Tax Court found that Pro-Mac's liability for these salaries and bonuses, like those of Putoma, were contingent on the financial condition of the company.

We conclude that the obligation of Putoma and Pro-Mac to pay the salaries was not a fixed obligation but was contingent and conditioned on future events, namely, the financial condition of the corporations and the determination of the same by their Boards of Directors. In addition to the authorities cited above that prohibit the deduction of contingent and conditional obligations, see this court's decision in *Burlington-Rock Island Railroad Co. v. United States*, 321 F.2d 817 (5 Cir. 1963), *cert. denied*, 377 U.S. 943, 84 S.Ct. 1349, 12 L.Ed.2d 306 (1964). In that case, the taxpayer sought to deduct accrued but unpaid interest on its debt to its shareholder-creditors. Under the terms of an agreement entered into with its creditors, the taxpayer was required to make the interest payments "from time to time, insofar as its cash situation will reasonably permit." In disallowing the claimed interest deductions, this Court pointed out that the agreement created only a conditional obligation to pay the interest and that the creditors could enforce payment only by showing that taxpayer had sufficient funds for that purpose. The court then went on to conclude:

"Burlington's [taxpayer's] duty to pay the statutory interest was thus contingent upon its financial situation, and no legal obligation could arise under the agreement until the occurrence of that contingency." 321 F.2d 821.

Also, see *Pierce Estates v. Commissioner*, 195 F.2d 475 (3 Cir. 1952). There, the taxpayer was obligated to pay annual interest at a fixed rate but only from its net income "as ascertained and declared by its board of directors." The court held that the taxpayer had correctly deducted the interest in the year of payment rather than accruing and deducting the interest each year because its legal duty to pay the interest was contingent on the actions of its directors. In so holding, the court stated:

"Because interest is compensation for the use or forbearance of money it ordinarily accrues as an item of expense from day to day even though its payment may be deferred until a latter date. But this is not true if the payment is not merely deferred but the obligation to pay at all is wholly contingent upon the happening of a later event as, for example, the subsequent earning of profits. In the latter case, the interest may not be regarded as an accrued expense until the year in which, by the earnings of the profits the contingency is satisfied and the obligation to pay becomes fixed and absolute." 195 F.2d 477.

We hold that the all-events test was not met as to salaries and bonuses of Purselley and Hunt and that the deductions of such items were improperly made by Putoma and Pro-Mac. (Footnote 7)

FOOTNOTE:

7. The Commissioner contends alternatively that if the salary and bonus deductions were properly made, Putoma and Pro-Mac should be required to restore them to their income under the tax benefit rule when they were forgiven by Purselley and Hunt. In view of our disposition of this part of the case, we do not reach that question.

Consider the following questions about *Putoma*.

1. Which of the prongs was at issue in this case?

2. Suppose a corporate employer established a plan that provided for the payment of bonuses to its key executives on the last day of the calendar year, December 31. But, the plan also provided that when the corporation's fiscal year ended on March 31, it would calculate corporate earnings for the year. If corporate earnings were equal to an amount set aside for dividends to its common holders and the amount of the bonuses, the employees could retain their bonuses. If, however, corporate earnings turned out to be insufficient to cover the amount of the bonuses, the key executives agreed to return all or part of their bonuses to the company.

Recall *Lewis* and our discussion following it. Suppose a cash basis employee receives her bonus on the last day of the calendar year, which is also her tax year. Whether she cashes the check or not, she will have to report income for that year. But, if the bonus plan requires that she repay all or part of the bonus in the following tax year if the corporation has insufficient earnings to support it, she will utilize section 1341 to correct for the return.

Will the payor, on the other hand, if it is an accrual basis taxpayer, be unable to deduct any amount until the following year? What policy would support this divergence in tax treatment, whereby the recipient must pay tax this year but the payor receives no deduction (reducing its tax) until the following year?

3. **Note the court's comments in footnote 7.** As one of his alternative arguments, the Commissioner asserted that if the taxpayer had properly accrued the unpaid salary and bonus, the tax benefit rule would require the company to include those amounts in income upon their forgiveness by the shareholders. **Recall our earlier discussion of the tax benefit rule in Part II.** Explain why the Commissioner made this alternative argument.

Now consider the following case, noting that the taxpayer was harmed both with respect to its income by the normal operation of the accrual method rules and with respect to its expenses by a strict statutory interpretation of the Code.

SPRING CITY FOUNDRY CO. v. COMMISSIONER
292 U.S. 182 (1934)

MR. CHIEF JUSTICE HUGHES delivered the opinion of the Court.

Petitions for writs of certiorari were granted, "limited to the question whether a debt ascertained to be partially worthless in 1920 was deductible in that year under either § 234(a)(4) or § 234(a)(5) [of the Revenue Act of 1918] and to the question whether the debt was returnable as taxable income in that year to the extent that it was then ascertained to be worthless." 291 U.S. 656.

Petitioner kept its books during the year 1920 and filed its income tax return for that year on the accrual basis. From March, 1920, to September, 1920, petitioner sold goods to the Cotta Transmission Company for which the latter became indebted in the amount of $39,983.27, represented by open account and unsecured notes. In the latter part of 1920 the Cotta Company found itself in financial straits. Efforts at settlement having failed, a petition in bankruptcy was filed against the Company on December 23, 1920, and a receiver was appointed. In the spring of 1922 the receiver paid to creditors, including petitioner, a dividend of 15 per cent. and, in 1923, a second and final dividend of 12 1/2 per cent.

Petitioner charged off on its books the entire debt on December 28, 1920, and claimed this amount as a deduction in its income tax return for that year. It included as income in its returns for 1922 and 1923 the dividends received in those years. The Commissioner disallowed the amount claimed as a deduction in 1920 but allowed a deduction in 1923 of $28,715.76, the difference between the full amount of the debt and the two dividends.

On review of the deficiency assessed by the Commissioner for 1920, the Board of Tax Appeals found that the debt was not entirely worthless at the time it was charged off. An offer had been made in November, 1920, to purchase the assets of the debtor at 33 1/3 per cent. of the creditors' claims and the offer had been declined. The Board concluded that in view of all the circumstances, including the probable expense of the receivership, the debt could be regarded as uncollectible, at the time of the charge-off, to the extent of $28,715.76, and allowed a deduction for 1920 of that amount. 25 B.T.A. 822. This ruling, contested by both the Commissioner and the taxpayer, was reversed by the Circuit Court of Appeals upon the ground that 'there was in 1920 no authority for a debt deduction unless the debt were worthless.' 67 F.(2d) 385, 387.... [T]his Court granted writs of certiorari limited as above stated.

1. Petitioner first contends that the debt, to the extent that it was ascertained in 1920 to be worthless was not returnable as gross income in that year, that is, apart from any

question of deductions, it was not to be regarded as taxable income at all. We see no merit in this contention. Keeping accounts and making returns on the accrual basis, as distinguished from the cash basis, import that it is the *right* to receive and not the actual receipt that determines the inclusion of the amount in gross income. When the right to receive an amount becomes fixed, the right accrues. When a merchandizing concern makes sales, its inventory is reduced and a claim for the purchase price arises. Article 35 of Regulations 45 under the Revenue Act of 1918 provided: "In the case of a manufacturing, merchandising, or mining business 'gross income' means the total sales, less the cost of goods sold, plus any income from investments and from incidental or outside operations or sources."

On an accrual basis, the "total sales," to which the regulation refers, are manifestly the accounts receivable arising from the sales, and these accounts receivable, less the cost of the goods sold, figure in the statement of gross income. If such accounts receivable become uncollectible, in whole or part, the question is one of the deduction which may be taken according to the applicable statute. *See United States v. Anderson*, 269 U.S. 422, 440, 441; ... *Brown v. Helvering*, 291 U.S. 193, 199.... That is the question here. It is not altered by the fact that the claim of loss relates to an item of gross income which had accrued in the same year.

2. Section 234(a)(5) of the Revenue Act of 1918 [predecessor to section 166(a)] provided for the deduction of worthless debts, in computing net income, as follows: "Debts ascertained to be worthless and charged off within the taxable year." Under this provision, the taxpayer could not establish a right to the deduction simply by charging off the debt. It must be ascertained to be worthless within the taxable year. In this instance, in 1920, the debt was in suspense by reason of the bankruptcy of the debtor but it was not a total loss. What eventually might be recovered upon it was uncertain, but recovery to some extent was reasonably to be expected. The receiver continued the business and substantial amounts were subsequently realized for the creditors. In this view, the Board of Tax Appeals decided that the petitioner did not sustain a loss in 1920 "equal to the total amount of the debt" and hence that the entire debt was not deductible in that year. The question, then, is whether petitioner was entitled to a deduction in 1920 for the portion of the debt which ultimately—on the winding up in bankruptcy—proved to be uncollectible. Such a deduction of a part of the debt, the Government contends and the Circuit Court of Appeals held, the Act of 1918 did not authorize. The Government points to the literal meaning of the words of the statute, to the established administrative construction, and to the action of the Congress in recognition of that construction. "Worthless," says the Government, means destitute of worth, of no value or use. This was the interpretation of the statute by the Treasury Department. Article 151 of Regulations 45 (made applicable to corporations by Article 561) provided that "An account merely written down" is not deductible. (Footnote 3) To the same effect was the corresponding provision of the regulations under the Revenue Act of 1916.

The right to charge off and deduct a *portion* of a debt where during the taxable year the debt was found to be recoverable only in part, was granted by the Act of 1921. By that Act, section 234(a)(5), 42 Stat. 254, was changed so as to read: "Debts ascertained to be worthless and charged off within the taxable year (or in the discretion of the Commissioner, a reasonable addition to a reserve for bad debts); and when satisfied that a debt is recoverable only in part, the Commissioner may allow such debt to be charged off in part." We think that the fair import of this provision, as contrasted with the earlier one, is that the Congress, recognizing the significance of the existing provision and its appropriate construction by the Treasury Department, deliberately intended a change in the law. . . .

This intent is shown clearly by the statement in the report of the Committee on Ways and Means of the House of Representatives in relation to the new provision. The Committee said explicitly:—"Under the present law worthless debts are deductible in full or not at all." (Footnote 5) While the change was struck out by the Finance Committee of the Senate, the provision was restored on the floor of the Senate and became a law as proposed by the House. Regulations 62 issued by the Treasury Department under the Act of 1921 made a corresponding change in Article 151. The Treasury Department consistently adhered to the former rule in dealing with deductions sought under the Act of 1918. (Footnote 7)

In numerous decisions the Board of Tax Appeals has taken the same view of the provision of the Act of 1918. (Footnote 8) ... The contrary result in the instant case was reached in deference to the opinion expressed by the Circuit Court of Appeals of the Second Circuit in *Sherman & Bryan, Inc., v. Commissioner*, 35 F.(2d) 713, 716, and by the Court of Appeals of the District of Columbia in *Davidson Grocery Co. v. Lucas*, ... 37 F.(2d) 806, 808—views which are opposed to those of the Circuit Courts of Appeals of the Eighth Circuit in *Minnehaha National Bank v. Commissioner*, 28 F. (2d) 763, 764, and of the Fifth Circuit in *Collin County National Bank v. Commissioner*, 48 F. (2d) 207, 208.

We are of opinion that section 234(a)(5) of the Act of 1918 authorized only the deduction of a debt ascertained to be worthless and charged off within the taxable year; that it did not authorize the deduction of a debt which was not then ascertained to be worthless but was recoverable in part, the amount that was not recoverable being still uncertain. Here, in 1923, on the winding up, the debt that then remained unpaid, after deducting the dividends received, was ascertained to be worthless and the Commissioner allowed deduction accordingly in that year.

3. Petitioner also claims the right of deduction under section § 234(a)(4) [predecessor to section 165(a)] of the Act of 1918 providing for the deduction of "losses sustained during the taxable year and not compensated for by insurance or otherwise." We agree with the decision below that this subdivision and the following subdivision (5) relating to debts are mutually exclusive. . . . The making of the specific provision as to debts indicates that these were to be considered as a special class and that losses on debts were not to be regarded as falling under the preceding general provision. What was excluded from deduction under subdivision (5) cannot be regarded as allowed under subdivision (4). If subdivision (4) could be considered as ambiguous in this respect, the administrative construction which has been followed from the enactment of the statute—that subdivision (4) did not refer to debts—would be entitled to great weight. We see no reason for disturbing that construction.

Petitioner insists that "good business practice" forbade the inclusion in the taxpayer's assets of the account receivable in question or at least the part of it which was subsequently found to be uncollectible. But that is not the question here. Questions relating to allowable deductions under the income tax act are quite distinct from matters which pertain to an appropriate showing upon which credit is sought. It would have been proper for the taxpayer to carry the debt in question in a suspense account awaiting the ultimate determination of the amount that could be realized upon it, and thus to indicate the status of the debt in financial statements of the taxpayer's condition. But that proper practice, in order to advise those from whom credit might be sought of uncertainties in the realization of assets, does not affect the construction of the statute, or make the debt deductible in 1920, when the entire debt was not worthless, when the amount which would prove uncollectible was not yet ascertained, rather than in 1923 when that amount was ascertained and its deduction allowed.

We conclude that the ruling of the Circuit Court of Appeals was correct.

Judgment affirmed.

FOOTNOTES:

3. Article 151 of Regulations 45 provided: "Bad debts.—An account merely written down or a debt recognized as worthless prior to the beginning of the taxable year is not deductible. Where all the surrounding and attendant circumstances indicate that a debt is worthless and uncollectible and that legal action to enforce payment would in all probability not result in the satisfaction of execution on a judgment, a showing of these facts will be sufficient evidence of the worthlessness of the debt for the purpose of deduction. Bankruptcy may or may not be an indication of the worthlessness of a debt, and actual determination of worthlessness in such a case is sometimes possible before and at other times only when a settlement in bankruptcy shall have been had...."

...

5. H.Rep. No. 350, 67th Cong., 1st sess., p. 11. The statement of the Committee is: "Under the present law worthless debts are deductible in full or not at all, but Section 214 would authorize the Commissioner to permit a deduction for debts recoverable only in part, or in his discretion to recognize a reserve for bad debts—a method of providing for bad debts much less subject to abuse than the method of writing off bad debts required by the present law." Section 214 related to deductions by individuals and contained the same new provision as that inserted in §234(a)(5), quoted in the text, with respect to deductions by corporations.

7. In Treasury decision 3262, I-1, Cumulative Bulletin, January–June, 1922, 152, 153, it was said: "No deduction shall be allowed for the part of a debt ascertained to be worthless and charged off prior to January 1, 1921, unless and until the debt is ascertained to be totally worthless and is finally charged off or charged down to a nominal amount, or the loss is determined in some other manner by a closed and completed transaction." ...

8. The members of the Board of Tax Appeals who dissented in the instant case pointed out that the Board had "consistently held in at least twenty-three cases that under the Revenue Act of 1918 no deduction may be taken where a taxpayer ascertains that a debt is recoverable only in part." 25 B.T.A., 834.

———

Consider the following questions.

1. What is a "receiver"?

2. In 1922 and 1923, the receiver paid a "dividend" of 15% and 12.5% respectively. What does that mean?

3. In what way does the tax accounting in this case deviate from the financial accounting? **You might also wish to refer back to** *RCA*. How did the court justify the divergence?

Note that the taxpayers in both *RCA* and *Spring City* were attempting to use experience to modify the normal rules of their method of tax accounting. It is interesting to note that in the Revenue Act of 1921, following the *Spring City* case, Congress authorized both deduction of partially worthless debts and the setting up of a reserve for bad debts for tax purposes. This latter provision remained in the Code until 1986. The Code continues to authorize deduction of partially worthless debts that arise in a trade or business.

4. Why does it matter if the proper deduction of the unpaid receivables should be treated as a bad debt rather than as a loss or vice versa? **Compare sections 165(a) with sections 166(a) and 166(d).**

5. Would this business have achieved a better result if it had used the cash method of accounting? What, if anything, would prevent a company like Spring City Foundry from using the cash method? **Read Treasury Regulation section 1.446-1(c)(2)(i).** What justifies this rule?

The Court stated that a business must accrue income equal to its sales less its "cost of goods sold." **Look at Treasury Regulation section 1.61-3.** What is the "cost of goods sold"? Cost of goods sold is the cost of inventory sold during the period. In determining the cost of inventory, a taxpayer must use his usual method of accounting.

> To compute the cost of the goods that have been sold during the period (the Cost of Goods Sold), you look at how much you had at the beginning of the period (Beginning Inventory) and how much you added during the period (Inventory Purchased or Manufactured), and compare that to what's left at the end of the period (Ending Inventory).... The difference is what you sold.
>
> **The Cost of Goods Sold**—the inventory sold during the period—is an expense. Selling those goods produced revenue and the cost of the goods must be subtracted from that revenue to determine the net income or loss arising from the sales.[11]

b. Economic Performance

Until the Deficit Reduction Act of 1984, the all-events test for accrual of deductions did not contain the requirement that economic performance occur before a taxpayer could accrue a deduction. Thus, in order to accrue a deduction, the taxpayer had only to show that the fact of the liability was established and that she could determine the amount with reasonable accuracy. Read the following case and determine how the taxpayer attempted to use those two requirements to its advantage.

MOONEY AIRCRAFT, INC. v. UNITED STATES
420 F.2d 400 (5th Cir. 1969)

CASSIBRY, District Judge.

Mooney Aircraft, Inc. (taxpayer) seeks refund of federal income taxes for the fiscal years ending September 30, 1959, October 31, 1962, and October 31, 1963. The district court granted the Government's motion for summary judgment and the taxpayer appeals.

---

11. C. Steven Bradford and Gary Adna Ames, *Basic Accounting Principles for Lawyers* 54 (1997).

This is yet another case in the continuing conflict between commercial accounting practice and the federal income tax. The facts, as accepted by the parties for the purpose of the motion for summary judgment, may be summarized as follows:

During the years 1961 through 1965 taxpayer was in the business of manufacturing and selling single-engine, executive aircraft. The taxpayer's practice was to sell exclusively to regional distributors throughout the United States and Canada. These distributors sold to more localized dealers who in turn sold to the ultimate consumers.

During the fiscal years ending October 31, 1961, 1963, 1964 and 1965 taxpayer issued, with each aircraft which it manufactured and sold, a document captioned "Mooney Bond" setting out an unconditional promise that taxpayer would pay to the bearer the sum of $1,000 when the corresponding aircraft should be permanently retired from service. (Footnote 1) By far the great majority of the "Mooney Bonds" issued by the taxpayer were retained by the distributors to whom they were originally issued, or by persons related to such distributors as the result of reorganizations, liquidations, etc. By October 31, 1965 many distributors had accumulated quite large holdings in the certificates; one distributor, for example, held no fewer than 122. (Footnote 2)

Taxpayer seeks to deduct from gross income the face value of either all Mooney Bonds, or those Mooney Bonds which it is estimated will ultimately be redeemed, (Footnote 3) in the year the instruments were issued. It is the Government's position that the Mooney Bonds may be deducted only in the year the aircraft to which they relate are in fact permanently retired from service. The Government has alleged, and the taxpayer has not denied, that perhaps 20 or more years may elapse between issuance of the Bonds and retirement of the aircraft. The district court sustained the Government's position and, for the reasons to be discussed, we affirm the judgment of the district court.

The issue in this case is whether the taxpayer's "accrual" system of accounting is acceptable for tax purposes. In order to better understand this issue it may be helpful to first discuss the purpose and techniques of accrual accounting as they relate to the federal income tax.

"Income" has been defined as "a net or resultant determined by matching revenues with related expenses." Since the Internal Revenue Code allows the deduction of substantially all business expenses it seems reasonably clear that Congress intended to tax only net business income. This objective, however, is complicated by the fact that the tax is exacted on an annual basis (Footnote 5) whereas business transactions are often spread over two or more years. A business may receive payment for goods or services in one tax year but incur the related expenses in subsequent tax years. The result is that the expenses cannot be used to offset the receipts, and the full amount of the receipts is taxed as though it were all net "profit." (Footnote 7)

The purpose of 'accrual' accounting in the taxation context is to try to alleviate this problem by matching, in the same taxable year, revenues with the expenses incurred in producing those revenues. Accurate matching of expenses against revenues in the same taxable year may occur either by "deferring" receipts until such time as the related expenses are incurred or by "accruing" estimated future expenses so as to offset revenue. Under the deferral concept present receipts are not recognized as "income" until they are "earned" by performing the related services or delivering goods. It is thus not the actual receipt but the *right* to receive which is controlling; and, from an accounting (if not from a tax) point of view, that "right" does not arise until the money is "earned." A corresponding principle states that expenses are to be reported in the year the related income is "earned" whether or not actually paid in that year.

Another accounting technique for matching expenses and revenues is the "accrual" of estimated future expenses which has been described as follows:

> "The professional accountant recognizes estimated future expenses when the current performance of a contract to deliver goods or render services creates an *incidental* obligation in the seller which may require him to incur additional expenses at some future time. Instead of deferring the recognition of a portion of the revenue from the sale transaction until such time as the future expenses are incurred, accepted accounting procedures require inclusion of the total revenue in the current determination of income when the contract has been substantially performed, and the simultaneous deduction of all the related expenses, including a reasonable estimate for future expenses." (Footnote 12)

The early Revenue Acts of 1909 and 1913 did not recognize accounting techniques designed to match receipts and expenses in the same taxable year, but required the reporting of income on the basis of actual receipts and disbursements. It was soon realized that such a requirement could seriously distort income — especially in a business of any complexity in which payment is frequently received in a different accounting period than that in which expenses attributable to such payment are incurred. In order to alleviate the situation the Commissioner of Internal Revenue permitted some departures from the strict receipts and disbursements basis. United States v. Anderson, 269 U.S. 422, 423, 440, ... (1926). Finally, in the Revenue Act of 1916, Congress provided that a corporation keeping its books upon any basis other than actual receipts and disbursements could report its income on the same basis, "unless such other basis does not clearly reflect its income...." The substance of this provision was carried forward into the Internal Revenue Code of 1939 and the present Internal Revenue Code of 1954. (Footnote 16) The 1954 code specifically permitted the reporting of income under the "accrual" (Footnote 17) method, unless the Commissioner determines that such method "does not clearly reflect income." (Footnote 18)

These provisions seemed designed to reconcile the tax laws with commercial accounting practice, (Footnote 19) but unfortunately they have failed to do so. The Commissioner has consistently opposed deferral of prepaid income, or accrual of estimated future expenses, on the ground that for tax purposes such methods do not clearly reflect income. In the "deferral" cases he has argued that when the taxpayer receives payment under "claim of right," — i.e., without restriction as to disposition — deferring such payments to a future year violates the annual accounting concept, and they must therefore be reported in the year received. Similarly, in the "accrual" cases, the Commissioner has maintained that it is equally violative of the annual accounting concept to allow present deduction of a future expense unless "all the events" (Footnote 22) fixing the fact and the amount of the liability occur in the taxable year. Both of these positions are legal crystalizations of the Commissioner's discretionary power under [the Code] to reject an accounting method when it does not clearly reflect income. The principal question in the present case is whether, in the light of the statutory policies these doctrines are intended to implement, the Commissioner was justified in disallowing a present deduction of the Mooney Bonds as "not clearly reflecting income."

Although the Government admits that the retirement of the aircraft in this case is inevitable, it contends, nevertheless, that taxpayer cannot deduct the bonds in the year of issuance because the obligation they represent is contingent upon the happening of a future event—retirement of the related aircraft. Therefore, "all the events" creating the liability have not occurred in the taxable year. We cannot agree. In all the cases cited by the Government there was uncertainty as to whether the future event would actually happen; here there is none. There is no contingency in this case as to the *fact* of liability itself; the only contingency relates to *when* the liability will arise. (Footnote 26) To be sure, technically, the liability is 'created' by the event of the retirement of a particular plane; if a plane lasted forever there would be no liability. But taxation has been called a "practical field," and we do not see how the technical position the Government takes is designed to further the purpose of the statute.... If there is any doubt whether the liability will occur courts have been loath to interfere with the Commissioner's discretion is disallowing a deduction.... But here there is no doubt at all that the liability will occur since airplanes, like human beings, regrettably must cease to function. (Footnote 28)

The "all events test," however, is not the only basis upon which the Commissioner can disallow a deduction. Under §446(b) he has discretion to disallow any accounting method which does not clearly reflect income. As previously stated, the Commissioner has often relied on the "claim of right test," ... to disallow a deduction or a deferral of income in cases where the taxpayer's receipt of the funds was unrestricted. He appears to be doing so here, for the Government says in its brief, "Taxpayer received the full economic benefit of these proceeds, without any restriction as to use or enjoyment, and without any duty to return or transfer any part of these proceeds." The claim of right doctrine, however, has not enjoyed universal acceptance in the courts, ... and in two recent major decisions in this area, American Automobile Assn. v. United States, 367 U.S. 687, ... (1961) (hereafter AAA) and Schlude v. Commissioner of Internal Revenue, 372 U.S. 128, ... (1963) (hereafter *Schlude*), the Supreme Court seems to have placed little if any reliance on the doctrine.

Both *AAA* and *Schlude* involved an attempt to defer prepaid receipts to the future years when they allegedly would be 'earned.' In *AAA* the association received membership dues a year in advance, and membership could be commenced in any month of the year. In return for the dues the association provided its members with certain services, such as road maps, highway repair service, etc., but the services were performed only on the demand of an individual member. Rather than reporting all of the dues from the tax year in which received, the association "prorated" them over a twelve month membership period, overlapping two tax years, according to estimates of future costs based on its past experience. The Supreme Court held that even though the taxpayer's accrual system was in accord with generally accepted commercial accounting principles, the Commissioner could reject it as "not clearly reflecting income" for tax purposes. Since the services involved were not performed on fixed dates after the tax year, but only on demand by an individual member, the dues of each member were being deferred to "a taxable period in which none, some, or all the services paid for by those dues may or may not be rendered." *AAA, supra*, 367 U.S. at 692,.... Even the detailed proof showing a correspondence between the deferral and the overall cost structure was rejected:

> "The Code exacts its revenue from the individual member's dues which, no one disputes, constitute income. When their receipt as earned income is recognized ratably over two calendar years, without regard to correspondingly fixed individual expense or performance justification, but consistently with overall experience, their accounting doubtless presents a rather accurate image of the total financial structure, but fails to respect the criteria of annual tax accounting and may be rejected by the Commissioner." *Id.*

Similarly, in *Schlude, supra,* the Supreme Court rejected deferral of prepaid income for dancing lessons. The dates for the dancing lessons were not fixed in advance but were to be arranged between student and instructor. Hence, since the student might not "demand" lessons, there was no assurance that any lessons would be given, and thus the corresponding "costs" incurred, on dates after the tax year. The Commissioner could thus disallow the deferral as not accurately reflecting income.

Insofar as *AAA* and *Schlude* concerned inaccurate matching of revenues and expenses, both seem distinguishable from the present case. For one thing, this case involves an attempt to deduct future expenses rather than to defer present receipts.... Although the net effect of deferral of income and deduction of future expenses is often identical, deferral creates a greater risk of loss of tax revenues since at least in the accrual of expenses situation income is reported and taxed when received.... But even if "deferral" and "accrual" are identical for tax purposes, there is no doubt in this case that taxpayer will incur the "costs" necessary to pay the bonds on dates after the tax year. The Government argues that *Schlude* and *AAA* require that these costs must arise on fixed dates. But we think that the relevance of the 'fixed dates' criteria in *Schlude* and *AAA* was that since there were no fixed dates on which services had to be performed, there was no assurance that services *would be performed* after the tax year. If it is certain that there will be services (or costs) after the tax year, why should it make any difference that the date of those services (or costs) is uncertain? All that *Schlude* and *AAA* would seem to require is that the deferred income is reported as the related costs do in fact occur. If this were a deferral case, the taxpayer would report the "income" represented by the bonds in the years they were redeemed and paid.

Schlude and *AAA,* however, have significance far beyond their particular facts. For in both these cases the Court announced an additional reason for its decision which indicated that even if the taxpayer's system did truly reflect income it still might be rejected. Sections 452 and 462 of the Internal Revenue Code of 1954 contained the first explicit legislative sanction of deferral of income and deduction of future estimated expenses. In 1955 these provisions were retroactively repealed. The Court construed the enactment and repeal of these sections as indicating Congressional disapproval of the practices they had authorized:

> "The fact is that §452 for the first time specifically declared petitioner's system of accounting to be acceptable for income tax purposes, and overruled the long-standing position of the Commissioner and courts to the contrary. And the repeal of the section the following year, upon insistence by the Treasury that the proposed endorsement of such tax accounting would have a disastrous impact on the Government's revenue, was just as clearly a mandate from Congress that petitioner's system was not acceptable for tax purposes." (Footnote 34)

This alternative ground, based on legislative intent, would seem to dispose of the entire question: *all* deferrals and accruals are bad unless specifically authorized by Congress. But the Court was careful to discuss the legislative history as dictum and restricted its holding to a finding that the Commissioner did not abuse his discretion in rejecting the *AAA*'s accounting system.... It seems, then, that the Court is for the present taking a middle ground pending Congressional reform and clarification in this extremely confused area of the law: While the repeal of §§452 and 462 does not absolutely preclude deferrals and accruals, it indicates that the Commissioner should have very broad discretion to disallow such accounting techniques when there is any reasonable basis for his action. This is the construction given these two Supreme Court cases by the United States Tax Court:

> "We suspect, because of its repeated emphasis on the Commissioner's discretion under Sec. 41 of the 1939 Code and Sec. 446 of the 1954 Code, and the

legislative history of Secs. 452 and 462, that the majority of the Supreme Court stand for the principle that, absent statutory sanction for it, unless the taxpayer can show that the Commissioner clearly abused his discretion in disallowing deferral of prepaid income or accrual of estimated future expenses, this exercise of the Commissioner's discretion will not be disturbed by the Court even though the taxpayer's method of accounting is in accord with generally accepted principles of commercial accounting. We also suspect that this principle, if such it be, will meet with some resistance in the courts. See the dissenting opinions of Mr. Justice Stewart in American Automobile Assn. v. United States, 367 U.S. 687, 698, ... (1961) and Schlude v. Commissioner..., 372 U.S. 128, 137, ... (1963).... The application of such a principle to the facts here would certainly require a decision for respondent on this issue. Simplified Tax Records, Inc. v. Commissioner, 41 T.C. 75, 81, ... (1963).

The question remains: Was there reasonable basis for the Commissioner's action in this case? It appears to us there was ample basis.

The most salient feature in this case is the fact that many or possibly most of the expenses which taxpayer wishes to presently deduct will not actually be paid for 15, 20 or even 30 years (the taxpayer has not attempted to deny this). In no other case coming to our attention have we found anything even comparable to the time span involved in this case. In virtually all these other cases, even though a taxpayer may have received money under "claim of right" and had unrestricted use of the funds, there was still some relationship between those funds and related expenses which, more or less proximately, had to be borne. If there were no actual strings there were at least invisible strings attached to the money. Taxpayers could not use the money without at least an eye to the upcoming expenses or services to be performed. In this case, however, the related expenditure is so distant from the time the money is received as to completely attenuate any relationship between the two. For all practical purposes the revenue taxpayer received from the sale of the planes is his to use as he pleases. Rather than being set up as a reserve to pay an impending expense it is far more probable that the money will be used as capital to expand the business. In what sense, then, is it an accurate reflection of income to regard it as an expense of doing business in the current year? To so regard it is to let an accounting fiction obscure the business and fiscal realities that are the heart of this case. In exercising his discretion the Commissioner need not close his eyes to these realities. We feel that from both a business and tax standpoint the accounting systems rejected by the Supreme Court in *Schlude* and *AAA* were much more reasonable than the one involved here, and that to allow a present deduction in this case would distort rather than reflect income. We therefore find no difficulty in concluding that the Commissioner had a reasonable basis for disallowing the deduction as not clearly reflecting income.

There is yet another reason why the time span is too long. The longer the time the less probable it becomes that the liability, though incurred, will ever in fact be *paid*. Some courts have held that the improbability of payment is not a ground for disallowing the accrual of a future expense. Yet under 452 of the Internal Revenue Code of 1954, note 31 *supra*, the first express legislative sanction of deferral of income (repealed in 1955, ...) Congress specifically limited the length of time income could be deferred to five years. Where the liability for prepaid income extends beyond five years from the time of receipt, or where the liability is to extend for an indeterminate period—e.g., in the case of coupon books or service tickets—any income attributable to liability extending beyond the five year period is required to be prorated over the year of receipt and the ensuing five year period. It seems to us that these time limits are founded on the need to protect tax revenues, since the longer the interval between receipt of the funds and imposition of the tax the greater the risk the funds will be dissipated or that the taxpayer will die or that a business will be dissolved. A similar risk of loss of revenues exists in the case of accruals. Indeed, the very purpose of the "all events test" is to make sure that the taxpayer will not deduct expenses that might never occur. Just as in the deferral situation, the longer the time interval between receipt of money and payment of the related expense the greater the chance that the money will be dissipated and never paid. If it is never paid, it is not an expense and should have been taxed. In the present case the taxpayer could in good faith use the monies it has received as capital to expand its business; if one day it became insolvent the expense might never be paid, yet the money would have been used as tax-free income. We repeat that because of the inordinate length of time involved in this case the Commissioner was clearly within his discretion in disallowing deduction of the "Mooney Bonds" as a *current* expense....

We affirm the judgment of the District Court.

Affirmed.

FOOTNOTES:

1. All private aircraft in the United States are required to be registered currently with the Federal Aviation Agency, which publishes a monthly report listing every aircraft in service in the country. A copy of this monthly report is regularly obtained by the taxpayer. Comparable registration requirements exist and reports are available in other countries in which aircraft manufactured and sold by the taxpayer operate.

2. The following table sets forth the face value, in thousands of dollars, of all Mooney Bonds redeemed and outstanding at the end of the relevant fiscal years:

Fiscal Years	Issued	Redeemed	Final Balance Outstanding
10/31/61	217	-	217
10/31/62	-	2	215
10/31/63	303	5	513
10/31/64	655	10	1,158
10/31/65	766	16	1,908

3. Taxpayer attempted to introduce an expert study estimating what number of the bonds would actually be presented for redemption.

5. Int. Rev. Code of 1954, § 441(a). See also Burnet v. Sanford & Brooks Co., 282 U.S. 359, 365, ... (1931).

7. The expenses incurred in a subsequent year can, of course, be used to offset receipts for that year; but there may be no receipts for that year, or the receipts may be less than the expenses. In other words, the relationship between expenses incurred in producing the revenues of an earlier year, and the revenues received in the year the expenses are incurred, may well be random and thus produce a distortion of "income" for that year.

12. Comment, 61 Mich.L.Rev. 148, 151 (1962).

16. 26 U.S.C.A. § 446:

"§ 446. General rule for methods of accounting

"(a) *General rule.*—Taxable income shall be computed under the method of accounting on the basis of which the taxpayer regularly computes his income in keeping his books.

"(b) *Exceptions.*—If no method of accounting has been regularly used by the taxpayer, or if the method used does not clearly reflect income, the computation of taxable income shall be made under such method as, in the opinion of the Secretary or his delegate, does clearly reflect income.

"(c) *Permissible methods.*—Subject to the provisions of subsections (a) and (b), a taxpayer may compute taxable income under any of the following methods of accounting—

"(1) the cash receipts and disbursements method;

"(2) an accrual method;

"(3) any other method permitted by this chapter; or

"(4) any combination of the foregoing methods permitted under regulations prescribed by the Secretary or his delegate."

17. §446(c)(2), note 16, *supra.*

18. §446(b), note 16, *supra.*

19. "A consideration of the difficulties involved in the preparation of an income account on a strict basis of receipts and disbursements for a business of any complexity, which had been experienced in the application of the Acts of 1909 and 1913 and which made it necessary to authorize by departmental regulation, a method of preparing returns not in terms provided for by those statutes, indicates with no uncertainty the purpose of sections 12(a) and 13(d) of the Act of 1916. It was to enable taxpayers to keep their books and make their returns according to scientific accounting principles, by charging against income earned during the taxable period, the expenses incurred in and properly attributable to the process of earning income during that period...."

(Justice Stone in United States v. Anderson, 269 U.S. 422, 440, 46 S.Ct. 131, 134, 70 L.Ed. 347 (1926)).

22. The "all events test," as it has come to be known, was originally formulated in United States v. Anderson, 269 U.S. 422, 441, ... (1926). The all events test has been expressly adopted by Treas. Reg. § 1.461-1(a)(2) (1964).

26. See, e.g., Revenue Ruling 57-105, 1957-1 Cum. Bull. 193:

" ... an obligation is considered contingent when the existence of any liability at all is uncertain or when its existence depends upon the happening of a future *contingent* event.

Although, strictly speaking, liability in the present case depends upon a future event, it does not depend upon a future *contingent* event, since retirement of the planes is certain.

28. Even if the fact of the liability seems certain or highly probable some decisions have disallowed a deduction if the *amount* is uncertain or at least cannot be reasonably estimated. See, e.g., Brown v. Helvering, 291 U.S. 193, ... (1934). Since there is no finding by the trial judge on this issue, and since, as appears below, its resolution is not necessary for the decision of this case, we do not reach it.

34. *AAA*, 367 U.S. 687, 695, ... (1961)....

———————

Consider the following questions about *Mooney Aircraft*.

1. What was a "Mooney Bond"? How did the taxpayer account for it?

Assume Mooney Aircraft pays the top marginal rate of corporate tax of 35%. A deduction of $1,000 in the year it issued a bond, would produce a tax savings of $350. Assume further that the airplane will have a useful life of 20 years before its purchaser retires it from service. Mooney will then have to pay the distributor $1,000 to redeem the bond at the end of the twentieth year. How much would Mooney have to deposit in an interest-bearing account today to satisfy its $1,000 obligation at the end of 20 years? How would you calculate the answer? Assume that an acceptable rate of return on a bond issued by a company of similar credit-worthiness would produce an interest rate of 8%, compounded monthly. **Consult the time value of money tables set forth in Part II following *Raytheon*.** You will quickly find that Mooney need only set aside $203 today to provide for its future retirement of the bond. Therefore, it captures a deduction of $1,000 worth $350 to it this year at a cost of only $203, a net profit to Mooney of $147. If it invests that $147 at the same interest rate, also compounded monthly, for the same 20 year period, it will have $1,476 at the end of the period! No wonder Mooney wanted to accelerate its deduction.

2. The court begins its opinion by observing that this is another case concerning the difference between financial accounting and tax accounting. What is the issue here?

3. What does the court mean when it says that to consider liability for payment on the bonds as an expense of doing business in the current year would be to "let an accounting fiction obscure the business and fiscal realities that are the heart of this case"?

4. Does the court adequately explain the basis for its denial of a deduction that meets the literal requirements of the all events test?

5. The court was clearly troubled by the fact that satisfaction of the liability was so far into the future. Could it have adopted an intermediate position and allowed Mooney to deduct the present value of the bond redemption price?

Compare *Mooney Aircraft* with the following case.

OHIO RIVER COLLIERIES COMPANY v. COMMISSIONER

77 T.C. 1369 (1981)

OPINION

NIMS, *Judge*: Respondent determined deficiencies in petitioner's income tax for the tax year ending June 30, 1975.... Petitioner claims an overpayment of income tax ... for such year.

Due to concessions by the petitioner, the only issue remaining for decision is whether petitioner, an accrual basis taxpayer, may deduct the reasonably estimated expenses necessary to satisfy its obligation under Ohio law to reclaim strip-mined land in the year it incurred the obligation.

The facts of this case are fully stipulated....

Petitioner, an Ohio corporation, maintained its principal office in Bannock, Ohio, at the time the petition in this case was filed.

Petitioner, at all relevant times, was an accrual basis taxpayer. It regularly kept its records using the accrual method of accounting.

Ohio River Collieries Co. (hereinafter petitioner) strip-mined coal exclusively in Ohio. Strip mining involves the removal of topsoil and the overburden from above the coal seam, followed by removal and sale of the coal and reclamation of the affected area.

In April 1972, Ohio enacted a comprehensive reclamation statute which regulated the strip mining of coal during the tax year before us. Operators needed a strip-mining license before they could strip-mine coal. The State issued a license only after it approved a plan for mining and reclamation and after the operator deposited a surety bond payable to the State if the operator failed to perform (inter alia) its reclamation duties.

The Ohio law details requirements for refilling, grading, resoiling, and planting mined areas. These activities, except planting, had to be completed within 12 months after mining ceased. Reclamation also was required as mining progressed, whenever possible. Planting had to occur in the next appropriate season following completion of refilling, grading, and resoiling. Status reports by the operator and periodic inspections by the State monitored compliance.

The operator's bond was for payment of an amount of money equal to the estimated cost to the State to perform the reclamation required by the statute. The bond would not be released until the State was satisfied that the operator had fulfilled its reclamation duties.

If an operator failed to perform any of its reclamation obligations, the State reclaimed the land and satisfied its costs from the fund created by the bond. If the costs exceeded the funds available from the bond, then the operator was personally liable for the amount of money required to complete the reclamation.

Operators violating the Ohio reclamation law also faced potential civil and criminal penalties.

Ohio has required full compliance with the law at all times since the statute's enactment.

Petitioner performed its reclamation duties within the time required by the law. Petitioner did substantially all of the reclamation work itself.

The petitioner's estimate of the cost of reclamation work required by the reclamation law, but not accomplished as of June 30, 1974, was $150,527.86. The petitioner's estimate of the cost of reclamation work required by the reclamation law, but not accomplished as of June 30, 1975, was $397,883. The parties stipulate that these estimates were determined with reasonable accuracy.

All of the reclamation work required by Ohio law, but not accomplished as of June 30, 1974, was completed by petitioner during the fiscal year ended June 30, 1975. Consequently, the estimate for work not accomplished as of June 30, 1975, is the unfinished reclamation obligation arising from the strip mining which occurred during the tax year ended June 30, 1975.

Petitioner accrued on its books, and claimed as a deduction for Federal income tax purposes, the estimated cost of reclamation work required by Ohio law but not accomplished as of the end of the pertinent fiscal years ended June 30, 1973, June 30, 1974, and June 30, 1975. Respondent disallowed the deduction for the tax year ended June 30, 1975.

The question presented to us is whether petitioner, an accrual basis taxpayer, may accrue and deduct as a section 162 business expense the reasonable estimate of the cost of fulfilling the reclamation obligation in the year in which the duty to reclaim arose. (Footnote 3) The parties agree that application of the "all of the events" test contained in section 1.461-1(a)(2), Income Tax Regs., determines the result in this case. (Footnote 4) The dispute concerns the interpretation of that test.

Section 461(a) states the general rule that a taxpayer is allowed a deduction in "the taxable year which is the proper taxable year under the method of accounting used in computing taxable income," and the regulations elaborate on this general provision. For accrual basis taxpayers, such as petitioner, section 1.461-1(a)(2), Income Tax Regs., provides in part as follows:

> Under an accrual method of accounting, an expense is deductible for the taxable year in which all the events have occurred which determine the fact of the liability and the amount thereof can be determined with reasonable accuracy.... While no accrual shall be made in any case in which all of the events have not occurred which fix the liability, the fact that the exact amount of the liability which has been incurred cannot be determined will not prevent the accrual within the taxable year of such part thereof as can be computed with reasonable accuracy.

The "all of the events" test appearing in the quoted portion of the regulations was first enunciated in *United States v. Anderson*, 269 U.S. 422 (1926)....

It is apparent from the *Anderson* holding and from the principles set forth in the regulations, that petitioner must satisfy two requirements before it properly may deduct the accrued reclamation expenses during the tax year ended June 30, 1975:

(1) All of the events which determine petitioner's reclamation liability must have occurred before the end of the tax year in issue.... This requirement prevents the deduction of an expenditure that might never be made.... *Mooney Aircraft, Inc. v. United States*, 420 F.2d 400, 406 (5th Cir. 1969).

(2) Petitioner must have been able to estimate with reasonable accuracy during the tax year ended June 30, 1975, the amount of the reclamation expenditure to be made in subsequent years.... This requirement provides an element of certainty, although it is not essential that the precise amount of the expenditure be definitely ascertained.... The failure to satisfy either requirement of the foregoing two-step test would be fatal to petitioner's claim....

Since the parties have stipulated that the petitioner's estimate of the cost of reclamation work required by the Ohio reclamation law as of June 30, 1975, was determined with reasonable accuracy, part two of the regulation's two-step test is satisfied....

...

We think it is essential to focus on the fact that the tax accounting problem confronting us results from two separate and distinct events: the *strip mining*, itself, which created this liability, and the *reclamation*, which created the cost. It is this factual distinctiveness which makes the problem unusual....

It may readily be seen, however, that having stipulated that reclamation costs were reasonably estimated, respondent has substantially circumscribed his area of maneuverability. By making this stipulation, respondent is precluded from arguing that events occurring in the succeeding year or years might substantially alter the cost of the reclamation. Apparently, fully accepting this constriction, he focuses his argument instead on petitioner's "liability to pay." Respondent's position is stated in the following manner in his brief: "It is respondent's position that this taxpayer's statutory duty to reclaim did not create any *liability to pay* and that the deduction claimed is therefore not allowable. Rather, the expense of reclamation will be deductible only when, as and if the reclamation is performed." ...

Respondent's liability-to-pay approach is, in actuality, an argument that the reclamation expenses are deductible only when, as, and if the reclamation is performed, as above quoted from his brief. Such an argument, however, flies in the face of the reality of the Ohio law which requires the strip miner to estimate his reclamation cost and post a surety bond to cover it. Accordingly, once these two acts have been performed, followed by a third, the intended strip mining, the liability becomes certain. Either the strip miner performs the reclamation or he forfeits the bond. There is nothing whatever in this record to support respondent's argument that petitioner might do neither....

... During the tax year, petitioner's obligation to reclaim, and thus its liability to pay reclamation expenditures, was fixed by the fact of strip mining and, by concession of the parties, fixed as to amount. The fact that the recipients of petitioner's reclamation payments and the relative portions that they would receive were not identified in the tax year is irrelevant. Petitioner need not wait until the reclamation work is done before it can accrue and deduct the anticipated reclamation expenses where, as here, the events fixing the fact of liability to pay these expenses occurred during the tax year....

In summary, we hold that petitioner has satisfied both facets of the all-events test of section 1.461-1(a)(2) of the Income Tax Regs. Accordingly, we hold for petitioner.... Furthermore, we deem it necessary to stress that the potential for abuse makes it essential that the all-events test of the regulations continues to be strictly construed in future cases of this nature before this Court, and that such cases are not viewed as occasions to judicially "reenact" the section 462 that the Congress repealed in 1955.

FOOTNOTES:

3. The parties agree that the reclamation costs are properly deductible as a business expense. The controversy concerns only the year in which petitioner may take the deduction.

4. Respondent does not argue that petitioner's accounting method does not clearly reflect income. See sec. 446(b).

Consider the following questions.

1. On what basis did the Secretary argue that the taxpayer had failed to satisfy the test for proper accrual of the liability?

2. Why did the Tax Court decide in favor of Ohio River Collieries after the Fifth Circuit decided against Mooney Aircraft? Didn't the taxpayer in *Mooney* have a better argument under the then-existing all events test because in *Mooney* the amount of the liability was fixed whereas in *Ohio River Collieries* it was only estimated?

Congress could have chosen one of two ways to address the abuse that the Commissioner and the *Mooney* court were worried about: (1) allow the taxpayer to deduct the present value of a fixed but deferred liability, or (2) require that the taxpayer defer deduction until payment actually occurred. In fact, it chose this latter approach by enacting section 461(h). **Read section 461(h). Read also the following excerpt from the "Blue Book"**[12] **describing the new provision:**

------

12. **Recall our explanation of the Blue Book in the footnotes, to Part II, Chapter 2.**

Reasons For Change

Congress believed that the rules relating to the time for accrual of a deduction by a taxpayer using the accrual method of accounting should be changed to take into account the time value of money and the time the deduction is economically incurred. Recent court decisions in some cases permitted accrual method taxpayers to deduct currently expenses that were not yet economically incurred (i.e., that were attributable to activities to be performed or amounts to be paid in the future). Allowing a taxpayer to take deductions currently for an amount to be paid in the future overstates the true cost of the expense to the extent that the time value of money is not taken into account; the deduction is overstated by the amount by which the face value exceeds the present value of the expense. The longer the period of time involved, the greater is the overstatement.

Congress was concerned about the potential revenue loss from such overstated deductions. In many everyday business transactions, taxpayers incur liabilities to pay expenses in the future. Congress believed that because of the large number of transactions in which deductions may be overstated and because of the high interest rates in recent years, the magnitude of the revenue loss could be significant....

Explanation of Provision

...

The Act provides that in determining whether an amount has been incurred with respect to any item during the taxable year by a taxpayer using the accrual method of accounting, all the events which establish liability for such amount generally are not to be treated as having occurred any earlier than the time economic performance occurs.[13]

What would be the result in *Mooney Aircraft* after its enactment? What about *Ohio River Collieries*?

---

13. Staff of Joint Comm. on Taxation, 98th Cong., 2d Sess., *General Explanation of the Revenue Provisions of the Deficit Reduction Act of 1984*, (H.R. 4170, Public Law 98-369) 260–61 (Joint Comm. Print 1984).

Chapter 2

Special Problems of Timing: Recovery of Capital

A. A Return to the Concept of Cost Recovery

Chapter 1 expanded your knowledge of the annual accounting period that began in Part II with our study of *Burnet v. Sanford and Brooks*. But is the annual accounting period the "proper" period for all items that affect taxable income? You cannot answer that question without first giving some thought to concepts of equity and economic reality.

Suppose, for example, that a business must purchase a major piece of equipment in order to complete a construction project. Assume that Danielle, on behalf of her construction company, DL, Inc., enters into a contract with the Chens to build a commercial building for them. The project will take two years and DL will receive "progress payments" as the work is done. The agreement between the Chens and DL provides that DL will submit quarterly invoices for its costs plus 10%. Upon completion of the project, the Chens will pay the remaining balance due under the contract, less the progress payments. You have certainly learned enough to surmise that the progress payments will in no way match the tax results during the construction period. For example, assume that the special piece of equipment DL will acquire will be useless for all other projects. For tax purposes, of course, the rules of section 168 will require DL to recover its capital through periodic depreciation deductions. What will it do for accounting purposes in order to bill the Chens? If the machine will, in fact, be worthless to DL when this project is complete, it will have to make an agreement with the Chens at the outset as to its cost, but for tax purposes, it may not be able to recover the bulk of the cost until the project ends and DL disposes of the equipment by sale or abandonment.

As another example, ABC Company manufactures widgets. In order to manufacture the widgets, it must purchase a drill press machine that costs $1 million and is expected to last for 10 years. How should ABC Company account for the cost of this machine? The cash method would require it to treat the expense as "paid" in the year ABC company actually pays for it. The accrual method would require ABC Company to treat the expense as "accrued" in the year its liability to pay for the machine is fixed. But whatever the treatment, the taxpayer may be unable to deduct the full expense in a single tax year. Recall again our earlier discussion of depreciation.

Section 168 represents, in effect, a special method of accounting for capital expenditures for trade or business or investment assets. While the taxpayer's normal method of accounting determines in which tax year the liability is fixed, the depreciation rules de-

termine the portion of the expense the taxpayer may deduct in each tax year until she
has recovered the entire cost of the item.

But, the treatment of capital expenditures is not the only problem with which the ordinary rules of cash or accrual basis accounting do not deal adequately in the context of
certain income-producing activities. Suppose that in order to begin the manufacture of
widgets, ABC Company must purchase extruded aluminum rods. The manufacturer of
these rods will only sell them by the ton. Of course, a ton of aluminum rods is quite a
few rods. It is unlikely that the start-up company will use all the rods in a single tax year.

If ABC Company used the cash method of accounting it would attribute the full cost
of the rods to the year it paid for them. But note the distortion in the results for the
ABC Company of such accounting: in year one, the expense of the rods could easily exceed the income from the sale of widgets (without even taking into account the other
expenses of manufacture); in year two, the income could greatly exceed the cost of production if no part of the cost of the rods appears on the books for the second year.

But, would the accrual method of accounting produce a less distorted effect? If ABC
Company's liability to pay for the full ton of rods accrued in year one, the accrual
method would also treat the expense as accrued in year one.

Thus, both the cash and accrual method of accounting might require that ABC
Company treat the cost of the rods as an expense in the year of acquisition.[1] Would either of these methods relate the expense of producing the product to the income from
its sale? What methods of accounting for the expense of acquiring the rods might you
suggest?[2] Would the likelihood that ABC Company will sell all the widgets it produces
from these rods in a single tax year affect your answer?

There are other problems that face taxpayers trying to account for the costs they have
paid or incurred in the production of income. These problems can occur either in computing basis on acquisition or in computing basis on disposition.

Suppose, for example, ABC Company itself constructs the equipment it will use in
producing the widgets from the rods. In doing so, it incurs a number of costs for labor
and materials. Should these costs produce current deductions? Read the following case.
As you are reading it, **recall** *Encyclopaedia Britannica* **in Part II, Chapter 3.**

COMMISSIONER v. IDAHO POWER CO.
418 U.S. 1 (1974)

MR. JUSTICE BLACKMUN delivered the opinion of the Court.

This case presents the sole issue whether, for federal income tax purposes, a taxpayer
is entitled to a deduction from gross income, under § 167(a) of the Internal Revenue

---

1. The cash method would require the expense to be recorded in the year ABC Company paid
for the rods and the accrual method would require the expense to be recorded in the year in which
the liability of ABC Company to pay for the rods became fixed, the amount could be determined
with reasonable certainty, and economic performance had occurred. That would certainly be the
year in which the buyer purchased and paid for the rods.

2. A detailed discussion of the methods of accounting for the costs of producing inventory, such
as the widgets, is beyond the scope of this basic introduction to federal income tax. In fact, the Code
contains complex rules for several methods of accounting for these costs. Our purpose here, in asking you to consider the possible methods of allocating the costs of the rods to the production of the
widgets is to encourage you to think as tax policy makers and be as creative as possible, rather than
simply studying what Congress, in fact, chose.

Code of 1954, ... (Footnote 1) for depreciation on equipment the taxpayer owns and uses in the construction of its own capital facilities, or whether the capitalization provision of § 263(a)(1) of the Code, ... (Footnote 2) bars the deduction.

The taxpayer claimed the deduction, but the Commissioner of Internal Revenue disallowed it. The Tax Court (Scott, J., in an opinion not reviewed by the full court) upheld the Commissioner's determination. 29 T.C.M. 383 (1970). The United States Court of Appeals for the Ninth Circuit, declining to follow a Court of Claims decision, *Southern Natural Gas Co. v. United States*, 188 Ct. Cl. 302, 372–380, 412 F.2d 1222, 1264–1269, (1969), reversed. 477 F.2d 688 (1973). We granted certiorari in order to resolve the apparent conflict between the Court of Claims and the Court of Appeals. 414 U.S. 999 (1973).

I

Nearly all the relevant facts are stipulated. The taxpayer-respondent, Idaho Power Company, is a Maine corporation organized in 1915, with its principal place of business at Boise, Idaho. It is a public utility engaged in the production, transmission, distribution, and sale of electric energy. The taxpayer keeps its books and files its federal income tax returns on the calendar year accrual basis. The tax years at issue are 1962 and 1963.

For many years, the taxpayer has used its own equipment and employees in the construction of improvements and additions to its capital facilities. (Footnote 3) The major work has consisted of transmission lines, transmission switching stations, distribution lines, distribution stations, and connecting facilities.

During 1962 and 1963, the tax years in question, taxpayer owned and used in its business a wide variety of automotive transportation equipment, including passenger cars, trucks of all descriptions, power-operated equipment, and trailers. Radio communication devices were affixed to the equipment and were used in its daily operations. The transportation equipment was used in part for operation and maintenance and in part for the construction of capital facilities having a useful life of more than one year.

On its books, the taxpayer used various methods of charging costs incurred in connection with its transportation equipment either to current expense or to capital accounts. To the extent the equipment was used in construction, the taxpayer charged depreciation of the equipment, as well as all operating and maintenance costs (other than pension contributions and social security and motor vehicle taxes) to the capital assets so constructed. This was done either directly or through clearing accounts in accordance with procedures prescribed by the Federal Power Commission and adopted by the Idaho Public Utilities Commission.

For federal income tax purposes, however, the taxpayer treated the depreciation on transportation equipment differently. It claimed as a deduction from gross income *all* the year's depreciation on such equipment, including that portion attributable to its use in constructing capital facilities. The depreciation was computed on a composite life of 10 years and under straight-line and declining-balance methods. The other operating and maintenance costs the taxpayer had charged on its books to capital were not claimed as current expenses and were not deducted.

To summarize: On its books, in accordance with Federal Power Commission—Idaho Public Utilities Commission prescribed methods, the taxpayer capitalized the construction-related depreciation, but for income tax purposes that depreciation incre-ment was claimed as a deduction under § 167(a). (Footnote 4)

Upon audit, the Commissioner of Internal Revenue disallowed the deduction for the construction-related depreciation. He ruled that that depreciation was a nondeductible capital expenditure to which § 263(a)(1) had application. He added the amount of the depreciation so disallowed to the taxpayer's adjusted basis in its capital facilities, and then allowed a deduction for an appropriate amount of depreciation on the addition, computed over the useful life (30 years or more) of the property constructed. A deduc-tion for depreciation of the transportation equipment to the extent of its use in day-to-day operation and maintenance was also allowed. The result of these adjustments was the disallowance of depreciation, as claimed by the taxpayer on its returns, in the net amounts of $140,429.75 and $96,811.95 for 1962 and 1963, respectively. This gave rise to asserted deficiencies in taxpayer's income taxes for those two years of $73,023.47 and $50,342.21.

The Tax Court agreed with the decision of the Court of Claims in *Southern Natural Gas, supra,* and described that holding as one to the effect that "depreciation allocable to the use of the equipment in the construction of capital improvements was not de-ductible in the year the equipment was so used but should be capitalized and recovered over the useful life of the assets constructed." 29 T.C.M., at 386. The Tax Court, accord-ingly, held that the Commissioner "properly disallowed as a deduction ... this allocable portion of depreciation and that such amount should be capitalized as part of [tax-payer's] basis in the permanent improvements in the construction of which the equip-ment was used." *Ibid.*

The Court of Appeals, on the other hand, perceived in the Internal Revenue Code of 1954 the presence of a liberal congressional policy toward depreciation, the underlying theory of which is that capital assets used in business should not be exhausted without provision for replacement. 477 F.2d, at 690–693. The court concluded that a deduction expressly enumerated in the Code, such as that for depreciation, may properly be taken and that "no exception is made should it relate to a capital item." *Id.,* at 693. Section 263(a)(1) of the Code was found not to be applicable because depreciation is not an "amount paid out," as required by that section. The court found *Southern Natural Gas* unpersuasive and felt "constrained to distinguish" it in reversing the Tax Court judg-ment. 477 F.2d, at 695–696.

The taxpayer asserts that its transportation equipment is used in its "trade or busi-ness" and that depreciation thereon is therefore deductible under § 167(a)(1) of the Code. The Commissioner concedes that § 167 may be said to have a literal application to depreciation on equipment used in capital construction, (Footnote 5) ... but con-tends that the provision must be read in light of § 263(a)(1) which specifically disallows any deduction for an amount "paid out for new buildings or for permanent improve-ments or betterments." He argues that § 263 takes precedence over § 167 by virtue of what he calls the "priority-ordering" terms (and what the taxpayer describes as "house-keeping" provisions) of § 161 of the Code, 26 U.S.C. § 161, (Footnote 6) and that sound principles of accounting and taxation mandate the capitalization of this depreciation.

It is worth noting the various items that are not at issue here. The mathematics, as such, is not in dispute. The taxpayer has capitalized, as part of its cost of acquisition of capital assets, the operating and maintenance costs (other than depreciation, pension contributions, and social security and motor vehicle taxes) of the transportation equip-ment attributable to construction. This is not contested. The Commissioner does not dispute that the portion of the transportation equipment's depreciation allocable to operation and maintenance of facilities, in contrast with construction thereof, qualifies as a deduction from gross income. There is no disagreement as to the allocation of depreciation between construction and maintenance. The issue, thus comes down primarily to a question of timing, as the Court of Appeals recognized, 477 F.2d, at 692, that is, whether the construction-related depreciation is to be amortized and deducted over the *shorter* life of the equipment or, instead, is to be amortized and deducted over the *longer* life of the capital facilities constructed.

II

Our primary concern is with the necessity to treat construction-related depreciation in a manner that comports with accounting and taxation realities. Over a period of time a capital asset is consumed and, correspondingly over that period, its theoretical value and utility are thereby reduced. Depreciation is an accounting device which recognizes that the physical consumption of a capital asset is a true cost, since the asset is being depleted. (Footnote 7) As the process of consumption continues, and depreciation is claimed and allowed, the asset's adjusted income tax basis is reduced to reflect the distribution of its cost over the accounting periods affected. The Court stated in *Hertz Corp. v. United States*, 364 U.S. 122, 126, ... (1960): "[T]he purpose of depreciation accounting is to allocate the expense of using an asset to the various periods which are benefited by that asset." ... When the asset is used to further the taxpayer's day-to-day business operations, the periods of benefit usually correlate with the production of income. Thus, to the extent that equipment is used in such operations, a current depreciation deduction is an appropriate offset to gross income currently produced. It is clear, however, that different principles are implicated when the consumption of the asset takes place in the construction of other assets that, in the future, will produce income themselves. In this latter situation, the cost represented by depreciation does not correlate with production of current income. Rather, the cost, although certainly presently incurred, is related to the future and is appropriately allocated as part of the cost of acquiring an income-producing capital asset.

The Court of Appeals opined that the purpose of the depreciation allowance under the Code was to provide a means of cost recovery, ... and that this Court's decisions, ... endorse a theory of replacement through "a fund to restore the property." 477 F.2d, at 691. Although tax-free replacement of a depreciating investment is one purpose of depreciation accounting, it alone does not require the result claimed by the taxpayer here. Only last Term, in *United States v. Chicago, B. & Q.R. Co.*, 412 U.S. 401, ... (1973), we rejected replacement as the strict and sole purpose of depreciation:

"Whatever may be the desirability of creating a depreciation reserve under these circumstances, as a matter of good business and accounting practice, the answer is ... [d]epreciation reflects the cost of an existing capital asset, not the cost of a potential replacement." *Id.*, at 415.

Even were we to look to replacement, it is the replacement of the constructed facilities, not the equipment used to build them, with which we would be concerned. If the taxpayer now were to decide not to construct any more capital facilities with its own equipment and employees, it, in theory, would have no occasion to replace its equipment to the extent that it was consumed in prior construction.

Accepted accounting practice (Footnote 8) and established tax principles require the capitalization of the cost of acquiring a capital asset. In *Woodward v. Commissioner*, 397

U.S. 572, ... (1970), the Court observed: "It has long been recognized, as a general matter, that costs incurred in the acquisition ... of a capital asset are to be treated as capital expenditures." This principle has obvious application to the acquisition of a capital asset by purchase, but it has been applied, as well, to the costs incurred in a taxpayer's construction of capital facilities. *See, e.g., Southern Natural Gas Co. v. United States, supra;....* (Footnote 9)

There can be little question that other construction-related expense items, such as tools, materials, and wages paid construction workers, are to be treated as part of the cost of acquisition of a capital asset. The taxpayer does not dispute this. Of course, reasonable wages paid in the carrying on of a trade or business qualify as a deduction from gross income. § 162(a)(1) of the 1954 Code.... But when wages are paid in connection with the construction or acquisition of a capital asset, they must be capitalized and are then entitled to be amortized over the life of the capital asset so acquired.... See Treas. Reg. § 1.266-1(e).

Construction-related depreciation is not unlike expenditures for wages for construction workers. The significant fact is that the exhaustion of construction equipment does not represent the final disposition of the taxpayer's investment in that equipment; rather, the investment in the equipment is assimilated into the cost of the capital asset constructed. Construction-related depreciation on the equipment is not an expense to the taxpayer of its day-to-day business. It is, however, appropriately recognized as a part of the taxpayer's cost or investment in the capital asset. The taxpayer's own accounting procedure reflects this treatment, for on its books the construction-related depreciation was capitalized by a credit to the equipment account and a debit to the capital facility account. By the same token, this capitalization prevents the distortion of income that would otherwise occur if depreciation properly allocable to asset acquisition were deducted from gross income currently realized....

An additional pertinent factor is that capitalization of construction-related depreciation by the taxpayer who does its own construction work maintains tax parity with the taxpayer who has its construction work done by an independent contractor. The depreciation on the contractor's equipment incurred during the performance of the job will be an element of cost charged by the contractor for his construction services, and the entire cost, of course, must be capitalized by the taxpayer having the construction work performed. The 'Court of Appeals' holding would lead to disparate treatment among taxpayers because it would allow the firm with sufficient resources to construct its own facilities and to obtain a current deduction, whereas another firm without such resources would be required to capitalize its entire cost including depreciation charged to it by the contractor....

The presence of § 263(a)(1) in the Code is of significance. Its literal language denies a deduction for "[a]ny amount paid out" for construction or permanent improvement of facilities. The taxpayer contends, and the Court of Appeals held, that depreciation of construction equipment represents merely a decrease in value and is not an amount "paid out," within the meaning of § 263(a)(1). We disagree.

The purpose of § 263 is to reflect the basic principle that a capital expenditure may not be deducted from current income. It serves to prevent a taxpayer from utilizing currently a deduction properly attributable, through amortization, to later tax years when the capital asset becomes income producing. The regulations state that the capital expenditures to which § 263(a) extends include the "cost of acquisition, construction, or erection of buildings." Treas. Reg. § 1.263(a)-2(a). This manifests an administrative understanding that for purposes of § 263(a)(1), "amount paid out" equates with "cost incurred." The Internal Revenue Service for some time has taken the position that construction-related depreciation is to be capitalized. Rev. Rul. 59-380, 1959-2 Cum. Bull. 87; Rev. Rul. 55-252, 1955-1 Cum. Bull. 319.

There is no question that the cost of the transportation equipment was a "paid out" in the same manner as the cost of supplies, materials, and other equipment, and the wages of construction workers. The taxpayer does not question the capitalization of these other items as elements of the cost of acquiring a capital asset. We see no reason to treat construction-related depreciation differently. In acquiring the transportation equipment, taxpayer "paid out" the equipment's purchase price; depreciation is simply the means of allocating the payment over the various accounting periods affected. As the Tax Court stated in *Brooks v. Commissioner*, 50 T.C., at 935, "depreciation—inasmuch as it represents a using up of capital—is as much an 'expenditure' as the using up of labor or other items of direct cost."

Finally, the priority-ordering directive of § 161—or, for that matter, § 261 of the Code ... (Footnote 12)—requires that the capitalization provision of § 263(a) take precedence, on the facts here, over § 167(a). Section 161 provides that deductions specified in Part VI of Subchapter B of the Income Tax Subtitle of the Code are "subject to the exceptions provided in part IX." Part VI includes § 167 and Part IX includes § 263. The clear import of § 161 is that, with stated exceptions set forth either in § 263 itself or provided for elsewhere ... none of which is applicable here, an expenditure incurred in acquiring capital assets must be capitalized even when the expenditure otherwise might be deemed deductible under Part VI.

The Court of Appeals concluded, without reference to § 161, that § 263 did not apply to a deduction, such as that for depreciation of property used in a trade or business, allowed by the Code even though incurred in the construction of capital assets. We think that the court erred in espousing so absolute a rule, and it obviously overlooked the contrary direction of § 161. To the extent that reliance was placed on the congressional intent, in the evolvement of the 1954 Code, to provide for "liberalization of depreciation," H.R. Rep. No. 1337, 83d Cong., 2d Sess., 22 (1954), that reliance is misplaced. The House Report also states that the depreciation provisions would "give the economy added stimulus and resilience without departing from realistic standards of depreciation accounting." *Id.*, at 24.... To be sure, the 1954 Code provided for new and accelerated methods for depreciation, resulting in the greater depreciation deductions currently available. These changes, however, relate primarily to computation of depreciation. Congress certainly did not intend that provisions for accelerated depreciation should be construed as enlarging the class of depreciable assets to which § 167(a) has application or as lessening the reach of § 263(a)....

We hold that the equipment depreciation allocable to taxpayer's construction of capital facilities is to be capitalized.

The judgment of the Court of Appeals is reversed....

FOOTNOTES:

1. "§ 167. Depreciation.

"(a) General rule.

"There shall be allowed as a depreciation deduction a reasonable allowance for the exhaustion, wear and tear (including a reasonable allowance for obsolescence)—

"(1) of property used in the trade or business, or

"(2) of property held for the production of income."

2. "§ 263. Capital expenditures.

"(a) General rule.

"No deduction shall be allowed for—

"(1) Any amount paid out for new buildings or for permanent improvements or betterments made to increase the value of any property or estate."

3. For a period near the end of World War II, the taxpayer constructed all its capital improvements. At other times, outside contractors have performed part of this work. At the time of the trial of this tax case, the taxpayer had 140 employees engaged in new construction; it has had as many as 300 employees so engaged.

4. For 1962 and 1963 the taxpayer's gross construction additions were $8,235,440.22 and $5,988,139.56, respectively. Of these amounts, the taxpayer itself constructed $7,139,940.72 and $5,642,342.79. The self-construction portion, therefore, obviously was a substantial part of the gross. The equipment depreciation for those years, to the extent allocated to use in construction and capitalized on the taxpayer's books, amounted to $150,047.42 and $130,523.99, respectively. These were the depreciation amounts deducted for income tax purposes, the major portions of which are presently at issue.

5. For purposes of the issue here presented, the key phrase of

§ 167(a)(1) is "property used in the trade or business." Construction of this phrase in the present context has been infrequent and not consistent. In *Great Northern R. Co. v. Commissioner*, 40 F.2d 372 (CA8), ... the court held that where a railroad transported men and equipment to a construction site, the depreciation of the train attributable to the construction work was to be capitalized. No consideration was given to whether the claimed deduction was available for property used in the taxpayer's trade or business....

In a subsequent case, *Great Northern R. Co. v. Commissioner*, 30 B.T.A. 691 (1934), the Board of Tax Appeals reached the contrary result on identical facts. The Board held that the train equipment, even though used in part for construction of branch lines of the railroad, was used in *a* trade or business, and that this satisfied the requirements of the statute. The depreciation, therefore, was held deductible. *Id.*, at 708. This appears to have been the prevailing view until the issuance of Rev. Rul. 59-380, 1959-2 Cum. Bull. 87, where it was stated:

"In the instant case the capital improvements constructed constitute property to be used in the trade or business or property held for the production of income. However, the building equipment used in the construction cannot be considered as property used in the regular trade or business of the taxpayer." *Id.* at 88.

Rev. Rul. 59-380 was in part the basis for the holding of the Court of Claims in *Southern Natural Gas Co. v. United States*, 188 Ct. Cl. 302, 378–379, 412 F.2d 1222, 1268 (1969). The Court of Claims rejected the "*a* trade or business" approach in favor of the rule that, to be deductible from current income, depreciation must be of property used in *the* trade or business of the taxpayer. Equipment, to the extent used by the taxpayer in construction of additional facilities, was not used in *the* trade or business of the natural gas company. Thus, no depreciation deduction was allowable and the contested amount of depreciation was to be capitalized.

In the instant case, the Court of Appeals concluded that transportation equipment used by the taxpayer to construct its own capital improvements was used in the trade or business of the taxpayer:

"The continuity and regularity of taxpayer's construction activities, the number of employees engaged in construction and the amounts expended on construction all point to the conclusion that construction of facilities is a major aspect of the taxpayer's trade or business. These activities are auxiliary operations incident to the taxpayer's principal trade or business of producing, transmitting, distributing and selling electrical energy within the meaning of section 167." 477 F.2d, at 696.

Since the Commissioner appears to have conceded the literal application of § 167(a) to Idaho Power's equipment depreciation, we need not reach the issue whether the Court of Appeals has given the phrase "used in the trade or business" a proper construction. For purposes of this case, we assume, without deciding, that § 167(a) does have a literal application to the depreciation of the taxpayer's transportation equipment used in the construction of its capital improvements.

6. "§ 161. Allowance of deductions.

"In computing taxable income under section 63(a), there shall be allowed as deductions the items specified in this part, subject to the exceptions provided in part IX (sec. 261 and following, relating to items not deductible)."

7. The Committee on Terminology of the American Institute of Certified Public Accountants has discussed various definitions of depreciation and concluded that:

"These definitions view depreciation, broadly speaking, as describing not downward changes of value regardless of their causes but a money cost incident to exhaustion of usefulness. The term is sometimes applied to the exhaustion itself, but the committee considers it desirable to emphasize the cost concept as the primary if not the sole accounting meaning of the term: thus, *depreciation* means the cost of such exhaustion, as wages means the cost of labor." 2 APB Accounting Principles, Accounting Terminology Bulletin No. 1 — Review and Resumé ¶ 48, p. 9512 (1973) (emphasis in original).

8. The general proposition that good accounting practice requires capitalization of the cost of acquiring a capital asset is not seriously open to question. The Commissioner urges, however, that accounting methods as a rule require the treatment of construction-related depreciation of equipment as a capital cost of the facility constructed. Indeed, there is accounting authority for this. See, *e.g.*, W. Paton, Asset Accounting 188, 192–193 (1952); H. Finney & H. Miller, Principles of Accounting — Introductory 246–247 (6th ed. 1963) (depreciation as an expense should be matched with the production of income); W. Paton, Accountants' Handbook 652 (3d ed. 1943); Note, 1973 Duke L.J. 1377, 1384; Note, 52 N.C.L.Rev. 684, 692 (1974).

9. Except for the Court of Appeals in the present case, the courts consistently have upheld the position of the Commissioner that construction-related depreciation is to be capitalized. *Great Northern R. Co. v. Commissioner*, 30 B.T.A. 691 (1934), upon which the Court of Appeals relied, is not to the contrary. In that case the Board concluded that construction-related depreciation was deductible under the Revenue Act of 1928, § 23(k), 45 Stat. 800 (the provision corresponding to § 167(a)(1) of the 1954 Code). The Commissioner in that case, however, had not argued for the capitalization of construction-related depreciation. 30 B.T.A., at 708.

12. "§ 261. General rule for disallowance of deductions.

"In computing taxable income no deduction shall in any case be allowed in respect of the items specified in this part."

MR. JUSTICE DOUGLAS, dissenting.

This Court has, to many, seemed particularly ill-equipped to resolve income tax disputes between the Commissioner and the taxpayers. The reasons are (1) that the field has become increasingly technical and complicated due to the expansions of the Code and the proliferation of decisions, and (2) that we seldom see enough of them to develop any expertise in the area. Indeed, we are called upon mostly to resolve conflicts between the circuits which more providently should go to the standing committee of the Congress for resolution....

... I disagree with the Court in disallowing the present claim for depreciation. A company truck has, let us say, a life of 10 years. If it cost $10,000, one would expect that "a reasonable allowance for the exhaustion, wear and tear" of the truck would be $1,000 a year within the meaning of 26 U.S.C. § 167(a). That was the provision in the House Report of the 1954 Code when it said that it provided for "a liberalization of depreciation with respect to both the estimate of useful life of property and the method of allocating the depreciable cost over the years of service." (Footnote 1) H.R. Rep. No. 1337, 83d Cong., 2d Sess., 22.

Not so, says the Government. Since the truck was used to build a plant for the taxpayer and the plant has a useful life of 40 years, a lower rate of depreciation must be used—a rate that would spread out the life of the truck for 40 years even though it would not last more than 10. Section 167 provides for a depreciation deduction with respect to property "used in the (taxpayer's) trade or business" or "held for the production of income" by the taxpayer. There is no intimation that § 167(a) is not satisfied. The argument is rested upon § 161 which allows the deductions specified in § 167(a) "subject to the exceptions" in § 263(a) which provides:

"No deduction shall be allowed for—

"(1) Any amount paid out for new buildings or for permanent improvements or for betterments made to increase the value of any property or estate...."

I agree with the Court of Appeals that depreciation claimed on a truck whose useful life is 10 years is not an amount "paid out" within the meaning of § 263(a)(1). If "payment" in the setting of § 263(a)(1) is to be read as including depreciation, Congress—not the courts—should make the decision.

I suspect that if the life of the vehicle were 40 years and the life of the building were 10 years the Internal Revenue Service would be here arguing persuasively that depreciation of the vehicle should be taken over a 40-year period. That is not to impugn the integrity of the IRS. It is only an illustration of the capricious character of how law is construed to get from the taxpayer the greatest possible return that is permissible under the Code.

The opinion of the Court of Appeals ... states my view of the law....

The IRS, however, has ruled that depreciation on construction equipment owned by a taxpayer and used in its construction work must be capitalized. (Footnote 3) That Revenue Ruling, as the Court of Appeals held, is a legal opinion within the agency, not a Regulation or Treasury decision. It is without force when it conflicts with an Act of Congress. (Footnote 4)....

If the test under § 263(a)(1) were the cost of capital improvements, the result would be different. But, as noted, the test is "any amount paid out," which certainly does not describe depreciation deductions unless words are to acquire esoteric meanings merely to accommodate the IRS. Congress is the lawmaker; and taking the law from it, we should affirm the Court of Appeals.

FOOTNOTES:

1. The Committee indicated that "reasonable" depreciation allowances include the straightline method, the declining-balance method, or any other method that on an annual basis does not exceed the allowances on the declining-balance method. H.R. Rep. No. 1337, 83d Cong., 2d Sess., 22–23.

The purpose of providing more liberal depreciation allowances was explicitly stated:

"More liberal depreciation allowances are anticipated to have far-reaching economic effects. The incentives resulting from the changes are well timed to help maintain the present high level of investment in plant and equipment. The acceleration in the speed of the tax-free recovery of costs is of critical importance in the decision of management to incur risk. The faster tax writeoff would increase available working capital and materially aid growing businesses in the financing of their expansion. For all segments of the American economy, liberalized depreciation policies should assist modernization and expansion of industrial capacity, with resulting economic growth, increased production and a higher standard of living.

"Small business and farmers particularly have a vital stake in a more liberal and constructive depreciation policy. They are especially dependent on their current earnings or short-term loans to obtain funds for expansion. The faster recovery of capital investment provided by this bill will permit them to secure short-term loans which would otherwise not be available." *Id.*, at 24.

3. Rev. Rul. 59-380, 1959-2 Cum. Bull. 87, 88.

"[D]epreciation sustained on construction equipment owned by a taxpayer and used in the erection of capital improvements for its own use is not an allowable deduction, but shall be added to and made a part of the cost of the capital improvements. So much thereof as is applicable to the cost of depreciable capital improvements is recoverable through deductions for depreciation over the useful life of such capital improvements.

"In the instant case the capital improvements constructed constitute property to be used in the trade or business or property held for the production of income. However, the building equipment used in the construction cannot be considered as property used in the regular trade or business of the taxpayer."

4. "[D]epartmental rulings not promulgated by the Secretary are of little aid in interpreting a tax statute...," *Biddle v. Commissioner*, 302 U.S. 573, 582. Indeed, each issue of the Internal Revenue Bulletin warns that "Revenue Rulings ... reported in the Bulletin do not have the force and effect of Treasury Department Regulations...."

Consider the following questions concerning *Idaho Power.*

1. How did the taxpayer's tax treatment of equipment it used in construction of its facilities differ from its financial accounting treatment of the item? Over how many years did the taxpayer depreciate the equipment?

2. What was the government's position in the case? Did the government contend that the equipment was not depreciable?

3. Review our discussion of depreciation in Part II. **Review section 263(a)(1). Does section 263(a)(1)** have application under both the taxpayer's and the government's theories of the case?

4. Is the cost of the equipment a capital expenditure? If both the taxpayer and the government would agree with this proposition, what is the nature of their difference? **Recall *Woodward* in Part II, Chapter 3.** Why does the Court cite *Woodward*?

5. In his dissent, Justice Douglas states: "I suspect that if the life of the vehicle were 40 years and the life of the building were 10 years the Internal Revenue Service would be here arguing persuasively that depreciation of the vehicle should be taken over a 40-year period." Is this a cynical view? Should the Service always take a position that will maximize the revenue?

6. **Look at section 263A(a).** Why didn't the Court cite this section?

In *Idaho Power* (and, earlier in *Encyclopaedia Britannica*), you saw one type of problem that taxpayers face in trying to account for the costs they have paid or incurred in acquiring or creating an asset. But once a taxpayer has calculated its investment, it may encounter another question: how to account for the recovery of that capital on disposition.

Now, recall our earlier discussion of section 1001 of the Code and the concept of adjusted basis under section 1016. But, the calculation of adjusted basis is only a first step in some instances. If there are multiple items of income to which that adjusted basis relates, how should the taxpayer allocate that basis?

Suppose, for example, Cecilia bought a 50-acre parcel of land, intending to subdivide it into 50 one-acre lots, which she will offer to the public for sale. She paid $500,000 for the 50 acres. She sells the first lot for $25,000. Suppose that she would prefer to postpone recognizing any gain until she has sold all 50 lots. Can she do so? **Look at Treasury Regulation section 1.61-6. Then, consider the following case.**

INAJA LAND COMPANY, LTD. v. COMMISSIONER
9 T.C. 727 (1947)

The issue is whether petitioner received taxable income of $48,945 under a certain indenture of August 11, 1939, whereby it granted the city of Los Angeles, California, certain easements over its land and settling all claims arising out of the release of foreign waters from the city's Mono Craters Tunnel project....

FINDINGS OF FACT.

Petitioner is a stock corporation, organized under the laws of California....

On or about January 26, 1928, petitioner acquired approximately 1,236 acres of land in Mono County, California, together with all water and water rights appurtenant or belonging thereto, at a cost of approximately $61,000. This property was located along the banks of the Owens River, which flows through and over petitioner's land, involved in this controversy. The land was 2 1/2 miles long and 1 1/2 miles wide at its farthest extremities and included the following classifications:

	Acres
Rocky hill lands	419
Irrigated rocky pasture	195
Dry rocky pasture	104
Irrigated meadows	358
Dry tillable brush	160
Total	1,236

When the property was acquired in 1928 there were two small cabins or shacks located thereon. In 1940 petitioner purchased and moved onto the property two cabins, one to replace the southwest cabin and the other as an addition to the caretaker's cabin. In the years prior to 1939, with the consent of the board of directors, four members, at their own expense, had each erected a cabin for his own use, and in 1940 two members at their own expense each purchased and moved onto the property an additional cabin.

Petitioner's purpose in acquiring its properties was to operate a private fishing club thereon, with incidental rental of its properties for grazing livestock. It has conducted these activities since the time of its incorporation to date.

Petitioner's organization consists of twenty-five members, each owning twenty shares of stock. It has a president, a vice president, a secretary-treasurer, an assistant secretary, and a board of five directors. The members pay no dues, but the stock is assessable. An annual assessment, with the exception of one or two years, has been levied to cover expenses and amortization of loans.

The principal value of petitioner's lands to petitioner arose from the fishing facilities offered by the Owens River as it flowed through and over petitioner's land; but it also had some value for grazing purposes. The property was not used for agricultural purposes, other than livestock grazing. Aside from the receipt of the amount in controversy, the only sources of income are, and have been, its receipts from guest card fees and its receipt of grazing rentals. The amounts of guest card fees received by petitioner in the years 1939 to 1946, inclusive, and the amount of grazing rentals for the years 1936 to 1946, inclusive, are as follows:

Year	Guest fees	Grazing rentals	Year	Guest fees	Grazing rentals
1936		$300	1942	$105	$550
1937		300	1943	145	1,000
1938		300	1944	110	1,000
1939	$330	300	1945	275	1,000
1940	310	300	1946	340	1,000
1941	130	550			

Each stockholder is entitled to the use of the properties for guests for not exceeding eight guest days a season, and each day or fraction of a day a guest uses the privileges of petitioner is counted as one guest day. The fee collectible, either from the stockholder or the guest, is $5 per day. Petitioner's rules regarding guests and guest card fees are designed to restrict the number of guests and not to develop a source of revenue. The decline in guest card fee receipts following 1939 was due in part to poor fishing on account of increased flow and muddy water and, in later years, to gasoline rationing. The increase in grazing rental following the year 1939 was not due to any increase in grazing area or the number of grazing cattle, but to the fact that higher prices for cattle and cattle fodder enabled petitioner to demand higher grazing rentals, and for the year 1943 and subsequent years the leases were revised to free the lessee from the requirement of maintaining two men to keep poachers off petitioner's property.

The Department of Water and Power of the City of Los Angeles, a municipal corporation, is responsible for the construction, operation, and maintenance of the water supply of that city. On or about September 25, 1934, the Department of Water and Power commenced the construction of Mono Craters Tunnel in Mono County (the west portal of this tunnel being in Mono Basin and the east portal being in the Owens River Drainage Basin.) On or about January 18, 1940, the westerly aqueduct connecting this tunnel with Grant Lake Storage Reservoir was completed. On or about April 4, 1940, the first diversion of Mono Basin waters into the west portal of the tunnel was commenced. The east portal of the Mono Craters Tunnel opens into the Owens River at a point approximately two miles up the river from petitioner's property. In the operation of the Mono Craters Tunnel the city of Los Angeles has stored waters in the Grant Lake Storage Reservoir and Walker Lake, and natural storage has occurred in unregulated lakes, all in the Mono Basin. The object of the tunnel project was, and the result accomplished is, to divert waters which would naturally remain in the Mono Basin into the Owens River at a point upstream from petitioner's lands. These waters flow through or over petitioner's lands. The waters are recaptured from the river by the city at a point below petitioner's lands and are diverted into the water supply system of the city of Los Angeles. The waters flowing out of or released from the east portal of the Mono Craters Tunnel are "foreign waters" (that is, waters brought into the watershed from another source by artificial means) with respect to the Owens River Drainage Basin, and would not naturally flow into this river if it were not for the tunnel.

During the entire period of the construction of the Mono Craters Tunnel, seepage waters from the tunnel in a substantial amount of between 10 and 15 cubic second feet flowed out of the east portal of the tunnel into the Owens River and through and over petitioner's lands. These seepage waters were polluted to a substantial extent by concrete dust, sediment, and foreign matter, which injured and killed fish and interfered with the fishing on petitioner's lands.

Prior to the settling of the rights of petitioner and the city of Los Angeles by the execution of an indenture dated August 11, 1939, except as hereinafter stated, the city was not possessed of, and had not acquired, either by way of condemnation, prescription, user, grant or license, any right to divert, release, or suffer the release of waters into the Owens River in such a manner that such waters would flow through or over petitioner's lands, or to deposit or permit the deposit of foreign matter in or to pollute the Owens River as it flowed through petitioner's land; nor had the city compensated petitioner in respect to these matters. Petitioner had not given the city any release or acquittance with respect thereto, except for the period from November 12 to December 2, 1935, when petitioner gave the city a revocable license to "dump" waters into the river, and the city engineer was given permission to enter on petitioner's lands for the purpose of making surveys.

Between September 25, 1934, the date the Mono Craters Tunnel project was commenced, and August 11, 1939, petitioner and its attorneys complained to the city and its officials concerning trespasses and invasions by the city and its employees and against unauthorized fishing and poaching by city employees upon petitioner's lands and rights. Petitioner threatened to institute injunctive and other legal proceedings. After extended negotiations, petitioner and the city entered into an arm's length agreement settling their differences on August 11, 1939. The indenture of August 11, 1939, after reciting that petitioner, grantor, is the owner of certain described lands and that the city of Los Angeles, as grantee, is constructing and intends to construct a tunnel known as Mono Craters Tunnel, contains the further recital, covenants and provisions material hereto, as follows:

(e) WHEREAS, a dispute has arisen between the parties hereto wherein Grantor claims that it has been and is being damaged by reason of the discharge into said Owens River, at a point upstream from Grantor's land, of foreign waters, and that such damage will continue henceforth, and in a greater degree when said tunnel is completed and in use, and said Grantor has threatened to sue for damages and for an injunction, and the Grantee desires to obtain from Grantor the right to discharge all such foreign water into said river in the future, and the parties hereto are desirous of settling their differences, and for these purposes the parties have executed, delivered and accepted this indenture for the hereinafter mentioned consideration, rights and covenants.

I. FOR AND IN CONSIDERATION of the sum of Fifty Thousand Dollars ($50,000.00), lawful money of the United States, paid by the Department of Water and Power of The City of Los Angeles, receipt of which is hereby acknowledged by Grantor, and of the covenants, conditions and promises on the part of Grantee herein contained:

(A) The Grantor has released and forever discharged and by these presents does for itself, its successors and assigns, release and forever discharge The City of Los Angeles and the said Department of Water and Power of said City of and from all manner of actions, causes of action, suits, controversies, trespasses, damages, claims and demands whatsoever, in law or in equity, which it now has, or ever had, or may have against said City and said Department of Water and Power by reason of the discharging, releasing and emptying of foreign waters from the easterly portal of the Mono Craters Tunnel into the Owens River at a point upstream from Grantor's lands resulting in the said waters flowing in and outside of the channel of the Owens River across and over grantor's land, and by reason of discharging, releasing and emptying waters from any and all other sources into said Owens River resulting in said waters flowing in and outside of the channel of the Owens River across and over Grantor's land and, further, by reason of any and all other acts of whatsoever kind or nature of said Department, its employees, officers, or agents, upon, in connection with or pertaining to Grantor's land, and any and all adjoining lands owned by Grantor, and for all time up to and including the date of the execution and delivery of this agreement, and its acceptance by Grantee.

(B) The Grantee, both for itself and for the Department of Water and Power of The City of Los Angeles, has released and forever discharged and by these presents does for itself, its successors and assigns, release and forever discharge the Grantor of and from all manner of actions, causes of action, suits, controversies, trespasses, damages, claims and demands whatsoever, in law or in equity, which said City or said Department of Water and Power may have for all time up to and including the date of the execution and delivery of this agreement, and its acceptance by Grantee.

(C) The Grantor does hereby and by these presents grant, convey and transfer unto the Grantee all those certain permanent and exclusive rights of way and easements at any time and from time to time to convey all foreign waters into the channel of the Owens River at a point therein near said easterly portal and upstream from Grantor's land, over, through and across said lands by natural gravity flow in the flood channel or channels of said Owens River and over, through and across such other portions of Grantor's land as may be inundated and overflowed at high stages of flow, without being materially diminished in quantity or being materially impaired in quality by any act of Grantor, its successors or assigns, for the purpose of being recaptured by Grantee and used at any time or place of diversion downstream from said hereinafter described lands; and said easement shall include the right so to convey said foreign waters even though, when combined with the natural waters flowing in said Owens River, they exceed the safe carrying capacity of said channel or channels of said Owens River as it now exists or as said channel or channels hereafter may exist upon said Grantor's lands, or damages or injuries [sic] said lands by inundation, flooding, overflowing the existing channel or channels, cutting a new channel or channels from time to time, silting, cutting, washing, raising the underground water level or in any other manner whatsoever or at all.

Reserving unto Grantor, its successors and assigns, the following:

1. The right and privilege, at its own expense, of directing the flow of said waters upon, over and across Grantor's lands and/or confining the area overflowed by said foreign waters and natural waters by dredging, deepening, cleaning out or straightening any existing channel of said Owens River, by dredging an additional channel or channels on Grantor's lands or by any other reasonable manner or method, provided that the same is consistent with good engineering practice in the operation of Grantee's municipal water system and does not interfere with the reasonable flowage of said discharged waters upon, over, across and off of Grantor's lands.

2. All waters and water rights, riparian, appropriated or of whatsoever kind or nature, now owned or possessed by Grantor.

3. The exclusive fishing, hunting and trapping rights and privileges in and about all waters, both foreign and natural, flowing in said Owens River, its branches, tributaries, flood waters and back waters, all rights to use said lands for the purpose of agriculture, horticulture, bee-raising, farming, ranching, raising and/or pasturing livestock, the erection or maintenance of structures incidental or convenient thereto, the use of said lands for the construction and maintenance of residential ranch or farm cabins or lodges, or structures incidental thereto, provided that the same does not interfere with the full, free and complete possession, use and enjoyment by grantee of all the rights herein granted.

The grantee also covenants to perform certain other conditions regulating and limiting the amount of water released by the grantee.

Petitioner expended in 1939 the sum of $1,055 for attorneys' fees and costs in connection with the settlement with the city.

Under the indenture of August 11, 1939, the petitioner reserved substantial beneficial interests in its properties and has continued to function and operate as a fishing club, with incidental leasing out of its lands for grazing livestock from the date of the indenture to the present time. The indenture permits the city to release foreign waters into the Owens River in such quantities that the total of the foreign and natural waters flowing into that river as it enters petitioner's lands shall not exceed 400 cubic feet per second. The Mono Craters Tunnel has a capacity of 365 cubic feet per second. The natural flow of the Owens River as it enters petitioner's lands was not less than 35 cubic feet per second for the years 1939 to 1946, inclusive. The natural flow of the Owens River through petitioner's lands in terms of mean annual cubic feet per second, and the highest daily average released from the east portal of the Mono Craters Tunnel, are as follows:

Year	Natural flow, feet per second	Released from tunnel, feet per second
1940	45.9	110.9
1941	56.1	266.
1942	64.	173.9
1943	61.3	169.5
1944	53.7	140.
1945	59.4	206.8
1946	60.3	19.8

The amounts of water released from the Mono Craters Tunnel into Owens River in the years 1939 to date have resulted in substantial injury and damage to petitioner and its properties in that (a) the quality and quantity of the fish have been reduced; (b) grazing lands have been damaged and grazing fodder reduced from 25 per cent to 35 per cent below its former quality and quantity; (c) irrigation ditches and intake gates have been damaged, necessitating repairs; (d) the river banks have been cut and undermined and the character of the stream altered; and (e) the meadow lands have been flooded for extended periods. Petitioner has been put to an expense of $13,800 in constructing a diversion ditch in an attempt to control the waters flowing through and over its property. It also expended $1,409.30 in 1939 and 1940 in restocking the Owens River with some 50,000 small fry and some 3,000 full sized fish in an attempt to replace fish destroyed by the Mono Craters Tunnel project. Petitioner has not used and does not have need to use the Mono Craters Tunnel waters or the diversion ditch for irrigation purposes.

The adjusted basis of petitioner's properties was more than $50,000 on January 1, 1939. Disregarding the sum in controversy, no event occurred in 1939 which would cause or require the adjusted basis of these properties to be reduced below $50,000 for the taxable year involved.

The petitioner's income and excess profits tax return for the taxable year 1939 did not report receipt of any income from the city of Los Angeles, but included a schedule which reported receipt of $50,000 from the city in connection with a certain written agreement and settlement of certain specified matters, wherein expenses amounted to $1,055, and petitioner received a net amount of $48,945. In his deficiency notice the respondent included the sum of $48,945 as taxable income to petitioner under section 22(a) of the Internal Revenue Code.

OPINION.

LEECH, *Judge*: The question presented is whether the net amount of $48,945 received by petitioner in the taxable year 1939 under a certain indenture constitutes taxable income under section 22(a), or is chargeable to capital account. The respondent contends: (a) That the $50,000, less $1,055 expenses incurred, which petitioner received from the city of Los Angeles under the indenture of August 11, 1939, represented compensation for loss of present and future income and consideration for release of many meritorious causes of action against the city, constituting ordinary income; and, (b) since petitioner has failed to allocate such sum between taxable and nontaxable income, it has not sustained its burden of showing error. Petitioner maintains that the language of the indenture and the circumstances leading up to its execution demonstrate that the consideration was paid for the easement granted to the city of Los Angeles and the consequent damage to its property rights; that the loss of past or future profits was not considered or involved; that the character of the easement rendered it impracticable to attempt to apportion a basis to the property affected; and, since the sum received is less than the basis of the entire property, taxation should be postponed until the final disposition of the property.

The recitals in the indenture of August 11, 1939, indicate its principal purpose was to convey to the city of Los Angeles a right of way and perpetual easements to discharge water upon and flood the lands of petitioner, in connection with the water supply of the city. Among its covenants are reciprocal releases by the respective parties. The respondent relies heavily on the language of the release by petitioner as grantor, contained in paragraph (A) of the indenture, which is set forth in full in our findings of fact. We think the respondent places too much emphasis upon the release provision of the indenture. It is usual and customary in agreements of this character to incorporate a provision for the release and discharge of any possible past, present, or future claims and demands. The mutuality of the releases indicates the purpose was precautionary and protective rather than descriptive and in recognition of asserted claims and demands. Paragraph (e) of the indenture recites that "a dispute has arisen between the parties hereto wherein Grantor claims that it has been and is being damaged by reason of the discharge into said Owens River ... of foreign waters, and that such damage will continue henceforth...." The character of the damage is not specified or otherwise indicated. The record reveals, through the testimony of petitioner's officers and its attorneys who carried on the negotiations culminating in the agreement, that no claim for damages for lost profits or income was ever asserted or considered. Of primary concern was the fact that, if the city were permitted to continue interference with petitioner's rights as riparian owner, the city might acquire, by prescription or user, the right to direct foreign waters into the Owens River, flooding petitioner's lands and interfering with its fishing rights by polluting the stream. The threat of an injunction suit was to protect petitioner against the city acquiring such rights without making proper compensation therefor. The evidence does not disclose any claim for or loss of income. There is some evidence that employees of the city, from time to time, engaged in unauthorized fishing and poaching upon petitioner's lands. The remedy of the petitioner for such wrongful acts would be against the individuals and not against the municipality, since clearly such tortious acts were not within the scope of their employment. Obviously, no part of the consideration received by petitioner from the city was paid for the release of such claims and demands. The recital in the indenture that petitioner, as grantor, released the city from all claims and demands "by reason of any and all other acts of whatsoever kind or nature of said Department, its employees, officers, or agents, upon, in connection with or pertaining to Grantor's land" embraces such acts as were within the scope of their employment. The record does not disclose the existence of such acts, if there were any. No claims or demands based on acts of that character had been made. We conclude that petitioner has satisfactorily established that the $50,000 it received in 1939 was consideration paid by the city for a right of way and easements and for resulting damages to its property and property rights.

The respondent further contends that petitioner has failed to allocate any portion of the $50,000 to nontaxable recovery of capital. He argues that the payment was a "lump sum" settlement related to many things which were not connected with petitioner's capital, such as loss of grazing rentals, guest card fees, and loss of fish from pollution. The record establishes that the grazing rentals were constant and that the guest fees were not intended to develop a source of operating revenue, but merely to restrict the number of guests. Pollution of the stream is an injury to property. The loss of fish as a result of the pollution of the river could form no basis for a claim, since fish in their wild state belong to the sovereign. In support of his position the respondent relies upon *Raytheon Production Corporation*, 1 T.C. 952; affd., 144 Fed.(2d) 110 ... *R. J. Durkee*, 6 T.C. 773; since reversed, 162 Fed.(2d) 184. In the *Durkee case*, the Circuit Court says:

It is settled that since profits from business are taxable, a sum received in settlement of litigation based upon a loss of profits is likewise taxable; but where the settlement represents damages for lost capital rather than for lost profits the money received is a return of capital and not taxable.... [Citing many cases.] The difficulty is in determining whether the recovery is for lost profits or for lost capital. The test is as stated by this Court in *Farmers' & Merchants' Bank v. Commissioner*, ... namely, "The fund involved must be considered in the light of the claim from which it was realized and which is reflected in the petition filed."

Upon this record we have concluded that no part of the recovery was paid for loss of profits, but was paid for the conveyance of a right of way and easements, and for damages to petitioner's land and its property rights as riparian owner. Hence, the respondent's contention has no merit. Capital recoveries in excess of cost do constitute taxable income. Petitioner has made no attempt to allocate a basis to that part of the property covered by the easements. It is conceded that all of petitioner's lands were not affected by the easements conveyed. Petitioner does not contest the rule that, where property is acquired for a lump sum and subsequently disposed of a portion at a time, there must be an allocation of the cost or other basis over the several units and gain or loss computed on the disposition of each part, except where apportionment would be wholly impracticable or impossible. *Nathan Blum*, 5 T.C. 702, 709. Petitioner argues that it would be impracticable and impossible to apportion a definite basis to the easements here involved, since they could not be described by metes and bounds; that the flow of the water has changed and will change the course of the river; that the extent of the flood was and is not predictable; and that to date the city has not released the full measure of water to which it is entitled. In *Strother v. Commissioner*, 55 Fed.(2d) 626, the court says:

... A taxpayer ... should not be charged with gain on pure conjecture unsupported by any foundation of ascertainable fact. *See Burnet v. Logan*, 283 U.S. 404....

... Apportionment with reasonable accuracy of the amount received not being possible, and this amount being less than petitioner's cost basis for the property, it can not be determined that petitioner has, in fact, realized gain in any amount. Applying the rule as above set out, no portion of the payment in question should be considered as income, but the full amount must be treated as a return of capital and applied in reduction of petitioner's cost basis. *Burnet v. Logan*, 283 U.S. 404....

Decision will be entered for the petitioner.

Consider the following questions concerning *Inaja Land*.

1. Why did the court make the finding of fact that "[t]he adjusted basis of petitioner's properties was more than $50,000 on January 1, 1939"?

2. If Inaja Land Company received the net amount of $48,945 from the City of Los Angeles, how could *all* of it be characterized as gross income as the government contended?

Recall *Raytheon* **in Part II.** What test must you apply in a situation such as this in order to characterize the proceeds? What test did the *Inaja Land* court apply?

3. What was Inaja Land Company's position in the case?

What does the concept "chargeable to capital account" mean? Where have you seen this language before? **Recall Revenue Ruling 81-277 (in Part II) and its discussion of section 1016(a)(1).** Under Inaja Land's theory of the case, would its receipt of the $48,945 have affected its basis in the land?

4. Inaja Land Company conceded that not all of its lands were affected by the easements it conveyed. Why didn't Inaja Land Company allocate its recovery and basis to the use of the land it lost, and report a gain or loss under section 1001? Has there been a "sale or other disposition"?

5. Suppose you bought 100 shares of stock for $1,000 on July 1, 1990. On July 1, 1999 you decide to sell 15 shares for $500. Do you realize gain or loss under section 1001?

Suppose you had bought an additional 100 shares of the same stock on July 1, 1995, for $5,000. Does this fact affect your answer with respect to the tax consequences of the sale of 15 shares for $500 on July 1, 1999? **Look at Treasury Regulation section 1.1012-1(c).**

An additional special method of accounting that frequently over-rides the normal rules is the installment method. Section 453 of the Code sets forth the treatment of installment payments that result when a taxpayer agrees to sell an asset with payments due over a period of time. Of course, we are all familiar with the type of installment sale that occurs when someone purchases a car or furniture "on time." Another common example is seller-financing of a home. The buyer makes a downpayment to the seller and the seller then "takes back a mortgage," that is, the seller makes a mortgage loan to the buyer equal to the unpaid portion of the purchase price and the buyer executes both a promissory note and a mortgage (security interest) to the seller. The buyer agrees to make a series of payments, each consisting of both principal and interest. How should the seller treat the payments? Of what does each consist?

Remember TOAD. Under the installment method, a part of each payment represents the return of the seller's basis. What about the balance? A portion of the balance represents interest on the unpaid amount and the rest represents the seller's profit on the transaction. Section 453 provides the rules for allocating the amounts between TOAD and profit after reduction for the interest amount.

In the simple example, allocation of basis to each payment creates no problems. If the total amount of payments is fixed and the payments represent the purchase of a single item, it is a simple matter to allocate basis ratably to each payment.

Suppose Peggy, who is a cash basis taxpayer, decides to sell the house she owns.[3] After months of listing it, the only willing purchaser is C.W., a recent law school graduate. Because he has student loans and has been employed for only a few months, he has been unable to secure a commitment from any bank to make a mortgage loan to him to buy Peggy's house. Peggy offers to give him a "purchase money mortgage" loan; that is,

---

3. Some of you may have heard that in some cases, taxpayers can "rollover" the proceeds from the sale of a principal residence to a new residence without the payment of tax. Congress repealed the rollover provision as part of the 1997 Tax Act and substituted a gain exclusion provision. We will take up discussion of this topic in Chapter 3. For the purpose of this hypothetical, assume that Peggy does not qualify for gain exclusion because the house she is selling is not her principal residence.

Peggy will allow C.W. to pay for the house over a period of time (for example, twenty years). In exchange, C.W. will give Peggy a note promising to make payments at regular intervals, including interest at an agreed-upon rate, and a "mortgage," that is, a security interest in the property.[4]

Many of you have probably entered into one or more installment sales: purchasing an automobile, buying a large consumer item like a television or stereo system,[5] or even buying clothes on layaway. These are all common examples of installment sales. Note that even though in the automobile sale the purchaser has the use of the car before the full balance is paid, while in the clothing layaway case, the buyer does not, they are both installment sales.

Suppose the sale by Peggy to C.W. was for $120,000 payable $20,000 upon the "closing"[6] and $100,000 over a period of 20 years with simple interest at the rate of 10% per annum. You may assume that the 10% interest rate exceeds the current applicable federal rate. Therefore, you need not be concerned in this problem with the more difficult calculations that result from a stated interest rate that is below the applicable federal rate. If an installment obligation provides for no interest or for a rate that is below the applicable federal rate at the time the sale occurs, the rules of sections 483 or 1274 will require the taxpayers to make a calculation of how much of the putative principal is, in fact, interest.[7] (The current rules require a calculation of the present value of the total of the payments due and comparison of it to the amount of the payments actually required. In calculating the present value, the taxpayer uses the applicable federal rate at the time of the transaction, compounded semi-annually.)

The temptation to understate interest often arises from the desire of the seller to increase the amount of his capital gain on the sale and minimize the amount of interest he will receive over the payment period. From the buyer's viewpoint, the conversion of interest to principal will deny her the full amount of the interest deduction she deserved. She will, however, have a higher basis in the asset. For some taxpayers this is a small sacrifice. For example, a taxpayer who does not itemize deductions would not be able to deduct the interest incurred in purchasing a personal residence; a taxpayer who does itemize deductions may, nevertheless, be unable to deduct the interest on purchases of other types of assets due to the limitation of section 163(h).

Assume the closing occurs on January 1 of the current year and C.W. is obligated to make each of his 20 payments on January 1st of each year, beginning January 1 of the next year. Suppose too that Peggy's basis in the house was $60,000. What will Peggy's total income from the sale be? When should she report the income? How many alternative methods can you suggest?

---

4. Peggy can record her security interest on the land records for the locality in which the house is located in order to give notice to any interested person that C.W. owes her a debt that is secured by the property. If at any time before full payment C.W. fails to make the payments specified in the note, Peggy can "foreclose" on her interest and either take back the property or force its sale.

5. Recall studying *Fuentes v. Shevin*, 407 U.S. 67 (1972).

6. "Closing" is the term used to describe the consummation of the sale, at which time the benefits and burdens of ownership pass from the seller to the buyer. Title may also pass at the same time; but, in some cases, title does not pass until the last installment payment has been made and the seller's (or other lender's) security interest in the property is discharged.

7. The rules of section 1274 govern most debt instruments issued for property, but the rules of section 483 govern the sale of a principal residence.

Congress has chosen as the applicable method of reporting most installment sales, one that allows the taxpayer to allocate each payment (excluding interest[8]) she receives between return of capital ("basis") and realized gain on the sale. **Look at section 453(a), (b)(1), and (c).** Code section 453 does not define "gross profit" or "total contract price." Where would you next look for these definitions?

Now consider the following questions.

1. Note that the Treasury regulation defining the terms used in Code section 453 is a "temporary" regulation. Do you recall the earlier discussion of the significance of that designation?

2. What is the difference between a "proposed regulation" and a "temporary regulation," if any?

3. What is Peggy's "gross profit" from the sale? What is the "total contract price" of the sale?

4. State as a formula how Peggy will compute her income for each tax year as required by section 453(c) of the Code. What term does the regulation apply to this formula?

5. Calculate the amount of interest income Peggy will have for the current year if she is a cash basis taxpayer.

6. Would your answer be different if she is an accrual basis taxpayer?

7. How much will C.W. pay Peggy the next year? How much will she include in gross income under which parts of section 61?[9]

Compare the consequences of Peggy's installment sale of her property to C.W. with what would happen if she sold the property for $110,000 in cash and placed the proceeds in a savings account.[10] First, note that when she engaged in the installment sale to C.W. she was not taxed on the full gain in the year of sale. As a consequence, the capital she had not yet been paid (the amount he continued to owe her), earned interest income without being reduced by tax. That is, until she receives a payment, she earns interest income on the gross amount. In contrast, if she sells her house, pays the full amount of tax, and places the remainder in a savings account, she will earn interest on a smaller amount of principal. Second, she may or may not receive any or all of the remaining payments due from C.W. In contrast, her savings account will likely be insured

---

8. Note that section 453, the installment sale provision, does not deal with interest. If the buyer and seller do specify the interest (and it equals or exceeds the applicable federal rate at the time of the sale), the calculation described above relates only to the profit and return of capital portions of any payments made by the buyer to the seller. Interest is accounted for separately by buyer and seller. If the buyer and seller fail to provide for interest, or if the rate they choose is too low, the Code will "impute" a standard rate of interest under either section 483 or section 1274. The rate at which the Code will "impute" interest, varies depending upon market rates. Treasury announces these rates by periodically issuing revenue procedures. (We will discuss imputed interest in more detail when we study the concept of original issue discount ("OID") in the next part of the chapter, and also in one of the transactional problems involving section 7872.)

9. At this point, it is too early to discuss the fact that part of the income she reports may be subject to a different rate of tax. We will discuss this part of her problem when we discuss capital gains and losses.

10. **See the time value of money tables we studied in connection with the Adams Adverts problem in Part II, Chapter 1.** Which table is applicable to this question?

by one of the federal insurance programs, like FDIC.[11] Third, until C.W. makes his final payment, her investment remains frozen in the mortgage loan obligation (unless she is able to sell it.[12]) In contrast, she can easily move her investment into one or more alternate forms from the savings account.

But suppose the total amount to be paid by the buyer is not determinable? The brief introduction to the problem of accounting for the costs of producing inventory may have led you to think about the problem of accounting for the costs of items when the number of items to which a given expenditure can be allocated is uncertain. Consider the following case:

BURNET v. LOGAN
283 U.S. 404 (1931)

MR. JUSTICE MCREYNOLDS delivered the opinion of the Court....

Prior to March, 1913, and until March 11, 1916, respondent, Mrs. Logan, owned 250 of the 4,000 capital shares issued by the Andrews & Hitchcock Iron Company. It held 12% of the stock of the Mahoning Ore & Steel Company, an operating concern. In 1895 the latter corporation procured a lease for 97 years upon the "Mahoning" mine and since then has regularly taken therefrom large, but varying, quantities of iron ore—in 1913, 1,515,428 tons; in 1914, 1,212,287 tons; in 1915, 2,311,940 tons; in 1919, 1,217,167 tons; in 1921, 303,020 tons; in 1923, 3,029,865 tons. The lease contract did not require production of either maximum or minimum tonnage or any definite payments. Through an agreement of stockholders (steel manufacturers) the Mahoning Company is obligated to apportion extracted ore among them according to their holdings.

On March 11, 1916, the owners of all the shares in Andrews & Hitchcock Company sold them to Youngstown Sheet & Tube Company, which thus acquired, among other things, 12% of the Mahoning Company's stock and the right to receive the same percentage of ore thereafter taken from the leased mine.

For the shares so acquired the Youngstown Company paid the holders $2,200,000 in money and agreed to pay annually thereafter for distribution among them 60 cents for each ton of ore apportioned to it. Of this cash Mrs. Logan received 250/4000ths— $137,500; and she became entitled to the same fraction of any annual payment thereafter made by the purchaser under the terms of sale.

Mrs. Logan's mother had long owned 1100 shares of the Andrews & Hitchcock Company. She died in 1917, leaving to the daughter one-half of her interest in payments thereafter made by the Youngstown Company. This bequest was appraised for federal estate tax purposes at $277,164.50.

During 1917, 1918, 1919 and 1920 the Youngstown Company paid large sums under the agreement. Out of these respondent received on account of her 250 shares $9,900.00 in 1917, $11,250.00 in 1918, $8,995.50 in 1919, $5,444.30 in 1920—$35,589.80. By rea-

---

11. Federal Deposit Insurance Corporation.

12. There is often a market for the sale of mortgage loans on personal residences but, in general, a purchase money mortgage is likely to be less "liquid," that is, easily convertible into some other form, than is a savings account. Curtis J. Berger and Quentin Johnstone, *Land Transfer and Finance: Cases and Materials* 139 (4th ed. 1993).

son of the interest from her mother's estate she received $19,790.10 in 1919, and $11,977.49 in 1920.

Reports of income for 1918, 1919 and 1920 were made by Mrs. Logan upon the basis of cash receipts and disbursements. They included no part of what she had obtained from annual payments by the Youngstown Company. She maintains that until the total amount actually received by her from the sale of her shares equals their value on March 1, 1913, no taxable income will arise from the transaction. Also that until she actually receives by reason of the right bequeathed to her a sum equal to its appraised value, there will be no taxable income therefrom.

On March 1, 1913, the value of the 250 shares then held by Mrs. Logan *exceeded* $173,089.80—the total of all sums actually received by her prior to 1921 from their sale ($137,500.00 cash in 1916 plus four annual payments amounting to $35,589.80). That value also exceeded original cost of the shares. The amount received on the interest devised by her mother was less than its valuation for estate taxation; also less than the value when acquired by Mrs. Logan.

The Commissioner ruled that the obligation of the Youngstown Company to pay 60 cents per ton had a fair market value of $1,942,111.46 on March 11, 1916; that this value should be treated as so much cash and the sale of the stock regarded as a closed transaction with no profit in 1916. He also used this valuation as the basis for apportioning subsequent annual receipts between income and return of capital. His calculations, based upon estimates and assumptions, are too intricate for brief statement. (Footnote 1) He made deficiency assessments according to the view just stated and the Board of Tax Appeals approved the result.

The Circuit Court of Appeals held that, in the circumstances, it was impossible to determine with fair certainty the market value of the agreement by the Youngstown Company to pay 60 cents per ton. Also, that respondent was entitled to the return of her capital—the value of 250 shares on March 1, 1913, and the assessed value of the interest derived from her mother—before she could be charged with any taxable income. As this had not in fact been returned, there was no taxable income.

We agree with the result reached by the Circuit Court of Appeals.

The 1916 transaction was a sale of stock—not an exchange of property. We are not dealing with royalties or deductions from gross income because of depletion of mining property. Nor does the situation demand that an effort be made to place according to the best available data some approximate value upon the contract for future payments. This probably was necessary in order to assess the mother's estate. As annual payments on account of extracted ore come in they can be readily apportioned first as return of capital and later as profit. The liability for income tax ultimately can be fairly determined without resort to mere estimates, assumptions and speculation. When the profit, if any, is actually realized, the taxpayer will be required to respond. The consideration for the sale was $2,200,000.00 in cash and the promise of future money payments wholly contingent upon facts and circumstances not possible to foretell with anything like fair certainty. The promise was in no proper sense equivalent to cash. It had no ascertainable fair market value. The transaction was not a closed one. Respondent might never recoup her capital investment from payments only conditionally promised. Prior to 1921 all receipts from the sale of her shares amounted to less than their value on March 1, 1913. She properly demanded the return of her capital investment before assessment of any taxable profit based on conjecture.

"In order to determine whether there has been gain or loss, and the amount of the gain, if any, we must withdraw from the gross proceeds an amount sufficient to restore the capital value that existed at the commencement of the period under consideration." *Doyle v. Mitchell Bros. Co.*, 247 U.S. 179....."Generally speaking, the income tax law is concerned only with realized losses, as with realized gains." *Lucas v. American Code Co.*, 280 U.S. 445, 449.

From her mother's estate Mrs. Logan obtained the right to share in possible proceeds of a contract thereafter to pay indefinite sums. The value of this was assumed to be $277,164.50 and its transfer was so taxed. Some valuation—speculative or otherwise—was necessary in order to close the estate. It may never yield as much, it may yield more. If a sum equal to the value thus ascertained had been invested in an annuity contract, payments thereunder would have been free from income tax until the owner had recouped his capital investment. We think a like rule should be applied here....

The judgments below are *Affirmed*.

FOOTNOTES:

1. In the brief for petitioner the following appears:

"The fair market value of the Youngstown contract on March 11, 1916, was found by the Commissioner to be $1,942,111.46. This was based upon an estimate that the ore reserves at the Mahoning mine amounted to 82,858,535 tons; that all such ore would be mined; that 12 per cent (or 9,942,564.2 tons) would be delivered to the Youngstown Company. The total amount to be received by all the vendors of stock would then be $5,965,814.52 at the rate of 60 cents per ton. The Commissioner's figure for the fair market value on March 11, 1916, was the then worth of $5,965,814.52, upon the assumption that the amount was to be received in equal annual installments during 45 years, discounted at 6 per cent, with a provision for a sinking fund at 4 per cent. For lack of evidence to the contrary this value was approved by the Board. The value of the 550/4000 interest which each acquired by bequest was fixed at $277,164.50 for purposes of Federal estate tax at the time of the mother's death.

"During the years here involved the Youngstown Company made payments in accordance with the terms of the contract, and respondents respectively received sums proportionate to the interests in the contract which they acquired by exchange of property and by bequest.

"The Board held that respondents' receipts from the contract, during the years in question, represented 'gross income'; that respondents should be allowed to deduct from said gross income a reasonable allowance for exhaustion of their contract interests; and that the balance of the receipts should be regarded as taxable income."

———

Consider the following questions concerning *Burnet v. Logan*.

1. Can you diagram the ownership interest that belonged to Mrs. Logan that led to the tax controversy?

2. What transaction created the tax controversy?

3. Why did Mrs. Logan maintain that "until the total amount actually received by her from the sale of her shares equals their value on March 1, 1913, no taxable income will arise from the transaction"? See case to appropriate language in case.

4. Does the date March 1, 1913 have the same significance with respect to the interest in Andrews & Hitchcock Iron Company that Mrs. Logan inherited from her mother?

5. How did the government attempt to treat the transaction for tax purposes?

6. Are there any timing differences that result to Mrs. Logan if her treatment of the transaction prevails, rather than the treatment proposed by the government?

Burnet v. Logan represents one of the more complicated examples of cases that deal with the treatment of so-called "installment" transactions. These transactions arise in many ways, including, sales of businesses where the total purchase price depends upon future events. Suppose for example, that Nicky decides to sell her law practice and retire to the South of France.[13] She advertises in her state bar journal and Francois decides to purchase her practice. It is relatively easy for the parties to come to an agreement as to the value, and, therefore, the sales price, of the office furniture and equipment. It is far more difficult to determine the value of the good will of the practice. **Recall the Adams' Adverts problem following the *Raytheon* case in Part II, Chapter 1.** Most importantly, there is no guarantee that even long-term clients will continue to patronize the practice.[14] In many cases, the parties will agree to a purchase price that is, at least partially, contingent on the earnings of the practice.

The Treasury Regulations forcefully express the view of the Treasury that open transaction treatment will be permitted only in "rare and extraordinary cases." **See Temp. Treas. Reg. section 15A.453-1(d)(2)(iii).** Therefore, the parties, in particular the seller, must account for the sales price using the installment method. The regulations provide that if there is a stated maximum price, the taxpayer must compute the gross profit ratio on the assumption that the maximum price will be paid.[15] If it is not paid, the seller is allowed a loss in the final year equal to the excess gain reported earlier. If the selling price is not fixed but there is a fixed period specified for payment, the seller recovers basis ratably over the specified period. If both the purchase price and the payment period are left open, in general, the seller recovers her basis over 15 years.[16]

B. Annuities, Pensions, IRA's

Another common type of investment also requires a taxpayer to allocate her basis to each payment she receives: annuities. There are several common forms of annuities; the most common requires an investor to pay a fixed sum of money to purchase the annuity.

---

13. Nicky is a great fan of the French. She has always wanted to improve her French fluency.

14. The same would, of course, be true, if the sale were of a medical or dental practice. Some patients will switch to the new service provider. But, it is impossible to estimate with any accuracy how many will remain. Moreover, service businesses, such as law, medical, or dental practices, do not generate a regular flow of income from each client as would be the case for a television cable company. And, even the cable company cannot be certain how many existing customers it will continue to serve and how many, if any, new customers will enroll.

15. Section 453(j)(2) directs the Secretary to prescribe regulations which "shall include regulations providing for ratable basis recovery in transactions where the gross profit or the total contract price (or both) cannot be readily ascertained." How would you characterize this regulation: interpretive or legislative?

16. Temp. Treas. Reg. sections 15A.453-1(c)(1) through (c)(4).

The investor may then select among several alternatives as to the number of payments and when they are to begin. For example, a taxpayer may purchase an annuity while she is still working to begin making payments to her upon retirement. She may select that these payments will continue for a fixed period, *e.g.*, 20 payments over 20 years, or she may select that they will continue for as long as she lives. Let us consider first the easier to value of these two options, the one in which the payments will continue for 20 years.

Suppose that Genevieve inherited $120,000 from her mother, which she uses to purchase an annuity contract that promises to make payments to her of $10,000 per year for 20 years, beginning on the anniversary of her purchase. Therefore, she will receive 20 payments of $10,000 from the seller of the annuity (probably an insurance company).[17] As soon as she purchases the annuity, the insurance company will begin earning a return (the amount of which will depend upon the type of investment the annuity company makes with her money).[18] Whether this investment is a wise one for Genevieve depends upon the rate of return she could earn if she invested the money herself. (**Consult Table 3: the future value after n periods of $1 invested today.**)

Genevieve will also need to know how to report the payments for tax purposes. Section 72 of the Code provides special rules for taxing the earnings on her investment (her initial investment has already been taxed). Section 72 dictates Genevieve's treatment of both the return of principal portion of the pay-out and the interest it earned during the period of the investment. In other words, section 72 apportions the periodic payouts from the annuity, which is a mixture of income from the investment and return of capital.

Read section 72(b)(1). That section requires Genevieve to calculate an "exclusion ratio." She will apply the exclusion ratio to each payment she receives in order to determine what portion of the payment represents a return of her original investment, which, as you recall, was TOAD. The balance represents the interest income that will be taxable. Compute Genevieve's exclusion ratio. Can you suggest a formula that expresses mathematically the method for determining her exclusion ratio?[19] What two variables in this formula require definition? **Look at section 72(c)(1) to determine Genevieve's investment in the contract.** (Assume section 72(c)(2) does not apply.) **Look at section 72(c)(3) to determine Genevieve's expected return under the contract.** (Also assume that section 72(c)(3)(A) does not apply.) Now you should be able to compute her exclusion ratio under section 72(b). Applying that ratio to each payment, you will readily be able to determine the amount of each payment that represents return of capital and the amount of each payment that represents interest.

---

17. Annuities may provide for various alternatives as to the disposition of remaining payments if Genevieve, the "annuitant," dies before receiving all 20 payments. Some investors choose annuities that are payable for the life of either the investor or her spouse, whichever survives longer. Some provide that in any event, there will be a minimum of a certain number of payments, for example 20. Each different option will affect the amount that the investor receives. Remember, like a life insurance policy, an annuity contract is, in fact, a wager by the insurer that the annuitant or beneficiary will receive fewer dollars than the total of the initial investment and its earnings, and the insurer will profit from the difference. The annuitant or insured is betting, however, that she will outlast the actuarial estimates of life expectancy and profit by doing so.

18. She could, of course, simply invest the money herself and not withdraw any of her investment (the principal) or the earnings until she reaches 65. As you consider the annuity provision, keep this alternative in mind and be prepared to discuss the tax consequences of self-investing as an alternative to purchasing an annuity.

19. Those of you with math phobia should not be scared off by the prospect of having to create a mathematical formula. It's not calculus; it's just a ratio!

Genevieve chose a fixed-term annuity. Has Genevieve made a wise investment if she lives exactly 20 years? (**Consult Table 1: The present value of an annuity of $1 payable at the end of each period for n periods.**) We know that she invested $120,000, the present value of which was $120,000. Therefore, assuming her annuity begins immediately, she would be receiving a return of between 5% and 6%. She might be quite satisfied with this return.

She might have chosen, as an alternative at the time she purchased the annuity, a contract that promised to pay her a fixed amount until her death. (In that event, the payments the company promised to make to her would likely have been less than the $10,000 per year for the fixed term.[20]) Suppose she had purchased this alternate form of contract. What would happen if she died before recovering her full investment in the contract, that is, the full $120,000 TOAD she initially invested? **Look at section 72(b)(3)(A).** What is the effect of that section?

Suppose Genevieve outlives her life expectancy, that is, she recovers all her investment in the contract. How does she treat additional payments? **Look at section 72(b)(2).**

Now recall Peggy. Suppose she made an installment sale of her property for $120,000, and the contract of sale provided for 20 payments of $6,000, plus interest of 5% compounded semi-annually, beginning on the anniversary of the sale.[21] Peggy's property had a present value of $120,000 which she chose to "invest" at the rate of 5% when she agreed to finance the buyer's purchase of her property. Compare the "return" on Peggy's investment with that of Genevieve.

Now compare the results for Peggy if she had insisted on being paid the full $120,000 in cash and she had invested it herself. (**Consult Table 3: the future value after n periods of $1 invested today.**) What factors might influence Peggy to choose either the installment sale or the cash payment?

Suppose, in contrast to Peggy and Genevieve, Reuben sold some stock that his mother bequeathed to him. (You may assume that the fair market value at her date of death was $120,000, and you may assume that there was no brokerage commission on the sale of the stock.) Reuben took the cash and invested it in a "zero coupon bond." What is that? Reuben's bond will mature in 20 years, at which time he will receive $318,396. (**Consult Table 2: the present value of $1 payable after n periods in the future, or Table 3: the future value after n periods of $1 invested today.**)

How would you characterize the difference between the $120,000 Reuben paid for the bond and the amount he will receive upon its maturity? How should Reuben account for

---

20. The amount of the annuity will relate directly to the annuitant's life expectancy at the time she purchases the policy. The shorter her expected remaining life span, the larger the annual payment; the longer her expected remaining life span, the smaller the payment. (Her life expectancy will be determined based on "actuarial tables.") Remember, the annuitant and the company are making a bet: how long will she live? If she outlives her life expectancy, she wins; if she does not live out her life expectancy, the company wins.

21. Remember that section 453 (the installment sale provision), requires the taxpayer to allocate each payment between return of capital, profit, and interest. If the installment sales contract provides for adequate interest, the calculation in a case like Peggy's is not difficult. She allocates first to interest. She allocates the balance between return of capital and profit by recovering her basis ratably over the total payments due, using her gross profit percentage. If the interest is below the applicable federal rate, however, the taxpayer must recalculate what the interest should be at the applicable federal rate, allocate that portion of the payment to interest, and allocate the balance to basis and profit. An increase in the amount of the payment characterized as interest will decrease the amount of the payment treated as profit.

the interest on this bond? You might argue that he should not have to report the interest income until he receives it on the maturity of the bond. That would mean that he can defer reporting the interest income and paying tax on it until he actually receives it. If he is a cash basis taxpayer, that should be the proper time to report the income. If, however, he were an accrual basis taxpayer, he would have to report the income as it is earned, year-by-year. Zero coupon bonds represent another case in which special rules of the Code depart from the general rules of accounting. Whether he is a cash or an accrual basis taxpayer, the Code now requires Reuben to report the interest income on a yearly basis.

The rules for calculating the amount of interest he must include in income each year appear in the sections of the Code that apply to items termed "original issue discount" or "OID."[22] The OID amount is equal to the difference between the amount that Reuben will receive on maturity and the amount he invested.[23] The rules might have required that he include 1/20th of this difference in his income each year as interest. This is the method that Code section 72 specifies for annuity interest reporting. Instead, the Code adopts the constant yield to maturity method (the "economic accrual method").[24] This method requires Reuben to include an amount of interest income that increases each year. Why does an increase occur?

Consider a savings account that provides for annual compounding. Assume that Janet places $1,000 in her savings account. At the end of year 1, the account has earned interest at the rate of 5%, or $50. She does not withdraw that amount from the account. (But, she must report $50 of interest income for income tax purposes.[25]) In year 2, she has $1,050 in her account. Therefore, her interest earnings in year 2 (assuming a constant rate of 5%), will be $52.50. (Again, she will report that amount in interest income for tax purposes.) At the beginning of year 3, she will have a total of $1,102.50 on deposit. So, again, her interest income will increase. Indeed, it will increase each year until she ultimately withdraws her original principal and the interest from the account. A zero coupon bond is very much like this scenario. But while Janet could have withdrawn the interest at any time, an investor in a zero coupon bond cannot. The investor in the zero coupon bond might, however, be able to sell the bond. If Reuben were to sell his zero coupon bond prior to maturity, he would expect to receive an amount that reflects the earned but unpaid interest from the date of original issue until the date of sale.

Original issue discount appears in other types of instruments (as well as in zero coupon bonds). For example, when a company like Kirby Lumber issues bonds (in order to borrow money), it generally must determine the appropriate rate of interest in advance of the actual offering of the bonds.

Suppose ABC Company decides to borrow $2 million. It will issue bonds in denominations of $1,000. At the time it was putting the deal together, the appropriate rate of interest for a company of its type was 5%. But, by the time the bonds are actually offered on an exchange, the interest rate for loans to companies of similar creditworthiness has risen to 5.5%. The bonds (and the bond indentures) have already been printed, providing for an interest rate of 5%. What happens is that there will be an adjustment down in the actual amount that lenders (investors) will pay the company for each bond

---

22. Sections 1271–1275.
23. Section 1273(a)(1).
24. Section 1272(a)(1).
25. She will have to report the interest income, even if she does not withdraw it, no matter what her method of accounting, cash or accrual. Why?

that will pay $1,000 at maturity. (Why?[26]) The difference between the face value of $1,000 and the lesser amount that the investor actually lends constitutes "OID."[27]

The OID rules also affect the timing of the interest deduction allowable to the payor. As noted above, the special rules applicable to receipt of OID income place all taxpayers, in effect, on the accrual method of accounting. So too, the OID rules require the payor of OID interest to deduct the payment of the interest on an accrual basis.[28]

In each of the cases we have seen, the investment has been affected by interest at a rate that was set at the outset of the investment. But that is not the case with all investments. These investments all shared the common characteristic that they were relatively long-term investments and the only way the investor could convert to an alternate form of investment would probably result in an additional cost to the investor. That additional cost would result in an overall lower rate of return than the return the investor expected at the outset. Moreover, these investors were "locked-in" to the rate of return to which they agreed at the outset. Would this be to the advantage or disadvantage of the investor if the rate of return on similar investments changed during the 20 year period? Does it depend on whether the interest rate on similar types of investments has increased or declined?

The complexity that Congress's recognition of the time value of money imposes on many transactions is often unrecognized by taxpayers (and their lawyers). Indeed, in many cases, taxpayers enter into arrangements with each other without any awareness that they have, unwittingly, created a transaction that should be generating reportable interest income.

Two additional types of favored investment whose timing rule diverge from the normal ones applicable to income deserve mention here. Many taxpayers now qualify for one of several types of tax-deferred retirement plans, either through employment or self-employment. A study of the many forms of pension plans available is beyond the scope of this book. But, it is important to note that all these options represent policy decisions to alter the normal timing of income in order to encourage savings. These special provisions allow taxpayers to invest income, sometimes without the payment of tax on that income, and, in some cases, allow the earnings on the invested income to grow without current taxation.[29] Whether the taxpayer qualifies for savings through an IRA or an employer-sponsored pension plan, Congress has blessed the deferral of income for the perceived benefit to the taxpayer and society.

These variations from the normal tax and timing rules all reflect congressional approval prompted by policy choices that over-ride tax or economic outcomes. Note that all of these variations require calculation of basis and a division between basis ("TOAD") and income. In some cases, for example, in the case of the OID rules, the al-

---

26. Of course, the reverse can occur: if interest rates decline prior to the offering. In that case, the selling price of the bond will be greater than $1,000.

27. If the investor pays more than the face amount on the initial offering of the bond, the difference is "bond premium."

28. Section 163(e).

29. In fact, so-called "Roth IRA's," named after William Roth, former Senator from Delaware and former Chairman of the Senate Finance Committee, allow the income to escape taxation forever. A Roth IRA allows the appreciation in the after-tax invested amount to escape taxation entirely if the taxpayer satisfies the requirements for making the investment.

location to each period harmonizes with economic reality; in other cases, for example, in the case of section 72, it does not. A mortgage loan requires periodic repayments, generally of equal amounts, of which a portion represents interest on the borrowing and the balance represents repayment of principal. In the early years, the largest portion of each payment represents interest (because the entire or almost the entire amount of the principal is outstanding). In later years, when payments have reduced the principal balance outstanding, the balance between interest payments and repayments of principal shifts. By the time the mortgage is nearly repaid, the remaining principal is small. Therefore, the portion of each payment attributable to interest is also small; the portion attributable to principal is large. This treatment comports with the economic reality of the accrual of interest over time. In contrast, section 453, the installment sale provision, and section 72, the annuity provision, artificially assign an equal amount of basis (return of capital) to each payment.

Whatever the capital recovery method commanded by the Code, the taxpayer must divide a payment between an already taxed portion ("TOAD") and one that is as yet untaxed. As you review these provisions and encounter new ones, consider what policy might have prompted Congress to provide the specific treatment accorded the item. Why has Congress decided to alter the normal timing rules, and which taxpayers benefit from the alteration?

Chapter 3

Nonrecognition Transactions

Recall the directive of section 1001(c) that "[e]xcept as otherwise provided in this subtitle, the entire amount of the gain or loss, determined under this section, on the sale or exchange of property shall be recognized." See section 1001(c). This general rule requires a taxpayer to recognize her gain or loss[1] on a sale or exchange of property. But, a number of provisions in the Code provide specific exceptions to the general rule. (You have already encountered, for example, section 1041.) Part III of Subchapter O, in fact, lists thirteen "common nontaxable exchanges." Two of these, sections 1033 and 1031, are of extraordinary importance to many taxpayers and warrant a detailed examination.

Recall Jeremiah, the Civil War buff we introduced you to in Part II, Chapter 3.A.1.b. Remember that Jeremiah suffered a terrible casualty to his favorite Civil War uniform that he had purchased for $1,000. Although it seems like a loss to him, he, in fact, had a casualty gain because he was smart enough to insure the uniform for its new fair market value of $5,000, rather than for the $1,000 he paid for it. How did he calculate the realized gain? Must he recognize that gain? Section 1001(c) proclaims "yes" unless he can find an "except as otherwise provided" section somewhere in the subtitle. (Note that if he cannot find a special rule, poor Jeremiah will have to report the gain, pay a tax out of his insurance proceeds, and then not have enough of the proceeds left to replace the lost uniform.) **Look at the list of common nontaxable exchanges in the Table of Contents under Part III of Subchapter O.** Does any one of the exceptions look, from its title, as though it might apply?

Examine sections 1033(a)(1), — (a)(2), — (a)(2)(A), and — (a)(2)(B). Suppose Jeremiah were lucky enough to find a replacement, a Civil War uniform that he liked even better that he was able to purchase with the $5,000 of insurance proceeds he received as a result of the destruction of his former uniform. Does section 1033 provide any relief from section 1001(c)? Are there any statutory words or phrases that require close examination in order to conclude that section 1033 will protect Jeremiah from having to recognize gain? Are those words or phrases clear on the face of the statute? Are they defined in the statute? If not, what is the next source to consult?[2] If no Treasury regulation or other Treasury publication satisfies your inquiry, what's next? What about consulting case law? Read the following case.

---

1. Remember, however, that section 165 must authorize the deduction of the loss.
2. Remember that if you find a statement in Treasury regulations that is favorable to your client, you need look no farther; you may rely absolutely on the regulation. (If, however, you find a regulation that is unfavorable to your client, you should probably rethink the transaction because it is almost impossible to overturn a regulation.)

MALOOF v. COMMISSIONER

65 T.C. 263 (1975)

TANNENWALD, *Judge*: Respondent determined a deficiency ... in petitioner's 1966 Federal income tax. Petitioner has conceded some of the issues raised in the notice of deficiency, leaving for our decision the question whether his taxable income included $83,456 recovered during the taxable year with respect to a war loss.

FINDINGS OF FACT

Virtually all of the material facts have been stipulated and are found accordingly....

From sometime in 1938 until December 7, 1941, when hostilities commenced between the United States and Japan, petitioner operated a sole proprietorship engaged in the general import and export business in China. His head office was at 98 Kialat Road, Swatow, China, which city was the center of the drawnwork business in China. Petitioner had an office and warehouse located at 150 Kialat Road, Swatow, China, and two branches—one in Shanghai, China, and the other in Hong Kong, China.

The business was conducted along traditional lines. Raw materials known in the trade as "piece goods," mostly Irish linens, were purchased in Belfast and other foreign markets and were shipped to China for manufacturing and processing. Some materials were purchased in the United States; others, principally silks, in China and Japan.

The processing and manufacture of the piece goods were preceded by the selection of the designs and colors were subject to frequent change as dictated by changing fashions and by competition. The designs were created by or under the direction of petitioner, at considerable cost, in some cases, and sent by him to his Swatow offices. By far the larger part of the business was the linen drawnwork business, such as handkerchiefs and tableware.

The piece goods, together with the designs, thread, yarn for embroidery, etc., were placed in the hands of Chinese "contractors" in the Swatow area who did the "manufacturing." The procedure was generally as follows:

(a) The designs were made and selected.

(b) The materials were measured on a frame and a thread was drawn to mark each dozen. Then more threads were drawn to square and mark each piece of handkerchief before cutting.

(c) After the handkerchiefs were cut, each one was stamped with a design and style number.

(d) After bargaining, the Chinese contractor or contractors who had submitted the lowest bid was given the contract to do the work. He then proceeded to his village with the cargo; he distributed as many dozens as his village workers could handle, and subcontracted the balance to others.

The petitioner's head office at 98 Kialat Road, Swatow, China, performed the following services: (a) Receiving and storing all piece goods, yarn for embroidery, etc., (b) supervising designs, (c) marking and preparing all materials for processing, (d) distributing and receiving work in process, (e) laundering, finishing, and shipping, (f) local buying, and (g) bookkeeping and general office work.

The petitioner's office at 150 Kialat Road performed the following services: (a) tailoring and finishing all wearing apparel, (b) receiving and storing piece goods, mostly silks, and (c) packing and preparing goods for shipment.

Petitioner's Shanghai office attended to: (a) purchasing Chinese-made silk piece goods, yarn, etc., for embroidery and sewing, (b) purchasing merchandise available in the Shanghai market for export, and (c) transshipment of cargo from Swatow to foreign ports, and from foreign ports to Swatow—"in transit" cargo.

Petitioner's Hong Kong office attended to the "in transit" cargo which went through Kong Kong.

On or about December 7, 1941, petitioner's business was confiscated by the Japanese, and he sustained a war loss under section 127, I.R.C. 1939. Petitioner's net investment in the business as of the date of the seizure consisted of:

Assets:

Accounts receivable	$100,553
Ascertainable inventories, at cost	342,543
Real estate, furniture, fixtures, and machinery	3,130
Miscellaneous other assets	303
Total assets	446,529

Liabilities:

Accounts payable	$105,207
Bank loans	86,351
Total liabilities	191,558

Net business investment 254,971

He deducted $254,971 as a war loss on his income tax return for the fiscal year ended July 31, 1942.

In 1945, petitioner recovered a portion of the seized assets, consisting of merchandise valued at $81,388 which had cost $71,981. He also obtained cancellation of bank loans of $41,825, resulting in a total recovery of $123,213. He elected, pursuant to subparagraphs (3) and (5) of section 127(c), I.R.C. 1939, to report his war loss recovery by reducing the war loss deduction to $131.758. The amount of the net war loss was subsequently fixed at $94,000 by agreement between petitioner and respondent's agents.

On July 2, 1964, pursuant to the War Claims Act of 1948, 50 U.S.C. app. sec. 2001 et seq. (1970), petitioner claimed that he sustained losses as follows:

(a) *Swatow losses*.—On December 8, 1941, the properties of the petitioner in Swatow, China, were taken over by the Japanese military forces. From time to time thereafter during the period of the war, the petitioner's large inventory was taken by the Japanese military authorities. Also confiscated were the contents of a five-room apartment located at 98 Kialat Road which was the personal residence of petitioner.

(b) *Shanghai losses*.—The losses in Shanghai consisted of an inventory of merchandise in stocks; 22 cases of drawnwork and embroidered articles which had been received at the Shanghai office a few days prior to Pearl Harbor day and which were awaiting transshipment to the United States; and some Chinese antiques which were the personal possessions of the petitioner.

(c) *Hong Kong losses*.—The losses in Hong Kong consisted of merchandise in transit stored in Holts Wharf and in the godown of the Hong Kong and Kowloon Wharf and Godown Co., Ltd., and some of petitioner's personal effects which were in the custody of petitioner's Hong Kong manager.

(d) *Ship cargo losses.*—In November of 1941, petitioner shipped 35 cases of linen goods from his Swatow offices to his Shanghai offices for transshipment to the United States. This cargo was loaded in Shanghai on the S.S. Bernadin de St. Pierre for transshipment via Manila to the United States and a bill of lading was issued therefor to petitioner. This cargo never reached its destination in the United States.

On June 1, 1966, the Foreign Claims Settlement Commission found that petitioner sustained war losses and awarded him $331,912.37 with respect to lost business property (consisting entirely of inventory items) and $22,090 with respect to his personal property. Petitioner determined that $83,456 of this amount should be treated as gain from an involuntary conversion of property ... (Footnote 3) and reported it accordingly on his 1966 return. Since the involuntary conversion involved herein occurred prior to January 1, 1951, he applied for and received the consent of the Internal Revenue Service to establish a fund to replace his business which was destroyed during the war. (Footnote 4) Including extensions of time, petitioner was allowed until July 1, 1969, to expend the fund in reestablishing his business.

On January 9, 1969, petitioner registered the Frederick Trading Co. in Hong Kong as a sole proprietorship engaged in general import-export and manufacturing. Petitioner had invested HK $728,087.74 in that business by April 30, 1969. The company's balance sheet as of that date showed the following assets at cost: (Footnote 5)

	HK$	US$
Current assets other than inventory	$136,848.01	$22,511.50
Inventory	90,816.59	14,939.33
Land and building (before depreciation)	356,100.00	58,578.45
Plant and machinery (before depreciation)	68,633.00	11,290.13
Furniture and fixtures (before depreciation)	35,574.90	5,852.07
	687,972.50	113,171.48

Schedule C of petitioner's 1969 return shows that Frederick Trading Co. had no opening inventory.

At least until June 30, 1969, the business of Frederick Trading Co. was conducted as follows: Cotton, silk, yarn, and synthetic fabrics were purchased in Hong Kong or were imported. The materials in some cases were knotted and in all cases were cut and sewn in the company's Hong Kong factory. Finished goods were sold and delivered to retail outlets, primarily in the United States.

Schedule C of petitioner's 1968 return shows that, during that year, he operated a sole proprietorship in Hong Kong under the designation Fortuna & Co., whose principal activity was manufacturing knitwear.

OPINION

... Under ... section [1033], where a taxpayer realizes a gain on the involuntary conversion of property used in his own trade or business, it is clear that the reinvestment must be made in substantially similar business property. *Ellis D. Wheeler*, 58 T.C. 459, 463 (1972). Stated differently, the statute requires a "reasonably similar continuation of the petitioner's prior commitment of capital and not a departure from it." *Harvey J. Johnson*, 43 T.C. 736, 741 (1965). While it is not necessary to acquire property which duplicates exactly that which was converted (*Loco Realty Co. v. Commissioner*, 306 F.2d 207 (8th Cir. 1962), revg. 35 T.C. 1059 (1961)), the fortuitous circumstance of involuntary conversion does not permit a taxpayer to change the character of his investment without tax consequences (*see Liant Record, Inc. v. Commissioner*, 303 F.2d 326 (2d Cir. 1962), revg. 36 T.C. 224 (1961). (Footnote 6)

The main point of contention between the parties is whether the conversion proceeds were reinvested in property "similar or related in service or use" to the converted property, a condition precedent to nonrecognition under section 1033(a)(2). Both parties agree that the appropriate test is one of "functional use." Petitioner argues that this test is satisfied without reference to the nature of particular assets, if the general character of the new business is substantially the same as that of the old. Respondent asks us to apply the test to the particular assets and to rule that because the 1966 award was received entirely with respect to merchandise, only that portion of the gain which was reinvested in inventory items is entitled to nonrecognition.

Where a taxpayer suffers a loss of business assets and uses the replacement property to continue or reenter the same business, opinion is divided as to whether different classes of assets must be considered separately or together for the application of section 1033. Compare *The International Boiler Works Co.*, 3 B.T.A. 283 (1926), Rev. Rul. 70-465, 1970-2 C.B. 162, and Rev. Rul. 70-501, 1970-2 C.B. 163, with *O. N. Bymaster*, 20 T.C. 649 (1953), *Massillon-Cleveland-Akron Sign Co.*, 15 T.C. 79 (1950), and Rev. Rul. 73-225, 1973-1 C.B. 32. Petitioner and respondent seek to utilize the authorities in this area to support their positions herein. We think they are both in error. Neither an aggregate nor an atomistic approach is adequate to determine in every case whether converted property has been replaced with other property which is similar or related in service or use. Section 1033 provides a means by which a taxpayer whose enjoyment of his property is interrupted without his consent may arrange to have that interruption ignored for tax purposes, by returning as closely as possible to his original position.... Granted that it is a relief provision entitled to liberal and realistic construction, still the taxpayer may claim its protection only if he does not "materially alter his type of business." *S. E. Ponticos, Inc.*, 40 T.C. 60, 64 (1963), revd. 338 F.2d 477 (6th Cir. 1964). (Footnote 7) ...

But, there are limits to the extent of the change which can be countenanced and we think petitioner has exceeded those limits. His old business consisted primarily of the acquisition of raw materials, design, and marketing of finished products. Over 99 percent of his investment was in inventory and accounts receivable. The business which he established in 1969, by contrast, included an entire manufacturing plant. Well over half of his investment went into fixed assets such as real and depreciable personal property. This disproportionate shift from current to fixed assets reflects a fundamental change in the nature of the business itself. The acquisition of a manufacturing operation cannot be equated with the reestablishment of petitioner's former enterprise; a substantial change from inventory to depreciable assets, such as is the case herein, cannot be regarded as satisfying the "similar or related in service or use" requirement of section 1033....

Our view that, in a situation such as the one before us, section 1033 requires a reasonable degree of continuity in the nature of the assets as well as in the general character of the business is confirmed by the legislative history of section 1033. Thus, when the involuntary conversion provision was first enacted as section 217 of the Revenue Act of 1921, the floor manager in the House spoke in terms of a situation where the taxpayer "immediately proceeds to invest the moneys received in *other similar property*." ... See 61 Cong. Rec. 5201 (1921). And when the provision was amended in 1951 (by which time it had become section 112(f) of the Internal Revenue Code of 1939), the then chairman of the House Ways and Means Committee observed on the House floor (see 97 Cong. Rec. 10348 (1951)):

Although proposals were received for broadening still further the relief granted by the bill, it was the unanimous decision of the Committee on Ways and Means that the relief should be granted within the basic framework of existing law requiring that the replacement property be similar or related in service or use to the property converted. *To permit the taxpayer to defer gain while changing the nature of his investment would be a serious departure from the policy of existing law which the Committee on Ways and Means believes should not be allowed....*

Again, when the provision (by this time, sec. 1033 of the Internal Revenue Code of 1954) was amended in 1958, the committee reports referred to the "purchase [of] other *property similar in nature to the property converted.*" (Emphasis added.) See H. Rept. No. 775, 85th Cong., 1st Sess. (1957), 1958-3 C.B. 811, 838; S. Rept. No. 1983, 85th Cong., 2d Sess. (1958), 1958-3 C.B. 922, 992. At that time, Congress also added subsection (g) to section 1033 in order to incorporate the more liberal "like kind" test of section 1031 but, in doing so, carefully limited its liberalization to real estate investments. See S. Rept. No. 1983, *supra*, 1958-3 C.B. at 994; Conf. Rept. No. 2632, 85th Cong., 2d Sess. (1958), 1958-3 C.B. 1188, 1219.

Petitioner did not replace an old manufacturing plant with one of modern design; rather, he replaced a business involving subcontracting most of the necessary labor over which he apparently exercised little control with one which has an integrated and mechanized operation of his own. Petitioner asks us to take judicial notice of advancing technology which rendered his former mode of operation impracticable. But, even if we were to accede to his request, it would be of no avail. The test of section 1033 would still not be satisfied, since difficulty of compliance does not make the requirements of the statute inapplicable to petitioner. *Fullilove v. United States*, 71 F.2d 852 (5th Cir. 1934); *United Development Co. v. United States, supra.*

Petitioner argues in the alternative that, in any event, no gain was realized in 1966 because his cost basis in the seized inventory items exceeded the amount of the award which he received. Respondent correctly states that petitioner has stipulated to the cost of the inventory included in his old business and to the recovery of a portion thereof in 1945 and that he may not now argue for a higher cost.

We hold that, except for purchases of inventory, petitioner did not replace his converted property with other property similar or related in use within the meaning of section 1033. Within this holding, however, we are left with one loose end. Respondent concedes that nonrecognition is proper with respect to $14,939.33 invested in inventory of Frederick Trading Co. by April 30, 1969. Petitioner is entitled to the same treatment of amounts expended from the replacement fund for the acquisition of inventory from May 1 to June 30, 1969, as well as amounts so expended for "similar or related" items in 1968. In this latter connection, it is also possible that the operations of Fortuna Co. in 1968 involved some qualifying reinvestment in inventory. As to these elements, the record is incomplete. We anticipate that the parties will be able to reach agreement under the Rule 155 computation, but, if they do not, we will, in accordance with out undertaking at the trial, reopen the record in order to take further evidence.

FOOTNOTES:

3. ...

The $83,456 figure results from reducing a net recovery of $305,021 by the following:

Losses for which no tax benefit was received:

Losses not claimed $89,807
War loss claimed $254,971
Less 1945 recovery at market value 123,213

                                          131,758
War loss allowed 94,000

                                                  37,758

                                                127,565
Loss previously allowed
    taxable at prior years' rates 94,000

                                                221,565

4. See sec. 1033(a)(2); sec. 1.1033(a)-4, Income Tax Regs.

5. Respondent and petitioner apparently agree on an exchange rate of HK $1 = US $.1645[.]

6. The two cited cases involved a type of situation not involved in this case; in any event, the basis of the reversals was accepted by this Court in *Harvey J. Johnson*, 43 T.C. 736, 741 (1965). Since the involuntary conversion occurred prior to Jan. 1, 1951, tracing of the funds is necessary (see sec. 1.1033(a)-3(c), Income Tax Regs.), a requirement not demanded under the current statutory provision (see sec. 1.1033(c)-1, Income Tax Regs.).

7. The basis of this reversal was also accepted by this Court in *Harvey J. Johnson, supra* n. 6.

Consider the following questions about *Maloof*.

1. What kind of property did Maloof lose?

2. With what did he replace it?

3. Was it "similar or related in service or use"? What is the test according to the court?

4. The court talks about "business property." Is there anything in the statute that limits its application solely to business property? Is Jeremiah's uniform "business property"? Does section 1033 apply to property held for personal use?

5. What do you make of the court's statement that "the fortuitous circumstance of involuntary conversion does not permit a taxpayer to change the character of his investment without tax consequences"? Do you think Mr. Maloof or Jeremiah considered his loss a "fortuitous circumstance"?

6. Does the strict construction of the requirement that the taxpayer replace the lost property with property that is similar or related in service or use accord with what you perceive to be the policy underlying this important exception to section 1001(c)?

Now, return to the question of Jeremiah's replacement of his uniform. Do you think it qualifies as similar or related in service or use? If so, how does Jeremiah qualify for relief? **Consult Treasury Regulation section 1.1033(a)-2(c).**

7. Are there any time limits on his purchase of the new uniform? **Examine section 1033(a)(2)(B).** (Also consult the regulation.) Suppose he does qualify under section 1033. Does Jeremiah escape gain recognition forever?

8. (The same regulation may help you answer the following questions.) What if he does not purchase the new uniform in the same tax year as the year in which he receives the insurance proceeds? What if he makes the election to replace the uniform but then decides the following tax year to use the insurance proceeds to go on a trip around the world?

9. If Jeremiah does purchase a replacement uniform for $5,000, within the allowable period, what will his basis be in the new uniform? **Consult section 1033(b).**[3] Which paragraph of subsection 1033(b) applies to Jeremiah? Can you express the basis rule as a formula? Can you prove that your formula works to preserve for later recognition the gain that Jeremiah did not have to recognize currently as a result of the application of section 1033?

10. What if his new uniform costs only $4,000? What result under section 1033(a)? What is his basis in the new uniform under section 1033(b)? Does the result here seem consistent with what you believe to be the underlying policy of section 1033? Do you have to modify the formula you used above to express the basis rule? Can you, once again, prove that your basis formula is correct?

11. What if his new uniform costs $6,000? Answer again the same questions as in Question 10.

12. Now suppose that he finds a new uniform for only $500. What result? What is his basis in the new uniform?

13. Suppose the new uniform is not a Civil War uniform, but, rather a Revolutionary War uniform. Would that qualify for section 1033 treatment? Suppose what he replaces the uniform with is a Civil War sword?

One other aspect of section 1033 deserves attention. **Look at section 1033(g)(1).**[4] It provides that in the case of condemnation of "real property ... held for productive use in trade or business or for investment" the replacement property must be "property of a like kind," rather than the narrower standard of "similar or related in service or use." Can you speculate on why Congress inserted this different standard for real property

---

3. Note that section 1033(a) provides for two methods of replacing property, each with its own rules: (1) a direct replacement, or (2) use of the money received as a result of the casualty to acquire replacement property. (Direct replacement might occur, for example, if a taxpayer exchanges property threatened with condemnation—a taking of private property for some governmental use—for other property owned or acquired for the purpose by the authority that is threatening condemnation.) Each of these two methods of replacing property has its own basis rule. See section 1033(b).

4. Congress enacted section 1033(g) in 1958 as a relief provision for certain taxpayers from the otherwise rigid rule of "similar or related in service or use." Prior to its enactment, frequent litigation involved real property used for rental purposes. The Service insisted that replacement property would not qualify unless its end use duplicated the end use of the replaced property, i.e., property rented to a hairdresser could not be replaced with property rented to a grocery store. A series of cases rejected this "end use" doctrine and substituted the "similar economic relationship" standard, under which qualification depended upon the taxpayer's use of her property, not the end use of it. *See, e.g., Liant Record, Inc. v. Commissioner,* 303 F.2d 326 (2d Cir. 1962). If the taxpayer continued to use her replacement property as commercial rental property, the type of end use carried on by her tenant was irrelevant.

that has been condemned?[5] What does "like kind" mean? Is it the same as "similar or related in service or use"?

***

Now Look at section 1031(a). Assume that Juan owns an apartment building in Chicago that he purchased in December 1990 for $400,000. He wants to sell the building so that he can purchase undeveloped farmland outside the city near Kankakee. He thinks that the suburbs will soon expand even farther south toward Kankakee and that he has a real opportunity to make a "killing." Suppose the apartment building has a current fair market value of $1,000,000. What result if Juan simply sells the building today?[6] How much will Juan have in hand after payment of taxes to invest in the farmland he wants to buy?

On a property-seeking trip to Kankakee, Juan meets Lilian at a coffee shop. Lilian owns a large farm she inherited from her parents. Since the recent death of her parents, she has been unable to operate the farm by herself and has had no luck finding reliable employees. Therefore, she is anxious to indulge her long-time yearning to move to Chicago.

Lilian is willing to sell 200 acres of the farm property (not including the house) to Juan for $1,000,000.[7] Juan explains to her that he will not have enough left on the sale of his apartment building, after paying the resulting taxes. But Lilian, anxious to make a quick sale, tells Juan that she read an article in *The Farm Journal* explaining how farmers can exchange their farms for other property without paying tax. She wonders if the same could be true for Juan. What do you advise?

Does section 1031(a) encompass this transaction? If so, which of the parties would it help? What terms or phrases are critical to satisfying the requirements of section 1031?

If Lilian agrees that she will exchange the 200 acres of farmland for Juan's apartment building, what result to both parties? Would such an exchange satisfy the requirements for application of section 1031(a)? **Look at Treasury Regulation sections 1.1031(a)-1(b) and 1.1031(a)-1(c)(2).**

Suppose Juan holds the apartment house as an investment.[8] Assume that Juan intends to farm the property for the foreseeable future, that is, he will use it in the trade of business of farming. Will the exchange qualify? **Look at Treasury Regulation section 1.1031(a)-1(a)(1).** What will be Juan's basis in the farm? **Look at section 1031(d).**

Why does the basis rule work this way? How can you prove that the basis you calculated is correct?

***

5. You may not be able to answer this question until you have studied the next section of the materials. But, make sure you return to it.

6. You may assume that Juan's tax rate is 15%. In Part V, soon to come, you will discover why his rate might only be 15%.

7. Lilian does not want to sell the whole farm, which was appraised at the time of her parents' recent death in an automobile accident, for $3,260,000. She wants to keep her family home and one of her neighbors wants to lease the balance of her acreage (her family originally owned a section of land), to produce hay for his farm animals. By the way, a "section" is 640 acres or one square mile.

8. You will learn more about how the holding of real property may be characterized in the section containing the commercial and residential real estate transactional problems. For now, note that most owners of apartment buildings are considered to hold their property for investment, rather than for use in a trade or business.

Now suppose that Juan intends to subdivide the property immediately into 200 one-acre lots that he plans to sell as quickly as possible. That is, Juan will hold the new property primarily for sale to customers who will build or arrange to have built their own houses. Will the exchange qualify? **Look at section 1031(a)(2)(A) and Treasury Regulation section 1.1031(a)-1(a)(1).**

Suppose instead that Juan makes the exchange of his apartment building for the farm, intending to farm it himself. But instead of beginning to farm it himself, he immediately gives the property to his son, a lawyer in Chicago, who wants a "gentleman's farm" to get away from the city on weekends and for vacations? Read the following case.[9]

CLICK V. COMMISSIONER
78 T.C. 225 (1982)

STERRETT, *Judge* ... [R]espondent determined a deficiency in petitioner's Federal income tax for the taxable year 1974....

The issues for our decision are (1) whether the nonrecognition provisions of section 1031, I.R.C. 1954, apply to petitioner's acquisition of two residential properties....

FINDINGS OF FACT

...

Petitioner Dollie H. Click resided in Fairfax, Va., at the time of filing her petition herein. Using a single filing status, she filed a Federal income tax return, Form 1040, for the calendar year 1974 with the Internal Revenue Service Center at Memphis, Tenn.

On December 30, 1964, petitioner and her husband purchased approximately 161.250 acres of farmland (hereinafter the farm) in Prince William County, for $110,000. The property was to be held for investment purposes. On September 19, 1967, petitioner and her husband conveyed approximately 4.085 acres of the farm (hereinafter parcel B) to their daughter and son-in-law, Mary and Carlton Highsmith. On June 27, 1967, petitioner and her husband conveyed approximately 2.080 acres of the farm (hereinafter parcel C) to their son and daughter-in-law, John and Sharon Click. Petitioner's remaining parcel consisted of approximately 155.085 acres (hereinafter parcel A).

Petitioner's husband died on September 21, 1972. During the last months of 1972, petitioner received a number of offers to purchase the farm. All of these offers were made by Manassas Realty, on behalf of Williams Properties, Inc., and an undisclosed principal. The undisclosed principal was later identified as the Marriott Corp. (hereinafter Marriott).

On January 9, 1973, petitioner entered into an agreement of lease and purchase option with Williams Properties, Inc., on behalf of its still undisclosed principal, Marriott. Although the agreement provided for the purchase of the entire farm, petitioner's children and their spouses, who owned parcels B and C, neither executed the agreement nor were named as parties to it.

---

9. You will find that diagramming the facts of this case will substantially aid in your understanding of the transactions.

Marriott hoped to acquire the entire farm and certain land adjacent to the farm in order to build a 515-acre amusement park that would contain, inter alia, shops, theaters, and carnival rides. As of June 9, 1973, Marriott had obtained options to purchase an additional 353.46 acres of land surrounding the farm. The farm was the largest single component of the proposed park site, and Marriott considered its acquisition to be a critical and inseparable part of its plans.

In June 1973, Marriott indicated its desire to renegotiate the terms of its January 9, 1973, purchase option because it was not binding on petitioner's children, it contained no subordination provision to allow Marriott to finance improvements, it contained no prepayment provisions, and it was difficult to administer. On June 9, 1973, petitioner and Mr. and Mrs. Highsmith executed with Marriott a 1-year lease and a revised purchase option agreement for parcels A and B. The option agreement gave Marriott until June 9, 1974, to inform the petitioner and Mr. and Mrs. Highsmith of its intention to purchase the property, and until July 9, 1974, to reach settlement on the purchase. In addition, the agreement contained a provision that permitted the sellers, petitioner and her daughter and son-in-law, to opt for partial or full payment through the receipt of "exchange" or "swap" property or properties which the sellers would have the right to designate. Also on June 9, 1973, Mr. and Mrs. John Click entered into a separate agreement with Marriott for the sale of parcel C with settlement to take place on or before July 9, 1974.

During this time, Mr. and Mrs. Highsmith owned and resided in a house on North Ninth Street in Arlington, Va. However, they wanted to move to a new house and so advised petitioner. On petitioner's suggestion, they began looking for a new home to use as "swap" property. Their condition for such property was that it contain a house larger than their house on North Ninth Street. They selected a home, also in Arlington, Va., that was owned by William C. and Bernice Gierisch (hereinafter the Gierisches).

Mr. and Mrs. John Click owned and resided in a house in Fairfax, Va., but they were interested in obtaining a house and more acreage. At petitioner's suggestion, they also began looking for "swap" property. Their condition for such property was that it contain a three-bedroom house with acreage sufficient to maintain a horse. They selected residential property in Clifton, Va., owned by Oscar W. and Margaret Ann Tinney (hereinafter the Tinneys).

The Tinney residence had previously been listed for sale in 1973. Mrs. Sharon Click saw the Tinneys' "for sale" sign and inspected the house several times in 1973. She liked the Tinney residence and wanted to purchase it at that time. However, the Tinneys decided not to sell their house and consequently took it off the market. Subsequently, the Tinneys once again listed their house for sale. Mrs. Click again visited the Tinney residence on several occasions in 1974 prior to the time of Marriott's offer to purchase the house.

On February 22, 1974, Marriott and the Gierisches entered into a purchase agreement for the Gierisch residence. On April 18, 1974, Marriott and the Tinneys entered into a purchase agreement for the Tinney residence. On June 5, 1974, Marriott notified petitioner and Mr. and Mrs. Highsmith of its intent to purchase parcels A and B.

Petitioner did not inspect the Tinney residence until after Marriott had made its offer to purchase and after the house was taken off the market.

On July 9, 1974, the Gierisches and the Tinneys conveyed their houses to Marriott. On the same day, Marriott exercised its option to purchase parcels A and B. Accordingly, petitioner and Mr. and Mrs. Highsmith received from Marriott a promissory note in the amount of $630,925.53, the Gierisch residence valued at $96,152.20, and the Tinney residence valued at $135,816.96 in exchange for parcels A and B. At closing, the three also received the first installment on the promissory note in the amount of $23,647.

Petitioner held all equity rights in the two residences which were received by her in partial satisfaction of the amount due her from the sale of parcel A to Marriott. Petitioner and Mr. and Mrs. Highsmith did not intend that the Highsmiths' legal interests in either the Gierisch residence or the Tinney residence would be in full or partial satisfaction of their conveyance of parcel B to Marriott. Instead, petitioner and the Highsmiths intended that 2.56 percent of the cash paid at closing on July 9, 1974, and a similar percentage of the principal and interest due under the note, would be in satisfaction of their conveyance of parcel B to Marriott.

On July 9, 1974, Mr. and Mrs. Highsmith together received a total of $619 as their pro rata share of Marriott's initial payment ($23,647) on its purchase of parcels A and B.

On or about July 9, 1974, Mr. and Mrs. Highsmith moved into the Gierisch residence, and Mr. and Mrs. John Click moved into the Tinney residence. The Highsmiths sold their North Ninth Street, Arlington, Va., home on or about July 12, 1974. Sometime in August or September 1974, Mr. and Mrs. John Click secured a purchaser for their Fairfax, Va., home. The closing, however, did not occur until December 27, 1974.

During the period from July 9, 1974, through February 8, 1975, Mr. and Mrs. Highsmith took out property damage insurance and paid property taxes on the Gierisch residence. During the same period, Mr. and Mrs. John Click made substantial improvements to the Tinney residence totaling over $5,000. The improvements included a fence for $593.75 to keep their horse enclosed on the property, an automatic garage door opener for $283.36, a well pump and other expenses related to the well for $239.48, a light fixture for $49.69, wall-to-wall carpeting for $1,440, custom draperies for $1,368.02, and wrought iron railings to replace wooden rails for $392. They also paid $781 to prune a tree, $129.71 for gravel for the driveway, and $30 for repair of a canvas awning. Mr. and Mrs. John Click paid for these improvements themselves and did not ask for petitioner's prior approval. At no time did either couple pay rent to petitioner for the respective houses in which they lived.

During this period, petitioner had other investment properties. It was her practice, with the advice and assistance of her attorneys, to take care of arrangements, such as obtaining property insurance, with respect to these properties.

On February 8, 1975, petitioner executed a deed of gift for the Tinney residence to John Click and a deed of gift for the Gierisch residence to Mary Highsmith.

On her 1974 income tax return, petitioner reported that she "exchanged approximately 43 acres of real property acquired in 1961 [sic] and held for investment purposes with a value of $231,968 for two pieces of residential real estate to be held for similar purposes of $ 231,968.00." She elected to report the remainder of the amount received pursuant to section 453.

In his statutory notice, respondent determined that petitioner's exchange of parcel A for the two residential properties and a note and cash does not qualify as a like-kind exchange under section 1031. In the alternative, respondent also determined that the sale and exchange constituted one transaction for purposes of section 453.

OPINION

We must determine whether petitioner's exchange of farmland for two residential properties, cash, and a note qualifies for nonrecognition treatment under section 1031.

Section 1031(a) provides that no gain or loss shall be recognized if property held for productive use in a trade or business or for investment is exchanged solely for property of a like kind which is also "to be held either for productive use in a trade or business or for investment." (Footnote 1)

To qualify for treatment under section 1031, three requirements must be satisfied: (1) The transaction must be an exchange; (2) the exchange must involve like-kind properties; and (3) both the properties transferred and the properties received must be held either for productive use in a trade or business or for investment. Sec. 1.1031(a)-1(a) and (c), Income Tax Regs.... The parties do not question that the transaction at issue constitutes an exchange. Furthermore, they appear to agree that the farmland and the two residences are like-kind properties because the nature and character of the properties, as distinguished from their grade or quality, are substantially the same. See generally sec. 1.1031(a)-1(b), Income Tax Regs.... The controversy, therefore, centers on whether the two residences received by petitioner Dollie H. Click in the exchange ... were held for investment.

A taxpayer's intent to hold property for investment must be determined as of the time of the exchange. We must examine the substance of the transaction, rather than the form in which it is cast, when analyzing a purported section 1031 exchange of property.... The petitioner bears the burden of proving that she had the requisite investment intent....

In the instant case, respondent proposes to disallow section 1031 nonrecognition treatment on the theory that petitioner's gifts of the residences were part of a pre-arranged plan. He alleges that petitioner's intent at the time of the exchange was not to hold the houses for investment, but eventually to gift them to her children. Petitioner counters with the assertion that she had no concrete plan to transfer the acquired property to her children at the time of the exchange. Rather, she stated that she took the property because she wanted "something that would grow in value." As such, she claims that she held the houses as an investment until 7 months after the exchange, at which time she decided to gift them to her children.

In *Wagensen v. Commissioner*, ... [74 T.C. 653 (1980)] we considered a factual setting that appears, at first glance, to be analogous to the case at hand. The taxpayer therein exchanged his ranch for another ranch and cash. Nine months later, he made a gift of the new ranch and some cash to his son and daughter. We held that the taxpayer had no concrete plans at the time of the like-kind exchange to make the later gift. First, the facts showed that he did not initiate discussions with his accountants about a gift until after the exchange. Second, he used the acquired ranch in his ranching business during the period between the exchange and the gift. Accordingly, while we found that the general desire to make a gift prior to the time of the exchange is not inconsistent with an intent to hold the acquired ranch for productive use in business or for investment, we also found that, considering the facts presented, the gift was not part of the exchange transaction. 74 T.C. at 659.

Respondent argues that the *Wagensen* opinion does not control in the instant case because petitioner intended to gift the residences to her children at the time of the exchange, and petitioner never had the requisite investment intent. Furthermore, respondent says that the ranch property exchanged in *Wagensen* was inherently investment or business property, while the houses received herein were personal. (Footnote 3) Respondent asserts that our holding in *Regals Realty Co. v. Commissioner*, [43 B.T.A. 194 (1940)] is apposite. In *Regals Realty*, the corporate taxpayer swapped real property used

542   NONRECOGNITION TRANSACTIONS

in its trade or business for like-kind real property. Approximately 2 weeks later, the corporation's board of directors decided to liquidate and sell the property. Although it was unsuccessful in finding a purchaser, the corporation eventually transferred property to a new corporation in exchange for the new corporation's stock, and such stock was distributed in liquidation to the taxpayer's shareholders. The Board of Tax Appeals there held that the transaction did not qualify for nonrecognition treatment under the predecessor to section 1031 because "It places an unbearable strain on the credulity to believe that under those circumstances the property acquired was 'to be held' for investment." 43 B.T.A. at 209.

In the instant case, the facts reveal that petitioner suggested to her son and daughter and their spouses as early as mid-1973 that they look for new homes to use as "swap" property. Mr. and Mrs. Highsmith located the Gierisch residence. Mr. and Mrs. John Click located the Tinney residence, which had been the focus of prior inquiry by Mrs. Click in 1973. Such homes suited the personal lifestyles of the two couples and satisfied their desires for larger homes and more land. Only after Marriott made its offer to purchase did petitioner visit the Tinney residence. We cannot believe that petitioner, who was an experienced investor, had an investment intent with respect to property that she did not personally select and had never seen prior to its selection.

Further, petitioner, now 72 years old, was working on an estate plan with her attorney in 1973 and 1974 at the same time that the idea for the exchange of properties developed and at the time of the transaction with Marriott. As a woman with a potentially substantial estate, petitioner had been advised with respect to estate and gift tax liabilities that might arise. Based on the evidence presented, we believe that petitioner's estate planning activities are highly indicative of an intent at the time of the exchange to gift the residences to her children.

Finally, petitioner's testimony indicates that she normally took care of her investments and obtained property insurance therefor. Here, the facts indicate that Mr. and Mrs. Highsmith took out property insurance and paid property taxes on the Gierisch residence for the period from July 9, 1974, through February 8, 1975. In addition, during the same period, Mr. and Mrs. John Click paid for a homeowner's insurance policy on the Tinney residence. They also made substantial expenditures for improvements on the Tinney residence. John Click testified that he treated the property as his own, although he knew he was not the owner. He lived in the house rent free during the 7-month period and spent money on the improvements purportedly to protect his mother's investment. A review of the expenditures indicates that many were for improvements that were more in the nature of personal custom features than for general maintenance. In addition, the fact that Mr. Click did not obtain his mother's approval before making the expenditures further belies petitioner's claim that her children lived in the houses as "caretakers" during the period between the exchange and the gift.

Accordingly, we cannot find that petitioner had an investment intent in accepting the homes as "swap" property. Rather, it appears that her primary purpose was to provide larger homes in which her children and grandchildren could reside. From all of the evidence, we believe that petitioner acquired the residences with the intent of making gifts of them to her children and not to hold as investments for eventual sale. While petitioner was certainly a generous and caring parent and grandparent, her concern for the welfare of her family does not qualify the exchange for nonrecognition treatment under section 1031.

Having determined that section 1031 does not apply to the transaction, we need not address the second issue.

FOOTNOTES:

1. If cash or other property that does not qualify as like-kind property is included in such an exchange, the recipient must recognize gain to the extent of the cash or fair market value of other property received. Sec. 1031(b).

3. Respondent further argues that the facts in the instant case would not qualify for sec. 1031 treatment based on the substance-over-form analysis put forth in *Wagensen v. Commissioner*, 74 T.C. 653, 660 (1980). There, the Court reasoned that if the form of the transaction had been altered so that the taxpayer gifted an interest in his ranch to his children prior to the exchange, the children's subsequent exchange of the ranch property would have qualified for nonrecognition treatment. Here, however, if petitioner Dollie Click had transferred a portion of her farm property to her children prior to the exchange, and they had exchanged investment farm property for personal residences (in which they planned to live immediately after the exchange), the children would not be entitled to sec. 1031 treatment.

Consider the following questions about *Click*.

1. Why did Marriot purchase the Gierisch and Tinney residences?

2. Were the properties that Mrs. Click exchanged with Marriott "like-kind" within the meaning of section 1031? How can farmland and residential property be "like-kind"? Cite your authority.

3. Why did the Tax Court hold that Mrs. Click lacked the requisite investment motive with respect to the Gierisch and Tinney residences? On what facts did the court rely?

4. Why did Mrs. Click wait until February 8, 1975, to execute a deed of gift to her children for the residences?

5. Would Mrs. Click have won the case if her children had waited until February 8, the date of the gift, to move into the residences?

6. How long must someone hold either the old or new property for the property to be considered "held" for use in a trade or business or for investment? How would you have advised a client like Mrs. Click to maximize her chance for success?

Now suppose Juan and Lilian make the exchange and Juan begins to farm the property. He reports a loss on his farming operations as a loss from the trade or business of farming. (**Recall "Farmer Smith," the Johnson & Johnson executive we encountered in Part II, Chapter 3.**) On audit, the Service contends that he is operating the farm as a hobby, rather than as a trade or business. What result to Juan?

Is Lilian's purpose in holding either the farm or the apartment building relevant to Juan's tax consequences on the exchange? Suppose, in fact, that Lilian does not want the apartment building at all. But, she agrees to the exchange in order to facilitate Juan's plan because she believes that she will quickly be able to sell the apartment building at a small profit. Any effect on Juan?

Suppose instead, that Lilian simply refuses to trade for the apartment building, even though Juan tells her that he has a buyer all lined up and that if she will only accommodate him, the buyer will give her a small premium when she sells the apartment building to him immediately after the exchange.[10] Is Juan simply out of luck or can you propose a different plan to accomplish Juan's desire for a section 1031 exchange? Does the court's discussion in *Click* of substance over form prevent the success of this type of exchange under section 1031?

———————

What happens if the apartment building is worth $100,000 more than the land. Could Juan and Lilian still make an exchange? Would Juan be willing to do so? (**Recall Revenue Ruling 79-24, the barter ruling, and *Philadelphia Park*.** How would you go about equalizing the values? What effect would your plan have on the tax consequences to each party? Is the exchange still of "like-kind" property? **Look at section 1031(b).** It refers to the receipt of "other property or money," commonly referred to as "boot." How would each calculate basis in their new properties? **Look again at section 1031(d).** Can you, once again, develop a formula for calculating basis in a case like this one? Can you explain the adjustments required by section 1031(d) in relation to TOAD?

Suppose that in the transaction described in the previous paragraph, Juan's basis in the apartment house was $950,000, instead of $400,000. All other facts remain the same. What result to Juan on the exchange?

———————

One final idea to consider: if Juan's basis in the apartment building was $1,500,000, would he want to enter into a like-kind exchange? Can he avoid the application of section 1031? Consider the following case.

JORDAN MARSH COMPANY v. COMMISSIONER
269 F.2d 453 (2d Cir. 1959)

HINCKS, Circuit Judge.

This is a petition to review an order of the Tax Court, which upheld the Commissioner's deficiency assessment of $2,101,823.39 in income and excess profits tax against the petitioner, Jordan Marsh Company. There is no dispute as to the facts, which were stipulated before the Tax Court and which are set forth in substance below.

The transactions giving rise to the dispute were conveyances by the petitioner in 1944 of the fee of two parcels of property in the city of Boston where the petitioner, then as now, operated a department store. In return for its conveyances the petitioner received $2,300,000 in cash which, concededly, represented the fair market value of the properties. The conveyances were unconditional, without provision of any option to repurchase. At the same time, the petitioner received back from the vendees leases of the same properties for terms of 30 years and 3 days, with options to renew for another 30 years if the petitioner-lessee should erect new buildings thereon. The vendees were in no way connected with the petitioner. The rentals to be paid under the leases concededly were full and normal rentals so that the leasehold interests which devolved upon the petitioner were of no capital value.

In its return for 1944, the petitioner, claiming the transaction was a sale under § 112(a), Internal Revenue Code of 1939 [predecessor to section 1001], sought to deduct from income the difference between the adjusted basis of the property and the

———————

10. This type of immediate sale is sometimes referred to as a "flip."

cash received. The Commissioner disallowed the deduction, taking the position that the transaction represented an exchange of property for other property of like kind. Under Section 112(b)(1) [predecessor to section 1031(a)] such exchanges are not occasions for the recognition of gain or loss; and even the receipt of cash or other property in the exchange of the properties of like kind is not enough to permit the taxpayer to recognize loss. Section 112(e) [predecessor to section 1031(c)]. Thus the Commissioner viewed the transaction, in substance, as an exchange of a fee interest for a long term lease, justifying his position by Treasury Regulation 111, § 29.112(b)(1)-1 [predecessor to Treasury Regulation section 1.1031(a)-1(c)], which provides that a leasehold of more than 30 years is the equivalent of a fee interest. Accordingly the Commissioner made the deficiency assessment stated above. The Tax Court upheld the Commissioner's determination....

Upon this appeal, we must decide whether the transaction in question here was a sale or an exchange of property for other property of like kind within the meaning of §§ 112(b) and 112(e) of the Internal Revenue Code cited above. If we should find that it is an exchange, we would then have to decide whether the Commissioner's regulation, declaring that a leasehold of property of 30 years or more is property "of like kind" to the fee in the same property, is a reasonable gloss to put upon the words of the statute. The judge in the Tax Court felt that Century Electric Co. v. Commissioner of Internal Rev., 8 Cir., 192 F.2d 155, ... affirming 15 T.C. 581, was dispositive of both questions. In the view which we take of the first question, we do not have to pass upon the second question. For we hold that the transaction here was a sale and not an exchange.

The controversy centers around the purposes of Congress in enacting § 112(b), dealing with non-taxable exchanges. The section represents an exception to the general rule, stated in § 112(e), that upon the sale or exchange of property the entire amount of gain or loss is to be recognized by the taxpayer. The first Congressional attempt to make certain exchanges of this kind non-taxable occurred in Section 202(c), Revenue Act of 1921, c. 135, 42 Stat. 227. Under this section, no gain or loss was recognized from an exchange of property unless the property received in exchange had a "readily realizable market value." In 1924, this section was amended to the form in which it is applicable here. Discussing the old section the House Committee observed:

> "The provision is so indefinite that it cannot be applied with accuracy or with consistency. It appears best to provide generally that gain or loss is recognized from all exchanges, and then except specifically and in definite terms those cases of exchanges in which it is not desired to tax the gain or allow the loss. This results in definiteness and accuracy and enables a taxpayer to determine prior to the consummation of a given transaction the tax liability that will result." (Committee Reports on Rev. Act of 1924, reprinted in Int. Rev. Cum. Bull. 1939-1 (Part 2), p. 250.)

Thus the "readily realizable market value" test disappeared from the statute. A later report, reviewing the section, expressed its purpose as follows:

> "The law has provided for 12 years that gain or loss is recognized on exchanges of property having a fair market value, such as stocks, bonds, and negotiable instruments; on exchanges of property held primarily for sale; or on exchanges of one kind of property for another kind of property; but not on other exchanges of property solely for property of like kind. In other words, profit or loss is recognized in the case of exchanges of notes or securities, which are essentially like money; or in the case of stock in trade; or in case the taxpayer ex-

changes the property comprising his original investment for a different kind of property; but *if the taxpayer's money is still tied up in the same kind of property* as that in which it was originally invested, he is not allowed to compute and deduct his theoretical loss on the exchange, nor is he charged with a tax upon his theoretical profit. The calculation of the profit or loss is deferred until it is realized in cash, marketable securities, or other property not of the same kind having a fair market value." (House Ways and Means Committee Report, reprinted in Int. Rev. Cum. Bull. 1939-1 (Part 2), p. 564.)

These passages lead us to accept as correct the petitioner's position with respect to the purposes of the section. Congress was primarily concerned with the inequity, in the case of an exchange, of forcing a taxpayer to recognize a paper gain which was still tied up in a continuing investment of the same sort. If such gains were not to be recognized, however, upon the ground that they were theoretical, neither should equally theoretical losses. And as to both gains and losses the taxpayer should not have it within his power to avoid the operation of the section by stipulating for the addition of cash, or boot, to the property received in exchange. These considerations, rather than concern for the difficulty of the administrative task of making the valuations necessary to compute gains and losses, were at the root of the Congressional purpose in enacting §§ 112(b)(1) and (e). Indeed, if these sections had been intended to obviate the necessity of making difficult valuations, one would have expected them to provide for nonrecognition of gains and losses in all exchanges, whether the property received in exchanges were "of a like kind" or *not* of a like kind. And if such had been the legislative objective, § 112(c) [predecessor to section 1031(b)], providing for the recognition of gain from exchanges not wholly in kind, would never have been enacted.

That such indeed was the legislative objective is supported by Portland Oil Co. v. Commissioner of Internal Revenue, 1 Cir., 109 F.2d 479. There Judge Magruder, in speaking of a cognate provision contained in § 112(b), said at page 488:

"It is the purpose of Section 112(b)(5) to save the taxpayer from an immediate recognition of a gain, or to intermit the claim of a loss, in certain transactions where gain or loss may have accrued in a constitutional sense, but where in a popular and economic sense there has been a mere change in the form of ownership and the taxpayer has not really 'cashed in' on the theoretical gain, or closed out a losing venture."

In conformity with this reading of the statute, we think the petitioner here, by its unconditional conveyances to a stranger, had done more than make a change in the *form of ownership*: it was a change as to the *quantum* of ownership whereby, in the words just quoted, it had "closed out a losing venture." By the transaction its capital invested in the real estate involved had been completely liquidated for cash to an amount fully equal to the value of the fee. This, we hold, was a sale—not an exchange within the purview of § 112(b).

The Tax Court apparently thought it of controlling importance that the transaction in question involved no change in the petitioner's possession of the premises: it felt that the decision in Century Electric Co. v. Commissioner of Internal Rev., supra, controlled the situation here. We think, however, that that case was distinguishable on the facts. For not with-standing the lengthy findings made with meticulous care by the Tax Court in that case, 15 T.C. 581, there was no finding that the cash received by the taxpayer was the full equivalent of the value of the fee which the taxpayer had conveyed to the vendee-lessor, and no finding that the lease back called for a rent which was fully equal to the rental value of the premises. Indeed, in its opinion the Court of Appeals pointed to evidence that the fee which the taxpayer had "exchanged" may have had a value substantially in excess of the cash received. And in the Century Electric case, the findings showed, at page 585, that the taxpayer-lessee, unlike the taxpayer here, was not required to pay "general state, city and school taxes" because its lessor was an educational institution which under its charter was exempt from such taxes. Thus the leasehold interest in Century Electric on this account may well have had a premium value. In the absence of findings as to the values of the properties allegedly "exchanged," necessarily there could be no finding of a loss. And without proof of a loss, of course, the taxpayer could not prevail. Indeed, in the Tax Court six of the judges expressly based their concurrences on that limited ground. 15 T.C. 596.

In the Century Electric opinion it was said, 192 F.2d at page 159:

> " ... Subsections 112(b)(1) and 112(e) indicate the controlling policy and purpose of the section, that is, the nonrecognition of gain or loss in transactions where neither is readily measured in terms of money, where in theory the taxpayer may have realized gain or loss but where in fact his economic situation is the same after as it was before the transaction. See Fairfield S.S. Corp. v. Commissioner, 2 Cir., 157 F.2d 321, 323; Trenton Cotton Oil Co. v. Commissioner, 6 Cir., 147 F.2d 33, 36."

But the Fairfield case referred to was one in which the only change in taxpayer's ownership was through the interposition of a corporate title accomplished by transfer to a corporation wholly owned by the taxpayer. And in the Trenton Cotton Oil case, the court expressly relied on Portland Oil Co. v. Commissioner of Internal Revenue, supra, as stating correctly the purpose of § 112(b), but quoted only the first of the two requisites stated in Portland. As we have already observed, in that case Judge Magruder said that it was the purpose of § 112(b) "to intermit the claim of a loss" not only where the economic situation of the taxpayer is unchanged but also "*where ... the taxpayer has not ... closed out a losing venture.*" Here plainly the petitioner by the transfer finally closed out a losing venture. And it cannot justly be said that the economic situation of the petitioner was unchanged by a transaction which substituted $2,300,000 in cash for its investment in real estate and left it under a liability to make annual payments of rent for upwards of thirty years. Many *bona fide* business purposes may be served by such a transaction....

In ordinary usage, an "exchange" means the giving of one piece of property in return for another—not, as the Commissioner urges here, the return of a lesser interest in a property received from another. It seems unlikely that Congress intended that an "exchange" should have the strained meaning for which the Commissioner contends. For the legislative history states expressly an intent to correct the indefiniteness of prior versions of the Act by excepting from the general rule "specifically and in definite terms those cases of exchanges in which it is not desired to tax the gain or allow the loss."

But even if under certain circumstances the return of a part of the property conveyed may constitute an exchange for purposes of § 112, we think that in this case, in which cash was received for the full value of the property conveyed, the transaction must be classified as a sale.... Reversed.

Consider the following questions concerning *Jordan Marsh*.

1. What was the form of the transaction that Jordan Marsh entered into with the other party to the transaction?

2. How did Jordan Marsh report the tax consequences of this transaction? Why did Jordan Marsh want the transaction treated in this manner?

3. How did the Service characterize the transaction? Why did the Service prefer its view of the transaction?

4. The rule that a lease for a period equalling or exceeding 30 years should be treated as the fee has long been a part of the Treasury regulations. Can you think of a rationale that justifies this treatment?

5. Can you identify one or more important factors that led the court to rule as it did that might aid you in advising a client seeking either to achieve or to avoid like-kind exchange treatment?

We earlier introduced you to some of the instances in which, like *Jordan Marsh*, the characterization of the transaction depended upon a close examination of the particular facts. As noted there, these cases arise in a variety of ways. You have now seen issues of sale vs. lease and sale vs. loan. In Part VI, we will return to these characterization issues when we read *Estate of Franklin*.

Now that you have examined both section 1033 and section 1031, can you suggest any justification for the difference in requirements between "similar or related in service or use" and "like-kind"? Taxpayers who suffer a casualty loss do not do so voluntarily. In contrast, most taxpayers who wish to engage in a section 1031 transaction do so voluntarily. To which type of exchange does the narrower test apply? Why?

Chapter 3 of this Part IV has done little more than introduce you to a few of the nonrecognition transactions that form exceptions to the general rule of section 1001(c).[11] But, you certainly have realized that none of the nonrecognition provisions we have examined thus far forgives the gain forever. Rather, they represent simply deferrals of gain until sometime in the future.[12] It is probably not an overstatement to suggest that the underlying policy for these provisions is to make the transformation of one type of property ownership into another without the imposition of tax less costly and troublesome. As stated by one of the regulations to former section 1002: "the underlying assumption of these exceptions is that the new property is substantially a continuation of the old investment still unliquidated."[13] If that is the reason, has Congress imposed appropriate conditions on when these exceptions apply so as to change the proper time for reporting and paying a tax?

Thus, the following scenario prompted Congressional action: suppose you received a house used as rental property in a section 1031 like-kind exchange. Section 1031 protected you from gain on the disposition of your old property that was held for investment. Sometime later, you decided to convert the property to your own personal use

---

11. Recall that you studied another nonrecognition provision in Part III. What was it?

12. We have already encountered two exceptions to the general rule that these nonrecognition provisions do no more than defer the proper time for paying a tax. One is the section 1014 step-up in basis at death you studied in Part II. In Part III, you encountered section 121, another exception of broad applicability that you will see again in the personal residence transactional problem. Section 121 forgives forever a certain amount of gain on the sale of a personal residence.

13. Treas. Reg. section 1.1002-1(c).

and move in, occupying it as your principal residence.[14] Two years later, you decide to sell your residence. Can you exclude up to $250,000 of gain from the sale ($500,000 if you are married and file a joint return), even if a portion of the gain accrued prior to your conversion of the property from property held for investment to property held for personal use? The 2004 Jobs Act prevents exclusion of the gain unless you have held the property for at least 5 years. **See section 121(d)(10).**

These few chapters have also introduced you to a few of the ways in which the issue of timing arises in tax law. There are many others (and many elaborations of the few you have studied.) But the theme that unites all the subtopics concerning timing might be said to be those twins that first appeared in Part II: realization and recognition. It is these two fundamental concepts of tax law that dictate the proper time for reporting. It is these fundamental concepts that sometimes prompt taxpayers to attempt to alter the proper timing of the tax effects of a transaction. Not all such attempts will fail; indeed, many succeed. The difference between success and failure often consists of knowing the rules, grounding the planning in motives other than purely tax ones, and not being too greedy.[15]

---

14. In other words, you were smarter than Mrs. Click and waited some period of time before converting the new investment property to personal use.

15. The "pig" theory of taxation says: "little piggies get fat, but hogs get slaughtered." Also remember that pigs don't smell very good. Often, purely tax-motivated transactions don't pass the "smell test." Tax lawyers commonly refer to the "smell test" when determining whether a planned transaction will pass muster for tax purposes.

V. The "Proper" Rate Revisited: Capital Gains and Losses

Introduction

In Part I we examined the rate structure of the federal income tax as set forth in section 1 of the Code. We noted that the current rate structure is progressive in that it consists, after the 2001 and 2003 Acts, of six rates ranging from 10 percent to 35 percent, which apply to increasing amounts of a taxpayer's taxable income.[1] In certain circumstances, however, section 1(h), which is entitled "Maximum Capital Gains Rate," imposes an alternative rate structure to the regular section 1 rates in situations in which a taxpayer has "net capital gain" ("NCG").

Beginning in 1987, Section 1(h) placed a cap on the tax rate applicable to the taxpayer's NCG by providing that NCG would be taxed at a rate no higher than 28 percent. Thus, for taxpayers whose taxable income placed them in the 31 percent or higher marginal tax brackets, section 1(h) provided a preferential rate no higher than 28 percent on their NCG, if they had any.

Congress amended section 1(h) in 1997 to effect an even further reduction in the tax rates applicable to certain NCG's. That version of section 1(h), effective for assets sold after July 28, 1997, is long and complex. (Professor Marvin Chirelstein has referred to it as "something of a reader's nightmare."[2]) In general, however, section 1(h) lowered the tax rate on certain most-favored capital gains to 20 percent (10 percent for taxpayers in the 15 percent bracket). The 1997 Act also added a new wrinkle to section 1(h): different rates for different types of assets. It created a new 25 percent rate for certain capital gains from depreciable real estate, and retained the 28 percent rate for other less-favored capital gains.[3]

The ink was barely dry on the 1997 amendments before complexities and technical problems became apparent. Of perhaps greatest concern was the difference in holding periods for capital assets introduced by the 1997 legislation. To obtain a favorable capital gains rate of tax, a taxpayer had to hold some assets for more than twelve months and others for more than eighteen. As a result, Congress again amended section 1(h) in 1998. The 1998 legislation repealed the eighteen month period. A taxpayer now is eligible for the favorable capital gains rates for assets held for more than one year.

---

1. For a discussion of the current rate structure and the gradual rate reductions effected by the 2001 and 2003 Acts, return to Part I, Chapter 2.

2. Marvin A. Chirelstein, *Federal Income Taxation* 349 (9th ed. 2002.)

3. Depreciable real estate is subject to a 25 percent rate on any gain attributable to straight line depreciation. (How does straight line depreciation cause gain?) Recall section 1016(a)(2). Gain in excess of that attributable to straight line depreciation was eligible for the lowest 20 (or 10) percent rate.

Certain capital assets, referred to as "collectibles," such as works of art, rugs, antiques, metals, gems, stamps, coins, and alcoholic beverages are still eligible only for a 28 percent rate. In addition, gain on "section 1202 stock" is also subject to the 28 percent rate. Look at section 1202(a). Can you explain why the effective rate of tax on gain from this special type of stock is 14 percent?

To complicate matters even further, beginning in the year 2001, net gains from sales of capital assets acquired and held for more than 5 years from 2001 were to be taxed at a maximum 18 percent rate. (For taxpayers in the 15 percent or lower ordinary income bracket, an 8 percent rate was to apply, beginning in 2001, to the sale of capital assets held for more than 5 years no matter when acquired.)

Dissatisfied with the complexity it had enacted in the 1997, 1998, and 2001 Acts, Congress made further changes to section 1(h) in the 2003 Act. For individual taxpayers (other than low-income individuals), the 20 percent rate fell to 15 percent through 2008. For lower-income individuals, the 10 percent fell to 5 percent through 2007, then to 0 percent for 2008. The special rules for 5-year property, that is the 18 and 8 percent rates, were repealed. In May, 2006, Congress extended these lower capital gains rates through 2010.[4]

Section 1(h) represents the current manifestation of the long-standing preference that Congress has afforded income that is characterized as "capital gain." Except for a brief period in the late 1980s, the Code has contained special provisions since 1921 that have taxed "capital gains" at a favorable tax rate.[5] Taxpayers have, therefore, coveted "capital gain" income over its counterpart, "ordinary income," which is taxed at the regular, higher rates.

The House Ways and Means Committee has explained that one of the purposes for the preferential rate for "capital gains" is its recognition that the gain on the sale of an investment asset is attributable to appreciation of the asset that has occurred over a long period of time, and it would be unfair to tax all the gain in one year.[6] This rationale for the capital gains preference is commonly referred to as addressing the "bunching" problem. Query whether a one year holding period is the appropriate choice to remedy this problem.

Another rationale that has been advanced over the years to support the preference is that it compensates for the effects of inflation in light of the fact that much of the appreciation in the value of an asset upon which taxpayer will be taxed results from inflation. Some people have suggested that a better way to deal with this problem would be to index the basis of assets for inflation similar to the manner in which the Code already requires various adjustments for inflation.

Still another rationale proponents put forward for the preference is that it encourages the free flow of capital into new investments by investors who, without the preference, would hesitate to cash in on their investments because of the tax they would incur on sale. This problem is commonly referred to as the "lock-in" problem.

In many instances, the capital gains preference has been used as a political football in election years. Many people believe that the preference benefits the wealthy only be-

---

4. In the Tax Increase Prevention and Reconciliation Act of 2005, Pub. L. No. 109-222, signed by President George W. Bush on May 17, 2006.(Hereinafter, referred to as "the 2005 Act.")

5. The structure of the current capital gains preference in section 1(h) was enacted as part of the Tax Reform Act of 1986. Prior to that time, the preference took the form of an above-the-line deduction of a percentage of the taxpayer's net long term capital gains. Thus, before the 1986 amendment, in calculating her tax, a taxpayer deducted 60 percent of her net long term capital gains above the line. After the deduction, only 40 percent of her gain remained in her taxable income ("TI"). As a consequence, taxpayers whose income was subject to the top marginal rate of 50 percent, paid tax only at the rate of 20 percent on their net long term capital gains (50 percent rate x 40 percent of the net long term capital gains).

6. H.R. Rep. No. 94-658 on the Tax Reform Act of 1976.

cause the wealthy are the ones who can afford to own investment assets, and thus, that the preference discriminates against wage earners who have to pay a higher rate of tax on their "ordinary" income from personal services. On the other hand, proponents of the preference maintain that it is the wealthy who create more jobs and wealth (and more tax revenue) by their ability to invest capital; thus, Congress should encourage, not discourage, such investments.

In contrast to favored capital gains, "capital losses" of taxpayers have been subject to special deductibility restrictions since 1924. Section 1211(b) limits the amount of "capital loss" that an individual may deduct during any particular tax year, although the Code has not traditionally restricted the deductibility of "ordinary losses."[7] Thus, just as taxpayers have coveted "capital gain" and avoided "ordinary income" on the gain side, on the loss side, taxpayers have coveted "ordinary loss" and avoided "capital loss."

Because of the preferred tax-rate treatment on the gain side and the restricted deductibility treatment on the loss side, the characterization of gains and losses under section 1001 as "capital" versus "ordinary" is, depending on the circumstances, of keen and conflicting interest to taxpayers and the government. The rules of the Code governing this process of characterization have been described as "[o]ne of the principal complicating features of the federal income tax structure."[8] The following materials provide a brief, and by no means comprehensive, overview of the provisions of the Code that set forth the basic rules governing this critical characterization process. The materials provide you with the basic framework for analysis of the issues involved in the characterization process.

---

7. "Ordinary losses" that currently have no restrictions on deductibility are above-the-line deductions as described in section 62(a)(1): losses incurred in a trade or business of a taxpayer who is not an employee, *i.e.*, a proprietor. Section 165(c) restricts the deductibility of losses by individuals. Even if a loss is allowed under section 165(c), it will be below-the-line if it is not an ordinary loss described in section 62(a)(1), or a capital loss described in section 62(a)(3). As you learned in Carole's problem, below-the-line deductions may also be subject to limits found in sections 67 and 68.

8. Boris I. Bittker and Martin J. McMahon, Jr., *Federal Income Taxation of Individuals* § 31.1 (2d ed. 1995).

Chapter 1

Policy Underlying the Capital Gains Preference

The United States Supreme Court long ago identified two arguments in favor of a different form of taxation for income from capital. It explained:

> Before the Act of 1921, gains realized from the sale of property were taxed at the same rates as other income, with the result that capital gains, often accruing over long periods of time, were taxed in the year of realization at the high rates resulting from their inclusion in the higher surtax brackets. The provisions of the 1921 revenue act for taxing capital gains at a lower rate, reënacted in 1924 without material change, were adopted to relieve the taxpayer from these excessive tax burdens on gains resulting from a conversion of capital investments, and to remove the deterrent effect of those burdens on such conversions.[1]

These have become just two of the claims justifying the continuation of the special treatment this type of income enjoys. Many politicians, tax experts, and economists have continued to claim that one of the purposes in conferring a preferential rate for capital gains is to recognize that the gain on the sale of an investment asset is attributable to appreciation in the value of the asset over a long period of time. Therefore, it would be unfair to tax all the gain in one year.[2] Moreover, subjecting this income to tax in one year may discourage asset owners from disposing of assets (and replacing them with other assets), thereby distorting the capital markets.

Other rationales advanced for a preferential rate include the argument that the increase in a long-held asset's value arises in large measure from inflation, rather than from a true increase in the value of the asset.[3] As the three articles that follow demonstrate, there is wide disagreement among politicians, tax experts, and economists concerning the proper treatment of income arising from sales or exchanges of capital assets. As you read them, consider both the propriety of adopting a preferential rate and the practical difficulties of defining the character and length of investment required by choosing special treatment for certain items of income. Also consider whether, in your view, capital gains are or are not income.

At the beginning of their long article, Professors Noel Cunningham and Deborah Schenk set forth the arguments that the proponents of a capital gains preference advance.

---

1. *Burnet v. Harmel*, 287 U.S. 103, 106 (1932). The Court cited House Report No. 350, Ways and Means Committee, 67th Cong., 1st Sess. on the Revenue Bill of 1921, p. 10.

2. H.R. Rep. No. 94-658.

3. *Hellermann v. Commissioner*, 77 T.C. 1361 (1981). In *Hellermann*, the Tax Court held that gain from the sale of property attributable solely to inflation is income within the meaning of the Sixteenth Amendment, and, therefore, subject to taxation.

The Case for a Capital Gains Preference[4]

...

III. CAPITAL GAINS IN A NORMATIVE INCOME TAX

Most of the plausible arguments in favor of a capital gains preference are directed at one or more of the flaws in the current treatment of capital assets. In this Section, we carefully consider the arguments advanced in favor of a capital gains preference as a means of addressing the problems caused by

deviations from the base....

...

A. Capital Gains Are Not Income

Several of the traditional arguments in favor of a preference essentially are definitional. They range from the conclusive ("capital gains are not income") to the completely specious ("people do not regard capital gains as income") to the slightly serious. Their gist is that capital gains are unexpected, nonrecurring receipts, wholly unlike wages or other payments for productive effort.

...

B. Consumption and Not Income Should be Taxed

Commentators sometimes argue that because the ideal tax base is consumption, and not income, a preference comes fairly close to the correct treatment of capital gains. Under a consumption tax, the income from capital would be taxed only if it were used for consumption and thus, would be excluded from the base if not consumed. Exclusion of a portion of the gain is, therefore, closer to the correct treatment than is full taxation. This argument often is supported by the observation that our current system is a hybrid with aspects of both a Haig-Simons base and a consumption tax base.

...

C. Bunching

Essentially, the bunching argument is that the realization rule forces a taxpayer to report in one year capital gains that have accrued over several years and may subject the gains to a higher marginal rate than would have applied had the gains been reported each year as they accrued. A preference acts as a crude averaging device to offset the telescoping effect of the realization requirement. To illustrate, consider the following:

> T purchased X stock 10 years ago for $10. During each of those 10 years, T was in the 25% tax bracket. This year T sold the stock for $510, recognizing a gain of $500. As a result of this gain, T is pushed into a higher bracket and must pay taxes on the gain at a 40% rate.

Bunching is a potential problem only in a system with graduated tax rates and only if the taxpayer is in a higher bracket on the disposition date than she was when the income accrued. Thus, for example, if the $500 gain is taxed at a 40%

---

4. Noel B. Cunningham and Deborah H. Schenk, "The Case for a Capital Gains Preference," 48 Tax L. Rev. 319 *passim* (1993).

rate, T would owe $200 in taxes, compared to the $125 she would have owed if the gain had accrued at $50 a year for 10 years and had been subjected to a 25% rate.

...

D. Double Taxation of Corporate Earnings

Under our current income tax system, corporate income is taxed twice, once at the corporate level when earned, and again at the shareholder level when distributed. This "classical system" of taxation is inconsistent with an ideal Haig-Simons income tax and has been the subject of much criticism. For decades, reformers have called for its elimination by integrating the corporate and individual income taxes.

...

Proponents of the preference for capital gains argue that, in the absence of integration, the preference can be justified as a second-best solution to the inefficiencies created by the double taxation of corporate earnings. Although a preference would not completely eliminate the problem created by the classical system, it would reduce its impact....

...

E. Inflation

One of the principal arguments used to support the preference is that capital gains are largely inflationary. To that extent, they do not represent economic income and should not be included in a base with Haig-Simons income as the norm....

...

F. Risk

Proponents argue that a preference is necessary to offset the negative effects on risk taking of an income tax, especially one with limitations on the deduction of realized losses. At least as a normative goal, a well-designed tax system should leave the taxpayer free to assume the same amount of risk that he would assume in a tax-free world. Commentators often argue that the mere existence of an income tax discourages risk taking because it reduces the expected return from a risky investment. This reduces economic welfare because investors may shift their portfolios toward less risky assets than they would retain in a nontax world. Proponents of a preference for capital gains argue that it is an effective way to reduce this distortion....

...

G. Lock-In Effect

1. The Lock-in Phenomenon

The most serious argument in favor of a capital gains preference is premised upon the so-called lock-in effect. The lock-in effect describes an investor's reluctance to incur a tax on realization of gains; it is a direct consequence of prior decisions to impose a realization requirement and not to tax gains at death. An investor who is not taxed until realization and who can avoid tax altogether by holding an asset until death, tends not to change investments, even though he may believe that higher returns are available elsewhere. For example, suppose T holds *Asset #1* with a basis of $100 and a value of $500 in a world with a flat 25% tax on income. The expected yield on this investment is 10%, or $50. T has the opportunity to invest in *Asset #2*, which has an expected yield of 12%. If T sold *Asset #1*, he would pay $100 in taxes, leaving only $400 to invest in *Asset #2*. Because a $400 investment in *Asset #2* has an expected yield of only $48, T will not change investments. The toll charge prevents T from diversifying his portfolio.

Although studies differ as to the extent of realizations, they all agree that a large percentage (approximately one-half) of capital gains are never subject to tax. This lock-in of accrued gains is said to create inefficiency that impedes the flow of capital to its most productive uses. An individual who wishes to diversify her portfolio or to sell to fund consumption may be unwilling to do so, thus reducing her utility. For example, an investor might want to reduce (or increase) the risk in her portfolio or sell stock to buy a home or enjoy other forms of consumption. This alteration of investment decisions is said to misallocate capital, especially in the case of an entrepreneur who might otherwise use capital for a new venture.

Whether the lock-in effect attributable to the tax burden imposes a significant onus on the economy as a whole is less clear. Although an individual may benefit greatly by changing her portfolio, it is not clear that it matters much to society who owns IBM stock. Trading in marketable securities (a significant source of capital gains), for example, has only marginal effects on the economy as a whole and is not likely to increase the total amount of investment.

. . .

Professor John Lee prepared an article for presentation at a time when Congress was once again considering retention or expansion of the capital gains preference. His article explores what he calls the "myths" supporting the continuation or extension of the preference.

Capital Gains Myths[5]

H.R. 1215, Contract with America Tax Relief Act of 1995 ("CWATRA"), passed along partisan lines by the House of Representatives on April 5, 1995, provides both (a) a 50-percent exclusion for realizations by noncorporate taxpayers of gains from capital assets (other than from collectibles) held for at least one year and (b) indexing for inflation of the basis of capital assets acquired by noncorporate taxpayers on or after January 1, 1995, and held for three or more years. H.R. Rep. 104-84, the accompanying House Ways and Means Committee Report, provides unusually detailed "Reasons for Change" in support of these provisions.... This article examines those reasons in the order set forth in the report, as amplified by the contentions of capital gains cuts proponents and opponents in the recent hearings and the House floor debate, concluding that most are either wrong or better answered through other techniques not on the table....

Myth No. 1: A Capital Gains Tax Cut Will Increase the Saving Rate of American Households

H.R. Rep. No. 84 points out that net personal savings in the United States averaged 4.8 percent of gross domestic product (GDP) in the 1980s, below the rate of our major trading partners, and further dropped to 3.5 percent of GDP in 1992.... According to the report, many economists testified that a reduction in capital gains taxation by increasing the rate of return on savings would increase savings. The actual theoretical and empirical economic literature conflicts as to whether an increase in rate of return

---

5. John Lee, "Capital Gains Myths," 67 Tax Notes 809 *passim* (May 8, 1995)(footnotes omitted).

increases savings. As Dr. Barry Bosworth, Senior Fellow at the Brookings Institute, put it at the January 11, 1995, Ways and Means Hearing on the Contract: "We [economists] don't agree on a damn thing about how to stimulate private savings and what will work and what won't work." Indeed, ... in the real world of the leveraged buyouts in the 1980s, ... over half of the proceeds were spent on consumption items.... The 1978 and 1981 capital gains cuts did not increase the individual savings rate despite claims at the time that they would. Indeed, household savings fell in the period following such cuts. From this, one could conclude that the savings incentives in the Contract will not lift the private savings rate. Rather, given that the decline in savings occurred as to Americans now 55 or older, other causes appear to have been at work. For example, the decline may be attributable to an increase in the availability of insurance and Social Security and Medicare benefits, reducing the necessity for private savings. The most direct way to increase private savings is likely to be to reduce the federal budget deficit.

Myth No. 2: A Capital Gains Tax Cut Will Encourage Risk Taking by Individuals Pursuing New Businesses Exploiting New Technologies

H.R. Rep. No. 84 reasons that risk taking is stifled if taxation of any resulting gain is high and the ability to claim losses is limited. Proponents of the capital gains cuts in the Contract steadfastly maintained in the 1995 hearings that a generic capital gains cut (some added indexing) is necessary either to unlock frozen capital assets for investment in starting up or expanding young businesses or to reward the entrepreneur and investors for the greater risk in new ventures. The opposing view is that entrepreneurs (who together with family and friends are the primary source of capital for new ventures) are motivated by the rewards of running their own business and not the capital gains tax rate on selling out. As Rep. Fortney Pete Stark, D-Calif., asserted ... "entrepreneurs are born, not made." Thus, "stifling" appears a myth, at least with a top capital gains rate of 28 percent, a top ordinary rate of 39.6 percent, and an existing preference of 50 percent for stock in certain small businesses under section 1202.... For most entrepreneurs, a capital gains preference appears to be a subsidy rewarding them for what they would have done anyway rather than an incentive to do what they otherwise would not have done.

The real myth is that the capital gains preference "essentially" benefits the small-business folks, farmers, and home owners, in whose interest congressional capital gains cuts proponents usually claim the need for the additional capital gains preferences.... Some congressional supporters of the current capital gains proposals ... might actually believe that the primary beneficiaries of the cuts are these interests. They are deluded. Small-business people and farmers together probably account for 5 to 10 percent of annual capital gains realizations at best; venture capital, around 1 percent; and the overwhelming number of sales of personal residences are not taxed.... In good stock market years 50 percent of the realizations are equity, overwhelmingly public stock, and the bulk of the rest of the realizations are improved real estate....

...

Myth No. 3: Lowering Capital Gains Rates Will Unblock Many Sales Permitting More Money to Flow to New, More Highly Valued Uses

The Ways and Means report states that a reduction in the capital gains tax should improve the efficiency of the capital markets; all economists agreed that a capital gains cut would reduce "lock-in" and increase realizations. The report concludes that such unblocking would permit money to flow to new, more highly valued uses, thus improving the efficiency of the capital market. For more than 50 years, capital gains cut proponents have claimed that unblocking would permit capital to flow from sales of public stock to new companies. That case has never been made.... [R]ealizations from public stock do not flow to new venture capital or to closely held businesses (unless they are of public stock held by the entrepreneur herself). As Sen. Dale Bumpers, D-Ark., ... stated ..."I have never understood what economic benefit this country derives when somebody sells General Electric and uses the money and buys DuPont stock." The Small Business Administration also regards a generic capital gains cut as "rewarding nonproductive speculation in real estate or the stock market...." The facts behind this rhetoric are that most mature corporations raise outside capital these days through debt and not common stock offerings.... [L]ess than 3 percent of the action on Wall Street consists of public offerings of new common stock. Initial public offerings make up one-third to one-half of new common stock offerings, most of which probably could qualify under section 1202 as to noncorporate purchasers and thus obtain a preference under current law....

Myth No. 4:   Unblocking Sales Will Have the Short-Term and Long-Term Effect of Increasing Revenues

The Ways and Means Committee report also claims that this unblocking of sales will have the short- and long-term effect of increasing revenues. Whether the proposed preferences would raise revenue is harder to predict since this is another economic question upon which economists cannot agree in theory or empirical studies. The issues are microeconomic (increased realizations through unblocking effects) and macroeconomic (growth in the economy) effects. The Joint Committee Staff estimates that increased realizations induced by ... capital gains cuts would lower the "static" loss in the five-year budget window by 60 percent. The catch is that the Joint Committee believes that after an initial surge in realizations (50 percent of the baseline during the initial five-year budget window) most taxpayers will settle into a permanent level of lower realizations yet higher than would be expected in the absence of a rate reduction. But this permanent level of realizations would still lose revenue over the five-year budget window and beyond.... [The Joint Committee] scored the capital gains proposals as modified on March 9, 1995, as losing only $31.7 billion over the first five years.... Treasury scored CWATRA's capital gains provisions considerably lower, ... losing only $11 billion over the five-year budget window and $91 billion over the 10-year window. Here too there was an experiment, the 1978 and 1981 capital gains tax cuts. Treasury and the Joint Committee both found that, over the long haul, these capital gains cuts lost revenue under a "timed series" analysis.

The big debate is over the macroeconomic or "feedback" effects. Neither Treasury nor the Joint Committee on Taxation takes such effects into account in estimating future revenue gains and losses, in part because there is wide disagreement among economists as to such effects.... It is very difficult to separate the effects of such tax cuts from other forces at work in the economy at that time. For instance, the increased capital gains realizations during 1978–1985 coincided with stock and real estate booms....

    ...

Clearly, more realizations and hence more revenue would result from taxation at death of unrealized appreciation (many more realizations would occur prior to death) or annual accrual of unrealized appreciation in public stock. Those who support additional capital gains preferences would give them up rather than be faced with income taxation at death.... Their opposition to annual accrual would be even more intense....

Myth No. 5: Many Americans Realizing Capital Gains Are Middle-Income Taxpayers Pushed into Top Brackets by a Once-in-a-Lifetime Sale

... Treasury's distribution tables showed the top 1 percent of families (700,000 families, beginning at $349,438) as receiving 45.9 percent of such tax benefits; the top 5 percent (2,300,000 families beginning at $145,412), 66.5 percent of such benefits; and the top 10 percent (3,500,000 families beginning at $108,704), 73.9 percent.... Proponents of a capital gains cut claimed that most capital gains are realized by middle-income taxpayers, some of whom are pushed into high-income status by the once-in-a-lifetime realization in just one tax year of gain that has accrued over a number of years, as in the case of a retirement sale of a small business, farm or residence. This is the "king-for-a-day" myth.

In 1990 then Rep. (now Sen.) Byron Dorgan, D-N.D., asked the Joint Committee on Taxation Staff to make a time-series study of a sample of capital gains realizations, which demonstrated that the 43.7 percent of the individual taxpayers in the sample who realized capital gains only once in the five-year period surveyed (1979–83) had an average capital gain of $2,000 and realized only 9.8 percent of all capital gains realized by individuals in the period. On the other hand, the 15.7 percent of the individuals who realized capital gains in all five years realized an average capital gain of $100,000 and 58.9 percent of total capital gains realized over the period. Those who realized such gains in at least four years out of the five-year period recognized 70.9 percent of the total dollar value of reported capital gains. The Staff of the Joint Committee on Taxation concluded in 1995 that "[h]igher-income taxpayers generally hold a larger proportion of corporate stock and other capital assets than do other taxpayers. Thus, while many taxpayers may benefit from an exclusion or indexing for capital gains, a larger proportion of the dollar value of any tax reduction will go to those higher-income taxpayers who realize the bulk of the dollar value of gains."

Some members of Congress may even believe the claims that 70 percent of capital assets are held by taxpayers with no more than $50,000 of AGI and that such taxpayers pay most of the capital gains taxes. They are deluded both as to the facts and as to patterns of wealth in this country. The opposite is more true: 70 percent of the benefits of a capital gains preference are realized year after year by the same top 10 percent of families and 50 percent of the capital gains realizations are enjoyed by the top 1 percent of families with the bulk of their gains being real and not inflationary. It could be no other way taking into account the sources of capital gains realizations (mostly public stock and investment real estate and concentration of ownership of such assets at the top.

Myth No. 6: There Is Substantial Economic Mobility in the United States So That a Lower-Income Taxpayer May Be Higher-Income a Decade Later (and Presumably Realize Her Share of Capital Gains)

H.R. Rep. No. 84 claimed as a further deficiency in traditional studies of benefits of a capital gains cut that they classify taxpayers only by their current economic condition; studies show that there is substantial economic mobility in the United States so that an individual classified as lower income may be higher income in a decade. "Substantial" income mobility is another misleading myth. Treasury under the Bush administration, to answer the Democratic charges of the failure of trickle down economics embodied in the 1978 and 1981 tax cuts, performed mobility studies concluding that as many as one-third of the taxpayers at the bottom of the income scale in 1979 moved up the scale during the 1980s and similarly as many as one-third in the top 20 percent moved down the income scale during this period. Much of the apparent upward mobility in income reflects, however, the young growing older and becoming part of a two-working-spouse household or reaching peak earning years; downward mobility, growing older and retiring. "Although the poor can 'make it' in America, and the wealthy can 'fall from grace', these events are neither very common nor more likely to occur today than in the 1970s."

Myth No. 7:   Reduction in Capital Gains Leads to Increased Investment and Thus Greater Productivity and Higher Wages

The Ways and Means Committee report stressed as the most important aspect of the benefits of a capital gains cut that it would lead to economic growth benefitting all Americans. Again, this experiment has been tried before and failed. The decline in wages at the middle and bottom over the past two decades indicates that the benefits of the capital gains cuts of 1978 and 1981 did not trickle down.... [P]retax income from 1978 to 1990 increased only at the top (where it almost doubled primarily due to speculative bubbles in the stock and real estate markets, while income remained stagnant at the middle and bottom as average wages fell and average hours worked by families increased, both in large part due to a greater percentage of working spouses. Contrary to the extreme rhetoric, the trickle down economics cuts did not cause the pretax income disparities, but they did make the after-tax disparities even wider.

While some of the discussion of capital gains focuses on whether the capital gains preference is the proper method for dealing with the effects described by Professors Cunningham and Schenk, some commentators have made a more fundamental argument concerning capital gains. Indeed, the capital gains preference represents the middle ground between two diametrically opposed views. One group of theorists argues that a pure Haig-Simons treatment of capital gains would result in reporting them as ordinary income on a yearly basis (without regard to realization). See Haig-Simons definition of income in Part II, Chapter 1.B. The other group argues that capital gains are not income at all. Former Treasury official Bruce Bartlett forcefully expresses the view that Congress should debate and decide the real issue.

Why the Correct Capital Gains Tax Rate Is Zero[6]

... Proponents of [a] change [in capital gains rates] cite economic studies showing increases in economic growth, realizations of gains, and even higher revenue for the government. Opponents dispute these points, but mainly argue that a capital gains tax cut is unfair because it benefits only the rich.

If history is any guide, neither of these arguments will be decisive. In the end, whether the capital gains tax rate is cut or not will be solely a function of politics....

Thus whether the capital gains tax is cut or not, it will remain a political football, as it has been almost continuously since 1921, when the first capital gains preference was enacted. It would be far better for Congress to resolve once and for all whether capital

---

6. Bruce Bartlett, "Why the Correct Capital Gains Tax Rate Is Zero," 84 Tax Notes 1411 *passim* (Sept. 6, 1999) (footnotes omitted).

gains are income like any other form of income—such as wages, dividends, rent, and interest—or are not income at all. If it accepts the former, it should move not only to tax capital gains as ordinary income, as was the case from 1914 to 1921 and from 1987 to 1990, but to tax accrued capital gains on an ongoing basis, regardless of whether such gains are realized. If it accepts the latter, then capital gains should be completely removed from the tax base and not taxed at all. The alternative is to keep raising and lowering the capital gains tax rate depending simply on which way the political winds are blowing.

...

... Do occasional, unexpected gains constitute "income" in a meaningful sense? Does not the concept of "income" imply regularity and consistency? This was certainly the view of many economists at the time the Supreme Court decided that capital gains were "income." For example, in his presidential address to the American Economic Association in 1923, Carl Plehn of the University of California stated that, "Income is essentially wealth available for recurrent consumption, recurrently (or periodically) received. Its three essential characteristics are: receipt, recurrence, and expendability."

Before 1921, lower courts also ruled that regularity was an essential quality of "income," which capital gains necessarily do not have. For example, in a 1918 case, Judge Learned Hand ruled that the discharge of a debt did not constitute taxable income because it lacked regularity. The term "income," he wrote, "unquestionably imports, at least so it seems to us, the current distinction between what is commonly treated as the increase or increment from the exercise of some economically productive power of one sort or another, and the power itself, and should not include such wealth as is honestly appropriated to what would customarily be regarded as the capital of the corporation taxed."

Since the 1920s, theoretical arguments about capital gains taxation have principally revolved around efforts by self-styled tax reformers to get rid of the capital gains preference. In general, the reformers have relied on a definition of income developed by Robert M. Haig and Henry Simons to press for full taxation of capital gains as ordinary income. Known as the Haig-Simons definition of income, it consists of all consumption during the course of a year plus the change in net worth. Thus, under Haig-Simons, even unrealized capital gains would be subject to taxation.

It is hard to say why the Haig-Simons definition of income achieved its status as the "official" definition universally used by economists and tax lawyers. Part of it has to do with its simplicity and part to the vigor with which some of its adherents have promoted it as the only theoretically pure definition of income....

The central problem with the Haig-Simons definition of income as it relates to capital gains is that it implicitly endorses the double taxation of capital. The fact is that capital gains arise only in the case of an income-producing asset. The value of the asset is simply the discounted present value of the future flow of income associated with that asset (rent in the case of real estate, interest in the case of bonds, and corporate profits in the case of stocks). Thus, if the income stream (rent, interest, profits/dividends) are taxed, then any additional tax on the underlying asset (real estate, bonds, stocks) must necessarily constitute a double tax on the same income.

Of course, asset values rise and fall all the time with no change in income. But permanent changes come about only because of a permanent increase in income flows. As the great economist E.R.A. Seligman put it, "Capital is a capitalization not simply of present or actual income but of the present worth of all future anticipated incomes.

There can be no permanent change in the value of the capital unless there is at least an anticipated change in future income." ...

...

Confirming the broad acceptance of the principle that capital gains do not constitute income, is the fact that the National Income and Product Accounts of the United States, from which the gross domestic product is calculated, have never included capital gains as part of the nation's economic income. Nobel Prize-winning economist Simon Kuznets, father of the national income accounts, explains, "Capital gains and losses are not increments to or drafts upon the heap of goods produced by the economic system for consumption or for stock destined for future use, and hence they should be excluded." In 1996, $249.5 billion of capital gains included in adjusted gross income for tax purposes were excluded from personal income in the national income accounts.

Neither Haig nor Simons ever addressed this argument. In truth, their rationalization for taxation of capital gains rested more on ideological grounds than scientific analysis. As Haig once put it, "an income tax which would allow capital gains to escape unscathed would, in this country at least, be an ethical monstrosity." Simons took the same basic view. "The main and decisive case for inclusion of capital gains rests on the fact that equity among individuals is impossible under an income tax which disregards such items of gain and loss," he wrote.

Thus, for all its presumed scientific precision, it turns out that the Haig-Simons definition of income is nothing more than an opinion based on ideological preferences for a more egalitarian society. In any event, the U.S. tax system does not remotely correspond to a pure Haig-Simons tax base....

Thus, one can argue that while a pure Haig-Simons approach might be an improvement — it would at least eliminate the lock-in effect, since the tax would no longer depend on whether an asset was held or sold — it makes no sense to argue that Haig-Simons demands full taxation of capital gains while ignoring all the other exceptions to a comprehensive tax base in our current tax system. If supporters of eliminating the preference for capital gains wish to cite Haig-Simons in support of their position, they must also be willing to accept all the rest of the definition as well, which would, among other things, require taxation of unrealized gains, taxation of imputed income (such as the rent one receives for living in one's own home).... One cannot pick and choose.

Finally, regarding capital gains, it is important to know that Haig and Simons both accepted the principle that all gains should be adjusted for inflation before being taxed. As Haig wrote in 1921:

> If income is defined as the total accretion in one's economic strength between two points of time, as valued in terms of money, it is clear that his income will reflect every change in the value of money between those two points of time in so far as the items entered on the balance sheets at those times affect the computation. If the level of prices goes up 10 percent the money value of my assets will ordinarily follow at a like rate. That particular increase in value does not really indicate an increase in my economic strength. My power to command economic goods and services has not increased, for the money-value of these goods and services has likewise increased.... If it were possible to modify the concept of taxable income so as to eliminate this variation it would certainly be desirable to do so.

Simons conceded that most capital gains are "largely fictitious" once inflation is taken into account. In principle, he said, tax law should adjust gains and losses for changes in the price level. "Considerations of justice demand that changes in monetary conditions be taken into account in the measurement of gain and loss," Simons wrote in 1938. Numerous studies have documented that failure to index capital gains for inflation has subjected taxpayers to significantly higher taxes.

- In 1973, taxpayers realized nominal gains of $4.5 billion, but a real loss of $1 billion.

    . . .

- In 1985, nominal gains amounted to $78.8 billion, but real gains came to just $63.5 billion.

    . . .

- In 1993, nominal gains of $81.4 billion fell to $39.5 billion when adjusted for inflation. (Disregarding current limits on the deductibility of losses would produce a nominal gain of $71.9 billion and a real loss of $19.4 billion.)

    . . .

. . . [T]he main argument for taxing gains from a theoretical point of view, Haig-Simons, is deeply flawed. Yet accepting Haig-Simons would at least require full adjustment of gains for inflation, which would virtually wipe out all taxable gains in the aggregate.

    . . .

After reading these representative excerpts, you should not be surprised when the capital gains debate continues for the foreseeable future. As earlier suggested, the current capital gains preference represents a middle-ground choice between the two extremes, a middle ground that Professors Cunningham and Schenk ultimately conclude in their article is a poor choice. But their, and others', suggestions for an alternative, rather than adoption of the "all or nothing" proposal by Mr. Bartlett, guarantee that the debate (and, probably, legislative changes) will continue.

Chapter 2

The Capital Gains Preference: Outline of the Relevant Code Sections

The capital gains preference represents a special way of taxing the gain on certain realization events. Recall that section 1001(c) requires that gain realized under section 1001(a) shall be recognized in the absence of some special provision of the Code. **Review section 1001(a) and (c).** Therefore, a taxpayer will not enjoy the preferential capital gains rate unless she has made a "sale or exchange" of a "capital asset."[1] We begin our examination of the capital gains preference by examining the important Code provisions. As you will see, the provisions require careful reading; each definition requires you to utilize one or more other statutory definitions in order to make your way to the identification of an NCG.

As we noted in the Introduction, section 1(h) sets forth an alternative tax calculation that contains a preferential rate of tax for taxpayers who have NCG. Thus, in order to qualify for the preferential rate, a taxpayer must have NCG. **Look at section 1(h)(1), first clause.** If a taxpayer has no NCG the alternative section 1(h) preferential rate does not apply.

Section 1222(11) defines NCG as "the excess of the net long-term capital gain for the taxable year over the net short-term capital loss for such year." (This may be expressed as follows: NCG = NLTCG - NSTCL.) **Read carefully section 1222(11).**

Section 1222(7) defines NLTCG as "the excess of long-term capital gains for the taxable year over the long-term capital losses for such year." (NLTCG = LTCG - LTCL) **Read carefully 1222(7).**

Section 1222(6) defines NSTCL as "the excess of short-term capital losses for the taxable year over the short-term capital gains for such year." (NSTCL = STCL - STCG) **Read carefully section 1222(6).**

Sections 1222(1)-(4) define STCG, STCL, LTCG, and LTCL as the "gains" or "losses" "from sales or exchanges of capital asset[s]." The dividing line between short-term and long-term gains and losses is a holding period of "not more than 1 year" for short-term and "more than 1 year" for long-term. **Read carefully sections 1222(1)-(4).**

The process requires beginning with section 1(h), moving to section 1222, and working backwards from section 1222(11) to 1222(1). Thus, the application of the capital gain and loss provisions of the Code requires three essential elements: (1) the "sale

---

1. Nor will a taxpayer suffer the limitation on capital losses if she does not sell or exchange a capital asset.

or exchange" of (2) a "capital asset" (3) held for more than one year or one year or less. Therefore, the actual starting point in capital gain/loss analysis requires you to determine whether the taxpayer has engaged in a "sale or exchange" of a "capital asset," and, if so, you must determine the holding period.

A. Identifying the Required Disposition Event: "Sale or Exchange"

Recall that the "sale or other disposition" of property triggers section 1001(a). A "capital gain" or "capital loss" occurs only when the taxpayer disposes of a "capital asset" by means of a "sale or exchange." Thus, if a taxpayer sells or otherwise disposes of a capital asset, she computes her realized and recognized gain or loss under the by-now familiar rules of sections 1001(a) and (c). But the gain or loss is characterized as capital gain or loss only if the disposition of the capital asset is by means of a "sale or exchange," which is a narrower category of disposition than is covered generally by section 1001. That is, "other disposition" of a capital asset that triggers realization and recognition of gain or loss under section 1001 is not necessarily considered a "sale or exchange."

Read the following case.

HELVERING v. WILLIAM FLACCUS OAK LEATHER CO.
313 U.S. 247 (1941)

MR. JUSTICE MURPHY delivered the opinion of the Court.

In September, 1935, respondent's plant was destroyed by fire. Later that year it received $73,132.50 from an insurance company as compensation for the loss of buildings, machinery, and equipment. The buildings, machinery, and equipment had been fully depreciated for income tax purposes prior to 1935, and no part of the insurance proceeds was used to acquire other property similar or related in service or use to the property destroyed, or to acquire control of a corporation owning such property, or to establish a fund to replace the property destroyed.

In its return for 1935, respondent reported the insurance proceeds as capital gain and added to that amount a gain, not in issue here, of $862.50 from sales of securities. During that same year, respondent had capital losses, also not in dispute, of $76,767.62 which it used to offset completely the total reported capital gains of $73,995. This left an excess of capital losses over capital gains of $2,772.62, and respondent deducted $2,000 of that amount from ordinary income.

The Commissioner held that the insurance proceeds were ordinary income rather than capital gain. Accordingly, he decreased respondent's capital gain and increased its ordinary income by $73,132.50, and allowed respondent capital losses of only $2,862.50, an amount equal to the gain from security sales plus $2,000. The Board of Tax Appeals affirmed.... The Circuit Court of Appeals reversed.... We granted certiorari....

It is conceded that respondent's losses resulted from sales or exchanges of capital assets. It is also conceded that the entire amount received from the insurance company must be included in respondent's income since the property had been fully depreciated for income tax purposes prior to 1935. Respondent contends, however, that that amount may be reported as capital gain, in order that capital losses may absorb it, rather than as an item of ordinary gross income.

Section 117(d) of the Revenue Act of 1934 (48 Stat. 680) provides in part: "Losses from sales or exchanges of capital assets shall be allowed only to the extent of $2,000 plus the gains from such sales or exchanges." Thus, the single question is whether the amount respondent received from the insurance company derived from the "sale or exchange" of a capital asset.

Generally speaking, the language in the Revenue Act, just as in any statute, is to be given its ordinary meaning, and the words "sale" and "exchange" are not to be read any differently.... Neither term is appropriate to characterize the demolition of property and subsequent compensation for its loss by an insurance company. Plainly that pair of events was not a sale. Nor can they be regarded as an exchange, for "exchange," as used in § 117(d), implies reciprocal transfers of capital assets, not a single transfer to compensate for the destruction of the transferee's asset.

The fact that § 112(f) characterizes destruction of property and indemnification for its loss as an involuntary conversion does not establish that the two events constituted a sale or exchange. That section provides: "If property (as a result of its destruction in whole or in part, theft or seizure, or an exercise of the power of requisition or condemnation, or the threat or imminence thereof) is compulsorily or involuntarily converted into property similar or related in service or use to the property so converted, or into money which is forthwith in good faith, under regulations prescribed by the Commissioner with the approval of the Secretary, expended in the acquisition of other property similar or related in service or use to the property so converted, or in the acquisition of control of a corporation owning such other property, or in the establishment of a replacement fund, no gain or loss shall be recognized. If any part of the money is not so expended, the gain, if any, shall be recognized, but in an amount not in excess of the money which is not so expended."

We can find nothing in this language or in other sections of the Act which indicates, either expressly or by implication, that Congress intended to classify as "sales or exchanges" the involuntary conversions enumerated in § 112(f). It is true that § 111(c) says that "in the case of a sale or exchange, the extent to which the gain or loss ... shall be recognized ... shall be determined under the provisions of section 112." It is also true that § 112(f) follows § 112(a) which provides that "upon the sale or exchange of property the entire amount of the gain or loss ... shall be recognized, except as hereinafter provided in this section."

The inference, drawn from the juxtaposition and cross referencing of these three sections, that the involuntary conversion of respondent's property is thus implicitly characterized as a sale or exchange ignores the fact that in the same Act Congress has chosen a particular method for classifying as sales or exchanges transactions which would not ordinarily be described by one of those terms. Thus § 115(c) provides: "Amounts distributed in complete liquidation of a corporation shall be treated as in full payment in exchange for the stock"....

... Section 117(f) provides: "For the purposes of this title, amounts received by the holder upon the retirement of bonds, debentures, notes, or certificates or other evidences of indebtedness issued by any corporation ... with interest coupons or in registered form, shall be considered as amounts received in exchange therefor." ...

These sections demonstrate that Congress has expressly specified the ambiguous transactions which are to be regarded as sales or exchanges for income tax purposes. They are convincing evidence that the involuntary conversion of respondent's property, which bears far less resemblance to a sale or exchange than the transactions embraced in

§§ 115(c) ... and 117(f), is not to be placed in one or the other of those categories by implication....

The judgment of the Circuit Court of Appeals is

Reversed.

Consider the following questions about the case.

1. How did the taxpayer report its receipt of the insurance proceeds?

2. Was there a "sale or other disposition" of taxpayer's property within the meaning of section 1001(a)?

3. What was the significance of the Court's statement that "no part of the insurance proceeds was used to acquire other property similar or related in service or use to the property destroyed"?

4. Was there a "sale or exchange" of taxpayer's property within the meaning of section 1222? What were the consequences of the answer to this question?

Some dispositions of capital assets that do not appear to be sales or exchanges, however, have been held to be. Read the following case.

HELVERING v. HAMMEL
311 U.S. 504 (1941)

MR. JUSTICE STONE delivered the opinion of the Court.

We are asked to say whether a loss sustained by an individual taxpayer upon the foreclosure sale of his interest in real estate, acquired for profit, ... is a capital loss deductible only to the limited extent provided in §§ 23(e)(2), (j), and 117.

In the computation of taxable income § 23(e)(2) of the 1934 Revenue Act permits the individual taxpayer to deduct losses sustained during the year incurred in any transaction for profit. Subsection (j) provides that "losses from sales or exchanges of capital assets" shall be allowed only to the extent of $2,000 plus gains from such sales or exchanges as provided by § 117(d). By § 117(b) it is declared that "capital assets" "means property held by the taxpayer ... but does not include stock in trade of the taxpayer ... or property held by the taxpayer primarily for sale to customers in the ordinary course of his trade or business."

Respondent taxpayers, with other members of a syndicate, purchased "on land contract" a plot of land in Oakland County, Michigan, for the sum of $96,000, upon a down payment of $20,000.... [P]ayments for the land were to be made in installments, and the vendor retained an interest in the land as security for payment of the balance of the purchase price. Before the purchase price was paid in full the syndicate defaulted on its payments. The vendor instituted foreclosure proceedings by suit in equity in a state court which resulted in a judicial sale of the property, the vendor becoming the purchaser, and in a deficiency judgment against the members of the syndicate. Respondents' contribution to the purchase money, some $4,000, was lost.

The commissioner, in computing respondents' taxable income for 1934, treated the taxpayers' interest in the land as a capital asset and allowed deduction of the loss from gross income only to the extent of $2,000 as provided by §§ 23(j) and 117(d), in the case of losses from sales of capital assets. The Board of Tax Appeals ruled that the loss was deductible in full. The circuit court of appeals affirmed, 108 F.2d 753, holding that the loss established by the foreclosure sale was not a loss from a "sale" within the meaning of § 23(j). We granted certiorari....

It is not denied that it was the foreclosure sale of respondents' interest in the land purchased by the syndicate for profit, which finally liquidated the capital investment made by its members and fixed the precise amount of the loss which respondents seek to deduct as such from gross income. But they argue that the "losses from sales" which by § 23(j) are made deductible only to the limited extent provided by § 117(d) are those losses resulting from sales voluntarily made by the taxpayer, and that losses resulting from forced sales like the present not being subject to the limitations of § 117(d) are deductible in full like other losses....

To read this qualification into the statute respondents rely on judicial decisions applying the familiar rule that a restrictive covenant against sale or assignment refers to the voluntary action of the covenantor and not to transfers by operation of law or judicial sales *in invitum*.... But here we are not concerned with a restrictive covenant of the taxpayer, but with a sale as an effective means of establishing a deductible loss for the purpose of computing his income tax. The term sale may have many meanings, depending on the context, see Webster's New International Dictionary. The meaning here depends on the purpose with which it is used in the statute and the legislative history of that use. Hence the respondents argue that the purpose of providing in the 1934 Act for a special treatment of gains or losses from capital assets was to prevent tax avoidance by depriving the taxpayer of the option allowed to him by the earlier acts, to effect losses deductible in full by sales of property at any time within two years after it was acquired, which until held for that period was not defined as a capital asset....

It is said that since losses from foreclosure sales not within the control of the taxpayer are not within the evil aimed at by the 1934 Act, they must be deemed to be excluded from the reach of its language. To support this contention respondents rely on the report of the Ways and Means Committee submitting to the House the bill which, with amendments not now material, became the Revenue Act of 1934. The Committee in pointing out a "defect" of the existing law said: "Taxpayers take their losses within the two year period and get full benefit therefrom and delay taking gains until the two-year period has expired, thereby reducing their taxes." ...

But the treatment of gains and losses from sales of capital assets on a different basis from ordinary gains and losses was not introduced into the revenue laws by the 1934 Act. That had been a feature of every revenue law beginning with the Act of 1921 ... and each had defined as capital losses "losses from sales or exchanges of capital assets." The 1934 Act made no change in this respect but for the first time it provided that "capital assets" should include all property acquired by the taxpayer for profit regardless of the length of time held by him and that capital gains and losses from sales of capital assets should be recognized in the computation of taxable income according to the length of time the capital assets are held by the taxpayer, varying from 100% if the capital asset is held for not more than a year to 30% if it is held more than ten years. § 117(a). Finally, for the first time, the statute provided that capital losses in excess of capital gains should be deducted from ordinary income only to the extent of $2,000. Thus by treating all property acquired by the taxpayer for profit as capital assets and limiting the deduction of capital losses in the manner indicated, the Act materially curtailed the advantages which the taxpayer had previously been able to gain by choosing the time of selling his property.

The definition of capital losses as losses from "sales" of capital assets, as we have pointed out, was not new. As will presently appear, the legislative history of this definition shows that it was not chosen to exclude from the capital assets provisions losses resulting from forced sales of taxpayers' property. And, if so construed, substantial loss of revenue would result under the 1934 Act, whose purpose was to avoid loss of revenue by the application of the capital assets provisions. In drafting the 1934 Act the Committee had before it proposals for stabilizing the revenue by the adoption of the British system under which neither capital gains nor losses enter into the computation of the tax. In declining to follow this system in its entirety the Committee said: "It is deemed wiser to attempt a step in this direction without letting capital gains go entirely untaxed." It accordingly reduced the tax burden on capital gains progressively with the increase of the period up to ten years, during which the taxpayer holds the capital asset, and permitted the deduction, on the same scale, of capital losses, but only to the extent that there are taxable capital gains, plus $2,000. In thus relieving capital gains from the tax imposed on other types of income, it cannot be assumed, in the absence of some clear indication to the contrary, that Congress intended to permit deductions in full of losses resulting from forced sales of the taxpayers' property, from either capital gains or ordinary gross income, while taxing only a fraction of the gains resulting from the sales of such property....

The taxation of capital gains after deduction of capital losses on a more favorable basis than other income, was provided for by ... the 1921 Revenue Act, as the means of encouraging profit-taking sales of capital investments.... In this section, as in later Acts, capital net gain was defined as "the excess of the total capital gain over the sum of capital deductions and capital losses"; capital losses being defined as the loss resulting from the sale or exchange of capital assets. In submitting the proposed Revenue Act of 1924, the House committee pointed out that the 1921 Act contained no provision for limiting deduction of capital losses where they exceeded the amount of capital gains.... This was remedied by providing ... that the amount by which the tax is reduced on account of a capital loss shall not exceed 12 1/2% of the capital loss. In commenting on this provision the Committee said, ... : "If the amount by which the tax is to be increased on account of capital gains is limited to 12 1/2% of the capital gain it follows logically that the amount by which the tax is reduced on account of capital losses shall be limited to the 12 1/2% of the loss." This provision was continued without changes now material until the 1934 Act....

Congress thus has given clear indication of a purpose to offset capital gains by losses from the sale of like property and upon the same percentage basis as that on which the gains are taxed.... This purpose to treat gains and deductible losses on a parity but with a further specific provision provided by § 117(d) of the 1934 Act, permitting specified percentages of capital losses to be deducted from ordinary income to the extent of $2,000, would be defeated in a most substantial way if only a percentage of the gains were taxed but losses on sales of like property could be deducted in full from gross income. This treatment of losses from sales of capital assets in the 1924 and later Acts and the reason given for adopting it afford convincing evidence that the "sales" referred to in the statute include forced sales such as have sufficed, under long accepted income tax practice, to establish a deductible loss in the case of non-capital assets. Such sales can equally be taken to establish the loss in the case of capital assets without infringing the declared policy of the statute to treat capital gains and losses on a parity.

We can find no basis in the language of the Act, its purpose or its legislative history, for saying that losses from sales of capital assets under the 1934 Act, more than its predecessors, were to be treated any differently whether they resulted from forced sales or voluntary sales. True, courts in the interpretation of a statute have some scope for adopting a restricted rather than a literal or usual meaning of its words where acceptance of that meaning would lead to absurd results.... But courts are not free to reject that meaning where no such consequences follow and where, as here, it appears to be consonant with the purposes of the Act as declared by Congress and plainly disclosed by its structure.

...

Now consider the following questions concerning *Hammel.*

1. What position did the Service take concerning the characterization of the foreclosure?

2. Compare the Service's position in *Hammel* with the position it took in *William Flaccus Oak Leather Co.* Can you speculate on why the Service did not take the same position in both cases?

Characterization of a "sale or other disposition" as a "sale or exchange" is only one of the requirements for obtaining special treatment of the gain on a sale.[2] Of course, as you have now seen, it also is a characterization a taxpayer may wish to escape if the disposition produces a loss. Characterization of the disposition is just the first step, however.

B. Identifying a "Capital Asset"

Section 1221 is entitled "Capital Asset Defined." **Read section 1221 carefully, focussing your attention particularly on subsections (a)(1) and (a)(2) of the section.** How does section 1221 define a "capital asset"? The section takes an "everything in the world but ..." approach. Thus, any asset that a taxpayer owns is a capital asset unless it is excluded by one of the eight subsections of section 1221.[3] The following case will provide some background on the definition of a "capital asset" under section 1221.

ARKANSAS BEST CORP. v. COMMISSIONER
485 U.S. 212 (1988)

JUSTICE MARSHALL delivered the opinion of the Court.

The issue presented in this case is whether capital stock held by petitioner Arkansas Best Corporation (Arkansas Best) is a "capital asset" as defined in § 1221 of the Internal Revenue Code regardless of whether the stock was purchased and held for a business purpose or for an investment purpose.

---

2. As the Supreme Court noted in *William Flaccus Oak Leather Co.*, the Code also, by legislative fiat, treats certain dispositions as "sales or exchanges." An exhaustive list is beyond the scope of this book. **But, look at sections 165(g)(1) and 166(d)(1)(B).** They represent examples of dispositions that Congress has designated as "sales or exchanges" even if they might not appear to be. Section 165(g)(1) requires sale or exchange treatment for worthless securities. The provision treats these as either long-term or short-term sales or exchanges, provided the securities were capital assets in the taxpayer's hands. Section 166(d)(1)(B) requires sale or exchange treatment for non-business bad debts. The provision characterizes these as short-term no matter how long the debt has been owed.

3. But *see* Section 1221(b)(3), discussed in footnote 5, *infra.*

I

Arkansas Best is a diversified holding company. In 1968 it acquired approximately 65% of the stock of the National Bank of Commerce (Bank) in Dallas, Texas. Between 1969 and 1974, Arkansas Best more than tripled the number of shares it owned in the Bank, although its percentage interest in the Bank remained relatively stable. These acquisitions were prompted principally by the Bank's need for added capital. Until 1972, the Bank appeared to be prosperous and growing, and the added capital was necessary to accommodate this growth. As the Dallas real estate market declined, however, so too did the financial health of the Bank, which had a heavy concentration of loans in the local real estate industry. In 1972, federal examiners classified the Bank as a problem bank. The infusion of capital after 1972 was prompted by the loan portfolio problems of the bank.

Petitioner sold the bulk of its Bank stock on June 30, 1975, leaving it with only a 14.7% stake in the Bank. On its federal income tax return for 1975, petitioner claimed a deduction for an ordinary loss of $9,995,688 resulting from the sale of the stock. The Commissioner of Internal Revenue disallowed the deduction, finding that the loss from the sale of stock was a capital loss, rather than an ordinary loss, and that it therefore was subject to the capital loss limitations in the Internal Revenue Code. (Footnote 1)

Arkansas Best challenged the Commissioner's determination in the United States Tax Court. The Tax Court, relying on cases interpreting *Corn Products Refining Co. v. Commissioner*, 350 U.S. 46 ... (1955), held that stock purchased with a substantial investment purpose is a capital asset which, when sold, gives rise to a capital gain or loss, whereas stock-purchased and held for a business purpose, without any substantial investment motive, is an ordinary asset whose sale gives rise to ordinary gains or losses. See 83 T.C. 640, 653–654 (1984). The court characterized Arkansas Best's acquisitions through 1972 as occurring during the Bank's "'growth' phase," and found that these acquisitions "were motivated primarily by investment purpose and only incidentally by some business purpose." ... The stock acquired during this period therefore constituted a capital asset, which gave rise to a capital loss when sold in 1975. The court determined, however, that the acquisitions after 1972 occurred during the Bank's "'problem' phase," *ibid.*, and, except for certain minor exceptions, "were made exclusively for business purposes and subsequently held for the same reasons." *Id.*, at 656. These acquisitions, the court found, were designed to preserve petitioner's business reputation, because without the added capital the Bank probably would have failed. *Id.*, at 656–657. The loss realized on the sale of this stock was thus held to be an ordinary loss.

The Court of Appeals for the Eighth Circuit reversed the Tax Court's determination that the loss realized on stock purchased after 1972 was subject to ordinary-loss treatment, holding that all of the Bank stock sold in 1975 was subject to capital-loss treatment. 800 F.2d 215 (1986). The court reasoned that the Bank stock clearly fell within the general definition of "capital asset" in Internal Revenue Code § 1221, and that the stock did not fall within any of the specific statutory exceptions to this definition. The court concluded that Arkansas Best's purpose in acquiring and holding the stock was irrelevant to the determination whether the stock was a capital asset. We granted certiorari, 480 U.S. 930, and now affirm.

II

Section 1221 of the Internal Revenue Code defines "capital asset" broadly as "property held by the taxpayer (whether or not connected with his trade or business)," and then excludes five specific classes of property from capital-asset status. In the statute's present form, … the classes of property exempted from the broad definition are (1) "property of a kind which would properly be included in the inventory of the taxpayer"; (2) real property or other depreciable property used in the taxpayer's trade or business; (3) "a copyright, a literary, musical, or artistic composition," or similar property; (4) "accounts or notes receivable acquired in the ordinary course of trade or business for services rendered" or from the sale of inventory; and (5) publications of the Federal Government. Arkansas Best acknowledges that the Bank stock falls within the literal definition of "capital asset" in § 1221, and is outside of the statutory exclusions. It asserts, however, that this determination does not end the inquiry. Petitioner argues that in *Corn Products Refining Co. v. Commissioner, supra,* this Court rejected a literal reading of § 1221, and concluded that assets acquired and sold for ordinary business purposes rather than for investment purposes should be given ordinary-asset treatment. Petitioner's reading of *Corn Products* finds much support in the academic literature and in the courts. Unfortunately for petitioner, this broad reading finds no support in the language of § 1221.

In essence, petitioner argues that "property held by the taxpayer (whether or not connected with his trade or business)" does not include property that is acquired and held for a business purpose. In petitioner's view an asset's status as "property" thus turns on the motivation behind its acquisition. This motive test, however, is not only nowhere mentioned in § 1221, but it is also in direct conflict with the parenthetical phrase "whether or not connected with his trade or business." The broad definition of the term "capital asset" explicitly makes irrelevant any consideration of the property's connection with the taxpayer's business, whereas petitioner's rule would make this factor dispositive. (Footnote 5)

In a related argument, petitioner contends that the five exceptions listed in § 1221 for certain kinds of property are illustrative, rather than exhaustive, and that courts are therefore free to fashion additional exceptions in order to further the general purposes of the capital-asset provisions. The language of the statute refutes petitioner's construction. Section 1221 provides that "capital asset" means "property held by the taxpayer[,] … but does not include" the five classes of property listed as exceptions. We believe this locution signifies that the listed exceptions are exclusive. The body of § 1221 establishes a general definition of the term "capital asset," and the phrase "does not include" takes out of that broad definition only the classes of property that are specifically mentioned. The legislative history of the capital-asset definition supports this interpretation, see H.R. Rep. No. 704, 73d Cong., 2d Sess., 31 (1934) ("[T]he definition includes all property, except as specifically excluded"); H.R. Rep. No. 1337, 83d Cong., 2d Sess., A273 (1954), ("[A] capital asset is property held by the taxpayer with certain exceptions"), as does the applicable Treasury Regulation, see 26 CFR § 1.1221-1(a) (1987) ("The term 'capital assets' includes all classes of property not specifically excluded by section 1221").

Petitioner's reading of the statute is also in tension with the exceptions listed in § 1221. These exclusions would be largely superfluous if assets acquired primarily or exclusively for business purposes were not capital assets. Inventory, real or depreciable property used in the taxpayer's trade or business, and accounts or notes receivable acquired in the ordinary course of business, would undoubtedly satisfy such a business-motive test. Yet these exceptions were created by Congress in separate enactments spanning 30 years. (Footnote 6) Without any express direction from Congress, we are unwilling to read § 1221 in a manner that makes surplusage of these statutory exclusions.

In the end, petitioner places all reliance on its reading of *Corn Products Refining Co. v. Commissioner*, 350 U.S. 46 (1955)—a reading we believe is too expansive. In *Corn Products,* the Court considered whether income arising from a taxpayer's dealings in corn futures was entitled to capital-gains treatment. The taxpayer was a company that converted corn into starches, sugars, and other products. After droughts in the 1930's caused sharp increases in corn prices, the company began a program of buying corn futures to assure itself an adequate supply of corn and protect against price increases. See *id.*, at 48. The company "would take delivery on such contracts as it found necessary to its manufacturing operations and sell the remainder in early summer if no shortage was imminent. If shortages appeared, however, it sold futures only as it bought spot corn for grinding." *Id.*, at 48–49. The Court characterized the company's dealing in corn futures as "hedging." *Id.*, at 51. As explained by the Court of Appeals in *Corn Products,* "[h]edging is a method of dealing in commodity futures whereby a person or business protects itself against price fluctuations at the time of delivery of the product which it sells or buys." 215 F.2d 513, 515 (CA2 1954). In evaluating the company's claim that the sales of corn futures resulted in capital gains and losses, this Court stated:

> "Nor can we find support for petitioner's contention that hedging is not within the exclusions of [§ 1221]. Admittedly, petitioner's corn futures do not come within the literal language of the exclusions set out in that section. They were not stock in trade, actual inventory, property held for sale to customers or depreciable property used in a trade or business. But the capital-asset provision of [§ 1221] must not be so broadly applied as to defeat rather than further the purpose of Congress. Congress intended that profits and losses arising from the everyday operation of a business be considered as ordinary income or loss rather than capital gain or loss.... Since this section is an exception from the normal tax requirements of the Internal Revenue Code, the definition of a capital asset must be narrowly applied and its exclusions interpreted broadly." 350 U.S., at 51–52, (citations omitted).

The Court went on to note that hedging transactions consistently had been considered to give rise to ordinary gains and losses, and then concluded that the corn futures were subject to ordinary-asset treatment. *Id.*, at 52–53.

The Court in *Corn Products* proffered the oft-quoted rule of construction that the definition of "capital asset" must be narrowly applied and its exclusions interpreted broadly, but it did not state explicitly whether the holding was based on a narrow reading of the phrase "property held by the taxpayer," or on a broad reading of the inventory exclusion of § 1221. In light of the stark language of § 1221, however, we believe that Corn Products is properly interpreted as involving an application of § 1221's inventory exception. Such a reading is consistent both with the Court's reasoning in that-case and with § 1221. The Court stated in *Corn Products* that the company's futures transactions were "an integral part of its business designed to protect its manufacturing operations against a "price increase in its principal raw material and to assure a ready supply for future manufacturing requirements." 350 U.S., at 50. The company bought, sold, and took delivery under the futures contracts as required by the company's manufacturing needs. As Professor Bittker notes, under these circumstances, the futures can "easily be viewed as surrogates for the raw material itself." 2 B. Bittker, Federal Taxation of Income, Estates and Gifts ¶ 51.10.3, p. 51–62 (1981). The Court of Appeals for the Second Circuit in *Corn Products* clearly took this approach. That court stated that when commodity futures are "utilized solely for the purpose of stabilizing inventory cost[,] ... [they] cannot reasonably be separated from the inventory items," and concluded that "property used in hedging transactions properly comes within the exclusions of [§ 1221]." 215 F.2d, at 516. This Court indicated its acceptance of the Second Circuit's reasoning when it began the central paragraph of its opinion: "Nor can we find support for petitioner's contention that hedging is not within the exclusions of [§ 1221]." 350 U.S., at 51. In the following paragraph, the Court argued that the Treasury had consistently viewed such hedging transactions as a form of insurance to stabilize the cost of inventory, and cited a Treasury ruling which concluded that the value of a manufacturer's raw-material inventory should be adjusted to take into account hedging transactions in futures contracts. See *id.*, at 52–53 (citing G.C.M. 17322, XV-2 Cum. Bull. 151 (1936)). This discussion, read in light of the Second Circuit's holding and the plain language of § 1221, convinces us that although the corn futures were not "actual inventory," their use as an integral part of the taxpayer's inventory-purchase system led the Court to treat them as substitutes for the corn inventory such that they came within a broad reading of "property of a kind which would properly be included in the inventory of the taxpayer" in § 1221.

Petitioner argues that by focusing attention on whether the asset was acquired and sold as an integral part of the taxpayer's everyday business operations, the Court in *Corn Products* intended to create a general exemption from capital-asset status for assets acquired for business purposes. We believe petitioner misunderstands the relevance of the Court's inquiry. A business connection, although irrelevant to the initial determination whether an item is a capital asset, is relevant in determining the applicability of certain of the statutory exceptions, including the inventory exception. The close connection between the futures transactions and the taxpayer's business in *Corn Products* was crucial to whether the corn futures could be considered surrogates for the stored inventory of raw corn. For if the futures dealings were not part of the company's inventory-purchase system, and instead amounted simply to speculation in corn futures, they could not be considered substitutes for the company's corn inventory, and would fall outside even a broad reading of the inventory exclusion. We conclude that *Corn Products* is properly interpreted as standing for the narrow proposition that hedging transactions that are an integral part of a business' inventory-purchase system fall within the inventory exclusion of § 1221. (Footnote 7) Arkansas Best, which is not a dealer in securities, has never suggested that the Bank stock falls within the inventory exclusion. *Corn Products* thus has no application to this case.

It is also important to note that the business-motive test advocated by petitioner is subject to the same kind of abuse that the Court condemned in *Corn Products*. The Court explained in *Corn Products* that unless hedging transactions were subject to ordinary gain and loss treatment, taxpayers engaged in such transactions could "transmute ordinary income into capital gain at will." 350 U.S., at 53–54. The hedger could garner capital-asset treatment by selling the future and purchasing the commodity on the spot market, or ordinary-asset treatment by taking delivery under the future contract. In a similar vein, if capital stock purchased and held for a business purpose is an ordinary asset, whereas the same stock purchased and held with an investment motive is a capital asset, a taxpayer such as Arkansas Best could have significant influence over whether the asset would receive capital or ordinary treatment. Because stock is most naturally viewed as a capital asset, the Internal Revenue Service would be hard pressed to challenge a taxpayer's claim that stock was acquired as an investment, and that a gain arising from the sale of such stock was therefore a capital gain. Indeed, we are unaware of a single decision that has applied the business-motive test so as to require a taxpayer to report a gain from the sale of stock as an ordinary gain. If the same stock is sold at a loss, however, the taxpayer may be able to garner ordinary-loss treatment by emphasizing the business purpose behind the stock's acquisition. The potential for such abuse was evidenced in this case by the fact that as late as 1974, when Arkansas Best still hoped to sell the Bank stock at a profit, Arkansas Best apparently expected to report the gain as a capital gain. See 83 T.C., at 647–648.

III

We conclude that a taxpayer's motivation in purchasing an asset is irrelevant to the question whether the asset is "property held by a taxpayer (whether or not connected with his business)" and is thus within § 1221's general definition of "capital asset." Because the capital stock held by petitioner falls within the broad definition of the term "capital asset" in § 1221 and is outside the classes of property excluded from capital-asset status, the loss arising from the sale of the stock is a capital loss. *Corn Products Refining Co. v. Commissioner, supra,* which we interpret as involving a broad reading of the inventory exclusion of § 1221, has no application in the present context. Accordingly, the judgment of the Court of Appeals is affirmed.

. . .

FOOTNOTES:

1. Title 26 U.S.C. § 1211(a) states that "[i]n the case of a corporation, losses from sales or exchanges of capital assets shall be allowed only to the extent of gains from such sales or exchanges." Section 1212(a) establishes rules governing carrybacks and carryovers of capital losses, permitting such losses to offset capital gains in certain earlier or later years.

5. Petitioner mistakenly relies on cases in which this Court, in narrowly applying the general definition of "capital asset," has "construed 'capital asset' to exclude property representing income items or accretions to the value of a capital asset themselves properly attributable to income," even though these items are property in the broad sense of the word.... See, *e.g., Commissioner v. Gillette Motor Co.,* 3 4 U.S. 130 (1960) ("capital asset" does not include compensation awarded taxpayer that represented fair rental value of its facilities); *Commissioner v. P.G. Lake, Inc.,* 356 U.S. 260 (1958) ("capital asset" does not include proceeds from sale of oil, rights); *Hort v. Commissioner,* 313 U.S. 28 (1941) ("capital asset" does not include payment to lessor for cancellation of unexpired portion of a lease). This line of cases, based on the premise that § 1221 "property" does not include claims or rights to ordinary income, has no application in the present context. Petitioner sold capital stock, not a claim to ordinary income.

6. The inventory exception was part of the original enactment of the capital-asset provision in 1924. See Revenue Act of 1924, ch. 234, § 208(a)(8), 43 Stat. 263. Depreciable property used in a trade or business was excluded in 1938, see Revenue Act of 1938, ch. 289, § 117(a)(1), 52 Stat. 500, and real property used in a trade or business was excluded in 1942, see Revenue Act of 1942, ch. 619, § 151(a), 56 Stat. 846. The exception for accounts and notes receivable acquired in the ordinary course of trade or business was added in 1954. Internal Revenue Code of 1954, § 1221(4), 68A Stat. 322.

7. Although congressional inaction is generally a poor measure of congressional intent, we are given some pause by the fact that over 25 years have passed since *Corn Products Refining Co. v. Commissioner* was initially interpreted as excluding assets acquired for business purposes from the definition of "capital asset," see *Booth Newspapers, Inc. v. United States,* 157 Ct. Cl. 886, 303 F.2d 916 (1962), without any sign of disfavor from Congress. We cannot ignore the unambiguous language of § 1221, however, no matter how reticent Congress has been. If a broad exclusion from capital asset status is to be created for assets acquired for business purposes, it must come from congressional action, not silence.

Consider the following questions about *Arkansas Best.*

1. What asset did the taxpayer sell that caused the controversy in the case?

2. Did the taxpayer realize a gain or loss on the asset?

3. What was the taxpayer's position with respect to its characterization?

4. The Court cites the case of *Corn Products Refining Co. v. Commissioner,* 350 U.S. 46 (1955). Why did the taxpayer rely on that case?

5. What are "corn futures"?

6. In *Corn Products* was it loss or gain that was at issue? Do you think that made a difference?

7. How did the Court reinterpret *Corn Products in Arkansas Best?*

8. After *Arkansas Best,* can an investment asset, like a share of stock, ever be anything other than a capital asset? **Look at section 1221(a)(7).** Congress added section 1221(a)(7) to the Code in 1999. What is its purpose?

Now, ask yourself the following question: Is a shoe a capital asset? Under section 1221 it is a capital asset unless it is excluded under one of the subsections. Thus, the shoe that you are currently wearing is a capital asset in your hands (or on your feet), but when the shoe store salesman owned that same shoe before he sold it to you, it was not a capital asset in his hands. Why? **Look at section 1221(a)(1).** At the shoe store, the shoe was part of the store owner's "stock in trade" or "inventory." Similarly, the car that you drive for personal purposes is a capital asset in your hands, but, if you used that same car exclusively for business purposes, it would not be a capital asset. Why? **Look at section 1221(a)(2).** If used in a trade or business, the car is a depreciable asset and is therefore not a capital asset.[4] Thus, whether or not a particular asset is a "capital asset" depends not on the intrinsic nature of the asset itself but on how the taxpayer uses it. You cannot identify whether something is a "capital asset" without asking about its use in the hands of a particular taxpayer.

In general, as you might surmise from reading sections 1221(a)(1) and (a)(2), a capital asset is something that a taxpayer holds for investment in order to realize long-term appreciation on the asset. It is not something that assists in the production of the taxpayer's everyday or "ordinary" income-producing trade or business activities.[5] Thus, the

---

4. The automobile example brings up a point that students often find confusing. When we covered "capital expenditures" in Part II, Chapter 3.B.4., you learned that certain capital expenditures, for example, those made for assets used in a trade or business, are subject to the allowance for depreciation under section 167(a). If the automobile that is used for business is characterized as a capital expenditure when it is acquired, why is it not a "capital asset"? The answer is that not all "capital expenditures" are made for "capital assets." It is critical for you to determine the difference between the two concepts. In common business parlance, people frequently use the term "capital assets" to describe the plant and equipment of a business. Although the purchase and construction of plant and equipment would be classified as "capital expenditures" under section 263(a) of the Code, they would not be "capital assets" under the definition in section 1221 because they are depreciable and are thus excluded from "capital asset" status under section 1221(a)(2).

5. But *see* section 1221(b)(3) of the Code, enacted in May, 2006, as part of the 2005 Act. (Act section 204.) Section 1221(b)(3) provides that, at the taxpayer's election, the sale or exchange of a musical composition or a copyright in a musical work created by a taxpayer's personal efforts is treated as the sale or exchange of a capital asset. Is this special treatment of musical compositions

distinction between "ordinary" income that is taxed at the usual section 1 rates and "capital gain" income that is taxed at a favorable rate is a factual issue. The quintessential "capital asset" would be a share of stock in the hands of an investor. Based on your reading of section 1221, why is this statement true? The same share of stock in the hands of a securities dealer would not be a capital asset. Why?

C. Identifying the Holding Period

As noted at the beginning of this Part, section 1(h) provides a special rate of tax only for the portion of a taxpayer's income that constitutes NCG. Your examination of section 1222(11) has undoubtedly illustrated that the only way a taxpayer can have an NCG is to have an LTCG. You have also learned that the taxpayer must have sold or exchanged an asset. The final requirement for achieving an LTCG is satisfaction of the holding period. The current rule requires the taxpayer to have "held [the asset] for more than 1 year." The one-year holding period reflects Congress's intent to provide a preferential rate for gains on "long-term" investments.

Defining what constitutes "long-term" has been a continuing source of controversy for legislators and tax policy experts. In the past, Congress has defined the required period to be as short as six months (from 1942 to 1976) or as long as eighteen (from July 28, 1997 to January 1, 1998, part of the 1997 Act). No matter what choice Congress makes, the period will be somewhat arbitrary in at least two respects: what is "long-term" for one investor may be a relatively short-term investment for another, and adoption of any period means that an investment held for exactly one day too few does not qualify, while one held for one day longer does. **Look at sections 1222(1) and (3).**

The case of *Fogel v. Commissioner*, 203 F.2d 347 (5th Cir. 1953), explains how to count the period. The general rule is to disregard the day of acquisition but include the day of sale. Therefore, in order to have held an asset acquired on June 1, 2002, for more than one year, the taxpayer who wishes to achieve a long-term capital gain cannot sell or exchange it until June 2, 2003.

In most cases, identification of the date of acquisition and the date of disposition of an asset involves no uncertainty. The general common law rule provides that a transfer occurs on the date that title or the benefits and burdens of ownership pass, whichever occurs first.[6] For example, for stock acquisitions or dispositions accomplished through a broker, the date of purchase or sale will appear on the customer's brokerage statement. The period begins on the day after the buy order is executed and ends on the date the sale order is executed.[7]

---

consistent with traditional notions of what constitutes a capital asset? Are writers or visual artists afforded the same treatment on the sale of their works? Why not? **Look at Section 1221(a)(3).**

6. In general, the date of passage of title and benefits and burdens will be the same date. An exception exists in cases where title does not pass on the same date as benefits and burdens pass. If the delay is one that requires merely the passage of time, the sale occurs on the date of passage of the benefits and burdens. If the delay requires the satisfaction of a condition that will not necessarily occur merely through the passage of time, the sale does not occur until satisfaction of the condition. For example, a requirement of approval of the sale by a government agency is a condition that will not be fulfilled merely by the passage of time. In this case, the sale will not occur until the approval is granted.

7. Revenue Ruling 93-84, 1993-2 C.B. 225.

There are some cases involving the sale of property where the date of acquisition or disposition may require some examination. A common example is an installment sale of property. Under normal practice, title does not pass until the final payment is made. Nevertheless, the holding period generally begins on the date the buyer and seller execute the installment sale contract.

Transactions in real property often involve differences in the time of passage of title and passage of the benefits and burdens. In addition to installment sales contract transactions, where the rule is the same as for personal property, other variations frequently occur. For example, a seller of real property who takes back a purchase money mortgage may retain technical title until the buyer retires the loan. Provided the benefits and burdens have passed to the purchaser, the delay in passage of title is irrelevant. Another common example results from the practice by which mortgagees in some states retain deeds of trust until the loan is fully paid.[8]

Questions occasionally occur concerning the treatment of options to purchase. Recall our discussion of form versus substance in Part III, Chapter 2. Then read the following case.

ESTATE OF FRANKLIN v. COMMISSIONER
64 T.C. 752 (1975)[9]

FEATHERSTON, *Judge:* ...

... [O]nly one issue remains for our resolution: Are petitioners entitled to deductions for their distributive share of the losses reported by a limited partnership which entered into a contract with respect to the acquisition of a motel and related property? The answer depends on whether the obligations undertaken by the partnership were sufficiently definite and unqualified to constitute "indebtedness" within the meaning of section 163(a) and cost basis for depreciation purposes as provided by section 167(g).

FINDINGS OF FACT

Charles T. Franklin (hereinafter referred to as decedent) ... and his wife filed a timely joint Federal income tax return for 1968 ... and for 1969....

Twenty-Fourth Property Associates (hereinafter the partnership or Twenty-Fourth) is a limited partnership formed on November 25, 1968, pursuant to the California Uniform Limited Partnership Act. The partnership was composed of one general partner, Jack R. Young & Associates (hereinafter JRYA), a California corporation, and eight limited partners. Decedent was one of these limited partners, who included seven medical doctors and one dentist.

The formation of Twenty-Fourth was evidenced by two documents, an "Agreement of Limited Partnership" (hereinafter the agreement) and a "Certificate of Limited Partnership of Twenty-Fourth Property Associates." ...

---

8. In a state that uses deeds of trust, the borrower executes a deed to a trustee who holds the property on behalf of the lender. In that event, if the mortgagor fails to make the required payments, the trustee generally need not utilize a formal foreclosure proceeding in order to sell the property.

9. *Aff'd*, 544 F.2d 1045 (9th Cir. 1976). We will discuss the Ninth Circuit's differing approach to the case in Part VI, Chapter 1.

The agreement recites that the purpose of the partnership was to acquire from Wayne L. and Joan E. Romney (hereinafter the Romneys or Wayne L. Romney singularly as Romney) real property, improvements, and certain personal property known as the Thunderbird Inn (sometimes referred to as the motel or property) in Williams, Ariz., and to lease the property back to the sellers or their nominee.

The agreement provides that six of the limited partners would contribute $10,000 each to the limited partnership, to be credited to their respective capital accounts, and a like amount towards the capital account of the general partner, JRYA. Two of the limited partners contributed $7,500 each to the partnership's capital and a similar amount to the capital account of JRYA. According to the agreement, contributions by the limited partners towards the capital account of JRYA, amounting to a total of $75,000 (which JRYA withdrew before the end of 1968), were compensation for services to be rendered by JRYA to the partnership during its life. The other $75,000 was paid to the Romneys as prepaid interest pursuant to a "Sales Agreement," described later herein.

· · ·

Of the $75,000 withdrawn by JRYA from its capital account,

$18,750 was paid by JRYA as commissions or finder's fees to the salesmen who arranged for the contributions of the limited partners, and approximately $50,000 was allocated by JRYA to services performed during the first year of the partnership. The amount left was to cover services to be performed over the remaining life of the partnership. These duties could include preparation of the partnership tax returns, any negotiations leading to a renewal of leases with respect to the acquired property or the refinancing of any mortgages, or any other disposition of the property owned by the partnership.

· · ·

JRYA, on behalf of Twenty-Fourth, executed a "Sales Agreement" with the Romneys, dated November 15, 1968. The sales agreement recites that: "Seller [the Romneys] has this date sold to Buyer [the partnership] and Buyer has purchased from Seller" the real property, together with the improvements and personal property, known as the Thunderbird Inn. According to the sales agreement, the conveyed property included all personal property located on the premises except the liquor license and certain inventory. The sales agreement did not cover the 17 acres adjacent to the motel.

In negotiating the sales agreement for the Thunderbird Inn, Romney and Jack R. Young, representative of JRYA (hereinafter Young), utilized an appraisal report, prepared in May 1968 at Romney's request, by Ralph W. Jenkins, who died several years prior to the trial. Young never had an independent appraisal made for the benefit of JRYA.

Young was not personally familiar with the property which he purported to purchase on behalf of Twenty-Fourth. He did not visit the property, but a Mr. Darling, then president of JRYA, who was not a real estate appraiser, visited the motel and gave Young a general report on its condition. Young did not make an effort to determine the age of the property improvements which are the subject of the sales agreement.

The total sales price stated in the sales agreement was $1,224,000, plus interest on the unpaid balance at the rate of 7 1/2 percent per annum, payable in monthly installments of principal and interest of $9,045.36 for a period of approximately 10 years.

The sales agreement also recites that a payment, described as prepaid interest and in the amount of $75,000, as mentioned in our earlier discussion of the partnership agreement, was payable upon the signing of the agreement, and this payment was made.

At the time of the execution of the sales agreement, there was a first mortgage on the property in the approximate amount of $235,000, and a second mortgage in the approximate amount of $550,000 was in the process of being placed on the property. These encumbrances remain the sole obligation of the Romneys under the sales agreement until the end of the 10-year period, at which time, if the transaction is completed, Twenty-Fourth is to assume them.

At the expiration on January 15, 1979, of the 10-year period, a payment equal to the "Seller's equity" will be due. The sales agreement defines "Seller's equity" as the difference between the outstanding encumbrances and the principal balance due and owing under the terms of that agreement. At the time of the execution of the sales agreement, it was estimated that at the end of the 10 years, the unpaid principal balance would equal approximately $975,000.

The sales agreement further provides:

> Buyer is purchasing the property described in Exhibit "A" together with the improvements situated thereon and the furnishings and fixtures located therein, subject to the existing indebtedness thereon, and is not assuming any of said indebtedness, and Buyer's liability and obligation hereunder shall be limited to its investment in the property in accordance with the terms and provisions of this Agreement, and there shall be no personal liability on the part of Buyer, nor may any deficiency be assessed against the Buyer, and Seller will be limited to forfeiting out Buyer's interest in the real property, improvements and personal property if the payments are not made by Buyer as called for under the terms and provisions of this Agreement, and nothing herein contained shall be construed as obligating Buyer to assume the mortgages or other obligations of record, as set forth in Schedule "A" nor is Buyer or Buyer's nominees or assignees assuming any mortgages, leases, notes or other obligations, and if Buyer fails to make the payments herein called for under Paragraph 2 hereof, Seller is limited to look solely to the real and personal property involved in this transaction, and Buyer, or Buyer's nominees or assigns shall have no personal liability or obligation hereunder.

> . . .

Twenty-Fourth, through its general partner, and the Romneys opened an escrow with Southern California First National Bank, San Diego, Calif., and deposited therein the sales agreement, a warranty deed from the Romneys to the partnership, a bill of sale from seller to buyer and one from buyer to seller covering the personal property located in the motel, and a quitclaim deed from the partnership to the Romneys, all of which were called for by the sales agreement. The sales agreement recites that upon full payment of the purchase price, all of these documents are to be delivered by the escrow agent to Twenty-Fourth. The sales agreement further states that upon a default by Twenty-Fourth under the sales agreement and upon the Romneys' electing to forfeit Twenty-Fourth's interest in said real property, all the documents are to be delivered by the escrow agent to the Romneys.

> . . .

Concurrently with the execution of the sales agreement, the parties executed a document entitled "Lease," which reflects that Twenty-Fourth as landlord leased the property, subject to the sales agreement, to the Romneys as tenants for a term of 10 years commencing on November 15, 1968. The lease authorizes the Romneys to use the premises "for any lawful purpose other than a dangerous or noxious trade or business."

The rental under the lease is $1,435 per month for the first 9 months, $2,532 for the 10th month, and $9,045 per month for the remaining term of the lease. These rental payments approximate the payments due for the same period under the sales agreement after the buyer is credited with the $75,000 described as prepaid interest in the sales agreement.

Under the terms of the lease, the Romneys are to pay all utilities and real property taxes and other taxes, assessments, rents, charges, and levies "(general and specific, ordinary and extraordinary, or [sic] every name, nature and kind whatsoever)." They are also, at their "sole cost and expense," to keep and maintain the premises in good repair, expressly "waiving any or all right or law to make repairs at the expense of Landlord," and "shall make all necessary or appropriate repairs, replacements, renewals and betterments of such improvements, structural and nonstructural, ordinary and extraordinary, and foreseen and unforeseen." In addition, the Romneys, at their "sole cost and expense," are to maintain fire, extended coverage, and other casualty insurance as well as liability insurance as to the subject property. The instrument, described as a "net lease," further provides that the Romneys are to hold the partnership harmless from all the foregoing or any other liabilities.

The lease recites the fact that Twenty-Fourth and the Romneys are also parties "to a Sales Agreement" in which they are buyer and seller, respectively. The lease provides that if the Romneys default on their obligations as seller under the sales agreement by failing to pay and discharge the underlying encumbrances according to the terms thereof, Twenty-Fourth at its option may consider the Romneys in default under the lease, may suspend its payments under the sales agreement, and may make payments on the underlying encumbrances directly for its own benefit and not that of the Romneys.

...

No payments have been actually made under either the sales agreement or the lease. Instead, entries have been made by both parties in books of account which are reconciled annually. Up to the date of the trial, no money other than Twenty-Fourth's original $75,000 payment to the Romneys had changed hands between the parties.

Young, the representative of JRYA who negotiated the agreements on behalf of Twenty-Fourth, was well acquainted with the Romneys. From 1967 to 1971, the Romneys and Young, or JRYA, were involved in approximately 49 transactions involving motor hotels and apartment houses. During November 1968, the same month as the various original agreements herein were executed, the Romneys and Young were involved in transactions involving two other motel properties. All of those transactions were structured in a manner similar to the transaction herein at issue.

Decedent purchased his percentage interest in Twenty-Fourth from Leo E. Shaw (hereinafter Shaw). Shaw sold partnership interests to six of the eight limited partners of Twenty-Fourth. He showed potential investors, including decedent, [a] ... projection prepared by an accounting firm....

This projection indicates that decedent's distributive share of the alleged losses of Twenty-Fourth would equal $78,684 by 1974 and would total $79,763 by 1978. No cash flow would be generated by the operations of Twenty-Fourth during the 10-year period covered by the lease.

Decedent and his wife reported $22,244 and $16,583 as their distributive share of the losses of Twenty-Fourth for 1968 and 1969, respectively. Respondent disallowed these deductions, determining in the notice of deficiency that petitioners had established neither the nature nor the extent of the losses.

OPINION

Petitioners contend that Dr. Franklin, as a member of the partnership, Twenty-Fourth, was entitled to deduct his distributive share of the partnership losses.... Those losses were composed of the annual excess of the interest on the stated gross purchase price plus the depreciation deductions claimed on the motel property over the rent specified in the lease. Respondent makes two arguments. First, he maintains that the purported sale and leaseback of the motel was a "sham" transaction without any legal or economic purpose or motive other than tax avoidance. (Footnote 3) Alternatively, respondent contends that the partnership could decide at the end of the 10 years whether to complete the purchase or "walk away" from the deal without any further liability and that the partnership thus obtained only an option to buy the motel property. Consequently, according to respondent's view, Dr. Franklin as a member of the partnership is not entitled to any partnership loss deductions during the years in issue.

Section 163(a) allows a deduction for "interest paid or accrued within the taxable year on *indebtedness.*" (Emphasis supplied.) An indebtedness is an existing, unconditional, and legally enforceable obligation for the payment of a principal sum.... Depreciation deductions are designed to compensate an investor in property for the economic loss attributable to the property's deterioration through exhaustion, wear and tear, and obsolescence. They are computed with reference to a taxpayer's adjusted basis for the purpose of determining gain or loss on the sale or other disposition of property.... Such adjusted basis, in a case like the present one, depends initially upon the cost of the property....

We hold for respondent. We think any obligations to pay the purchase price stated in the sales agreement signed November 15, 1968, when read in the light of the contemporaneously executed lease and the surrounding circumstances, were not legally enforceable or were too indefinite and tentative to create "indebtedness" within the meaning of section 163(a) or give the partnership a cost basis under section 167(g) and related provisions. At best, the substance of the transaction here in dispute was to give the partnership an option to buy the motel property on January 15, 1979, and no earlier, at a computable price. Consequently, petitioners are not entitled to the claimed deductions.

An option to purchase property does not create an enforceable obligation to pay the purchase price or give the taxpayer a cost basis for the property. "It is simply a contract by which the owner of property agrees with another person that the latter shall have the right to purchase the property at a fixed price within a certain time." ... It gives the optionee no present estate, ... and imposes on him no obligation to consummate the transaction. He has the choice of exercising the option or allowing it to lapse.... If an option is not exercised, the optionor becomes entitled to keep only the amount paid as consideration for granting the option ... and has no enforceable right of action against the optionee for damages....

A contract of sale, in contrast, carries mutual obligations on the part of the seller to sell and the buyer to buy.... It "is a contract 'to pass rights of property for money,— which the buyer pays or promises to pay to the seller.'" ... The purchaser in such a bilateral contract is liable for full contract damages if he fails to perform.... Accordingly, a contract of sale imposes an enforceable obligation to pay the purchase price, which will support interest deductions and give the purchaser a cost basis in the property on which depreciation is allowable.

Whether the several agreements in the instant case are to be construed as constituting an option or a contract of sale depends not upon any particular phraseology used in the documents but rather upon what the parties actually did, gleaned from a consideration of the written instruments (both the sales agreement and the lease) in their entirety and the surrounding circumstances.... True, the sales agreement contains language ordinarily found in a contract of sale, but the technical niceties of conveyancing will not suffice. When the sales agreement is read with the contemporaneously executed lease, in the light of the record as a whole, the arrangement has the characteristics of an option. We think those characteristics clearly predominate. We base our conclusion on the *totality* of the following considerations:

First, the sales agreement purports to create an obligation on the partnership to pay a sales price of $1,224,000 but, in fact, the true price is to be computed according to a carefully prescribed formula as of January 15, 1979. On that date the partnership may elect to consummate the transaction or withdraw from it....

    ...

The monthly "payments," which were to serve to reduce the purchase price, have never been made and, we infer, were never intended to be made. The partnership has no funds of any sort with which to make the monthly payments. (Footnote 8) The contemporaneously executed lease called for rental payments equal to the amortization payments under the sales agreement. (Footnote 9) Instead of actually making the so-called rental payments and purported amortization payments, however, the Romneys and the partnership merely made offsetting bookkeeping entries on their respective records, reflecting monthly payments of the rent under the lease and monthly "installments" under the sales agreement. Not since the initial $75,000 prepaid interest payment has any money changed hands between the parties.

Thus, the only economic effect (other than claimed tax consequences) between December 15, 1968, the due date of the first payment, and January 15, 1979, of the so-called rental payments and purported amortization payments is to provide a mathematical formula for computing the price for which the partnership will be entitled to elect or not to purchase the motel on the latter date. A wide variety of figures could have been used in that formula for the interest rate, monthly amortization, and corresponding rental payment factors in order to produce the January 1979 option price. Since the purported rental and amortization payment figures actually used were only bookkeeping entries, the stated purchase price of $1,224,000 is meaningless. The only price of any legal or economic significance is the figure computable as of January 1979 under the prescribed formula.

Second, and of major importance, neither the sales agreement nor the lease obligates the partnership to buy the motel or pay anything in the way of damages if it fails to do so. In one provision the sales agreement appears to obligate the partnership to make the $9,045.36 monthly amortization payments beginning on December 15, 1968, and to pay the "principal balance due and owing" on January 15, 1979. But a further provision, quoted in our Findings, makes it explicitly clear that the partnership's liability is limited to a forfeiture of its rights under the sales agreement and that the partnership shall have no other liability of any kind. Thus, if the partnership fails to consummate the sale, it will lose only its rights under the contract to buy the motel property on January 15, 1979, at the computable price. It cannot be compelled to assume the mortgages or pay any other portion of the option price. These facts bring the case within the rule of numerous decisions holding that a distinguishing characteristic of an option is that it imposes no obligation on the optionee to complete the transaction....

Petitioners argue that the partnership acquired equitable title to the motel property which the partnership is required to forfeit if it "defaulted" and that the transaction was no different from any other nonrecourse purchase. True, the sales agreement required the Romneys to deposit with an escrow agent a warranty deed covering the real property and a bill of sale covering the personalty. But the partnership was to deliver to the escrow agent documents which canceled the warranty deed and bill of sale: a quitclaim deed and a bill of sale reconveying the personalty to the Romneys and the sales agreement, which provides that "in the event Buyer's interest in the property should hereafter be forfeited out, Seller will be entitled to retain all of the personal property, ... in the premises at the time such forfeiture may become effective." Only the sales agreement was to be recorded, and in case the partnership does not complete the transaction, all of these documents, including the quitclaim deed, are to be delivered to the Romneys. No evidence of title is to be delivered to the partnership unless and until the purchase price is paid in January 1979.

True, also, the sales agreement refers to the Romneys as the "Seller" and to the partnership as the "Buyer" and recites that "Seller has this date sold to Buyer and Buyer has purchased from Seller" the real and personal property, including improvements, comprising the motel. Language of this sort is ordinarily used only in bilateral sales agreements.... But where such language appears in an instrument, and other provisions of the agreement permit the buyer to withdraw and incur no liability other than his initial payment, the agreement may constitute an option....

Moreover, as a matter of economic reality, petitioners have not shown they had anything of value to forfeit, other than the option rights. As discussed above no actual payments, except the $75,000 initial prepaid interest payment, were ever made to the Romneys. The "equity" buildup allegedly attributable to the amortization payments was illusory. Petitioners have not shown that the purported sales price of $1,224,000 (or any other price) had any relationship to the actual market value of the motel property or that the purported rent had any realistic relationship to the fair rental value of the motel property. (Footnote 13)

Also, petitioners presented no expert testimony as to the value of the motel property. Nor did they show its earnings history or evidence of comparable sales on which the Court could base an independent valuation. The record shows that during the period from February through August 1968, the Romneys had bought the stock of two corporations, one of which owned the motel, for approximately $800,000 and that about $660,000 of that purchase price was allocable to the assets purportedly sold to the partnership. The previous owner, Thunderbird Inn, Inc., the Romneys, and their successor-in-interest have maintained insurance policies on the property in the respective amounts of $583,200, $700,000, and $614,000, covering periods from May 1967 to January 1, 1974. From those raw facts, however, we cannot estimate the property's value.

Indeed, the parties proceeded as if they had no concern about whether the purchase price or rental rate accurately reflected the value of the property or its use. Shaw and Young, who sold the deal to Dr. Franklin and the other limited partners, never visited the premises, and it was not shown that Dr. Franklin or any of the other limited partners did so either or that any of them engaged legal counsel or consulted experts before entering into this huge transaction. The record contains no indication that the partners ever attempted to formulate a judgment as to the probable January 15, 1979, value of the motel or even inquired as to the age of the building in 1968, the suitability of its location for motel use, the prospective highway construction and its effect on the motel, the effect of 10 years of additional use and deterioration, the motel's earnings history, and the like. We are not satisfied, as a matter of economic reality, that the partnership has any equity to forfeit in the case of its failure to pay the purchase price or that the partners ever intended to complete the purchase.

Third, the sales agreement and the lease did not transfer the burdens and benefits of ownership of the motel.... Possession of the motel property was never actually transferred to the partnership. The 10-year lease, executed contemporaneously with the sales agreement, left the Romneys in possession of the property with the right to use the premises "for any lawful purpose other than a dangerous or noxious trade or business." To the same extent as any owner, the Romneys continue to be liable under the lease for the payment of taxes, assessments, charges, and levies of all kinds. They are required, at their own expense, to keep and maintain the premises in good order, condition, and repair, "waiving any or all right or law to make repairs at the expense of Landlord [the partnership]." They are also required, at their own expense, to maintain casualty and liability insurance and to save the partnership "harmless from and against all ... obligations of every kind and nature whatsoever related to the said premises or the improvements thereon which may arise or become due during the term of this Lease." (Footnote 14) And they have no right to terminate the lease by reason of any "event, occurrence, or situation during the term of this Lease whether foreseen or unforeseen, and however extraordinary." (Footnote 15)

...

In summary, as we view the entire record, the sales agreement and the lease—when read together and in the light of all the facts—are incompatible with a sale. At most they give the partnership an option to buy the motel property on January 15, 1979.... We are not satisfied that the partnership has any investment in the motel property or that it will suffer any economic loss as that property deteriorates over the 10-year period covered by the purported sales agreement and lease. Accordingly, the estate of Dr. Franklin, who was a member of the Twenty-Fourth partnership, and his surviving spouse are not entitled to deductions ... for their distributive share of an alleged partnership loss.

...

FOOTNOTES:

3. While the tax savings sought by petitioners are considerable, respondent errs in placing such heavy emphasis on the tax results Dr. Franklin and the other limited partners sought to achieve.... They were entitled to take advantage of the tax-saving opportunities offered by the statute dealing with partnership losses. *See Gregory v. Helvering....* However, they must show that, in substance and not merely in form, they actually did what they purported to do.

...

8. The $75,000 prepayment of interest to the Romneys and the withdrawal by JRYA of the $75,000 credited to its account completely exhausted the $150,000 invested in the limited partnership by the eight limited partners. The partnership agreement contained no provision obligating the partners to make any further contributions.

9. As detailed in our Findings, the sales agreement called for an initial $75,000 payment to the Romneys, the only payment they ever received from the partnership, and provided that such payment "shall be construed and accepted by Seller as a prepayment

and an advance payment of interest." The rental payments called for in the lease for the first 10 months were adjusted by this $75,000 so that, over the entire term of the lease, the total rental payments and the total amortization payments were about the same. The record does not explain why the rent payable by the Romneys for the first 10 months should have been adjusted by this $75,000 if it was, in fact, merely a prepayment of interest on the purported purchase price of the motel property.

13. Petitioners offered an error-filled, sketchy appraisal report prepared for Romney at his expense by one Ralph W. Jenkins, now deceased, but Jenkins' opinions could not be subjected to the purifying tests of cross-examination. The report is obviously suspect because of Romney's participation with Young or JRYA in approximately 48 other similar transactions. The report was admitted for the limited purpose of showing that Young had the appraisal report when he and Shaw sold the transaction to the limited partners. Young testified that a Mr. Darling, one of his associates, visited the property, but Darling is not an appraiser. And, significantly, he did not testify at the trial.... Young's summary of the information obtained by Darling was very general. Petitioners offered no credible evidence on this important issue as to the correlation of the purported purchase price of $1,224,000 with the value of the property....

14. Petitioners contend that the Romneys gave up the benefits of ownership of the motel property, "the most important of which is the right to dispose of the property and participate in any appreciation in value of the property." But any optionor, by granting the option, relinquishes the same rights.

15. Petitioners seek to dismiss these provisions on the ground that the arrangement was a so-called net lease. But that argument ignores the fact that the lease was actually part of the contemporaneously executed purported sales agreement. The two instruments are interdependent and, as a matter of reality, cannot be separated. The argument thus assumes the point in issue. The rights, powers, and obligations retained by the Romneys far exceed those customarily granted in a net lease.

Now consider the following questions about the Tax Court's opinion in *Estate of Franklin.*

1. How did the taxpayer's partnership structure its deal with the Romneys?

2. Was the motel property a capital asset in the hands of the partnership?[10]

3. Where did you earlier see this kind of deal?

4. Why did the court conclude in *Frank Lyon Co.* that the structure of the transaction coincided with its form, while the court here did not?

5. How did the court characterize the structure of the transaction in this case?

6. When did the partnership's holding period begin on this piece of property? (Remember that the date of acquisition is important for calculating depreciation as well as for measuring the period of ownership. Of course, in the case of depreciation, the buyer must acquire the property and place it in service in order to be entitled to claim depreciation. But, the buyer may not claim depreciation if he has placed the property in service but has not "acquired" it.)

---

10. You may want to review the earlier material dealing with partnerships in Part III, Chapter 1.B.2.a.

One other aspect of identifying the proper holding period requires discussion. When we introduced you to some of the nonrecognition provisions, you learned that one of the consequences of nonrecognition was the need to account for the basis of the old property in the basis of the new property in order to preserve the possibility of recognition of the gain or loss in the future. Recall, for example, section 1031. Section 1031(d) requires a taxpayer to calculate her basis in the property she receives on the exchange by beginning with her basis in the old property. She then makes adjustments for boot and any gain that is recognized on the exchange. The result is that the difference between the basis of the new property and its fair market value at the time of the exchange preserves the unrecognized gain or loss.[11]

When a taxpayer uses the basis of one piece of property in order to determine the basis of an alternative piece of property, the Code refers to this as a "substituted basis." **Read section 7701(a)(42).** What other provision can you identify that also requires the taxpayer to use a "substituted basis"? **Recall** *Taft v. Bowers.*

When a nonrecognition transaction occurs, the taxpayer must also consider her holding period in the new property. If the rationale for nonrecognition is continuity of investment and the rationale for section 1015 is continuity of investor (typically within the family), then how should a taxpayer determine the holding period of property she acquires through either a nonrecognition transaction or a gift of property? The Code provides a solution in section 1223. **Read section 1223.** Which part of section 1223 covers a section 1031 transaction? Which covers a gift under section 1015? In effect, in the case of exchange property, the Code allows the taxpayer to "tack" the holding period of the old asset onto that of her new property. In the case of a gift, the Code allows the taxpayer to "tack" the holding period of the donor onto hers.

A taxpayer's acquisition of property from a decedent does not constitute what one thinks of as a nonrecognition transaction. In fact, until 2010, the recipient will enjoy a "stepped-up" basis or suffer a "stepped-down" basis, a basis equal to the fair market value of the property on the date of the decedent's death (or on the alternate valuation date).[12] But what is the recipient's holding period in the asset? **Look at section 1223(9).**

---

11. The mechanics of section 1033 work a little differently. But, the effect is the same. The basis in the new property still includes the TOAD invested in the old property.

12. The 2001 Act changed the rules of section 1014. By 2010, when the estate tax is completely repealed, section 1014 will also be repealed and will no longer permit a step-up or require a step-down in basis to fair market value as it did before the Act. **Locate in the footnotes to Part II, Chapter 2.A., the explanation of the 2001 Act changes.**

Chapter 3

The Limitation on the Deductibility of Capital Losses

Recall that, upon the "sale or other disposition" of property, if the taxpayer's amount realized is less than his adjusted basis, he realizes a loss under section 1001(a). **Review section 1001(a).** Section 1001(c) requires recognition of the loss in the absence of a relevant nonrecognition provision. **Review section 1001(c).** In the case of losses of individual taxpayers, however, you learned that you must make an additional inquiry: whether the loss is "allowed" under section 165(c). **Review section 165(c).** Once you have determined that a loss is "allowed" under section 165(c), you must proceed to section 165(f). **Read section 165(f).** Section 165(f) then sends you to section 1211. **Read section 1211(b).** Thus, in the case of individuals, two restrictions limit the deductibility of losses. First, section 165(c) imposes a general limit on all losses of individuals to the three stated categories. If the taxpayer's loss passes the hurdle of section 165(c), but it is a capital loss, section 165(f) directs the taxpayer to the second limitation that appears in section 1211.

Since 1924, the Code has limited the ability of taxpayers to deduct "capital losses." The current version of this restriction appears in section 1211. Section 1211 reflects Congress's concern that taxpayers might manipulate the timing of capital gains and losses to minimize overall income. Taxpayers can choose when to realize gains or losses under section 1001 because that section requires a "sale or other disposition." Without the restriction of section 1211, taxpayers might be tempted to retain appreciated assets but dispose of assets that have declined in value, in order to offset ordinary income with capital losses.

Section 1211(a) restricts the deductibility of capital losses by corporations,[1] and section 1211(b) restricts the deductibility of capital losses by individuals. **Compare sections 1211(a) and 1211(b).** How do sections 1211(a) and 1211(b) differ? Read each of the subsections carefully. Note that section 1211 does not distinguish between long-term and short-term capital losses.

Suppose this year a taxpayer has capital gain (whether long-term, or short-term) in the amount of $15,000 and total capital losses (whether long-term or short-term) in the amount of $60,000. How much capital loss could the taxpayer deduct if it were a corporation? An individual? Is the deduction by the individual above or below the line? **Look at section 62(a)(3).**

If section 1211 limits the taxpayer's deduction, what happens to the amount of the capital loss the taxpayer cannot deduct this year? **Look at section 1212.** For now, notice

---

1. Note that there is no preferential tax rate for corporate capital gains, but section 1211(a) limits the deductibility of corporate capital losses.

the organization of the section. Do not try to do the kind of detailed reading yet that is your normal practice in examining a new Code section.

Section 1212(a) contains the rules for corporations. In general, corporations may carry capital losses back for three years and forward for five years. The carryback rule may require the corporation to file an amended return in order to claim the losses. The corporate taxpayer may not decide to carry the losses forward rather than backward in order to escape the filing of an amended return. If the corporate taxpayer had capital gains in any of the five preceding tax years against which to deduct the current year's capital losses, it must carry them first to the earliest of the five years, then to the next earliest, and so on. It then carries any remaining capital losses forward until they are exhausted or the ten-year period expires.

In contrast, section 1212(b), applicable to individuals, does not contain a provision allowing for carrybacks. But, an individual taxpayer may carry her losses forward indefinitely (or until her death, whichever occurs first). **Now look carefully at section 1212(b).** The only way to comply accurately with section 1212(b) is to write it out and carefully plug in each of the amounts, using the definitions you learned in section 1222.

Capital Gains and Losses Problems — Jon and Melissa

The following problems will assist you in understanding the rudiments of the structure of the basic capital gain/loss provisions.

———————

I. Jon is an unmarried, cash basis taxpayer. He is a lawyer in solo private practice. He has gross receipts from his law practice in the amount of $300,000. He also has dividend income in the amount of $5,000, and interest income in the amount of $10,000. He has ordinary and necessary business expenses in the amount of $125,000, and depreciation expense in connection with business equipment in the amount of $15,000. He pays alimony in the amount of $25,000 per year.

In addition, Jon had capital gains and losses from stock market transactions as indicated in the following alternatives below:

   (a) LTCG = $6,000 and STCL = $2,000

   (b) STCG = $6,000 and LTCL = $2,000

   (c) LTCG = $4,000 and STCG = $1,000

   (d) LTCG = $6,000, STCG = $2,000, and LTCL = $3,000

   (e) LTCG = $6,000, STCG = $2,000, and STCL = $3,000

   (f) LTCG = $5,000 and LTCL = $10,000

   (g) STCG = $2,000 and LTCL = $10,000

   (h) LTCG = $20,000, LTCL = $12,000, STCG = $4,000, and STCL = $2,000

   (i) LTCG = $600,000, LTCL = $20,000, STCG = $60,000, and STCL = $140,000

1. For *each* of the alternatives, determine Jon's AGI. Query: must you concern yourself with whether Jon has NCG for purposes of this question? At what point in the taxing formula does the concept of NCG become relevant?

2. For *each* alternative, determine whether Jon has NCG.

II. Melissa is a researcher for a legal publishing company with a salary of $83,000 for the current tax year. Melissa decided to purchase a house. In order to do so, she made the following sales in the current year:

(a) 1000 shares of Dandy Computer Corp. for $100 per share on June 30th of the current year. She had acquired the stock as a gift from her mother (who had acquired the stock on January 16th of last year) on May 1st of this year. Her mother's basis in the stock was $50 per share; the fair market value of the stock on the date of the gift was $100 per share.

(b) 500 shares of Legalese Publishing Co. (her employer) on June 15th of the current year at a price of $52 per share. She had acquired the stock on June 15th of last year at $47 per share. Its value at the time she acquired the stock was $50 per share.

(c) A red Miata convertible for $20,000 on March 30 of the current year. She had purchased the automobile for $26,000 on a "whim" on March 24 of last year, to use on weekends for fun. When she discovered that she had no time for fun, and no other use for the car, she decided that she had better sell it.

(d) 10,000 shares of Hytek.com stock for $1 per share on February 28th of the current year. She had inherited the stock from her father who had purchased it for $200 per share in 1998 (it was one of those high-flying "tech" stocks). But, by the time her father died in June of last year, its value had declined to $4 per share (so that his estate was too small to have to file an estate tax return).

1. Does Melissa have any capital gains or losses? If so, are they long-term or short-term?

2. Does Melissa qualify for the preferential tax rate on capital gains provided by section 1(h)? Why?

As we noted in the Introduction to this Part V, commentators have referred to the current version of section 1(h) as a "reader's nightmare." We agree. We also believe, and history suggests, that section 1(h) will not remain in its current incarnation for long. Therefore, rather than spending an inordinate amount of time analyzing the provision in its current form, of greater value is an examination of Schedule D, the current version of the schedule taxpayers use to report capital gains and losses. Having completed Schedule D, a taxpayer then attaches it to his Form 1040 and transfers the results of the schedule to the appropriate line on the 1040. The result of these efforts, under current law, will, in general, limit the tax on the NCG of a taxpayer whose ordinary income is taxed at a more than 15% rate to a maximum rate of 15%, and, for a taxpayer whose ordinary income is taxed at a rate below 15%, to a maximum rate of 5 (0% in 2008).[2]

As you examine Schedule D, consider the "bad rap" that the Service often receives from taxpayers (who forget that it is Congress and the President who make the tax laws, and the Service which simply must carry them out). While we have relieved you of the burden of untangling the current version of section 1(h), not so for the worker(s) in the

---

2. *But see* footnote 3 and accompanying text in the Introduction to this Part V.

Service charged with the responsibility of drafting Schedule D. In addition to the form itself, the Service must also create instructions. The instructions for the 2005 version of Schedule D encompass 9 pages!

SCHEDULE D
(Form 1040)

Department of the Treasury
Internal Revenue Service   (99)

Capital Gains and Losses

► Attach to Form 1040.   ► See Instructions for Schedule D (Form 1040).
► Use Schedule D-1 to list additional transactions for lines 1 and 8.

OMB No. 1545-0074

2005

Attachment
Sequence No. **12**

Name(s) shown on Form 1040

Your social security number

Part I   Short-Term Capital Gains and Losses—Assets Held One Year or Less

	(a) Description of property (Example: 100 sh. XYZ Co.)	(b) Date acquired (Mo., day, yr.)	(c) Date sold (Mo., day, yr.)	(d) Sales price (see page D-6 of the instructions)	(e) Cost or other basis (see page D-6 of the instructions)	(f) Gain or (loss) Subtract (e) from (d)
1						

2	Enter your short-term totals, if any, from Schedule D-1, line 2	**2**	
3	**Total short-term sales price amounts.** Add lines 1 and 2 in column (d)	**3**	
4	Short-term gain from Form 6252 and short-term gain or (loss) from Forms 4684, 6781, and 8824	**4**	
5	Net short-term gain or (loss) from partnerships, S corporations, estates, and trusts from Schedule(s) K-1	**5**	
6	Short-term capital loss carryover. Enter the amount, if any, from line 8 of your **Capital Loss Carryover Worksheet** on page D-6 of the instructions	**6**	( )
7	**Net short-term capital gain or (loss).** Combine lines 1 through 6 in column (f)	**7**	

Part II   Long-Term Capital Gains and Losses—Assets Held More Than One Year

	(a) Description of property (Example: 100 sh. XYZ Co.)	(b) Date acquired (Mo., day, yr.)	(c) Date sold (Mo., day, yr.)	(d) Sales price (see page D-6 of the instructions)	(e) Cost or other basis (see page D-6 of the instructions)	(f) Gain or (loss) Subtract (e) from (d)
8						

9	Enter your long-term totals, if any, from Schedule D-1, line 9	**9**	
10	**Total long-term sales price amounts.** Add lines 8 and 9 in column (d)	**10**	
11	Gain from Form 4797, Part I; long-term gain from Forms 2439 and 6252; and long-term gain or (loss) from Forms 4684, 6781, and 8824	**11**	
12	Net long-term gain or (loss) from partnerships, S corporations, estates, and trusts from Schedule(s) K-1	**12**	
13	Capital gain distributions. See page D-1 of the instructions	**13**	
14	Long-term capital loss carryover. Enter the amount, if any, from line 13 of your **Capital Loss Carryover Worksheet** on page D-6 of the instructions	**14**	( )
15	**Net long-term capital gain or (loss).** Combine lines 8 through 14 in column (f). Then go to Part III on the back	**15**	

For Paperwork Reduction Act Notice, see Form 1040 instructions.   Cat. No. 11338H   Schedule D (Form 1040) 2005

Part III   **Summary**

16	Combine lines 7 and 15 and enter the result. If line 16 is a loss, skip lines 17 through 20, and go to line 21. If a gain, enter the gain on Form 1040, line 13, and then go to line 17 below . .	**16**	

17   Are lines 15 and 16 **both** gains?
☐ **Yes.** Go to line 18.
☐ **No.** Skip lines 18 through 21, and go to line 22.

18   Enter the amount, if any, from line 7 of the **28% Rate Gain Worksheet** on page D-7 of the instructions . . . . ▶   **18**

19   Enter the amount, if any, from line 18 of the **Unrecaptured Section 1250 Gain Worksheet** on page D-8 of the instructions . . . . ▶   **19**

20   Are lines 18 and 19 **both** zero or blank?
☐ **Yes.** Complete Form 1040 through line 43, and then complete the **Qualified Dividends and Capital Gain Tax Worksheet** on page 38 of the Instructions for Form 1040. **Do not** complete lines 21 and 22 below.
☐ **No.** Complete Form 1040 through line 43, and then complete the **Schedule D Tax Worksheet** on page D-9 of the instructions. **Do not** complete lines 21 and 22 below.

21   If line 16 is a loss, enter here and on Form 1040, line 13, the **smaller** of:

● The loss on line 16 or
● ($3,000), or if married filing separately, ($1,500)   } . . . .   **21**   ( )

Note. When figuring which amount is smaller, treat both amounts as positive numbers.

22   Do you have qualified dividends on Form 1040, line 9b?
☐ **Yes.** Complete Form 1040 through line 43, and then complete the **Qualified Dividends and Capital Gain Tax Worksheet** on page 38 of the Instructions for Form 1040.
☐ **No.** Complete the rest of Form 1040.

Chapter 4

Sections 1231 and 1245: The Yin/Yang of Capital Gains Analysis

When a taxpayer realizes and recognizes gain or loss under section 1001, she first determines whether the gain or loss will be characterized as capital gain or loss under sections 1221 and 1222. As we saw in the last chapter, a gain or loss under section 1001 will be characterized as capital gain or loss if there has been a "sale or exchange" of a "capital asset." If there has been *either* no "sale or exchange," *or*, if there has been a "sale or exchange," but it is of something that is not a "capital asset" under section 1221, there is no capital gain or loss.

The taxpayer's characterization process does not end with the application of sections 1221 and 1222, however. If the section 1001 gain or loss is the result of the sale or exchange or involuntary conversion of certain types of business or investment property, the taxpayer must move next to section 1231 to determine whether that section characterizes such gain or loss as capital or ordinary.[1]

A. The Section 1231 Hotchpot: Special Treatment of "Property Used in the Trade or Business"

Read section 1221(a)(2) again. Section 1221(a)(2) excludes from capital asset status "property, used in [the] trade or business, of a character which is subject to the allowance for depreciation provided in section 167, or real property used in [the] trade or business." Congress added the predecessor of this exclusion to the Code in 1938 during the Great Depression. Falling property values created the likelihood of large capital losses for the many businesses forced to sell business assets at that time. Without the new exception, sales of these assets would have created capital losses. As you learned

---

1. As you will see in the next section, however, later historical developments resulted in the enactment of section 1245, which applies to characterize certain gain on the sale or other disposition of depreciable property as ordinary income. Any gain attributable to depreciation deductions the taxpayer has taken will be characterized under section 1245 as ordinary income before the application of section 1231.

earlier, the Code limits the deductibility of capital losses. Therefore, Congress created the exclusion to ensure that losses sustained on depreciable business property would be characterized as ordinary, and thus deductible in full without limitation.

By the early 1940's, however, the Depression was over and World War II had begun. The exclusion from capital asset status for depreciable business assets became a problem. What had been enacted to assist business taxpayers now turned into a problem for them; the inflation-affected war economy produced gains that were now taxed as ordinary income rather than as capital gains.

The wartime inflation affected most owners of business assets. Whether their assets were appropriated for the war effort or loaned to the government and later destroyed, the amount realized through either government buy-outs or insurance compensation greatly exceeded the business owners' bases.

Shipowners, in particular, whose ships had been appropriated by the United States government for use in the war effort, were affected. Their ships were depreciable business assets, non-capital assets by definition under the predecessor to section 1221(a)(2). Therefore the compensation they received on appropriation or sale resulted in significant gains taxed at ordinary income rates.

Congress enacted the predecessor to section 1231 against this historical backdrop. The theory of section 1231 is to create capital gain if non-capital-asset business property produces a gain upon a sale or exchange, but to continue to provide favorable ordinary loss treatment if sale or exchange of this property produces a loss. Moreover, section 1231 solved the difficulty encountered during the war years when the disposition of business assets was often not by means of a sale or exchange. Section 1231 in effect creates a sale or exchange for business assets and capital assets held in connection with an investment activity if their disposition is the result of an involuntary conversion such as a casualty or condemnation.

Turn now to section 1231 and follow along as we describe its operation. Sections 1231(a)(1) and (2) provide that if the "section 1231 gains" for any taxable year exceed the "section 1231 losses" for that year, all of those gains and losses shall be treated as long-term capital gains and losses. On the other hand, if the taxpayer's "section 1231 losses" exceed her "section 1231 gains" for the year, all of those gains and losses shall not be treated as gains and losses from the sale or exchange of capital assets. Thus, they will be characterized as ordinary gains and losses.

Based on the foregoing description of the history and operation of sections 1231(a)(1) and (2), can you explain why this section has been described as providing taxpayers with the "best of all possible worlds"?[2]

At the outset of your closer examination of section 1231 it is important for you to remember that the section *does not create* gain or loss; it merely *characterizes*, as ordinary or capital, gains and losses that a taxpayer has already realized and recognized under section 1001. Section 1231 is just the next stop on the characterization journey.

---

2. Little did Candide realize that his naive quest for "the best of all possible worlds" would end in the Internal Revenue Code!

Read carefully sections 1231(a)(1)-(4) and (b)(1). Section 1231 applies to the following *disposition events* and *properties*, which comprise the statutory definition of "Section 1231 Gains and Losses" found in section 1231(a)(3):

1. Sale or exchange of "property used in the trade or business," Section 1231(a)(3)(A)(i); and

2. The compulsory or involuntary conversion of "property used in the trade or business," or of any capital asset held for more than 1 year in connection with a trade or business *or* a transaction entered into for profit, Section 1231(a)(3)(A)(ii).

Section 1231(b) sets forth the critical definition of "property used in the trade or business." **Look again at section 1231(b)(1). Compare it to section 1221(a).** What is the relationship between the two sections? Which subsection of section 1221 does the definition of "property used in the trade or business" parallel? What is the difference between the definition of "property used in the trade or business" and the parallel provision appearing in section 1221? Why are they different? (Hint: recall the definition of NCG which is required for application of the favorable capital gain rate.)

Once the taxpayer has identified whether she has recognized gain or loss created by the disposition events with respect to property described in section 1231(a)(3)(A)(i) or (ii), she then nets those gains and losses as required by sections 1231(a)(1) and (2) to determine the character of the gains or losses in question. Tax experts frequently affectionately refer to the netting process as the "hotchpot" in that the relevant gains and losses are jumbled together in one pot to determine whether gains exceed losses or vice-versa. A taxpayer's desired result is for property that would not be a capital asset under the definition of 1221(a)(2) or property that is a capital asset but not disposed of in "sale or exchange" will (1) qualify for preferential capital gain treatment on the up side,[3] or (2) for ordinary loss treatment on the down side. The netting process sets up an all-or-nothing proposition; gains and losses covered under section 1231 will be characterized either as all capital or all ordinary. If gains exceed losses, all gains and losses will be characterized as capital; if losses exceed gains, all losses and gains will be characterized as ordinary.

Examine section 1231(a)(4)(C). It adds a slight bit of complication to the netting process. Before the taxpayer nets her section 1231 gains and losses in the hotchpot, she must do a preliminary netting of certain gains and losses. Tax experts frequently affectionately refer to the preliminary netting process as the "firepot." This process, which appears in section 1231(a)(4)(C), requires taxpayers to net gains and losses from certain involuntary conversions—fire, storm, shipwreck, other casualty, or theft (but not condemnation).[4] The taxpayer must first separate out her gains and losses from involuntary

---

3. Because section 1231 creates capital gain from assets that are either not capital assets or capital assets that have not been disposed of by a sale or exchange transaction, the assets governed by section 1231 are frequently referred to as "quasi-capital assets." Such assets are not capital assets, however.

4. Professors Bittker and MacMahon in their treatise *Federal Income Tax of Individuals* comment as follows about their characterization of the preliminary hotchpot under section 1231 (a)(4)(C) as the "firepot": "Because destruction by fire is probably the most common occasion for a preliminary hotchpot, it is called 'the firepot' by aficionados of New York University Law School's LL.M. program in taxation—a crowd much addicted to insider code words." Bittker and McMahon, *supra* at §33.2. Hence, the authors' affection for this characterization.

Note that property disposed of by condemnation, even though an involuntary conversion, is not netted in the firepot; it is netted in the hotchpot only.

conversions and net them against each other in the firepot. If the losses exceed the gains, section 1231 does not apply to them. Both gains and losses will be treated as ordinary. If the gains exceed the losses, all gains and losses become part of the hotchpot for another round of netting.

Although the firepot adds a bit more complexity to an already complex code section, its operation is favorable to the taxpayer in that involuntary conversions qualify for special treatment by themselves. Thus, a taxpayer characterizes losses from such conversions as ordinary without netting them against other dispositions of business assets, which may be more likely to produce gain.

Follow along (carefully and slowly) with this example that demonstrates how the section 1231 hotchpot and firepot work. Assume Gail, who is engaged in a trade or business as a sole proprietor (she is a free-lance musician), has the following items of gain or loss that she must recognize under section 1001(c):

1. $10,000 gain on the sale of a violin held 2 years and used in her business to teach students;

2. $2,000 loss on the uninsured theft of a guitar held 13 months and used in her business to perform solo concerts;

3. $5,000 gain on the insured fire loss of a coin collection held 5 years for investment; and,

4. $9,000 gain on the condemnation of rental property held 7 years.

Step 1: Determine whether each gain or loss is a "section 1231 gain" or "section 1231 loss" within the meaning of sections 1231(a)(3)(A) or (B). Why is each of the four items a section 1231 gain or loss? What is your authority?

Step 2: Identify which of the four items go into the firepot of section 1231(a)(4)(C) for preliminary netting. Why do items 2 and 3 go into the firepot, but 1 and 4 do not?

Step 3: Net items 2 and 3 in the firepot. The $5,000 gain of item 3 exceeds the $2,000 loss of item 2. Thus, gains exceed losses so both items 2 and 3 go into the hotchpot along with items 1 and 4.

Step 4: Net all four items in the hotchpot of sections 1231 (a)(1) and (2). Gains total $24,000 (the total of items 1, 3, and 4); losses total $2,000 (item 2). Thus, gains exceed losses and all four items are individually characterized as long-term capital gain and loss.

Now test your understanding of section 1231 by assuming that item 2 is a gain of $2,000 and item 3 is a loss of $5,000. How do the new assumptions change, if at all, the characterization of the four items?

As we observed earlier, section 1231 offers taxpayers the best of both worlds: capital gain when gains exceed losses and ordinary loss when losses exceeds gains. A smart taxpayer might think: "Hey, why don't I sell all my loss assets this year so I can report ordinary loss and all my gain assets next year so I can report capital gain?" You've learned enough by this point to suspect that Congress may have addressed this type of tax-avoidance-manipulation. **Look at section 1231(c).** What result for the "smart" taxpayer if in year 1 he has a net section 1231(a)(2) loss of $6,000 and in year 2 he has a net section 1231(a)(1) gain of $7,000? Does your answer change if his gain occurred in year 1 and his loss occurred in year 2?

B. Section 1245:
The Yang to Section 1231's Yin

The alchemy of section 1231, which creates, in certain circumstances, capital gain from assets that are defined specifically as non-capital assets under section 1221, created a problem for the government's revenues. Recall that section 1221(a)(2) provides that property used in a trade or business of a character subject to depreciation is not a capital asset. But if it is held for more than one year, it is "property used in the trade or business" within the meaning of section 1231(b). It is thus eligible for capital gain treatment under the special rule of section 1231(a). The following simple example illustrates the government's problem.

Brian's Problem Revisited

Recall Brian's rotator cuff machine that he bought for his business for $10,000. We depreciated the machine under section 168. By the end of the applicable recovery period, Brian had taken a total of $10,000 in depreciation deductions under section 167. Because these were trade or business deductions of a sole proprietor, they were above-the-line deductions under section 62(a)(1). Each $1 of depreciation deduction reduced Brian's ordinary business income by $1. Assuming that Brian was in the top section 1 tax bracket of 35%, and using a marginal rate analysis, each $1 of depreciation deduction saved him 35 cents in tax. Assuming Brian was in the 35% tax bracket during the applicable recovery period, he would have saved a total of $3,500 in tax over the period. At the end of the recovery period, his adjusted basis in the machine was $0 because section 1016(a)(2) required Brian to reduce his basis each year by the amount of depreciation deduction allowed.

Now assume Brian is able to sell the machine the following year for $10,000. Under section 1001 he will have a realized and recognized gain of $10,000. (A/R $10,000 less A/B $0 equals gain in the amount of $10,000.) What is the character of that gain? Well, the machine is not a capital asset; it is excluded from that status under section 1221(a)(2) because it is property used in the trade or business subject to depreciation.

If the sale were Brian's only tax-significant transaction for the year, the $10,000 would be a section 1231 gain because it is derived from the sale or exchange of property used in the trade or business as defined by section 1231(b). His section 1231 gain of $10,000 would exceed the section 1231 losses of $0 and section 1231(a) would characterize the gain as long-term capital gain. This gain would be eligible for the favorable 15% top tax rate on NCG. Thus, Brian would have to pay tax of only $1,500 on the $10,000 capital gain. This would result in a net tax gain to Brian (and a loss to the government in the same amount) on the use of the machine. The gain to Brian would equal the difference between what he saved in taxes on his business machine by claiming depreciation deductions, $3,500, and the amount he paid in tax upon disposition, $1,500. That is, Brian saved tax of $2,000, and the government suffered a loss in that amount.[5] The government was caught between the Scylla of section 167 and the Charybdis of section 1231! Consider the following case.

FRIBOURG NAVIGATION CO. INC. v. COMMISSIONER
383 U.S. 272 (1966)

MR. CHIEF JUSTICE WARREN delivered the opinion of the Court.

The question presented for determination is whether, as a matter of law, the sale of a depreciable asset for an amount in excess of its adjusted basis at the beginning of the year of sale bars deduction of depreciation for that year.

On December 21, 1955, the taxpayer, Fribourg Navigation Co., Inc., purchased the S.S. *Joseph Feuer*, a used Liberty ship, for $469,000. Prior to the acquisition, the taxpayer obtained a letter ruling from the Internal Revenue Service advising that the Service would accept straight-line depreciation of the ship over a useful economic life of three years, subject to change if

warranted by subsequent experience. The letter ruling also advised that the Service would accept a salvage value on the *Feuer* of $5 per dead-weight ton, amounting to $54,000. Acting in accordance with the ruling the taxpayer computed allowable depreciation, and in its income tax returns for 1955 and 1956 claimed ratable depreciation deductions for the 10-day period from the date of purchase to the end of 1955 and for the full year 1956. The Internal Revenue Service audited the returns for each of these years and accepted the depreciation deductions claimed without adjustment. As a result of these depreciation deductions, the adjusted basis of the ship at the beginning of 1957 was $326,627.73.

In July of 1956, Egypt seized the Suez Canal. During the ensuing hostilities the canal became blocked by sunken vessels, thus forcing ships to take longer routes to ports otherwise reached by going through the canal. The resulting scarcity of available ships to carry cargoes caused sales prices of ships to rise sharply. In January and February of 1957, even the outmoded Liberty ships brought as much as $1,000,000 on the market. In June 1957, the taxpayer accepted an offer to sell the *Feuer* for $700,000. Delivery was accomplished on December 23, 1957, under modified contract terms which reduced the sale price to $695,500.... As it developed, the taxpayer's timing was impeccable—by December 1957, the shipping shortage had abated and Liberty ships were being scrapped for amounts nearly identical to the $54,000 which the taxpayer and the Service had originally predicted for salvage value.

On its 1957 income tax return ... the taxpayer reported a capital gain of $504,239.51 on the disposition of the ship, measured by the selling price less the adjusted basis after taking a depreciation allowance of $135,367.24 for 357 1/2 days of 1957. The taxpayer's deductions from gross income for 1957 included the depreciation taken on the *Feuer*. Although the Commissioner did not question the original ruling as to the useful life and salvage value of the *Feuer* and did not reconsider the allowance of depreciation for 1955 and 1956, he disallowed the entire depreciation deduction for 1957. His position was sustained by a single judge in the Tax Court and, with one dissent, by a panel of the Court of Appeals for the Second Circuit.... We reverse.

---

5. This amount of tax savings does not take into account the additional savings that Brian enjoyed by means of the time-value-of-money advantage he gained through deducting the greater amount over the earlier period.

I.

The Commissioner takes the position here and in a Revenue Ruling first published the day before the trial of this case in the Tax Court (Footnote 1) that the deduction for depreciation in the year of sale of a depreciable asset is limited to the amount by which the adjusted basis of the asset at the beginning of the year exceeds the amount realized from the sale. The Commissioner argues that depreciation deductions are designed to give a taxpayer deductions equal to the "actual net cost" of the asset to the taxpayer, and since the sale price of the *Feuer* exceeded the adjusted basis as of the first of the year, the use of the ship during 1957 'cost' the taxpayer 'nothing.' By tying depreciation to sale price in this manner, the Commissioner has commingled two distinct and established concepts of tax accounting—depreciation of an asset through wear and tear or gradual expiration of useful life and fluctuations in the value of that asset through changes in price levels or market values.

Section 167(a) of the Internal Revenue Code of 1954 provides, in language substantially unchanged in over 50 years of revenue statutes: 'There shall be allowed as a depreciation deduction a reasonable allowance for the exhaustion, wear and tear (including a reasonable allowance for obsolescence)—(1) of property used in the trade or business, or (2) of property held for the production of income.' In *United States v. Ludey* . . . , the Court described depreciation as follows:

> "The depreciation charge permitted as a deduction from the gross income in determining the taxable income of a business for any year represents the reduction, during the year, of the capital assets through wear and tear of the plant used. The amount of the allowance for depreciation is the sum which should be set aside for the taxable year, in order that, at the end of the useful life of the plant in the business, the aggregate of the sums set aside will (with the salvage value) suffice to provide an amount equal to the original cost."

. . . In so defining depreciation, tax law has long recognized the accounting concept that depreciation is a process of estimated allocation which does not take account of fluctuations in valuation through market appreciation.

It is, of course, undisputed that the Commissioner may require redetermination of useful life or salvage value when it becomes apparent that either of these factors has been miscalculated. The fact of sale of an asset at an amount greater than its depreciated basis may be evidence of such a

miscalculation. . . . But the fact alone of sale above adjusted basis does not establish an error in allocation. That is certainly true when, as here, the profit on sale resulted from an unexpected and shortlived, but spectacular, change in the world market.

. . .

II.

This concept of depreciation is reflected in the Commissioner's own regulations. The reasonable allowance provided for in § 167 is explained in Treas. Reg. §1.167(a)-1 as 'that amount which should be set aside for the taxable year in accordance with a reasonably consistent plan . . . so that the aggregate of the amounts set aside, plus the salvage value, will, at the end of the estimated useful life of the depreciable property, equal the cost or other basis of the property. . . . The allowance shall not reflect amounts representing a mere reduction in market value.' Treas. Reg. §1.167(a)-1(c) defines salvage value as the amount, determined at the time of acquisition, which is estimated will be realizable upon sale or when it is no longer useful in the taxpayer's trade or business.

That section continues: "Salvage value shall not be changed at any time after the determination made at the time of acquisition merely because of changes in price levels. However, if there is a redetermination of useful life ... salvage value may be redetermined based upon facts known at the time of such redetermination of useful life." Useful life may be redetermined "only when the change in the useful life is significant and there is a clear and convincing basis for the redetermination." Treas. Reg. §1.167(a)-1(b). This carefully constructed regulatory scheme provides no basis for disallowances of depreciation when no challenge has been made to the reasonableness or accuracy of the original estimates of useful life or salvage value....

The Commissioner relies heavily on Treas. Reg. §1.167(b)-0 providing that the reasonableness of a claim for depreciation shall be determined "upon the basis of conditions known to exist at the end of the period for which the return is made." He contends that after the sale the taxpayer 'knew' that the *Feuer* had "cost" him "nothing" in 1957. This again ignores the distinction between depreciation and gains through market appreciation. The court below admitted that the increase in the value of the ship resulted from circumstances "normally associated with capital gain." The intended interplay of §167 and the capital gains provisions is clearly reflected in Treas. Reg. §1.167(a)-8(a)(1), which provides:

> "Where an asset is retired by sale at arm's length, recognition of gain or loss will be subject to the provisions of sections 1002, 1231, and other applicable provisions of law."

III.

The Commissioner's position represents a sudden and unwarranted about-face from a consistent administrative and judicial practice followed prior to 1962. The taxpayer has cited a wealth of litigated cases and several rulings in which the Commissioner unhesitatingly allowed depreciation in the year of favorable sale. Against this array of authority, the Commissioner contends that he did not "focus" on the issue in most of these instances. This is hardly a persuasive response to the overwhelmingly consistent display of his position. One might well speculate that the Commissioner did not 'focus' on the issue in many cases because he treated it as too well settled for consideration. Moreover, in several instances, the Commissioner did not merely consent to depreciation in the year of sale, but insisted over the taxpayer's objection that it be taken.

. . .

The Commissioner attempts further to explain away the authority aligned against him by stating that most of the cases and rulings prior to 1942 (when capital gain treatment was provided for sales above adjusted basis) are irrelevant since the gain on sale was taxed at the same ordinary income rate that would have been applied had depreciation been disallowed. This contention does not explain away the Commissioner's sudden decision that allowance of such depreciation involves a fundamental error in the basic concept of depreciation. Further, other than his lack of 'focus,' the Commissioner has had no explanation for those cases in which capital gain on sale *was* involved. Even in those cases before this Court upon which the Commissioner relies for support of his theory, depreciation was willingly allowed in the year of sale....

. . .

IV.

Over the same extended period of years during which the foregoing administrative and judicial precedent was accumulating, Congress repeatedly re-enacted the depreciation provision without significant change. Thus, beyond the generally understood scope of the depreciation provision itself, the Commissioner's prior long-standing and consistent administrative practice must be deemed to have received congressional approval....

The legislative history in this area makes it abundantly clear that Congress was cognizant of the revenue possibilities in sales above depreciated cost. In 1942 Congress restored capital gain treatment to sales of depreciable assets. (Footnote 11) The accompanying House Report stated that it would be 'an undue hardship' on taxpayers who were able to sell depreciable property at a gain over depreciated cost to treat such gain as ordinary income. H.R.Rep.No. 2333, 77th Cong., 2d Sess., 54 (1942). This, of course, is *pro tanto* the effect of disallowing depreciation in the year of sale above adjusted basis. It would be strange indeed, especially in light of the House Report, to conclude that Congress labored to create a tax provision which, in application to depreciable property, could by administrative fiat be made applicable only to sales of assets for amounts exceeding their basis at the beginning of the year of sale, and then only to the excess. In succeeding years Congress was repeatedly asked to enact legislation treating gains on sales of depreciated property as ordinary income; (Footnote 12) it declined to do so until 1962.

In 1961, in his Tax Message to Congress, the President observed that existing law permitted taxpayers to depreciate assets below their market value and, upon sale, to treat the difference as capital gain. (Footnote 13) The Secretary of the

Treasury concurred in this position. The exhibits appended not only contain no mention of the Commissioner's power to require recalculation of depreciation in the year of sale, but refute the existence of such power. In example after example cited by the Treasury, the taxpayer had depreciated an asset, sold it for an amount in excess of its depreciated basis, and treated the difference as capital gain. The Treasury asserted that existing law permitted this practice, and made no mention of the power which the Commissioner now alleges he possesses to disallow year-of-sale depreciation.

In 1962 Congress enacted § 1245 of the Internal Revenue Code of 1954, providing that gain on future dispositions of depreciable personal property be treated as ordinary income to the extent of depreciation taken. For post-1962 transactions § 1245 applies to the situation which occurred in the instant case and would produce greater revenue. The taxpayer must report as ordinary income *all* depreciation recouped on sale....

V.

Finally, the Commissioner's position contains inconsistencies.... [T]he Commissioner apparently will not extend his new theory to situations where it would benefit the taxpayer. If a depreciable asset is sold for *less* than its adjusted basis, it would seem to follow from the Commissioner's construction that the asset has "cost" the taxpayer an additional amount and that further depreciation should be permitted. However, Revenue Ruling 69-92 does not extend to such a case and the Commissioner has expressly refused to make it do so. (Footnote 17)

...

In light of the foregoing, we conclude that the depreciation claimed by the taxpayer for 1957 was erroneously disallowed.

Reversed.

FOOTNOTES:

1. Rev. Rul. 62-92, 1962-1 Cum. Bull. 29.... That Ruling provides in part:

" ... the deduction for depreciation of an asset used in the trade or business or in the production of income shall be adjusted in the year of disposition so that the deduction, otherwise properly allowable for such year under the taxpayer's method of accounting for depreciation, is limited to the amount, if any, by which the adjusted basis of the property at the beginning of such year exceeds the amount realized from sale or exchange."

11. Int. Rev. Code, 1939, § 117(j), 56 Stat. 846 (now Int. Rev.

Code, 1954, § 1231).

12. See, e.g., Hearings before the House Ways and Means Committee, 80th Cong., 1st Sess., on Revenue Revisions, pt. 5, p. 3756 (1948), at which the Treasury recommended that gains on sales of depreciable assets should be subject to ordinary income taxation to the extent the gains arose from accelerated depreciation; Hearings before the Senate Finance Committee, 83d

Cong., 2d Sess., on H. R. 8300, pt. 3, p. 1324 (1954), at which Congress was asked by the American Institute of Accountants to enact that all gains on sales of depreciable assets be treated as ordinary income. See also Treasury Department Release A-761, February 15, 1960.

13. The President stated:

"Another flaw which should be corrected at this time relates to the taxation of gains on the sale of depreciable business property. Such gains are now taxed at the preferential rate applicable to capital gains, even though they represent ordinary income.

"This situation arises because the statutory rate of depreciation may not coincide with the actual decline in the value of the asset. While the taxpayer holds the property, depreciation is taken as a deduction from ordinary income. Upon its resale, where the amount of depreciation allowable exceeds the decline in the actual value of the asset so that a gain occurs, this gain under present law is taxed at the preferential capital gains rate. The advantages resulting from this practice have been increased by the liberalization of depreciation rates.

"I therefore recommend that capital gains treatment be withdrawn from gains on the disposition of depreciable property, both personal and real property, to the extent that depreciation has been deducted for such property by the seller in previous years, permitting only the excess of the sales price over the original cost to be treated as a capital gain." Message on Taxation, Hearings before the Committee on Ways and Means, House of Representatives, H. R. Doc. No. 140, 87th Cong., 1st Sess., 11 (1961).

17. *In Engineers Limited Pipeline Co.*, 44 T. C. 226 (1965), the

taxpayer contended that he should get a further depreciation deduction on assets which he sold for less than their depreciated basis. The Commissioner disallowed the additional deduction....

Now consider the following questions concerning *Fribourg Navigation*.

1. What is a Liberty ship?

2. Was the ship a capital asset in the taxpayer's hands?

3. How did the taxpayer characterize the gain it realized on disposition of the ship in 1957? What was the taxpayer's authority for its position?

4. The taxpayer had structured the transaction to conform to a provision applicable to corporations that provided for non-recognition of gain. Therefore, it reported the gain on its return for information purposes only. If the taxpayer did not have to report gain on the transaction, why would the Service take the position it took in the case?

5. Suppose the transaction had been one in which the taxpayer would have to recognize gain. Would there have been a benefit to the taxpayer in claiming depreciation in the year of sale?

As the Supreme Court noted in *Fribourg Navigation Co., Inc,* in 1962 Congress acted to stop the whipsaw effect of depreciation by enacting section 1245. Although section 1245 appears on its face to be complicated, its principle is simply stated: to the extent that the gain realized on the sale or other disposition of a depreciable asset represents recovery of previously taken depreciation deductions, that gain must be characterized as ordinary income rather than as capital gain. To the extent that the gain on disposition merely reflects previously taken depreciation deductions, the gain must be "recaptured" as ordinary. A reversal of the process, as it were. Thus, in the case of Brian's rotator cuff machine, if he sells the machine for $10,000, all of his gain of $10,000 represents previously-taken depreciation deductions, and all of the $10,000 gain will be characterized as ordinary under section 1245.

What if Brian sells the machine for more than $10,000? The recognized gain in excess of his original purchase price of $10,000 will be eligible for characterization under section 1231. Thus, if Brian sells the machine for $15,000, $10,000 of the gain will be characterized as ordinary under section 1245 and the remaining $5,000 of gain will go into the section 1231 hotchpot for netting.

Look at sections 1245(a)(1)-(3). Assume that Brian sells his machine at the end of year 3. What result under the terms of section 1245 if: (1) he had elected to use accelerated cost recovery and he sold the machine for: (a) $8,000; (b) $11,000; or (c) $2,000; or (2) he elected the straight line method and he sold the machine for the same three alternative amounts. Is the machine "section 1245 property"? What is its "recomputed basis"? What is the final result for all six alternatives?

One final point. Does section 1245 apply to depreciable real property? Is a building "section 1245 property"? **Look at sections 1245(a)(3), and 1250(a)(1), (b)(1), and (c).** What result to Brian under sections 1250 and 1231 if he bought a building for $500,000 in January 1998, to house his business, and he sold it for $600,000 in December 2002? (Assume $100,000 is allocable to the land on purchase and sale.)

C. Ben's Problem: Placing Capital Gains and Losses into "The Big Picture"

Work on the following final problem to test your understanding of the relationship among all the capital gains and losses provisions that you have just studied. Assume for purposes of the problem that all sales of assets occurred in the current year.

Ben works as a nurse for Gotham Hospital. His salary is $75,000 per year. Ben sold the car he used to drive to and from work. He bought it five years ago for

$12,000; he sold it for $2,500. He then leased a new car for $275 per month to drive to and from work.

In his spare time, Ben also refinishes floors. To drive to his floor jobs, he bought a used van three years ago for $12,000. He uses the van exclusively for his floor refinishing business. In the current year, he earned $15,500 and incurred $3,500 in ordinary and necessary expenses. He sold an electronic floor sander for $12,000. He had bought it at a bargain for $10,000. His basis at the time of sale was $4,000. He also sold a hand sander for $1,000. He had acquired this sander for $5,000 and his basis at the time of sale was $1,920. Ben also suffered an uninsured theft loss of a fine-dust vacuum cleaner in the amount of $2,500.

Ben also sold some stock. He sold BigCo, Inc. stock for $5,000 that he had purchased more than 10 years ago for $1,000. He sold Technocrat, Inc. stock for $1,000 that he had purchased several years ago for $15,000.

Ben also had stock in OhMy Corp. that he had purchased for $10,000 four years ago. The stock became worthless in the current year.

1. Determine Ben's gains and losses for the current year.

Which are capital, which are ordinary?

2. Determine Ben's gross income for the current year.

3. Determine Ben's adjusted gross income for the year. You may assume that depreciation deductions for the truck, sanders, and fine-dust vacuum total $15,130.

4. Does Ben have NCG?

We have revisited the "proper" rate in this Part V by focusing exclusively on the special treatment of capital gains and losses of individuals. Although the issue appears in other forms in the Code, for individuals, this is the most important occasion for a reexamination.

Almost from the beginning of the income tax there has been widespread agreement that certain types of income should produce a different rate of tax. Since 1921, the tax law has provided for preferential rates on items of income termed "capital gains." The difference in the rate of tax on these items of income from the rates applicable to other income items have added enormous complexity to the tax law and have often enticed taxpayers to attempt to fit their items of income into the favorable rate schedule and their losses into the higher regular rate schedule.

VI. Some Consequences of Debt

Introduction

Most asset acquisitions in modern day commerce involve debt. It is frequently necessary for a taxpayer to incur debt in order to finance the acquisition of property—not only to acquire trade or business or investment property, but personal-use property as well. Thus, it is important for you to come away from a basic income tax course knowing some of the fundamentals with respect to the issues involved when a taxpayer incurs debt to acquire an asset. The following materials are intended to give you a brief overview of the consequences of debt in the context of the acquisition and ownership of various assets, including real estate.

Several important issues pervade the treatment of debt: what constitutes debt, and when and whether a taxpayer should be able to deduct the cost incurred for the use of money ("interest"). Issues concerning debt arise in both profit-seeking activities and property transfers. From the borrower's viewpoint, the issues often arise from the desire to deduct an amount of purported interest in order to protect income from tax; from the lender's viewpoint, the issues often arise from the desire to convert ordinary income into capital gain or into income that is not taxable at all.

Debt involves two components: principal and interest. You must analyze the components from the viewpoints of both borrower and lender. We first saw some fundamentals of debt when we studied the *Glenshaw Glass* test for gross income. When the borrower borrows money, she has no income because she has no true dominion and control in the *Glenshaw Glass* sense; she must repay the loan. Of course, during the life of the loan, the borrower must pay the lender for the right to use the money, a sort of "rent," which we call interest. Therefore, we must also examine interest in the context of its payment by the borrower to the lender, and its receipt by the lender from the borrower. Interest is gross income to the lender (under *Glenshaw Glass*). For the lender, the issues are of identification and timing of inclusion (remember OID). For the borrower, the primary issue is deductibility. We must also examine the consequences if the borrower fails to repay the loan, or fails to make the required payments of interest. If the borrower fails to repay, she is enriched; (and, for that reason, relief from debt is gross income).[1] While the lender has no income if the borrower repays, (repayment is simply a return of capital),[2] what result to the lender if the borrower does not repay the princi-

---

1. Recall section 61(a)(12). But remember, too, section 108.
2. You can prove, once again, these principles to yourself by creating balance sheets for both borrower and lender. If Aaron borrows $500 from Tempti Finance Co., promising to repay the loan at the end of one year with 6% simple interest, he has no income when the loan is made. His net worth does not change. Nor does it change when he repays the principal to the bank. But, what about his payment of the 6% interest? Payment of the 6% interest does diminish his net worth; it is an expense. Is the expense deductible? When? There were also no income consequences to the bank when Aaron borrowed the money. Its net worth also did not change. When Aaron repays the loan,

pal or the interest? If the borrower fails to make a complete repayment, the lender should be entitled to account for the diminishment in his net worth in some fashion; for him it is the opposite of enrichment in the *Glenshaw Glass* sense. The Code accomplishes this by allowing the lender to claim a deduction for the bad debt.[3]

As noted, the borrower has no gross income when she borrows. But, suppose she buys a machine with the borrowed money. How many TOADs has she invested? Can she take a deduction for depreciation if she uses the machine in a trade or business? Recall Brian. If Brian had borrowed $9,000 of the $10,000 he invested in his rotator cuff machine, what would have been his basis for calculating depreciation? What the taxpayer does with borrowed money raises several issues: basis in the asset (apparent conflict with the TOAD principle), and a related question: will he be able to deduct interest?

Of course, the interest that borrowing produces is merely one expense associated with the ownership of property. What about other expenses associated with owning property? One of the best illustrative examples of the consequences of debt for federal income tax purposes is in real estate transactions. Real estate transactions are also a good way to examine the treatment of other expenses associated with the ownership of property. So, we will employ two typical real estate transactions to demonstrate many of the issues of debt; to act as a review of many of the other topics we have examined (and hark back to Carole's problem); and to introduce you to a few more common tax issues.

These materials place you at the threshold of more advanced tax issues. You should view the problems as an opportunity to apply all the basic rules and Code-reading skills that you have worked hard to master in this course. After examining the two real estate problems, you will have an opportunity to see how these transactions fit into the entire tax calculation outline with which we began in the Introduction to this book.

---

the bank is enriched, but only by the amount of interest he pays. The bank, therefore, has interest income. When and how should it report the income?

3. **Read section 166 of the Code, which provides the rules.**

Chapter 1

What Is Debt?

There is generally no issue concerning the existence of debt. In the common borrowing transaction of the type noted in footnote 2 of the Introduction to this Part VI, there is rarely any question of whether a true debt exists. During the "heyday" of tax shelters, however, promoters often structured investments to create large deductions for limited partners (who were protected from the general liabilities of the partnership). These deductions often took the form of pre-payments of interest and fees of various kinds, generally deductible by cash basis taxpayers. The ingenuity of taxpayers (and their advisers) was unbounded. Taxpayers pursued extremely creative plans to produce tax deductions at little or no real risk to their capital. Read the following case.

KNETSCH v. UNITED STATES
364 U.S. 361 (1960)

Mr. Justice BRENNAN delivered the opinion of the Court.

This case presents the question of whether deductions from gross income claimed on petitioners' 1953 and 1954 joint federal income tax returns, of $143,465 in 1953 and of $147,105 in 1954, for payments made by petitioner, Karl F. Knetsch, to Sam Houston Life Insurance Company, constituted "interest paid ... on indebtedness" within the meaning of §23(b) of the Internal Revenue Code of 1939, and §163(a) of the Internal Revenue Code of 1954. (Footnote 1) The Commissioner of Internal Revenue disallowed the deductions and determined a deficiency for each year. The petitioners paid the deficiencies and brought this action for refund in the District Court for the Southern District of California. The District Court rendered judgment for the United States, and the Court of Appeals for the Ninth Circuit affirmed....

On December 11, 1953, the insurance company sold Knetsch ten 30-year maturity deferred annuity savings bonds, each in the face amount of $400,000 and bearing interest at 2 1/2% compounded annually. The purchase price was $4,004,000. Knetsch gave the company his check for $4,000, and signed $4,000,000 of nonrecourse annuity loan notes for the balance. The notes bore 3 1/2% interest and were secured by the annuity bonds. The interest was payable in advance, and Knetsch on the same day prepaid the first year's interest, which was $140,000. Under the Table of Cash and Loan Values made part of the bonds, their cash or loan value at December 11, 1954, the end of the first contract year, was to be $4,100,000. The contract terms, however, permitted Knetsch to borrow any excess of this value above his indebtedness without waiting until December 11, 1954. Knetsch took advantage of this provision only five days after the purchase. On December 16, 1953, he received from the company $99,000 of the $100,000 excess over his $4,000,000 indebtedness, for which he gave his notes bearing 3 1/2% interest. This interest was also payable in advance and on the same day he prepaid the first year's interest of $3,465. In their joint return for 1953, the petitioners deducted the sum of the two interest payments, that is $143,465, as "interest paid ... within the taxable year on indebtedness," under § 23(b) of the 1939 Code.

The second contract year began on December 11, 1954, when interest in advance of $143,465 was payable by Knetsch on his aggregate indebtedness of $4,099,000. Knetsch paid this amount on December 27, 1954. Three days later, on December 30, he received from the company cash in the amount of $104,000, the difference less $1,000 between his then $4,099,000 indebtedness and the cash or loan value of the bonds of $4,204,000 on December 11, 1955. He gave the company appropriate notes and prepaid the interest thereon of $3,640. In their joint return for the taxable year 1954 the petitioners deducted the sum of the two interest payments, that is $147,105, as "interest paid ... within the taxable year on indebtedness," under § 163(a) of the 1954 Code.

The tax years 1955 and 1956 are not involved in this proceeding, but a recital of the events of those years is necessary to complete the story of the transaction. On December 11, 1955, the start of the third contract year, Knetsch became obligated to pay $147,105 as prepaid interest on an indebtedness which now totalled $4,203,000. He paid this interest on December 28, 1955. On the same date he received $104,000 from the company. This was $1,000 less than the difference between his indebtedness and the cash or loan value of the bonds of $4,308,000 at December 11, 1956. Again he gave the company notes upon which he prepaid interest of $3,640. Petitioners claimed a deduction on their 1955 joint return for the aggregate of the payments, or $150,745.

Knetsch did not go on with the transaction for the fourth contract year beginning December 11, 1956, but terminated it on December 27, 1956. His indebtedness at that time totalled $4,307,000. The cash or loan value of the bonds was the $4,308,000 value at December 11, 1956, which had been the basis of the "loan" of December 28, 1955. He surrendered the bonds and his indebtedness was canceled. He received the difference of $1,000 in cash.

The contract called for a monthly annuity of $90,171 at maturity (when Knetsch would be 90 years of age) or for such smaller amount as would be produced by the cash or loan value after deduction of the then existing indebtedness. It was stipulated that if Knetsch had held the bonds to maturity and continued annually to borrow the net cash value less $1,000, the sum available for the annuity at maturity would be $1,000 ($8,388,000 cash or loan value less $8,387,000 of indebtedness), enough to provide an annuity of only $43 per month.

The trial judge made findings that "[t]here was no commercial economic substance to the ... transaction," that the parties did not intend that Knetsch "become indebted to Sam Houston," that "[n]o indebtedness of [Knetsch] was created by any of the ... transactions," and that "[n]o economic gain could be achieved from the purchase of these bonds without regard to the tax consequences...." His conclusion of law ... was that "[w]hile in form the payments to Sam Houston were compensation for the use or forbearance of money, they were not in substance. As a payment of interest, the transaction was a sham."

We first examine the transaction between Knetsch and the insurance company to determine whether it created an "indebtedness" within the meaning of § 23(b) of the 1939 Code and § 163(a) of the 1954 Code, or whether, as the trial court found, it was a sham. We put aside a finding by the District Court that Knetsch's "only motive in purchasing these 10 bonds was to attempt to secure an interest deduction." As was said in *Gregory v. Helvering*, 293 U.S. 465, 469...."The legal right of a taxpayer to decrease the amount of what otherwise would be his taxes, or altogether avoid them, by means which the law permits, cannot be doubted.... But the question for determination is whether what was done, apart from the tax motive, was the thing which the statute intended."

When we examine "what was done" here, we see that Knetsch paid the insurance company $294,570 during the two taxable years involved and received $203,000 back in the form of "loans." What did Knetsch get for the out-of-pocket difference of $91,570? In form he had an annuity contract with a so-called guaranteed cash value at maturity of $8,388,000, which would produce monthly annuity payments of $90,171, or substantial life insurance proceeds in the event of his death before maturity.

This, as we have seen, was a fiction, because each year Knetsch's annual borrowings kept the net cash value, on which any annuity or insurance payments would depend, at the relative pittance of $1,000. (Footnote 3) Plainly, therefore, Knetsch transaction with the insurance company did "not appreciably affect his beneficial interest except to reduce his tax...." ... For it is patent that there was nothing of substance to be realized by Knetsch from this transaction beyond a tax deduction. What he was ostensibly "lent" back was in reality only the rebate of a substantial part of the so-called "interest" payments. The $91,570 difference retained by the company was its fee for providing the facade of "loans" whereby the petitioners sought to reduce their 1953 and 1954 taxes in the total sum of $233,297.68. There may well be single premium annuity arrangements with nontax substance which create an "indebtedness" for the purposes of §23(b) of the 1939 Code and §163(a) of the 1954 Code. But this one is a sham.

...

The judgment of the Court of Appeals is

Affirmed.

FOOTNOTES:

1. The relevant words of the two sections are the same, namely that there shall be allowed as a deduction "All interest paid or accrued within the taxable year on indebtedness...."

3. Petitioners argue further that in 10 years the net cash value of the bonds would have exceeded the amounts Knetsch paid as "interest." This contention, however, is predicated on the wholly unlikely assumption that Knetsch would have paid off in cash the original $4,000,000 "loan."

Now consider the following questions concerning *Knetsch.*

1. Describe the arrangement between Mr. Knetsch and the Sam Houston Life Insurance Co.

2. Why did Mr. Knetsch enter into this arrangement?

3. Why did the insurance company enter into this arrangement?

4. After reading *Knetsch,* can you define "indebtedness" for the purpose of section 163? Did the Court?

5. Note that the Court in *Knetsch* referred approvingly to the famous observation in *Gregory v. Helvering* that a taxpayer has a right to attempt to minimize taxes. Then why did the plan engaged in by Knetsch and the insurance company not succeed?

Now, return to Part V. There you read the decision of the Tax Court in the case of *Estate of Franklin*. Recall that the partnership had entered into a transaction with the Romneys which it attempted to characterize as a purchase by the partnership, using non-recourse debt. The Tax Court recharacterized the transaction as an option to purchase in the future. How else might the court have characterized the transaction? Read the opinion of the appeals court in the same case.

ESTATE OF FRANKLIN v. COMMISSIONER
544 F.2d 1045 (9th Cir. 1976)

SNEED, Circuit Judge:

This case involves another effort on the part of the commissioner to curb the use of real estate tax shelters. (Footnote 1) In this instance he seeks to disallow deductions for the taxpayers' distributive share of losses reported by a limited partnership with respect to its acquisition of a motel and related property. These "losses" have their origin in deductions for depreciation and interest claimed with respect to the motel and related property. These deductions were disallowed by the Commissioner on the ground either that the acquisition was a sham or that the entire acquisition transaction was in substance the purchase by the partnership of an option to acquire the motel and related property on January 15, 1979. The Tax court held that the transaction constituted an option exercisable in 1979 and disallowed the taxpayers' deductions. *Estate of Charles T. Franklin*, 64 T.C. 752 (1975). We affirm this disallowance although our approach differs somewhat from that of the Tax Court.

The interest and depreciation deductions were taken by Twenty-Fourth Property Associates (hereinafter referred to as Associates), a California limited partnership of which Charles T. Franklin and seven other doctors were the limited partners. The deductions flowed from the purported "purchase" by Associates of the Thunderbird Inn, an Arizona motel, from Wayne L. Romney and Joan E. Romney (hereinafter referred to as the Romneys) on November 15, 1968.

Under a document entitled "Sales Agreement," the Romneys agreed to "sell" the Thunderbird Inn to Associates for $1,224,000. The property would be paid for over a period of ten years, with interest on any unpaid balance of seven and one-half percent per annum. "Prepaid interest" in the amount of $75,000 was payable immediately; monthly principal and interest installments of $9,045.36 would be paid for approximately the first ten years, with Associates required to make a balloon payment at the end of the ten years of the difference between the remaining purchase price, forecast as $975,000, and any mortgages then outstanding against the property.

The purchase obligation of Associates to the Romneys was nonrecourse; the Romneys' only remedy in the event of default would be forfeiture of the partnership's interest. The sales agreement was recorded in the local county. A warranty deed was placed in an escrow account, along with a quitclaim deed from Associates to the Romneys, both documents to be delivered either to Associates upon full payment of the purchase price, or to the Romneys upon default.

The sale was combined with a leaseback of the property by Associates to the Romneys; Associates therefore never took physical possession. The lease payments were designed to approximate closely the principal and interest payments with the consequence that with the exception of the $75,000 prepaid interest payment no cash would cross between Associates and Romneys until the balloon payment. The lease was on a net basis;

thus, the Romneys were responsible for all of the typical expenses of owning the motel property including all utility costs, taxes, assessments, rents, charges, and levies of "every name, nature and kind whatsoever." The Romneys also were to be responsible for the first and second mortgages until the final purchase installment was made; the Romneys could, and indeed did, place additional mortgages on the property without the permission of Associates. Finally, the Romneys were allowed to propose new capital improvements which Associates would be required to either build themselves or allow the Romneys to construct with compensating modifications in rent or purchase price.

In holding that the transaction between Associates and the Romneys more nearly resembled an option than a sale, the Tax Court emphasized that Associates had the power at the end of ten years to walk away from the transaction and merely lose its $75,000 "prepaid interest payment." It also pointed out that a deed was never recorded and that the "benefits and burdens of ownership" appeared to remain with the Romneys. Thus, the sale was combined with a leaseback in which no cash would pass; the Romneys remained responsible under the mortgages, which they could increase; and the Romneys could make capital improvements. (Footnote 2) The Tax Court further justified its "option" characterization by reference to the nonrecourse nature of the purchase money debt and the nice balance between the rental and purchase money payments.

Our emphasis is different from that of the Tax Court. We believe the characteristics set out above can exist in a situation in which the sale imposes upon the purchaser a genuine indebtedness within the meaning of section 167(a), Internal Revenue Code of 1954, which will support both interest and depreciation deductions. (Footnote 3) They substantially so existed in *Hudspeth v. Commissioner*, 509 F.2d 1224 (9th Cir. 1975) in which parents entered into sale-leaseback transactions with their children. The children paid for the property by executing nonnegotiable notes and mortgages equal to the fair market value of the property; state law proscribed deficiency judgments in case of default, limiting the parents' remedy to foreclosure of the property. The children had no funds with which to make mortgage payments; instead, the payments were offset in part by the rental payments, with the difference met by gifts from the parents to their children. Despite these characteristics this court held that there was a bona fide indebtedness on which the children, to the extent of the rental payments, could base interest deductions....

In none of these cases, however, did the taxpayer fail to demonstrate that the purchase price was at least approximately equivalent to the fair market value of the property. Just such a failure occurred here. The Tax Court explicitly found that on the basis of the facts before it the value of the property could not be estimated. 64 T.C. at 767–768. (Footnote 4) In our view this defect in the taxpayers' proof is fatal.

Reason supports our perception. An acquisition such as that of Associates if at a price approximately equal to the fair market value of the property under ordinary circumstances would rather quickly yield an equity in the property which the purchaser could not prudently abandon. This is the stuff of substance. It meshes with the form of the transaction and constitutes a sale.

No such meshing occurs when the purchase price exceeds a demonstrably reasonable estimate of the fair market value. Payments on the principal of the purchase price yield no equity so long as the unpaid balance of the purchase price exceeds the then existing fair market value. Under these circumstances the purchaser by abandoning the transaction can lose no more than a mere chance to acquire an equity in the future should the value of the acquired property increase. While this chance undoubtedly influenced the

Tax Court's determination that the transaction before us constitutes an option, we need only point out that its existence fails to supply the substance necessary to justify treating the transaction as a sale *ab initio*. It is not necessary to the disposition of this case to decide the tax consequences of a transaction such as that before us if in a subsequent year the fair market value of the property increases to an extent that permits the purchaser to acquire an equity. (Footnote 5)

Authority also supports our perception. It is fundamental that "depreciation is not predicated upon ownership of property *but rather upon an investment in property. Gladding Dry Goods Co.*, 2 BTA 336 (1925)." *Mayerson, supra* at 350 (italics added). No such investment exists when payments of the purchase price in accordance with the design of the parties yield no equity to the purchaser.... In the transaction before us and during the taxable years in question the purchase price payments by Associates have not been shown to constitute an *investment in the property*. Depreciation was properly disallowed. Only the Romneys had an investment in the property.

Authority also supports disallowance of the interest deductions. This is said even though it has long been recognized that the absence of personal liability for the purchase money debt secured by a mortgage on the acquired property does not deprive the debt of its character as a bona fide debt obligation able to support an interest deduction. *Mayerson, supra* at 352. However, this is no longer true when it appears that the debt has economic significance only if the property substantially appreciates in value prior to the date at which a very large portion of the purchase price is to be discharged. Under these circumstances the purchaser has not secured "the use or forbearance of money." ... Nor has the seller advanced money or forborne its use.... Prior to the date at which the balloon payment on the purchase price is required, and assuming no substantial increase in the fair market value of the property, the absence of personal liability on the debt reduces the transaction in economic terms to a mere chance that a genuine debt obligation may arise. This is not enough to justify an interest deduction. To justify the deduction the debt must exist; potential existence will not do. For debt to exist, the purchaser, in the absence of personal liability, must confront a situation in which it is presently reasonable from an economic point of view for him to make a capital investment in the amount of the unpaid purchase price. *See Mayerson, supra* at 352. Associates, during the taxable years in question, confronted no such situation. Compare *Crane v. Commissioner*, 331 U.S. 1, 11–12, ... (1947).

Our focus on the relationship of the fair market value of the property to the unpaid purchase price should not be read as premised upon the belief that a sale is not a sale if the purchaser pays too much. Bad bargains from the buyer's point of view as well as sensible bargains from buyer's, but exceptionally good from the seller's point of view do not thereby cease to be sales.... We intend our holding and explanation thereof to be understood as limited to transactions substantially similar to that now before us.

AFFIRMED

FOOTNOTES:

1. An early skirmish in this particular effort appears in *Manuel D. Mayerson*, 47 T.C. 340 (1966), which the Commissioner lost. The Commissioner attacked the substance of a nonrecourse sale, but based his attack on the nonrecourse and long-term nature of the purchase money note, without focusing on whether the sale was made at an unrealistically high price. In his acquiescence to *Mayerson*, 1969-2 Cum.Bull. xxiv, the Commissioner recognized that the fundamental issue in these cases generally will be whether the property has been "acquired" at an artificially high price, having little relation to its fair market value. "The Service emphasizes that its acquiescence in *Mayerson* is based on the

particular facts in the case and will not be relied upon in the disposition of other cases except where it is clear that the property has been acquired at its fair market value in an arm's length transaction creating a bona fide purchase and a bona fide debt obligation." Rev.Rul. 69-77, 1969-1 Cum.Bull. 59.

2. There was evidence that not all of the benefits and burdens of ownership remained with the Romneys. Thus, for example, the leaseback agreement appears to provide that any condemnation award will go to Associates. Exhibit 6-F, at p. 5.

3. Counsel differed as to whether the Tax Court's decision that the transaction was not a sale, but at best only an option, is reviewable by this court as a question of law or of fact. We agree with other circuits that, while the characteristics of a transaction are questions of fact, whether those characteristics constitute a sale *for tax purposes* is a question of law....

4. The Tax Court found that appellants had "not shown that the purported sales price of $1,224,000 (or any other price) had any relationship to the actual market value of the motel property...." 64 T.C. at 767.

Petitioners spent a substantial amount of time at trial attempting to establish that, whatever the actual market value of the property, Associates acted in the good faith *belief* that the market value of the property approximated the selling price. However, this evidence only goes to the issue of sham and does not supply substance to this transaction. "Save in those instances where the statute itself turns on intent, a matter so real as taxation must depend on objective realities, not on the varying subjective beliefs of individual taxpayers." ...

In oral argument it was suggested by the appellants that neither the Tax Court nor they recognized the importance of fair market value during the presentation of evidence and that this hampered the full and open development of this issue. However, upon an examination of the record, we are satisfied that the taxpayers recognized the importance of presenting objective evidence of the fair market value and were awarded ample opportunity to present their proof; appellants merely failed to present clear and admissible evidence that fair market value did indeed approximate the purchase price. Such evidence of fair market value as was relied upon by the appellants, *viz.* two appraisals, one completed in 1968 and a second in 1971, even if fully admissible as evidence of the truth of the estimates of value appearing therein, does not require us to set aside the Tax Court's finding. As the Tax Court found, the 1968 appraisal was "error-filled, sketchy" and "obviously suspect." 64 T.C. at 767 n. 13. The 1971 appraisal had little relevancy as to 1968 values. On the other side, there existed cogent evidence indicating that the fair market value was substantially less than the purchase price. This evidence included (i) the Romneys' purchase of the stock of two corporations, one of which wholly-owned the motel, for approximately $800,000 in the year preceding the "sale" to Associates ($660,000 of which was allocable to the sale property, according to Mr. Romney's estimate), and (ii) insurance policies on the property from 1967 through 1974 of only $583,200, $700,000, and $614,000. 64 T.C. at 767–768.

Given that it was the appellants' burden to present evidence showing that the purchase price did not exceed the fair market value and that he had a fair opportunity to do so, we see no reason to remand this case for further proceedings.

5. These consequences would include a determination of the property basis of the acquired property at the date the increments to the purchaser's equity commenced.

Now consider the following questions concerning the Ninth Circuit's decision in *Estate of Franklin*.

1. How does the view of the Ninth Circuit differ from the view of the Tax Court?

2. What is the significance of the declaration of the court that: "It is not necessary to the disposition of this case to decide the tax consequences of a transaction such as that before us if in a subsequent year the fair market value of the property increases to an extent that permits the purchaser to acquire an equity"? Does the observation suggest that if the transaction remains in place, the taxpayers might be able to claim depreciation and interest deductions in a future year?

3. Is the concept of "equity" used by the court in this case the same as the concept of "equity" you first encountered in Part II when we considered Larry's balance sheet?

4. What is the significance of the fact that there was no third-party lender? Would a third-party lender have made this non-recourse loan?[1]

5. Would the partnership have entered into the same transaction if the loan had been made with recourse?

6. Was the insurance company in *Knetsch* in the same position as the Romneys?

As you learned in Part IV, Congress has now greatly limited some of these creative opportunities for tax savings through, for example, passage of limits on the deductibility of pre-paid interest by cash basis taxpayers. But even when there is no issue as to the existence of debt, other issues arise. Identification of the existence of indebtedness marks only the beginning of the necessary careful examination of the relationship between borrower and lender and the terms to which they have agreed.

---

1. Note that the court observed: "The purchase obligation of Associates to the Romneys was nonrecourse; the Romneys' only remedy in the event of default would be forfeiture of the partnership's interest." Therefore, the partnership (and the partners) never risked other assets if the partnership failed to make payments on the non-recourse loan.

Chapter 2

What Is Deductible Interest?

Calculation of the appropriate amount of interest marks the beginning of another stage in the analysis of the deal into which borrower and seller have entered. Several important examples of these issues appear earlier in the book: below-market loans and original issue discount. Once the amount of interest is known, the questions of how much income the lender must report and how much, if any, the borrower may claim as a deduction, remain. Should a borrower always be entitled to deduct the interest? Read the following case.

GOLDSTEIN v. COMMISSIONER
364 F.2d 734 (2d Cir. 1966)

WATERMAN, Circuit Judge.

Tillie Goldstein and her husband (Footnote 1) petition to review a decision of the Tax Court disallowing as deductions for federal income tax purposes payments totaling $81,396.61 made by petitioner to certain banks, which payments petitioner claimed were payments of interest on indebtedness within Section 163(a) of the 1954 Internal Revenue Code. This section provides that "There shall be allowed as a deduction all interest paid or accrued within the taxable year on indebtedness." Int. Rev. Code of 1954 § 163(a). A majority of the Tax Court held for several reasons to be considered in the body of this opinion that these payments were not deductible. Goldstein v. Commissioner, 44 T.C. 284 (1965). We affirm on one of the grounds mentioned by the Tax Court.

During the latter part of 1958 petitioner received the good news that she held a winning Irish Sweepstakes ticket and would shortly receive $140,218.75. This windfall significantly improved petitioner's financial situation, for she was a housewife approximately 70 years old and her husband was a retired garment worker who received a $780 pension each year. In 1958 the couple's only income, aside from this pension and the unexpected Sweepstakes proceeds, was $124.75, which represented interest on several small savings bank accounts. The petitioner received the Sweepstakes proceeds in December 1958 and she deposited the money in a New York bank. She included this amount as gross income in the joint return she and her husband filed for 1958 on the cash receipts and disbursements basis.

Petitioner's son, Bernard Goldstein, was a certified public accountant, practicing in New York in 1958. In November of that year Bernard either volunteered or was enlisted to assist petitioner in investing the Sweepstakes proceeds, and in minimizing the 1958 tax consequences to petitioner of the sudden increase in her income for that year. A series of consultations between Bernard and an attorney resulted in the adoption of a plan, which, as implemented, can be summarized as follows: During the latter part of December 1958 petitioner contacted several brokerage houses that bought and sold securities for clients and also arranged collateral loans. With the assistance of one of these brokerage houses, Garvin, Bantel & Co., petitioner borrowed $465,000 from the First

National Bank of Jersey City. With the money thus acquired, and the active assistance of Garvin, Bantel, petitioner purchased $500,000 face amount of United States Treasury 1/2% notes, due to mature on October 1, 1962. Petitioner promptly pledged the Treasury notes so purchased as collateral to secure the loan with the Jersey City Bank. At approximately the same time in 1958 Bernard secured for petitioner a $480,000 loan from the Royal State Bank of New York. With the assistance of the Royal State Bank petitioner purchased a second block of $500,000 face amount of United States Treasury 1 1/2% notes, due to mature on October 1, 1961. Again the notes were pledged as collateral with this bank to secure the loan. Bernard testified that the petitioner purchased the Treasury notes because he believed "the time was ripe" to invest in this kind of government obligation. Also, pursuant to the prearranged plan, petitioner prepaid to the First National Bank of Jersey City and to the Royal State Bank the interest that would be due on the loans she had received if they remained outstanding for 1 1/2 to 2 1/2 years. These interest prepayments, made in late December of 1958, totaled $81,396.61. Petitioner then claimed this sum as a Section 163(a) deduction on the 1958 income tax return she filed jointly with her husband.

After reviewing these transactions in detail the Tax Court held the $81,396.61 was not deductible as "interest paid or accrued" on "indebtedness" under Section 163(a). In large part this holding rested on the court's conclusion that both loan transactions were "shams" that created "no genuine indebtedness." To support this conclusion the court stressed that, even though petitioner was borrowing approximately one half million dollars from each bank, the banks had agreed to the loans without any of their officers or employees having met petitioner or having investigated her financial position. The court noted that in each of the loan transactions petitioner was not required to commit any of her funds toward the purchase of the Treasury notes in their principal amount. And at several points the court appears to have attached great weight to the fact that most of the relevant transactions were apparently conducted by Garvin, Bantel and the Jersey City Bank, or by Bernard and the Royal State Bank, without petitioner's close supervision. Taking all these factors together, the Tax Court decided that, in fact, each transaction was "… an investment *by the bank* in Treasury obligations; wherein the bank, in consideration for prepayment to it of 'interest' by a customer … would carry such Treasury notes in the customer's name as purported collateral for the 'loan.'" … The court went on to say that "… if it is necessary to characterize the customer's payment, we would say that it was a fee to the bank for providing the 'façade' of a loan transaction." *Ibid.*

There is a certain force to the foregoing analysis. Quite clearly the First National Bank of Jersey City and the Royal State Bank of New York preferred to engage in the transactions they engaged in here rather than invest funds directly in Treasury notes because petitioner's loans bore interest at an appreciably higher rate than that yielded by the government obligations. This fact, combined with the impeccable property pledged as security for the loans, may have induced these banks to enter into these transactions without all the panoply that the court indicates usually accompanies loan transactions of such size. Indeed, while on its face purporting to be a debtor-creditor transaction between a taxpayer and a bank, in fact there can be a situation where the bank itself is, in effect, directly investing in the securities purportedly pledged by taxpayer as collateral to taxpayer's obligation; in such a transaction the taxpayer truly can be said to have paid a certain sum to the bank in return for the "facade" of a loan transaction. For Section 163(a) purposes such transactions are properly described as "shams" creating no "genuine indebtedness" and no deduction for the payment of "interest" to the bank should be allowed. See cases cited note 5 *infra*. Cf. Knetsch v. United States, 364 U.S. 361, 81 S. Ct. 132, 5 L. Ed. 2d 128 (1960).

In our view, however, the facts of the two loan arrangements now before us fail in several significant respects to establish that these transactions were clearly shams. We agree with the dissent below that the record indicates these loan arrangements were "... regular and, moreover, indistinguishable from any other legitimate loan transaction contracted for the purchase of Government securities." ... In the first place, the Jersey City Bank and the Royal State Bank were independent financial institutions; it cannot be said that their sole function was to finance transactions such as those before us.... Second, the two loan transactions here did not within a few days return all the parties to the position from which they had started. *Ibid.* Here the Royal State Bank loan remained outstanding, and, significantly, that Bank retained the Treasury obligations pledged as security until June 10, 1960, at which time petitioner instructed the bank to sell the notes, apply the proceeds to the loan, and credit any remaining balance to her account. The facts relating to the Jersey City Bank loan are slightly different: this loan was closed in June 1959 when the brokerage house of Gruntal & Co. was substituted for the Jersey City Bank as creditor. Gruntal received and retained the 1962 Treasury 1 1/2's originally pledged as security for the loan until December 1, 1959 when, pursuant to instructions from petitioner and her advisors, these notes were sold, and $500,000 face amount of United States Treasury 2 1/2% bonds were purchased to replace them as security. Petitioner's account with Gruntal was not finally closed until June 13, 1960 when the last of these substituted bonds were sold, the petitioner's note was marked fully paid, and the balance was credited to petitioner. Third, the independent financial institutions from which petitioner borrowed the funds she needed to acquire the Treasury obligations possessed significant control over the future of their respective loan arrangements: for example, the petitioner's promissory note to the Jersey City Bank explicitly gave either party the right to accelerate the maturity of the note after 30 days, and it was the Jersey City Bank's utilization of this clause that necessitated recourse to Gruntal; the Royal State Bank had the right at any time to demand that petitioner increase her collateral or liquidate the loan, and on several occasions it made such a demand. Fourth, the notes signed by petitioner in favor of both banks were signed with recourse. If either of the independent lending institutions here involved had lost money on these transactions because of the depreciation of the collateral pledged to secure the loans we are certain that, upon petitioner's default of payment, they would have without hesitation proceeded against petitioner to recover their losses.... Moreover, all things being equal, the banks' chances of judgments in their favor would have been excellent. In view of this combination of facts we think it was error for the Tax Court to conclude that these two transactions were "shams" which created no genuine indebtedness. Were this the only ground on which the decision reached below could be supported we would be compelled to reverse.

...

One ground advanced by the Tax Court seems capable of reasoned development to support the result reached in this case by that court. The Tax Court found as an ultimate fact that petitioner's purpose in entering into the Jersey City Bank and Royal State Bank transactions "was not to derive any economic gain or to improve here [sic] beneficial interest; but was *solely* an attempt to obtain an interest deduction as an offset to her sweepstake winnings." ... This finding of ultimate fact was based in part on a set of computations made by Bernard Goldstein shortly after the Jersey City Bank and Royal State Bank loan transactions had been concluded. These computations were introduced by the Commissioner below and they indicated that petitioner and her financial advisors then estimated that the transactions would produce an economic loss in excess of $18,500 inasmuch as petitioner was out of pocket the 4% interest she had prepaid and could expect to receive 1 1/2% interest on the Treasury obligations she had just purchased plus a modest capital gain when the obligations were sold. This computation also reflected Bernard's realization that if the plan was successful this economic loss would be more than offset by the substantial reduction in petitioner's 1958 income tax liability due to the large deduction for interest "paid or accrued" taken in that year. The memorandum drawn up by Bernard is set out in full in the opinion of the Tax Court. 44 T.C. at 292–293. In fact, petitioner sustained a $25,091.01 economic loss on these transactions for some of the Treasury obligations were ultimately sold for less than the price that had been originally anticipated by petitioner's advisors.

Before the Tax Court, and before us, petitioner has argued that she realistically anticipated an economic gain on the loan transactions due to anticipated appreciation in the value of the Treasury obligations, and that this gain would more than offset the loss that was bound to result because of the unfavorable interest rate differential. In support of this position, Bernard testified, and documentary evidence was introduced, to the effect that in December 1958 the market for Treasury obligations was unreasonably depressed, and that many investors at that time were favorably disposed toward their purchase. In short, petitioner argued that she intended a sophisticated, speculative, sortie into the market for government securities.

In holding that petitioner's "sole" purpose in entering into the Jersey City Bank and Royal State Bank transactions was to obtain an interest deduction, the Tax Court rejected this explanation of her purpose in entering into these transactions. For several reasons we hold that this rejection was proper. First, petitioner's evidence tending to establish that she anticipated an economic profit on these transactions due to a rising market for Treasury obligations is flatly contradicted by the computations made by Bernard contemporaneously with the commencement of these transactions and introduced by the Commissioner at trial. These computations almost conclusively establish that petitioner and her advisors from the outset anticipated an economic loss. Petitioner's answer to this damaging evidence is that the set of Bernard's computations introduced by the Commissioner was only one of several arithmetic projections made at the same time by Bernard, and that Bernard intended the computations introduced by the Commissioner to represent the worst that could befall the plan if prices for government obligations continued to decline. The petitioner introduced several exhibits that purported to be reconstructions of the other arithmetic projections made by Bernard contemporaneously with the computations introduced by the Commissioner. Exhibit 83, introduced by petitioner, purported to be an arithmetic projection of petitioner's expected profit on the assumption that the market for Treasury obligations remained at the level it had reached at the close of 1958; this exhibit showed an economic profit on both transactions over a two-year period totaling a meager $2,075.00. Exhibit 84, also introduced by petitioner, purported to be an arithmetic projection of petitioner's expected profit on the assumption that the market for Treasury obligations reverted to previous highs; this exhibit projected an economic profit on both transactions over a two year period totaling $22,875.00. The Tax Court's ground (or grounds) for refusing to credit these exhibits and related evidence does not clearly appear in its opinion, but sufficient grounds are not hard to find. First, unlike the computations made by Bernard that the Commissioner introduced, Exhibits 83 and 84 purported only to be reconstructions of calculations made by Bernard in late December 1958. The originals of Exhibits 83 and 84 were not produced; no explanation of petitioner's failure to do so was given. On this ground the Tax Court might have decided that Exhibits 83 and 84 were especially prepared for this litigation and had not entered into Tillie's calculations at the outset. Second, even if we assume Exhibits 83 and 84 represent computations made con temporaneously with petitioner's entrance into these transactions, they far from establish that the transactions were undertaken with a realistic expectation of economic profit. For example, Exhibit 83 purports to establish that, assuming the market for Treasury obligations remained constant, petitioner and her advisors anticipated an economic profit of $2,075.00 over a two year period on these transactions. But Exhibit 83 fails to reflect the $6,500 fee paid to Bernard and tax counsel for their work in planning these transactions. Once this fee is included in these computations all economic profit disappears. Inclusion of this $6,500 item similarly reduces the total economic profit as computed in Exhibit 84. Furthermore, although petitioner made an outlay of "prepaid interest" on the Royal State Bank loan for a period of 1 1/2 years, Exhibits 83 and 84 compute the outlay on this loan as if there had been an interest payment for only one year. The payment of interest on the Jersey City Bank loan similarly is computed on a two-year basis instead of the basis of the actual outlay, which extended for two years, nine and one half months. Such computations presuppose petitioner could, at her option, terminate the loans prior to their due dates, sell the securities, and be reimbursed for the portions of the prepaid interest not yet earned by the banks. However, neither loan agreement contains a provision entitling petitioner to be reimbursed for any unearned portion of the prepaid interest if the loan is terminated *by the petitioner* prior to the due date. And, in the case of the Royal State Bank transaction, it is not even clear that petitioner had the power to prepay the principal of the loan prior to its maturity date. This uncertainty in the consequences of a sale by petitioner of the Treasury obligations prior to their due date might have led the Tax Court to conclude that petitioner and her advisors could not have entertained a realistic hope of economic profit when these loan transactions were commenced. Finally, Exhibit 84 is predicated on the remote possibility that the Treasury obligations could be sold considerably in excess of par, thereby yielding an effective rate of interest well below 1 1/2%, even though it would be unlikely that investors would purchase them for such a small return when they were to mature at par in the near future.

For all of the above reasons the Tax Court was justified in concluding that petitioner entered into the Jersey City Bank and Royal State Bank transactions without any realistic expectation of economic profit and "solely" in order to secure a large interest deduction in 1958 which could be deducted from her sweepstakes winnings in that year. This conclusion points the way to affirmance in the present case.

We hold, for reasons set forth hereinafter, that Section 163(a) of the 1954 Internal Revenue Code does not permit a deduction for interest paid or accrued in loan arrangements, like those now before us, that can not with reason be said to have purpose, substance, or utility apart from their anticipated tax consequences. See Knetsch v. United States, 364 U.S. 361, 366, 81 S.Ct. 132, 5 L.Ed.2d 128 (1960).... (Footnote 5) ... [I]t is frequently stated that deductions from "gross income" are a matter of "legislative grace." E. g., Deputy v. DuPont, 308 U.S. 488, 493, 60 S.Ct. 363, 84 L.Ed. 416 (1940). There is at least this much truth in this oft-repeated maxim: a close question whether a particular Code provision authorizes the deduction of a certain item is best resolved by reference to the underlying Congressional purpose of the deduction provision in question. (Footnote 6)

Admittedly, the underlying purpose of Section 163(a) permitting the deduction of "all interest paid or accrued within the taxable year on indebtedness" is difficult to articulate because this provision is extremely broad: there is no requirement that deductible interest serve a business purpose, that it be ordinary and necessary, or even that it be reasonable.... Nevertheless, it is fair to say that Section 163(a) is not entirely unlimited in its application and that such limits as there are stem from the Section's underlying notion that if an individual or corporation desires to engage in purposive activity, there is no reason why a taxpayer who borrows for that purpose should fare worse from an income tax standpoint than one who finances the venture with capital that otherwise would have been yielding income.

In order fully to implement this Congressional policy of encouraging purposive activity to be financed through borrowing, Section 163(a) should be construed to permit the deductibility of interest when a taxpayer has borrowed funds and incurred an obligation to pay interest in order to engage in what with reason can be termed purposive activity, even though he decided to borrow in order to gain an interest deduction rather than to finance the activity in some other way. In other words, the interest deduction should be permitted whenever it can be said that the taxpayer's desire to secure an interest deduction is only one of mixed motives that prompts the taxpayer to borrow funds; or, put a third way, the deduction is proper if there is some substance to the loan arrangement beyond the taxpayer's desire to secure the deduction. After all, we are frequently told that a taxpayer has the right to decrease the amount of what otherwise would be his taxes, or altogether avoid them, by any means the law permits. E. g., Gregory v. Helvering.... (Footnote 7) On the other hand, and notwithstanding Section 163(a)'s broad scope this provision should not be construed to permit an interest deduction when it objectively appears that a taxpayer has borrowed funds in order to engage in a transaction that has no substance or purpose aside from the taxpayer's desire to obtain the tax benefit of an interest deduction: and a good example of such purposeless activity is the borrowing of funds at 4% in order to purchase property that returns less than 2% and holds out no prospect of appreciation sufficient to counter the unfavorable interest rate differential. Certainly the statutory provision's underlying purpose, as we understand it, does not require that a deduction be allowed in such a case. Indeed, to allow a deduction for interest paid on funds borrowed for no purposive reason, other than the securing of a deduction from income, would frustrate Section 163(a)'s purpose; allowing it would encourage transactions that have no economic utility and that would not be engaged in but for the system of taxes imposed by Congress. When it enacted Section 163(a) Congress could not have intended to permit a taxpayer to reduce his taxes by means of an interest deduction that arose from a transaction that had no substance, utility, or purpose beyond the tax deduction. See Knetsch v. United States....

In many instances transactions that lack all substance, utility, and purpose, and which can only be explained on the ground the taxpayer sought an interest deduction in order to reduce his taxes, will also be so transparently arranged that they can candidly be labeled "shams." ... The present case makes plain, however, ... that a court need not always first label a loan transaction a "sham" in order to deny a deduction for interest paid in connection with the loan.

In Knetsch v. United States, ... the Supreme Court cautions us, by reiteration there of what the Court had said in Gregory v. Helvering, ... that in cases like the present "the question for determination is whether what was done, apart from the tax motive, was the thing which the statute intended." We here decide that Section 163(a) does not "intend" that taxpayers should be permitted deductions for interest paid on debts that were entered into solely in order to obtain a deduction. It follows therefore from the foregoing, and from the

Tax Court's finding as a matter of "ultimate" fact that petitioner entered into the Jersey City Bank and Royal State Bank transactions without any expectation of profit and without any other purpose except to obtain an interest deduction, and that the Tax Court's disallowance of the deductions in this case must be affirmed.

FOOTNOTES:

1. Tillie Goldstein, whose income is involved here, filed a joint return with her husband, Kapel Goldstein, for the calender year 1958. Therefore, though husband and wife are joint petitioners in the case, we use "petitioner" throughout this opinion to indicate this fact and to show that Kapel Goldstein is involved only because of the filing of the joint return.

5. We confine our discussion of transactions inspired by tax avoidance motives to those transactions inspired by the lure of Section 163(a)—a section that has proved to be the Internal Revenue Code's counterpart of the mythical Sirens of the Surrentine promontory....

6. The proposition that because deductions are a matter of "legislative grace" they should be strictly construed is much more doubtful as an interpretative guide....

7. This area of the law is particularly full of black-letter maxims that prove singularly unhelpful when it comes to deciding cases.

Now answer the following questions concerning *Goldstein*.

1. Why did the Tax Court refuse to honor the taxpayer's treatment of the prepaid interest?

2. Why did the Court of Appeals refuse to honor the taxpayer's treatment of the prepaid interest?

3. Based on the opinion of the Court of Appeals, could the taxpayer have been more effective in presenting her case to the court and thereby have succeeded in deducting the prepaid interest?

4. Did the Court of Appeals cite a provision of the Code that permitted the Service to disallow the deduction?

The current Code contains a provision that prevents a cash method taxpayer from deducting prepaid interest. **Look at section 461(g).** Congress added section 461(g) to the Code as part of the Tax Reform Act of 1976. That provision requires a cash method taxpayer to report the deduction over the period to which it applies, in other words, in the same manner as an accrual method taxpayer would report it.

Even when debt is incurred to engage in "purposive activities," other issues may arise. For example, the following case illustrates the issue of whether a taxpayer may deduct the interest regardless of what method she chooses to use in order to pay it.

BATTELSTEIN v. INTERNAL REVENUE SERVICE
631 F.2d 1182 (5TH Cir 1980)

FRANK M. JOHNSON, Jr., Circuit Judge

This case arose out of Chapter XI petitions in bankruptcy filed by Barry L. Battelstein and Jerry E. Battelstein in the United States District Court for the Southern District of Texas. In the ensuing proceedings, the Internal Revenue Service (IRS) filed proof of claims against each. The Battelsteins objected to the claims and their objections were consolidated for trial. The bankruptcy judge denied the IRS claims after trial and the denial was affirmed by the district court. In response to an appeal filed by the IRS, a panel of this Court reversed the district court's decision denying the IRS claims.... The panel's decision was vacated when the Court granted the Battelsteins' petition for rehearing en banc.... The case was taken under submission by the Court en banc following additional briefing by the parties.

The facts are not in dispute. As the panel opinion explained, the Battelsteins were land developers. Gibraltar Savings Association was their lender. In 1971, Gibraltar agreed to loan the Battelsteins more than three million dollars to cover the purchase of a piece of property known as Sharpstown. Gibraltar also agreed to make to the Battelsteins, if desired, future advances of the interest costs on this loan as they became due. The Battelsteins never paid interest except by way of these advances. Each quarter, Gibraltar would notify the Battelsteins of the amount of interest currently due. The Battelsteins would then send Gibraltar a check in this amount, and, on its receipt, Gibraltar would send the Battelsteins its check in the identical amount.

The controversy stems from the Battelsteins' deduction of the amount of these checks under authority of Internal Revenue Code § 163(a).... Section 163(a) allows cash basis taxpayers such as the Battelsteins to take a deduction for interest paid within the taxable year on indebtedness. The issue in this case is whether the Gibraltar-Battelstein check exchanges resulted in interest being paid within the taxable year. The bankruptcy judge and the district court decided that the exchanges had such a result. We conclude, as did the panel, that this decision was incorrect.

It is plain that the check exchanges relied on by the Battelsteins could not themselves extinguish the Battelsteins' interest obligations to Gibraltar. What happened at the time of each of the exchanges, as the Battelsteins now concede, is that the Battelsteins gave Gibraltar their note promising to pay the amount of interest then due, plus interest, in the future. It is well established, however, that such a surrender of notes does not constitute the current payment of interest that Section 163(a) requires. The Supreme Court has repeatedly held, as long ago as 1931 and as recently as 1977, that payment for tax purposes must be made in cash or its equivalent. *Don E. Williams Co. v. Commissioner, 429 U.S. 569....* The 1977 decision explained that, "The reasoning is apparent: the note may never be paid, and if it is not paid, 'the taxpayer has parted with nothing more than his promise to pay.'" ... The Battelsteins attempted to avoid such a characterization of their interest transactions here by adding to their surrender of notes the inconsequential exchanges of identical amount checks. (Footnote 1) In ignoring these exchanges, we merely follow a well-established principle of law, viz., that in tax cases it is axiomatic that we look through the form in which the taxpayer has cloaked a transaction to the substance of the transaction.... The check exchanges notwithstanding, the Battelsteins satisfied their interest obligations to Gibraltar by giving Gibraltar notes promising future payment. The law leaves no doubt that such a surrender of notes does not constitute payment for tax purposes entitling a taxpayer to a deduction.

As the panel concluded, the Battelsteins' reliance on the line of Tax Court cases beginning with *Burgess v. Commissioner, 8 T.C. 47 (1947),* is misplaced, even assuming that the *Burgess* cases constitute good law. In the *Burgess* cases, the Tax Court was faced with situations in which taxpayers had obtained first one loan and then another from the same lender, and then had attempted to claim a deduction for interest paid on the first loan, even though the interest was possibly paid with funds obtained as part of the second loan. Under the Code, a taxpayer may be entitled to a deduction in such a situation only if the second loan was not for the purpose of financing the interest due on the first loan. If the second loan was for the purpose of financing the interest due on the first loan, then the taxpayer's interest obligation on the first loan has not been paid as Section 163(a) requires; it has merely been postponed. (Footnote 3) In many cases, it is not apparent what the purpose of a subsequent loan payment was—whether it was to finance the interest payments on a previous loan for which deductions are being claimed, or whether it was to fulfill some other unrelated objective. In the *Burgess* cases, the Tax Court attempted to establish a formula to be used in making such a determination. (Footnote 4) The formula has been subject to criticism for being too easy to manipulate by taxpayers and thus as unduly inviting tax evasion. Whether or not this criticism is valid, it is clear that it is unnecessary to apply the formula here, or that if applied here in light of its purpose it could yield only one result. This is because the subsequent loans made by Gibraltar to the Battelsteins—the checks issued by Gibraltar to the Battelsteins as part of the check exchanges, in the exact amount of the Battelsteins' current interest obligations—were plainly for no purpose other than to finance the Battelsteins' current interest obligations to Gibraltar.... Even under *Burgess*, the Battelsteins' check exchanges cannot be said to have resulted in the payment of interest required for a deduction by Section 163(a).

In announcing our decision, we note that, contrary to what has been suggested, neither the Court nor, for that matter, the panel has considered the Battelsteins' 'entrepreneurial style' to be an issue in this case. For business men to defer payment of interest obligations in the way the Battelsteins have done may well be a sensible way in which to do business. Whether it is or is not, what is relevant here is that interest obligations so deferred cannot be claimed for tax purposes as interest obligations paid. Under the Code, cash basis taxpayers such as the Battelsteins are entitled to a deduction for interest paid on indebtedness only if that interest is paid within the taxable year. The Battelsteins simply do not qualify.

...

The only question before us is whether the Battelsteins' check exchange scheme resulted in the payment of interest Section 163(a) requires. A review of the scheme under the familiar standards of appraisal mandated by the Supreme Court permits no conclusion other than that no interest was paid, and thus that no deduction may be allowed.

REVERSED AND REMANDED FOR A CALCULATION OF TAX LIABILITY.

FOOTNOTES:

1. The Battelsteins do not assert, nor do we find it possible to infer, any other purpose for the check exchanges.

3. In other words, the obligation as between the taxpayer and the lender remains but—like a note promising payment in the future, which does not qualify for a deduction, *see supra*—merely in another form. Compare the situation in which a taxpayer borrows money from a certain lender, and then borrows money from a third party in order to pay the original lender the interest. In such a situation the interest is considered paid and deductible because the obligation as between the taxpayer and the original lender has not been postponed, it has been extinguished. *See, e.g., Crain v. Commissioner,* 75 F.2d 962, 964 (8th Cir. *1935); McAdams v. Commissioner,* 15 T.C. 231, 235 (1950).

4. In *Burgess* and its progeny, the Tax Court held that interest may be considered paid even though the taxpayer may have paid it with money subsequently borrowed from the initial lender, so long as the money subsequently borrowed actually passed into the hands or bank account of the taxpayer, was commingled with other funds of the taxpayer and thus became subject to the taxpayer's unrestricted control. *Burgess v. Commissioner,* 8 T.C. at 49–50....

POLITZ, Circuit Judge, with whom BROWN, RONEY, GEE, JAMES C. HILL, FAY, VANCE, GARZA, REAVLEY and RANDALL, Circuit Judges, join, dissenting:

Respectfully, I dissent. The Battelstein loan arrangement is precisely the type of transaction covered by the *Burgess* rule. In 1971 the Battelsteins borrowed in excess of three million dollars from the Gibraltar Savings Association to finance the Sharpstown project. They took additional loans from Gibraltar in 1973 and 1974. It is beyond dispute that a § 163(a) deduction is not available to the Battelsteins if notes alone, rather than cash or its equivalent, were given in payment of the accrued interest on the initial loan. But I cannot agree with the narrow characterization of this overall transaction as a paper shuffling sham composed of surrendered notes with check exchanges flying CAP. By declining to apply and raising the spectre of criticism of *Burgess*, the majority registers its objection to a 33 year old tax law precedent which is both logical and meritorious. I believe this rejection unjustified.

There is no question but that the § 163(a) interest deduction may be claimed in instances in which the interest is paid with the proceeds of a loan. If the Battelsteins had borrowed the money to pay the interest to Gibraltar from a different lender, no challenge would apparently be made to the interest deduction. It is only because the Battelsteins secured additional loans from Gibraltar, equal to the interest paid, that they forfeit the deduction. It is this dimension of the majority opinion with which we take issue, and for which the *Burgess* rule is particularly apropos. Its rejection causes the taxpayers of this circuit to run through a legal minefield they ought not have to cross. Today's decision portends the day when the ' 163(a) deduction is put in jeopardy whenever a taxpayer borrows from a lender a sum at least equal to the interest paid that same lender that tax year.

It is not difficult to envision completely unacceptable consequences of the rule of this case. Let us suppose that a homeowner/taxpayer has a $30,000 mortgage required $300 monthly payments of principal and interest. Let us also suppose that he has an automatic $1,000 line of credit available if he should overdraw his personal account. The mortgage loan and the checking account, with the protective line of credit, are with the same bank. Let us further suppose that at various times during the year our hypothetical taxpayer either owes up to $1,000 or has several thousands of dollars on demand deposit, depending on transitory seasonal fluctuations. Throughout the entire year his assets exceed $100,000 which, for his own reasons, he chooses not to liquidate during the "deficit" periods but opts to rely on borrowing in order to maintain financial flexibility. Under today's decision the deductibility of the mortgage interest is endangered because funds drawn on the line of credit may have been used to make the monthly mortgage payments. The risk is created simply because both loans came from the same lender. Proper application of the *Burgess* rule would assure this taxpayer safe passage.

The only credible distinction between the Battelsteins' predicament and that of our hypothetical taxpayer is that the former is structured and the latter is not. The Battelsteins appear to have designed their transaction to conform with existing case law and regulatory precedents. Our hypothetical taxpayer is in a quite common situation very probably affecting a substantial number of taxpayers. I am compelled to the conclusion that the Battelsteins are being penalized for trying to carefully fashion a tax-oriented transaction designed to maximize tax advantages. Surely this effort is not proscribed....

The *Burgess* formulation, which I believe should govern disposition of this case, is a time tested amalgamation of various factors that aid courts in determining whether a taxpayer is perpetrating a dual loan transaction sham or is legitimately entitled to the interest deduction. To qualify for the tax deduction under the *Burgess* test it is necessary that: (1) there be valid and legitimate reasons for the second loan other than to repay interest on the first loan, (2) proceeds of the second loan are commingled with the taxpayer's other funds, (3) the taxpayer have funds or available resources to cover the interest payment, and (4) the lending institution loses control of the proceeds of the second loan....

Factor one is satisfied because valid reasons existed for the subsequent loans, other than merely making interest payments on the first loan. Funds were required to finance development of the Sharpstown project which was a multi-million dollar long-range venture; roads were not in, utilities were not installed. The controversial subsequent loan agreement was really a clause contained in the Battelstein-Gibraltar loan accord that stated:

> After execution of the agreement Gibraltar will, pursuant to the terms thereof, from time to time, advance to Owners ... an additional sum or sums of money equal to the Owners' actual out-of-pocket costs incurred and paid on said property subsequent to the execution of the agreement, including, but not being limited to debt services, taxes ...

In return for this long-term financing clause, Gibraltar was to be repaid the loans plus interest and receive a 19% interest in the net proceeds when the land was sold. Jerry Battelstein was eager to obtain this type of financing because it did not tie up his own liquid assets; he testified that he firmly believed an astute businessman could make money with borrowed money. Advances were in fact made to the Battelsteins in 1973 and 1974 for sums equal to the ad valorem taxes paid on the land and for debt service or interest owed to Gibraltar on the initial loan.

It is clear that the subsequent loans were intended to place the full cost of acquisition and development of the Sharpstown property on Gilbraltar in order to give the Battelsteins added financial flexibility. The majority's position focuses, in isolation, on the funds borrowed to pay interest charges on the first loan. No mention is made of the funds borrowed to pay the ad valorem taxes, the payment of which had been originally rejected as a deduction by the I.R.S. for the same reason, *i.e.*, the funds used for payment had been borrowed from Gibraltar. This focusing obscures the business purpose of the subsequent loans, the underwriting of *all* "out-of-pocket" expenses associated with the Sharpstown parcel.

Factors (2) and (3) of *Burgess* are met. Proceeds of the second loan were commingled with personal Battelstein funds in their bank accounts (which were not with Gibraltar). Additionally, in each of the eight challenged instances of payment (quarterly during the two-year period under scrutiny) the Battelsteins had ample assets to cover taxes and interest payments independent of the subsequent loan proceeds. During the years 1973, 1974 and 1975, Jerry Battelstein's average monthly checking account balances were $24,000, $75,000 and $35,000 respectively. Barry Battelstein's monthly averages during those years were $36,000, $44,000 and $40,000. Jerry Battelstein's approximate net worth exceeded four million dollars in 1973 and was over five million in 1974. Similarly, Barry Battelstein had substantial assets upon which to draw for payments. For example, in 1973 he had $1,300,000 worth of Certificates of Deposit that could have been liquidated to pay accruing ad valorem taxes and interest charges on the first loan. During the years in question accruing interest paid with funds borrowed under the second loan accord fluctuated between $4,991.06 and $48,728.10. It cannot be disputed that the Battelsteins had more than adequate funds to pay the quarterly interest, independent of any monies received on later advances from Gibraltar.

Finally, *Burgess* requires that Gibraltar relinquish total control of the questioned loan proceeds. From the majority's perspective, the sequencing of checks between the Battelsteins and Gibraltar conclusively proved that the bank's control of these funds was not extinguished because an "inconsequential exchange of surrendered notes" occurred rather than a cash payment of interest. Emphasis is placed on the fact that the Battelsteins first sent their checks for the quarterly interest payments at which time Gibraltar sent the Battelsteins a like check which they deposited in their general bank accounts. I find this significant, but reach a conclusion exactly opposite from that of the majority. Upon receipt of the Battelsteins' check, Gibraltar had made more than a mere promise to pay (such as would be evidenced by a note). When Gibraltar received the checks the Battelsteins had paid. Had Gibraltar chosen for some reason not to loan an amount equal to the particular payment, the Battelsteins would have been obliged to see that the check was honored out of their own substantial personal funds. Sending those checks was the equivalent of sending cash. The record reflects that in some instances the funds on deposit when Gibraltar received the checks were sufficient to cover the checks before Gibraltar made any further loan; and in every instance, the Battelsteins had more than adequate resources available. The record also reflects that in some instances the check to Gibraltar was debited before the proceeds from the Gibraltar check were deposited.

It is apparent that in many, if not most "dual loan" cases the *Burgess* requirements would preclude the taxpayer from taking the interest deduction. That is all the more reason to support the application of Burgess in a proper case. I view this as just such a case. The Tax Court continues to support the rule in appropriate cases....

The majority opinion occasions further comments which perhaps might best be stated in the form of inquiries. Setting aside for the moment the permutation of cash versus accrual basis and date of crediting in determining taxable income we inquire, in general terms, about the tax posture of Gibraltar. What may we safely assume to be the position of the I.R.S. as respects the Battelsteins' interest payments? Was that reportable income to Gibraltar? When did it become so? May Gibraltar insist that it did not receive the interest payments due on the initial loan because it made other loans at different rates of interest and with different due dates?

Viewing the total transaction from the standpoint of the Battelsteins we must also inquire. The development envisioned the sale of the property, presumably at a handsome profit. One would assume that was the early expectation. What would have been the position of the I.R.S. had the Battelsteins borrowed from Gibraltar (and other institutions) all sums necessary to make the quarterly interest payments over a several year period, and timed or extended the subsequent loans so that all came due in the year of the sale, to be used in a lump sum against the profit realized? One need hardly doubt the reception that program would have gotten.

The essential predicate for the majority opinion is that the subsequent loans came from the same lender. How far do we extend the "sameness"? What about a loan from a subsidiary or affiliated lending institution or from a sibling bank which happens to be a member of the growing bancshare-type organization? Will we not be compelled to articulate a *Burgess* type rubric?

I am convinced beyond peradventure that the *Burgess* test is applicable to this case and should be endorsed. I would affirm the decisions of the bankruptcy court and the district court allowing the interest deduction. I therefore respectfully DISSENT.

Now consider the following questions concerning *Battelstein*.

1. Would the Battelsteins' plan have succeeded if they had borrowed from a second bank in order to make payment of the interest to Gibraltar Savings? Can you point to language in the decision that supports your answer?

2. Suppose they had merely used the additional advance from Gibraltar to repay the loan from the second bank?

3. Is the plan outlined in question 2 different from one in which the Battelsteins obtain a second loan from Gibraltar and use the proceeds to pay the interest on the first loan? In that case, would the interest be deductible?

4. Which decision makes more sense to you: the majority or the dissent?

5. If the Battelsteins' payment of interest had been recognized as interest when they borrowed additional amounts to pay the interest on their loan, their indebtedness principal would have increased. What happens to the amount of their indebtedness as a consequence of the court's holding in the case?

These two cases have been no more than a brief glimpse at some of the issues that have arisen concerning what is deductible interest. Of course, in most cases, there is little doubt as to what constitutes interest and whether it has been paid. But, because debt is such an important part of property ownership and operation, it is important to know that characterization issues arise here, as they did in other contexts you have seen. Here, as before, courts often look to see if the substance of the transaction conforms to its form.

Real estate transactions have been an important area for the application of both the technical rules of tax and the common law doctrines that courts have formulated. But, in order to solve the real estate problems that conclude this Part, we must introduce you to some additional key concepts.

Chapter 3

Property Ownership and Transfers

A. The Fundamentals: Classification of Ownership

The two primary forms of lending for the acquisition of assets are referred to as "recourse" and "nonrecourse," denoting the presence or absence of personal liability on the part of the borrower for the amounts borrowed.[1] When an individual wishes to acquire an asset without paying the full cost in cash, he will arrange to borrow the portion of the funds needed. He will generally memorialize the borrowing by executing a promissory note that sets forth the terms for repayment. The note will often be secured by a lien on the purchased asset. In the case of real property, that lien usually takes the form of either a mortgage or a deed of trust. There is little difference between a mortgage and a deed of trust (and, in fact, the Restatement of Property Law—Mortgages refers to both as "mortgages"). In some communities, a mortgage is more common; in others, a deed of trust. In either case, the lien document provides the security for the loan; the promissory note provides the terms for repayment.

In the promissory note, the borrower promises to repay the amount borrowed. The terms of the promissory note may require payments of a specific amount (a "level-payment") at regular intervals until the total balance of the loan and interest are discharged. The specific payment amount is referred to as the "debt service," consisting of the total of principal and interest to be paid at regular intervals. Most promissory notes associated with home mortgages require this type of repayment. In some home mortgages, the amount of the debt service may change, if, for example, the terms of the note permit a change in interest rate based on market conditions (an "adjustable loan").

---

1. There are many variations in the agreements that lenders make with their borrowers. Some include provisions that allow the lender to participate in the anticipated profits its lending produces; others involve variations in the normal arrangements for repayment. As you learned by reading *Frank Lyon* and *Estate of Franklin*, however, the most important issues for tax lawyers involve identification of the true owner of the property and the substance of the transaction for tax purposes.

The terms of many loans secured by home mortgages may also allow the mortgagor to make additional payments at will.[2] But, the additional payments generally do not reduce the total payment due under the note (although they may shorten the term).

The repayment terms of the promissory notes for certain other loans may require regular payments for a specific period of time, at the end of which the remaining balance is due (a "balloon"). Balloon financing is more common in commercial borrowing. It is especially attractive at times of high interest rates because it allows the borrower to refinance the balloon (remaining balance) at a rate the borrower hopes will be lower at the time the balloon is due. Of course, rates could go in the opposite direction!

Level-payment and balloon arrangements are only two of the most common schedules for repayment. In fact, lenders and borrowers, particularly commercial lenders and borrowers, may fashion an unlimited number of variations that suit their particular circumstances. They may, for example, provide for payment of varying amounts at different times in an attempt to match expected events in the life of the asset or the business cycle. Despite these variations, however, the function of the two fundamental documents, the promissory note and the mortgage, remains the same.

In many commercial and virtually all residential loans, the promissory note will require the borrower to assume personal liability for repayment of the loan. If a default occurs, the lender may seek to collect unpaid principal and interest by "recourse" to the borrower's other assets. In contrast, in some commercial transactions, the lender will agree to make the loan without recourse to the borrower's other assets. That is, the lender may agree to look only to the asset itself for security for the loan. This latter type of arrangement is termed "nonrecourse." A lender's willingness to make a loan without recourse often arises from a combination of factors including the general creditworthiness of the borrower, the value of the asset, and market conditions. In some cases, the fact that the asset will be owned by a single-purpose entity, for example, a corporation, LLC, or partnership formed solely to own a single piece of real estate, may influence the lender. If the entity has no other significant assets, recourse is meaningless.[3] In that case, the lender may, nevertheless, be willing to make the loan because of the nature of the project and familiarity with the principals involved.

The mortgagor might decide to sell or otherwise dispose of his interest in the property before retiring the loan. If he fails to ask for and receive the permission of the mortgagee, the sale may constitute a default under the terms of the loan agreement, requiring immediate repayment of the total balance (and any interest) outstanding. Even if he seeks and obtains permission to transfer his interest, he will not escape liability on the loan if the mortgage was made with recourse.

The initial inquiry must be the relationship between the original borrower and the transferee. What kind of an agreement did the parties make at the time the transferee

---

2. Many mortgage loans, both residential and commercial, have provisions that prohibit an early prepayment of the balance due on the mortgage, or impose a substantial penalty for early repayment. If they are enforceable, these provisions put at least some control over repayment in the hands of the lender. At a time when interest rates are rising, however, the lender may be happy to give the borrower permission to repay early, enabling the lender to relend to someone else at a higher interest rate.

3. The lender may, however, seek to insure a greater likelihood of repayment by demanding a personal guarantee from one or more of the partners (making the loan, in effect, "recourse" as to the guaranteeing partner(s)).

purchased the original borrower's equity in the property? Did the transferee promise the seller that she would pay the debt? If so, she is said to have "assumed" the mortgage and has become an "assuming grantee." If she did not make the promise to pay, she is a "non-assuming grantee." What difference does her promise make?

If the original borrower was personally liable on the original debt, that is, the loan was with recourse, both the original borrower and his buyer will be personally liable if there is a default and a mortgage foreclosure sale fails to produce sufficient funds to retire the entire debt outstanding. If, however, the buyer does not assume, that is the buyer is a non-assuming grantee, she will not be personally liable for a shortfall between the sale price and the debt outstanding (a "deficiency"). But, in the event of a foreclosure, she will lose her interest in the land, and, thus, any equity for which she paid the seller or has built up since the sale.

Suppose, however, that the original borrower was not personally liable for the loan, that is, the loan was a nonrecourse one. In that event, a non-assuming grantee will also not incur personal liability. But if the grantee does assume, there is a division among the cases as to how to treat the assuming grantee. Does the break in the chain (of personal liability) between the original mortgagor and the grantee prevent the enforcement of personal liability against the grantee? In some cases it does; in others it does not.

The ability to borrow on a nonrecourse basis, coupled with the ability to deduct the noncash expense of depreciation, and, for cash basis taxpayers, to accelerate interest deductions, produced a torrent of so-called "tax shelter" investments beginning with the building boom that followed World War II. Wealthy taxpayers were eager to invest their money to obtain deductions, often far in excess of their cash investments, in order to shield income from other sources from high taxation. In order to understand how tax shelters worked, you will have to learn more about debt. Congress has sharply limited the ability of taxpayers to accomplish the type of sheltering that was widespread. Various sections of the Code now short-circuit a taxpayer's ability to produce large deductions in excess of the amount an investor is at risk to lose. Nevertheless, the fundamentals of debt remain of interest.

Many investments in both real estate and other assets require a careful analysis of both the tax and non-tax consequences that will flow from the investment. As a starting point, it is often critical to determine the nature of the taxpayer's ownership of property. The particular classification often dictates which tax (as well as non-tax) rules apply to the owner. Therefore, consider first the various classifications of property ownership.

For tax purposes, the Code generally recognizes four classifications of ownership: (1) property held for personal use; (2) property held for the production of income; (3) property held for use in a trade or business; and (4) property held as inventory, which, in the case of real property is referred to as "property held primarily for sale to customers."

1. Property Held for Personal Use

This category encompasses all kinds of property, including a taxpayer's personal residence, that the taxpayer holds without an intention to use the property to make a profit. Therefore, deduction of the expenses associated with this type of property are allowable, if at all, for purely policy reasons identified by Congress. For example, a homeowner may deduct (within limits), the interest on the mortgage borrowing she incurs to purchase her principal residence. Most of these deductions have been part of the Code for long periods of time; taxpayers have come to expect their availability. When Congress debated repeal of the deduction for personal interest, for example, taxpayers' voices joined those in the real estate and banking industries to preserve, at least, the deduction for the interest on a home mortgage. Congress agreed, in part, because of the almost universally accepted idea that home ownership is a desirable goal for Americans. Of course, deduction of the interest paid on a home mortgage is not the only favorable tax provision that Congress continues to authorize for homeowners.[4]

2. Property Held for the Production of Income

Also referred to as "investment property," this category encompasses assets like stocks and bonds held by a taxpayer for investment, and real estate held by an investor who is not in the trade or business of owning real estate. Real property held for investment includes both raw land held for future use and developed property. Because the expenses associated with this type of property are generally deductible, Congress became increasingly concerned that taxpayers were entering these activities and incurring expenses in connection with them in order to produce losses that could offset income from other sources, particularly ordinary earned income. To limit the availability of these deductions, Congress enacted a series of provisions. Some, like the provision that alters the ability of cash-basis taxpayers to claim deductions for interest paid early, simply place the taxpayer in the position she would have been in had she elected a different method of accounting (the accrual method). Others require taxpayers to sort certain types of activities into the equivalent of separate baskets. Expenses associated with these activities can only be deducted against income from the same type of activity. Section 163(d) contains a limitation of this type. Because Congress was concerned that taxpayers were incurring interest expenses associated with investment activities that offset income from other types of activities, it enacted this section. Section 163(d) requires, in effect, that investors isolate their investment income and investment interest expense and allows a deduction for the interest expense only up to the amount of the income.

It is sometimes difficult to distinguish property held for investment from property held for other purposes. You have already encountered the tension between property held for use in a trade or business and property held as a hobby. **Recall Farmer Smith's case in Part II, Chapter 3.** The same tension can exist between property held for investment and that used in a hobby. Another example concerns the issue of when a personal residence becomes property held for investment. Because different benefits flow from each type of ownership, the distinction is often critical to the taxpayer. Suppose you own a resort condominium that you finance, in part, through periodic rentals. Is the condominium property held for personal use or property held for investment? Consider the following case.

---

4. Condominium owners enjoy the same benefits as those who own traditional houses. Moreover, Congress authorized a special provision to grant analogous benefits to the owners of cooperative dwellings. Should renters be granted similar benefits? As part of their rent payments, renters arguably pay, at least indirectly, the same expenses for mortgage interest and real estate taxes as do home owners. Does granting these deductions to homeowners but not to renters disrupt horizontal equity?

NEWCOMBE v. COMMISSIONER

54 T.C. 1298 (1970)

OPINION

TANNENWALD, *Judge:* Respondent determined a deficiency of

$2,059.95 in petitioners' income taxes for their taxable year 1966. The only issue is the deductibility of expenses incurred during the period in which a house, previously used by petitioners as their residence, was held for sale.

...

Until December 1, 1965, petitioner Frank A. Newcombe (hereinafter referred to as Frank) was employed and he and his wife resided in a house at Pine Bluff, Ark.

Petitioners' total adjusted cost basis in the house on December 1, 1965, was $70,887.39, allocated $3,500 to the land and $67,387.39 to the house. The total fair market value on that date was $60,000, allocated $52,000 to the house and improvements and $ 8,000 to the land.

On December 1, 1965, Frank retired and shortly thereafter he and his wife moved to Naples, Fla. In Naples, they purchased a residence in which they have since continuously resided. After this move, petitioners never again occupied the Pine Bluff house. It remained unoccupied from December 1, 1965, until it was sold. Frank did return to Pine Bluff three times during 1966 to attend certain board meetings, but each of these times he stayed at a motel or with his adult daughter, who resided in her own home in Pine Bluff.

Petitioners listed their Pine Bluff house for sale on or about December 1, 1965, with a local realtor. They never attempted to rent the house. The price at which it was initially listed for sale was $70,000. Continuing efforts to sell during all of 1966 were unsuccessful. It was finally sold for $50,000 on or about February 1, 1967.

During 1966, petitioners incurred and paid the following maintenance expenses, totaling $1,146, in connection with their Pine Bluff house:

Expense	Amount
Maid and yard service	$451
Telephone	71
Gas	234
Electricity	132
Sanitation	25
Water	46
Painting white trim on house	178
Plumbing repair	9

On their 1966 income tax return, petitioners claimed these expenses as deductions and also claimed $2,600 in depreciation as a deduction, utilizing a $52,000 basis, a 20-year life, and the straight-line method.

The threshold question involved herein is whether, during 1966, petitioners' former residence at Pine Bluff, Ark., constituted "property held for the production of income" so as to entitle them to deductions for maintenance expenses and depreciation under sections 212(2) and 167(a)(2).... The quoted phrase in both sections stems from the Revenue Act of 1942, 56 Stat. 798, 819. Since the two sections have the same purpose, the phrase should be given the same construction in one as in the other and neither party has argued otherwise....

Each of the parties seeks the adoption of a single standard for determination. Petitioners argue that the mere abandonment of personal use of property plus offering it for sale is sufficient to satisfy the statutory requirements. Respondent disagrees and urges that we hold that there can be a conversion of a personal residence to an income-producing use only where the property is rented or offered for rent. We do not share the penchant for polarization which the arguments of the parties reflect. Rather, we believe that a variety of factors must be weighed and, on this basis, we have concluded that petitioners' deductions should not be sustained.

In reaching this conclusion, we have taken into account the following considerations:

(1) Petitioners actually occupied the Pine Bluff house as their personal residence for a substantial period of time. This factor has been emphasized in the decided cases as indicative of the personal nature of the expenses subsequently incurred while holding the property for postoccupancy sale.... Similarly, the total absence or limited presence of this factor has made it easier to find that the statutory requirements have been met, e.g., with respect to inherited property or property acquired by purchase, which is then offered for sale....

(2) The house was not occupied during the period between its abandonment as the petitioners' residence and its ultimate disposition. Under such circumstances, the house was potentially available to petitioners for their personal use.... To be sure, the facts herein show that petitioners did not reoccupy the house, even temporarily, and it appears that realistically it would have been difficult for Frank to do so during trips to Pine Bluff. As a consequence, this element is of minor significance herein.

(3) Some of the decided cases have emphasized the recreational character of the property as militating against the taxpayer's position and there is some indication that buildings not being personally used may, without more, qualify as property "held for the production of income." ... While recreational property such as the yacht involved in *May v. Commissioner*, 299 F.2d 725 (4th Cir. 1962) may make the decisional task easier, it does not necessarily follow that buildings fall automatically into a preferred category....

(4) Offers to rent are an important element in the taxpayer's favor.... We are not inclined, however, to

accept respondent's position that the presence or the absence of rental offers should be the focal point. In some cases, their presence may be of minimal significance because of the adverse state of the market for rental property. (Footnote 7) Moreover, the absence of offers to rent may sometimes be explainable in terms of their adverse impact on efforts to sell the property....

(5) Another element is the presence of offers for sale. Merely offering property for sale does not, as petitioners argue, *necessarily* work a conversion into "property held for the production of income." ... But it does not follow, as respondent argues, that offers for sale can *never* effect such a conversion. There is no requirement under section 212(2) that the income be recurrent in nature, as rent normally is. On particular facts, property held solely for sale may be "property held for the production of income." So say the committee reports to the 1942 Act. H. Rept. No. 2333, 77th Cong., 2d Sess., p. 75 (1942); S. Rept. No. 1631, 77th Cong., 2d Sess., p. 87 (1942). (Footnote 8) The regulations echo those reports....

If the taxpayer is merely seeking to recover his investment or a part thereof, it will be difficult to find that the property was "held for the production of income." ... Any sale under such conditions will not produce a profit since the taxpayer's basis for determining gain will be his cost. Section 61 describes income, among other things, as "(3) *Gains* derived from dealings in property." (Emphasis added.) And the committee reports at the time the predecessors of sections 167(a)(2) and 212(2) were enacted state that income is "not confined to recurring income but applies as well to *gain* from the disposition of property." (Emphasis added.) See fn. 8 *supra*. Consequently, it would appear that the property is being held simply for the production of loss and the expenses would not be deductible....

We are, of course, aware of the provision of respondent's regulations that "Expenses paid or incurred in managing, conserving, or maintaining property held for investment may be deductible under section 212 even though the property is not currently productive and there is no likelihood that the property will be sold at a profit or will otherwise be productive of income and even though the property is held merely to minimize a loss with respect thereto." Sec. 1.212-1(b), Income Tax Regs. See also fn. 8 *supra*. But a precondition to the applicability of this provision is a determination that the property is "held for investment," i.e., for the production of income. Once that condition is attained, the subsequent absence of the economic indicators of profit, during any given period of time, will not preclude a deduction. In the initial determination whether the "investment" status exists, such absence of economic indicators may appropriately be considered.

The taxpayer must also be seeking to realize a profit representing postconversion appreciation in the market value of the property. Clearly, where the profit represents only the appreciation which took place during the period of occupancy as a personal residence, it cannot be said that the property was "held for the production of income." ... Additionally, the determination of the taxpayer's purpose will require taking into account the facts that offers for sale often reflect merely a bargaining stance and that selling commissions and other expenses of sale must be treated as offsets against the selling price....

The placing of the property on the market for immediate sale, at or shortly after the time of its abandonment as a residence, will ordinarily be strong evidence that a taxpayer is not holding the property for postconversion appreciation in value. Under such circumstances, only a most exceptional situation will permit a finding that the statutory requirement has been satisfied. On the other hand, if a taxpayer believes that the value of the property may appreciate and decides to *hold* it for some period in order to realize upon such anticipated appreciation, as well as an excess over his investment, it can be said that the property is being "held for the production of income." And this would be true regardless of whether his expectation of gain was reasonable.

The key question, in cases of the type involved herein, is the purpose or intention of the taxpayer in light of all the facts and circumstances.... In this respect, the approach is not unlike that of the so-called hobby loss cases where a similar question, namely, "expectation of profit," is the critical inquiry....

Clearly, petitioners herein do not meet the necessary criteria. Their only action was to offer the Pine Bluff house for sale. This they did immediately upon its abandonment. To be sure, the property was offered at a price in excess of the then market value, but, under the circumstances herein, we cannot say that this reflected an attempt to realize on postconversion appreciation in value rather than a bargaining stance and an offset against commissions and expenses. Moreover, it does not appear that petitioners were seeking to obtain an amount in excess of their investment. Petitioners' adjusted cost basis on the date of conversion was $70,887.39, the fair market value on that date was $60,000, and the property was offered for sale on or about that date at $70,000.

We hold that, during the taxable year 1966, petitioners did not hold the Pine Bluff residence for the production of income....

...

FOOTNOTES:

7. Such a market evaluation should not be equated with the test for determining the bona fides of rental efforts because of the range of good faith differences of opinion as to the likelihood of rental either within a given dollar range or at all.

8. "Ordinary and necessary expenses so paid or incurred are deductible under section 23(a)(2) [now sec. 212(2)] even though they are not paid or incurred for the production or collection of income of the taxable year or for the management, conservation, or maintenance of property held for the production of such income. The term 'income' for the purpose comprehends not merely income of the taxable year but also income which the taxpayer has realized in a prior taxable year or may realize in subsequent taxable years, *and is not confined to recurring income but applies as well to gain from the disposition of property*. Expenses incurred in managing or conserving property held for investment may be deductible under this provision even though there is no likelihood that the property will be sold at a profit or will otherwise be productive of income, and even though the property is held merely to minimize a loss with respect thereto." (Emphasis supplied.) The language of the House report is almost identical.

DRENNEN, J., concurring: I agree with the conclusion of the majority opinion on the facts here presented; however, I am not certain how the legal premises stated in the body of the opinion will be interpreted and applied under different factual circumstances. Hence, I feel constrained to voice my views on the legal premises to be used in determining the intent of the taxpayer in holding the property, which I agree is the basic question in these cases.

In my view in order for a taxpayer to be entitled to deduct expenses incurred with respect to holding property formerly occupied as his residence he must either rent the property or bona fide offer the property for rent after he moves out and before he sells it, or he must hold the property for appreciation in value subsequent to the time he abandons it as his residence. I do not agree that the taxpayer must prove that he was holding the property for sale at a price which would exceed his cost or tax basis in the property, i.e., at a price which would produce a tax gain, but I do believe he must show that he was holding the property after abandoning it as his residence for sale at a value that would reflect an appreciation in value over the value of the property at the time it was abandoned as taxpayer's residence.

...

FORRESTER, J., concurring: I think that the majority has reached the correct result and that that result is entirely supported by the ultimate finding "it is clear that [petitioners] were not seeking to realize on possible *post-conversion* appreciation in value." (Emphasis supplied.)

The time when the conversion occurred is obviously the key, and any appreciation prior thereto would not have grown while the property was being "held for investment," (sec. 1.212-1(b), Income Tax Regs.) but while the property was being held as taxpayers' personal residence.

The foregoing raises the question, Appreciation over what basis? I believe that the only sensible answer is appreciation over the fair market value of the property at the time of conversion, for otherwise the owner of a residence which had declined in value during his occupancy would be precluded from any tax benefits in attempting to minimize his loss even though it were quite apparent that the property would appreciate in value after he had abandoned it as a residence unless he could also prove that he reasonably expected the appreciation to carry through his original tax base.

By way of dictum the majority seems to require just such excessive (for want of a better term) postconversion appreciation and I think that this dictum is wrong.

...

———————

Now consider the following questions concerning *Newcombe*:

1. What expenses did the taxpayers seek to deduct? Would any of those expenses have been deductible if they were incurred in connection with a personal residence?

2. Describe the arguments made respectively by the taxpayers and the Service. Which argument did the court adopt?

3. What kind of test does the court adopt for determining the nature of the taxpayers' ownership of the property?

4. Why does the determination of the nature of the taxpayer's ownership matter? Couldn't a taxpayer argue that he is holding his personal residence for appreciation in value even while occupying it? Does the opinion provide an answer?

———————

Suppose the Newcombes had rented their residence for some period prior to its sale. Would that have altered the result in the case? Consider the following case.

BOLARIS v. COMMISSIONER
776 F.2d 1428 (9th Cir. 1985)

CYNTHIA HOLCOMB HALL, Circuit Judge:

I. FACTS

The taxpayers, Stephen and Valerie H. Bolaris (the "Bolarises"), purchased a home in San Jose, California, in April 1975 for $44,000 and used it as their principal residence until October 1977, when they moved into a new home they had constructed at a cost of $107,040. They attempted to sell their old home continuously from July 1977 until it was sold in August 1978 for $70,000.

In the beginning, the Bolarises tried unsuccessfully for 90 days to sell their old home. At that point they rented the home on a month-to-month basis (to "lessen the burden of carrying the property") at a fair rental value in an arm's length transaction. After eight months the Bolarises asked the tenant to leave in the hopes of improving the saleability of the house. To that end they cleaned and repainted the home. About six weeks after the original tenant left, and after the house was improved, the Bolarises received their first offer to buy the old home, which the Bolarises accepted. Because the purchasers were having difficulty obtaining financing, the Bolarises agreed to rent the old home to the buyers until they obtained financing. The buyers rented the home for about one month, and finally bought it on August 14, 1978 for $70,000.

The Bolarises filed joint income tax returns reporting salaries of $29,021 and interest of $281 in 1977 and salaries of $33,355 and interest of $286 in 1978. In addition, they received rent from their old home of $1,271 in 1977 and $2,717 in 1978. From this income they deducted depreciation of $373 in 1977 and $1,120 in 1978 and rental expenses of $1,365 in 1977 and $3,607 in 1978. The IRS disallowed the depreciation and rental expense (except interest and real estate taxes of $486 in 1977 and $2,915 in 1978). (Footnote 1) The reason given in the statutory notice for disallowing the depreciation and rental expenses was that the rental of the home "was not entered into as a trade or business or for the production of income." These disallowances, along with a disallowed IRA deduction and California State Disability Insurance deduction, resulted in deficiencies of $486 in 1977 and $408 in 1978.

The Bolarises filed a *pro se* petition in the Tax Court.... On the day of trial the IRS filed an amended answer asserting an increased deficiency of $3,339 and raising for the first time the issue of whether the Bolarises were entitled to deferred recognition of the gain from the sale of their old home under I.R.C. section 1034. (Footnote 2) The IRS contended that if the Bolarises were entitled to deferred gain on the sale of their old home under § 1034, they were not entitled to depreciation or rental expenses on the old home under §§ 167 and 212. As far as we have been able to determine, this is an issue of first impression. The Tax Court, in a reviewed decision, permitted deferred recognition of the gain from the sale of the old home, but denied the Bolarises' claimed depreciation and rental expense under I.R.C. sections 167 and 212, accepting the IRS's theory that depreciation and rental expenses, and deferred recognition of gain were mutually exclusive as a matter of law. The Bolarises appealed *pro se* to this Circuit.

II. DELAYED RECOGNITION OF GAIN.

The first issue is whether the Bolarises are entitled to delayed recognition of gain on the sale of their old home under section 1034. As the Tax Court stated, the IRS "does not seriously challenge the applicability of section 1034 to the sale in question, stating that 'the best view of the facts of this case is that [the Bolarises] qualify for section 1034 treatment. [Section 1034] is available because [the Bolarises] never converted the house from personal use.'" ... The Tax Court held that the Bolarises rental of their old residence prior to its sale did not preclude the applicability of section 1034....

The Tax Court's findings regarding whether the Bolarises were entitled to nonrecognition of gain on the sale of their old home are subject to a clearly erroneous standard of review. *See Crocker v. Commissioner*, 571 F.2d 338, 338 (6th Cir. 1978). We agree for the reasons stated by the Tax Court that the rental of the Bolarises' old home prior to its sale does not preclude the nonrecognition of gain realized on the sale of the old home.... The legislative history of section 1034 supports the nonrecognition of gain in this case by stating:

> The term "residence" is used in contradistinction to property used in trade or business and property held for the production of income. Nevertheless, the mere fact that the taxpayer temporarily rents out either the old or the new residence may not, in the light of all the facts and circumstances in the case, prevent the gain from being not recognized. For example, if the taxpayer purchases his new residence before he sells his old residence, the fact that he rents

out the new residence during the period before he vacates the old residence will not prevent the application of this subsection.

H.R. Rep. No. 586, 82d Cong., 1st Sess. 109.... We affirm the Tax Court's decision permitting deferred recognition of gain from the sale of the Bolarises' old home.

III. DEDUCTIONS FOR PROPERTY HELD FOR THE PRODUCTION OF INCOME.

A more difficult question is raised by the Tax Court's denial of depreciation and other rental expense deductions. Section 167 permits depreciation deductions for "property held for the production of income." I.R.C. § 167(a)(2). Section 212 permits deductions for insurance and miscellaneous maintenance

expenses. *See id.* § 212 (permitting deductions for "ordinary and necessary expenses" relating to "the management, conservation, or maintenance of property held for the production of income").

A. Effect of Nonrecognition of Gain.

The Tax Court accepted the IRS's argument that a residence which qualifies for nonrecognition of gain under section 1034 cannot, as a matter of law, also be held for the production of income under sections 167 or 212. *Bolaris*, 81 T.C. at 848–49. We review *de novo* this legal question involving statutory interpretation....

The IRS's argument isolates the sentence in the legislative history of section 1034 quoted above that "[t]he term 'residence' is used in contradistinction to property used in trade or business and property held for the production of income." H.R. Rep. No. 586, *supra*. However, this sentence must be read in context with the remainder of the legislative history and in light of the historical background of sections 167, 212, and 1034. In 1942 Congress enacted the statutory predecessors to sections 167 and 212 which for the first time permitted deductions for expenses involving property held for the production of income.... The following year the Tax Court held that property which has been abandoned as a residence and which has been diligently listed for rent or sale qualifies as property held for the production of income for purposes of obtaining rental expense deductions. *See Robinson v. Commissioner*, 2 T.C. 305, 307 (1943). This was true even though the property in *Robinson* was never rented. *Id.* at 307, 309.

Section 1034 was enacted in 1951. Congress was presumably aware of the *Robinson* decision at the time section 1034 was enacted. As noted above, the legislative history of section 1034 begins by stating that "'residence' is used in contradistinction to ... property held for the production of income." H.R.Rep. No. 586, *supra*. However, despite Congress' presumed awareness that an abandoned residence which was rented could qualify as property held for the production of income, the legislative history further states that "*[n]evertheless*, the mere fact that the taxpayer temporarily rents out either the old or the new residence may not, in light of all of the facts and circumstances in the case, prevent the gain from being not recognized." *Id.* (emphasis added). Thus, we read the legislative history of section 1034 as stating that a former residence could qualify for nonrecognition of gain even if the residence was temporarily rented and also qualified as being held for the production of income. This interpretation has never been questioned until this lawsuit.

The IRS apparently has now come to the conclusion that permitting both rental expense deductions and nonrecognition of gain provides an improper "windfall" to taxpayers. Our response is three-fold. First, not all rentals of former residences will qualify for rental expense deductions. For example, a rental for less than fair market value will most likely not qualify as property being held for the production of income.... Second, to the extent any "windfall" exists it is limited to a period of two years, the time within which the old residence must be sold to qualify for nonrecognition of gain. See I.R.C. § 1034(a). Third, if Congress had intended to prevent a "windfall" to taxpayers, it easily could have included a provision stating that application of section 1034 precluded rental expense deductions under sections 167 and 212. Congress did not draft such a provision and we refuse to imply one. We therefore reject the IRS's argument that a residence which qualifies for nonrecognition of gain cannot also be held for the production of income. If the IRS wants such a rule, it should ask Congress to enact it.

B. Entitlement to Rental Expense Deductions.

The remaining issue is whether the Bolarises are entitled to the claimed deductions in this case. An individual is entitled to deductions under sections 167 and 212 if "the individual [engaged] in the activity with the predominant purpose and intention of making a profit." ... See I.R.C. § 183. The burden of proving a profit motive is on the petitioner.... The existence of a profit motive is a factual question subject to clearly erroneous review....

The Tax Court recently set forth a non-exhaustive list of five factors to be considered in determining whether an individual has converted his residence to property held for the production of income. See Grant v. Commissioner, 84 T.C. 809 (1985). The five factors, which we adopt, are as follows:

> (1) the length of time the house was occupied by the individual as his residence before placing it on the market for sale; (2) whether the individual premanently [sic] abandoned all further personal use of the house; (3) the character of the property (recreational or otherwise); (4) offers to rent; and (5) offers to sell.

Id. at 825. See also Newcombe v. Commissioner, 54 T.C. 1298, 1300–01 (1970). No one factor is determinative and all of the facts and circumstances of a particular case must be considered....

Several factors strongly support the conclusion that the Bolarises possessed the requisite profit-motive based upon their rental of the old home. First, this case involves both offers to rent and offers to sell. More importantly, the Bolarises actually rented their old home at fair market rental. As the Tax Court's majority opinion recognized, "renting the residence at its fair market value would normally suggest that the taxpayer had the requisite profit objective." ...

Second, the Bolarises permanently abandoned the old home when they moved to their new residence. Even if the Bolarises had wanted to return to the old home, they would have been unentitled legally to do so because the home was rented almost continually from the time they vacated the home until it was sold....

Third, the old home offered no elements of personal recreation.... (Footnote 7)

We view the Bolarises' ancillary desire to sell the old home as an insignificant factor in determining their profit-motive....

The IRS argues that the Bolarises could not have intended to make a profit because the rental payments they received were less than their mortgage payments. Sustained unexplained losses are probative of a lack of profit motive but they present only one non-determinative factor to be considered.... We believe that the other factors discussed above outweigh the existence of short-term losses experienced by the Bolarises.

In denying the Bolarises' rental expense deductions, the Tax Court relied upon the IRS's new theory that a residence which qualifies for nonrecognition of gain cannot also be held for the production of income. In light of the factors discussed above indicating that the Bolarises possessed the requisite profit motive, we conclude that the Tax Court clearly erred in denying the deductions claimed under sections 167 and 212.

. . .

FOOTNOTES:

1. Interest and real estate taxes qualified as itemized deductions under §§ 163 and 164 of the Internal Revenue Code of 1954, 26 U.S.C. §§ 163 and 164 (further references to the Internal Revenue Code of 1954 cited as "I.R.C.") whether or not the old residence was held for production of income.

2. During the tax years in question section 1034 provided in part:

(a) **Nonrecognition of gain**

If property (in this section called "old residence") used by the taxpayer as his principal residence is sold by him and, within a period beginning 18 months before the date of such sale and ending 18 months after such date, property (in this section called "new residence") is purchased and used by the taxpayer as his principal residence, gain (if any) from such sale shall be recognized only to the extent that the taxpayer's adjusted sales price (as defined in subsection (b)) of the old residence exceeds the taxpayer's cost of purchasing the new residence.

(b) **Adjusted sales price defined**

(1) **In general**

For purposes of this section, "adjusted sales price" means the amount realized, reduced by the aggregate of the expenses for work performed on the old residence in order to assist in its sale.

(2) **Limitations**

The reduction provided in paragraph (1) applies only to expenses—

(A) for work performed during the 90-day period ending on the day on which the contract to sell the old residence is entered into;

(B) which are paid on or before the 30th day after the date of the sale of the old residence;

and

(C) which are—

(i) not allowable as deductions in computing taxable income under section 63(a) (defining taxable income), and

(ii) not taken into account in computing the amount realized from the sale of the old residence.

Section 1034 has since been amended to allow non-recognition of gain if the new residence is purchased within two years before or after the date of sale of the old residence. . . . find the remaining *Grant* factor, the length of time the house was occupied as a residence before placing it on the market for sale, to be unhelpful in this case. The Bolarises occupied the old home as their principal residence from August 1975 to October 1977. This length of occupancy is too short to adequately indicate "the personal nature of expenses subsequently incurred while holding the property for postoccupancy sale" but is too long to adequately indicate that such expenses are non-personal. *Newcombe*, 54 T.C. at 1300.

REINHARDT, Circuit Judge, concurring and dissenting:

While I agree that the Bolarises are entitled to deferred recognition of the gain on the sale of their home under I.R.C. § 1034, I cannot agree that they are also entitled to take deductions under I.R.C. §§ 167 and 212 for the period during which they were attempting to sell that property. Under section 1034, deferred recognition of gain is allowed only if the property sold is the taxpayer's "principal residence." § 1034; Treas.Reg. § 1.1034-1(c)(3). On the other hand, under sections 167 and 212 deductions can be taken for depreciation and maintenance expenses only if the property is "held for the production of income." The two phrases are mutually exclusive as are the respective forms of tax treatment.

Courts have long recognized the difference between a residence and income producing property. It has been well-established law for over 40 years that deductions are not allowable under sections 167 and 212 for expenses incurred with respect to a taxpayer's residence, whether principal or not....

It would seem that the words of the statute as well as the interpretations of the courts compel the conclusion that if the sale of a "principal residence" results in a deferral of gain under section 1034, then the seller is barred from taking deductions under sections 167 and 212 for expenses incurred with respect to that property. Given the clarity of statutory language and the consistency of judicial interpretation, there would seem to be no reason to turn, as the majority does, to the legislative history.

In any event, the legislative history is plain and unambiguous. It states: "[t]he term 'residence' is used in contradistinction to ... property held for production of income." H.R.Rep. No. 586, 82d Cong. 1st Sess. 109....

Thus, the legislative history confirms what we have already noted: "residence" and "property held for the production of income" are mutually exclusive terms.

The legislative history also states that the fact that the taxpayer rents out his old house may not, in light of all the facts and circumstances, be inconsistent with a finding that the old house is still the taxpayer's residence. *Id. See* Treas.Reg. § 1.1034-1(c)(3). The majority seizes on the statement that the temporary renting out of a home does not deprive it of its character as the taxpayer's principal residence. On the basis of this rather benign proposition and without any particular further explanation, the majority leaps to the conclusion that a taxpayer's home can at once be *both* a residence and property held for the production of income. In fact, as has been demonstrated above, the legislative history provides compelling support for precisely the opposite conclusion. Contrary to the majority's assertion, the proposition that a "residence" and "income producing property" are antithetical terms is not novel: it has been advanced by the Commissioner and accepted by the Tax Court, either expressly or impliedly, on a number of occasions....

Moreover, a holding that the Bolarises cannot take deductions under sections 167 and 212 does not mean that they are not entitled to any deductions at all for expenses relating to their home. Under sections 163, 164, and 183(b)(1) the

Bolarises were entitled to, and did, deduct in full the mortgage interest and real estate taxes that they paid. In addition, section 183(b)(2) [now section 280A] authorizes the deduction of the depreciation and maintenance expenses to the extent that the income from the rental of the house exceeds the amount of the mortgage interest and real estate tax payments. It is only because the Bolarises' rental income was less than the

amount of those payments that they cannot deduct at least some portion of the maintenance and depreciation expenses they incurred.

...

———————————

Now consider these questions concerning *Bolaris*.

1. Why did the taxpayers want the property to continue to be classified as a personal residence?

Note that section 1034 no longer appears in the Code. Congress replaced it as part of the 1997 Act with section 121. Prior to its repeal and replacement by section 121, section 1034 allowed a taxpayer to defer gain on the sale of a principal residence provided the taxpayer reinvested the sales proceeds in a new residence.[5] New section 121 is more flexible than old section 1034; under new section 121, the taxpayer need only have used the home as a principal residence for 2 of the last 5 years preceding the sale, and it permits an exclusion of gain (rather than simply its deferral).

2. Why did the Service file an amended answer on the day of trial?

Note that the taxpayers were *pro se*. In general, the Tax Court does not often grant continuances. Does the ability of the government to alter its view of the case on the brink of trial seem unfair when the taxpayer is not represented by experienced counsel? But also note, that at the time of the case, Tax Court Rule 142(a) provided as follows:

> Rule 142. Burden of Proof. (a) *General*. The burden of proof shall be upon the petitioner, except as otherwise provided by statute or determined by the Court; and except that, in respect of any new matter, increases in deficiency, and affirmative defenses pleaded in the answer, it shall be upon the respondent.

From your reading of the case, would you argue that the change in the government's position represented introduction of a "new matter" causing a shift in the burden of proof to the government?

The standard for what is a "new matter" is far from clear. In *Achiro v. Commissioner*, 77 T.C. 881 (1981), the same judge, Judge Hall, who wrote the opinion for the Ninth Circuit in *Bolaris*, wrote (in a case before the Tax Court):

> The assertion of a new theory which merely clarifies or develops the original determination without being inconsistent or increasing the amount of the deficiency is not a new matter requiring the shifting of the burden of proof.... However, if the assertion in the amended answer either alters the original deficiency or requires the presentation of different evidence, then respondent has introduced a new matter.... The factual bases and rationale required to establish that the amounts paid by [the taxpayer's corporation] as management fees were expended for that purpose and were ordinary and necessary business expenses are entirely different from the factual bases and rationale necessary to establish that sections 482, 269, 61, and 414(b) do not apply to the present situation.... Respondent's new positions raised in his amended answer require the presentation of new evidence and do not simply clarify or develop his original position.

77 T.C. at 890.

———————————

5. What other provisions have you encountered that allow a similar deferral of gain?

3. How can a piece of property be both a personal residence and property held for the production of income?

The problem of conversion of personal use property to property held for the production of income, or vice versa, arises frequently with respect to residences. As the previous case illustrates, the outcome is highly factually dependent. Among the important consequences of the distinction are the availability of the deduction for depreciation and the ability of the taxpayer to claim a loss on a sale.[6] When a taxpayer forms the intent to convert the property, she can begin to claim depreciation, even if the property is not yet rented because section 167(a)(2) allows the deduction for depreciation of "property held for the production of income." (The taxpayer's basis for depreciation will be the lesser of its fair market value at the time she begins to "hold" it as rental property or its adjusted basis at the time. **Read Treasury Regulation section 1.167(g)-1.**)

To claim a loss on the sale of investment property, however, the taxpayer must survive the hurdle of section 165, specifically, section 165(c)(2). Section 165(c)(2) requires the taxpayer to have "losses incurred in any transaction entered into for profit, though not connected with a trade or business." Treasury Regulation section 1.165-9(b) interprets section 165(c)(2). **Read Treasury Regulation section 1.165-9(b).** The Regulation provides that a taxpayer seeking to convert her personal residence to property held for the production of income actually rent or otherwise appropriate the property to income-producing purposes and use it for such purposes up to the time of its sale in order to claim a loss. (That Regulation also includes a rule for determining the basis the taxpayer must use for calculating the loss. Section 1.165-9(b)(2) provides that the adjusted basis shall be the lesser of the fair market value at the time of conversion or the adjusted basis for loss at the time of conversion, adjusted for depreciation.)

The difference in the basis rules can have an undesirable effect on the taxpayer at the time of sale of loss property if the property declines further in value between the date she begins claiming depreciation and the date she actually commences renting it. Assume, for example, that the taxpayer's adjusted basis in her residence prior to conversion is $150,000. At the time she converts it to rental property for depreciation purposes, the value is $100,000. That is the basis she will use for depreciation. But if the value continues to decline prior to the actual date of rental, to $75,000 for example, that will be its starting point in the calculation of its basis for the purpose of determining loss. From that amount, she will have to further reduce the basis for any depreciation she claims prior to the sale. **Study Treasury Regulation section 1.165-9(c), Examples 1 and 2.**

In both *Newcombe* and *Bolaris*, the issue concerned whether the taxpayers had successfully converted the use of their properties from personal use to investment use. In both cases, you saw the difficulty the courts had in resolving the nature of the taxpayer's ownership. Now recall the question concerning your occasional rental of your condominium. The same problems of characterization can also arise in connection with "mixed" use property. When a taxpayer purchases a condominium, intending to rent it off and on to help finance the purchase, the use of the condo is mixed: in part personal, in part property held for the production of income. But, if a court must apply a factual

---

6. Whether the taxpayer holds the property as a personal residence or as rental property, she may claim deductions for mortgage interest and property taxes. What difference does the nature of her ownership of the property make in entering these deductions into the tax calculation outline?

test, as in *Newcombe* and *Bolaris*, the taxpayer will have no certainty that he has reported the income and expenses properly until the time for an audit has expired. (Remember, in Part II, we encountered the problem of trying to distinguish between business and personal elements in claiming deductions for such items as education, clothing, travel, child care, and the operation of a farm?)

Congress eventually responded by enacting section 280A. **Read section 280A.** What kind of test does section 280A establish? What are the advantages and disadvantages of this type of test?

In effect, section 280A creates three alternatives, depending upon the actual amount of time the taxpayer uses the property for personal or rental use:

- If the taxpayer's use of the property as a residence is merely incidental (defined as the lesser of no more than 14 days or 10% of the number of days the property is rented at a fair rental value), the use is treated as property held for the production of income. But, the taxpayer must allocate the expenses between the number of days used for personal use and the number of days rented at fair rental value.

- If the taxpayer's rental use of the property is merely incidental (defined as rented for less than 15 days during the taxable year), the property is treated as wholly for personal use and the taxpayer need not include the rental income in gross income. In that case, the taxpayer may deduct the usual below-the-line deductions associated with residential property ownership.

- The third category recognizes the mixed use of the property and requires the taxpayer to include rental income in gross income but allows the taxpayer to claim deductions. The taxpayer may claim all below-the-line deductions to which she would be entitled in the case of personal use property. Similar to the method you first encountered in section 183, she may also claim additional deductions in an amount equal to the difference between the rental income and the below-the-line deductions. Unlike section 183, however, these additional deductions are characterized in part as "above-the-line" deductions and in part as below-the-line deductions. The allocation depends upon the proportion of the total days of usage represented by rental days at fair rental.

As in the case of the distinction between property held for personal use and property held for investment, the distinction between property held for investment and property held for other income-producing purposes has produced frequent litigation. When does "investment" become a different category of ownership?

3. Property Held for Use in a Trade or Business

A taxpayer who owns an operating business, for example, a dry cleaning business, owns equipment used in that "trade or business." Thus, in many cases, identification of this classification of property will follow naturally from identifying the nature of the taxpayer's activity as a trade or business. But, in other cases, identification is less clear. Consider, for example, the taxpayer who initially purchases a two-family house, intending to live in one-half of the house and rent out the other half. One-half the house is surely property held for personal use; the other half is property held for investment. When the taxpayer buys a second two-family house, intending to rent both halves, has the taxpayer converted his investment activity into a trade or business? In general, activities that require ongoing active management have crossed the line from investment to trade or business activities. **Recall** *Groetzinger*. Thus, the taxpayer who owns and manages a hotel that provides normal hotel services is in a trade or business, whereas a taxpayer who owns a rental apartment building that requires merely the engagement of a rental agent and a superintendant to perform janitorial services is not.

4. Inventory (Property Held Primarily for Sale to Customers)

The final category, inventory, is also denoted as "property held primarily for sale to customers in the ordinary course of a taxpayer's trade or business." This latter designation is used for real estate, rather than the term "inventory." Once again, the distinction between this category of property and property held for other purposes is probably most difficult in the case of real property and has produced frequent litigation. Consider, for example, the following case.

MALAT v. RIDDELL

383 U.S. 569 (1966)

PER CURIAM.

Petitioner was a participant in a joint venture which acquired a 45-acre parcel of land, the intended use for which is somewhat in dispute. Petitioner contends that the venturers' intention was to develop and operate an apartment project on the land; the respondent's position is that there was a "dual purpose" of developing the property for rental purposes or selling, whichever proved to be the more profitable. In any event, difficulties in obtaining the necessary financing were encountered, and the interior lots of the tract were subdivided and sold. The profit from those sales was reported and taxed as ordinary income.

The joint venturers continued to explore the possibility of commercially developing the remaining exterior parcels. Additional frustrations in the form of zoning restrictions were encountered. These difficulties persuaded petitioner and another of the joint venturers of the desirability of terminating the venture; accordingly, they sold out their interests in the remaining property. Petitioner contends that he is entitled to treat the profits from this last sale as capital gains; the respondent takes the position that this was "property held by the taxpayer primarily for sale to customers in the ordinary course of his trade or business," (Footnote 2) and thus subject to taxation as ordinary income.

The District Court made the following finding:

"The members of (the joint venture), as of the date the 44.901 acres were acquired, intended either to sell the property or develop it for rental, depending upon which course appeared to be most profitable. The venturers realized that they had made a good purchase price-wise and, if they were unable to obtain acceptable construction financing or rezoning ... which would be prerequisite to commercial development, they would sell the property in bulk so they wouldn't get hurt. The purpose of either selling or developing the property continued during the period in which [the joint venture] held the property."

The District Court ruled that petitioner had failed to establish that the property was not held primarily for sale to customers in the ordinary course of business, and thus rejected petitioner's claim to capital gain treatment for the profits derived from the property's resale. The Court of Appeals affirmed, 347 F.2d 23. We granted certiorari ... to resolve a conflict among the courts of appeals (Footnote 3) with regard to the meaning of the term 'primarily' as it is used in § 1221(1) of the Internal Revenue Code of 1954.

The statute denies capital gain treatment to profits reaped from the sale of "property held by the taxpayer *primarily* for sale to customers in the ordinary course of his trade or business." (Emphasis added.) The respondent urges upon us a construction of "primarily" as meaning that a purpose may be "primary" if it is a "substantial" one.

As we have often said, "the words of statutes—including revenue acts—should be interpreted where possible in their ordinary, everyday senses." *Crane v. Commissioner of Internal Revenue*, 331 U.S. 1, 6.... Departure from a literal reading of statutory language may, on occasion, be indicated by relevant internal evidence of the statute itself and necessary in order to effect the legislative purpose. See, e.g., *Board of Governors of Federal Reserve System v. Agnew*, 329 U.S. 441, 446–448. But this is not such an occasion. The purpose of the statutory provision with which we deal is to differentiate between the "profits and losses arising from the everyday operation of a business" on the one hand (Corn Products Refining Co. v. Commissioner, 350 U.S. 46, 52 ...) and "the realization of appreciation in value accrued over a substantial period of time" on the other. (*Commissioner of Internal Revenue v. Gillette Motor Transport, Inc.*, 364 U.S. 130, 134.). A literal reading of the statute is consistent with this legislative purpose. We hold that, as used in § 1221(1), "primarily" means "of first importance" or "principally."

Since the courts below applied an incorrect legal standard, we do not consider whether the result would be supportable on the facts of this case had the correct one been applied. We believe, moreover, that the appropriate disposition is to remand the case to the District Court, for fresh fact-findings, addressed to the statute as we have now construed it.

Vacated and remanded.

FOOTNOTES:

2. Internal Revenue Code of 1954, § 1221(1), ..."For purposes of this subtitle, the term 'capital asset' means property held by the taxpayer (whether or not connected with his trade or business), but does not include—

"(1) ... property held by the taxpayer primarily for sale to customers in the ordinary course of his trade or business."

3. *Compare Rollingwood Corp. v. Commissioner*, 190 F.2d 263, 266 (C.A.9th Cir.); *American Can Co. v. Commissioner*, 317 F.2d 604, 605 (C.A.2d Cir.), with *United States v. Bennett*, 186 F.2d 407, 410–411 (C.A.5th Cir.); *Municipal Bond Corp. v. Commissioner*, 341 F.2d 683, 688–689 (C.A.8th Cir.). Cf. *Recordak Corp. v. United States*, 163 Ct.Cl. 294, 300–301, 325 F.2d 460, 463–464.

Now consider the following questions concerning *Malat v. Riddell*.

1. What was the government's position as to the meaning of "primarily"? Why did it take this position?

2. How did the Court reach its conclusion? Where else did you see the Court interpreting the words of a tax statute in a similar fashion? **Recall *Welch v. Helvering.***

Once again, you see a court establishing a facts and circumstances test for deciding a tax issue. How useful do you think this test will be when applied to future cases? Read the following two cases.

BIEDENHARN REALTY COMPANY, INC. v. UNITED STATES
526 F.2d 409 (5th Cir. 1976)

GOLDBERG, Circuit Judge:

The taxpayer-plaintiff, Biedenharn Realty Company, Inc. [Biedenharn], filed suit against the United States in May, 1971, claiming a refund for the tax years 1964, 1965, and 1966. In its original tax returns for the three years, Biedenharn listed profits of $254,409.47 from the sale of 38 residential lots.

Taxpayer divided this gain, attributing 60% to ordinary income and 40% to capital gains. Later, having determined that the profits from these sales were entirely ordinary income, the Internal Revenue Service assessed and collected additional taxes and interest. In its present action, plaintiff asserts that the whole real estate profit represents gain from the sale of capital assets and consequently that the Government is indebted to taxpayer for $32,006.86 in overpaid taxes. Reviewing the facts of this case in the light of our previous holdings and the directions set forth in this opinion; we reject plaintiff's claim and in so doing reverse the opinion of the District Court.

...

A. *The Realty Company.* Joseph Biedenharn organized the Biedenharn Realty Company in 1923 as a vehicle for holding and managing the Biedenharn family's numerous investments. The original stockholders were all family members. The investment company controls, among other interests, valuable commercial properties, a substantial stock portfolio, a motel, warehouses, a shopping center, residential real property, and farm property.

B. *Taxpayer's Real Property Sales—The Hardtimes Plantation.* Taxpayer's suit most directly involves its ownership and sale of lots from the 973 acre tract located near Monroe, Louisiana, known as the Hardtimes Plantation. The plaintiff purchased the estate in 1935 for $50,000.00. B. W. Biedenharn, the Realty Company's president, testified that taxpayer acquired Hardtimes as a "good buy" for the purpose of farming and as a future investment. The plaintiff farmed the land for several years. Thereafter, Biedenharn rented part of the acreage to a farmer who Mr. Biedenharn suggested may presently be engaged in farming operations.

1. *The Three Basic Subdivisions.* Between 1939 and 1966, taxpayer carved three basic subdivisions from Hardtimes—Biedenharn Estates, Bayou DeSiard Country Club Addition, and Oak Park Addition—covering approximately 185 acres. During these years, Biedenharn sold 208 subdivided Hardtimes lots in 158 sales, making a profit in excess of $800,000.00. These three basic subdivisions are the source of the contested 37 sales of 38 lots. (Footnote 7) Their development and disposition are more fully discussed below.

a) Biedenharn Estates Unit 1, including 41.9 acres, was platted in 1938. Between 1939 and 1956, taxpayer apparently sold 21 lots in 9 sales. Unit 2, containing 8.91 acres, was sold in 9 transactions between 1960 and 1965 and involved 10 lots.

b) Bayou DeSiard Country Club Addition, covering 61 acres, was subdivided in 1951, with remaining lots resubdivided in 1964. Approximately 73 lots were purchased in 64 sales from 1951 to 1966.

c) Oak Park Units 1 and 2 encompassed 75 acres. After subdivision in 1955 and re-subdivision in 1960, plaintiff sold approximately 104 lots in 76 sales.

2. *Additional Hardtimes Sales.* Plaintiff lists at least 12 additional Hardtimes sales other than lots vended from the three basic subdivisions. The earliest of these dispositions occurred in November, 1935, thirteen days after the Plantation's purchase. Ultimately totaling approximately 275 acres, most, but not all, of these sales involved large parcels of nonsubdivided land.

C. *Taxpayer's Real Property Activity: Non-Hardtimes Sales.* The 208 lots marketed from the three Hardtimes subdivisions represent only part of Biedenharn's total real property sales activities. Although the record does not in every instance permit exactitude, plaintiff's own submissions make clear that the Biedenharn Realty Company effectuated numerous non-Hardtimes retail real estate transactions. From the Company's formation in 1923 through 1966, the last year for which taxes are contested, taxpayer sold 934 lots. Of this total, plaintiff disposed of 249 lots before 1935 when it acquired Hardtimes. Thus, in the years 1935 to 1966, taxpayer sold 477 lots apart from its efforts with respect to the basic Hardtimes subdivisions. Biedenharn's year by year sales breakdown is attached as Appendix I of this opinion. That chart shows real estate sales in all but two years, 1932 and 1970, since the Realty Company's 1923 inception.

Unfortunately, the record does not unambiguously reveal the number of *sales* as opposed to the number of *lots* involved in these dispositions. Although some doubt exists as to the actual *sales* totals, even the most conservative reading of the figures convinces us of the frequency and abundance of the non-Hardtimes sales. For example, from 1925 to 1958, Biedenharn consummated from its subdivided Owens tract a minimum of 125, but perhaps upwards of 300, sales (338 lots). Eighteen sales accounted for 20 lots sold between 1923 and 1958 from Biedenharn's Cornwall property. Taxpayer's disposition from 1927 to 1960 of its Corey and Cabeen property resulted in at least 50 sales. Plaintiff made 14 sales from its Thomas Street lots between 1937 and 1955. Moreover, Biedenharn has sold over 20 other properties, a few of them piecemeal, since 1923.

Each of these parcels has its own history. Joseph Biedenharn transferred much of the land to the Realty Company in 1923. The company acquired other property through purchases and various forms of foreclosure. Before sale, Biedenharn held some tracts for commercial or residential rental. Taxpayer originally had slated the Owens acreage for transfer in bulk to the Owens-Illinois Company. Also, the length of time between acquisition and disposition differed significantly among pieces of realty. However, these variations in the background of each plot and the length of time and original purpose for which each was obtained do not alter the fact that the Biedenharn Realty Company regularly sold substantial amounts of subdivided and improved real property, and further, that these sales were not confined to the basic Hardtimes subdivisions.

D. *Real Property Improvements.* Before selling the Hardtimes lots, Biedenharn improved the land, adding in most instances streets, drainage, water, sewerage, and electricity. The total cost of bettering the Plantation acreage exceeded $200,000 and included $9,519.17 for Biedenharn Estates Unit 2, $56,879.12 for Bayou DeSiard County Club Addition, and $141,579.25 for the Oak Park Addition.

E. *Sale of the Hardtimes Subdivisions.* Bernard Biedenharn testified that at the time of the Hardtimes purchase, no one foresaw that the land would be sold as residential property in the future. Accordingly, the District Court found, and we do not disagree, that Biedenharn bought Hardtimes for investment. Later, as the City of Monroe expanded northward, the Plantation became valuable residential property. The Realty Company staked off the Bayou DeSiard subdivision so that prospective purchasers could see what the lots "looked like." As demand increased, taxpayer opened the Oak Park and Biedenharn Estates Unit 2 subdivisions and resubdivided the Bayou DeSiard section. Taxpayer handled all Biedenharn Estates and Bayou DeSiard sales. Independent realtors disposed of many of the Oak Park lots. Mr. Herbert Rosenhein, a local broker, sold Oak Park Unit 1 lots. Gilbert Faulk, a real estate agent, sold from Oak Park Unit 2. Of the 37 sales consummated between 1964 and 1966, Henry

Biedenharn handled at least nine transactions (Biedenharn Estates (2) and Bayou DeSiard (7)) while "independent realtors" effected some, if not all, of the other 28 transactions (Oak Park Unit 2). Taxpayer delegated significant responsibilities to these brokers. In its dealings with Faulk, Biedenharn set the prices, general credit terms, and signed the deeds. Details, including specific credit decisions and advertising, devolved to Faulk, who utilized on-site signs and newspapers to publicize the lots.

In contrast to these broker induced dispositions, plaintiff's non-brokered sales resulted after unsolicited individuals approached Realty Company employees with inquiries about prospective purchases. At no time did the plaintiff hire its own real state salesmen or engage in formal advertising.

Apparently, the lands' prime location and plaintiff's subdivision activities constituted sufficient notice to interested persons of the availability of Hardtimes lots. Henry Biedenharn testified:

> [Once] we started improving and putting roads and streets in people would call us up and ask you about buying a lot and we would sell a lot if they wanted it.

The Realty Company does not maintain a separate place of business but instead offices at the Biedenharn family's Ouachita Coca-Cola bottling plant. A telephone, listed in plaintiff's name, rings at the Coca-Cola building. Biedenharn has four employees: a camp caretaker, a tenant farmer, a bookkeeper and a manager. The manager, Henry Biedenharn, Jr., devotes approximately 10% of his time to the Realty Company, mostly collecting rents and overseeing the maintenance of various properties. The bookkeeper also works only part-time for plaintiff. Having set out these facts, we now discuss the relevant legal standard for resolving this controversy.

II.

The determination of gain as capital or ordinary is controlled by the language of the Internal Revenue Code. The Code defines capital asset, the profitable sale or exchange of which generally results in capital gains, as "property held by the taxpayer." 26 U.S.C. § 1221. Many exceptions limit the enormous breadth of this congressional description and consequently remove large numbers of transactions from the privileged realm of capital gains. In this case, we confront the question whether or not Biedenharn's real estate sales should be taxed at ordinary rates because they fall within the exception covering "property held by the taxpayer primarily for sale to customers in the ordinary course of his trade or business." 26 U.S.C. § 1221(1).

The problem we struggle with here is not novel. We have become accustomed to the frequency with which taxpayers litigate this troublesome question. Chief Judge Brown appropriately described the real estate capital gains-ordinary income issue as "old, familiar, recurring, vexing and ofttimes elusive." ... The difficulty in large part stems from ad-hoc application of the numerous permissible criteria set forth in our multitudinous prior opinions. Over the past 40 years, this case by case approach with its concentration on the facts of each suit has resulted in a collection of decisions not always reconcilable. Recognizing the situation, we have warned that efforts to distinguish and thereby make consistent the Court's previous holdings must necessarily be "foreboding and unrewarding." ... Litigants are cautioned that "each case must be decided on its own peculiar facts.... Specific factors, or combinations of them are not necessarily controlling." ... Nor are these factors the equivalent of the philosopher's stone, separating "sellers garlanded with capital gains from those beflowered in the garden of ordinary income." ...

Assuredly, we would much prefer one or two clearly defined, easily employed tests which lead to predictable, perhaps automatic, conclusions. However, the nature of the congressional "capital asset" definition and the myriad situations to which we must apply that standard make impossible any easy escape from the task before us. No one set of criteria is applicable to all economic structures. Moreover, within a collection of tests, individual factors have varying weights and magnitudes, depending on the facts of the case. The relationship among the factors and their mutual interaction is altered as each criteria increases or diminishes in strength, sometimes changing the controversy's outcome. As such, there can be no mathematical formula capable of finding the X of capital gains or ordinary income in this complicated field.

Yet our inability to proffer a panaceatic guide to the perplexed with respect to this subject does not preclude our setting forth some general, albeit inexact, guidelines for the resolution of many of the §1221(1) cases we confront. This opinion does not purport to reconcile all past precedents or assure conflict-free future decisions. Nor do we hereby obviate the need for ad-hoc adjustments when confronted with close cases and changing factual circumstances. Instead, with the hope of clarifying a few of the area's mysteries, we more precisely define and suggest points of emphasis for the major *Winthrop* delineated factors (Footnote 22) as they appear in the instant controversy. In so doing, we devote particular attention to the Court's recent opinions in order that our analysis will reflect, insofar as possible, the Circuit's present trends.

III.

We begin our task by evaluating in the light of *Biedenharn's* facts the main *Winthrop* factors—substantiality and frequency of sales, improvements, solicitation and advertising efforts, and brokers' activities—as well as a few miscellaneous contentions. A separate section follows discussing the keenly contested role of prior investment intent. Finally, we consider the significance of the Supreme Court's decision in *Malat v. Riddell.*

A. *Frequency and Substantiality of Sales*

Scrutinizing closely the record and briefs, we find that plaintiff's real property sales activities compel an ordinary income conclusion. In arriving at this result, we examine first the most important of *Winthrop's* factors—the frequency and substantiality of taxpayer's sales. Although frequency and substantiality of sales are not usually conclusive, they occupy the preeminent ground in our analysis. The recent trend of Fifth Circuit decisions indicates that when dispositions of subdivided property extend over a long period of time and are especially numerous, the likelihood of capital gains is very slight indeed.... Conversely, when sales are few and isolated, the taxpayer's claim to capital gain is accorded greater deference....

On the present facts, taxpayer could not claim "isolated" sales or a passive and gradual liquidation.... Although only three years and 37 sales (38 lots) are in controversy here, taxpayer's pre-1964 sales from the Hardtimes acreage as well as similar dispositions from other properties are probative of the existence of sales "in the ordinary course of his trade or business." ... As Appendix I indicates, Biedenharn sold property, usually a substantial number of lots, in every year, save one, from 1923 to 1966....

The frequency and substantiality of Biedenharn's sales go not only to its holding purpose and the existence of a trade or business but also support our finding of the ordinariness with which the Realty Company disposed of its lots. These sales easily meet the criteria of normalcy set forth in *Winthrop*....

... [O]ne could fairly infer that the income accruing to the Biedenharn Realty Company from its pre-1935 sales helped support the purchase of the Hardtimes Plantation. Even if taxpayer made no significant acquisitions after Hardtimes, the "purpose, system, and continuity" of Biedenharn's efforts easily constitute a business....

...

B. *Improvements*

Although we place greatest emphasis on the frequency and substantiality of sales over an extended time period, our decision in this instance is aided by the presence of taxpayer activity—particularly improvements—in the other *Winthrop* areas. Biedenharn vigorously improved its subdivisions, generally adding streets, drainage, sewerage, and utilities. These alterations are comparable to those in *Winthrop*, ... except that in the latter case taxpayer built five houses. We do not think that the construction of five houses in the context of *Winthrop*'s 456 lot sales significantly distinguishes that taxpayer from Biedenharn....

C. *Solicitation and Advertising Efforts*

Substantial, frequent sales and improvements such as we have encountered in this case will usually conclude the capital gains issue against taxpayer.... Thus, on the basis of our analysis to this point, we would have little hesitation in finding that taxpayer held "primarily for sale" in the "ordinary course of [his] trade or business." "[The] flexing of commercial muscles with frequency and continuity, design and effect" of which *Winthrop* spoke, *supra* at 911, is here a reality. This reality is further buttressed by Biedenharn's sales efforts, including those carried on through brokers. Minimizing the importance of its own sales activities, taxpayer points repeatedly to its steady avoidance of advertising or other solicitation of customers. Plaintiff directs our attention to stipulations detailing the population growth of Monroe and testimony outlining the economic forces which made Hardtimes Plantation attractive residential property and presumably eliminated the need for sales exertions. We have no quarrel with plaintiff's description of this familiar process of suburban expansion, but we cannot accept the legal inferences which taxpayer would have us draw.

The Circuit's recent decisions ... implicitly recognize that even one inarguably in the real estate business need not engage in promotional exertions in the face of a favorable market. As such, we do not always require a showing of active solicitation where "business ... [is] good, indeed brisk,".... Plainly, this represents a sensible approach. In cases such as *Biedenharn*, the sale of a few lots and the construction of the first homes, albeit not, as in *Winthrop*, by the taxpayer, as well as the building of roads, addition of utilities, and staking off of the other subdivided parcels constitute a highly visible form of advertising. Prospective home buyers drive by the advantageously located property, see the development activities, and are as surely put on notice of the availability of lots as if the owner had erected large signs announcing "residential property for sale." We do not by this evaluation automatically neutralize advertising or solicitation as a factor in our analysis. This form of inherent notice is not present in all land sales, especially where the property is not so valuably located, is not subdivided into small lots, and is not improved. Moreover, inherent notice represents only one band of the solicitation spectrum. Media utilization and personal initiatives remain material components of this criterion. When present, they call for greater Government oriented emphasis on *Winthrop's* solicitation factor.

D. *Brokerage Activities*

In evaluating Biedenharn's solicitation activities, ... the Realty Company hired brokers who, using media and on site advertising, worked vigorously on taxpayer's behalf. We do not believe that the employment of brokers should shield plaintiff from ordinary income treatment.... Their activities should at least in discounted form be attributed to Biedenharn. To the contrary, taxpayer argues that "one who is not already in the trade or business of selling real estate does not enter such business when he employs a broker who acts as an independent contractor...." ... Biedenharn determined original prices and general credit policy. Moreover, the Realty Company did not make all the sales in question through brokers.... Biedenharn sold the Bayou DeSiard and Biedenharn Estates lots and may well have sold some of the Oak Park land. In other words, ... Biedenharn's brokers did not so completely take charge of the whole of the Hardtimes sales as to permit the Realty Company to wall itself off legally from their activities.

E. *Additional Taxpayer Contentions*

Plaintiff presents a number of other contentions and supporting facts for our consideration. Although we set out these arguments and briefly discuss them, their impact, in the face of those factors examined above, must be minimal. Taxpayer emphasizes that its profits from real estate sales averaged only 11.1% in each of the years in controversy, compared to 52.4% in *Winthrop*. Whatever the percentage, plaintiff would be hard pressed to deny the substantiality of its Hardtimes sales in absolute terms (the subdivided lots alone brought in overone million dollars) or, most importantly, to assert that its real estate business was too insignificant to constitute a separate trade or business.

The relatively modest income share represented by Biedenharn's real property dispositions stems not from a failure to engage in real estate sales activities but rather from the comparatively large profit attributable to the Company's 1965 ($649,231.34) and 1966 ($688,840.82) stock sales. The fact of Biedenharn's holding, managing, and selling stock is not inconsistent with the existence of a separate realty business. If in the face of taxpayer's numerous real estate dealings this Court held otherwise, we would be sanctioning special treatment for those individuals and companies arranging their business activities so that the income accruing to real estate sales represents only a small fraction of the taxpaying entity's total gains.

Similarly, taxpayer observes that Biedenharn's manager devoted only 10% of his time to real estate dealings and then mostly to the company's rental properties. This fact does not negate the existence of sales activities. Taxpayer had a telephone listing, a shared business office, and a few part-time employees. Because, as discussed before, a strong seller's market existed, Biedenharn's sales required less than the usual solicitation efforts and therefore less than the usual time. Moreover, plaintiff, unlike taxpayers in *Winthrop*, *supra* and *Thompson*, *supra*, hired brokers to handle many aspects of the Hardtimes transactions—thus further reducing the activity and time required of Biedenharn's employees.

Finally, taxpayer argues that it is entitled to capital gains since its enormous profits (74% to 97%) demonstrate a return based principally on capital appreciation and not on taxpayer's "merchandising" efforts. We decline the opportunity to allocate plaintiff's gain between long-term market appreciation and improvement related activities.... Even if we undertook such an analysis and found the former element predominant, we would on the authority of *Winthrop*, ... reject plaintiff's contention which, in effect, is merely taxpayer's version of the Government's unsuccessful argument in that case.

IV.

The District Court found that "[taxpayer] is merely liquidating over a long period of time a substantial investment in the most advantageous method possible." ... In this view, the original investment intent is crucial, for it preserves the capital gains character of the transaction even in the face of normal real estate sales activities.

The Government asserts that Biedenharn Realty Company did not merely "liquidate" an investment but instead entered the real estate business in an effort to dispose of what was formerly investment property. Claiming that Biedenharn's activities would result in ordinary income if the Hardtimes Plantation had been purchased with the intent to divide and resell the property, and finding no reason why a different prior intent should influence this outcome, the Government concludes that original investment purpose is irrelevant. Instead, the Government would have us focus exclusively on taxpayer's intent and the level of sales activity during the period commencing with subdivision and improvement and lasting through final sales. Under this theory, every individual who improves and frequently sells substantial numbers of land parcels would receive ordinary income.

While the facts of this case dictate our agreement with the Internal Revenue Service's ultimate conclusion of taxpayer liability, they do not require our acquiescence in the Government's entreated total elimination of *Winthrop*'s first criterion, "the nature and purpose of the acquisition."

Undoubtedly, in most subdivided-improvement situations, an investment purpose of antecedent origin will not survive into a present era of intense retail selling. The antiquated purpose, when overborne by later, but substantial and frequent selling activity, will not prevent ordinary income from being visited upon the taxpayer.... Generally, investment purpose has no built-in perpetuity nor a guarantee of capital gains forever more. Precedents, however, in certain circumstances have permitted landowners with earlier investment intent to sell subdivided property and remain subject to capital gains treatment....

    ...

We reject the Government's sweeping contention that prior investment intent is always irrelevant. There will be instances where an initial investment purpose endures in controlling fashion notwithstanding continuing sales activity. We doubt that this aperture, where an active subdivider and improver receives capital gains, is very wide; yet we believe it exists. We would most generally find such an opening where the change from investment holding to sales activity results from unanticipated, externally induced factors which make impossible the continued pre-existing use of the realty.... Acts of God, condemnation of part of one's property, new and unfavorable zoning regulations, or other events forcing alteration of taxpayer's plans create situations making possible subdivision and improvement as a part of a capital gains disposition.

However, cases of the ilk of … *Winthrop*, … remain unaffected in their ordinary income conclusion. There, the transformations in purpose were not coerced. Rather, the changes ensued from taxpayers' purely *voluntary* responses to increased economic opportunity—albeit at times externally created—in order to enhance their gain through the subdivision, improvement, and sale of lots. Thus reinforced by the trend of these recent decisions, we gravitate toward the Government's view in instances of willful taxpayer change of purpose and grant the taxpayer little, if any, benefit from *Winthrop's* first criterion in such cases.

The distinction drawn above reflects our belief that Congress did not intend to automatically disqualify from capital gains bona fide investors forced to abandon prior purposes for reasons beyond their control. At times, the Code may be severe, and this Court may construe it strictly, but neither Code nor

Court is so tyrannical as to mandate the absolute rule urged by the Government. However, we caution that although permitting a land owner substantial sales flexibility where there is a forced change from original investment purpose, we do not absolutely shield the constrained taxpayer from ordinary income. That taxpayer is not granted *carte blanche* to undertake intensely all aspects of a full blown real estate business. Instead, in cases of forced change of purpose, we will continue to utilize the *Winthrop* analysis discussed earlier but will place unusually strong taxpayer-favored emphasis on *Winthrop's* first factor.

Clearly, under the facts in this case, the distinction just elaborated undermines Biedenharn's reliance on original investment purpose. Taxpayer's change of purpose was entirely voluntary and therefore does not fall within the protected area. Moreover, taxpayer's original investment intent, *even if* considered a factor sharply supporting capital gains treatment, is so overwhelmed by the other *Winthrop* factors discussed *supra*, that that element can have no decisive effect. However wide the capital gains passageway through which a subdivider with former investment intent could squeeze, the Biedenharn Realty Company will never fit.

V.

The District Court, citing *Malat v. Riddell*, … stated that "the lots were not held … primarily for sale as that phrase was interpreted … in *Malat*.…" … Finding that Biedenharn's primary purpose became holding for sale and consequently that *Malat* in no way alters our analysis here, we disagree with the District Court's conclusion. *Malat* was a brief per curiam in which the Supreme Court decided only that as used in Internal Revenue Code § 1221(1) the word "primarily" means "principally," "of first importance." The Supreme Court, remanding the case, did not analyze the facts or resolve the controversy which involved a real estate dealer who had purchased land and held it at the time of sale with the dual intention of developing it as rental property or selling it, depending on whichever proved to be the more profitable.… In contrast, having substantially abandoned its investment and farming intent, Biedenharn was cloaked primarily in the garb of sales purpose when it disposed of the 38 lots here in controversy. With this change, the Realty Company lost the opportunity of coming within any dual purpose analysis.

We do not hereby condemn to ordinary income a taxpayer merely because, as is usually true, his principal intent at the exact moment of disposition is sales. Rather, we refuse capital gains treatment in those instances where over time there has been such a thoroughgoing change of purpose, ... as to make untenable a claim either of twin intent or continued primacy of investment purpose.

VI.

Having surveyed the Hardtimes terrain, we find no escape from ordinary income. The frequency and substantiality of sales over an extended time, the significant improvement of the basic subdivisions, the acquisition of additional properties, the use of brokers, and other less important factors persuasively combine to doom taxpayer's cause. Applying *Winthrop*'s criteria, this case clearly falls within the ordinary income category delineated in that decision. In so concluding, we note that *Winthrop* does not represent the most extreme application of the overriding principle that "the definition of a capital asset must be narrowly applied and its exclusions interpreted broadly." *Corn Products Refining Co. v. Commissioner of Internal Revenue....*

We cannot write black letter law for all realty subdividers and for all times, but we do caution in words of red that once an investment does not mean always an investment. A simon-pure investor forty years ago could by his subsequent activities become a seller in the ordinary course four decades later.

The period of Biedenharn's passivity is in the distant past; and the taxpayer has since undertaken the role of real estate protagonist. The Hardtimes Plantation in its day may have been one thing, but as the plantation was developed and sold, Hardtimes became by the very fact of change and activity a different holding than it had been at its inception. No longer could resort to initial purpose preserve taxpayer's once upon a time opportunity for favored treatment. The opinion of the District Court is reversed.

APPENDIX I

(Plaintiff's Answers to Interrogatory 26)

YEAR	GROSS SALES	NUMBER LOTS
1923	1,900.00	4
1924	1,050.00	2
1925	7,442.38	18

YEAR	GROSS SALES	NUMBER LOTS
1926	11,184.00	29
1927	9,619.25	52
1928	49,390.55	37
1929	35,810.25	55
1930	8,473.00	24
1931	5,930.00	18
1932	none	none
1933	520.00	2
1934	5,970.00	8
1935	2,639.00	7
1936	2,264.00	3
1937	14,071.00	8

1938	1,009.00	3
1939	5,558.00	10
1940	3,252.00	4
1941	2,490.00	3
1942	6,714.00	9
1943	6,250.00	12
1944	9,250.00	38
1945	15,495.00	20
1946	12,732.58	29
1947	38,310.00	169
1948	23,850.00	22
1949	8,830.00	26
1950	9,370.00	19
1951	55,222.99	16
1952	38,134.29	16
1953	123,007.22	17
1954	235,396.04	10
1955	76,805.00	20
1956	100,593.25	61
1957	133,448.10	36
1958	110,369.00	27
1959	44,400.00	12
1960	130,610.19	21
1961	48,729.60	25
1962	6,720.00	1
1963	7,475.00	1
1964	77,650.00	10
1965	75,759.00	10
1966	155,950.00	20

		NUMBER
YEAR	GROSS SALES	LOTS
1967	75,380.00	9
1968	89,447.50	10
1969	31,010.00	3
1970	none	none
1971	130,000.00	139

...

FOOTNOTES:

7. The 37 sales (1964–1966) break down as follows:

Biedenharn Estates Unit 2	2
Bayou DeSiard Country Club Addition	7
Oak Park Addition	28 (29 lots)

In 1965, Biedenharn effected the sale of two additional properties, the Keller house and lot and 1.958 acres from Hardtimes. These sales are not in controversy here. All subdivisions except Biedenharn Estates Unit 1 are restricted to single family residences of at least 60% masonry construction and of not less than 1200 square feet exclusive of porches and carport.

22. In *United States v. Winthrop*, 5 Cir. 1969, 417 F.2d 905,

910, the Court enumerated the following factors:

> (1) the nature and purpose of the acquisition of the property and the duration of the ownership; (2) the extent and nature of the taxpayer's efforts to sell the property; (3) the number, extent, continuity and substantiality of the sales; (4) the extent of subdividing, developing, and advertising to increase sales; (5) the use of a business office for the sale of the property; (6) the character and degree of supervision or control exercised by the taxpayer over any representative selling the property; and (7) the time and effort the taxpayer habitually devoted to the sales.

The numbering indicates no hierarchy of importance.

Consider some questions concerning *Biedenharn*.

1. What does the court say about the cases that have arisen since *Malat*?

2. What did the court say about the *Malat* case? Did the Supreme Court enunciate a rule in *Malat* that provided sufficient guidance for the resolution of future cases?

3. What factors did the Fifth Circuit adopt? Were they consistent with the discussion by the Supreme Court in *Malat*?

4. Do the factors adopted by the Fifth Circuit in *Biedenharn* provide greater predictability of result?

Now read the following case, also decided by the Fifth Circuit. How did the *Biedenharn* factors fare in the four years that elapsed between the two cases?

SUBURBAN REALTY COMPANY v. UNITED STATES
615 F.2d 171 (5th Cir. 1980)

GOLDBERG, Circuit Judge:

We must today answer the riddle at once adumbrated and apparently foreclosed by the false dichotomy created by the United States Supreme Court in *Malat v. Riddell*, ... when profits have "aris[en] from the [ordinary] operation of a business" on the one hand and are *also* "the realization of appreciation in value over a substantial period of time" on the other, are these profits treated as ordinary income or capital gain? Lacking any clear guidance but the language of the capital asset statute itself, we turn to that language for the answer. Before we can arrive at this interesting and important question, however, we must once again tramp along (but not trample on) that time—and precedent—worn path which separates capital gains from ordinary income. By the time we emerge into the light at the far edge of the forest, we will find that the *Riddell* riddle has seemingly answered itself, and all that will remain will be a brief reassessment of our answer. In our peregrinations, we of necessity wander into virgin territory. We hope that we shed new light onto this murky terrain; at the least, we think we have neither riddled the cases nor muddled the issues.

I.

Suburban Realty Company was formed in November, 1937 to acquire an undivided one-fourth interest in 1,742.6 acres of land located in Harris County, Texas ("the property").... Suburban's corporate charter states that it was formed to erect or repair any building or improvement, and to accumulate and lend money for such purposes, and to purchase, sell, and subdivide real property, and to accumulate and lend money for that purpose.

The five transactions whose characterization is in dispute here concern six tracts of unimproved real estate sold from the property by Suburban between 1968 and 1971. (Footnote 4) On its tax returns, Suburban originally reported profits from these sales, as well as all of its other real estate sales, as ordinary income. Later, Suburban filed a claim for refund asserting that these six tracts, as well as three similar tracts sold later, were capital assets, and that profits from these sales were entitled to capital gain treatment. The Internal Revenue Service denied Suburban's claim as to the sales here in issue. Suburban then instituted this action for a refund of $102,754.50. The district court, in a non-jury trial, rendered a decision against Suburban and entered a judgment dismissing Suburban's complaint. Suburban appealed.

The parties' legal contentions are closely bound to the facts. It is undisputed that, at the time of sale, the tracts at issue here were subject to a grass lease which apparently covered much of the property. Except for this grass lease, the six tracts, as well as much of the rest of the property, were never put to any substantial use. However, certain other portions of the property were the subject of greater activity. The parties disagree to some degree concerning the extent of, and appropriate characterization of, the activities conducted relating to these other portions of the property, and they fundamentally dispute the weight such activities carry in properly characterizing the sales at issue here. We will first discuss Suburban's overall activities with respect to the entire property, and then turn to those portions of the property singled out by the parties as being the subject of greater activity.

A. Overall activities.

1. *Total Sales Activity From the Property.*

Between 1939 and 1971, Suburban made at least 244 individual sales of real estate out of the property. Of these, approximately 95 sales were unplatted and unimproved property legally suitable for commercial development for any other purpose, and at least 149 sales were from platted property restricted to residential development. (Footnote 7) In each of these 33 years, Suburban concluded at least one sale; in most years, there were four or more sales. Suburban's total proceeds from real estate sales over this period were $2,353,935. Proceeds from all other sources of income amounted to $474,845. Thus, eighty-three percent of Suburban's proceeds emanated from real estate sales; only seventeen percent flowed from all other sources.

2. *North Loop Freeway.*

In 1957, the Texas Highway Department proposed that the limited access superhighway now known as the North Loop would be located from east to west across the property. In 1959 and 1960, Suburban sold at least two parcels out of the property to the Texas Highway Department for the purpose of constructing this highway. The location of the highway had a dramatic effect on the price of land in the area. Land which had been selling for between three and five thousand dollars per acre prior to announcement of the highway rose in value to between seven and twelve thousand dollars per acre.

3. *Corporate Discussions and Investments.*

Starting not later than 1959, Suburban's officers, directors and stockholders began discussing liquidation of the corporation. Many of these discussions occurred after 1961, when Rice University became a stockholder of Suburban and the Treasurer of Rice University became a member of the board of directors.

Because Rice University desired investments in income-producing assets rather than raw land, discussions concerning liquidation of Suburban's real estate holdings and the possibility of a partition of its holding among its stockholders were common. Starting in 1966, Suburban made substantial investments in stocks and bonds and began receiving substantial income from these investments.

B. Specific portions.

1. *Houston Gardens.* In 1938, Suburban and the other owners of the property formed a separate corporation, Houston Gardens Annex, Inc. ("Houston Gardens"), to plat and sell a parcel in the northeast quadrant of the property.... Houston Gardens owned approximately 200 or 250 lots, which were generally sold in bulk to builders. These sales covered as many as 20, 30, or even 50 lots at a time. By 1961, Houston Gardens had sold all but two of its lots, and it was then liquidated. Houston Gardens never engaged in advertising, used brokers or real estate agents, or employed a sales organization at any time during its existence.

2. *Homestead Addition.* Certain portions of the property, located near its center, were designated as Homestead Addition Sections One, Two, Three, and Four. Little was done with Homestead Addition Section One except for platting it and running a few utility lines up to it.

Homestead Addition Section Two, however, was the primary subject of Suburban's activities. In July, 1948, Suburban acquired 100 percent ownership of Homestead Addition Section Two.... Immediately thereafter, Suburban commenced development of Homestead Addition Section Two. The area was platted, streets and sewers were put in, and a sewage disposal plant was built nearby. Suburban also built a lumberyard in Section Two. At the instance of one of the individuals whom Suburban hired to collect water bills and notes on houses and to manage the lumberyard, Suburban also built eleven houses in Section Two in the early 1950's. The last was built by 1955, and none was sold later than 1958. Between 1948 and 1966, Suburban sold 252 subdivided lots out of Section Two. About half of these lots were sold in bulk to builders—10, 15, or 20 lots at a time. (Footnote 14)

Homestead Addition Sections Three and Four were platted for residential use by Suburban in 1951. This area was never developed by Suburban, however. In 1961 the plats were withdrawn and cancelled. This had the effect of eliminating restrictions which prevented commercial use of the land. Subsequently, the real estate within Sections Three and Four was sold to commercial and industrial users.

3. *Other Parcels.* The remainder of the property appears to have been treated as one undifferentiated bulk by Suburban. It is from this undifferentiated, undeveloped remainder that the sales at issue here were made. There are no specific findings by the trial court, and there appears to be no evidence of record from which we could ourselves make findings, concerning the number and frequency of sales of real estate from other parts of the property. Rather, the evidence concerning annual sales groups all sales made by Suburban, including sales from the Homestead Addition Sections, together. However, it is clear that throughout the period 1939–1971, sales were being made from the remainder of the property.

II.

Our analysis of this case must begin with *Biedenharn Realty Co., Inc. v. United States*, 526 F.2d 409 (5th Cir.) (en banc), *cert. denied*, 429 U.S. 819, 97 S.Ct. 64, 50 L.Ed.2d 79 (1976). *Biedenharn* is this Court's latest (and only) *en banc* pronouncement concerning the characterization of profits of a real estate business as ordinary income or capital gain. The decision answers the characterization question by evaluating certain "factors" often present in cases of this ilk. (Footnote 16) *Biedenharn* attempts to guide the analysis in this area by assigning different levels of importance to various of the "factors." Substantiality and frequency of sales is called the most important factor. *Biedenharn*, 526 F.2d at 416. Improvements to the land, solicitation and advertising efforts, and brokerage activities also play an important part in the *Biedenharn* analysis.

The question before us today, put into the *Biedenharn* framework, can be stated as follows: when a taxpayer engages in frequent and substantial sales over a period of years, but undertakes no development activity with respect to parts of a parcel of land, and engages in no solicitation or advertising efforts or brokerage activities, under what circumstances is income derived from sales of undeveloped parts of the parcel ordinary income?

The *Biedenharn* framework allows us to ask the question, but gives us little guidance in answering it. In the principal recent cases, there has always been a conjunction of frequent and substantial sales with development activity relating to the properties in dispute.... The conjunction of these two factors "will usually conclude the capital gains issue against [the] taxpayer." ... Judge Wisdom has recently written that "ordinary income tax rates usually apply when dispositions of subdivided property over a period of time are continuous and substantial rather than few and isolated." ... Also, it has been explicitly stated that the factor which will receive greatest emphasis is frequency and substantiality of sales over an extended time period.... However, substantial and frequent sales activity, standing alone, has never been held to be automatically sufficient to trigger ordinary income treatment. In fact, we have continual reminders of the fact that "specific factors, or combinations of them are not necessarily controlling,"....

...

Today, we must go into territory as yet unmapped in this Circuit. Suburban's case is at once more favorable to the taxpayer than Biedenharn's and less so. It is more favorable because, *with respect to the particular parcels of land here at issue*, it is undisputed that Suburban undertook no development or subdivision activity. It is less favorable because Biedenharn was continually engaged in business activities other than real estate sales, whereas Suburban was for many years doing little else. Following the *Biedenharn* framework alone, we would be left with yet another essentially *ad hoc* decision to be made. We could justify a decision for either party, yet remain confident that we were being fully consistent with the analysis in *Biedenharn*. However, although there will always remain a certain irreducible *ad hoc*-ishness in this area, we are now firmly convinced that the uncertainty can be substantially reduced by turning to the divining rod of capital gains versus ordinary income—the statute itself.

III.

The jurisprudence of the "real estate capital gains-ordinary income issue" in this Circuit has at times been cast somewhat loose of its statutory mooring. The ultimate inquiry in cases of this nature is whether the property at issue was "property held by the taxpayer primarily for sale to customers in the ordinary course of his trade or business." ... In our focus on the "tests" developed to resolve this question, we have on occasion almost lost sight entirely of the statutory framework. The "tests" or "factors," ... have seemingly acquired an independent meaning of their own, only loosely tied to their statutory pier. Some years ago, Judge Brown cautioned us against this tendency:

> Essential as they are in the adjudication of cases, we must take guard lest we be so carried away by the proliferation of tests that we forget that the statute excludes from capital assets 'property held by the taxpayer primarily for sale to customers in the ordinary course of his trade or business.'

...

The tendency to overemphasize the independent meaning of the "factors" has been accompanied by, perhaps even caused by, a tendency to view the statutory language as posing only one question: whether the property was held by the taxpayer "primarily for sale to customers in the ordinary course of his trade or business." This determination was correctly seen as equivalent to the question whether the gain was to be treated as ordinary or capital. However, probably because the question "is the gain ordinary" is a single question which demands an answer of yes or no, the courts have on occasion lost sight of the fact that the statutory language requires the court to make not one determination, but several separate determinations. In statutory construction cases, our most important task is to ask the proper questions. In the context of cases like the one before us, the principal inquiries demanded by the statute are:

1) was taxpayer engaged in a trade or business, and, if so, what business?

2) was taxpayer holding the property primarily for sale in that business?

3) were the sales contemplated by taxpayer "ordinary" in the course of that business?

...

In fact, once the inquiry is redirected towards the statutory inquiries, the ultimate relevance of the *Biedenharn* factors becomes apparent. It will remain true that the frequency and substantiality of sales will be the most important factor. But the reason for the importance of this factor is now clear: the presence of frequent and substantial sales is highly relevant to each of the principal statutory inquiries listed above. A taxpayer who engages in frequent and substantial sales is almost inevitably engaged in the real estate business. The frequency and substantiality of sales are highly probative on the issue of holding purpose because the presence of frequent sales ordinarily belies the contention that property is being held "for investment" rather than "for sale." And the frequency of sales may often be a key factor in determining the "ordinariness" question.

The extent of development activity and improvements is highly relevant to the question of whether taxpayer is a real estate developer. Development activity and improvements may also be relevant to the taxpayer's holding purpose, but, standing alone, some degree of development activity is not inconsistent with holding property for purposes other than sale. (Footnote 22) The extent of development activity also seems to be only peripherally relevant to the "ordinariness" question. Thus, under the statutory framework, ... the extent of development activity and improvements, although an important factor, is less conclusive than the substantiality and frequency of sales.

Solicitation and advertising efforts are quite relevant both to the existence of a trade or business and to taxpayer's holding purpose. Thus, their presence can strengthen the case for ordinary income treatment.... However, ... their absence is not conclusive on either of these statutory questions for, as we noted [in *Biederharn*], "even one inarguably in the real estate business need not engage in promotional exertions in the face of a favorable market." ...

We need not comment individually on each of the other *Biedenharn-Winthrop* factors. It should be apparent that each factor is relevant, to a greater or lesser extent, to one or more of the questions posed by the statute along the path to the ultimate conclusion.

IV.

Having laid the framework for the requisite analysis, we must now apply that framework to the facts here. We must decide whether Suburban was engaged in a trade or business, and, if so, what business; whether Suburban was holding the properties at issue here primarily for sale; and whether Suburban's contemplated sales were "ordinary" in the course of Suburban's business.

Before we commence this analysis, we must ascertain the appropriate standard of appellate review.... This Circuit has often faced the question whether the characterization of property as "primarily held for sale to customers in the ordinary course of [taxpayer's] trade or business" is a question of law or a question of fact. This characterization is of course crucial to the outcome of many cases — if the characterization is a question of fact, the factfinder's answer must be accepted unless clearly erroneous, but, if a question of law is presented, plenary review on appeal is appropriate....

We need not here psychoanalyze the nightmares of characterization that have fascinated professors of civil procedure: the distinctions between historical, evidentiary, subsidiary, and ultimate facts are too fine for useful discussion. Once it is perceived that the ultimate legal conclusion of capital gain or ordinary income involves several independent determinations, it can be easily seen that some of the determinations are predominantly legal conclusions or are "mixed questions of fact and law," whereas others are essentially questions of fact. Thus, the question of taxpayer's purpose or purposes for holding the property is primarily factual, as is the question of which purpose predominates. Similarly, the "ordinariness" of the contemplated sales is mainly a fact question. The question of whether taxpayer was engaged in a trade or business involves the application of legal standards concerning what constitutes a trade or business to the facts concerning taxpayer's activities, and therefore is best characterized as a "mixed question of fact and law", The ultimate legal conclusion, based on these factual and legal conclusions, of whether the property was "held primarily for sale to customers in the ordinary course of his trade or business" cannot be appropriately characterized in this scheme at all because, as noted above, there are several subsidiary questions which, separately answered, lead to the ultimate conclusion. (Footnote 28)

A. Was Suburban in the real estate business?

This is a relatively simple issue. The question is whether taxpayer has engaged in a sufficient quantum of focused activity to be considered to be engaged in a trade or business. The precise quantum necessary will be difficult to establish, and cases close to the line on this issue will arise.

Happily, we need not here define that line. It is clear to us that Suburban engaged in a sufficient quantity of activity to be in the business of selling real estate. Suburban's sales were continuous and substantial. It completed at least 244 sales transactions over the 33-year period 1939–1971. This averages to over 7 transactions per year. Proceeds from these sales exceeded 2.3 million dollars.

Suburban does not claim to have been engaged in any business other than real estate; rather, it claims that during the periods at issue it simply "did not carry on a trade or business." ...

Suburban relies heavily on the insignificance of its subdivision and development activity and the total absence of any advertising or sales solicitation activity on its part. However, the first two absences do not concern us at all....

The presence of any sales solicitation or advertising activity would certainly be relevant to the issue of whether Suburban was in the business of selling real estate. Strenuous, but largely unsuccessful, attempts to sell might compel the conclusion that a taxpayer with very few sales transactions was nonetheless in the business of selling. But the absence of such activity does not compel the opposite conclusion....

Suburban also seeks solace from the fact that it never purchased any additional real estate to replenish acreage it sold. As is the case with the presence of sales activity, the presence of such purchases tends to demonstrate that a taxpayer is engaged in a real estate business, but their absence is not conclusive:

> The fact that [taxpayer] bought no additional lands during this period does not prevent his activity being a business. [Taxpayer] merely had enough land to do a large business without buying any more.

> ...

Additionally, Suburban points to its commencement of an investment program in securities in 1966. By itself, this cannot affect our conclusion that Suburban was in the real estate business. It merely demonstrates that, commencing in 1966, Suburban was also engaged in investing in securities. As stated earlier, the presence of other types of activities does not prevent taxpayer's real estate activities from being considered a business.

Suburban also contends that, if it was ever in the real estate business, it had exited that business long before 1968, the time of the first transaction here at issue. Even if this is true, it cannot affect our ultimate conclusion. The statutory language does not demand that property actually be sold while a taxpayer is still actively engaged in its trade or business for ordinary income treatment to be required. Rather, it demands that the property have been held primarily for sale in that business. (Footnote 33) To that inquiry we now turn.

B. What was Suburban's primary purpose for holding the properties whose characterization is here in dispute?

Put into the framework being used here, Suburban's contention concerning holding purpose is two-fold. Principally, it argues that, at the time of the sales in dispute, the properties were not being held for sale. Alternatively, it contends that it "originally acquired its property as an investment..., and it continued to hold it for investment purposes." ...

We reject Suburban's statement of the legal principle upon which its first argument is premised. It simply cannot be true that "the decisive question is the purpose for which [the property] 'primarily' was held when sold." ... At the very moment of sale, the property is certainly being held "for sale." The appropriate question certainly must be the taxpayer's primary holding purpose at some point before he decided to make the sale in dispute.

> ...

... [N]either party has cited any Supreme Court or Fifth Circuit precedent which states the proposition that the relevant holding purpose is that existing at the moment of sale. Suburban relies on *Malat v. Riddell*.... *Malat* does not address this issue at all, but concerns the meaning of the word "primarily" in 26 U.S.C. § 1221(1)....

...

The "holding purpose" inquiry may appropriately be conducted by attempting to trace the taxpayer's primary holding purpose over the entire course of his ownership of the property. *See Malat v. Riddell*.... (Footnote 36) Thus, the inquiry should start at the time the property is acquired. We seek to divine the taxpayer's primary purpose for acquiring the property. In this case, we are willing to assume, as Suburban argues, that the property was acquired principally as an investment. We then seek evidence of a change in taxpayer's primary holding purpose. Here, such evidence is plentiful and convincing.

The property was acquired in December, 1937. Houston Gardens Annex, Inc. was formed in 1938 to plat and sell a portion of the property. Sales commenced by 1939, and sales were transacted in each year thereafter. From 1946 through 1956, approximately 17 sales per year occurred. Proceeds from sales exceeded $8,500 each year, and were as high as $69,000 (in 1952). Also during this period, the development activity pertaining to Homestead Addition Two was occurring.... This development activity clearly contemplated, and was accompanied by, sales.

All of these factors convince us that, by the mid-1940's at the latest, and probably much earlier, Suburban's primary holding purpose was "for sale." We need not decide the precise moment. Were it necessary to our decision, we quite likely would be unwilling to accept Suburban's contention that the property was initially acquired for investment....

With its primary holding purpose through the 1940's and 1950's fixed at "for sale," Suburban is then entitled to show that its primary purpose changed to, or back to, "for investment." Suburban claims that this shift occurred either in 1959, when its officers and directors discussed liquidation; in 1961, when Rice University became a stockholder of Suburban, further liquidation discussions were held, and the plats were withdrawn; or, at the latest, in 1966, when further liquidation discussions were held and Suburban began investing in securities.

We view this determination to be a closer call than any of the others in this case. The frequency of sales did drop off after the late 1950's. Suburban had discontinued its development activities. Also, 1961 was the year the plats for Homestead Additions Three and Four were withdrawn.

This withdrawal of plats could be quite significant. Unlike liquidation discussions, which were apparently a dime a dozen for Suburban, withdrawal of the plats was an action taken by Suburban which may evince a different relationship to its land. The critical question is whether this withdrawal indicated that henceforth the land was being held principally as an investment or simply showed that Suburban was attempting to maximize sales profits by selling to commercial users.

The continuing sales activity is strong evidence that the latter interpretation is the correct one. Moreover, the trial court found that the withdrawal evinced "an attempt to maximize profits from the sale of real estate and to capitalize on the new North Loop Freeway which would cross [Suburban's] property." Thus, we conclude that Suburban's primary purpose for holding the property remained "for sale" at the time of the transactions here disputed. (Footnote 42)

Suburban does not explicitly contend that its primary purpose for holding the specific parcels at issue here was different from its purpose for holding the property as a whole. However, it does attempt to rely to some degree on the lack of development activity relating to the parcels here at issue. Although in some circumstances a taxpayer in the real estate business may be able to establish that certain parcels were held primarily for investment, ... the burden is on the taxpayer to establish that the parcels held primarily for investment were segregated from other properties held primarily for sale. The mere lack of development activity with respect to parts of a large property does not sufficiently separate those parts from the whole to meet the taxpayer's burden.... The lack of development activity with respect to the parts of the property here at issue is at least equally consistent with a primary motivation to maximize immediate sales profits as it is with a primary motivation to hold for investment.

C.   Were the Sales Contemplated by Suburban "Ordinary" in the Course of Suburban's Business?

We need say no more on this question than quote from the discussion of this issue in *Winthrop, supra*:

> The concept of normalcy requires for its application a chronology and a history to determine if the sales of lots to customers were the usual or a departure from the norm. History and chronology here combine to demonstrate that [taxpayer] did not sell his lots as an abnormal or unexpected event. [Taxpayer] began selling shortly after he acquired the land; he never used the land for any other purpose; and he continued this course of conduct over a number of years. Thus, the sales were ... ordinary.

...

V.

Having relied on the language of § 1221 itself to determine that the assets here at issue were not capital assets, we must return for a moment to the query posed at the outset. In this case, as we have demonstrated, sales of the type here in dispute were precisely what Suburban's business was directed towards.

In other words, the profits garnered from these sales arose from the ordinary operation of Suburban's business.

At the same time, however, these profits did not arise principally from the efforts of Suburban. Rather, they arose from the same historical, demographic, and market forces that have caused the City of Houston to grow enormously during the years Suburban held the land. Shrewdly, Suburban held on to much of its land. It only sold relatively small portions year by year. Thus, by 1968, market forces and the location of the North Loop Freeway had driven up the value of Suburban's land. We must decide whether the policies motivating lower tax rates on capital gains and the controlling precedents expressing those policies require that we ignore the plain language of § 1221 and hold for Suburban.

The key cases we must explore here number three. First is *Malat v. Riddell*, ... It lends us no aid. As we have previously stated, it suggests that profits cannot arise from both "the [ordinary] operation of a business" and "appreciation in value accrued over a substantial period of time." Yet here we have profits which fall squarely into both categories.

We thus turn to the two cases from which the *Malat* court quotations are taken, *Commissioner v. Gillette Motor Transport, Inc.*, 364 U.S. 130 ... and *Corn Products Refining Company v. Commissioner*, 350 U.S. 46 ... (1955). In *Gillette*, the Supreme Court said:

This Court has long held that the term "capital asset" is to be construed narrowly in accordance with the purpose of Congress to afford capital-gains treatment only in situations typically involving the realization of appreciation in value accrued over a substantial period of time, and thus to ameliorate the hardship of taxation and the entire gain in one year.

... We note that the quoted language does not state that all gains emanating from appreciation in value over a substantial period of time are to be treated as capital gains. Rather, it states the logical converse of that proposition; *i.e.*, that capital gain treatment will be proper only if the gain emanates from appreciation in value. Instances of gain emanating from appreciation being treated as ordinary income are not inconsistent with this proposition.

We also note the Supreme Court's recognition of the attempt by Congress to avoid taxing income earned over a period of years in one year. In Suburban's case, although it is true that with respect to each individual parcel of land there is a "bunching" effect, taxation of the overall gains from the property as a whole has been spread over a long period of years. Thus, the "bunching" effect has been minimized. Last, we note the Supreme Court's admonition to construe the term "capital asset" narrowly. *Id.*

Further support for a narrow construction of the term "capital asset" and a broad interpretation of its exclusions comes from *Corn Products*, the third key case in this area....

More importantly, the Supreme Court in *Corn Products* squarely stated:

> Congress intended that profits and losses arising from the everyday operation of a business be considered as ordinary income or loss rather than capital gain or loss.

... It is this type of profit that is before us today.

We thus conclude that § 1221(1) should be construed in accord with its plain meaning, and that, if the other requirements of § 1221(1) are met, when the ordinary business of a business is to make profits from appreciation in value caused by market forces, those profits are to be treated as ordinary income. Such is the case here.

VI.

Our journey over, we have nothing more to add. The decision of the district court dismissing Suburban's complaint is AFFIRMED.

APPENDIX

Date	Number Commercial Sales	Number Residential Sales	Total Number Sales
1939	4	0	4
1940	3	? *	3+ *
1941	1	?	1+
1942	2	?	2+
1943	1	?	1+
1944	3	?	3+
1945	5	?	5+
1946	11	6	17
1947	3	12	15

1948	0	21	21
1949	3	6	9
1950	6	46	52
1951	1	6	7
1952	4	14	18
1953	2	6	8
1954	0	5	5
1955	1	16	17
1956	1	6	7
1957	1	1	2
1958	1	3	4
1959	3	1	4
1960	1	0	2
1961	2	0	2
1962	1	0	1
1963	4	0	3
1964	6	0	4
1965	4	0	6
1966	7	0	5
1967	4	0	4
1968	1	0	3
1969	4	0	3
1970	1	0	1
1971	4	0	4
TOTAL	95	149+	244+

* Records incomplete for 1940–1945.

FOOTNOTES:

4. The parties stipulated that the sales were as follows:

Date	Acreage	Sales Price
December 31, 1968	4.5	$ 56,250
July 31, 1969	6.25	93,285
July 31, 1969	6.0225	90,225
July 31, 1969	17.50	262,282
1970 [*sic*]	5.6944	39,799
April 14, 1971	4.375	65,675

7. See Appendix, *infra*.

14. There is no finding by the court below, or any record evidence that we can locate, concerning the number of individual transactions employed to sell the 252 lots. This lack of evidence may be attributable to Suburban's failure to record separately transactions from the various Homestead Addition Sections or even to separate Homestead Addition sales from non-Homestead sales. Alternatively, the paucity of evidence may merely reflect incompleteness of the records submitted to the district court.

16. In the *United States v. Winthrop*, 417 F.2d 905, 910 (5th Cir. 1969), the following factors were enumerated:

(1) the nature and purpose of the acquisition of the property and the duration of the ownership; (2) the extent and nature of the taxpayer's efforts to sell the property; (3) the number, extent, continuity and substantiality of the sales; (4)

the extent of subdividing, developing, and advertising to increase sales; (5) the use of a business office for the sale of the property; (6) the character and degree of supervision or control exercised by the taxpayer over any representative selling the property; and (7) the time and effort the taxpayer habitually devoted to the sales.

22. For example, a taxpayer might clear trees and conduct some grading and filling activities in preparation for farming the land.

28. It should be apparent that appellate review of a trial court's application of the answers to the subsidiary questions to arrive at the ultimate conclusion is plenary.

33. The question of exit from a business is intimately tied to, although independent of, the "holding purpose" inquiry. Exit from active business can be strong evidence of a change in holding purpose. The holding purpose question, as well as the timing of its inquiry, are discussed immediately below.

36. It is not clear to us from the *Malat* decision whether "primarily" means "predominates at a certain point of time" or "predominates over the life of taxpayer's ownership of the asset." This could be critical if, for example, a taxpayer held a piece of property primarily for sale over many years, but then, shortly but not immediately before sale, switched his primary holding purpose to one of investment. If the appropriate measure of "primarily" is at a fixed instant of time, this taxpayer would be entitled to capital gain treatment if the other requirements of § 1221 are met. However, taxpayer's "primary holding purpose" over the length of his ownership of the asset would still be "for sale," and, if this is the proper test, ordinary income treatment would be mandated.

. . .

42. Some of our skepticism over Suburban's claim to have changed its holding purpose stems from the fact that it points to so many separate times when its purpose may have changed. This leads us to believe that Suburban was merely gradually shifting its strategies as market conditions changed in an effort to maximize sales profits. We do not reject outright the possibility that a sequence of events separate in time may indicate a gradual change in holding purpose from "for sale" to "for investment." However, we would be more likely to find a "change of purpose" argument convincing if a discrete event were followed by a string of zero's in the annual sales column figures, especially if this were followed by a sale of the remainder of taxpayer's property in a small number of transactions.

———————

Now consider the following questions concerning *Suburban Realty*.

1. Does the Fifth Circuit abandon the factors set forth in *Biedenharn*?

2. Does the court grant greater importance to the Supreme Court's decision in *Malat* than it had when deciding *Biedenharn*?

3. How did the court refocus the analysis of the issue between *Biedenharn* and *Suburban Realty*?

4. The presentation in these materials of these cases proceeds in the order of their decision. Can you formulate the advice you would give to a client who wants to be sure that her ownership of property will be treated as property held for use in a trade or business? Property held for investment?

B. The Fundamentals: Basis and Debt

Before tackling the real estate transactional problems in Chapter 4 of this Part VI, several foundation cases will introduce you to the issue of a taxpayer's basis in real estate financed through nonrecourse borrowing.

First, read the following case involving the famous Mrs. Crane. As you read, think about what she was trying to accomplish and why the Supreme Court thwarted her plan.

CRANE v. COMMISSIONER
331 U.S. 1 (1947)

MR. CHIEF JUSTICE VINSON delivered the opinion of the Court.

The question here is how a taxpayer who acquires depreciable property subject to an unassumed mortgage, holds it for a period, and finally sells it still so encumbered, must compute her taxable gain.

Petitioner was the sole beneficiary and the executrix of the will of her husband, who died January 11, 1932. He then owned an apartment building and lot subject to a mortgage,(Footnote 1) which secured a principal debt of $255,000.00 and interest in default of $7,042.50. As of that date, the property was appraised for federal estate tax purposes at a value exactly equal to the total amount of this encumbrance. Shortly after her husband's death, petitioner entered into an agreement with the mortgagee whereby she was to continue to operate the property — collecting the rents, paying for necessary repairs, labor, and other operating expenses, and reserving $200.00 monthly for taxes — and was to remit the net rentals to the mortgagee. This plan was followed for nearly seven years, during which period petitioner reported the gross rentals as income, and claimed and was allowed deductions for taxes and operating expenses paid on the property, for interest paid on the mortgage, and for the physical exhaustion of the building. Meanwhile, the arrearage of interest increased to $15,857.71. On November 29, 1938, with the mortgagee threatening foreclosure, petitioner sold to a third party for $3,000.00 cash, subject to the mortgage, and paid $500.00 expenses of sale.

Petitioner reported a taxable gain of $1,250.00. Her theory was that the "property" which she had acquired in 1932 and sold in 1938 was only the equity, or the excess in the value of the apartment building and lot over the amount of the mortgage. This equity was of zero value when she acquired it. No depreciation could be taken on a zero value. (Footnote 2) Neither she nor her vendee ever assumed the mortgage, so, when she sold the equity, the amount she realized on the sale was the net cash received, or $2,500.00. This sum less the zero basis constituted her gain, of which she reported half as taxable on the assumption that the entire property was a "capital asset." (Footnote 3)

The Commissioner, however, determined that petitioner realized a net taxable gain of $23,767.03. His theory was that the "property" acquired and sold was not the equity, as petitioner claimed, but rather the physical property itself, or the owner's rights to possess, use, and dispose of it, undiminished by the mortgage. The original basis thereof was $262,042.50, its appraised value in 1932. Of this value $55,000.00 was allocable to land and $207,042.50 to building. (Footnote 4) During the period that petitioner held the property, there was an allowable depreciation of $28,045.10 on the building, (Footnote 5) so that the adjusted basis of the building at the time of sale was $178,997.40. The amount realized on the sale was said to include not only the $2,500.00 net cash receipts, but also the principal amount (Footnote 6) of the mortgage subject to which the property was sold, both totaling $257,500.00. The selling price was allocable in the proportion, $54,471.15 to the land and $203,028.85 to the building. (Footnote 7) The Commissioner agreed that the land was a "capital asset," but thought that the building was not. Thus, he determined that petitioner sustained a capital loss of $528.85 on the land, of which 50% or $264.42 was taken into account, and an ordinary gain of $24,031.45 on the building, or a net taxable gain as indicated.

The Tax Court agreed with the Commissioner that the building was not a "capital asset." In all other respects it adopted petitioner's contentions, and expunged the deficiency. Petitioner did not appeal from the part of the ruling adverse to her, and these questions are no longer at issue. On the Commissioner's appeal, the Circuit Court of Appeals reversed, one judge dissenting. We granted certiorari because of the importance of the questions raised as to the proper construction of the gain and loss provisions of the Internal Revenue Code.

The 1938 Act, §111(a), defines the gain from "the sale or other disposition of property" as "the excess of the amount realized therefrom over the adjusted basis provided in section 113(b)...." It proceeds, §111(b), to define "the amount realized from the sale or other disposition of property" as "the sum of any money received plus the fair market value of the property (other than money) received." Further, in §113(b), the "adjusted basis for determining the gain or loss from the sale or other disposition of property" is declared to be "the basis determined under subsection (a), adjusted ... [(1)(B)] ... for exhaustion, wear and tear, obsolescence, amortization ... to the extent allowed (but not less than the amount allowable)...." The basis under subsection (a) "if the property was acquired by ... devise ... or by the decedent's estate from the decedent," §113(a)(5), is "the fair market value of such property at the time of such acquisition."

Logically, the first step under this scheme is to determine the unadjusted basis of the property, ... and the dispute in this case is as to the construction to be given the term "property." If "property," as used in that provision, means the same thing as "equity," it would necessarily follow that the basis of petitioner's property was zero, as she contends. If, on the contrary, it means the land and building themselves, or the owner's legal rights in them, undiminished by the mortgage, the basis was $262,042.50.

We think that the reasons for favoring one of the latter constructions are of overwhelming weight. In the first place, the words of statutes—including revenue acts—should be interpreted where possible in their ordinary, everyday senses. (Footnote 13) The only relevant definitions of "property" to be found in the principal standard dictionaries (Footnote 14) are the two favored by the Commissioner, i.e., either that "property" is the physical thing which is a subject of ownership, or that it is the aggregate of the owner's rights to control and dispose of that thing. "Equity" is not given as a synonym, nor do either of the foregoing definitions suggest that it could be correctly so used. Indeed, "equity" is defined as "the value of a property ... above the total of the liens...." (Footnote 15) The contradistinction could hardly be more pointed. Strong countervailing considerations would be required to support a contention that Congress, in using the word "property," meant "equity," or that we should impute to it the intent to convey that meaning.

...

A further reason why the word "property" in §113(a) should not be construed to mean "equity" is the bearing such construction would have on the allowance of deductions for depreciation and on the collateral adjustments of basis.

Section 23(l) permits deduction from gross income of "a reasonable allowance for the exhaustion, wear and tear of property...." Sections 23(n) and 114(a) declare that the "basis upon which exhaustion, wear and tear ... are to be allowed" is the basis "provided in section 113(b) for the purpose of determining the gain upon the sale" of the property, which is the §113(a) basis "adjusted ... for exhaustion, wear and tear ... to the extent allowed (but not less than the amount allowable)...."

Under these provisions, if the mortgagor's equity were the §113(a) basis, it would also be the original basis from which depreciation allowances are deducted. If it is, and if the amount of the annual allowances were to be computed on that value, as would then seem to be required, they will represent only a fraction of the cost of the corresponding physical exhaustion, and any recoupment by the mortgagor of the remainder of that cost can be effected only by the reduction of his taxable gain in the year of sale. If, however, the amount of the annual allowances were to be computed on the value of the property, and then deducted from an equity basis, we would in some instances have to accept deductions from a minus basis or deny deductions altogether. The Commissioner also argues that taking the mortgagor's equity as the §113(a) basis would require the basis to be changed with each payment on the mortgage, and that the attendant problem of repeatedly recomputing basis and annual allowances would be a tremendous accounting burden on both the Commissioner and the taxpayer. Moreover, the mortgagor would acquire control over the timing of his depreciation allowances.

Thus it appears that the applicable provisions of the Act expressly preclude an equity basis, and the use of it is contrary to certain implicit principles of income tax depreciation, and entails very great administrative difficulties. It may be added that the Treasury has never furnished a guide through the maze of problems that arise in connection with depreciating an equity basis, but, on the contrary, has consistently permitted the amount of depreciation allowances to be computed on the full value of the property, and subtracted from it as a basis. Surely, Congress' long-continued acceptance of this situation gives it full legislative endorsement.

We conclude that the proper basis under §113(a)(5) is the value of the property, undiminished by mortgages thereon, and that the correct basis here was $262,042.50. The next step is to ascertain what adjustments are required under §113(b). As the depreciation rate was stipulated, the only question at this point is whether the Commissioner was warranted in making any depreciation adjustments whatsoever.

Section 113(b)(1)(B) provides that "proper adjustment in respect of the property *shall in all cases be made* ... for exhaustion, wear and tear ... to the extent allowed (but not less than the amount allowable)...." (Italics supplied.) The Tax Court found on adequate evidence that the apartment house was property of a kind subject to physical exhaustion, that it was used in taxpayer's trade or business, and consequently that the taxpayer would have been entitled to a depreciation allowance under §23(l), except that, in the opinion of that Court, the basis of the property was zero, and it was thought that depreciation could not be taken on a zero basis. As we have just decided that the correct basis of the property was not zero, but $262,042.50, we avoid this difficulty, and conclude that an adjustment should be made as the Commissioner determined.

Petitioner urges to the contrary that she was not entitled to depreciation deductions, whatever the basis of the property, because the law allows them only to one who actually bears the capital loss, and here the loss was not hers but the mortgagee's. We do not see, however, that she has established her factual premise. There was no finding of the Tax Court to that effect, nor to the effect that the value of the property was ever less than the amount of the lien. Nor was there evidence in the record, or any indication that petitioner could produce evidence, that this was so. The facts that the value of the property was only equal to the lien in 1932 and that during the next six and one-half years the physical condition of the building deteriorated and the amount of the lien increased, are entirely inconclusive, particularly in the light of the buyer's willingness in 1938 to take subject to the increased lien and pay a substantial amount of cash to boot....

At last we come to the problem of determining the "amount realized" on the 1938 sale. Section 111(b), it will be recalled, defines the "amount realized" from "the sale ... of property" as "the sum of any money received plus the fair market value of the property (other than money) received," and § 111(a) defines the gain on "the sale ... of property" as the excess of the amount realized over the basis. Quite obviously, the word "property," used here with reference to a sale, must mean "property" in the same ordinary sense intended by the use of the word with reference to acquisition and depreciation in § 113, both for certain of the reasons stated heretofore in discussing its meaning in § 113, and also because the functional relation of the two sections requires that the word mean the same in one section that it does in the other. If the "property" to be valued on the date of acquisition is the property free of liens, the "property" to be priced on a subsequent sale must be the same thing.

We are not troubled by petitioner's argument that her contract of sale expressly provided for the conveyance of the equity only. She actually conveyed title to the property, and the buyer took the same property that petitioner had acquired in 1932 and used in her trade or business until its sale.

Starting from this point, we could not accept petitioner's contention that the $2,500.00 net cash was all she realized on the sale except on the absurdity that she sold a quarter-of-a-million dollar property for roughly one per cent of its value, and took a 99 per cent loss. Actually, petitioner does not urge this. She argues, conversely, that because only $2,500.00 was realized on the sale, the "property" sold must have been the equity only, and that consequently we are forced to accept her contention as to the meaning of "property" in § 113. We adhere, however, to what we have already said on the meaning of "property," and we find that the absurdity is avoided by our conclusion that the amount of the mortgage is properly included in the "amount realized" on the sale.

Petitioner concedes that if she had been personally liable on the mortgage and the purchaser had either paid or assumed it, the amount so paid or assumed would be considered a part of the "amount realized" within the meaning of § 111(b). The cases so deciding have already repudiated the notion that there must be an actual receipt by the seller himself of "money" or "other property," in their narrowest senses. It was thought to be decisive that one section of the Act must be construed so as not to defeat the intention of another or to frustrate the Act as a whole, and that the taxpayer was the "beneficiary" of the payment in "as real and substantial [a sense] as if the money had been paid it and then paid over by it to its creditors."

Both these points apply to this case. The first has been mentioned already. As for the second, we think that a mortgagor, not personally liable on the debt, who sells the property subject to the mortgage and for additional consideration, realizes a benefit in the amount of the mortgage as well as the boot. (Footnote 37) If a purchaser pays boot, it is immaterial as to our problem whether the mortgagor is also to receive money from the purchaser to discharge the mortgage prior to sale, or whether he is merely to transfer subject to the mortgage—it may make a difference to the purchaser and to the mortgagee, but not to the mortgagor. Or put in another way, we are no more concerned with whether the mortgagor is, strictly speaking, a debtor on the mortgage, than we are with whether the benefit to him is, strictly speaking, a receipt of money or property. We are rather concerned with the reality that an owner of property, mortgaged at a figure less than that at which the property will sell, must and will treat the conditions of the mortgage exactly as if they were his personal obligations.

Therefore we conclude that the Commissioner was right in determining that petitioner realized $257,500.00 on the sale of this property.

The Tax Court's contrary determinations, that "property," as used in §113 (a) and related sections, means "equity," and that the amount of a mortgage subject to which property is sold is not the measure of a benefit realized, within the meaning of §111 (b), announced rules of general applicability on clear-cut questions of law. The Circuit Court of Appeals therefore had jurisdiction to review them.

Petitioner contends that the result we have reached taxes her on what is not income within the meaning of the Sixteenth Amendment. If this is because only the direct receipt of cash is thought to be income in the constitutional sense, her contention is wholly without merit. If it is because the entire transaction is thought to have been "by all dictates of common sense ... a ruinous disaster," as it was termed in her brief, we disagree with her premise. She was entitled to depreciation deductions for a period of nearly seven years, and she actually took them in almost the allowable amount. The crux of this case, really, is whether the law permits her to exclude allowable deductions from consideration in computing gain. We have already showed that, if it does, the taxpayer can enjoy a double deduction, in effect, on the same loss of assets. The Sixteenth Amendment does not require that result any more than does the Act itself.

Affirmed.

FOOTNOTES:

1. The record does not show whether he was personally liable for the debt.

2. This position is, of course, inconsistent with her practice in claiming such deductions in each of the years the property was held. The deductions so claimed and allowed by the Commissioner were in the total amount of $25,500.00.

3.... only 50% of the gain realized on the sale of a "capital asset" need be taken into account, if the property had been held more than two years.

4. The parties stipulated as to the relative parts of the 1932 appraised value and of the 1938 sales price which were allocable to land and building.

5. The parties stipulated that the rate of depreciation applicable to the building was 2% per annum.

6. The Commissioner explains that only the principal amount, rather than the total present debt secured by the mortgage, was deemed to be a measure of the amount realized, because the difference was attributable to interest due, a deductible item.

7. See *supra*, note 4.

13. *Old Colony R. Co. v. Commissioner*, 284 U.S. 552, 560.

14. See Webster's New International Dictionary, Unabridged, 2d Ed.; Funk & Wagnalls' New Standard Dictionary; Oxford English Dictionary.

15. See Webster's New International Dictionary, *supra*.

37. Obviously, if the value of the property is less than the amount of the mortgage, a mortgagor who is not personally liable cannot realize a benefit equal to the mortgage. Consequently, a different problem might be encountered where a mortgagor abandoned the property or transferred it subject to the mortgage without receiving boot. That is not this case.

Consider the following questions about Mrs. Crane's real estate transactions.

1. Can you diagram the transaction in *Crane*? Hint: begin with the ownership of the property by Mrs. Crane's husband, indicating his relationship with the lender. Then, show the transfer from Mr. Crane (through his estate) to Mrs. Crane.

2. What was the real estate that was the subject of the case?

3. How did Mrs. Crane acquire it?

4. What was the property's value at the time Mrs. Crane acquired it?

5. What is a mortgage? What does owning property "subject to" a mortgage mean?

6. What is a mortgagee?

7. What was Mrs. Crane's arrangement with the mortgagee?

8. How could Mrs. Crane not have been personally liable for repayment of the debt that was secured by the mortgage on the property?

9. What types of deductions was Mrs. Crane entitled to during her period of ownership of the building?

10. Would the building have been a "capital asset" under the current definition in section 1221(a)(2)?

11. What does the Court mean by the term "boot"?

12. There were two principal issues in the case. Can you identify them?

13. Can you explain the two holdings of the case that are applicable generally upon the acquisition and disposition of property of any kind?

Footnote 37 in *Crane* sparked lively discussions in the tax community concerning the likely outcome if, in fact, the value of the property subject to nonrecourse financing, had fallen below the amount of the outstanding debt. The answer would not come until 1983. In the meantime, however, other questions remained. Consider the following case.

WOODSAM ASSOCIATES, INC. v. COMMISSIONER
198 F.2d 357 (2d Cir. 1952)

CHASE, Circuit Judge.

The petitioner paid its income and ... excess profits taxes for 1943 as computed upon returns it filed which included as part of its gross income $146,058.10 as gain realized upon the mortgage foreclosure sale in that year of improved real estate which it owned and which was bid in by the mortgagee for a nominal sum. It filed a timely claim for refund on the ground that its adjusted basis for the property had been understated and its taxable gain, therefore, was less than that reported. The refund claim was denied and a deficiency in both its income taxes and ... excess profits taxes was determined which was affirmed, without dissent, in a decision reviewed by the entire Tax Court. The decisive issue now presented is whether the basis for determining gain or loss upon the sale or other disposition of property is increased when, subsequent to the acquisition of the property, the owner receives a loan in an amount greater than his adjusted basis which is secured by a mortgage on the property upon which he is not personally liable. If so, it is agreed that part of the income taxes and all of the ... excess profits taxes paid for 1943 should be refunded.

A comparatively brief statement of the admitted facts and their obvious, and conceded, tax consequences will suffice by way of introduction.

On December 29, 1934, Samuel J. Wood and his wife organized the petitioner and each transferred to it certain property in return for one-half of its capital stock. One piece of property so transferred by Mrs. Wood was the above mentioned parcel of improved real estate consisting of land in the City of New York and a brick building thereon divided into units suitable for use, and used, in retail business. The property was subject to a $400,000 mortgage on which Mrs. Wood was not personally liable and on which the petitioner never became personally liable. Having, thus, acquired the property in a tax free exchange, I.R.C. [Sec. 351(a)] ... the petitioner took the basis of Mrs. Wood for tax purposes. I.R.C.... [Sec. 362(a)]. Upon the final disposition of the property at the foreclosure sale there was still due upon the mortgage the principal amount of $381,000 and, as the petitioner concedes, the extent to which the amount of the mortgage exceeds its adjusted basis was income taxable to it even though it was not personally liable upon the mortgage. Crane v. C.I.R., 331 U.S. 1....

Turning now to the one item whose effect upon the calculation of the petitioner's adjusted basis is disputed, the following admitted facts need to be stated. Mrs. Wood bought the property on January 20, 1922 at a total cost of $296,400. She paid $101,400 in cash, took the title subject to an existing mortgage for $120,000 and gave a purchase money bond and second mortgage for $75,000. She had made payments on the first mortgage reducing it to $112,500, when, on December 30, 1925, both of the mortgages were assigned to the Title Guarantee and Trust Company. On January 4, 1926 Mrs. Wood borrowed $137,500 from the Title Guarantee & Trust Company and gave it a bond and mortgage for $325,000 on which she was personally liable, that being the amount of the two existing mortgages, which were consolidated into the new one, plus the amount of the cash borrowed. On June 9, 1931 this consolidated mortgage was assigned to the East River Savings Bank and, shortly thereafter, Mrs. Wood borrowed an additional $75,000 from that bank which she received upon the execution of a second consolidated mortgage for $400,000 comprising the principal amount due on the first consolidated mortgage plus the additional loan. However, this transaction was carried out through the use of a "dummy" so that, under New York law, Mrs. Wood was not personally liable on this bond and mortgage.... This was the mortgage, reduced as above stated, which was foreclosed.

The contention of the petitioner may now be stated quite simply. It is that, when the borrowings of Mrs. Wood subsequent to her acquisition of the property became charges solely upon the property itself, the cash she received for the repayment of which she was not personally liable was a gain then taxable to her as income to the extent that the mortgage indebtedness exceeded her adjusted basis in the property. That being so, it is argued that her tax basis was, under familiar principles of tax law, increased by the amount of such taxable gain and that this stepped up basis carried over to the petitioner in the tax free exchange by which it acquired the property.

While this conclusion would be sound if the premise on which it is based were correct, we cannot accept the premise. It is that the petitioner's transferor made a taxable disposition of the property, within the meaning of I.R.C.... [Sec. 1001(a)] when the second consolidated mortgage was executed, because she had, by then, dealt with it in such a way that she had received cash, in excess of her basis, which, at that time, she was freed from any personal obligation to repay. Nevertheless, whether or nor personally liable on the mortgage, "The mortgagee is a creditor, and in effect nothing more than a preferred creditor, even though the mortgagor is not liable for the debt. He is not the less a creditor because he has recourse only to the land, unless we are to deny the term to one who may levy upon only a part of his debtor's assets." C.I.R. v. Crane, 2 Cir., 153 F.2d 504, 506. Mrs. Wood merely augmented the existing mortgage indebtedness when she borrowed each time and, far from closing the venture, remained in a position to borrow more if and when circumstances permitted and she so desired. And so, she never "disposed" of the property to create a taxable event which Sec. [1001(a)] ... I.R.C. makes a condition precedent to the taxation of gain. 'Disposition,' within the meaning of Sec. [1001(a)], is the 'getting rid, or making over, of anything; relinquishment'. Herber's Estate v. Commissioner, 3 Cir., 139 F.2d 756, 758, certiorari denied 322 U.S. 752, 64 S.Ct. 1263, 88 L.Ed. 1582. Nothing of that nature was done here by the mere execution of the second consolidated mortgage; Mrs. Wood was the owner of this property in the same sense after the execution of this mortgage that she was before. As was pointed out in our decision in the Crane case, supra, 153 F.2d at 505–506, "... the lien of a mortgage does not make the mortgagee a cotenant; the mortgagor is the owner for all purposes; indeed that is why the 'gage' is 'mort,' as distinguished from a '*vivum vadium*.' Kortright v. Cady, 21 N.Y. 343, 344.... He has all the income from the property; he manages it; he may sell it; any increase in its value goes to him; any decrease falls on him, until the value goes below the amount of the lien." Realization of gain was, therefore, postponed for taxation until there was a final disposition of the property at the time of the foreclosure sale.... Therefore, Mrs. Wood's borrowings did not change the basis for the computation of gain or loss.

Affirmed.

Now consider the following questions concerning *Woodsam Associates.*

1. Can you diagram the transaction is *Woodsam Associates*?

2. What was Mrs. Woodsam trying to accomplish?

3. What, if anything, does *Woodsam Associates* add to *Crane*?

As noted above, footnote 37 in *Crane* continued to spark lively discussions among tax aficionados: what would the Supreme Court do when it faced (as it no doubt would soon) a case in which the fair market value of the property had declined below the balance on a non-recourse mortgage. The day finally arrived. Read the following case.

COMMISSIONER v. TUFTS
461 U.S. 300 (1983)

JUSTICE BLACKMUN delivered the opinion of the Court.

Over 35 years ago, in *Crane v. Commissioner*, 331 U.S. 1 (1947), this Court ruled that a taxpayer, who sold property encumbered by a nonrecourse mortgage (the amount of the mortgage being less than the property's value), must include the unpaid balance of the mortgage in the computation of the amount the taxpayer realized on the sale. The case now before us presents the question whether the same rule applies when the unpaid amount of the nonrecourse mortgage exceeds the fair market value of the property sold.

I

On August 1, 1970, respondent Clark Pelt, a builder, and his wholly owned corporation, respondent Clark, Inc., formed a general partnership. The purpose of the partnership was to construct a 120-unit apartment complex in Duncanville, Tex., a Dallas suburb. Neither Pelt nor Clark, Inc., made any capital contribution to the partnership. Six days later, the partnership entered into a mortgage loan agreement with the Farm & Home Savings Association (F&H). Under the agreement, F&H was committed for a $1,851,500 loan for the complex. In return, the partnership executed a note and a deed of trust in favor of F&H. The partnership obtained the loan on a nonrecourse basis: neither the partnership nor its partners assumed any personal liability for repayment of the loan. Pelt later admitted four friends and relatives, respondents Tufts, Steger, Stephens, and Austin, as general partners. None of them contributed capital upon entering the partnership.

The construction of the complex was completed in August 1971. During 1971, each partner made small capital contributions to the partnership; in 1972, however, only Pelt made a contribution. The total of the partners' capital contributions was $44,212. In each tax year, all partners claimed as income tax deductions their allocable shares of ordinary losses and depreciation. The deductions taken by the partners in 1971 and 1972 totalled $439,972. Due to these contributions and deductions, the partnership's adjusted basis in the property in August 1972 was $1,455,740.

In 1971 and 1972, major employers in the Duncanville area laid off significant numbers of workers. As a result, the partnership's rental income was less than expected, and it was unable to make the payments due on the mortgage. Each partner, on August 28, 1972, sold his partnership interest to an unrelated third party, Fred Bayles. As consideration, Bayles agreed to reimburse each partner's sale expenses up to $250; he also assumed the nonrecourse mortgage.

On the date of transfer, the fair market value of the property did not exceed $1,400,000. Each partner reported the sale on his federal income tax return and indicated that a partnership loss of $55,740 had been sustained. (Footnote 1) The Commissioner of Internal Revenue, on audit, determined that the sale resulted in a partnership ... gain of approximately $400,000. His theory was that the partnership had realized the full amount of the nonrecourse obligation. (Footnote 2)

Relying on *Millar v. Commissioner*, 577 F.2d 212, 215 (CA3) ... the United States Tax Court, in an unreviewed decision, upheld the asserted deficiencies.... The United States Court of Appeals for the Fifth Circuit reversed. 651 F. 2d 1058 (1981). That court expressly disagreed with the *Millar* analysis, and, in limiting *Crane v. Commissioner, supra*, to its facts, questioned the theoretical underpinnings of the *Crane* decision. We granted certiorari to resolve the conflict....

II

... Section 1001 governs the determination of gains and losses on the disposition of property. Under § 1001(a), the gain or loss from a sale or other disposition of property is defined as the difference between "the amount realized" on the disposition and the property's adjusted basis. Subsection (b) of § 1001 defines "amount realized": "The amount realized from the sale or other disposition of property shall be the sum of any money received plus the fair market value of the property (other than money) received." At issue is the application of the latter provision to the disposition of property encumbered by a nonrecourse mortgage of an amount in excess of the property's fair market value.

A

In *Crane v. Commissioner, supra,* this Court took the first and controlling step toward the resolution of this issue. Beulah B. Crane was the sole beneficiary under the will of her deceased husband. At his death in January 1932, he owned an apartment building that was then mortgaged for an amount which proved to be equal to its fair market value, as determined for federal estate tax purposes. The widow, of course, was not personally liable on the mortgage. She operated the building for nearly seven years, hoping to turn it into a profitable venture; during that period, she claimed income tax deductions for depreciation, property taxes, interest, and operating expenses, but did not make payments upon the mortgage principal. In computing her basis for the depreciation deductions, she included the full amount of the mortgage debt. In November 1938, with her hopes unfulfilled and the mortgagee threatening foreclosure, Mrs. Crane sold the building. The purchaser took the property subject to the mortgage and paid Crane $3,000; of that amount, $500 went for the expenses of the sale.

Crane reported a gain of $2,500 on the transaction. She reasoned that her basis in the property was zero (despite her earlier depreciation deductions based on including the amount of the mortgage) and that the amount she realized from the sale was simply the cash she received. The Commissioner disputed this claim. He asserted that Crane's basis in the property, under ... [the predecessor to section] was the property's fair market value at the time of her husband's death, adjusted for depreciation in the interim, and that the amount realized was the net cash received plus the amount of the outstanding mortgage assumed by the purchaser.

In upholding the Commissioner's interpretation ... (Footnote 3) the Court observed that to regard merely the taxpayer's equity in the property as her basis would lead to depreciation deductions less than the actual physical deterioration of the property, and would require the basis to be recomputed with each payment on the mortgage. 331 U.S., at 9–10. The Court rejected Crane's claim that any loss due to depreciation belonged to the mortgagee. The effect of the Court's ruling was that the taxpayer's basis was the value of the property undiminished by the mortgage. *Id.*, at 11.

The Court next proceeded to determine the amount realized under ... [the predecessor to] § 1001(b).... In order to avoid the "absurdity," see 331 U.S., at 13, of Crane's realizing only $2,500 on the sale of property worth over a quarter of a million dollars, the Court treated the amount realized as it had treated basis, that is, by including the outstanding value of the mortgage. To do otherwise would have permitted Crane to recognize a tax loss unconnected with any actual economic loss. The Court refused to construe one section of the Revenue Act so as "to frustrate the Act as a whole." *Ibid.*

Crane, however, insisted that the nonrecourse nature of the mortgage required different treatment. The Court, for two reasons, disagreed. First, excluding the nonrecourse debt from the amount realized would result in the same absurdity and frustration of the Code. *Id.*, at 13–14. Second, the Court concluded that Crane obtained an economic benefit from the purchaser's assumption of the mortgage identical to the benefit conferred by the cancellation of personal debt. Because the value of the property in that case exceeded the amount of the mortgage, it was in Crane's economic interest to treat the mortgage as a personal obligation; only by so doing could she realize upon sale the appreciation in her equity represented by the $2,500 boot. The purchaser's assumption of the liability thus resulted in a taxable economic benefit to her, just as if she had been given, in addition to the boot, a sum of cash sufficient to satisfy the mortgage. (Footnote 4)

In a footnote, pertinent to the present case, the Court observed:

> "Obviously, if the value of the property is less than the amount of the mortgage, a mortgagor who is not personally liable cannot realize a benefit equal to the mortgage. Consequently, a different problem might be encountered where a mortgagor abandoned the property or transferred it subject to the mortgage without receiving boot. That is not this case." *Id.*, at 14, n. 37.

B

This case presents that unresolved issue. We are disinclined to overrule *Crane*, and we conclude that the same rule applies when the unpaid amount of the nonrecourse mortgage exceeds the value of the property transferred. *Crane* ultimately does not rest on its limited theory of economic benefit; instead, we read *Crane* to have approved the Commissioner's decision to treat a nonrecourse mortgage in this context as a true loan. This approval underlies *Crane*'s holdings that the amount of the nonrecourse liability is to be included in calculating both the basis and the amount realized on disposition. That the amount of the loan exceeds the fair market value of the property thus becomes irrelevant.

When a taxpayer receives a loan, he incurs an obligation to repay that loan at some future date. Because of this obligation, the loan proceeds do not qualify as income to the taxpayer. When he fulfills the obligation, the repayment of the loan likewise has no effect on his tax liability.

Another consequence to the taxpayer from this obligation occurs when the taxpayer applies the loan proceeds to the purchase price of property used to secure the loan. Because of the obligation to repay, the taxpayer is entitled to include the amount of the loan in computing his basis in the property; the loan, under § 1012, is part of the taxpayer's cost of the property. Although a different approach might have been taken with respect to a nonrecourse mortgage loan, (Footnote 5) the Commissioner has chosen to accord it the same treatment he gives to a recourse mortgage loan. The Court approved that choice in *Crane*, and the respondents do not challenge it here. The choice and its resultant benefits to the taxpayer are predicated on the assumption that the mortgage will be repaid in full.

When encumbered property is sold or otherwise disposed of and the purchaser assumes the mortgage, the associated extinguishment of the mortgagor's obligation to repay is accounted for in the computation of the amount realized. (Footnote 6) ... Because no difference between recourse and nonrecourse obligations is recognized in calculating basis, (Footnote 7) *Crane* teaches that the Commissioner may ignore the nonrecourse nature of the obligation in determining the amount realized upon disposition of the encumbered property. He thus may include in the amount realized the amount of the nonrecourse mortgage assumed by the purchaser. The rationale for this treatment is that the original inclusion of the amount of the mortgage in basis rested on the assumption that the mortgagor incurred an obligation to repay. Moreover, this treatment balances the fact that the mortgagor originally received the proceeds of the nonrecourse loan tax-free on the same assumption. Unless the outstanding amount of the mortgage is deemed to be realized, the mortgagor effectively will have received untaxed income at the time the loan was extended and will have received an unwarranted increase in the basis of his property. The Commissioner's interpretation of § 1001(b) in this fashion cannot be said to be unreasonable.

C

The Commissioner in fact has applied this rule even when the fair market value of the property falls below the amount of the nonrecourse obligation. Treas. Reg. § 1.1001-2(b) ... (Footnote 9) Rev. Rul. 76-111, 1976-1 Cum. Bull. 214. Because the theory on which the rule is based applies equally in this situation, ... we have no reason, after *Crane*, to question this treatment. (Footnote 11)

...

Respondents received a mortgage loan with the concomitant obligation to repay by the year 2012. The only difference between that mortgage and one on which the borrower is personally liable is that the mortgagee's remedy is limited to foreclosing on the securing property. This difference does not alter the nature of the obligation; its only effect is to shift from the borrower to the lender any potential loss caused by devaluation of the property. (Footnote 12) If the fair market value of the property falls below the amount of the outstanding obligation, the mortgagee's ability to protect its interests is impaired, for the mortgagor is free to abandon the property to the mortgagee and be relieved of his obligation.

This, however, does not erase the fact that the mortgagor received the loan proceeds tax-free and included them in his basis on the understanding that he had an obligation to repay the full amount. See *Woodsam Associates, Inc. v. Commissioner*, 198 F. 2d 357, 359 (CA2 1952).... When the obligation is canceled, the mortgagor is relieved of his responsibility to repay the sum he originally received and thus realizes value to that extent within the meaning of § 1001(b). From the mortgagor's point of view, when his obligation is assumed by a third party who purchases the encumbered property, it is as if the mortgagor first had been paid with cash borrowed by the third party from the mortgagee on a nonrecourse basis, and then had used the cash to satisfy his obligation to the mortgagee.

Moreover, this approach avoids the absurdity the Court recognized in *Crane*. Because of the remedy accompanying the mortgage in the nonrecourse situation, the depreciation in the fair market value of the property is relevant economically only to the mortgagee, who by lending on a nonrecourse basis remains at risk. To permit the taxpayer to limit his realization to the fair market value of the property would be to recognize a tax loss for which he has suffered no corresponding economic loss. (Footnote 13) Such a result would be to construe "one section of the Act ... so as ... to defeat the intention of another or to frustrate the Act as a whole." 331 U.S., at 13.

In the specific circumstances of *Crane*, the economic benefit theory did support the Commissioner's treatment of the nonrecourse mortgage as a personal obligation. The footnote in *Crane* acknowledged the limitations of that theory when applied to a different set of facts. *Crane* also stands for the broader proposition, however, that a nonrecourse loan should be treated as a true loan. We therefore hold that a taxpayer must account for the proceeds of obligations he has received tax-free and included in basis.

Nothing in either § 1001(b) or in the Court's prior decisions requires the Commissioner to permit a taxpayer to treat a sale of encumbered property asymmetrically, by including the proceeds of the nonrecourse obligation in basis but not accounting for the proceeds upon transfer of the encumbered property....

...

IV

When a taxpayer sells or disposes of property encumbered by a nonrecourse obligation, the Commissioner properly requires him to include among the assets realized the outstanding amount of the obligation. The fair market value of the property is irrelevant to this calculation. We find this interpretation to be consistent with *Crane v. Commissioner*, 331 U.S. 1 (1947), and to implement the statutory mandate in a reasonable manner....

The judgment of the Court of Appeals is therefore reversed.

FOOTNOTES:

1. The loss was the difference between the adjusted basis, $1,455,740, and the fair market value of the property, $1,400,000. On their individual tax returns, the partners did not claim deductions for their respective shares of this loss. In their petitions to the Tax Court, however, the partners did claim the loss.

2. The Commissioner determined the partnership's gain on the sale by subtracting the adjusted basis, $1,455,740, from the liability assumed by Bayles, $1,851,500....

3.... The Court interpreted the term "property" [in the predecessor to section 1014] to refer to the physical land and buildings owned by Crane or the aggregate of her rights to control and dispose of them. 331 U.S., at 6....

4. Crane also argued that even if the statute required the inclusion of the amount of the nonrecourse debt, that amount was not Sixteenth Amendment income because the overall transaction had been "by all dictates of common sense ... a ruinous disaster." ... The Court noted, however, that Crane had been entitled to and actually took depreciation deductions for nearly seven years. To allow her to exclude sums on which those deductions were based from the calculation of her taxable gain would permit her "a double deduction ... on the same loss of assets." The Sixteenth Amendment, it was said, did not require that result. 331 U.S., at 15–16.

5. The Commissioner might have adopted the theory, implicit in Crane's contentions, that a nonrecourse mortgage is not true debt, but, instead, is a form of joint investment by the mortgagor and the mortgagee. On this approach, nonrecourse debt would be considered a contingent liability, under which the mortgagor's payments on the debt gradually increase his interest in the property while decreasing that of the mortgagee.... Because the taxpayer's investment in the property would not include the nonrecourse debt, the taxpayer would not be permitted to include that debt in basis....

We express no view as to whether such an approach would be consistent with the statutory structure and, if so, and *Crane* were not on the books, whether that approach would be preferred over *Crane's* analysis. We note only that the *Crane* Court's resolution of the basis issue presumed that when property is purchased with proceeds from a nonrecourse mortgage, the purchaser becomes the sole owner of the property. 331 U.S., at

6. Under the *Crane* approach, the mortgagee is entitled to no portion of the basis. *Id.*, at 10, n. 28. The nonrecourse mortgage is part of the mortgagor's investment in the property, and does not constitute a coinvestment by the mortgagee....

7. The Commissioner's choice in *Crane* "laid the foundation stone of most tax shelters," Bittker, Tax Shelters, Nonrecourse Debt, and the *Crane* Case, 33 Tax.L.Rev. 277, 283 (1978), by permitting taxpayers who bear no risk to take deductions on depreciable property. Congress recently has acted to curb this avoidance device by forbidding a taxpayer to take depreciation deductions in excess of amounts he has at risk in the investment.... Real estate investments, however, are exempt from this prohibition. § 465(c)(3)(D).... Although this congressional action may foreshadow a day when non-recourse and recourse debts will be treated differently, neither Congress nor the Commissioner has sought to alter *Crane's* rule of including nonrecourse liability in both basis and the amount realized.

9. The regulation was promulgated while this case was pending before the Court of Appeals for the Fifth Circuit. T. D. 7741, 45 Fed. Reg. 81743, 1981-1 Cum. Bull. 430 (1980). It merely formalized the Commissioner's prior interpretation, however.

11. Professor Wayne G. Barnett, as *amicus* in the present case, argues that the liability and property portions of the transaction should be accounted for separately. Under his view, there was a transfer of the property for $1.4 million, and there was a cancellation of the $1.85 million obligation for a payment of $1.4 million. The former resulted in a capital loss of $50,000, and the latter in the realization of $450,000 of ordinary income. Taxation of the ordinary income might be deferred under § 108....

   Although this indeed could be a justifiable mode of analysis, it has not been adopted by the Commissioner. Nor is there anything to indicate that the Code requires the Commissioner to adopt it. We note that Professor Barnett's approach does assume that recourse and nonrecourse debt may be treated identically.

   ...

12. In his opinion for the Court of Appeals in *Crane*, Judge Learned Hand observed:

"[The mortgagor] has all the income from the property; he manages it; he may sell it; any increase in its value goes to him; any decrease falls on him, until the value goes below the amount of the lien.... When therefore upon a sale the mortgagor makes an allowance to the vendee of the amount of the lien, he secures a release from a charge upon his property quite as though the vendee had paid him the full price on condition that before he took title the lien should be cleared...." 153 F. 2d 504, 506 (CA2 1945).

13. In the present case, the Government bore the ultimate loss. The nonrecourse mortgage was extended to respondents only after the planned complex was endorsed for mortgage insurance under §§ 221(b) and (d)(4) of the National Housing Act, 12 U.S.C. §§ 1715(l)(b) and (d)(4).... After acquiring the complex from respondents, Bayles operated it for a few years, but was unable to make it profitable. In 1974, F&H foreclosed, and the Department of Housing and Urban Development paid off the lender to obtain title. In 1976, the Department sold the complex to another developer for $1,502,000. The sale was financed by the Department's taking back a note for $1,314,800 and a non-recourse mortgage. To fail to recognize the value of the nonrecourse loan in the amount realized, therefore, would permit respondents to compound the Government's loss by claiming the tax benefits of that loss for themselves.

JUSTICE O'CONNOR, concurring.

I concur in the opinion of the Court, accepting the view of the Commissioner. I do not, however, endorse the Commissioner's view. Indeed, were we writing on a slate clean except for the decision in *Crane v. Commissioner*, I would take quite a different approach—that urged upon us by Professor Barnett as *amicus*.

Crane established that a taxpayer could treat property as entirely his own, in spite of the "coinvestment" provided by his mortgagee in the form of a nonrecourse loan. That is, the full basis of the property, with all its tax consequences, belongs to the mortgagor. That rule alone, though, does not in any way tie nonrecourse debt to the cost of property or to the proceeds upon disposition. I see no reason to treat the purchase, ownership, and eventual disposition of property differently because the taxpayer also takes out a mortgage, an independent transaction. In this case, the taxpayer purchased property, using nonrecourse financing, and sold it after it declined in value to a buyer who assumed the mortgage. There is no economic difference between the events in this case and a case in which the taxpayer buys property with cash; later obtains a nonrecourse loan by pledging the property as security; still later, using cash on hand, buys off the mortgage for the market value of the devalued property; and finally sells the property to a third party for its market value.

The logical way to treat both this case and the hypothesized case is to separate the two aspects of these events and to consider, first, the ownership and sale of the property, and, second, the arrangement and retirement of the loan. Under Crane, the fair market value of the property on the date of acquisition—the purchase price—represents the taxpayer's basis in the property, and the fair market value on the date of disposition represents the proceeds on sale. The benefit received by the taxpayer in return for the property is the cancellation of a mortgage that is worth no more than the fair market value of the property, for that is all the mortgagee can expect to collect on the mortgage. His gain or loss on the disposition of the property equals the difference between the proceeds and the cost of acquisition. Thus, the taxation of the transaction *in property* reflects the economic fate of the *property*. If the property has declined in value, as was the case here, the taxpayer recognizes a loss on the disposition of the property. The new purchaser then takes as his basis the fair market value as of the date of the sale. See, *e.g.*, *United States v. Davis*, 370 U.S. 65, 72 (1962)....

In the separate borrowing transaction, the taxpayer acquires cash from the mortgagee. He need not recognize income at that time, of course, because he also incurs an obligation to repay the money. Later, though, when he is able to satisfy the debt by surrendering property that is worth less than the face amount of the debt, we have a classic situation of cancellation of indebtedness, requiring the taxpayer to recognize income in the amount of the difference between the proceeds of the loan and the amount for which he is able to satisfy his creditor.... §61(a)(12). The taxation of the financing transaction then reflects the economic fate of the loan.

The reason that separation of the two aspects of the events in this case is important is, of course, that the Code treats different sorts of income differently. A gain on the sale of the property may qualify for capital gains treatment ... while the cancellation of indebtedness is ordinary income, but income that the taxpayer may be able to defer. §§ 108, 1017.... Not only does Professor Barnett's theory permit us to accord appropriate treatment to each of the two types of income or loss present in these sorts of transactions, it also restores continuity to the system by making the taxpayer-seller's proceeds on the disposition of property equal to the purchaser's basis in the property. Further, and most important, it allows us to tax the events in this case in the same way that we tax the economically identical hypothesized transaction.

Persuaded though I am by the logical coherence and internal consistency of this approach, I agree with the Court's decision not to adopt it judicially. We do not write on a slate marked only by *Crane*. The Commissioner's longstanding position, Rev.Rul. 76-111, 1976-1 Cum. Bull. 214, is now reflected in the regulations. Treas. Reg. § 1.1001-2 ... (1982). In the light of the numerous cases in the lower courts including the amount of the unrepaid proceeds of the mortgage in the proceeds on sale or disposition, ... it is difficult to conclude that the Commissioner's interpretation of the statute exceeds the bounds of his discretion. As the Court's opinion demonstrates, his interpretation is defensible. One can reasonably read § 1001(b)'s reference to "the amount realized *from* the sale or other disposition of property" (emphasis added) to permit the Commissioner to collapse the two aspects of the transaction. As long as his view is a reasonable reading of § 1001(b), we should defer to the regulations promulgated by the agency charged with interpretation of the statute.... Accordingly, I concur.

Consider these questions concerning *Tufts*.

1. What is the significance of the Supreme Court's adoption of footnote 37 in *Crane*?

2. Did the decision in *Crane* require the Court to conclude as it did in *Tufts*? Or, can you articulate a way in which the Court might have distinguished the two cases?

3. In his *amicus* brief, Professor Wayne Barnett began by noting that according to the government the amount released as a consequence of the foreclosure must be realized or the taxpayer will escape gain recognition on the portion in excess of the property's fair market value. Professor Barnett argues that the government's statement is incorrect; that it "presents a false dilemma." (Br. at 2.) Rather, the amount realized should represent only the amount released as a result of the foreclosure, with the balance treated as income from the discharge of indebtedness (similar to the result in *Kirby Lumber*). As Professor Barnett expressed his argument:

> The prior loan proceeds must indeed be accounted for, but the proper way to account for them is to treat them not as an amount received for the *asset* but as what they are: an amount received for the note the taxpayers issued and hence for the *liability* they thereby accepted. A taxpayer who buys in a note for less than he receives for issuing it (his "basis" for the liability) has a gain equal to the difference—what the statute calls "income from the discharge of indebtedness" ... but what will here be called simply a "liability gain". And it is specifically in the computation of *such* gains, not of asset gains, that one properly accounts for receipts for accepting liabilities.
>
> It is evident too that, since the asset was all that they gave up for it, the taxpayers cannot be deemed to have *expended* for their relief from the liability any more than they are deemed to have *received* for the asset. If, then, ... they are deemed to have received for their asset only an amount equal to its value—$1.4 million—then $1.4 million is also the only amount they can be deemed to have paid to be relieved of the liability. And since their basis for the liability was $1.85 million, that would mean they realized a *liability gain* of $450,000. The result, it may be seen, is that the *total* gain the taxpayers realized (their asset gain or loss plus their liability gain or loss) will be the same

however the amount of the deemed receipt (for the asset) and expenditure (for the liability relief) is fixed. What turns on the issue mooted by the parties, then, is not *how much* gain the taxpayers realized but only *what kind* of gain it was.[7]

But, did the Court's general statements in *Crane* make it more difficult for it to adopt Professor Barnett's view in *Tufts*? Can you identify statements in the majority opinion in *Tufts* that help answer this question? In Justice O'Connor's concurrence?

Recall the hypothetical we posed to you early in this course. Suppose a friend comes to you and you loan her $1,000. She gives you an unsecured promissory note for the $1,000. Now suppose that on the date the note is due, your friend tells you that she is unable to pay more than $750. You accept the $750 in full payment. What result to your friend? Now suppose that she comes to you and tells you that she cannot pay anything in cash, but she can give you a painting worth $750 for which she paid $200. Her delivery to you of the painting is certainly treated as a sale or other disposition of the painting. But what is her amount realized? It must be $750, creating a gain under section 1001 of $550.[8] But, if you then forgive the balance of her debt, the remaining $250, what tax consequence to her? It is just as clearly income from the discharge of indebtedness, includible in gross income under section 61(a)(12), as in the case in which she gave you only $750 in cash and you forgave the balance.[9] Why is the result different in *Tufts*?

After the Supreme Court's decision in *Crane*, but before its 1983 decision in *Tufts*, the Treasury issued Treasury Regulation section 1.1001-2. **Read Treasury Regulation section 1.1001-2.** That regulation, cited by Professor Barnett in his *amicus* brief, supports a bifurcated treatment of a foreclosure where the value of property has declined below the balance of its financing in the case of recourse financing. But in the case of non-recourse financing, it supports the argument the government was simultaneously making before the courts in *Tufts*.[10] Did Treasury attempt to bolster its position in *Tufts* through promulgation of this regulation?

The Service issued the following Revenue Ruling after the Supreme Court's decision in *Tufts*.

REVENUE RULING 90-16
1990-1 C.B. 12

ISSUE

A taxpayer transfers to a creditor a residential subdivision that has a fair market value in excess of the taxpayer's basis in satisfaction of a debt for which the taxpayer was personally liable. Is the transfer a sale or disposition resulting in the realization and recognition of gain by the taxpayer under section 1001(c) and 61(a)(3) of the Internal Revenue Code?

---

7. *Brief for Amicus Curiae* at 2, *Commissioner v. Tufts*, 461 U.S. 300 (1983) (No. 81-1536).

8. It has been clear since at least 1943, when the Second Circuit decided *International Freighting Corp. v. Commissioner*, 135 F.2d 310 (2d Cir. 1943), that satisfaction of an obligation through delivery of property constitutes a "sale or other disposition" within the meaning of section 1001(a). Even though the taxpayer does not technically receive money or other property, she is considered as having received "money's worth" equal to the value of the property transferred. 135 F.2d at 313. In other words, the tax law treats the transaction as if the taxpayer had sold the property for cash and then used the cash to satisfy the obligation.

9. This is, in effect, Professor Barnett's argument in his *amicus* brief.

10. **See Treasury Regulation section 1.1001-2(c), examples 7 and 8.**

FACTS

X was the owner and developer of a residential subdivision. To finance the development of the subdivision, *X* obtained a loan from an unrelated bank. *X* was unconditionally liable for repayment of the debt. The debt was secured by a mortgage on the subdivision.

X became insolvent (within the meaning of section 108(d)(3) of the Code) and defaulted on the debt. *X* negotiated an agreement with the bank whereby the subdivision was transferred to the bank and the bank released *X* from all liability for the amounts due on the debt. When the subdivision was transferred pursuant to the agreement, its fair market value was 10,000x dollars, *X*'s adjusted basis in the subdivision was 8,000x dollars, and the amount due on the debt was 12,000x dollars, which did not represent any accrued but unpaid interest. After the transaction *X* was still insolvent.

LAW AND ANALYSIS

Sections 61(a)(3) and 61(a)(12) of the Code provide that, except as otherwise provided, gross income means all income from whatever source derived, including (but not limited to) gains from dealings in property and income from discharge of indebtedness.

Section 108(a)(1)(B) of the Code provides that gross income does not include any amount that would otherwise be includible in gross income by reason of discharge (in whole or in part) of indebtedness of the taxpayer if the discharge occurs when the taxpayer is insolvent. Section 108(a)(3) provides that, in the case of a discharge to which section 108(a)(1)(B) applies, the amount excluded under section 108(a)(1)(B) shall not exceed the amount by which the taxpayer is insolvent (as defined in section 108(d)(3)).

Section 1.61-6(a) of the Income Tax Regulations provides that the specific rules for computing the amount of gain or loss from dealings in property under section 61(a)(3) are contained in section 1001 and the regulations thereunder.

Section 1001(a) of the Code provides that gain from the sale or other disposition of property shall be the excess of the amount realized therefrom over the adjusted basis provided in section 1011 for determining gain.

Section 1001(b) of the Code provides that the amount realized from the sale or other disposition of property shall be the sum of any money received plus the fair market value of the property (other than money) received.

Section 1001(c) of the Code provides that, except as otherwise provided in subtitle A, the entire amount of the gain or loss, determined under section 1001, on the sale or exchange of property shall be recognized.

Section 1.1001-2(a)(1) of the regulations provides that, except as provided in section 1.1001-2(a)(2) and (3), the amount realized from a sale or other disposition of property includes the amount of liabilities from which the transferor is discharged as a result of the sale or disposition. Section 1.1001-2(a)(2) provides that the amount realized on a sale or other disposition of property that secures a recourse liability does not include amounts that are (or would be if realized and recognized) income from the discharge of indebtedness under section 61(a)(12). *Example (8)* under section 1.1001-2(c) illustrates these rules as follows:

> *Example (8)*. In 1980, F transfers to a creditor an asset with a fair market value of $6,000 and the creditor discharges $7,500 of indebtedness for which F is personally liable. The amount realized on the disposition of the asset is its fair market value ($6,000). In addition, F has income from the discharge of indebtedness of $1,500 ($7,500–$6,000).

In the present situation, X transferred the subdivision to the bank in satisfaction of the 12,000x dollar debt. To the extent of the fair market value of the property transferred to the creditor, the transfer of the subdivision is treated as a sale or disposition upon which gain is recognized under section 1001(c) of the Code. To the extent the fair market value of the subdivision, 10,000x dollars, exceeds its adjusted basis, 8,000x dollars, X realizes and recognizes gain on the transfer. X thus recognizes 2,000x dollars of gain.

To the extent the amount of debt, 12,000x dollars, exceeds the fair market value of the subdivision, 10,000x dollars, X realizes income from the discharge of indebtedness. However, under section 108(a)(1)(B) of the Code, the full amount of X's discharge of indebtedness income is excluded from gross income because that amount does not exceed the amount by which X was insolvent.

If the subdivision had been transferred to the bank as a result of a foreclosure proceeding in which the outstanding balance of the debt was discharged (rather than having been transferred pursuant to the settlement agreement), the result would be the same. A mortgage foreclosure, like a voluntary sale, is a "disposition" within the scope of the gain or loss provisions of section 1001 of the Code. *See Helvering v. Hammel*, 311 U.S. 504 (1941)....

HOLDING

The transfer of the subdivision by X to the bank in satisfaction of a debt on which X was personally liable is a sale or disposition upon which gain is realized and recognized by X under sections 1001(c) and 61(a)(3) of the Code to the extent the fair market value of the subdivision transferred exceeds X's adjusted basis. Subject to the application of section 108 of the Code, to the extent the amount of debt exceeds the fair market value of the subdivision, X would also realize income from the discharge of indebtedness.

Note that in Revenue Ruling 90-16, the Treasury cites Example 8 from Treasury Regulation section 1.1001-2(c). The Service also cited Example 8 in the following technical advice memorandum.

TECHNICAL ADVICE MEMORANDUM 199935002

DATE: May 3, 1999

. . .

ISSUE

For purposes of section 108(d)(3) of the Internal Revenue Code, which, if any, of the taxpayers' assets are not included in a determination of whether the taxpayers are insolvent?

. . .

FACTS

On October 9, 1984, the taxpayers purchased their residence for 130x dollars. On October 7, 1987, the mortgagee foreclosed on the residence using a non-judicial foreclosure proceeding. At the time of the foreclosure, the residence had a fair market value of 100x dollars and was subject to a mortgage with an outstanding balance of 122x dollars. Due to the Alaska antideficiency statute, the mortgagee is barred from attempting to collect from the mortgagor a deficiency resulting from the nonjudicial foreclosure of a residence whose fair market value has fallen below the outstanding mortgage balance. Therefore, the deficiency of 22x was discharged by the non-judicial foreclosure. It is represented that the taxpayers were insolvent on the date of the foreclosure if assets exempt from the claims of creditors under Alaska state law are not included in the insolvency determination. The taxpayers have not filed bankruptcy.

APPLICABLE LAW AND RATIONALE

Under section 61(a)(12) of the Code, except as otherwise provided, gross income means all income including income from the discharge of indebtedness.

Example 8 of section 1.1001-2(c) of the Income Tax Regulations provides that when property subject to a recourse liability is transferred to a creditor in satisfaction of the liability, the taxpayer has capital gain or loss of the difference between the fair market value of the property and the taxpayer's basis in the property and discharge of indebtedness income of the difference between the outstanding amount of the indebtedness and the fair market value of the property.

Section 108(a)(1)(B) of the Code provides that discharge of indebtedness income is excluded from gross income if the discharge occurs when the taxpayer is insolvent. Section 108(a)(3) provides that the amount excluded by section 108(a)(1)(B) does not exceed the amount by which the taxpayer is insolvent.

Section 108(d)(3) of the Code defines "insolvent" to mean the excess of liabilities over the fair market value of assets determined immediately before the discharge.

The Bankruptcy Tax Act of 1980, Pub. L. No. 96-589, ... substantially amended section 108 of the Code, and (among other things) codified in section 108(a)(1)(B) the judicially developed insolvency exception to the general rule that income is realized upon the discharge of indebtedness. See H.R. Rep. No. 833, 96th Cong., 2d Sess. 7 (1980); S. Rep. No. 1035, 96th Cong., 2d Sess. 8 (1980).... The Bankruptcy Tax Act also added section 108(e)(1) of the Code, which provides that the insolvency exception in section 108(a)(1)(B) is the exclusive insolvency exception.

The statutory language of section 108(d)(3) of the Code does not specify which assets and which liabilities are taken into consideration for determining the definition of "insolvent," and the committee reports to the Bankruptcy Tax Act do not clarify this definition. Although case law interpreting the judicial insolvency exclusion that was in effect prior to the enactment of the Bankruptcy Tax Act of 1980 excluded assets exempt from creditors under state law ... the statutory language places no limitation on assets that are taken into account in determining a taxpayer's solvency. The plain meaning of the term asset in section 108(d)(3) would include all of the taxpayer's assets in the insolvency calculation. Generally, where the language of a statute is clear and unambiguous, no further inquiry into the meaning of the statute is needed. 1 Mertens Law of Federal Taxation section 3.05 (1991). Further, section 108, as an exclusion from income, is to be construed narrowly. *U.S. v. Centennial Savings Bank FSB*, 499 U.S. 573, 583 (1991).

Further, the legislative history provides no clear guidance regarding the treatment of exempt assets for purposes of the insolvency definition....

...

The legislative history underlying section 108 indicates that a bankrupt debtor and an insolvent debtor should be provided with a fresh start in that they should not be burdened with current taxation on the discharge of indebtedness. S. Rep. No. 96-1035, 96th Cong., 2d Sess. 9-10 (1980).... This rationale was based upon the fact that such debtors would not have assets available to pay a tax liability that would arise upon the discharge of their debts. However, excluding exempt assets from the measure of insolvency would provide taxpayers who are economically solvent, i.e. whose total assets exceed their liabilities, the opportunity to defer a current tax in instances where they have the ability to pay the tax. Such taxpayers would have assets available to pay a tax liability (although the assets would be exempt from the reach of creditors under state law).

For the reasons discussed above, we conclude that assets exempt from creditor's claims under state law should be included in determining a taxpayer's solvency for purposes of sections 108(d) and 108(a)(1)(B).

In this case, the taxpayers have discharge of indebtedness income as a result of the mortgagee's non-judicial foreclosure on their residence since State's anti-deficiency statute relieved them of their liability for any deficiency on the mortgage note. The taxpayers in this case may not exclude assets exempt from the claims of their creditors under State law from the calculation of their total assets for purposes of determining whether they are insolvent under section 108 of the Code.

A copy of this technical advice memorandum is to be given to the taxpayer. Section 6110[k](3) of the Code provides that it may not be used or cited as precedent.

Notice the form of the technical advice memorandum. As noted earlier in this book, auditors (when examining a tax return), often seek guidance on the proper tax treatment of a taxpayer's transactions by asking for such a ruling. Of course, the ruling does not have the same effect as issuance of a regulation or even a revenue ruling. It is personal to the taxpayer and may not be relied upon by others. Nevertheless, since the outset of publication of these memoranda (and their "twins," private letter rulings) in the 1980's (thanks in large measure to the efforts of Tax Analysts), they have served as important indications of the current position of the Service on particular issues.[11]

Now answer the following questions comparing *Tufts* to Revenue Ruling 90-16 and TAM 199935002.

1. Using the actual numbers from the case and the rulings, respectively, explain all relevant tax consequences of each.

2. What would have been the tax consequences in *Tufts* if the debt had been recourse?

3. What would have been the respective tax consequences in Revenue Ruling 90-16 and TAM 199935002 if the debts had been nonrecourse? (Note that the taxpayers in TAM 199935002 lived in a state that had an "anti-deficiency statute." What is that? Why did the Service still treat the debt as recourse?)

4. Does the difference in treatment between nonrecourse and recourse debt create opportunities for tax planning (or avoidance) by taxpayers?[12]

---

11. A recent article argues that despite the limitation contained in section 6110(k)(3), courts and taxpayers are treating private letter rulings and technical advice memoranda as persuasive (though not controlling). William H. Volz, Deborah Jones, and Rachel E. Wisley, "Practitioner Reliance on Private Letter Rulings as Legal Authority," 88 Tax Notes 1035 (Aug. 21, 2000).

12. *See* Fred T. Witt, Jr. and William H. Lyons, "An Examination of the Tax Consequences of Discharge of Indebtedness," 10 Va. Tax. Rev. 1, 61–63 (1990).

5. Is there any justification for the difference?[13]

From the beginning of the course, you learned that the starting point for basis is TOAD. This Chapter 3.B. has illustrated some of the problems that arise when taxpayers finance the acquisition of assets using borrowed funds. Borrowed money does not constitute TOAD, but at the same time, the taxpayer is treated as owning an asset which, if used in a trade or business or an investment activity, is subject to the allowance for depreciation. The Supreme Court's decision in *Crane* addressed this conundrum by adopting the position that a taxpayer can acquire basis using borrowed funds based on the assumption that he will eventually repay the borrowed funds with TOAD. To the extent that upon disposition of the asset, he does so, the assumption is justified. When, however, he does not do so, the assumption underlying the inclusion in basis of the borrowed funds ceases to work well.[14] But the alternative, highlighted in *Crane*, that of a constantly changing basis, created other problems. Therefore, as a practical matter, the Court almost certainly made the better choice with respect to basis. But the ongoing controversy concerning the Court's corollary conclusion of including the borrowed funds in the amount realized as applied in *Tufts* suggests that there may well be more to this puzzle in the future.

C. Some Additional Considerations on the "Sale or Other Disposition" of Property

In an earlier section of this book, you studied the general rule for sales or other dispositions of property. Suppose, however, that the lender to an owner of property financed through mortgage borrowing forecloses its loan? How should the borrower treat his loss of the property? It is first necessary to learn a little more about mortgages. We have already encountered the concepts of recourse and nonrecourse borrowing. In either case, the lender makes the loan and the borrower delivers to the lender a note promising to repay the loan and a document representing the lender's security interest in the property. In many cases that security interest takes the form of a "mortgage." In the case of a mortgage, the borrower does not surrender ownership of the property to the lender unless and until there is a default in the borrower's compliance with the terms of the note. In that case, the lender may "foreclose" on the mortgage. In other cases, the lender's security interest takes the form of a "deed of trust" by which the bor-

---

13. For a discussion of the rationale in favor of different treatment, see Douglas A. Kahn, *Federal Income Tax, A Student's Guide to the Internal Revenue Code* § 16.1511-1B (3d ed., Foundation Press 1994). For the contrary view, see Deborah A. Geier, "Tufts and the Evolution of Debt Discharge Theory," 1 Fla. Tax Rev. 115 (1992).

14. It worked satisfactorily in *Crane* because the value of the asset continued to exceed the amount of the indebtedness. Mrs. Crane could be treated as repaying the full amount of her borrowed funds because the purchaser of her property took subject to the existing debt and, again, the assumption was that he would repay it. It did not work well in *Tufts*, however, because of the decline in the value of the property to an amount that was less than the balance outstanding on the loan. In that event, the difference between the loan balance and the value of the property will never be paid with TOAD.

rower transfers ownership of the property to a trustee for the lender until the debt is discharged.[15]

1. Foreclosures and Abandonments

YARBRO v. COMMISSIONER

737 F.2d 479 (5th Cir. 1984)

JOHN R. BROWN, Circuit Judge:

This case presents the question of whether an individual taxpayer's loss resulting from the abandonment of unimproved real estate subject to a non-recourse mortgage exceeding the market value is an ordinary loss or a capital loss. Because the Commissioner may change an earlier interpretation of the law to another reasonable interpretation, we affirm the Tax Court's holding that an abandonment of real property subject to non-recourse debt is a "sale or exchange" for purposes of determining whether a loss is a capital loss.

Facts

James W. Yarbro (Taxpayer) has been a self-employed financial and tax consultant since 1969. In 1972, he acquired a real estate broker's license. In that year, he formed three joint ventures and negotiated a separate land purchase for each of the ventures. Only the land purchase for the last of the three joint ventures is at issue here.

The venture was formed by Taxpayer, together with five other persons, for the purpose of acquiring about 132 acres of undeveloped land on the northern limits of the city of Fort Worth, Texas. The purchase price was $362,132.08. About 10% was paid in cash, and the balance was covered by four non-recourse promissory notes secured by deeds of trust on the property. Taxpayer took title to the property as trustee, and under the terms of the joint venture agreement, was responsible for managing the property. For his services as trustee and manager, Taxpayer received a one-time fee of $4,000. Taxpayer was also entitled to receive a 3% sales commission if the property were sold.

Each participant in the joint venture was required to contribute $4,100 in cash for each ten-percent interest purchased. One investor purchased a 50-percent interest, while the other investors, including taxpayer herein, each purchased a ten-percent interest. About six months after the joint venture was organized, taxpayer bought out one of the other ten-percent investors for $6,150, making his total investment in the joint venture a little over $10,000.

At the time the property was acquired, it was subject to a livestock grazing lease, and during the years the joint venture owned the property (1972 through 1976), it continued to be rented for grazing purposes at a rental of approximately $1,000 per year. The joint venture's only other income during those years was a small amount of interest. During that same period of time, the joint venture incurred expenses of

---

15. The Restatement 2nd of Mortgages refers to both of these methods as "mortgages," as does this book. The specific methodology applicable to the process by which the lender terminates the interest of the borrower will not be important until a later point in this part, and then only for limited purposes.

about $23,000 each year for interest, taxes and insurance. Because these expenses greatly exceeded the income generated by the land, the participants were required to make annual pro-rata contributions to the venture. Taxpayer's contributions were about $4,500 per year.

Taxpayer acknowledged at trial that one of the primary purposes in purchasing the property was the expectation that the property would appreciate in value and that it could be sold at a later date for a substantial profit. Although the possibility of developing the property was considered, no definite development plans were drawn up, no improvements were ever made, and the joint venture participants were never asked to advance any funds for that purpose. (Footnote 2)

In the summer of 1976, the City of Fort Worth decided to raise the real estate taxes on the joint venture's property by 435% from $770 per year to approximately $3,350 per year. At about the same time, real estate activity in the area completely dried up. As a consequence, by November of 1976, the property's fair market value had dropped below the face amount of the non-recourse mortgage to which it was subject. When confronted with these facts, the joint venture participants decided to abandon the property and not to pay the real estate taxes for 1976 or the $22,811 annual interest payment for that year. Accordingly, on November 15, 1976, Taxpayer, as trustee, notified the Fort Worth National Bank (the trustee of the mortgages) that he was abandoning the property. Although the bank requested Taxpayer to reconvey the property to it, Taxpayer refused to do so, reasoning that he "had nothing to convey and would have nothing to do ... with the property from that point on."

In June, 1977, the bank obtained title to the property pursuant to foreclosure proceedings. None of the joint venture participants received any consideration from the foreclosure sale.

The Tax

On his 1976 federal income tax return, Taxpayer claimed an ordinary loss of $10,376 from the abandonment of the joint venture property. The Commissioner, however, determined that Taxpayer's loss was not an ordinary loss, but, rather, constituted a long-term capital loss. The Commissioner took the position that Taxpayer's abandonment of the property constituted a "sale or exchange" within the meaning of Sections 1211 and 1222 of the Code. The Commissioner further contended that Taxpayer held his own interest in the land as an investment and not for use in taxpayer's "trade or business" or "primarily for sale to customers in the ordinary course of business." Thus, the Commissioner contended that the abandonment was a "sale or exchange" of a "capital asset."

The Tax Court agreed with the Commissioner's analysis. Determining that Taxpayer acquired his interest in the property "primarily for investment purposes" the Tax Court held that the property was not used in Taxpayer's financial consulting and property management business within the meaning of Section 1231 of the Code. The Tax Court also concluded that the "casual" rental of the land for grazing purposes at a nominal fee did not evidence use of the land in a bona fide rental business, and that the evidence did not support a finding that the land was held primarily for sale to customers in the ordinary course of business. Finally, the Tax Court, following the course charted in *Freeland v. Commissioner*, 74 T.C. 970 (1980), and *Middleton v. Commissioner*, 77 T.C. 310 (1981), *aff'd* per curiam, 693 F.2d 124 (11th Cir.1982), held that an abandonment of property constituted a "sale or exchange" for purposes of Code Sections 1211 and 1222.

Statutory Context

Section 165(a) of the Internal Revenue Code of 1954 provides, as a general rule, that taxpayers may deduct "any loss sustained during the taxable year and not compensated for by insurance or otherwise." 26 U.S.C. § 165(a). The application of this general rule, however, is limited by Section 165(f), which provides that "losses from *sales or exchanges* of *capital assets* shall be allowed only to the extent allowed in §§ 1211 and 1212." 26 U.S.C. § 165(f) (emphasis added). Taxpayer, by arguing that the abandonment was not a "sale or exchange," and that the land in the hands of the joint venture was not a "capital asset," seeks to establish that the loss was an ordinary loss. If accepted, this position would allow Taxpayer to avoid the limitations imposed by §§ 1211 and 1212 on the deduction that may be taken for capital losses. (Footnote 3)

"Sale or Exchange" by Abandonment

Taxpayer first argues that the Tax Court's decision that the abandonment of property subject to a non-recourse mortgage is a "sale or exchange" must be rejected because it is a reversal of the position previously taken by the Commissioner, the Tax Court, and other courts. Taxpayer adds that he relied on their earlier positions. In support of this proposition, Taxpayer cites *Commissioner v. Hoffman*, 117 F.2d 987 (2d Cir. 1941); *A.J. Industries v. United States*, 503 F.2d 660 (9th Cir. 1974); *Blum v. Commissioner*, 133 F.2d 447, 448 (2d Cir. 1943); *Bickerstaff v. Commissioner*, 128 F.2d 366 (5th Cir. 1942); *Helvering v. Gordon*, 134 F.2d 685 (4th Cir. 1943); *Denman v. Brumback*, 58 F.2d 128 (6th Cir. 1932).

We point out that in these cases—except for *Blum*—the issue was not whether an abandonment is a "sale or exchange" for determining whether the loss is capital or ordinary. Instead, these cases decided in which year the loss is appropriately taken. The cases held that the loss was sustained in the year in which the property became worthless and was abandoned, rather than the year in which the taxpayer was technically divested of title. *Blum* held that the transaction in question was indeed a sale and not an abandonment, and concluded that there was a capital loss. In *Commissioner v. Green*, 126 F.2d 70 (3d Cir. 1941) and *Helvering v. Jones*, 120 F.2d 828 (8th Cir. 1941), the courts seem to assume that an abandonment was not a "sale or exchange," but nevertheless held that the loss was a capital loss because the taxpayers' interests in the property were not cut off until the later foreclosure sales, which themselves are "sales or exchanges." *Helvering v. Hammel*, 311 U.S. 504 ... (1941).

More recently, the Tax Court, in a case identical in material respects to this case, held that an abandonment of property subject to non-recourse debt is a "sale or exchange" resulting in capital loss treatment, and the Eleventh Circuit affirmed. *Middleton v. Commissioner*, 77 T.C. 310 (1981), *aff'd*, 693 F.2d 124 (11th Cir. 1982). Assuming that *Middleton* was a departure from the prior position of the Commissioner and the Tax Court, we reject Taxpayer's argument that such a departure is improperly applied retroactively. The Supreme Court has recently held that the Commissioner may change an earlier interpretation of the law, even if such change is made retroactive in effect, and even though a taxpayer may have relied to his detriment upon the Commissioner's prior position. *Dickman v. Commissioner*, [465 U.S. 330] ... (1984); *Dixon v. United States*, 381 U.S. 68 ... (1965). The Commissioner is not required to assert a particular position as soon as the statute authorizes such an interpretation. *Id.*

The interpretation of an agency charged with the administration of a statute is entitled to a substantial degree of deference. *Aluminum Co. of America v. Central Lincoln*

Peoples' Utility District, [467 U.S. 380] ... (1984). To uphold an agency's interpretation, "we need not find that its construction is the only reasonable one.... We need only conclude that it is a reasonable interpretation of the relevant provisions." *Id., quoting Unemployment Compensation Comm'n v. Aragon*, 329 U.S. 143 ... (1946). As our discussion below indicates, the Commissioner in *Middleton* and in this case has given the statutory term "sale or exchange" a reasonable and practical interpretation in light of decisions more recent than the *Hoffman, Bickerstaff, Denman* line of cases. Moreover, the Tax Court, with its own expertise, has accepted that interpretation.

The term "exchange," in its most common, ordinary meaning implies an act of giving one thing in return for another thing regarded as an equivalent. Webster's New International Dictionary (2d ed. 1954). Thus, three things are required: a giving, a receipt, and a causal connection between the two. In the case of abandonment of property subject to nonrecourse debt, the owner gives up legal title to the property. The mortgagee, who has a legal interest in the property, is the beneficiary of this gift, because the mortgagee's interest is no longer subject to the abandoning owner's rights.

In Middleton, as in this case, the taxpayer argued that, because the debt was nonrecourse and he therefore had no personal liability for the debt, he received nothing in exchange for his relinquishment of title. In essence, the argument is that because the taxpayer personally had no obligation to repay the debt, the abandonment could not have relieved him of any obligation. This argument is inconsistent with several Supreme Court decisions.

The Supreme Court has held that regardless of the nonrecourse nature of the debt, the taxpayer does receive a benefit from the disposition of the property: he is relieved of his obligation to pay the debt and taxes and assessments against the property. In *Crane v. Commissioner*, 331 U.S. 1 ... (1947), the Supreme Court established that, in computing the *amount* of gain on the disposition, the outstanding debt must be included in the "amount realized" by the taxpayer, whether the debt is recourse or non-recourse. However, in that case Mrs. Crane, besides having the vendee take over the loan payments, received $2500 in cash (boot) on the sale. This left open the question of whether the non-recourse debt would be treated the same as recourse debt in situations where the outstanding debt exceeds the fair market value of the property. In such case, the owner-debtor would not obtain any boot by abandoning the property or transferring it subject to the mortgage. (Footnote 4)

In *Commissioner v. Tufts*, 461 U.S. 300 ... (1983), the Supreme Court answered this unanswered question by holding that where the debt exceeded the market value, the entire non-recourse debt—not just the fair market value—was the "amount realized" by the taxpayer on the disposition of the property. The *Tufts* court explained:

> We read Crane to have approved the Commissioner's decision to treat a nonrecourse mortgage in this context as a true loan.
>
> ...
>
> When a taxpayer receives a loan, he incurs an obligation to repay that loan at some future date.
>
> ...
>
> Because of the obligation to repay, the taxpayer is entitled to include the amount of the loan in computing his basis in that property;
>
> ...

Because there is no difference between recourse and nonrecourse obligations in calculating bases, Crane teaches that the Commissioner may ignore the nonrecourse nature of the obligation in determining the amount realized upon disposition of the incumbered property.

...

When the obligation is cancelled, the mortgagor is relieved of his responsibility to repay the sum he originally received and thus realizes value to that extent....

...

Although *Crane* and *Tufts* concerned the amount of the gain or loss and not the *character* of the gain or loss, their rationales support the Commissioner's position in the instant case to the extent that the concept of "amount realized" for computing gain or loss may be equated with the concept of consideration for "sale or exchange" purposes.

Indeed, the Supreme Court in two decisions has followed the same approach of *Crane* and *Tufts* in the "sale or exchange" context.

In *Helvering v. Hammel*, 311 U.S. 504 ... (1941), and *Helvering v. Nebraska Bridge Supply & Lumber Co.*, 312 U.S. 666 ... (1941), the Court held that there had been a "sale or exchange" and a capital loss even though the taxpayer had received no boot or other consideration, other than relief from a debt. In *Hammel*, the Court looked to the legislative purpose and history of the capital gain and loss provisions and held that "sale or exchange" included foreclosure sales. The involuntary nature of the transaction and the lack of any surplus from the sale to be returned to the owner did not make the foreclosure any less a "sale or exchange." Soon after *Hammel*, the Supreme Court rendered a decision, the relevance of which to the recourse-nonrecourse "sale or exchange" issue was aptly explained by the Seventh Circuit:

> In *Helvering v. Nebraska Bridge Supply & Lumber Co.*, 312 U.S. 666 ... (per curiam), the rationale of *Hammel* was extended. The taxpayer in *Nebraska Bridge Supply* owned property on which the real estate taxes were delinquent. The delinquency created no personal liability. The tax lien was thus like a nonrecourse mortgage. Arkansas bid in the property at a tax sale, acquiring it without paying anything. The state was thus like the holder of a nonrecourse mortgage foreclosing on property worth less than the mortgage. The Eighth Circuit had allowed the taxpayer to take an ordinary loss deduction because "[t]he transfer of title to the State is not only involuntary, but is without any consideration moving to the transferor." 115 F.2d 288, 291 (1940). The Supreme Court summarily reversed.

Laport v. Commissioner, 671 F.2d 1028 (7th Cir. 1982). Based on the Supreme Court's reasoning in *Crane*, *Tufts* and *Nebraska Bridge Supply*, we approve the Tax Court's acceptance of the Commissioner's interpretation that one who abandons property subject to non-recourse debt receives a relief from the debt obligation when he gives up legal title. Moreover, it is clear that the relief from the debt is what causes the abandonment. It was advantageous, in the view of the Supreme Court, for the Taxpayer to relinquish title only because the debt of which he was relieved was greater than the market value. Thus, under the Supreme Court precedents, the abandonment in this case involved a giving in order to receive something in return as the equivalent, (Footnote 5) and therefore fit within the ordinary meaning of "sale or exchange."

Moreover, an abandonment of property subject to non-recourse debts has the same *practical effect* as several other transactions which have each been held to be a "sale or exchange." The Supreme Court has held that an involuntary foreclosure sale of real estate was a "sale or exchange" and the loss a capital loss. *Helvering v. Hammel*, 311 U.S. 504 ... (1941). In *Nebraska Bridge Supply*, the Court held a tax forfeiture to be a "sale or exchange." In *Laport v. Commissioner*, 671 F.2d 1028 (7th Cir. 1982), the Court held that the taxpayer's conveyance to the mortgagee by quitclaim deed in lieu of foreclosure was a "sale or exchange." In *Freeland v. Commissioner*, 74 T.C. 970 (1980), the Tax Court held that where the value of land sunk below the amount of a nonrecourse debt and the owner conveyed the land to the mortgagee by quitclaim, there was a "sale or exchange" and an ordinary loss.

The abandonment followed by the mortgagee's foreclosure in this case is the functional equivalent of the foreclosure sale in *Hammel*, the tax forfeiture in *Nebraska Bridge Supply*, and the quitclaims in lieu of foreclosure in *Laport* and *Freeland*. In all these transactions, the taxpayer-owner is relieved of his obligation to repay the debt and is relieved of title of the property. Because the mortgagee is legally entitled to recover title to the property in any of these cases, the fact that out of prudence he concludes he must go through foreclosure proceedings to formalize his interest in the land is not a rational basis for altering the character of the gain or loss realized by the taxpayer on the transaction. The differences in these transactions is not a difference in substance, but only in form.

The taxpayer who has decided that he cannot or should not make further payment on the nonrecourse loan can manipulate the form of the change in ownership of the property simply by either quitclaiming or abandoning the land before the mortgagee forecloses. Thus, the question is "whether a taxpayer can avoid the tax consequences of *Hammel* and *Nebraska Bridge Supply* by the simple expedient of [abandoning] the property before the mortgagee can foreclose. The *Freeland* Court saw no reason, nor do we, to put such a premium on artful timing." *Laport v. Commissioner*, 671 F.2d at 1033. *Cf. Diedrich v. Commissioner*, 457 U.S. 191, 102 S.Ct. 2414, 72 L.Ed.2d 777 (1982) (ignoring form of transaction in favor of the substance of the transaction).

Allowing taxpayers to manipulate the character of their losses from capital to ordinary by hastening to abandon rather than allowing foreclosure would frustrate the congressional purpose to treat capital gains and losses on a parity. As explained by the Supreme Court in *Hammel*, the *quid pro quo* of allowing generous tax treatment on capital gains is the limitation imposed on deductions for capital losses. 311 U.S. at 509–10.... Thus, where the taxpayer would be eligible for capital gains treatment upon the sale of property had it appreciated in value, he should not be allowed to avoid the limitations on deductions for capital losses by using an artfully timed abandonment rather than a sale, voluntary reconveyance, or foreclosure. Accordingly, we affirm the Tax Court's holding that the Commissioner's interpretation of "sale or exchange" as including an abandonment of property subject to nonrecourse debt is a reasonable one.

...

Capital Asset

Taxpayer argues alternatively that even if the abandonment is a sale or exchange, his loss was still ordinary because the land was not a "capital asset" in his hands. 26 U.S.C. § 1221. (Footnote 6) Specifically, he argues that the land was not held for investment, but instead was "used in his trade or business" of renting property.

This Court has recently held that our review on the question of a taxpayer's holding purpose is narrowly confined by the Rule 52(a) "clearly erroneous" rule, even though it is an ultimate question of fact in deciding "capital asset" status. *Byram v. United States*, 705 F.2d 1418 (5th Cir. 1983). "The choice of a standard will determine the outcome of many cases," and this is one such case. 705 F.2d at 1421.

The Tax Court held that Taxpayer was not in the trade or business of renting property, and his interest in the land was not bought or held for that purpose. The Court declared: "We think petitioner acquired his interest primarily for investment purposes.... We are not persuaded that the casual rental converts the tract into property used in a trade or business within the meaning of the statute." This finding was supported by Taxpayer's testimony acknowledging that one of the primary purposes in purchasing the property was to realize an appreciation in value of the land expected to occur as a result of the growth of nearby Fort Worth. The only rental of the land was for grazing, which brought in approximately $1000 annually. That income covered only a minute part of the partnership's yearly expenses of approximately $71,470 (taxes, insurance, and primarily interest) incurred in owning the land during the same period. Even ignoring these expenses, the $1000 yearly rental would represent a rate of return of far less than 1% on the $362,132 investment in the property. Moreover, there were no improvements made on the land, nor any definite plans to make improvements in the future.

The Tax Court also held that the Taxpayer's interest in the land was not property used in his trade or business of tax and financial consulting, stating that the connection between the business and the owning of the interest in the land was too tenuous and conjectural. Taxpayer argued that he participated in the venture "to show [to his partner-clients] good faith belief that it was a worthy investment." However, that position means only that he was showing his clients that it was a good investment by choosing it for himself *as a good investment*. Taxpayer's assertion, therefore, supports the Tax Court's finding that he held the property for investment, rather than for *use* in his trade or business.

The Tax Court's position is further supported by another admission by the Taxpayer. Shortly after the joint venture was formed, all of the participants elected to be excluded from the partnership provisions of the Internal Revenue Code pursuant to Section 761(a) of the Code, which provides that an unincorporated organization may elect to be excluded from the partnership provisions of the Code if it is availed of "for investment purposes only and not for the active conduct of a business." On February 15, 1973, Taxpayer herein, as trustee, filed the Section 761 election, reciting that the joint venture "qualifies for the election as an investing partnership." Thus, although there was some evidence that Taxpayer's ownership of the property was somewhat related to his consulting business and that some rental income was received, we are not left, after reviewing the record, with a definite and firm conviction that a mistake has been made.... Accordingly, the tax court's finding that the property was a capital asset in Taxpayer's hands was not clearly erroneous, and must stand.

AFFIRMED.

FOOTNOTES:

2. Other reasons taxpayer gave for purchasing the property were: (1) to further his property management business and to earn a $4,000 management fee, (2) to have the opportunity to earn a three-percent real estate commission if the property were ever sold, (3) to earn rental income, and (4) to become associated with Lawson Ridgeway, a local real estate developer who purchased a 50-percent interest in the joint venture.

3. There are two requirements for the capital gain and loss provisions to be applicable: (1) there must be a "capital asset" or property that is treated like a capital asset under

§ 1231, and (2) there must be a "sale or exchange." 29 U.S.C. §§ 165(a), (f), 1211, 1212.... Thus, in order to affirm the holding that the loss was a capital loss, we must affirm that there was both (1) a "sale or exchange," and (2) a "capital asset."

4. In the now famous footnote 37, the *Crane* Court observed:

> Obviously, if the value of the property is less than the amount of the mortgage, a mortgagor who is not personally liable cannot realize a benefit equal to the mortgage. Consequently, a different problem might be encountered where a mortgagor abandoned the property or transferred it subject to the mortgage without receiving boot. That is not this case.

Id. at 14....

5. The mortgage agreement effectively treated the property and the debt as being equivalent in value.

6. Section 1221 of the Code, in pertinent part provides that a capital asset is "property held by the taxpayer (whether or not connected with his trade or business)." Excluded from the definition of a capital asset, however, is "property held by the taxpayer primarily for sale to customers in the ordinary course of his trade or business" and "real property used in his trade or business."

Consider the following questions about *Yarbro*.

1. Under what section of the Code did the taxpayer determine the amount of his loss on the abandonment of the property? Is this treatment consistent with the wording of section 1001?

2. What is the relationship between section 1001 and section 165(a)? Once the taxpayer has made a "sale or other disposition" of property, the Code does not immediately allow him to deduct a loss (in contrast to the specific language of section 1001(c) in the case of a gain). Rather, the taxpayer must conquer several additional hurdles.

3. Is characterization of the transaction as a "sale or other disposition" sufficient for the Service to require the taxpayer to claim a capital loss rather than an ordinary loss?

4. Suppose the property had been unencumbered by a mortgage. Would the abandonment have constituted a "sale or exchange" in the view of the Fifth Circuit? Would there, nevertheless, be a "sale or other disposition"? What would be the tax consequence to the taxpayer?

When a lender forecloses on a mortgage and sells the property at a foreclosure sale, the transaction is clearly a "sale or other disposition" within the meaning of section 1001. **Recall *Helvering v. Hammel*.** And, as you learned from *Crane* and *Tufts*, in the case of nonrecourse financing, the gain or loss equals the difference between the debtor's basis in the property and the amount of debt forgiven. So too, as you now know, when a debtor abandons the property or surrenders it to his creditor to avoid foreclosure, the event is clearly a disposition to which section 1001 applies.

In contrast, when property is destroyed by fire, or lost through theft or expropriation, it is more difficult to justify characterizing the transaction as a "sale or other disposition" for tax purposes. Unlike the usual sale or disposition, these events do not involve a voluntary act.[16] In the case of, for example, loss of the property (or its value) through fire, obsolescence, or physical deterioration, there is neither a voluntary act nor a clear "sale or other disposition." Nevertheless, as you first learned through the study of involuntary conversions, these events do constitute "sales or other dispositions" that may produce gains or losses.[17]

You may also have noticed when we examined involuntary conversions, that section 165(a) allows a deduction for losses when "sustained" (and does not require a sale or other disposition). Also note that section 61(a)(3) requires the inclusion in gross income of "gains derived from dealings in property" and section 62(a)(3) allows the taxpayer to deduct the "deductions allowed by part VI (sec. 161 and following) *as* losses from the sale or exchange of property." (Emphasis added.) Nevertheless, review of these provisions does not satisfactorily bridge the gap from the "sale or other disposition" requirement of section 1001 to the definitions in section 1222 that require the "sale or exchange" of a capital asset. Thus, for these events, the rules developed by the courts finesse the usual requirement of section 1222 that there be a "sale or exchange." (In other cases, the Code specifically provides that the event shall be treated as a "sale or exchange."[18])

But when a lender forecloses on a mortgage and auctions off the property at a foreclosure sale, the transaction is clearly a sale or other disposition within the meaning of section 1001. And, despite the criticism of *Tufts*, the debtor's gain or loss when the mortgage is nonrecourse is the difference between the adjusted basis of the property and the amount of the canceled debt. So too, when a debtor surrenders the property to his creditor to avoid foreclosure, the transaction is a disposition to which section 1001 applies. Thus, the statutory phrase "sale or other disposition" does not, in fact, imply that the transfer must be voluntary; merely that a sale or disposition occurs. Whether by judicial sale or power of sale, a foreclosure does produce a sale or other disposition.

What tax treatment should result when the lender acquires the borrower's property or sells it to a purchaser at a foreclosure sale or in connection with a deed of trust? Suppose that, rather than wait for the foreclosure sale, the borrower surrenders the property to the lender (a so-called "deed in lieu of foreclosure")? Suppose the borrower simply abandons the property? In all these cases, the borrower has "disposed" of his interest in the property. Are these dispositions the type of disposition that section 1001 is intended to address?[19] Yes, according to *Yarbro*. Did the *Woodsam* case help answer this question?

---

16. In the case of a foreclosure, the justification for characterizing the event as having a volitional element is that the mortgagor incurred the debt (or acquired the property subject to the debt) voluntarily.

17. Recall that in Part V., Chapter 2.A., you learned that the phrase "sale or other disposition" is not the same thing as a "sale or exchange." In order to have a capital gain or loss, the taxpayer must have a "sale or exchange." *See William Flaccus Oak Leather Co.*

18. *See, e.g.*, section 165(g).

19. Recall our earlier discussion of casualty losses in Part II, Chapter 3 A.1.b. What section provided the tax rule for the treatment of a casualty loss? Recall also that the gradual deterioration of property would not constitute a casualty and would not, therefore, produce a casualty loss. How different is a sudden catastrophe in which a building is totally destroyed by fire from a gradual deterioration of the building by termites until it is also totally destroyed? In one, the casualty loss rules apply; in the other they do not. Nevertheless, the total destruction of the property by termites may make the property useless, creating the perfect circumstances for nonpayment of a mortgage debt leading to a foreclosure, a deed in lieu of foreclosure, or an abandonment.

In contrast, when property is destroyed by fire, or lost through theft or expropriation it is more difficult to rationalize treatment as a "sale or other disposition" especially if the owner is not compensated by insurance or otherwise for the calamity. The statutory language also does not clearly comprehend events such as the physical disintegration of property, a loss of value attributable to obsolescence, the termination of an asset's legal life, or the revocation of a license. Nevertheless, as you first learned through the study of involuntary conversions, these events do constitute "sales or other dispositions" that may produce gains or losses.

2. Year of Gain or Loss

Because the Code treats a foreclosure sale for tax purposes as a voluntary sale, gain or loss is realized in the year the sale becomes final. The finality of the sale depends on local law.

Most of modern American foreclosure law has its roots in the common law of England. The original common law rule concerning the rights of the mortgagor in the event of a nonpayment, provided, in fact, no rights to the mortgagor. In the case of a default in payment, the property automatically became the property of the mortgagee. The harshness of this rule led to the establishment of the doctrine of "equity of redemption." That doctrine gave the mortgagor a last chance to pay the debt in full prior to its becoming the property of the mortgagee. But the mortgagee needed to be able to bring the period during which the mortgagor could redeem to an end. The answer was "foreclosure," and the equity of redemption period would end when the foreclosure was complete.

This doctrine of a right of redemption was adopted in the United States virtually intact.[20] All states in the United States now provide this right of redemption. The original doctrine of the equity of redemption required that the Chancellor,

> at the mortgagee's request, ... fix a reasonable redemption period for the mortgagor. If the mortgagor failed to redeem within that period, the redemption right was forever barred and both legal and equitable title to the real estate vested in the mortgagee. This type of foreclosure was and is known as strict foreclosure.[21]

Two states, Connecticut and Vermont, continue to allow this strict foreclosure method. The more common method for terminating the right of the mortgagor to redeem, however, is by auction sale, a method available in all states.[22] All states provide the debtor with this last chance to redeem. The length of the period varies, however, from state to state.[23]

As noted, the basic rules, as amended through the development of the law of mortgages in England, became the foundation for practice in all the states. In more than half the states, however, this debtor's equity of redemption is still not his last chance. In these states, the law provides the debtor with an additional last chance to regain the property. This state-created right is termed a "statutory right of redemption." In states

---

20. *Restatement of the Law of Property: Mortgages* § 3.1 cmt. a (1997).

21. *Id.* at 99.

22. *Id.* at 100. For a discussion of the alternative methods by which mortgagees hold security interests in property, *see* the Restatement, *supra*, §§ 3.1–3.5. In addition to the mortgagor, creditors whose interests in the property arose after that of the mortgagee also have the right to redeem.

23. In addition to the mortgagor, creditors whose interest in the property arouse after that of the mortgagee also have the rights to redeem.

where the statutory right of redemption is available, the mortgagor has the right to regain the property even after the foreclosure sale. The general rule is that the redemption amount is the price paid at the foreclosure sale. The reasoning appears to be that this rule will hinder attempts by the mortgagee (or others) to buy the property at the foreclosure sale at a below-market price in hopes of reselling at a profit. The length of the period during which the debtor may exercise the right of redemption also varies from state to state.[24] Even this brief description should suggest why "statutory rights of redemption" are controversial.

These rules provide another example of the interplay between the tax law and rules relating to other areas of law. Tax rules have determined that a foreclosure constitutes a "sale or other disposition" for tax purposes, but it is state real estate law that determines when that sale actually occurs (becomes final).

If the mortgagor retains a right of redemption after the foreclosure sale, the sale is not final for tax purposes until the right of redemption expires.[25] If local law provides no right of redemption, gain or loss will be realized in the year of the foreclosure sale.

In those jurisdictions granting mortgagors a right of redemption, the mortgagor may be able to exercise control over the year of realization. If the mortgagor prefers the gain or loss to be realized in the year of foreclosure and the right of redemption expires in the following year, he may accelerate realization by releasing his right of redemption.

Once again, to apply the proper tax rules, you must begin with an understanding of the real estate rules. To the extent that there is a foreclosure by sale,[26] the tax rules should treat that sale no differently than any other sale or disposition. Several other real estate concepts are important, however, and may affect the tax treatment of the foreclosure.

As noted, all states retain the common law "equity of redemption." This doctrine, traceable to the 13th and 14th centuries in England, gave a mortgagor the right to repay the whole debt until the so-called "law day."[27] In modern practice, as described earlier, the borrower has the right to repay until the date of the foreclosure sale.[28] If he exercises the right, the debt will be discharged in full, and the mortgagor will not have engaged in a "sale or other disposition" of the property.

---

24. In some states, parties other than the debtor, who had an interest in the property that arose after the mortgage that was foreclosed, can redeem. Where that is the case, state law also dictates either the order in which various people can redeem or that they may all "scramble." The general rule is that the redeemer must pay the foreclosure sale price.

25. *R. O'Dell and Sons Co. v. Commissioner,* 8 T.C. 1165 (1947), *aff'd,* 169 F.2d 247 (3d Cir. 1948); *Hawkings v. Commissioner,* 34 B.T.A. 918 (1936), *aff'd,* 91 F.2d 354 (5th Cir. 1937).

26. Two states, Connecticut and Vermont, continue to provide for "strict foreclosure," foreclosure without sale in which the lender simply takes the property. For tax purposes, this procedure, as in the case of a foreclosure by sale, constitutes a disposition of the property.

27. "Law Day" remains important in Connecticut and Vermont because they retain the "strict foreclosure" procedure.

28. In some states, a mortgage may grant the lender a "power of sale," allowing the lender to sell the property without the formal supervision of a court. Most, however, require a judicially supervised sale. The theory is that judicial supervision will more likely assure the borrower that the sale will receive sufficient advance publicity to attract competing buyers who will, in bidding against each other, more likely protect any equity the borrower has in the property. In the absence of sufficient publicity, few potential buyers may attend the sale and the sales price might be substantially lower. Only if the successful bidder at the sale bids more than the outstanding debt (principal and unpaid interest) owed to the lender, will the borrower have a chance to recoup some or all of his equity.

Or, the right may be exercised by a creditor whose interest is subordinate to that of the lender who is foreclosing. In that event, no sale has occurred so, again, the original mortgagor has not made a "sale or other disposition" of the property (as would have been the case absent a redemption by the mortgagor or a third party). Rather, the subordinated creditor is subrogated to the position of the mortgagee. That is, the debt is treated as still existing for the benefit of the creditor who redeems.

As noted, however, in some states, the mortgagor-borrower has a second chance. Where state law provides the borrower with a statutory "right to redeem" after the foreclosure sale, the length of the period depends upon state law. How does such a right affect the tax rules applicable?

Suppose the mortgagor chooses to redeem. What is the effect of the redemption for tax purposes? It is clear that the redemption nullifies the sale. But, it is necessary to consider the various prices at which the redemption might occur. As noted earlier in this chapter, in most jurisdictions, the redemption price is the price at which the property sold at the foreclosure sale; in others, the mortgagor must pay the entire balance outstanding in order to redeem.[29] Consider each possibility separately.

a. Redemption at the Foreclosure Price

If the mortgagor is able to redeem by paying only the price paid at the foreclosure sale, it is clear that the redemption totally nullifies the sale. And if there is no sale, there can be no gain or loss to the mortgagor as a consequence. But what happens to the difference between the remaining outstanding balance of the debt and the amount discharged through the redemption? If that amount remains owing, it may or may not be secured by the property; states vary. Whether it remains owing depends initially on whether the mortgage was a recourse or nonrecourse mortgage. Can you suggest the difference the nature of the mortgage might make?

If a third party redeems, the outcome also varies depending upon the nature of the mortgage. The basic consequence is the same for the debtor. Redemption by a junior lienor does not nullify the foreclosure sale. But, the existence and enforceability of a deficiency depends upon the nature of the mortgage: if the mortgage was with recourse, the mortgagor continues to owe the unpaid portion of the debt not satisfied through the foreclosure; if the mortgage was nonrecourse, the mortgagor is discharged from the balance. How should that discharge be characterized for tax purposes?

It is clearly an accession to wealth, and hence income. But, should it constitute part of the amount realized on the "sale or other disposition" or should it constitute income from the discharge of indebtedness? Recall the discussion following *Tufts*.

If the mortgagor remains liable for the deficiency (no longer secured by the property, no matter who redeemed), what happens if he pays it off? What happens if the creditor ultimately decides to write-off the deficiency as a bad debt?

b. Redemption for the Total Amount of the Debt

Here the whole debt is clearly discharged; the lender no longer has a security interest in the property. If the party who redeemed was the owner of the property, she now

---

29. *See* Grant S. Nelson and Dale A. Whitman, *Real Estate Finance Law* 689 (West 2001). In addition, the redeeming mortgagor generally will have to pay interest and possibly costs.

owns the property free of the original lender's lien (although she may have had to create a lien in favor of a different third party in order to secure funds to complete the redemption). There are no tax consequences in this type of redemption; there has been no "sale or other disposition."

If a different party redeems, however, the interest of the original debtor is severed (just as it would have been without the redemption). In that event, the results to the mortgagor/debtor are the same as if there had been no redemption.

Now that you have learned the fundamental rules, the next step is to apply them to the two real estate problems that appear in Chapter 4 of this Part VI. These problems will enable you to apply the general principles you have already learned and will introduce you to some additional provisions of the Code, some of which are peculiar to real estate transactions; but others of which apply frequently in both real estate and other transactions.

Chapter 4

Some Common Real Estate Problems

These problems describe several transactions and ask a series of questions, most of which concern the tax consequences of the transactions. Assume for purposes of the problems that the provisions of the current version of the Internal Revenue Code apply to all transactions.

In the absence of a contrary indication, assume that all loans (1) are with recourse as between the original borrower and the original lender, and (2) call for (a) simple interest and (b) equal annual debt service payments. In all of your calculations, round all of the numbers off to the nearest dollar.

You should (1) provide the specific numerical and other answers that the questions call for, and (2) support your answers by citing the appropriate provisions of the Code or the other materials in this chapter. You should be able to use these problems to draft one or more memoranda to your client, explaining, step by step, each of your answers.

In working through the relevant tax provisions, it is a wise idea to remember the myth of Theseus and the labyrinth. In the myth, Daedalus constructed a labyrinth for King Minor of Crete, in which the Minotaur was confined. Daedalus's work was so skillful that no person enclosed in the labyrinth could find a way out without guidance. The Minotaur roamed its corridors, killing and consuming young Athenian men and maidens sent to Crete as tributes to the king. Theseus arrived on Crete as one of these young men, and Ariadne, the daughter of the king of Crete, fell in love with him. She gave him a ball of golden thread to enable him to escape from the labyrinth. After fastening one end to the door of the labyrinth, Theseus unrolled the thread as he went along the corridors until he found and killed the Minotaur. He then followed the thread back to the door and made his escape.[1]

This unrolling of the golden thread is exactly what you should be doing with the Code. You begin at a certain point and proceed through the twisting paths, as did Theseus. And then, like him, you must retrace your steps.

---

1. Jesse Dukeminier, "A Modern Guide To Perpetuities," 74 Cal. L. Rev. 1867 (1986).

A. A Common Residential Real Estate Problem

Consider the investment that almost 70% of Americans have made: an investment in a home. If it is the owner's personal residence, a home certainly constitutes property held for personal use. But, even with property held for personal use, the tax consequences can be significant, often making homeownership possible at all. As you consider the following problem, also consider the tax policy issues. Do the tax benefits Congress has provided to home owners create an unfair advantage for those who can afford to buy over those who must pay rent?

Meghan and her husband, Jake, bought their first home four years ago for $100,000. They paid $25,000 from their own funds and borrowed $75,000 from the Barker National Bank, giving Barker a note and a first mortgage on the property.

In June of last year, Meghan and Jake spent $2,500 on redecorating to make the home look, as Jake put it, "more conventional." They paid for the work as soon as it was completed. One month later, they made a contract to sell the home to Delta for $120,000. Sixty days after the signing of the contract, the closing took place: Meghan and Jake conveyed the property to Delta and she paid them and took possession. Meghan and Jake paid off their debt to Barker, which released them from their obligation on the note and discharged the mortgage, and they also paid a brokerage commission of $7,200 and legal fees of $800. Thirty days later, they bought and moved into a larger home, for which they paid $150,000. This time they paid $30,000 from their own funds and borrowed $120,000 from the Littleton National Bank, giving Littleton a note and a first mortgage on the property.

---

1. What are the tax consequences to Meghan and Jake of their sale of one home and purchase of another?

The following two authorities will help you answer this question.

TREASURY REGULATION SECTION 1.1034-1[2]

§ 1.1034-1 Sale or exchange of residence. —

...

(b) *Definitions.* The following definitions of frequently used terms are applicable for purposes of section 1034 ...

(1) "Old residence" means property used by the taxpayer as his principal residence which is the subject of a sale by him after December 31, 1953 (section 1034(a); for detailed explanation see paragraph (C)(3) of this section).

---

2. Although Congress has repealed section 1034, replacing it with section 121, this regulation will provide you with guidance in answering question 1. (See also Treasury Regulation section 1.263(a)-2(e).) **Is this regulation of any aid in calculating Meghan's and Jakes's gain on the sale of their home?**

(2) "New residence" means property used by the taxpayer as his principal residence which is the subject of a purchase by him (section 1034(a); for detailed explanation and limitations see paragraphs (c)(3) and (d)(1) of this section).

...

(4) "Amount realized" is to be computed by subtracting

(i) The amount of the items which, in determining

the gain from the sale of the old residence, are properly an offset against the consideration received upon the sale (such as commissions and expenses of advertising the property for sale, of preparing the deed, and of other legal services in connection with the sale); from

(ii) The amount of the consideration so received, determined (in accordance with section 1001(b) and regulations issued thereunder) by adding to the sum of any money so received, the fair market value of the property (other than money) so received. If, as part of the consideration for the sale, the purchaser either assumes a liability of the taxpayer or acquires the old residence subject to a liability (whether or not the taxpayer is personally liable on the debt), such assumption or acquisition, in the amount of the liability, shall be treated as money received by the taxpayer in computing the "amount realized."

(5) "Gain realized" is the excess (if any) of the amount realized over the adjusted basis of the old residence (see also section 1001(a) and regulations issued thereunder).

...

(c) *Rules for application of section 1034-*

...

(2) *Computation and examples.* In applying the general rule stated in subparagraph (1) of this paragraph, the taxpayer should first subtract the commissions and other selling expenses from the selling price of his old residence, to determine the amount realized. A comparison of the amount realized with the cost or other basis of the old residence will then indicate whether there is any gain realized on the sale. Unless the amount realized is greater than the cost or other basis, no gain is realized.... If the amount realized exceeds the cost or other basis, the amount of such excess constitutes the gain realized.... The application of the general rule stated above may be illustrated by the following examples:

Example (1). A taxpayer decides to sell his residence, which has a basis of $17,500. To make it more attractive to buyers, he paints the outside at a cost of $300 in April, 1954. He pays for the painting when the work is finished. In May, 1954, he sells the house for $20,000. Brokers' commissions and other selling expenses are $1,000. In October, 1954, the taxpayer buys a new residence for $18,000. The amount realized, the gain realized, the adjusted sales price, and the gain to be recognized are computed as follows:

Selling price $20,000
Less: Commissions and other selling expenses 1,000
Amount realized 19,000
Less: Basis 17,500
Gain realized 1,500

...

Example (2). The facts are the same as in example (1), except that the selling price of the old residence is $18,500. The computations are as follows:

Selling price $18,500
Less: Commissions and other selling expenses   1,000
Amount realized 17,500
Less: Basis 17,500
Gain realized 0

...

REVENUE RULING 72-456
1972-2 C.B. 468

Advice has been requested concerning the proper treatment to be accorded broker-age commissions paid in connection with exchanges of properties that result in nontax-able or partially nontaxable exchanges under section 1031 of the Internal Revenue Code of 1954 in the situations described below.

Situation 1.   A taxpayer exchanged his property, land held

for productive use in trade or business or for investment, with an adjusted basis of $12,000, for property of a like kind, to be held for productive use in trade or business or for investment, with a fair market value of $20,000 and $10,000 in cash. He paid a commission of $2,000 to a real estate broker.

Situation 2.   A taxpayer exchanged his property, land held

for productive use in trade or business or for investment, with an adjusted basis of $29,500, for property of a like kind, to be held for productive use in trade or business or for investment, with a fair market value of $20,000 and $10,000 in cash. He paid a commission of $2,000 to a real estate broker.

Situation 3.   A taxpayer exchanged his property, land held

for productive use in trade or business or for investment, with an adjusted basis of $10,000, for property of a like kind, to be held for productive use in trade or business or for investment, with a fair market value of $20,000. He paid a commission of $2,000 to a real estate broker.

Section 1031(a) of the Code provides, in part, that no gain or loss shall be recognized if property held for productive use in trade or business or for investment is exchanged solely for property of a like kind to be held either for productive use in trade or business or for investment.

Section 1031(b) of the Code provides, in part, that if an exchange would be within the provisions of section 1031(a) if it were not for the fact that the property received in exchange consists not only of property permitted by such provisions to be received without the recognition of gain, but also of other property or money, then the gain, if any, to the recipient shall be recognized, but in an amount not in excess of the sum of such money and the fair market value of such other property.

Section 1031(c) of the Code provides, in part, that if an exchange would be within the provisions of section 1031(a) if it were not for the fact that the property received in exchange consists not only of property permitted by such provisions to be received without the recognition of gain or loss, but also of other property or money, then no loss from the exchange shall be recognized.

Section 1.1031(d)-1(c) of the Income Tax Regulations provides, in part, that if, upon an exchange of properties of the type described in section 1031 of the Code, the taxpayer received other property (not permitted to be received without the recognition of gain) and gain from the transaction was recognized as required under section 1031(b) of the Code, the basis of the property transferred by the taxpayer, decreased by the amount of any money received and increased by the amount of gain recognized, must be allocated to and is the basis of the properties (other than money) received on the exchange.

Section 1.1031(d)-2 of the regulations, example (2), indicates that money paid out in connection with an exchange under section 1031 of the Code is offset against money received in computing gain realized and gain recognized and is also added in determining the basis of the acquired property.

Accordingly, it is held that the three factual situations presented result in the following:

SIITUATIONS

	1	2	3
Received:			
Land—F.M.V.	$20,000.00	$20,000.00	$20,000.00
Cash	10,000.00	10,000.00	- 0 -
Total	$30,000.00	$30,000.00	$20,000.00
Less:			
Brokerage commission	2,000.00	2,000.00	2,000.00
Amount realized	$28,000.00	$28,000.00	$18,000.00
Given up:			
Land—basis	12,000.00	29,500.00	10,000.00
Realized gain (loss)	$16,000.00	$(1,500.00)	$ 8,000.00
Recognized gain			
(lesser of realized gain or net cash received)	$ 8,000.00	$ - 0 -	$ - 0 -
Basis:			
Land given up—basis	$12,000.00	$29,500.00	$10,000.00
Less cash received	(10,000.00)	(10,000.00)	- 0 -
Plus recognized gain	8,000.00	- 0 -	- 0 -
Plus brokerage commission	2,000.00	2,000.00	2,000.00
Basis of land received	$12,000.00	$21,500.00	$12,000.00

2. What is Meghan's and Jake's basis in their new home?

3. How, if at all, would your answers to 1 and 2 above be different if the sale price of the first home was $750,000 and Meghan and Jake paid a commission of $45,000 and legal fees of $800?

4. What are the tax consequences, if any, to Meghan and Jake of their mortgage payments on their new home? **Read carefully section 163.** (Do not discuss section 163(h)(3)(D).) What is the location in the tax calculation outline of any deductions that Meghan and Jake are entitled to claim?

5. If Meghan and Jake took a cash advance in the amount of $20,000 on one of their credit cards and used the funds to go on a second honeymoon to Bora Bora, would they be able to deduct the interest on that loan?

6. How, if at all, would your answer to question 5 change if, instead of taking the cash advance on the credit card, Meghan and Jake borrowed the $20,000 from the Harwood Savings Bank, giving the bank a note and a second mortgage on their new home?

If your answer would change, what policy justifies the difference in the tax treatment of the two transactions?

7. Would Meghan and Jake's choice between the two ways of financing their vacation affect their basis in their new home?

8. Suppose instead of purchasing their first home four years ago, Meghan and Jake acquired it by exchanging property held for investment for this property, intending to use the new property as property held for investment. On the exchange, Meghan and Jake did not recognize realized gain on the old property. As a consequence, their basis in the new property is currently $100,000 (the carryover basis in the property received in the section 1031 exchange less depreciation during the period they used the property as property held for investment). Just one year after the exchange, however, they converted the new property to personal use property and began using it as their principal residence. Do they qualify for exclusion of gain when they sell the residence 3 years later?

9. What, if any, difference would it make if Meghan and Jake completed the section 1031 exchange 7 years ago and converted the property to personal use property 6 years ago?

B. A Common Rental Real Estate Problem

In March of this year (Year 1) Meghan and Jake decided to invest in an apartment building located a few blocks from their home. Farmers Savings Bank held a mortgage on the building in the principal amount of $107,000. The interest rate was 12% per year, the annual debt service was $13,000, and the next payment was due on July 1 of this year (Year 1). The tenants paid a total of $35,000 per year in rent, real estate taxes were $10,000 per year, and the cost of maintenance was $7,000 per year.

Polly, the owner of the building, had bought the property from Elmer, taking subject to the Farmers mortgage. Polly was willing to sell, and after she and Meghan and Jake reached a tentative agreement on the basic terms of the transaction, she introduced them to her lawyer, Aidalia. Aidalia prepared a proposed sales contract, which provided that the closing date was October 1 of this year (Year 1) and the price was $200,000. Meghan and Jake were to pay $40,000 in cash when the parties signed the agreement. At the closing, they were to pay $27,660 more in cash, and Polly was to accept a note from them for $25,500, secured by a mortgage, with interest of 11% per year and debt service of $3,000 per year, the first payment being due on September 30 of next year (Year 2).

---

1. Do the numbers that Aidalia put in her proposed contract add up? What adjustment, other than for rent, real estate taxes, and utilities, will the parties need to make at the closing? Calculate the adjustment.

To calculate the adjustment, you will need to consider what expenses the seller may already have paid in connection with his ownership of the property. (In a normal transaction, you would have to calculate adjustments for rent, paid or unpaid; real estate taxes; utilities; and any other expenses that may be past due or prepaid, including, for example, the cost of the oil in the oil tank.) You will then have to construct a mortgage reduction schedule (also called an amortization schedule) of the first mortgage. To do so, you must complete as much of the following chart as you need to answer the question. (You will need to complete more of the first mortgage amortization schedule, and complete a portion of an additional one for the second mortgage, to answer the questions that follow.)

Loan Amortization Schedules[3]

First Mortgage

Payment Date	Debt Service	Interest	Principal	Remaining Principal Balance
7/1/Year 1	$13,000			

Second Mortgage (Purchase Money Mortgage)

Payment Date	Debt Service	Interest	Principal	Remaining Principal Balance
9/30/Year 2	$3,000			

Meghan and Jake signed the contract and paid Polly $40,000 in cash. They then completed the closing on October 1 of this year (Year 1) paying her the additional $27,660 in cash and giving her the $25,500 note and mortgage that the contract required, as well as an assumption of the Farmers loan. The tenants continued to pay a total of $35,000 per year in rent, the real estate taxes remained $10,000 per year, and maintenance costs remained $7,000 per year. Meghan and Jake took the appropriate depreciation deductions for the year of acquisition and the next three years. You may assume that they were not taxpayers "in [the] real property business" within the meaning of Code section 469(c)(7), and that their total adjusted gross income for Year 3 less than $100,000. They held the property "for the production of income" within the meaning of Code section 167(a)(2).

---

3. A typical loan amortization schedule specifies a fixed monthly payment over the term of the loan. The monthly payment consists of an interest component and a principal component. The amounts of interest and principal vary each month and are computed based on the outstanding principal balance at the beginning of the month. Thus, during the early period of the loan, because the outstanding principal balance is large, the amount of interest is large but declines each month during the loan period. As the interest payment declines each month, the portion of the payment that constitutes principal increases.

The amounts set forth in Meghan and Jake's amortization schedule would be computed as follows: For year 1, the outstanding principal balance of the loan was $107,000. Twelve percent (simple interest) on a debt of $107,000 would produce interest due of $12,840 for the year. The difference between the total payment of $13,000 and the interest component of $12,840, or $160, is the portion of the payment that is the principal repayment component. You must then subtract the principal repayment amount from the original outstanding principal balance to arrive at $106,840, the outstanding principal balance as of the beginning of year 2.

Note how the interest figures decline slightly and the principal repayment figures increase slightly each year. As noted above, this results from the fact that the outstanding principal balance of the loan declines each year and, thus, the interest due declines each year. Toward the end of the amortization period, the interest amounts will be quite small and the principal repayments will be quite large.

2. What were the tax consequences to Meghan and Jake of their ownership and operation of the property during Year 3? Answer the following questions.

a. What was their gross income from the activity?

b. How much interest did Meghan and Jake pay during Year 3? (Do you need to consult your reduction schedules for the mortgages?)

c. Did Meghan and Jake have any other cash outlay with respect to the building during Year 3?

d. What deductions were they allowed to take with respect to this property?[4] (Support those deductions by citing specific Code sections.)

e. What is the location in the income tax calculation outline of the deductions they are allowed to take that are attributable to the building?

f. What was their taxable income for year 3 from the property?

3. How did their taxable income from the property compare to the net cash flow that it produced? (To make this comparison, you will have to make a separate calculation based on their cash receipts and disbursements, and compare it to your answer in part d. of question 2 above. Think of the concept of the "cash flow" as relating to the excess of cash received from the investment less cash paid out for its operation.) What is the significance of the difference, if any?

Now look at section 469. What purpose does section 469 serve? Congress enacted section 469 as part of the Tax Reform Act of 1986 out of concern over the proliferation of "tax shelter" investments. Read the following excerpt from the legislative history of section 469.[5]

Present Law

In general, no limitations are placed on the ability of a taxpayer to use deductions from a particular activity to offset income from other activities. Similarly, most tax credits may be used to offset tax attributable to income from any of the taxpayer's activities.

There are some exceptions to this general rule. For example, deductions for capital losses are limited to the extent that there are not offsetting capital gains....

In the absence of more broadly applicable limitations on the use of deductions and credits from one activity to reduce tax liability attributable to other activities, taxpayers with substantial sources of positive income are able to eliminate or sharply reduce tax liability by using deductions and credits from other activities, frequently by investing in tax shelters. Tax shelters commonly offer the opportunity to reduce or avoid tax liability with respect to salary or other positive income, by making available deductions and credits, possibly exceeding real economic costs or losses currently borne by the taxpayer, in excess or in advance of income from the shelters.

Reasons for Change

In recent years, it has become increasingly clear that taxpayers are losing faith in the Federal income tax system. This loss of confidence has resulted in large part from the

---

4. For the sake of computational simplicity, you need not allocate the purchase price between the land and the building.

5. Report of the Senate Finance Committee, S. Rep. No. 99-313 at 713–719, 99th Cong., 2d Sess. (1986).

interaction of two of the system's principal features: its high marginal rates (in 1986, 50 percent for a single individual with taxable income in excess of $88,270), and the opportunities it provides for taxpayers to offset income from one source with tax shelter deductions and credits from another.

The prevalence of tax shelters in recent years — even after the highest marginal rate for individuals were reduced in 1981 from 70 percent to 50 percent — has been well documented. For example, a recent Treasury study revealed that in 1983, out of 260,000 tax returns reporting "total positive income" in excess of $250,000, 11 percent paid taxes equaling 5 percent or less of total positive income, and 21 percent paid taxes equaling 10 percent or less of total positive income. Similarly, in the case of tax returns reporting total positive income in excess of $1 million, 11 percent paid tax equaling less than 5 percent of total positive income, and 19 percent paid tax equaling less than 10 percent of total positive income.

Such patterns give rise to a number of undesirable consequences, even aside from their effect in reducing Federal tax revenues. Extensive shelter activity contributes to public concerns that the tax system is unfair, and to the belief that tax is paid only by the naive and the unsophisticated. This, in turn, not only undermines compliance, but encourages further expansion of the tax shelter market, in many cases diverting investment capital from productive activities to those principally or exclusively serving tax avoidance goals.

The committee believes that the most important sources of support for the Federal income tax system are the average citizens who simply report their income (typically consisting predominantly of items such as salaries, wages, pensions, interest, and dividends) and pay tax under the general rules. To the extent that these citizens feel that they are bearing a disproportionate burden with regard to the costs of government because of their unwillingness or inability to engage in tax-oriented investment activity, the tax system itself is threatened.

Under these circumstances, the committee believes that decisive action is needed to curb the expansion of tax sheltering and to restore to the tax system the degree of equity that is a necessary precondition to a beneficial and widely desired reduction in rates. So long as tax shelters are permitted to erode the Federal tax base, a low-rate system can provide neither sufficient revenues, nor sufficient progressivity, to satisfy the general public that tax liability bears a fair relationship to the ability to pay. In particular a provision significantly limiting the use of tax shelter losses is unavoidable if substantial rate reductions are to be provided to high-income taxpayers without disproportionately reducing the share of total liability under the individual income tax that is borne by high-income taxpayers as a group.

. . .

The question of what constitutes a tax shelter that should be subject to limitations is closely related to the question of who Congress intends to benefit when it enacts tax preferences. For example, in providing preferential depreciation for real estate or favorable accounting rules for farming, it was not Congress's primary intent to permit outside investors to avoid tax liability with respect to their salaries by investing in limited partnership syndications. Rather, Congress intends to benefit and provide incentives to taxpayers active in the businesses to which the preferences were directed.

In some cases, the availability of tax preferences to nonparticipating investors has even harmed the industries that the preferences were intended to benefit. For example, in the case of farming, credits and favorable deductions have often encouraged investments by wealthy individuals whose principal or only interest in farming is to receive an investment return, largely in the form of tax benefits to offset tax on positive sources of income. Since such investors may not need a positive cash return from farming in order to profit from their investments, they have a substantial competitive advantage in relation to active farmers, who commonly are not in a position to use excess tax benefits to shelter unrelated income. This has significantly contributed to the serious economic difficulties presently being experienced by many active farmers.

The availability of tax benefits to shelter positive sources of income also has harmed the economy generally, by providing a non-economic return on capital for certain investments. This has encouraged a flow of capital away from activities that may provide a higher pre-tax economic return, thus retarding the growth of the sectors of the economy with the greatest potential for expansion.

The committee believes that, in order for tax preferences to function as intended, their benefit must be directed primarily to taxpayers with a substantial and *bona fide* involvement in the activities to which the preferences relate. The committee also believes that it is appropriate to encourage nonparticipating investors to invest in particular activities, by permitting the use of preferences to reduce the rate of tax on income from those activities; however, such investors should not be permitted to use tax benefits to shelter unrelated income.

There are several reasons why it is appropriate to examine the materiality of a taxpayer's participation in an activity in determining the extent to which such taxpayer should be permitted to use tax benefits from the activity. A taxpayer who materially participates in an activity is more likely than a passive investor to approach the activity with a significant nontax economic profit motive, and to form a sound judgment as to whether the activity has genuine economic significance and value.

A material participation standard identifies an important distinction between different types of taxpayer activities. In general, the more passive investor is seeking a return on capital invested, including returns in the form of reductions in the taxes owed on unrelated income, rather than an ongoing source of livelihood. A material participation standard reduces the importance, for such investors, of the tax-reduction features of an investment, and thus increases the importance of the economic features in an investor's decision about where to invest his funds.

Moreover, the committee believes that restricting the use of losses from business activities in which the taxpayer does not materially participate against other sources of positive income (such as salary and portfolio income) addresses a fundamental aspect of the tax shelter problem.... Such transactions commonly are marketed to investors who do not intend to participate in the transactions, as devices for sheltering unrelated sources of positive income (*e.g.*, salary and portfolio income). Accordingly, by creating a bar against the use of losses from business activities in which the taxpayer does not materially participate to offset positive income sources such as salary and portfolio income, the committee believes that it is possible significantly to reduce the tax shelter problem.

   ...

Explanation of Provisions

1. Overview

The bill provides that deductions from passive trade or business activities, to the extent they exceed income from all such passive activities (exclusive of portfolio income), generally may not be deducted against other income. Similarly, credits from passive activities generally are limited to the tax allocable to the passive activities. Suspended losses and credits are carried forward and treated as deductions and credits from passive trade or business activities in the next year. Suspended losses from an activity are allowed in full when the taxpayer disposes of his entire interest in the activity.

...

Losses and credits from a passive activity (taking into account expenses such as interest attributable to acquiring or carrying an interest in the activity) may be applied against income for the taxable year from other passive activities or against income subsequently generated by any passive activity. Such losses (and credits) generally cannot be applied to shelter other income, such as compensation for services or portfolio income (including interest, dividends, royalties, and gains from the sale of property held for investment)....

Salary and portfolio income are separated from passive activity losses and credits because the former generally are positive income sources that do not bear, at least to the same extent as other items, deductible expenses. Since salary and portfolio income are likely to be positive, they are susceptible to sheltering by means of investments in activities that give rise to tax benefits. The passive loss provision ensures that salary and portfolio income, along with other non-passive income sources, cannot be offset by tax losses from passive activities until the amount of such losses is determined upon disposition.

Under the provision, suspended losses attributable to passive trade or business activities are allowed in full upon a taxable disposition of the taxpayer's entire interest in the activity. The full amount of gain or loss from the activity can then be ascertained. To the extent the taxpayer's basis in the activity has been reduced by suspended deductions, resulting in gain on disposition, the remaining suspended deductions will, in effect, offset such gain....

---

4. Does section 469 limit Meghan's and Jake's loss from the building?

Examine sections 469(i)(1) and (i)(2). To qualify for relief under these provisions, an individual must "actively participate" in rental real estate activity. Because "active" participation is so important, one would expect the statute to define it. Does it do so?

Now look at section 469(i)(6)(A). It contains one of those negative definitions; it defines "active participation" by what it is not. A taxpayer does not actively participate if he and his spouse have an interest of less than 10 percent (by value) of all interests in the activity. Why this limit? The assumption appears to be that someone with a less-than-10 percent interest performs services primarily for his co-owners, not primarily for his own account. **Now consider section 469(i)(6)(C).** Again, it contains a negative definition. An interest of a limited partner cannot constitute an interest with respect to which he actively participates.

Yet, we still have found no specific definition of "active participation" in the Code. But, the Senate Finance Committee Report provides some guidance.[6] It makes clear that

---

6. The Senate Finance Committee report explains the reason for the relief provisions under section 469(i) as follows:

Active participation in a rental
real estate activity
Allowance of $25,000 of losses and credits against other income specified circumstances
For purposes of the passive loss provision, rental activities are treated as passive without out regard to whether the taxpayer materially participates.

"active participation" differs from "material participation" (required by section 469(h)). In fact, "active participation" requires a lesser degree of participation than does "material participation" (which, after all, allows unlimited deductibility of losses). The Report states that active participation may exist without regular, continuous, and substantial involvement in day-to-day operations, provided that the taxpayer participates in making management decisions, such as the selection of tenants, the setting of rental terms, the approval of capital or repair expenditures, and other similar decisions. Or, the taxpayer may arrange for others to provide services in a significant and bona fide way.

5. Does section 469(i) provide relief to Meghan and Jake?

6. How, if at all, would your answer to question 5 be different if Meghan's and Jake's total adjusted gross income for year 2 had been more than $100,000?

But, even if a taxpayer qualifies as actively participating in the activity, the complications of the section continue! What more must Meghan and Jake show in order to claim a deduction of a passive activity loss? And, what will happen if they are unable to claim the loss this tax year? Suppose they can claim the loss this year after application of all the limits that appear in section 469, but they do not have sufficient income from other sources to make the passive activity loss useful?

In the early part of Year 3, although the tenants continued to pay rent, Meghan and Jake encountered financial problems. They paid Polly the remaining principal balance on her note, but on July 1 of Year 5, they failed to make the required $13,000 payment to Farmers. The bank accelerated the obligation and foreclosed pursuant to a power of sale in its mortgage, purchasing the property at a sale in October for the outstanding principal amount of the debt. Neither the bank's conduct of the sale nor its purchase of the property violated applicable state law. The jurisdiction had no statutory redemption period. Meghan and Jake did claim the appropriate amount of depreciation for for Year 5.

7.a. What were the tax consequences of the foreclosure to Meghan and Jake?

b. How, if at all, would your answer to 7.a. be different if Meghan and Jake had taken a total of $110,000 in depreciation by the time of the sale?

c. How, if at all, would your answer to 7.a. be different if, by the time of the foreclosure, the fair market value of the property had declined to $80,000? **Recall *Tufts* and Revenue Ruling 90-16.**

8. Disregard the assumptions stated in 7.b. and 7.c. above.

In the case of rental real estate, however, some specifically targeted relief has been provided because rental real estate is held, in many instances, to provide financial security to individuals with moderate incomes. In some cases, for example, an individual may hold for rental a residence that he uses part-time, or that previously was and at some future time may be his primary residence. Even absent any such residential use of the property by the taxpayer, the committee believes that a rental real estate investment in which the taxpayer has significant responsibilities with respect to providing necessary services, and which serves significant nontax purposes of the taxpayer, is different in some respects from the activities that are meant to be fully subject to limitation under the passive loss provision.

Id. at 736.

How, if at all, would your answer to 7.a. be different if the bank had bought the property at the foreclosure for $60,000?

In order to answer this question, you should **review Revenue Ruling 90-16 in Chapter 3 and read the following additional revenue ruling.**

REVENUE RULING 91-31
1991-1 C.B. 19

ISSUE

If the principal amount of an undersecured nonrecourse debt is reduced by the holder of the debt who was not the seller of the property securing the debt, does this debt reduction result in the realization of discharge of indebtedness income for the year of the reduction under section 61(a)(12) of the Internal Revenue Code or in the reduction of the basis in the property securing the debt?

FACTS

In 1998, individual *A* borrowed $1,000,000 from *C* and signed a note payable to *C* for $1,000,000 that bore interest at a fixed market rate payable annually. *A* had no personal liability with respect to the note, which was secured by an office building valued at $1,000,000 that *A* acquired from *B* with the proceeds of the nonrecourse financing. In 1989, when the value of the office building was $800,000 and the outstanding principal on the note was $1,000,000, *C* agreed to modify the terms of the note by reducing the note's principal amount to $800,000. The modified note bore adequate stated interest within the meaning of section 1274(c)(2).

The facts here do not involve the bankruptcy, insolvency, or qualified farm indebtedness of the taxpayer. Thus, the specific exclusions provided by section 108(a) do not apply.

LAW AND ANALYSIS

Section 61(a)(12) of the Code provides that gross income includes income from the discharge of indebtedness. Section 1.61-12(a) of the Income Tax Regulations provides that the discharge of indebtedness, in whole or in part, may result in the realization of income.

In Rev. Rul. 82-292, 1982-2 C.B. 35, a taxpayer prepaid the mortgage held by a third party lender on the taxpayer's residence for less than the principal balance of the mortgage. At the time of the prepayment, the fair market value of the residence was greater than the principal balance of the mortgage. The revenue ruling holds that the taxpayer realizes discharge of indebtedness income under section 61(a)(12) of the Code, whether the mortgage is recourse or nonrecourse and whether it is partially or fully prepaid. Rev. Rul. 82-292 relies on *United States v. Kirby Lumber Co.*, 284 U.S. 1 (1931), ... in which the United States Supreme Court held that a taxpayer realized ordinary income upon the purchase of its own bonds in an arm's length transaction at less than their face amount.

In *Commissioner v. Tufts*, 461 U.S. 300 (1983), 1983-120, the Supreme Court held that when a taxpayer sold property encumbered by a nonrecourse obligation that exceeded the fair market value of the property sold, the amount realized included the amount of the obligation discharged. The Court reasoned that because a nonrecourse note is treated as a true debt upon inception (so that the loan proceeds are not taken into income at that time), a taxpayer is bound to treat the nonrecourse note as a true debt when the taxpayer is discharged from the liability upon disposition of the collateral, notwithstanding the lesser fair market value of the collateral. *See* section 1.001-2(c) Example 7, of the Income Tax Regulations.

In *Gershkowitz v. Commissioner*, 88 T.C. 984 (1987), the Tax Court, in a reviewed opinion, concluded, in part, that the settlement of a nonrecourse debt of $250,000 for a $40,000 cash payment (rather than surrender of the $2,500 collateral) resulted in $210,000 of discharge of indebtedness income. The court, following the *Tufts* holding that income results when a taxpayer is discharged from liability for an undersecured nonrecourse obligation upon the disposition of the collateral, held that the discharge from a portion of the liability for an undersecured nonrecourse obligation through a cash settlement must also result in income.

The Service will follow the holding in *Gershkowitz* where a taxpayer is discharged from all or a portion of a nonrecourse liability when there is no disposition of the collateral. Thus, the present case, *A* realizes $200,000 of discharge of indebtedness income in 1989 as a result of the modification of *A*'s note payable to *C*.

In an earlier Board of Tax Appeals decision, *Fulton Gold Corp. v. Commissioner*, 31 B.T.A. 519 (1934), a taxpayer purchased property without assuming an outstanding mortgage and subsequently satisfied the mortgage for less than its face amount. In a decision based on unclear facts, the Board of Tax Appeals, for purposes of determining the taxpayer's gain or loss upon the sale of the property in a later year, held that the taxpayer's basis in the property should have been reduced by the amount of the mortgage debt forgiven in the earlier year.

The *Tufts* and *Gershkowitz* decisions implicitly reject any interpretation of *Fulton Gold* that a reduction in the amount of a nonrecourse liability by the holder of the debt who was not the seller of the property securing the liability results in a reduction of the basis in that property, rather than discharge of indebtedness income for the year of the reduction. *Fulton Gold*, interpreted in this manner, is inconsistent with *Tufts* and *Gershkowitz*. Therefore, that interpretation is rejected and will not be followed.

HOLDING

The reduction of the principal amount of an undersecured nonrecourse debt by the holder of a debt who was not the seller of the property securing the debt results in the realization of discharge of indebtedness income under section 61(a)(12) of the Code.

EFFECT ON OTHER REVENUE RULINGS

Rev. Rul. 82-202 is amplified to apply whether the fair market value of the residence is greater or less than the principal balance of the mortgage at the time of the refinancing.

---

9. How, if at all, would your answer to 7.a. be different if the bank had bought the property at the foreclosure sale for the amount of the debt owed to it, but Meghan and Jake had not paid off Polly's note before the foreclosure?

---

10. Disregard the assumptions stated in 7, 8, and 9 above. Suppose the jurisdiction had a statutory redemption period and Meghan and Jake redeemed, paying the purchase price which was $10,000 less than the debt. What were the tax consequences to them of the redemption? Assume that they did not pay off their debt to Polly before the foreclosure.

VII. Additional Transactional Problems

Note

The following transactional problems illustrate a variety of tax issues in context. Some of the sections you have seen before; others will be new. In some cases, we have guided you to the applicable section; in others we have not. But, the skill you have gained throughout the course in locating, reading, and applying sections of the Code will enable you to answer the questions, while demonstrating the pervasiveness of tax, about which we have been telling you throughout the course.

Notice how many of the everyday activities in which taxpayers of all income levels engage can involve one or even multiple tax issues. Even students must be aware of the many tax pitfalls awaiting them!

Problem 1. Some Problems of Middle-Income Taxpayers

More than three-quarters of married women under age 55 with children are now employed outside their homes. For many, this is an economic necessity despite the possibility that a wife's earnings will produce the so-called marriage penalty. See marriage penalty materials in Part III. The couple may also face other tax issues, not necessarily limited to middle-income taxpayers. But some of these tax issues are of particular significance to middle-income taxpayers; moderate-income taxpayers do not have sufficient earnings for these issues to arise and higher-income taxpayers do not qualify for certain benefits. For example, the nonrefundable Hope and Lifetime Learning credits will be available only to those taxpayers who can pay at least some of the costs of education, but taxpayers with high adjusted gross incomes will not qualify. The problems below will help you learn more about some of the provisions we have discussed earlier and introduce you to some new provisions of the Code.

I. Leo and Fatima live in a state that does not have a state income tax. They have four children, two, Abdul and Hannan, are from Leo's previous marriage.[1] Both Leo and Fatima are employed: Leo works part-time for a law firm as a paralegal (while pursuing a law degree part-time), and Fatima is an executive with a publishing company, Ajax Comics. As part of her employment package, Fatima is entitled to use the company-subsidized child-care facilities at Ajax headquarters. Because the two youngest children, Sophie and Magdalena, ages 2 and 3, are not yet in school, this is a valuable benefit that enables Leo to work, go to school, and study without having full-time child-care responsibilities. (The other two children are older; one, Abdul, is a senior, age 17, at the local public high school, the other, Hannan, is 20 years old and is a full-time student in her second year at a private college.)

Leo's income from the law firm is $10,000; Fatima's income is $70,000. They rent a house at a cost of $1,500 per month. They also have additional expenses in connection with the house of $100 per month for telephone and $250 for utilities.

1. Are Leo and Fatima eligible to file a joint return? Could they file a joint return if they have never formally married? **Study sections 7703 and 6013.** Assuming they do qualify, do you need additional information in order to help Leo and Fatima decide if they should file a joint return? See discussion in Part III. Chapter 1.C.1. concerning joint and several liability. (Sometimes married couples find that they will owe less total tax if they file separate returns.)

2. May Leo and Fatima claim any personal exemptions? If so, how many? **Study sections 151 and 152.**

3. Assuming they are married and have no other tax-relevant items (other than the items described above), compute their gross income, adjusted gross income, taxable income, and tentative tax liability if they choose to file a joint return.

---

1. The divorce decree provides that the children will live with Leo but will visit their mother for a month each summer at her new home in Colorado. Leo's ex-wife pays for the children's plane fares to visit her, but provides no other support for them other than the cost of their care during their summer visits to her. The cost of the plane fares varies from $450 to $550 for both children, round-trip.

4. Suppose they decide to compare the results of filing a joint return with the results of filing separate returns. Who may claim the children as dependents? Is there a clear answer in either section 151 or 152? In the regulations? Anywhere else?

5. If Leo and Fatima are not legally married according to the state where they live, what would be each one's filing status? **Study section 2.** May both Leo and Fatima claim to be "heads-of-household"? Who may claim dependency exemptions for the children? **Look again at sections 151 and 152.**

You have now encountered some of the complexity of the sections of the Code that apply to all taxpayers: filing status and entitlement to dependents, sections that are, in fact, critical to proper filing by every taxpayer. Can the average taxpayer make an informed choice as to her filing status and right to claim dependents? Does the complexity, in effect, force even low-income taxpayers to hire a return preparer or accountant? As you continue with this problem, examining some of the many credits that may apply to Leo and Fatima, keep this question in mind.

Look at the Table of Contents of the Code and find Part IV of Subchapter A of the Code containing the "nonrefundable personal credits" in Subpart A. These credits, when applicable, offset a taxpayer's tax liability dollar for dollar. **Re-examine the income tax calculation outline in the Introduction to this book.** Based on your review, which is more valuable to a taxpayer, a deduction or a credit? Does the location in the taxing formula of each, deductions and credits, suggest the answer?

In the case of nonrefundable credits, the taxpayer calculates her tentative tax liability and then offsets it with any applicable credits. If the tentative tax exceeds the amount of her credits, she owes the remainder to which she adds any additional taxes, such as alternative minimum tax or self-employment tax. But, if her nonrefundable credits exceed her tentative tax, she owes no regular tax, but her excess credits are lost. (She may still owe, for example, alternative minimum tax and/or self-employment tax, however.[2]) Unlike a nonrefundable credit, a taxpayer may receive a refund of a portion of a "refundable credit" (contained in Subpart C of Subchapter A, Part IV.) if her credits exceed her tax liability.

Note that many of these credits are directed toward taxpayers with children.[3] What policy arguments might you make for and against the inclusion in the tax code of this type of provision? Re-read the quote in Part I, Chapter 1, from McIntyre et al. Why would Congress make some credits nonrefundable and others refundable? If Congress chooses to aid parents, what alternatives might it choose instead of a credit?

Assuming once again, that they are, in fact, legally married, which of these credits might be applicable to Leo and Fatima? **Study sections 21, 24, and 25A.**

Fatima generally brings the two children to the day-care center when she arrives at work and picks them up when she is ready to go home. For these services, Fatima pays $150 per week but the value of the services is $300 per week. Fatima must pay for all weeks during which her children are enrolled, whether she uses the center or not. In other words, she must continue to pay when she is on vacation or the children are absent.

---

2. Note that a special rule in effect for tax years 2000–2006 allows taxpayers to offset both their regular and alternative minimum tax liabilities with nonrefundable credits. *See* section 26(a)(2).

3. In addition, many of these credits require married taxpayers to choose to file a joint return in order to obtain the credit.

6. What are the tax consequences, if any, to Leo and Fatima of using the company-subsidized day-care facility? **Study Code sections 129 and 21.** May they exclude from income all or part of the benefit they receive from using the subsidized day-care facility? **Examine section 129(a)(2).**

7. Do you need any additional information to decide whether Leo and Fatima will qualify for a child care credit? **Examine section 21(e).**[4]

8. Now study section 24. What is the difference between this credit and the credit you just studied in section 21? Which taxpayers are eligible for the credit provided by section 24? Suppose the total credits provided by sections 21 and 24 exceed Leo and Fatima's tentative tax liability. Does the excess benefit them? **Look at section 24(d).**

———

Suppose Leo pays $6,000 per year for tuition for his daughter, Hannan. Hannan's college costs include $20,000 for tuition, $6,000 for room and board and $1,000 for miscellaneous costs of books, notebooks, and other supplies. Toward these costs, she receives a scholarship from her college of $15,000, a scholarship from the Girl Scouts of $1,000, and $1,000 from her mother. Leo and Fatima must pay the balance other than what she can finance through loans and summer and part-time earnings. This year, Hannan received federally subsidized loans (that is, no interest accrues until graduation), of $3,000. She contributed her summer earnings of $1,000 and she has a part-time job on campus that pays $500 which she uses for her clothes, sundries, and telephone. Leo's part-time program at law school costs $10,000 for tuition and he spends $1,000 for books and supplies.

9. **Study Code section 25A.** Will Leo and Fatima qualify for either or both the Hope or the Lifetime Learning credit for the portion of Hannan's tuition they pay? (You may assume that Hannan qualifies as a "student who meet[s] the requirements of section 484(a)(1) of the Higher Education Act of 1965" and that the educational institution she attends is described in section 481 of the Higher Education Act of 1965 and is eligible to participate in a program under title IV of the Act.) What will happen next year when Hannan is a junior, assuming all other facts remain the same?

10. If Leo is enrolled in a regular part-time program of 10 credits per semester at a accredited law school, does his tuition qualify for either credit under section 25A? What will Leo have to demonstrate if he wishes to deduct his educational expenses as business expenses? **Study section 162 and Treasury Regulation section 1.162-5. Study especially sections 1.162-5(b)(3)(i) and 1.162-5(b)(3)(ii), examples 1 and 2. Look at section 222.** Does section 222 change your answer?

11. Suppose Leo and Fatima make a gift of their share of her expenses to Hannan and she is responsible for all expenses. Will Leo and Fatima incur a gift tax as a result? If Hannan pays her own expenses, will she qualify for either or both the Hope and Life-

———

4. Section 21 requires *both* that they file a joint return to be eligible for the credit, *and* that they supply identifying information with respect to the provider. *See* section 21(e)(2) and (e)(9). What can a taxpayer do if the babysitter refuses to give her social security number, as is all too often the case? Child care has, unfortunately, been an area of tax evasion; when service providers are paid in cash, there is a temptation to fail to report income. The identifying information requirement of section 21(e)(9) serves the same function as the identifying information required for the deduction of alimony payments. *See* section 215(c).

time Learning credits? Would having Hannan become responsible for her own expenses have any other effect on Leo and Fatima?

Taxpayers like Leo and Fatima often maintain an office at home. Suppose Leo and Fatima have set aside a room in their house that he uses to study for law school and she uses for work she brings home from her office at Ajax. (The room represents one tenth of the floor space in the house.) Fatima also uses the room to meet with authors or perspective authors of comics in the evenings or on weekends. (They do not use the room for any other purpose.) What are the requirements for deducting the cost of a home office? **Study section 280A(c).** Do you need additional information? Note that Congress, at the urging of the Treasury,[5] has made it difficult for a taxpayer to deduct a portion of the costs of her home because she uses part of the home as an office. Why does Treasury view the deductibility of a home office as an attractive tax shelter that deserves close scrutiny?

12. What other Code section have you studied that refers to the "convenience of the employer?" **Recall section 119 materials in Part II, Chapter 2.**

13. Assume that Leo and Fatima are legally married, do not deduct educational expenses or a home office, and claim all four children as dependents, what would be their gross income, adjusted gross income, taxable income, tentative federal income tax liability, tax credits, and final tax for the current year? (Watch out for phase-outs that may apply limit credits for which they might otherwise qualify.) What is their effective tax rate? Suppose Fatima were to receive a raise that brought her gross income to $80,000. Would her raise affect any of the calculations you have made?

II. Suppose Leo made the mistake of loaning his brother, Sal, $10,500, when Sal wanted to buy into a franchise with his friend. Sal did not sign a note. As is too often the case, the franchise operation was unsuccessful and Sal has been unable to repay Leo. In fact, Sal has decided to seek bankruptcy protection.

1. Will Sal's debt to Leo be discharged as a consequence of the bankruptcy proceeding? If Sal's debt is discharged, will he have gross income? **Recall sections 61(a)(12) and 108.**

2. As an unsecured creditor, Leo will never be repaid. How does the Code treat this type of unpaid debt? **Look at section 166.** Recall the dentist in Part II, Chapter 1 whose patient was unable to pay the full amount of what he owed for the dentist's services. **Read the discussion before** *Kirby Lumber.* If the patient does not pay, can the dentist look to section 166 for some relief? **Look at Treasury Regulation section 1.166-1(e).**

III. Suppose that Leo and Fatima move to the high tax state of Connecticut. Leo has finished school and is practicing law as an associate at a law firm; Fatima has had several promotions and raises. Both Leo's children from his previous marriage are full-time students, but they live at home with Leo and Fatima. Leo contributes $6,000 to each

5. Treasury communicates its legislative agenda to Congress through both formal and informal channels, including the Tax Legislative Counsel's office.

one's tuition costs. They are 23 and 21 years old respectively. Leo and Fatima's other two children are 6 and 7 and attend the local public school.

Leo earns $60,000; Fatima earns $140,000. They have purchased a house, using as a down payment a legacy that Fatima received from her mother and borrowing the balance. They pay Peninsula Trust Bank mortgage interest on their first mortgage of $10,000 (all of which is deductible under section 163(h)). **Read the material on section 163 in the residential real estate problem in Part VI, Chapter 4.** In addition, they have a home equity loan on which they pay interest to The Southside Bank of $8,000, all of which is deductible under section 163(h)(3). Their real property tax for the house is $8,000; their personal property tax on their cars is $1,800; and their state income taxes are $9,000. Together they have $9,000 of unreimbursed employee business expenses, after the application of the 2% limitation in section 67. **Read section 67 material in Carole's problem in Part II, Chapter 3.** They make an annual $5,000 contribution to the alumni fund of Leo's law school which qualifies as a charitable contribution under section 170(c).

Calculate Leo and Fatima's gross income, adjusted gross income, taxable income, tentative tax, and credits using the regular method you used in the previous problem. (Again, watch out for limitations on deductions and personal exemptions and for any phase-outs that may apply to their credits.) **Now, study section 55.** What does this section do? Why has Congress, in effect, enacted what appears to be a separate, parallel system of taxation? The Senate Report states:

> [T]he minimum tax should serve one overriding objective: to insure that no taxpayer with substantial economic income can avoid insignificant tax liability by using exclusions, deductions, and credits. Although these provisions may provide incentives for worthy goals, they become counterproductive when taxpayers are allowed to use them to avoid virtually all tax liability. The ability of high-income individuals and highly profitable corporations to pay little or no tax undermines respect for the entire tax system and, thus, for the incentive provisions themselves. In addition, even aside from public perceptions, the committee believes that it is inherently unfair for high-income individuals and highly profitable corporations to pay little or no tax due to their ability to utilize various tax preferences.[6]

In broad outline, after determining regular tax liability, a taxpayer then must determine what his tax would be using the alternative method. He then compares his regular tax liability with the alternative minimum tax ("AMT") liability. If regular tax liability exceeds alternative tax liability, he pays only his regular tax liability. But, if the AMT is larger, he must add the difference to his regular tax liability.

Of course, you know by now that this explanation of the outcome is far simpler than the actual steps you must take as you work your way through these sections. In brief, the taxpayer first calculates "alternative minimum taxable income" ("AMTI")[7] by making certain adjustments to his regular taxable income ("TI") as required by sections 56 and 58,[8] and adds the items of tax preference listed in section 57.[9] From AMTI, the tax-

---

6. S. Rep. No. 313, 99th Cong., 2d Sess. 518–19 (1986).
7. Section 55(b)(2) defines AMTI.
8. These adjustments may either increase or decrease TI.
9. These items of tax preference always increase TI.

payer subtracts the relevant exemption amount,[10] and applies the relevant AMT rate to the remainder.[11]

How would Leo and Fatima determine if they owe any additional tax as a result of the application of section 55? In order to determine their AMT, you will have to examine sections 56 and 58 to calculate any "adjustments" that you must add to or subtract from Leo and Fatima's taxable income. You must also examine section 57 to determine whether there are any items of tax preference to add to their taxable income.[12] Do Leo and Fatima have any AMT liability?

Are Leo and Fatima the type of taxpayer described in the Senate Report?[13] Does the AMT unfairly discriminate against taxpayers who live in high tax states, particularly if those are states with relatively high costs of living as well? Does the AMT unfairly discriminate against taxpayers who have large families? Is the imposition of the AMT in such cases consistent with the apparent Congressional intent in providing for dependency exemptions and enacting the many credits that benefit taxpayers with children?[14] Read the following letter that a taxpayer wrote to President Clinton:[15]

Dear President Clinton:

Discrimination comes in many forms and from many sources, but I never thought it would come from our own federal government. How so, you ask. In our case, it's the federal alternative minimum tax ("AMT").

For the current tax year 1998, our family has fallen prey to the AMT in the amount of $1,332.43. Our regular federal income tax liability is $27,568.13, but our AMT liability is $28,900.56.

After an analysis of the mechanics of this tax, we have concluded that there are two reasons why we are subject to this tax in 1998. They are:

1. We have four dependent children.

2. We live in a state ... which has a relatively higher state tax burden than other states in the U.S.

---

10. Section 55(d) prescribes the exemption amount. The exemption amount phases out as AMTI increases.

11. Section 55(b)(1)(A) prescribes two rates: 26% of the amount of the remainder that does not exceed $175,000 and 28% of any amount over $175,000.

12. For tax years 2000–2006, you must also examine section 26 in order to determine whether they may claim any nonrefundable credits to offset alternative minimum tax. *See* footnote 2, *supra*, and accompanying text.

13. David Cay Johnston has reported that by the year 2010, the AMT—the "stealth tax" as he calls it—will affect 35 million taxpayers, particularly families with three or more children and incomes of $100,000 or more. Johnston quoted W. Val Oveson, former National Taxpayer Advocate for the Service, who described the AMT as "absolutely, asininely stupid." *See* David Cay Johnston, "A 'Stealth Tax' is Creeping Up on Growing Numbers of Americans," *The New York Times* C17, Feb. 17, 2002.

14. Note that Leo and Fatima will not qualify for most of the tax credits they qualified for in the earlier problem because of the substantial increase in their income and their new deductions. Note in addition to the credits you have already examined, the credit section 23 provides to taxpayers who adopt children. Does the section 23 credit also include a phase-out provision?

15. Letter dated Feb. 15, 1999. Treasury released the letter on Apr. 15, 1999, after removing identifying information. 1999 TNT 72-59, Apr. 15, 1999

With regard to the first point, we are paying AMT while our neighbors with similar economic income do not simply because we have four children and they have two children. If we only had two children and reported four exemptions on our tax return instead of six, we would not have been required to pay any AMT. As you know, personal exemptions are disallowed for the AMT calculation.

With regard to the second point, we are paying AMT because we live in a state that requires relatively higher state taxes to be paid. Other taxpayers, again with similar economic income do not pay AMT simply because they live in lower tax states such as Nevada, Tennessee, Texas and Florida. As you know, the deduction for state taxes (i.e., income and real and personal property taxes) is disallowed for the AMT calculation.

We do not understand why this AMT tax is occurring in our lives. We thought that the AMT tax was put into place to tax people who were using special tactics to avoid paying their fair share of REGULAR taxes. We simply do not understand how we fall into that category.

Please let us know if you received this letter and if you agree or disagree with our opinion. If you agree with our opinion, please let us know what you will do in the near future to correct this problem. If you do not agree with our opinion, please explain to us why we are targeted to carry the burden of additional AMT taxes when others are not.

Our tax system should be consistent, and non-discriminatory. I ask that you make a real difference in our lives by helping to change this inequality.

Thank you.

Sincerely,

* * *

IV. Suppose that Leo becomes disabled and is unable to work. Because he and Fatima did not anticipate his disability by purchasing a disability insurance policy, he will receive only the minimal amount provided by Social Security for those who are disabled. Fatima is unable to earn enough to compensate for their great reduction in income. And, like many Americans, they have little savings.

1. Suppose they are unable to pay their income taxes for the year. What will be the consequences if they fail to file a return and pay the tax? **Consult section 6651. Compare section 6662.** When does it apply? Could the Service assert a penalty for civil fraud? **Compare section 6651(f) with 6663.**

2. Suppose the Service prepares a return for them. **See section 6020.** Will the Service prepare a joint return? Can it? Once the return is prepared and filed, what are the steps necessary for the unpaid tax to be entered ("assessed") on the records of the Service as a "deficiency"? **Recall our discussion of federal tax procedure following *Old Colony* in Part II, Chapter 1.**

3. After the tax has been assessed, the Service may make a demand for payment. If the taxpayer fails to respond to that demand, the Service may begin collection action. Can the taxpayer seek to have a lien for unpaid taxes discharged in bankruptcy? Will you find your answer in the Internal Revenue Code?

4. Suppose Leo and Fatima were "lucky" and their entire tax liability, like that of many employees, was satisfied through withholding: the employer withheld an esti-

mated amount of income tax on a regular basis and pays it over on behalf of the employee. But Leo and Fatima are not as lucky with their other creditors. Indeed, they owe a total of $164,000. Their only substantial assets are their home, with an adjusted basis of $130,000 and a fair market value of $150,000, but encumbered by a recourse mortgage in the amount of $120,000, and an automobile with a value that is $1,000 less than the remaining balance on the installment loan it secures. What tax result if the bankruptcy frees Leo and Fatima from $44,000 of debt? Suppose the bankruptcy also reduces the amount of debt encumbering their residence from $120,000 to $100,000. What, if any, tax effect would that reduction produce? **Review section 108.**

Problem 2. Some Problems of Low- and Moderate-Income Taxpayers

You have already encountered some of the issues that are important to low- and moderate-income taxpayers in the earlier materials and in the problems of middle-income taxpayers. Taxpayers at all income levels share the same problems of identifying proper filing status and entitlement to personal and dependency exemptions. Moreover, as you observed in the case of middle-income taxpayers, some tax credits are available to taxpayers whose incomes substantially exceed what might commonly be considered moderate income. For taxpayers with low—or moderate-incomes, however, the earned income tax credit (the "EITC") probably constitutes the most important of the credits. As one of the refundable tax credits, it can result in a payment by the government to a taxpayer who does not, in fact, owe any tax. In other words, it is, in effect, a negative income tax. Consider the EITC and its relationship to the other credits by analyzing the following problems.

Cyril is a cash basis single taxpayer. He has two children, Isabel and Lucinda, ages 8 and 10, who live with him. Their mother abandoned them five years ago and left the state. Cyril obtained a divorce based on her desertion and a court order that she pay weekly child support in an amount equal to the state's guidelines. She sends payments only sporadically (this year totaling $300) but Cyril has not been successful in securing effective legal representation to obtain out-of-state enforcement of his court order.

Cyril works during the day as a security guard. He could work more hours and obtain a higher hourly rate if he were willing to work the midnight shift but that would require him to hire a child-care person to take care of his children. Instead, he works a part-time schedule and earns $7 per hour for 30 hours per week, or $210 per week, $10,920 per year. By working during the day and limiting his hours to 30 hours per week, or 6 hours per day, he can take his children to school; be at work by 10 a.m. and only need a babysitter for 2 hours in the afternoons to meet the children at school and stay at home with them until he gets home at 4:30 p.m. (In this manner, he believes that he nets more on a part-time work schedule than he would if he went on the night shift and had to pay a babysitter for the night hours.)

Instead of hiring a regular babysitter, he asked his widowed mother if she would be willing to do this for him. He told her that he would pay her $30 per week during the year (50 weeks) and, in addition, would work in her yard on weekends, as needed. (The value of his landscaping services is $1,000.) In the summer, his children attend a full-time day camp run by his church, for which he pays a token fee of $20 per week for 11 weeks. His mother continues to pick up the children and take care of them for 2 hours per day. He will take his vacation for the final 2 weeks of summer before the children go back to school.

Thus, Cyril is one of the "working poor." He and his children live in federally subsidized housing that has a fair market value of $750 but for which he pays only $250 per month, including heat. He pays $40 per month for electricity, and he has telephone expenses of $25, and tries never to make long distance calls. He would like to have cable television but it is just too expensive. He has no car and spends $20 per week to take the bus to work. He used to receive welfare benefits (before he secured his current job), but the recent welfare reforms have limited the number of years of welfare for which he can qualify and he is afraid to use those years up as long as he has at least a part-time job. He does qualify for and receives $300 per month in food stamps, however.

———————

1. What is Cyril's filing status? How many personal and dependency exemptions may he claim? Does Cyril's receipt of child support, housing benefits, and food stamps affect your answer? What is the amount of his standard deduction? **Review section 63.** Suppose one of the children is legally blind. Would that alter your answers to any of these questions? **Study section 63(f).**

2. What is Cyril's gross income, adjusted gross income, taxable income, tentative income tax, and FICA/SECA tax? **Read discussion of FICA and SECA taxes in Part I, Chapter 2.**

3. Does Cyril qualify for the dependent care, child, or earned income credit(s)? **Examine sections 21, 24, and 32(a), -(b), and -(j).** Does the Code make clear in what order you should perform your analysis to determine eligibility for and the amount of the credits?

4. Begin with the dependent care credit and assume that Cyril does not qualify for the section 24 or 32 credits. **Study section 21.** What would be the amount of the credit? Does this credit appear to benefit Cyril? In other words, does Cyril have any regular tentative income tax liability? Can he use the credit to offset his FICA/SECA tax? **Look at section 26(a).** What is its function?

5. **Next, examine section 24.** Assuming again that Cyril does not qualify for a credit pursuant to section 32, is he entitled to a section 24 credit? If so, in what amount? Does Cyril's eligibility for the section 24 credit depend on whether he has any regular tentative income tax liability? **Look at section 24(b)(3). Now look at section 24(d).** Are these two subsection contradictory? Does either subsection, or both, apply to Cyril? What result under these subsections if Cyril had three or more children?

6. **Now turn to section 32.** Does Cyril qualify for the EITC and, if so, in what amount? (Note both the basic allowance in section 32(a) and possible adjustments pursuant to section 32(j). What function does section 32(j) perform? How do you determine whether there are any applicable adjustments under section 32(j)? Does Cyril's eligibility for the EITC depend on whether he has any regular tentative income tax liability? Notice that section 32 appears in Subpart C of Part IV of Subchapter A of Chapter 1 of the Code. What is the significance of this location? Why isn't section 24 in the same subpart as section 32?

7. Now suppose that Cyril's income from his security guard job is $25,000 for the year but all other facts remain the same.[16] What is his gross income, adjusted gross income, taxable income, tentative income tax, and FICA/SECA tax? Does he qualify for tax credits under sections 21, 24, and/or 32?

———————

You can see that calculating the EITC using the words of the statute can be extremely complicated. In section 32(f) Congress has directed (presumably, because of the high incidence of error) that taxpayers must determine the amount of their EITC under tables prescribed by the Secretary of the Treasury. In addition, the Service includes, as part of the Form 1040 (or 1040A and 1040EZ) tax package, a worksheet for taxpayers to

———————

16. Of course, such a dramatic increase in income would certainly alter his eligibility for food stamps and affect the amount of his rent in subsidized housing. For purposes of this problem, however, ignore these changes because they do not affect his income tax liability.

use to determine eligibility for, and to compute the amount of, the EITC. At the end of this problem you will find the fourteen pages comprising the eligibility/computation worksheet and tables from the instruction book for the Form 1040 for tax year 2005. **Take a moment to examine the worksheet and tables.**

Now that you have examined the worksheet, think about whether it may be too difficult for many unsophisticated taxpayers for whose benefit Congress adopted the credit. **Look at section 32(k).** Does it surprise you to learn that taxpayers claiming the EITC are the most frequently audited group?[17] Does the complexity of the credits that are designed to aid taxpayers of low or moderate income, some of whom do not speak or read English, in effect, force them to seek out the services of a paid return preparer?[18] What are the positive and negative aspects of effectuating income-transfer payments to low-income persons through the federal income tax system?[19]

---

17. David Cay Johnston of *The New York Times* has recently reported that, for returns filed for tax year 2000, the Service audited 403,506 returns filed by low-income taxpayers who applied for the EITC, but only 295,000 filed by other individuals. *See* David Cay Johnston, "I.R.S. Audits of Working Poor Increase," *The New York Times* C2, Mar. 1, 2002. He also reported that low-income taxpayers who applied for the EITC had a 1 in 47 chance of being audited for tax year 2000, whereas taxpayers with adjusted gross incomes from $50,000 to $100,000 had only a 1 in 435 chance, and taxpayers with adjusted gross incomes over $100,000 had only a 1 in 145 chance. *See* David Cay Johnston, "Affluent Avoid Scrutiny on Taxes even as I.R.S. Warns of Cheating," *The New York Times* A1, Apr. 7, 2002.

18. In 2002, the Brookings Institution and The Progressive Policy Institute published a study reporting that 68 percent of low-income taxpayers who receive the EITC hire a commercial tax-preparation service to prepare their returns. The study also reported that tax-preparation firms that file returns electronically and that offer their customers refund anticipation loans ("RALs") "are carving out a profitable niche" for themselves, fueling the growth of these services. But the fees the firms charge for return preparation, electronic filing, and the RALs are "exact[ing] a steep price in low-income communities." The report estimated that some $1.75 billion of the $30 billion in EITCs, which Congress intended to go to low-income taxpayers to lift them out of poverty, instead goes to commercial tax-preparation services and related financial institutions. *See* "Brookings Study Tallies Cost of Tax Preparation, Refund Loan Fees to EITC," 2002 TNT 99-25 (May 22, 2002).

19. *See* Anne L. Alstott, "The Earned Income Tax Credit and the Limitations of Tax-Based Welfare Reform," 108 Harv. L. Rev. 533 (1995).

Lines 66a and 66b—
Earned Income Credit (EIC)

What Is the EIC?

The EIC is a credit for certain people who work. The credit may give you a refund even if you do not owe any tax.

 You may be able to elect to use your 2004 earned income to figure your EIC if (a) your 2004 earned income is more than your 2005 earned income, and (b) your main home was in the Hurricane Katrina disaster area on August 25, 2005. Also, special rules may apply for people who had to relocate because of Hurricane Katrina. For details, see Pub. 4492.

To Take the EIC:

- Follow the steps below.
- Complete the worksheet that applies to you or let the IRS figure the credit for you.
- If you have a qualifying child, complete and attach Schedule EIC.

For help in determining if you are eligible for the EIC, go to *www. irs.gov/eitc* and click on "EITC Assistant." This service is available in English and Spanish.

 If you take the EIC even though you are not eligible and it is determined that your error is due to reckless or intentional disregard of the EIC rules, you will not be allowed to take the credit for 2 years even if you are otherwise eligible to do so. If you fraudulently take the EIC, you will not be allowed to take the credit for 10 years. See Form 8862, Who must file, on page 48. You may also have to pay penalties.

Step 1   All Filers

1. If, in 2005:
   - 2 children lived with you, is the amount on Form 1040, line 38, less than $35,263 ($37,263 if married filing jointly)?
   - 1 child lived with you, is the amount on Form 1040, line 38, less than $31,030 ($33,030 if married filing jointly)?
   - No children lived with you, is the amount on Form 1040, line 38, less than $11,750 ($13,750 if married filing jointly)?

   ☐ **Yes.** Continue ↘   ☐ **No.** (STOP)
   You cannot take the credit.

2. Do you, and your spouse if filing a joint return, have a social security number that allows you to work or is valid for EIC purposes (see page 48)?

   ☐ **Yes.** Go to question 3.   ☐ **No.** (STOP)
   You cannot take the credit. Put "No" on the dotted line next to line 66.

3. Is your filing status married filing separately?

   ☐ **Yes.** (STOP)   ☐ **No.** Continue ↘
   You cannot take the credit.

4. Are you filing Form 2555 or 2555-EZ (relating to foreign earned income)?

   ☐ **Yes.** (STOP)   ☐ **No.** Continue ↘
   You cannot take the credit.

5. Were you or your spouse a nonresident alien for any part of 2005?

   ☐ **Yes.** See *Nonresident aliens* on page 48.   ☐ **No.** Go to Step 2.

Step 2   Investment Income

1. Add the amounts from Form 1040:

Line 8a		_____
Line 8b	+	_____
Line 9a	+	_____
Line 13*	+	_____

   Investment Income = [_____]

   *Do not include if line 13 is a loss.

2. Is your investment income more than $2,700?

   ☐ **Yes.** Continue ↘   ☐ **No.** Skip question 3; go to question 4.

3. Are you filing Form 4797 (relating to sales of business property)?

   ☐ **Yes.** See *Form 4797 filers* on page 48.   ☐ **No.** (STOP)
   You cannot take the credit.

4. Do any of the following apply for 2005?
   - You are filing Schedule E.
   - You are reporting income or a loss from the rental of personal property not used in a trade or business.
   - You are reporting income on Form 1040, line 21, from Form 8814 (relating to election to report child's interest and dividends).

   ☐ **Yes.** You must use Worksheet 1 in Pub. 596 to see if you can take the credit. To get Pub. 596, see page 7.   ☐ **No.** Continue ↘

5. Did a child live with you in 2005?

   ☐ **Yes.** Go to Step 3 on page 46.   ☐ **No.** Go to Step 4 on page 46.

Need more information or forms? See page 7.

Form 1040—Lines 66a and 66b

Continued from page 45

Step 3   **Qualifying Child**

A qualifying child for the EIC is a child who is your...

Son, daughter, stepchild, foster child, brother, sister, stepbrother, stepsister, or a descendant of any of them (for example, your grandchild, niece, or nephew)

was ...

Under age 19 at the end of 2005

or

Under age 24 at the end of 2005 and a student (see page 48)

or

Any age and permanently and totally disabled (see page 48)

who...

Lived with you in the United States for more than half of 2005.
If the child did not live with you for the required time, see *Exception to time lived with you* on page 48.

⚠️ *If the child meets the conditions to be a qualifying child of any other person (other than your spouse if filing a joint return) for 2005, or the child was married, see page 48.*

1. Could you, or your spouse if filing a joint return, be a qualifying child of another person in 2005?

☐ **Yes.** (STOP)   ☐ **No.** Go to question 2.

You cannot take the credit. Put "No" on the dotted line next to line 66a.

2. Do you have at least one child who meets the conditions to be your qualifying child?

☐ **Yes.** The child must have a valid social security number as defined on page 48 unless the child was born and died in 2005. Skip Step 4; go to Step 5 on page 47.

☐ **No.** Go to Step 4, question 2, if the amount on Form 1040, line 38, is less than $11,750 ($13,750 if married filing jointly).

Step 4   **Filers Without a Qualifying Child**

1. Could you, or your spouse if filing a joint return, be a qualifying child of another person in 2005? See Step 3.

☐ **Yes.** (STOP)   ☐ **No.** Continue ↘

You cannot take the credit. Put "No" on the dotted line next to line 66a.

2. Can you, or your spouse if filing a joint return, be claimed as a dependent on someone else's 2005 tax return?

☐ **Yes.** (STOP)   ☐ **No.** Continue ↘

You cannot take the credit.

3. Were you, or your spouse if filing a joint return, at least age 25 but under age 65 at the end of 2005?

☐ **Yes.** Continue ↘   ☐ **No.** (STOP)

You cannot take the credit.

4. Was your home, and your spouse's if filing a joint return, in the United States for more than half of 2005? Members of the military stationed outside the United States, see page 48 before you answer.

☐ **Yes.** Go to Step 5 on page 47.

☐ **No.** (STOP)

You cannot take the credit. Put "No" on the dotted line next to line 66a.

Need more information or forms? See page 7.   **- 46 -**

Form 1040—Lines 66a and 66b

Continued from page 46

Step 5 Earned Income

1. Are you filing Schedule SE because you were a member of the clergy or you had church employee income of $108.28 or more?

☐ **Yes.** See *Clergy* or *Church employees,* whichever applies, on this page.   ☐ **No.** Continue ⬇

2. Figure earned income:

Form 1040, line 7 _____

Subtract, if included on line 7, any:

- Taxable scholarship or fellowship grant not reported on a Form W-2.
- Amount received for work performed while an inmate in a penal institution (put "PRI" and the amount subtracted on the dotted line next to Form 1040, line 7).
- Amount received as a pension or annuity from a nonqualified deferred compensation plan or a nongovernmental section 457 plan (put "DFC" and the amount subtracted on the dotted line next to Form 1040, line 7). This amount may be shown in Form W-2, box 11. If you received such an amount but box 11 is blank, contact your employer for the amount received as a pension or annuity.

       − _____

Add all of your nontaxable combat pay if you elect to include it in earned income. Also enter this amount on Form 1040, line 66b. See *Combat pay, Nontaxable* on this page.

       + _____

⚠ **CAUTION** *Electing to include nontaxable combat pay may increase or decrease your EIC. Figure the credit with and without your nontaxable combat pay before making the election.*

Earned Income* = ☐_____

*You may be able to elect to use your 2004 earned income to figure your EIC if (a) your 2004 earned income is more than your 2005 earned income, and (b) your main home was in the Hurricane Katrina disaster area on August 25, 2005. For details, see Pub. 4492. If you make this election, skip question 3 and go to question 4.

⚠ **CAUTION** *Electing to use your 2004 earned income may increase or decrease your EIC. Figure the credit using your 2005 earned income. Then figure the credit using your 2004 earned income. Compare the two amounts before making the election.*

3. Were you self-employed, or are you filing Schedule SE because you were a member of the clergy or you had church employee income, or are you filing Schedule C or C-EZ as a statutory employee?

☐ **Yes.** Skip question 4 and Step 6; go to Worksheet B on page 50.   ☐ **No.** Continue ⬇

4. If you have:

- 2 or more qualifying children, is your earned income* less than $35,263 ($37,263 if married filing jointly)?
- 1 qualifying child, is your earned income* less than $31,030 ($33,030 if married filing jointly)?
- No qualifying children, is your earned income* less than $11,750 ($13,750 if married filing jointly)?

☐ **Yes.** Go to Step 6.   ☐ **No.** 🛑 You cannot take the credit.

Step 6 How To Figure the Credit

1. Do you want the IRS to figure the credit for you?

☐ **Yes.** See *Credit figured by the IRS* on page 48.   ☐ **No.** Go to Worksheet A on page 49.

Definitions and Special Rules

(listed in alphabetical order)

Adopted child. An adopted child is always treated as your own child. An adopted child includes a child lawfully placed with you for legal adoption.

Church employees. Determine how much of the amount on Form 1040, line 7, was also reported on Schedule SE, line 5a. Subtract that amount from the amount on Form 1040, line 7, and enter the result in the first space of Step 5, line 2. Be sure to answer "Yes" to question 3 in Step 5.

Clergy. The following instructions apply to ministers, members of religious orders who have not taken a vow of poverty, and Christian Science practitioners. If you are filing Schedule SE and the amount on line 2 of that schedule includes an amount that was also reported on Form 1040, line 7:

1. Put "Clergy" on the dotted line next to Form 1040, line 66a.
2. Determine how much of the amount on Form 1040, line 7, was also reported on Schedule SE, line 2.
3. Subtract that amount from the amount on Form 1040, line 7. Enter the result in the first space of Step 5, line 2.
4. Be sure to answer "Yes" to question 3 in Step 5.

Combat pay, Nontaxable. If you were a member of the U.S. Armed Forces who served in a combat zone, certain pay is excluded from your income. See *Combat Zone Exclusion* in Pub. 3. You can elect to include this pay in your earned income when figuring the EIC. The amount of your nontaxable combat pay should be shown in Form(s) W-2, box 12, with code Q. If you are filing a joint return and both you and your spouse received nontaxable combat pay, you can each make your own election.

Need more information or forms? See page 7.

Form 1040—Lines 66a and 66b

Credit figured by the IRS. To have the IRS figure your EIC:

1. Put "EIC" on the dotted line next to Form 1040, line 66a.

2. Be sure you enter the nontaxable combat pay you elect to include in earned income on Form 1040, line 66b. See *Combat pay, Nontaxable* on page 47.

3. If you have a qualifying child, complete and attach Schedule EIC. If your EIC for a year after 1996 was reduced or disallowed, see *Form 8862, Who must file* below.

Exception to time lived with you. A child is considered to have lived with you for all of 2005 if the child was born or died in 2005 and your home was this child's home for the entire time he or she was alive in 2005. Temporary absences for special circumstances, such as for school, vacation, medical care, military service, or detention in a juvenile facility, count as time lived at home. Also see *Kidnapped child* on page 21 or *Members of the military* below.

Form 4797 filers. If the amount on Form 1040, line 13, includes an amount from Form 4797, you must use Worksheet 1 in Pub. 596 to see if you can take the EIC. To get Pub. 596, see page 7. Otherwise, stop; you cannot take the EIC.

Form 8862, Who must file. You must file Form 8862 if your EIC for a year after 1996 was reduced or disallowed for any reason other than a math or clerical error. But do not file Form 8862 if either of the following applies.

- You filed Form 8862 for another year, the EIC was allowed for that year, and your EIC has not been reduced or disallowed again for any reason other than a math or clerical error.

- You are taking the EIC without a qualifying child and the only reason your EIC was reduced or disallowed in the other year was because it was determined that a child listed on Schedule EIC was not your qualifying child.

  Also, do not file Form 8862 or take the credit for the:

- 2 years after the most recent tax year for which there was a final determination that your EIC was reduced or disallowed due to reckless or intentional disregard of the EIC rules, or

- 10 years after the most recent tax year for which there was a final determination that your EIC was reduced or disallowed due to fraud.

Foster child. A foster child is any child placed with you by an authorized placement agency or by judgment, decree, or other order of any court of competent jurisdiction. For more details on authorized placement agencies, see Pub. 596.

Married child. A child who was married at the end of 2005 is a qualifying child only if (a) you can claim him or her as your dependent on Form 1040, line 6c, or (b) you could have claimed him or her as your dependent except for the rules for *Children of divorced or separated parents* on page 20.

Members of the military. If you were on extended active duty outside the United States, your home is considered to be in the United States during that duty period. Extended active duty is military duty ordered for an indefinite period or for a period of more than 90 days. Once you begin serving extended active duty, you are considered to be on extended active duty even if you serve fewer than 90 days.

Nonresident aliens. If your filing status is married filing jointly, go to Step 2 on page 45. Otherwise, stop; you cannot take the EIC.

Permanently and totally disabled. A person who, at any time in 2005, cannot engage in any substantial gainful activity because of a physical or mental condition and a doctor has determined that this condition (a) has lasted or can be expected to last continuously for at least a year, or (b) can be expected to lead to death.

Qualifying child of more than one person. If the child is the qualifying child of more than one person, only one person can claim the child as a qualifying child for all of the following tax benefits, unless the rules for *Children of divorced or separated parents* on page 20 apply.

1. Dependency exemption (line 6c).
2. Child tax credits (lines 52 and 68).
3. Head of household filing status (line 4).
4. Credit for child and dependent care expenses (line 48).
5. Earned income credit (lines 66a and 66b).

No other person can take any of the five tax benefits listed above unless he or she has a different qualifying child. If you and any other person claim the child as a qualifying child, the IRS will apply the following rules.

- If only one of the persons is the child's parent, the child will be treated as the qualifying child of the parent.

- If two of the persons are the child's parents, the child will be treated as the qualifying child of the parent with whom the child lived for the longer period of time in 2005. If the child lived with each parent for the same amount of time, the child will be treated as the qualifying child of the parent who had the higher adjusted gross income (AGI) for 2005.

- If none of the persons is the child's parent, the child will be treated as the qualifying child of the person who had the highest AGI for 2005.

Example. Your daughter meets the conditions to be a qualifying child for both you and your mother. If you and your mother both claim tax benefits based on the child, the rules above apply. Under these rules, you are entitled to treat your daughter as a qualifying child for any of the five tax benefits listed above for which you otherwise qualify. Your mother would not be entitled to take any of the five tax benefits listed above unless she has a different qualifying child.

If you will not be taking the EIC with a qualifying child, put "No" on the dotted line next to line 66a. Otherwise, go to Step 3, question 1, on page 46.

Social security number (SSN). For the EIC, a valid SSN is a number issued by the Social Security Administration unless "Not Valid for Employment" is printed on the social security card and the number was issued solely to apply for or receive a federally funded benefit.

To find out how to get an SSN, see page 16. If you will not have an SSN by April 17, 2006, see *What if You Cannot File on Time?* on page 12.

Student. A child who during any part of 5 calendar months of 2005 was enrolled as a full-time student at a school, or took a full-time, on-farm training course given by a school or a state, county, or local government agency. A school includes a technical, trade, or mechanical school. It does not include an on-the-job training course, correspondence school, or Internet school.

Welfare benefits, Effect of credit on. Any refund you receive as a result of taking the EIC will not be used to determine if you are eligible for the following programs or how much you can receive from them. But if the refund you receive because of the EIC is not spent within a certain period of time, it can count as an asset (or resource) and affect your eligibility.

- Temporary Assistance for Needy Families (TANF).
- Medicaid and supplemental security income (SSI).
- Food stamps and low-income housing.

Need more information or forms? See page 7.   - 48 -

Worksheet A—Earned Income Credit (EIC)—Lines 66a and 66b   *Keep for Your Records*

Before you begin: ✓ Be sure you are using the correct worksheet. Use this worksheet only if you answered "No" to Step 5, question 3, on page 47, or you elect to use your 2004 earned income to figure your EIC (see page 47). Otherwise, use Worksheet B that begins on page 50.

Part 1 **All Filers Using Worksheet A**	1.	Enter your earned income from Step 5 on page 47. But if you elect to use your 2004 earned income (see page 47), enter that amount instead.	**1**
	2.	Look up the amount on line 1 above in the EIC Table on pages 52–58 to find the credit. Be sure you use the correct column for your filing status and the number of children you have. Enter the credit here. If line 2 is zero, (STOP) You cannot take the credit. Put "No" on the dotted line next to line 66a.	**2**
	3.	Enter the amount from Form 1040, line 38.	**3**
	4.	Are the amounts on lines 3 and 1 the same? ☐ **Yes.** Skip line 5; enter the amount from line 2 on line 6. ☐ **No.** Go to line 5.	

| **Part 2** **Filers Who Answered "No" on Line 4** | 5. | If you have:
• No qualifying children, is the amount on line 3 less than $6,550 ($8,550 if married filing jointly)?
• 1 or more qualifying children, is the amount on line 3 less than $14,400 ($16,400 if married filing jointly)?

☐ **Yes.** Leave line 5 blank; enter the amount from line 2 on line 6.

☐ **No.** Look up the amount on line 3 in the EIC Table on pages 52–58 to find the credit. Be sure you use the correct column for your filing status and the number of children you have. Enter the credit here.
Look at the amounts on lines 5 and 2. Then, enter the **smaller** amount on line 6. | **5** |

| **Part 3** **Your Earned Income Credit** | 6. | **This is your earned income credit.** If you elect to use your 2004 earned income (see page 47), enter "PYEI" and the amount of your 2004 earned income on the dotted line next to line 66a. | **6**
Enter this amount on Form 1040, line 66a. |

Reminder—

✓ If you have a qualifying child, complete and attach Schedule EIC.

⚠ CAUTION *If your EIC for a year after 1996 was reduced or disallowed, see page 48 to find out if you must file Form 8862 to take the credit for 2005.*

Form 1040—Lines 66a and 66b

Worksheet **B**—Earned Income Credit (EIC)—Lines 66a and 66b   *Keep for Your Records*

Use this worksheet if you answered "Yes" to Step 5, question 3, on page 47, and you do not elect to use your 2004 earned income to figure your EIC (see page 47).

✓   Complete the parts below (Parts 1 through 3) that apply to you. Then, continue to Part 4.

✓   If you are married filing a joint return, include your spouse's amounts, if any, with yours to figure the amounts to enter in Parts 1 through 3.

Part 1 **Self-Employed, Members of the Clergy, and People With Church Employee Income Filing Schedule SE**	**1a.** Enter the amount from Schedule SE, Section A, line 3, or Section B, line 3, whichever applies.	**1a**
	b. Enter any amount from Schedule SE, Section B, line 4b, and line 5a.	+ **1b**
	c. Combine lines 1a and 1b.	= **1c**
	d. Enter the amount from Schedule SE, Section A, line 6, or Section B, line 13, whichever applies.	– **1d**
	e. Subtract line 1d from 1c.	= **1e**

Part 2 **Self-Employed NOT Required To File Schedule SE** For example, your net earnings from self-employment were less than $400.	**2.** Do not include on these lines any statutory employee income or any amount exempt from self-employment tax as the result of the filing and approval of Form 4029 or Form 4361.	
	a. Enter any net farm profit or (loss) from Schedule F, line 36, and from farm partnerships, Schedule K-1 (Form 1065), box 14, code A*.	**2a**
	b. Enter any net profit or (loss) from Schedule C, line 31; Schedule C-EZ, line 3; Schedule K-1 (Form 1065), box 14, code A (other than farming); and Schedule K-1 (Form 1065-B), box 9*.	+ **2b**
	c. Combine lines 2a and 2b.	= **2c**
	*Reduce any Schedule K-1 amounts by any partnership section 179 expense deduction claimed, unreimbursed partnership expenses claimed, and depletion claimed on oil and gas properties. If you have any Schedule K-1 amounts, complete the appropriate line(s) of Schedule SE, Section A. Put your name and social security number on Schedule SE and attach it to your return.	

Part 3 **Statutory Employees Filing Schedule C or C-EZ**	**3.** Enter the amount from Schedule C, line 1, or Schedule C-EZ, line 1, that you are filing as a statutory employee.	**3**

Part 4 **All Filers Using Worksheet B** **Note.** If line 4b includes income on which you should have paid self-employment tax but did not, we may reduce your credit by the amount of self-employment tax not paid.	**4a.** Enter your earned income from Step 5 on page 47.	**4a**
	b. Combine lines 1e, 2c, 3, and 4a. **This is your total earned income.**	**4b**

If line 4b is zero or less, (STOP) You cannot take the credit. Put "No" on the dotted line next to line 66a.

5.   If you have:
   ● 2 or more qualifying children, is line 4b less than $35,263 ($37,263 if married filing jointly)?
   ● 1 qualifying child, is line 4b less than $31,030 ($33,030 if married filing jointly)?
   ● No qualifying children, is line 4b less than $11,750 ($13,750 if married filing jointly)?

☐ **Yes.** If you want the IRS to figure your credit, see page 48. If you want to figure the credit yourself, enter the amount from line 4b on line 6 (page 51).

☐ **No.** (STOP)   You cannot take the credit. Put "No" on the dotted line next to line 66a.

Need more information or forms? See page 7.   **- 50 -**

Worksheet B—Continued from page 50

Keep for Your Records

Part 5		
All Filers Using Worksheet B	**6.** Enter your total earned income from Part 4, line 4b, on page 50.	**6**
	7. Look up the amount on line 6 above in the EIC Table on pages 52–58 to find the credit. Be sure you use the correct column for your filing status and the number of children you have. Enter the credit here.	**7**
	If line 7 is zero, **(STOP)** You cannot take the credit. Put "No" on the dotted line next to line 66a.	
	8. Enter the amount from Form 1040, line 38.	**8**
	9. Are the amounts on lines 8 and 6 the same?	
	☐ **Yes.** Skip line 10; enter the amount from line 7 on line 11.	
	☐ **No.** Go to line 10.	

Part 6		
Filers Who Answered "No" on Line 9	**10.** If you have:	
	• No qualifying children, is the amount on line 8 less than $6,550 ($8,550 if married filing jointly)?	
	• 1 or more qualifying children, is the amount on line 8 less than $14,400 ($16,400 if married filing jointly)?	
	☐ **Yes.** Leave line 10 blank; enter the amount from line 7 on line 11.	
	☐ **No.** Look up the amount on line 8 in the EIC Table on pages 52–58 to find the credit. Be sure you use the correct column for your filing status and the number of children you have. Enter the credit here. Look at the amounts on lines 10 and 7. Then, enter the **smaller** amount on line 11.	**10**

Part 7		
Your Earned Income Credit	**11. This is your earned income credit.**	**11**
		Enter this amount on Form 1040, line 66a.
	Reminder—	
	✓ If you have a qualifying child, complete and attach Schedule EIC.	

⚠ **CAUTION** *If your EIC for a year after 1996 was reduced or disallowed, see page 48 to find out if you must file Form 8862 to take the credit for 2005.*

Need more information or forms? See page 7.

2005 Earned Income Credit (EIC) Table

Caution. This is **not** a tax table.

1. To find your credit, read down the "At least – But less than" columns and find the line that includes the amount you were told to look up from your EIC Worksheet.

2. Then, go to the column that includes your filing status and the number of qualifying children you have. Enter the credit from that column on your EIC Worksheet.

Example. If your filing status is single, you have one qualifying child, and the amount you are looking up from your EIC Worksheet is $2,455, you would enter $842.

If the amount you are looking up from the worksheet is—		And your filing status is— Single, head of household, or qualifying widow(er) and you have—		
At least	But less than	No children	One child	Two children
		Your credit is—		
2,400	2,450	186	825	970
2,450	2,500	189	842	990

If the amount you are looking up from the worksheet is—		And your filing status is—					
		Single, head of household, or qualifying widow(er) and you have—			Married filing jointly and you have—		
At least	But less than	No children	One child	Two children	No children	One child	Two children
		Your credit is—			Your credit is—		
$1	$50	$2	$9	$10	$2	$9	$10
50	100	6	26	30	6	26	30
100	150	10	43	50	10	43	50
150	200	13	60	70	13	60	70
200	250	17	77	90	17	77	90
250	300	21	94	110	21	94	110
300	350	25	111	130	25	111	130
350	400	29	128	150	29	128	150
400	450	33	145	170	33	145	170
450	500	36	162	190	36	162	190
500	550	40	179	210	40	179	210
550	600	44	196	230	44	196	230
600	650	48	213	250	48	213	250
650	700	52	230	270	52	230	270
700	750	55	247	290	55	247	290
750	800	59	264	310	59	264	310
800	850	63	281	330	63	281	330
850	900	67	298	350	67	298	350
900	950	71	315	370	71	315	370
950	1,000	75	332	390	75	332	390
1,000	1,050	78	349	410	78	349	410
1,050	1,100	82	366	430	82	366	430
1,100	1,150	86	383	450	86	383	450
1,150	1,200	90	400	470	90	400	470
1,200	1,250	94	417	490	94	417	490
1,250	1,300	98	434	510	98	434	510
1,300	1,350	101	451	530	101	451	530
1,350	1,400	105	468	550	105	468	550
1,400	1,450	109	485	570	109	485	570
1,450	1,500	113	502	590	113	502	590
1,500	1,550	117	519	610	117	519	610
1,550	1,600	120	536	630	120	536	630
1,600	1,650	124	553	650	124	553	650
1,650	1,700	128	570	670	128	570	670
1,700	1,750	132	587	690	132	587	690
1,750	1,800	136	604	710	136	604	710
1,800	1,850	140	621	730	140	621	730
1,850	1,900	143	638	750	143	638	750
1,900	1,950	147	655	770	147	655	770
1,950	2,000	151	672	790	151	672	790
2,000	2,050	155	689	810	155	689	810
2,050	2,100	159	706	830	159	706	830
2,100	2,150	163	723	850	163	723	850
2,150	2,200	166	740	870	166	740	870
2,200	2,250	170	757	890	170	757	890
2,250	2,300	174	774	910	174	774	910
2,300	2,350	178	791	930	178	791	930
2,350	2,400	182	808	950	182	808	950
2,400	2,450	186	825	970	186	825	970
2,450	2,500	189	842	990	189	842	990
2,500	2,550	193	859	1,010	193	859	1,010
2,550	2,600	197	876	1,030	197	876	1,030
2,600	2,650	201	893	1,050	201	893	1,050
2,650	2,700	205	910	1,070	205	910	1,070
2,700	2,750	208	927	1,090	208	927	1,090

If the amount you are looking up from the worksheet is—		And your filing status is—					
		Single, head of household, or qualifying widow(er) and you have—			Married filing jointly and you have—		
At least	But less than	No children	One child	Two children	No children	One child	Two children
		Your credit is—			Your credit is—		
2,750	2,800	212	944	1,110	212	944	1,110
2,800	2,850	216	961	1,130	216	961	1,130
2,850	2,900	220	978	1,150	220	978	1,150
2,900	2,950	224	995	1,170	224	995	1,170
2,950	3,000	228	1,012	1,190	228	1,012	1,190
3,000	3,050	231	1,029	1,210	231	1,029	1,210
3,050	3,100	235	1,046	1,230	235	1,046	1,230
3,100	3,150	239	1,063	1,250	239	1,063	1,250
3,150	3,200	243	1,080	1,270	243	1,080	1,270
3,200	3,250	247	1,097	1,290	247	1,097	1,290
3,250	3,300	251	1,114	1,310	251	1,114	1,310
3,300	3,350	254	1,131	1,330	254	1,131	1,330
3,350	3,400	258	1,148	1,350	258	1,148	1,350
3,400	3,450	262	1,165	1,370	262	1,165	1,370
3,450	3,500	266	1,182	1,390	266	1,182	1,390
3,500	3,550	270	1,199	1,410	270	1,199	1,410
3,550	3,600	273	1,216	1,430	273	1,216	1,430
3,600	3,650	277	1,233	1,450	277	1,233	1,450
3,650	3,700	281	1,250	1,470	281	1,250	1,470
3,700	3,750	285	1,267	1,490	285	1,267	1,490
3,750	3,800	289	1,284	1,510	289	1,284	1,510
3,800	3,850	293	1,301	1,530	293	1,301	1,530
3,850	3,900	296	1,318	1,550	296	1,318	1,550
3,900	3,950	300	1,335	1,570	300	1,335	1,570
3,950	4,000	304	1,352	1,590	304	1,352	1,590
4,000	4,050	308	1,369	1,610	308	1,369	1,610
4,050	4,100	312	1,386	1,630	312	1,386	1,630
4,100	4,150	316	1,403	1,650	316	1,403	1,650
4,150	4,200	319	1,420	1,670	319	1,420	1,670
4,200	4,250	323	1,437	1,690	323	1,437	1,690
4,250	4,300	327	1,454	1,710	327	1,454	1,710
4,300	4,350	331	1,471	1,730	331	1,471	1,730
4,350	4,400	335	1,488	1,750	335	1,488	1,750
4,400	4,450	339	1,505	1,770	339	1,505	1,770
4,450	4,500	342	1,522	1,790	342	1,522	1,790
4,500	4,550	346	1,539	1,810	346	1,539	1,810
4,550	4,600	350	1,556	1,830	350	1,556	1,830
4,600	4,650	354	1,573	1,850	354	1,573	1,850
4,650	4,700	358	1,590	1,870	358	1,590	1,870
4,700	4,750	361	1,607	1,890	361	1,607	1,890
4,750	4,800	365	1,624	1,910	365	1,624	1,910
4,800	4,850	369	1,641	1,930	369	1,641	1,930
4,850	4,900	373	1,658	1,950	373	1,658	1,950
4,900	4,950	377	1,675	1,970	377	1,675	1,970
4,950	5,000	381	1,692	1,990	381	1,692	1,990
5,000	5,050	384	1,709	2,010	384	1,709	2,010
5,050	5,100	388	1,726	2,030	388	1,726	2,030
5,100	5,150	392	1,743	2,050	392	1,743	2,050
5,150	5,200	396	1,760	2,070	396	1,760	2,070
5,200	5,250	399	1,777	2,090	399	1,777	2,090
5,250	5,300	399	1,794	2,110	399	1,794	2,110
5,300	5,350	399	1,811	2,130	399	1,811	2,130
5,350	5,400	399	1,828	2,150	399	1,828	2,150
5,400	5,450	399	1,845	2,170	399	1,845	2,170
5,450	5,500	399	1,862	2,190	399	1,862	2,190

(Continued on page 53)

2005 Earned Income Credit (EIC) Table—*Continued* (Caution. This is **not** a tax table.)

If the amount you are looking up from the worksheet is— At least	But less than	Single, head of household, or qualifying widow(er) and you have— No children	One child	Two children	Married filing jointly and you have— No children	One child	Two children
5,500	5,550	399	1,879	2,210	399	1,879	2,210
5,550	5,600	399	1,896	2,230	399	1,896	2,230
5,600	5,650	399	1,913	2,250	399	1,913	2,250
5,650	5,700	399	1,930	2,270	399	1,930	2,270
5,700	5,750	399	1,947	2,290	399	1,947	2,290
5,750	5,800	399	1,964	2,310	399	1,964	2,310
5,800	5,850	399	1,981	2,330	399	1,981	2,330
5,850	5,900	399	1,998	2,350	399	1,998	2,350
5,900	5,950	399	2,015	2,370	399	2,015	2,370
5,950	6,000	399	2,032	2,390	399	2,032	2,390
6,000	6,050	399	2,049	2,410	399	2,049	2,410
6,050	6,100	399	2,066	2,430	399	2,066	2,430
6,100	6,150	399	2,083	2,450	399	2,083	2,450
6,150	6,200	399	2,100	2,470	399	2,100	2,470
6,200	6,250	399	2,117	2,490	399	2,117	2,490
6,250	6,300	399	2,134	2,510	399	2,134	2,510
6,300	6,350	399	2,151	2,530	399	2,151	2,530
6,350	6,400	399	2,168	2,550	399	2,168	2,550
6,400	6,450	399	2,185	2,570	399	2,185	2,570
6,450	6,500	399	2,202	2,590	399	2,202	2,590
6,500	6,550	399	2,219	2,610	399	2,219	2,610
6,550	6,600	396	2,236	2,630	399	2,236	2,630
6,600	6,650	392	2,253	2,650	399	2,253	2,650
6,650	6,700	388	2,270	2,670	399	2,270	2,670
6,700	6,750	384	2,287	2,690	399	2,287	2,690
6,750	6,800	381	2,304	2,710	399	2,304	2,710
6,800	6,850	377	2,321	2,730	399	2,321	2,730
6,850	6,900	373	2,338	2,750	399	2,338	2,750
6,900	6,950	369	2,355	2,770	399	2,355	2,770
6,950	7,000	365	2,372	2,790	399	2,372	2,790
7,000	7,050	361	2,389	2,810	399	2,389	2,810
7,050	7,100	358	2,406	2,830	399	2,406	2,830
7,100	7,150	354	2,423	2,850	399	2,423	2,850
7,150	7,200	350	2,440	2,870	399	2,440	2,870
7,200	7,250	346	2,457	2,890	399	2,457	2,890
7,250	7,300	342	2,474	2,910	399	2,474	2,910
7,300	7,350	339	2,491	2,930	399	2,491	2,930
7,350	7,400	335	2,508	2,950	399	2,508	2,950
7,400	7,450	331	2,525	2,970	399	2,525	2,970
7,450	7,500	327	2,542	2,990	399	2,542	2,990
7,500	7,550	323	2,559	3,010	399	2,559	3,010
7,550	7,600	319	2,576	3,030	399	2,576	3,030
7,600	7,650	316	2,593	3,050	399	2,593	3,050
7,650	7,700	312	2,610	3,070	399	2,610	3,070
7,700	7,750	308	2,627	3,090	399	2,627	3,090
7,750	7,800	304	2,644	3,110	399	2,644	3,110
7,800	7,850	300	2,662	3,130	399	2,662	3,130
7,850	7,900	296	2,662	3,150	399	2,662	3,150
7,900	7,950	293	2,662	3,170	399	2,662	3,170
7,950	8,000	289	2,662	3,190	399	2,662	3,190
8,000	8,050	285	2,662	3,210	399	2,662	3,210
8,050	8,100	281	2,662	3,230	399	2,662	3,230
8,100	8,150	277	2,662	3,250	399	2,662	3,250
8,150	8,200	273	2,662	3,270	399	2,662	3,270
8,200	8,250	270	2,662	3,290	399	2,662	3,290
8,250	8,300	266	2,662	3,310	399	2,662	3,310
8,300	8,350	262	2,662	3,330	399	2,662	3,330
8,350	8,400	258	2,662	3,350	399	2,662	3,350
8,400	8,450	254	2,662	3,370	399	2,662	3,370
8,450	8,500	251	2,662	3,390	399	2,662	3,390

If the amount you are looking up from the worksheet is— At least	But less than	Single, head of household, or qualifying widow(er) and you have— No children	One child	Two children	Married filing jointly and you have— No children	One child	Two children
8,500	8,550	247	2,662	3,410	399	2,662	3,410
8,550	8,600	243	2,662	3,430	396	2,662	3,430
8,600	8,650	239	2,662	3,450	392	2,662	3,450
8,650	8,700	235	2,662	3,470	388	2,662	3,470
8,700	8,750	231	2,662	3,490	384	2,662	3,490
8,750	8,800	228	2,662	3,510	381	2,662	3,510
8,800	8,850	224	2,662	3,530	377	2,662	3,530
8,850	8,900	220	2,662	3,550	373	2,662	3,550
8,900	8,950	216	2,662	3,570	369	2,662	3,570
8,950	9,000	212	2,662	3,590	365	2,662	3,590
9,000	9,050	208	2,662	3,610	361	2,662	3,610
9,050	9,100	205	2,662	3,630	358	2,662	3,630
9,100	9,150	201	2,662	3,650	354	2,662	3,650
9,150	9,200	197	2,662	3,670	350	2,662	3,670
9,200	9,250	193	2,662	3,690	346	2,662	3,690
9,250	9,300	189	2,662	3,710	342	2,662	3,710
9,300	9,350	186	2,662	3,730	339	2,662	3,730
9,350	9,400	182	2,662	3,750	335	2,662	3,750
9,400	9,450	178	2,662	3,770	331	2,662	3,770
9,450	9,500	174	2,662	3,790	327	2,662	3,790
9,500	9,550	170	2,662	3,810	323	2,662	3,810
9,550	9,600	166	2,662	3,830	319	2,662	3,830
9,600	9,650	163	2,662	3,850	316	2,662	3,850
9,650	9,700	159	2,662	3,870	312	2,662	3,870
9,700	9,750	155	2,662	3,890	308	2,662	3,890
9,750	9,800	151	2,662	3,910	304	2,662	3,910
9,800	9,850	147	2,662	3,930	300	2,662	3,930
9,850	9,900	143	2,662	3,950	296	2,662	3,950
9,900	9,950	140	2,662	3,970	293	2,662	3,970
9,950	10,000	136	2,662	3,990	289	2,662	3,990
10,000	10,050	132	2,662	4,010	285	2,662	4,010
10,050	10,100	128	2,662	4,030	281	2,662	4,030
10,100	10,150	124	2,662	4,050	277	2,662	4,050
10,150	10,200	120	2,662	4,070	273	2,662	4,070
10,200	10,250	117	2,662	4,090	270	2,662	4,090
10,250	10,300	113	2,662	4,110	266	2,662	4,110
10,300	10,350	109	2,662	4,130	262	2,662	4,130
10,350	10,400	105	2,662	4,150	258	2,662	4,150
10,400	10,450	101	2,662	4,170	254	2,662	4,170
10,450	10,500	98	2,662	4,190	251	2,662	4,190
10,500	10,550	94	2,662	4,210	247	2,662	4,210
10,550	10,600	90	2,662	4,230	243	2,662	4,230
10,600	10,650	86	2,662	4,250	239	2,662	4,250
10,650	10,700	82	2,662	4,270	235	2,662	4,270
10,700	10,750	78	2,662	4,290	231	2,662	4,290
10,750	10,800	75	2,662	4,310	228	2,662	4,310
10,800	10,850	71	2,662	4,330	224	2,662	4,330
10,850	10,900	67	2,662	4,350	220	2,662	4,350
10,900	10,950	63	2,662	4,370	216	2,662	4,370
10,950	11,000	59	2,662	4,390	212	2,662	4,390
11,000	11,050	55	2,662	4,400	208	2,662	4,400
11,050	11,100	52	2,662	4,400	205	2,662	4,400
11,100	11,150	48	2,662	4,400	201	2,662	4,400
11,150	11,200	44	2,662	4,400	197	2,662	4,400
11,200	11,250	40	2,662	4,400	193	2,662	4,400
11,250	11,300	36	2,662	4,400	189	2,662	4,400
11,300	11,350	33	2,662	4,400	186	2,662	4,400
11,350	11,400	29	2,662	4,400	182	2,662	4,400
11,400	11,450	25	2,662	4,400	178	2,662	4,400
11,450	11,500	21	2,662	4,400	174	2,662	4,400

(Continued on page 54)

- 53 -

Need more information or forms? See page 7.

2005 Earned Income Credit (EIC) Table—Continued (Caution. This is **not** a tax table.)

And your filing status is— *(Single, head of household, or qualifying widow(er) and you have— / Married filing jointly and you have—)*

If the amount you are looking up from the worksheet is— At least	But less than	Single — No children	Single — One child	Single — Two children	Married — No children	Married — One child	Married — Two children
11,500	11,550	17	2,662	4,400	170	2,662	4,400
11,550	11,600	13	2,662	4,400	166	2,662	4,400
11,600	11,650	10	2,662	4,400	163	2,662	4,400
11,650	11,700	6	2,662	4,400	159	2,662	4,400
11,700	11,750	2	2,662	4,400	155	2,662	4,400
11,750	11,800	0	2,662	4,400	151	2,662	4,400
11,800	11,850	0	2,662	4,400	147	2,662	4,400
11,850	11,900	0	2,662	4,400	143	2,662	4,400
11,900	11,950	0	2,662	4,400	140	2,662	4,400
11,950	12,000	0	2,662	4,400	136	2,662	4,400
12,000	12,050	0	2,662	4,400	132	2,662	4,400
12,050	12,100	0	2,662	4,400	128	2,662	4,400
12,100	12,150	0	2,662	4,400	124	2,662	4,400
12,150	12,200	0	2,662	4,400	120	2,662	4,400
12,200	12,250	0	2,662	4,400	117	2,662	4,400
12,250	12,300	0	2,662	4,400	113	2,662	4,400
12,300	12,350	0	2,662	4,400	109	2,662	4,400
12,350	12,400	0	2,662	4,400	105	2,662	4,400
12,400	12,450	0	2,662	4,400	101	2,662	4,400
12,450	12,500	0	2,662	4,400	98	2,662	4,400
12,500	12,550	0	2,662	4,400	94	2,662	4,400
12,550	12,600	0	2,662	4,400	90	2,662	4,400
12,600	12,650	0	2,662	4,400	86	2,662	4,400
12,650	12,700	0	2,662	4,400	82	2,662	4,400
12,700	12,750	0	2,662	4,400	78	2,662	4,400
12,750	12,800	0	2,662	4,400	75	2,662	4,400
12,800	12,850	0	2,662	4,400	71	2,662	4,400
12,850	12,900	0	2,662	4,400	67	2,662	4,400
12,900	12,950	0	2,662	4,400	63	2,662	4,400
12,950	13,000	0	2,662	4,400	59	2,662	4,400
13,000	13,050	0	2,662	4,400	55	2,662	4,400
13,050	13,100	0	2,662	4,400	52	2,662	4,400
13,100	13,150	0	2,662	4,400	48	2,662	4,400
13,150	13,200	0	2,662	4,400	44	2,662	4,400
13,200	13,250	0	2,662	4,400	40	2,662	4,400
13,250	13,300	0	2,662	4,400	36	2,662	4,400
13,300	13,350	0	2,662	4,400	33	2,662	4,400
13,350	13,400	0	2,662	4,400	29	2,662	4,400
13,400	13,450	0	2,662	4,400	25	2,662	4,400
13,450	13,500	0	2,662	4,400	21	2,662	4,400
13,500	13,550	0	2,662	4,400	17	2,662	4,400
13,550	13,600	0	2,662	4,400	13	2,662	4,400
13,600	13,650	0	2,662	4,400	10	2,662	4,400
13,650	13,700	0	2,662	4,400	6	2,662	4,400
13,700	13,750	0	2,662	4,400	2	2,662	4,400
13,750	14,400	0	2,662	4,400	0	2,662	4,400
14,400	14,450	0	2,653	4,388	0	2,662	4,400
14,450	14,500	0	2,645	4,378	0	2,662	4,400
14,500	14,550	0	2,637	4,367	0	2,662	4,400
14,550	14,600	0	2,629	4,357	0	2,662	4,400
14,600	14,650	0	2,621	4,346	0	2,662	4,400
14,650	14,700	0	2,613	4,336	0	2,662	4,400
14,700	14,750	0	2,605	4,325	0	2,662	4,400
14,750	14,800	0	2,597	4,315	0	2,662	4,400
14,800	14,850	0	2,589	4,304	0	2,662	4,400
14,850	14,900	0	2,582	4,294	0	2,662	4,400
14,900	14,950	0	2,574	4,283	0	2,662	4,400
14,950	15,000	0	2,566	4,273	0	2,662	4,400
15,000	15,050	0	2,558	4,262	0	2,662	4,400
15,050	15,100	0	2,550	4,252	0	2,662	4,400

And your filing status is— *(Single, head of household, or qualifying widow(er) and you have— / Married filing jointly and you have—)*

If the amount you are looking up from the worksheet is— At least	But less than	Single — No children	Single — One child	Single — Two children	Married — No children	Married — One child	Married — Two children
15,100	15,150	0	2,542	4,241	0	2,662	4,400
15,150	15,200	0	2,534	4,230	0	2,662	4,400
15,200	15,250	0	2,526	4,220	0	2,662	4,400
15,250	15,300	0	2,518	4,209	0	2,662	4,400
15,300	15,350	0	2,510	4,199	0	2,662	4,400
15,350	15,400	0	2,502	4,188	0	2,662	4,400
15,400	15,450	0	2,494	4,178	0	2,662	4,400
15,450	15,500	0	2,486	4,167	0	2,662	4,400
15,500	15,550	0	2,478	4,157	0	2,662	4,400
15,550	15,600	0	2,470	4,146	0	2,662	4,400
15,600	15,650	0	2,462	4,136	0	2,662	4,400
15,650	15,700	0	2,454	4,125	0	2,662	4,400
15,700	15,750	0	2,446	4,115	0	2,662	4,400
15,750	15,800	0	2,438	4,104	0	2,662	4,400
15,800	15,850	0	2,430	4,094	0	2,662	4,400
15,850	15,900	0	2,422	4,083	0	2,662	4,400
15,900	15,950	0	2,414	4,073	0	2,662	4,400
15,950	16,000	0	2,406	4,062	0	2,662	4,400
16,000	16,050	0	2,398	4,051	0	2,662	4,400
16,050	16,100	0	2,390	4,041	0	2,662	4,400
16,100	16,150	0	2,382	4,030	0	2,662	4,400
16,150	16,200	0	2,374	4,020	0	2,662	4,400
16,200	16,250	0	2,366	4,009	0	2,662	4,400
16,250	16,300	0	2,358	3,999	0	2,662	4,400
16,300	16,350	0	2,350	3,988	0	2,662	4,400
16,350	16,400	0	2,342	3,978	0	2,662	4,400
16,400	16,450	0	2,334	3,967	0	2,653	4,388
16,450	16,500	0	2,326	3,957	0	2,645	4,378
16,500	16,550	0	2,318	3,946	0	2,637	4,367
16,550	16,600	0	2,310	3,936	0	2,629	4,357
16,600	16,650	0	2,302	3,925	0	2,621	4,346
16,650	16,700	0	2,294	3,915	0	2,613	4,336
16,700	16,750	0	2,286	3,904	0	2,605	4,325
16,750	16,800	0	2,278	3,894	0	2,597	4,315
16,800	16,850	0	2,270	3,883	0	2,589	4,304
16,850	16,900	0	2,262	3,872	0	2,582	4,294
16,900	16,950	0	2,254	3,862	0	2,574	4,283
16,950	17,000	0	2,246	3,851	0	2,566	4,273
17,000	17,050	0	2,238	3,841	0	2,558	4,262
17,050	17,100	0	2,230	3,830	0	2,550	4,252
17,100	17,150	0	2,222	3,820	0	2,542	4,241
17,150	17,200	0	2,214	3,809	0	2,534	4,230
17,200	17,250	0	2,206	3,799	0	2,526	4,220
17,250	17,300	0	2,198	3,788	0	2,518	4,209
17,300	17,350	0	2,190	3,778	0	2,510	4,199
17,350	17,400	0	2,182	3,767	0	2,502	4,188
17,400	17,450	0	2,174	3,757	0	2,494	4,178
17,450	17,500	0	2,166	3,746	0	2,486	4,167
17,500	17,550	0	2,158	3,736	0	2,478	4,157
17,550	17,600	0	2,150	3,725	0	2,470	4,146
17,600	17,650	0	2,142	3,714	0	2,462	4,136
17,650	17,700	0	2,134	3,704	0	2,454	4,125
17,700	17,750	0	2,126	3,693	0	2,446	4,115
17,750	17,800	0	2,118	3,683	0	2,438	4,104
17,800	17,850	0	2,110	3,672	0	2,430	4,094
17,850	17,900	0	2,102	3,662	0	2,422	4,083
17,900	17,950	0	2,094	3,651	0	2,414	4,073
17,950	18,000	0	2,086	3,641	0	2,406	4,062
18,000	18,050	0	2,078	3,630	0	2,398	4,051
18,050	18,100	0	2,070	3,620	0	2,390	4,041

(Continued on page 55)

2005 Earned Income Credit (EIC) Table—Continued (Caution. This is not a tax table.)

If the amount you are looking up from the worksheet is—		Single, head of household, or qualifying widow(er) and you have—			Married filing jointly and you have—		
At least	But less than	No children	One child	Two children	No children	One child	Two children
18,100	18,150	0	2,062	3,609	0	2,382	4,030
18,150	18,200	0	2,054	3,599	0	2,374	4,020
18,200	18,250	0	2,046	3,588	0	2,366	4,009
18,250	18,300	0	2,038	3,578	0	2,358	3,999
18,300	18,350	0	2,030	3,567	0	2,350	3,988
18,350	18,400	0	2,022	3,557	0	2,342	3,978
18,400	18,450	0	2,014	3,546	0	2,334	3,967
18,450	18,500	0	2,006	3,535	0	2,326	3,957
18,500	18,550	0	1,998	3,525	0	2,318	3,946
18,550	18,600	0	1,990	3,514	0	2,310	3,936
18,600	18,650	0	1,982	3,504	0	2,302	3,925
18,650	18,700	0	1,974	3,493	0	2,294	3,915
18,700	18,750	0	1,966	3,483	0	2,286	3,904
18,750	18,800	0	1,958	3,472	0	2,278	3,894
18,800	18,850	0	1,950	3,462	0	2,270	3,883
18,850	18,900	0	1,942	3,451	0	2,262	3,872
18,900	18,950	0	1,934	3,441	0	2,254	3,862
18,950	19,000	0	1,926	3,430	0	2,246	3,851
19,000	19,050	0	1,918	3,420	0	2,238	3,841
19,050	19,100	0	1,910	3,409	0	2,230	3,830
19,100	19,150	0	1,902	3,399	0	2,222	3,820
19,150	19,200	0	1,894	3,388	0	2,214	3,809
19,200	19,250	0	1,886	3,378	0	2,206	3,799
19,250	19,300	0	1,878	3,367	0	2,198	3,788
19,300	19,350	0	1,870	3,356	0	2,190	3,778
19,350	19,400	0	1,862	3,346	0	2,182	3,767
19,400	19,450	0	1,854	3,335	0	2,174	3,757
19,450	19,500	0	1,846	3,325	0	2,166	3,746
19,500	19,550	0	1,838	3,314	0	2,158	3,736
19,550	19,600	0	1,830	3,304	0	2,150	3,725
19,600	19,650	0	1,822	3,293	0	2,142	3,714
19,650	19,700	0	1,814	3,283	0	2,134	3,704
19,700	19,750	0	1,806	3,272	0	2,126	3,693
19,750	19,800	0	1,798	3,262	0	2,118	3,683
19,800	19,850	0	1,790	3,251	0	2,110	3,672
19,850	19,900	0	1,783	3,241	0	2,102	3,662
19,900	19,950	0	1,775	3,230	0	2,094	3,651
19,950	20,000	0	1,767	3,220	0	2,086	3,641
20,000	20,050	0	1,759	3,209	0	2,078	3,630
20,050	20,100	0	1,751	3,199	0	2,070	3,620
20,100	20,150	0	1,743	3,188	0	2,062	3,609
20,150	20,200	0	1,735	3,177	0	2,054	3,599
20,200	20,250	0	1,727	3,167	0	2,046	3,588
20,250	20,300	0	1,719	3,156	0	2,038	3,578
20,300	20,350	0	1,711	3,146	0	2,030	3,567
20,350	20,400	0	1,703	3,135	0	2,022	3,557
20,400	20,450	0	1,695	3,125	0	2,014	3,546
20,450	20,500	0	1,687	3,114	0	2,006	3,535
20,500	20,550	0	1,679	3,104	0	1,998	3,525
20,550	20,600	0	1,671	3,093	0	1,990	3,514
20,600	20,650	0	1,663	3,083	0	1,982	3,504
20,650	20,700	0	1,655	3,072	0	1,974	3,493
20,700	20,750	0	1,647	3,062	0	1,966	3,483
20,750	20,800	0	1,639	3,051	0	1,958	3,472
20,800	20,850	0	1,631	3,041	0	1,950	3,462
20,850	20,900	0	1,623	3,030	0	1,942	3,451
20,900	20,950	0	1,615	3,020	0	1,934	3,441
20,950	21,000	0	1,607	3,009	0	1,926	3,430
21,000	21,050	0	1,599	2,998	0	1,918	3,420
21,050	21,100	0	1,591	2,988	0	1,910	3,409

If the amount you are looking up from the worksheet is—		Single, head of household, or qualifying widow(er) and you have—			Married filing jointly and you have—		
At least	But less than	No children	One child	Two children	No children	One child	Two children
21,100	21,150	0	1,583	2,977	0	1,902	3,399
21,150	21,200	0	1,575	2,967	0	1,894	3,388
21,200	21,250	0	1,567	2,956	0	1,886	3,378
21,250	21,300	0	1,559	2,946	0	1,878	3,367
21,300	21,350	0	1,551	2,935	0	1,870	3,356
21,350	21,400	0	1,543	2,925	0	1,862	3,346
21,400	21,450	0	1,535	2,914	0	1,854	3,335
21,450	21,500	0	1,527	2,904	0	1,846	3,325
21,500	21,550	0	1,519	2,893	0	1,838	3,314
21,550	21,600	0	1,511	2,883	0	1,830	3,304
21,600	21,650	0	1,503	2,872	0	1,822	3,293
21,650	21,700	0	1,495	2,862	0	1,814	3,283
21,700	21,750	0	1,487	2,851	0	1,806	3,272
21,750	21,800	0	1,479	2,841	0	1,798	3,262
21,800	21,850	0	1,471	2,830	0	1,790	3,251
21,850	21,900	0	1,463	2,819	0	1,783	3,241
21,900	21,950	0	1,455	2,809	0	1,775	3,230
21,950	22,000	0	1,447	2,798	0	1,767	3,220
22,000	22,050	0	1,439	2,788	0	1,759	3,209
22,050	22,100	0	1,431	2,777	0	1,751	3,199
22,100	22,150	0	1,423	2,767	0	1,743	3,188
22,150	22,200	0	1,415	2,756	0	1,735	3,177
22,200	22,250	0	1,407	2,746	0	1,727	3,167
22,250	22,300	0	1,399	2,735	0	1,719	3,156
22,300	22,350	0	1,391	2,725	0	1,711	3,146
22,350	22,400	0	1,383	2,714	0	1,703	3,135
22,400	22,450	0	1,375	2,704	0	1,695	3,125
22,450	22,500	0	1,367	2,693	0	1,687	3,114
22,500	22,550	0	1,359	2,683	0	1,679	3,104
22,550	22,600	0	1,351	2,672	0	1,671	3,093
22,600	22,650	0	1,343	2,661	0	1,663	3,083
22,650	22,700	0	1,335	2,651	0	1,655	3,072
22,700	22,750	0	1,327	2,640	0	1,647	3,062
22,750	22,800	0	1,319	2,630	0	1,639	3,051
22,800	22,850	0	1,311	2,619	0	1,631	3,041
22,850	22,900	0	1,303	2,609	0	1,623	3,030
22,900	22,950	0	1,295	2,598	0	1,615	3,020
22,950	23,000	0	1,287	2,588	0	1,607	3,009
23,000	23,050	0	1,279	2,577	0	1,599	2,998
23,050	23,100	0	1,271	2,567	0	1,591	2,988
23,100	23,150	0	1,263	2,556	0	1,583	2,977
23,150	23,200	0	1,255	2,546	0	1,575	2,967
23,200	23,250	0	1,247	2,535	0	1,567	2,956
23,250	23,300	0	1,239	2,525	0	1,559	2,946
23,300	23,350	0	1,231	2,514	0	1,551	2,935
23,350	23,400	0	1,223	2,504	0	1,543	2,925
23,400	23,450	0	1,215	2,493	0	1,535	2,914
23,450	23,500	0	1,207	2,482	0	1,527	2,904
23,500	23,550	0	1,199	2,472	0	1,519	2,893
23,550	23,600	0	1,191	2,461	0	1,511	2,883
23,600	23,650	0	1,183	2,451	0	1,503	2,872
23,650	23,700	0	1,175	2,440	0	1,495	2,862
23,700	23,750	0	1,167	2,430	0	1,487	2,851
23,750	23,800	0	1,159	2,419	0	1,479	2,841
23,800	23,850	0	1,151	2,409	0	1,471	2,830
23,850	23,900	0	1,143	2,398	0	1,463	2,819
23,900	23,950	0	1,135	2,388	0	1,455	2,809
23,950	24,000	0	1,127	2,377	0	1,447	2,798
24,000	24,050	0	1,119	2,367	0	1,439	2,788
24,050	24,100	0	1,111	2,356	0	1,431	2,777

(Continued on page 56)

Need more information or forms? See page 7.

2005 Earned Income Credit (EIC) Table—Continued (Caution. This is not a tax table.)

If the amount you are looking up from the worksheet is—		Single, head of household, or qualifying widow(er) and you have—			Married filing jointly and you have—		
At least	But less than	No children	One child	Two children	No children	One child	Two children
		Your credit is—			Your credit is—		
24,100	24,150	0	1,103	2,346	0	1,423	2,767
24,150	24,200	0	1,095	2,335	0	1,415	2,756
24,200	24,250	0	1,087	2,325	0	1,407	2,746
24,250	24,300	0	1,079	2,314	0	1,399	2,735
24,300	24,350	0	1,071	2,303	0	1,391	2,725
24,350	24,400	0	1,063	2,293	0	1,383	2,714
24,400	24,450	0	1,055	2,282	0	1,375	2,704
24,450	24,500	0	1,047	2,272	0	1,367	2,693
24,500	24,550	0	1,039	2,261	0	1,359	2,683
24,550	24,600	0	1,031	2,251	0	1,351	2,672
24,600	24,650	0	1,023	2,240	0	1,343	2,661
24,650	24,700	0	1,015	2,230	0	1,335	2,651
24,700	24,750	0	1,007	2,219	0	1,327	2,640
24,750	24,800	0	999	2,209	0	1,319	2,630
24,800	24,850	0	991	2,198	0	1,311	2,619
24,850	24,900	0	984	2,188	0	1,303	2,609
24,900	24,950	0	976	2,177	0	1,295	2,598
24,950	25,000	0	968	2,167	0	1,287	2,588
25,000	25,050	0	960	2,156	0	1,279	2,577
25,050	25,100	0	952	2,146	0	1,271	2,567
25,100	25,150	0	944	2,135	0	1,263	2,556
25,150	25,200	0	936	2,124	0	1,255	2,546
25,200	25,250	0	928	2,114	0	1,247	2,535
25,250	25,300	0	920	2,103	0	1,239	2,525
25,300	25,350	0	912	2,093	0	1,231	2,514
25,350	25,400	0	904	2,082	0	1,223	2,504
25,400	25,450	0	896	2,072	0	1,215	2,493
25,450	25,500	0	888	2,061	0	1,207	2,482
25,500	25,550	0	880	2,051	0	1,199	2,472
25,550	25,600	0	872	2,040	0	1,191	2,461
25,600	25,650	0	864	2,030	0	1,183	2,451
25,650	25,700	0	856	2,019	0	1,175	2,440
25,700	25,750	0	848	2,009	0	1,167	2,430
25,750	25,800	0	840	1,998	0	1,159	2,419
25,800	25,850	0	832	1,988	0	1,151	2,409
25,850	25,900	0	824	1,977	0	1,143	2,398
25,900	25,950	0	816	1,967	0	1,135	2,388
25,950	26,000	0	808	1,956	0	1,127	2,377
26,000	26,050	0	800	1,945	0	1,119	2,367
26,050	26,100	0	792	1,935	0	1,111	2,356
26,100	26,150	0	784	1,924	0	1,103	2,346
26,150	26,200	0	776	1,914	0	1,095	2,335
26,200	26,250	0	768	1,903	0	1,087	2,325
26,250	26,300	0	760	1,893	0	1,079	2,314
26,300	26,350	0	752	1,882	0	1,071	2,303
26,350	26,400	0	744	1,872	0	1,063	2,293
26,400	26,450	0	736	1,861	0	1,055	2,282
26,450	26,500	0	728	1,851	0	1,047	2,272
26,500	26,550	0	720	1,840	0	1,039	2,261
26,550	26,600	0	712	1,830	0	1,031	2,251
26,600	26,650	0	704	1,819	0	1,023	2,240
26,650	26,700	0	696	1,809	0	1,015	2,230
26,700	26,750	0	688	1,798	0	1,007	2,219
26,750	26,800	0	680	1,788	0	999	2,209
26,800	26,850	0	672	1,777	0	991	2,198
26,850	26,900	0	664	1,766	0	984	2,188
26,900	26,950	0	656	1,756	0	976	2,177
26,950	27,000	0	648	1,745	0	968	2,167
27,000	27,050	0	640	1,735	0	960	2,156
27,050	27,100	0	632	1,724	0	952	2,146

If the amount you are looking up from the worksheet is—		Single, head of household, or qualifying widow(er) and you have—			Married filing jointly and you have—		
At least	But less than	No children	One child	Two children	No children	One child	Two children
		Your credit is—			Your credit is—		
27,100	27,150	0	624	1,714	0	944	2,135
27,150	27,200	0	616	1,703	0	936	2,124
27,200	27,250	0	608	1,693	0	928	2,114
27,250	27,300	0	600	1,682	0	920	2,103
27,300	27,350	0	592	1,672	0	912	2,093
27,350	27,400	0	584	1,661	0	904	2,082
27,400	27,450	0	576	1,651	0	896	2,072
27,450	27,500	0	568	1,640	0	888	2,061
27,500	27,550	0	560	1,630	0	880	2,051
27,550	27,600	0	552	1,619	0	872	2,040
27,600	27,650	0	544	1,608	0	864	2,030
27,650	27,700	0	536	1,598	0	856	2,019
27,700	27,750	0	528	1,587	0	848	2,009
27,750	27,800	0	520	1,577	0	840	1,998
27,800	27,850	0	512	1,566	0	832	1,988
27,850	27,900	0	504	1,556	0	824	1,977
27,900	27,950	0	496	1,545	0	816	1,967
27,950	28,000	0	488	1,535	0	808	1,956
28,000	28,050	0	480	1,524	0	800	1,945
28,050	28,100	0	472	1,514	0	792	1,935
28,100	28,150	0	464	1,503	0	784	1,924
28,150	28,200	0	456	1,493	0	776	1,914
28,200	28,250	0	448	1,482	0	768	1,903
28,250	28,300	0	440	1,472	0	760	1,893
28,300	28,350	0	432	1,461	0	752	1,882
28,350	28,400	0	424	1,451	0	744	1,872
28,400	28,450	0	416	1,440	0	736	1,861
28,450	28,500	0	408	1,429	0	728	1,851
28,500	28,550	0	400	1,419	0	720	1,840
28,550	28,600	0	392	1,408	0	712	1,830
28,600	28,650	0	384	1,398	0	704	1,819
28,650	28,700	0	376	1,387	0	696	1,809
28,700	28,750	0	368	1,377	0	688	1,798
28,750	28,800	0	360	1,366	0	680	1,788
28,800	28,850	0	352	1,356	0	672	1,777
28,850	28,900	0	344	1,345	0	664	1,766
28,900	28,950	0	336	1,335	0	656	1,756
28,950	29,000	0	328	1,324	0	648	1,745
29,000	29,050	0	320	1,314	0	640	1,735
29,050	29,100	0	312	1,303	0	632	1,724
29,100	29,150	0	304	1,293	0	624	1,714
29,150	29,200	0	296	1,282	0	616	1,703
29,200	29,250	0	288	1,272	0	608	1,693
29,250	29,300	0	280	1,261	0	600	1,682
29,300	29,350	0	272	1,250	0	592	1,672
29,350	29,400	0	264	1,240	0	584	1,661
29,400	29,450	0	256	1,229	0	576	1,651
29,450	29,500	0	248	1,219	0	568	1,640
29,500	29,550	0	240	1,208	0	560	1,630
29,550	29,600	0	232	1,198	0	552	1,619
29,600	29,650	0	224	1,187	0	544	1,608
29,650	29,700	0	216	1,177	0	536	1,598
29,700	29,750	0	208	1,166	0	528	1,587
29,750	29,800	0	200	1,156	0	520	1,577
29,800	29,850	0	192	1,145	0	512	1,566
29,850	29,900	0	185	1,135	0	504	1,556
29,900	29,950	0	177	1,124	0	496	1,545
29,950	30,000	0	169	1,114	0	488	1,535
30,000	30,050	0	161	1,103	0	480	1,524
30,050	30,100	0	153	1,093	0	472	1,514

(Continued on page 57)

2005 Earned Income Credit (EIC) Table—Continued (Caution. This is **not** a tax table.)

If the amount you are looking up from the worksheet is—		Single, head of household, or qualifying widow(er) and you have—			Married filing jointly and you have—		
At least	But less than	No children	One child	Two children	No children	One child	Two children
		Your credit is—			Your credit is—		
30,100	30,150	0	145	1,082	0	464	1,503
30,150	30,200	0	137	1,071	0	456	1,493
30,200	30,250	0	129	1,061	0	448	1,482
30,250	30,300	0	121	1,050	0	440	1,472
30,300	30,350	0	113	1,040	0	432	1,461
30,350	30,400	0	105	1,029	0	424	1,451
30,400	30,450	0	97	1,019	0	416	1,440
30,450	30,500	0	89	1,008	0	408	1,429
30,500	30,550	0	81	998	0	400	1,419
30,550	30,600	0	73	987	0	392	1,408
30,600	30,650	0	65	977	0	384	1,398
30,650	30,700	0	57	966	0	376	1,387
30,700	30,750	0	49	956	0	368	1,377
30,750	30,800	0	41	945	0	360	1,366
30,800	30,850	0	33	935	0	352	1,356
30,850	30,900	0	25	924	0	344	1,345
30,900	30,950	0	17	914	0	336	1,335
30,950	31,000	0	9	903	0	328	1,324
31,000	31,050	0	*	892	0	320	1,314
31,050	31,100	0	0	882	0	312	1,303
31,100	31,150	0	0	871	0	304	1,293
31,150	31,200	0	0	861	0	296	1,282
31,200	31,250	0	0	850	0	288	1,272
31,250	31,300	0	0	840	0	280	1,261
31,300	31,350	0	0	829	0	272	1,250
31,350	31,400	0	0	819	0	264	1,240
31,400	31,450	0	0	808	0	256	1,229
31,450	31,500	0	0	798	0	248	1,219
31,500	31,550	0	0	787	0	240	1,208
31,550	31,600	0	0	777	0	232	1,198
31,600	31,650	0	0	766	0	224	1,187
31,650	31,700	0	0	756	0	216	1,177
31,700	31,750	0	0	745	0	208	1,166
31,750	31,800	0	0	735	0	200	1,156
31,800	31,850	0	0	724	0	192	1,145
31,850	31,900	0	0	713	0	185	1,135
31,900	31,950	0	0	703	0	177	1,124
31,950	32,000	0	0	692	0	169	1,114
32,000	32,050	0	0	682	0	161	1,103
32,050	32,100	0	0	671	0	153	1,093
32,100	32,150	0	0	661	0	145	1,082
32,150	32,200	0	0	650	0	137	1,071
32,200	32,250	0	0	640	0	129	1,061
32,250	32,300	0	0	629	0	121	1,050
32,300	32,350	0	0	619	0	113	1,040
32,350	32,400	0	0	608	0	105	1,029
32,400	32,450	0	0	598	0	97	1,019
32,450	32,500	0	0	587	0	89	1,008
32,500	32,550	0	0	577	0	81	998
32,550	32,600	0	0	566	0	73	987
32,600	32,650	0	0	555	0	65	977
32,650	32,700	0	0	545	0	57	966
32,700	32,750	0	0	534	0	49	956
32,750	32,800	0	0	524	0	41	945
32,800	32,850	0	0	513	0	33	935
32,850	32,900	0	0	503	0	25	924
32,900	32,950	0	0	492	0	17	914
32,950	33,000	0	0	482	0	9	903
33,000	33,050	0	0	471	0	*	892
33,050	33,100	0	0	461	0	0	882

If the amount you are looking up from the worksheet is—		Single, head of household, or qualifying widow(er) and you have—			Married filing jointly and you have—		
At least	But less than	No children	One child	Two children	No children	One child	Two children
		Your credit is—			Your credit is—		
33,100	33,150	0	0	450	0	0	871
33,150	33,200	0	0	440	0	0	861
33,200	33,250	0	0	429	0	0	850
33,250	33,300	0	0	419	0	0	840
33,300	33,350	0	0	408	0	0	829
33,350	33,400	0	0	398	0	0	819
33,400	33,450	0	0	387	0	0	808
33,450	33,500	0	0	376	0	0	798
33,500	33,550	0	0	366	0	0	787
33,550	33,600	0	0	355	0	0	777
33,600	33,650	0	0	345	0	0	766
33,650	33,700	0	0	334	0	0	756
33,700	33,750	0	0	324	0	0	745
33,750	33,800	0	0	313	0	0	735
33,800	33,850	0	0	303	0	0	724
33,850	33,900	0	0	292	0	0	713
33,900	33,950	0	0	282	0	0	703
33,950	34,000	0	0	271	0	0	692
34,000	34,050	0	0	261	0	0	682
34,050	34,100	0	0	250	0	0	671
34,100	34,150	0	0	240	0	0	661
34,150	34,200	0	0	229	0	0	650
34,200	34,250	0	0	219	0	0	640
34,250	34,300	0	0	208	0	0	629
34,300	34,350	0	0	197	0	0	619
34,350	34,400	0	0	187	0	0	608
34,400	34,450	0	0	176	0	0	598
34,450	34,500	0	0	166	0	0	587
34,500	34,550	0	0	155	0	0	577
34,550	34,600	0	0	145	0	0	566
34,600	34,650	0	0	134	0	0	555
34,650	34,700	0	0	124	0	0	545
34,700	34,750	0	0	113	0	0	534
34,750	34,800	0	0	103	0	0	524
34,800	34,850	0	0	92	0	0	513
34,850	34,900	0	0	82	0	0	503
34,900	34,950	0	0	71	0	0	492
34,950	35,000	0	0	61	0	0	482
35,000	35,050	0	0	50	0	0	471
35,050	35,100	0	0	40	0	0	461
35,100	35,150	0	0	29	0	0	450
35,150	35,200	0	0	18	0	0	440
35,200	35,250	0	0	8	0	0	429
35,250	35,300	0	0	**	0	0	419
35,300	35,350	0	0	0	0	0	408
35,350	35,400	0	0	0	0	0	398
35,400	35,450	0	0	0	0	0	387
35,450	35,500	0	0	0	0	0	376
35,500	35,550	0	0	0	0	0	366
35,550	35,600	0	0	0	0	0	355
35,600	35,650	0	0	0	0	0	345
35,650	35,700	0	0	0	0	0	334
35,700	35,750	0	0	0	0	0	324
35,750	35,800	0	0	0	0	0	313
35,800	35,850	0	0	0	0	0	303
35,850	35,900	0	0	0	0	0	292
35,900	35,950	0	0	0	0	0	282
35,950	36,000	0	0	0	0	0	271
36,000	36,050	0	0	0	0	0	261
36,050	36,100	0	0	0	0	0	250

*If the amount you are looking up from the worksheet is at least $31,000 ($33,000 if married filing jointly) but less than $31,030 ($33,030 if married filing jointly), your credit is $2. Otherwise, you cannot take the credit.

**If the amount you are looking up from the worksheet is at least $35,250 but less than $35,263, your credit is $1. Otherwise, you cannot take the credit.

(Continued on page 58)

Need more information or forms? See page 7.

2005 Earned Income Credit (EIC) Table—*Continued*   (**Caution.** This is **not** a tax table.)

If the amount you are looking up from the worksheet is—		And your filing status is—						If the amount you are looking up from the worksheet is—		And your filing status is—					
		Single, head of household, or qualifying widow(er) and you have—			Married filing jointly and you have—					Single, head of household, or qualifying widow(er) and you have—			Married filing jointly and you have—		
		No children	One child	Two children	No children	One child	Two children			No children	One child	Two children	No children	One child	Two children
At least	But less than	Your credit is—			Your credit is—			At least	But less than	Your credit is—			Your credit is—		
36,100	36,150	0	0	0	0	0	240	36,850	36,900	0	0	0	0	0	82
36,150	36,200	0	0	0	0	0	229	36,900	36,950	0	0	0	0	0	71
36,200	36,250	0	0	0	0	0	219	36,950	37,000	0	0	0	0	0	61
36,250	36,300	0	0	0	0	0	208	37,000	37,050	0	0	0	0	0	50
36,300	36,350	0	0	0	0	0	197	37,050	37,100	0	0	0	0	0	40
36,350	36,400	0	0	0	0	0	187	37,100	37,150	0	0	0	0	0	29
36,400	36,450	0	0	0	0	0	176	37,150	37,200	0	0	0	0	0	18
36,450	36,500	0	0	0	0	0	166	37,200	37,250	0	0	0	0	0	8
36,500	36,550	0	0	0	0	0	155	37,250	37,263	0	0	0	0	0	1
36,550	36,600	0	0	0	0	0	145	37,263 or more		0	0	0	0	0	0
36,600	36,650	0	0	0	0	0	134								
36,650	36,700	0	0	0	0	0	124								
36,700	36,750	0	0	0	0	0	113								
36,750	36,800	0	0	0	0	0	103								
36,800	36,850	0	0	0	0	0	92								

Problem 3. Some Problems of Investors

Many Americans are investors in various kinds of assets, either directly or indirectly through retirement plans. The most important investment for many of these investors is, of course, their homes. (You learned about some of the issues concerning ownership of a personal residence in Chapter 4.A. of Part VI.) But, in addition, more and more of us also have a variety of financial assets, ranging from bank savings accounts to extremely sophisticated (and risky) investments.

Many of us are investors in this wide variety of assets indirectly through retirement plans. But, many of us have also ventured into direct investing as well. Indeed, the growth of on-line brokerage firms has attracted many millions of people who previously invested, if at all, only through retirement plans, or, perhaps, through mutual funds managed by professionals. The rapid growth in the types of investment made by taxpayers of many income levels demands some discussion of the tax consequences of at the least some of the various types of investments that have become popular.

The tax consequences of these investments are frequently surprising to the investor and vary depending upon the type of investment. For example, you learned in an earlier part of this book that cash basis taxpayers must report income when they have constructively received the income (even if there has been no actual receipt). Therefore, a cash basis taxpayer who owns a passbook savings account must report the interest income she has earned as of the end of her tax year, even if she has not had her passbook "stamped" to reflect the interest and has not withdrawn it. What about some other types of investment that have become common? Consider the following problems. These problems are not intended to present an exhaustive survey of all types of investments; rather, they are meant to highlight some common types, and by doing so, introduce you to some of the tax consequences that result. By examining these samples, you should be better able to examine closely all the alternative types of investment your client might choose.

---

1. Laurie is an unmarried cash basis taxpayer employed by a company that allows its employees to participate in a tax-deferred retirement plan after completing one year of full-time employment. To participate, the employee agrees to contribute a percentage of her earnings and the employer agrees to contribute an equal amount. The information sheet provided to Laurie by her employer informs her that she may exclude her contribution from her gross income (making her contribution tax-free), and she may also exclude her employer's contribution from her gross income (although the employer's contribution is clearly additional compensation). (You may assume that the plan qualifies for tax deferral pursuant to section 401(k) of the Code.) When, if ever, will Laurie be subject to tax on her contribution, her employer's contribution, and the income earned by these contributions?

---

2. Laurie also wishes to invest on her own. She has arranged with her employer to have $250 (after-tax) withheld from each of her bi-monthly paychecks and deposited in her employer's credit union plan. The credit union pays interest at a modest rate, equal to the rate paid by savings banks in the same community, and her deposits are federally insured. Laurie reports the interest yearly on her income tax return, based on the Form 1099 she receives from the credit union. Is this the proper treatment of the interest?

At the end of each calendar year, Laurie withdraws the balance from her credit union account and invests it in a mutual fund. She has chosen a "no-load" fund because she does not want to pay a commission at the start.[20] What is Laurie's basis in the mutual fund shares?

Unlike her money market account, the value of Laurie's shares in the mutual fund fluctuates daily based on variations in the values of the stocks and bonds owned by the fund. Laurie's mutual fund, like the majority of mutual funds by both number and the value of their assets, is an "open-ended" fund. That means that there is no limit on the number of investors who can become shareholders. As the number of investors increases, the fund managers use the new investments to acquire additional assets for the fund.

As is the case with all open-ended mutual funds, Laurie receives a Form 1099 at the end of each year, reporting her share of the dividends declared by the fund for the year. She does not receive these dividends in cash; rather, she is credited with additional shares in the fund based on the "net asset value" of the fund as of the date the fund declares the dividends. The fund calculates the "net asset value" by subtracting the fund's liabilities from the market values of its assets on that date, and dividing by the number of shares outstanding. Suppose at the end of this tax year, Laurie receives a Form 1099 showing dividends in the amount of $460, entitling her to 23 additional shares in the fund. Does Laurie have income for tax purposes (although she did not receive an actual cash distribution)? What is her basis in the new shares?

---

3. Laurie and her friend, Mary-Elizabeth, decide to start a small business, which they will conduct part-time. An attorney they know, Basil, suggests that they utilize the corporate form in order to avoid personal liability. Basil also suggests to them that they elect to have the stock of the corporation treated as "section 1244" stock. They agree and each invests $10,000 by contributing it to the LT Corp. in exchange for 100% of the corporate stock with a par value of $1 per share. Each receives 10,000 shares. They also elect to operate LT Corp. as an "S" corporation. So, when LT Corp. loses all $20,000, the losses "flow through" to them in the amount of $10,000 each and reduce each of their bases to 0. Suppose they liquidate the corporation. What tax result to each of them?

---

4. Michael is a cash basis, calendar year taxpayer. Michael's assets, other than his personal residence, consist of a money market account and an investment in a mutual fund. Michael owns 1000 shares of the money market fund which he purchased for $1 per share. The value of his shares in the money market fund does not vary and he may redeem at any time, simply by writing a check on the account. So long as he does not withdraw his investment, however, he is entitled to interest at the simple rate of 6%. The financial institution in which he has the account credits his account with interest at the rate of $60 per year (which he may either invest in additional shares of the fund at the rate of $1 per share or withdraw). What tax result? Should the results here be different from the basic rule you learned concerning a passbook savings account?

---

20. No-load funds reward fund managers yearly, or more frequently, through payments based on a percentage of the fund's capital, a percentage of the fund's earnings, or a combination. Front-load funds allow the managers to collect a fee at the time of initial investment, but the ongoing fees may be set at a lower rate than the fees in a no-load fund.

5. Michael also owns shares in a mutual fund. Suppose Michael's original investment in the mutual fund was in the amount of $10,000 and at the time of his investment, the net asset value was $50 per share. He acquired those shares on January 14 four years ago. On December 31 of that year he received a notice of a dividend of $460 that was automatically reinvested in additional shares. At the time of the dividend, the net asset value of the shares of the fund was $46 per share. Therefore, his dividend produced an additional 10 shares of the mutual fund for Michael. On December 31 of the following year he received a notice that the dividends for year 2 equaled $480 and the net asset value on that date was $48 per share. Therefore, his dividend for that year purchased an additional 48 shares for him.

Shortly after receiving the notice of his dividend at the end of the second year, Michael wanted to sell some of his shares. He decided to sell 40 shares of stock. Would it matter to Michael which shares of the fund he sold? Why? If so, is there a procedure that allows him to identify from which group of shares the 40 he sells came?

6. Michael is a senior vice president of a growing, publicly-traded corporation. As part of the inducement offered to him by his employer, Michael was granted "non-qualified" options to purchase 10,000 shares of stock at the price at which the shares were selling on the date Michael joined the company, $9. Were there any tax consequences to Michael as a result of his receipt of the options? **Consult section 83.**

Michael watched the stock price rise and finally decided to exercise 5,000 of his options when the price reached $25 per share. To exercise these options, Michael had to borrow money. He borrowed $25,000 and paid the balance of the "strike" price ($20,000) out of his savings. What tax effect, if any, did Michael's exercise of the options produce?

Suppose that for that tax year, Michael paid $2,500 in interest on the debt he incurred to buy the stock. Can he deduct the interest?

Michael's decision to exercise the options was quite untimely. Indeed, shortly after his exercise, the price of the stock fell precipitously (due to bad corporate news and a turn-around in the general economic outlook for the country). By the time Michael realized that he would have to sell the stock (or some of it) to pay the tax resulting from his exercise, the price of the stock had fallen to $5 per share. (And, he still owed the $25,000 he borrowed to exercise his option on which he paid $2,500 in interest.) What tax advice would you give Michael?

7. Suppose that Michael's employer had granted "incentive stock options" (sometimes called "qualified" options) to him (rather than the non-qualified ones in question 6). What would be the tax consequences to Michael on the issuance of the options? **Consult section 422.** Suppose he later exercised the options at a time when the stock was trading at $25 per share. What tax consequences to him then?

8. Not content with his misfortune in investing in the stock of his own company, Michael decides to subscribe to the Wall Street Journal online and Institutional Investor Magazine at a cost of $59 and $200 respectively. Can he deduct the cost of these subscriptions?

9. Michael decides to "play it safe" by investing in some bonds. He decides that he would like to purchase bonds issued by the Connecticut Higher Education Funding Authority. He has been told that these bonds were issued pursuant to a prospectus that described them as having the full backing of the State of Connecticut and as being free of both federal and Connecticut income tax. If Michael is a resident of Virginia, what tax advice would you give him? If he borrows to purchase these bonds, will he be able to deduct the interest expense he incurs?

Suppose that Michael paid $1,003 for each bond with a redemption price of $1,000. What will be the tax consequence to him when the Connecticut Higher Education Funding Authority redeems its bonds in two years?

Suppose, instead, that Michael purchases 10 "zero coupon" bonds for $820 each, issued by Autopak, Inc., a new corporation that offers franchises similar to Mail Boxes, Inc. The bonds have a face value of $1,000, payable in two years. What will be the tax consequences to Michael during the 24 months that he owns the bonds and at the time of their redemption? (Part V, Chapter 1P, Subtitle A of Title 26, includes some special rules relevant to bonds that you might wish to consult.)

Suppose Autopak is unable to redeem the bonds for $1,000 or to repay Michael his $820. What tax result to Michael?

---

10. Michael also had in his portfolio 1000 shares of Optimum Computer Corp. which he purchased in 1998 for $8 per share. Although the price of the stock had fallen to $3 per share, he still had faith in the long-term prospects for the company. But on December 30, 2000, he decided to sell the stock at $3 per share. What tax result if he did so and then repurchased the stock at $3.25 per share on January 15, 2001?

After repurchasing the stock on January 15, 2001, Michael's expectations proved correct; the price of the stock has risen steadily since that time. By November, 2001, it was selling at $9 per share. He wanted to sell it then, but he thought he would wait until he could claim a long-term capital gain. What is the earliest date on which he could recognize a long-term gain? If he waits until January 16, 2002 and sells it then at a price of $10 per share, what tax result?

Suppose Michael purchases a "put option" that allows him to require some other investor to purchase the 100 shares of the Optimum Computer Corp. stock no later than March 1, 2002, at a price of $12 per share. Michael paid $1.50 per share for the option. Under what circumstances would Michael exercise this option? What would be the tax consequences of his exercise?

---

11. Suppose that Michael decided to retire early. After his retirement, he spent a good part of every day managing his investments. He decided that he needed a special place in his home that he would reserve solely for his investing activities. He spent $1,500 remodeling a small child's room, and $4,500

installing a digital computer line and acquiring a new computer, copier, and fax machine. What tax result?

Suppose that Michael wants to deduct the cost of the new phone line he has installed to serve his office, and a portion of the regular household expenses, e.g., heat, electricity, property taxes. Can he do so? Would your answer be the same if Michael had not retired from his regular employment?

12. Suppose Laurie decides that she wants to start her own business. She has accumulated $330,000 in her mutual fund in which she has a basis of $300,000. What tax result to her if she redeems all her shares in the mutual fund in order to start her business?

13. Suppose Laurie also has accumulated $240,000 in her tax-deferred retirement plan. (Recall that she paid no tax on the contributions she made and no tax on the contributions her employer made to this fund.) She is considering also withdrawing this amount for use in starting her business. What will be the tax consequences to her if she is currently 44 years old?

Problem 4. Some Problems of Debt

Recall the cases of *Crane v. Commissioner* and *Estate of Franklin*. In studying these cases, you began to learn both about basis and about two common types of mortgage loan: recourse and nonrecourse. In reading these cases, you could also see the interaction between the tax and non-tax aspects of the transactions. *Crane* in particular illustrates the necessity for understanding the non-tax consequences of a transaction in order to be able to understand the tax consequences.

For example, one of the frequent motives for using borrowed money is to increase the possible return on investment through the use of what is called "leverage." Investors often borrow because they do not have sufficient capital to make a particular investment without the use of borrowed funds. An investor who does have sufficient capital may, nevertheless, prefer to borrow a portion of her investment in order to maximize the use of her capital for additional projects and to increase the return on the investment. Consider, for example, an investor who wishes to buy a particular government bond with a face value of $1,000 and a coupon rate of 6%. If she invests $1,000 of her capital, her return will be exactly 6%. But if she borrows a portion of the $1,000, her return will be calculated based on her actual investment, the $60 interest paid on the bond, and the cost of her borrowing.

Assume, for example, that she is able to borrow $500 of her $1,000 purchase price at a simple interest rate of 5%. She would then have to invest only $500 of her own funds to purchase the bond. But, at the end of the annual period, she would owe $25 interest to her lender. Subtracting this from her bond interest return of $60, would leave her with a net of $35 on her $500 investment, a return of 7%. So, by borrowing a portion of her investment, she has used leverage to increase her possible return. In fact, when leverage works, the more one borrows, the higher the return on an investment. You might view the transaction as one in which the lender is willing to accept a lower but fixed rate of return on the borrowed money while the borrower earns a return on both her own investment and that of the lender to the extent that she can invest the borrowed funds at a higher rate than the cost of the borrowing.

That is, leverage only produces a favorable result if one can borrow at a lower cost than the return the borrowed funds will produce. Recall *Goldstein*. And that is one of the points at which tax treatment becomes important to the equation. In order to assess the desirability of borrowing, you must compare the possible after-tax return on the borrowed money with the after-tax cost of the borrowing.

Leverage prompts investors in stocks and other securities to use borrowed funds in making investments. It is also an important factor in real estate investments. As you already have learned, the common real estate mortgage, either recourse or nonrecourse, creates a security interest in the real estate for which the borrowing is used. (In addition to the "mortgage" itself, the document that creates the security interest, the borrower will give the lender a promissory note that recites the terms of the loan: the principal amount, interest rate, date payments are due, and so forth.) (Second, or "equity," mortgages are often also this common garden variety of mortgage. The important distinction between a first and a second or equity mortgage being that the first mortgagee has the senior claim to the security. Recall that we examined the relationship between first and second mortgage lenders in the commercial real estate problem.)

But creative lenders and borrowers have invented new and more complex arrangements, some of which may not, at first, appear to be lending transactions at all. For example, consider a landowner who "leases" a piece of property to a developer for a down payment plus an obligation to pay rent (called a "ground lease") for 99 years. Is the transaction really very different from a loan? Suppose the developer has the right to "purchase" the property for a nominal price at the end of the lease term? The lump sum payment and ground rental payments are at least analogous enough to a mortgage to ask some of the same questions as the transaction in *Estate of Franklin* created. Who is the real owner of the property? Is the financial transaction a loan or an installment sale?[21] These questions simply highlight the need for careful detective work to determine the non-tax character of a transaction in order to determine its tax consequences.

With that as background, consider what happens in the case of a taxpayer who loses his home in a foreclosure. As you may know, most home mortgage loans are made with recourse. Therefore, as a theoretical matter at least, if the amount of the loan exceeds either the fair market value of the property (in the case of a strict foreclosure) or the sale price of the property (in the case of a foreclosure sale), the borrower will continue to owe the balance. The lender may continue to attempt to collect the unpaid balance, although it is no longer secured by the property. (In the case of a non-recourse loan, the lender will, of course, no longer be able to attempt to collect any excess of the loan balance over the fair market value or the sale price.[22])

As you learned in Part III, one of the long-standing issues created by loans was the treatment of the no-interest or low-interest loan made between parties who are somehow related. Long before the Code dictated special treatment for these loans, there was almost universal agreement that they represented beneficial transfers. For example, when a parent made an interest-free loan to a child, it was generally assumed that the forgiveness of interest should be characterized as a gift. So too, a no-interest or low-interest loan made by an employer to an employee almost certainly represented additional compensation to the employee.

After years of discussion, Congress added section 7872 to the Code in 1984. This complicated, multi-part provision offers you an opportunity to practice the Code-reading skills you have been developing. While you are working through the problem below, consider the likelihood that the average taxpayer can follow the rules without the aid of a sophisticated tax advisor, and whether it is likely that most taxpayers are aware that some everyday loan transactions might have complex tax repercussions.

Read section 7872 carefully. Note that is covers more than the no-interest and low-interest intrafamily loans that were its genesis. But also note Congress' attempt to carve out safe harbors for some small transactions where the amounts involved are relatively small and do not warrant the complex calculations and reporting application of section 7872 requires.

---

21. *See, Starr's Estate v. Commissioner,* 274 F.2d 294 (9th Cir. 1959); and *Judson Mills v. Commissioner,* 11 T.C. 25 (1948).

22. It is for that reason that some commentators have suggested that the lender is, in effect, in partnership with the borrower in the case of a non-recourse loan; the borrower is at risk up to the amount of his equity; the lender is at risk in an amount equal to the amount, if any, by which the amount of the loan exceeds the value of the property. *See e.g., Commissioner v. Tufts,* 461 U.S. 300, 317 (1983) (O'Connor, concurrence). Even a careful lender might find itself in this situation in an period of falling real estate values.

Titania desires to make an interest-free loan to Morgan. She makes the loan on January 1 of this year. Morgan's only income, other than described below, is a salary of $20,000. You may assume the following facts:

(1) The applicable federal rate is 10%.

(2) The present value of all payments on the $75,000 loan, discounted at the applicable federal rate, is $45,000. The present value of all payments on the $400,000 loan, discounted at the applicable federal rate, is $210,000.

(3) Interest on the $75,000 loan, calculated at the applicable federal rate, accrues at $22 per day. Interest on the $400,000 loan, calculated at the applicable federal rate, accrues at $120 per day.

Describe the income tax consequences to Titania and Morgan, that is, their respective items of income and deduction, gross income, adjusted gross income, and taxable income, in the following hypotheticals:

A. Titania and Morgan are mother and son. The loan is intended as a gift to Morgan.

1. The terms and conditions of the loan are as follow:

a. The loan is in the principal amount of $75,000.

b. It is a term loan payable in equal annual installments of $15,000 beginning December 31 of this year.

c. Morgan uses the money to purchase a gold-plated Jacuzzi.

2. Are your answers any different if the loan, instead of being payable in equal annual installments, is payable on demand, but if no demand is made, on December 31 of year 5?

3. Same facts as in number 2, plus, in the alternative:

a. Morgan has net investment income of $800;

b. Morgan has net investment income of $5,000; and

c. Morgan has net investment income of $10,000.

4. Same facts as number 2 (that is, the loan is a demand loan), except that the loan is in the principal amount of $400,000.

5. Same facts as number 2, except the loan is for $9,000.

B. Instead of Titania being Morgan's mother, it is Titania, Inc. Their relationship is that of employer/employee. The loan is intended as additional compensation to Morgan.

1. The terms and conditions of the loan are as follow:

a. The loan is in the amount of $75,000.

b. It is a term loan payable in equal annual installments of $15,000 beginning December 31 of this year.

c. Morgan uses the money to purchase a gold-plated jacuzzi.

2. Are your answers any different if the loan, instead of being payable in equal annual installments, is payable on demand, but if no demand is made, on December 31 of year 5?

3. Same facts as number 2, except that the loan is in the principal amount of $400,000.

4. Same facts as number 2, except the loan is in the principal amount of $9,000.

5. Is your answer in 4 any different if the corporation was in the 35% bracket and Morgan is in the 28% bracket?

C. Instead of being an employee of Titania, Morgan is the sole shareholder of Titania, Inc. Titania, Inc. makes the loan to Morgan in his capacity as a shareholder.

  1. The terms and conditions of the loan are as follow:

    a. The loan is in the principal amount of $75,000.

    b. It is a term loan payable in equal annual installments of $15,000 beginning December 31 of this year.

    c. Morgan uses the money to purchase a gold-plated jacuzzi.

  2. Are your answers any different if the loan, instead of being payable in equal annual installments, is payable on demand, but if no demand is made, on December 31 of year 5?

Problem 5. Some Problems of Divorce, Separation, and Child Support

When two people seek to dissolve a personal relationship, whether of formal marriage or some other type of commitment, they are often forced to unwind an economic as well as an emotional relationship. All too often, the decisions they will make, at a time of emotional turmoil that generally makes good planning more difficult, will produce federal tax consequences. You have already encountered the rules concerning the tax treatment of alimony and child support payments and the transfer of jointly-owned property. See Part III, Chapter 1.C.

But, as is often the case in the practice of law, you will find that knowing the technical rules is only the foundation on which you will build a plan that must satisfy your client's nonlegal aspirations. So too, as a tax lawyer, the tax rules are merely the foundation to which you must add the non-tax technical rules and, finally, the non-legal considerations. The two problems below will give you an opportunity to review the tax rules you have already learned in realistic planning scenarios. As you go through these problems, try to imagine what besides the "numbers" might be important to each of the parties. Beware, there are no right answers! So, you will not have the satisfaction of flipping to the back and finding out if you were correct. In fact, for fun, we suggest you try these problems with a partner; each of you should represent one of the parties.

I. Mario and Julia are having marital difficulties. They have agreed to seek a divorce. You are provided with the following facts: Mario is 50, in fine health, and has a steady income as an executive of a large enterprise. He currently earns $200,000 a year, and is expected to be gainfully employed for the foreseeable future. (He also has a qualified pension plan with a balance of $550,000, all of which will be taxable when he begins withdrawing it. But, he will not begin receiving distributions until he retires.) Julia, 43, daughter of a sports team owner and a former socialite, has not worked in years, but could get employment as a player scout. Her income would be $20,000 per year. Mario and Julia have two children, Dimitri, born nine years ago, on November 1, and Davara, born four years ago, on April 1. The family lives on a farm in Connecticut.

The parties have agreed that Julia will have custody of the two children. Mario owns the following assets, all of which were purchased nine years ago, except the car, which he bought new last year:

Asset	Basis	FMV
200 shares of Technocrat stock	$ 1,000	$ 300,000
100 shares of Yahoo Motors stock	330,000	51,000
300 acre farm in Connecticut	400,000	1,750,000
Bulletproof Mercedes	94,000	94,000
Cash	180,000	180,000

Mario is willing to pay Julia a total of $30,000 per year for her support and the support of Dimitri and Davara. Mario wants to reduce the amount of support by $5,000 per year when each child reaches the age of 18. Mario and Julia have agreed to split the property equally, based on their agreed upon fair market values.

Advise the parties as to the best method of effectuating the divorce from a tax perspective; specifically, who should get what property, how should the decree for divorce be worded to maximize Mario's deductions, or alternatively, minimize Julia's income, and who should get the personal exemptions for the children.

————————

II. Jonas and Eugenie are contemplating a separation. Jonas has been employed for 7 years as the chief executive of a large enterprise. Although Eugenie has been employed in the past, during the last seven years, she has not been gainfully employed, serving instead as a typical corporate wife: planning their social lives (including entertaining on Jonas's behalf when he is not available), supervising their staff of household employees, and caring for their only child, Ian, a son of 15 who is now away at prep school in California.

Eugenie has informed Jonas that she intends to seek a job in another city at the end of next year. She hopes he will accompany her. But if he is unwilling to do so, she will go without him. Jonas's reply is that he does not know at this time what opportunities he will have at the end of next year. But if she goes without him, he will seek some kind of official separation (he does not "believe in" divorce).

1. Without regard to the division of any property that Jonas and Eugenie may own, advise them on the outlines of the types of arrangements, short of divorce, that are available to them and the tax consequences of each.

————————

A year has passed without a resolution of their dilemma. The time has now arrived for a decision and Jonas has decided to pursue an opportunity in California, close to their son's prep school. (Jonas feels somewhat guilty for not spending more time with the boy over the last eight years and wants to make an effort to repair his relationship with his son before his son graduates from prep school and college and is likely to be involved in building his own career.)

————————

Jonas and Eugenie have the following assets:

Asset	Basis	FMV
Townhouse in the city	$ 150,000	$ 550,000
Furnishings	100,000	100,000
Infiniti Q45 (this year's model)	50,000	40,000
Jonas's 401(k)	-0-	800,000
Eugenie's IRA	-0-	100,000
Zydeco Graphics common stock	25,000	200,000
Webco Internet, Inc. common stock	300,000	10,000

Eugenie's new job will pay her $82,000 per year and she will be entitled to many fringe benefits of her employment. She will, however, have to do a great deal of traveling and may have to maintain a second home in the city in which they now reside. (But the parties agree that they cannot plan on retaining their present residence.) In addition to her salary, Eugenie will be entitled to a travel allowance of $10,000 per year, a clothing allowance of $10,000 per year, medical insurance for herself and any minor children she wishes to cover, a 401(k) plan for which she will be eligible immediately if she agrees to contribute 5% of her base salary (her employer will then contribute 10%), and life insurance in an amount equal to twice her base salary.

2. Which, if any of the benefits will be includible in Eugenie's income?

3. Excluding the availability of a dependency exemption for her son, and assuming she uses the standard deduction and files "married, filing separately," what will be her marginal rate of tax?

4. Although Jonas is unwilling to grant her a divorce, is there any other filing status that might be available to her and if so, will its use change her marginal rate?

Assume that Jonas has agreed to pay Eugenie child support for ten years only in the amount of $20,000 per year. He expects her to use some of this to pay $10,000 of their son's school tuition for as long as he remains a full-time student, (Jonas will pay an equal amount). She must also pay for clothing for Ian, for his travel expenses when he visit her, and for incidental expenses (food, entertainment, etc.) while he is visiting her. (But, she does not have to account to Jonas for the actual use of the support money.) They both expect Ian to finance the balance of his yearly costs through full-time summer and part-time winter employment, loans, and a small trust fund set up by his maternal grandfather some years ago.

Jonas has not, as yet, secured employment, but he is entitled to a pension that will begin paying him $78,000 per year on the first of next year.

5. Advise Jonas on the tax treatment of the yearly payments he will make to Eugenie.

6. Eugenie insists that Jonas's pension plan be used to secure payment to her of the amount Jonas has agreed to pay her for ten years. Will such a guarantee alter the tax treatment of the payments?

7. Could the payments for Ian's support be structured to satisfy the definition of "alimony?" Should the parties do so? In the alternative, can the parties structure the payments so that they are not treated as alimony?

8. Is the dependency exemption available to either parent? If so, who will benefit most from utilizing it? What will happen when Ian reaches the age of 18? Does his decision to enroll in college full-time affect the answer? Suppose when he graduates at age 22, he decides to pursue a graduate degree?

9. Suppose that while they were married, Jonas and Eugenie invested in a land speculation deal in West Virginia. Although a number of years have passed and they had all but forgotten the deal, they have just been informed that they are being audited by the Service for the last year in which their tax return included losses from the deal ("Blackwater Canyon"). The Service is claiming that Jonas and Eugenie owe additional taxes in the amount of $30,000 plus interest and penalties. Assuming the statute of limitations is not available to them as a defense and that Jonas has agreed to assume financial responsibility for any additions to tax (and interest and penalties), can Jonas indemnify Eugenie? What will the lawyers need to include in their separation agreement? Should the same terms be in the decree if they seek a decree of separation from the court?

10. Omitting the assumption contained in question 9, but assuming the parties agree that their current residence will be sold, that Jonas will make yearly payments of $20,000 to Eugenie, and that Ian will live more than 6 months at the residence of either parent, recommend an equitable distribution of their assets. Would your position be different depending upon which spouse you represent?

11. Omitting all assumptions above, what would be the tax treatment to Jonas if he is also entitled to an annuity from an insurance company for which he paid $600,000 on which he had been taxed, if he will receive $75,000 per year for (a) 20 years, or (b) for his remaining life, beginning at age 60?

Problem 6. Some Problems of Law Students[23]

Among the most troublesome problems for students and their families are: (1) the impact of financial aid on a student's individual income tax obligations, (2) the impact of financial aid on the ability of others to claim a student as a dependent, (3) the tax treatment of employer-provided educational benefits to employees and the children of employees, and (4) the availability of the various credits, including the earned income tax credit and the lifetime learning credit. But, these are, by no means, the only tax issues. The following series of problems explores these and many others. Early consideration of them may help parents and children decide, among other important decisions, when to emancipate children, rather than continuing to claim them as dependents, and whether it makes tax sense for a student to accept a low-paying summer job, rather than doing the volunteer work she might prefer.

A surprising number of tax issues are relevant to law students, even to someone who is a full-time law student, certainly to someone who is a part-time law student and is also employed. For example, a full-time student is sometimes entitled to claim the earned income credit? What are the rules and how will the claim by the student affect the parents' tax return (or returns)? When does a part-time student have gross income if his employer reimburses him for the tuition he paid if he attains a certain grade? Suppose a student is an editor of the law review and receives a $1,000 stipend for the work she performs for the law review during the summer. Does she have gross income.

———————

1. Assume that Ling is a full-time student at an accredited law school. The Public Interest Law Project ("PILP")(a qualified 501(c)(3), not-for-profit corporation), awards Ling a $5,000 summer stipend to perform work for a non-profit legal foundation for the summer. In the alternative, she has a job offer from a firm in a distant city. If she accepts the stipend from PILP, she will be able to remain in her current apartment (for which she pays $600 per month rent). If she accepts the law firm job, she will still have to pay her rent for her current apartment; she has a lease that would be difficult to break and she paid the landlord two months security when she signed it. She will also have to pay for an apartment in the new city, and she will have to spend additional amounts on new clothes that would not be necessary if she works at the non-profit. She is certain that she will have to spend a minimum of $1,500 for new clothes. She visited that city (at the expense of the law firm) and could not find an apartment for less than $1,000 per month. But, the firm will pay her $1,000 per week for 8 weeks and will reimburse her for the cost of her plane fare to get to the distant city. Her summer earnings will constitute her only earnings for the year. Help Ling evaluate which opportunity she should accept. **Read sections 74 and 117. Also review the materials concerning "away from home" expenses, section 162 and its regulations, and section 132.**

2. Suppose Ling's earnings for this tax year totaled $12,000. She also received $10,000 from her parents as a gift to help with her law school and living expenses. She borrowed the balance that she needed to pay her tuition of $20,000 and her room, board, and book expenses of $12,000. She did not live with her parents. As a full-time law student, would she qualify for any credits or deductions? **Consult sections 25A and 222.**

———————

23. Of course, these problems are equally shared by non-law and undergraduate students. The focus here, however, is primarily on the tax issues that confront students at the graduate level.

3. Assume that Esteban is an engineer, employed full-time by a defense contractor. His employer pays for his law school courses (provided he attains a grade of "B" or better), and the assigned texts. In his first and second years as a part-time student, Esteban took only required courses. His employer reimbursed him last year for his tuition and his books in the amount of $10,600. Did he have gross income? Did he have any offsetting deductions? **Study sections 74 and 127.**

This year he is taking (as electives) antitrust and patents. If his employer reimburses him for tuition and books in the amount of $3,100 for each of these courses, will he have gross income? If he has income, can he claim offsetting deductions? Or, can he capitalize the costs and amortize them over some period of time? Do any credits apply? **Look at sections 25A, 127, and 132.**

---

4. Tamika is a full-time law student. Her future employer has agreed to pay the cost of her bar review course. Income? If so, does she have an offsetting deduction? **Review section 162 and its regulations.**

---

5. Jeffrey is a full-time, unmarried, first-year law student. He is 24 years old. He lived at home with his parents until the beginning of law school in this fall. He completed college last spring. His total earnings for the year, $3,500, came from working as a life guard for the summer. He now lives in the dormitory at his school. His parents pay the full cost of his tuition, room, board, and books. Can his parents claim him as a dependent? Can he also claim his own personal exemption on this own tax return? Does he have to file a tax return? **Review sections 151, 152, and 6012.**

Jeffrey certainly does not think of himself as part of the "working poor." May he, nevertheless, claim an earned income tax credit? **Consult section 32.**

Suppose Jeffrey is 25 years old. Does that change any of your answers? Would it change any of your answers if Jeffrey used his own savings plus money that he borrowed through his law school to pay his tuition and other expenses?

6. One of Jeffrey's fellow students offers him $1,000 for the excellent outline she hears he has made for contracts. If he accepts, does he have income? Does it change any of your answers to question 4? Does it matter if Jeffrey is 24 or 25?

7. Suppose Jeffrey's girl friend, Calli, offers to trade her civil procedure outline for his contract outline. What result to Jeffrey? What result to Calli? Suppose instead, Calli offers to tutor Jeffrey in civil procedure in exchange for his contracts outline. Again, what result to each?

---

8. Suppose Clive graduated from law school several years ago. He has been working for a public interest law firm where his salary is $45,000. He has been making regular payments of principal and interest on time on his federally guaranteed student loans. Last year he paid $3,600 in interest on the loans. Did he properly deduct the interest expense? **Consult section 221.** (You may assume that his adjusted gross income equals his gross income. And, you may assume that his "modified adjusted gross income" equals his adjusted gross income.)

This year, Clive lost his job. He has been unable to make the payments. He was shocked to learn that the Service was applying his $550 refund from last year's taxes to his unpaid student loan. Does he have a legitimate objection? **Look at section 6402(d).**

9. Suppose that Clive works for a not-for-profit law firm. As a result of his law school's loan forgiveness program, $10,000 of Clive's student loan is forgiven at a time when he is not insolvent. Does he have income? **Recall *Kirby Lumber*.** Would the result change if he were insolvent? **Look at section 108.**

10. Can Clive obtain relief from his law school loans by seeking voluntary bankruptcy? Suppose that in Problem 9, Clive has gross income under section 61(a)(12) as a result of the cancellation of his debt. Can Clive obtain relief from the resulting tax liability by seeking voluntary bankruptcy?

————————

11. Sylvia is a full-time law student. She lives at home with her parents. She has only a part-time job that provides her with a small amount of income (about $1,500 per year), just enough to pay for the insurance on her car and pay for gas. Her parents pay for her tuition and books. She is 23 years old.

For the current school year, her second year of law school, she was awarded a scholarship of $4,000 based on her academic performance in her first year. Her parents have paid the remainder of the cost of her tuition and books from their savings, $22,800 for the year. What are the tax consequences to Sylvia of her scholarship? **Read section 117.**

May her parents claim her as a dependent? **Look again at sections 151 and 152.** Is Sylvia entitled to a life-time learning credit? Are her parents? You may assume that Sylvia's parents have "modified adjusted gross income" of $85,000 and they file a joint return. **Read section 25A.**

Would any of your answers change if Sylvia were 25 years old?

How would your answer be affected, if at all, if Sylvia cashes in $2,000 of mature United States savings bonds for which her grandparents paid $1,200 in 1990? Suppose her grandparents purchased the bonds in 1988? **Study section 135.**

Problem 7. Some Problems Arising from Personal Injuries

One night, while driving home from a party, Renata and her husband, Alexander, were hit from behind by Mohammed. The impact caused Renata, who was driving, to swerve off the road. The impact was so great that her car went through the guardrail and slammed into a tree at the bottom of a ravine. Renata was seriously injured; Alexander suffered damage to his right rotator cuff.

After months in intensive care and rehabilitation, Renata went home from the hospital, although she was still in need of continuing physical therapy. Most of Renata's medical expenses were covered by the excellent group policy her employer made available to her. Her employer's medical insurer paid $38,500 in medical and hospital expenses for Renata. She did not pay the cost of this insurance; rather, her employer paid the full premium of $4,000 per year. Renata did pay $500 of her medical expenses herself from savings.

1. Does Renata have to include the cost of her medical insurance, paid by her employer, in her gross income?

2. How should Renata treat the medical expenses that are paid directly by the medical insurance company to the providers? What about the $500 she paid herself?

———————————

Renata and Alexander had never taken advantage of her ability to add Alexander to the policy if she would agree to pay the cost of the additional coverage. They were young, without much disposable income, and thought that at some point they would acquire an individual major medical plan for Alexander with a high deductible. Therefore, when they learned that Alexander would need surgery to repair a tear in his rotator cuff, they decided to sue the other driver for the deductible portion of Renata's expenses not covered by insurance ($500), her pain and suffering ($1 million), and the cost of Alexander's surgery.

They retained Shannon, an outstanding personal injury attorney in their town. She agreed to represent them for a contingent fee of one-third of their recovery plus expenses.

Shannon drafted the complaint and served Mohammed, who was represented by an attorney for his insurance company.

3. Suppose to avoid litigation, the insurance company offers to settle for $600,000 plus Shannon's expenses (which at that point were minimal) and Renata and Alexander decide to accept. What are the tax consequences to them of the settlement? Is the portion the insurance company pays Shannon directly for her expenses income to Renata? What about the portion that represents the contingency fee?

4. Would your answer be different if, rather than physical injury, the damages settlement was to settle a lawsuit brought by Renata claiming defamation? Consider the following case.

KENSETH v. COMMISSIONER[24]

114 T.C. 399 (2000)

RUWE, *Judge*:(Footnote *) Respondent determined a deficiency of $55,037 in petitioners' 1993 Federal income tax. The sole issue for decision is whether petitioners'

———————————

24. *Aff'd.*, 259 F.3d 881 (7th Cir. 2001).

gross income includes the portion of the settlement proceeds of a Federal age discrimination claim that was paid as the attorney's fees of Eldon R. Kenseth (petitioner) pursuant to a contingent fee agreement.

FINDINGS OF FACT

In a complaint filed with the Wisconsin Department of Industry, Labor, and Human Relations (DILHR) in October 1991, petitioner alleged that on March 27, 1991, APV Crepaco, Inc. (APV), terminated his employment. The complaint also alleged that, at the time of his discharge, petitioner was 45 years old, held the position of master scheduler, was earning $ 33,480 per year, and had been employed by APV for 21 years. It further alleged that, around the time of petitioner's discharge, APV did not terminate younger employees also acting as master schedulers but did terminate other employees over age 40.

Prior to filing the DILHR complaint, petitioner and 16 other former employees of APV (the class) retained the law firm of Fox & Fox, S.C. (Fox & Fox), to seek redress against APV. In July 1991, petitioner executed a contingent fee agreement with Fox & Fox that provided for legal representation in his case against APV. Each member of the class entered into an identical contingent fee agreement with Fox & Fox.

The contingent fee agreement was a form contract prepared and routinely used by Fox & Fox; the client's name was manually typed in, but the names of Fox & Fox and APV had already been included in preparing the form used for all the class members. Fox & Fox would have declined to represent petitioner if he had not entered into the contingent fee agreement and agreed to the attorney's lien provided therein.

The contingent fee agreement provided in relevant part:

FOX & FOX, S.C.

CONTINGENT FEE AGREEMENT: (Case involving Statutory Fees)

. . .

II. CLIENT TO PAY LITIGATION EXPENSES

The client will pay all expenses incurred in connection with the case, including charges for transcripts, witness fees, mileage, service of process, filing fees, long distance telephone calls, reproduction costs, investigation fees, expert witness fees and all other expenses and out-of-pocket disbursements for these expenses according to the billing policies and procedures of FOX & FOX, S.C. The client agrees to make payments against these bills in accordance with the firm's billing policies.

III. THE ATTORNEYS' FEES WHERE THERE IS NO SEPARATE PAYMENT OF ATTORNEYS' FEES

In the event that there is recovered in the case a single sum of money or property including a job that can be valued in monetary advantage to the client, either by settlement or by litigation, the attorneys' fees shall be the greater of:

A. A reasonable attorney's fee in a contingent case, which shall be defined as the attorneys' fees computed at their regular hourly rates, plus accrued interest at their regular rate, plus a risk enhancer of 100% of the regular hourly rates (but in no event greater than the total recovery), or:

B. A contingency fee, which shall be defined as:

Forty percent (40%) of the recovery if it is recovered before any appeal is taken;

Forty-Six percent (46%) of the recovery if it is recovered after an appeal is taken.

Any settlement offer of a fixed sum which includes a division proposed by the offeror between damages and attorneys' fees shall be treated by the client and the attorneys as an offer of a single sum of money and, if accepted, shall be treated as the recovery of a single sum of money to be apportioned between the client and the attorneys according to this section. Any division of such an offer into damages and attorneys' fees shall be completely disregarded by the client and the attorneys.

...

VI. CLIENT NOT TO SETTLE WITHOUT ATTORNEYS' CONSENT

The client will not compromise or settle the case without the written consent of the attorneys. The client agrees not to waive the right to attorneys' fees as part of a settlement unless the client has reached an agreement with the attorney for an alternative method of payment that would compensate the attorneys in accordance with Section III of this agreement.

VII. WIN OR LOSE RETAINER

The client agrees to pay a Five Hundred ($500.00) Dollar win or lose retainer. This amount will be credited to the attorney fees set forth in Section III in the event a recovery is made. If no recovery is made, this amount is non-refundable to the client.

VIII. LIEN

The client agrees that the attorney shall have a lien against any damages, proceeds, costs and fees recovered in the client's action for the fees and costs due the attorney under this agreement and said lien shall be satisfied before or concurrent with the dispersal of any such proceeds and fees.

IX. CHANGE OF ATTORNEY

In the event the client chooses to terminate the contract for legal services with Fox & Fox, S.C., said firm will have a lien upon any recovery eventually obtained. Said lien will be for the fees set forth in Section III of this agreement.

In the event the client chooses to terminate the contract for legal services with Fox & Fox, S.C., the client will further make immediate payment of all outstanding costs and disbursements to the firm of Fox & Fox, S.C. and will do so within ten (10) days of the termination of the contract.

In entering into this contract Fox & Fox, S.C. has relied on the factual representations made to the firm by the client. In the event such representations are intentionally false, Fox & Fox, S.C. reserves the right to unilaterally terminate this agreement and to charge the client for services to the date of termination rendered on an hourly basis plus all costs dispersed and said amount shall be due within ten (10) days of termination.

At the time of entering into the contingent fee agreement, petitioner had paid only the $500 "win or lose" retainer to Fox & Fox. This amount was to be credited against the contingent fee that would be payable if there should be a recovery on the claim; if there should be no recovery, this amount was nonrefundable. Under section II of the agreement, petitioner expressly agreed to reimburse Fox & Fox for out-of-pocket expenses, in accordance with the firm's normal billing policies and procedures. In contrast, under section III of the agreement (which set forth the contingent fee agreement), petitioner did not expressly agree to pay anything. Instead, section III provided how the amount of the contingent fee was to be calculated if there should be a recovery. Other sections of the agreement summarized below provided for the attorney's lien.

The contingent fee agreement required aggregation of the elements of any settlement offer divided between damages and attorney's fees and provided that any division of such an offer into damages and attorney's fees would be disregarded by Fox & Fox and petitioner. The contingent fee agreement provided that petitioner could not settle his case against APV without the consent of Fox & Fox. Under the contingent fee agreement, petitioner agreed that Fox & Fox "shall have a lien" for its fees and costs against any recovery in petitioner's action against APV. This lien by its terms was to be satisfied before or concurrently with the disbursement of the recovery. The contingent fee agreement further provided that, if petitioner should terminate his representation by Fox & Fox, the firm would have a lien for the fees set forth in section III of the agreement, and all costs and disbursements that had been expended by Fox & Fox would become due and payable by petitioner within 10 days of his termination of his representation by Fox & Fox.

. . .

. . . The total settlement that Fox & Fox negotiated on behalf of the claimants amounted to $2,650,000, which was apportioned as follows pursuant to the contingent fee agreements:

Total recovery to class members $1,590,000
Total fee to Fox & Fox 1,060,000

Total settlement 2,650,000

On February 15, 1993, the dispute between petitioner and APV was resolved by their execution of a "Settlement Agreement and Full and Final Release of Claims" (settlement agreement). Each member of the class entered into an identical settlement agreement. The entire amount received by the members of the class under their settlement agreements represented a recovery under ADEA. However, the settlement agreements required petitioner and the other members of the class to relinquish all their claims against APV, including claims for attorney's fees and expenses but did not specifically allocate any amount of the recovery to attorney's fees. . . .

Petitioner's allocated share of the gross settlement amount of $2,650,000 was $229,501.37. Of this amount, $32,476.61 was paid as lost wages by an APV check issued directly to petitioner. APV withheld applicable Federal and State employment taxes from this portion of the settlement; the actual net amount of the check to the order of petitioner was $21,246.20.

The portion of the settlement proceeds allocated to petitioner and not designated as lost wages was $197,024.76. . . . APV issued a check for this amount directly to the Fox & Fox trust account. Fox & Fox calculated its fee, pursuant to the contingent fee agreement, using 40 percent of the gross settlement amount of $229,501.37 allocated to petitioner. After deducting its fee of $91,800.54 and crediting petitioner with the $500 "win or lose" retainer payment, Fox & Fox issued a check for $105,724.22 from the Fox & Fox trust account to petitioner.

. . .

Petitioner and the other members of the class relied on the guidance and expertise of Fox & Fox in . . . seeking redress against APV. . . . Fox & Fox made all strategic and tactical decisions in the management and pursuit of the age discrimination claims of petitioner and the other class members against APV that led to the settlement agreement and the recovery from APV.

Fox & Fox was aware of the relationship between any gross settlement amount and the resulting fee that Fox & Fox would receive. In the effort to ensure that the amounts ultimately received by petitioner and the other class members would approximate the full value of their claims, Fox & Fox factored in an amount for the attorney's fee portion of the settlement in preparing for and conducting their negotiations with APV and its attorneys.

...

OPINION

Petitioners concede that the proceeds from the settlement are includable in gross income except for the portion of the settlement used to pay Fox & Fox under the contingent fee agreement. Specifically, petitioners argue that they exercised insufficient control over the settlement proceeds used to pay

Fox & Fox and should, therefore, not be taxed on amounts to which they had no "legal" right and could not, and did not, receive. Conversely, respondent argues that (1) the amount petitioners paid or incurred as attorney's fees must be included in petitioners' gross income and (2) the contingent fee is deductible as a miscellaneous itemized deduction, subject to the 2-percent floor under section 67 and the overall limitation under section 68 and also nondeductible in computing the alternative minimum tax (AMT) under section 56.

This controversy is driven by the substantial difference in the amount of tax burden that may result from the parties' approaches. (Footnote 3) The difference, of course, is a consequence of the plain language of sections 56, 67, and 68, so the characterization of the attorney's fees as excludable or deductible becomes critical. There have been attempts to provide relief from the resulting tax burden by creative approaches, including attempts to modify longstanding tax principles. This Court believes that it is Congress' imposition of the AMT and limitations on personal itemized deductions that cause the tax burden here. We perceive dangers in the ad hoc modification of established tax law principles or doctrines to counteract hardship in specific cases.... Despite this potential for unfairness, however, these policy issues are in the province of Congress, and we are not authorized to rewrite the statute....

There is a split of authority among the Federal Courts of Appeals on this issue. The U.S. Court of Appeals for the Fifth Circuit reversed this Court and held that amounts awarded in Alabama litigation that were assigned and paid directly to cover attorney's fees pursuant to a contingent fee agreement are excludable from gross income. See *Cotnam v. Commissioner*, 263 F.2d 119 (5th Cir. 1959), affg. in part and revg. in part 28 T.C. 947 (1957). In *Cotnam*, the taxpayer entered into a contingent fee agreement to pay her attorney 40 percent of any amount recovered on a claim prosecuted for the taxpayer's behalf. A judgment was obtained on the claim, and a check in the amount of the judgment was made jointly payable to the taxpayer and her attorney. The attorney retained his share of the proceeds and remitted the balance to the taxpayer. The Commissioner treated the total amount of the judgment as includable in the taxpayer's gross income and allowed the attorney's fees as an itemized deduction. This Court agreed with the Commissioner, holding that the taxpayer realized income in the full amount of the judgment, even though the attorney received 40 percent in accordance with the contingent fee agreement.

... The U.S. Court of Appeals for the Fifth Circuit's reversal was based on two legal grounds. An opinion by Judge Wisdom on behalf of the panel reasoned that, under the

Alabama attorney lien statute, an attorney has an equitable assignment or lien enabling the attorney to hold an equity interest in the cause of action to the extent of the contracted for fee. See 263 F.2d at 125. Under the Alabama statute, attorneys had the same right to enforce their lien as clients have or had for the amount due the clients. See *id*.

The other judges in *Cotnam*, Rives and Brown, in a separate opinion, stated that the claim involved was far from being perfected and that it was the attorney's efforts that perfected or converted the claim into a judgment. Judge Wisdom, in the second of his opinions, dissented, reasoning that the taxpayer had a right to the already-earned income and that it could not be assigned to the attorneys without tax consequence to the assignor. The *Cotnam* holding with respect to the Alabama attorney lien statutes has been distinguished by this Court from cases interpreting the statutes of numerous other states. Significantly, this Court has, for nearly 40 years, not followed *Cotnam* with respect to the analysis in the opinion of Judges Rives and Brown that the attorney's fee came within an exception to the assignment of income doctrine....

Addressing the assignment of income question in similar circumstances, the U.S. Court of Appeals for the Federal Circuit reached a result opposite from that reached in *Cotnam*. See *Baylin v. United States*, 43 F.3d 1451, 1454–1455 (Fed. Cir. 1995). In *Baylin*, a tax matters partner entered into a contingent fee agreement with the partnership's attorney in a condemnation proceeding. When the litigants entered into a settlement, the attorney received his one-third contingency fee directly from the court in accordance with the fee agreement....

[T]he taxpayer argued that the portion of the recovery used to pay attorney's fees was never a part of the partnership's gross income and should be excluded from gross income. The Federal Circuit, rejecting the taxpayer's argument, held that even though the partnership did not take possession of the funds that were paid to the attorney, it "received the benefit of those funds in that the funds served to discharge the obligation of the partnership owing to the attorney as a result of the attorney's efforts to increase the settlement amount." *Id*. at 1454. The Court of Appeals for the Federal Circuit sought to prohibit taxpayers in contingency fee cases from avoiding Federal income tax with "skillfully devised" fee agreements. See *id*.

. . .

In a recent holding, the U.S. Court of Appeals for the Sixth Circuit reached a result based on similar reasoning to that used in *Cotnam*. See *Estate of Clarks v. United States*, 202 F.3d 854 (6th Cir. 2000). In Estate of Clarks, after a jury awarded the taxpayer personal injury damages and interest, the judgment debtor paid the taxpayer's lawyer the amount called for in the contingent fee agreement. Because the portion of the attorney's fee that was attributable to the recovery of taxable interest was paid directly to the attorney, the taxpayer excluded that amount from gross income on the estate's Federal income tax return. The Commissioner determined that the portion of the attorney's fees attributable to interest was deductible as a miscellaneous itemized deduction and was not excludable from gross income....

. . .

The U.S. Court of Appeals for the Sixth Circuit ... employ[ed] reasoning similar to that used in *Cotnam*. The Court of Appeals held that, under Michigan law, the taxpayer's contingent fee agreement with the lawyer operated as a lien on the portion of the judgment to be recovered and transferred ownership of that portion of the judgment to the attorney. The court seemed to place greater emphasis on the fact that the taxpayer's claim was speculative and dependent upon the services of counsel when it was assigned.

In that respect, the court held that the assignment was no different from a joint venture between the taxpayer and the attorney. The court explained that this case was distinguishable from other assignment of income cases in that there was "no vested interest, only a hope to receive money from the lawyer's efforts and the client's right, a right yet to be determined by judge and jury." *Id.* at 857. The court stated:

> Here the client as assignor has transferred some of the trees in his orchard, not merely the fruit from the trees. The lawyer has become a tenant in common of the orchard owner and must cultivate and care for and harvest the fruit of the entire tract. Here the lawyer's income is the result of his own personal skill and judgment, not the skill or largess of a family member who wants to split his income to avoid taxation. The income should be charged to the one who earned it and received it, not as under the government's theory of the case, to one who neither received it nor earned it.... [*Id.* at 858.]

This Court has, for an extended period of time, held the view that taxable recoveries in lawsuits are gross income in their entirety to the party-client and that associated legal fees—contingent or otherwise—are to be treated as deductions. (Footnote 5) See ... *O'Brien v. Commissioner*, 38 T.C. 707, 712 (1962), aff'd. per curiam 319 F.2d 532 (3d Cir. 1963).... In *O'Brien*, we held that "even if the taxpayer had made an irrevocable assignment of a portion of his future recovery to his attorney to such an extent that he never thereafter became entitled thereto even for a split second, it would still be gross income to him under" assignment of income principles. *O'Brien v. Commissioner, supra* at 712. "Although there may be considerable equity to the taxpayer's position, that is not the way the statute is written." *Id.* at 710. In reaching this conclusion, we rejected the distinction made in *Cotnam v. Commissioner, supra*, with respect to the Alabama attorney's lien statute, stating that it is "doubtful that the Internal Revenue Code was intended to turn upon such refinements." *O'Brien v. Commissioner, supra* at 712. Numerous decisions of this Court have reached the same result as *O'Brien* by distinguishing other States' attorney's lien statutes from the Alabama statute considered in *Cotnam*....

After further reflection on *Cotnam* and now *Estate of Clarks v. United States, supra*, we continue to adhere to our holding in O'Brien that contingent fee agreements, such as the one we consider here, come within the ambit of the assignment of income doctrine and do not serve, for purposes of Federal taxation, to exclude the fee from the assignor's gross income. We also decline to decide this case based on the possible effect of various States' attorney's lien statutes. (Footnote 6)

Section 61(a) provides that "gross income means all income from whatever source derived," and typically, all gains are taxed unless specifically excluded. See *James v. United States*, 366 U.S. 213, 219 ... (1961). We can identify no specific exclusion from gross income for the payment made to Fox & Fox. While it is true that petitioner did not physically receive the portion of the settlement proceeds used to pay the attorney's fees, he did receive the full benefit of those funds in the form of payment for the services required to obtain the settlement. At the time that petitioner entered into the contingent fee agreement, he had already been discriminated against in the form of his wrongful termination from employment. In other words, petitioner was owed damages, and the attorney was willing to enter into a contingent fee agreement to recover the damages owed to petitioner. Therefore, petitioner must recognize as income the amount of the judgment.

In coming to this conclusion, we reject the significance placed by the U.S. Court of Appeals for the Sixth Circuit on the speculative nature of the claim and/or that the claim was dependent upon the assistance of counsel. Despite characterizing petitioner's right to recovery as speculative, his cause of action had value in the very beginning; otherwise, it is unlikely that Fox & Fox would have agreed to represent petitioner on a contingent basis. We find no meaningful distinction in the fact that the assistance of counsel was necessary to pursue the claim. Attorney's fees, contingent or otherwise, are merely a cost of litigation in pursuing a client's personal rights. Attorneys represent the interests of clients in a fiduciary capacity. It is difficult, in theory or fact, to convert that relationship into a joint venture or partnership. The entire ADEA award was "earned" by and owed to petitioner, and his attorney merely provided a service and assisted in realizing the value already inherent in the cause of action.

An anticipatory assignment of the proceeds of a cause of action does not allow a taxpayer to avoid the inclusion of income for the amount assigned. A taxpayer who enters into an agreement for the rendering of services that assists in the recovery from a third party must include the amount recovered (compensation) in gross income, irrespective of whether it is received by the taxpayer.... This Court, relying on Lucas v. Earl, 281 U.S. 111 ... (1930), has consistently held that a taxpayer cannot avoid taxation on his income by an anticipatory assignment of that income to another. See *id.* Thus, any anticipatory assignment by the taxpayer of the proceeds of the lawsuit must be included in the taxpayer's gross income.

We reject petitioner's contention that he had insufficient control over his cause of action to be taxable on a recovery of a portion of the settlement proceeds that was diverted to or paid to Fox & Fox under the contingent fee agreement. There is no evidence supporting petitioner's contention that he had no control over his claim. In Wisconsin, a lawyer cannot acquire a proprietary interest that would enable the attorney to continue to press a cause of action despite the client's wish to settle. Indeed, the Supreme Court of Wisconsin has stated that "The claim belongs to the client and not the attorney, the client has the right to compromise or even abandon his claim if he sees fit to do so." *Goldman v. Home Mut. Ins. Co.*, 22 Wis. 2d 334, 341 ... (1964).

Likewise, petitioner has not waived his right to settle his claim at any time, and it would be an ethical violation for his attorney to press forward with such a case against the will of the client. Wisconsin Supreme Court rule 20:1.2(a) provides:

> A lawyer shall abide by a client's decisions concerning the objectives of representation, ... and shall consult with the client as to the means by which they are to be pursued. A lawyer shall inform a client of all offers of settlement and abide by a client's decision whether to accept an offer of settlement of a matter. * * *

Although petitioner may have entrusted Fox & Fox with the details of his litigation, ultimate control was not relinquished. If petitioner wanted to proceed without Fox & Fox, he could have obtained new representation.

The assignment of income doctrine was originated by the Supreme Court and has evolved over the past 70 years. See *Helvering v. Eubank*, 311 U.S. 122 ... (1940); *Helvering v. Horst*, 311 U.S. 112 ... (1940); *Lucas v. Earl, supra.* Although legislation may result in anomalous or inequitable results with respect to particular taxpayers, we are not in a position to address those policy questions. So, for example, if the AMT computation effectively renders de minimis a taxpayer's recovery due to the nondeductibility of the attorney's fees, we should not be tempted to modify established assignment of income principles to remedy the situation. That could result in a certain class of taxpayer's (those who receive reportable income from judgments) being treated differently from all other taxpayers who are subject to the AMT. These are matters within Congress' authority to decide. Congress, not the Courts, is the final arbiter of how the tax burden is to be borne by taxpayers.

Even if we were willing to follow the *Cotnam* and/or *Estate of Clarks* "attorney's lien" rationale, our analysis of the Wisconsin statutes and case law would not result in excluding the attorney's fee from petitioners' gross income here. In *Cotnam*, the Alabama statute provided that "attorneys at law shall have the same right and power over said suits, judgments and decrees, to enforce their liens, as their clients had or may have for the amount due thereon to them." ... The relevant Wisconsin statute does not recognize the same right and power in favor of attorneys that was identified in the Alabama attorney's lien statute. The Wisconsin statute provides:

> Any person having or claiming a right of action, sounding in tort or for unliquidated damages on contract, may contract with any attorney to prosecute the action and give the attorney a lien upon the cause of action and upon the proceeds or damages derived in any action brought for the enforcement of the cause of action, as security for fees in the conduct of the litigation; when such agreement is made and notice thereof given to the opposite party or his or her attorney, no settlement or adjustment of the action may be valid as against the lien so created, provided the agreement for fees is fair and reasonable. This section shall not be construed as changing the law in respect to champertous contracts. [Wis. Stat. Ann. sec. 757.36 (West 1981).]

This statute provides for an attorney's lien upon the cause of action or upon the proceeds or damages from such cause of action to secure compensation, but it does not give attorneys the same rights as their clients over the proceeds of suits, judgments, and decrees. Accordingly, the Wisconsin statute contains obvious differences and is distinguishable from the Alabama statute.

...

We conclude that petitioner's award, undiminished by the amount that he paid to Fox & Fox, is includable in his 1993 gross income. The amount paid to Fox & Fox is deductible subject to certain statutory limitations as determined by respondent....

Reviewed by the Court.

...

FOOTNOTES:

* This case was reassigned to Judge Robert P. Ruwe by order of the Chief Judge.

3. Under respondent's position in this case, the settlement proceeds are included in petitioners' gross income in full, but the itemized deduction is subject to limitations and is not available in computing the alternative minimum tax (AMT). Under these circumstances, it is possible that the attorney's fees and tax burden could consume a substantial portion (possibly all) of the damages received by a taxpayer. It is noted, however, that if the recovery or income was received in a trade or business setting, the attorney's fees may be fully deductible in arriving at adjusted gross income, thereby obviating the perceived unfairness that may be occasioned in the circumstances we consider in this case. Commentators and courts have long observed this potential for unfairness in the operation of the AMT in this and other areas of adjustments and tax preference items. See, e.g., "State Bar of California tax section, Partial Deduction of Attorneys' Fees Proposed for computing AMT", 1999 TNT 125-45 (June 30, 1999); Wood, "The Plight of the Plaintiff: The Tax Treatment of Legal fees", 98 TNT 220-101 (Nov. 16, 1998).

BEGHE, J., dissenting: As presiding judge at the trial of this case, my disagreement with the majority is neither

a dispute about evidentiary facts nor a doctrinal dispute as such. What divides me from the majority—notwithstanding the majority have adopted my proposed factual findings pretty much verbatim—is a disagreement about the significance of those facts. In my view, those facts do not call for application of the assignment of income doctrine.

...

FINDINGS AND RESULTING INFERENCES

I would find the ultimate fact that the elements of control over the prosecution of the ADEA claims ceded by Mr. Kenseth and assumed and exercised by Fox & Fox under the contingent fee agreement make it reasonable to include in petitioners' gross income only Mr. Kenseth's net share of the settlement proceeds, $138,201. This means that, in computing Mr. Kenseth's gross income from the settlement, his share of the proceeds should be offset by the $91,800 portion of Fox & Fox's $ 1,060,000 contingent fee that reduced his share of such proceeds, *not* by including $229,501 in his gross income and treating his share of the fee as an itemized deduction, subject to the alternative minimum tax (AMT).

The following evidentiary facts and inferences therefrom support this ultimate finding.

The contingent fee agreement was a standardized form contract prepared by Fox & Fox. Fox & Fox would have declined to represent Mr. Kenseth if he had not entered into the contingent fee agreement and agreed to the attorney's lien provided therein.

Mr. Kenseth and the 16 other members of the class had a common grievance arising from APV's terminations of their employment. That grievance impelled them to retain the same law firm to advise them and prosecute their claims for redress. Once that law firm had entered an identical contingent fee agreement with each claimant, there was a substantial additional practical impediment—as compared with a sole plaintiff who enters into a contingent fee agreement—to Mr. Kenseth or any other class member firing Fox & Fox and hiring other attorneys....

In contrast to the unconditional personal liability Mr. Kenseth assumed to pay his share of out-of-pocket expenses, he did not agree to pay a fee, only to the modes of computation and payment of the contingent fee to which Fox & Fox would be entitled from the proceeds of any recovery. If there had been no recovery, Fox & Fox would have received nothing.

The contingent fee agreement required aggregation of the elements of any settlement offer divided between damages and attorney's fees and provided that any division of such an offer into damages and attorney's fees would be disregarded by Fox & Fox and Mr. Kenseth. This means that, if either the defendant's settlement offer or the court's decision had provided for a separate award of attorney's fees, the award of attorney's fees and the damages would have been grossed up to determine the fee that Fox & Fox would be entitled to under the terms of the contingent fee agreement.

The contingent fee agreement provided that Mr. Kenseth could not settle his case against APV without the consent of Fox & Fox. Under Section VIII of the contingent fee agreement, Mr. Kenseth agreed that Fox & Fox "shall have a lien" for its fees and costs against any recovery in Mr. Kenseth's action against APV. This lien by its terms was to be satisfied before or concurrently with the disbursement of the recovery. The contingent fee agreement further provided that if Mr. Kenseth should terminate his representation by Fox & Fox, the firm would have a lien for the fees set forth in Section III of the agreement, and all out-of-pocket expenses that had been disbursed by Fox & Fox would become due and payable by Mr. Kenseth within 10 days of his termination of Fox & Fox as his attorneys.

Mr. Kenseth and the other members of the class relied on the guidance and expertise of Fox & Fox in signing the separation agreement tendered to them by APV and then seeking redress against APV.... Fox & Fox made all strategic and tactical decisions in the management and pursuit of the age discrimination claims of Mr. Kenseth and the other class members against APV.

Fox & Fox was well aware of the relationship between any gross settlement amount and the resulting fee that Fox & Fox would be entitled to. In preparing for and conducting negotiations with APV and its attorneys, Fox & Fox tried to ensure that the amounts actually received by Mr. Kenseth and the other class members would approximate the full value of their claims. Fox & Fox did this by including in their demands on behalf of the claimants an amount for attorney's fees that would be included in and paid out of the settlement proceeds.

The bulk of the settlement proceeds was paid by APV directly to the Fox & Fox trust account, by prearrangement between APV and Fox & Fox. From the gross amount so paid, Fox & Fox paid itself its agreed upon contingent fee of $1,060,000 and computed and apportioned the remaining amount for distribution to Mr. Kenseth and the other class members.

Discussion

My task is to persuade the reader that the governing law permits—indeed compels—the ultimate finding that Mr. Kenseth did not retain enough control over his claim to justify including in his gross income any part of the contingent fee paid to his attorneys.

1. *Issue Is Ripe for Reexamination*

My dissatisfaction with the results of recent cases, antedating publication of *Estate of Clarks* ... impelled me to ride the case at hand as the vehicle to reexamine the Tax Court's treatment of

contingent fees paid to obtain taxable recoveries. Although this case is not the most egregious recent example, the mechanical interplay of the itemized deduction rules with the AMT can result—in cases in which the contingent fee exceeds 50 percent of the recovery—in an overall effective rate of Federal income tax and AMT on the net recovery exceeding 50 percent; in cases in which the aggregate fees exceed 72–73 percent of the recovery, the tax can exceed the net recovery, resulting in an overall effective rate of tax that exceeds 100 percent of the net recovery.

Even if *Estate of Clarks* ... had not recently been decided in the taxpayer's favor by the Court of Appeals for the Sixth Circuit, it would be appropriate to revisit this issue. That Congress has not yet responded to comments that the itemized deduction and AMT provisions are working in unanticipated and inappropriate ways that support revision or repeal does not mean that courts are powerless to step in on a case-by-case basis....

[T]he assignment of income doctrine ... is judge-made law, not a rule of statutory interpretation of the more recently enacted itemized deduction and AMT provisions. Contrary to the claims of the majority ... we need not wait for Congress to change those provisions. We're dealing with a problem under the common law of taxation;

what the courts have created and applied, courts can interpret, refine, and distinguish to determine whether in changed circumstances the conditions for application of the doctrine have been satisfied.

...

4. Cotnam and Estate of Clarks

The inquiry continues with a review of the opinion[] of the Court of Appeals for the Fifth Circuit in *Cotnam v. Commissioner*.... The handling of the matter by the Court of Appeals discloses both a narrow ground and a broader ground for its decision. The numerous occasions we have distinguished *Cotnam* on the narrow ground have obscured the broader ground and contributed to our failure to grapple with the issue in a broad-gauged, principled way under the Federal common law of taxation as adopted by the Supreme Court....

...

... On the ... question, whether the contingent legal fee was excluded from the ... [taxpayer's income], Judge Wisdom, writing for the panel, made clear that he disagreed with the outcome in the taxpayer's favor, stating as follows:

> A majority of the Court, Judges Rives and Brown, hold that the $50,365.83 paid Mrs. Cotnam's attorneys should not be included in her gross income. This sum as income to the attorneys but not to Mrs. Cotnam.

> * * * * * * *

> The facts in this unusual case, taken with the Alabama statute, put the taxpayer in a position where she did not realize income as to her attorneys' interests of 40% in her cause of action and judgement.

[*Cotnam v. Commissioner*, 263 F.2d at 125.]

This is the narrow holding of the Court of Appeals' decision in *Cotman* discussed below in subpart i.

There then followed a statement of the broad ground of the panel's decision, introduced by the following statement: "Judges RIVES and BROWN add to the foregoing, the following", 263 F.2d at 125, and concluding: "Accordingly, the attorneys' fee of $50,365.83 should not have been included in the taxpayer's gross income", 263 F.2d at 126. Then came the dissenting opinion of Judge Wisdom, who had written the opinion for the panel embodying the narrow holding. The disagreement [in Cotnam] between the additional statement of Judges Rives and Brown and Judge Wisdom's dissent is a disagreement about the application of traditional assignment of income principles. The broader holding, which, the majority and I agree, frames the issue on which the case at hand and other contingent fee cases should be decided as discussed in subpart ii. Of course, the majority agree with Judge Wisdom and I agree with Judges Rives and Brown.

...

i. Narrow Ground — Significance of State Law

In deciding *Cotnam v. Commissioner, supra*, the majority of the Court of Appeals, in the portion of the panel's opinion written by Judge Wisdom (hereinafter majority opinion), relied heavily on two unusual characteristics of attorney's liens under Alabama law. The majority opinion noted that the Alabama attorney's lien statute gave an attorney *an interest in the client's suit or cause of action,* as well as the usual security interest in any judgment or settlement the client might eventually win or receive....

When we have not followed *Cotnam*, we have usually relied on differences between the attorney's lien law for the State in issue and Alabama law....

Wisconsin law governed the attorney-client relationship between Fox & Fox and Mr. Kenseth. Wisconsin law arguably gives attorneys the two unusual interests in their clients' lawsuits relied on by the majority opinion in *Cotnam v. Commissioner*....

...

ii *Broader Ground—Federal Standard*

The primary point made by Judges Rives and Brown was that in a practical sense the taxpayer never had control over the portion of the recovery that was retained by her attorneys. In my view, this broader ground disposes of the case at hand in petitioners' favor, independently of the narrow ground.

Judge Wisdom's dissent was very much in the vein that the transaction was governed by the classic assignment of income cases that he cited and relied upon: *Helvering v. Eubank*; ... *Helvering v. Horst*; ... and *Lucas v. Earl*.... After quoting at length from Helvering v. Horst, supra, Judge Wisdom concluded:

> This case is stronger than Horst or Eubank, since Mrs. Cotnam assigned the right to income already earned. She controlled the disposition of the entire amount and diverted part of the payment from herself to the attorneys. By virtue of the assignment Mrs. Cotnam enjoyed the economic benefit of being able to fight her case through the courts and discharged her obligation to her attorneys (in itself equivalent to receipt of income, under *Old Colony Trust Co. v. Commissioner*....
>
> [*Cotnam v. Commissioner*, 263 F.2d at 127.]

The majority in *Cotnam* also rejected the Commissioner's and Judge Wisdom's reliance on *Old Colony Trust Co. v. Commissioner* ... because a contingent fee agreement creates no personal obligation. The only source of payment is the recovery; if there is no recovery, the client pays nothing and the attorney receives nothing. I agree with this additional point of the Court of Appeals majority in *Cotnam*.

The points made by the Courts of Appeals in *Cotnam* and *Estate of Clarks* ... are not in complete agreement, but their differences don't invalidate the essential on which they do agree. The Courts of Appeals in *Cotnam* and *Clarks* agree that the value of the claim was speculative and dependent on the services of counsel who was willing to take it on a contingent fee basis to try to bring it to fruition. They also agree that the only benefit the taxpayer could obtain from his or her claim was to assign the right to receive a portion of it (the contingent fee percentage) to an attorney in an effort to collect the remainder and that such benefit does not amount to full enjoyment that justifies including the fee portion in the assignor's gross income. The Courts of Appeals in *Cotnam* and *Clarks* also agree that the proper treatment is to divide the gross income between the client and the attorney, rather than to include the entire recovery in the client's income and to relegate the client to a deduction that is not fully usable.

I am in complete agreement with Judges Rives and Brown and the panel in *Estate of Clarks* that the assignment of income doctrine should not apply to contingent fee agreements. A contingent fee agreement is not an intrafamily donative transaction, or even a transaction within an economic family, such as parent-subsidiary.... Notwithstanding the attorneys' fiduciary responsibilities to their client, a contingent fee agreement is a commercial transaction between parties with no preexisting common interest that sharply reduces or eliminates the client's dominion and control over both the cause of action and any recovery. Our decisions distinguishing (or just not following) the decision of the Court of Appeals in *Cotnam v. Commissioner,* *supra,* have not adequately considered the characteristics of contingent fee agreements or the effect those characteristics should have in deciding whether such agreements should be treated as assignments of income to be disregarded for Federal income tax purposes.

...

5. *Significance of Control In Supreme Court's Assignment of Income Jurisprudence*

The transfers of income or property at issue in the classic cases on which the dissent of Judge Wisdom and this Court have relied — cases such as *Lucas v. Earl* ... and *Helvering v. Horst* ... were intrafamily donative transfers. If given effect for tax purposes, such intrafamily transfers would permit family members to "split" their incomes and avoid the progressive rate structure (a less pressing concern these days). In addition, because the transferred item never leaves the family group, the transferor may continue to enjoy the economic benefits of the item as though the transfer had never occurred.... Contingent fee agreements between client and attorney do not present these problems.

Equally importantly, in *Lucas v. Earl* ... and *Helvering v. Horst* ... the transferor — in part due to the family relationship — was found to have retained a substantial and significant measure of control after the transfer over the income rights or property transferred. The presence of such continuing control is undoubtedly important in deciding whether a transfer should be treated as an invalid assignment of income.... [A]s the Supreme Court wrote in *Corliss v. Bowers,* 281 U.S. 376 ... (1930) (revocable trust created by husband for benefit of wife and children treated as invalid assignment of income):

> taxation is not so much concerned with the refinements of title as it is with actual command over the property taxed.... The income that is subject to a man's unfettered command and that he is free to enjoy at his own option may be taxed to him as his income, whether he sees fit to enjoy it or not....

...

I ... acknowledge that the assignor's lack of retained control may be trumped if the subject of the assignment is personal service income. Unlike the trust and property cases, *Lucas v. Earl,* ... can be rationalized not so much on the service provider's retained control over whether or not he works, "but on the more basic policy to 'tax salaries to those who earned them'".

My response is that Mr. Kenseth's claim did not generate personal service income. Even though the loss of past earnings as well as future income and benefits were taken into account in computing his settlement recovery, Mr. Kenseth's claim had its origin in the rights inhering in a constitutionally or statutorily protected status (e.g., age, sex, race, disability) rather than a free bargain for services under an ongoing employment relationship or personal service contract. Such rights are no less alienable than other types of property rights that may be bought and sold and otherwise compromised by payments of money. Indeed, where a claim based on status, such as an ADEA claim, is the subject of a contingent fee agreement, the amount paid the attorney as a result of his successful prosecution of the claim is much more personal service income of the attorney than personal service income of the claimant, however the claimant's share of the income might be characterized for tax purposes....

6. *Substantial Reduction of Claimant's Control by Contingent Fee Agreement*

When Mr. Kenseth executed the contingent fee agreement, he gave up substantial control over the conduct of his age discrimination claim. He also gave up total control of the portion of the recovery that was ultimately received and retained by Fox & Fox.

The contingent fee agreement provided that Mr. Kenseth could not settle his case without the consent of Fox & Fox. It further provided that, if Mr. Kenseth had terminated his representation by Fox & Fox, that firm would still have a lien for the contingent fee called for by the agreement, and all costs and disbursements would become due and payable within 10 days. Moreover, Mr. Kenseth was just one member of the class of claimants represented by Fox & Fox. All these factors contributed, as a practical matter, to the creation of substantial barriers to Mr. Kenseth's ability to fire Fox & Fox and to hire other attorneys or to try to settle his case himself.

Mr. Kenseth instead relied on the guidance and expertise of Fox & Fox, and Fox & Fox made all strategic and tactical decisions in the management and pursuit of Mr. Kenseth's age discrimination claim. Fox & Fox negotiated a net recovery (after reduction by the contingent fee) that substantially exceeded

the settlement that the EEOC had recommended.

i. *"Contract of Adhesion"*

For all these reasons it is clear, when Mr. Kenseth signed the contingent fee agreement, that he gave up substantial control—perhaps all effective control—over the future conduct of his age discrimination claim. This is not surprising; a contingent fee agreement in all significant respects amounts to a "contract of adhesion", defined by Black's Law Dictionary 318–319 (7th ed. 1999) as: "A standard-form contract prepared by one party, to be signed by the party in a weaker position, usu. a consumer, who has little choice about the terms."

I'm not suggesting that the contingent fee agreement would be unenforceable; contracts of adhesion are prima facie enforceable as written…. Nor do I suggest that the contingent fee agreement in the case at hand operated unfairly so as to make it unenforceable. I do suggest that the character of the agreement as a contract of adhesion supports my ultimate finding that Mr. Kenseth as the adhering party gave up substantial control over his claim, which was the subject matter of the agreement.

ii. *American Bar Foundation Contingent Fee Study*

My ultimate finding in this case is not just the sympathetic response of a "romantic judge" or an idiosyncratic reaction divorced from the practical realities of the operation of contingent fee agreements. My findings on Mr. Kenseth's reduced control over the prosecution and recovery of his claim are supported by the recurring comments to the same effect in the study by MacKinnon, Contingent Fees for Legal Services: A Study of Professional Economics and Liabilities (American Bar Foundation 1964). What is striking about the MacKinnon study, which makes no mention of any tax questions, are its repeated references to the high degree of practical control that attorneys acquire under contingent fee agreements over the prosecution, settlement, and recovery of plaintiffs' claims.

After Mr. Kenseth signed the contingent fee agreement, he had absolutely *no* control over the portion of the recovery from his claim that was assigned to and received by Fox & Fox as its legal fee. The agreement provided that, even if Mr. Kenseth fired Fox & Fox, Fox & Fox would receive the greater of 40 percent of any recovery on Mr. Kenseth's claim or their regular hourly time charges, plus accrued interest of 1 percent per month, plus a risk enhancer of 100 percent of their regular hourly charges (not exceeding the total recovery). The agreement also stated that Mr. Kenseth gave Fox & Fox a lien on any recovery or settlement. The agreement also provided that Mr. Kenseth would not settle the claim without first obtaining the approval of Fox & Fox.

As noted above, the contingent fee agreement between Mr. Kenseth and Fox & Fox was not an intrafamily donative transaction and did not occur within an economic group of related parties. In addition, Mr. Kenseth's control of his claim (and of any recovery therefrom) was sharply reduced or eliminated by the contingent fee agreement. For all these reasons, the broader ground of the decisions of the Courts of Appeals in *Cotnam* ... and *Estate of Clarks* ... applies to the case at hand. The contingent fee agreement did not effect an assignment of income that must be disregarded for income tax purposes under *Helvering v. Eubank*, ... *Helvering v. Horst*, ... and *Lucas v. Earl*....

This conclusion provides an independent and sufficient ground for the holding, decoupled from the narrow ground of *Cotnam* and *Estate of Clarks* regarding attorneys' ownership interests in lawsuits under State law, that Mr. Kenseth's gross income in the case at hand does not include any part of the settlement proceeds paid to the Fox & Fox trust account and retained by Fox & Fox as its contingent fee.

...

9. Preventing Tax Avoidance By Other Transferors

The majority state ... : "We perceive dangers in the ad hoc modification of established tax law principles or doctrines to counteract hardship in specific cases, and, accordingly, we have not acquiesced in such approaches". Although the majority opinion does not spell out those dangers, concerns have been expressed that adoption of my findings and conclusion would open the door to tax avoidance. My response to such concerns is that the contingent fee agreement is a peculiar situation, far removed from the intrafamily and other related party transfers, including commercial assignments within economic units, that generated and continue to sustain the assignment of income doctrine. The result I espouse can be confined to the contingent fee situation; the tools of legal reasoning remain alive and well to enable the Commissioner and the courts to defend the fisc against transferors who in other contexts might seize upon my proposed result in this case to try to extend it beyond its proper limits.

10. Cropsharing ... Analogy

...

One way to think of the contingent fee agreement, which brings us back to the metaphor about fruits and trees, is to analogize it to a cropsharing arrangement. Cropsharing is strikingly similar to the contingent fee agreement. The attorney is in the position of the tenant farmer, who bears all his direct and overhead expenses incurred in earning the contingent fee (and the contingent fees under all such arrangements to which he is a party with other clients). The client is in the position of the landowner (lessee-sub-lessor), who bears none of the operating expenses, but is responsible for paying the carrying charges on his land, such as mortgage interest and real estate taxes. These charges are analogous to court costs, which the client under a contingent fee agreement is usually responsible for, and which the attorney can only advance to or on behalf of the client.

It is apparently so clear that there is no direct authority that cropsharing arrangements result in a division of the crops and the total gross revenue from their sale in the agreed upon percentages. See IRS Publication 225, Farmer's Tax Guide 15–16 (1999). This income is characterized as rental income to the owner or lessee of the land and farm income to the tenant-farmer.

...

The analogy of contingent fee agreements to crop sharing arrangements is suggestive and helpful. It solves the problem under the attorney's ethics rule that says the attorney is not supposed to acquire an ownership interest in the cause of action that is the subject of such an agreement. The client, like the owner or lessee of farmland who rents it to the tenant farmer, transfers to the attorney an interest in the recovery that is analogous to the tenant farmer's share of the crop generated by his farming activities on the land leased or made available to him by the non-active owner or sublessor.

CONCLUSION

The assignment of income cases decided by the Supreme Court for the most part have arisen in intrafamily donative transfers. Assignment of income cases arising in commercial contexts have concerned attempts at income tax avoidance between related parties. The touchstone of these cases has been the retained control over the subject matter of the assignment by the assignor.

The control retained by Mr. Kenseth in this case was much less than the control retained by the assignor in any of the cases in which the assignment of income doctrine has been properly applied. Indeed, the control retained by Mr. Kenseth was so much less as to make it unreasonable to charge him with the full amount of his share of the total settlement, without offset of the attorney's fee apportioned against his share. From the inception of the contingent fee agreement, a substantial portion of any recovery that might be obtained was dedicated to Fox & Fox, who through the mixture of their labor with the claims of Mr. Kenseth and his colleagues, first, caused the claims to be realized under a settlement agreement, and, second, added substantially to whatever speculative value those claims might have had when the contingent fee agreements were entered into.

The Bankruptcy Court for the Middle District of Alabama said it very well in recently applying *Cotnam in Hamilton v. United States*, 212 B.R. 384 (Bankr. M.D. Ala. 1997) ..."This decision does not limit taxation of the total amount of the judgment as income. It merely apportions the income to the proper entities".

...

---

5. Why did the Chief Judge of the Tax Court reassign the case to Judge Ruwe? (*See* the first footnote of the case, designated "*".)

6. Until the end of 2004, the Supreme Court had refused to grant certiorari to resolve this conflict among the circuits. *See, Sinyard v. Commissioner*, 268 F.3d 756 (9th Cir. 2001), *cert. denied*, 122 S.Ct. 2357 (2002); and *Hukkanen-Campbell v. Commissioner*, 274 F.3d 1312 (10th Cir. 2001), *cert. denied*, 122 S.Ct. 1915 (2002).

The Supreme Court finally agreed to hear two cases in which the government appealed victories by taxpayers based on differing state laws. Read the following case. As you do, recall Judge Beghe's dissent in *Kenseth*.

COMMISSIONER v. BANKS

543 U.S. 426 (2005)

Justice Kennedy delivered the opinion of the Court.

The question in these consolidated cases is whether the portion of a money judgment or settlement paid to a plaintiff's attorney under a contingent-fee agreement is income to the plaintiff under the Internal Revenue Code, 26 U.S.C. § 1 et seq.... The issue divides the courts of appeals. In one of the instant cases, *Banks v. Comm'r, 345 F.3d 373 (2003)*, the Court of Appeals for the Sixth Circuit held the contingent-fee portion of a litigation recovery is not included in the plaintiff's gross income. The Courts of Appeals for the Fifth and Eleventh Circuits also adhere to this view, relying on the holding, over Judge Wisdom's dissent, in *Cotnam v. Commissioner, 263 F.2d 119, 125–126 (CA5 1959)*. *Srivastava v. Commissioner, 220 F.3d 353, 363–365 (CA5 2000)*; *Foster v. United States, 249 F.3d 1275, 1279–1280 (CA11 2001)*. In the other case under review, *Banaitis v. Comm'r, 340 F.3d 1074 (2003)*, the Court of Appeals for the Ninth Circuit held that the portion of the recovery paid to the attorney as a contingent fee is excluded from the plaintiff's gross income if state law gives the plaintiff's attorney a special property interest in the fee, but not otherwise. Six Courts of Appeals have held the entire litigation recovery, including the portion paid to an attorney as a contingent fee, is income to the plaintiff. Some of these Courts of Appeals discuss state law, but little of their analysis appears to turn on this factor. *Raymond v. United States, 355 F.3d 107, 113–116 (CA2 2004)*; *Kenseth v. Comm'r, 259 F.3d 881, 883–884 (CA7 2001)*; *Baylin v. United States, 43 F.3d 1451, 1454–1455 (CA Fed. 1995)*. Other Courts of Appeals have been explicit that the fee portion of the recovery is always income to the plaintiff regardless of the nuances of state law. *O'Brien v. Commissioner, 38 T. C. 707, 712 (1962)*, aff'd, *319 F.2d 532 (CA3 1963)* (per curiam); *Young v. Comm'r, 240 F.3d 369, 377–379 (CA4 2001)*; *Hukkanen-Campbell v. Comm'r, 274 F.3d 1312, 1313–1314 (CA10 2001)*. We granted certiorari to resolve the conflict....

We hold that, as a general rule, when a litigant's recovery constitutes income, the litigant's income includes the portion of the recovery paid to the attorney as a contingent fee. We reverse the decisions of the Courts of Appeals for the Sixth and Ninth Circuits.

I

A. *Commissioner v Banks*

In 1986, respondent John W. Banks, II, was fired from his job as an educational consultant with the California Department of Education. He retained an attorney on a contingent-fee basis and filed a civil suit against the employer in a United States District Court. The complaint alleged employment discrimination in violation of *42 U.S.C. §§ 1981 and 1983 [42 USCS §§ 1981 and 1983]*, *Title VII of the Civil Rights Act of 1964*, as amended, *42 U.S.C. § 2000e et seq. [42 USCS §§ 2000e et seq.]*, and *Cal. Govt. Code Ann. § 12965* (West 1986). The original complaint asserted various additional claims under state law, but Banks later abandoned these. After trial commenced in 1990, the parties settled for $464,000. Banks paid $150,000 of this amount to his attorney pursuant to the fee agreement.

Banks did not include any of the $464,000 in settlement proceeds as gross income in his 1990 federal income tax return. In 1997 the Commissioner of Internal Revenue issued Banks a notice of deficiency for the 1990 tax year. The Tax Court upheld the Commissioner's determination, finding that all the settlement proceeds, including the $150,000 Banks had paid to his attorney, must be included in Banks' gross income.

The Court of Appeals for the Sixth Circuit reversed in part. *345 F.3d 373 (2003)*. It agreed the net amount received by Banks was included in gross income but not the amount paid to the attorney. Relying on its prior decision in *Estate of Clarks v. United States, 202 F.3d 854 (2000)*, the court held the contingent-fee agreement was not an anticipatory assignment of Banks' income because the litigation recovery was not already earned, vested, or even relatively certain to be paid when the contingent-fee contract was made. A contingent-fee arrangement, the court reasoned, is more like a partial assignment of income-producing property than an assignment of income. The attorney is not the mere beneficiary of the client's largess, but rather earns his fee through skill and diligence. *345 F.3d, at 384–385* (quoting *Estate of Clarks, supra, at 857–858*). This reasoning, the court held, applies whether or not state law grants the attorney any special property interest (*e.g.,* a superior lien) in part of the judgment or settlement proceeds.

B. *Commissioner v Banaitis*

After leaving his job as a vice president and loan officer at the Bank of California in 1987, Sigitas J. Banaitis retained an attorney on a contingent-fee basis and brought suit in Oregon state court against the Bank of California and its successor in ownership, the Mitsubishi Bank. The complaint alleged that Mitsubishi Bank willfully interfered with Banaitis' employment contract, and that the Bank of California attempted to induce Banaitis to breach his fiduciary duties to customers and discharged him when he refused. The jury awarded Banaitis compensatory and punitive damages. After resolution of all appeals and post-trial motions, the parties settled. The defendants paid $4,864,547 to Banaitis; and, following the formula set forth in the contingent-fee contract, the defendants paid an additional $3,864,012 directly to Banaitis' attorney.

Banaitis did not include the amount paid to his attorney in gross income on his federal income tax return, and the Commissioner issued a notice of deficiency. The Tax Court upheld the Commissioner's determination, but the Court of Appeals for the Ninth Circuit reversed. *340 F.3d 1074 (2003)*. In contrast to the Court of Appeals for the Sixth Circuit, the *Banaitis* court viewed state law as pivotal. Where state law confers on the attorney no special property rights in his fee, the court said, the whole amount of the judgment or settlement ordinarily is included in the plaintiff's gross income. *Id., at 1081*. Oregon state law, however, like the law of some other States, grants attorneys a superior lien in the contingent-fee portion of any recovery. As a result, the court held, contingent-fee agreements under Oregon law operate not as an anticipatory assignment of the client's income but as a partial transfer to the attorney of some of the client's property in the lawsuit.

II

To clarify why the issue here is of any consequence for tax purposes, two preliminary observations are useful. The first concerns the general issue of deductibility. For the tax years in question the legal expenses in these cases could have been taken as miscellaneous itemized deductions subject to the ordinary requirements, *26 U.S.C. §§ 67–68…,* but doing so would have been of no help to respondents because of the operation of the Alternative Minimum Tax (AMT). For noncorporate individual taxpayers, the AMT establishes a tax liability floor equal to 26 percent of the taxpayer's "alternative minimum taxable income" (minus specified exemptions) up to $175,000, plus 28 percent of alternative minimum taxable income over $175,000. *§§ 55(a), (b)....* Alternative minimum taxable income, unlike ordinary gross income, does not allow any miscellaneous itemized deductions. *§§ 56(b)(1)(A)(i).*

Second, after these cases arose Congress enacted the American Jobs Creation Act of 2004, 118 Stat 1418. Section 703 of the Act amended the Code by adding *§ 62(a)(19) Id., at 1546.* The amendment allows a taxpayer, in computing adjusted gross income, to deduct "attorney fees and court costs paid by, or on behalf of, the taxpayer in connection with any action involving a claim of unlawful discrimination." *Ibid.* The Act defines "unlawful discrimination" to include a number of specific federal statutes, *§§ 62(e)(1) to (16),* any federal whistle-blower statute, *§ 62(e)(17),* and any federal, state, or local law "providing for the enforcement of civil rights" or "regulating any aspect of the employment relationship ... or prohibiting the discharge of an employee, the discrimination against an employee, or any other form of retaliation or reprisal against an employee for asserting rights or taking other actions permitted by law," *§ 62(e)(18) Id., at 1547–1548.* These deductions are permissible even when the AMT applies. Had the Act been in force for the transactions now under review, these cases likely would not have arisen. The Act is not retroactive, however, so while it may cover future taxpayers in respondents' position, it does not pertain here.

III

The Internal Revenue Code defines "gross income" for federal tax purposes as "all income from whatever source derived." *26 U.S.C. § 61(a)....* The definition extends broadly to all economic gains not otherwise exempted. *Commissioner v. Glenshaw Glass Co., 348 U.S. 426, 429–30 ... (1955); Commissioner v. Jacobson, 336 U.S. 28, 49 ... (1949).* A taxpayer cannot exclude an economic gain from gross income by assigning the gain in advance to another party. *Lucas v. Earl ... (1930); Comm'r v. Sunnen, 333 U.S. 591, 604 ... 92 L. Ed. 898, 68 S. Ct. 715 (1948); Helvering v. Horst, 311 U.S. 112, 116–117 ... (1940).* The rationale for the so-called anticipatory assignment of income doctrine is the principle that gains should be taxed "to those who earn them," *Lucas, supra, at 114 ...* a maxim we have called "the first principle of income taxation," *Comm'r v. Culbertson, 337 U.S. 733, 739–740 ... (1949).* The anticipatory assignment doctrine is meant to prevent taxpayers from avoiding taxation through "arrangements and contracts however skillfully devised to prevent [income] when paid from vesting even for a second in the man who earned it." *Lucas, 281 U.S. at 115....* The rule is preventative and motivated by administrative as well as substantive concerns, so we do not inquire whether any particular assignment has a discernible tax avoidance purpose. As *Lucas* explained, "no distinction can be taken according to the motives leading to the arrangement by which the fruits are attributed to a different tree from that on which they grew." *Ibid.*

Respondents argue that the anticipatory assignment doctrine is a judge-made antifraud rule with no relevance to contingent-fee contracts of the sort at issue here. The Commissioner maintains that a contingent-fee agreement should be viewed as an anticipatory assignment to the attorney of a portion of the client's income from any litigation recovery. We agree with the Commissioner.

In an ordinary case attribution of income is resolved by asking whether a taxpayer exercises complete dominion over the income in question. *Glenshaw Glass Co., supra, at 431 ...* ; see also *Commissioner v. Indianapolis Power & Light Co., 493 U.S. 203, 209 ...*

(1990); *Commissioner v. First Security Bank of Utah, N. A., 405 U.S. 394, 403 ... (1972)*. In the context of anticipatory assignments, however, the assignor often does not have dominion over the income at the moment of receipt. In that instance the question becomes whether the assignor retains dominion over the income-generating asset, because the taxpayer "who owns or controls the source of the income, also controls the disposition of that which he could have received himself and diverts the payment from himself to others as the means of procuring the satisfaction of his wants." *Horst, supra,* at 116–117.... See also *Lucas, supra, at 114–115 ...* ; *Helvering v. Eubank, 311 U.S. 122, 124–125 ... (1940)*; *Sunnen, supra, at 604....* Looking to control over the income-generating asset, then, preserves the principle that income should be taxed to the party who earns the income and enjoys the consequent benefits.

In the case of a litigation recovery the income-generating asset is the cause of action that derives from the plaintiff's legal injury. The plaintiff retains dominion over this asset throughout the litigation. We do not understand respondents to argue otherwise. Rather, respondents advance two counterarguments. First, they say that, in contrast to the bond coupons assigned in *Horst,* the value of a legal claim is speculative at the moment of assignment, and may be worth nothing at all. Second, respondents insist that the claimant's legal injury is not the only source of the ultimate recovery. The attorney, according to respondents, also contributes income-generating assets—effort and expertise—without which the claimant likely could not prevail. On these premises respondents urge us to treat a contingent-fee agreement as establishing, for tax purposes, something like a joint venture or partnership in which the client and attorney combine their respective assets—the client's claim and the attorney's skill—and apportion any resulting profits.

We reject respondents' arguments. Though the value of the plaintiff's claim may be speculative at the moment the fee agreement is signed, the anticipatory assignment doctrine is not limited to instances when the precise dollar value of the assigned income is known in advance. *Lucas, supra*; *United States v. Basye, 410 U.S. 441, 445, 450–452 ... (1973)*. Though *Horst* involved an anticipatory assignment of a predetermined sum to be paid on a specific date, the holding in that case did not depend on ascertaining a liquidated amount at the time of assignment. In the cases before us, as in *Horst,* the taxpayer retained control over the income-generating asset, diverted some of the income produced to another party, and realized a benefit by doing so. As Judge Wesley correctly concluded in a recent case, the rationale of *Horst* applies fully to a contingent-fee contract. *Raymond v. United States, 355 F.3d, at 115–116.* That the amount of income the asset would produce was uncertain at the moment of assignment is of no consequence.

We further reject the suggestion to treat the attorney-client relationship as a sort of business partnership or joint venture for tax purposes. The relationship between client and attorney, regardless of the variations in particular compensation agreements or the amount of skill and effort the attorney contributes, is a quintessential principal-agent relationship. *Restatement (Second) of Agency § 1, Comment e (1957)* (hereinafter Restatement); ABA Model Rules of Professional Conduct Rule 1.3, Comments 1, 1.7 1 (2002). The client may rely on the attorney's expertise and special skills to achieve a result the client could not achieve alone. That, however, is true of most principal-agent relationships, and it does not alter the fact that the client retains ultimate dominion and control over the underlying claim. The control is evident when it is noted that, although the attorney can make tactical decisions without consulting the client, the plaintiff still must determine whether to settle or proceed to judgment and make, as well, other critical decisions. Even where the attorney exercises independent judgment without supervision by, or consultation with, the client, the attorney, as an agent, is obligated to act solely on behalf of, and for the exclusive benefit of, the client-principal, rather than for the benefit of the attorney or any other party. Restatement §§ 13, 39, 387.

The attorney is an agent who is duty bound to act only in the interests of the principal, and so it is appropriate to treat the full amount of the recovery as income to the principal. In this respect Judge Posner's observation is apt: "[T]he contingent-fee lawyer [is not] a joint owner of his client's claim in the legal sense any more than the commission salesman is a joint owner of his employer's accounts receivable." *Kenseth, 259 F.3d, at 883.* In both cases a principal relies on an agent to realize an economic gain, and the gain realized by the agent's efforts is income to the principal. The portion paid to the agent may be deductible, but absent some other provision of law it is not excludable from the principal's gross income.

This rule applies whether or not the attorney-client contract or state law confers any special rights or protections on the attorney, so long as these protections do not alter the fundamental principal-agent character of the relationship. Cf. Restatement § 13, *Comment b*, and § 14G, *Comment a* (an agency relationship is created where a principal assigns a chose in action to an assignee for collection and grants the assignee a security interest in the claim against the assignor's debtor in order to compensate the assignee for his collection efforts). State laws vary with respect to the strength of an attorney's security interest in a contingent fee and the remedies available to an attorney should the client discharge or attempt to defraud the attorney. No state laws of which we are aware, however, even those that purport to give attorneys an "ownership" interest in their fees, e.g., *340 F.3d, at 1082–1083* (discussing Oregon law); *Cotnam, 263 F.2d, at 125* (discussing Alabama law), convert the attorney from an agent to a partner.

Respondents and their *amici* propose other theories to exclude fees from income or permit deductibility. These suggestions include: (1) The contingent-fee agreement establishes a Subchapter K partnership under *26 U.S.C. §§ 702, 704*, and *761 …* ; (2) litigation recoveries are proceeds from disposition of property, so the attorney's fee should be subtracted as a capital expense pursuant to *§§ 1001, 1012*, and *1016 …* ; and (3) the fees are deductible reimbursed employee business expenses under *§ 62(a)(2)(A)…*. These arguments, it appears, are being presented for the first time to this Court. We are especially reluctant to entertain novel propositions of law with broad implications for the tax system that were not advanced in earlier stages of the litigation and not examined by the Courts of Appeals. We decline comment on these supplementary theories….

IV

The foregoing suffices to dispose of Banaitis' case. Banks' case, however, involves a further consideration. Banks brought his claims under federal statutes that authorize fee awards to prevailing plaintiffs' attorneys. He contends that application of the anticipatory assignment principle would be inconsistent with the purpose of statutory fee shifting provisions. See *Venegas v. Mitchell, 495 U.S. 82, 86 … (1990)* (observing that statutory fees enable "plaintiffs to employ reasonably competent lawyers without cost to themselves if they prevail"). In the federal system statutory fees are typically awarded by the court under the lodestar approach, *Hensley v. Eckerhart, 461 U.S. 424, 433 … (1983)*, and the plaintiff usually has little control over the amount awarded. Sometimes, as when the plaintiff seeks only injunctive relief, or when the statute caps plaintiffs' recoveries, or when for other reasons damages are substantially less than attorney's fees, court-awarded attorney's fees can exceed a plaintiff's monetary recovery. See, e.g., *Riverside v. Rivera, 477 U.S. 561 … (1986)*

(compensatory and punitive damages of $33,350; attorney's fee award of $245,456.25). Treating the fee award as income to the plaintiff in such cases, it is argued, can lead to the perverse result that the plaintiff loses money by winning the suit. Furthermore, it is urged that treating statutory fee awards as income to plaintiffs would undermine the effectiveness of fee-shifting statutes in deputizing plaintiffs and their lawyers to act as private attorneys general.

We need not address these claims. After Banks settled his case, the fee paid to his attorney was calculated solely on the basis of the private contingent-fee contract. There was no court-ordered fee award, nor was there any indication in Banks' contract with his attorney, or in the settlement agreement with the defendant, that the contingent fee paid to Banks' attorney was in lieu of statutory fees Banks might otherwise have been entitled to recover. Also, the amendment added by the American Jobs Creation Act redresses the concern for many, perhaps most, claims governed by fee-shifting statutes.

For the reasons stated, the judgments of the Courts of Appeals for the Sixth and Ninth Circuits are reversed, and the cases are remanded for further proceedings consistent with this opinion.

It is so ordered.

––––––––––––

7. Do you agree with the Supreme Court majority? Has the majority dealt adequately with the points raised by Judge Beghe in his dissent in *Kenseth*?

While the Supreme Court case was pending Congress, sympathetic to taxpayers who had been reported as paying more in tax on damage awards or settlements than the amount they retained, sought to remedy the problem. As part of the 2004 Jobs Act, it added a new subsection to section 62 of the Code. The primary reason for the perceived overtaxation resulting from the old rules was the fact that when a taxpayer included the portion of damages paid to an attorney in income, the taxpayer could deduct it only "below-the-line" under section 212. Deducting the payment below the line exposed it to both the limitation of section 67 and required the taxpayer to add the deduction back in calculating alternative minimum tax. Thus, the interplay of the regular tax and alternative minimum tax rules, could produce a total tax that was greater than the portion of the damages remaining to the plaintiff after paying her attorney. As the remedy, Congress made the portion of an award or settlement paid over to a lawyer deductible in certain cases. **Read Code section 62(a)(20).**[25]

––––––––––––

Alexander's case did not end as quickly and easily as did Renata's case. When he entered Emporia Hospital for surgery to repair the tear to his rotator cuff, he was advised that the surgery was simple and routine. It did not prove to be so. Once again, Renata and Alexander turned to Shannon, who prepared and served the following complaint.

––––––––––––

25. For a time, odd numbering resulted from the amendment made by section 703(a). Congress added "new" subsection 62(a)(19), but there was already a subsection 62(a)(19). American Jobs Creation Act of 2004, P.L. 108-357.Congress corrected its error, redesignating the new section as 62(a)(20) as part of the Gulf Opportunity Zone Act of 2005. P.L. 109-135, §412(Q)(1)(A)-(B).

STATE OF MATHEWS
IN THE CIRCUIT COURT OF GREYSTONE
ALEXANDER M. SMITH
     Plaintiff,

                                              Case No.:

     v.

EMPORIA HOSPITAL CORPORATION,
MATHEWS COMMUNITY HEALTH SYSTEMS, INC.,
GREYSTONE MEMORIAL HOSPITAL,
CENTER FOR ORTHOPEDIC SURGERY, INC., and
JOSHUA SINGH, M.D.
     Defendants.

COMPLAINT

The plaintiff, Alexander M. Smith ("Mr. Smith"), by counsel, for his Complaint against the defendants, Emporia Hospital Corporation, Mathews Community Health Systems Inc., Greystone Memorial Hospital, Center for Orthopaedic Surgery, Inc., and Joshua Singh, M.D. states as follows:

Count One

1. At all times relevant to this action, Emporia Hospital Corporation and Mathews Community Health Systems, Inc. owned andoperated Greystone Memorial Hospital in the City of Emporia, State of Mathews.

2. On April 6, 2000, Mr. Smith was admitted as a patient to Greystone Memorial Hospital for the purpose of undergoing surgical repair of a right rotator cuff tear.

3. On April 6, 2000, Dr. Joshua Singh undertook to surgically repair Mr. Smith's right rotator cuff tear at Greystone Memorial Hospital.

4. Subsequent to the surgical procedure, Dr. Singh ordered that Demerol, agents, fluids, and other substances via a PCA (Patient Controlled Analgesia) machine be administered by Mr. Smith for the purpose of postoperative pain management.

5. Following the surgical repair of the right rotator cuff, Greystone Memorial Hospital, acting by and through its employees who were acting within the scope of their employment by Greystone Memorial Hospital, undertook to deliver Demerol, agents and fluids via PCA machine to Mr. Smith.

6. As a direct consequence of the PCA machine, the manner it was used and the medications, agents, fluids, and substances used in conjunction with the PCA machine, Mr. Smith sustained severe injuries to his person, leaving him permanently paralyzed.

7. The injury described in paragraph 5 would not normally have occurred if the equipment, materials, medications, agents, fluids, and substances used in conjunction with the PCA machine had been properly used.

8. From the time the employees of Greystone Memorial Hospital commenced the actions described in paragraph 4 and continuing until the PCA was discontinued, the equipment, materials, medications, agents, fluids, and substances utilized in conjunction with the PCA were owned, completely possessed, exclusively controlled, and maintained by Greystone Memorial Hospital, and Greystone Memorial Hospital has exclu-

sive knowledge of the way the equipment, materials, medications, agents, fluids, and substances were used.

9. Greystone Memorial Hospital and its employees, acting within the scope of their employment, during the course of providing health care to Mr. Smith, owed Mr. Smith the duty to exercise ordinary care and to comply with the standard of care set forth in §8.01-581.20 of the Code of Mathews.

10. Greystone Memorial Hospital and its agents, servants and employees, acting within the scope of their employment, and other persons for whose conduct Greystone Memorial Hospital is responsible, were negligent and breached the duties owed to Mr. Smith and were negligent by:

a. Failing to appropriately evaluate Mr. Smith's condition.
b. Failing to report Mr. Smith's declining condition to Dr. Singh.
c. Failing to call Dr. Amy Barton in a timely manner to evaluate Mr. Smith's condition.
d. Failing to properly program the PCA Pump.
e. Failing to properly train nurses to enter PCA prescriptions.
f. Failing to properly operate the PCA Machine.
g. Administering Demerol to Mr. Smith who had a known history of allergic reaction to the medication.
h. Failing to monitor Mr. Smith's vital signs.
i. Failing to maintain the PCA equipment.
j. Failing to get a physician into the hospital to evaluate Mr. Smith for his declining neurologic condition.
k. Failing to take steps to prevent serious injury.
l. Failing to recognize hypotension and hypertension and take steps to get medical intervention.
m. Failing to question the dosage of the Narcan ordered by Dr. Singh.

11. As a direct and proximate result of the negligence of Greystone Memorial Hospital and its employees acting within the scope of their employment by Greystone Memorial Hospital, and others for whose conduct Greystone Memorial Hospital is legally responsible, Mr. Smith sustained injuries, has suffered and will continue to suffer great physical and mental pain and suffering, and has been otherwise injured.

12. As a direct and proximate result of the negligence of

Greystone Memorial Hospital, its agents, servants, and employees, acting within the scope of their employment by Greystone Memorial Hospital, and others for whose conduct Greystone Memorial Hospital is legally responsible, Mr. Smith has incurred, and will be compelled to incur in the future, expenses for hospital, doctor, and other medical professionals' bills in an effort to be cured of his injuries and be relieved of his pain and suffering; sustained and will sustain loss of income and diminishment of earning capacity; and suffered other damages.

Count Two

Mr. Smith repeats and restates the allegations contained in paragraphs 1 though 12 of Count One with the same force and effect as if fully set forth herein.

13. At all times relevant to this action, Dr. Singh was licensed to practice medicine in the State of Mathews and engaged in the practice of orthopedic surgery.

14. At all times relevant to this action, Dr. Singh was an agent, servant, and employee of Center for Orthopedic Surgery, Inc. acting within the scope of his employment, and for whose conduct the Center for Orthopedic Surgery, Inc. is legally responsible.

15. On April 6, 2002, Dr. Singh undertook to serve as the orthopedic surgeon for Mr. Smith and to provide health care to Mr. Smith while he was hospitalized at Greystone Memorial Hospital following surgical repair of his torn rotator cuff.

16. In his capacity as the orthopedic surgeon caring for Mr. Smith, Dr. Singh assumed responsibility for the administration, management, and monitoring of Demerol, agents and fluids via a PCA machine, including selection of the medications, agents and fluids.

17. Dr. Singh and his employees and borrowed servants, acting within the scope of their employment, and other persons for whom Dr. Singh is responsible during the course of providing health care to Mr. Smith, owed Mr. Smith the duty to exercise ordinary care and to comply with the standard of care set forth in § 8.01-581.20 of the Code of Mathews.

18. Dr. Singh and his employees and borrowed servants, acting within the scope of their employment, and other persons for whom Dr. Singh is responsible, were negligent and breached the duties owed to Mr. Smith, and were negligent by:

    a. Failing to appropriately observe and evaluate Mr. Smith's condition.
    b. Failing to get a neurological consult in timely manner to evaluate Mr. Smith's declining condition.
    c. Failing to call Dr. Amy Barton in a timely manner to evaluate Mr. Smith's condition.
    d. Ordering and administering Narcan in an inappropriate dosage.
    e. Failing to see Mr. Smith and evaluate his condition.
    f. Failing to monitor Mr. Smith's vital signs.
    g. Ordering Demerol for Mr. Smith with a known history of allergic reaction.
    h. Failing to get Mr. Smith transferred to Mathews Central Hospital in a timely manner to treat his neurological condition.
    i. Failing to take steps to prevent serious injury.
    j. Failing to recognize hypotension and hypertension and take steps to prevent hypoxia.
    k. Failing to treat Mr. Smith's declining neurological condition.
    l. Failing to recognize that Mr. Smith was at increased risk of an ischemic event because of his existing medical problems.

19. As a direct and proximate result of the negligence of Dr. Singh and his employees and borrowed servants, acting within the scope of their employment, and other persons for whom Dr. Singh is responsible, Mr. Smith sustained injuries, has suffered and will continue to suffer great physical and mental pain and suffering, and has been otherwise injured.

20. As a direct and proximate result of the negligence of Dr. Singh and his employees and borrowed servants, acting within the scope of their employment, and other persons for whom Dr. Singh is responsible, Mr. Smith has incurred, and will be compelled to incur in the future, expenses for hospital, doctor and other medical professionals' bills in an effort to be cured of his injuries and be relieved of his pain and suffering, sustained and will sustain loss of income and diminishment of earning capacity, and suffered other damages.

WHEREFORE, plaintiff, by counsel, demands judgment against the defendants, jointly and severally, in the amount of One Million Five Hundred Thousand Dollars ($1,500,000.00), his costs expended in this action, and interest from April 6, 2002.

PLAINTIFF REQUESTS TRIAL BY JURY.

Alexander M. Smith

By _____

Counsel

Shannon V. Daily, MSB#4025
Chad B. Shriver MSB#6930
DAILY & SHRIVER, L.L.P.
1600 West 12th Street, Suite 201
Emporia, Mathews
Counsel for Plaintiff

---

8. Suppose after trial, the jury awards Alexander $1,500,000. How would you advise him to treat the award for tax purposes? Does the complaint provide a sufficient basis for determining how much, if any, of the award is excludible from gross income? Remember that attorneys often can guide the jury in allocating an award between categories of payment and participate in the drafting of the court order that memorializes that award.

9. Suppose the hospital's insurance company offers to pay Alexander $2 million if he will agree to accept payment ratably over a period of 5 years. How would you advise him: is the greater amount worth more if he only receives one-fifth per year? Does his agreement to accept installment payments change the tax treatment of the award?

10. Suppose that Alexander's suit had been based upon a claim of race discrimination and after trial, the jury had awarded him $1,5000,000 in actual damages (based on lost income) and $1,500,000 punitive damages. Alexander paid his attorney $1,000,000. What were the tax consequences to Alexander and his attorney?

11. Suppose Alexander's claim was for breach of contract and the jury awarded him $1,500,000 actual damages and $1,500,000 punitive damages. If he paid his attorney $1,000,000, what would be the tax consequences to Alexander and his attorney?

Problem 8. Some Problems on the Sale of a Business

You have already encountered some of the tax problems involved in the sale of a business. **Recall *Raytheon* and the Adams Adverts problem that followed.** We used the Adams Adverts problem as part of our consideration of the parameters of gross income. Now that you have a more comprehensive understanding of all the components of the tax calculation outline, it is time to delve more deeply into several additional tax issues that arise on the sale of a proprietorship. Consider the following problem.

Mack is an unmarried, cash basis taxpayer who, until August of the current year, lived in New York City, and now lives in sunny Florida. Mack is a former certified public accountant who got tired of dealing with balance sheets all day. He decided to leave public accounting to embark on a new venture: he became an itinerant knife sharpener. He decided to do it because he wanted to go back to the simpler way of life when the Fuller Brush man and the Avon lady (there were definite gender roles in those days) came to your door to find out what you needed. He thought there was enough renewed interest in door-to-door service to support his new venture.

Mack commenced his new venture four years ago. First, he walked around his neighborhood, asking his neighbors whether he could sharpen their knives for a small fee. When he realized the level of enthusiasm for his service, he decided to purchase, for use strictly in the business, a minivan (under 5,000 pounds) for $35,000, and a state-of-the-art grinding machine (which had a class life of four years) for $20,000. He had his van specially painted with a logo he designed showing Excalibur piercing the rock with his business name—"Mack the Knife (sharpener)"—under it. He also had the van specially fitted with a musical horn that tooted a distinctive theme he composed and copyrighted. (No, not the Kurt Weill song that Bobby Darrin made famous; Mack's was even more catchy.) He paid $10,000 for the special paint job, the horn, and customized fittings for installation of the grinding machine.

When he drove through the neighborhoods of the five boroughs of New York City, the residents knew that Mack "was back in town" ready to sharpen those dull knives they had always intended to, but had put off, sharpening. (Mack was the Mr. Softee of the knife-sharpening business.) Mack's business was soon incredibly successful. He was so successful that he was written up in newspaper and magazine articles. Everyone in the five boroughs got their knives and scissors out when they heard that catchy tune of his. They loved the quaint idea of door-to-door personal service.

But Mack was so successful that he found himself working sixteen-hour days and six-day weeks. By the beginning of the current year he was burned out and decided that he had to slow down. He started to think about selling his business. Mack contacted an appraiser to get an idea of what his business assets were worth. The appraiser determined that the value of Mack's business property as follows:

- The specially fitted van: $30,000

- The grinding machine: $25,000 (The appraiser told Mack that the machine had gone up in value because its manufacturer had gone out of business, but its machines were still sought after.)

- Accounts receivable: $5,000

- Jingle copyright: $50,000

- Inventory of German knives: $10,000 (Mack's basis in the knife inventory was $4,000. He carried the knife merchandise to sell to customers, who trusted his judgment in good knives.)

Mack found a buyer. On July 1 of the current year, Big-Blade, Inc. offered to purchase Mack's business for $750,000 in cash and 2,500 shares of Big-Blade stock that had a fair market value of $250,000. (Payment to be made in a lump sum.) Big-Blade believed that Mack's business would fit nicely with its diversified holdings in blades of all sorts. Mack decided to accept Big-Blade's offer. Under the terms of the agreement, the parties agreed that Big-Blade will continue to use the name "Mack the Knife(sharpener);" Mack's logo, and his jingle. They also agreed that Mack will not operate a knife sharpening business within the five boroughs of New York City for five years.

---

1. How did the parties arrive at the value of Mack's business? Recall our discussion in connection with the Adams Adverts problem.

2. Why would Big Blade pay so much more for Mack's business than the $120,000 value of the assets that the appraiser determined?

3. Assuming Mack takes Big-Blade's offer, what are the tax consequences of the sale and purchase to both parties? Before you answer the question, read the following case.

WILLIAMS v. McGOWAN
152 F.2d 570 (2d Cir. 1945)

HAND, Circuit Judge

...

Williams, the taxpayer, and one, Reynolds, had for many years been engaged in the hardware business in the City of Corning, New York. On the 20th of January, 1926, they formed a partnership, of which Williams was entitled to two-thirds of the profits, and Reynolds, one-third. They agreed that on February 1, 1925, the capital invested in the business had been $118,082.05, of which Reynolds had a credit of $29,029.03, and Williams, the balance—$89,053.02. At the end of every business year, on February 1st, Reynolds was to pay to Williams, interest upon the amount of the difference between his share of the capital and one-third of the total as shown by the inventory; and upon withdrawal of one party the other was to have the privilege of buying the other's interest as it appeared on the books. The business was carried on through the firm's fiscal year, ending January 31, 1940, in accordance with this agreement, and thereafter until Reynolds' death on July 18th of that year. Williams settled with Reynolds' executrix on September 6th in an agreement by which he promised to pay her $12,187.90, and to assume all liabilities of the business; and he did pay her $2,187.98 in cash at once, and $10,000 on the 10th of the following October. On September 17th of the same year, Williams sold the business as a whole to the Corning Building Company for $63,926.28—its agreed value as of February 1, 1940—'plus an amount to be computed by multiplying the gross sales of the business from the first day of February, 1940 to the 28th day of September, 1940,' by an agreed fraction. This value was made up of cash of about $8100, receivables of about $7000, fixtures of about $800, and a merchandise inventory of about $49,000, less some $1000 for bills payable. To this was added about $6,000 credited to Williams for profits under the language just quoted, making a total of nearly $70,000. Upon this sale Williams suffered a loss upon his original two-thirds of the business but he made a small gain upon the one-third which he had bought from Reynolds' executrix; and in his income tax return he entered both as items of 'ordinary income,' and not as transactions in 'capital assets.' This the Commissioner disallowed and recomputed the tax accordingly; Williams paid the deficiency and sued to recover it in this action. The only question is whether the business was 'capital assets'....

... When Williams bought out Reynolds' interest, he became the sole owner of the business, the firm had ended upon any theory, and the situation for tax purposes was no other than if Reynolds had never been a partner at all, except that to the extent of one-third of the 'amount realized' on Williams' sale to the Corning Company, his 'basis' was different. The judge thought that, because upon that sale both parties fixed the price at the liquidation value of the business while Reynolds was alive, 'plus' its estimated earnings thereafter, it was as though Williams had sold his interest in the firm during its existence. But the method by which the parties agreed upon the price was irrelevant to the computation of Williams' income. The Treasury, if that served its interest, need not heed any fiction which the parties found it convenient to adopt; nor need Williams do the same in his dealings with the Treasury. We have to decide only whether upon the sale of a going business it is to be comminuted into its fragments, and these are to be separately matched against the definition [of "capital assets"], or whether the whole business is to be treated as if it were a single piece of property.

Our law has been sparing in the creation of juristic entities; it has never, for example, taken over the Roman 'universitas facti'; (Footnote 1) and indeed for many years it fumbled uncertainly with the concept of a corporation. (Footnote 2) One might have supposed that partnership would have been an especially promising field in which to raise up an entity, particularly since merchants have always kept their accounts upon that basis. Yet there too our law resisted at the price of great continuing confusion; and, even when it might be thought that a statute admitted, if it did not demand, recognition of the firm as an entity, the old concepts prevailed.... And so, even though we might agree that under the influence of the Uniform Partnership Act a partner's interest in the firm should be treated as indivisible, and for that reason a 'capital asset'... we should be chary about extending further so exotic a jural concept. Be that as it may, in this instance the section [that defines capital assets, section 1221] itself furnishes the answer. It starts in the broadest way by declaring that all 'property' is 'capital assets,' and then makes three exceptions. The first is 'stock in trade * * * or other property of a kind which would properly be included in the inventory'; next comes 'property held * * * primarily for sale to customers'; and finally, property 'used in the trade or business of a character which is subject to * * * allowance for depreciation.' In the face of this language, although it may be true that a 'stock in trade,' taken by itself, should be treated as a 'universitas facti,' by no possibility can a whole business be so treated; and the same is true as to any property within the other exceptions. Congress plainly did mean to comminute the elements of a business; plainly it did not regard the whole as 'capital assets.'

As has already appeared, Williams transferred to the Corning Company 'cash,' 'receivables,' 'fixtures' and a 'merchandise inventory.' 'Fixtures' are not capital because they are subject to a depreciation allowance; the inventory, as we have just seen, is expressly excluded. So far as appears, no allowance was made for 'good-will'.... There can of course be no gain or loss in the transfer of cash; and, although Williams does appear to have made a gain of $ 1072.71 upon the 'receivables,' the point has not been argued that they are not subject to a depreciation allowance. That we leave open for decision by the district court, if the parties cannot agree. The gain or loss upon every other item should be computed as an item in ordinary income.

Judgment reversed.

FOOTNOTES:

1. By *universitas facti* is meant a number of things of the same kind which are regarded as a whole; e.g. 'a herd, a stock of wares.' Mackeldey, Roman Law Sec. 162.

2. 'To the 'church' modern law owes its conception of a juristic person, and the clear line that it draws between 'the corporation aggregate' and the sum of its members.' Pollack & Maitland, Vol. 1, . 489.

FRANK, Circuit Judge (dissenting in part).

...

... I do not agree that we should ignore what the parties to the sale, Williams and the Corning Company, actually did. They did not arrange for a transfer to the buyer, as if in separate bundles, of the several ingredients of the business. They contracted for the sale of the entire business as a going concern. Here is what they said in their agreement: 'The party of the first part agrees to sell and the party of the second part agrees to buy, all of the right, title and interest of the said party of the first part in and to the hardware business now being conducted by the said party of the first part, including cash on hand and on deposit in the First National Bank & Trust Company of Corning in the A. F. Williams Hardward Store account, in accounts receivable, bills receivable, notes receivable, merchandise and fixtures, including two G.M. trucks, good will and all other assets of every kind and description used in and about said business.... Said party of the first part agrees not to engage in the hardware business within a radius of twenty-five miles from the City of Corning, New York, for a period of ten years from the 1st day of October 1940.'

To carve up this transaction into distinct sales—of cash, receivables, fixtures, trucks, merchandise, and good will—is to do violence to the realities.... Where a business is sold as a unit, the whole is greater than its parts. Businessmen so recognize; so, too, I think, did Congress. Interpretation of our complicated tax statutes is seldom aided by saying that taxation is an eminently practical matter (or the like). But this is one instance where, it seems to me, the practical aspects of the matter should guide our guess as to what Congress meant. I believe Congress had those aspects in mind and was not thinking of the nice distinctions between Roman and Anglo-American legal theories about legal entities.

Now look at section 1060 and Treasury Regulation section 1.1060-1.

Now that you have read *Williams v. McGowan*, section 1060, and Treasury Regulation section 1.1060-1, can you answer question 3 above? Do you need to know any further information?

4. Does section 1060 require that the parties agree to an allocation of the purchase price?

5. How might Mack report the sale on his tax return? What is Mack's basis in his 2,500 shares of Big-Blade stock?

6. Why might Big Blade want to report something different from what Mack reports?

Forms Appendix

Form **1040** Department of the Treasury—Internal Revenue Service
U.S. Individual Income Tax Return **2005** (99) IRS Use Only—Do not write or staple in this space.

| For the year Jan. 1–Dec. 31, 2005, or other tax year beginning | , 2005, ending | , 20 | OMB No. 1545-0074 |

Label
(See instructions on page 16.)
Use the IRS label.
Otherwise, please print or type.

	Your first name and initial	Last name	Your social security number
L A B E L	If a joint return, spouse's first name and initial	Last name	Spouse's social security number
H E R E	Home address (number and street). If you have a P.O. box, see page 16.	Apt. no.	▲ **You must enter your SSN(s) above.** ▲
	City, town or post office, state, and ZIP code. If you have a foreign address, see page 16.		Checking a box below will not change your tax or refund.

Presidential Election Campaign ▶ Check here if you, or your spouse if filing jointly, want $3 to go to this fund (see page 16) ▶ ☐ You ☐ Spouse

Filing Status
Check only one box.

1 ☐ Single
2 ☐ Married filing jointly (even if only one had income)
3 ☐ Married filing separately. Enter spouse's SSN above and full name here. ▶
4 ☐ Head of household (with qualifying person). (See page 17.) If the qualifying person is a child but not your dependent, enter this child's name here. ▶
5 ☐ Qualifying widow(er) with dependent child (see page 17)

Exemptions

6a ☐ **Yourself.** If someone can claim you as a dependent, **do not** check box 6a
b ☐ **Spouse**
c Dependents:

(1) First name Last name	(2) Dependent's social security number	(3) Dependent's relationship to you	(4) ✓ if qualifying child for child tax credit (see page 19)
			☐
			☐
			☐
			☐

If more than four dependents, see page 19.

| Boxes checked on 6a and 6b |
| No. of children on 6c who: • lived with you • did not live with you due to divorce or separation (see page 20) |
| Dependents on 6c not entered above |
| Add numbers on lines above ▶ |

d Total number of exemptions claimed

Income

Attach Form(s) W-2 here. Also attach Forms W-2G and 1099-R if tax was withheld.

If you did not get a W-2, see page 22.

Enclose, but do not attach, any payment. Also, please use Form 1040-V.

7 Wages, salaries, tips, etc. Attach Form(s) W-2 | 7
8a Taxable interest. Attach Schedule B if required | 8a
b Tax-exempt interest. **Do not** include on line 8a | 8b |
9a Ordinary dividends. Attach Schedule B if required | 9a
b Qualified dividends (see page 23) | 9b |
10 Taxable refunds, credits, or offsets of state and local income taxes (see page 23) | 10
11 Alimony received | 11
12 Business income or (loss). Attach Schedule C or C-EZ | 12
13 Capital gain or (loss). Attach Schedule D if required. If not required, check here ▶ ☐ | 13
14 Other gains or (losses). Attach Form 4797 | 14
15a IRA distributions | 15a | b Taxable amount (see page 25) | 15b
16a Pensions and annuities | 16a | b Taxable amount (see page 25) | 16b
17 Rental real estate, royalties, partnerships, S corporations, trusts, etc. Attach Schedule E | 17
18 Farm income or (loss). Attach Schedule F | 18
19 Unemployment compensation | 19
20a Social security benefits | 20a | b Taxable amount (see page 27) | 20b
21 Other income. List type and amount (see page 29) | 21
22 Add the amounts in the far right column for lines 7 through 21. This is your **total income** ▶ | 22

Adjusted Gross Income

23 Educator expenses (see page 29) | 23
24 Certain business expenses of reservists, performing artists, and fee-basis government officials. Attach Form 2106 or 2106-EZ | 24
25 Health savings account deduction. Attach Form 8889 | 25
26 Moving expenses. Attach Form 3903 | 26
27 One-half of self-employment tax. Attach Schedule SE | 27
28 Self-employed SEP, SIMPLE, and qualified plans | 28
29 Self-employed health insurance deduction (see page 30) | 29
30 Penalty on early withdrawal of savings | 30
31a Alimony paid b Recipient's SSN ▶ | 31a
32 IRA deduction (see page 31) | 32
33 Student loan interest deduction (see page 33) | 33
34 Tuition and fees deduction (see page 34) | 34
35 Domestic production activities deduction. Attach Form 8903 | 35
36 Add lines 23 through 31a and 32 through 35 | 36
37 Subtract line 36 from line 22. This is your **adjusted gross income** ▶ | 37

For Disclosure, Privacy Act, and Paperwork Reduction Act Notice, see page 78. Cat. No. 11320B Form **1040** (2005)

Form 1040 (2005)   Page **2**

Tax and Credits	38	Amount from line 37 (adjusted gross income)	38	
	39a	Check if: ☐ **You** were born before January 2, 1941, ☐ Blind. ☐ **Spouse** was born before January 2, 1941, ☐ Blind. Total boxes checked ▶ 39a		
Standard Deduction for—	b	If your spouse itemizes on a separate return or you were a dual-status alien, see page 35 and check here ▶39b ☐		
	40	**Itemized deductions** (from Schedule A) **or** your **standard deduction** (see left margin) . .	40	
	41	Subtract line 40 from line 38	41	
• People who checked any box on line 39a or 39b **or** who can be claimed as a dependent, see page 36.	42	If line 38 is over $109,475, or you provided housing to a person displaced by Hurricane Katrina, see page 37. Otherwise, multiply $3,200 by the total number of exemptions claimed on line 6d	42	
	43	**Taxable income.** Subtract line 42 from line 41. If line 42 is more than line 41, enter -0-	43	
	44	**Tax** (see page 37). Check if any tax is from: **a** ☐ Form(s) 8814 **b** ☐ Form 4972 . . .	44	
• All others:	45	**Alternative minimum tax** (see page 39). Attach Form 6251	45	
Single or Married filing separately, $5,000	46	Add lines 44 and 45 . . . . ▶	46	
	47	Foreign tax credit. Attach Form 1116 if required	47		
	48	Credit for child and dependent care expenses. Attach Form 2441	48		
	49	Credit for the elderly or the disabled. Attach Schedule R . .	49		
Married filing jointly or Qualifying widow(er), $10,000	50	Education credits. Attach Form 8863	50		
	51	Retirement savings contributions credit. Attach Form 8880 . .	51		
	52	Child tax credit (see page 41). Attach Form 8901 if required .	52		
	53	Adoption credit. Attach Form 8839	53		
Head of household, $7,300	54	Credits from: **a** ☐ Form 8396 **b** ☐ Form 8859 . . .	54		
	55	Other credits. Check applicable box(es): **a** ☐ Form 3800 **b** ☐ Form 8801 **c** ☐ Form _____	55		
	56	Add lines 47 through 55. These are your **total credits**	56	
	57	Subtract line 56 from line 46. If line 56 is more than line 46, enter -0- . . . . . . ▶	57	
Other Taxes	58	Self-employment tax. Attach Schedule SE	58	
	59	Social security and Medicare tax on tip income not reported to employer. Attach Form 4137 . .	59	
	60	Additional tax on IRAs, other qualified retirement plans, etc. Attach Form 5329 if required .	60	
	61	Advance earned income credit payments from Form(s) W-2	61	
	62	Household employment taxes. Attach Schedule H	62	
	63	Add lines 57 through 62. This is your **total tax** . . . . ▶	63	
Payments	64	Federal income tax withheld from Forms W-2 and 1099 . .	64		
	65	2005 estimated tax payments and amount applied from 2004 return	65		
If you have a qualifying child, attach Schedule EIC.	66a	**Earned income credit (EIC)**	66a		
	b	Nontaxable combat pay election ▶ 66b			
	67	Excess social security and tier 1 RRTA tax withheld (see page 59)	67		
	68	Additional child tax credit. Attach Form 8812	68		
	69	Amount paid with request for extension to file (see page 59)	69		
	70	Payments from: **a** ☐ Form 2439 **b** ☐ Form 4136 **c** ☐ Form 8885 .	70		
	71	Add lines 64, 65, 66a, and 67 through 70. These are your **total payments** . . . . ▶	71	
Refund	72	If line 71 is more than line 63, subtract line 63 from line 71. This is the amount you **overpaid**	72	
Direct deposit? See page 59 and fill in 73b, 73c, and 73d.	73a	Amount of line 72 you want **refunded to you** . . . . ▶	73a	
	▶ b	Routing number			▶ c Type: ☐ Checking ☐ Savings
	▶ d	Account number			
	74	Amount of line 72 you want **applied to your 2006 estimated tax** ▶	74		
Amount You Owe	75	**Amount you owe.** Subtract line 71 from line 63. For details on how to pay, see page 60 ▶	75	
	76	Estimated tax penalty (see page 60)	76		

Third Party Designee

Do you want to allow another person to discuss this return with the IRS (see page 61)? ☐ **Yes.** Complete the following. ☐ **No**

Designee's name ▶ _____ Phone no. ▶ ( )_____ Personal identification number (PIN) ▶ _____

Sign Here

Under penalties of perjury, I declare that I have examined this return and accompanying schedules and statements, and to the best of my knowledge and belief, they are true, correct, and complete. Declaration of preparer (other than taxpayer) is based on all information of which preparer has any knowledge.

Joint return? See page 17.

Keep a copy for your records.

Your signature _____ Date _____ Your occupation _____ Daytime phone number ( )_____

Spouse's signature. If a joint return, **both** must sign. _____ Date _____ Spouse's occupation _____

Paid Preparer's Use Only

Preparer's signature ▶ _____ Date _____ Check if self-employed ☐ Preparer's SSN or PTIN _____

Firm's name (or yours if self-employed), address, and ZIP code ▶ _____ EIN _____ Phone no. ( )_____

Form **1040** (2005)

☻ *Printed on recycled paper*

F–3

SCHEDULES A&B
(Form 1040)
Department of the Treasury
Internal Revenue Service (99)

Schedule A—Itemized Deductions

(Schedule B is on back)

▶ **Attach to Form 1040.**   ▶ **See Instructions for Schedules A&B (Form 1040).**

OMB No. 1545-0074

2005

Attachment
Sequence No. **07**

Name(s) shown on Form 1040

Your social security number

Medical and Dental Expenses		**Caution.** Do not include expenses reimbursed or paid by others.		
	1	Medical and dental expenses (see page A-2) . . .	1	
	2	Enter amount from Form 1040, line 38 ⌊ 2 ⌋		
	3	Multiply line 2 by 7.5% (.075).	3	
	4	Subtract line 3 from line 1. If line 3 is more than line 1, enter -0-		4
Taxes You Paid (See page A-2.)	5	State and local **(check only one box)**: a ☐ Income taxes, **or** b ☐ General sales taxes (see page A-3)	5	
	6	Real estate taxes (see page A-5)	6	
	7	Personal property taxes	7	
	8	Other taxes. List type and amount ▶	8	
	9	Add lines 5 through 8		9
Interest You Paid (See page A-5.)	10	Home mortgage interest and points reported to you on Form 1098	10	
	11	Home mortgage interest not reported to you on Form 1098. If paid to the person from whom you bought the home, see page A-6 and show that person's name, identifying no., and address ▶	11	
Note. Personal interest is not deductible.	12	Points not reported to you on Form 1098. See page A-6 for special rules	12	
	13	Investment interest. Attach Form 4952 if required. (See page A-6.)	13	
	14	Add lines 10 through 13		14
Gifts to Charity If you made a gift and got a benefit for it, see page A-7.	15a	Total gifts by cash or check. If you made any gift of $250 or more, see page A-7	15a	
	b	Gifts by cash or check after August 27, 2005, that you elect to treat as qualified contributions (see page A-7) ⌊ **15b** ⌋		
	16	Other than by cash or check. If any gift of $250 or more, see page A-7. You **must** attach Form 8283 if over $500	16	
	17	Carryover from prior year	17	
	18	Add lines 15a, 16, and 17		18
Casualty and Theft Losses	19	Casualty or theft loss(es). Attach Form 4684. (See page A-8.)		19
Job Expenses and Certain Miscellaneous Deductions (See page A-8.)	20	Unreimbursed employee expenses—job travel, union dues, job education, etc. Attach Form 2106 or 2106-EZ if required. (See page A-8.) ▶	20	
	21	Tax preparation fees.	21	
	22	Other expenses—investment, safe deposit box, etc. List type and amount ▶	22	
	23	Add lines 20 through 22	23	
	24	Enter amount from Form 1040, line 38 ⌊ **24** ⌋		
	25	Multiply line 24 by 2% (.02)	25	
	26	Subtract line 25 from line 23. If line 25 is more than line 23, enter -0-		26
Other Miscellaneous Deductions	27	Other—from list on page A-9. List type and amount ▶		27
Total Itemized Deductions	28	Is Form 1040, line 38, over $145,950 (over $72,975 if married filing separately)? ☐ **No.** Your deduction is not limited. Add the amounts in the far right column for lines 4 through 27. Also, enter this amount on Form 1040, line 40. ☐ **Yes.** Your deduction may be limited. See page A-9 for the amount to enter.	▶	28
	29	If you elect to itemize deductions even though they are less than your standard deduction, check here ▶ ☐		

For Paperwork Reduction Act Notice, see Form 1040 instructions.   Cat. No. 11330X   **Schedule A (Form 1040) 2005**

Schedules A&B (Form 1040) 2005

OMB No. 1545-0074 Page **2**

Name(s) shown on Form 1040. Do not enter name and social security number if shown on other side.

Your social security number

Schedule B—Interest and Ordinary Dividends

Attachment
Sequence No. **08**

			Amount
Part I **Interest** (See page B-1 and the instructions for Form 1040, line 8a.) **Note.** If you received a Form 1099-INT, Form 1099-OID, or substitute statement from a brokerage firm, list the firm's name as the payer and enter the total interest shown on that form.	**1**	List name of payer. If any interest is from a seller-financed mortgage and the buyer used the property as a personal residence, see page B-1 and list this interest first. Also, show that buyer's social security number and address ▶	**1**
	2	Add the amounts on line 1	**2**
	3	Excludable interest on series EE and I U.S. savings bonds issued after 1989. Attach Form 8815	**3**
	4	Subtract line 3 from line 2. Enter the result here and on Form 1040, line 8a ▶	**4**

Note. If line 4 is over $1,500, you must complete Part III.

			Amount
Part II **Ordinary Dividends** (See page B-1 and the instructions for Form 1040, line 9a.) **Note.** If you received a Form 1099-DIV or substitute statement from a brokerage firm, list the firm's name as the payer and enter the ordinary dividends shown on that form.	**5**	List name of payer ▶	**5**
	6	Add the amounts on line 5. Enter the total here and on Form 1040, line 9a ▶	**6**

Note. If line 6 is over $1,500, you must complete Part III.

		Yes	No
Part III **Foreign Accounts and Trusts** (See page B-2.)	You must complete this part if you **(a)** had over $1,500 of taxable interest or ordinary dividends; or **(b)** had a foreign account; or **(c)** received a distribution from, or were a grantor of, or a transferor to, a foreign trust.		
	7a At any time during 2005, did you have an interest in or a signature or other authority over a financial account in a foreign country, such as a bank account, securities account, or other financial account? See page B-2 for exceptions and filing requirements for Form TD F 90-22.1.		
	b If "Yes," enter the name of the foreign country ▶		
	8 During 2005, did you receive a distribution from, or were you the grantor of, or transferor to, a foreign trust? If "Yes," you may have to file Form 3520. See page B-2		

For Paperwork Reduction Act Notice, see Form 1040 instructions.

Schedule B (Form 1040) 2005

F-5

SCHEDULE C
(Form 1040)

Department of the Treasury
Internal Revenue Service   (99)

Profit or Loss From Business

(Sole Proprietorship)

▶ Partnerships, joint ventures, etc., must file Form 1065 or 1065-B.

▶ Attach to Form 1040 or 1041.   ▶ See Instructions for Schedule C (Form 1040).

OMB No. 1545-0074

2005

Attachment
Sequence No. **09**

Name of proprietor

Social security number (SSN)

A Principal business or profession, including product or service (see page C-2 of the instructions)	**B** Enter code from pages C-8, 9, & 10 ▶
C Business name. If no separate business name, leave blank.	**D** Employer ID number (EIN), if any

E Business address (including suite or room no.) ▶ ....
City, town or post office, state, and ZIP code

F Accounting method: **(1)** ☐ Cash   **(2)** ☐ Accrual   **(3)** ☐ Other (specify) ▶ ....

G Did you "materially participate" in the operation of this business during 2005? If "No," see page C-3 for limit on losses   ☐ Yes   ☐ No

H If you started or acquired this business during 2005, check here   .   .   .   .   ▶ ☐

Part I   Income

1	Gross receipts or sales. **Caution.** If this income was reported to you on Form W-2 and the "Statutory employee" box on that form was checked, see page C-3 and check here . . . . . . ▶ ☐	**1**
2	Returns and allowances	**2**
3	Subtract line 2 from line 1	**3**
4	Cost of goods sold (from line 42 on page 2)	**4**
5	**Gross profit.** Subtract line 4 from line 3	**5**
6	Other income, including Federal and state gasoline or fuel tax credit or refund (see page C-3) . . .	**6**
7	**Gross income.** Add lines 5 and 6 . . . . ▶	**7**

Part II   Expenses. Enter expenses for business use of your home **only** on line 30.

8	Advertising	**8**	**18**	Office expense	**18**
9	Car and truck expenses (see page C-3)	**9**	**19**	Pension and profit-sharing plans	**19**
10	Commissions and fees . .	**10**	**20**	Rent or lease (see page C-5):	
11	Contract labor (see page C-4)	**11**	**a**	Vehicles, machinery, and equipment .	**20a**
12	Depletion	**12**	**b**	Other business property . . .	**20b**
13	Depreciation and section 179 expense deduction (not included in Part III) (see page C-4)	**13**	**21**	Repairs and maintenance . .	**21**
			22	Supplies (not included in Part III) .	**22**
			23	Taxes and licenses	**23**
			24	Travel, meals, and entertainment:	
			a	Travel	**24a**
14	Employee benefit programs (other than on line 19) . .	**14**	**b**	Deductible meals and entertainment (see page C-5)	**24b**
15	Insurance (other than health) .	**15**	**25**	Utilities	**25**
16	Interest:		**26**	Wages (less employment credits) .	**26**
a	Mortgage (paid to banks, etc.) .	**16a**	**27**	Other expenses (from line 48 on page 2)	**27**
b	Other	**16b**			
17	Legal and professional services	**17**			

28	**Total expenses** before expenses for business use of home. Add lines 8 through 27 in columns . ▶	**28**
29	Tentative profit (loss). Subtract line 28 from line 7	**29**
30	Expenses for business use of your home. Attach **Form 8829**	**30**
31	**Net profit or (loss).** Subtract line 30 from line 29.	
	● If a profit, enter on **Form 1040, line 12,** and **also** on **Schedule SE, line 2** (statutory employees, see page C-6). Estates and trusts, enter on Form 1041, line 3.	**31**
	● If a loss, you **must** go to line 32.	
32	If you have a loss, check the box that describes your investment in this activity (see page C-6).	
	● If you checked 32a, enter the loss on **Form 1040, line 12,** and **also** on **Schedule SE, line 2** (statutory employees, see page C-6). Estates and trusts, enter on Form 1041, line 3.	**32a** ☐ All investment is at risk.
	● If you checked 32b, you **must** attach **Form 6198.** Your loss may be limited.	**32b** ☐ Some investment is not at risk.

For Paperwork Reduction Act Notice, see page C-7 of the instructions.   Cat. No. 11334P   Schedule C (Form 1040) 2005

Schedule C (Form 1040) 2005   Page **2**

Part III   **Cost of Goods Sold** (see page C-6)

33   Method(s) used to
value closing inventory: **a** ☐ Cost   **b** ☐ Lower of cost or market   **c** ☐ Other (attach explanation)

34   Was there any change in determining quantities, costs, or valuations between opening and closing inventory? If
"Yes," attach explanation . . . . ☐ **Yes**   ☐ **No**

35 Inventory at beginning of year. If different from last year's closing inventory, attach explanation . .	**35**	
36 Purchases less cost of items withdrawn for personal use	**36**	
37 Cost of labor. Do not include any amounts paid to yourself	**37**	
38 Materials and supplies	**38**	
39 Other costs	**39**	
40 Add lines 35 through 39	**40**	
41 Inventory at end of year	**41**	
42 **Cost of goods sold.** Subtract line 41 from line 40. Enter the result here and on page 1, line 4 . .	**42**	

Part IV   **Information on Your Vehicle.** Complete this part **only** if you are claiming car or truck expenses on
line 9 and are not required to file Form 4562 for this business. See the instructions for line 13 on page
C-4 to find out if you must file Form 4562.

43   When did you place your vehicle in service for business purposes? (month, day, year) ▶ ....../....../...... .

44   Of the total number of miles you drove your vehicle during 2005, enter the number of miles you used your vehicle for:

a   Business ....   **b** Commuting (see instructions) ....   **c** Other ....

45   Do you (or your spouse) have another vehicle available for personal use?. . . . . ☐ **Yes**   ☐ **No**

46   Was your vehicle available for personal use during off-duty hours? . . . . ☐ **Yes**   ☐ **No**

47a   Do you have evidence to support your deduction? . . . . ☐ **Yes**   ☐ **No**

b   If "Yes," is the evidence written? . . . . ☐ **Yes**   ☐ **No**

Part V   **Other Expenses.** List below business expenses not included on lines 8–26 or line 30.

....		
....		
....		
....		
....		
....		
....		
....		
48 **Total other expenses.** Enter here and on page 1, line 27	**48**	

♻ *Printed on recycled paper*   **Schedule C (Form 1040) 2005** F–7

SCHEDULE SE
(Form 1040)

Department of the Treasury
Internal Revenue Service   (99)

Self-Employment Tax

► **Attach to Form 1040.** ► **See Instructions for Schedule SE (Form 1040).**

OMB No. 1545-0074

2005

Attachment
Sequence No. **17**

Name of person with **self-employment** income (as shown on Form 1040)

Social security number of person
with **self-employment** income ►

Who Must File Schedule SE

You must file Schedule SE if:

● You had net earnings from self-employment from **other than** church employee income (line 4 of Short Schedule SE or line 4c of Long Schedule SE) of $400 or more, **or**

● You had church employee income of $108.28 or more. Income from services you performed as a minister or a member of a religious order **is not** church employee income (see page SE-1).

Note. Even if you had a loss or a small amount of income from self-employment, it may be to your benefit to file Schedule SE and use either "optional method" in Part II of Long Schedule SE (see page SE-3).

Exception. If your only self-employment income was from earnings as a minister, member of a religious order, or Christian Science practitioner **and** you filed Form 4361 and received IRS approval not to be taxed on those earnings, **do not** file Schedule SE. Instead, write "Exempt–Form 4361" on Form 1040, line 58.

May I Use Short Schedule SE or Must I Use Long Schedule SE?

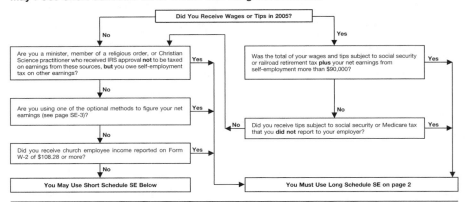

Section A—Short Schedule SE. Caution. Read above to see if you can use Short Schedule SE.

1	Net farm profit or (loss) from Schedule F, line 36, and farm partnerships, Schedule K-1 (Form 1065), box 14, code A	**1**	
2	Net profit or (loss) from Schedule C, line 31; Schedule C-EZ, line 3; Schedule K-1 (Form 1065), box 14, code A (other than farming); and Schedule K-1 (Form 1065-B), box 9. Ministers and members of religious orders, see page SE-1 for amounts to report on this line. See page SE-2 for other income to report	**2**	
3	Combine lines 1 and 2	**3**	
4	**Net earnings from self-employment.** Multiply line 3 by 92.35% (.9235). If less than $400, **do not** file this schedule; you do not owe self-employment tax . . . . ►	**4**	
5	**Self-employment tax.** If the amount on line 4 is: ● $90,000 or less, multiply line 4 by 15.3% (.153). Enter the result here and on **Form 1040, line 58.** ● More than $90,000, multiply line 4 by 2.9% (.029). Then, add $11,160.00 to the result. Enter the total here and on **Form 1040, line 58.**	**5**	
6	**Deduction for one-half of self-employment tax.** Multiply line 5 by 50% (.5). Enter the result here and on **Form 1040, line 27**	**6**	

For Paperwork Reduction Act Notice, see Form 1040 instructions.   Cat. No. 11358Z   Schedule SE (Form 1040) 2005   F–8

Name of person with **self-employment** income (as shown on Form 1040)	Social security number of person with **self-employment** income ▶		

Section B—Long Schedule SE

Part I   Self-Employment Tax

Note. If your only income subject to self-employment tax is **church employee income,** skip lines 1 through 4b. Enter -0- on line 4c and go to line 5a. Income from services you performed as a minister or a member of a religious order **is not** church employee income. See page SE-1.

A   If you are a minister, member of a religious order, or Christian Science practitioner **and** you filed Form 4361, but you had $400 or more of **other** net earnings from self-employment, check here and continue with Part I . . . . . . ▶ ☐

1	Net farm profit or (loss) from Schedule F, line 36, and farm partnerships, Schedule K-1 (Form 1065), box 14, code A. **Note.** Skip this line if you use the farm optional method (see page SE-4)	**1**		
2	Net profit or (loss) from Schedule C, line 31; Schedule C-EZ, line 3; Schedule K-1 (Form 1065), box 14, code A (other than farming); and Schedule K-1 (Form 1065-B), box 9. Ministers and members of religious orders, see page SE-1 for amounts to report on this line. See page SE-2 for other income to report. **Note.** Skip this line if you use the nonfarm optional method (see page SE-4)	**2**		
3	Combine lines 1 and 2	**3**		
4a	If line 3 is more than zero, multiply line 3 by 92.35% (.9235). Otherwise, enter amount from line 3	**4a**		
b	If you elect one or both of the optional methods, enter the total of lines 15 and 17 here . . .	**4b**		
c	Combine lines 4a and 4b. If less than $400, **stop;** you do not owe self-employment tax. **Exception.** If less than $400 and you had **church employee income,** enter -0- and continue. . . . . . ▶	**4c**		
5a	Enter your **church employee income** from Form W-2. See page SE-1 for definition of church employee income **5a**	**5b**		
b	Multiply line 5a by 92.35% (.9235). If less than $100, enter -0-	**5b**		
6	**Net earnings from self-employment.** Add lines 4c and 5b	**6**		
7	Maximum amount of combined wages and self-employment earnings subject to social security tax or the 6.2% portion of the 7.65% railroad retirement (tier 1) tax for 2005	**7**	90,000	00
8a	Total social security wages and tips (total of boxes 3 and 7 on Form(s) W-2) and railroad retirement (tier 1) compensation. If $90,000 or more, skip lines 8b through 10, and go to line 11 . . . . **8a**			
b	Unreported tips subject to social security tax (from Form 4137, line 9) **8b**			
c	Add lines 8a and 8b . . . . ▶	**8c**		
9	Subtract line 8c from line 7. If zero or less, enter -0- here and on line 10 and go to line 11 . ▶	**9**		
10	Multiply the **smaller** of line 6 or line 9 by 12.4% (.124)	**10**		
11	Multiply line 6 by 2.9% (.029)	**11**		
12	**Self-employment tax.** Add lines 10 and 11. Enter here and on **Form 1040, line 58**	**12**		
13	**Deduction for one-half of self-employment tax.** Multiply line 12 by 50% (.5). Enter the result here and on **Form 1040, line 27** **13**			

Part II   Optional Methods To Figure Net Earnings (see page SE-3)

Farm Optional Method. You may use this method only if **(a)** your gross farm income[1] was not more than $2,400 **or (b)** your net farm profits[2] were less than $1,733.

14	Maximum income for optional methods	**14**	1,600	00
15	Enter the **smaller** of: two-thirds (⅔) of gross farm income[1] (not less than zero) **or** $1,600. Also include this amount on line 4b above	**15**		

Nonfarm Optional Method. You may use this method only if **(a)** your net nonfarm profits[3] were less than $1,733 and also less than 72.189% of your gross nonfarm income[4] **and (b)** you had net earnings from self-employment of at least $400 in 2 of the prior 3 years.

Caution. You may use this method no more than five times.

16	Subtract line 15 from line 14	**16**		
17	Enter the **smaller** of: two-thirds (⅔) of gross nonfarm income[4] (not less than zero) **or** the amount on line 16. Also include this amount on line 4b above	**17**		

[1] From Sch. F, line 11, and Sch. K-1 (Form 1065), box 14, code B.

[2] From Sch. F, line 36, and Sch. K-1 (Form 1065), box 14, code A.

[3] From Sch. C, line 31; Sch. C-EZ, line 3; Sch. K-1 (Form 1065), box 14, code A; and Sch. K-1 (Form 1065-B), box 9.

[4] From Sch. C, line 7; Sch. C-EZ, line 1; Sch. K-1 (Form 1065), box 14, code C; and Sch. K-1 (Form 1065-B), box 9.

Form
1040A

Department of the Treasury—Internal Revenue Service

U.S. Individual Income Tax Return (99) **2005**   IRS Use Only—Do not write or staple in this space.

Label (See page 18.)	L A B E L	Your first name and initial	Last name		OMB No. 1545-0074
					Your social security number
Use the IRS label.	H E R E	If a joint return, spouse's first name and initial	Last name		**Spouse's social security number**
Otherwise, please print or type.		Home address (number and street). If you have a P.O. box, see page 18.		Apt. no.	▲ You **must** enter your SSN(s) above. ▲
		City, town or post office, state, and ZIP code. If you have a foreign address, see page 18.			Checking a box below will not change your tax or refund.

Presidential Election Campaign ▶ Check here if you, or your spouse if filing jointly, want $3 to go to this fund (see page 18) ▶ ☐ **You** ☐ **Spouse**

Filing status
Check only one box.

1 ☐ Single
2 ☐ Married filing jointly (even if only one had income)
3 ☐ Married filing separately. Enter spouse's SSN above and full name here. ▶
4 ☐ Head of household (with qualifying person). (See page 19.) If the qualifying person is a child but not your dependent, enter this child's name here. ▶
5 ☐ Qualifying widow(er) with dependent child (see page 19)

Exemptions

6a ☐ **Yourself.** If someone can claim you as a dependent, **do not** check box 6a.

b ☐ **Spouse**

c **Dependents:**

(1) First name Last name	**(2)** Dependent's social security number	**(3)** Dependent's relationship to you	**(4)** ✔ if qualifying child for child tax credit (see page 21)
	:		☐
	:		☐
	:		☐
	:		☐
	:		☐
	:		☐

If more than six dependents, see page 21.

Boxes checked on 6a and 6b ____

No. of children on 6c who:
• lived with you ____
• did not live with you due to divorce or separation (see page 22) ____

Dependents on 6c not entered above ____

Add numbers on lines above ▶ ☐

d Total number of exemptions claimed.

Income

Attach Form(s) W-2 here. Also attach Form(s) 1099-R if tax was withheld.

If you did not get a W-2, see page 24.

Enclose, but do not attach, any payment.

7 Wages, salaries, tips, etc. Attach Form(s) W-2.   **7**

8a **Taxable** interest. Attach Schedule 1 if required.   **8a**
b **Tax-exempt** interest. **Do not** include on line 8a.   8b

9a Ordinary dividends. Attach Schedule 1 if required.   **9a**
b Qualified dividends (see page 25).   9b

10 Capital gain distributions (see page 25).   **10**

11a IRA distributions. 11a   11b Taxable amount (see page 25). **11b**

12a Pensions and annuities. 12a   12b Taxable amount (see page 26). **12b**

13 Unemployment compensation and Alaska Permanent Fund dividends.   **13**

14a Social security benefits. 14a   14b Taxable amount (see page 28). **14b**

15 Add lines 7 through 14b (far right column). This is your **total income.** ▶ **15**

Adjusted gross income

16 Educator expenses (see page 28).   16
17 IRA deduction (see page 28).   17
18 Student loan interest deduction (see page 31). 18
19 Tuition and fees deduction (see page 32).   19
20 Add lines 16 through 19. These are your **total adjustments.**   **20**

21 Subtract line 20 from line 15. This is your **adjusted gross income.** ▶ **21**

For Disclosure, Privacy Act, and Paperwork Reduction Act Notice, see page 58.   Cat. No. 11327A   Form **1040A** (2005)

Form 1040A (2005) Page **2**

Tax, credits, and payments	**22**	Enter the amount from line 21 (adjusted gross income).	22	

Standard Deduction for—

• People who checked any box on line 23a or 23b **or** who can be claimed as a dependent, see page 32.

• All others:

Single or Married filing separately, $5,000

Married filing jointly or Qualifying widow(er), $10,000

Head of household, $7,300

23a	Check if:	☐ **You** were born before January 2, 1941, ☐ Blind ☐ **Spouse** was born before January 2, 1941, ☐ Blind } **Total boxes** checked ▶ 23a		
b		If you are married filing separately and your spouse itemizes deductions, see page 32 and check here ▶ 23b	☐	
24		Enter your **standard deduction** (see left margin).	24	
25		Subtract line 24 from line 22. If line 24 is more than line 22, enter -0-.	25	
26		If line 22 is over $109,475, or you provided housing to a person displaced by Hurricane Katrina, see page 33. Otherwise, multiply $3,200 by the total number of exemptions claimed on line 6d.	26	
27		Subtract line 26 from line 25. If line 26 is more than line 25, enter -0-. This is your **taxable income.** ▶	27	
28		**Tax,** including any alternative minimum tax (see page 34).	28	
29		Credit for child and dependent care expenses. Attach Schedule 2. 29		
30		Credit for the elderly or the disabled. Attach Schedule 3. 30		
31		Education credits. Attach Form 8863. 31		
32		Retirement savings contributions credit. Attach Form 8880. 32		
33		Child tax credit (see page 38). Attach Form 8901 if required. 33		
34		Adoption credit. Attach Form 8839. 34		
35		Add lines 29 through 34. These are your **total credits.**	35	
36		Subtract line 35 from line 28. If line 35 is more than line 28, enter -0-.	36	
37		Advance earned income credit payments from Form(s) W-2.	37	
38		Add lines 36 and 37. This is your **total tax.** ▶	38	

If you have a qualifying child, attach Schedule EIC.	**39**	Federal income tax withheld from Forms W-2 and 1099. 39		
	40	2005 estimated tax payments and amount applied from 2004 return. 40		
	41a	**Earned income credit (EIC).** 41a		
	b	Nontaxable combat pay election. 41b		
	42	Additional child tax credit. Attach Form 8812. 42		
	43	Add lines 39, 40, 41a, and 42. These are your **total payments.** ▶	43	

Refund	**44**	If line 43 is more than line 38, subtract line 38 from line 43. This is the amount you **overpaid.**	44	
Direct deposit? See page 53 and fill in 45b, 45c, and 45d.	**45a**	Amount of line 44 you want **refunded to you.** ▶	45a	
	▶ **b**	Routing number		
		▶ **c** Type: ☐ Checking ☐ Savings		
	▶ **d**	Account number		
	46	Amount of line 44 you want **applied to your 2006 estimated tax.** 46		

Amount you owe	**47**	**Amount you owe.** Subtract line 43 from line 38. For details on how to pay, see page 54. ▶	47	
	48	Estimated tax penalty (see page 54). 48		

Third party designee	Do you want to allow another person to discuss this return with the IRS (see page 55)? ☐ **Yes.** Complete the following. ☐ **No**
	Designee's name ▶ _____ Phone no. ▶ ( ) _____ Personal identification number (PIN) ▶ _____

Sign here

Joint return? See page 18.

Keep a copy for your records.

Under penalties of perjury, I declare that I have examined this return and accompanying schedules and statements, and to the best of my knowledge and belief, they are true, correct, and accurately list all amounts and sources of income I received during the tax year. Declaration of preparer (other than the taxpayer) is based on all information of which the preparer has any knowledge.

Your signature	Date	Your occupation	Daytime phone number ( )
Spouse's signature. If a joint return, **both** must sign.	Date	Spouse's occupation	

Paid preparer's use only	Preparer's signature ▶	Date	Check if self-employed ☐	Preparer's SSN or PTIN
	Firm's name (or yours if self-employed), address, and ZIP code ▶		EIN
			Phone no. ( )

Form **1040A** (2005)

Department of the Treasury—Internal Revenue Service

Form 1040EZ

Income Tax Return for Single and Joint Filers With No Dependents (99) **2005**

OMB No. 1545-0074

Label

(See page 11.)

Use the IRS label.
Otherwise, please print or type.

L A B E L   H E R E

Your first name and initial	Last name		Your social security number
If a joint return, spouse's first name and initial	Last name		Spouse's social security number
Home address (number and street). If you have a P.O. box, see page 11.		Apt. no.	▲ You **must** enter your SSN(s) above. ▲
City, town or post office, state, and ZIP code. If you have a foreign address, see page 11.			

Checking a box below will not change your tax or refund.

Presidential Election Campaign (page 12) ▶

Check here if you, or your spouse if a joint return, want $3 to go to this fund? . . . ▶ ☐ **You**   ☐ **Spouse**

Income

Attach Form(s) W-2 here.
Enclose, but do not attach, any payment.

1 Wages, salaries, and tips. This should be shown in box 1 of your Form(s) W-2. Attach your Form(s) W-2. | 1 |

2 Taxable interest. If the total is over $1,500, you cannot use Form 1040EZ. | 2 |

3 Unemployment compensation and Alaska Permanent Fund dividends (see page 13). | 3 |

4 Add lines 1, 2, and 3. This is your **adjusted gross income.** | 4 |

5 If someone can claim you (or your spouse if a joint return) as a dependent, check the applicable box(es) below and enter the amount from the worksheet on back.

☐ **You**   ☐ **Spouse**

If someone cannot claim you (or your spouse if a joint return), enter $8,200 if **single;** $16,400 if **married filing jointly.** See back for explanation. | 5 |

6 Subtract line 5 from line 4. If line 5 is larger than line 4, enter -0-. This is your **taxable income.** ▶ | 6 |

Payments and tax

7 Federal income tax withheld from box 2 of your Form(s) W-2. | 7 |

8a **Earned income credit (EIC).** | 8a |

b Nontaxable combat pay election. | 8b |

9 Add lines 7 and 8a. These are your **total payments.** ▶ | 9 |

10 **Tax.** Use the amount on **line 6 above** to find your tax in the tax table on pages 24–32 of the booklet. Then, enter the tax from the table on this line. | 10 |

Refund

Have it directly deposited! See page 18 and fill in 11b, 11c, and 11d.

11a If line 9 is larger than line 10, subtract line 10 from line 9. This is your **refund.** ▶ | 11a |

▶ **b** Routing number |__|__|__|__|__|__|__|__|__| ▶ **c** Type: ☐ Checking ☐ Savings

▶ **d** Account number |__|__|__|__|__|__|__|__|__|__|__|__|__|__|__|__|__|

Amount you owe

12 If line 10 is larger than line 9, subtract line 9 from line 10. This is the **amount you owe.** For details on how to pay, see page 19. ▶ | 12 |

Third party designee

Do you want to allow another person to discuss this return with the IRS (see page 19)? ☐ **Yes.** Complete the following. ☐ **No**

Designee's name ▶   Phone no. ▶ (   )   Personal identification number (PIN) ▶ |__|__|__|__|__|

Sign here

Joint return? See page 11.
Keep a copy for your records.

Under penalties of perjury, I declare that I have examined this return, and to the best of my knowledge and belief, it is true, correct, and accurately lists all amounts and sources of income I received during the tax year. Declaration of preparer (other than the taxpayer) is based on all information of which the preparer has any knowledge.

Your signature	Date	Your occupation	Daytime phone number
			( )
Spouse's signature. If a joint return, **both** must sign.	Date	Spouse's occupation	

Paid preparer's use only

Preparer's signature ▶		Date	Check if self-employed ☐	Preparer's SSN or PTIN
Firm's name (or yours if self-employed), address, and ZIP code ▶			EIN	
			Phone no.	( )

For Disclosure, Privacy Act, and Paperwork Reduction Act Notice, see page 23.   Cat. No. 11329W   Form **1040EZ** (2005)

Use this form if

- Your filing status is single or married filing jointly. If you are not sure about your filing status, see page 11.
- You (and your spouse if married filing jointly) were under age 65 and not blind at the end of 2005. If you were born on January 1, 1941, you are considered to be age 65 at the end of 2005.
- You do not claim any dependents. For information on dependents, use TeleTax topic 354 (see page 6).
- Your taxable income (line 6) is less than $100,000.
- You do not claim any adjustments to income. For information on adjustments to income, use TeleTax topics 451-458 (see page 6).
- The only tax credit you can claim is the earned income credit. For information on credits, use TeleTax topics 601-608 and 610 (see page 6).
- You had only wages, salaries, tips, taxable scholarship or fellowship grants, unemployment compensation, or Alaska Permanent Fund dividends, and your taxable interest was not over $1,500. But if you earned tips, including allocated tips, that are not included in box 5 and box 7 of your Form W-2, you may not be able to use Form 1040EZ (see page 12). If you are planning to use Form 1040EZ for a child who received Alaska Permanent Fund dividends, see page 13.
- You did not receive any advance earned income credit payments.
  If you cannot use this form, use TeleTax topic 352 (see page 6).

Filling in your return

If you received a scholarship or fellowship grant or tax-exempt interest income, such as on municipal bonds, see the booklet before filling in the form. Also, see the booklet if you received a Form 1099-INT showing federal income tax withheld or if federal income tax was withheld from your unemployment compensation or Alaska Permanent Fund dividends.

For tips on how to avoid common mistakes, see page 20.

Remember, you must report all wages, salaries, and tips even if you do not get a Form W-2 from your employer. You must also report all your taxable interest, including interest from banks, savings and loans, credit unions, etc., even if you do not get a Form 1099-INT.

Worksheet for dependents who checked one or both boxes on line 5

(keep a copy for your records)

Use this worksheet to figure the amount to enter on line 5 if someone can claim you (or your spouse if married filing jointly) as a dependent, even if that person chooses not to do so. To find out if someone can claim you as a dependent, use TeleTax topic 354 (see page 6).

A. Amount, if any, from line 1 on front . . . . **A.** _____

B. Is line A more than $550?
    ☐ **Yes.** Add $250 to line A. Enter the total. ⎫
    ☐ **No.** Enter $800. ⎭ . . . . **B.** _____

C. If **single**, enter $5,000; if **married filing jointly,** enter $10,000 . . **C.** _____

D. Enter the **smaller** of line B or line C here. This is your standard deduction . . . . **D.** _____

E. Exemption amount.
- If single, enter -0-.
- If married filing jointly and you checked—
   —both boxes on line 5, enter -0-.
   —only one box on line 5, enter $3,200. ⎱ **E.** _____

F. Add lines D and E. Enter the total here and on line 5 on the front . **F.** _____

If you did not check any boxes on line 5, enter on line 5 the amount shown below that applies to you.

- Single, enter $8,200. This is the total of your standard deduction ($5,000) and your exemption ($3,200).
- Married filing jointly, enter $16,400. This is the total of your standard deduction ($10,000), your exemption ($3,200), and your spouse's exemption ($3,200).

Mailing return

Mail your return by **April 17, 2006.** Use the envelope that came with your booklet. If you do not have that envelope or if you moved during the year, see the back cover for the address to use.

Form **1040EZ** (2005)

Form **1040X**
(Rev. November 2005)

Department of the Treasury—Internal Revenue Service

Amended U.S. Individual Income Tax Return

► See separate instructions.

OMB No. 1545-0074

This return is for calendar year ►   **, or fiscal year ended ►**

Please print or type

| Your first name and initial | Last name | Your social security number |
| If a joint return, spouse's first name and initial | Last name | Spouse's social security number |

| Home address (no. and street) or P.O. box if mail is not delivered to your home | Apt. no. | Phone number |

| City, town or post office, state, and ZIP code. If you have a foreign address, see page 2 of the instructions. | For Paperwork Reduction Act Notice, see page 6. |

A If the address shown above is different from that shown on your last return filed with the IRS and you would like us to change it, check here . . . . ► ☐

B Filing status. Be sure to complete this line. **Note.** You cannot change from joint to separate returns after the due date.

On original return ► ☐ Single ☐ Married filing jointly ☐ Married filing separately ☐ Head of household ☐ Qualifying widow(er)

On this return ► ☐ Single ☐ Married filing jointly ☐ Married filing separately ☐ Head of household* ☐ Qualifying widow(er)

* If the qualifying person is a child but not your dependent, see page 2 of the instructions.

Use Part II on the back to explain any changes

			A. Original amount or as previously adjusted (see page 3)	**B. Net change—** amount of increase or (decrease)— explain in Part II	**C. Correct amount**
	Income and Deductions (see instructions)				
1	Adjusted gross income (see page 3)	1			
2	Itemized deductions or standard deduction (see page 3). .	2			
3	Subtract line 2 from line 1	3			
4	Exemptions. If changing, fill in Parts I and II on the back (see page 3)	4			
5	Taxable income. Subtract line 4 from line 3	5			
6	Tax (see page 4). Method used in col. C	6			
7	Credits (see page 4)	7			
8	Subtract line 7 from line 6. Enter the result but not less than zero .	8			
9	Other taxes (see page 4)	9			
10	Total tax. Add lines 8 and 9	10			
11	Federal income tax withheld and excess social security and tier 1 RRTA tax withheld. If changing, see page 4 . . .	11			
12	Estimated tax payments, including amount applied from prior year's return	12			
13	Earned income credit (EIC)	13			
14	Additional child tax credit from Form 8812	14			
15	Credits from Form 2439, Form 4136, or Form 8885 . . .	15			
16	Amount paid with request for extension of time to file (see page 4)			16	
17	Amount of tax paid with original return plus additional tax paid after it was filed			17	
18	Total payments. Add lines 11 through 17 in column C			18	

Refund or Amount You Owe

19	Overpayment, if any, as shown on original return or as previously adjusted by the IRS . . .			19	
20	Subtract line 19 from line 18 (see page 5)			20	
21	**Amount you owe.** If line 10, column C, is more than line 20, enter the difference and see page 5 .			21	
22	If line 10, column C, is less than line 20, enter the difference			22	
23	Amount of line 22 you want **refunded to you**			23	
24	Amount of line 22 you want **applied to your** **estimated tax**	24			

Sign Here

Joint return? See page 2.

Keep a copy for your records.

Under penalties of perjury, I declare that I have filed an original return and that I have examined this amended return, including accompanying schedules and statements, and to the best of my knowledge and belief, this amended return is true, correct, and complete. Declaration of preparer (other than taxpayer) is based on all information of which the preparer has any knowledge.

► Your signature   Date

► Spouse's signature. If a joint return, **both** must sign.   Date

Paid Preparer's Use Only

Preparer's signature ►	Date	Check if self-employed ☐	Preparer's SSN or PTIN
Firm's name (or yours if self-employed), address, and ZIP code ►		EIN	
		Phone no. ( )	

Cat. No. 11360L

Form **1040X** (Rev. 11-2005)

F–14

Form 1040X (Rev. 11-2005) Page **2**

Part I	**Exemptions.** See Form 1040 or 1040A instructions.	**A. Original number** of exemptions reported or as previously adjusted	**B. Net change**	**C. Correct number** of exemptions

Complete this part **only** if you are:
- Increasing or decreasing the number of exemptions claimed on line 6d of the return you are amending, or
- Increasing or decreasing the exemption amount for housing individuals displaced by Hurricane Katrina.

25	Yourself and spouse **25**			
	Caution. If someone can claim you as a dependent, you cannot claim an exemption for yourself.			
26	Your dependent children who lived with you **26**			
27	Your dependent children who did not live with you due to divorce or separation **27**			
28	Other dependents **28**			
29	Total number of exemptions. Add lines 25 through 28 . . . **29**			
30	Multiply the number of exemptions claimed on line 29 by the amount listed below for the tax year you are amending. Enter the result here and on line 4.			

Tax year	Exemption amount	But see the instructions for line 4 on page 3 if the amount on line 1 is over:
2005	$3,200	$109,475
2004	3,100	107,025
2003	3,050	104,625
2002	3,000	103,000

		30		
31	If you are claiming an exemption amount for housing individuals displaced by Hurricane Katrina, enter the amount from Form 8914, line 2 (see instructions for line 4) **31**			
32	Add lines 30 and 31. Enter the result here and on line 4 . . . . . **32**			

33 Dependents (children and other) not claimed on original (or adjusted) return:

(a) First name	Last name	(b) Dependent's social security number	(c) Dependent's relationship to you	(d) ✓ if qualifying child for child tax credit (see page 5)
		: :		☐
		: :		☐
		: :		☐
		: :		☐
		: :		☐

No. of children on 33 who:
- lived with you . . . ► ☐
- **did not** live with you due to divorce or separation (see page 5) . ► ☐

Dependents on 33 not entered above ► ☐

Part II	**Explanation of Changes**

Enter the line number from the front of the form for each item you are changing and give the reason for each change. Attach only the supporting forms and schedules for the items changed. If you do not attach the required information, your Form 1040X may be returned. Be sure to include your name and social security number on any attachments.

If the change relates to a net operating loss carryback or a general business credit carryback, attach the schedule or form that shows the year in which the loss or credit occurred. See page 2 of the instructions. Also, check here. . . . . . ► ☐

Part III	**Presidential Election Campaign Fund.** Checking below will not increase your tax or reduce your refund.

If you did not previously want $3 to go to the fund but now want to, check here . . . . ► ☐
If a joint return and your spouse did not previously want $3 to go to the fund but now wants to, check here . . . . ► ☐

Form **1040X** (Rev. 11-2005) F–15

Form **870** (Rev. March 1992)	Department of the Treasury—Internal Revenue Service **Waiver of Restrictions on Assessment and Collection of Deficiency in Tax and Acceptance of Overassessment**	Date received by Internal Revenue Service

Names and address of taxpayers *(Number, street, city or town, State, ZIP code)*	Social security or employer identification number

Increase (Decrease) in Tax and Penalties

Tax year ended	Tax	Penalties

(For instructions, see back of form)

Consent to Assessment and Collection

I consent to the immediate assessment and collection of any deficiencies *(increase in tax and penalties)* and accept any overassessment *(decrease in tax and penalties)* shown above, plus any interest provided by law. I understand that by signing this waiver, I will not be able to contest these years in the United States Tax Court, unless additional deficiencies are determined for these years.

YOUR SIGNATURE HERE ➤		Date
SPOUSE'S SIGNATURE ➤		Date
TAXPAYER'S REPRESENTATIVE HERE ➤		Date
CORPORATE NAME ➤		
CORPORATE OFFICER(S) SIGN HERE ➤		Title	Date
		Title	Date

Catalog Number 16894U   Form **870** (Rev. 3-1992) F-16

Name of Taxpayer:

Identification Number:

Form 870 page 2

Instructions

General Information

If you consent to the assessment of the deficiencies shown in this waiver, please sign and return the form in order to limit any interest charge and expedite the adjustment to your account. Your consent will not prevent you from filing a claim for refund *(after you have paid the tax)* if you later believe you are so entitled. It will not prevent us from later determining, if necessary, that you owe additional tax; nor extend the time provided by law for either action.

We have agreements with State tax agencies under which information about Federal tax, including increases or decreases, is exchanged with the States. If this change affects the amount of your State income tax, you should file the required State form.

If you later file a claim and the Service disallows it, you may file suit for refund in a district court or in the United States Claims Court, but you may not file a petition with the United States Tax Court.

We will consider this waiver a valid claim for refund or credit of any overpayment due you resulting from any decrease in tax and penalties shown above, provided you sign and file it within the period established by law for making such a claim.

Who Must Sign

If you filed jointly, both you and your spouse must sign. If this waiver is for a corporation, it should be signed with the corporation name, followed by the signatures and titles of the corporate officers authorized to sign. An attorney or agent may sign this waiver provided such action is specifically authorized by a power of attorney which, if not previously filed, must accompany this form.

If this waiver is signed by a person acting in a fiduciary capacity *(for example, an* executor, *administrator, or a trustee)* Form 56, Notice Concerning Fiduciary Relationship, should, unless previously filed, accompany this form.

Form **8275**

(Rev. May 2001)

Department of the Treasury
Internal Revenue Service

Disclosure Statement

Do not use this form to disclose items or positions that are contrary to Treasury
regulations. Instead, use Form 8275-R, Regulation Disclosure Statement.
See separate instructions.

▶ **Attach to your tax return.**

OMB No. 1545-0889

Attachment
Sequence No. **92**

Name(s) shown on return	Identifying number shown on return

Part I   **General Information** (see instructions)

(a) Rev. Rul., Rev. Proc., etc.	(b) Item or Group of Items	(c) Detailed Description of Items	(d) Form or Schedule	(e) Line No.	(f) Amount
1					
2					
3					

Part II   **Detailed Explanation** (see instructions)

1

2

3

Part III   **Information About Pass-Through Entity.** To be completed by partners, shareholders, beneficiaries, or residual interest holders.

Complete this part only if you are making adequate disclosure for a pass-through item.

Note: *A pass-through entity is a partnership, S corporation, estate, trust, regulated investment company (RIC), real estate investment trust (REIT), or real estate mortgage investment conduit (REMIC).*

1 Name, address, and ZIP code of pass-through entity	**2** Identifying number of pass-through entity
	3 Tax year of pass-through entity / / to / /
	4 Internal Revenue Service Center where the pass-through entity filed its return

For Paperwork Reduction Act Notice, see separate instructions.   Cat. No. 61935M   Form **8275** (Rev. 5-2001)

Form 8275 (Rev. 5-2001)

Page **2**

Part IV	Explanations *(continued from Parts I and/or II)*

Form **8275** (Rev. 5-2001)

Department of the Treasury
Internal Revenue Service

Letter Number: 3219 (SC/CG)

Letter Date:

Taxpayer Identifying Number:

Tax Form:

Tax Year Ended and Deficiency:

Person to Contact:

Employee Identification Number:

Contact Telephone Number:

Hours to Call:

Last Day to File a Petition With
the United States Tax Court:

Notice of Deficiency

Penalties or Additions to Tax

IRC Section	Deficiency

Dear Taxpayer:

We have determined that there is a deficiency (increase) in your income tax as shown above. This letter is your NOTICE OF DEFICIENCY, as required by law. The enclosed statement shows how we figured the deficiency.

If you want to contest this determination in court before making any payment, you have until the **Last Date to Petition Tax Court** (90 days from the date of this letter or 150 days if the letter is addressed to you outside of the United States) to file a petition with the United States Tax Court for a redetermination of the amount of your tax. You can get a petition form and the rules for filing a petition from the Tax Court. You should file the petition with the **United States Tax Court, 400 Second Street NW, Washington, D.C. 20217.** Attach a copy of this letter to the petition.

The time in which you must file a petition with the court (90 or 150 days as the case may be) is fixed by law and the Court cannot consider your case if your petition is filed late. As required by law, separate notices are sent to spouses. If this letter is addressed to both a husband and wife, and both want to petition the Tax Court, both must sign the petition or each must file a separate, signed petition.

The Tax Court has a simplified procedure for small tax cases when the amount in dispute is $50,000 or less for any one tax year. You can also get information about this procedure, as well as a petition form you can use, by writing to the Clerk of the United States Tax Court at 400 Second Street NW., Washington D.C. 20217. You should write promptly if you intend to file a petition with the Tax Court.

Letter 3219 (SC/CG) (Rev. 2-2001)
Catalog Number 27500P

F-20

If you decide *not* to file a petition with the Tax Court, please sign and return the enclosed waiver form to us. This will permit us to assess the deficiency quickly and will limit the accumulation of interest. We've enclosed an envelope you can use. If you decide not to sign and return the waiver and you do not petition the Tax Court, the law requires us to assess and bill you for the deficiency after 90 days from the date of this letter (150 days if this letter is addressed to you outside the United States).

If you have questions about this letter, you may call the contact person whose name and telephone number are shown in the heading of this letter. If this number is outside your local calling area, there will be a long distance charge to you. If you prefer, you can call the Internal Revenue Service (IRS) telephone number in your local directory. An IRS employee there may be able to help you, but the office at the address shown on this letter is most familiar with your case.

When you send information we requested or if you write to us about this letter, please provide a telephone number and the best time for us to call you if we need more information. Please attach this letter to your correspondence to help us identify your case. Keep the copy for your records.

The person whose name and telephone number are shown in the heading of this letter can access your tax information and help get you answers. You also have the right to contact the Taxpayer Advocate. You can call 1-877-777-4778 and ask for Taxpayer Advocate Assistance. Or you can contact the Taxpayer Advocate for the IRS Office that issued this Notice of Deficiency by calling or writing to:

Taxpayer Advocate

Taxpayer Advocate assistance is not a substitute for established IRS procedures such as the formal appeals process. The Taxpayer Advocate is not able to reverse legally correct tax determinations, nor extend the time fixed by law that you have to file a petition in the United States Tax Court. The Taxpayer Advocate can, however, see that a tax matter that may not have been resolved through normal channels gets prompt and proper handling.

Thank you for your cooperation.

Sincerely yours,

Commissioner
By

Enclosures:
Copy of this letter
Statement
Waiver
Envelope
☐ Publication 3498-A
☐ Publication 1
☐ Publication 5
☐ Publication 594
☐ Notice 609

Letter 3219 (SC/CG) (Rev. 2-2001)
Catalog Number 27500P

F-21

Form **5564-A** (October 1999)	Department of the Treasury — Internal Revenue Service **Notice of Deficiency-Waiver**	Symbols

Name and address of taxpayer(s)   Social Security or Employer Identification Number

Kind of tax   ☐ Copy to authorized representative

DEFICIENCY — Increase in Tax and Penalties

Tax Year Ended:

Deficiency:
Increase in tax

I consent to the immediate assessment and collection of the deficiencies (increase in tax and penalties) shown above, plus any interest. Also, I waive the requirement under section 6532 (a) (1) of the Internal Revenue Code that a notice of claim disallowance be sent to me by certified mail for any overpayment shown on the attached report.

I understand that the filing of this waiver is irrevocable and it will begin the 2-year period for filing suit for refund of the claims disallowed as if the notice of disallowance had been sent by certified or registered mail.

Your Signature ➤	_(Signature)_	_(Date signed)_
Spouse's Signature **(If A Joint Return** **Was Filed)** ➤	_(Signature)_	_(Date signed)_
Taxpayer's **Representative** **Sign Here** ➤	_(Signature)_ _(Title)_	_(Date signed)_

(For instructions, please see the next page)

If you agree, please sign one copy of this form and return it; keep the other copy for your records.

Cat. No. 29001P   www.irs.gov   Form **5564-A** (10-1999)   F–22

Instructions for Form 5564-A

Note:

If you consent to the assessment of the deficiencies shown in this waiver, please sign and return this form to limit the interest charge and expedite our bill to you. Please do not sign and return any prior notices you may have received. Your consent signature is required on this waiver, even if fully paid.

Your consent will not prevent you from filing a claim for refund (after you have paid the tax) if you later believe you are so entitled; nor prevent us from later determining, if necessary, that you owe additional tax; nor will it extend the time provided by law for each action.

If you later file a claim and the Internal Revenue Service disallows it, you may file suit for refund in a District Court or in the United States Claims Court, but you may not file a petition with the United States Tax Court.

Who Must Sign

If you filed a joint return, both you and your spouse must sign. the original and duplicate of this form Your attorney or agent may sign this waiver provided that the action is specifically authorized by a power of attorney which, if not previously filed, must accompany this form.

If this waiver is signed by a person acting in a fiduciary capacity (for example, an executor, administrator, or a trustee), Form 56, Notice Concerning Fiduciary Relationship, should, unless previously filed, accompany this form.

Optional Paragraphs

A check in the block to the left of a paragraph below indicates that the paragraph applies to your situation.

☐ The amount shown as the deficiency may not be billed, since all or part of the refund due has been held to offset all or a portion of the amount of the deficiency. The amount that will be billed, if any, is shown on the attached examination report.

☐ The amount shown as a deficiency may not be billed, since the refund due will be reduced by the amount of the deficiency. The net refund due is shown on the attached examination report.

Form **4549** (Rev. March 2005)	Department of the Treasury-Internal Revenue Service **Income Tax Examination Changes**	Page _____ of _____
Name and Address of Taxpayer	Taxpayer Identification Number	Return Form No.:
	Person with whom examination changes were discussed.	Name and Title:

1. **Adjustments to Income**	Period End	Period End	Period End
a.			
b.			
c.			
d.			
e.			
f.			
g.			
h.			
i.			
j.			
k.			
l.			
m.			
n.			
o.			
p.			
2. **Total Adjustments**			
3. Taxable Income Per Return or as Previously Adjusted			
4. **Corrected Taxable Income** Tax Method Filing Status			
5. **Tax**			
6. Additional Taxes / Alternative Minimum Tax			
7. Corrected Tax Liability			

8. **Less**   a.
   Credits   b.
         c.
         d.			

9. **Balance** *(Line 7 less Lines 8a through 8d)*			

10. Plus   a.
   Other   b.
   Taxes   c.
        d.			

11. Total Corrected Tax Liability *(Line 9 plus Lines 10a through 10d)*			
12. Total Tax Shown on Return or as Previously Adjusted			
13. Adjustments to: a. b.			
14. Deficiency-Increase in Tax or *(Overassessment-Decrease in Tax)* *(Line 11 less Line 12 adjusted by Lines 13a plus 13b)*			
15. Adjustments to Prepayment Credits - Increase *(Decrease)*			
16. **Balance Due or *(Overpayment)*** - *(Line 14 adjusted by Line 15)* *(Excluding interest and penalties)*			

The Internal Revenue Service has agreements with state tax agencies under which information about federal tax, including increases or decreases, is exchanged with the states. If this change affects the amount of your state income tax, you should amend your state return by filing the necessary forms.

You may be subject to backup withholding if you underreport your interest, dividend, or patronage dividend income you earned and do not pay the required tax. The IRS may order backup withholding *(withholding of a percentage of your dividend and/or interest income)* if the tax remains unpaid after it has been assessed and four notices have been issued to you over a 120-day period.

Catalog Number 23105A   www.irs.gov   Form **4549** (Rev. 3-2005)   F-24

Form **4549** (Rev. March 2005)	Department of the Treasury-Internal Revenue Service **Income Tax Examination Changes**		Page_____ of _____
Name of Taxpayer		Taxpayer Identification Number	Return Form No.:

17. Penalties/ Code Sections	**Period End**	**Period End**	**Period End**
a.			
b.			
c.			
d.			
e.			
f.			
g.			
h.			
i.			
j.			
k.			
l.			
m.			
18. Total Penalties			
Underreporter attributable to negligence: *(1981-1987)* *A tax addition of 50 percent of the interest due on the underpayment will accrue until it is paid or assessed.*			
Underreporter attributable to fraud: *(1981-1987)* *A tax addition of 50 percent of the interest due on the underpayment will accrue until it is paid or assessed.*			
Underreporter attributable to Tax Motivated Transactions *(TMT).* The interest will accrue and be assessed at 120% of the under-payment rate in accordance with IRC §6621(c)			
19. Summary of Taxes, Penalties and Interest:			
a. Balance due or *(Overpayment)* Taxes - *(Line 16, Page 1)*			
b. Penalties *(Line 18)* - computed to			
c. Interest *(IRC § 6601)* - computed to			
d. TMT Interest - computed to *(on TMT underpayment)*			
e. Amount due or *(refund)* - *(sum of Lines a, b, c and d)*			

Other Information:

Examiner's Signature:	Employee ID:	Office:	Date:

Consent to Assessment and Collection- I do not wish to exercise my appeal rights with the Internal Revenue Service or to contest in the United States Tax Court the findings in this report. Therefore, I give my consent to the immediate assessment and collection of any increase in tax and penalties, and accept any decrease in tax and penalties shown above, plus additional interest as provided by law. It is understood that this report is subject to acceptance by the Area Director, Area Manager, Specialty Tax Program Chief, or Director of Field Operations.

PLEASE NOTE: *If a joint return was filed.* **BOTH** *taxpayers must sign*

Signature of Taxpayer	Date:	Signature of Taxpayer	Date:
By:		Title:	Date:

Catalog Number 23105A   www.irs.gov   Form **4549** (Rev. 3-2005) F−25

Form **886-A** (Rev. January 1994)	**EXPLANATIONS OF ITEMS**	Schedule number or exhibit
Name of taxpayer	Tax Identification Number	Year/Period ended

FORM 1

PETITION (Other Than In Small Tax Case)

(See Rules 30 through 34)

UNITED STATES TAX COURT

....

Petitioner(s)

v.

COMMISSIONER OF INTERNAL REVENUE,

Respondent

} Docket No.

PETITION

The petitioner hereby petitions for a redetermination of the deficiency (or liability) set forth by the Commissioner of Internal Revenue in the Commissioner's notice of deficiency (or liability) [Service symbols] dated ...., and as the basis for the petitioner's case alleges as follows:

1. The petitioner is [set forth whether an individual, fiduciary, corporation, etc., as provided in Rule 60] with mailing address now at

....

Street   City   State   Zip Code

and with legal residence (or principal office) now at [if different from the mailing address]

....

Street   City   State   Zip Code

Petitioner's taxpayer identification number (e.g., Social Security or employer identification number) is ....

The return for the period here involved was filed with the Office of the Internal Revenue Service at ....

City   State

2. The notice of deficiency (or liability) (a copy of which, including so much of the statement and schedules accompanying the notice as is material, is attached and marked Exhibit A) was mailed to the petitioner on ...., and was issued by the Office of the Internal Revenue Service at ....

City   State

3. The deficiencies (or liabilities) as determined by the Commissioner are in income (estate, gift, or certain excise) taxes for the calendar (or fiscal) year ...., in the amount of $..............., of which $.............. is in dispute.

4. The determination of the tax set forth in the said notice of deficiency (or liability) is based upon the following errors: [Here set forth specifically in lettered subparagraphs the assignments of error in a concise manner. Do not plead facts, which properly belong in the succeeding paragraph.]

(6/30/03)   198

(6/30/03)   199

5. The facts upon which the petitioner relies, as the basis of the petitioner's case, are as follows: [Here set forth allegations of fact, but not the evidence, sufficient to inform the Court and the Commissioner of the positions taken and the bases therefor. Set forth the allegations in orderly and logical sequence, with subparagraphs lettered, so as to enable the Commissioner to admit or deny each allegation. See Rules 31(a) and 34(b)(5).]

WHEREFORE, petitioner prays that [here set forth the relief desired].

(Signed) ....
                                        Petitioner or Counsel

....
                    Present address—City, State, Zip Code

Dated: ....
....
                        Telephone (include area code)

....
                     Counsel's Tax Court Bar Number

F–28

FORM 2

PETITION (Small Tax Case)
(Deficiency, Employment Status, Relief from Joint and Several Liability, or
Lien or Levy)
(Available—Ask for Form 2)
(See Rules 170 through 175, 291(c), 321(c), 331(c))

UNITED STATES TAX COURT

www.ustaxcourt.gov

(FIRST) (MIDDLE) (LAST)

....
(PLEASE TYPE OR PRINT)   Petitioner(s)
v.   Docket No. ....
COMMISSIONER OF INTERNAL REVENUE,
                              Respondent

PETITION

1. Petitioner(s) hereby file(s) a (PLACE AN **"X"** IN THE APPROPRIATE BOX):

☐ Petition for Redetermination of a   ☐ Petition for Determination of Relief
    Deficiency   from Joint and Several Liability on a
                                                   Joint Return

☐ Petition for Lien or Levy Action   ☐ Petition for Redetermination of
    (Collection Action)   Employment Status (Worker
                                                   Classification)

2. Petitioner(s) disagree(s) with the determination contained in the notice issued
by the Internal Revenue Service for the year(s) or period(s) ...., as set forth
in such notice dated ...., A COPY OF WHICH IS ATTACHED. DO
NOT ATTACH ANY OTHER DOCUMENTS TO THIS PETITION.

3. Petitioner(s)' taxpayer identification (e.g., Social Security) number(s) is (are)
....

4. Set forth the relief requested and the reasons why you believe you are entitled
to such relief.
....
....
....
....

Petitioner(s) request(s) that this case be conducted under the "small tax case" procedures. The amount in dispute or any overpayment claimed is $50,000 or less. A
decision in a "small tax case" is final and cannot be appealed to a Court of Appeals
by the Internal Revenue Service or the Petitioner(s). If you do **NOT** want this case
conducted as a "small tax case", place an **"X"** in the following box. ☐

....
Signature of Petitioner   Date   (Print) Mailing Address

                                                              ....
                                                              City, State, Zip Code, (Area Code) Telephone No.

....
Signature of Petitioner (e.g., Spouse)   Date   (Print) Mailing Address
   (If Named in the Final Notice)

                                                              ....
                                                              City, State, Zip Code, (Area Code) Telephone No.

....
Signature, Name, Address, Telephone No. and Tax Court Bar Number of Counsel, if Retained by Petitioner(s)

(6/30/03)   200

F-29

Publications Appendix

Department of the Treasury
Internal Revenue Service

Publication 1
(Rev. May 2005)

Catalog Number 64731W

www.irs.gov

Your Rights as a Taxpayer

The first part of this publication explains some of your most important rights as a taxpayer. The second part explains the examination, appeal, collection, and refund processes. This publication is also available in Spanish.

Declaration of Taxpayer Rights

I. Protection of Your Rights

IRS employees will explain and protect your rights as a taxpayer throughout your contact with us.

II. Privacy and Confidentiality

The IRS will not disclose to anyone the information you give us, except as authorized by law. You have the right to know why we are asking you for information, how we will use it, and what happens if you do not provide requested information.

III. Professional and Courteous Service

If you believe that an IRS employee has not treated you in a professional, fair, and courteous manner, you should tell that employee's supervisor. If the supervisor's response is not satisfactory, you should write to the IRS director for your area or the center where you file your return.

IV. Representation

You may either represent yourself or, with proper written authorization, have someone else represent you in your place. Your representative must be a person allowed to practice before the IRS, such as an attorney, certified public accountant, or enrolled agent. If you are in an interview and ask to consult such a person, then we must stop and reschedule the interview in most cases.

You can have someone accompany you at an interview. You may make sound recordings of any meetings with our examination, appeal, or collection personnel, provided you tell us in writing 10 days before the meeting.

V. Payment of Only the Correct Amount of Tax

You are responsible for paying only the correct amount of tax due under the law—no more, no less. If you cannot pay all of your tax when it is due, you may be able to make monthly installment payments.

VI. Help With Unresolved Tax Problems

The Taxpayer Advocate Service can help you if you have tried unsuccessfully to resolve a problem with the IRS. Your local Taxpayer Advocate can offer you special help if you have a significant hardship as a result of a tax problem. For more information, call toll free 1–877–777–4778 (1–800–829–4059 for TTY/TDD) or write to the Taxpayer Advocate at the IRS office that last contacted you.

VII. Appeals and Judicial Review

If you disagree with us about the amount of your tax liability or certain collection actions, you have the right to ask the Appeals Office to review your case. You may also ask a court to review your case.

VIII. Relief From Certain Penalties and Interest

The IRS will waive penalties when allowed by law if you can show you acted reasonably and in good faith or relied on the incorrect advice of an IRS employee. We will waive interest that is the result of certain errors or delays caused by an IRS employee.

THE IRS MISSION

PROVIDE AMERICA'S TAXPAYERS TOP QUALITY SERVICE BY HELPING THEM UNDERSTAND AND MEET THEIR TAX RESPONSIBILITIES AND BY APPLYING THE TAX LAW WITH INTEGRITY AND FAIRNESS TO ALL.

Examinations, Appeals, Collections, and Refunds

Examinations (Audits)

We accept most taxpayers' returns as filed. If we inquire about your return or select it for examination, it does not suggest that you are dishonest. The inquiry or examination may or may not result in more tax. We may close your case without change; or, you may receive a refund.

The process of selecting a return for examination usually begins in one of two ways. First, we use computer programs to identify returns that may have incorrect amounts. These programs may be based on information returns, such as Forms 1099 and W-2, on studies of past examinations, or on certain issues identified by compliance projects. Second, we use information from outside sources that indicates that a return may have incorrect amounts. These sources may include newspapers, public records, and individuals. If we determine that the information is accurate and reliable, we may use it to select a return for examination.

Publication 556, Examination of Returns, Appeal Rights, and Claims for Refund, explains the rules and procedures that we follow in examinations. The following sections give an overview of how we conduct examinations.

By Mail

We handle many examinations and inquiries by mail. We will send you a letter with either a request for more information or a reason why we believe a change to your return may be needed. You can respond by mail or you can request a personal interview with an examiner. If you mail us the requested information or provide an explanation, we may or may not agree with you, and we will explain the reasons for any changes. Please do not hesitate to write to us about anything you do not understand.

By Interview

If we notify you that we will conduct your examination through a personal interview, or you request such an interview, you have the right to ask that the examination take place at a reasonable time and place that is convenient for both you and the IRS. If our examiner proposes any changes to your return, he or she will explain the reasons for the changes. If you do not agree with these changes, you can meet with the examiner's supervisor.

Repeat Examinations

If we examined your return for the same items in either of the 2 previous years and proposed no change to your tax liability, please contact us as soon as possible so we can see if we should discontinue the examination.

Appeals

If you do not agree with the examiner's proposed changes, you can appeal them to the Appeals Office of IRS. Most differences can be settled without expensive and time-consuming court trials. Your appeal rights are explained in detail in both Publication 5, Your Appeal Rights and How To Prepare a Protest If You Don't Agree, and Publication 556, Examination of Returns, Appeal Rights, and Claims for Refund.

If you do not wish to use the Appeals Office or disagree with its findings, you may be able to take your case to the U.S. Tax Court, U.S. Court of Federal Claims, or the U.S. District Court where you live. If you take your case to court, the IRS will have the burden of proving certain facts if you kept adequate records to show your tax liability, cooperated with the IRS, and meet certain other conditions. If the court agrees with you on most issues in your case and finds that our position was largely unjustified, you may be able to recover some of your administrative and litigation costs. You will not be eligible to recover these costs unless you tried to resolve your case administratively, including going through the appeals system, and you gave us the information necessary to resolve the case.

Collections

Publication 594, The IRS Collection Process, explains your rights and responsibilities regarding payment of federal taxes. It describes:

- What to do when you owe taxes. It describes what to do if you get a tax bill and what to do if you think your bill is wrong. It also covers making installment payments, delaying collection action, and submitting an offer in compromise.

- IRS collection actions. It covers liens, releasing a lien, levies, releasing a levy, seizures and sales, and release of property.

Your collection appeal rights are explained in detail in Publication 1660, Collection Appeal Rights.

Innocent Spouse Relief

Generally, both you and your spouse are each responsible for paying the full amount of tax, interest, and penalties due on your joint return. However, if you qualify for innocent spouse relief, you may be relieved of part or all of the joint liability. To request relief, you must file Form 8857, Request for Innocent Spouse Relief no later than 2 years after the date on which the IRS first attempted to collect the tax from you. For example, the two-year period for filing your claim may start if the IRS applies your tax refund from one year to the taxes that you and your spouse owe for another year. For more information on innocent spouse relief, see Publication 971, Innocent Spouse Relief, and Form 8857.

Potential Third Party Contacts

Generally, the IRS will deal directly with you or your duly authorized representative. However, we sometimes talk with other persons if we need information that you have been unable to provide, or to verify information we have received. If we do contact other persons, such as a neighbor, bank, employer, or employees, we will generally need to tell them limited information, such as your name. The law prohibits us from disclosing any more information than is necessary to obtain or verify the information we are seeking. Our need to contact other persons may continue as long as there is activity in your case. If we do contact other persons, you have a right to request a list of those contacted.

Refunds

You may file a claim for refund if you think you paid too much tax. You must generally file the claim within 3 years from the date you filed your original return or 2 years from the date you paid the tax, whichever is later. The law generally provides for interest on your refund if it is not paid within 45 days of the date you filed your return or claim for refund. Publication 556, Examination of Returns, Appeal Rights, and Claims for Refund, has more information on refunds.

If you were due a refund but you did not file a return, you generally must file your return within 3 years from the date the return was due (including extensions) to get that refund.

Tax Information

The IRS provides the following sources for forms, publications, and additional information.

- *Tax Questions:* 1–800–829–1040 (1–800–829–4059 for TTY/TDD)

- *Forms and Publications:* 1–800–829–3676 (1–800–829–4059 for TTY/TDD)

- *Internet: www.irs.gov*

- *Small Business Ombudsman:* A small business entity can participate in the regulatory process and comment on enforcement actions of IRS by calling 1-888-REG-FAIR.

- *Treasury Inspector General for Tax Administration:* You can confidentially report misconduct, waste, fraud, or abuse by an IRS employee by calling 1–800–366–4484 (1–800–877–8339 for TTY/TDD). You can remain anonymous.

Your Appeal Rights and How To Prepare a Protest If You Don't Agree

IRS

Department of the Treasury
Internal Revenue Service

www.irs.ustreas.gov

Publication 5 (Rev. 01-1999)
Catalog Number 46074I

Introduction

This Publication tells you how to appeal your tax case if you don't agree with the Internal Revenue Service (IRS) findings.

If You Don't Agree

If you don't agree with any or all of the IRS findings given you, you may request a meeting or a telephone conference with the supervisor of the person who issued the findings. If you still don't agree, you may appeal your case to the Appeals Office of IRS.

If you decide to do nothing and your case involves an examination of your income, estate, gift, and certain excise taxes or penalties, you will receive a formal Notice of Deficiency. The Notice of Deficiency allows you to go to the Tax Court and tells you the procedure to follow. If you do not go to the Tax Court, we will send you a bill for the amount due.

If you decide to do nothing and your case involves a trust fund recovery penalty, or certain employment tax liabilities, the IRS will send you a bill for the penalty. If you do not appeal a denial of an offer in compromise or a denial of a penalty abatement, the IRS will continue collection action.

If you don't agree, we urge you to appeal your case to the Appeals Office of IRS. The Office of Appeals can settle most differences without expensive and time-consuming court trials. [Note: Appeals can not consider your reasons for not agreeing if they don't come within the scope of the tax laws (for example, if you disagree solely on moral, religious, political, constitutional, conscientious, or similar grounds.)]

The following general rules tell you how to appeal your case.

Appeals Within the IRS

Appeals is the administrative appeals office for the IRS. You may appeal most IRS decisions with your local Appeals Office. The Appeals Office is separate from - and independent of - the IRS Office taking the action you disagree with. The Appeals Office is the only level of administrative appeal within the IRS.

Conferences with Appeals Office personnel are held in an informal manner by correspondence, by telephone or at a personal conference. There is no need for you to have representation for an Appeals conference, but if you choose to have a representative, see the requirements under **Representation.**

If you want an Appeals conference, follow the instructions in our letter to you. Your request will be sent to the Appeals Office to arrange a conference at a convenient time and place. You or your representative should prepare to discuss all issues you don't agree with at the conference. Most differences are settled at this level.

In most instances, you may be eligible to take your case to court if you don't reach an agreement at your Appeals conference, or if you don't want to appeal your case to the IRS Office of Appeals. See the later section Appeals To The Courts.

Protests

When you request an appeals conference, you may also need to file a formal written protest or a small case request with the office named in our letter to you. Also, see the special appeal request procedures in Publication 1660, Collection Appeal Rights, if you disagree with lien, levy, seizure, or denial or termination of an installment agreement.

You need to file a written protest:

- In all employee plan and exempt organization cases without regard to the dollar amount at issue.

- In all partnership and S corporation cases without regard to the dollar amount at issue.

- In all other cases, unless you qualify for the small case request procedure, or other special appeal procedures such as requesting Appeals consideration of liens, levies, seizures, or installment agreements. See Publication 1660.

How to prepare a protest:

When a protest is required, **send it within the time limit specified in the letter you received.** Include in your protest:

1) Your name and address, and a daytime telephone number,

2) A statement that you want to appeal the IRS findings to the Appeals Office,

3) A copy of the letter showing the proposed changes and findings you don't agree with (or the date and symbols from the letter),

4) The tax periods or years involved,

5) A list of the changes that you don't agree with, and why you don't agree.

6) The facts supporting your position on any issue that you don't agree with,

7) The law or authority, if any, on which you are relying.

8) You must sign the written protest, stating that it is true, under the penalties of perjury as follows:

"Under the penalties of perjury, I declare that I examined the facts stated in this protest, including any accompanying documents, and, to the best of my knowledge and belief, they are true, correct, and complete."

If your representative prepares and signs the protest for you, he or she must substitute a declaration stating:

1) That he or she submitted the protest and accompanying documents and

2) Whether he or she knows personally that the facts stated in the protest and accompanying documents are true and correct.

We urge you to provide as much information as you can, as this will help us speed up your appeal. This will save you both time and money.

Small Case Request:

If the total amount for any tax period is not more than $25,000, you may make a small case request instead of filing a formal written protest. In computing the total amount, include a proposed increase or decrease in tax (including penalties), or claimed refund. For an offer in compromise, in calculating the total amount, include total unpaid tax, penalty and interest due. For a small case request, follow the instructions in our letter to you by: sending a letter requesting Appeals consideration, indicating the changes you don't agree with, and the reasons why you don't agree.

Representation

You may represent yourself at your appeals conference, or you may have an attorney, certified public accountant, or an individual enrolled to practice before the IRS represent you. Your representative must be qualified to practice before the IRS. If you want your representative to appear without you, you must provide a properly completed power of attorney to the IRS before the representative can receive or inspect confidential information. Form 2848, Power of Attorney and Declaration of Representative, or any other properly written power of attorney or authorization may be used for this

P–4

purpose. You can get copies of Form 2848 from an IRS office, or by calling 1-800-TAX-FORM (1-800-829-3676).

You may also bring another person(s) with you to support your position.

Appeals To The Courts

If you and Appeals don't agree on some or all of the issues after your Appeals conference, or if you skipped our appeals system, you may take your case to the United States Tax Court, the United States Court of Federal Claims, or your United States District Court, after satisfying certain procedural and jurisdictional requirements as described below under each court. (However, if you are a nonresident alien, you cannot take your case to a United States District Court.) These courts are independent judicial bodies and have no connection with the IRS.

Tax Court

If your disagreement with the IRS is over whether you owe additional income tax, estate tax, gift tax, certain excise taxes or penalties related to these proposed liabilities, you can go to the United States Tax Court. (Other types of tax controversies, such as those involving some employment tax issues or manufacturers' excise taxes, cannot be heard by the Tax Court.) You can do this after the IRS issues a formal letter, stating the amounts that the IRS believes you owe. This letter is called a notice of deficiency. You have 90 days from the date this notice is mailed to you to file a petition with the Tax Court (or 150 days if the notice is addressed to you outside the United States). The last date to file your petition will be entered on the notice of deficiency issued to you by the IRS. If you don't file the petition within the 90-day period (or 150 days, as the case may be), we will assess the proposed liability and send you a bill. You may also have the right to take your case to the Tax Court in some other situations, for example, following collection action by the IRS in certain cases. See Publication 1660.

If you discuss your case with the IRS during the 90-day period (150-day period), the discussion will not extend the period in which you may file a petition with the Tax Court.

The court will schedule your case for trial at a location convenient to you. You may represent yourself before the Tax Court, or you may be represented by anyone permitted to practice before that court.

Note: If you don't choose to go to the IRS Appeals Office before going to court, normally you will have an opportunity to attempt settlement with Appeals before your trial date.

If you dispute not more than $50,000 for any one tax year, there are simplified procedures. You can get information about these procedures and other matters from the Clerk of the Tax Court, 400 Second St. NW, Washington, DC 20217.

Frivolous Filing Penalty

Caution: If the Tax Court determines that your case is intended primarily to cause a delay, or that your position is frivolous or groundless, the Tax Court may award a penalty of up to $25,000 to the United States in its decision.

District Court and Court of Federal Claims

If your claim is for a refund of any type of tax, you may take your case to your United States District Court or to the United States Court of Federal Claims. Certain types of cases, such as those involving some employment tax issues or manufacturers' excise taxes, can be heard only by these courts.

Generally, your District Court and the Court of Federal Claims hear tax cases only after you have paid the tax and filed a claim for refund with the IRS. You can get information about procedures for filing suit in either court by contacting the Clerk of your District Court or the Clerk of the Court of Federal Claims.

If you file a formal refund claim with the IRS, and we haven't responded to you on your claim within 6 months from the date you filed it, you may file suit for a refund immediately in your District Court or the Court of Federal Claims. If we send you a letter that proposes disallowing or disallows your claim, you may request Appeals review of the disallowance. If you wish to file a refund suit, you must file your suit no later than 2 years from the date of our notice of claim disallowance letter.

Note: Appeals review of a disallowed claim doesn't extend the 2 year period for filing suit. However, it may be extended by mutual agreement.

Recovering Administrative and Litigation Costs

You may be able to recover your reasonable litigation and administrative costs if you are the prevailing party, and if you meet the other requirements. You must exhaust your administrative remedies within the IRS to receive reasonable litigation costs. You must not unreasonably delay the administrative or court proceedings.

Administrative costs include costs incurred on or after the date you receive the Appeals decision letter, the date of the first letter of proposed deficiency, or the date of the notice of deficiency, whichever is earliest.

Recoverable litigation or administrative costs may include:

- Attorney fees that generally do not exceed $125 per hour. This amount will be indexed for a cost of living adjustment.

- Reasonable amounts for court costs or any administrative fees or similar charges by the IRS.

- Reasonable expenses of expert witnesses.

- Reasonable costs of studies, analyses, tests, or engineering reports that are necessary to prepare your case.

You are the prevailing party if you meet all the following requirements:

- You substantially prevailed on the amount in controversy, or on the most significant tax issue or issues in question.

- You meet the net worth requirement. For individuals or estates, the net worth cannot exceed $2,000,000 on the date from which costs are recoverable. Charities and certain cooperatives must not have more than 500 employees on the date from which costs are recoverable. And taxpayers other than the two categories listed above must not have net worth exceeding $7,000,000 and cannot have more than 500 employees on the date from which costs are recoverable.

You are not the prevailing party if:

- The United States establishes that its position was substantially justified. If the IRS does not follow applicable published guidance, the United States is presumed to not be substantially justified. This presumption is rebuttable. Applicable published guidance means regulations, revenue rulings, revenue procedures, information releases, notices, announcements, and, if they are issued to you, private letter rulings, technical advice memoranda and determination letters. The court will also take into account whether the Government has won or lost in the courts of appeals for other circuits on substantially similar issues, in determining if the United States is substantially justified.

You are also the prevailing party if:

- The final judgment on your case is less than or equal to a "qualified offer" which the IRS rejected, and if you meet the net worth requirements referred to above.

A court will generally decide who is the prevailing party, but the IRS makes a final determination of liability at the administrative level. This means you may receive administrative costs from the IRS without going to court. You must file your claim for administrative costs no later than the 90th day after the final determination of tax, penalty or interest is mailed to you. The Appeals Office makes determinations for the IRS on administrative costs. A denial of administrative costs may be appealed to the Tax Court no later than the 90th day after the denial.   P–5

Index